ISBN 978-1-5280-0140-3
PIBN 10929079

FB &c Ltd, Dalton House, 60 Windsor Avenue, London, SW19 2RR.
Company number 08720141. Registered in England and Wales.

For support please visit www.forgottenbooks.com

THE

The Parliamentary History

OF

ENGLAND,

FROM

THE EARLIEST PERIOD

TO

THE YEAR

1803.

FROM WHICH LAST-MENTIONED EPOCH IT IS CONTINUED DOWNWARDS IN THE WORK ENTITLED, "THE PARLIAMENTARY DEBATES."

VOL. IV.

A.D. 1660—1668.

LONDON:

PRINTED BY T. C. HANSARD, PETERBOROUGH-COURT, FLEET-STREET:

FOR LONGMAN, HURST, REES, ORME, & BROWN; J. RICHARDSON; BLACK, PARRY, & CO.; J. HATCHARD; J. RIDGWAY; E. JEFFERY; J. BOOKER; J. BODWELL; CRADOCK & JOY; R. H. EVANS; J. BUDD; J. BOOTH; AND T. C. HANSARD.

1808.

ADVERTISEMENT.

THE present Volume embraces that period of our Parliamentary History, which is, perhaps, the most interesting of any; namely, from the Restoration of Charles the Second in the year 1660, to the Revolution, in 1688. For this period, the Proceedings and Debates, in both Houses, have been, for the most part, collected from the following works: 1. The Journals of the House of Lords; 2. The Journals of the House of Commons; 3. That portion of the Parliamentary, or Constitutional History of England, which contains the proceedings of the Convention Parliament, from its meeting on the 25th of April, 1660, to its dissolution, on the 24th of December following, at which epoch the editors of this able performance conclude their labours; 4. The Life of the Earl of Clarendon, written by himself, containing some interesting Debates, in both Houses, during the period between the Restoration of the King and the banishment of the said Earl, in the year 1667, which Debates never yet found their way into any Collection; 5. The Proceedings of the House of Commons touching the Impeachment of the Earl of Clarendon, with the many Debates in that House upon the subject; 6. The Works of the celebrated Andrew Marvell, who, from 1660 to 1678, regularly transmitted to his constituents of Hull, a faithful account of each day's proceedings; 7. The Debates of the House of Commons, from 1667 to 1694, collected by the Honourable Anchitell Grey, who was thirty years a member for the town of Derby; 8. The Debates in the House of Commons on the Bill of Exclusion, in the year 1680, first published in 1681, in a small duodecimo volume, and afterwards republished in 1716, and again in 1807, with the addition of the Debates in the Short Parliament held at Oxford, in the month of March, 1680-1, the proceedings of which related chiefly to the same subject; that is to say, the Exclusion of the Duke of York from the succession to the crown; 9. Timberland's History and Proceedings of the House of Lords; and, 10. Chandler's History and Proceedings of the House of Commons.

ADVERTISEMENT.

It will, doubtless, have been observed by most persons who have much attended to the matter, that, for the period from the Restoration to the year 1743, the two last mentioned works, that is to say, those of Timberland and Chandler, have hitherto been regarded as a regular and complete collection, and the only regular and complete collection, of the Proceedings in Parliament; and that, as such, they have been introduced into, and enjoyed a distinguished place in, almost every public and great private library in the kingdom. Therefore, in preparing the present volume for the press, it might naturally have been expected, that considerable assistance would have been afforded by these works. It is, however, a remarkable fact, which may be verified by a reference to the proceedings of any single session, that very little assistance indeed has been received from them. To say the truth, a discovery of the extreme imperfectness of these works produced one of the motives which led to the present undertaking. On comparing their contents with those of the authentic works before enumerated, they were found to be so extremely defective and incorrect, that they could, in hardly any case, be relied upon with safety. In them, King's Speeches are, in numerous instances, either wholly omitted, or very much curtailed. Scarcely any of the Speeches of the different Lord Chancellors, delivered at the opening of the several Sessions, though those speeches generally contain an outline of the state of the national affairs, are preserved. The Journals appear to have been rarely consulted. Scarcely a Motion or Resolution, is given as it stands in those authentic records. Explanatory notes there are none; and, in only one or two instances have the compilers deemed it necessary to favour the reader with information as to the source, whence they have drawn their materials; which would seem, indeed, to have been moulded into the form of volumes for the mere purpose of filling up a chasm in a book-case.

Besides resorting to the above-recited works, recourse has been had to the best historians, and contemporary writers. From Burnet, Echard, Kennet, Oldmixon, Rapin, North, Ralph, Marvell, Reresby, Temple, Walpole, and the Work of the late Mr. Fox, recently published, many Notes, historical and biographical, have been introduced; and, for the sake of connection, a short account of the principal Occurrences, during each recess of Parliament, has, where necessary, been inserted.

ADVERTISEMENT.

By way of Appendix to this volume, is subjoined a Collection of scarce and valuable Tracts, purely parliamentary, taken from the State Tracts, privately printed in the reign of Charles II. and James II.; from the Harleian Miscellany; and from the noble Collections of Lord Somers. Through these, a more lively image of the times is conveyed, than could be received from any general description, from however eloquent a pen it might proceed. From their scarceness, it is impossible that they should, in their separate state, be generally known; and, as the utility of them, when accompanying the Parliamentary History of the times in which they were written, must be manifest to every one, the compiler does certainly consider them as not the least valuable part of his work.

June 24, 1808.

TABLE OF CONTENTS

TO

VOLUME IV.

A. D. 1660.

12 CHARLES II.

First Session of the Second Parliament of King Charles II. commonly called the Pensionary Parliament.

SECOND SESSION OF THE SECOND PARLIAMENT.

THIRD SESSION OF THE SECOND PARLIAMENT.

FOURTH SESSION OF THE SECOND PARLIAMENT.

FIFTH SESSION OF THE SECOND PARLIAMENT: HELD AT OXFORD.

SIXTH SESSION OF THE SECOND PARLIAMENT.

SEVENTH SESSION OF THE SECOND PARLIAMENT.

EIGHTH SESSION OF THE SECOND PARLIAMENT.

NINTH SESSION OF THE SECOND PARLIAMENT.

TENTH SESSION OF THE SECOND PARLIAMENT.

Eleventh Session of the Second Parliament.

Twelfth Session of the Second Parliament.

Thirteenth Session of the Second Parliament.

Fourteenth Session of the Second Parliament.

Fifteenth Session of the Second Parliament.

Page

SIXTEENTH SESSION OF THE SECOND PARLIAMENT.

SEVENTEENTH SESSION OF THE SECOND PARLIAMENT.

First Session of the Third Parliament.

Second Session of the Third Parliament.

First Session of the Fourth Parliament.

JAMES II.

THE FIRST AND ONLY PARLIAMENT IN THE REIGN OF JAMES II.

PARLIAMENTARY PAPERS:

CONSISTING OF

I. ARTICLES OF IMPEACHMENT.

II. ADDRESSES.

ADDRESSES, *continued.*

III. DECLARATIONS.

IV. KING'S LETTERS.

Charles II.

V. KING'S MESSAGES.

Charles II.

James II.

VI. KING'S SPEECHES.

Charles II.

PARLIAMENTARY PAPERS.

XI. PERSONS FILLING THE HIGH OFFICES OF STATE FROM 1660 TO 1688.

Archbishops of Canterbury.

1660. William Juxon, translated from London.
1663. Gilbert Sheldon, translated from London.
1667. William Sancroft, Dean of St. Pauls. Deprived for not taking the Oaths to King William and Queen Mary.

Lord High Chancellors.

1660. Sir Edward Hyde, knt. and bart. Keeper (Created Lord Hyde) Jan. 13, 1658; instituted Lord High Chancellor, Jan. 29; and created Earl of Clarendon.
1667. Sir Orlando Bridgman, knt. and bart. Lord Keeper, August 30.
1672. Anthony Ashley, Earl of Shaftsbury, November 5.
1673. Sir Heneage Finch, knt. (Created Baron of Daventry, Jan. 10, 1674) Lord Keeper.
1675. Sir Heneage Finch, made Lord High Chancellor, and created Earl of Nottingham.
1682. Sir Francis North, knt. Lord Keeper (Created Lord Guilford in 1683.)
1685. Sir George Jeffereys, knt. Lord Jeffereys.

Speakers of the House of Commons.—King Charles II.

1660.	April 25.	Sir Harbottle Grimstone, bart. Member for Colchester.
1661.	May 16.	Sir Edward Turner, bart. Hereford town. On his being appointed Chief Baron of the Exchequer, May 23, 1671, the House chose, at their next meeting,
1672-3.	Feb. 4.	Sir Job Charlton, bart. Ludlow, Salop; but he desiring leave to resign on account of his health,
	15.	Edward Seymour, Esq. Hindon, Wilts, was elected in his place.
1678-9.	Mar. 6.	Sir Edward Seymour, Bart. Hindon, Wilts. The King refused his consent, and the Commons, after several days debate and a Prorogation, chose,
	15.	Mr. Serjeant Gregory. Weobly, Herefordshire.
1680.	Oct. 21.	William Williams, Esq. Serjeant at Law. Chester City.
1680-1.	Mar. 21.	

King James II.

1685.	May 19.	Sir John Trevor, knt. Member for Denbigh Town.

Masters of the Rolls.

1660.	Nov. 3.	Sir Harbottle Grimstone, baronet.
1684.	Jan. 12.	Sir John Churchill, knight.
1685.	Oct. 20.	Sir John Trevor, knight.

Attorneys General.

1660.	May 31.	Jefferey Palmer, Esq.
1670.		Sir Heneage Finch, knt. and bart. afterwards Lord Finch.
1673.	Nov. 12.	Sir Francis North, knight, afterwards Lord Guildford.
1674.		Sir William Jones, knight.
1679.	Oct. 27.	Sir Cresvil Levinz, knight.
1680.	Feb. 14.	Sir Robert Sawyer, knight.
1687.	Dec. 13.	Sir Thomas Powis.

Solicitors General.

1660.	June 6.	Heneage Finch, Esq.
1670.	May 11.	Sir Edward Turner, knight.
1671.	May 20.	Francis North, Esq.
1673.	Nov. 14.	Sir William Jones, knight.
1678.		Sir Francis Winnington, knight.
	Jan. 13.	Heneage Finch, Esq.
1686.	April 26.	Sir Thomas Powis, knight.
1687.	Dec. 13.	Sir William Williams, knight.

XII. CONTENTS OF THE APPENDIX.

PARLIAMENTARY PAPERS.

XIII.

INDEX

OF THE NAMES OF THE SEVERAL SPEAKERS IN BOTH HOUSES OF PARLIAMENT.

Parliamentary History.

COBBETT'S

Parliamentary History.

Meeting of the Convention Parliament.] April 25, 1660. This day, the New Parliament met according to appointment. The Journals of both Houses now begin again; but before we enter upon the Proceedings of this ever-memorable Convention of two Estates, we shall present the reader with the names of those members who composed the lower of them, viz. the House of Commons; reserving a List of the Peers to another place, when more of them were assembled together, with their King in the midst of them:

A List of the Names of the Knights, Citizens, Burgesses, and Barons of the Cinque Ports, of England and Wales, as they were returned to the Crown-Office, for the Parliament begun at Westminster, April 25, 1660, commonly called the Convention Parliament, which was sitting at the Return of King Charles, and voted his Restoration.*

*** Where there was a double Return, those in the Italic Character were not allowed to sit.

Bedfordshire,
Robert lord Bruce,
Samuel Brown.
Bedford,
Sir Samuel Luke,
Humphrey Winch.
Berkshire,
Sir Robert Pye,
Richard Powell.
New Windsor,
Alexander Blake,
Roger Palmer,
Richard Winwood.
Reading,
Thomas Rich,
John Blagrave.
Abingdon,
Sir John Stonehouse,
Sir John Lenthall.
Wallingford,
Hun. Dunch, made his Election for Cricklade,
Thomas Saunders.
Buckinghamshire,
Thos. Tyrrel, Serjeant at Law, one of the Lords Commissioners,
William Boyer.
Buckingham,
Sir R. Temple,
John Dormer.
Wicomb,
Edmund Petty,
Richard Brown,
Thomas Scott.
Aylesbury,
Richard Ingoldsby,
Thomas Lee.
Amersham,
Charles Cheyne,
Thomas Proby.
Wendover,
Richard Hampden,
John Baldwin.
Marlow,
Peregrine Hoby,
William Borlace.
Cambridgeshire,
Thomas Wendy,
Isaac Thornton.
Cambridge-University,
Gen. Monk, made his Election for Devonshire.
Thomas Crouch.
Cambridge,
Sir Dudley North,
Sir Tho. Willis.
Cheshire,
Sir George Booth,
Thomas Manwaring.
Chester,
John Ratcliff,
William Ince.
Cornwall,
Sir John Carew,
Hugh Boscawen.
Dunchevit, alias Launceston,
Thomas Gewen,
Sir John Clobery,
Edward Elliot.
Leskard,
John Connock,
John Robinson.
Thomas Johnson.
Lestwithiel,
John Clayton,
Walter Moyle.
Henry Ford.
Truro,
Walter Vincent,
Edward Boscawen,
Henry Roberts.
Bodmyn,
Henry Roberts,
John Scilly,
Sir Peter Killegrew,
Helston,
Thomas Robinson,
——Godolphin,
Sir Peter Killegrew.
Camelford,
Sir Peter Killegrew,
William Cotton,
Henry Nicol,
Samuel Trelawney.
Westlow,
John Buller,
John Keneal.
Grampound,
Hugh Boscawen, made his Election for Cornwall.
Thomas Herle.
Eastlow,
Henry Seymour,
John Trelawney,
George Strelley,
Nathaniel Moyle.
Penryn,
Samuel Enys,
James Cobins.
Tregony,
Edw. Boscawen, made his Election for Truro
John Temple,
William Tredinham,
Dr. Clargis.
Bossiney,
Francis Gerrard,
Charles Pym.

* From a pamphlet of the times, which has been carefully compared with the Journals.

St. Ives,
John St. Aubin,
Edward Nosworthy,
James Pread,
Peter Cely.
Fowey,
Edward Herle,
John Barton,
St. Germains,
John Elliot,
Richard Knightley.
Michel,
Thomas Carew,
Henage Finch, made his Election for Canterbury.
Humphrey Burace.
Newport,
Sir Francis Drake,
Wm. Morrice, made his Election for Plymouth.
St. Mawes,
William Tredingham,
Arthur Spry,
John Clobery.
Kellington,
Robert Roll,
Edw. Herle, made his Election for Fowey.
Cumberland,
Lord Charles Haward,
Sir Wilfrid Lawson.
Carlisle,
William Brisco,
Jeremy Tolhur.
Cockermouth,
Richard Tolson,
Wilfrid Lawson.
Derbyshire,
Henry Cavendish, vis. Mansfield,
John Ferrers.
Derby,
John Dalton,
Roger Aleby.
Devonshire,
Lord General Monk,
Sir John Northcott.
Exeter,
John Maynard,
Thomas Bampfield,
Richard Ford.
Totness.
Thomas Chafe,
Thomas Clifford.
Plymouth,
Samuel Tralawney,
William Morrice, Secretary of State.
John Maynard,
Edmund Vowel.
Barnstaple,
John Roll,
Nicholas Dennis.
Plumpton,
William Strode,
Christopher Martyn
Tavistock,
William Russell,
George Howard,
Ellis Crimes.
Clifton, Dartmouth,
Hardness,
John Hale,
—— Frederick.
Beralstone,
Geo. Howard, made his Election for Tavistock.
John Maynard,
Sir Francis Drake,
Tiverton,
Tho. Bampfield, made his Election for Exeter.
Robert Shapcot.
Ashburton,
Sir William Courtney,
John Fowel.
Honyton,
Sir John Young,
Samuel Serle.
Okehampton,
Edward Wise,
Josias Calmady,
Robert Reynolds.
Dorsetshire,
John Fitz-James,
Robert Coker.
Poole.
Sir Walter Erle,
George Cooper.
Dorchester,
Denzil Hollis,
John Whiteway.
Lyme-Regis,
Walter Young,
Tho. Moor, made his Election for Heytesbury.
Weymouth.
Gen. Edw. Montagu,
Sir William Penn.
Melcomb-Regis,
Henry Weltham,
Samuel Bond,
Peter Middleton.
Bridport,
John Drake,
Henry Henly.
Shaftsbury,
Thomas Grove,
James Baker.
Wareham,
George Pitt,
Robert Colleford.
Corfe-Castle,
Ralph Banks,
John Tregonwell.
Essex,
John Bramston,
Edward Turner.
Colchester,
Sir Harbottle Grimston, Speaker,
John Shaw.
Malden,
Tristam Conyers,
Henry Mildmay, declared void,
Edward Harris.
Harwich,
Capel Luckyn,
Henry Wright.
Gloucestershire,
Matthew Hale,
Edward Stephens.
Gloucester,
Edward Masse,
James Stephens.
Cirencester.
Thomas Master,
Henry Powell.
Tewkesbury,
Henry Capell,
Richard Dawdeswell.
Herefordshire,
Edward Harley,
William Hinson, alias Powell, made his Election for Dover.
Hertford,
Roger Bosworth,
Herbert Wastfailing.
Weobly,
James Pitts,
Richard Weston,
Both declared void.
Leominster,
John Birch,
Edward Pytt.
Hertfordshire,
Rowland Litton,
Henry Cæsar.
St. Albans,
Richard Jennings,
William Foxwist,
Col. Alban Cox.
Hertford.
James Cooper,
Arthur Spark.
Huntingdonshire,
Rob. Lord Mandevil,
Henry Cromwell.
Huntingdon,
John Bernard,
Nicholas Pedley.
Kent,
Sir John Tufton,
Sir Edw. Deering.
Canterbury,
Sir Anth. Archer,
Heneage Finch.
Rochester,
John Mansham,
Peter Petit.
Maidstone,
Thomas Twisden,
Robert Barnham.
Queenborough,
James Herbert,
Sir Wm. Wheeler.
Lancashire,
Sir Robert Bindlos,
Roger Bradshaigh,
Lancaster,
Sir Gilbert Gerrard,
William West.
Preston,
Richard Standish,
Alexander Rigby, declared void.
Newton,
Richard Leigh,
William Banks.
Wigan.
William Gardiner.
Hugh Forth.
Clithero,
Sir Ralph Ashton,
William Hulton.
Liverpool,
William Stanley,
Gilbert Ireland.
Leicestershire,
Thomas Merry,
Jathew Babinton.
Leicester.
John Grey,
Thomas Armstrong.
Lincolnshire,
Edward Rossiter,
Sir Geo. Saunderson.
Lincoln,
John Monson,
Thomas Meeres.
Boston,
Sir Anthony Irby,
Thomas Hatcher.
Great Grimsby,
William Wray,
Edward King.
Stamford,
John Hatcher,
Francis Wingfield,
John Weaver.
Grantham,
Thomas Skipwith,
John Newton,
William Ellis.
Middlesex,
Sir Wm. Waller,
Lancelot Leke.
Westminster,
Gilbert Gerrard,
Thomas Clargis.
London,
Wm. Wild, Recorder.
Major-gen. Brown,
John Robinson,
William Vincent.
Monmouthshire,
Henry lord Herbert,
William Morgan.
Monmouth,
Sir Trevor Williams.

Norfolk,
Sir Horn. Townshend,
T. Richardson, Baron of Cramond.
Norwich,
William Barnham
Thomas Rant.
Lynn-Regis,
Sir Ralph Hare,
Edward Walpole.
Yarmouth,
John Potts,
Sir Wm. D'Oyley,
Sir John Palgrave,
Miles Corbet.
Thetford,
Sir Philip Wodehouse,
Robert Paston.
Castle-Rising,
Sir John Holland,
John Spelman.
Northamptonshire,
Sir Henry Yelverton,
John Crew.
Peterborough,
C. lord de le Spencer,
Humphrey Orme.
Francis St. John,
Northampton,
Sir John Norwich,
Richard Rainsford.
Brackley,
Thomas Crewe,
William Lisle, jun.
Higham-Ferrers,
Sir Thomas Dacres,
Edward Harvey.
Northumberland,
Sir William Fenwick,
Ralph Delaval.
Newcastle upon-Tyne,
Robert Ellison,
William Calverley.
Berwick,
Sir Thomas Widdrington, one of the Lords Commissioners of the Great Seal of England. Made his Election for York.
John Rushworth.
Morpeth.
Thomas Widdrington,
Col. Ralph Knight.
Nottinghamshire,
William Pierepoint,
Gilbert lord Haughton.
Nottingham,
Arthur Stanhope,
Col. John Hutchinson, expelled the House June 9, and rendered incapable of bearing any Office of public Trust.
East-Retford.
William Hickman,
Wentworth Fitzgerald, earl of Kildare.
Oxfordshire,
Sir Tho. Wenman, afterwards viscount Wenman,
James Fiennes.
Oxford University,
Thomas Clayton,
John Mills.
Oxford,
Henry Carey, viscount Falkland.
James Haxley.
Woodstock,
Sir Tho. Spencer,
Edward Atkins,
Banbury,
Sir Anthony Cope.
Rutlandshire,
Philip Sherard,
Samuel Brown.
Shropshire,
Sir Wm. Whitmore,
Henry Vernon.
Shrewsbury,
Samuel Jones,
Thomas Jones.
Bridgenorth,
Walter Acton,
John Bennet.
Ludlow,
Tim. Lyttleton,
John Charlton.
Great Wenlock,
Sir Francis Lawley,
Thomas Whitmore.
Bishops-Castle.
William Oakley,
Edmund Waring.
Somersetshire,
George Horner,
Hugh Smith.
Bristol,
John Stephens,
John Knight, sen.
Bath,
Alexander Popham,
William Prynne.
Wells,
Thomas White,
Henry Bull.
Taunton,
William Windham,
Thomas Gorger.
Bridgewater,
Sir Tho. Wroth,
Francis Rolle.
Minehead,
Francis Luttrel,
Charles Prymme.
Ilchester,
Robert Hunt,
Henry Dunster.
Milborn-Port,
William Milborn,
Michael Maller.
Southamptonshire,
Richard Norton,
John Buckley.
Winchester,
Tho. Cole, made his Election for Petersfield,
John Hooke.
Southampton,
William Stanley,
Robert Richbell.
Portsmouth,
Rd. Norton, made his Election for Southamptonshire,
Henry Whitehead.
Yarmouth,
Sir George Leigh,
Richard Lucy.
Petersfield,
Thomas Cole,
Arthur Bold.
Newport,
Robert Dillington,
William Oglander.
Stockbridge,
Francis Rivet,
Sir John Evelin.
Newton,
Sir John Barrington,
Sir Henry Worsley.
Christ-Church,
John Hildesley,
Henry Fulse.
Whitchurch,
Robert Wallop, He was expelled the House June 11, and excepted out of the Act of general Pardon and Oblivion, in respect only of such Pains, Penalties and Forfeitures, (not extending to Life) as should be thought fit to be inflicted on him,
Giles Hungerford.
Lymington,
John Button,
Henry Bromfield.
Andover,
John Trott,
John Collins.
Staffordshire,
Edward Bagot,
William Snead.
Litchfield,
Michael Biddolph,
Thomas Manners.
Stafford,
Sir Charles Wolseley,
John Swinfen.
Newcastle under Line,
John Bowyer,
Samuel Terrick.
Tamworth,
Rd. Newdigate, lord chief justice of the Upper Bench.
Thomas Fox.
Suffolk,
Sir Henry Felton,
Henry North.
Ipswich,
Nathaniel Bacon,
Francis Bacon.
Dunwich,
John Rous,
Henry Beddingfield.
Orford,
Walter Devereux,
Allen Broderick.
Aldborough,
Robert Brook,
Thomas Bacon.
Sudbury,
John Gurdon,
Joseph Brand,
Robert Cordel.
Eye,
Charles Cornwallis,
George Reeve.
St. Edmunsbury,
Sir Henry Crofts,
Sir John Duncombe,
Thomas Chaplin,
Thomas Clarke.
Surrey,
Francis Angier, baron of Langford.
Daniel Harvey.
Southwark,
John Langham,
Thomas Bludworth.
Blechingley,
Sir John Evelin,
John Goodwyn.
Ryegate,
John Hele,
Edward Thurland.
Guildford,
Sir Rd. Onslow,
Arthur Onslow.
Gatton,
Thomas Turgis,
William Oldfield,
Roger James,
Rob. Wood. Declared void.
Haslemere,
John Westbrook,
Richard West.
Sussex,
Sir John Pelham,
Henry Goring.
Chichester,
Henry Peckham,
John Farrington,
William Cawley.
Horsham,
Thomas Middleton,
Hall. Ravenscroft.

Midhurst,
Will. Willoughby,
John Steward.
Lewes,
John Staple,
Nisel Rivers.
Shoreham,
Herbert Springet,
Edward Blaker.
Brambert
John Byne,
Edward Eversfield,
Steyning,
H. Goring, made his Election for Sussex,
John Fagg.
East-Grinstead,
Marmaduke Gresham,
George Courthop.
Arundel,
Roger lord Broghill,
Henry visc. Falkland, made his Election for Oxford City.
Warwickshire,
George Brown,
Thomas Archer.
Coventry,
John Beake,
Richard Hopkins, Declared void.
Warwick,
Clem. Throckmorton, jun.
John Rous.
Westmoreland,
Sir John Lowther,
Sir Thomas Wharton.
Appulby,
Sir Henry Cholmley,
Christ. Clapham.
Wiltshire,
Sir A. Ashley Cooper,
John Earnely.
Salisbury,
Henry Eyre,
Edward Tooker.
Wilton,
John Swanton,
W. Hughes, his election declared void.
Francis Swanton,
Rd. Grobham Howe.
Dounton,
Gyles Eyre, jun.
John Elliot.
Thomas Fitz-James,
William Coles.
Hindon,
Sir Tho. Thyn,
Geo. Grobham Howe,
Edmund Ludlow.
Heytesbury,
Thomas Moore,
John Jolliffe.
Westbury,
Richard Lewes,
William Brunker.
Calne,
Edward Bainton,
William Ducket.
Devizes,
William Lewis,
Robert Aldworth,
John Norden.
Chippenham,
Edw. Hungerford,
Edw. Poole.
Malmsbury,
Robert Danvers,
Sir Fran. Hen. Lee.
Cricklade,
Hungerford Dunch,
Nevil Maskeline.
Bedwin,
Robert Spencer,
Thomas Gape,
Sir Walter St. John,
Sir Ralph Varney.
Ludgershall,
William Prynne, made his Election for Bath,
William Thomas,
Sir John Evelin.
Old Sarum,
Seymour Bowman,
John Norden,
Algernon Cecil.
Wooton Basset,
John Pleydell,
Henry lord Herbert, made his Election for Monmouthshire.
Marlborough,
Henry Hungerford,
Jeffrey Daniel.
Worcestershire,
Henry Bromley,
John Talbot.
Worcester,
Thomas Street,
Thomas Hall.
Droitwich,
Samuel Sandys,
Thomas Coventry.
Evesham,
Sir Thomas Rous,
John Egiocke.
Bewdley,
Thomas Foley.
Yorkshire,
Thomas lord Fairfax,
John Dawnay.
York,
Sir Tho. Widdrington, one of the Lords Commissioners of the Great Seal,
Metcalf Robinson.
Kingston on Hull,
John Ramsden,
Andrew Marvel.
Knaresborough,
William Stockdale,
Henry Bethell.
Scarbrough,
William Thompson,
L. Robinson, June 21, 1660, Mr. Robinson was discharged by an Order of the House from sitting, and a Writ ordered to be issued to elect another in his room; but the Journals do not give us the Reason for this Expulsion.
John Legard.
Ripon,
Henry Arthington,
Edmund Jennings,
John Lambert.
Richmond,
James D'Arcy,
Sir Christ. Wyvell.
Heydon,
Col. Hugh Bethell,
J. Clobery, made his Election for Launceston.
Boroughbridge,
Conyers D'Arcy,
Henry Stapylton.
Thirsk,
Barring Bourchier,
Wm. Stanley, made his Election for Liverpool.
Thomas Harrison.
Aldborough,
Solomon Swale,
Francis Goodrick.
Beverley,
Sir John Hotham,
Col. H. Bethell, made his Election for Heydon.
Pontefract,
Sir George Savile,
William Lowther,
John Hewly,
Lionel Copley.
Malton,
Philip Howard,
Thomas Heblethwayt.
Allerton,
Francis Lascelles, expelled the House June 9, rendered incapable of bearing any Office of public Trust; and it was resolved that he should not be within that Clause of Exception in the Act of general Pardon, as to any Fine or Forfeiture of any Part of his Estate not purchased of, or belonging to, the Public.
Thomas Lascelles.

CINQUE PORTS.

Hastings,
Denny Ashburnham,
Nicholas Delves.
Romney,
Sir Nor. Knatchbull,
John Knatchbull.
Hythe,
P. ld. visc. Strangford,
Phineas Andrews.
Dover,
Edward Montagu,
Arnold Braimes.
Sandwich,
Henry Oxenden,
James Thurbarne.
Seaford,
Sir Thomas Dike,
George Parker.
Rye,
Herbert Morley,
William Hay.
Winchelsea,
Wm. Howard, second son of Edward lord Howard, of Escrick,
Samuel Gott.

WALES.

Anglesey,
Rt. lord visc. Bulkley.
Beaumaris,
Griffith Bodurda.
Brecon,
Sir Wm. Lewis.
Brecon T.
Sir Henry Williams.
Cardigan,
John Vaughan.
Cardigan T.
Wm. Griffiths.
Carmarthen,
John Lloyd.
Carmarthen T.
Arthur Annesley,
Carnarvon,
John Glynn.
Carnarvon T.
Wm. Glynn.
Denbigh,
Sir Tho. Middleton.
Denbigh T
Sir John Carter.
Flint,
Sir T. Hanmer.
Flint T.
Roger Whitley.
Glamorgan,
Sir Edward Mansel.

Cardiff,	*Pembroke* T.
Bussey Mansel.	Sir Hugh Owen, declared void. New writ ordered to be issued June 29.
Merioneth,	*Haverford-West,*
Edmund Merrick.	Wm. Phillips.
Montgomery,	*Radnor,*
John Pursell.	George Gwin,
Montgomery T.	*Radnor* T.
Thomas Middleton.	Robert Harley.
Pembroke,	
Arthur Owen.	

Proceedings of the House of Lords.] April 25. This day the house of lords met. As we have been long strangers to them, we think it proper to give their first five days proceedings, as they are entered on the Journals. The lords present were, the earl of Manchester, appointed to be Speaker pro tempore, the earls of Northumberland, Lincoln, Suffolk, and Denbigh, viscount Say and Sele, lords Wharton, Hunsdon, Grey de Werk, and Maynard.

Ordered, That Monday next be appointed to be kept, by this house, as a day of Fasting and Humiliation, for seeking a Blessing from God by prayer, upon the Meeting of both Houses of Parliament, in order to a Settlement of this Nation; and the place to be the Abbey Church in Westminster for the Peers, wherein the house of commons are to be desired to do the like for their house. A message was sent to the commons, to let them know that the lords have appointed to keep Monday next as a Fast-Day, for seeking of God for a Blessing upon the meeting of both houses, in order to a Settlement of this nation, and to desire their concurrence for the same day to be kept as a Fast by their house.

The earls of Northumberland and Lincoln, the lords Wharton, Hunsdon, and Grey de Werk, were appointed to consider of the Draught of an Order for Henry Scobell, esq. to deliver all Acts, Records, and Journal-Books, and all Papers and Writings whatsoever, that are in his custody, belonging to the Peers, to John Brown, esq. clerk of the parliament, and likewise the Stone Tower and dwelling-house belonging thereunto, and report the same to this house. Their lordships to meet presently.

Resolved, That George Monk, esq. is nominated and appointed, by this house, to be Captain-General of all Land Forces in England, Scotland, and Ireland, and the concurrence of the commons be desired therein.

The earl of Lincoln reported from the committee, the Order concerning the Records of this house, which was read and approved of, and ordered to be signed by the Speaker of this house, viz.

"Whereas Henry Scobell, esq. is now in the possession of the dwelling-house in the Old Palace Yard, at Westminster, belonging to the clerk of the parliament, who attends as clerk to the house of peers, and hath in his custody the Acts, Journals, and other Records of that house: it is ordered by the lords in parliament, That the said Henry Scobell shall, upon sight hereof, forthwith deliver unto John Brown, esq. clerk of the parliament, or his assigns, the possession of a certain stone building, standing within the said dwelling house, commonly called the Tower, wherein the Records were usually kept, and the keys and other things belonging to the same: as also the Acts, Ordinances, Journals, Records, Writings, and Papers appertaining, or any wise belonging to the said office. And lastly, That the said Henry Scobell shall deliver the quiet possession of the said dwelling-house, with the appurtenances, unto the said John Brown, or his assigns, within 14 days next after the date of this Order, and hereunto obedience is required accordingly."

The earl of Northumberland, lord visc. Say and Sele, with the lords Wharton and Hunsdon, were appointed to consider of such lords as shall have Letters written to them, to desire their attendance on this house. To meet presently in the Prince's Lodgings.—The lord Wharton reported the Names of those lords, and likewise a Draught of the Letter, which were read and agreed to, viz. "My lord; I am commanded by the house of peers, hereby to signify their pleasures, that you do repair to attend the house with what convenient speed you can: and so rest, Your, &c. Manchester. Speaker pro tempore."

The earls of Northumberland, Suffolk, and Manchester, viscount Say and Sele, and the lords Hunsdon, Grey de Werk, and Maynard, were appointed by the house to go to the lord-general Monk, to deliver this Message to him, from the lords in parliament, and the earl of Manchester, Speaker, was to speak it, viz. "The peers in parliament assembled, have commanded me to own your lordship's valour and prudence in managing the great affairs in trusted to you; and they likewise return your lordship their acknowledgements for the care and respects which you have expressed to the peers, in restoring them to their antient and undoubted rights. And they hope that God will still bless you in the use of all means for the procuring a safe and well-grounded peace, according to the antient fundamental government of this nation, wherein they shall employ their councils and utmost endeavours in concurrence with you."

April 25, p. m. Ordered, That Dr. Reynolds and Mr. Hardy are appointed to preach before the lords on the Fast-Day; and that the house be called to-morrow.

April 26. The messengers sent yesterday to the house of commons return with the Answer, That they concur with this house in keeping Monday next a Fast-Day.

Ordered, That the antient Order of this house be revived for the Lords to pay coming after Prayers, viz. every earl 2*s*. and every baron 1*s*.

The earls of Northumberland, Lincoln, Dorset, &c. were ordered to prepare an Ordinance in pursuance of the Vote made yesterday by this house, concerning the lord-general Monk. Their lordships, or any four of them, to meet to-morrow morning at 8 of the clock, and Mr. Rich and Mr. Eltonhead to be assistants.

The Roll of the standing Orders of this house was read.

The earl of Manchester reported, that his lordship and the rest of the lords committees delivered to general Monk what this house had directed yesterday; and the general expressed himself to this effect: "That he took it for a great honour and civility from the house of peers; and said he would be ready to carry on all things that tend to the Safety and Settlement of this nation; and desired that their lordships would be pleased to look forward and not backward, in transacting of affairs."

A Message was brought from the commons by James Herbert, esq. who said, "He was commanded by the knights, citizens, and burgesses of the house of commons in parliament assembled, to acquaint this house, that they have resolved that this day fortnight be set apart for a Day of Thanksgiving to the Lord, for raising up his excellency the Lord-General, and other eminent persons who have been instrumental in the delivery of this nation from thraldom. Also they have resolved, That this day fortnight be the day set apart for a Day of Thanksgiving for that house, and within the cities of London and Westminster, and the late lines of communication; and this day month for the whole nation. To all which the house of commons desire their lordships concurrence."—The Answer returned to this Message was, That the Lords do, with thankful hearts, acknowledge God's great mercy in delivering them out of their long thraldom, confusion, and misery, and do fully concur with you in setting apart those public Days of Thanksgiving.

April 27. Ordered, That Mr. Hodges is appointed to preach before the Lords, the next Day of Thanksgiving, in the Abbey-Church.

Signification being given to the house, that divers Lords were in the lobby, ready to attend the service of this house, having never sat in parliament since the death of their ancestors, the house gave the gentleman usher authority to call them in to sit in their places in this house. The names of the aforesaid lords were, the earls of Oxon, Derby, and Strafford, lord viscount Conway, and the lords Cromwell, Gerrard, Tenham, and Capell.

Ordered, That the Speaker of this house do write several and respective Letters to the earls of Leicester, Bedford, and Clare, and lord Paget, to give their attendance on this house as peers.

The earls of Oxon, Northumberland, Rutland, &c. were ordered to frame an Ordinance for the constituting of a Committee of Safety of both houses, and to report the same to this house.

Resolved, That the earl of Manchester is hereby nominated and appointed one of the Commissioners of the Great Seal of England, and to send to the house of commons for their concurrence.

Lords Committees appointed to consider of the Privileges of this house, viz. Earls of Oxon, Northumberland, Derby, &c. Their lordships, or any 9 of them, to meet in the Prince's Lodgings when they please, and to adjourn from time to time, as they shall see cause.—Ordered, That it is referred to the Lords Committees for Privileges to consider of the different cases of those lords that have late come to sit in this house, and those that do not; and also what assistants that formerly sat in this house, and are now alive and capable of being admitted, to be assistants to this house.

Ordered, That a conference be had with the house of commons, to consider of some way and means to be found out to make up the Breaches and Distractions of this kingdom. This conference to be on Tuesday next in the Painted Chamber: and the earls of Oxon, Northumberland, Bedford, &c. were appointed to consider and draw up Heads for this conference.—A Message was sent to the commons by Mr. Rich and Mr. Eltonhead, to desire a conference on Tuesday next, at ten of the clock, in the Painted-Chamber, in order to the Settlement of the great Affairs of this kingdom.

April 30. Ordered, That the Lords of this house do receive Sacrament in the Abbey Church of Westminster; and, as concerning the time, it is referred to the committee of privileges to consider of it, and report the same to this house.

The lords, before they went to the Fast Sermons, made a Collection for the Poor, which was to be distributed as the house should thereafter appoint. Then the Lords went from this house together, in their order, to keep the Fast in the Abbey Church.

Proceedings of the House of Commons.] April 25. The Journals of the house of commons begin with acquainting us, That on this day the members of that house first went to Margaret's Church, Westminster, to hear a Sermon, and then repaired to their own house; where, on a motion made by Mr. Pierepoint, sir Harbottle Grimston was chosen Speaker,* and placed in the chair by the lord-general

* "Sir Harbottle Grimston had been a member of the Long Parliament, and continued, rather than concurred, with them till after the Treaty of the Isle of Wight; where he was one of the Commissioners sent to treat with that king, and behaved himself so well, that his majesty was well satisfied with him; and after his return from thence, he pressed the King's Concessions; and was thereupon in the number of those who were by force excluded the house. His election to be Speaker at this time was contrived by those who meant well to the King; and he submitted to it out of a hope and confidence that the designs it was laid for would succeed." Lord Clarendon, vol. vi. p. 755.

Monk,* Mr. Hollis, and the said Mr. Pierepoint. Next Wm. Jessop, esq. James Northfolk, esq. and Ralph Darnall, esq. were chosen clerk, serjeant at arms, and clerk assistant.

The Clerk of the Crown attended with a Book, containing an account of the members chosen to serve in this present parliament, by which the house was called over; and those members who were present did, upon their naming, withdraw into the committee chambers and gallery above. Afterwards, when the Book was gone through, they returned and took their places in the house.

On a Message from the lords, the house agreed to hold a Fast on Monday the 30th; and that Mr. Calamy, Dr. Gauden, and Mr. Baxter, be desired to assist in carrying on the work of Fasting and Humiliation, on that day, at Margaret's Church, Westminster, in order to seek the Lord for a blessing on these distracted nations.

A large Committee for Privileges and Elections was appointed, with full powers for that purpose.—A Day of Thanksgiving to the Lord was appointed, for raising up his excellency the Lord General, and other eminent persons, who have been instrumental in the delivery of this nation from thraldom and misery. May the 10th to be the day, and that the lords concurrence be desired herein. Ordered also, That Mr. Price, the Lord-General's Chaplain, be desired to carry on the Work of Thanksgiving, before this house, at Margaret's Church, Westminster; and that Dr. Clargis do give him notice thereof.

Solemn Thanks given to General Monk.] Resolved, That his excellency the Lord-General Monk have the Recognition, Acknowledgment, and hearty Thanks of this house, for his eminent and unparalleled services done to these nations. Accordingly, the Speaker gave the Thanks of the house to the Lord-General, standing in his place, to the effect following: "That he was commanded by this house to take notice of his eminent services, his wisdom being such, and God having so blessed him in his great affairs, that he hath made a conquest of those who are enemies and disaffected to the government, happiness, and welfare of this church and state, without a bloody nose: That this hath much advanced the honour of his services, having been effected without the expence of blood or treasure, of both which the nation had been so much exhausted, that nothing but a necessity could rationally have satisfied any man to draw out more: that his lordship hath been our physician; and hath cured us with his lenitives: that statues have heretofore been set up for persons meriting much of their country; but his lordship hath a statue set up higher, and in another place, as high as may be, in the hearts of all well-wishers to the good of this nation, and a crown of glory, he doubts not, laid up for him in heaven: that God hath made him instrumental, by his helping hand, to keep the nation from sinking, when no way was represented to our understanding, whence deliverance should arise; so that God's raising him up, accompanying, blessing, and assisting him in his counsels, in such sort as to accomplish his work to that height, cannot be otherwise owned by those that look upon him, and his actions, than as a miracle: and therefore, in the name of the house, he returns to his lordship the hearty Thanks of this house; adding, he was sure his lordship would believe it if he had not said so."

Then it was resolved, That col. Ingoldsby should have the Thanks of the house, for his former and late great and eminent services done for this nation, which the Speaker accordingly gave him to the effect following: "That he is commanded by the house to take notice of his former services, and of his late action, wherein God hath made him instrumental to do so great and eminent a service to the nation, for which he returns him their hearty Thanks; having made him as high in favour as he is in his own merit, for adventuring himself so far in the public cause; and that the house's good acceptance thereof is the more valuable, being taken notice of on the same day with the great services performed for the nation by his excellency the Lord-General."

April 27. Ordered, That the great business, touching the Settlement of these Nations, be taken into consideration on Tuesday the 1st of May, at 8 o'clock; to which day the house adjourned itself, reserving power to all Committees to sit and act in the mean time, notwithstanding this adjournment.

During this short interval of the Commons, for the Lords did not adjourn at all, there happened an affair, which Dr. Price has given us, and is a piece of secret history very necessary to be known previous to their next meeting. This author tells us, "That, in this short recess, the General and sir John Grenville consulted together about the delivery of his Message, Letters, &c. from his majesty to both houses. That which was superscribed to the General, to be by him communicated to the Army and Council of State, was, by his appointment, delivered to him at the door of the Council-Chamber, where Grenville attended, and into which, as col. Birch, one of the Members of it, was entering, Grenville requested him (but unknown) that he might speak with my Lord-General; who, upon Birch's intimation, came to the door, and there, in the sight of his guards attending, received Grenville's Letters, but not with much regard either to his person or his business; of which the General seemed to understand somewhat by the seal, and asked him if he would stay there till

* "The general was elected a member, unanimously, by the university of Cambridge; which honour, Dr. Gumble says, he ever remembered with thankfulness. But being at the same time returned one of the knights of the shire for the county of Devon, he chose to represent the latter as his native country."—Dr. Gumble's Life of General Monk, p. 288.

he had his Answer, otherwise his guards should secure him, commanding them to look to him. So his excellency produceth his Letters to the Council of State, Grenville is sent for in, and Birch protested that he neither knew the gentleman nor his business. The lord-president of the council examined Grenville from whence those Letters came, whose they were, and how he came by them, (for as yet they were not opened) he told the president that the King, his master, gave him them with his own hands at Breda: so the opening of them was deferred till the Parliament sat. Grenville was to have been sent into custody, but the General was his bail, who said he knew the gentleman, (being his near kinsman) and would take his parole to appear before the parliament."

The King's Letter to the House of Peers.] May 1. The two houses met. After the Lords had done some other business, and ordered a call of their house to be on the 3d instant, they were informed, That there was a gentleman, sir John Grenville, in the lobby, who had a Letter to deliver to this house from the King; the house thereupon was adjourned during pleasure, and the Speaker was appointed to go to the lower end of the house, and receive it at the hands of the messenger. The house being resumed, the Speaker reported, "That sir John Grenville delivered to him a Letter, which he said he received from the King, his master, to deliver to the house of peers." Hereupon, the house commanded the said Letter, with a Declaration inclosed therein, to be read twice; which was done accordingly, and are as follow:

"To the Speaker of the House of Peers, and to the Lords there assembled.

"C. R. Right trusty and right well-beloved cousins, and right trusty and well-beloved, we greet you well: We cannot have a better reason to promise ourself an end of our common sufferings and calamities, and that our own just power and authority will, with God's blessing, be restored to us, than that we hear you are again acknowledged to have that authority and jurisdiction which hath always belonged to you by your birth, and the fundamental laws of the land: and we have thought it very fit and safe for us to call to you for your help in the composing the confounding distempers and distractions of the kingdom, in which your sufferings are next to those we have undergone ourself; and therefore you cannot but be the most proper counsellors for removing those mischiefs, and for preventing the like for the future. How great a trust we repose in you, for the procuring and establishing a blessed Peace and Security for the Kingdom, will appear to you by our inclosed Declaration; which trust, we are most confident, you will discharge with that justice and wisdom that becomes you, and must always be expected from you; and that, upon your experience how one violation succeeds another, when the known relations and rules of justice are once transgressed, you will be as jealous for the rights of the crown, and for the honour of your king, as for yourselves, and then you cannot but discharge your trust with good success, and provide for and establish the peace, happiness, and honour of king, lords, and commons, upon that foundation which can only support it, and we shall be all happy in each other: and as the whole kingdom will bless God for you all, so we shall hold ourself obliged, in an especial manner, to thank you in particular, according to the affection you shall express towards us. We need the less enlarge to you upon this subject, because we have likewise writ to the house of commons, which we suppose they will communicate to you; and we pray God to bless your joint endeavours for the good of us all: and so we bid you very heartily farewell. Given at our Court at Breda, this 14th day of April, 1660, in the 12th year of our reign."

The King's Declaration.] His majesty's Declaration from Breda to all his loving Subjects, inclosed in the foregoing, was as follows:

"C. R. "Charles, by the Grace of God, King of England, Scotland, France, and Ireland, Defender of the Faith, &c. To all our loving subjects, of what degree or quality soever, greeting: If the general distraction and confusion which is spread over the whole kingdom, doth not awaken all men to a desire and longing that those wounds, which have so many years together been kept bleeding, may be bound up, all we can say will be to no purpose; however, after this long silence, we have thought it our duty to declare how much we desire to contribute thereunto; and that as we can never give over the hope, in good time, to obtain the possession of that right which God and nature hath made our due; so we do make it our daily suit to the Divine Providence, that he will, in compassion to us and our subjects, after so long misery and sufferings, remit, and put us into a quiet and peaceable possession of that our right, with as little blood and damage to our people as is possible; nor do we desire more to enjoy what is ours, than that all our subjects may enjoy what by law is theirs, by a full and entire administration of justice throughout the land, and by extending our mercy where it is wanted and deserved.—And to the end that the fear of punishment may not engage any, conscious to themselves of what is past, to a perseverance in guilt for the future, by opposing the quiet and happiness of their country, in the Restoration both of king, peers, and people to their just, antient, and fundamental rights, we do, by these presents, declare, That we do grant a free and general Pardon, which we are ready, upon demand, to pass under our Great Seal of England, to all our subjects, of what degree or quality soever, who, within 40 days after the publishing hereof, shall lay hold upon this our grace and favour, and shall, by any public act, declare their doing so, and that they return to the loyalty and obedience of good subjects; excepting only such persons as shall hereafter be excepted by parliament, those only to be excepted. Let all our subjects, how faulty soever, rely upon the word of a king, solemnly given by this present Declaration, That no crime whatsoever, committed against us or our royal father before the publication of this, shall ever rise in judgment, or be brought in question, against any of them, to the least endamagement of them, either in their lives, liberties, or estates, or (as far forth as lies in our power) so much as to the prejudice of their reputations, by any reproach or term of distinction from the rest of our best subjects; we desiring and ordaining, that henceforth all notes of discord, separation, and difference of parties be utterly abolished among all our subjects, whom we invite and conjure to a perfect union among themselves, under our protection, for the Re-settlement of our just Rights and theirs, in a Free Parliament, by which, upon the word of a king, we will be advised.—And because the passion and uncharitableness of the times have produced several opinions in Religion, by which men are engaged in parties and animosities against each other, (which, when they shall hereafter unite in a freedom of conversation, will be composed, or better understood) we do declare a Liberty to tender Consciences, and that no man shall be disquieted or called in question, for differences of opinion in matter of Religion, which do not disturb the peace of the kingdom; and that we shall be ready to consent to such an act of parliament, as, upon mature deliberation, shall be offered to us, for the full granting that indulgence.—And because, in the continued distractions of so many years, and so many and great revolutions, many grants and purchases of estates have been made to, and by, many officers, soldiers, and others, who are now possessed of the same, and who may be liable to actions at law upon several titles, we are likewise willing that all such differences, and all things relating to such grants, sales, and purchases, shall be determined in parliament; which can best provide for the just satisfaction of all men who are concerned.—And we do further declare, That we will be ready to consent to any act or acts of parliament to the purposes aforesaid, and for the full satisfaction of all Arrears due to the officers and soldiers of the Army under the command of general Monk, and that they shall be received into our service upon as good pay and conditions as they now enjoy. Given under our Sign Manual and Privy-Signet, at our Court at Breda, this 14th day of April, 1660, in the 12th year of our reign."

The King's Letter to the House of Commons.] May 1. In the house of commons, Mr. Annesley reported from the Council of State, a Letter from the King, unopened, directed, 'To our Trusty and Well-beloved General 'Monk, to be communicated to the President 'and Council of State, and to the Officers of 'the Armies under his command,' being received from the hands of sir John Grenville. The house being informed that sir John Grenville, a messenger from the King, was at the door, it was resolved that he should be called in; which being done, and he at the bar, after obeisance made, he said, 'Mr. Speaker, I am 'commanded by the King, my master, to deliver this Letter to you, and his desires that 'you would communicate it to the house.' The messenger being withdrawn, the Letter was read to the house by Mr. Speaker, and was as follows:

"To our Right Trusty and Well-beloved the SPEAKER of the House of Commons:

"C. R. Trusty and Well-beloved, we greet you well: In these great and insupportable afflictions and calamities under which the poor nation hath been so long exercised, and by which it is so near exhausted, we cannot think of a more natural and proper Remedy, than to resort to those for council and advice, who have seen and observed the first beginning of our miseries, the progress from bad to worse, and the mistakes and misunderstandings which have produced and contributed to inconveniences which were not intended; and after so many revolutions, and the observation of what hath attended them, are now trusted by our good subjects to repair the breaches which are made, and to provide proper Remedies for those Evils, and for the lasting Peace, Happiness, and Security of the kingdom.—We do assure you, upon our royal word, that none of our predecessors have had a greater esteem of parliaments than we have; in our judgment, as well as from our obligation, we do believe them to be so vital a part of the constitution of the kingdom, and so necessary for the government of it, that we well know, neither prince nor people can be, in any tolerable degree, happy without them: and therefore you may be confident, that we shall always look upon their counsels as the best we can receive, and shall be as tender of their Privileges, and as careful to preserve and protect them, as of that which is most near to ourself, and most necessary for our own preservation.—And as this is our opinion of Parliaments, that their authority is most necessary for the government of the kingdom, so we are most confident that you believe and find, that the preservation of the King's Authority is as necessary for the preservation of parliaments; and that it is not the name, but the right constitution of them, which can prepare and apply proper Remedies for those evils which are grievous to the people, and which can thereby establish their Peace and Security: and therefore we have not the least doubt but that you will be as tender in, and as jealous of, any thing that may infringe our honour, or impair our authority, as of your own liberty and property, which is best preserved by preserving the other.—How far we have trusted you in this great affair, and how much it is in your power to restore the nation to all that it hath lost, and to redeem it from any infamy it hath undergone, and to make king and people as happy as they ought to be, you will find by our inclosed Declaration, a copy of which we have likewise sent to the house of peers, (see p. 16): and you will easily believe that we would not voluntarily, and of ourself, have reposed so great a trust in you, but upon an entire confidence that you will not abuse it, and that you will proceed in such a manner, and with such due consideration of us who have trusted you, that we shall not be ashamed of declining other assistance, (which we have assurance of) and repairing to you for more natural and proper Remedies for the evils we would be freed from; nor sorry that we have bound up our own interest so intirely with that of our subjects, as that we refer it to the same persons to take care of us, who are trusted to provide for them. We look upon you as wise and dispassionate men, and good patriots, who will raise up those banks and fences which have been cast down, and who will most reasonably hope, that the same prosperity will again spring from those roots from which it hath heretofore and always grown. Nor can we apprehend that you will propose any thing to us, or expect any thing from us, but that we are as ready to give as you to receive.—If you desire the advancement and propagation of the Protestant Religion, we have, by our constant profession and practice of it, given sufficient testimony to the world, that neither the unkindness of those of the same faith towards us, nor the civilities and obligations from those of a contrary profession, (of both which we have had abundant evidence) could in the least degree startle us, or make us swerve from it. And nothing can be proposed to manifest our zeal and affection for it, to which we will not readily consent. And we hope in due time ourself to propose somewhat to you for the propagation of it, that will satisfy the world that we have always made it both our care and our study, and have enough observed what is most like to bring disadvantage to it.—If you desire Security for those, who, in these calamitous times, either wilfully or weakly have transgressed those bounds which were prescribed, and have invaded each other's rights, we have left to you to provide for their Security and Indemnity, and in such a way as you shall think just and reasonable; and, by a just computation of what men have done and suffered, as near as is possible, to take care that all men be satisfied; which is the surest way to suppress and extirpate all such uncharitableness and animosity, as might hereafter shake and threaten that Peace, which, for the present, might seem established. If there be a crying sin, for which the nation may be involved in the infamy that attends it, we cannot doubt but that you will be as solicitous to redeem and vindicate the nation from that guilt and infamy as we can be.—If you desire that reverence and obedience may be paid to the fundamental Laws of the Land, and that Justice may be equally and impartially administered to all men, it is that which we desire to be sworn to ourself, and that all persons in power and authority should be so too.—In a word; there is nothing that you can propose, that may make the kingdom happy, which we will not contend with you to compass; and, upon this confidence and assurance, we have thought fit to send you this Declaration, that you may, as much as is possible, at this distance, see our heart; which when God shall bring us nearer together, (as we hope he will do shortly) will appear to you very agreeable to what we have professed. And we hope that we have made that right Christian use of our affliction, and that the observation and experience we have had in other countries hath been such, as that we, and we hope all our subjects, shall be the better for what we have seen and suffered.—We shall add no more but our prayers to Almighty God, that he will so bless your counsels, and direct your endeavours, that his Glory and Worship may be provided for, and the Peace, Honour, and Happiness of the nation may be established upon those foundations which can best support it. And so we bid you farewell. Given at our Court at Breda this 14th day of April, 1660, in the 12th year of our reign."

The King's Letter to Gen. Monk, and the Council of State.] After reading the foregoing, with the Declaration inclosed, the following Letter from his majesty to general Monk was also read:

"To our Trusty and Well-beloved General MONK, to be by him communicated to the President and Council of State, and to the Officers of the Armies under his Command.

"C. R. Trusty and Well-beloved, we greet you well: It cannot be believed but that we have been, are, and ever must be, as solicitous as we can, by all endeavours, to improve the affections of our good subjects at home, and to procure the assistance of our friends and allies abroad, for the recovery of that Right, which, by the laws of God and man, is unquestionable, and of which we have been so long dispossessed by such force, and with those circumstances, as we do not desire to aggravate by any sharp expressions; but rather wish that the memory of what is past may be buried to the world. That we have more endeavoured to prepare and to improve the affections of our subjects at home for our Restoration, than to procure assistance from abroad to invade either of our kingdoms, is as manifest to the world: and we cannot give a better evidence that we are still of the same mind than in this conjuncture, when common reason must satisfy all men that we cannot be without assistance from abroad, we chuse rather to send to you, who have it in your own power to prevent that ruin and desolation which a war would bring upon the nation, and to make the whole kingdom owe the Peace, Happiness, Security, and Glory it shall enjoy, to your virtue; and to acknowledge that your armies have complied with their obligations for which they were first raised, for the preservation of the Protestant Religion, the Honour and Dignity of the King, the Privileges of Parliament, the Liberty and Property of the Subject, and the Fundamental Laws of the Land; and that you have vindicated that trust which others most perfidiously abused and betrayed. How much we desire and resolve to contribute to those good ends, will appear to you by our inclosed Declaration, which we desire you to cause to be published for the information and satisfaction of all good subjects, who do not desire a further effusion of precious Christian blood; but to have their Peace and Security founded upon that which can only support it, an Unity of Affections amongst ourselves, an equal Administration of Justice to men, restoring Parliaments to a full capacity of providing for all that is amiss, and the Laws of the Land to their due veneration.—You have been yourselves witnesses of so many Revolutions, and have had so much experience how far any power and authority, that is only assumed by passion and appetite, and not supported by justice, is from providing for the happiness and peace of the people, or from receiving any obedience from them, without which no government can provide for them, that you may very reasonably believe that God hath not been well pleased with the attempts that have been made, since he hath usually increased the confusion, by giving all the success that hath been desired, and brought that to pass without effect, which the designers have proposed as the best means to settle and compose the nation; and therefore we cannot but hope and believe that you will concur with us in the Remedy we have applied; which, to human understanding, is only proper for the ills we all groan under; and that you will make yourselves the blessed instruments to bring this blessing of Peace and Reconciliation upon king and people, it being the usual method in which Divine Providence delighteth itself to use and sanctify those very means which ill men design for the satisfaction of private and particular ends and ambition, and other wicked purposes, to wholesome and public ends, and to establish that good which is most contrary to the designers; which is the greatest manifestation of God's peculiar kindness to a nation that can be given in this world. How far we resolve to preserve your interests and reward your services, we refer to our Declaration; and we hope God will inspire you to perform your duty to us and to your native country, whose happiness cannot be separated from each other.—We have intrusted our well-beloved servant sir John Grenville, one of the gentlemen of our bed-chamber, to deliver this unto you, and to give us an account of your reception of it, and to desire you, in our name, that it may be published; and so we bid you farewell. Given at our Court at Breda this 14th of April, 1660, in the 12th year of our reign."

The King's Letter to the Lord Mayor and City of London.] Besides the foregoing, the following Letter from the King was sent to the Lord Mayor, Aldermen, and Common Council of the City of London:

"To our Trusty and Well-beloved the Lord Mayor, Aldermen, and Common Council of our City of London.

"C. R. Trusty and Well-beloved, we greet you well: In these great Revolutions which of late have happened in that our kingdom, to the wonder and amazement of all the world, there is none that we have looked upon with more comfort than the so frequent and public manifestations of their affections to us in the city of London, which hath exceedingly raised our spirits, and which, no doubt, hath proceeded from the Spirit of God, and his extraordinary mercy to the nation, which hath been encouraged by you, and your good example, to assert that government, under which it hath so many hundred years enjoyed as great felicity as any nation in Europe, and to discountenance the imaginations of those who would subject our subjects to a government they have not yet devised; and, to satisfy the pride and ambition of a few ill men, would introduce the most arbitrary and tyrannical power that was ever yet heard of. How long we have all suffered under those and the like devices, all the world takes notice, to the no-small reproach of the English nation, which we hope is now providing for its own security and redemption, and will be no longer bewitched by those inventions. How desirous we are to contribute to the obtaining the peace and happiness of our subjects without further effusion of blood, and how far we are from desiring to recover what belongs to us by a war, if it can be otherwise done, will appear to you by the inclosed Declaration; which, together with this our Letter, we have intrusted our right trusty and well-beloved cousin the lord viscount Mordaunt, and our trusty and well-beloved servant sir John Greuville, knt. one of the gentlemen of our bed-chamber, to deliver to you, to the end that you, and all the rest of our good subjects of that our city of London, (to whom we desire it should be published) may know how far we are from the desire of revenge, or that the Peace, Happiness, and Security of the kingdom should be raised upon any other foundation than the affection and hearts of our subjects, and their own consents. We have not the least doubt of your just sense of those our condescensions, or of your zeal to advance and promote the same good end, by disposing all men to meet us with the same affection and tenderness, in restoring the fundamental laws to that reverence that is due to them, and upon the preservation whereof all our happiness depends: and you will have no reason to doubt of enjoying your full share in that happiness, and of the improving it by our particular affection to you. It is very natural for all men to do all the good they can for their native country, and to advance the honour of it: and as we have that full affection for the kingdom in general, so we would not be thought to be without some extraordinary kindness for our native city in particular, which we shall manifest on all occasions, not only by renewing their Charter, and confirming all those Privileges which they have received from our predecessors, but by adding and granting any new favours which may advance the trade, wealth, and honour of that our native city; for which we will be so solicitous, that we doubt not but that it will, in due time, receive some benefit and advantage in all those respects, even from our own observation and experience abroad: and we are most confident we shall never be disappointed in our expectation of all possible service from your affections; and so we bid you farewell. Given at our Court at Breda the 14th day of April, 1660, in the 12th year of our reign."

After reading these Letters, with the Declaration, in the two houses, the Lords ordered sir John Grenville to be called in again, and the Speaker, by direction of the house, gave him Thanks, in their name, for his care in bringing this gracious Message from the King. They also ordered, That the King's Letter to them and the Declaration should be forthwith printed and published, with this title, 'His Majesty's 'gracious Letter and Declaration, sent to 'the House of Peers by sir John Grenville, 'knt.' Lastly, the Lords appointed a Committee to consider of a Letter of Thanks to the King for his gracious Message sent, this day, to the house, and to present it for their lordships consideration.

Mr. Rich, and Mr. Eltonhead, Masters of the Chancery, being sent by the Lords, with a Message, desiring a conference with the Commons this day (May 1) at 11 o'clock, in the Painted-Chamber, in order to the Settlement of the great Affairs of the Kingdom, the messengers were called in, and the Speaker acquainted them, That the house had considered their Message, and would return an Answer by messengers of their own.

Then it was resolved, nem. con. "That an Answer be prepared to his Majesty's Letter, expressing the great and joyful sense of this house of his gracious offers, and their humble and hearty Thanks to his majesty for the same, with professions of their loyalty and duty to his majesty; and that this house will give a speedy Answer to his majesty's gracious proposals."—Mr. Finch, Mr. Annesley, sir Anth. Ashley Cooper, the Lord-General, sir Wm. Lewis, Mr. Morris, and Mr. Hollis, were ordered to prepare the said Answer.

It was also resolved, nem. con. "That the sum of 50,000*l.* be presented to the King's majesty from this house; and the Committee appointed to draw up the Answer to the King's Letter were ordered to go to the lord mayor, aldermen, and commons of the city of London, to consider with them how the said sum of 50,000*l.* may be raised; what security they will desire for the repayment thereof with interest after the rate of 6*l.* per cent. and to offer such security as they shall think fit, for repayment thereof to the persons who shall advance the same."—Resolved, That it be referred to the same Committee appointed to consider with the lord mayor, aldermen, and commons of the city of London, about a further sum to be raised and applied for the paying of the Army, and to consider how the Arrears of the Army may be satisfied.

A Conference having been desired by the lords with the other house, the commons sent up sir George Booth to let them know, that they were ready for it as they desired. The committee appointed by the commons to manage this conference, were, Mr. Annesley, Mr. Finch, Mr. Turner, lord Falkland, Mr. Piercpoint, serjeants Hales and Brown. The subject was the Settlement of the Government of these Nations.

May 1, p. m. Mr. Annesley reported the Conference had with the lords: That the earl of Manchester had acquainted the committee of this house with the lords' receipt of a Letter from his majesty, and of a Declaration inclosed. He told us, it was a maxim, "Where the Word of a King is, there is power;" and where the Word of our King is, as it is now received, there is truth; and Power and Truth are the best supports of government: he wished us to consider the mistaken maxims of some politicians, that distrust and jealousies are the nerves and sinews of wisdom; but he hopes, that we will rather consider that Wisdom from above, which is first pure, * *, easy to be intreated; and that all distrust and jealousy might be laid aside: he took notice of some new State-Builders, that had been framing imaginary states of government; which brought into consideration our antient government, the best in the world: and thereupon took notice of a Vote in the lords' house, concerning the Government of this kingdom, to the tenor following, viz. The lords do own and declare, 'That, according to the antient and fundamental laws of this kingdom, the government 'is, and ought to be, by King, Lords, and 'Commons.'—Then he proceeded further, and took notice of the great revolutions and changes that have been, and the occasion of them to be, the separation of the head from the members; and therefore he acquainted the committee with another Vote of the lords, viz. 'That the lords, having a deep sense of the 'miseries and distractions that this kingdom 'hath been involved in, since the violent attempts to dissolve the established government; and conceiving that the separating the 'head from the members hath been the chiefest occasion of all our disorders and confusions, they desire that some ways may be considered how to make up these breaches, and 'to obtain the King's Return again to his people.' And that he also acquainted them with a third Vote of the lords, in order to a further proceeding on the former, viz. 'That a committee of the house of commons may be appointed to meet with a committee of the 'lords, to prepare such things as may be in 'order to these good and necessary ends; and 'to frame a Letter of Thanks and Acknowledgments to his majesty for his gracious

'Letter and Declaration.' And, lastly, his majesty's said Letter and Declaration, sent to the lords, was read there; and that they had intrusted the committee with them, that they might also be read here, and a Resolution given upon the whole.

After hearing this Report, the commons ordered the King's Letter to the lords, with his majesty's Declaration there inclosed, to be read; and then it was Resolved, "That this house doth agree with the lords, and do own and declare, that, according to the antient and fundamental laws of this kingdom, the Government is, and ought to be, by King, Lords, and Commons."—Ordered also, That the following committee be appointed to peruse the Journals and Records, and to examine what pretended Acts or Orders have passed, which are inconsistent with the Government by King, Lords, and Commons, and report them, with their opinion thereon, to this house; and also to offer such expedients, as may carry on the Courts of Justice of this kingdom; and how fines, recoveries, assurances, judgments, and decrees, passed, may be confirmed and made good. Mr. Prynne, Mr. Finch, lord Falkland, Mr. Turner, sir Wm. Lewis, serjeant Hales, sir Walter Erle, sir Anth. Ash. Cooper, lord commissioner Tyrrel, sir A. Cope, serjeant Glynn, lord commissioner Widdrington, sir John Courtop, and all the gentlemen of the long robe.

May 2. The commons were busy, this day, in altering and correcting the form of an Answer to the King's Letter to them; which, being all read, was agreed to, and ordered to be superscribed, 'To the King's Most Excellent Majesty.'—Ordered, that sir John Grenville be called to the bar, and that the Speaker return him Thanks for his care, moreover the house voted him 500*l.* to buy him a Jewel, as a testimony of their respects to him, and as a badge of honour, for bringing so gracious a Letter from the king's majesty to this house.

Alderman Robinson informed the house, That he was commanded, by the lord mayor, aldermen, and common council of the city of London, to acquaint them that they had received a Letter, (see p. 21) and Declaration from the king's majesty, by the hands of the lord visc. Mordaunt and sir John Grenville; and that they desire the leave of this house to give an Answer to them; to which the house agreed.

The Answer of the House of Lords to the King's Letter.] May 3. This day, in the house of lords, the earl of Manchester reported the draught of an Answer to the King's gracious Letter to their house; which, being read, was approved of, and ordered to be sent to the king by the earls of Oxford, Warwick, Middlesex, viscount Hereford, lord Berkeley, and lord Brooke; who were to consider what time they desire to prepare themselves to go. A Message was sent down to the commons, to acquaint them with this Vote. The Letter of the Lords to the King was as follows:

"For the KING's Most Excellent Majesty,

"Most gracious Sovereign; Your loyal subjects the Peers, now assembled, do, with all humility and thankfulness, return their acknowledgments to your majesty for your gracious Letter and Declaration; and do esteem it their greatest honour that your majesty is pleased to express a confidence of their counsels and endeavours for the composing the sad and unhappy distractions of your kingdoms; and they own this as their great advantage, that they may now act in discharge of their own duty by your maj.'s command. Your majesty's great and many sufferings have long affected their hearts with deep resentments of trouble and sorrow; but the same power that usurped and profaned your sceptre, divested them of their rights and privileges, and kept them under such pressures and difficulties, as they were rendered incapable of serving your majesty in order to those ends, to which their duty and allegiance did engage them. It hath been their constant desire that the nation had continued happy and innocent; but your majesty's piety and wisdom hath shewed you to what degree your clemency is to be extended; and we hope all your subjects will answer your majesty's grace and favour to the utmost point of fidelity and obedience. The peers have a just ground to own a more particular dependence and subserviency to the throne of majesty, not only by the prescriptions of law, but by that affection and duty which is fixed in their hearts upon the foundations of loyalty, which gives them the privilege to stile themselves Your majesty's most loyal, most dutiful, and most obedient Subjects and Servants.—Signed in the name, and by the command, of the said House of Peers, by E. MANCHESTER, Speaker of the House of Peers pro tempore. Westminster, May 3, 1660."

This day, the lords made an Order, That the Statues of the late king's majesty be set up again in all the places from whence they were pulled down: and that the Arms of the Commonwealth be demolished and taken away wherever they are, and the King's Arms be put up in their stead: That the king's majesty be publicly prayed for by all ministers in their churches: and, lastly, that some place be considered of where general Monk's Statue may be set up. All which particulars were referred to the committee of privileges to consider of and make report to the house.

May 3. A Committee of the Commons had been appointed to go to the city of London, to borrow Money of them for the present occasions; who returning, Mr. Annesley reported from them, That they had treated with the lord mayor, &c. for a Loan of 100,000*l.* which the city was willing to advance on the security of an Ordinance for 3 months assessment; the money arising from it to be paid into the Chamber of London; and that their Chamberlain should be receiver for the whole. The house agreed to this proposal; and also voted 6 per cent. interest, from the time of receiving to the paying in the sum. An Ordinance for 3 months Assessment was ordered to be brought in the next morning. The Committee were also to consider how the 50,000*l.* which was voted to be presented to his majesty may be remitted to him, to his best advantage, and so that there be no loss upon the exchange.

Sir John Grenville thanked by the Speaker of the H. of Commons.] The commons being informed that sir John Greaville, who brought the King's Letter, was at the door, he was called in to receive the Thanks of this house, according to the order of yesterday; who, standing at the bar, the Speaker said to him, in effect, as followeth: "Sir John Grenville, I need not tell you with what grateful and thankful hearts the commons, now assembled in parliament, have received his majesty's gracious Letter: 'res ipse loquitur:' you yourself have been 'ocularis & auricularis testis de rei veritate:' our bells and our bonfires have already proclaimed his majesty's goodness, and our joys. We have told the people that our king, the glory of England, is coming home again; and they have resounded it back again in our ears, that they are ready, and their hearts are open, to receive him. Both parliament and people have cried aloud to the King of Kings, in their prayers, 'Long live King Charles the Second!'—Sir, I am likewise to tell you, that this house doth not think it fit that you should return back to our royal sovereign, without some testimony of respect to yourself: they have therefore ordered and appointed that 500*l.* shall be delivered to you to buy a Jewel, as a badge of that honour which is due to a person whom the king hath honoured to be messenger of so gracious a message: and I am commanded, in the name of the house, to return you their very hearty Thanks." *

The Answer of the House of Commons to the King's Letter.] After this, the house sent a message to the lords by sir Wm. Lewis, to acquaint their lordships, That they had prepared an Answer to his majesty's gracious Letter sent to their house, and that they intended to send the same by some members of their own.—Resolved, That, for determining what members of this house shall carry the Letter to his majesty, the several members of it shall put in papers of names; and that it be referred to a committee to view those papers, and make report to the house who have the greatest number of voices.—Ordered, also, That the Letter agreed to by this house, in Answer to his majesty's gracious Letter, shall be kept by the clerk, under such privacy, that no copy thereof may come to any hand, till it hath been communicated to his majesty.—The Letter was as follows:*

To the KING's Most Excellent Majesty,

"Most Royal Sovereign; We your majesty's most loyal subjects, the commons of England assembled in parliament, do with all humbleness, present unto your majesty the unfeigned thankfulness of our hearts, for those gracious expressions of piety and goodness, and love to us and the nations under your dominion, which your majesty's Letter of April 14th, dated from Breda, together with the Declaration inclosed in it, of the same date, do so evidently contain; for which we do, in the first place, look up to the great King of Kings, and bless his name, who hath put these thoughts into the heart of our king, to make him glorious in the eyes of his people, as those great deliverances which that divine majesty hath afforded unto your royal person from many dangers, and the support which he hath given unto your heroic and princely mind, under various trials, make it appear to all the world, that you are precious in his sight.—And give us leave to say, That as your majesty is pleased to declare your confidence in parliaments, your esteem of them, and this your judgment and character of them, That they are so necessary for the Government of the kingdom, that neither prince nor people can be in any tolerable degree happy without them; and therefore say, that you will hearken unto their counsels, be tender of their privileges, and careful to preserve and protect them: so we trust, and will with all humility be bold to affirm, That your majesty will not be deceived in us, and that we will never depart from that fidelity which we owe unto your majesty, that zeal which we bear unto your service, and a constant endeavour to advance your honour and greatness.—And we beseech your majesty we may add this further, for the vindication of parliaments, and even of the last parliament convened unto your royal father, of happy memory; when, as your majesty well observes, through mistakes and misunderstandings, many inconveniences were produced which were not intended: that those very inconveniences could not have been brought upon us by those persons who had designed them, without first violating the parliament

* "So great and sudden a change was this, that a servant of the King's, who, for near ten years together, had been in prisons, and under confinements, only for being the King's servant, and would, but three months before, have been put to have undergone a shameful death, if he had been known to have seen the King, should be now rewarded for bringing a Message from him! From this time there was such an emulation and impatience in Lords, Commons, and City, and generally over the kingdom, who should make the most lively expressions of their duty and of their joy, that a man could not but wonder where those people dwelt who had done all the mischief, and kept the King so many years from enjoying the comfort and support of such excellent subjects." Lord Clarendon, vol. vi. p. 761.

* The above Letter is not entered in the Journals, but it was printed by order of the commons, by Edward Husbands and Thomas Newcomb.

itself; for they well knew it was not possible to do a violence to that sacred person, whilst the parliament, which had vowed and covenanted for the defence and safety of that person, remained entire. Surely, sir, as the persons of our kings have ever been dear unto parliaments, so we cannot think of that horrid act committed against the precious life of our late sovereign, but with such a detestation and abhorrency as we want words to express it.—And, next to wishing it had never been, we wish it may never be remembered by your majesty, to be unto you an occasion of sorrow, as it will never be remembered by us, but with that grief and trouble of mind which it deserves, being the greatest reproach that ever was incurred by any of the English nation; an offence to all the Protestant Churches abroad, and a scandal to the profession of the truth of Religion here at home; though both profession and true professors, and the nation itself, as well as the parliament, were most innocent of it, having been only the contrivance and act of some few ambitious and bloody persons, and such others as, by their influence, were misled.—And as we hope and pray that God will not impute the guilt of it, nor of all the evil consequences thereof unto the land, whose divine justice never involves the guiltless with the guilty, so we cannot but give due praise to your majesty's goodness, who are pleased to entertain such reconciled and reconciling thoughts; and with them not only meet, but, as it were, prevent your parliament and people; proposing yourself, in a great measure, and inviting the parliament to consider further, and advise your majesty what may be necessary to restore the nation to what it hath lost, raise up again the banks and fences of it, and make the kingdoms happy, by the advancement of religion, the securing our laws, liberties, and estates, and the removing of all jealousies and animosities which may render our peace less certain and durable; wherein your majesty gives a large evidence of your great wisdom judging aright; that, after so high a distemper, and such an universal shaking of the very foundations, great care must be had to repair the breaches, and much circumspection and industry used to provide things necessary for the strengthening of those repairs, and preventing whatever may disturb and weaken them.—We shall immediately apply ourselves to the preparing of these things; and in a very short time, we hope, be able to present them unto your majesty; and, for the present, do, with all humble thankfulness, acknowledge your grace and favour, in assuring us of your royal concurrence with us, and saying, That we shall not expect any thing from you, but what you will be as ready to give as we to receive. And we cannot doubt of your majesty's effectual performance, since your own princely judgment hath prompted unto you the necessity of doing such things; and your piety and goodness hath carried you to a free tender of them to your faithful parliament. You speak as a gracious king, and we will do what befits dutiful, loving, and loyal subjects, who are yet more engaged to honour, and highly esteem your majesty for your declining, as you are pleased to say, all foreign assistance, and rather trust to your people, who, we do assure your majesty, will, and do, open their arms and hearts to receive you, and will spare neither their estates nor their lives, when your service shall require it of them.—And we have yet more cause to enlarge our praises and our prayers to God for your majesty, that you have continued unshaken in your faith: that neither the temptation of allurements, persuasions, and promises from seducing papists on the one hand, nor the persecution and hard usage from some seduced and misguided professors of the protestant religion on the other hand, could at all prevail upon your majesty to make you forsake the Rock of Israel, the God of your Fathers, the true Protestant Religion, in which your majesty hath been bred; but you have still been as a rock yourself, firm to your covenant with your and our God, even now expressing your zeal and affection for the Protestant Religion, and your care and study for the propagation thereof. This hath been a rejoicing of heart to all the faithful of the land, and an assurance to them that God would not forsake you; but after many trials, which should but make you more precious, as gold out of the fire, restore your majesty unto your patrimony and people with more splendour and dignity, and make you the glory of kings, and the joy of your subjects; which is, and ever shall be, the prayer of your majesty's most loyal subjects the commons of England assembled in parliament. Signed HARBOTTLE GRIMSTON, Speaker."

'Resolved, That a committee of this house be appointed to consider of the king's majesty's Letter and Declaration, and for preparing of Bills accordingly. This committee have power to prepare a Bill for taking away Tenures in Capite, and by Knights Service, and Socage in Capite, and also of the Court of Wards; and to consider and propound to this house, how 100,000*l.* a year may be raised and settled on his majesty, in compensation for Wardships and Liveries, and the Court of Wards.

May 4. The committee, according to order, had now began to prepare Bills, to be offered to the king on his return, for the Security of the Parliament itself, and of their properties who had purchased lands, &c. under titles depending wholly on the late revolutions. And, first, Mr. Finch did this day exhibit a Bill to the house, declaring the Continuance of this present parliament, which was read a 1st and 2nd time, and committed. The said gentleman also brought another Bill, concerning Lands purchased from the trustees of the late parliament, which was likewise read twice and committed.

A Declaration was ordered to be prepared, to give notice to the people, That there will be no proceedings in Westminster-Hall next

Easter-Term, upon causes depending in any of the courts, till the two last returns of the said term. Agreed to by the lords.

The Recorder of London, aldermen Vincent, Robinson, and Bludworth, had leave given them by the house to go to the King, with a Letter from the City, in Answer to the one the City had received from his majesty.

A Declaration of Parliament for keeping the Peace, &c.] May 5. Mr. Annesley, from the Council of State, informed the house, That there were many distemperatures in several parts of the kingdom; and that unquiet spirits might make an advantage to foment new troubles and distractions, by pretence and colour that the sheriffs, and other public ministers of justice, are not impowered, in this present juncture of affairs, with sufficient authority to dispense the ordinary acts of justice belonging to their respective places, for preserving of the public peace. The council of state did desire, That a Declaration should be set forth, for requiring all officers of justice to attend their places, and the duties thereof, as by commission they are enjoined; that so the public peace may be secured, and the justice of the nation carried on without any interruption. The commons appointed a committee to draw up a Declaration accordingly, which was done and agreed to by the lords, as follows:

"The lords and commons assembled in parliament, having received several informations that there hath been divers tumults, riots, outrages, and misdemeanors, lately committed in sundry parts of this realm, by unquiet and discontented spirits, to the disturbance of the public peace, and fomenting of new troubles, do hereby order and declare, That all sheriffs, justices of the peace, mayors, constables, and other ministers of public justice, that were in office the 25th of April, 1660, shall be continued in their respective offices, and shall exercise the same in the king's majesty's name and style, and shall use their best endeavours to suppress and prevent all riots, tumults, unlawful assemblies and misdemeanors whatsoever against the laws and peace of the realm; and all treasonable and seditious words, reports, and rumours against his majesty's royal person and authority, and proceed against all offenders therein according to law and justice: and all military officers and soldiers, and all others, are to be aiding and assisting to them therein."

The house proceeded to the election of 12 of their members, who were to go to the King, with their Letter, which was done by ballot in the same manner they used to elect their Council of State. The number of the members then in the house were 408, of which 4 were appointed for tellers, who received a paper from each member in a glass, with 12 names wrote in it; all which were delivered to the committee, who were to examine and report the greatest number of voices at their meeting on Monday next.

May 7. The lord Howard brought in the numbers, when it appeared, that sir George Booth, lord Falkland, Mr. Hollis, sir John Holland, sir Anth. Ashley Cooper, lord Bruce, sir Horatio Townshend, lord Herbert, lord Castleton, lord Fairfax, sir Henry Cholmley, and lord Mandeville, were duly elected by a majority, to carry the Answer to the King's Letter from the house, who were all separately put to the vote, and approved on by them.

This day both houses agreed, that the King should be proclaimed on the next; but, previous to this ceremony, a committee of 4 Lords and 8 of the commons were agreed on to meet to consider of the manner, time, and other circumstances, to be observed on that occasion. The report of this to be made the first thing the next morning.

Another Committee had been appointed to draw up some Orders, relating to Ministers praying for the King, &c. and this day Mr. Finch reported two Votes, which were agreed to, viz. "Resolved, That all and every the Ministers throughout the kingdoms of England and Ireland, the Dominion of Wales, and Town of Berwick upon Tweed, do, and are hereby required and enjoined, in their public prayers, to pray for the king's most excellent majesty, by the name of our sovereign lord Charles, by the grace of God, of England, Scotland, France, and Ireland, King, Defender of the Faith, &c. and for the most illustrious prince James, duke of York, and the rest of the royal progeny."—"Resolved, That the Ministers who are appointed to officiate before this house upon Thursday next, being the day appointed for a public Thanksgiving, and all other ministers within the cities of London and Westminster, and the late lines of communication, who in their several churches and chapels are to carry on the duties of that day; and also all other ministers who are, on that day fortnight, to perform the like duty throughout the kingdom of England, the dominion of Wales, and town of Berwick upon Tweed, shall be, and are hereby enjoined, to return Thanks to Almighty God, for his majesty's several gracious Letters to both houses of parliament, and to the commanders in chief of the forces both by land and sea, and to the lord mayor and common council of the city of London, together with the Declarations inclosed, and the just and honourable concessions therein contained; and for the hearty, loyal, and dutiful conjunction of the lords and commons now assembled in parliament, and the universal concurrence of all the commanders and forces both by land and sea, to receive his majesty into his dominions and government; according to their bounden duty and the laws of the land; and that the Ministers upon Thursday fortnight be enjoined to read his majesty's Letters and Declarations to both houses, in their several churches and chapels at the same time."—These Votes being communicated to the lords, were agreed to by them.

Form of a Proclamation of the King.] May 8. A Form of a Proclamation, agreed on by a committee of lords and commons, was read and approved of by both houses, as follows:

"Although it can no way be doubted but that his majesty's right and title to this crown and kingdoms is, and was every way, completed by the death of his most royal father, of glorious memory, without the ceremony or solemnity of a Proclamation; yet, since Proclamations in such cases have been always used, to the end that all good subjects might, upon this occasion, testify their duty and respect; and since the armed violence and other the calamities of many years last past, have hitherto deprived us of any such opportunity, wherein we might express our loyalty and allegiance to his majesty: we, therefore, the lords and commons now assembled in parliament, together with the lord mayor, aldermen, and commons of the city of London, and other freemen of this kingdom, now present, do, according to our duty and allegiance, heartily, joyfully, and unanimously, acknowledge and proclaim, That, immediately upon the decease of our late sovereign lord king Charles the imperial crown of the realm of England, and of all the kingdoms, dominions, and rights belonging to the same, did, by inherent birth-right, and lawful and undoubted succession, descend and come to his most excellent majesty Charles II. as being lineally, justly, and lawfully, next heir of the blood-royal of this realm; and that, by the goodness and providence of Almighty God, he is of England, Scotland, France, and Ireland, the most potent, mighty, and undoubted king; and thereunto we do most humbly and faithfully submit and oblige ourselves, our heirs, and posterities for ever. God save the King."

The King proclaimed.] Ordered, That a copy of this Proclamation, to be signed by the Speakers of both houses, be forthwith sent to the lord mayor of the city of London; and that the members of the house of commons, who serve for the several counties, cities, and boroughs, in England, Wales, and the town of Berwick upon Tweed, do take care, forthwith, to send the sheriffs, mayors, bailiffs, and other head officers of these counties, &c. for which they served, the Proclamation for proclaiming the king's majesty, that it might be done accordingly.—At the same time was sent down a Declaration, touching Acts which were preparing to be passed, to be read along with the Proclamation.—It was then ordered, That the lords commissioners of the great seal, in their gowns, with the purse and mace before them; the lord president of the council of state, with his mace, should attend the Proclamation, next after the Speaker of the house of commons. And both houses, with their Speakers, went in their coaches, in procession, at the solemnity; which was performed this day, with great pomp and ceremony; and all imaginable demonstrations of joy, first at Whitehall, then at Temple-Bar, where they met the lord mayor, sheriffs, aldermen, common council, and other officers, &c. of the city; as also at the Fleet, Conduit in Cheapside, and the Royal Exchange. The same Proclamation was soon after made over all the three kingdoms.

May 9. Both houses received Letters from admiral Montagu at sea, intimating, That he had received his majesty's Declaration, and a Letter directed to general Monk and himself, to be communicated to the Fleet, which he had done accordingly. That all the commanders, officers, and seamen, were desirous that they should express to his majesty their great joyfulness of heart for the Declaration, and favours to them, in the said Letter; as also their loyalty and duty to him. Therefore they humbly intreated the houses to know their pleasure, whether such an Answer should be returned to his majesty or not. Both the Speakers were ordered to write to the admirals, to give them Thanks for their respects shewn to them, and gave them leave to send such an Answer, either jointly or severally, as they should think fit.

Mr. Prynne, from the house of commons, brought up several Votes, which they had passed, and desired their lordships concurrence to them, viz. That the king's majesty be desired to make a speedy return to his parliament, and to the exercise of his kingly office.—Votes enjoining all Ministers to pray for the King.—A Bill, intitled, 'An Act for removing and preventing all Questions and Disputes concerning the Assembling and Sitting of this present Parliament.'—That the Arms of the Commonwealth, wherever they are standing, be forthwith taken down, and that the King's Arms be set up in their stead: the commons having lead the way, by altering the Arms over their Speaker's chair, in the same manner. All which the lords ratified and confirmed.

The lords appointed a Committee to consider and take information where any of the King's Goods, Jewels, or Pictures, were placed; and to advise of some course how the same might be restored to his majesty.

The house of commons had resolved, That all Proceedings should go in the King's Name, from the 1st of May inclusive; and that in all cases where the Great Seal shall be necessary to be used, all proceedings do pass accordingly. Also, that for carrying on and expediting the Justice of the kingdom, the Great Seal, now remaining in the custody of the earl of Manchester, and the rest of the commissioners, be used till further orders. In like manner all the Seals belonging to any other courts should be so used; and all process and proceedings there run in the King's Name. The lords agreed to the last part of this Vote; but, as to the Seals, they ordered it to be laid aside.

The lords appointed a Committee to consider how the King was to be received on his Return; and when to be sent for, and by whom. Both houses also ordered, That admiral Montagu do observe such commands as the king's majesty shall please to give him, for the disposal of the Fleet, or any part thereof, in order to his return. A committee of 12 lords and 24 commoners was appointed to meet and prepare Instructions for those who were to go with the Letters from both houses to his majesty, and they were ordered to set forward on Friday the 11th instant.

Instructions for the Commissioners of both Houses, appointed to go to the King.] May 10. This being the day appointed for the Thanksgiving, both houses attended their devotions in the forenoon; but, in the afternoon, they both met again to do business. The commons sent up a copy of the Instructions for the Commissioners who were to go to the King; which being read, some alterations were made in them, concerning the Arms of the Commonwealth, and then they were agreed to by the commons. They were in these words:

INSTRUCTIONS for Aubrey earl of Oxford, Charles earl of Warwick, Lionel earl of Middlesex, Leicester viscount Hereford, George lord Berkeley, Robert lord Brooke, the lord Herbert, the lord Mandevile, the lord Bruce, the lord Castleton, the lord Falkland, the lord Fairfax, Denzil Hollis, esq. sir Horatio Townsend, sir John Holland, sir Anthony Ashley-Cooper, sir Geo. Booth, and sir Henry Cholmley.

"You are to begin your Journey towards his majesty on Friday next (May 18) and make a speedy repair to such place where his majesty shall be, and humbly to present the Letters wherewith you are respectively intrusted by both houses of parliament.—You are to acquaint his majesty with what great joy and acclamation he was proclaimed, in and about the cities of London and Westminster, upon the 8th day of May instant, and present the Proclamation itself to his majesty; and to acquaint him with the Orders of both houses to have the same proclaimed throughout the kingdoms of England and Ireland, dominion of Wales, and the town of Berwick upon Tweed; and that both houses have ordered, That all and every the Ministers throughout the kingdoms of England and Ireland be enjoined in their public Prayers to pray for his most excellent majesty, and for the most illustrious prince James duke of York, and the rest of the royal progeny. And also that they have ordered, That the assumed Arms of the late pretended Commonwealth, wherever they are standing, be taken down, and that his majesty's arms be set up instead thereof: and you are to communicate to his majesty the Resolutions of both houses relating to this Instruction.—You are to acquaint his majesty with the earnest desire of both houses, That his majesty will be pleased to make a speedy Return to his parliament, and to the exercise of his Kingly Office, and that in order thereunto both houses have given directions to general Montague, one of the generals at sea, and other officers of the Fleet, to observe such commands as his majesty shall please to give him or them for disposal of the Fleet, in order to his majesty's return: and you are to communicate to his majesty the Resolutions of both houses relating to this Instruction.—That the Committee from both houses do beseech his majesty that they may know where he purposeth to take shipping, and to land at his coming over, that preparation may be made for his reception; and which of his majesty's houses he intendeth to make use of at his first coming to London, and whether he will come all the way by land after he comes on shore, or whether he will please to come by water from Gravesend to London; and that his majesty will declare in what manner he is pleased to be received."

Mr. Denzil Hollis's Speech to the King at Breda.] When the commissioners arrived at Breda, they were immediately admitted to an Audience of the King. Upon this occasion, Mr. Denzil Hollis* addressed his majesty as follows:

"Dread Sovereign; Your faithful subjects, the commons of England, assembled in parliament, have sent us hither, twelve of their number, to wait upon your majesty, and, by their commands, we are here prostrate at your royal feet, where themselves are all of them present with us in the sincere and most loyal affections and desires of their hearts, and would have been in their persons, if your majesty's service, and the trust reposed in them by all the several parts of the kingdom did not necessarily require their attendance and continuance in the place where they now are, and where all their thoughts and endeavours are wholly taken up and employed in those two great and main works, which are the proper and genuine ends of all parliaments, the advancement of their king's service, and the discharge of their country's trust.—And certainly, sir, we can speak it with a great deal of joy, and with no less of truth, that never parliament made greater demonstrations of zeal, affection and loyalty to any of the kings of England than this parliament hath done, and doth, and we hope, and doubt not, nay we know it, that it ever will do, unto your majesty, our liege lord and king. Their hearts are filled with a veneration of you, longings for you, confidence in you, and desires

* "Hollis was a man of great courage, and of as great pride: he was counted for many years the head of the Presbyterian Party. He was faithful and firm to his side, and never changed through the whole course of his life. He was well versed in the records of Parliament, and argued well, but too vehemently; for he could not bear contradiction. He had the soul of an old stubborn Roman in him. He was a faithful but a rough friend, and a severe but fair enemy. He had a true sense of religion, and was a man of an unblameable life, and of a sound judgment when it was not biassed by passion. He was made a lord for his merits in bringing about the Restoration." Burnet, vol. i. p. 98.

to see and serve you; and their tongues do, upon all occasions, express it, and in so doing they are (according to the nature of Parliaments) the true representative of the whole nation; for they but do that in a more contracted and regular way, which the generality of the people of the land, from one end of it to the other, do in a more confused and disorderly manner, yet as heartily and as affectionately, all degrees, and ages, and sexes, high and low, rich and poor (as I may say) men, women, and children, join in sending up this prayer to Heaven, 'God bless king Charles! long live 'king Charles!' So as our English air is not susceptible of any other sound, and echoes out nothing else; our bells, bonfires, peals of ordnance, vollies of shot, the shouts and acclamations of the people, bear no other moral, have no other signification but to triumph, in the triumphs of our king in the hearts of his people.—Your majesty cannot imagine nor can any man conceive it but he who was present to see and hear it, with what joy, what chearfulness, what lettings out of the soul, what expressions of transported minds, a stupendous concourse of people attended the Proclaiming of your majesty, in your cities of London and Westminster, to be our most potent, mighty, and undoubted king: the oldest man living never saw the like before, nor is it probable, scarce possible, that he who hath longest to live will ever see the like again, especially (and God forbid he should) upon such an occasion, for we wish and heartily pray that your majesty may be the last of men of the generation now in being, who shall leave his place to a successor.—We have here the Proclamation itself to present unto your majesty and the Order of the two houses enjoining it to be proclaimed throughout England, Ireland, and your dominions of Wales; and, likewise, their Orders for all Ministers in their public Prayers to pray for your majesty, and for the illustrious Prince the duke of York your majesty's brother, and for the rest of the royal progeny; and another Order of theirs for taking down every where the assumed Arms of the late pretended Commonwealth, and setting up the arms of your majesty in their stead."—[Here he tendered the Proclamation and the several Orders unto his majesty, offered to read them, but then said, he thought that his majesty had already received them from the Lords, and that, therefore, it would be but a trouble to his majesty to hear them again. To which his majesty answering, that he had received them, was pleased further to enlarge himself in some discourse to this effect; expressing his sense of the miseries which his people had suffered under those unlawful governors which had ruled over them, and of his gladness for their returning unto him, with those good affections, which they now shewed towards him; adding, that he had always made it his study, and ever would, to make them as happy as himself; which was the sum and substance of what his majesty said.—To which was replied, with humble thanks for those gracious expressions,*] "That his majesty would ever find both parliament and people to be full of loyalty and obedience unto his majesty; as his majesty was of grace and goodness towards them." [And then he went on with his Speech relating to those Orders and Proceedings of parliament; and said,] "These are some testimonies of their love and affection unto your majesty, such as can as yet be expressed by them, which are but as a picture in little, of a great and large

* "The King was at this time thirty years of age, and, as might have been supposed, past the levities of youth and the extravagance of pleasure. He had a very good understanding. He knew well the affairs of state both at home and abroad. He had a softness of temper that charmed all who came near him, till they found how little they could depend on good looks, kind words, and fair promises; in which he was liberal to excess, because he intended nothing by them but to get rid of importunities and to silence all farther pressing upon him. He seemed to have no sense of Religion: both at prayers and sacrament he, as it were, took care to satisfy people, that he was in no sort concerned in that about which he was employed. So that he was very far from being an hypocrite, unless his assisting at those performances was a sort of hypocrisy, (as no doubt it was:) but he was sure not to encrease that by any the least appearance of Religion. He said once to myself, he was no atheist, but he could not think God would make a man miserable only for taking a little pleasure out of the way. He said often, he thought government was a much safer and easier thing where the authority was believed infallible, and the faith and submission of the people was implicit: about which I had once much discourse with him. He was affable and easy, and loved to be made so by all about him. The great art of keeping him long, was the being easy, and the making every thing easy to him. He had made such observations on the French government, that he thought a king who might be checked, or have his ministers called to account by a parliament, was but a king in name. He had a great compass of knowledge, though he was never capable of much application or study. He understood the mechanics and physic; and was a good chymist, and much set on several preparations of mercury, chiefly the fixing it. He understood navigation well; but, above all, he knew the architecture of ships so perfectly, that in that respect he was exact rather more than became a prince. His apprehension was quick, and his memory good. He was an everlasting talker. He told his stories with a good grace; but they came in his way too often. He hated business, and could not be easily brought to mind any: but when it was necessary, and he was set to it, he would stay as long as his ministers had work for him." Burnet, vol. 1. p. 93.

body, which far exceeds in its true and natural dimensions, the whole compass of a small piece of cloth, on which, notwithstanding, it is drawn and represented to the life.—And may it please your majesty to give us leave to say, that as the affection, so your subjects expectations of you are high, and their longings after you great and vehement. And both expectations and longings have increased by the long time that your majesty hath been kept from them.—Hope deferred makes the heart sick; and the sickness still augments till the thing hoped for be obtained.—You who are the light of their eyes, and the breath of their nostrils, their delight and all their hope, to have been so long banished from them into a strange land, it is no wonder that the news of your return should put a new life into them: what then will it be when their eyes shall be blessed with the sight of your royal person? And, therefore, are we commanded humbly to acquaint your majesty with the earnest desire of both houses for your speedy return unto your parliament, and the exercise of your Kingly Office; and that, in order to it, they have given directions to general Montagu, one of the generals at sea, and to the other officers at sea, to observe such commands, as your majesty shall please to give them for the disposal of the Fleet: and we have it in our Instructions further to beseech your majesty to let your parliament know when, and where, your majesty purposeth to take shipping, and where to land; and after your coming on shore, whether to come all the way to London by Land, or by water from Gravesend; and which of your houses your majesty intends to make use of at your coming to London; that, accordingly, provision may be made for your majesty's reception: for then, and, not till then, will be the completing of your subjects rejoicing.—True it is (as your majesty was pleased just now to touch upon it) that, in your absence, other lords have had dominion over them, have reigned and ruled over their bodies, and estates; but their better part, their hearts and minds and souls were free, and did abhor such rulers, and still continued faithful and loyal to your majesty, their rightful lord and sovereign; and with you, and under you, they now expect to re-enter into the possession of their antient Rights and Privileges, to enjoy again their laws, and liberties: and, which is above all, their religion in purity, and truth; of all which those lords (who called themselves so, and made themselves so, that is, to be so called, but in truth were not so, for they were nothing less) those kind of lords, I say, had so long deprived them. This is our expectation from your majesty, and we are more than confident, we shall not be deceived in it, but that your majesty will answer and go beyond all that can be expected from you: a king of so many vows, and of so many prayers, cannot but crown the desires of his people.—Sir, to tell you what men think, and say, and wish, and even are assured of in relation to your majesty and the happiness which your government will produce, would seem a description of the Golden Age, that poets fancy. Truly we dare not undertake it, in your majesty's presence, lest we should be thought to flatter, and should offend the sacred modesty of your ears, and of your princely mind. Though it would all be but a real truth; yet looking like that, which you do not like, we fear you would dislike it for the look's sake; great princes will not be flattered, but really and truly served, and we desire to serve your majesty in your own way.—Your majesty hath been pleased to declare your royal intentions unto your parliament, in your gracious Letters to either house, and the two houses have severally given unto your majesty a faithful account of that grateful sense, wherewith they have received them, and of their humble submission unto and compliance with, all your majesty's desires, which by their Letters, in answer unto your majesty's, they make bold to signify. That from the house of peers hath been already presented, and we who are before your majesty, are intrusted by the house of commons with the delivery of theirs; an honour not more conferred upon us beyond our deservings, than embraced and received by us, with an excess of joy, and with all due respect, which is the errand upon which we are now come. That Letter and the Proclamation and the several Orders, together with ourselves, our lives and fortunes, and the vows and services of those who sent us, we do with all humbleness lay at your majesty's feet, lifting up our hearts and hands to the God of heaven, for your majesty's long and happy reign over us, and speedy return unto us."

This day, the commons voted the sum of 5000*l.* for the duke of York, and the same sum to the duke of Gloucester, for their present supply and accommodation; but afterwards, that of the duke of York's was made 10,000*l.*

Necessaries to be provided for the King's Household.] Mr. Annesley reported, from the Committee appointed to consider of the Manner of the King's Return and Reception, and of Preparations requisite to those ends, three Lists of Things necessary to be provided for his majesty's Service, viz.

I. Things necessary to be provided for his Majesty's Service, and his Brothers, the Dukes of York and Gloucester.

"A rich Bed, to be of velvet, either embroidered with gold or laced, and lined with cloth of silver or sattin, as shall be best approved of; with a high chair of state, two high stools, one foot-stool, and two cushions, all suitable to the bed. Two great quilts or mattresses of sattin, suitable to the lining of the bed. Two thick fustian quilts, to lie under the sattin quilts; one down bolster, one pair of fustian blankets, and one pair of Spanish blankets. One close-stool suitable to the bed. Six pair of Holland sheets, having 24 ells of Holland in a pair, at 10, 11, or 12*s.* the ell. Two beds more for the king's majesty, to be removing beds, either of scarlet cloth or of velvet, all lined with sattin; and all necessaries to each bed as to the former bed, except sheets. And for the present, two beds, of the like goodness, to be made for the duke of York and the duke of Gloucester, with all particulars as the others, and 6 pair of sheets for each of the duke's beds. For the present 20 large pallet beds, with bolsters, 20 large tapestry counterpains, 20 pair of good large blankets, 40 pair of good Holland sheets, of 18 ells in each pair, being of Holland of 3*s.* 6*d.* per ell for those beds. 20 good double yellow ground carpets, of Turkey making, and 6 hides, 6 cart canvasses. There must be provided also tenter-hooks, hammers, tacks, and such like necessaries for the wardrobe. For Table Linen for his majesty, 12 damask table-cloths for his majesty's own table, as many towels, and 6 napkins for every table cloth. The like for each duke, if they eat asunder; but if they eat together, half the proportion. For other diets for the great lords, though table linen was allowed them, yet they used their own linen. Inferior diets had Holland or flaxen table-cloths, but no napkins.—A rich Coach also, the inside crimson velvet, richly laced and fringed; Liveries for two coachmen and two postillions suitable. The footmen should have liveries and coats suitable.

II. A Particular of what is at present necessary to be provided for his Majesty's Service, humbly offered to the consideration of this Honourable Board.

"Two Coaches, the one for travelling, the other to be a rich one. Two sets of coach horses. Liveries for 2 coachmen, 2 postillions, 6 grooms, and 10 footmen. Two rich saddles for the great horse: 6 pad-saddles: 4 sumpter-horses and cloaths to them. 2 horses for the great saddle. Provisions of all sorts to be laid into the Mews against his majesty's coming.

III. "A Memorial of Flags, &c. for the Fleet.

Naseby,
- A Standard, - - - - } Silk,
- A Jack, - - - - - } Silk,
- An Ensign - - - - - } Silk,
- A Suit of Pendants - - } Silk,
- Waist Clothes, Scarlet.
- A rich Barge, of the same Dimension as this we have, of 33 feet, with a Standard.

Vice-Admiral. Rear-Admiral.
- Flags, - - - - } Silk.
- Jacks, - - - - } Silk.
- Ensigns, - - - } Silk.
- A Suit of good Kersey Waist Clothes.

In most of the Frigates there will need the king's Arms, either carved or in painted cloth. Carvers, painters, and a glazier, for every flag ship will be necessary. The general's cabbin to be new glazed with square glass. Wardrobe men and upholsterers to be brought down. Mr. Kennersley will be very useful to confer with about what is necessary herein. Beal's Galley, and a Standard. Beale and Simpson, and a choice noise of trumpets. Singleton's Music."

Resolved, That this house doth agree with the Committee, that the Particulars, contained in the three Lists now presented, be forthwith provided and furnished for the Service and Accommodation of his majesty. Ordered, That it be referred to the Council of State, to cause the same to be provided and furnished accordingly; and that they are impowered to charge any part of the public revenue, for raising of monies to pay for the same.*

An Act of General Pardon, Indemnity, and Oblivion, was this day read a 2nd time in the house, and some Votes in the Journal of Dec. 12, 1650, concerning the Trial of the late king, were also read, as also a record, intituled, 'A 'Journal of the Proceedings of the High 'Court of Justice, erected by an Act of the 'Commons of England, for the trying and 'judging of Charles Stuart, King of England,' was read. After which, divers members of the house, then present, who were named commissioners in the said Act, stood up in their places; and did severally express how far they were concerned in the said proceedings, and their sense thereupon.

Mr. Lenthall severely reprimanded by the Speaker.] One Mr. Lenthall, a member of the house, happening to speak in the debate on the Bill of Indemnity, said, 'He that drew his sword against the King committed as high an offence as he that cut off the King's Head.' Exception was taken at these words, and Mr. Lenthall was ordered to the bar; when the Speaker, by order of the house, gave him the following Reprimand: "Mr. Lenthall, The house hath taken very great offence at some words you have let fall, upon debate of this business of the Bill of Indemnity; which, in the judgment of this house, hath as high a reflection on the justice and proceedings of the lords and commons, in the last parliament, in their actings before 1648, as could be expressed. They apprehend there is much of poison in the words, and that they were spoken out of design to set this house on fire; they tending to render them that drew the sword to bring delinquents to condign punishment, and to vindicate their just liberties, into balance with them that cut

* The celebrated Andrew Marvell, who was a member of the Convention Parliament, alludes to these resolutions in the following lines:

"Of a tall stature, and of sable hue,
Much like the son of Kish, that lofty Jew;
Twelve years compleat he suffer'd in exile,
And kept his father's asses all the while.
At length, by wonderful impulse of fate,
The people call him home to help the state:
And what is more, they send him money too,
And cloath him all, from head to foot, anew:
Nor did he such small favours then disdain,
Who in his thirtieth year began his reign:"

Marvell's Works, vol. iii. p. 330.

off the king's head; of which act they express their abhorrence and detestation, appealing to God, and their conscience bearing them witness, that they had no thoughts against his person, much less against his life. Therefore I am commanded to let you know, That had these words fallen out at any other time but in this parliament, or at any time in this parliament but when they had considerations of mercy, pardon, and indemnity, you might have expected a sharper and severer sentence than I am now to pronounce: but the disposition of his majesty is to mercy; he hath invited his people to accept it, and it is the disposition of the body of this house to be healers of breaches, and to hold forth mercy to men of all conditions, so far as may stand with justice, and the justification of themselves before God and man. I am therefore commanded to let you know, that that being their disposition, and the present subject of this day's debate being mercy, you shall therefore taste of mercy; yet I am to give you a sharp reprehension; and I do as sharply and severely as I can (for so I am commanded) reprehend you for it."

May 14. The house of commons began at this time to question the Regicides, and an Order was made, That all those persons, who sat in Judgment upon the late King's majesty, when the Sentence was pronounced for his condemnation, should be forthwith secured: also that Mr. John Cooke, Andrew Broughton, John Phelpes, and Edward Dendy; those two persons who were employed for the Execution of his majesty, and one Matthew, who boasted that he was an instrument in the said Execution, and had a reward of 300*l.* for it: likewise Cornet Joice,* who seized upon the person of his late majesty at Holmby, should be all secured.—A List of the Names of those who sat in Judgment on the late King, was ordered to be delivered to the serjeant at arms attending this house; and all officers both civil and military, were required to be assistants to the serjeant, or his deputies, in securing those persons, or such others as are named above. The house being informed that Mr. John Cooke was in custody in Ireland, they ordered him to be sent over hither with all speed.—Resolved, on the question, That the number of seven, of those who sat in the Judgment, when Sentence was given upon the late King, shall be excepted, for life and estate, out of the Act for General Pardon and Oblivion.—The commons ordered secretary Thurloe to be secured by the serjeant at arms, on a charge of High Treason exhibited against him; and appointed a committee to take his Examination that afternoon.

Ordered, "That sir Henry Mildmay, Mr. Cornelius Holland, and Mr. Nicholas Love, do attend the Committee for the King's Reception; to give an account what was become of the crowns, robes, sceptres, and jewels, belonging to his majesty; and that such other robes, or sceptres, as have been provided at the public charge, be forthwith brought to the said committee, by such persons as have them in their custody." It is probable these Regalia were not easily found: for the commons, this day, appointed Thomas Langhorn, citizen and skinner, of London, to provide new Robes of Ermines for his majesty; and alderman Vyner to provide a crown and sceptre, the estimate of which amounted to about 900*l.* To which the lords also agreed.

The commons next resumed the debate upon the Bill for a General Pardon, Indemnity, and Oblivion: and, after some time spent therein, it was resolved, "That John Bradshaw, deceased, late serjeant at law, Oliver Cromwell, deceased, Henry Ireton, deceased, and Thomas Pride, deceased, be some of those who shall be attainted, by act of parliament, for the Murder of the late king's majesty: and that their attainders shall take place from the 1st of Jan. 1648."

The late King's Statue, now at Charing Cross, discovered.] May 16. The lords were informed, that the earl of Portland had lately discovered where a Brass Horse, with his late majesty's Figure upon it, was hid; which, in justice, the earl supposes belongs to him; and there being no courts of justice now open, wherein he can sue for it, doth humbly desire the lords to order it to be removed from the place where it now is; not defaced nor otherways disposed of, till the title be determined at law to whom it belongs. The lords ordered accordingly. This was the famous Statue since set up at Charing-Cross.

Expence of the King's Reception.] The earl of Dorset reported, from the committee for the King's Reception, that yesterday they had before them several of the king's servants, who gave in these Estimates following, viz.

	£.	s.	d.
For necessaries for the King's present Reception, as silver plates of several sorts and sizes	2,200	0	0
For Table Linen of all sorts -	300	0	0
For a Week's Diet at 53*l.* per diem - - - - - - - - -	350	0	0
For Coaches and Stables - -	2,950	0	0
For furnishing his Majesty's Bed-Chamber, &c. - - -	1,801	19	0
For repairing the Mews - -	1,000	0	0
Repair of Whitehall, St. James's and Somerset-House, estimated at - - - - - - -	5,000	0	0
The Crown and Sceptre, besides Robes - - - - -	900	0	0
	£.14,501	19	0

This Report was confirmed by the House.

An Order was made by the commons, that James Northfolk, esq. serjeant at arms, should forthwith seize upon, and secure, all the goods, &c. late belonging to John Bradshaw, serjeant at law, wherever he can find them: and that, in case of resistance, he be impowered to break

* See vol. iii. p. 589.

open any doors and locks for the more effectual execution of this service. Also, that the Records, Books, Papers, and other writings, relating to the public, in the hands of Mr. John Phelpes, be forthwith secured by Mr. Prynne and col. Bowyer, members of this house, and such as have been removed and secured, in whose hands soever they may be found. An Order was made likewise, That all the Books and Papers belonging to the Library of the abp. of Canterbury, and now, or lately, in the hands of Hugh Peters, be forthwith secured.

Charge on the Revenue by the Council of State.] Mr. Annesley, lord president of the Council of State, reported, from them, a Particular of the Sums of Money charged by Order and Warrants of the Council of State upon the several Treasuries therein named, from Feb. 25th, 1659, to May 15th, 1660, which was as follows:

A PARTICULAR of the Sums of Money, charged by Orders and Warrants from the Council of State, upon the several Treasuries after-named, from Feb. 25, 1659, to May 15, 1660, viz.

Charged on the Receipt of the public Exchequer.

	l.	s.	d.
For his excellency the lord-General Monk, on an Act of the late Parliament, of which there is yet unpaid 4,856*l.*	20,000	0	0
For Dunkirk Garrison -	19,006	8	10
For Savoy and Ely-House Hospitals - - - - - - - - -	2,000	0	0
For the Council's Contingencies - - - - - - - - -	8,400	0	0
For Mr. Martin Noell, to enable him to strike a tally, for so much paid by him, on Orders of the former Council of State, to Gen. Montagu, and for the Commissioners Plenipotentiaries of this Commonwealth at the Sound - - - - - - - - -	7,252	6	2
For Alderman Tho. Vynes and Ald. Christ. Packe, treasurers for the Collection-Money for Piedmont and Poland, for so much ordered from them by the late parliament, into the Exchequer, none of which is paid -	7,978	8	9
And for so much deposited in the Exchequer, of clipp'd Brass Money, part of the said Collection-Money - - - - - - -	475	19	10
For the earl and countess of Nottingham, on Pensions from his late majesty, and confirmed by Parliament, viz.			
To the said earl, all unpaid -	300	0	0
To the said countess, all unpaid - - - - - - - - -	200	0	0
For the Gentleman Porter, Warders, and Gunners at the Tower, for two quarters ended March 25, 1660, no part paid -	1,160	4	4½
For Christ. Piercehay, esq. Receiver-General for Yorkshire, to enable him to strike a tally for so much paid by him out of his receipt, on Order of the late Council, to col. Sam. Clarke, for pay of his Regiment on their march to Scotland -	1,500	0	0
	68,273	7	11½
Of which sum there is paid but - - - - - - -	34,386	13	3½
So there is unpaid thereof	33,886	14	8½
And of what was paid, there came into the Council's Contingencies no more than - - -	3,000	0	0

Charged on the Council's Contingencies.

	l.	s.	d.
By Warrant on Mr. Wm. Jessop, on the 1,000*l.* by him received at the Receipt of Exchequer - - - - - - - - - -	1,000	0	0

Charged on Mr. Tho. Parry, Treasurer of the Council's Contingencies.

	l.	s.	d.
For several public Services	1,427	14	10
For Salaries and Disbursements to Officers in arrear - -	1,901	17	3
To several persons, on account for Repairs - - - -	710	0	0
To the Officers of the late Parliament, on their orders -	1,438	15	0
To the officers of the present Council - - - - - - -	1,132	0	4
For Dunkirk - - - -	1,650	10	3
For Bills of Exchange from public Ministers abroad - -	1,700	0	0
For Repair of Garrisons - -	800	0	0
For Relief, To lady Inchequin, not paid	20	0	0
To Ann Hopkins, not paid	10	0	0
For the Army, To col. Stretter, to pay off Gunners, &c. not pd	60	0	0
To lt. col. Peppar, for Fire and Candle at Bury St. Edmond's -	5	13	3
By Order of the present Parliament, To sir J. Grenville, by so much borrow'd of Mr. Forth - - -	500	0	0
To gen. Edw. Montagu, not paid - - - -	500	0	0
So the Total charged on the Council's Contingencies is, - - - - - - -	12,065	10	11

	l.	s.	d.
By Warrants charged on Mr. Jessop - - - - - - - - -	1,000	0	0
On Mr. Parry	11,865	0	0
	12,865	0	0

	£.	s.	d.
Whereof paid by Mr. Jessop, being the whole received by him - - - - - -	1,000	0	0
By Mr Parry, part of 2,000*l.* by him received, with the 500*l.* advanced by Mr. Forth - - - - - -	2,460	13	3
Total paid is - - - - - -	3,460	13	3
So rests unpaid - - - -	9,404	6	9

Charged on the Committee for the Army.

For the Forces in England -	8,938	4	6
For the Forces in Scotland	13,329	8	0
For the Forces in, and belonging to, Ireland - - -	23,350	0	0
For transporting 70 Recruits to Dunkirk - - - - - -	40	0	0
	45,657	12	6

Charged on the Almoner, Dr. Barnard.

For lady Inchequin, not paid	100	0	0
For Inhabitants of Dover, for quartering sick and wounded Soldiers sent from Dunkirk, not paid	300	0	0
For Mr. Sam. Hartlib, in part of his arrears of what was allowed him by the State, not paid -	200	0	0
	600	0	0

Charged on the Treasury of the Navy.

For gen. Montagu, advanced on his going to sea - - - -	500	0	0
For gen. Penn, for a special service - - - - - - - - -	100	0	0
Charged on the Treasurers for the Piedmont Collection-Money	156	0	0
Charged on the Revenue in Scotland, &c. - - - - - - -	4,500	0	0
Charged on the Prize-Office	45	0	0
Charged on Sherwood-Forest	20	0	0
	5,321	0	0

Pensions charged by Order of the Council of State.

On the Exchequer, per Week	17	5	0
On the Council's Contingencies, per week - - - - - -	10	0	0

The house approved of this Account, in all its particulars; and ordered, That the Monies charged by the respective Warrants be paid accordingly: and the Thanks of the house were ordered also to be returned by the Speaker to the Council, for their great and careful service.

List of the Navy of England at this time.] A List of such of his majesty's Ships of the Navy-Royal, now in pay, and not of the Summer's Guard; with an Account of the Wages due to them to the 1st of May 1660, and the Charge they are at, was read as followeth:

Rates.	Ships.	Men.	Guns.	Wages due to May 1 £.	s.	d.
3.	Lamport - - -	210	50	8,854	1	9
	Torrington - -	210	52	9,286	3	9
4.	Kentish - - -	150	40	3,025	6	0
	Maidstone - -	140	40	6,386	14	3
	Centurion - -	150	40	4,432	8	8
	Dover - - -	140	40	5,206	11	9
	Hampshire - -	130	38	2,163	14	3
	Nampwich - -	140	40	4,430	14	3
	Preston - - -	140	40	3,785	14	3
	Portland - - -	156	40	6,578	11	9
	Taunton - - -	140	40	5,220	0	3
	Dragon - - -	130	38	4,370	6	0
	Elias - - - -	110	36	5,175	4	8
	Success - - -	100	34	3,310	10	3
	President - -	130	38	3,167	3	0
	Const. Warwick	115	32	2,619	10	3
	Tyger - - - -	130	38	5,147	7	6
	Marmaduke - -	110	32	2,629	18	6
5.	Sorlings - - -	100	22	5,811	18	0
	Forester - - -	100	22	2,787	7	2
	Coventry - -	90	20	3,579	8	10
	Convert - - -	90	26	4,604	19	0
	Hector - - -	85	20	2,480	12	0
	Greyhound - -	85	20	3,512	3	9
	Lizard - - -	60	16	1,619	0	0
6.	Weymouth - -	60	14	1,415	10	0
	Wolfo - - -	60	16	3,452	15	0
	Francis - - -	45	10	1,007	6	4
	Cygnet - - -	35	6	840	14	0
	Lilly - - - -	35	6	833	2	6
	Roe - - - -	35	8	1,545	19	6
	Hunter - - -	30	6	881	7	6
6.	Griffin - - -	40	12	1,693	11	8
	Chesnut - - -	40	10	1,440	14	0
	Cagway - - -	35	8	648	9	8
	Pearl - - - -	25	4	1,985	9	9
	Dolphin - - -	25	4	620	17	3
	Truelove } Henrietta } - -	60	12	1,179	17	6
	Hart - - - -	35	8	1,260	19	6
Ships 40—Men 3681—Wages				128,982	4	0

Mem. The Charge of these 40 Ships, which are unnecessarily kept abroad, will for every month they continue unpaid, amount to 11,085*l.*

May 17. The lords heard a Report, from their Committee of Privileges, by the lord Roberts, That it was their opinion, that when a Message is brought from the commons, the Speaker of this house is to go to the bar alone, and receive the Message; the rest of the lords sitting in their places; which the house approved of, and ordered it to be added to the Roll of the Orders of this house.

The Commons ordered, That all the Titles of Honour received from the late Protectors, Oliver and Richard, or from Henry Cromwell, son of the said Oliver, by any person named a commissioner in the Ordinance for 3 months Assessment, be omitted and struck out of the said Ordinance.

Proceedings against the late King's Judges.] May 18. A Message was brought from the commons, by Mr. Prynne and others, with several Votes, whereunto he desired their lordships concurrence, viz. "Resolved, upon the question, by the and commons assembled in parliament, That all the persons who sat in Judgment upon the late King's majesty, when Sentence of Death was pronounced against him, and the estates, both real and personal, of all and every the said persons (whether in their own hands, or any other in trust for their or any of their uses) who are fled, be forthwith seized and secured, and the respective sheriffs and other officers whom this may concern are to take effectual order accordingly.—2. That nothing in the Orders touching the seizing of the persons or estates of those who sat in Judgment upon the late King, do in anywise extend to colonel Matthew Tomlinson or his estate.—3. That the Council of State do forthwith take Order for stopping of all the ports, to the end that none of those who are ordered to be apprehended, as having sat in Judgment upon the late king's majesty, may make his escape beyond the seas.—4. That these Votes, with a List of the Names of those who are to be secured, be sent up to the lords and their concurrence desired, viz.

John Bradshaw, serj. at law, president of the pretended High Court of Justice.	John Okey, John Hewson, William Goff, Cornelius Holland,
John Lisle,	John Carew,
William Say,	John Jones,
Oliver Cromwell,	Miles Corbet,
Colonel Henry Ireton,	Francis Allen,
Sir Hardress Waller,	Peregrine Pelham,
Valentine Wauton,	John Moore,
Thomas Harrison,	John Alured,
Edward Whaley,	Henry Smyth,
Thomas Pride,	Humphrey Edwards,
Isaac Ewer,	Gregory Clements,
Lord Grey, of Grooby,	Thomas Wogan,
Sir John Danvers,	Sir Gregory Norton,
Sir Tho. Maleverer,	Edmund Harvey,
Sir John Bourchier,	John Penn,
Wm. Heveningham,	Thomas Scott,
Alderm. Pennington,	Thomas Andrews,
Wm. Purefoy,	William Cawley,
Henry Marten,	Anthony Stapley,
John Barkstead,	John Downes,
Matthew Tomlinson,	Thomas Horton,
John Blakiston,	Thomas Hammond,
Gilbert Millington,	Augustin Garland,
Sir Wm. Constable,	George Fleetwood,
Edmund Ludlow,	James Temple,
John Hutchinson,	Daniel Blagrave,
Sir Michael Livesay,	Thomas Wayte,
Robert Tichborne,	Nicholas Love,
Owen Rowe,	Vincent Potter,
Robert Lilburne,	John Dixwell,
Adrian Scrope,	Simon Mayne,
Richard Deane,	Peter Temple."

The earl of Lincoln, visc. Say and Sele, and lord Roberts being appointed by the house to consider of the said Votes, with the List of the Names, they went out of the house presently to consider of the same.—Lord Roberts reported, That the committee thought fit, instead of the first Vote, to have this Order following to be made, viz. "Upon complaint made this day, by the commons in parliament assembled, That all these persons, viz. John Bradshaw, John Lisle, and the rest, (except Matthew Tomlinson) who sat in Judgment upon the late King's majesty when Sentence of Death was pronounced against him; and the estates, both real and personal, of all and every the said persons (whether in their own hands, or in the hands of any in trust for their or any of their uses) who are fled, be forthwith seized and secured; and the respective sheriffs and other officers whom this may concern, are to take effectual order accordingly."

The house, after some consideration of the said Report, consented unto the Order accordingly; and ordered, that the same, with the List aforesaid, shall be printed and published. And touching the rest of the said matters in the Votes, the lords sent a Message to the commons for a conference to be had with them the next morning in the Painted-Chamber.

May 19. This day the said conference was held between the two houses, when the earl of Manchester, deputed by the lords, offered the following Reasons: He was to let the commons know, "That their lordships do not agree to these Votes as they were brought up, in respect they do intrench upon the antient privileges of this house; Judicature in parliament being solely in the lords house, and the Votes brought up were such. That, notwithstanding, their lordships were so careful of the matter as they would not lose time for the manner, and therefore have issued out an Order of their own for doing that which was desired; in which Order colonel Tomlinson is omitted, according to the desire of the commons. That the 3rd Vote relates to a Council of State, which the lords conceive not in being, and therefore have resolved that such emergencies as shall necessarily arise during his majesty's absence, and until his pleasure be further known, for his majesty's service and the peace of the kingdom, shall be transacted henceforth by the committee of lords and commons appointed for the Reception of his majesty, wherein their lordships desire the concurrence of the commons."

The commons, in a grand committee, went upon Ways and Means for the speedy raising of a considerable sum of money, for the satisfaction of the Arrears due to the Army and Navy; and came to a Resolution, That a Poll-Bill should be brought in for raising 400,000*l.* for that purpose.

May 21. The commons heard the Report of the late conference with the lords, concerning their Votes for securing the persons and estates of the King's Judges; and appointed a committee to peruse their own Journal-Books, state the matter of fact upon the whole, and prepare Heads for a free conference with the lords about it. They also ordered that all the ports should be stopped, and that none of those persons should make their escape beyond the seas: and that no money or bullion be exported without the approbation of parliament.

May 22. Another Conference was held between the two houses, on the subject of the last, and of which we find this Entry in the Lords Journals. The earl of Manchester reported the effect of the free Conference this morning, which his lordship said was managed by Mr. Annesley; who said, The commons had an earnest desire to continue a fair correspondency between both the houses; and they were sensible what distempers have been for many years past; and they desired that all breaches might be healed; that this conference was to preserve a good understanding. The commons said, "That they had seen a printed Paper, which was printed and published from their lordships, without their concurrence or a conference, or taking notice of it: the Paper is dated the 18th instant, which mentions, That, upon complaint made by the commons in parliament, it is ordered, by the lords in parliament, That divers persons should be secured, who sat in Judgment upon the late King's majesty, when Sentence of Death was pronounced; which Order leaves them out, contrary to their Resolution, as they presented it to this house for concurrence. The commons take notice that there was no Complaint in this case made by the commons, nor is there any Entry thereof in their Journals. If there had been a Complaint preceding, the lords could not have proceeded as they have, in a judicial way, without consent of the commons. —As this case is, the point of Judicature is not in question. 1. The Order sent by the commons to the lords for their concurrence, is not in a judicial, but in an extraordinary way, and for a notorious and transcendent crime. 2. The law allowed no such proceedings regularly before conviction. 3. This was in order only to bring them to a judicial proceeding. 4. The lords sent several Orders to the commons in the cases of sales, securing rents, and hindering of cutting or selling of wood or timber; wherein the commons concurred, and this before the parties heard: and this is a case of members of the lords house, all being assented unto as cases of extremity.—The commons say they cannot admit the lords Judicature so largely as they assert it; but judicature, as aforesaid, not being in question, they decline this dispute. They conceive the lords intrench upon the commons privileges; for col. Hutchinson, a member of the commons, could not be under such an Order of the lords, upon any account, unless the commons Order had been consented to. By this way, if allowed, the lords may vary from any Orders sent up by the commons, without a conference, and ground their variation upon pretended Complaint of the commons when there is none. The printing of the lords Order before the conference with the commons, or their assent, is a further intrenching upon the privilege of the commons.'"

Hereupon the lords appointed a committee to consider what Answer is fit to be returned to the commons, upon the matter of this free conference, whereby a good correspondency may be kept between the houses, and the privileges of this house preserved.

Several peers had leave given them to attend the King on his Landing; the same leave was given to general Monk by the commons, and to such other members of that house as he should desire to accompany him.

Letter from the Committee of Lords sent to the King.] May 23. The following Letter from the lords who were sent by their house to his majesty, was read:

For the right hon. the earl of MANCHESTER, Speaker of the House of Peers,

"My lord; We have delivered the Letters and Message intrusted to us by the house of peers, and found a most gracious reception from his majesty, who is pleased to declare (which we desire your lordships to communicate to the house) that he intends to depart from hence on Monday next, being the 21st of this month, to land at Dover; and, after a short stay at Canterbury, to continue his journey to London, and there to reside with his Court at Whitehall. This we are commanded to impart to your lordships from his majesty, and remain, Your, &c. Oxford, Middlesex, visc. Hertford, Berkley, Brook."

Another Letter was sent, of the same date, to the house of commons, from their members sent to the King, but it is not entered in their Journals.

Another Letter from the Speaker of the House of Lords to the King.] May 25. Both houses agreed to send congratulatory Letters to their committees with the King, to deliver to his majesty on his landing in England; which he was now very near doing, as the reader will find by a subsequent Letter from admiral Montagu to the lords. The Letter from the house of commons to the King is only mentioned in their Journals, as reported and approved of by that house, but not entered: that from the lords ran in these words:

"To the KING's Most Excellent Majesty;

"May it please your Majesty; The sense your faithful subjects the peers, now assembled, have of your majesty's safe arrival into this your realm of England is so great, as obligeth them, by all dutiful acknowledgments, to express the same by these lines, before they have the honour and happiness to do it personally to your majesty; which they intend to perform so soon as they shall receive signification of your majesty's pleasure when, where, and in what manner they shall wait upon you. And, as your faithful council, do humbly offer to your majesty's deliberation so to consult the safety of your royal person, wherein they are highly concerned, that, in your return to London, the security thereof be preferred to all external considerations; which, out of our zeal to your majesty, is humbly offered by, Your majesty's most humble, faithful, and obedient Subjects and Servants. Signed in the Names, and by the command, of the said House of

Peers, by E. MANCHESTER, Speaker pro tempore. Westminster, May 25, 1660."

The Letter from general Montagu was as follows:

"To the right hon. the SPEAKER of the House of Peers.

"About ten leagues from Scheveling, May 23, 1660.

"My lord; Having appointed a rendezvous of as many ships as could be got together in the Bay of Scheveling, that I might the better receive his majesty's commands, in order to his happy return to England, it pleased his most gracious majesty, this day about noon, to embark himself in the Nazeby, riding before Scheveling. Their royal highnesses the dukes of York and Gloucester, the princess royal, queen of Bohemia, and the prince of Orange, accompanied his majesty on board; and, about 3 hours after, the duke of York embarking in the London, the duke of Gloucester in the Swiftsure, the princess royal, the queen of Bohemia, and prince of Orange, returned to Scheveling; and the fleet set sail, by his majesty's command, bound for the port of Dover, whither I trust God will give us a speedy and prosperous passage. I apprehend it my duty to give your lordships the soonest advertisement thereof I could, and so remain, Your, &c.

"E. MONTAGU."

The commons read a 2nd time, and committed, a Bill for taking away the Court of Wards and Liveries, and all Tenures in capite, or by Knights Service; and, on the question, resolved, "That the sum of 100,000*l.* a-year be settled on the king's majesty, in lieu of the said Court and Tenures."

The King's Letter to the Lords after landing.] May 28. The Speaker of the house of lords acquainted their lordships with a Letter he had received by the hands of Mr. Berkeley; which, being opened, appeared to be a Letter from the King, and was read as follows:

"To our Trusty and right Well-beloved the SPEAKER of our House of Peers, to be communicated to the Lords there assembled;

"C. R. Right Trusty and intirely-beloved cousins, right trusty and right well-beloved cousins, and right trusty and well-beloved, we greet you well: After we had received your invitation, we made all possible expedition to embark, and return to our native kingdom. It hath pleased God to bring us safe to land, and we hope that peace and happiness shall be brought to our kingdoms with us. We know our own heart to have nothing but affection to the good of all our people; and we cannot doubt of God's blessing on our councils and endeavours, for the advancing the honour and happiness of our kingdoms. We cannot distrust but that you will answer the professions you have made of your loyalty and affection to our service; and, you may be sure, that we will be deficient in nothing that becomes a gracious prince to his faithful subjects. We hope shortly to see you, and do intend to set forward from hence on Monday next, and we hope to arrive at London on Tuesday in the afternoon, and will then give you timely notice where, and when, to attend us; and, in the mean time, we bid you heartily farewell. Given at our Court at Canterbury, this 26th day of May, 1660, in the 12th year of our reign."

After the foregoing Letter was read, the lord Berkley, one of the Commissioners sent over to the king, acquainted the house, That he was commanded by his majesty to let their lordships know, the King intended to be the next day at Whitehall, at 12 o'clock, where he expected their lordships to attend him in a full assembly.

Another Letter, to the same purport as the last to the lords, from the King, was presented to the commons by lord Falkland, and was read by their Speaker.

The late lords commissioners of the Great Seal, according to the Order of the house, did this day bring the Great Seal, in their custody, to the clerk's table, and delivered the same to the Speaker: and a smith being sent for forthwith, he was ordered to deface and break in pieces the said Seal at the bar, the house then sitting, which was done accordingly, and the pieces thereof were delivered to the late Commissioners as their fees.

Both Houses wait upon the King at Whitehall.] May 29, p. m. The lords met for the purpose of going in the forenoon of this day from their own house, in procession, to wait upon the King at Whitehall. The earl of Manchester was appointed to speak what his lordship thought fit, to express the joy of that house for his majesty's safe return to his throne.

The commons did nothing material in the forenoon of this day, but resolve, nem. con. "That the king's majesty be pleased to give order, that the Oaths of Supremacy and Allegiance be administered according to the laws and statutes of this realm now in force."

In the afternoon they met again, read and committed a Bill for Confirmation of the Privileges of Parliament, Magna Charta, Statutum de Talagio non concedendo, the Petition of Rights, and other Acts: after which we find the following Entry in their Journals: "The King's majesty having, by Letter to this house, signified his pleasure to be at Whitehall this day, and the lord Herbert having communicated his majesty's intentions to give a meeting to this house there, the house did, after their adjournment, walk on foot from Westminster to Whitehall, divers gentlemen going before Mr. Speaker; and, after them, the clerk, and clerk-assistant of this house; and next, before Mr. Speaker, the serjeant at arms attending this house bearing his mace, (being all uncovered) the members of this house following Mr. Speaker three in a rank; and, being come to Whitehall, they went up into the Banquetting-House, and there attended his majesty's coming to Whitehall;

which being about 7 of the clock, his majesty, about half an hour after, came into the Banquetting-House, and there placed himself in his chair of state: whereupon Mr. Speaker, being before retired to the lower part of the room, and the way being clear to the chair of state, did, after his humble obeisance, walk up towards his majesty; two members of the house going, one on one hand, and another on the other hand of him, and divers other members following him, the serjeant going immediately before him, with the mace turned downwards; and, in his way, made two other obeisances to his majesty; and, coming up to his majesty, he did address himself to him, in the name of this house, by an eloquent oration, to which his majesty gave a gracious Answer: which being performed, the members of this house, then attending, kissed his majesty's hand: and, after that, his majesty retired out of the Banquetting-House; and Mr. Speaker, and the rest, thereupon departed."

Speech of the Speaker of the House of Lords to the King at Whitehall.] May 30. The two houses having congratulated his majesty on his Return to his dominions and the exercise of his kingly office, by the mouths of their distinct Speakers, they met again this day to proceed in national affairs, which were now to be carried on according to the antient government of this realm, by king, lords, and commons. The Speech the earl of Manchester, Speaker of the house of lords, till a lord chancellor, or lord keeper of the great seal could be created, made to the king, is entered in the proceedings of this day, in their Journals, as follows:

"That this day may prove happy to your majesty, is the hope, the expectation, and the earnest desire of my lords the peers, whose commands are upon me to make this humble tender to your majesty, of their loyal joy for your majesty's safe Return to your native kingdom, and for this happy Restoration of your majesty to your crown and dignity, after so long, and so severe, a suppression of your just right and title.—I shall not reflect upon your majesty's sufferings, which have been your people's miseries; yet I cannot omit to say, that as the nation in general, so the peers, with a more personal and particular sense, have felt the stroke that cut the gordian knot, which fastened your majesty to your kingdom, and your kingdom to your majesty.—For since those strange and various fluctuations and discomposures in government, since those horrid and unparalleled violations of all order and justice, strangers have ruled over us, even with a rod of iron: but now, with satisfaction of heart, we own and see your majesty, our native king, a son of the wise, a son of the antient king's, whose hand holds forth a golden scepter.—Great King! Give me leave to speak the confidence, as well as the desires, of the peers of England. Be you the powerful Defender of the true Protestant Faith; the just asserter and maintainer of the Laws and Liberties of your subjects; so shall 'judgment run down like a river, and justice 'like a mighty stream;' and God, the God of your mercy, who hath so miraculously preserved you, will establish your throne in righteousness and in peace.—Dread Sovereign! I offer no flattering titles, but speak the words of truth. You are the desire of three kingdoms, the strength and the stay of the tribes of the people, for the moderating of extremities, the reconciling of differences, the satisfying of all interests, and for the restoring of the collapsed honour of these nations. Their eyes are toward your majesty, their tongues, with loud acclamations of joy, speak the thoughts and loyal intentions of their hearts; their hands are lift up to Heaven with prayers and praises: and what oral triumph can equal this your pomp and glory?—Long may your majesty live and reign; a support to your friends, a terror to your enemies, an honour to your nation, and an example to kings of piety, justice, prudence, and power; that this prophetic expression may be verified in your majesty, 'King Charles the Second shall be greater than ever was the greatest of that name.'"

The King's Answer.] To the above speech his majesty made the following Answer:

"My lord; I am so disordered by my journey, and with the noise still sounding in my ears, (which I confess was pleasing to me, because it expressed the affections of my people) as I am unfit at the present to make such a reply as I desire; yet thus much I shall say unto you, That I take no greater satisfaction to myself in this my change, than that I find my heart really set to endeavour, by all means, for the restoring of this nation to their freedom and happiness: and I hope, by the advice of my parliament, to effect it. Of this also you may be confident, that, next to the honour of God, from whom principally I shall ever own this Restoration to my crown, I shall study the welfare of my people; and shall not only be a true Defender of the Faith, but a just asserter of the Laws and Liberties of my Subjects."

Speech of the Speaker of the House of Commons to the King at Whitehall.] The Speech of the Speaker of the House of Commons on this occasion is not entered in the Journals. It was, however, afterwards printed, as follows:

The Speech of Sir HARBOTTLE GRIMSTON, Bart. Speaker of the Honourable House of Commons, to the King's Most Excellent Majesty, delivered in the Banquetting-House, at Whitehall, May 29, 1660, the Members of that House being then present.

"Most gracious and dread Sovereign; If all the reason and eloquence that is dispersed in so many several heads and tongues as are in the whole world, were conveyed into my brain, and united in my tongue, yet I should want sufficiency to discharge that great task I am now enjoined.—The restitution of your majesty to the exercise of your just and most indubitable native right of sovereignty, and the deliverance of your people from bondage and slavery, hath been wrought out and brought to pass, by a miraculous way of Divine Providence, beyond and above the reach and comprehension of our understandings, and therefore to be admired; impossible to be expressed. —God hath been pleased to train your majesty up in the school of affliction, where you have learned that excellent lesson of patience so well, and improved it so much for the good of your people, that we have all just cause for ever to bless God for it, and we doubt not but your name is registered in the records of Heaven, to have a place in the highest form amongst those glorious martyrs of whom it is reported, that, through faith in Christ and patience in their sufferings, they converted their very tormenters, and conquered those barbarous bloody tyrants, under whom they then suffered, insomuch as they themselves were many times inforced to confess and cry out, 'Sat est vicisti Gallilæus,' they had their 'vicisti,' and that deservedly; but your majesty must have a treble vicisti, for with the same weapons, faith and patience, you have overcome and conquered the hearts and affections of all your people in three great nations, the hearts and affections of all that are worthy the name of good Christians, or reasonable men—It is God, and God alone, to whom be the glory, that hath made your majesty so great a conqueror; indeed your conquest is incomparable, no story can instance the like, or furnish us with an example to parallel it withal. It was a use and custom amongst the Romans, when any of their commanders had done eminent services abroad, at their returns, to honour them with triumphs, and riding through their streets; there they received the praises and applauses of the people, with this inscription upon their laurel crowns. 'Vincenti dabitur.' But your majesty's victory is of another nature; and as it differs much from theirs in the quality of it, so your triumph must differ as much from theirs in the manner of it. They conquered bodies, but your majesty hath conquered souls; they conquered for the honour and good of themselves, but your majesty hath conquered for the honour and good of your people; they conquered with force, but your majesty hath conquered with faith; they conquered with power, but your majesty hath conquered with patience; and therefore God himself hath written your Motto, and inscribed it upon your royal crown, 'Patienti dabitur.' Their triumphs were in narrow streets, but your majesty's triumph must be in large hearts; their triumphs lasted but for a day, but your majesty's triumph must last for all your days, and after that to triumph in Heaven to all eternity.—I have read of a duke of Burgundy, who was called Carolus Audax, the Historian tells us that his father was called Carolus Bonus: an Observator hath this Note upon it, 'That goodness doth ever produce boldness.' Sir, you are the true son of such a good father; and so long as you serve our good God, he, who is goodness itself, will give you boldness, a princely virtue, and the best foil your majesty can use, to set out the true lustre of all your other most eminent and lovely graces.—Most Royal Sovereign, I have yet a few words more, and to doubt your patience, who is the mirror of patience, were to commit a crime unpardonable and fit to be excepted out of that Act of Oblivion, which your majesty hath so graciously tendered unto your people; therefore, with an humble confidence, I shall presume to acquaint your majesty, that I have it further in command to present you, at this time, with a Petition of Right, and humbly, upon my bended knees, to beg your royal assent thereunto. Sir, it hath already passed two great houses, Heaven and Earth, and I have Vox Populi, and Vox Dei, to warrant this bold demand. It is, That your majesty would be pleased to remove your throne of state, and to set it up in the hearts of your people; and as you are deservedly the king of hearts, there to receive from your people a crown of hearts. Sir, this crown hath three excellent and rare properties, it is a sweet crown, it is a fast crown, and it is a lasting crown; it is a sweet crown, for it is perfumed with nothing but the incense of prayers and praises; it is a fast crown, for it is set upon your royal head, by him who only hath the power of hearts, the King of Kings; and it is a lasting crown, your majesty can never wear it out, for the longer you wear this crown, it will be the better for the wearing; and it is the hearty desires and most earnest prayers of all your loyal, loving, and faithful subjects, that you may never change that crown till you change it for a better, a crown of eternal glory in the highest heavens; and the Lord say Amen."

The King's Answer.] To this harangue the King returned the following Answer:

"I shall not trouble you with many words, for really I am so weary that I am scarce able to speak: But I desire you may know thus much, That whatsoever may concern the good of this people, the defence and confirmation of your Laws, and the establishment of your Religion, I shall be as ready to grant as you shall be to ask: And I shall study nothing more than to make them as happy as myself."

Account of the King's Entry into London.] Before we go on with the Proceedings of both Houses of Parliament, we shall revert a little, to give some Account of the King's Landing at Dover, and the public Entry he afterwards made into his City of London, and to that palace to which he was then so great a stranger. The Author we shall quote from is Dr. Gumble, who wrote the Life of General Monk, and who accompanied his master down to Dover, to meet and receive the King on his Landing.—"On Saturday, May 26, his majesty landed at the beach on Dover Pier, with the dukes of York and Gloucester, and many other noblemen and gentlemen: The General received him with an affection so absolutely entire and vehement, as higher could not be expressed from a prince to his subject; he embraced and kissed him. Our Author says, he had the honour to be at the General's back when this happened, and was the third person that kissed the hem of his majesty's garments after he set foot in England: That he set himself to observe his majesty's countenance on his first Landing, where he did see a mixture of other passions besides joy in his face. Certainly, adds this Author, he had the remembrance of the cruel persecutions of both his father and himself, besides the numbers of people shouting, the great guns from the ships in the road, and from the Castle, thundering with all the expressions of glory that were possible: these, with a reflection of things past not many years before might as well amaze as rejoice his royal heart."—We shall not trace this Author any further in the King's Journey from Dover* to London, where he says, "his majesty pressed to be, that he might enter his capital on May 29, the day of his birth; on which day, being got as near Blackheath, he found the Army drawn up, and there expressed their dutiful allegiance in an humble Address, offering to sacrifice their lives, or whatsoever could be more dear to them, for his service, against whatsoever opposers; and would shew their obedience better in their actions than in words. This sight did please his majesty very much, and he took a full view of them. They were as brave Troops as the world could shew, appearing to be soldiers well disciplined, and seemed to be men of one age and one mind. His majesty did like rather to have them loyal subjects, as they now protested, than (what some of them had been formerly) violent enemies. These men had bought wit at the hazard of their souls, as well as by the loss of some blood, and now resolved loyalty into their nature and principles, and, I hope,

* "The first mortification the king met with was as soon as he arrived at Canterbury, which was within three hours after he had landed at Dover; and where he found many of those who were justly looked upon, from their own sufferings or those of their fathers, and their constant adhering to the same principles, as of the king's party, who with joy waited to kiss his hand, and were received by him with those open arms and flowing expressions of grace, calling all those by their names who were known to him, that they easily assured themselves of the accomplishment of all their desires from such a generous prince. And some of them, that they might not lose the first opportunity, forced him to give them present audience, in which they reckoned up the insupportable losses undergone by themselves or their fathers, and some services of their own; and thereupon demanded the present grant or promise of such or such an office. Some, for the real small value of one though of the first classis, pressed for two or three with such confidence and importunity, and with such tedious discourses, that the king was extremely nauseated with their suits, though his modesty knew not how to break from them; that he no sooner got into his chamber, which for some hours he was not able to do, than he lamented the condition to which he found he must be subject, and did in truth from that minute contract such a prejudice against the persons of some of those, though of the greatest quality, for the indecency and incongruity of their pretences, that he never afterwards received their addresses with his usual grace or patience, and rarely granted any thing they desired, though the matter was more reasonable, and the manner of asking much more modest. But there was another mortification which immediately succeeded this, that gave him much more trouble, and in which he knew not how to comport himself. The general, after he had given all necessary orders to his troops, and sent a short dispatch to the parliament of the king's being come to Canterbury, and of his purpose to stay there two days till the next Sunday was past, he came to the king in his chamber, and in a short secret audience, and without any preamble or apology, as he was not a man of a graceful elocution, he told him "that he could not do him better service, than by recommending to him such persons, who were most grateful to the people, and in respect of their parts and interests were best able to serve him:" and thereupon gave him a large paper full of names, which the king in disorder enough received, and without reading put it into his pocket that he might not enter into any particular debate upon the persons, and told him "that he would be always ready to receive his advice, and willing to gratify him in any thing he should desire, and which would not be prejudicial to his service." The king, as soon as he could, took an opportunity when there remained no more in his chamber, to inform the chancellor of the first assaults he had encountered as soon as he alighted out of his coach, and afterwards of what the general had said to him; and thereupon took the paper out of his pocket and read it. It contained the names of at least threescore and ten persons, who were thought fittest to be made privy counsellors; in the whole number whereof, there were only two, who had ever served the king, or been looked upon as zealously affected to his service, the marquis of Hertford, and the earl of Southampton, who were both of so universal reputation and interest, and so well known to have the very particular esteem of the king, that they needed no much recommendation. All the rest were either those counsellors who had served the king, and deserted him by adhering to the parliament; or of those who had most eminently disserved him in the beginning of the rebellion, and in the carrying it on with all fierceness and animosity until the new model, and dismissing the earl of Essex: then indeed Cromwell had grown terrible to them and disposed them to wish the king were again possessed of his regal power, and which they did but wish. There were then the names of the principal persons of the Presby-

keep this resolution to this day. At St. George's Fields the lord mayor and aldermen had pitched a glorious tent, and provided a sumptuous collation, and there, upon their knees, did their duties; and the lord mayor delivered his sword, and received it again. After a short stay his majesty hastened to see Whitehall, being glutted with the ceremonies of the day. Princes need their solitudes and retirements, and certainly he must be wise to a miracle, that is never alone and always himself.—All the streets were richly adorned with tapestry, the conduits flowing with the richest wines, every window filled with numbers of spectators, and upon scaffolds built for that purpose, and all other places of conveniency. There were ranked, in good order, the Trained Band forces on the one side of the streets, and the several companies in their liveries on the other. From Temple-Bar to Whitehall the Trained Bands of Westminster and the parts adjacent on one side, and some companies of the Army on the other, to whom was joined a company of the late king's officers, commanded by sir John Stowel. This was one of the pleasantest sights that ever England beheld, to see a good prince and an obedient people striving who should exceed in love and affection. May there never be other contention between them. —The procession was led by major-general Brown, who had a troop of 300, all in cloth of silver-doublets; then followed 1200 in velvet coats, with footmen in purple liveries attending them; then another troop, in buff coats, led by sir John Robinson, with sleeves of cloth of silver, and very rich green scarfs: After

---

terian party, to which the general was thought to be most inclined, at least to satisfy the foolish and unruly inclinations of his wife. There were likewise the names of some who were most notorious in all the other factions; and of some who in respect of their mean qualities and meaner qualifications, no body could imagine how they could come to be named, except that, by the very odd mixture, any sober and wise resolutions and concurrence might be prevented.—The king was in more than ordinary confusion with the reading this paper, and knew not well what to think of the general, in whose absolute power he now was. However, he resolved in the entrance upon his government not to consent to such impositions, which might prove perpetual fetters and chains upon him ever after. He gave the paper therefore to the chancellor, and bade him "take the first opportunity to discourse the matter with the general" (whom he had not yet saluted) "or rather with Mr. Morrice his most intimate friend," whom he had newly presented to the king, and "with both whom he presumed he would shortly be acquainted," though for the present both were equally unknown to him. Shortly after, when mutual visits had passed between them, and such professions as naturally are made between persons who were like to have much to do with each other; and Mr. Morrice being in private with him, the chancellor told him "how much the king was surprised with the paper he had received from the general, which at least recommended (and which would have always great authority with him) some such persons to his trust, in whom he could not yet, till they were better known to him, repose any confidence." And thereupon he read many of their names, and said, "that if such men were made privy counsellors, it would either be imputed to the king's own election, which would cause a very ill measure to be taken of his majesty's nature and judgment; or (which more probably would be the case) to the inclination and power of the general, which would be attended with as ill effects." Mr. Morrice seemed much troubled at the apprehension, and said, "the paper was of his handwriting, by the general's order, who he was assured had no such intention; but that he would presently speak with him and return," which he did within less than an hour, and expressed "the trouble the general was in upon the king's very just exception; and that the truth was, he had been obliged to have much communication with men of all humours and inclinations, and so had promised to do them good offices to the king, and could not therefore avoid inserting their names in that paper, without any imaginations that the king would accept them: that he had done his part, and all that could be expected from him, and left the king to do what he had thought best for his own service, which he would always desire him to do, whatever proposition he should at any time presume to make to his majesty, which he would not promise should be always reasonable. However, he did still heartily wish, that his majesty would make use of some of those persons," whom he named, and said, "he knew most of them were not his friends, and that his service would be more advanced by admitting them, than by leaving them out."—The king was abundantly pleased with this good temper of the general, and less disliked those, who he discerned would be grateful to him, than any of the rest: and so the next day, he made the general knight of the Garter, and admitted him of the council, and likewise at the same time gave the signet to Mr. Morrice, who was sworn of the council and secretary of state; and sir Anthony Ashley Cooper, who had been presented by the general under a special recommendation, was then too sworn of the council, and the rather because having lately married the niece of the earl of Southampton (who was then likewise present and received the Garter to which he had been elected some years before) it was believed that his slippery humour would be easily restrained and fixed by the uncle. All this was transacted during his majesty's stay at Canterbury." Lord Clarendon's Life, written by himself, p. 5.

these a troop of 150, with blue liveries, laced with silver lace, with 6 trumpeters and 7 footmen in sea-green and silver. Then a troop of 220, with 30 footmen in grey and silver liveries, and 4 trumpeters richly cloathed; then another troop of 105, with grey liveries, and 6 trumpets; and another of 70, with 5 trumpets. Then 3 troops more, two of 300, and one of 100, all richly habited and bravely mounted; after these came two trumpets with his majesty's arms; the sheriffs men in red cloaks, richly laced with silver lace, to the number of 80, with pikes in their hands. Then followed 600 of the several companies of London, on horseback, in black velvet coats with gold chains, each company having footmen in rich Liveries attending.—After these came a kettle-drum, 5 trumpets, 3 streamers, and many rich red liveries with silver lace: After these 12 ministers, and then another kettle-drum and 4 trumpets, with his majesty's life-guard of horse, commanded by the lord Gerrard. Then 3 trumpets in rich coats and sattin doublets, and the city marshal with 8 footmen in French green, trimmed with crimson and white, the city waits, and all the city officers in order; then the two sheriffs, and all the aldermen in their scarlet gowns and rich trappings, with footmen in liveries, red coats laced with silver, and cloth of gold and silver, the heralds and maces in rich coats; then the lord mayor carrying the sword bare, and next to him the duke of Buckingham and the General, and then the king's majesty betwixt the dukes of York and Gloucester; after which followed a great troop of his majesty's servants; then followed a troop of horse with white colours; then the General's life-guard, commanded by sir Philip Howard; wherein, beside the established number, rode several noble persons; in the first rank were such as had 100,000*l.* per ann. of inheritance among them; after them 5 regiments of the Army Horse, led by col. Knight; and then two troops of noblemen and gentlemen to close the procession*."

May 31. The earl of Berkshire acquainted the lords, That he was commanded by his majesty to signify his desire to this house, that those who were created peers by patent, by his late majesty at Oxford, should sit in the house. On which the lords ordered the same lord to attend the king, and acquaint him, That matters of honour did belong to his majesty, and this house did acquiesce in his pleasure. And agreed, That the Order formerly passed, for excluding any lords made at Oxford from sitting in the house, should be cancelled, nulled, and made void, and that the lords sub-committee for Privileges, &c. should see this done and executed accordingly. Also, that the said lords should meet to consider of placing the seats and forms of the house, for making more room for the peers.

The King comes to the House.] June 1. The King came to the house of lords for the first time, and, sending for the commons, his majesty made a short speech to both houses, and then commanded the lord chancellor (Hyde) to deliver his mind further to them, which he accordingly did, say the Journals, in a large one; but neither of them are entered in those authorities. Nor have we met with them, at length, elsewhere; there is only a short abstract of the chancellor's Speech preserved in history*, which he made after the king had given his royal assent to these 3 Bills, viz. 1. "An Act for preventing and removing all Questions and Disputes, concerning the Assembling and Sitting of this present Parliament. 2. An Act for putting in Execution an Ordinance mentioned in the said Act. 3. An Act for Continuance of Process, and all judicial Proceedings. After which,

The *Lord Chancellor* told both houses, "With how much readiness his majesty had passed these important Acts, and how willing they should at all times hereafter find him, to pass any other that might tend to the advantage and benefit of the people; in a particular manner desiring, in his majesty's behalf, That the Bill of Oblivion, in which they had made so good a progress, might be expedited: that the people might see and know his majesty's extraordinary gracious care to ease and free them from their doubts and fears; and that he had not forgotten his gracious Declaration made at Breda, but that he would in all points make good the same."

Thanks returned to the Committee sent to the King.] The Commons resolved, That the gentlemen, the members of this house, who were sent to his majesty with a Letter from this house, have the thanks of this house, for their eminent service. Accordingly, the Speaker said, "Gentlemen, I shall not need to tell you what notice the house hath taken of the eminent service you have performed in your late employment to his majesty; you have brought home the ark, the glory of England, his majesty's person, in safety; and truly, if ever a service deserved to be called a service of ever-blessed memory, this is such a service: therefore the house hath commanded this service to be singled out from all your former eminent and worthy services, and to do it per excellentiam, as much exceeding all that ever hath been done before for

* "The concourse was so great, that the king rode in a crowd from the Bridge to Whitehall; all the Companies of the City standing in order on both sides, and giving loud thanks to God for his majesty's presence. He no sooner came to Whitehall but the two Houses of Parliament solemnly cast themselves at his feet, with all vows of affection to the world's end. In a word, the joy was so unexpressible and so universal, that his majesty said smiling to some about him, 'he doubted it had been his own 'fault he had been absent so long; for he saw 'nobody that did not protest he had ever 'wished his return." Clarendon, v. vi. p. 773.

* See Echard's History of England, p. 773.

this nation. And since the merit thereof is such, that no thanks can be proportionable thereunto, but the thanks of this house, I am therefore commanded, in the name of this house, and of all those they represent, the commons of England, to return you their very hearty Thanks."

At the same time, Mr. Hollis informed the house, That he having been sent, with the other worthy members, to the king, some aspersions had been cast upon him, as if he had, in his Speech to the king, (see p. 36) transgressed the Instructions given him by the house: on which the house ordered, 'That he should have leave to print the Speech he made to his majesty, as also the King's Answer to it, for which he had the king's leave, as well as the Instructions of the house, for his own vindication.

June 4. The commons sent up Mr. Prynne, and others, to the lords, to desire their concurrence in sending to his majesty, to desire him to issue out his Proclamation, against those that had a hand in the horrid Murder of his late majesty. The lords agreed to this, and the king consenting, a Proclamation was published accordingly.

Oaths of Supremacy and Allegiance to be taken by the Members, &c.] The commons were busy most of this day in taking the Oaths to the new government, or rather to the old one re-established. The right hon. James, marquis and earl of Ormond, lord lieutenant of Ireland, and lord steward of his majesty's household, came into the lobby at the door of the house of commons, where a table being set, and a chair prepared, being attended by the clerk of the crown, and the clerk of the commons house, with the Rolls of such members as were returned to serve in this parliament, his lordship gave the Oaths of Supremacy and Allegiance to several members, whom he had, by his commission, deputed to administer the same to other members in his absence.

Form of the Oath of Supremacy.

"I, A. B. do utterly testify and declare in my conscience, That our sovereign lord king Charles II. is the only supreme governor of this realm, and of all other his majesty's dominions and countries, as well in all spiritual or ecclesiastical things, or causes, as temporal; and that no foreign prince, person, prelate, state, or potentate, hath, or ought to have, any jurisdiction, power, superiority, pre-eminence, or authority, ecclesiastical or spiritual, within this realm: and therefore I do utterly renounce and forsake all foreign jurisdictions, powers, superiorities, and authorities; and do promise, that from henceforth I shall bear faith and true allegiance to the king's majesty, his heirs and lawful successors; and, to my power, shall assist and defend all jurisdictions, privileges, pre-eminences, and authorities, granted or belonging to the king's majesty, his heirs and successors; or united or annexed to the imperial crown of this realm: So help me God, and by the contents of this book."

Form of the Oath of Allegiance.

"I, A. B. do truly and sincerely acknowledge, profess, testify, and declare, in my conscience, before God and the world, That our sovereign lord king Charles II. is lawful and rightful king of this realm, and of all other his majesty's dominions and countries; and that the Pope, neither of himself, nor by any authority of the Church or See of Rome, or by any other means, with any other, hath any power or authority to depose the king, or to dispose of any of his majesty's kingdoms or dominions, or to authorize any foreign prince to invade or annoy him, or his countries; or to discharge any of his majesty's subjects of their allegiance and obedience to his majesty; or to give licence or leave to any of them to bear arms, raise tumults, or to offer any violence or hurt to his majesty's royal person, state, or government, or to any of his majesty's subjects, within his majesty's dominions.—Also, I do swear from my heart, That, notwithstanding any declaration, or sentence of excommunication or deprivation, made or granted, or to be made or granted, by the Pope, or his successors, or by any authority derived, or pretended to be derived, from him, or his see, against the said king, his heirs or successors, or any absolution of the said subjects from their obedience, I will bear faith and true allegiance to his majesty, his heirs and successors; and him and them will defend, to the uttermost of my power, against all conspiracies and attempts whatsoever, which shall be made against his or their persons, their crown and dignity, by reason or colour of any such sentence or declaration, or otherwise; and will do my best endeavour to disclose and make known unto his majesty, his heirs and successors, all treasons, and traiterous conspiracies, which I shall know, or hear of, to be against him, or any of them.—And I do further swear, That I do, from my heart, abhor, detest, and abjure, as impious and heretical, this damnable doctrine and position, That princes, which be excommunicated or deprived by the Pope, may be deposed or murdered by their subjects, or any other whatsoever. And I do believe, and in conscience am resolved, that neither the Pope, nor any person whatsoever, hath power to absolve me of this Oath, or any part thereof; which I acknowledge, by good and full authority, to be lawfully ministered unto me; and do renounce all pardons and dispensations to the contrary: and all these things I do plainly and sincerely acknowledge and swear, according to these express words by me spoken, and according to the plain and common sense and understanding of the same words, without any equivocation, or mental evasion, or secret reservation whatsoever: and I do make this recognition and acknowledgment heartily, willingly, and truly, upon the true faith of a Christian. So help me God."

June 5. The commons were still busy in carrying on the Act of Indemnity and general Pardon, and this day it was proposed to except seven persons for life and estate. And it being likewise proposed, That they should be then named, Thomas Harrison, Wm. Say, John Jones, Thomas Scott, Cornelius Holland, John Lisle, and John Barkstead, were agreed on for that purpose.

June 8. The commons proceeded to except more persons out of their Act of Pardon, when John Cooke, Andrew Broughton, and Edward Dendy, solicitors and agents at the late King's Trial, were excepted both as to life and estates. And having examined some Witnesses, touching the person who executed the late King, they resolved, That those two persons, who were upon the scaffold in disguise, when the detestable and traiterous sentence upon the late King was executed, be excepted out of the general Act of Pardon for life and estate.

The commons, in carrying on the Act of Oblivion, were still seeking out for such as were to be excepted out of it, and had appointed a committee to inform themselves, by perusing the Journal of the pretended High Court of Justice, for the Trial of the late King, what persons not sitting at the said Trial on the 27th of Jan. 1648, did sit at the said trial, in Westminster-Hall, any of the days preceding, and to report their Names to the House.

June 9. Accordingly, Mr. Prynne, from the committee, brought in several Names of such persons, with the times of their sitting at the Trial; on which the house resolved, That Wm. lord Munson, Thomas Challoner, James Challoner, John Fry, Francis Lascelles, sir H. Mildmay, Rob. Wallop, sir Gilbert Pickering, sir James Harrington, Tho. Lister, and John Phelpes, one of the clerks under the pretended High Court of Justice, should all be excepted out of the Act of general Pardon and Oblivion, for and in respect only of such pains, penalties, and forfeitures, (not extending to life) as shall be thought fit to be inflicted on them by another Act, intended to be hereafter passed for that purpose.—At the same time, the following persons were voted to be spared for life, though all sat in Judgment on the late King; the lord Grey of Grooby, sir Hardress Waller, Valentine Wauton, Edw. Whalley, Isaac Ewer, sir John Danvers, sir Tho. Maleverer, sir John Bourchier, Wm. Heveningham, Isaac Pennington, Henry Marten, Wm. Purefoy, John Blakiston, Gilbert Millington, sir Wm. Constable, Edm. Ludlow, sir Michael Livesay, Rob. Tichborne, Owen Rowe, Robert Lilburne, Richard Deane, John Okey, John Hughson, Wm. Goffe, John Carew, Miles Corbett, Francis Allen, Peregrine Pelham, John Moore, John Allured, Henry Smyth, Humphry Edwards, Gregory Clement, Tho. Wogan, sir Gregory Norton, Edm. Harvey, John Venn, Thomas Andrews, alderman of London, Wm. Cawley, Anthony Stapely, John Downes, Tho. Horton, Thomas Horton, Tho. Hammond, Nich. Love, Vincent Potter, Augustin Garland, John Dixwell, Geo. Fleetwood, Simon Mayne, James Temple, Peter Temple, Daniel Blagrave, and Thomas Wayte.

June. The house resumed the debate on the Act of general Pardon and Oblivion, when a Letter from William Lenthall, esq. the Speaker of the Long Parliament, was read, and the question being put, That he be one of the 20 persons to be excepted out of the general Act of Pardon, to suffer such pains and penalties, life only excepted, as should be thought proper to inflict upon him? The house divided, and it was carried against him by 215 to 126. Sir Henry Vane was also voted to lie under the same dilemma, without any division.—The above-mentioned Letter was addressed to the Speaker, and was as follows:

"Mr. Speaker; I find it not possible for me to take off the misapprehensions of some persons, misled by arguments, of my great gains which I got when I sat in your chair, and especially that of Compositions, where it is thought I had 5*l.* of every compounder. It is true, both houses did so order it, but very shortly it was again disannulled; so that what I received of that was very inconsiderable, as may appear by examination of the books of the house, and the serjeant at arms; and the clerks first reserving their parts, paid mine unto me, which is a check upon me. And as to the profit concerning passing of private Bills, as it is paid by the clerks, so it is checked as aforesaid.—Before his late majesty's going from London, the house took into consideration my great and extraordinary charge and loss, and gave me, by vote, 6,000*l.* but I never to this day received the one half of it; besides which I never had gift of land or money, nor any part of that 5*l.* per diem which is due to the Speaker, as Speaker, whilst he so continues. I shall desire you, sir, to offer so much of this as shall be necessary to express me, with all humility, to the house; but not as a justification of myself, but to shew the truth of my condition. And this will very much oblige, Mr. Speaker, W. LENTHALL.*"

* William Lenthall, esq. died Sept. 3, 1662, and very penitent, as appears from the following Account, in a Letter from Dr. Ralph Bridcock, who visited him in his last sickness.—"When," says he, "I came to his presence, he told me he was very glad to see me, for he had two great works to do, and I must assist him in both; to fit his body for the earth, and his soul for heaven; to which purpose he desired me to pray with him: I told him the Church had appointed an Office at the Visitation of the Sick, and I must use that; and he said, 'Yes, he chiefly 'desired the Prayers of the Church,' wherein he joined with great fervency and devotion. After prayers he desired absolution; I told him I was ready and willing to pronounce it, but he must first come to a Christian confession and contrition for the sins and failings of his life. 'Well, sir,' said he, 'then instruct me 'to my duty.' I desired him to examine his

The lords had had an affair of their own Privilege before them for some time, relating to the Choice of their own Speaker in some cases: and, a committee being appointed to examine into this business, the lord Roberts reported their result to the house: "That it is the duty of the lord-chancellor, or lord-keeper of the great seal, of England, ordinarily to attend the lords house of parliament; and that in case those great officers be absent from the house, and that there be none authorized, under the great seal, by the king, to supply that place in the house of peers, the lords may then chuse their own Speaker during that vacancy." The house confirmed this report, and ordered it to be entered in the Roll amongst the standing Orders of the house: and, soon after, the king thought proper to grant a commission, under his great seal, to sir Orlando Bridgman, lord chief baron of the exchequer, to execute that place whenever the lord chancellor should be absent.—The lords also appointed a committee to consider of the great Violation that hath been committed upon the Peers of this realm, by restraining their persons, burning them in the hand, refusing their Privileges when they have been claimed, and many other Breaches: and that the said committee have power to send for all offenders in those kinds, and after examination thereof, to report it to the house.

June 13. The commons agreed that the following persons should be of the 20 who were to be excepted out of the Act of Pardon, for pains and penalties not extending to life, viz. Wm. Burton, serj. Rd. Keeble, Oliver St. John, John Ireton, sir Arthur Haslerig, col. Wm. Sydenham, John Desborough, and Daniel Axtell. The Trial of Bulstrode Whitlocke, a person well known in these and former times, came also on; and the question being put, Whether the main question be now put, it passed in the negative, 175 against 134; so

---

life by the Ten Commandments, and wherein he found his failings, to fly to the Gospel for mercy. Then I read the Ten Commandments to him in order, mentioning the principal sins against each commandment. To pass by other things, (under the seal of the office) when I came to the fifth commandment, and remembered him, That disobedience, rebellion, and schism, were the great sins, against this commandment, 'Yes, sir,' said he, 'there is my trouble;' my 'disobedience, not to my natural parents, but 'against the pater patriæ, our deceased sovereign. I confess, with Saul, I held their 'cloaths whilst they murdered him; but herein 'I was not so criminal as Saul was, for, God 'thou knowest, I never consented to his death; 'I ever prayed and endeavoured what I could 'against it, but I did too much, God forgive 'me!' I then desired him to deal freely and openly in that business, and if he knew any of those villains that plotted or contrived that horrid murder, who were not yet detected, he would now discover them. He answered, 'He 'was a stranger to that business, his soul never 'entered into that secret; but what concerns 'myself,' said he, 'I will confess freely. Three 'things are especially laid to my charge, 'wherein, indeed, I am too guilty: That I 'went from the parliament to the Army; that 'I proposed the bloody question for trying the 'king; and that I sat after the king's death. 'To the first I give this Answer, That Cromwell, and his agents, deceived a wiser man 'than myself; that excellent king, and then 'might well deceive me also, as they did. I 'knew the Presbyterians would never restore 'the king to his just rights, as those men swore 'they would. For the second, no excuse can 'be made, but I have the king's pardon, and I 'hope Almighty God will shew me his mercy 'also; yet, sir,' said he, 'even then, when I 'put the question, I hoped the very putting 'the question would have cleared him, because 'I believed there were four to one against it; 'but they deceived me also. To the third, I 'make this candid confession, That it was my 'own baseness, cowardice, and unworthy fear, 'to submit my life and estate to the mercy of 'those men that murdered the king, that hurried me on against my own conscience to act 'with them; yet then I thought also I might 'do some good, and hinder some ill. Something I did for the Church and the Universities; something for the king when I broke 'the Oath of Abjuration, as sir O. B. and 'yourself know; something for his Return 'also too, as my lord G. M. J. T. and yourself, 'know: but the ill I did over-weighed the 'little good I would have done. God forgive 'me for this also.' After this I remembered him, That the Fathers of the Church had also been murdered and ruined, and asked, Whether he had any hand, or gave any consent therein? He answered, 'No; for I always 'did believe that was the primitive and best 'government of the Church;' and said, 'I die 'a dutiful son of the Church of England, as it 'was established before those times; for I 'have not seen the alteration of the Liturgy.' After this office, wherein, indeed, he shewed himself a very hearty penitent, he again desired the Absolution of the Church, which I then pronounced, and which he received with much content and satisfaction; 'For,' said he, 'now, 'indeed, do I feel the joy and benefit of the 'Office which Christ hath left in his Church.' Then praying for the king that he might long and happily reign over us, and for the peace of the Church, he again desired prayers. The next day he received the Sacrament; and after that work I desired him to express himself to Mr. Dickerson, (a learned physician, fellow of Merton College, who received the Sacrament with him) concerning the King's Death, because he had only done it to me in confession; which he did, to the same effect as he had done to me. The rest of his time was spent in devotion and penitential meditations to his very last." From an Original in Dr. William's MS. Collections, vol. viii. No 127.

that Mr. Whitlocke was respited for that time. —The commons continued to except persons out of their Act of Pardon, but though it had been voted to except no more than 20, yet they went on with their exceptions for Pains and Penalties, and col. John. Lambert, Christ. Pack, alderman of London, and John Blackwell, of Mortlack, were named for that purpose.

The celebrated John Milton comes next to be questioned for writing two Books, one intituled, "Johannis Miltoni Angli pro Populo Anglicano Defensio, contra Claudii Anonimi, alias Salmasii Defensionem Regiam;" the other, an Answer to a Book called, "The Portraiture of his late Majesty in his Solitude and Sufferings." At the same time, one John Goodwin was mentioned for writing another Book, intituled, "The Obstructors of Justice," in defence of the traiterous Sentence against the late king. These two persons were ordered to be taken into custody by the serjeant at arms, to be prosecuted by the attorney-general; and, lastly, the king was desired to issue out his proclamation to recall their Books, along with such other Books as should be presented to his majesty, in a schedule from the house, in order to their being burnt by the hands of the common hangman.

The King's Message relative to the Act of Indemnity.] This day, Mr. Secretary Morrice* acquainted the commons that he had a Message from his majesty in writing; which he was commanded to deliver to that house, and desired it might be read. It was as follows:

"C. R. We have had too ample a manifestation of your affection and duty toward us, the good effect whereof is notorious to the world, to make the least doubt of the continuance and improvement thereof, or in the least degree to dislike what you have done, or to complain of what you have left undone. We know well the weight of those affairs, which depend upon your counsels, and the time that must unavoidably be spent in debates, where there must naturally be difference of opinion and judgment, amongst those whose desires of the public peace and safety are the same; and, neither we nor you must be overmuch troubled, if we find our good intentions, and the unwearied pains we take to reduce those good intentions into real acts, for the quiet and security of the nation, mis-represented and mis-interpreted by those who are, in truth, afflicted to see the public distractions, by God's blessing, so near an end; and, by others, upon whose weakness, fears, and jealousies, the activity and cunning of those ill men have too great an influence.—How wonderful and miraculous soever the great harmony of affections between us and our good subjects is, (and that is so visible and manifest to the world, that there scarce appears the view of any cloud to overshadow or disturb it) yet, we must not think that God Almighty hath wrought the miracle to that degree, that a nation so miserably divided for so many years, is so soon and entirely united in their affections and endeavours, as were to be wished; but that the evil consciences of many men continue so awake for mischief, that they are not willing to take rest themselves, or to suffer others to take it: and we have all had too sad experience of the unhappy effects of fears and jealousies, how groundless and unreasonable soever, not to think it very necessary to apply all timely and proper remedies to those distempers, and to prevent the inconveniences and mischiefs which too naturally flow from thence: we well foresaw, that the great violation, which the laws of the land had for so many years sustained, had filled the hearts of the people with a terrible apprehension of insecurity to themselves, if all they had said and done should be liable to be examined and punished by those laws which had been so violated; and that nothing could establish the security of king and people, but a full provision, that the returning to the reverence and obedience of the law, which is good for us all, should not turn to the ruin of any, who are willing and fit to receive that protection hereafter from the law, and to pay that subjection to it that is just and necessary; and, therefore, we made that free offer of a general Pardon, in such a manner, as is expressed in our Declaration; and how ready and desirous we are to make good the same, appears by our Proclamation, which we have issued out upon, and according to, your desire.—However, it is evident, that all we have, or do offer, doth not enough compose the minds of our people, nor, in their opinions, can their security be provided for, till the Act of Indemnity and Oblivion be passed; and we find great industry is used by those, who do not wish that peace to the kingdom they ought to do, to persuade our good subjects, that we have no mind to make good our promises, which, in truth, we desire to perform for our own sake as well as theirs: and we do therefore very earnestly recommend it to you, that all possible expedition be used in the passing that most necessary Act, whereby our good subjects generally will be satisfied, that their ecurity is in their own hands, and

* "Sir William Morrice, who was allied to general Monk, was, for his own merit, and that of his illustrious kinsman, preferred to the office of Secretary of State. He was a man of learning and good abilities, but was not completely qualified for his great employment, as he knew but little of foreign languages, and less of foreign affairs. The Secretary spoke Latin fluently, understood Greek, and acquitted himself during the seven years that he continued in office without reproach. He died Dec. 12, 1676. He was author of a Book entitled, 'The Common Right to the Lord's Supper asserted.' One singularity is recorded of him, That he would never suffer any man to say grace in his own house beside himself; there, he said, he was both priest and king." Grainger, vol. iii. p. 350.

depends upon their future actions, and that they are free for all that is past, and so all the endeavours of ill men will be disappointed, which would persuade them not to do well now, because they have heretofore done amiss. And we are the more engaged to this our recommendation, because, upon the reflection of your eminent zeal and affection for our service, and hearty concurrence with us in all we have desired from you, men are apt to persuade others, though they do not believe it themselves, that the passing the Act is therefore deferred, because we do not enough press the dispatch of it, which we do desire from our heart, and are confident you will the sooner do, upon this our earnest recommendation."

After the reading of the above Remonstrance from the king, the commons desired the Secretary to return their humble Thanks to his majesty for his gracious Message; and to acquaint him, That the house would make it their endeavour to give a speedy dispatch to what is mentioned in the Message; and to all other matters relating to the public.

Debate on the Act of Indemnity.] Accordingly, the house resumed the Act of Indemnity; when, after debate, it was resolved, That Charles Fleetwood, John Pyne, Richard Dean, major Richard Creed, Philip Nye, John Goodwin, clerk, colonel Ralph Cobbet, William Hewet, and Hugh Peters, should be excepted out of the act of general pardon and oblivion; the two last for life.

A curious Manuscript, * which has certainly been the Note-Book of some member of this parliament, and which was sent in to the Editors of the 'Parliamentary or Constitutional History of England,' informs us, That when this debate was entered into, at this time, sir Henry Cholmley moved, That all such members as had sat in any High Court of Justice should withdraw, but refused to name any. This motion was seconded by sir Wm. Vincent; to which Mr. Charlton and Mr. Prynne added, all those that abjured, or signed the Instrument of Government. Mr. Goodrick spoke to lay that business aside; and sir George Booth, not to question them now, but to go to the business of the day. Lord Falkland moved to exclude them; as did also sir George Ryves, and col. King. Some other speakers are named in the MS. for and against the motion: the house did not divide upon it, but went to the business of the day, which was to name the 20 persons who were to be excepted out of the general Pardon. Mr. Prynne moved first against col. Fleetwood, which was answered by sir Ralph Knight, for him; but Mr. Palmer and col. King, speaking also against him, he was voted to be excepted; making the 14th man. Lord Falkland named col. Pyne; which Mr. Swanton and Mr. Chafe, seconding, saying, He was called the King of the West, and was a great tyrant, upon the question, he was voted to be excepted, being the 15th man. Mr. Philip Jones was named next; but, on reading a Petition from him, justifying himself that he was not guilty of the king's death, and Mr. Annesley and Mr. Finch speaking for him, his affair was dropt. Mr. Prynne moved against Richard Cromwell; but, no one seconding, the house proceeded no farther against him at that time. The same member named major Salway, but Mr. Doleswell delivering a Petition from the major, and he and Mr. Knightley speaking for him, he was also passed by. Sir Tho. Clarges moved against Rd. Dean; saying, There was a suspicion that he had lately dispersed dangerous papers in Scotland, and was an Anabaptist; upon which he was voted amongst the excepted, and made the 16th man.

The case of Mr. Whitlocke, the Memorialist, who had acted in high stations in every revolution since the late king's death, came on again this day. Mr. Prynne first moved the house against him, which was seconded by sir Ralph Ashton and sir Henry Finch, who said Whitlocke was as much an ambassador as St. John was; was for fining him, but not to exceed the value of two years income of his estate. Mr. Annesley was for not quitting him, but to set some mark of disfavour upon him only, by reason of his numerous family. Mr. Charlton also spoke against him, but moderately; and Mr. Palmer moved to spare his estate for his children's sake. For Whitlocke spoke Mr. Willoughby, sir Henry Cholmley, Mr. Turner, lord Howard, sir Geo. Booth, sir John Robinson, and sir Rd. Brown, who said, Mr. Whitlocke preserved him from being taken; and sir John Holland, who urged his sending the king over 500*l*. and his securing Lyme for him, of which his son was governor. On the whole, Mr. Whitlocke was again acquitted.

The next person who was named was major Creed, and only major Archer spoke for him; however, the house divided twice on this affair; first, Whether the question should be then put; which was carried, 147 against 101; and the main question being put, Creed was cast by 133 to 103: so he made the 17th man.

Sir William Wylde moved the house against Philip Nye, a minister: he was seconded by sir Henry Finch; who said, Nye had enriched himself very much in those times of plunder and rapine; and that there needed no particular charge, since the hue-and-cry was general against him. Mr. Turner also urged it home against Nye, and said, That he being the grandee at the committee for bestowing Benefices, a young man of learning and merit

* This Manuscript is by way of Diary, and begins with June 18, 1660; but is broken into sometimes by lacerations, &c. It is written in the hand of the times, coincides exactly with the Journals of the commons, but is much more particular in the names of the Speakers in each debate. It was communicated to the Editors of the 'Parliamentary or Constitutional History of England' by the Rev. Charles Lyttelton, LL.D. Dean of Exeter.

would not pass with him, when a worthless good-for-nothing fellow was always preferred. Sir Rd. Temple moved to charge Nye with some capital crime; but the house was more moderate, and one Mr. Folie speaking for him, he was only excepted as above, and made the 18th man.—John Goodwin, the Author before-mentioned, was next named by Mr. Prynne, and voted to be the 19th man.*

Col. Cobbett was moved against by Mr. Hopkins; sir Henry Finch seconded; but not to put him on the list of the 20, but except him by himself as capital: but this not being agreed to, it was resolved, That Cobbett should only stand for pains and penalties, and he made the 20th man.

Judge Thorpe was named at the same time with Cobbett, by col. King, seconded by Mr. Winfield and Mr. Prynne; who mentioned one Thorpe, that was a judge in Edw. 2nd's time, who, for taking bribes and other misdemeanors, was punished; and therefore desired that this Judge Thorpe might also suffer the same: but several members speaking in behalf of Thorpe, he was acquitted, and Cobbett taken in his place.

The case of Hugh Peters, the pulpit incendiary, came next to be considered. Serjeant Tyrrel produced an information against him, from one Dr. Young, a physician in Wales: that Peters, being very sick and like to die, told him, that it was he and Cromwell consulted together how to dispose of the late king. Hewlett, the man suspected to have cut off the king's head, was also named with Peters, there being two witnesses ready to swear against him: on which the house thought proper to except them out of the Act for life, and leave them to the law.

July 2. The business of raising money for the present exigencies of the State came first on the carpet, in the house of commons, the beginning of this month: which, the MS. Diary acquaints us, was first moved for by Mr. secretary Morrice, in an excellent speech for that purpose. This motion was seconded by Mr. Stevens, and Mr. Annesley, who were for doing of it speedily. But sir Wm. Lewis argued, That it was best to proceed with the Act of Indemnity first, that people might be more ready to pay. Sir John Northcot spoke on the same side, as did also Mr. Prynne and Mr. Knightley. However, lord Falkland, speaking in behalf of the first motion, which was to raise money speedily to pay the Debts of the Nation; and Mr. Pierepoint saying, That the charge of the Army and Navy, and the interest, came to 6000*l.* a day; that it was inconsistent for an army and parliament to subsist together, and that the Trained-Bands were sufficient: To all which, col. Birch adding, That the people's liberties were not safe with such an army; that, though he was a member of it himself, yet he moved it might be paid off; and said, that 260,000*l.* would disband ten regiments of foot; the house agreed to set aside every Tuesday, Thursday, and Saturday, to go upon means to raise money for that purpose.

The same day, the house went upon the Act of Indemnity; in which a strong debate and a division upon it ensued, which we give from the authority of the aforementioned MS. Diary. A proviso was put into the house by some unknown member, to be added to the Bill; which was, to disable all the persons of the High Court of Justice; all decimators, major-generals, abjurors, and all those that petitioned against the king. Hereupon a hot debate began; Mr. Annesley moved to have it thrown out, which was seconded by sir John Northcot; Mr. Goodrick to throw it out, saying, It was as dangerous as a hand-granado in a barrel of gunpowder. Sir Henry Finch for throwing it out; saying, It did include all men. Sir Tho. Clarges for the same, adding, That it was a most dangerous thing, and an indulgence not to inquire who brought it in, for he deserved to be called to the bar. On the other side, there were several members who spoke for the whole proviso, and others to mitigate and take part. Mr. Prynne was for the whole, seconded by Mr. Charlton, who added, That he who said the person who brought it in deserved to be called to the bar, deserved it himself; and moved against those that petitioned against the king, or sat in parliament in the years 1647 and 48, and in the High Court of Justice: Also, against all those who were the contrivers of the Instrument of Government, those that were imposers of taxes under Oliver, major-generals, and decimators; adding, That though he never pressed the death of any man, yet, to secure the future peace of the nation, he could not be silent. Col. King was likewise for receiving the proviso; saying, It was not prudence to set up those in power that now lay under their feet: nor that any in the house who were guilty of such crimes, should plead their own causes.—The mitigators were, first sir Henry Chomley, who moved to take in the Proviso in part. Mr. Trelany was only against major-generals and decimators. Mr. Palmer against all abjurors, major-generals, and High Court of Justice men. Sir Wm. D'Oiley was for referring the proviso to a committee. Mr. Knight urged, That the proviso was too large and not to be mended. Sir Thomas Meeres to amend it, if possible; but he feared it was

* Nye was a leading Independent preacher: "He was put into Dr. Featly's living at Acton, and rode thither every Lord's day in triumph, in a coach drawn with four horses, to exercise there." See Levite's Scourge, 1644, p. 61. "At the Restoration it was debated several hours together, whether Philip Nye and John Goodwin should not be excepted for life, because they had acted so highly (none more so, except Hugh Peters) against the King; and it came at last to this result, That if, after the 1st of September, the same year, they should accept any preferment, they should in law stand as if they had been excepted totally for life." Wood's Athen. Oxon. vol. ii. col. 369.

impossible. But serj. Hales, being for rejecting the whole Proviso, argued, That it was contrary to the king's desire, and even the Act itself, which excepted but 20 persons for pains and penalties; and therefore moved, in order to cement all differences, to reject it. And Mr. Young saying, That though he was not concerned in the proviso, yet he was against it, because it was against the king's desire. Mr. Thomas concluding, That this ought to be laid aside, and to take another something like it. At last the proviso was ordered to be laid aside. But this debate begat another, for col. White immediately moved the house, That any Proviso brought in, read, and nobody owning it, might be laid aside. This was seconded by col. Shapcot and sir George Booth. Mr. Knightley was for owning of it the first time of reading it; Mr. Stevens, to subscribe their names; Mr. Trelany, to cast it out the first reading, if none spoke to it; and though Mr. Charlton argued, That if the gentleman that brought in the Proviso be out of the house, and no one speak to it, then to reject it, yet no Order was made on this motion, says the Diary, nor is there any such thing in the Journals.

The commons resuming the affair of the Bill of Indemnity, another Proviso was offered; the debate on which was stronger than any we have yet met with; lasting, as the MS. says, above two hours. Col. Jones spoke first, very strongly, to it, in every particular. This Proviso was to cause all Officers, during the Protectorate, to refund their salaries. Particularly aimed against Mr. Prideaux for the post-office; likewise against the High Court of Justice men, the Council and Committee of Safety, commissioners for excise and customs, the trustees for king and queen's lands, dean and chapter's commissioners, with all those that were commissioners of sequestrations, or concerned in the Prize-Office. This motion was seconded by Mr. Prynne, in all its articles; who said also, That he knew those persons had received above 250,000*l.* for their iniquitous doings, and therefore moved that they might be made to refund it. Col. King spoke on the same side very warmly, saying amongst other things, It was fit such spunges should be squeezed.—But this motion for refunding met with a very warm repulse. Sir Tho. Widdrington was the first who pleaded strongly against it. He ended his arguments by saying, That if he was included in the Proviso, he had much better have been wholly excluded the Act. Sir Heneage Finch said, That most of these complaints were already named in the Act, and particularly Accountants excepted, but not their heirs, which this proviso would include. Mr. Stevens said, That those were not accountants, but might be included in the proviso notwithstanding the Act, if some little amendments were made in it. Mr. Charlton said, The proviso might be amended, and moved that it might stand. Sir Wm. D'Oiley was also for receiving the proviso, but to refer it to two or three persons to word it better, and to leave out the Judges. Some other members, spoke for the proviso; but all ineffectual: for several members spoke on the other side of the question, as sir Tho. Clarges, Mr. Young, serj. Littleton, Mr. Bodardo, and Mr. Briscoe, who said, Such rigour would confound men, whereas mercy would convert them. To which Mr. Goodrick, on the same, argued, That the refunding would be to some a greater punishment, than to be one of the 20 excepted persons; and that all the soldiers were included: and, lastly, sir Anth. Ashley Cooper closed the debate, with saying, He might freely speak, because he never received any salary; but he looked upon the proviso as dangerous to the peace of the nation; adding, That it reached gen. Monk, and admiral Montagu, after the house had given them thanks, and thousands besides. On all which the question being called and put, Whether the Proviso should stand or be laid aside, the house divided, when the numbers were, for standing, 151, for the latter, 181.

The last Proviso offered this day, was against such as shall not take the Oaths of Allegiance and Supremacy; to which Mr. Turner added, 'or shall refuse them.' A great debate followed on this also, many members speaking for and against this Proviso. The most remarkable on each side were these, Mr. Trevor, in behalf of the Papists, said It was not fit to make an Oath the price of pardon. Mr. Bamfield was for not imposing the oaths so rigorously; for then, he said, they would force persons, for saving their lives and estates, to damn their souls. Mr. Knight moved to leave out the Oath of Supremacy, and then none would stick at the other. Mr. Hollis moved to consider more of this motion, and to be very tender in imposing oaths; asking, Whether this was intended to destroy all Catholics, which it would infallibly do; that he was as much against Papists as any man, but thought this Proviso was better laid aside.—There were many advocates for the motion; on which side sir Wm. Morrice speaking, said, There seemed to be something lay hid in the opposition to it: which words Mr. Hollis took exception at, because he had spoken against it. On the whole, this proviso was rejected, without a division.

July 6. Another warm debate took place on a Proviso offered to the Bill of Indemnity, which was, To question any Attorney or Solicitor, that acted for the Protector, or in any high court of justice. This was first spoken to by Mr. Prynne, who was for questioning them, and then to leave them to the law for recovery of damages. Several members spoke against this proviso to have it laid aside: till Mr. Charlton moved not to reject it, but to amend it; and particularly moved against one Mr. Ellis, who was solicitor at Dr. Hewitt's Trial. Col. Shapcot spoke against the proviso, and in favour of the Solicitor, and said, Dr. Hewitt did not refer himself in time to the court; for sentence being once given, the solicitor told the doctor the court could not hear him then: to which Mr. Raynesford answered, in behalf of the Solicitor, That he never sat in court but one day, and never said any such word as was laid to his charge. To which Mr. Grey added, That he heard Dr. Hewitt say, If any judge or counsel would say he ought to plead, he would have done it. At last, the question being put, Whether the Proviso should be laid aside, the Speaker gave it for the Ayes; but sir Rob. Brook said the Noes had it; upon which the house dividing, sir Tho. Widdrington said, There were two gentlemen gone out. Several motions ensued on this, to divide the house notwithstanding; and after that it took up an half an hour's debate, Whether the Ayes or Noes should go out; but the Speaker saying the Ayes should, although several old members in the house said the contrary, their numbers were 138 for the Proviso, and 163 against it; so that this also was laid aside.

Debate in the Commons on Religion.] July 9. The grand committee for Religion sat according to order; the debate on which we shall give at large, from the MS. Diary, observing, that now was the contest whether the Presbyterian Church Government, or the Church of England formerly established, should reign.

Sir *Trevor Williams* opened the debate, by moving for the established Religion, according to the 39 Articles; which he said was not only according to the Old and New Testament, but was as much as all that own Christianity profess.—Several members after him spoke for and against this motion; as, Mr. Gower, Dr. Clayton, col. King, Mr. Broderick, Mr. Stevens, and Mr. Throgmorton; who said, All Protestant Churches did profess according to the Scripture, and moved that the 39 Articles should be inserted in the Bill. Lord Richardson and sir John Northcot, for the same.

Serj. *Hales* said he was for the 39 Articles; but thought it not fitting to join them with the Old and New Testament, in the same paragraph, but in some other.

Mr. *Broderick* was for the Articles; saying, He had often conversed with those of several churches abroad, and, that all professed Religions were according to the Scriptures; and moved for a National Synod.

Lord *Falkland* spoke on the same side, and said, It was not fit to debate the whole Bill in that house, but to leave the doctrinal part to a Synod.

Mr. *Peckham* was not for altering our Religion without proper judges of it, as by a Synod; and urged a case in a trial in Westminster-Hall, where the judges sent for a falconer about a hawk; saying, 'Quilibet in arte sua;' and therefore moved for a Synod in this case, lest, going further, they should be like little [boys], who, learning to swim, go out of their [dep]th and are drowned.

[S]ir *Heneage Finch* spoke most excellently [con]cerning this subject, and said, That not one letter of the Bill made good the title of it; that the Religion of our church was not to seek, but we have enjoyed it long; and therefore should not now be inquiring for it. However, he moved this should be referred to an Assembly of Divines, for which they ought to petition the king; for he knew no law for altering the government of the Church by Bishops. And, lastly, as for liberty for tender consciences, he said no man knew what it was.

Mr. *Prynne* spoke very honestly and passionately for the paragraph in the Bill; and concluded with saying, The determination of the Synod must be confirmed by the king and parliament. To whom.

Sir *Heneage Finch* again said, That the original of the paragraph was from Cromwell, and he did hope they would not cant after him; but that, if the faith grounded upon Scripture, and the discipline according to the laws, were put in the paragraph, he then would give his consent to it.

Several more members spoke, till at last it was moved to adjourn it to another time, which was opposed by others; and the committee sat an hour in the dark, before candles were suffered to be brought in, and then they were twice blown out, but the third time they were preserved, though with great disorder; till at last, adds our authority, about ten at night it was voted, "That the king should be desired to convene a select number of Divines to treat concerning that affair, and the committee not to sit again till the 23d of Oct. next."

The Act of Indemnity passes the Commons.] July 11. This day the long-expected Act of Indemnity passed the commons; it was intituled, 'An Act of free and general Pardon, Indemnity, and Oblivion;' and was ordered to be sent up to the lords.

Debate on the Bill of Sales.] Another Bill of great consequence had been brought into the commons, and read once, called, 'A Bill of Sales.' This was to consider the cases of those who had been purchasers of the king's, queen's, and church's Lands, during the late times of plunder and devastation. And this day the said Bill coming to be read a 2nd time, a Debate arose, of which the MS. Diary gives this abstract:—It was opened by col. Jones, who moved the house against those who had bought the king's Lands and Woods, as also of Deans and Chapters; to examine what money the purchasers had paid for them; but to consider the Soldiers under general Monk at the same time. A Petition from the purchasers of St. James's, and St. Martin's in the Fields, being offered to the house by sir Anth. Irby, col. Shapcot opposed the reading of it there; but moved for a committee to receive Petitions.

Mr. *Palmer* spoke very high and excellently against the whole Bill; and moved that the king's Lands, as well as those of others, should be restored to them implicitly.

Sir *Tho. Wroth* seconded this motion, and said, That, as to his own case, whatever he had bought, he did freely give back again, though he had paid 18 years purchase for them.

Mr. *Prynne* said, That no compensation should be made to those who had bought the king's Lands; that it was against their oaths to suffer it, except to those who were antient tenants, who had bought the same in order to preserve themselves and titles; and, in that case, to petition the king: also to consider those who had purchased land in and about Westminster, which then was worth nought; but, having now built fair houses upon them, the rents amount to a considerable value, and will be so for the future.

Mr. *Goodrick* spoke also for the old tenants that were forced to buy or be turned out, and to commit the bill. Mr. Barton and Mr. Gewen for a commitment also; but the former was not for confirming any Sale to those who sat after 1648, or High Court of Justice men: the latter urged, That it was the king's interest to have the bill committed. Whether it was that this last assertion stirred up the zeal of another member, or from some other cause,

Mr. *Calmady* moved to have the bill cast out; or else, if they would commit it, to commit it to the *necessary-house* above. Which *motion*, as it might properly enough be called, Mr. Annesley rebuked, as unbefitting such an assembly.

Mr *Stephens* argued against the bill, saying, That they ought not to encourage evil-doers; but, instead of confirming estates, to punish the purchasers: he moved also for an act of resumption, wherein they were to be left to the king's mercy; but was for committing the bill.

Mr. *Knight* was against it; saying, He could not in conscience consent to it, as he should answer at the day of judgment.

Sir *Anth. Cope* would have all persons in the house to imitate sir Tho. Wroth, and restore their purchased Lands; which, he said, would be a good example to others without.

Mr. *Lowther* was against the bill; saying, The old proverb was, 'That he that eats the king's goose should be choaked with the feathers;' and that he was against the bill by reason of his oath.

Sir *Tho. Meres* desired the house not to have a greater care of the king than they had of the church; and said, The purchasers had already paid themselves; and moved for resumption and a grand committee.

Several members were for committing the bill; the last to have all major-generals and rumpers excepted out of the bill: not one member speaking directly in defence of it, except sir Tho. Widdrington, who might be a person deeply interested in its consequences.—Lord Falkland moved the house in behalf of the Queen, and to refer her case to a committee. Sir Geo. Ryves spoke also in behalf of the Queen, and against the Purchasers; and said, It was not fit the French, who all this while durst not demand the Queen's jointure, should now be suffered to do it; but that they should prevent them, and give her it themselves.—Upon the whole, it was ordered, That all the king's and queen's Lands, Rents and Profits, be left out of the bill; and to be referred to a grand committee of the whole house.

General Monk created Duke of Albemarle.] July 13. The lord-chancellor informed the house of lords, That his majesty had conferred the honour and title of Duke of Albemarle on the lord-general Monk; whereupon the house ordered, That he should be introduced between the duke of Buckingham and the marquis of Winchester, the lord great-chamberlain, without robes, Garter king at arms going before him. Being thus brought in, he delivered his patent, on his knees, to the lord-chancellor, who delivering the same to the clerk of parliament, it was publickly read; after which Garter king at arms delivered back the patent to the lord-general Monk; who, by this grant from his majesty, was created 'Baro de Potheridge, Beauchamp et Teys, comes Torrington, et Dux Albemarliæ.' The ceremony aforesaid being ended, the duke was placed, by Garter, between the duke of Buckingham and the marquis of Winchester. The lords ordered also, That the lord great-chamberlain and the lord Berkley should wait upon his majesty to give him Thanks, from that house, for the honour he had been pleased to confer on the duke of Albemarle; and that he be added to the committee of privileges.

Debate in the Commons on Religion.] July 16. We have already given, from a MS. Diary, the substance of a debate on Religion, by a Committee of the commons appointed for that purpose. The same authority gives us another, which happened this day.

Sir *John Northcot* began the debate, by speaking very highly against Deans and Chapters; but spared the Bishops, saying, The former did nothing 'but eat and drink and rise up to play,' or something worse: upon which Mr. —— stood up and reproved him; but he was justified by sir Walter Erle.

Mr. *Prynne* said, He could not be for bishops, unless they would derive their power from the king, and not vaunt themselves to be Jure Divino.

Mr. *Walpole* was for putting the question, Which was the Protestant Faith, according to the scriptures and the government of the Church, and according to law.

Mr. *Knightley* was for the clergy in general, saying, The faults of private persons ought not to make the function criminal.

Sir *Tho. Widdrington* said, The question, as it was, was not for a committee, or even a parliament; but moved to make two questions of it.

Mr. *Grove* said, The question was complicated, and desired that the first part might be put; adding, That the king was then consulting with divines about the discipline of the Church.

Dr. *Clayton* said, That discipline was as necessary with doctrine, as life in a natural body.

Mr. *Stephens* said, The first part of the question they should all agree in; but, for the second, not to anticipate the king, who was, at that time, consulting about it.

Mr. *Howard*, argued for the whole question. He said, That as monarchy had been so long interrupted by rebellion and faction, so had episcopacy by schism and heresy; and that no one that spoke against episcopacy offered any thing better.

Mr. *Young* was for dividing, and not to mix the doctrine and discipline together; yet, he said, he was for episcopacy, though he did not think it an article of faith: and urged the king's Declaration for tender consciences formerly, and his present endeavours for settling of peace amongst all people.

Sir *John Temple* argued for a division of the question, saying, the former discipline was the occasion of their former troubles; and moved for a synod.

Col. *King* said, That no man could tell what the discipline according to law was; and therefore moved to divide the question.

Mr. *Throgmorton* spoke highly for Bishops, saying, That, except Scotland, there was scarce any Reformed Church but what had Bishops.

Mr. *Bunckley* said, He thought a moderate episcopacy might take in the good of both parties; and urged the king's present inclinations and endeavours for it: that episcopacy, in its extent, was more boundless than monarchy; adding, That some of the Bishops gloried in putting down all lectures in a country, and it was a fault to preach twice a day; but concluded, That government by episcopacy, if circumscribed, was to be wished; and moved to divide the question.

Sir *Heneage Finch* said, The first part was not to be put singly, after 140 years practice.

Sir *John Talbot* said, Those that formerly desired to hasten the Settlement of Religion, now strove to obstruct the question.

Sir *Gilbert Gerrard* said, He could not give his vote for the question, until he knew whether it was against the Covenant. This was seconded by col. Shapcot, who argued, That many things in the Liturgy might be amended; and hoped that men would not be imposing on other's consciences: that he was not against Bishops, but their power; and moved to divide the question.

Sir *Tho. Wharton* said, He was in his judgment episcopal; but moved the question might not be put at present, because the king was in consultation about it.

Mr. *Bunckley*, again, was now for laying the whole question aside; because, he said, If it was put and carried, all ministers made since 1648 would be abolished.

Sir *John Northcot* again moved in behalf of the ministry, and said, Many of those who were ordained by Presbyters, were active in bringing in the king.

Sir *Anthony Ashley Cooper* said, Our Religion was too much mixed with interest; neither was it ripe enough now to handle that subject; and moved that this debate be now laid aside, and the whole committee adjourned for 3 months.—After 7 hours debate, about 10 at night, it was at last agreed to refer the matter to the king, and to such divines as he should please to chuse; and, to adjourn this Committee to the 23d of October next.

The Earl of Bristol's Speech on the Bill of Indemnity.] July 20. The lords adjourned themselves into a committee, to consider of the Bill of Indemnity; and, after some time, the house was resumed, but no report was made of their proceedings therein as yet.—At the same time, the lords received a quickening Message from the commons to hasten the dispatch of that Bill; and another for Confirmation of Judicial Proceedings: alledging these two reasons for it, That, unless the latter Bill be passed, there can be no Assizes kept, tho' they are appointed; and, unless the former be the same, the animosities of the people will be increased, and thereby the peace of the kingdom greatly disturbed.—On the receipt of this Message the lords went again into a committee on the Bill of Indemnity; and the house being resumed, the lord Roberts reported the opinion of the committee was, That all those persons who gave Sentence of Death upon the late king, or signed the Warrant for his murder, shall be excepted out of the Bill of Indemnity: and, that to know who those persons are, the original evidences shall be desired from the house of commons for their lordships information: which opinion the house confirmed.—In the debate, this day, on the above Bill,

The Earl of *Bristol*[*] addressed their lordships in these words: "My lords; Being to speak unto your lordships somewhat more extendedly than what is my use, and upon a subject wherein there may be, perhaps, not only difference, but even fervour of opinions, I find myself obliged, by somewhat that happened to me here the other day, to beg a favour of your

* London, printed in the year 1660. "The earl of Bristol was a man of courage and learning, of a bold temper, and a lively wit, but of no judgment nor steadiness. He was in the queen's interest during the war at Oxford. And he studied to drive things past the possibility of a treaty, or any reconciliation; fancying that nothing would make the military men so sure to the king, as his being sure to them, and giving them hopes of sharing the confiscated estates among them, whereas, he thought, all discourses of treaty made them feeble and fearful. When he went beyond sea he turned Papist. But it was after a way of his own: for he loved to magnify the difference between the Church and the Court of Rome. He was esteemed a very good speaker; but he was too copious, and too florid. He was set at the head of the Popish party, and was a violent enemy of the earl of Clarendon." Burnet, vol. i. p. 101.

lordships, that, if I should chance to err in forms and orders of the house, or that there should slip from me, unawares, any expression that may be dissonant to the ears of those who understand better than I the force and propriety of words, you will not be severe unto me; but be pleased to consider, that I have been 16 years out of my country, and in a profession far different from what I am now a-doing: in confidence of this indulgence I shall proceed.—My lords; you have here before you, in this Bill of Indemnity, the most important business that, perhaps, the house of peers hath at any time had in deliberation; it is that upon which the honour or eternal reproach of the nation abroad, and its happiness or confusion at home, seems (next under God's inscrutable providence) most principally to depend: for, on the one side, how abhorred a nation must we be to all others, if the infamy of our sovereign's murder should not be thoroughly washed away, by justice, in the blood of the guilty? And, on the other, what happiness or quiet can we hope for at home; nay, what new combustions ought we not to apprehend, if the criminal and the misled, (between whom the eye of the law can make little distinction) making up so numerous a part of the nation, their fears, which might urge them to new crimes, should not be secured, by the firmest assurances of impunity? Punishing and securing are, certainly, the two principal ends of this Bill; and wherein, as certainly, every one of your lordships doth concur; but whether the means of attaining those ends have been sufficiently lighted upon by the house of commons, in this Bill, that, I suppose, is the present question; and wherein I think myself in duty obliged to express unto your lordships, with freedom and sincerity, my judgment, in all humble submission unto yours. —As for that part of the Bill which relates to our sovereign's murder, I find it so short, and so much out of the way of what we owe, both to the severity and solemnity of that revenge, that I cannot but think it, in some sort, (pardon the expression) a profanation of the due right of that sacred expiation, to handle it in the same Bill, promiscuously, with other more vulgar things. My motion therefore shall be, That there be forthwith a committee appointed, to consider of all things fit to be done, for the washing away of that stain from the nation, and from the age wherein we live; and to draw up an Act purposely and solely for that end. In confidence that this motion will either be embraced by your lordships, or that, if it be opposed, I shall have the liberty to fortify it by my reasons, I shall set that business apart, and apply my discourse to what concerns this bill, in all other relations; in which I shall not make nice to tell your lordships, that I think it defective in many things reasonable, and redundant in some things unreasonable; and yet, notwithstanding, not only my humble motion, but my most earnest pressure, as far as with humility I may, shall be, That we may proceed immediately to the passing of this Bill, with little or no alteration.—This, my lords, may appear a surprising motion from a person thought to be, as indeed I am, as much inflamed as any man living with indignation at the detestable proceedings of the late usurped power, so pernicious to the public, and so injurious to my own particular; in whom the motion may seem yet more surprising, when I shall have told you, with truth, that I am irreparably ruined in my fortune for my loyalty, if this Bill of Indemnity to others for their disloyalty, should pass as it is here offered unto your lordships: but the ground I go upon is this received maxim, as to all public sanctions, Better a mischief than an inconvenience; yea, better innumerable mischiefs to particular persons and families, than one heavy inconvenience to the public.—My lords; I profess unto you I find myself set on fire, when I think that the blood of so many virtuous and meritorious peers, and persons, and others of all ranks, so cruelly and impiously shed, should cry so loud for vengeance, and not find it from us. That many of the wickedest and meanest of the people should remain, as it were, rewarded for their treasons, rich and triumphant in the spoils of the most eminent in virtue and loyalty, of all the nobility and gentry of the kingdom. What generous spirit can make reflection on these things, and not find his heart burn into rage within him? Here it is, my lords, that we sufferers have need of all our philosophy. But when I consider that these are mischiefs only to the sufferers, and that, to insist upon a remedy, might perhaps expose the public to an irreparable inconvenience, I thank God I find, in an instant, all my resentments calmed and submitted to my primary duty.—My lords; we have here in our view a kingdom tossed, and rolling still with the effects of past tempests; and though, God be thanked, the storm be miraculously ceased, we cannot say that the danger is, until we get into still water: that still, that smooth water is only to be found in the generality's security from their guilty fears, and in the two houses' union between themselves, and with their sovereign. Whether the latter may not be endangered, if we should enter into controversy upon the particulars of this Bill, I leave unto your lordships to judge. But, certainly, as to the former, there can be hopes of raising monies, or disbanding armies, or of settling that happiness and tranquillity which we all sigh for, of being governed under our gracious sovereign by the antient and known laws of the land, whilst universal fears shall subsist by the delay in passing this Bill.—My lords; I shall sum up unto your lordships my whole drift in a few words. I think that, in this Bill, there are many things wanting, which solid and important reasons would require to be added, and many things inserted into it, which justice to his majesty's interest, and to particular persons, would require to be omitted, or rectified: but, I conceive, at the same time, that the mischiefs of the delay in passing it, do far outweigh all the advantages of improving it. My lords, I shall conclude my discourse, and your lordships trouble, with the application, to this purpose, of a memorable saying of that illustrious minister, the cardinal Mazarine, at a council in the wars of France, whereunto I had the honour to be called. It was, That in the great affairs of the world, he had not known any thing do more hurt than these two words, *faisons mieux*, let us do better: for, said he, whilst good wits endeavour, by debates, to bring good councils to a greater perfection, they do, for the most part, lose the opportunity of timing things rightly; which, in great actions, is of far more importance than the preference, according to refined reason, betwixt good and better. Upon this ground, my conclusion is, That that part which concerns the king's death, being put in the way proposed, we should proceed to the speedy passing of this Bill, without losing any time in emendations; but if we be destined to so fatal a loss, by ravelling into particulars, I shall, in that case, desire leave to offer unto your lordships therein my reflections also."

July 23. The lords made an Order, That the lieutenant of the Tower should examine colonel Hacker, touching the original Warrant* for execution of the late king, who soon after came down to the house, and acquainted their lordships, That he had examined the colonel, and that he confessed he had the Warrant at his house in the country, and that he believes it agrees with what was printed. But his wife and family being in town, he could not get it, without sending her down to fetch it. Hereupon the lords ordered, That the wife should go into the country to fetch the Warrant, and that the gentleman-usher of that house should send a man with her for that purpose.—The lieutenant of the Tower also acquainted the lords, That he had asked colonel Hacker if he knew the person that executed the late king, and he told him he heard it was a major, but did not know his name; but he would endeavour to find it out.

The lords ordered Lists to be made out from the Journal that came from the house of commons, of all those persons concerned in the Murder of the late king. After the reading of the said Lists, an Order was made, That all those in the beforesaid Lists should be absolutely excepted out of the Act of Indemnity; and that all their persons should be forthwith secured.

July 27. The duke of Ormond † was introduced into the house of lords, by the stile and title of baron of Lanthony, and earl of Brecknock.

The King's Speech to the Lords relative to the Act of Indemnity.] This day, the King came down the house of lords, and made the following Speech to them:

"My lords: When I came first hither to you, which was within two or three days after I came to Whitehall, I did, with as much earnestness as I could, both by myself and the chancellor, recommend to you and the house of commons, the speedy dispatch of the Act of Indemnity, as a necessary foundation of that security we all pray for. I did since, by a particular Message to the house of commons, again press them to hasten that important work; and did likewise, by a Proclamation, publish to all the kingdom, That I did with impatience expect, that that Act should be presented to me for my assent, as the most reasonable and solid foundation of that peace, happiness, and security, I hope and pray for, to myself, and all my dominions. I will not deny it to you, I thought the house of commons too long about that work, and therefore, now it is come up to you, I would not have you guilty of the same delay. I thank God, I have the same intentions and resolutions now I am here with you, which I had at Breda; and I believe that I owe my being here to God's blessing upon the intentions and resolutions I then expressed to have. I will read to you what I then said. 'And to the end 'that the fear of punishment may not engage 'any, conscious to themselves of what is passed, to a perseverance in guilt for the future, 'by opposing the quiet and happiness of their 'country in the Restoration both of king, peers, 'and people, to their just, antient, and fundamental rights, we do by these presents, declare, That we do grant a free and general 'Pardon, which we are ready, upon demand, 'to pass under our great seal of England, to 'all our subjects, of what degree or quality 'soever, who, within 40 days after the pub-

* For a Copy of the Warrant, see vol. iii. p. 1280.

† "After the earl of Clarendon, the man next in favour with the king, was the duke of Ormond; a man every way fitted for a Court: of a graceful appearance, a lively wit, and a chearful temper: a man of great expence, decent even in his vices, for he always kept up the form of religion. He had gone through many transactions in Ireland with more fidelity than success. He had made a treaty with the Irish, which was broken by the great body of them, though some few of them adhered still to him. But the whole Irish nation did still pretend, that, though they had broke the agreement first, yet he, or rather the king in whose name he had treated with them, was bound to perform all the articles of the treaty. He had miscarried so in the siege of Dublin, that it very much lessened the opinion of his military conduct. Yet his constant attendance on his master, his easiness to him, and his great sufferings for him, raised him to be Lord Steward of the Household, and Lord Lieutenant of Ireland. He was firm to the Protestant Religion, and so firm to the laws, that he always gave good advices: but when bad ones were followed, he was not for complaining too much of them." Burnet, vol. i. p. 95.

'lishing hereof, shall lay hold upon this our 'grace and favour, and shall, by any public 'Act, declare their doing so: and that they 'return to the loyalty and obedience of good 'subjects, excepting only such persons as shall 'hereafter be excepted by parliament. Those 'only excepted, let all our loving subjects, 'how faulty soever, rely upon the word of a 'king, solemnly given by this present Declaration, That no crime whatsoever committed against us or our royal father, before the 'publication of this, shall ever rise in judgment, or be brought in question, against any 'of them, to the least endamagement of them, 'either in their lives, liberties, or estates, or '(as far forth as lays in our power) so much 'as to the prejudice of their reputations, by 'any reproach, or term of distinction from the 'rest of our best subjects. We desiring and 'ordaining, that henceforward all notes of discord, separation, and difference of parties 'be utterly abolished among all our subjects, 'whom we invite and conjure to a perfect 'union among themselves under our protection, for the re-settlement of our just rights 'and theirs, in a free parliament; by which, 'upon the word of a king, we will be advised.' My lords, if you do not join with me in extinguishing this fear, which keeps the hearts of men awake, and apprehensive of safety and security, you keep me from performing my promise, which if I had not made, I am persuaded neither I nor you had been now here. I pray let us not deceive those who brought, or permitted, us to come together. I knew well there were some men who could neither forgive themselves, or be forgiven by us; and I thank you for your justice towards those, the immediate murderers of my father: and I will deal truly with you, I never thought of excepting any other. I pray think well upon what I have offered, and the benefit you and I have received from that offer, and encourage and oblige all other persons, by not excluding them from the benefit of this Act. This mercy and indulgence is the best way to bring them to a true repentance, and to make them more severe to themselves, when they find we are not so to them. It will make them good subjects to me, and good friends and neighbours to you; and then we have all our ends, and you shall find this the securest expedient to prevent future mischief. Therefore I do earnestly desire and conjure you to depart from all particular animosities and revenge, or memory of past provocations, and that you will pass this Act, without other exceptions, than of those who were immediately guilty of that murder of my father.—My lords, I have told you my opinion, and I hope you will be of the same. If any persons appear of such dangerous and obstinate principles, that the peace of the kingdom cannot be preserved whilst they have liberty in it, some other course may be taken, that they shall not be able to do hurt; and I assure you, there is nothing can enable them to do so much harm, as the deferring the passing this Act—I hope I need say nothing of Ireland, and that they alone shall not be without the benefit of my mercy. They have shewed much affection to me abroad, and you will have a care of my honour, and of what I have promised to them. I do again conjure you, that you will use all expedition in the dispatch of this Bill."

July 28. The king came again to the house of lords in order to pass some Bills that then lay ready for the royal assent. The commons being sent for as usual, and come up, their Speaker presented his majesty with two Bills; one, For a Grant of Tonnage and Poundage; the other, For a Continuance of Excise. After which, he made a short speech to the king, to this effect: "That it never was the custom of parliaments to charge the people with payments, until their liberties and grievances were first confirmed and redressed; yet, out of the greatest trust and confidence that ever subjects had in a prince, the house of commons did now go out of their old way, and had now supplied his majesty's necessities with the greatest gift that ever prince of this kingdom had ever given him by his people."—The Bills where then read by the clerk of parliament, and passed the royal assent.

The King's Message releasing all Arrears to the Crown.] July 30. The lords continuing to go into a committee every day, on the Bill of Indemnity, it was ordered, That the lord-chamberlain should go and acquaint his majesty with the great sums of money in Arrears in the Court of Wards, which are mentioned in the Act of Indemnity; and to know his majesty's pleasure therein. The next day, the said lord brought back from the king the following Answer in writing:

"C. R. His majesty is very well informed of the value of these Concessions, which are to pass in the Act of Indemnity, which relate intirely to his majesty's profit, and which have little or no relation to the war: he knows well that the Arrears of the wars, the Licences of Alienation, and Alienations without Licence, Purveyance, Respite of Homage, the Arrears of Rent still in the hands of the tenants, and the other particulars, amount to a great and vast sum; all which are released and discharged by this Act. But his majesty is so well satisfied of the good affection of his house of commons, and of their intentions and resolutions to settle such a Revenue upon his majesty as may preserve the crown from want, and from being undervalued by his neighbours; that he is resolved not to insist upon any particulars which the house of commons desired his majesty should release: and therefore, as his majesty thanks the house of peers for the information they have given him, and for the care they have expressed of his majesty's profit, so he is well contented that that clause shall pass in such manner as the house of commons hath set down: and continues his earnest desire, that all expedition be used in passing the said Act in the manner he hath formerly expressed.

Given at our Court at Whitehall, this 30th day of July in the 12th year of our reign. By his majesty's command, EDWARD NICHOLAS." *

This Answer the lords thought proper to communicate to the commons at a conference; who immediately appointed a large committee to sit and consider of settling such a Revenue on his majesty, as should maintain the splendour and grandeur of his kingly office, and preserve the crown from want, and from being undervalued by his neighbours.

Further Proceedings of the Lords on the Bill of Indemnity.] Aug. 1. The lords continued to scrutinize very closely into the principal actors of the late King's death; and this day col. Tomlinson, who commanded the guard at St. James's, and conducted the king to Whitehall, was examined; but by the evidence of Mr. Seymour, a member of the other house, who said that the late king told him, That the colonel did carry himself civilly towards his majesty in all respects, therefore their lordships, because it did not appear that the said col. signed the bloody Warrant; acquitted him, and ordered him to be left out of the List of excepted names in the Act of Indemnity.

The lord Roberts reported, from the committee on the said Act, That it was their opinion that col. Hacker, sir Henry Vane, sir Arthur Haslerig, col. Lambert, and col. Axtell, should be wholly exempted out of the Bill of Indemnity. Then was read the rest of the Clause, wherein the aforesaid persons were named in the Bill; and the question being put, Whether this clause should be left out of the Bill, it was carried in the affirmative.

August 2. The lords reported, from the committee on the Bill of Indemnity, that their further opinion was, That if any of the persons following, viz. Wm. Lenthall, Wm. Burton, Oliver St. John, col. Wm. Sydenham, col. Desborough, John Blackwell, Christ. Pack, Rd. Keeble, Ch. Fleetwood, John Pyne, Rd. Deane, maj. Creed, Philip Nye, John Goodwin, col. Corbet, and John Ireton, shall hereafter accept, or exercise, any office, ecclesiastical, civil, or military, or any other public employment, within this kingdom, dominion of Wales, or town of Berwick upon Tweed, or in Ireland, that then such person or persons that do so accept or execute as aforesaid, shall, to all intents and purposes in law, stand as if he or they had been totally excepted by name in this house.—All which the lords agreed to.

August 9. The lord Roberts reported from the above committee, That it was their opinion all those who sat in any High Court of Justice shall be made incapable of bearing any office, ecclesiastical, civil, or military, within this kingdom, &c. And that all such persons shall be liable to such further penalties as by any future act of parliament may be inflicted upon them, not extending to life; which the house confirmed.

The Commons urge the Lords again to pass it.] Notwithstanding the diligence the lords used to finish this business, yet the king and the house of commons thought them very slow in the matter. This day the commons sent up a Message to the lords to desire a conference with them on matters of importance: which being granted, and the lords returned, the lord-chancellor made the following Report of it, viz.—"That the house of commons desired earnestly the keeping of a good correspondency between the two houses, and to acquaint their lordships, That they had sent up several Bills to charge the people of this kingdom with Payments, contrary to former precedents of parliaments before Acts of Grace; for, as yet, there had been no such Act of Grace and Pardon to satisfy their representatives: and as we had a king, exceeding his predecessors in goodness and grace towards his people, so, the house of commons say, they have exceeded in their duty and proceedings beyond all former parliaments: that they had brought up divers Bills of great and public concernment to the king and the whole kingdom; as, the Bill of Indemnity, the Bill of Judicial Proceedings, one for Confirmation of Magna Charta; and the subjects cannot go on in chearfully paying their taxes, until the passing these Bills, especially that of Indemnity, which the houses have been so pressed for; first, by his majesty's Letter from Breda, and his Speech and Message, to give Expedition to.—And the house of commons further say, That they have such great and urgent occasions for present Monies, that they must be forced to desire a Loan of 100,000*l.* of the city of London, wherein they desire their lordships concurrence; but they had little hopes to obtain it, in regard of their fears, by the not passing the aforesaid Bill: that they had that day received a Message from the King concerning providing of Money speedily, for the Army and the Navy, who are in great necessity for money; there being 24 ships lately come into harbour for want of provisions, which cannot be got without money; also, for want of passing the Bill of Judicial Proceedings, the Judges cannot go their circuits, whereby the subjects suffer in their properties, estates, and lives; therefore the commons desired their lordships to give all possible expedition to the aforesaid Bills."

* "Secretary Nicholas was a man of general good reputation with all men, of unquestionable integrity and long experience in the service of the crown; whom the late king trusted as much as any man to his death. He was one of those who were excepted by the parliament from pardon or composition, and so was compelled to leave the kingdom shortly after Oxford was delivered up, when the king was in the hands of the Scots. The present king continued him in the office of secretary of state, which he had so long held under his father. He was a man of great gravity, and without any ambitious or private designs; and had a just friendship with the chancellor (Clarendon) for many years." Lord Clarendon's Life, p. 4.

After the hearing of this Remonstrance, the lords went into a committee on the Indemnity Bill; and, being resumed, the lord Roberts reported from them, That the opinion of the committee was, That, for the more speedy dispatch of this Bill, no further Addition or Exception shall be made to it, unless in the business of Ireland; which opinion was confirmed by the house.

The Lords pass the Indemnity Bill, with many Amendments.] August 10. The lords passed the Bill of Indemnity, with divers Amendments and Alterations; and ordered it to be sent down to the commons for their concurrence; as were, a few days after, the Bills for Poll Money and for Confirmation of all Judicial Proceedings.

Debate in the Commons, whether the Money Bill should precede the Act of Grace.] Before we proceed with the business of the house of lords, it is necessary to look back a little into the proceedings of the commons, after they had sent up the Bill of Indemnity.—And, first, we find in the MS. Diary so often quoted, That, on the 27th ult. when the commons had prepared the Money Bill, and it only waited for the royal assent, a motion was made by Mr. Annesley, for carrying it up; on which

Sir *John Northcot* said, That his duty to his king, and his love for his country, made a conflict within him; and desired the Bill for Money might not be carried up before the Act of Indemnity was passed: to which

Mr. *Pierepoint* answered. That, notwithstanding the lords delay, yet they ought not to stop the Money Bill; considering the great occasion the state had for money; and moved, rather to desire the king to quicken the lords.

Sir *George Downing* said, That it was not proper to distrust the king, but to pass the Bill for Money, without making conditions with him; and leave it to his majesty to hasten on the Bill of Indemnity.—Col. King and col. Jones spoke for sending up the Money Bill, and to trust the king.

Mr Secretary *Morrice* said, That they were afraid of their own fears; for fear did take things as they might happen; that they should have charity; and charity with reverence to princes; that, after having the king home without conditions, they should not then distrust him: adding, that confidence was the greatest obligation; that he had commands from the king to speed the Bill of Indemnity; but that they should shew their duty, and trust their king.

Sir *Henry Hungerford* said, He could not be jealous of his majesty, but the lords gave great cause for jealousy, in retarding the Bill so long; and desired the king might be moved to quicken them.

Mr. *Hollis* next said, If he thought the stopping the Bill of Indemnity, at present, was meant to injure the subject, he would not open his mouth for the Money Bill; but, as he was assured the king would do, and had done, all he could to hasten the Bill of Indemnity, if, after this, it stop only at the house of lords, the commons had acquitted themselves.

Mr. *Prynne* moved against the delay of the lords in other bills, as well as the last; especially in that against priests and jesuits: and, after all, it was voted, That the Bill for Money should pass; and the king be desired to appoint a time when the house should wait upon him with this and other Bills for the royal assent. At the same time, the members of the privy council and others, who were appointed to carry up this Message, were also to represent to his majesty, "That although Acts of Grace ever preceded Acts for Money, yet the house of commons had such confidence and assurance in his majesty's grace and goodness, that they do present the Bill for Money first, and shall wait his majesty's pleasure for speeding the Act of Grace."

This Message was carried to the king by Mr. Hollis, and others; and, at their return, Mr. Hollis reported the King's Answer to the Message, which was in these words: "That, if he knew his own heart, he took this kindness of the house so kindly, that he knew not how to be revenged of it; and, for the confidence they had in him, he only desired this, that they would retain it until he deceived them." And then he appointed the next day at 11 o'clock. (What was then done, at the king's coming to the house of lords, is already given at p. 90).

Debate in the Commons on the Ministers' Bill.] July 30. A Bill for settling and restoring Ministers in their Ecclesiastical Livings and Promotions, was read a 2nd time; and on which a long debate ensued, for which we are solely indebted, as well as for the former, to our MS. Diary.

Serj. *Littleton* moved against this bill, because, he said, it was to continue all scandalous Ministers out, and not remove all scandalous ones that were in.

Sir *Wm. Wheeler* was for committing the bill, and to refer the consideration of their characters to the justices of the peace in their respective counties.

Mr. *Palmer* was for stopping all extravagant preaching.

Sir *Tho. Clarges* moved against one Bond, a preacher, that writ a Book to justify the King's Murder, and produced the book.

Mr. *Prynne* moved to send for Bond; which was ordered.

Mr. *Thurland* moved, that all those who were to be continued, should read the 39 Articles.

Sir *Tho. Meres* seconded this motion; and spoke against the Triers at Whitehall, who put persons of anabaptistical principles into good livings; saying, They would put any body into mean livings; but none but those of their own humour into a great one.

Mr. *Swinfen* spoke for the bill; and that those who have now two livings may have but one; the present possessor to enjoy till Michaelmas; and not to impose all the Articles upon them; but only such as concern doctrine and not discipline; saying, It was too grating to the conscience. He moved also to bring the Bill in again by a committee speedily.

Sir *Heneage Finch* said, The Bill was not brought in according to the Votes of the committee; and moved against all such Ministers as will not conform to the laws of the land; saying, They could not punish the papists with any justice, if they did not punish their own Ministers for refusing to be regulated according to law. He added, That there was not a line in the Bill which provided against the scandalous, who were then incumbents; but that there was one against the ejected, and against those also who had two benefices. Lastly, he moved against all those Ministers who were presented against the consent of the patron, and were allowed to have grace but no allegiance: not to confirm any such; nor abate one of the 39 Articles, or the Oaths, to those that should stay in, but to leave them to their several patrons to be prosecuted according to law.

Mr. *Prynne* was for all Ministers to take the oaths; but their presentations to be good throughout, though not by the right patrons, in times of trouble.

Sir *John Masham* was for setting aside the whole Bill, or bringing in another; saying, That it was needless, or unjust, to confirm those persons in their livings against the patrons; and, having voted the king all his lands and appurtenances, this confirmation would contradict that act.

Mr. *Allen* was not for taking care of the patron if he neglected to present within six months; but, if he did, he said it was fitting there should be care taken to name very choice men, in the respective counties, to examine the matter, what sort of men they presented.

Sir *John Bowyer* said, There was before the house what was fit and what was just to be done; that he was for the just; and moved for the Oaths and the 39 Articles to be taken and subscribed by all priests; but moved, more especially, against those who were instrumental against the king.

Mr. *Trevor* spoke next, for mixing prudence with justice, and restoring all those who were truly deserving to their benefices: but yet to consider those who are in, that were as deserving too. He moved also against patrons, pro hac vice, and said, There was no provision in the Bill against those who are scandalous, and were then in.

Mr. *Charlton* spoke against the referring the Bill to a committee, but to refer it to the law; so as to let every man then in possession continue so, if he can prove the right owner scandalous; but, if he do not, then to be liable to arrears. He hoped the house would not be more cruel than Harry 8th, who allowed his turned-out priests maintenance for their lives; and therefore moved for all arrears of fifths only to be restored; but that no one man that was a Trier, and had a living then given him, should enjoy it.

Mr. *Hungerford* was for prudence and moderation, and committing the bill.

Mr. *Thomas* was for none to have the benefit of their livings that would not conform to the law; nor that justices or commissioners should be any judges of this business, but refer all to the law.

Mr. *Stephens*, was for restoring the orthodox, and against the scandalous; saying, He knew one that said, 'The Devil take the flock so he had the fleece;' and was for having six orthodox divines to join with the commissioners.

Mr. *Barton* was for having all to take the Oaths and read the Articles; but none to stay in that would not conform to the law; also to have some divines joined to the commissioners.

The Indemnity Bill sent down by the Lords to the Commons: Their Debate upon it.] August 11. After a long debate, the Bill of Indemnity was brought down from the lords with several Amendments and Alterations. The commons went immediately upon it; and, first, voted to agree with the lords for pardoning the Arrears of Papists on Sequestration, and Mr. Thurloe. Upon the lords excepting all the King's Judges, sir George Booth stood up in behalf of those who came in upon the Proclamation: he produced two Papers in favour of the lord Grey of Grooby, to testify his penitence for his being against the king, and moved to have his name left out of the Bill. Col. King moved to agree with the lords in excepting all. Sir John Bowyer was for adhering to his former vote. Sir Heneage Finch was not for adhering wholly, nor for agreeing; but, to salve all, he was for banishing those who were not executed. Sir Anth. Irby moved for a conference with the lords, concerning those that surrendered. Mr. Annesley was for adhering to those that came in, and a conference for the rest. In the end, it was voted to adhere to those that surrendered.

Aug. 13. The debate was re-assumed. The house agreed with the lords in pardoning sir Gilbert Pickering and Tho. Lister, esq.; and for the other 24 in that classis, it was carried to adhere to their former Vote about them, as to pains, &c. Voted also, To agree with the lords to except col. Hacker for life; which they had added to the Bill. A question was put, Whether to agree with the lords in pardoning Mr. Lenthall, and the other 15 in that classis, the house divided upon it; when the Yeas carried it by 197 against 102.—Another question was then started, Whether to agree with the lords about the excepting of Lambert, Vane, Haslerig, and Axtell, or to adhere to their former Vote, as to pains and penalties not extending to life; voted to adhere. Col. Scrope, whom the lords had also excepted, was voted to come off for a year's value of his estate. Col. Wauton, with the others of that classis, whom the lords had condemned for life, the commons reprieved for pains and penalties: but then they voted, That all the foregoing persons, as well as those who sat in any high court of justice, should never bear any office, civil or military, in the kingdom. In this debate the Diary informs us, That col. Shapcot, speaking in favour of the High Court of Justice men, was charged by col. Jones with being one himself. To which Shapcot replied, That if col. Jones was not careful of other men's credit, he desired he would be so of his own; and denied that he ever sat in any.

Conference between the two Houses, concerning the Indemnity Bill.] Aug. 16. The Bill of Indemnity, with such Alterations as the commons thought fit to make in the Amendments of the lords, had been returned to that house; and this day their lordships sent to desire a free and speedy conference about it: which being agreed to and ended, the commons ordered, That the Report of this conference should be made to them the next day. Accordingly,

Aug. 17. Sir Heneage Finch reported, That according to the commands of this house, the committee attended the lords at a Conference yesterday; and that the substance of the said Conference was as followeth:

"That the matter thereof was about the Bill of Indemnity: to shew wherein they did adhere to their former Amendments; and wherein they do agree with the Alterations made by this house.—That the lord Finch did manage the conference for the house of peers; and was pleased to tell us, in the first place, That in the Clause concerning Ireland they were willing to agree with this house, with some amendments;—(which the reporter did particularly open; and are specified in a Paper, then delivered to be communicated to this house;)—and these being agreed, it will comprehend their agreeing to some other words in the Bill, touching his majesty's dominions.—His lordship told us, That, to that clause, which concerns several persons that were Judges of his late majesty, they adhered, as they formerly sent it down; that is, to the blotting out of that Clause, whereby they were reserved to future penalties; and to the excepting of them for life, for which he offered some reasons, That though it be true we are now upon an Act of Indemnity and Oblivion, yet, they hoped, we would not make it an Act of Oblivion of our duty to God, the king, and the safety and honour of the kingdom.—He took notice, That this kingdom having now arrived to a miracle of preservation when the pit of destruction was open, and the privileges thereof, in all the parts of them, invaded; when the Murder of the King had been committed, against all the laws of God and man: this ought to stir up in us a sense more than ordinary; and, therefore, he thought it fit for us to consider our duty to the king, a gracious prince, and a prince endeared to us by the miraculous preservation of his person by the hand of Heaven; a prince that had suffered great afflictions, like Joseph in Egypt, lying long in fetters; and that such as entered into his soul, like David, when he was hunted as a partridge in the wilderness; and that had received deliverance like to that of David's and Joseph's, being both in the 30th year of their age: and the afflictions that befel this good king, were the effects of the counsels of these men that are now in question.—He said, We are next to consider the Safety of the kingdom: their lordships did not think it fit nor safe for this kingdom, that they should live: here they cannot live, nor abroad with safety; for danger to a kingdom is not always within doors: their life may give them opportunity of tampering to the working of mischief abroad. Then for the honour of the kingdom; first, in point of justice, blood requires blood; and he instanced in the Gibeonites, the shedding of their blood could not be expiated but by the shedding of blood.—He took notice, That his majesty's honour was concerned in the infamy, which the shedding of that royal blood hath brought upon this nation, in the eyes of foreign nations; and that this is the only opportunity to take it off.—He took notice of an objection, from the Proclamation, issued by his majesty, on the desire of both houses; and, before he gave Answer to that, he observed the wonderful moderation the king and house of peers had shewed in their proceeding towards the punishment of offenders at this time. His lordship observed, That to petition to bring a king to justice; to summon him to justice; to sit upon him, when he was summoned to justice; and to abuse the people by suggestions that might lead them to approve this action, made them so criminal, as none could excuse them: these proceedings were all high treason in themselves; and yet all these are pretermitted in the Act of Oblivion: these are those who murdered his royal father; those that sentenced him, and signed the Warrant: which moderation he made use of to shew, that they might have been more strict in this case. And to the objection from the Proclamation, he said, Something sure was intended by it: but, first, the Proclamation was but negative in the words of it; and that which can be gathered from it, is only implications out of a negative. He took notice how the Proclamation runs; first, 'That because divers persons are fled from justice, that they cannot be brought to a legal trial, therefore they are summoned to render themselves:' Whence it was argued, that the meaning thereof was suitable to the recital, 'To bring them to Justice.' He observed, That this Proclamation calls in, among the rest, Lisle and Say: it might have added Baxter and Scott; and yet none will say it intended to pardon them: therefore, he gathered, there could not be supposed an absolute intention in that Proclamation to pardon all that came in upon it: for the very persons instanced in, had they come in, had yet not been pardoned. He observed, That the Proclamation says, they must come in, under pain of being excepted from pardon and indemnity, for life and estate; and that we ourselves had resolved to confiscate their estates, notwithstanding the rendering of themselves: and thence his lordship argued thus: If it be just to take away their estates, it is as just to take away their Lives: If it be not just to take away their lives, then it is not just to take away their estates.—His lordship said farther, If these persons, thus excepted for life and estate, should, by us, be not excepted for life, but subjected only to future penalties, then the consequence would be, that we shall adhere to the pardon of some to life, who are more guilty a great deal than some of the persons whom we have excepted for life; some of them having been at all the sittings on the king, diligent attendants thereon all the while; some of them designing the place of slaughter before his own house. It is true, he said, the thrones of kings are established by judgment and mercy; but mercy had been shewed already, and nothing remains now for support of his throne but justice: And therefore his lordship concluded this point with advice, 'Let the wickedness of these men fall 'on their own heads; but let the throne of our 'king be established for ever.'—To the exception of the 4 perons that follow in the Clause concerning Vane, Lambert, &c. they also adhere, that they should stand excepted for life: His lordship said, indeed they were not excepted as murderers; but he took notice, that the king, of whose wisdom none can or doth doubt, and of whose wisdom, he knows, this house hath as great a veneration as any, his majesty himself, sitting the parliament, (who could not but take notice of it) thought fit to commit these persons to the Tower of London * * intimated, by some Letters of his majesty's in print, 'If there be persons dangerous to the safety of the nation;'—and, as such, he looked on these: but he said withal, if they were capable of mercy, no question but the king, the fountain of mercy, would extend it to them. In the mean time, their lordships thought it fit to leave them to the mercy of the king, and so he hoped this house will too.—To the Exception of those other 4 persons, that sat in the several high courts of justice, their lordships also adhere. He observed, It was some moderation in the house of peers, that they take no more than one a-piece. He said this was done among them suddenly, and at the table, without conference with any other persons, or meditating a revenge, to shew the candour and plainness of their proceedings: he confessed, it was equal and just, there should be a like expiation for the breach made on the privilege of the commons, and that some persons should be excepted on their account: But their lordships were as careful of the privileges of this house as of their own, and having more reason to expect it from us, than to send it to us, therefore they omitted that.—To the Proviso, whereby the 26 are sent down under an incapacity of all public employment, their lordships do agree, being content to acquiesce in their incapacitating only; and to omit the adjourning of them to future pains and penalties."

Debate thereon.] After the hearing of this Report, the commons read over the Amendments the lords had a second time made in the Bill, and a long debate ensued upon them, which we give from the Diary.

Sir *Wm. Wylde*, Recorder of London, said, That he was not convinced by what had been read, nor could he concur with the lords, so as to except all the King's Judges for life, because of the Proclamation.—Mr. Stevens, col. Shapcot, Mr. Trevor, and Sir John Bowyer, moved to adhere to their former Vote. Sir John Northcot, to petition the king. On the other side, sir A. Broderick was for agreeing with the lords.

Mr. *Charlton* said, He did not understand how a Vote of the house should be a contract, because they broke it as to Vane and Lambert, Haslerig and Axtell; and was for agreeing with the lords.

Sir *Edw. Turner* said, They were between two rocks, the honour of that house, and the desire of the lords; that they were masters of their own votes, and had pardoned Thurloe, whom before we condemned, and added Hacker, whom they never thought on: he also was for agreeing.

Mr. *Annesley* said, He would willingly do justice for the king's blood, and yet preserve the honour of the house, and moved for a committee to recollect and state all that had been done in it before.

Sir *Heneage Finch* put a question to the house, Whether it was better to venture the shipwreck of the whole vessel, or throw a few over-board? And said, That if they spared their lives they could not take one acre of their estates by the Proclamation. He added, That if any one of them should fly to a foreign prince, the war would be just if that prince would not render him up: that it was for the safety of the nation to throw Sheba's head over the wall: and, lastly, that the sparing of these people was the way to lose the Act of Oblivion to all; for who would think themselves obliged, when every one was pardoned; therefore he was for agreeing with the lords.

Mr. *Prynne* argued, That he was for excepting all at first, and was so still; and if they were not all so, they themselves must be guilty of the king's blood, those being such horrid traitors as never yet were known: that our oaths bound us much more than our votes, which we alter daily: what would the world say of us, adds he, but call us regicides? And said, they were bound, in conscience and honour, to agree with the lords.

Sir *Rd. Temple*, intimated a desire to agree with the lords; but did not conclude positively, but left it to the judgment of the house.

Col. *King* said, Though they passed a Vote for seven, the lords did not; and moved to have a greater regard for their own safeties than for such men, and therefore to agree with the lords.

Sir *Dudley North* spoke for the same; lest it should retard the whole Bill; but then to enter the Vote in the Journal, that it was only done for that end; and to petition the king to extend mercy to those that came in upon the Proclamation.

Serj. *Hales* said, That there never was so high a crime committed: that, if there was a cause shewn by the lords, they must alter their Vote; but the question was, Whether the lords had shewn that cause? But the case, he said, was here, That now they were in their power they could not let them go; and moved to have a *true* representation of the matter of fact, and then to judge.—Upon which, a committee was ordered accordingly.

The next day this debate was resumed; when sir Wm. Wylde, from the committee, made a Report concerning the Bill of Indemnity, and the Examination of the passages therein. To which,

Mr. *Allen* said, That he was not in the house when the first Vote was made: but that the fact of taking off the king was most barbarous, and the not bringing those men to justice would retard the Act: but then, on the other side, the honour of the house was to be preserved by reason of the Proclamation; and yet neither the Vote nor Proclamation were so binding, but the house might agree with the lords; for the Proclamation did not express mercy to those that came in: yet, he added, they did come in upon that Proclamation, and therefore he moved to have those pardoned; so was for adhering.

Sir *Henry North* replied and said, That had he a brother or an only son, he would not spare him in such a case: that the Vote was not binding, because it was relative as to the lords; and, for the proclamation, he said, they should be favoured in their estates for their wives and children, but not for their lives; and concluded for agreeing with the lords.

Mr. *Knight* spoke for an Agreement also, saying, That these people's lives were but as a bucket of water to the ocean, in regard of so many more as were to receive benefit by the Act of Pardon.

Mr. *Young* said, It would be a miserable thing if the act should be hindered by not agreeing with the lords; but yet, the vote of the house being passed, he thought it was obligatory, especially as the general himself had moved so earnestly in their behalfs: that he could not recede from his vote; but desired to have another conference with the lords.

Mr. *Thurland* said, The Votes of the house were alterable, without breach of honour or trust: and, for the Proclamation, it was no law nor a contract, and their coming in was but ex debito justitiæ; and moved for taking their lives, but to be favourable to their estates.

Col. *King* said, Their coming in upon the Proclamation was, that God had infatuated them to bring them to justice; 'qui Jupiter vult perdere prius dementat,' and that they were not injured by the house.

Mr. *Swinfen* said, That he desired to be rightly understood, that no one who spoke in behalf of these men, should be thought to allow of their fact; but what he spoke was for the honour of the house: that the Proclamation was obligatory, though there was no positive promise in it; yet it was as much security as that house could give; and that it would discourage all for the future from trusting to any such thing: he therefore moved for another conference with the lords, and to put the question, To agree with them or not.—On the contrary was

Col. *Jones* saying, What will the world think of those that speak for the king's murderers?

Sir *John Northcot* got up, and desired he might be called to the bar, or explain himself: Upon which the colonel stood up again and said, He did not reflect upon any person.

Sir *Rd. Brown*, the younger, said, He was for mercy; but it was for all the people in the land, and not for such horrid murderers as these were.

Sir *John Northcot* moved to have a free conference; and if the lords would not agree with them, then to agree with the lords as to their exceptions.

Serj. *Hales* said, That the Proclamation did not imply that those who came in should be pardoned, though they did presume upon it; nor would he plead for such offenders, but for the honour of the king and the houses. Adding, that if they had not been invited by the Proclamation they had been safe, which now they were not; and to refer them to the king was but to take a thorn out of their own foot, and put it into his.

Sir *Heneage Finch* said, It was only honour to observe the Vote, which pleaded against justice. He was for agreeing with the lords.

Col. *Birch* argued for sticking to the Proclamation; saying, That if he should give Articles to a garrison, he should think himself very unworthy to break them.

Sir *Edw. Turner* answered the colonel, and said, The king might summons any person that went beyond the sea to come over, and he was not bound to pardon him if he did.—At length a Conference was agreed to.

Second Conference between the two Houses, concerning the Indemnity Bill.] Aug. 21. A Report was made in the house of lords, of the effect of the free Conference yesterday had with the commons, concerning the Bill of Indemnity. viz. "The house of commons say, That they abhor and detest the horrid Murder of the late king; but they hold themselves bound to insist upon the number of 7 to be excepted for life and estate, because they conceive that many came in upon the king's Proclamation, and they are obliged to consider those persons that came in upon the public faith, and the king's honour is concerned in it. They said further, That the king's Message from Breda was intended to pardon all, excepting such persons as should be excepted by parliament: That the commons do propound an expedient, that those that came in upon the Proclamation should stand in the Bills as they are brought up from the commons, and a Bill to be brought in hereafter to proceed against them as the parliament shall think fit, both for life and estate. Concerning their lordships excepting Vane, Haslerig, Lambert, and Axtell, for life and estate, the commons say there is nothing appears to them to give that sentence upon them; therefore they desire that those 4 persons may stand in the classis as they came up in the Bill. Concerning the 4 persons their lordships had excepted for life and estate, upon account of sentencing to death the 4 peers, the commons say that one of those 4 is dead, and another is as good as dead; and they do not insist upon the shedding of blood upon the account of the death of commoners, and they hope their lordships would not have the sacrifice of the king's blood to be mingled with any other blood. Concerning the business touching Ireland; the commons do agree to their lordship's Alterations, and they desire that their lordships would concur with them in the aforesaid particulars, as they are brought from the commons."—And, after a long and serious debate of this business, it was ordered, That the lord who managed this free Conference with the commons, with the Addition of the Duke of Gloucester, earl of Southampton, and the lord Seymour, shall meet and consider of Reasons, according to the sense of this debate, to be offered at a Conference with the commons to-morrow morning, to fortify their lordships Resolutions herein, and to offer such expedients as they conceive may tend to a good conclusion of this business between the two houses; and to report the same to this house to-morrow morning.

Third Conference between the two Houses, concerning the Indemnity Bill.] Aug. 22. The lords sent a message to the commons, to desire a present free Conference with them, on the matter of the last, relating to the Bill of Indemnity; which being passed on the following day, sir Heneage Finch reported the substance of the said Conference as follows:—"The Conference," he said, "was managed by the lord chancellor (Hyde,) who applied his Reasons to these heads: 1. To the persons involved in the Exception for life and estate, as murderers of his late majesty: 2. To the 4 that are excepted for life and estate, viz. Vane, Haselrig, Lambert, and Axtell: 3. To those who sat in high courts of justice upon the peers. He told us the lords had weighed the Reasons offered from this house, with a great desire of concurrence, and willingness to retract from their own reason, if they had found cause. His lordship observed, the Reasons urged were taken partly from his majesty's Declaration, and partly from the Proclamation issued by advice of both houses. He took notice, that his majesty had frequently interposed, and been solicitous, for the dispatch of this bill; yea so far that (as he expressed himself) no guilty person in the kingdom did more desire the passing of it than himself: and, for the Declaration at Breda, he said it was not to be doubted but his majesty would most religiously observe it. But whereas it had been offered that his majesty tendered an absolute pardon to all persons, and that the exception mentioned was in the nature of a defeazance thereunto, and that, if a bill had been tendered, without an exception, his majesty had been obliged to pass it. To that his lordship answered, True it was so; and had a Bill been tendered to the king, without any exception at all, he had been much absolved by concurring with the houses, though much against his judgment: But his majesty was confident, when he sent that Message, that we would be as forward to do him and the nation justice, as he to desire it: And, withal, he desired us to take notice, that Declaration came inclosed in a letter, which reposed an intire confidence in the houses of parliament; and in which there is this clause: 'If there be a crying sin in which the nation may be involved in the infamy that attended it, we cannot doubt but that you will be as solicitous to redeem and vindicate the nation from that guilt and infamy, as we can be:' And his lordship said, His majesty could never doubt but the parliament could have as great resentment of that parricide, as the honour and justice of the nation is greatly concerned in it. He told us, His majesty (who was duly sensible of the great wound he received in that fatal day, when the news of it came to the Hague) bore but one part of the tragedy, for the whole world was sensible of it; and particularly instanced, that a woman at the Hague, hearing of it, fell down dead with astonishment*. His lordship told us, by the way, He had the honour to be then employed as the minister of his publicaffairs, in the court of Spain; and that the king's majesty, that now is, gave him in special command, and as part of his Instructions in that negotiation, that, when he treated with the king of Spain, he should avow and declare, that the Murder of his father was not looked upon, by him, as the act of the parliament or the people of England, but of a very wretched and very little company of miscreants in this kingdom: and that his majesty hath the same opinion still; not doubting but, if no Letter had been sent with the said Declaration, to intimate by way of restriction, what use should be made of his Declaration, yet the parliament of England would be as forward to except his father's murderers from pardon, as the thing merits: And he desired us to consider, if God had wrought this miracle of restitution within a month, or year, or another short time after the fact committed, how full of zeal, how full of vengeance, had the spirit of the nation likely to have been. His lordship took notice: That his majesty's Proclamation was pressed, by us, out of a ten-

* "The barbarous stroke," says lord Clarendon, "so surprised the king, that he was in all the confusion imaginable, and all about him were almost bereft of their understanding. The truth is, it can hardly be conceived, with what a consternation this terrible news was received by all, even by the common people of that country. There was a woman at the Hague, of the middling rank, who, being with child, with the horror of the mention of it, fell into travail, and in it died." Vol. v. p. 276.

derness we had to the honour of the nation, the king, and both houses of parliament, which are involved in it; and out of a desire that public invitations might not prove snares: To which his lordship said, That the lords themselves, being involved in the same honour with us, (aye, and the king too) hope the Reasons, which did satisfy their lordships, and had satisfied his majesty, would satisfy this house. He did profess, that the peers never had any other sense of this Proclamation, than as a process or summons, under pain of being excepted from any pardon of life or estate, if they came not in. He said, It was the sense of the king too; and it was not credible any man could imagine that the king would ever have joined with the houses in such a Proclamation, unless he had been confident the houses would have meant so likewise. His lordship pressed further, That, let the world judge of this Proclamation, they cannot but believe it was the sense of this house too; for it could not be imagined, that if Lisle, Say, Barkstead, and Scott, who were all inserted into the Proclamation, had come in, they should have had the benefit of their lives. It is true (his lordship observed) the Exception of these men, by our votes, was before the publishing of the Proclamation; but he desires pardon, if that seems not, to the peers, of any great weight; for, whatsoever our Votes were, the snare was the same upon such of the persons concerned, who took notice of our Votes, not of the Proclamation; as Scott pleads, he heard of the Proclamation, not of the Votes. He pressed us duly to consider the honour and justice of the nation; and what a reproach it would be if such offenders should escape justice, after such a crime. He put us in mind of some circumstances of aggravation: First, A libel is lately spread abroad, that justifies the Murder of the King with a bare face; yea, justifies it, as necessary; and that on such wicked grounds and arguments, as, in the logic of it, extends to the person of our sacred king that now is, should he fall into their hands. He told us, one of the persons we contend for lurks still; and that a serjeant at arms being sent to apprehend him, he rescued himself; yea, the sheriff of that county being required to give assistance therein, he refused. For the expedeint offered; the lords look upon it as that which tends to the making of these men's conditions better than now they are; an expedient to put off the discourse, and to make the Reasons, their lordships had given, of less weight hereafter than now.—To the other part, wherein they do adhere, as to the excepting for life Vane, Lambert, Haselrig, and Axtell, his lordship said, He did not believe that we of this house looked on these persons as innocent men; or as men so happy as not to have any crime laid to their charge. He thinks that, had we that good opinion of them, we should not ourselves have excepted them for future pains and penalties. He took notice to us, That the king's Speech to the House of lords, when they had passed this Act of Indemnity as far as they could, and included all these men, his father's murderers, in that fatal exception, gave them thanks for their justice on the immediate murderers of his father; and that, in that speech, there was a subsequent clause, which, if any persons be dangerous to the state, recommended it to the lords to have a care of them also. Now, for one of them, that is Axtell; the ground of excepting him was this: they had received information from Ireland, (where he is best known) which was first presented to the council, and by them to their lordships, that in the year 1648, while the Murder was acting and carrying on, he pressed the soldiers, with violence, to cry and clamour for justice; and when the violence had gone so far that the bloody Sentence was pronounced, he urged them to cry out, 'Execution! Execution!' For Lambert, his lordship intimated, That we could not but take notice how near he was to give a turn to all the present settlement we enjoy. For Haslerig and Vane, his lordship observed, That they were persons whom the secluded members, after their restitution, and when they were preparing the way for the great and good work, which is now effected, looked upon as fit to be secured and confined: That, after the king was come in, these gentlemen, notwithstanding the censure on them by the secluded members, and the blessed end of the Long Parliament, returned to town; never applying themselves to the king, but lurked up and down, without giving any account of themselves: and his lordship added, That they look on them as persons of a mischievous activity; and therefore their lordships desire to leave them to the mercy of the king; with this further intimation, That they would be ready to join with this house in a Petition to the king, that mercy might be shewed them; and that his severity might not extend to their lives; and he did not doubt but the intercession of the houses would be effectual for that. For the last four, who sat in the High Courts of Justice; his lordship observed, That we, of the house of commons, had departed very much from our own passion and provocation, in urging it as a reason why we could not agree, because we could not mingle the expiation of the blood of peers with the expiation of the blood of the king: but that, he said, was not the motive, but justice itself upon so high a breach of the law: and offered to consideration, whether it would not amount to justify those courts, if some severity was not used: but this was not much pressed, nor long insisted on."

"When his lordship had made an end, some worthy gentlemen, that attended the Conference, offered something of Reply; and I may do them some wrong in repeating it: but they are here, and can do right to themselves. It was observed, That this Proclamation was but in the nature of a process: to which it was said, Then at least they should have been heard before they were excepted; which they were not.—Secondly, In the summoning part of the Proclamation, there is not one word relating to a Trial; but the parliament were busy in proceeding upon the Act of Oblivion, and issued the Proclamation, that they might know in what rank to place these men: and admitting that this Proclamation, as to the holding forth of benefit to those that came in, amounts at highest to an implication; yet, being an implication, on which men have put their lives, it was dishonourable (as a worthy member enforced it) to retract the benefit held forth by the Proclamation. It was likewise observed, by the same worthy member, That to except them as to a trial signifies nothing; for they that do not come in are, however, excepted as to a trial. To which his lordship answered, It is true, that in the consequence of it, and as things now stand, it is so: those that come not in will have the benefit of a trial if they be taken, as well as those that do come in: but, at the time of the Proclamation, it might have been expected to be otherwise; and that those who did not render themselves should have been, ipso facto, attainted, and executed whensoever found. His lordship instanced the example of Scott, who professed, for himself, that he rendered on the account of the Proclamation, though his render will not serve his turn: for that render, which will save his life, must be a render to the Speaker or sheriff; to which he cannot pretend. But his lordship added, That if that be the meaning of the Proclamation, to extend benefit of life to all that rendered themselves, the equity is the same, as to him: for if a man hear of the Proclamation, and that he should have the benefit of it if he rendered himself to the Speaker or sheriff, and hastens to do it, but, being not able to do it within the time, renders himself to a public minister, it would be hard to make him incapable of the benefit intended by the Proclamation. Therefore his lordship observed, those that rendered themselves must not necessarily have the benefit of their lives. —It was then urged, that their lordships had excepted persons that are dead; Constable, Mauleverer, Danvers, and others; and that the excepting of them out of the Act of Oblivion signifies nothing: but the place where the commons had put them, was, that their estates should be subject to future penalties: a bare exception subjects not their estates to future penalties; but, when the Act passes, the heir and executor is discharged, though the ancestor be excepted. To which his lordship replied, They knew the exception of itself operated nothing; but they supposed and believed the persons excepted by this Act would (as well as Bradshaw and Cromwell) be attainted, for their guilt was equal, and they might deserve alike. For the 4 persons; it was observed, That to except Vane and the rest, so as to involve them in the danger of life and estate, and in the mean time to petition for their pardon, was repugnant in itself. To which his lordship made no reply, other than that still they were at the king's mercy, which way soever the proceedings passed."

Debate thereon.] After this Report was ended, the commons fell again into a debate on the question, Whether they should agree or not agree with the lords in this matter.—Mr. Prynne moved first for agreeing, and was seconded by sir Roger Palmer.—Mr. Howard said, That the late king cloathed them in scarlet, and had turned their iron into brass, their brass into silver, and themselves into gold: that this prince should be murdered at his own door, would make them seek out such a punishment for it, as the exquisiteness of a woman could invent: but the honour of the house being engaged, he moved to adhere; and to banish or immure them, that they should never see the sun more, which would be worse than death.—Sir Heneage Finch could not agree with the lords as to those who were dead; nor with them, as to those who sat upon the lords; and was willing to leave Vane, Haselrig, Lambert, and Axtell, to the king.—Sir George Booth moved for another conference with the lords, in hopes there might be some other expedient offered.—Mr. Baynton was for reading all petitions that came from these men.—Mr. Trevor was for adhering, and not to violate the public faith which had been given.—Mr. Gott was for adhering also, because he did advise some friends to come in.—Sir Gilbert Gerrard said, that he invited several to come in on the Proclamation; and therefore could never give his vote to agree.—Both these last gentlemen moving, also, for another free Conference with the lords, it was voted; the same managers as at the last, were deputed for this also.

But before this last Conference was desired, the Heads of it, as drawn up by the committee, were read in the house and approved of by them. These Heads are entered in the Journals of the commons; but since they will be better understood by the Report of them made afterwards in the upper house, and from the MS. Diary, we postpone them. Observing, that the commons, in order to bend somewhat to the lords, and that this last Conference might be made final and conclude this affair, entered previously into the following debate about it:—Mr. Trevor, who reported some things to be offered at the next Conference with the lords, said, That such of the king's judges as were excepted against might be banished, never to return. If that was not yielded to, then to refer them to another act for life, but to spare them in this. Sir Heneage Finch told the house, That if they spared Vane, Haslerig, Lambert, and Axtell, they did it not out of favour, but to leave them as living monuments of their villainy, and the houses dislike: urging that saying of David, 'Slay them not lest my people forget it.'—After this, the house voted to agree with the lords, as to except Axtell for life.

Mr. Thomas moved to have somebody die for the kingdom as well as for the king, and named sir Henry Vane. Sir Ralph Ashton said, That sir H. Vane told him, after the battle of Worcester, when the king escaped, and sir Ralph Ashton asked him, 'Where is your 'Providence now, which you have so oft spoke 'of, since the king is escaped?' To which he replied, 'If the man was above ground they 'would have him.' Sir Anth. Irby said, That since they had taken all he had, they might well spare his life. Mr. Hollis said, It was his majesty's pleasure to except only those who were his father's Judges, which Vane was not.—But one Mr. Lowther speaking against Vane, it was voted, To agree with the lords, as to except him for life.

Next, came on the trial of gen. Lambert, who was also excepted by the Lords; when it was moved by sir Allen Broderick to put him to a short question; Mr. Annesley moved, To read his Petition first. Sir George Booth spoke in Lambert's behalf. Mr. Swinfen moved to agree with the lords; but to petition the king to be merciful to them.—The question being called for, and put, it was voted, That Lambert should also be excepted.

Lastly, a motion was made against sir A. Haslerig. Mr. Tomkins said, That sir Arthur told him, when the first short parliament was dissolved, That the king should repent that day's work with every vein in his body. On the other hand, the knight had many speakers in his behalf. Mr. Petty moved for him, because the General engaged for him. Mr. Annesley spoke also in behalf of him, and to hear his Petition before the question was put. Mr. Young for him, alledging his rashness, which made him not a dangerous person.—Lord Ancram said, He was the main man that stirred up the Vote of no more Addresses to the late king; saying to the Speaker, 'Shall we believe that man of no faith?' and moved to put him to the question. Sir Roger Palmer said, That sir Arthur told him, 'If Charles Stuart do come in, it was but three wry mouths and a swing,' and therefore moved against him.—Sir A. A. Cooper was for executing nobody but those who were guilty of the king's blood, and said, He thought this man not considerable enough; but moved to put him with the rest. Col. Birch, by desire of the general, spoke for him. Sir John Bowyer was for having him walk to the gallows with the rest, and then come back again. However, at last, the question being put, the house divided upon it, Whether sir A. Haslerig should be included with the rest? The numbers on the division, were 116 to 141.

After this last Vote was passed, and sir Arthur spared, Mr. Pierepoint moved, That the king might be petitioned, that Lambert and Vane should not be tried for their lives by law; which was agreed to.

The last Conference between the two Houses on the Indemnity Bill.] Aug. 25. The lords sending to desire another Conference with the commons, they met accordingly, and the Report of it was made in that house afterwards, by sir Heneage Finch, in these words:—"The lord-chancellor told us, how unhappy soever former conferences have been, this, he doubted not, would be happy to the king and kingdom, and beget a chearful submission of all people to the determination of the parliament: he said he would repeat nothing of what he had formerly said; for though the lords might have insisted, in the Reasons they formerly offered, yet they have now complied with this house in effect, though not in form. The expedient for a final conclusion of the difference was this; That those gentlemen that rendered themselves on his majesty's proclamation, should stand in the same classes as in the lords Amendments formerly sent down; that is, as persons generally excepted for life and estate: but, to qualify that, they offered a clause to be added by way of Amendment, wherein the names of those persons who rendered themselves (their lordships know them not, and so have left the Paper with a Blank for that) upon an opinion, that they might safely do so, and have not fled to avoid the justice of the parliament, (who, he conceived, will be looked upon otherwise, as persons that have lost the benefit of the Proclamation) may be inserted by this house; and, he supposed, a special care would be had of securing their persons."

And then the reporter read the said Clause, being as followeth: "But in regard the said have personally appeared, and rendered themselves according to the Proclamation, bearing date the 6th of June, 1660, to summon the persons therein named, who gave judgment, and assisted in the said horrid and detestable Murder of our said late sovereign, to appear and render themselves; and do pretend thereby to some favour, upon some conceived doubtful words in the said Proclamation: be it enacted by this present parliament, and the authority of the same, (upon the humble desires of the lords and commons assembled in parliament) That if the said , or any of them, shall be legally attainted for the horrid treason and murder aforesaid, that then, nevertheless, the execution of the said person and persons, so attainted, shall be suspended until his majesty, by the advice and assent of the lords and commons in parliament, shall order the execution, by act of parliament to be passed for that purpose."

The Reporter proceeded: "For that, relating to the persons dead, (whom their lordships had put in that fatal clause, with an expectation that we would pass an Act for the future attainder) their lordships have departed from their resolution in that point, and permit them to continue in the classes wherein we placed them; whereby they are adjourned to the penalties which shall be inflicted on them by a future act; expecting only a bill of attainder of Cromwell, Bradshaw, Ireton, and Pryde.—For the other part, wherein we have agreed for excepting Axtell without further expectation, and Vane and Lambert with expectation of a further address on their behalf, their lordships agree in that. For that wherein we differed about sir Arthur Haslerig, upon what was offered by a member of our house, and since, by the duke of Albemarle, they found his case distinguished from the other two, and agree with us as to him.—And for the last 4; though their lordships saw very great reason to adhere to that for justice and example sake; yet, having taken our Reasons into consideration, and believing the good report we gave of some of them, their lordships departed from that reason in that point, and leave them to disability only, as we propounded."—Resolved, That this house doth agree with the lords in the matters communicated by the lords at the said Conference. Ordered, That it be referred to a committee to dispose the Alterations, made by the lords this day, into their proper places in the Act of Indemnity; and to inform themselves, which of the Judges of the late king's majesty rendered themselves upon his majesty's Proclamation; and which of them are now in the serjeant's custody; or how they are otherwise disposed.

The Bill of Indemnity concluded.] All obstacles being now removed, and matters entirely settled between the two houses, concerning the Bill of Indemnity, Mr. Hollis was ordered to return it to the lords. At the same time to desire the lords humbly to intreat his majesty, that he would please to come to the house the next morning, to pass it and the other Bills which were ready for the royal assent. To which Mr. Hollis brought Answer, That the lords would do as desired.

The Speaker's Speech to the King on presenting the Bill of Indemnity, &c.] Aug. 29. This day the King came to the house of lords, and his majesty, sitting in his chair of state, commanded the gentleman-usher of the black rod to give notice to the house of commons, that it is his majesty's pleasure they come up, who being come up, their Speaker addressed his majesty in the following terms:

"Most Gracious Sovereign; Not many months since England was but a great prison, where the worst of men were our governors, and their vilest lusts the laws by which they governed. The great and most wise God conveyed divine intelligence into your patient and pious soul, and taught you how, by suffering for us, to deliver us from our sufferings; to knock off our shackles, and set your people at liberty, when neither power nor policy could effect it. So soon as your majesty set your foot upon your English shore, our prison was turned into a paradise of pleasure, and the whole nation filled with joy, and love, and peace.—Sir, this great blessing is already registered in your people's thankful hearts, and they desire that the memory thereof may be perpetuated; and therefore they have laid it up amongst their choicest jewels, and annexed it to their Magna Charta; which they are willing to pawn unto your majesty, upon condition, when they forget this, to forfeit that and all.—Sir; amongst your many illustrious titles, which, like fair and beautiful flowers, do adorn and bedeck your royal crown, there is one exceeds and excells all the rest, as well in virtue as in beauty, and that is your title of 'Defender of the Faith.' Sir, as that title is your honour, so the truth of it is our happiness. Neither the highest provocations, nor the strongest temptations, that ever prince met withal, have been able to shake your victorious faith, nor abate your holy zeal; witness your first Act, after your return to the exercise of your regal power, in your early and timely suppressing profaneness, and discountenancing debauched persons, who know not how to express their thankfulness unto God for mercies, but by a sinful drinking them away; a practice your soul abhors.—And as it is your highest honour to be the Defender of that Faith which we profess; so it is the greatest interest, prerogative, and privilege your majesty can be endowed and invested withall in this world, and will be your most lasting comfort in the world to come, that God, who hath hitherto been a sun to direct you, will be a shield to protect you; and that faith which you defend will defend you against all your enemies, maugre the malice of the Devil and all his wicked instruments—Royal Sir, your eminent virtues, and those excellent qualifications that God hath bestowed upon you, to make you every way worthy and fit for government, invites us at this time, with joyful hearts, to make our humble addresses unto your majesty, and to give you a chearful account of our proceedings this parliament, wherein we have spent our whole time upon public Bills; some, we must confess, of very great concernment to your majesty and all your people, are not yet ripe, nor brought to perfection: but though, like an after-crop, yet, with the fair weather of your majesty's wonted patience, we hope likewise to inn them well at last, to your majesty's full satisfaction, and the great contentment of all your loyal and faithful subjects.—Some Bills are passed both houses, and already lodged here, which attend and wait for your majesty's royal assent, and I shall humbly beg the favour only but to touch upon some of those of most public concernment by the way, and in transitu, to that Bill here in my hand.—Sir, there is one bill now before you, intituled, 'An Act for the Confirmation of Judicial Proceedings.' The scope and intendment of that bill is to settle men's estates, which is the way to quiet their minds; and, when their minds are at rest, there will be no fear of their breaking the peace, or forfeiting their good behaviour any more in time to come.—There is another Bill, intituled, 'An Act to prevent the taking of excessive Usury.' The restraining men of avaricious minds, whose consciences are as large as their bags, will be a great ease to your people, and an enablement to your merchants the better to go on with their trades. They are the laborious bees, that bring in honey into your majesty's hive; and userers are the lazy idle drones that rob your hive of the honey.—There is another Bill, intituled, 'An Act for a perpetual Anniversary Thanksgiving to be observed and kept upon the 29th of May:' A day that God himself was pleased to honour and adorn with a new additional star, never seen before nor since; a star of rare aspect, which declared, to all the world at once, the happy news of your majesty's blessed nativity: and as it was your majesty's birth-day, so it was the day of your Restoration to your kingdoms, parliament, and people; and likewise the day of your people's re-creation out of a chaos of confusion and misery: and therefore they humbly pray, That not only we (for there would need no act for that so long as we live) but that our posterity, and the ages that shall succeed us, might for ever be obliged to set apart that day as a holiday, to dedicate their praises and thanksgivings up unto Almighty God for his miraculous deliverance of this poor nation, when it lay in dust and ashes, in a most miserable, desperate, forlorn, and deplorable condition. There is another Bill, intituled, 'An Act of free and general Pardon, Indemnity, and Oblivion.' It may well be called a free Pardon; for your majesty was pleased to offer it before we had confidence enough to ask it, and at a time when your people had most need of it: And it may as truly be called a general Pardon, in respect of the extensiveness of it. But looking over a long, black, prodigious, dismal roll and catalogue of malefactors, we there meet not with men but monsters, guilty of blood, precious blood, precious royal blood, never to be remembered without tears; incomparable in all the kinds of villainy that ever was acted by the worst of miscreants, perverters of religion; subverters of government; false to God; disloyal to the best of kings: and perfidious to their country: and therefore we found an absolute and indispensible necessity incumbent upon us, to except and set some apart for treacle, to expel the poison of sin and rebellion out of others, and that they might be made sacrifices to appease God's wrath, and satisfy divine justice. And now I am come to that Bill here in my hand, which I am commanded humbly to present your majesty withal.—Royal Sir, Your commons, the knights, citizens, and burgesses, now assembled in parliament, taking into consideration the great and insupportable burden of the Army and Navy, that your people do now groan under; and knowing, as Money is the sinews of war, so, as the state of affairs now stand, that it is likewise the best medium that can be used, in order to the attaining that end we have all so much desired and so long prayed for, the Settlement of a happy Peace: and therefore they have passed this Bill, intituled, 'An Act for a speedy Provision of Money to pay off and disband all the Forces of this Kingdom both by Sea and Land,' upon which they hope such a sum will be advanced and brought in, as may be sufficient fully to discharge and dispatch that work: And they humbly pray your majesty's gracious acceptance thereof, and your royal assent thereunto:—I am further to inform and assure your majesty, that your people have passed another Supply and Revenue unto your majesty, which far surmounteth all they have already done in value, and that is, their hearts and affections; having their hearts, your majesty may command their Purses.—Most royal sovereign, We have nothing more to offer, or to ask, at this time, but your majesty's gracious favour, so soon as your service and the public affairs will permit, that we might have leave to go into our countries, where we shall make your people sensible of their happiness, in having such a king to govern and rule over them; and as we praise your majesty, so likewise to pray for your majesty, that you may live long, and reign prosperously."

The King's Speech.] Then his majesty was pleased to give his royal assent to the said Bills; after which, he made the following very gracious Speech:

"My lords and gentlemen of the house of commons; I have been here some times before with you, but never with more willingness than I am at this time; and there be few men in the kingdom who have longed more impatiently to have these bills passed, than I have done to pass them; and, I hope, they will be the foundation of much security and happiness to us all. I do very willingly pardon all that is pardoned by this Act of Indemnity, to that time which is mentioned in the bill; nay, I will tell you, that, from that time to this day, I will not use great severity, except in such cases where the malice is notorious, and the public peace exceedingly concerned. But, for the time to come, the same discretion and conscience which disposed me to the clemency I have expressed, which is most agreeable to my nature, will oblige me to all rigour and severity, how contrary soever it be to my nature, towards those who shall not now acquiesce, but continue to manifest their sedition and dislike to the government, either in action or words. And I must conjure you all, my lords and gentlemen, to concur with me in this just and necessary severity; and that you will, in your several stations, be so jealous of the public peace, and of my particular honour, that you will cause exemplary justice to be done upon those who are guilty of seditious speeches or writings, as well as those who break out into seditious actions: And that you will believe those, who delight in reproaching and traducing my person, not to be well-affected to you and the public peace. Never king valued himself more upon the affections of his people, than I do; nor do I know a better way to make myself sure of your affections than by being just and kind to you all; and whilst I am so, I pray let the world see that I am possessed of your affections.—For your Poll Bill, I do thank you as much as if the money were to come into my own coffers; and wish, with all my heart, that it may amount to as great a sum as you reckon upon. If the work be well and orderly done to which it is designed, I am sure I shall be the richer by it in the end; and, upon my word, if I had wherewithal, I would myself help you, so much I desire the business done. I pray very earnestly, as fast as money comes in, discharge that great Burden of the Navy, and disband the Army as fast as you can; and, till you can disband the rest, make a provision for their support.—I do conjure you, as you love me, let me not hear the noise of Free-Quarter, which will be imputed to my want of care and government, how innocent soever I am; and therefore be sure you prevent it.—I am so confident of your affections, that I will not move you in any thing that immediately relates to myself; and yet I must tell you I am not richer; that is, I have not so much money in my purse as when I came to you. The truth is, I have lived principally, ever since, upon what I brought with me; which was indeed your money, for you sent it to me, and I thank you for it. The weekly expence of the Navy eats up all you have given me by the Bill of Tonnage and Poundage. Nor have I been able to give my brothers one shilling since I came into England, nor to keep any table in my house but what I eat myself: And that which troubles me most is, to see many of you come to me at Whitehall, and to think that you must go somewhere else to seek your dinner.—I do not mention this to you as any thing that troubles me; do but take care of the public, and for what is necessary for the peace and quiet of the kingdom, and take your own time for my own particular; which I am sure you will provide for with as much affection and frankness as I can desire."

The Lord General's Plan for disbanding the Army.] Aug. 30. Sir Wm. D'Oiley made a report from the Committee for the Army, and delivered in a Paper, sent to them by the lord-general as a Plan for disbanding the Army; which was read in the house, and is entered in the Journals, as follows;

1. "That the Officers and Soldiers who were in pay, in army or garrison, the 25th April, 1660, shall have their just Arrear, paying or defalking for their Quarters, in prosecution of his Majesty's Declaration, and my Engagement to the Army, upon the Address by them made, to acquiesce in the judgment of the parliament. 2. That for the present subsistence of the Army, the month's pay, appointed by ordinance of parliament, in part of the 6 weeks pay now due upon the new account, may be forthwith issued; that so the Army and Garrisons may be put into a condition of subsistence, until so many of them shall be disbanded, as shall be thought fit by his majesty and the parliament. 3. That the forces, that of necessity for the present must be continued for defence of the garrisons in Scotland, are 3 regiments of foot, and one troop of horse: the residue now there, are 3 regiments of foot, and 11 troops of horse; which may be disposed of as shall be thought fit. 4. As to the forces in field and garrison within this kingdom, appearing upon the List annexed, so many of them may forthwith be disbanded as shall be thought fit. 5. And, for the manner of disbanding, the money being prepared, I shall, upon notice from the commissioners appointed for that purpose, draw the regiments to the most convenient places and nearest to their quarters, where the arms may be secured for his majesty's service, (that is to say) the foot arms, except swords, which are their own; and for the horse to deliver up what defensive arms they have; their horses, swords, and pistols, being their own likewise.—This being done, the field officers of every regiment, to give passes under their hands and seals, to all under their command, to go into their respective countries.—As to the last part of the Order, I have already given direction, that no soldiers be henceforth listed in any troops or companies; and I shall take care that no officers be from henceforth commissioned into the room of any that shall die, or be removed."

Debate thereon.] After the reading of this Paper, the house fell into a debate on this important point, in which there were many difficulties to get over.

Mr. *Prynne* moved to pay no Arrears to those that were with Lambert and others, and did not submit.

Sir *John Northcot* argued, That Scotland should pay towards the disbanding of the Army.

Sir *Wm. Morrice* was for having the Army disbanded on all accounts, and said, That gunpowder was made of the same ingredients that caused an earthquake; and that, as long as the soldiery continued, there would be a perpetual trembling in the nation: that they were inconsistent with the happiness of any kingdom; and compared the keeping of an Army on foot to a sheep's skin and a wolf's skin; which, if they lie together, the former would lose its wool. And again: if a sheep and a wolf be put into two several grates, by one another, the sheep would pine and die at the sight of the other. Neither, said he, could the nation appear like itself, whilst the sword was over them; and moved to pay off and disband the army.

On which, the house came to the following Resolutions: 1. "That all the forces now of the English establishment, whether in England, Scotland, or elsewhere, be disbanded with all convenient speed. 2. That such of the officers and soldiers in army or garrison, who were in actual service on the 25th April, 1660, and not discharged since for not taking the oaths of allegiance and supremacy, shall have their just Arrear; paying or defalking for their quarters, in prosecution of his majesty's Declaration, and the lord-general's Engagement to the Army, upon the Address by them made to acquiesce in the judgment of the parliament."—Ordered, That it be referred to the Committee of the Army to prepare a Bill for disbanding of the Army, and bring it in to-morrow morning.

Message from the King concerning a Recess.] Aug. 31. A message from the lords came down to the commons, to desire a conference; which being agreed to, the lords communicated the following Message to them, which they had received from the King:

"C. R. His majesty being frequently desired, by several members of the house of peers, to dispense with their absence from the service of the house, and to give them leave to go into the country for their healths and their affairs: and finding that the circuits will carry many of the members of the house of commons into their several countries; where, he doubts not, they will much advance his majesty's service, and the peace of the kingdom; and the house of commons having, by their Speaker, desired his majesty's leave to go into the country, his majesty is graciously pleased that both houses shall have a recess upon Saturday the 8th of next month: In which time he doubts not care will be taken for the raising such money as shall be necessary for the payment of the debts of the Navy, disbanding the Army, and supporting it till it shall be disbanded; which his majesty desires as much as any man. And his majesty intends that both houses shall meet again upon Tuesday the 6th of Nov. next."

On the reading of this Message the commons ordered, That no private business, depending in their house, be proceeded in till the day of adjournment. But, at the same time, several debates arose concerning the word 'Recess' in the king's Message; whether to adjourn or no; or what the word meant; to adjourn, or to determine; and ordered another conference with the Lords, about it. But that house being risen before the message was sent, this matter was dropped for that time. However, two days after, a conference was held; when the lord-chancellor declared it was his majesty's pleasure that the parliament should be adjourned according to former usage; and not that he meant, by the word 'Recess,' a dissolution.

Sept. 4. The commons resolved, That his majesty should be desired not to dispose of any of the Manors or Lands of the persons excepted from pardon by the late act, until his brothers, the dukes of York and Gloucester, were provided for. At the same time, they ordered the sum of 10,000*l.* to be charged on the receipt of the excise, for the use of the duke of York, and 7000*l.* for the duke of Gloucester, to be paid for their present necessities; also 5000*l.* more for the repair of his majesty's houses.

State of the Revenue of the Crown.] A committee had been appointed to consider the State of the present Revenue of the Crown; and this day, sir Heneage Finch reported from the Committee to whom it was referred to consider of a Revenue to be settled on the king's majesty, and the State of the late king's Revenues, an Estimate of the present Revenue of his majesty, and several Resolves of the said committee; that is to say, "That, according to the best information the committee could receive from the officers heretofore employed about the Revenue, the total of the revenue which came unto his late majesty amounted, from the year 1637 to 1641 inclusive, communibus annis, unto 895,819*l.* 5*s.* whereof 210,493*l.* 17*s.* 4*d.* did arise by Payments, partly not warranted by law, and partly expired: and that the Expences of his said late majesty's government did amount, communibus annis, to about 200,000*l.* a-year above the Receipt; in which computation the incomes arising by Ship-Money are not comprehended: and that, by Estimate, the present Revenue of his now majesty may be computed at 819,398*l.* or thereabouts; that is to say, by

	£.
The Customs - - - - - - - -	400,000
The Composition for the Court of Wards - - - - - - - - - -	100,000
The Revenues of Farms and Rents	263,598
The Office of Postage - - - - -	21,500
The Proceeds of Deane Forest - -	4,000
The Imposition on Sea-Coal exported - - - - - - - - - -	8,000
Wine Licences, and other Additions	22,300
	819,398

"Of which sum 45,698*l.* 18*s.* 7*d.* part of the said 263,598*l.* for Farms and Rents, is casual, and, for the most part, lost; viz. for the Mint, Allum, Transportation of Gold, New-Years-Gifts, and installed Debts."

He also reported some Resolves of the said Committee, viz. "That a Bill be tendered to the house, for establishing and regulation of the office of Post-master: That the like Bill be tendered to the house, for Wine Licenses: That a Bill be prepared for settling the Lands of the Crown, so that no grant of the inheritance shall be good in law; nor any lease more than for 3 lives, or thirty one years, where a third part of the true yearly value is reserved for a rent, as it shall appear upon the return of a survey; which that Act is to take order for, that it may be speedily had and taken: that the house be desired to move his majesty, that there be a forbearance to make Leases of Lands, or other grants of the Revenue, till the said Act be passed: and That the said committee think fit that the Revenue, for the constant yearly support of his majesty, be a Revenue of 1,200,000*l.* a-year."

The question being propounded, That the present king's Revenue shall be made up 1,200,000*l.* a-year: it was put, and passed in the affirmative.

Resolved, That this house doth agree with the Committee, that a bill be brought in for establishing and regulation of the office of Wine Licenses; and that another bill be brought in for settling the Lands of the Crown, so as that no grant of the inheritance shall be good in law; nor any lease for more than 3 lives, or 31 years, where a third part of the true yearly value is reserved for a rent, as it shall appear upon the return of a survey, which that Act is to take order for, to be speedily had and taken.—Resolved, That this house doth agree with the Committee, that the king's majesty be humbly moved, to forbear to make any Leases of Lands, or other grants of the Revenue of the crown, till the said last mentioned Act be passed.—Resolved, That his majesty be humbly moved that he will be pleased to forbear the exercise of his prerogative, in making use of his Tenures, till this house shall have settled a Revenue in compensation thereof; which is already in an effectual way of settling.

Petition to the King from both Houses, on behalf of Vane and Lambert.] Sept. 5. A Petition was drawn up, and read in the house, to be presented to the king, from both houses, in these words:

To the King's Most Excellent Majesty: The Humble PETITION of the Lords and Commons in Parliament assembled,

"Sheweth; That your majesty having declared your gracious pleasure to proceed only against the immediate murderers of your royal father, we your majesty's most humble subjects, the lords and commons assembled in parliament, not finding sir Henry Vane or col. Lambert to be of that number, are humble suitors to your majesty, if they shall be attainted, yet execution, as to their lives, may be remitted. And, as in duty bound, we shall ever pray, &c."

Mr. Prynne was ordered by the house to carry up this Petition to the lords for their concurrence. To which their lordships agreed; and, on presenting it to his majesty, he was also graciously pleased to grant the same.

Debate in the Commons, relative to the King's Marriage.] Sept. 12. This day, a remarkable debate took place in the house of commons, of which the Journals take not the least notice, nor any historian that we know of. We are indebted to the MS. Diary so often quoted, for this piece of intelligence.

Mr. *Bamfield* moved, That the king should be desired to marry, and that it should be to a Protestant.

Mr. *Annesley* said, That he thought this motion was not timely offered; and that when queen Elizabeth was put in mind of such a thing, she said, They ought to look to matters that concerned themselves.—Sir Gilbert Gerrard spoke for the motion, as also Mr. Bunckley, for marrying a Protestant, and that the Speaker should move this matter when he went up with the Bills to the house of lords.

Sir *Samuel Jones* desired it might be left to the king's own choice.

Serj. *Hales* said, It was not reasonable to confine his majesty; urging how much the peace and good of the nation was bound up in him.

Sir *Heneage Finch* argued, That the motion was very sudden, and wished they might not be too sudden in their resolves upon it: that they had no reason to think the king would marry a Papist, being then at liberty to make his own choice, when before he was under Catholic princes, and might have been induced to marry amongst them. He desired to be satisfied, whether any one could propose a convenient Protestant match, and said, the world would think strangely of them, if they confined his majesty to a Protestant: that the cause of the late troubles was said to be the marriage of the king's father to a Papist, which he did not believe. And that now, to propose such a thing to him, when he had no time to consider of it, would savour very ill. He added, that he did not know the ambassadors, which were then come over, came to offer the king any match; but, if they did, he believed his majesty would be very wary in accepting one; though he might be induced, for the advantages which might be made to the kingdom, to hearken unto them.

Mr. *Boscawen* was for referring it to a committee to draw up a Petition for it. Mr. Hollis said, It was better to refer it to their next meeting; and Mr. Annesley, Sir John Temple, and Mr. Prynne, saying, That it was not seasonable at that time, the affair intirely dropped. The last member said, That the king having lived so many years unmarried, and had not yet thought of it, it was not fit to prescribe rules to him, but leave it to himself.

The Speaker's Speech to the King at the Adjournment, on presenting the Bills.] Sept. 13. His majesty came to the house of lords this day; and, sitting in his chair of state, commanded the gentleman-usher of the black rod to give notice to the house of commons, that they speedily attend his majesty, who being come up, their Speaker made the following Speech:

"Most Gracious and Royal Sovereign, Your commons, the knights, citizens, and burgesses, have commanded me to present your majesty with the sacrifices of their hearts, most humble thanks, for their often and frequent admissions unto your royal presence; and for the freedom you have been pleased to allow them, upon all occasions, of making their wants and desires known unto your majesty.—Sir, this royal favour and fatherly kindness unto your people hath naturalized their affections to your person, and their obedience to your precepts: And as it is their duty, so it is their desires to manifest and evidence the truth and reality thereof, by supporting and upholding that grandeur and splendour which is due to the majesty of so meritorious a prince as you yourself: And therefore they have resolved, uno flatu, et nemine contradicente, to make up your royal majesty's constant and ordinary Revenue 1,200,000*l.* per annum.—But finding as to some part of the settlement of that Revenue, that there will be a necessity of making use of the legislative power; and that the Bills, already brought into the house for that purpose, cannot possibly be perfected, dispatched, and made ready, for your royal assent, until the next meeting of your houses of parliament again; therefore they have taken into their consideration your majesty's present Supply; and, first, how to raise it in the most expeditious way, to answer your majesty's present occasions; and then how to lay it, with the most ease and equality, upon your people; and at last wrapp'd up their affections to your majesty, and the trust reposed in them by the people, in one of these Bills here in my hand, intituled, 'An Act for the speedy raising of '100,000*l.* for the present Supply of your majesty,' to be levied by way of Land-Rate, within the space of one month, to begin the 29th of this instant Sept. and to be paid in to your majesty's exchequer before the end of Oct. following. Sir, They have likewise passed another Bill, with Rules and Instructions, to impower and direct your commissioners how, and in what manner, to disband your Army and Garrisons, and to pay off some part of your Fleet, and to begin with those ships now in harbour: But not knowing for certain what the monies upon the Poll Bill, which is designed for that purpose, will be sufficient fully to defray that charge: and being unwilling that any thing should be wanting on their parts to perfect and complete so good a work, so acceptable to your majesty, and so grateful to all your people, they have passed another Act for raising 140,000*l.* 70,000*l.* per mensem, to begin the 1st Nov. and to be paid to your majesty's treasurers, in that Bill nominated and appointed, before the 15th of Dec. next ensuing: both which Bills I am commanded, in the name of your commons, humbly to present your majesty withal; and to pray your gracious acceptance thereof and your royal assent thereunto. Sir, there are other Bills likewise which wait and attend for your royal assent; one, intituled, 'An Act for regulating the Trade of Bays;' which is the only way to keep up the credit of that, which at this time is in some danger to be lost. When the credit of trade begins to decline, the trade itself decays with it, and is never long-lived after it.—Sir, many thousands of your people depend wholly upon that trade for their livelihood, and sustenance of them and their families: and as the loss of that trade would be a great damage unto your people, so your majesty would likewise find the loss of it in your customs; for that commodity hath its vent in Spain and Portugal, from whence we have always rich and quick returns: And, to prevent the loss of both, both to prince and people, that Bill is humbly tendered to your majesty.—Sir, there is another Bill, intituled, 'An Act for encouraging and encreasing Shipping and Navigation;' which will enable your majesty to give the law to foreign princes abroad as your royal predecessors have done before you: and it is the only way to enlarge your majesty's dominions all over the world; for so long as your majesty is master at sea, your merchants will be welcome wherever they come; and that is the easiest way of conquering, and the chiefest way of making, whatsoever is theirs; and when it is ours your majesty cannot want it.—Sir, there is another Bill, intituled, 'An Act for restoring some Ministers 'into their Places out of which they have been 'long and injuriously ejected and exposed; and 'for the confirming others in vacant Places.' Crazy titles need your majesty's help, as much as crazy bodies need the help of physicians: and by what your majesty hath already done, in that kind, to this parliament, and what you are now about to do, and what you have ever expressed your readiness, if we could be as ready to receive as your majesty is to give, we hope to vanish and banish all fears and jealousies out of men's minds for the future; and teach them how, with much confidence and contentedness, to rest and wholly rely upon your majesty's grace and goodness for what may be thought further necessary to be done hereafter, when a fitting opportunity shall be offered, at the next meeting of your houses of parliament.—Royal sir, We humbly beg your pardon for making thus bold with your patience; and therefore, to pretermit and pass over some other such Bills, which are not of such public concernment as those I have already mentioned, we most humbly crave your majesty's favour and leave to conclude all our work, at this time, with that which is our delight as well as our duty, to pray for your majesty's long life, and happy, blessed, and prosperous reign over us.'

The King's Speech to both Houses on the Adjournment.] His majesty having given the royal assent to the Bills presented to him, made the following Speech to both houses:

"My lords and gentlemen; If my presence here had not been requisite for the passing these many Bills, I did always intend to see you together before your adjournment, that I might again thank you for the many good things you have done for me and the kingdom; and, in truth, I do thank you more for what you have done for the public, than what you have done for my own particular; and yet I do thank you too for that, with all my heart. But, I confess to you, I do thank you more for the provision you have made to prevent Free-Quarter during the time the Army shall be disbanding, (which I take to be given for my satisfaction) than I do the other present you have made me for my own particular occasions: And I do promise you, which is the best way I can take to gratify you, I will not apply one penny of that money to my own particular occasions, what shift soever I make, till it is evident to me that the public will not stand in need of it; and, if it do, every penny of it shall be disbursed that way, and I dare say I shall not be the poorer for it.—I cannot but take notice of one particular Bill I have passed, which may seem of an extraordinary nature, that concerning the duke of Somerset; but you all know it is for an extraordinary person, who hath merited as much of the king my father and myself, as a subject can do; and I am none of those who think that subjects, by performing their duties in an extraordinary manner, do not oblige their princes to reward them in an extraordinary manner. There can be no danger from such a precedent; and I hope no man will envy him, because I have done what a good master should do to such a servant.—My lords and gentlemen; I will not deny to you that I had some inclination, when I consented, upon your desire, to your recess, to have made a session, which I thought most agreeable to the ancient order of parliaments; and I hope you will all join with me in reducing the proceedings of parliaments to the antient rules and orders of parliaments, the deviation from which hath done us no good, and I think there were never so many Bills passed together, as I have this day given my assent to, without a session: But upon the desire and reasons given by the house of commons, for an adjournment without a session, I did very willingly depart from that inclination, and do as willingly give you leave, and direct you, that you adjourn yourselves till the 6th day of Nov. when I hope you will all meet again; and, in the mean time, that you will be all welcome to your countries, and do me much service there.—I have many other particulars to say and recommend to you, in which I cannot enough trust my own memory, and therefore I shall command the chancellor to say the rest to you."

The Lord Chancellor's Speech.] After his majesty had ended his speech, the Lord Chancellor Hyde said as followeth:

"My lords and gentlemen; The king tells you that he hath commanded me to say many particulars to you; and, the truth is, he hath charged me with so many, that I have great reason to fear that I shall stand in much need of his mercy, for omitting many things he hath given me in command; at least for delivering them in more disorder and confusion than matters of such moment and importance ought to be to such an assembly, for which the king himself hath even a kind of reverence, as well as an extraordinary kindness. I am to mention some things he hath done already, and many things he intends to do during this recess, that you may see, how well content soever he is that you should have ease, and pleasure, and refreshment, he hath designed work enough for himself.—The king hath thanked you for the provision you have made, that there be no Free-Quarter during the time the Army shall be disbanding; and hath told you what he will do with that money you have given him, if there should want wherewithall to disband it. And now I hope you will all believe that his majesty will consent to the Disbanding: He will do so; and yet he does not take it unkindly at their hands, who have thought that his majesty would not disband this Army; it was a sober and a rational jealousy; no other prince in Europe would be willing to disband such an army: an army to which victory is entailed; and which, humanly speaking, could hardly fail of conquest wheresoever he should lead it. And if God had not restored his majesty to that rare felicity, as to be without apprehension of danger at home or from abroad, and without any ambition of taking from his neighbours what they are possessed of, himself would never disband this army; an army, whose order and discipline, whose sobriety and manners, whose courage and success, hath made it famous and terrible over the world; an army of which the king and his two royal brothers may say, as the noble Grecian said of Æneas,

> Stetimus tela aspera contra,
> Contulimusque manus, experto credite, quantus
> In Clypeum assergat, quo turbine torqueat hastam.

They have all three, in several countries, found themselves engaged, in the midst of these troops, in the heat and rage of battle; and if any common soldier (as no doubt many may) will demand the old Romans privilege for having encountered princes single, upon my conscience, he will find both favour and preferment. They have all three observed the discipline, and felt, and admired, and loved the courage of this Army, when they were the worse for it: and I have seen them in a season when there was little else of comfort in their view, refresh themselves with joy, that the English had done the great work, the English had got the day, and then please themselves with the imagination what wonders they should perform at the head of such an army: and therefore, when his majesty is so intirely possessed of the affection and obedience of this army, and when it hath merited so much from him, can it be believed or imagined that he can, without some regret, part with them? No, my lords and gentlemen, he will never part with them; and the only sure way never to part with them is to disband them: should it be otherwise, they must be exposed to the daily importunity of his great neighbours and allies; and how could he refuse to lend them his troops, of which he hath no use himself? His majesty knows they are too good Englishmen to wish that a Standing Army should be kept up in the bowels of their own country; that they who did but 'in Bello pacis gerere negotium;' and who, whilst an army, lived like good husbandmen in the country, and good citizens in the city, will now become really such, and take delight in the benefit of that peace they have so honestly and so wonderfully brought to pass. The king will part with them, as the most indulgent parents part with their children for their education, and for their preferment. He will prefer them to disbanding, and prefer them by disbanding; and will always retain such a kindness for them, and such a memory of the service they have done him, that both officers and soldiers, after they are disbanded, shall always find such countenance, favour, and reward from his majesty, that he doubts not but, if he should have occasion to use their service, they will again resort to him with the same alacrity, as if they had never been disbanded. And if there be any so ill amongst them (as there can but be very few, if any) who will forfeit that favour and protection they may have from him, by any withstanding his majesty's commands, and the full and declared sense of the kingdom, his majesty is confident they will be as odious to their companions, as they can be to any other honest men.—My lords and gentlemen; I am, in the next place, by the king's command, to put you in mind of the Act of Indemnity; not of any grants or concessions, or releases he made to you in that Act; I have nothing of that in charge; no prince hath so excellent a memory to forget the favours he doth; but of what be hath done against you in that act, how you may be undone by that act, if you are not very careful to perform the obligations he hath laid upon you in it. The Clause I am to put you in mind of is this: 'And to the intent and purpose that all names and terms of distinction may be likewise put into utter oblivion, be it further enacted, by the authority aforesaid, That if any person or persons, within the space of 3 years next ensuing, shall presume, maliciously, to call, or alledge, or object against any other person or persons any name or names, or other words of reproach, any way leading to revive the memory of the late differences, or the occasion thereof, that then every such person, so as aforesaid offending, shall forfeit, &c.' It is no matter for the penalty, it is too cheap a one; the king wishes it had been greater, and therefore hath, by his just prerogative (and it is well for us he hath such a prerogative) added another penalty more insupportable, even his high displeasure, against all who shall swerve from this clause in the Act. Give me leave to tell you, That as any name or names, or other words of reproach, are expressly against the letter, and punishable accordingly: so evil and envious looks, murmuring and discontented hearts, are as directly against the equity of this statute, a direct breach of the Act of Indemnity, and ought to be punished too; and I believe they may be so. You know kings are, in some sense, called Gods, and so they may in some degree be able to look into men's hearts; and God hath given us a king who can look as far into men's hearts as any prince alive: and he hath great skill in physiognomy too; you would wonder what calculations he hath made from thence; and, no doubt, if he be provoked by evil looks, to make a further inquiry into men's hearts, and finds those corrupted with the passions of envy and uncharitableness, he will never chuse those hearts to trust and rely upon. He hath given us a noble and princely example, by opening and stretching his arms to all who are worthy to be his subjects, worthy to be thought Englishmen, by extending his heart, with a pious and grateful joy, to find all his subjects at once in his arms, and himself in theirs; and shall we fold our arms towards one another, and contract our hearts with envy and malice to each other, by any sharp memory of what hath been unneighbourly or unkindly done heretofore? What is this but to rebel against the person of the king, against the excellent example and virtue of the king, against the known law of the land, this blessed Act of Oblivion?—My Lords and Gentlemen, the king is a suitor to you, makes it his suit very heartily, That you will join with him in restoring the whole nation to its primitive temper and integrity, to its old good manners, its old good humour, and its old good nature. Good nature, a virtue so peculiar to you, so appropriated by God Almighty to this nation, that it can be translated into no other language, hardly practised by any other people; and that you will, by your example, by the candour of your conversation, by your precepts, and by your practice, and by all your interest, teach your neighbours and your friends how to pay a full obedience to this clause of the statute, how to learn this excellent art of forgetfulness.—Let them remember, and let us all remember, how ungracious, how indecent, how ugly, the insolence, the fierceness, the brutishness of their enemies appeared to them, and we may piously and reasonably believe, that God's indignation against them, for their want of bowels, for their not being Englishmen, (for they had the hearts of pagans and infidels) sent a whirlwind in a moment to blow them out of the world, that is, out of a capacity to do more mischief in the world, except we practise their vices, and do that ourselves which we pretend to detest them for.—Let us not be too much ashamed, as if what hath been done amis proceeded from the humour and the temper of the nature of our nation. The astrologers have made us a fair excuse, and truly I hope a true one: all the motions of these last 20 years have been unnatural, and have proceeded from the evil influence of a malignant star; and let us not too much despise the influence of the stars. And the same astrologers assure us, that the malignity of that star is expired: the good genius of this kingdom is become superior, and hath mastered that malignity, and our own good old stars govern us again; and their influence is so strong, that with your help they will repair in a year what hath been decaying in 20, and they only shall have no excuse from the star who continue their malignity, and own all the ill that is past to be their own, by continuing and improving it for the time to come.—If any body here, or any where else, be too much exalted with what he hath done, or what he hath suffered, and from thence thinks himself warranted to reproach others, let him remember the story of Nicephorus: it is an excellent story, and very applicable to such distempers: he was a pious and religious man, and, for his piety and religion, was condemned to the fire. When he was led to execution, and when an old friend, who had done him injury enough, fell at his feet and asked his pardon, the poor man was so elated with the triumph he was going unto, with the Glory of Martyrdom, that he refused to be reconciled unto him; upon which he was disappointed of his end, and for this uncharitableness the spirit of God immediately forsook him, and he apostatized from the faith.—Let all those who are too proud of having been, as they think, less faulty than other men, and so are unwilling to be reconciled to those who have offended them, take heed of the apostacy of Nicephorus, and that those fumes of envy and uncharitableness, and murmuring, do not so far transport and intoxicate them, that they fall into those very crimes they value themselves for having hitherto declined.—But, my lords and gentlemen, whilst we conspire together to execute faithfully this part of the Bill, to put all old names and terms of distinction into utter Oblivion, let us not find new names and terms to keep up the same, or a worse distinction. If the old reproaches of Cavalier, and Round-Head, and Malignant, be committed to the grave, let us not find more significant and better words, to signify worse things; let not piety and godliness grow into terms of reproach, and distinguish between the court, and the city, and the country; and let not piety and godliness be measured by a morosity in manners, an affectation of gesture, a new mode and tone of speaking; at least, let not our constitutions and complexions make us be thought of a contrary party; and because we have not an affected austerity in our looks, that we have not piety in our hearts. Very merry men have been very godly men; and if a good conscience be a continual feast, there is no reason but men may be very merry at it.—You, Mr. Speaker, have this day made a noble present to the king. Do you think that if you and your worthy companions had brought it up with folded arms, down-cast looks, with sighs and other instances of desperation, it would not have been a very melancholic present? Have not your frank and dutiful expressions, that chearfulness and vivacity in your looks, rendered it much more acceptable, much more valuable? No prince in christendom loves a chearful giver so well as God Almighty does; and he, of all gifts, a chearful heart. And therefore, I pray, let not a cloudy and disconsolate face be the only or the best sign of piety and devotion in the heart.—I must ask your pardon for misplacing much of this discourse, which I should have mentioned when I came to speak of the Ministers Bill; they, I hope, will endeavour to remove these new marks of distinction and reproaches, and keep their auditories from being imposed upon by such characters and descriptions. The king hath passed this Act very willingly, and hath done much to the end of this act before; yet hath willingly admitted you to be sharers and partners with him in the obligation. I may say, confidently, his majesty hath never denied his confirmation to any man in possession who hath asked it; and they have all had the effect of it, except such who, upon examination and inquiry, appeared not worthy of it; and such who, though they are pardoned, cannot yet think themselves worthy to be preferred. His majesty well knows that, by this Act, he hath gratified and obliged many worthy and pious men, who have contributed much to his Restoration, and who shall always receive fresh evidence of his majesty's favour and kindness; but he is not sure that he may not likewise have gratified some, who did neither contribute to his coming in, nor are yet glad that he is in: how comes it else to pass, that he receives such frequent information of seditious Sermons in the city and in the country, in which all industry is used to alienate the affections of the people, and to infuse jealousies into them of the king and his government. They talk of introducing Popery, of evil counsellors, and such other old calumnies as are pardoned by this Act of Indemnity.—His majesty told you when he was last here, what rigour and severity he will hereafter use, how contrary soever it is to his nature, in these cases, and conjured you, my lords and gentlemen, to concur with him in this just and necessary severity: which I am sure you will do with your utmost vigilance, and that you will believe that too much ill cannot befall those who do the best they can to corrupt his majesty's nature, and to extinguish his mercy.—My Lords and Gentlemen; I told you I was to acquaint you with some things his majesty intends to do during this recess, that you may see he will give no intermission to his own thoughts for the public good, though for a time he dispenses with your assistance. He doth consider the infinite importance the improvement of Trade must be to this kingdom, and therefore his majesty intends, forthwith, to establish a Council for Trade, consisting of some principal merchants of the several Companies, to which he will add some gentlemen of quality and experience; and, for their greater honour and encouragement, some of my lords of his own privy council.—In the next place, his majesty hopes that, by a well-settled Peace, and God's great blessing upon him and you, this nation will in a short time flourish to that degree, that the land of Canaan did, when Esau found it necessary to part from his brother. 'For their riches were more than that they might dwell together, and the land wherein they were could not bear them, because of their cattle.' We have been ourselves very near this pinnacle of happiness, and the hope and contemplation that we may be so again, disposes the king to be very solicitous for the improvement and prosperity of his Plantations abroad, where there is such large room for the industry and reception of such who shall desire to go thither. And therefore his majesty likewise intends to erect and establish a Council for those Plantations, in which persons, well qualified, shall be wholly intent upon the good and advancement of those plantations.—There are two other particulars which I am commanded to mention, which were both mentioned and recommended to you by his majesty, in his Declaration from Breda: the one for the Confirmation of Sales, or other recompence for Purchasers; the other, for the composing those differences and distempers in Religion, which have too much disturbed the peace of the kingdom. Two very weighty particulars, in which his majesty knows you have spent much time, and concerning which he should have heard from you before this time, if you had not met with great difficulties in the disquisition of either.—For the first; his majesty hath not been without much thought upon the argument, and hath done much towards the accommodation of many particular persons; and you shall not be at your journey's end, before his majesty will put that business, concerning Sales, into such a way of dispatch, that he doubts not you will find a good progress made in it before your coming together again; and I believe the persons concerned will be very much to blame, if they receive not good satisfaction. And some of you who stay in town shall be advised and consulted with in that settlement.—The other, of Religion, is a sad argument indeed. It is a consideration that must make every religious heart to bleed, to see Religion, which should be the strongest obligation and cement of affection, and brotherly-kindness and compassion, made now, by the perverse wranglings of passionate and froward men, the ground of all animosity, hatred, malice, and revenge. And this unruly and unmanly passion (which no question the divine nature exceedingly abhors) sometimes, and I fear too frequently, transports those who are in the right, as well as those who are in the wrong, and leaves the latter more excusable than the former, when men, who find their manners and dispositions very conformable in all the necessary obligations of human nature, avoid one another's conversation, and grow first unsociable, and then uncharitable to each other, because one cannot think as the other doth. And from this separation we intitle God to the patronage of, and concernment in, our fancies and distinction, and purely for his sake hate one another heartily. It was not so of old, when one of the most antient Fathers of the church tells us, That love and charity was so signal and eminent in the Primitive Christians, that it even drew admiration and envy from their adversaries. 'Vide, inquiunt, ut invicem se diligunt!' Their adversaries in that in which they most agreed, in their very prosecution of them, had their passions and animosities amongst themselves: they were only Christians that loved, and cherished, and comforted, and were ready to die for one another; 'quid nunc illi dicerent Christiani, si nostra viderent tempora?' says the incomparable Grotius. How would they look upon our sharp and virulent contentions in the debates of Christian Religion, and the bloody wars that have proceeded from those contentions, whilst every one pretended to all the marks which are to attend upon the true Church, except only that which is inseparable from it, charity to one another.—My Lords and Gentlemen, This disquisition hath cost the king many a sigh, many a sad hour, when he hath considered the almost irreparable reproach the Protestant Religion hath undergone, from the divisions and distractions which have been so notorious within this kingdom. What pains he hath taken to compose them, after several discourses with learned and pious men of different persuasions, you will shortly see by a Declaration he will publish upon that occasion; by which you will see his great indulgence to those who can have any protection from conscience to differ with their brethren. And I hope God will so bless the candour of his majesty in the condescensions he makes, that the Church, as well as the State, will return to that unity and unanimity which will make both king and people as happy as they can hope to be in this world.—My Lords and Gentlemen, I shall conclude with the king's hearty thanks to you not only for what you have done towards him, which hath been very signal; but for what you have done towards each other; for the excellent correspondence you have maintained; for the very seasonable deference and condescension you have had for each other, which will restore parliaments to the veneration they ought to have. And since his majesty knows that you all desire to please him, you have given him ample evidence that you do so; he hath appointed me to give you a sure receipt to attain that good end; it is a receipt of his own prescribing, and therefore is not like to fail: be but pleased yourselves, and persuade others to be so; contrive all the ways imaginable for your own happiness, and you will make him the best pleased, and the most happy prince in the world."

The Lord Chancellor having concluded his Speech, both houses adjourned to the 6th of November.*

* "During the recess of parliament, the object, which chiefly interested the public, was the trial and condemnation of the Regicides. The general indignation attending the enormous crime of which these men had been guilty, made their sufferings the subject of joy to the people: but in the peculiar circumstances of that action, in the prejudices of the times, as well as in the behaviour of the criminals, a mind, seasoned with humanity, will find a plentiful source of compassion and indulgence. Can any one, without concern for human blindness and ignorance, consider the demeanor of general Harrison, who was first brought to trial? With great courage and elevation of sentiment, he told the court, that the pretended crime, of which he stood accused, was not a deed performed in a corner; the sound of it had gone forth to most nations; and in the singular and marvellous conduct of it had chiefly

The King's Declaration concerning Ecclesiastical Affairs.] During the recess of parliament, the king issued the following Declaration:

"His Majesty's DECLARATION to all his loving Subjects of his Kingdom of England and Dominion of Wales, concerning Ecclesiastical Affairs.

"C. R. How much the peace of the State is concerned in the peace of the Church, and how difficult a thing it is to preserve order and government in Civil, whilst there is no order or government in Ecclesiastical affairs, is evident to the world; and this little part of the world, our own dominions, hath had so late experience of it, that we may very well acquiesce in the conclusion, without enlarging ourself in discourse upon it, it being a subject we have had frequent occasion to contemplate upon, and to lament abroad, as well as at home.—In our Letter to the Speaker of the house of commons from Breda (p. 17), we declared how much we desired the advancement and propagation of the Protestant Religion: that neither the unkindness of those of the same faith towards us, nor the civilities and obligations from those of a contrary profession (of both which we have had abundant evidence) could, in the least degree, startle us, or make us swerve from it; and that nothing can be proposed to manifest our zeal and affection for it, to which we will not readily consent: and we said then, That we did hope, in due time, ourself to propose somewhat for the propagation of it, that will satisfy the world, that we have always made it both our care and our study, and have enough observed what is most like to bring disadvantage to it. And, the truth is, we do think ourself the more competent to propose, and, with God's assistance, to determine, many things now in difference, from the time we have spent, and the experience we have had, in most of the Reformed Churches abroad, in France, in the Low Countries, and in Germany; where we have had frequent conferences with the most learned men, who have unanimously lamented the great reproach the Protestant Religion undergoes from the distempers and too notorious schisms in matters of Religion in England: and as the most learned amongst them have always, with great submission and reverence, acknowledged and magnified the established government of the Church of England, and the great countenance and shelter the Protestant Religion received from it, before these unhappy times; so many of them have, with great ingenuity and sorrow, confessed, that they were too easily misled by misinformation and prejudice, into some disesteem of it, as if it had too much complied with the church of Rome; whereas, they now acknowledge it to be the best fence God hath yet raised against Popery in the world: and we are persuaded they do, with great zeal, wish it restored to its old dignity and veneration.—When we were in Holland, we were

appeared the sovereign power of heaven. That he himself, agitated by doubts, had often, with passionate tears, offered up his addresses to the divine majesty, and earnestly sought for light and conviction: he had still received assurance of a heavenly sanction, and returned from these devout supplications with more serene tranquillity and satisfaction. That all the nations of the earth were, in the eyes of their Creator, less than a drop of water in the bucket; nor were their erroneous judgments aught but darkness, compared with divine illuminations. That these frequent illapses of the divine spirit he could not suspect to be interested illusions; since he was conscious, that for no temporal advantage, would he offer injury to the poorest man or woman that trod upon the earth. That all the allurements of ambition, all the terrors of imprisonment, had not been able, during the usurpation of Cromwell, to shake his steady resolution, or bend him to a compliance with that deceitful tyrant. And that when invited by him to sit on the right hand of the throne, when offered riches and splendour and dominion, he had disdainedly rejected all temptations; and neglecting the tears of his friends and family, had still, through every danger, held fast his principles and his integrity.—Scot, who was more a republican than a fanatic, had said a little before the Restoration, that he desired no other epitaph to be inscribed on his tomb-stone than this; 'Here lies Tho. Scot, who adjudged the king to death.' He supported the same spirit upon his trial.—Carew, a Millenarian, submitted to his trial, 'saving to our Lord Jesus Christ his right to the government of these kingdoms.' Some scrupled to say, according to form, that they would be tried by God and their country; because God was not visibly present to judge them. Others said, that they would be tried by the word of God.—No more than six of the late king's judges, Harrison, Scot, Carew, Clement, Jones, and Scrope, were executed: Scrope alone, of all those who came in upon the king's proclamation. He was a gentleman of good family and of a decent character: but it was proved, that he had a little before, in conversation, expressed himself as if he were no-wise convinced of any guilt in condemning the king. Axtel, who had guarded the high court of justice, Hacker, who commanded on the day of the king's execution, Coke, the solicitor for the people of England, and Hugh Peters, the fanatical preacher, who inflamed the army and impelled them to regicide: all these were tried, and condemned, and suffered with the king's judges. No saint or confessor ever went to martyrdom with more assured confidence of heaven than was expressed by those criminals, even when the terrors of immediate death, joined to many indignities, were set before them. The rest of the king's judges, by an unexampled lenity, were reprieved; and they were dispersed into several prisons." Hume.

attended by many grave and learned ministers from hence, who were looked upon as the most able and principal asserters of the Presbyterian opinions, with whom we had as much conference, as the multitude of affairs, which were then upon us, would permit us to have; and, to our great satisfaction and comfort, found them persons full of affection to us, of zeal for the peace of the Church and State, and neither enemies (as they have been given out to be) to Episcopacy or Liturgy; but modestly to desire such alterations in either, as, without shaking foundations, might best allay the present distempers, which the indisposition of the time, and the tenderness of some men's consciences, had contracted: for the better doing whereof, we did intend, upon our first arrival in this kingdom, to call a Synod of Divines, as the most proper expedient to provide a proper remedy for all those differences and dissatisfactions which had, or should arise in matters of Religion; and, in the mean time, we published, in our Declaration from Breda, a liberty to tender consciences; and that no man should be disquieted or called in question for differences of opinion in matter of religion, which do not disturb the peace of the kingdom; and that we shall be ready to consent to such an act of parliament as, upon mature deliberation, shall be offered to us for the full granting of that indulgence.—Whilst we continued in this temper of mind and resolution, and have so far complied with the persuasion of particular persons, and the distemper of the times, as to be contented with the exercise of our religion in our own chapel, according to the constant practice and laws established, without enjoining that practice, and the observation of those laws, in the churches of the kingdom, in which we have undergone the censure of many, as if we were without that zeal for the church which we ought to have, and which by God's grace, we shall always retain, we have found ourself not so candidly dealt with as we have deserved; and that there are unquiet and restless spirits, who, without abating any of their own distemper, in recompence of the moderation they find in us, continue their bitterness against the church, and endeavour to raise jealousies of us, and to lessen our reputation by their reproaches, as if we were not true to the professions we have made. And, in order thereunto, they have very unseasonably caused to be printed, published, and dispersed throughout the kingdom, a Declaration heretofore printed in our name, during the time of our being in Scotland, of which we shall say no more than that the circumstances, by which we were enforced to sign that Declaration, are enough known to the world; and that the worthiest and greatest part of that nation did even then detest and abhor the ill usage of us in that particular, when the same tyranny was exercised there by the power of a few ill men, which, at that time, had spread itself over this kingdom; and therefore we had no reason to expect that we should, at this season, when we are doing all we can to wipe out the memory of all that hath been done amiss by other men, and, we thank God, have wiped it out of our own remembrance, have been ourself assaulted with those reproaches, which we will likewise forget.—Since the printing this Declaration, several seditious Pamphlets and Queries have been published and scattered abroad, to infuse dislike and jealousies into the hearts of the people, and of the army; and some, who ought rather to have repented the former mischief they have wrought, than to have endeavoured to improve it, have had the hardiness to publish, That the doctrine of the Church, against which no man with whom we have conferred hath excepted, ought to be reformed as well as the discipline.—This over-passionate and turbulent way of proceeding, and the impatience we find in many for some speedy determination in these matters, whereby the minds of men may be composed, and the peace of the Church established, hath prevailed with us to invert the method we had proposed to ourself, and even, in order to the better calling and composing of a Synod (which the present jealousies will hardly agree upon) by the assistance of God's blessed spirit, which we daily invoke and supplicate, to give some determination ourself to the matters in difference, until such a Synod may be called as may, without passion or prejudice, give us such farther assistance towards a perfect union of affections, as well as submission to authority, as is necessary: and we are the rather induced to take this upon us, by finding, upon the full conference we have had with the learned men of several persuasions, that the mischiefs, under which both the Church and State do at present suffer, do not result from any formed doctrine or conclusion which either party maintains or avows; but from the passion, appetite, and interest of particular persons, who contract greater prejudice to each other from those affections, than would naturally rise from their opinions; and those distempers must be in some degree allayed, before the meeting in a Synod can be attended with better success than their meeting in other places, and their discourses in pulpits have hitherto been; and till all thoughts of victory are laid aside, the humble and necessary thoughts for the vindication of truth cannot be enough entertained.—We must, for the honour of all those of either persuasion with whom we have conferred, declare, That the professions and desires of all, for the advancement of piety and true godliness, are the same; their professions of zeal for the peace of the church, the same; of affection and duty to us, the same: they all approve Episcopacy; they all approve a set Form of Liturgy; and they all disapprove and dislike the sin of sacrilege, and the alienation of the revenue of the Church. And if upon these excellent foundations, in submission to which there is such a harmony of affections, any superstructures should be raised, to the shaking those foundations, and to the contracting and lessening the blessed gift of charity, which is a vital part of Christian religion, we shall think ourself very unfortunate, and even suspect that we are defective in that administration of government with which God hath entrusted us.—We need not profess the high affection and esteem we have for the Church of England, as it is established by law, the reverence to which hath supported us, with God's blessing, against many temptations; nor do we think that reverence in the least degree diminished by our condescensions, not peremptorily to insist on some particulars of ceremony; which, however introduced by the piety, devotion, and order of former times, may not be so agreeable to the present; but may even lessen that piety and devotion, for the improvement whereof they might haply be first introduced, and consequently may well be dispensed with: and we hope this charitable compliance of ours will dispose the minds of all men to a chearful submission to that authority, the preservation whereof is so necessary for the unity and peace of the Church, and that they will acknowledge the support of the Episcopal authority to be the best support of Religion, by being the best means to contain the minds of men within the rules of government. And they who would restrain the exercise of that holy function within the rules which were observed in the primitive times, must remember and consider, that the ecclesiastical power, being in those blessed times always subordinate and subject to the civil, it was likewise proportioned to such an extent of jurisdiction as was most agreeable to that. And as the sanctity, simplicity, and resignation of that age, did then refer many things to the Bishops, which the policy of succeeding ages would not admit, at least did otherwise provide for; so it can be no reproach to primitive Episcopacy, if, where there have been great alterations in the civil government from what was then, there have been likewise some difference and alteration in the ecclesiastical, the essence and foundation being still preserved. And upon this ground, without taking upon us to censure the government of the church in other countries, where the government of the state is different from what it is here, or enlarging ourself upon the reasons why, whilst there was an imagination of erecting a democratical government here in the state, they should be willing to continue an aristocratical government in the church; it shall suffice to say, that since, by the wonderful blessing of God, the hearts of this whole nation are returned to an obedience to monarchial government in the state, it must be very reasonable to support that government in the church which is established by law, and with which the monarchy hath flourished through so many ages, and which is in truth as antient in this island as the Christian monarchy thereof; and which hath always, in some respects or degrees, been enlarged or restrained, as hath been thought most conducing to the peace and happiness of the kingdom: and therefore we have not the least doubt but that the present Bishops will think the present concessions, now made by us to allay the present distempers, very just and reasonable, and will very chearfully conform themselves thereunto.—1. We do in the first place declare our purpose and resolution is, and shall be, to promote the power of godliness, to encourage the exercises of Religion both public and private, and to take care that the Lord's Day be applied to holy exercises, without unnecessary divertisements; and that insufficient, negligent, and scandalous ministers, be not permitted in the Church. And that as the present Bishops are known to be men of great and exemplary piety in their lives, which they have manifested in their notorious and unexampled sufferings during these late distempers, and of great and known sufficiency of learning; so we shall take special care, by the assistance of God, to prefer no men to that office and charge, but men of learning, virtue, and piety, who may be themselves the best examples to those who are to be governed by them; and we shall expect, and provide the best we can, that the Bishops be frequent preachers, and that they do very often preach themselves in some church of their diocese, except they be hindered by sickness or other bodily infirmities, or some other justifiable occasion; which shall not be thought justifiable if it be frequent.—2. Because the Dioceses, especially some of them, are thought to be of too large extent, we will appoint such a number of Suffragan Bishops in every diocese, as shall be sufficient for the due performance of their work.—3. No Bishop shall ordain, or exercise any part of jurisdiction, which appertains to the censures of the Church, without the advice and assistance of the presbyters; and no chancellor, commissary, or official, as such, shall exercise any act of spiritual jurisdiction in these cases, viz. excommunication, absolution, or wherein any of the ministry are concerned, with reference to their pastoral charge. However, our intent and meaning is, to uphold and maintain the profession of the civil law, so far, and in such matters, as it hath been of use and practice within our kingdoms and dominions: albeit, as to excommunication, our will and pleasure is, That no chancellor, commissary, or official, shall decree any sentence of excommunication or absolution, or be judges in those things wherein any of the ministry are concerned, as is aforesaid. Nor shall the archdeacon exercise any jurisdiction without the advice and assistance of six ministers of his archdeaconry, whereof 3 to be nominated by the bishop, and 3 by the election of the major part of the presbyters within the archdeaconry.—4. To the end that the Deans and Chapters may be the better fitted to afford counsel and assistance to the bishops, both in ordination and the other offices mentioned before, we will take care that those preferments be given to the most learned and pious presbyters of the diocese;

and moreover, that an equal number (to those of the Chapter) of the most learned, pious, and discreet presbyters of the same diocese, annually chosen by the major vote of all the presbyters of that diocese present at such elections, shall be always advising and assisting, together with those of the chapter, in all ordinations, and in every part of jurisdiction which appertains to the censures of the church, and at all other solemn and important actions, in the exercise of the ecclesiastical jurisdiction, wherein any of the ministry are concerned: Provided, That at all such meetings, the number of the ministers so elected, and those present of the Chapter, shall be equal, and not exceed one the other; and that, to make the number equal, the juniors of the exceeding numbers be withdrawn, that the most antient may take place. Nor shall any Suffragan Bishop ordain, or exercise the fore-mentioned offices and acts of spiritual jurisdiction, but with the advice and assistance of a sufficient number of the most judicious and pious presbyters, annually chosen as aforesaid, within his precincts. And our will is, That the great work of Ordination be constantly and solemnly performed by the bishop and his aforesaid presbytery, at the four set times and seasons appointed by the church for that purpose.—5. We will take care that Confirmation be rightly and solemnly performed, by the information, and with the consent, of the minister of the place, who shall admit none to the Lord's Supper, till they have made a credible profession of their faith, and promised obedience to the will of God, according as is expressed in the considerations of the Rubrick before the catechism; and that all possible diligence be used for the instruction and reformation of scandalous offenders, whom the minister shall not suffer to partake of the Lord's Table, until they have openly declared themselves to have truly repented, and amended their former naughty lives, as is partly expressed in the Rubrick, and more fully in the Canons; provided there be place for due appeals to superior powers. But besides the Suffragans and their Presbytery, every Rural Dean, (those deans, as heretofore, to be nominated by the bishop of the diocese) together with three or four ministers of that deanry, chosen by the major part of all the ministers within the same, shall meet once in every month, to receive such complaints as shall be presented to them by the ministers or churchwardens of the respective parishes; and also to compose all such differences betwixt party and party, as shall be referred unto them by way of arbitration; and to convince offenders, and reform all such things as they find amiss, by their pastoral reproofs and admonitions, if they may be so reformed. And such matters as they cannot, by this pastoral and persuasive way, compose and reform, are by them to be prepared for, and presented to, the Bishop; at which meeting any other ministers of that deanry may, if they please, be present and assist. Moreover, the rural dean and his assistants are, in their respective divisions, to see that the children and younger sort be carefully instructed by the respective ministers of every parish, in the grounds of Christian Religion, and be able to give a good account of their faith and knowledge, and also of their Christian conversation conformable thereunto, before they be confirmed by the bishop, or admitted to the sacrament of the Lord's Supper.—6. No Bishop shall exercise any arbitrary power, or do or impose any thing upon the clergy or the people, but what is according to the known law of the land.—7. We are very glad to find, that all with whom we have conferred, do, in their judgments, approve a Liturgy, or set form of public worship, to be lawful; which, in our judgment, for the preservation of unity and uniformity, we conceive to be very necessary. And though we do esteem the Liturgy of the Church of England, contained in the Book of Common Prayer, and by law established, to be the best we have seen, and we believe that we have seen all that are extant and used in this part of the world) and well know what reverence most of the Reformed Churches, or at least the most learned men in those churches, have for it; yet, since we find some exceptions made against several things therein, we will appoint an equal number of learned divines, of both persuasions, to review the same, and to make such alterations as shall be thought most necessary, and some additional forms (in the Scripture phrase as near as may be) suited unto the nature of the several parts of worship; and that it be left to the minister's choice to use one or other at his discretion. In the mean time, and till this be done, although we do heartily wish and desire that the ministers, in their several churches, because they dislike some clauses and expressions, would not totally lay aside the use of the Book of Common Prayer; but read those parts against which there can be no exception, which would be the best instance of declining those marks of distinction, which we so much labour and desire to remove; yet, in compassion to divers of our good subjects, who scruple the use of it as now it is, our will and pleasure is, that none be punished or troubled for not using it, until it be reviewed and effectually reformed as aforesaid.—8. Lastly, concerning Ceremonies (which have administered so much matter of difference and contention, and which have been introduced by the wisdom and authority of the Church, for edification and the improvement of piety); we shall say no more, but that we have the more esteem of all, and reverence for many of them, by having been present in many of those churches where they are most abolished or discountenanced: and it cannot be doubted but that, as the Universal Church cannot introduce one ceremony in the worship of God, that is contrary to God's word expressed in the Scripture, so every National Church, with the approbation and consent of the sovereign power, may, and hath always introduced such particular Ceremonies, as, in that conjuncture of time, are thought most proper for edification, and the necessary improvement of piety and devotion in the people, though the necessary practice thereof cannot be deduced from scripture: and that which before was, and in itself is, indifferent, ceases to be indifferent after it is once established by law; and therefore our present consideration and work is, to gratify the private consciences of those who are grieved with the use of some Ceremonies, by indulging to, and dispensing with their omitting those ceremonies, not utterly to abolish any which are established by law, (if any are practised contrary to law, the same shall cease) which would be unjust and of ill example, and to impose upon the consciences of some, for the satisfaction of the consciences of others, which is otherwise provided for. As it could not be reasonable that men should expect that we should ourself decline, or enjoin others to do so, to receive the blessed sacrament upon our knees, which, in our conscience, is the most humble, most devout, and most agreeable posture for that holy duty, because some other men, upon reasons best, if not only, known to themselves, chuse rather to do it sitting or standing. We shall leave all decisions and determinations of that kind, if they shall be thought necessary for a perfect and entire unity and uniformity throughout the nation, to the advice of a national synod, which shall be duly called, after a little time and a mutual conversation between persons of different persuasions hath mollified those distempers, abated those sharpnesses, and extinguished those jealousies which make men unfit for those consultations. And upon such advice we shall use our best endeavour that such laws may be established, as may best provide for the peace of the church and state. Provided, That none shall be denied the Sacrament of the Lord's Supper, though they do not use the gesture of kneeling in the act of receiving.—In the mean time, out of compassion and compliance towards those who would forbear the Cross in Baptism, we are content that no man shall be compelled to use the same, or suffer for not doing it: But if any parent desires to have his child christened according to the form used, and the minister will not use the sign, it shall be lawful for that parent to procure another minister to do it; and if the proper minister shall refuse to omit that ceremony of the Cross, it shall be lawful for the parent, who would not have his child so baptized, to procure another minister to do it, who will do it according to his desire.—No man shall be compelled to bow at the name of Jesus, or suffer in any degree for not doing it; without reproaching those who, out of their devotion, continue that antient ceremony of the church.—For the use of the Surplice; we are contented that all men be left to their liberty to do as they shall think fit, without suffering in the least degree for wearing or not wearing it. Provided, That this liberty does not extend to our own chapel, cathedral, or collegiate churches, or to any college in either of our Universities; but that the several statutes and customs for the use thereof in the said places, be there observed as formerly.—And because some men, otherwise pious and learned, say they cannot conform unto the Subscription required by the Canon, nor take the Oath of Canonical Obedience, we are content, and it is our will and pleasure, (so they take the Oaths of Allegiance and Supremacy) that they shall receive ordination, institution, and induction, and shall be permitted to exercise their function, and to enjoy the profits of their livings, without the said Subscription or Oath of Canonical Obedience. And moreover, That no persons in the Universities shall, for the want of such Subscription, be hindered in the taking of their degrees. Lastly, That none be judged to forfeit his Presentation or Benefice, or be deprived of it, upon the statute of the 13th Eliz. c. 12. so he read and declare his assent to all the Articles of Religion, which only concern the confession of the true Christian Faith, and the doctrine of the Sacraments, comprised in the Book of Articles, in the said statute mentioned. In a word; we do again renew what we have formerly said in our Declaration from Breda, for the liberty of tender consciences, That no man shall be disquieted or called in question for differences of opinion in matters of religion, which do not disturb the peace of the kingdom; and if any have been disturbed in that kind since our arrival here, it hath not proceeded from any direction of ours.—To conclude, and in this place to explain what we mentioned before, and said in our Letter to the house of commons from Breda, That we hoped, in due time, ourself to propose somewhat for the propagation of the Protestant Religion, that will satisfy the world that we have always made it both our care and our study, and have enough observed what is most like to bring disadvantage to it: we do conjure all our loving subjects to acquiesce in, and submit to, this our Declaration, concerning those differences which have so much disquieted the nation at home, and given such offence to the Protestant Churches abroad, and brought such reproach upon the Protestant Religion in general, from the enemies thereof, as if, upon obscure notions of faith and fancy, it did admit the practice of Christian duties and obedience to be discountenanced and suspended, and introduce a licence in opinions and manners, to the prejudice of the Christian Faith. And let us all endeavour, and emulate each other in those endeavours, to countenance and advance the Protestant Religion abroad, which will be best done by supporting the dignity and reverence due to the best Reformed Protestant Church at home; and which, being once freed from the calumnies and reproaches it hath undergone from these late ill times, will be the best shelter for those abroad, which will, by that countenance, both be the better protected against their enemies, and be the more easily induced to compose the differences amongst themselves, which give their enemies more advantage against them. And we hope and expect, that all men will henceforward forbear to vent any such doctrine in the pulpit, or to endeavour to work in such manner upon the affections of the people, as may dispose them to an ill opinion of us and the government, and to disturb the peace of the kingdom; which if all men will, in their several vocations, endeavour to preserve with the same affection and zeal we ourself will do, all our good subjects will, by God's blessing upon us, enjoy as great a measure of felicity, as this nation hath ever done, and which we shall constantly labour to procure for them, as the greatest blessing God can bestow upon us in this world.—Given at our Court at Whitehall, this 25th of October, 1660."

Nov. 6. This day both houses met pursuant to adjournment. The house of lords being informed that, since their recess, the king had been pleased to confer the honour of peerage on the lord-chancellor Hyde, their lordships ordered his introduction in the usual manner; and, being created baron of Hindon, he was placed on the barons seat as the youngest baron, where he sat a-while, and afterwards resumed his place again, on the woolsack, as Speaker.

The first thing the commons did, after their meeting, was to vote the sum of 10,000*l.* to be presented to the princess Henrietta, the king's sister; who, since their recess, had come over with the queen-mother from France; the latter after an absence of 19 years. It was also moved, by Mr. Stroud, to congratulate the Queen's safe arrival. Both which were agreed to by the lords.

The King thanked for his Declaration concerning Ecclesiastical Affairs.] Sir Anth. Irby moved to return the King most hearty Thanks for his great care of the Church-Government, in his late gracious Declaration concerning Ecclesiastical Affairs, and to make an Act for confirming it. This motion was seconded by Mr. Bamfield and Mr. Stevens; which last said, They might see by this, that when the king was separated from his people in body, yet he was not so in heart. Mr. Lowther moved, That the whole house might go to the king to give him thanks; which was voted, nem. con. to be done that afternoon. Mr. Barton was not for making a law, as yet, upon the King's Declaration, because it referred to the calling of a Synod. Seconded by Mr. Chafe and Mr. Harris; and that the Book of Common Prayer should be read in the house. Sir Tho. Clarges said, That he was not against the last motion, but that the Common Prayer was never read in the house, and moved to have a law to confirm the Declaration. Mr. Annesley was for referring it to a committee to consider of it, and present it to the house. Mr. Allen, for appointing a day purposely to take this matter into consideration, and not to do it too suddenly. Sir Tho. Meres was against making any Act at all, but to leave it to a Synod. Sir John Masham, against taking it now into consideration. Mr. Bodurda was for it. However, Mr. Prynne and Mr. Jo. Stevens moving for a reference to a committee, it was voted accordingly.—Mr. Tomkins resumed the other argument about the Common Prayer, and was for having it read in the house, in which he was seconded by Mr. Finch. The Speaker said, He never heard it read in the house; but added, There was a form of Prayer in the Journal-Book, which was used to be read by the Speaker. The lord Bruce moved for having the Common Prayer read in the house, or some other set form, and not to leave it to the spirit of men. Sir Walter Erle reproved his lordship for speaking so meanly of those who prayed by the Spirit. Mr. Bamfield said, He found nothing amiss in the minister's prayers. Mr. Clayton, for a set form; and Mr. Prynne moving for the old form, it was voted to refer it to a committee to inquire out the old Form, and present it to the house.

Nov. 7. The last affair was renewed. After the minister had officiated, Mr. Bamfield moved, That a Form of Prayer might not be enjoined him till the committee had made their report; and said, That the Mass might be introduced as well as a good Form, if it was done without order. Upon this, the Speaker excused the minister from any more service till the Form was ordered.

Sir Heneage Finch brought in a Bill for an Anniversary Fast on the 30th of Jan. unless of a Sunday, for ever. Also, to attaint Oliver Cromwell, and divers others, actors in the horrid Murder of the late King, who had already suffered, or were dead. This bill was read a first time; and Mr. Prynne saying, That since the traitors heretofore read their Act for the Trial of the King twice together, he desired this might be read again, which was done and committed. Mr. Prynne also moved, That it should be referred to this committee, Whether the rest that are condemned should be executed. Sir Anth. Irby moved, That all their just debts should be considered and satisfied; but that their estates might remain to the crown for ever.

Debate on the Lord's Day Bill.] Nov. 10. Sir Wm. Wheeler reported some amendments in the Bill for the better Observation of the Lord's Day. Sir John Masham moved not to engross the bill, because it was taken care of in the King's Declaration. Sir Walter Erle spoke for it; and said, That in a former parliament, he knew a gentleman who, denying such a bill, fell down dead in the house, he giving his voice first for it, and afterwards against it. Upon which, the bill was ordered to be engrossed without any more debate about it.

Mr. Bamfield moved to have the bill read against profane Cursing and Swearing; which was done. Mr. Stevens approved it, and desired there might be a course taken against drinking of Healths.

Debate on the Alimony of Wives living apart from their Husbands.] Mr. Ferrers brought in a Bill for preventing the voluntary Separation, and living apart, of Women from their Husbands: that they should not be allowed Alimony, or have their debts paid, if they went away without consent; which was read a first time, and on which a debate ensued, as given in the MS. Diary.—Sir John Northcot said, It was not improper for an old man to speak in behalf of the women; that perhaps a young man, marrying a rich old woman, might also take it into his head to part from her, and so the woman might be ruined; therefore he moved to throw out the bill. Sir John Potts was not for falling too hastily on this matter. Mr. Knight moved for casting out the bill, because there were laws already against it; and said they ought not to be so severe to the female kind. Mr. Stevens, That the Bishops Court would take care of such things; and moved to do nothing in this matter. Mr. Hoskins, to read it again; saying, He knew a gentleman who paid 500*l.* for his wife's debts in 6 months time. Mr. Bamfield said, That it was fit women should have a livelihood; and yet not to have power to ruin their husbands by their own debts. Mr. Knightley moved to lay the bill aside; but Mr. Prynne humorously saying, That if they did, those that had ill wives would call for it again within a day or two, the question was put, Whether this bill should be read a 2nd time on the 15th inst. the house divided, Yeas 116, Noes 96.

State of the Public Debt.] Nov. 12. Sir Tho. Clarges reported the State of the Public Debt; of which he gave in an Estimate as follows:

The Estimate of the Debts of the Navy, in Charge before his majesty's coming in.

For Discharge of the Officers and Mariners Wages, Provision of Victuals and Stores, and to the Office of the Ordnance, and the extraordinary and extraordinary Expences of the several yards, the Account is estimated to 678,000*l.* Whereof the Officers and Mariners Wages, to the 10th Nov. is exactly stated (over and above the 25 ships now under consideration, and besides that number of ships his majesty receives into his pay) to amount to 248,049*l.* 8*s.* The Commissioners for disbanding the Army have estimated what money they conceive will be brought in upon the bill for Poll Money, and the Assessments; and compute that there will be wanting, to disband the remaining part of the Army, and such of the 25 ships which are not yet discharged, the sum of 422,819*l.*—His majesty's commissioners for managing the Affairs of the Navy do also offer, to be humbly represented to the consideration of the house, that all his majesty's stores are now empty, both of victual and all other necessaries for the fleet; and that the charge of renewing them will amount to 200,000*l.* Which raises the whole sum to 1,300,819*l.* 8*s.* Of which sum that which will require a present supply and advancement, to pay off the officers and mariners, and totally disband the Army, is 670,868*l.* 8*s.*

Debate thereon.] A debate arose on the stating this Account, which the MS. Diary gives in this manner: Mr. Knight first moved to raise money to pay these debts by a six-months Assessment. Mr. Prynne said, The Poll Bill had not yet raised 210,000*l.* and moved to nominate a committee to find out some other way to raise Money to pay the Public Debts. Sir John Northcot moved to borrow money of the Hollanders, and give the excise for security at 6 per cent. Mr. Stevens was for having every member examined, whether he had paid to the Poll Bill, according to his degree and estate. Sir Wm. Morrice, in a set speech, said, The Debts of the Public would be like that serpent in America, which would eat a cow at a meal, and, falling asleep, the birds of prey devour him; but if they break not the bones of him he grows as big as before: so would the debts of the nation, he said, if not fully satisfied and paid off together: or like the woman's hen which she roasted with a faggot, stick by stick till the faggot was spent, and the hen still raw. But said it was fitter to do as one did in Spain to the inquisitor, who, sending to him for a dish of his pears, the man sent him the whole tree, because he would not be troubled with the inquisitor again. He concluded with moving for a year's Assessment, at 70,000*l.* a month, to do it all with credit: for the city he said, was too backward in lending money though they had got more since the king came in, than in some years before.—This motion was seconded by Mr. Pierpoint and Mr. Annesley; the latter urging, That it should be set forth that no more such tax should be laid upon the people. Mr. Young argued against borrowing the money from the Hollanders, to the dishonour of the nation. Several members beside speaking for a Grand Committee, the same was ordered to be the next morning.

Nov. 13. The house resolved into a Grand Committee for consideration of the Public Debts. Mr. Knight moved to raise money by a Land-Tax. Sir John Northcot was for not paying any of Cromwell's debts; and to leave the raising money by a land-tax to the last way of all. Serj. Maynard moved for a land-rate; Mr. Trevor, for a monthly tax; and Mr. Annesley, for a year's tax. Mr. Eyre moved to raise 800,000*l.* half by the excise, and the other half by a land-rate; and all that would advance money to be allowed 8 per cent. Mr. Palmer urged the stating the Debts; which Mr. Prynne did, but could not state them all; on which the further consideration of this business was again referred to the next morning.

A Book, then printed, intituled, "The Long Parliament revived, by Thomas Phillips, Gent." was offered to the consideration of the house as a matter wherein their privileges were much concerned. Ordered, That the said

Phillips be sent for into custody, and the matter referred to the committee for privileges.

Nov. 14. The Bill against Women, for refusing to cohabit with their Husbands, if desired, was read a 2nd time. Mr. Ferrers spoke in behalf of it, and offered a proviso to it. Sir Wm. Lewis was for casting it out. Mr. Prynne said he was for the bill, though he never had a good or bad wife in his life. Mr. Walpole, That this was so severe a bill upon the Women, that, if a bridge was made from Dover to Calais, the women would all leave this kingdom: that it therefore inverted the proverb; and England, that was formerly the heaven, would be now the hell for women. However, the bill was committed.

Debate on the Militia Bill.] Nov. 16. Mr. Knightley brought in a bill for settling the Militia of this kingdom; which was read a first time, and on which a debate ensued, which we give from the Diary.—Mr. Pierepoint moved for casting out this bill, because there was martial law provided in it; which, he said, would be a strange grievance laid upon the people, and desired another bill might be drawn without it.—Sir Heneage Finch said, That whoever brought in martial law deserved to be made the first example of it. Neither could he ever consent to bring themselves to be wards to an army, when they were endeavouring to free themselves from being so to the king: but was for a 2nd reading, for the better understanding of this bill.—Sir Walter Erle said, He never knew any bill that ever intrenched so far upon the subject's privilege as this did, and moved for another bill. Mr. Knight spoke for this bill.—Mr. Goodrick said, It was one of the best and worst bills that could be made, and moved for an alteration. Sir Edw. Turner said, That it was fitting there should be great care taken for the settlement of the Militia; but could not agree to set up such a martial law as Mr. Pierepoint spoke of. Lord Falkland said, That the settling of the Militia heretofore occasioned all their last mischief, and therefore advised a 2nd reading.—Sir Wm. Lewis moved that the bill might be read again on that day se'nnight, since many objections might arise, the bill being of so great importance as to require much consideration about it. Serj. Charlton said, There was reason for compulsory justice for those who refuse to obey orders; and therefore moved to amend the bill speedily, and read it the next morning.

Mr. Drake questioned for writing a Book called, "THE LONG PARLIAMENT REVIVED."] Nov. 17. Mr. Secretary Morrice acquainted the house, That he had found out and examined the Author of the dangerous Book, called 'The Long Parliament revived.'* That his name was William Drake; that he had confessed to him he wrote the said Book, which struck at the root of their proceedings; and that he was in custody at the door.—Captain Titus said, That he knew the man to be a loyalist, and a great sufferer for the king, but did not believe he wrote the Book, though he had the vanity to own it. This was seconded by Mr. Hollis. And Mr. Bamfield moved for slighting the business, as the best way to get rid of it. However, the prisoner was ordered to be called in, and being at the bar, the Speaker asked him, Whether he wrote that Book which was then shewn him? He confessed he did write it, but said, It was out of his depth of loyalty and integrity to the king, and for the benefit of the kingdom: that he had been a great sufferer already for the royal cause, and it would be hard indeed to make him now suffer again for doing what, he thought, was right for his sovereign. The Speaker again asked him, Whether he had the help of any one else in it? He answered, No, he had no help but only of the lord Coke's Books; and that he had put the name of Phillips to the Book, because he himself, being a merchant, could not be thought to write such a book. Mr. Drake being withdrawn, sir John Frederick and sir Edw. Massey both spoke in his favour. Mr. Prynne moved to refer it to a committee. Sir Heneage Finch said, That he could not think any thing more dangerous than the writing this Book at such a time; that it blew up this parliament totally, and damned the Act of Oblivion; and the author had shewed himself the greatest incendiary that could be, and all his former merits could not countervail this action. Therefore he moved to proceed to justice with him, and that he should stand committed, and the business be referred to the committee of privileges. All which was ordered; and that they should read over the said Book, examine and state the material points that are offensive there, and report them to the house.

Debate on the Court of Wards.] Nov. 19. This day, the commons fell into a debate on the business of the Court of Wards, and the Settlement on the King in lieu thereof. Sir Henry Cholmley said, That if the king's present Revenue was made up 1,200,000*l.* a year, the Court of Wards might be spared, without any further trouble. Sir Samuel Jones and sir Tho. Widdrington moved to raise it by the Excise. Mr. Knight was for laying 2d. in the pound on all the Lands in England. Mr. Pierepoint against a Land Rate; but to lay it on the Excise of Ale and Beer. Sir Tho. Bludworth against the Excise, and for a Land Rate. Mr. Annesley was for placing the tax upon Land; which, he said, ought to pay, and not to charge it upon the poor people, by way of Excise. Sir Heneage Finch moved for referring it to a committee, to propose a method for raising the sum required. Mr. Knightley and sir Walter Erle spoke for a Land Rate; which was objected to by serj. Charlton, who said, He never knew a land

* As this Pamphlet is purely parliamentary, and is not to be met with but in some old Collections, a copy thereof is given in the APPENDIX to the present Volume, No. I.

rate perpetual, as this must be. Sir George Reeves was rather for regulating the Court of Wards, than burden the people with taxes. Sir John Frederick for laying it upon the land, which ought to pay it.—Upon the whole, it was resolved to adjourn the debate till the 21st instant.

Resolutions against Mr. Drake's Book.] Nov. 20. Serjeant Raynesford reported that the committee appointed to examine Mr. Drake's Book had come to the following Resolutions: 1. "That the pamphlet, intituled 'The Long Parliament revived,' &c. is seditious in those particulars which were alledged at the committee. 2. That the house be moved to order, that the said Pamphlet be publickly burnt by the hands of the common hangman. 3. That the house be desired to appoint a committee for the drawing up an Impeachment, in the name of all the commons of England, against Wm. Drake, for penning and publishing of this seditious Pamphlet, to be presented to the lords. 4. That the house be moved, That the said Wm. Drake may be kept under such restraint, that none may have access to speak with him."

Debate thereon.] The MS. Diary tells us, that sir Edw. Massey presented a Petition to the house, from Mr. Drake, acknowledging his faults as a rash and inconsiderate action; that he had ever retained his loyalty, and humbly begged the king's pardon and the favour of the house. Sir Edward spoke also in his behalf, saying, That he looked upon him to be distempered, and therefore desired the favour of the house for him. Mr. Secretary Morrice said, That punishment in the Greek was the same as example, and that he ought to be made one, because he did not own their power; and moved to agree with the committee. Captain Titus spoke highly in his favour, saying, He did not think him infallible, though he knew him to be extremely loyal; but he wanted that temper of mind which he ought to have; and added, that his former merits should compensate for his present slip. Lord Falkland was for condemning him first, and then leave him to the king's mercy. Sir Harry North said, It was true he had been loyal, but did not know whether he was so then; and was for agreeing with the committee. Mr. Hyde moved to examine him again, whether any one saw this Book, and approved it before it was published, and was for agreeing with the committee. Mr. Palmer was for making him an example. Sir Heneage Finch said, The price of the book was raised, and that every one hoped all would be turned up-side down again; that the burning the book was too tame a punishment; that no man had merit enough to expiate the setting the kingdom in a flame again; and moved to agree in all with the committee. Mr. Annesley said, He did agree that the Book was seditious, but the man repented of it, and had formerly merited; that it was hard to ruin a man for the first fault, and moved to forbear a while the severity of his punishment, but to burn the book. Sir John Northcot said, It was not safe nor honourable for them to spare him; and moved to agree in all with the committee but the imprisonment. Mr. Howard, That, he was a person who was writing a 'Mene Tekel' upon the wall against them, and that they would not so much as rap him upon the fingers; that he ought to be severely punished, by being tied up to the gallows, whilst his Book was burning below it; for if he, being a friend, wrote in that manner, what would their enemies do? Sir John Potts moved to have him make a public recantation whilst his book was burning. Mr. Knight, to make an example of him, notwithstanding his former merits.—At last Mr. Harris moving to put the Resolves of the committee, singly, to the question, it was voted, nem. con. That the Book was seditious; that an Impeachment be drawn against Mr. Drake; and that sir Heneage Finch go up to the lords with it, the next morning, and carry the Book along with him.—But though this prosecution against Mr. Drake was ordered in so warm a manner, we do not find that the commons made any great haste in it. For, though the Impeachment was brought in, read, and ordered to be ingrossed, on the 26th instant, and the manner of presenting it to the lords ordered to be considered of on the 29th, we hear no more of the matter till the 4th of the next month, when the Impeachment was actually sent up to the lords by the lord Falkland; as will shortly be seen.

Further Debate on the Court of Wards.] Nov. 21. The commons went again on the business of the Court of Wards, when sir Heneage Finch opened the debate, by moving, That the annual Income to be settled on the king, in lieu thereof, might be raised by an Excise on Beer and Ale, and to take away Purveyance also. And that half of this Excise might be settled for the king's life, and the other half for ever on the crown. This motion was seconded by Mr. Bunckley and Mr. Pierepoint; but sir John Frederick, Mr. Jolliffe, sir Wm. Vincent, Mr. Annesley, and some others, spoke against it. The last-named gentleman saying, That if this bill was carried, every man who earns his bread by the sweat of his brow must pay Excise, to excuse the Court of Wards, which would be a greater grievance upon all, than the Court of Wards was to a few. Sir A. A. Cooper spoke against the Court of Wards, and for the Excise. Mr. Prynne, against the Excise, saying, It was not fit to make all house-keepers hold in capite, and to free the nobility: and inveighed passionately, says the Diary, against the Excise; adding, That those Lands which ought to pay, being held in capite, should pay still. Mr. Bamfield said, He was against an everlasting Excise, and for laying the tax on lands in capite. Mr. Bainton also was against an Excise, saying, If it was carried so, they might expect that, one time or other, there would be some strange commotions by the common people about it; that he was rather for keeping the Court of Wards, regulated in its proceedings, than submit to an Excise, which, if it was kept up, an army must be so to sustain it. Sir Tho. Clarges was against the Excise, saying, That the rebellion in Naples came from impositions and excises.—This debate was ended by serj. Maynard and Mr. Trevor, who both spoke for an Excise, though the last said, that nothing but the Court of Wards taking away should have moved him to it. At last, the question being called for, the house divided, the numbers 151 against 149, when it was resolved, "That the Moiety of the Excise of Beer, Ale, Cyder, Perry, and Strong Waters, at the Rate it was now levied, shall be settled on the king's majesty, his heirs and successors, in full recompence and satisfaction for all tenures in capite, and by knights service; and of the Court of Wards and Liveries; and all emoluments thereby accruing, and in full satisfaction of all Purveyance.* Resolved also, That the further consideration of settling a Revenue of 1,200,000*l.* a year, on the king's majesty, be adjourned to the 23d instant."

Message from the King concerning a Dissolution.] Nov. 22. The commons received a Message from the lords desiring a present conference in the Painted-Chamber, about a Message they received yesterday from his majesty; which being agreed to, Mr. Hollis reported the substance of the Conference as follows, viz. That the lord-chancellor was pleased to acquaint them, That, in order to that good correspondence which hath been continued, and which he desires may ever be held, between the two houses, that house had been careful to acquaint the house of commons with all matters of consequence which did occur: and that the lords having received a Message from the king's majesty yesterday, which they desired then to have presently communicated to you, and sent their messengers to that purpose; but the important business of the house not then permitting, the lords had therefore desired this conference with them, to communicate his majesty's Message to them; which Message was as followeth:

"C. R. In consideration of the season of the year, and the approach of Christmas, when members of parliament will desire to be at their houses in the country; and, in regard of his majesty's Coronation within a month after Christmas, the preparation for which will take up much of his majesty's thoughts and time, and the time of the servants, which

* "Soon after the Restoration," says Mr. John Hampden, in a Tract intitled 'Some 'Considerations about the most proper way 'of Raising Money in the present Conjuncture,' "the house of commons expressed a desire, as their predecessors had often done, to take away the Court of Wards, and they had long deliberations how to settle upon the crown a recompence for it; many ways were proposed (as is usual in such cases) but at last it was thought best to lay it on Land; and they agreed the sum to be 100,000*l.* per ann. and appointed a committee to settle an equal rate upon every county towards it. This would have procured another great advantage to the nation, and especially to the associated counties and others, that are over-taxed in the Monthly Assessment, by bringing in a just and equal way of taxing all the lands of England, according to their true value. The committee, in pursuance of the order of the house, having taken great pains in settling a new Rate, at length agreed upon one, and reported it to the house, and it is entered in the Journal. But while they were taking all these pains, the court was privately informed, by some self-designing men, that it would be of much greater advantage to them, to get a Grant of the Excise upon Beer and Ale, since the value of that was unknown; and they assured them, that it would amount to a sum vastly beyond what the parliament intended them in lieu of the Court of Wards. These men encouraged the court to undertake this work, and promised their assistance and endeavours for the success of their proposal: hereupon the court resolved to push for the settling of the whole Excise, and by threatening privately the members of that house with a dissolution; and by giving to some considerable places, they got a question put, to settle one Moiety of the Excise (which had been invented and raised on evident necessity, in the time of civil war, and not granted longer than a few months) upon the crown in fee, in lieu of the Court of Wards, and the other moiety on the king for his life. The former part, to give the moiety in fee in recompence of the Wardships, was carryed in the affirmative, though in truth, it was the giving 300,000*l.* a year for one, for which that house is justly blamed, and will be so, as ill husbands for the kingdom, and unfaithful to their trust. A great parliament-man, late deceased, undertook to make out, it was the giving away the Barley-Land of England. The other part, viz. to give the other Moiety for Life (as much as that house was influenced by the court) was first carried in the negative, which enraged them to such a degree, that, the next day, a Message was sent to the house, to let them know they were to be dissolved a month after. This was a strange and unusual Message; they might have been quickened to dispatch public Bills, and told, the session would be but short; but the Message, as sent, put men throughout the kingdom on supplanting them. If the members staid in town (and go they could not without leave of the house) their several interests in their counties, were endangered. If they went down, the settling the Excise, for life, might be carryed in their absence. This was the dilemma the court had brought them to, and accordingly it was granted before that session ended." See APPENDIX to the present Volume.

therefore should be vacant from other business, his majesty hath thought fit to declare, That he resolves to dissolve this parliament on the 20th day of the next month, and to call another with convenient speed; and that this his purpose may be forthwith communicated to his houses of parliament, that they may the more vigorously apply themselves to the Dispatch of the most important business that depends before them. Given at our Court at Whitehall, the 20th Nov. 1660."

Further Debate on the Court of Wards.] Nov. 27. The state of the King's Revenue, and the Settlement for the Court of Wards, was again taken up. Mr. Prynne began the debate, by moving the house to consider, first, what legal things might be offered to make up the king's Revenue, before they fell upon the Excise; and named the Customs of Ireland and Scotland, the Post-Office, and several others. Sir George Downing said, The Customs did not amount to 400,000*l.* a-year; and, for the improvement of the King's Parks, there were divers grants made by the late king to his servants, which were then claimed; so that those could not be valued till they were surveyed and settled; and therefore moved to settle the other Moiety of the Excise upon the king. Col. King and Mr. Boscawen moved for inquiring into the state of the king's present Revenue first, and what was wanting there, before they voted an addition. Serj. Charlton said, It was scarce possible to know exactly the value of the king's Revenue, and therefore moved for putting the question for the Excise. Hereupon, an Estimate was read of the value of the king's Revenue; which, by computation, came to 819,000*l.* odd money. To this col. Birch said, That, by his computation, he could not make it amount to more than 110,000*l.* and therefore moved to refer it to a committee to examine. Sir John Northcot said, The king's Revenue was under-rated; and moved that the Excise might be settled in full for the Revenue. Sir Heneage Finch said, It was not material whether the words 'in full,' or 'in part,' were inserted, and moved for the question; which being called for, the house, without dividing, voted, "That the other Moiety of the Excise on Beer, Ale, Cyder, Perry, Strong Waters, Chocolet, Coffee, Sherbet, and Metheglin, be settled upon the king during his life, in full of the 1,200,000*l.* per ann. revenue resolved to be settled on his majesty."—1. Resolved, "That the several particulars of Chocolet, Coffee, Sherbet, and Metheglin, be added to the former Vote for settling a Moiety of the Excise of Beer and Ale on his majesty, in compensation for the Court of Wards and Purveyances. 2. That the time for commencement of that part of his majesty's Revenue, which is to arise from the Excise of Beer, Ale, &c. be the 25th Dec. 1660. 3. That the Committee for his majesty's Revenue be revived; and that they do meet, de die in diem, in the Queen's Court."

On a motion of the lord Valentia,* it was resolved, "That it be referred to the Committee for his majesty's Revenue to state the several particular Heads from which the yearly Revenue of 1,200,000*l.* for his majesty is to arise; and to prepare Bills, as they shall find necessary, for the settling and making the same effectual, and to report the whole to the house:"

Debate on the Lord's Day Bill.] Nov. 28. Two religious Bills were read a 2nd time, one against the Profanation of the Lord's Day, the other against profane Cursing and Swearing, &c. Sir John Masham spoke against the former, and was for throwing it out, not being satisfied which day in the week was the Lord's Day, that ought to be kept holier than the rest, but said, It was novelty. On which Mr. Prynne got up and spoke for the Bill, alledging several reasons, and vouching divers authorities for the antiquity of the custom. Sir Ralph Ashton moved, That the Speaker should reprove sir John Masham, for what he said relating to the Sabbath. Sir John said, He spoke against the bill only because it was a transcript of one in Oliver's time, and therefore he could not consent to any thing that was done by him. To which sir George Booth answered, That the Devil spoke Scripture sometimes; and moved for both the bills to pass; which was ordered accordingly.

Debate on the King's Declaration concerning Ecclesiastical Affairs.] The same day, a Bill for making the king's Declaration touching Ecclesiastical Affairs, effectual, was read a first time; on which a long debate ensued, which we give also from the MS. Diary.—Sir Allen Broderick moved to lay the bill aside, saying, The king would suddenly call a new parliament, and with them a Synod; and moved to let this alone till then. Mr. Stevens was for having the bill read again, as it would not stand with the honour of the parliament to lay it aside. Sir George Reeves was against the bill, and to be satisfied with the king's Declaration. Sir Clement Throckmorton said, That the bill gave too great a toleration, and made the Bishops no more than 'vox et preterea nihil.' Mr.

* Arthur Annesley, esq. who, by the death of his father, was then viscount Valentia, afterwards earl of Anglesey. "He was very learned, chiefly in the law. He had the faculty of speaking indefatigably upon every subject; but he spoke ungracefully, and did not know that he was not good at raillery, for he was always attempting it. He understood our government well, and had examined far into the original of our constitution. He was capable of great application, and was a man of grave deportment, but stuck at nothing, and was ashamed of nothing. He was neither loved nor trusted by any man on any side, and he seemed to have no regard to common decencies, but sold every thing that was in his power: and sold himself so often that at last the price fell so low that he grew useless." Burnet, vol. i. p. 97.

Buckley said, That without a bill the Declaration would be insignificant; that it was very fitting that many things in the Liturgy should be altered. He produced a Book, printed in 1641, which was the Opinions of the bishops of Armagh and Lincoln, Dr. Prideaux, Dr. Ward, Dr. Featly, and Dr. Hacket, that several things in the Liturgy should be rectified; and moved for another reading of the bill. Mr. Henry Hungerford moved, That all those, who pretended to so much loyalty, should agree with the king's desire, that they might all go down into the country, and be well accepted there; which, he said, they could not better deserve, than by setting this great affair in order before their dissolution.—Mr. Howard said, That the present business was of the highest concernment that ever yet was brought before them, wherein the honour of God was so much concerned, as well as the peace of the nation. He moved, therefore, that the bill should be read again in 3 days. Sir Rd. Temple said, That there was no repugnancy between the Declaration and the bill; and moved for having it read again at the same time.—Sir Tho. Meres spoke against the bill, and said, That to make this bill a law was the way to make all papists and other heretics, rejoice, since it would wholly remove all conformity in the church; and therefore moved to lay the bill aside, and leave it to another parliament and a Synod. Mr. John Stevens said, The King had taken much time and deliberation to consider it well, before he published his Declaration. To this Mr. Secretary Morrice added, That the same man who was sick might be cured with a medicine at one time, which would not help at another; and that some things are seasonable now, which were not so at another. That matters were not only to be done, but well done. Sometimes a wound would heal of itself, if you applied nothing to it; and added, that time would rather do that good which they desired, than to have it enforced by a bill; and therefore he was for laying it aside.—Mr. Young said, He had rather the bill had never been brought in, than that it should now be laid aside; that the Ceremonies of the Church were not of that great weight, as to embroil us again in a new war: but that some indulgence ought to be given to such as had ventured their lives for the good of all. He said, he could not hope for any benefit to be had by a Synod, because the spirits of the clergy, for their late sufferings, would be much higher in resentment than the minds of the house were there; and moved for a 2nd reading. Sir Solomon Swale spoke against the bill, but for the Declaration, saying, That since the government of the Church was despised, how were they fallen into confusion? And moved, that the laws established might suffice, and not frame this into a new one. Mr. Bodurda said, The king, by his Declaration, having desired an indulgence, he hoped they would not resist it; and therefore he moved the bill might pass, till the first session of the next parliament. Sir John Masham said, They had before them an excellent Declaration, metamorphosed into a very ugly bill; that the king's intention was for a settlement of Religion amongst us, which surely this bill did thwart; and moved to throw it out. Mr. Prynne answered the last speaker, and said, The Declaration was to settle peace in the kingdom only, which the bill did not confirm; and what a wonder would it be, after they had given the king thanks, to throw out the bill. Mr. Thurland said, It was very disputable, whether such an excellent Declaration would make an excellent law: he thought not, giving so great a toleration, and endeavouring to lessen the Liturgy. He added, that he never knew a Declaration, by wholesale, voted into an act; and moved to lay this aside for the present. Col. Shapcot said, That the king's honour and the honour of the house, were both concerned in this bill. That Ireland was highly pleased with the Declaration, and begged for bowels of mercy one towards another; and was for the bill. Sir Heneage Finch was as much for indulgence to tender consciences as any; but said, It must then be used and allowed to such as could not consent to such a liberty as the bill offered: neither did he think it was the king's desire to have it put into a bill; that the Catholics would upbraid them with doing injury to them, for so many years, for not going to Church, when we were going, says he, by an act, to tolerate it in others. He was not for taking away the rule of conformity, nor yet for throwing out the bill; but he wished it had never been brought in, and moved for a 2nd reading some other time, rather on that day se'nnight.—Mr. Swinfen was for having the bill read again in 3 days, saying, Nothing was more hoped by the people, than the passing this bill; and therefore they ought not to deceive them: that he thought it would not grate the Bishops at all, because they were with the king at the framing the Declaration. Lord Bruce said, They might as well make every act of grace from the king into a law as this, which he was utterly against; and moved to adjourn the debate. Serj. Maynard concluded this long debate, in saying, He was against passing the bill, because it gave too great a liberty, yet would not seem to reject it by a vote, because the king's Declaration, on which the bill was built, was so pleasing to every one. He moved rather to put the question, Whether the bill should be read a 2nd time? The house dividing upon it, the numbers were 157 for, and 183 against, a 2nd reading.

Debate on the Restitution of the Title of Duke of Norfolk.] Dec. 3. The bill for the Restitution of the Earl of Arundel, &c. to the Title of Duke of Norfolk, was brought from the committee to whom it was referred, unaltered, and was read a 3rd time.

The MS. Diary informs us, that Mr. Stevens spoke very earnestly against passing the bill, saying, That the earl was always bred amongst those who were enemies to the protestants;

that the earl was distracted; and that if he was here, it was a question whether they would confirm the Title; for, in his opinion, it was giving honour to the man in the moon. Sir Robert Paston said, That the earl's want of senses should rather gain him more advocates than enemies; that the lords had already examined witnesses concerning his present condition of mind, and were satisfied with it; that he himself was not satisfied fully concerning the death of the late duke of Norfolk, but thought the restoration of the honour could be no prejudice to any one; and therefore moved to have the bill pass. Mr. Prynne spoke against the bill, saying, It was nonsense, because it did not express from whence the first honour came, nor to whom given; that here was no patent produced, nor any form how the late duke was attainted; and said, the earl ought to have petitioned for his honour; but that here was no such thing. Sir Rd. Onslow moved for the bill, saying, That he was one of the guardians, and thought it very fit it should pass. Mr. Thomas moved to have that part of the bill, which reflected upon queen Elizabeth, amended at the table, and then to pass it. Serj. Charlton said, The house was not ready yet for passing the bill, without examining the record and the indictment of the late duke; that it was fitting the earl himself should be here, but if he was so far distracted, it was better to take his honour from him, and bestow it upon the next worthy person in the family; adding, that it was fitter to use the earl as Nebuchadnezzar was, to send him amongst beasts, for he had not the ordinary cleanliness of one; and moved to re-commit the bill.—Mr. Bamfield said, he did not understand why they should confer honour upon a mad man; neither was it fit to give an act of grace to those of the Popish religion.—Serj. Raynesford was against bestowing honours upon any of the Popish religion, which he understood this family was of; and unless they took the oaths he was against the bill. But, lastly, Mr. Trevor and sir George Reeves, speaking for the bill, the question was called for, and, being put, the house divided upon it, yeas 187, noes 116.

Debate on the Bill of Attainder.] Dec. 4. Mr. Thomas reported to the house, from the committee, some amendments and three provisoes to the bill of Attainder, which were read. Mr. Ratcliffe moved for an allowance to be made of just debts, legacies, and funeral expences, out of this Forfeiture of those four persons estates who have been attainted after their deaths, viz. Cromwell, Pride, Bradshaw, and Ireton. Sir John Northcot was against paying the Funeral Expences of Cromwell and Bradshaw. Mr. Allen and lord Valentia moved in favour of the executors, That they might not be ruined for what they had paid, because they were compelled to pay the legacies by law; but that a proviso might be added to the bill concerning it. Sir Heneage Finch said, That this bill was the prime sacrifice to justice that the parliament had made; that neither the queen, nor any of the royal family, had the least relief from those people, but were left to starve in exile; and moved that, if the debts on bond be allowed them, the book-debts should be so too; that the bill should be engrossed, and such provisoes taken care for as were proper to be received. Mr. Hollis said, He had as great an abhorrence of that black crew as any one; and therefore moved rather to consider the poor creditors, their wives and children, and the executors, by a proviso. Serj. Charlton said, That, in Scripture, we are told that the whole families of traitors were destroyed: that the case was not alike in private bonds, as it was in this, where the persons were attainted. He moved to leave it to the law, whether to allow any legacies or not; but added, It was reasonable the legatee should refund. Sir A. A. Cooper said, There was reason to allow Settlements before marriage, or as far retrospect as 1647. Col. Shapcot said, That to deny the payment of their debts, was to punish the honest creditors, not the offenders; and therefore moved to consider those poor people, by a proviso large enough for the purpose. Mr. Prynne spoke against any proviso, saying, There were none for the Gunpowder Traitors, nor any else that ever were traitors before. Captain Titus ended this debate, by observing, That execution did not leave traitors at their graves, but followed them beyond it: and that, since the heads and limbs of some were already put upon the gates, he hoped the house would order that the carcasses of those devils, who were buried at Westminster, Cromwell, Bradshaw, Ireton, and Pride, might be torn out of their graves, dragged to Tyburn, there to hang for some time, and afterwards be buried under the gallows.—This motion was agreed to, says the Diary, nem. con.: this is confirmed by the Journals, where the Order is entered at large. Ordered also, That James Norfolk, esq. serjeant at arms, should see execution done upon the bodies; and that capt. Titus do carry up the Order to the Lords for their concurrence; which was agreed to the same day.*—The Bill to be engrossed.

Articles of Impeachment against Drake for publishing a Pamphlet intitled the "LONG

* This Order was not executed till January 30, after the dissolution of this parliament, when a chronological Historian of these Times gives us this Account of it: "This day, Jan. 30, 1660-1, the odious Carcasses of Oliver Cromwell, Henry Ireton, and John Bradshaw, were taken out of their graves, drawn upon sledges to Tyburn, and being pulled out of their coffins, there hanged at the several angles of the triple tree, till sun-set; then taken down, beheaded, and their loathsome trunks thrown into a deep hole under the gallows. Their heads were afterwards set upon poles on the top of Westminster-Hall." Gesta Britannorum: or a succinct Chronology, &c. By sir George Wharton. London, 1667.

PARLIAMENT RESTORED."] This day, also, the long-designed Impeachment against William Drake was ordered to be carried up to the lords, by the lord Falkland, and delivered at the bar of that house, in the name of the house of commons, and of all the commons in England. This Impeachment is entered in both the Journals, as follows:

"The Knights, Citizens, and Burgesses of the House of Commons, in the name of themselves and all the commons of England, do hereby declare, complain and shew, against William Drake, citizen and merchant of London;

"That whereas this present parliament, through the blessing of God upon their endeavours, and the incomparable grace and goodness of his majesty's royal condescensions, have proved the happy instruments of repairing the breaches of this kingdom, restoring the antient foundations, and passing many good and wholesome laws for the safety and quiet of the people, and are daily preparing such others as may yet seem to be wanting.—Nevertheless the said Wm. Drake, in contempt of his majesty's crown and dignity, and of the laws and government of this kingdom, and out of a wicked and malicious intention to scandalize and subvert the authority and being of this present parliament, and to raise and stir up sedition and division in this kingdom, and against the peace of our sovereign lord the king, hath lately, that is to say, upon or before the 18th day of Nov. last at Westminster, in the county of Middlesex, written, printed, and published, in the name of one Thomas Phillips, gentleman, a certain false, wicked, malicious, and seditious Pamphlet, intituled, 'The Long 'Parliament revived; or An Act for Continu-'ation, and the not dissolving the Long Par-'liament, called by king Charles the First, in 'the year 1640, but by an act of parliament, 'with undeniable Reasons deduced from the 'said Act, to prove, that That Parliament is 'not yet dissolved. Also Mr. William Prynne's 'five Arguments fully answered, whereby he 'endeavours to prove it to be dissolved by the 'King's Death, &c. By Thomas Phillips, 'Gentleman, a sincere Lover of the King and 'Country." In which said scandalous and seditious Pamphlet the said Drake, amongst many other wicked expressions, clauses, and assertions therein contained, doth falsely, maliciously, and seditiously affirm and declare, 1. That all other Parliaments have no legal capacity, till this (meaning the Long Parliament, called in the year 1640) be legally dissolved. 2. The Act (meaning the Act of Parliament to which the title of the Pamphlet refers) is herein express, That by no other way or means, but by an act of parliament, it shall be dissolved; which, as it cannot be done by the dead king, but may be done by the successor, it ought to be so dissolved; or else it must and doth by virtue of this act, still remain legally in full being and authority. 3. How much it were to be wished, that the legislative authority might revert into that channel (meaning the Long Parliament aforesaid) by which the peace and settlement of the nation, through his majesty's most gracious influence, might durably, and without question, be provided for and preserved. 4. If that be a lawful parliament, (speaking of the Long Parliament aforesaid which he elsewhere affirmed to be in being) then this can be none, nor no other, till this be legally dissolved.—All which practices for stirring up of sedition, the commons are ready to prove, not only by the general scope of the said Book, but likewise by several clauses therein contained, besides these before-mentioned, and such other proofs as the cause, according to the course of parliament, shall require. And do pray, that the said Wm. Drake may be put to answer all and every of the premises; and that such proceeding, examination, trial, judgment, and exemplary punishment, may be thereupon had and executed as is agreeable to law and justice."

The lords ordered this Impeachment to be read, after which they made another Order That the said Wm. Drake should be apprehended as a delinquent, by the serjeant at arms, and brought before them the next morning, to answer to his charge; which being done, and he confessing his fault, the lords, in consideration of the shortness of time for proceeding further in this business, left him to be prosecuted in the King's Bench by the attorney-general; where what further was done with him we know not.

Debate on the Bill of Attainder renewed.] Dec. 7. This day, Sir Heneage Finch delivered in the Bill of Attainder engrossed. Mr. Prynne observed upon the providence of God, That the bill should be brought in at the very time, which was upon the same day 12 years, that the King's Trial was agreed on. He therefore moved, that some others of the regicides, who had surrendered themselves, should be put into this bill and now executed, particularly the lawyers, and named Garland. Captain Titus seconded this motion, and named sir Hardress Waller, who, he said, was a pensioner to the late king, saying, The Turks would not eat the bread of any man they meant to betray; and that a Roman servant, who betrayed his master, though for the publick good, was executed. —After some further debate the Bill passed. The title of it was, 'An Act for the Attainder of several Persons guilty of the horrid Murder of his late sacred majesty king Charles I.'

Resolutions for taking up the Bodies of Cromwell, &c.] Dec. 8. The lords returned the Order sent up to them before, for taking up the Bodies of Cromwell, &c. with a small addition to it, which was agreed to. The Order, as entered in both the Journals, stands thus, viz. "Resolved, by the lords and commons assembled in parliament, That the Carcasses of Oliver Cromwell, Henry Ireton, John Bradshaw, Tho. Pride, (whether buried in Westminster-Abbey, or elsewhere) be, with all expedition, taken up, and drawn upon a hurdle to Tyburn, and there hanged up in their coffins for some time; and, after that, buried under the said gallows: and that James Norfolk, esq. serjeant at arms, do take care that this Order be put in effectual execution by the common executioner for the county of Middlesex; and all such others, to whom it shall respectively appertain, who are required, in their several places, to conform to, and observe, this Order, with effect; and the sheriff of Middlesex is to give his assistance herein, as there shall be occasion; and the dean of Westminster is desired to give directions to his officers of the Abbey to be assistant in the execution of this Order."

Protest on a Bill to vacate certain Fines.] Dec. 13. An Act to vacate certain Fines unduely procured to be levied by sir Edw. Powel, knt. and bart. and dame Mary his wife, was read a 3rd time. The question being put, whether this Bill shall pass for a law? It was resolved in the affirmative. Upon which the following Protest was entered:

"Whereas before the question was put for passing the said Bill, leave was desired for entering Protestations in the behalf of the lords here underwritten, in case the vote upon the said Act should be carried in the affirmative, we, in pursuance thereof, do enter our Protests against the said Act for these reasons following: That Fines are the foundations of the assurances of the realm, upon which so many titles do depend, and therefore ought not to be shaken; nor hath there any precedent occurred to us, wherein any Fines have been vacated by judgment or act of parliament, or otherwise, without consent of the parties; the eye of the law looking upon Fines as things always transacted with consent, and with that reverence, that no averment whatsoever shall be good against them when they are perfected; and farther, we conceive, that by a future law to vacate assurances, which are good by the standing law, is unreasonable and of a dangerous consequence, especially in this case, where Skinner and Chute, purchasers of a considerable part of the lands comprized in the said Fines, have petitioned, and yet have not been heard upon the merits of their case, which is contrary, as we conceive, to the statute of 28 Edw. 3. c. 3. which saith, 'No man shall be put out of his land or tenement, nor disinherited, without being brought to answer by due process of law.' (Signed) Edw. Hyde, C, F. Montague, W. Say and Seale, T. Culpeper, T. Willoughby, Portland, Sandys, Will. Petre, Cha. Hatton, Ch. Richmond and Lenox, Manchester, Tho. Coventry, W. Roberts, Brecknock, Norwich, Brudenell, L. Howard, W. Grey, Albemarle, Berkshire. A. Capell, Ro. Lexington, Suffolk, Stafford, Fr. Dacre, P. Wharton."

Debate on the Bill for settling the Excise on the King for Life.] Dec. 14. Sir Heneage Finch brought in a bill from the Committee, for settling on the King, during his life, the other Moiety of the Excise on Beer, Ale, and other liquors;* which was read twice, and ordered to be referred to a Grand Committee, who were to sit de die in diem till that business was dispatched.—As it has ever been the custom of parliament to go upon Grievances whenever subsidial Bills were in agitation, so now, when this grand Settlement on the Crown was before the commons, this old affair was resumed, but it was somewhat singular to talk of Grievances in a government so newly established, though upon its old foundation. On this occasion, Sir Walter Erle moved to do somewhat for the good of the people, in lieu of these great payments, and complained of some disorders in the Army. He said, That soldiers had come into some houses he knew of, and calling the people 'Roundheads, had done much mischief; which he moved might be taken care of. This

* The celebrated Andrew Marvell, in his first Letter to the Corporation of Hull, writes thus: "The Excise bill for longer continuance (I wish it prove not too long) will come in next week. And I foresee we shall be called upon shortly to effect our vote made the former sitting of raising his majesty's Revenue to 1,200,000*l.* per ann. I do not love to write so much of this money news, but I think you have observed that Parliaments have been always made use of to that purpose, and though we may buy gold too dear, yet we must at any rate be glad of peace, freedom, and a good conscience." Vol. i. p. 4.

Dr. Granger in his Biographical History of England speaks thus of Marvell: "He was an admirable master of ridicule, which he exerted with great freedom in the cause of liberty and virtue. He never respected vice for being dignified, and dared to attack it wherever be found it, though on the throne itself. There never was a more honest satirist. His pen was always properly directed, and had some effect upon such as were under no check or restraint from any laws human or divine. He hated corruption more than he dreaded poverty; and was so far from being venal, that he could not be bribed by the king into silence, when he scarce knew how to procure a dinner. He was chosen member of parliament for Kingston upon Hull, before and after the Restoration. The people of that place, who honoured his abilities, but pitied his poverty, raised a contribution for his support. This was probably the last borough in England that paid a representative. As even trivial anecdotes of so ingenious and so honest a man are worth preserving, I shall subjoin the following, taken from a MS. of Mr. John Aubrey, who personally knew him: 'He was of a middling 'stature, pretty strong set, roundish faced, 'cherry-cheeked, hazel eyed, brown haired. 'He was, in his conversation, very modest and 'of very few words. He was wont to say, he 'would not drink high or freely with any one, 'with whom he would not trust his life.'" Vol. iii. p. 357 and vol. iv. p. 49.

motion was seconded by sir John Northcot, who moved for a Committee to consider of it, and present the Grievances to the lords; and if they would not redress them, then this house to remonstrate to the king. Col. King complained against the arbitrary power of lord-lieutenants, particularly the lord Derby. Mr. Stevens said, That as he had lived an Englishman, he desired to die so, and not to leave his posterity slaves. He spoke also against the lord-lieutenants, and moved for a Committee to examine all Abuses. Sir George Booth for the same; saying, There were very great abuses abroad. Mr. Palmer moved to check col. King, who mistook his information concerning lord Derby. Mr. Harry Hungerford spoke also against the exorbitancies; averring, That, to his knowledge, in some places, 2*s.* 9*d.* a-day was exacted for each trooper, and this especially whilst the parliament is sitting; and moved to acquaint the king with these Grievances.—Sir Heneage Finch said, The remedy was to be had without going out of the door; it was but to resume the Debate of the Militia, whereby all these abuses might be regulated. He moved against any Remonstrance; which, he said, was the wilderness in which at first they wandered to destruction; and was not for having them sully the glory of their offering, the Revenue, with a complaint to the king at the same time.—The debate still continuing, lord Howard said, That these complaints were not so universal as some would make them. He justified the district where he had to do from any such thing; but that it all might be remedied by resuming the Militia bill. Mr. Bunckley was satisfied that there were such Abuses done; but said, That in his county all was quiet, by the care of the lord-lieutenant there; yet was for a bill to restrain all. Mr. Bamfield acquainted the house, That he had a petition given him, by one, against the lord Derby, about a minister kept out of his church, whilst another was put into it by lord Derby's soldiers, who had taken possession of the minister's house: that they knocked him down several times, crying, 'Is the rogue living still?' That they also knocked down his wife, which made her miscarry; and, after thus injuring them, turned them both out of doors. But yet, he said, That, in all these complaints, there was no reflection thrown upon his majesty, but on those employed under him. He thought the bill for the Militia could not now be finished in time; but moved to acquaint the king with these matters, and desire his care and reproof therein. In answer to this charge against the lord Derby's soldiers, Mr. Rigby stood up and said, That he came through the town where the minister lived, and dwelt himself not far from thence, and he heard nothing of this great complaint made by Mr. Bamfield: since he got to town, he heard that this minister, Mr. Jessop, refused to give obedience to a replevin, which caused a great opposition by the sheriff's officers, and some violence was offered him on that account: that he got guns into his house to oppose the lawful minister, who was come to take possession; and therefore left it to the house to consider of this complaint.—Sir Samuel Jones moved for the Militia bill, that they might know, he said, how to govern and be governed. Lord Falkland told the house, That the king had taken care for all these things; and moved to go to the business of the day. Sir A. A. Cooper said, Those things had no approbation from his majesty, but checks; and moved for a law to know how to walk by a rule; but to pass over such things as could not be justified. At last, Serj. Maynard moving for some Amendments to be made to the old Militia bill, it was ordered, That the grand committee do meet that afternoon about it.

Dec. 14. This day somewhat remarkable happened, in regard to the Rules of the house of commons. Serj. Maynard moved, That the Speaker would reprove all persons that he observed talking, or but whispering, or reading a paper. Very soon after, and whilst a bill was reading, the Speaker took notice of some gentlemen that were talking near the bar; whereupon it was ordered, "That every member of this house, who shall stand in the passage by the door of this house, shall forfeit 12d. to be paid to the serjeant to the use of the Poor of Westminster."

Dec. 15. The first Bill for settling an Equivalent on the king for taking away the Court of Wards, was passed in the commons, after a great number of additions, alterations, and amendments made to it. The Bill for settling the other Moiety, &c. was referred to Monday.

Dec. 17. The celebrated Mr. John Milton having now laid long in custody of the serjeant at arms, was released by order of the house. Soon after, Mr. Andrew Marvel complained that the serjeant had exacted 150*l.* fees of Mr. Milton; which was seconded by col. King and col. Shapcot. On the contrary, sir Heneage Finch observed, That Milton was Latin secretary to Cromwell, and deserved hanging. However, this matter was referred to the committee of privileges to examine and decide the difference.

The second Bill of Settlement passed.] This day, also, the bill for the other Settlement on the King was read and passed.

Sir John Northcot made a motion, That there might be 5 or 6000*l.* given to the king to buy Jewels for the Crown, the rest being stolen from it; seconded by the lord Valentia, and to make it up 10,000*l.* as a mark of the favour of the house, having taken away such a jewel from the crown as the Court of Wards. Mr. Prynne was also for the motion; but for sir Henry Mildmay to pay it, having, as he said, stolen the former.—Lord Howard was for the motion, as also sir Wm. Lewis, who moved for laying a Month's Assessment to raise the money, rather than charge it on the Excise, according to others. Sir Heneage Finch seconded this last motion; and, accordingly, it was ordered, "That a Month's Assessment, after the rate of 70,000*l.* per mensem, be granted to the king towards the charges of his majesty's Coronation, and to buy Jewels for the crown, suitable to his honour and grandeur, and as a memorial of the respect and affection of this house to his sacred majesty."

Debate on the Post Office Bill.] Captain Titus reported the bill for the Settlement of the Post-Office, with the amendments; which were agreed to. Sir Walter Erle delivered a Proviso for the letters of all members of parliament to go free during their sitting. Sir Heneage Finch said, It was a poor mendicant Proviso, and below the honour of the house. Mr. Prynne spoke also againt the proviso. Mr. Bunckley, Mr. Boscawen, sir Geo. Downing, and serj. Charlton, for it; the latter saying, The council's letters went free. The question being called for, the Speaker was unwilling to put it, saying, He was ashamed of it; nevertheless the Proviso was carried and made part of the Bill.

Dec. 21. Mr. Hollis acquainted the house, That he had just met the lord chancellor, who told him the king had expected, ever since yesterday, to hear from the house that their business was ready, that he might dissolve the parliament: therefore he moved, That this day and to-morrow all might be dispatched, so as they might have nothing to do on the next, but wait upon the king.

An accident happened this day in the house of commons, which occasioned some merriment amongst them. The lords sent down two messengers with some bills they had passed, with some amendments; to which the bearers said, The lords humbly desired the concurrence of that house. When these were withdrawn, the MS. Diary says, a hearty laughter ensued at the word *humbly*, and some moved to have it so put down in the Journals, as a precedent.

Dec. 22. The lords sent down the Post-Office Bill with an alteration, That the letters of the members of the house of commons should not go free; to which that house assented.

Message from the King concerning a Dissolution.] Dec. 22. A Conference was desired by the lords concerning a Message from the King; which, at their meeting, the lord chancellor reported, That he had delivered the King's Message to the commons, which ran in these words, viz.

"His majesty hath expected, ever since Thursday morning, to be informed, that his two houses of parliament had been ready to present such Bills to him as they had prepared for his royal assent, and hath continued ever since in the same expectation, and hoped that he might, this day, have finished the work, and dissolved them according to his signification; but being informed that there are yet depending in both houses some few Bills of great importance to his and the public service, which are not yet ready to be presented to him; and being desirous to part with his two houses of parliament, who have deserved so well of him, in such a manner, that they may not be obliged to use more expedition in the dispatch, than is agreeable to the affairs which are to be dispatched, his majesty is graciously pleased to declare, That he will be ready to pass such Bills as are necessary, in point of time, to be passed, on Monday morning; and then that the houses adjourn till Thursday, so that they may have that day and Friday to put an end to those most public Bills which are not yet finished; and his majesty will on the next day, being Saturday the 29th of this month, be present with them, and dissolve the parliament; and his majesty desires both houses, against that time, to lay aside all business of private concernment to finish all public Bills."

Dec. 24. The commons received a Message from the King, commanding the Speaker and the house to attend him in the house of lords: on which they all went up; when the Speaker, as the Diary says, presented his majesty, in a handsome speech, with the Bill for taking away the Court of Wards and Purveyance, to which the king gave his consent: likewise the Bill for settling the Moiety of the Excise on Ale, Beer, and other Liquors, for increase of his majesty's Revenue during Life. For which the king, in very few words, gave thanks at present; but said he would enlarge himself on Saturday following, the day appointed for dissolving the parliament.—On the return of the Commons to their own house, sir Heneage Finch moved to adjourn to the 27th, in regard the lords did so. Mr. Pierepoint desired that the King's last Letter might not be entered in the Journals, lest it should be thought the house adjourned solely upon that Message, which might be construed a Breach of Privilege (though he himself did wholly submit and comply with the king's desire); for, he said, That the king could not adjourn the house, though he could dissolve it; but that the house must adjourn, as an act only of itself. This was the reason the Letter was not entered as usual.

The King dissolves the Parliament.] After this, the commons reassumed, once more, the Bill on the Arrears of Excise, and had proceeded in the debate so far as to order the blanks in the bill to be filled up; when the usher of the black rod came to the door, and the house being informed of it, the Speaker, with the rest of the members, went up to the house of peers.

The Speaker of the House of Commons' Speech to the King.] His majesty being seated on the throne, the Speaker addressed himself to him as follows:

"Most gracious and dread sovereign; The knights, citizens, and burgesses, now assembled in parliament, being the representative body of your commons of England, are, as conduit-pipes, or quills, to convey the streams of your people's dutiful affections and humble desires into your royal presence; and that being done, they need no other Speaker but yourself, for they know your skill, and have had experience of your will: and yet, royal sir, though they have no cause to complain, they cannot but take notice of your partiality; for when any thing in point of right, or but conveniency, hath fallen out to be, as we use to say, a measuring cast, a disputable case, between yourself and your people, without any regard or respect had to your own right, or the advantage that might accrue to yourself by asserting the same, if the good of your people hath come in competition with it, you have always cast it against yourself, and given it on your people's side.—Royal sir; thus to undo yourself to do your people good, is not to do as you would be done unto; and can we do less than, by a grateful retribution, chearfully to pay your majesty the just tribute of our dutiful obedience unto all your royal commands; and, upon all occasions, ready to sacrifice, se et sua, all that we have or enjoy, lives and fortunes, in the service of such an incomparable sovereign?—But, royal sir, it becomes not me to fill your majesty's ears with air: loquere ut te videam is the only rhetoric the people ought to use to such a king of kindness, and a prince so full of good works; and therefore, as I am commanded, I must humbly assure your majesty that the many healing expedients propounded by yourself, in your several most gracious Declarations, have been the subject-matter upon which your commons have wrought all this parliament: and, in the first place, they took into consideration the great and growing charges which then lay upon your people for the Pay of your Army and Navy; and they conceived it necessary to begin with that part thereof next at hand, wherein your people would receive the most ease and the greatest security and satisfaction, which was the disbanding your majesty's forces by land, and the paying off 25 of your ships then in the harbour, and of no use; and this led them to the consideration of such Ways and Means as were to be used to raise money for that purpose; and that for Poll-Money being propounded and passed, some were of opinion that that alone would have over-done the work, others having had experience of a former bill of the same nature, and upon the like occasion, fearing it might not answer expectation, and being unwilling to be deceived the second time, especially in such a business as this, wherein a mistake was like to prove so penal, moved for a further supply (which, after some debate, was agreed upon) of a two-months Assessment, at 70,000*l.* per month; and both have not yet fully done the work for which they were designed; but with the help of two other Bills here in my hand, the one intituled, 'An Act for the levying the Arrears of the 12 months Assessment, commencing June 24, 1659, and the 6 months Assessment, commencing Dec. 25, 1659;' and the other intituled, 'An Act for the speedy provision of Money, for disbanding and paying off the Forces of this kingdom, both by land and sea,' they hope this account will be fully cleared off at last.—Sir, your commons have likewise taken into their consideration the charge of your Summer Fleet; which, besides that part thereof, your majesty is pleased to take upon yourself for your ordinary guard of the seas, will amount to a very great sum; and as it is a great debt, so it is a growing debt: in a few months it doubles. There is a saying, 'qui cito dat, bis dat;' I am sure it must be true in this case, qui cito solvit, bis solvit,' to pay his debt readily is the way to pay but once; and to take time to pay it is the sure way to pay it twice; and therefore your commons, laying aside the sad thoughts of their long sufferings, and those miserable devastations and pressures they have lain under for many years last past; and looking upon the necessity of affairs, which call importunately, and must be answered effectually, hath passed another bill here in my hand, intituled, 'An Act for 6 months Assessment of 70,000*l.* per mensem, to begin the 1st of Jan. and to be paid in, the one moiety thereof before the 1st of Feb. and the other moiety, being the remaining part, by the 1st of April next ensuing:' which is to be applied wholly in paying off the Arrears of your majesty's Army and Navy.—I have three other Bills in my hand, which have relation to your majesty's Revenue, and are branches thereof; the one intituled, 'An Act for the better ordering the selling of Wines by retail, and for preventing of abuses in mingling, corrupting, and vitiating of Wines, and for settling and limiting the prices of the same:' and the bill is tendered unto your majesty for preventing all further disputes touching the legality thereof, for we know it is your majesty's desire, that nothing might be done by any of your officers or ministers that act under you, sine figura justitiæ et warranto legis. Another is intituled, 'An Act for erecting and establishing a Post-Office:' and this being likewise legally settled, will be of very great use to all your majesty's people, and especially your merchants, for holding intelligence with their correspondents, factors, and agents, in foreign parts, literæ sunt indices animi; and without the safe and speedy dispatch and conveyance of their letters, they will never be able to time their business, nor carry on their trade to an equal advantage with the merchants of other countries. The other Bill provides for the increase of your majesty's ordinary and constant Revenue, by the grant of an impost to be taken upon Ale, Beer, and other beverages therein particularly mentioned and expressed, to hold to your majesty for life, which God long continue. And as it is the desire of your commons that your majesty might never be necessitated to resort to any extraordinary or unparliamentary Ways and Means, for the raising of Money upon your people, so they likewise acknowledge it to be their desires to support and uphold, to the utmost of their powers, the honour and grandeur of your majesty's royal state and dignity.—And for a further evidence of your commons dutiful affections to your majesty's most dear and royal person, they have passed another Bill for the raising of 70,000*l.* for your majesty's further Supply; all which bills I am commanded humbly to present your majesty withal, and to pray your gracious acceptance thereof, and your royal assent thereunto.—There are other bills likewise, of public concernment, which have passed both houses, and do now attend upon your majesty, waiting for your royal assent; the one is intituled, 'An Act for the Attainder of several persons guilty of the horrid Murder of his late sacred majesty, your royal father of ever blessed memory.' There is another Bill, intituled, 'An Act for the confirmation of Leases and Grants from Colleges and Hospitals;' this will tend much to the quitting many men's estates that in the late unhappy times were inforced to renew and change their estates much for the worse, were it not for the favour your majesty intends them in this Bill: there is another bill to prohibit the exportation of Wool, Wool-Fells, Fullers Earth, or any other scouring earth: woollen manufactures, besides the duties they pay for your majesty's customs here at home, have great impositions laid upon them in foreign parts where they are vended, in the Low Countries 16 or 17 per cent. and in Portugal 20 per cent. at least; but those who, for their own filthy lucre sake, having no regard or respect to the public good, that steal over the materials of which those manufactures are made, pay not one penny here or there, and by that means strangers do make those manufactures of our wool upon such easy terms, that they can afford, and do undersell your merchants; which is the occasion of a double loss, first, to your majesty in your customs, and, in the next place, to your people, who are thereby disheartened and discouraged; and in a short time, if not prevented, will be utterly beaten out of that antient native staple trade, upon which many thousand families do wholly depend for all their livelihood and subsistence. —There is another Bill, intituled, 'An Act to prohibit the planting, setting, or sowing of Tobacco in England and Ireland.' This climate is so cold that it never comes to any maturity or perfection; for we find, by experience, though it be ever so well healed, and made up with the greatest art and skill that can be possible, yet it is impossible, after it is made up into the roll, to keep and preserve it from putrifying above 3 or 4 months at the most; and therefore physicians, even those that love it best and use it most, conclude, generally, that it is unwholesome for men's bodies; besides many other great damages and inconveniences will follow upon it, if it should be permitted, the abatement of your majesty's customs, the destruction of your plantations abroad, the discouragement of navigation, and so consequently the decay of shipping, which are the walls and bulwarks of your majesty's kingdom.—There is another bill, intituled, 'An Act for taking away the Court of Wards and Liveries, together with Tenures in capite, Knight's Service, Tenures, and Purveyances.' This bill, ex re nata, may properly be called a bill of exchange; for as care is therein taken for the ease of your people, so the supply of that part of your majesty's revenue, which formerly came into your treasury by your tenures, and for your purveyances is thereby likewise full provided for by the grant of another imposition, to be taken upon ale, beer, and other liquors, to hold to your majesty, your heirs and successors for ever; and that they should not look upon the considerations, mentioned in this bill, as a full compensation and recompence for your majesty's parting with two such royal prerogatives and antient flowers of the crown, if more were not implied than is expressed; for, royal sir, your tenures *in capite* are not only turned into a tenure of socage, (though that alone will for ever give your majesty a just right and title to the labour of your ploughs and the sweat of our brows) but they are likewise turned into a tenure *in corde.* What your majesty had before in your Court of Wards, you will be sure to find it hereafter in the exchequer of your people's hearts. The king of Spain's mines will sooner deceive him than this revenue will fail you, for his mines have bottoms; but the deeper your majesty sinks yourself into the hearts and affections of your people, the greater you will find your wealth to be, and the more invincible your strength.—Royal sir; we have nothing more to offer or to ask, but must conclude all our work this parliament with an humble and thankful acknowledgment of God's infinite goodness and mercy, in restoring your majesty to your royal and imperial crown, throne, and dignity, and for making you the restorer of that which is dearer unto us than our lives, our religion; in which, through God's blessing and gracious assistance, we are resolved to live and die: as likewise for restoring us to our Magna Charta liberties, having taken the charge and care of them into your own heart, which is our greatest security, and more than a thousand confirmations.—Royal sir; you have denied us nothing we have asked this parliament; indeed you have out-done your parliament, by doing much more for us than we could agree amongst ourselves to ask, and therefore must needs be a happy parliament: this is a healing parliament, a reconciling peace-making parliament, a blessed parliament; a parliament propter excellentiam, that may truly be called, 'Parliamentissimum Parliamentum.' No man can say, that hath made the most curious search into books and records, that there ever was such a parliament as this; and it is our unspeakable joy and comfort that no man can say, so long as your majesty lives, but we may have such another, for you have set your royal heart upon it to do your people good.—And as we have nothing more to say, so we have nothing more to do, but that which will be a-doing as long as we have a being, the pouring out of our souls unto Almighty God for your majesty's long, long, long, and most happy, blessed, glorious, and prosperous reign over us."

The King's Speech.] After which, the Speaker presented his majesty with 11 public, and 21 private bills. All these Bills being passed, the King was pleased to make the following Speech to both houses:

"My lords and gentlemen; I will not entertain you with a long discourse, the sum of all I have to say to you being but to give you thanks, and I assure you I find it a very difficult work to satisfy myself in my own expressions of those thanks; perfunctory thanks, ordinary thanks, for ordinary civilities are easily given, but when the heart is as full as mine is, it is a labour to thank you; you have taken great pains to oblige me, and therefore it cannot be easy for me to express the sense I have of it.—I will enlarge no further on this occasion than to tell you that, when God brought me hither, I brought with me an extraordinary affection and esteem for parliaments. I need not tell you how much it is improved by your carriage towards me; you have out-done all the good and obliging acts of your predecessors towards the crown; and, therefore, you cannot but believe my heart is exceedingly enlarged with the acknowledgement. Many former parliaments have had particular denominations from what they have done; they have been stiled learned and unlearned, and sometimes have had worse epithets; I pray let us all resolve that this be for ever called 'The Healing and Blessed Parliament.'—As I thank you, though not enough, for what you have done, so I have not the least doubt, by the blessing of God, but when I shall call the next parliament, which I shall do as soon as you can reasonably expect, or desire, I shall receive your thanks for what I have done since I parted from you, for I deal truly with you. I shall not more propose any one real good to myself in my actions and in my councils than this, What is a parliament like to think of this action or this council? and it shall be for want of understanding in me, if it will not bear that test.—I shall conclude with this, which I cannot say too often, nor you too often where you go, That, next to the miraculous blessing of God Almighty, and, indeed, as an immediate effect of that blessing, I do impute the good disposition and security we are all in, to the happy Act of Indemnity and Oblivion, which is the principal corner-stone that supports this excellent building, and creates kindness in us to each other; confidence being our joint and common security. You may be sure I will not only observe, religiously and inviolably, myself, but also exact the observation of it from others; and if any person should ever have the boldness to attempt to persuade me to the contrary, he will find such an acceptation from me as he would have who should persuade me to burn Magna Charta, cancel all the old laws, and to erect a new government after my own invention and appetite.—There are many other particulars which I will not trust my own memory with, but will require the Chancellor to say the rest to you."

The Lord Chancellor's Speech.] After his majesty had done, the lord chancellor Hyde came from his place and kneeled down close by his majesty's chair, and received his majesty's directions what to say further; and being returned to his place, he said as followeth:

"My lords, and you the knights, citizens, and burgesses of the house of commons; There cannot be a greater manifestation of an excellent temper and harmony of affections throughout the nation, than that the king and his two houses of parliament meet with the same affections and chearfulness, the same alacrity in their countenance, at the dissolution, as when they met at the convention of parliament. It is an unquestionable evidence that they are exceedingly satisfied in what they have done towards each other, that they have very well done all the business they came about; this is now your case, you have so well satisfied your own consciences, that you are sure you have satisfied the king's expectation and his hope, and the desire and wishes of the country.—It was very justly observed by you, Mr. Speaker, that you have never asked any one thing of the king which he hath not (with all imaginable chearfulness) granted; in truth, his majesty doth, with great comfort, acknowledge that you have been so far from denying him any thing he hath asked, that he hath scarce wished any thing that you have not granted; and it is no wonder that, having so fully complied with your obligations, and having so well composed the minds of the nation, you are willing to be relieved from this extraordinary fatigue you have submitted so long to, and to return to the consideration of your own particular affairs, which you have so long sacrificed to the public; and this reasonable wish and desire hath brought the king to comply with you, and, which nothing else could do, to part with you with an equal chearfulness; and he makes no doubt but all succeeding parliaments will pay you their thanks for all you have done, and look upon your actions and your example with all possible approbation and reverence.—The king and you have given such earnest to one another of your mutual affection; you have been so exact and punctual in your proceedings towards each other, that you have made no promise, no profession to each other, of making good, to the performing of which the world is not witness. You declared at the adjournment, in Sept. last, your resolution to settle a noble Revenue on the crown; you have done it with all the circumstances of affection and prudence: the king promised you to establish a Council of Trade, a Council for the foreign Plantations, a Commission for composing all differences upon Sales; all this he did before your coming together, and with very good effect, and you shall hear that the proceedings in every one of them are more vigorous and effectual after your dissolution. His majesty then promised you that he will give up all his endeavours to compose the unhappy differences in matters of Religion, and to restore the languishing Church to peace and order: Constantine himself spent so much of his own time in private and public conferences; to that purpose his majesty, in private, conferred with the learned men, and heard all that could be said upon several opinions and interests apart; and that, in the presence of both parties, himself moderating in the debates; and less care, and diligence, and authority would not have done that work; and God hath so blessed his labour, and made his determination in that affair so generally agreeable, that he hath received Thanks from his houses of parliament; that is, from the whole kingdom: if, after all this, his majesty doth not reap the full harvest he expected from those condescensions; if some men, by their writing and their preaching, endeavour to continue those breaches, and very rashly, and I think unconscientiously, keep up the distinctions, and publicly justify and maintain what hath heretofore been done amiss, and for which the Act of Indemnity was the best defence, I shall say no more than that I hope their want of modesty and obedience will cause them to be disclaimed by all pious and peaceable men; who cannot but be well contented to see them reduced by laws, to the obedience they owe to law: and his majesty is confident that this his beloved city, towards which his heart is so gracious and so full of princely designs to improve their honour, their wealth, and their beauty, will discountenance all these seditious designs; and, by returning and fixing themselves upon their good old foundations, make themselves the great example of piety, of loyalty, and of hearty affection to the whole kingdom.—This discourse puts me in mind to say to you, that though the king wonders much more at the many great things you have done than that you left any thing undone, yet he could have wished, and would have been glad, that your other weighty affairs had given you time to have published your opinion and advice in the business of the Militia; that the people, after so many disputes upon that argument, might have discerned that the king and his two houses of parliament are as much in the same mind in that as in all other things, as no doubt they are; but since that could not be done, you may all assure yourselves that the king will proceed therein with all imaginable care and circumspection, for the ease, quiet, and security of his people; and as he did before the last recess, by the unanimous advice of his privy council, issue out his commission of lieutenancy for the settling the Militia in the several counties, to prevent any disorders which many apprehended might arise upon the disbanding the Army, so he will now again recommend it to themselves to put it in such a posture, as may disappoint any seditious designs which are now on foot; and there cannot be too much circumspection and vigilance to frustrate those designs.—You have heard of many suspected and dangerous persons which have lately been clapt up; and it was high time to look about. His majesty hath spent many hours himself in the examination of this business, and some of the principal officers, who, before they came to his majesty's presence, could not be brought to acknowledge any thing, after the king himself had spoken to them, confessed that their spirits were insensibly prevailed upon and subdued, and that it was not in their power to conceal their guilt from him: they have confessed that there is a party of the late disbanded officers and soldiers, and others, full of discontent and seditious purposes, and a resolution to attempt the change of the present government, and to erect the republic: they acknowledge that they did purpose to have made their attempt for the rescue of those wretches who were so justly condemned at Newgate, and so worthily executed, and that Ludlow should have then appeared at the head of them; that they made themselves sure at the same time, by parties and confederacy, to have surprized the Tower of London and the Castle of Windsor, but that they found, or at least apprehended, that their design was discovered; which so broke their spirits, that they concluded they must acquiesce for the present, and stay till the Army should be disbanded; which, they said, was generally debauched; that is, returned to an honest and fast obedience to the king; and that it is evident they were betrayed by those who were most intirely trusted by them, and they were in the right. The king had notice of all their designs, what progress they made, and the night they intended to surprise the Tower and Windsor, and gave notice to the several governors; and so, without any noise, that mischief was, by God's goodness, prevented. They acknowledge that they have since recovered their courage and resolution, and were about this time to make their full attempt. They have been promised some considerable rising in the West under Ludlow, and in the North under others; but this place was the scene of greatest hopes; they made sure of a body here, I think they say of 2500 men, with which they resolved, in the first place, to secure (you know what that security is) the person of the General the duke of Albemarle, with whom they have so much reason to be angry, and at the same time to possess themselves of Whitehall: you know the method used in such possession, kill and take possession. And this insupportable calamity God hath again diverted from us; though I must tell you the poor men, who seem to speak honestly, and upon the impulsion of conscience, are very far from being confident that there will not be some desperate insurrection and attempts in several parts of this kingdom, within a short time, which all possible care will be taken to prevent; and, in truth, this very good city so well requires the king's abundant grace and kindness to it, that not only by the unwearied pains and diligence of the worthy lord mayor, but by the general temper and constitution of the whole city, the discontented and seditious party (which can never be totally extirpated out of such a metropolis) is like to have little encouragement to pursue their desperate councils.—The king doth not believe that all those persons, who, at present, are apprehended and in custody, will be found guilty of this treason; it is a vulgar and known artifice to corrupt inferior persons, by persuading them that better men are engaged in the same enterprize, and the king will make as much haste as he can to set those at liberty, against whom the evidence or suspicion is not too treasonable. In the mean time, they who, in truth, are innocent, must confess, that the proceedings towards them hath been very natural and full of clemency; and no man will wonder if his majesty be very desirous that, in this conjuncture, and in order to prevent or suppress these two visible distempers and machinations, his majesty in all places be in good order and preparation; and you may assure yourselves that, in the forming and conduct of it, he will have so great a care for the ease and quiet of his people, that if any person trusted by him shall, through want of skill or want of temper, satisfy his own passion, or appetite, in grieving or vexing his neighbours, his majesty will be so sensible of it, that, if it can be cured no other way, his trust shall be quickly determined: and he is not at all reserved in giving those animadversions and reprehensions when there is occasion, and his ears will be always open to receive those complaints.—My lords and gentlemen; You are now returning to your countries, to receive the thanks and acknowledgements of your friends and neighbours for the great things you have done; and to make the burden you have laid upon them easy, by convincing them of the inevitable necessity of their submitting to them. You will make them see that you have proceeded very far towards the separation, and even divorce, of that necessity from them, to which they have been so long married; that they are now restored to that blessed temper of government, under which their ancestors enjoyed, so many hundred years, that full measure of felicity, and the misery of being deprived of which they have so sensibly felt; that they are now free from those midnight alarms with which they have been so terrified, and rise off their beds, at their own healthy houses, without being saluted with the death of a husband, a son, and friend, miserably killed the night or day before, and with such circumstances killed, as improved the misery beyond the loss itself. This infranchisement is worth all they pay for it. Your lordships will easily recover that estimation and reverence that is due to your high condition, by the exercise and practice of that virtue from whence your honours first sprang; the example of your justice and piety will inflame the hearts of the people towards you, and from your practice they will make a judgment of the king himself. They know very well that you are not only admitted to his presence, but to his conversation, and even in a degree to his friendship, for you are his great council; by your example they will form their own manners, and by yours they will make a guess at the king's; therefore, under that obligation, you will cause your piety, your justice, your affability, and your charity, to shine as bright as is possible before them. They are too much in love with England, too partial to it, who believe it the best country in the world; there is a better earth, and a better air, and better, that is a warmer, sun in other countries; but we are no more than just when we say, that England is an inclosure of the best people in the world, when they are well informed and instructed; a people, in sobriety of conscience, the most devoted to God Almighty; in the integrity of their affections, the most dutiful to the king; in their good manners and inclinations, most regardful and loving to the nobility; no nobility in Europe so intirely beloved by the people; there may be more awe, and fear, and terror of them, but no such respect towards them as in England. I beseech your lordships do not undervalue this love; they have looked upon your lordships, and they will look upon your lordships again, as the greatest example and patron of duty; to the king, as their greatest security and protection from injury and injustice, and for their enjoying whatsoever is due to them by the law; and as the most proper mediators and interposers to the king, if, by any failure of justice, they should be exposed to any oppression and violence; and this exercise of your justice and kindness towards them will make them the more abhor and abominate that party upon which a commonwealth must be founded, because it would extirpate, or suppress, or deprive them of their beloved nobility, which are such a support and security to their full happiness.—And you gentlemen of the house of commons, who are now returning to your country, laden with a trust not inferior or less weighty than that you brought from thence: you came up their deputies to the king, and he returns you now his deputies to them; his plenipotentiaries to inform and assure them, that he thinks himself the happiest and greatest prince in the world, not from the situation of his dominions, and the power of his great navy, with which he can visit his neighbours, and keep them from visiting him; or from the noble revenue you have settled upon him, which he will improve with all good husbandry; but being possessed of the affections and hearts of such subjects, that he doth so intirely love them and depend upon them, that all his actions and all his councils shall tend to no other end but to make them happy and prosperous; that he thinks his honour and his interest principally to consist in providing for, and advancing the honour and interest of, the nation.—That you may have the more credit in what you say, he will not take it unkindly if you publish his defects and infirmities; you may tell them that he is so confident in the multitude of his very good and faithful subjects, that he is very hard to be persuaded that his few ill and unfaithful subjects can do him much harm; that he so much depends on the affections of honest men, and their zeal for his security, that he is not so solicitous and vigilant for his own safety as he ought to be, amidst so many combinations of which he is so well informed, that his servants, who with grief and anguish importune him not to take so little care of his own safety, can obtain no other answer from him, than what Cæsar heretofore gave to his zealous friends, 'mori me malle quam timere:' he will die any death rather than live in fear of his own subjects, or that they should be in fear of him. You may tell them, as a great infirmity, that a troubled and discontented countenance so afflicts him, that he would remove it from them at his own charge, as if he himself were in the fault: and when he hath been informed of any less kind or jealous thing said amongst you, (as your windows are never so close shut, but that the sound of your words goes to the several corners of the town) his majesty hath been heard to say no more but, 'What have I done? I wish that gentleman 'and I were acquainted, that he knew me 'better.' Oh! gentlemen, you cannot be yourselves, nor you cannot make yourselves too zealous or too jealous for such a prince's safety, or too solicitous for such a prince's satisfaction and content, to whom we may very justly say, as the king of Tyre writ to Solomon, 'Because God hath loved his people, 'he hath made thee king over them:' even his own defects and infirmities are very necessary towards the full measure of your prosperity.—My lords and gentlemen; God hath enabled us to invert one argument, which I hope may, to a good degree, repair the much mischief it hath heretofore done: it hath been urged very unreasonably, yet successfully urged, in the worst times, that it was not faith, but presumption, to expect that God would restore a family, with which he seemed to have a controversy, and hath humbled so far; that he would countenance a party that he had so much discountenanced, and almost destroyed. We may here much more reasonably, and therefore, I hope, as effectually, press the miracles that God Almighty hath lately wrought for king and people, as an evidence that he will not again easily forsake them. We may tell those who are using all their endeavours to embroil the nation in new troubles, that it is not probable that a nation, against which God hath seemed, these late years, to have pronounced his judgments in the very language of the prophets, 'Go ye swift messengers to a nation scattered and peeled; to a 'people terrible from the beginning hitherto; 'to a nation rooted out and trodden down, 'whose lands the rivers have spoiled; the Lord 'hath mingled a perverse spirit in the midst 'thereof;' that he should reduce that perverseness to the greatest meekness and resignation; that he should withdraw his judgment from this nation, and, in a moment, restore it to all the happiness it can wish, and to no other end but to expose it to the mercy and fury of a few discontented persons, the worst of the nation, is not easy to be believed.—We may tell those who still contrive the ruin of the Church, (the best and best reformed church in the Christian world, reformed by that authority, and with those circumstances, as a reformation ought to be made) that God would not so miraculously have snatched this church as a brand out of the fire; would not have raised it from the grave after he had suffered it to be buried so many years, by the boisterous hands of profane and sacrilegious persons, under its own rubbish, to expose it again to the same rapine, reproach, and impiety. That Church which delights itself in being called catholic, was never so near expiration, never had such a resurrection. That so small a pittance of meal and oil should be sufficient to preserve and nourish the poor widow and her family so long, is very little more miraculous than that such a number of pious, learned, and very aged bishops should so many years be preserved, in such wonderful straits and oppressions, until they should plentifully provide for their own succession. That after such a deep deluge of sacrilege, profaneness, and impiety had covered, and, to common understanding, swallowed it up; that that church should again appear above the waters, God be again served in that church, and served as he ought to be, and there should be some revenue left to support and encourage those who serve him; nay, that many of those who seemed to thirst after that revenue till they had possessed it, should conscientiously restore what they had taken away, and become good sons and willing tenants to that church they had so lately spoiled, may make us all piously believe that God Almighty would not have been at the expence and charge of such a deliverance; but, in the behalf of a church, very acceptable to him, and which shall continue to the end of the world, and against which the gates of hell shall not be able to prevail.—We may tell those desperate wretches who still harbour in their thoughts wicked designs against the sacred person of the king, in order to the compassing of their own imaginations, that God Almighty would not have led him through so many wildernesses of afflictions of all kinds, conducted him through so many perils at sea, and perils by land, snatched him out of the midst of this kingdom when it was not worthy of him, and when the hands of his enemies were even upon him, when they thought themselves so sure of him that they would bid so cheap and so vile a price for him; he could not, in that article, have so covered him with a cloud, that he travelled, even with some pleasure and great observation, through the midst of his enemies. He would not so wonderfully have new modelled that army, so inspired their hearts and the hearts of the whole nation, with an honest and impatient longing for the return of their dear sovereign; and, in the mean time, have so tried him (which had little less providence in it than the other) with these unnatural, or at least unusual, disrespects and reproaches abroad, that he might have a harmless and an innocent appetite to his own country, and return to his own people with a full value, and the whole unwasted bulk of his affections, without being corrupted or biassed by extraordinary foreign obligations. God Almighty would not have done all this but for a servant, whom he will always preserve as the apple of his own eye, and always defend from the most secret imaginations of his enemies.—If these argumentations, gentlemen, urged with that vivacity as is most natural to your own gratitude and affections, recover as many (and it would be strange if they should not) as have been corrupted by the other logic, the hearts of the whole nation, even to a man, will insensibly be so devoted to the king, as the only conservator and protector of all that is dear and precious to them; and will be so zealous to please him, whose greatest pleasure is to see them pleased, that when they make choice of persons again to serve in parliament, they will not chuse such as they wish should oppose the king, but therefore chuse because they have, and because they are to like to serve the king with their whole hearts; and, since he desires what is best for his people, to gratify him in all his desires. This blessed harmony would raise us to the highest pinnacle of honour and happiness in this world: a pinnacle without a point, upon which king and people may securely rest and repose themseves, against all the gusts, and storms, and temptations which all the malice of this world can raise against us: and I am sure you will all contend to be at the top of this pinnacle.—I have no more to add but the words of custom, That the king declares this present parliament to be dissolved; and this parliament is dissolved accordingly."*

* "Thus ended the famous Convention, about eight months after the first meeting, and seven after the Restoration, when it received the royal stamp of Parliament: an assembly that began with the greatest expectation, and ended with the greatest satisfaction of all people. Never was so glorious a harmony between the king and parliament of England for many years before. And here we may observe, with an ingenuous modern writer, that it looks as if Heaven took a more than ordinary care of the English, that they did not throw up all their liberties at once, upon the Restoration of the King; for, though some were for bringing him back upon terms, yet after he was once come, he so intirely possessed the hearts of his people, that they thought nothing too much for them to grant, or for him to receive. Among other designs to oblige him, there was one formed to settle such a Revenue upon him for life, as should place him beyond the necessity of asking more, except in the case of a war, or some such emergency. And as to particulars, another Writer informs us, That Mr. Alex. Popham, a man of intrigue and great capacity, offered the king, with the assistance of a party he had in the parliament, to procure an Act for settling on him and his successors, above two millions a year by way of Subsidy; which, with the Revenue of the Excise and other duties, must have made him a very rich prince. The king was well pleased with the proposal, especially since the want of money had occasioned his father's unfortunate projects; but advising about it with chancellor Hyde, that minister told him, 'That the best 'Revenue he could have, would be the gaining 'the hearts of his subjects; that if he would 'trust to them, he would find such Supplies as 'should never fail him in time of need.' Therefore it may be added, with another Writer, It is to his memory, that we owe our being a free people; for he, with his two great friends, the duke of Ormond and the earl of Southampton, checked the forwardness of some who were desirous to load the crown with prerogative and revenue. He put a stop to all this, which being afterwards odiously represented, brought on that great and lasting, but honourable disgrace." Echard, p. 783.

FIRST SESSION OF THE SECOND PARLIAMENT OF KING CHARLES II. COMMONLY CALLED THE LONG OR PENSIONARY PARLIAMENT.

The King's Speech.] May 8. 1661. This day the New Parliament met. The King, being arrayed in his regal robes with his crown on his head, ascended his seat of state; the Peers being in their robes, and the Commons being below the bar, his majesty made a short Speech, declaring the cause and the reasons for his summoning the present parliament as followeth:

"My lords and gentlemen of the house of commons:—I will not spend the time in telling you why I called you hither; I am sure I am glad to see you here. I do value myself much upon keeping my word, upon making good whatsoever I promise to my subjects: and I well remember when I was last in this place, I promised that I would call a parliament as soon as could be reasonably expected or desired; and truly, considering the season of the year, and all that has been done since we parted, you could not reasonably expect to meet sooner than now we do. If it might have been a week sooner, you will confess there was some reason to defer it to this day, for this day: we may without superstition love one day, prefer one day before another, for the memory of some blessings that befel us that day; and then you will not wonder that the memory of the great affection the whole kingdom shewed to me this day twelve-month, made me desirous to meet you again this day, when I dare swear you are full of the same spirit, and that it will be lasting in you. I think there are not many of you who are not particularly known to me; there are very few of whom I have not heard so much good, that I am sure, as I can be of any thing that is to come, that you will all concur with me, and that I shall concur with you in all things which may advance the peace, plenty, and prosperity of the nation: I shall be exceedingly deceived else.—My lords and gentlemen; you will find what method I think best for your proceeding, by two Bills I have caused to be prepared for you, which are for confirmation of all that was enacted at our last meeting: and above all, I must repeat what I said when I was last here; 'That next to the miraculous 'blessing of God Almighty, and indeed, as an 'immediate effect of that blessing, I do impute 'the good disposition and security we are all 'in, to the happy Act of Indemnity and Oblivion: that is the principal corner-stone, which 'supports this excellent building, that creates 'kindness in us to each other, and confidence 'in our joint and common security.' I am sure I am still of the same opinion, and more, if it be possible, of that opinion, than I was, by the experience I have of the benefit of it, and from the unreasonableness of what some men say against it, though I assure you not in my hearing. In God's name, provide full remedies for any future mischiefs; be as severe as you will against new offenders, especially if they be so upon old principles, and pull up those principles by the roots. But I shall never think him a wise man who would endeavour to undermine or shake that foundation of our public peace, by infringing that Act in the least degree; or that he can be my friend, or wish me well, who would persuade me ever to consent to the breach of a promise I so solemnly made when I was abroad, and performed with that solemnity; because, and after I promised it, I cannot suspect any attempts of that kind by any men of merit and virtue. *—I will not conclude without telling you some news; that I think will be very acceptable to you; and therefore I should think myself unkind and ill-natured, if I should not impart it to you. I have been often put in mind by my friends, That it was now high time to marry; and I have thought so myself ever since I came into England: but there appeared difficulties enough in the choice, though many overtures have been made to me: and if I should never marry till I could make such a choice, against which there could be no foresight of any inconvenience that may ensue, you would live to see me an old bachelor, which I think you do not desire to do. I can now tell you, not only that I am resolved to marry, but to whom I resolve to marry, if God please: and towards my resolution, I have used that deliberation, and taken that advice, as I ought to do in an affair of that importance; and, trust me, with a full consideration of the good of my subjects in general, as of myself: it is with the daughter of Portugal. When I had, as well as I could, weighed all that occurred to me, the first resolution I took, was to state the whole overtures which had been made to me, and, in truth, all that had been said against it to my privy-council; without hearing whose advice, I never did, nor ever will, resolve any thing of public importance. And I tell you with great satisfaction and comfort to myself, that after many hours debate in a full council, for I think there was not above one absent; and truly, I believe, upon all that can be said upon that subject, for or against it, my lords, without one dissenting voice, yet there were very few sate silent, advised me with all imaginable chearfulness to this Marriage; which I looked upon as very wonderful, and even as some instance of the approbation of God himself; and so took up my own resolution, and concluded all with the ambassador of Portugal, who is departing with the whole Treaty signed, which you will find

* Lord Clarendon, in the Continuation of his Life, p. 96. says, "That this warmth of his majesty upon this subject was not then more than needful: for the armies being now disbanded, there were great combinations entered into, not to confirm the Act of Oblivion; which they knew without confirmation would signify nothing. Men were well enough contented that the king should grant indemnity to all men that had rebelled against him; that he should grant their lives and fortunes to them, who had forfeited them to him: but they thought it very unreasonable and unjust, that the king should release those debts which were immediately due to them, and forgive those trespasses which had been committed to their particular damage. They could not endure to meet the same men in the king's highway, now it was the king's highway again, who had heretofore affronted them in those ways, because they were not the king's, and only because they knew they could obtain no justice against them. They could not with any patience see those men, who not only during the war had oppressed them, plundered their houses, and had their own adorned with the furniture they had robbed them of, ride upon the same horses which they had then taken from them upon no other pretence, but because they were better than their own; but, after the war was ended, had committed many insolent trespasses upon them wantonly, and to shew their power of Justice of Peace or Committee men, and had from the lowest beggars raised great estates, out of which they were well able to satisfy, at least in some degree, the damages the other had sustained. And those and other passions of this kind, which must have invalidated the whole Act of Indemnity, could not have been extinguished without the king's influence, and indeed his immediate interposition and industry."

to contain many great advantages to the kingdom: and I make all the haste I can to fetch you a queen hither, who, I doubt not, will bring great blessings with her, to me and you. I will add no more, but refer the rest to the Chancellor."

The Lord Chancellor's Speech.] After his majesty had finished his Speech, the Lord Chancellor (the earl of Clarendon), having first conferred with his majesty, spake as followeth:

"My lords; and you the knights, citizens, and burgesses, of the house of commons;—The king hath called you hither by his writ, to assist him, with your information and advice, in the greatest and weightiest affairs of the kingdom; by his writ, which is the only good and lawful way to the meeting of a parliament; and the pursuing that writ, the remembering how and why they came together, is the only way to bring a happy end to parliaments. There was no such writ as this, no such presence as this, in the year 1649, when this unhappy kingdom was dishonoured and exposed to the mirth and reproach of their neighbours, in the government of a Commonwealth. There was no such writ as this, no such presence as this, in Dec 1653, when that infant Commonwealth, when the three kingdoms of England, Scotland, and Ireland, and the dominions thereunto belonging, were delivered up into the bloody and merciless hands of a devouring Protector, and sacrificed to his lust and appetite. There was no such writ as this, no such presence as this, in the year 1656, when that Protector was more solemnly invested and installed, and the liberty of the three nations submitted to his absolute tyranny by the humble Petition and Advice. When people came together by such exorbitant means, it is no wonder that their consultations and conclusions were so disproportioned from any rules of justice or sobriety. God be thanked, that he hath reserved us to this day, a day that many good men have died praying for; that, after all those prodigies in church and state, we have lived to see the king at the opening of the parliament; that we have lived to see our king anointed and crowned, and crowned by the hands of an archbishop, as his predecessors have been, and that we are come hither this day in obedience to his writ.—The king tells you, he hath caused a Bill or two to be prepared for the Confirmation of all that was enacted in the last parliament, and commends the dispatch of those to you with some earnestness. The truth is, it is a great part of the business of this parliament, to celebrate the memory of the last, by confirming or re-enacting all that was done by that parliament, which, though it was not called by the king's writ, may be reasonably thought to have been called by God himself, upon the supplication and prayer of the king and the whole nation, as the only means to restore the nation to its happiness, to itself, to its honour, and even to its innocence. How glad the king was of it, appears by what he writ to them from Breda, when he referred more to them than ever was referred to parliament: he referred in truth (upon the matter) all that concerned himself, all that concerned religion, all that concerned the peace and happiness of the kingdom, to them; and to their honour be it spoken, and to their honour be it ever remembered, that the king, religion, and the kingdom, have no reason to be sorry that so much was intrusted to them, nor they to be ashamed of the discharge of their trust. It would have been a very unseasonable scruple in any man, who should have refused to bear his part in the excellent transactions of that parliament, because he was not called thither by the king's writ; and it would be a more unreasonable scruple now, in any man, after we have all received the fruit and benefit of their councils and conclusions, when in truth we owe our orderly and regular meeting at this time to their extraordinary meeting then, to their wisdom in laying hold upon the king's promises, and to the king's justice in performing all he promised, and to the kingdom's submission and acquiescence in those promises; I say, it would be very unseasonable and unreasonable now, to endeavour to shake that foundation, which, if you will take the king's judgment, supports the whole fabric of our peace and security. He tells you what he shall think of any who goes about to undermine that foundation; which is a zeal no prince could be transported with but himself. It might have seemed enough for a king who had received so many injuries so hardly to be forgotten, undergone so many losses so impossible to be repaired, to have been willing to confirm and to re-enact the Act of Oblivion and Indemnity, when you should present it to him; but to prepare such an act for you, to conjure you by all that is precious by your friendship to him, to dispatch those acts with expedition, is such a piece of fatherly tenderness and piety, as could proceed from no heart but such a one in which God hath treasured up a stock of mercy and justice and wisdom to redeem a nation. And truly, my lords and gentlemen, for ourselves, if we will consider how much we owe to those who with all the faculties of their souls contributed to and contrived the blessed change, the restoring the king to his people and his people to the king, and then how much we owe to those who gave no opposition to the virtuous activity of the other (and God knows a little opposition might have done much harm), whether we look upon the public, or upon our own private provocations, there will remain so few who do not deserve to be forgiven by us, that we may very well submit to the king's advice and his example; of whom we may very justly say, as a very good Historian said of a very great emperor, and I am sure it could never be so truly said of any emperor as of ours, 'Facere recte cives suos, princeps 'optimus faciendo docet; cumque sit imperio 'maximus, exemplo major est:' nor indeed hath he yet given us, or have we yet felt, any other instances of his greatness, and power, and superiority, and dominion over us, 'nisi' (as he said) 'aut levatione periculi, aut accessione dignitatis;' by giving us peace, honour, and security, which we could not have without him; by desiring nothing for himself, but what is as good for us as for himself; and therefore, I hope, we shall make no scruple of obeying him in this particular.—My Lords and Gentlemen; Though the last parliament did great and wonderful things, indeed as much as in that time they could, yet they have left very great things for you to do: you are to finish the structure, of which they but laid the foundation; indeed they left some things undone, which it may be they thought they had finished: you will find the Revenue they intended to raise for the king very much short of what they promised: you will find the Public Debts for the Discharge of the Army and the Navy, which they thought they had provided for sufficiently, to be still in arrear and unpaid: and here I am, by the king's special command, to commend the poor Seamen to you, who, by the rules which were prescribed for their payment, are in much worse condition than (without question) was foreseen they would be; for, by appointing them to be paid but from 1658 (which was a safe rule to the Army), very many are still in Arrear for 2, 3, or 4 years service; and so his majesty's promise to them from Breda remains unperformed. Some other losses, which resulted from other rules given for their payment, have been supplied to them by the king's own bounty. They are a people very worthy of your particular care and cherishing; upon whose courage and fidelity very much of the happiness and honour and security of the nation depends; and therefore his majesty doubts not you will see justice done towards them with favour.—My Lords and Gentlemen; You are now the great physicians of the kingdom; and God knows, you have many wayward, and froward, and distempered patients, who are in truth very sick, and patients, who think themselves sicker than they are; and some who think themselves in health, and are most sick of all. You must, therefore, use all the diligence, and patience, and compassion, which good physicians have for their patients; all the chearfulness, and complacency, and indulgence, their several habits, and constitutions, and distempers of body and mind, may require. Be not too melancholic with your patients, nor suffer them to be too melancholic, by believing that every little distemper will presently turn to a violent fever, and that fever will presently turn to the plague; that every little trespass, every little swerving from the known rule, must insensibly grow to a neglect of the law, and that neglect introduce an absolute confusion; that every little difference in opinion, or practice in Conscience or Religion, must presently destroy Conscience and Religion. Be not too severe and rough towards your patients, in prescribing remedies, how well compounded soever, too nauseous and offensive to their stomachs and appetite, or to their very fancy. Allay and correct those humours, which corrupt their stomachs and their appetites: if the good old known tried laws be for the present too heavy for their necks, which have been so many years without any yoke at all, make a temporary provision of an easier and a lighter yoke, till, by living in a wholesome air, by the benefit of a soberer conversation, by keeping a better diet, by the experience of a good and just government, they recover strength enough to bear, and discretion enough to discern, the benefit and the ease of those laws they disliked. If the present Oaths have any terms or expressions in them that a tender conscience honestly makes scruple of submitting to, in God's name let other oaths be formed in their places, as comprehensive of all those obligations which the policy of government must exact: but still let there be a yoke: let there be an Oath, let there be some law, that may be the rule to that indulgence, that, under pretence of Liberty of Conscience, men may not be absolved from all the obligations of law and conscience.—I have besought your good-nature and indulgence towards some of your weak patients, if by it they can be brought to follow and submit to your prescriptions for their health; nor is it reasonable to imagine that the distemper of 20 years can be rectified and subdued in 12 months. There must be a natural time, and natural applications, allowed for it. But there are a sort of patients that I must recommend to your utmost vigilance, utmost severity, and to no part of your lenity or indulgence; such who are so far from valuing your prescriptions that they look not upon you as their physicians, but their patients; such who, instead of repenting any thing that they have done amiss, repeat every day the same crimes for the Indemnity whereof the Act of Oblivion was provided. These are the seditious Preachers, who cannot be contented to be dispensed with for their full obedience to some laws established, without reproaching and inveighing against those laws, how established soever; who tell their auditories, that the Apostle meant, when he bid them stand to their liberties, that they should stand to their arms; and who, by repeating the very expressions, and teaching the very doctrine, they set on-foot in the year 1640, sufficiently declare that they have no mind that 20 years should put an end to the miseries we have undergone.—What good christian can think without horrour of these Ministers of the Gospel, who by their function should be the messengers of peace, and are in their practice the only trumpets of war, and incendiaries towards rebellion! How much more Christian was that Athenian nun in Plutarch, and how shall she rise up in judgment against these men, who, when Alcibiades was condemned by the public justice of the state, and a decree made, that the religious, the priests, and the nuns, should revile and curse him, stoutly refused to perform that office, saying, 'That she was professed religious, to pray and to bless, not to 'curse and ban!' And if the person and the place can improve and aggravate the offence, as no doubt it doth before God and man, methinks the preaching rebellion and treason out of the pulpit should be as much worse than the advancing it in the market, as the poisoning a man at the Communion would be worse than killing him at a tavern: and it may be, in the catalogue of those sins which the zeal of some men declares to be against the Holy Ghost, there may not be any one more reasonably thought to be such, than a Minister of Christ's turning rebel against his prince, which is a most notorious apostacy from his order; and his preaching rebellion to the people as the doctrine of Christ, adding blasphemy and pertinacy to his apostacy, hath all the marks by which good men are taught to know and avoid that sin against the Holy Ghost. If you do not provide for the thorough quenching these firebrands; king, lords, and commons, shall be their meanest subjects, and the whole kingdom kindled into one general flame.—My Lords and Gentlemen; When the king spake last in this place before this day, He said, 'When he should 'call the next parliament, he should receive 'their thanks for what he had done since he 'had dissolved the last; for he said, he should 'not more propose any one rule to himself, in 'his actions or his councils, than this, What is 'a parliament like to think of this action, or of 'that council? and that it should be want of 'understanding in him, if it would not bear 'that test:' He told you but now, 'That he 'values himself much upon keeping his word, 'upon performing all that he promises to his 'people.' And he hath the worst luck in the world, if he hath not complied with this promise, and if his understanding hath failed him in it. It was in a very little time after the Dissolution of that parliament, his majesty giving himself a few days to accompany his royal mother to the sea side, the only time he hath slept out of this town near these 12 months, that the most desperate, and prodigious Rebellion brake out in this city, that hath been heard of in any age; which continued two or three nights together, with the murder of several honest citizens. Let no man undervalue the treason because of the contemptibleness of the number engaged in it. No man knows the number; but, by the multitude of intercepted letters from and to all the counties of England, in which the time was set down wherein the work of the Lord was to be done, by the desperate carriage of the traitors themselves, and their bragging of their friends, we may conclude the combination reached very far. And in truth we may reasonably believe, that if the undaunted courage and the indefatigable industry of the lord mayor, who deserves to be mentioned before king, lords, and commons, and to be esteemed by them, had not prevented it; I say, it is probable this fury would have not been extinguished, before this famous city, or a great part of it, had been turned into ashes.*—If you

* The Chancellor alludes to the Insurrection of the Fifth Monarchy Men, under Venner, of which Insurrection archdeacon Echard gives us the following account? "While the affairs of the nation seemed to be in peace and tranquility, in the beginning of the new year 1660-1, there happened a strange and unparalleled action in London, which strengthened the belief of those secret Plots and Conspiracies mentioned by the lord chancellor. This was occasioned by a small body of Fifth-Monarchy Men, who hating all monarchy, and the appearance of it, had formerly made an attempt against Cromwell's government, but escaped beyond expectation. The head of them was one Thomas Venner, sometime a wine-cooper, who by the king's indulgence held a conventicle in Coleman-street, where he, and others, used to preach to them out of the Prophecies of Daniel and the Revelations, and from thence drew strange inferences, persuading their congregations 'to take up arms for King Jesus, 'against the powers of the earth, the king, the 'duke of York, general Monk, &c.' assuring them, 'That no weapons formed against them 'should prosper, nor a hair of their heads be 'touched; for one should chace a thousand, 'and two put ten thousand to flight.' Upon which they got a Declaration printed, entitled, 'A Door of Hope opened;' in which they said, and declared, 'That they would never 'sheath their swords till Babylon, as they 'called monarchy, became a hissing and a 'curse, and there be left neither Remnant, 'Son, nor Nephew: that when they had led 'captivity captive in England, they would go 'into France, Spain, Germany, &c. and rather 'die than take the wicked Oaths of Supremacy and Allegiance: that they would not 'make any leagues with monarchists, but 'would rise up against the carnal, to possess 'the Gate, or the world, to bind their kings in 'chains, and their nobles in fetters of iron.' And so to accomplish this heroic design, they observed so much policy as to put it in execution when the king was attending his mother and sister to embark at Portsmouth, for their return into France. Accordingly on Sunday the 6th of Jan. being fully animated by the sermon, which hinted to them, 'that they had been praying and preaching, but not acting for God,' they sallied out well armed from their Meeting-House, and marched to St. Paul's Church-Yard in the dark of the evening. Here they mustered their party, amounting to above 50, and placed their centinels for the time, one of whom killed a poor innocent man, who upon demand had answered, 'He was for God and 'king Charles!' This gave an alarm to the city, and the lord-mayor, sir Rd. Brown, and the trained-bands being upon the guard, some files of men were sent against them, whom these

enquire what the king did upon this unheard-of provocation, what vengeance he took upon those whose professed and avowed principle was not to distinguish between him and another man, nay, to kill him sooner than any other man, you will find, as was said of Cæsar, that 'libentius vitam victor jam daret, quam victi acciperent;' that his mercy hath been no less obstinate than their malice and wickedness; that few persons have suffered; and that he hath restrained the law from being severe to many, who at the same time continue their guilt, and undervalue his compassion; that there hath not been a week since that time, in which there hath not been combinations and conspiracies formed against his person, and against the peace of the kingdom, which before this time would have taken effect, if God had not put it into the hearts of some who were trusted in the councils, to discover the design, time enough for prevention. And upon all these alarms, and the interception of

---

desperate men quickly routed, and so marched on to Bishops-gate, where they passed without opposition, and from thence to Cripple-gate, where they came into the city again, and so to Alders-gate. Here threatening the constable, who was weakly attended, they were let out again. Then they declared themselves for King Jesus, and thus proceeded to Beech-Lane, where they killed a Headborough that opposed them, and so hastened to Cane-Wood, between Highgate and Hampstead, where they reposed themselves for that night.—The noise of this strange Insurrection caused the General to send a party of horse and foot the next day, who drove them out of the wood, and took some of them prisoners, who were committed to the Gate-House. The rest having rallied again, on Wednesday morning returned to London, with assurance by Venner their leader, 'That no weapon formed against them 'should prosper: therefore they might look 'upon the example of Gideon: it was the 'same thing to God, whether he saved by a 'few or a multitude.' Their first appearance was in Threadneedle-street, behind the Exchange, where they beat back a party sent by the guard there. But, upon the advance of more forces, they retreated to Bishops-gate-street; where after a sharp encounter, two of each side being slain, they gradually slipt away and disappeared. A while after, like the gathering of clouds, they were seen again at College-Hill and Maiden-Lane, where they designed to sacrifice the lord-mayor. But missing of him, they crossed Cheapside, and passed into Wood-street. Here began a cruel fight, wherein they shewed skill as well as great valour; and having ruffled some trained-bands, and repelled the horse-guards that came to assist them, they did not give way till Venner was knocked down and severely wounded, and Tuffney and Cragg, two of their fiercest preachers and combatants, were slain. Whereupon the greatest part of them retreated to Cripple-gate, firing in good order in their rear upon the trained-bands, who were in close pursuit of them. Col. Cox, who commanded, lodged ten of them in an ale-house near the postern, which house they obstinately maintained. The house being surrounded, some of the soldiers untiled the next house, and shot in upon them, being in the upper room, who still refused quarter: at the same time another party of musketeers got up the stairs, broke down the door, and entered their garrison. Six of them were killed before, another refusing quarter was first knocked down, and then shot with a musket. The rest being demanded why they did not ask quarter before, answered 'They durst not for fear their own fellows should have shot them.' In this Insurrection 20 of the king's men were slain, and as many of the rebels. Those taken were Venner himself, Hodgkins, Gowler, Allen, Pym, Ashton, Prichard, Fall, Hopkins, Wells, and about as many more, not much worth the naming; who blasphemously alledged, 'That if they were deceived or mis-led, it was God that deceived them.'—These, to the number of 20, were soon after arraigned at the Old Bailey for treason and murder; which being fully proved, with all the forementioned particulars, they were all found guilty, except Hopkins and Wells, against whom the evidence was not full, and against one Patshul only a single witness: wherefore they were acquitted by their jury. When sentence was pronounced against them, and the lord chief justice Foster seriously charged Venner with the blood of his unhappy accomplices, he impudently replied, 'It was not he, but Jesus that led them.' Three of them confessed their crime, and craved mercy, but the rest continued obstinate. Being sentenced to be hanged, drawn, and quartered, Venner and Hodgkins were on the 19th of Jan. executed over-against their Meeting-House in Coleman-street. The former spoke little but in vindication of himself and his fact, and something of his opinion, with an assurance 'That the time was at hand when other judgment would be;' highly reflecting upon the present government. Hodgkins raved and cursed in the manner of praying, 'calling down vengeance from Heaven upon the king, the judges, and the city of London;' nor would he desist, till the executioner put an end to all his extravagancies. Two days after nine more were executed in five several places of the city, without being quartered, as the two first were. All persisted, like the Regicides, in justifying their crimes, except one young man, who shewed great signs of repentance.—Thus ended a Rebellion of a very strange nature, which was begun and carried on with such infernal rage, that if their numbers had been equal to their spirits, they would have overturned the city, and the nation, and the world, which in their imagination they had divided among themselves." P. 784.

such letters as would in all other countries have produced the rack for further discoveries, and under the late government in this would have erected high courts of justice for their punishment, he hath left the offenders to the judges of the law, and those judges to the precise forms and ordinary rules of the law.—My Lords and Gentlemen; If the new licence and corruption of this time hath exceeded the wickedness of former ages, that the old laws have not enough provided for the punishment of wickedness they could not foresee or imagine; it will become your wisdoms to provide new Remedies for new diseases, and to secure the precious person of our dear sovereign from the first approaches of villany, and the peace of the kingdom from the first overtures of sedition.—If you will not provide laws to do it, the king will not do any thing extraordinary, even towards his own preservation. You see the rule by which he hath walked; and as he hath made good his promise to you, so, I doubt not, you will make good his prophecy, and that he shall receive thanks for what he hath done since he was last here.—He hath told you now what he hath done; that he is resolved to marry, and resolved whom to marry: which, I believe, is the most grateful news that the whole kingdom hath longed for, or could receive, from the first day of his landing here. And when they shall know the great deliberation he hath used before that resolution, and the circumstances in resolving it, they will surely have cause to confess, that never king, in the disposal of himself in marriage, took so great care for the good and felicity of his people.—Within a very short time after his landing in this kingdom, he was moved by the ambassador of Portugal, to renew a Treaty lately made between that crown and the Usurper; a treaty in very many respects the most advantageous to this nation that ever was entered into with any prince or people; a treaty by which, at this time, that crown is paying the penalty (which the Usurper exacted from it) for the most noble and heroic act of honour and friendship, performed by that king to our master, that ever was performed by any prince towards another prince in distress. And yet the king was nothing forward to ratify this Treaty; though it is very true, every Article in it but one was entirely for the benefit of this nation, for the extraordinary advancement of Trade, for the good of Religion, and for the honour of the crown: yet there was one, one single Article, that must oblige the king, as it did the Usurper, to supply Portugal with an army for his assistance, when he should require it; that is, Portugal should have power to make levies of 10,000 men for their service. This, the king foresaw, might produce a war with Spain, which he was very unwilling to undergo for that engagement; and yet his Council represented unto him how heart-breaking a thing it would be to his people, to lose the possession of so great a trade, and those other immense advantages they had by that Treaty; and that it would be judged an irrecoverable error in policy, if Portugal should be suffered again to be swallowed up by Spain. However, the king was resolved, not precipitately to engage himself in such a treaty as might be attended with such an inconvenience; but to take time, fully to consider of it; and this delay the Portugal could not be pleased with, and so the ambassador returned home to his master. About this time, the house of commons sent up a Bill to the lords, for the annexing Dunkirk and Jamaica to the crown of England, which seemed to have the most universal consent and approbation from the whole nation that ever any bill could be attended with: yet the same consideration which retarded the Treaty with Portugal made the king less warm towards the advancing of that Bill; and the Spanish ambassador was as solicitous to obstruct it, as he hath been since to obstruct the Match with Portugal. This being the case, and the Portugal ambassador returning with such particular overtures to the king for a Marriage with the daughter of that crown, that, both in respect of portion, and many other transcendent advantages for the advancement of the trade and empire of this kingdom, the like hath not been offered in this age; and his majesty having received as full information and satisfaction in the beauty and excellency of that renowned princess as can be had without a personal interview (a circumstance very rarely admitted to princes), it was not in his majesty's power to be without some approbation and inclination to this alliance: yet even then he would not trust himself in this great affair, which so nearly and so dearly concerns himself, and himself above all others. Though the benefit and advantage could but appear the same upon further consultation, yet there might possibly be some mischiefs, or some inconveniencies be discerned, which he had not foreseen. He resolves, therefore, to call his council; tells them some days before, that he had an affair of great importance to impart to them, and to receive their advice in; and therefore appointed an extraordinary day, that they might all appear (and truly, I think, there was but one lord absent, who was then indisposed in his health). In this council he stated the whole matter, all that was offered of benefit and advantage, all that occurred of hazard or inconvenience, without the least discovery of his own inclinations, further than that you would have believed he had seen the picture of his mistress; it having been a speech he hath often accustomed himself to, that he would not marry a woman he had not some reason to believe he could love, though she could bring him the empire of the world. He did not conceal from my lords what the Spanish ambassador had offered against this Marriage (who is not over-reserved in giving counsel, nor in communicating the counsel he gives), what proffers he had made of others, what threats of war in one case, what advantage of dowry in another; that he is so sollicitous for the advancement of the Protestant Religion, that be had offered several Protestant princesses to whom his master shall give a portion, as with the Infanta of Spain; and truly, less than the universal monarch could not dispose of so many princesses without the least consent or privity of their own. His majesty commanded all my lords to deliver their counsel and advice freely, upon a full prospect of what might appear good and happy for his people as well as for himself; assuring them, as he hath done you now this day, that, as he never did, so he never will do, any thing of great importance, without consulting with them. You will believe that my lords of the council are solicitous enough for the advancement of the Protestant Religion, upon which the welfare of this kingdom so much depends. But they were very apprehensive, that the first Protestant daughter that ever any king of Spain had, would not probably bring so great advantages to it as was pretended. They have no mind to encourage the king to a war; we have had war enough: but they do not think he should so much fear a war, as, out of the dread of it, to be at the disposal of any other prince; and that when he hath freed his own subjects from Wardships and from Liveries, that he should himself become a Ward to the king of Spain, and not marry without his approbation and consent. They observed, that in the same Memorials (I do not mean that which he last printed, but a former) in which the Spanish ambassador threatens war if the king marries with Portugal, he presseth very earnestly the delivering up of Dunkirk and Jamaica; and it is plain enough, he would have that recompence for the portion he would give. And, in truth, whosoever is against the Match with Portugal, is for the delivery of Dunkirk and Jamaica; war being as sure to follow from the latter as the former, and from neither till the king of Spain find it convenient for himself, which I hope he will not yet do. I will not enlarge upon the many reasons. The king hath told you the conclusion. There was never a more unanimous advice from any council, not any dissenting voice, in the beseeching his majesty to make this Marriage, and to finish it with all the expedition imaginable. Upon this, he sent for the Portugal ambassador, declared his resolution to him, hath writ himself to Portugal, and is preparing his fleet to fetch home our queen. And I hope now he hath deserved all your thanks, both for the matter and the manner; and that not only ourselves, but the ages that are to succeed us, shall have cause to bless God and his majesty for this resolution that he hath taken, and that he hath declared to us this day, and hath reserved for this day, having obliged his council to secrecy, that he might himself communicate it to his whole kingdom at once.—There are some other particulars of weight; but he will not mingle them with this great important one, which must so much fill your hearts and your heads; but will reserve them till he sees you again after you have chosen your Speaker, which he now leaves you to do, and to repair to your house for that purpose, that you may present your Speaker to him at 4 of the clock upon Friday."

Before we enter upon the Proceedings of this New Parliament, we think it proper to present our readers with the following Lists of the Members of both Houses:

LIST OF THE HOUSE OF LORDS.

The NAMES of the Lords Temporal in this present Parliament, begun at Westminster the 8th day of May, in the 13th year of the Reign of our most gracious Sovereign Lord King Charles II. 1661.*

DUKES *of the Blood-Royal.*

James, d. of York and Albany, l. high admiral of England,
Rupert, duke of Cumberland.

These take place in respect of their Offices.

Edward, earl of Clarendon, lord chancellor of England,
Thomas, earl of Southampton, lord treasurer of England.

DUKES.

George, duke of Buckingham,
Chas. d. of Richmond
George, duke of Albemarle, general of the armies.

MARQUISSES.

John, m. of Winchester
Edw. m. of Worcester
Wm. m. of Newcastle
Hen. m. of Dorchester

EARLS.

Montagu, e. of Lindsay, lord high chamberlain of England
James, earl of Brecknock, lord steward of his maj.'s household
Edw. e. of Manchester, lord chamberlain of the household
Aubrey, e. of Oxford
Algernon, e. of Northumberland
Fran. e. of Shrewsbury
Charles, e. of Derby
John, e. of Rutland
Wm. e. of Bedford
Philip, e. of Pembroke and Montgomery
Theoph. e. of Lincoln
Cha. e. of Nottingham
James, e. of Suffolk
Richard, e. of Dorset
Wm. e. Salisbury
John, e. of Exeter
John, e. of Bridgwater
Robert, e. of Leicester
Ja. e. of Northampton
Charles, e. of Warwick
Wm. e. of Devonshire
Basil, e. of Denbigh
George, e. of Bristol
Lionel, e. of Middlesex and Holland
John, e. of Clare
Oliv. e. of Bolingbroke
Mildmay, e. of Westmoreland
Thos. e. of Berkshire
Thos. e. of Cleveland
Edw. e. of Mulgrave
Hen. e. of Monmouth
Jas. e. of Marlborough
Thomas, e. of Rivers
Henry, earl of Dover
Henry, e. of Peterbro'
Henry, e. of Stamford
Hen. e. of Winchelsea
Chas. e. of Carnarvon
Mountj. e. of Newport
Phil. e. of Chesterfield
John, e. of Thanet.
Jeremy, e. of Portland
Wm. e. of Stafford
Rob. e. of Sunderland
James, e. of Sussex
George, e. of Norwich
Nicho. e. of Scarsdale
Hen. e. of St. Albans
Edw. e. of Sandwich
Edw. e. of Clarendon
Arthur, e. of Essex
Thos. e. of Cardigan
Arthur, e. of Anglesea
John, earl of Bath
Charles, e. of Carlisle

* Lord Somers's Collection.

VISCOUNTS.
Leicester, visc. Hereford
Francis, v. Montague
Wm. v. Say and Seal
Edward, v. Conway
Baptist, v. Cambden
William, v. Stafford
Thos. v. Falconberge
John, v. Mordant.

BARONS.
John lord Nevill, of Abergavenny
James lord Touchet of Audley
Charles lord West Delaware
George lord Berkley, of Berkley
Thomas lord Parker, of Morley and Montegle
Francis lord Dacres
Coovers lord Darcy, of Darcy
Wm. lord Stourton, of Stourton
William lord Sandys, Delevyne
Edward lord Vaux, of Harrowden
Thomas lord Windsor
Thos. lord Wentworth
Wingfield lord Cromwell
George lord Bruce
Philip lord Wharton, of Wharton
Francis lord Willoughby, of Parham
William lord Paget, of Beaudesert
Dudley lord North
William lord Chandos, of Sudeley
John lord Carey, of Hunsdon
William lord Peter
—— lord Gerrard, of Gerards Bromley
Charles lord Stanhope, of Harrington
Henry lord Arundel, of Wardour
Christopher lord Roper, of Tenham
Robert lord Brooke
Edw. lord Montague, of Boughton
Charles lord Howard, of Charlton
William lord Grey, of Warke
John lord Roberts, of Truro
Wm. lord Craven, of Hampstead Marshal
John lord Lovelace, of Hurley
John lord Paulet, of Hinton St. George
Wm. lord Maynard
Thos. lord Coventry, of Aylesborough
Edward lord Howard, of Escrick
Warwick lord Mohun
Peircy lord Herbert, of Poole
Edward lord Herbert, of Cherbury
Francis lord Seymour, of Trowbridge, chancellor of the dutchy of Lancaster
Thomas lord Bruce, of Wharlton
Francis lord Newport, of Highnrcall
Thomas lord Leigh
Christopher lord Hatton
Henry lord Hastings, of Loughborough
Richard lord Byron
Richard lord Vaughan
Charles lord Smith, of Carrington
William lord Widdrington
Humble lord Ward
Thos. lord Colepeper, of Thoresway
Isaac lord Astley, of Bramford
Richard lord Boyle, of Clifford
John lord Lucas.
John lord Bellasis
Lodowick ld. Watson, of Rockingham
Charles lord Gerard, of Brandon
Robert lord Sutton, of Lexington
Charles ld. Kirkhoven, of Wotton
Marmaduke ld. Langdale, of Holme
Wm. lord Crofts
John lord Berkley, of Stretton.
Denzil lord Hollis, of Ifield
Frederick lord Cornwallis, of Eye
George lord Delamere, of Dunham Massey
Horatio ld. Townsend, of Lynn Regis
Anth. lord Ashley, de Winborn St. Giles
John lord Crew de Stene

LIST OF THE HOUSE OF COMMONS,
In the Long, or Pensionary Parliament, which met on the 8th of May, 1661.*

Abington,	*Andover,*
George Stonehouse.	Sir John Trott,
Agmondesham,	John Collins.
Sir Henry Proby,	*Anglesea,*
William Drake.	Rd. lord visc. Bulkley
St. Albans,	*Apulby,*
Thomas Arras,	John Lowther,
Richard Jennings.	John Dalston.
Aldborough (Suffolk)	*Arundel,*
Robert Brook,	Lord Orrery,
Thomas Bacon.	Lord Falkland.
Aldborough (Yorksh.)	*Ashburton,*
Solomon Swale,	John Powel,
Francis Goodrick.	Sir George Sondes.
Allerton-North,	*Aylsbury,*
Fran. and T. Lascells.	Richard Ingoldsby,

* "The representatives," says Rapin, "for the most part, were elected agreeably to the wishes, and without doubt by the influence of the court. The greatest part were high-churchmen, that is, violent enemies of the presbyterians, great assertors of the minutest ceremonies of the church, and most devoted to the king and the royal prerogative. This parliament may be said to be composed by chancellor Hyde, prime minister, and on the 20th of April, created earl of Clarendon. Let it also be added, that it was called the 'Pensionary Parliament,' because it was afterwards discovered, that many of the members received pensions from the court. It is true, many will not allow that this was so at first, but pretend, that by length of time, and changes upon death, the new members suffered themselves to be bribed. I cannot, however, help remarking, that, at the very beginning, this parliament did things in favour of the king, which no other had ever done, and that it was not till afterwards that they retracted their extravagant maxims, concerning the royal prerogative. It may be judged how favourable this parliament was to the king, since it continued almost 18 years, on which account it was more justly called the Long Parliament, than that of 1640." Vol. xi. p. 213.

A short time previous to the dissolution of this parliament, a curious Tract was published, entitled, 'A Seasonable Argument to persuade 'all the Grand Juries in England to petition 'for a New Parliament: or a List of the Prin- 'cipal Labourers in the great design of Po- 'pery and Arbitrary Power, who have betrayed 'their country to the Conspirators, and bar- 'gained with them to maintain a Standing 'Army in England, under the command of the 'bigoted Popish D. who, by the assistance of 'the L. L.'s Scotch army, the forces in Ire- 'land, and those in France, hope to bring all 'back to Rome.' A Reward of 200*l.* was offered, by Proclamation, to such as would discover the Author of this piece. As it is now very scarce, a copy thereof is preserved in the APPENDIX to the present Volume, No. II.

Thomas Lee.
Bambury,
Sir John Holman.
Barnstaple,
John Rolle,
Nicholas Denny.
Bath,
Alex. Popham,
William Prynn.
Beaumaris,
Griffith Bodurda.
Bedfordshire,
Sir Humphry Winch,
Lord Bruce.
Bedford Town,
John Keyling,
Richard Taylor.
Bedwyn,
D. Stonehouse,
Thomas Gape.
Berkshire,
John Lovelace,
Richard Powle.
Berwick,
Sir Ralp Grey,
Sir Tho. Widrington.
Beverly,
Michael Wharton,
Sir John Hotham.
Bewdly,
Sir Henry Herbert.
Bishops Castle,
William Oakley,
Edmond Warring.
Bletchingly,
Sir Wm. Hayward,
Edward Bish.
Bodmin,
Sir John Carew,
Hender Roberts.
Boralston,
Sir Joseph Maynard,
John Maynard.
Boroughbridge,
Robert Lucy,
John Nicholas.
Bossiney,
Robert Roberts,
Richard Rous.
Boston,
Lord Willoby,
Anthony Irby.
Brackly,
Robert Spencer,
Sir Wm. Farmer.
Brumber,
Peter Goring,
John Pine.
Brecon County,
Sir Henry Williams.
Brecon Town.
Sir Henry Price.
Bridgwater,
Edmund Wyndham,
John Tynt.
Bridport,
Humphry Bishop,
John Strangeways.
Bristol,
Thomas Earl,
John Knight.
Bridgeworth,
Walter Acton,
John Bennet.
Buckinghamshire,
Sir Wm. Terringham,
Wm. Boyer.
Buckingham Town.
Sir Richard Temple,
William Smith.
Calne,
George Lee,
William Ducket.
Cambridgeshire,
Thomas Chichley,
Thomas Wendy.
Cambridge Town,
Sir Wm. Compton,
Roger Pepys.
Cambridge University,
Sir Richard Fenshaw,
Thomas Crouch.
Camelford,
J. Coventry,
Wm. Godolphin.
Canterbury,
Sir Edward Masters,
Thomas Lovelace.
Cardiff,
Bussey Mansel.
Cardigan County,
John Vaughan.
Cardigan Town,
Wm. Griffith
Carlisle,
Sir Philip Howard,
Sir Christ. Musgrave.
Caermarthen County,
John Lloyd.
Caermarthen Town,
Lord Vaughan.
Caernarvon County,
John Glynn.
Caernarvon Town,
Wm. Glynn.
Castle-rising,
Sir Robert Paston,
Robert Steward.
Chester County,
Lord Brereton,
Peter Venables.
Chester City,
Sir Thomas Smith,
John Ratcliff.
Chichester,
Wm. Garraway,
Henry Pecham.
Chippenham,
Edward Bainton,
Edward Hungerford.
Chipping,
Sir John Borlace,
Sir Edmund Pye.
Christ's Church,
Hugh Weld,
Henry Tulse.
Cirencester,
Richard Honour,
John George.
Clifton,
Thomas Southcot,
Henry Herbert.
Clithero,
Sir Ralph Ashton,
John Heath.
Cockermouth,
Richard Tolson,
Wilfrid Lawson.
Colchester,
Sir Henry Grimston,
John Shaw.
Corfcastle,
Sir Ralph Banks,
John Tregonel.
Cornwall,
John Trelawny,
John Coriton.
Coventry,
Sir Clement Fisher,
Thomas Flint.
Cricklade,
Henry Dunch,
Edward Masklyn.
Cumberland,
Sir Peter Curwin,
Sir George Fletcher.
Denbighshire,
Sir Thos. Middleton.
Denbigh Town,
Sir John Salisbury.
Derbyshire,
Lord Cavendish,
Philip Frechnill.
Derby Town,
Roger Alestree,
John Dalton.
Devises,
Wm. York,
John Kent.
Devonshire,
Sir Hugh Pollard,
Sir John Rolle.
Dorchester,
James Gould,
Daniel Hollis.
Dorsetshire,
George Strangeways,
John Strode.
Dover,
Sir Francis Vincent,
George Montagu.
Downton,
Giles Eyre,
John Elliot.
Droitwich,
Samuel Sandys,
Henry Coventry.
Dunwich,
Sir John Rouse,
Richard Cook.
Eastlow,
Henry Seymour,
Robert Atkins.
Edmundsbury,
Sir Henry Pooley,
Sir John Duncomb.
Essex,
Sir Benjamin Ayloff,
John Brampton.
Evesham,
Richard Cullen,
John Sandys.
Exeter,
Sir James Smith,
Robert Walker
Eye,
Charles Cornwallis,
George Reeve.
Flintshire,
Sir Thomas Hanmer.
Flint Town,
Roger Whitley.
Fowey,
Jon. and John Rashleigh.
Gatten,
Sir Nicholas Carew,
Thomas Sturgis.
Germans, (St.)
John and Edw. Elliot.
Glamorgan,
Sir Edward Mansel.
Gloucestershire,
Benj. Throgmorton,
John How.
Gloucester City,
Sir Edward Massey,
Edward Seymour.
Grampound,
Charles Trevanion,
John Tanner.
Grantham,
Anthony Thorold,
John Newton.
Grimsby,
William Wray,
Edward King.
Grimstead,
Lord Buckhurst,
George Corthop.
Guildford,
Sir Richard Onslow,
Arthur Onslow.
Harwich,
Capel Lukin,
Henry Wright.
Haslemere,
John Westbrook,
Richard West.
Hastings,
Edmund Waller,
John Ashburnham.
Haverford West,
Sir Frederick Hyde.
Helstone,
Sir Peter Killegrew,
Thomas Robertson

Herefordshire,
John Scudamore,
Thomas Price.
Hereford City,
Sir Henry Lingen,
Sir Edward Hopton.
Hertfordshire,
Sir Thomas Fenshaw,
Sir Richard Fleming.
Hertford Town.
Sir Edward Turner,
Thomas Fenshaw.
Heydon,
John Appleyard,
Hugh Bethel.
Heytesbury,
Sir Charles Berkley,
Henry Coker.
Higham,
Lewis Palmer.
Hindon,
Edmund Ludlow,
George How.
Honiton,
Charles Pool,
Peter Prideaux.
Horsham,
Sir John Covert,
John Cheney.
Huntingdonshire,
Lord Mandeville,
Henry Cromwell.
Huntingdon Town,
John Barnard,
Nicholas Pedley.
Hythe,
John Harvey,
Peter Andrews.
Ilcester,
Edward Philips,
Henry Dunster.
Ipswich,
John Siclemore,
William Blois.
Ives, (St.)
James Praed,
Edward Noseworthy.
Kellington,
Sir Cyril Wyche,
Anthony Buller.
Kent,
Sir Thomas Peyton,
Sir John Tufton.
Kingstone,
Andrew Marvel,
Abraham Gilby.
Knaresborough,
Sir John Crosland,
Wm. Thompson.
Lancaster County,
Sir Roger Bradshaw,
Edward Stanley.
Lancaster Town,
Sir John Harrison,
Richard Kirkby.
Lanceston,
Sir Charles Harwood,
Richard Edgcomb.
Leicestershire,
Lord Rooes,
George Fount.
Leicester Town,
Sir Wm. Hartop,
Wm. Billingham.
Leominster,
Richard Grimes,
Hugh Cornwall.
Leskard,
John Harris,
Benjamin Greville.
Lestwithiel,
Sir Charles Wray,
John Bulteel.
Lewes,
Thomas Woodcock,
John Staple.
Lincolnshire,
Charles Hussey,
Sir George Castleton,
Lincoln City,
Sir Robert Bowles,
Thomas Meers.
Litchfield,
Anthony Dicey,
John Lane.
Liverpool,
William Stanley,
Sir Gilbert Ireland.
London,
John Toke,
William Thompson,
Christopher Love,
John Jones.
Ludlow,
Thomas Littleton,
Francis Carlton.
Luggershall,
Sir Jeffery Palmer,
William Ash.
Lyme,
Sir John Shaw,
Henry Henley.
Lymington,
Sir Wm. Lewis,
John Bunkley.
Lynn,
Sir Wm. Howel,
Edward Walpole.
Maidstone,
Sir Edmund Pierce,
Robert Barnham.
Malden,
Sir John Tyrrel,
Sir Richard Wiseman.
Malmsbury,
Laurence Wallington,
Henry Dean.
Malton,
Thomas Gower,
James Danby.
Marlborough,
Lord Seymour,
Jeffery Daniel.
Marlow,
Peter Hobby,
William Borlace.
Mawes,
Sir Wm. Tredenham,
Arthur Spry.
Melcomb,
Benjamin Remes,
John Penn.
Merioneth,
Henry Meyrick.
Midhurst,
John Lukner,
John Steward.
Middlesex,
Sir Thomas Allen,
Lancelot Lake.
Milbourn,
Sir Francis Wyndham,
Michael Mallet.
Minehead,
Sir Hugh Wyndham,
Francis Lutterel.
Michael, (St.)
Matthew Wren,
John Borlace.
Monmouthshire,
Lord Herbert,
William Morgan.
Monmouth Town,
Sir Trevor Williams.
Morpeth,
Lord Morpeth,
Sir George Downing.
Montgomeryshire,
John Purcel.
Montgomery Town.
Edward Vaughan.
Newark,
Sir Robert Markham,
Richard Rothwell.
Newcastle (Staffordsh.)
Sir Cæsar Colcow,
Edward Manwaring.
Newcastle (Northum.)
Sir Francis Anderson,
Sir John Morley.
Newport (Cornwall)
Sir Francis Drake,
John Specott.
Newport (Hants.)
Sir Robert Dillington,
Wm. Glascock.
Newton (Lancashire.)
Richard Gorges,
Richard Leigh.
Newton (Hants.)
Sir John Barrington,
Sir Joseph Worsley.
Norfolk County,
Sir Ralph Hare,
Lord Richardson.
Northamptonshire,
Sir Justinian Isham,
John Park.
Northampton Town,
Francis Harvey,
Richard Raynsford.
Northumberland.
Lord Mansfield,
John Fenwick.
Norwich,
Francis Corey,
Christopher Jay.
Nottinghamshire,
Sir John Clifton,
John Eyres
Nottingham Town,
John Hutchinson,
Arthur Stanhope.
Okehampton,
Sir Thomas Hale,
Edward Wise.
Orford,
Walter Devereux,
Henry Broderick.
Oxfordshire,
Lord Faulkland,
Sir Anthony Cope.
Oxford City,
Benj. Whorwood,
Richard Crook.
Oxford University,
Sir Heneage Finch,
Sir Laurence Hyde.
Pembrokeshire,
Arthur Owen.
Pembroke Town,
Sir Hugh Owen.
Penryn,
Wm. Pendarvis,
John Birch.
Peterborough,
Lord Spencer,
Hugh Orme.
Petersfield,
Thomas Neal,
Arthur Bold.
Plymouth,
John Maynard,
William Morris.
Plimpton,
Thomas Hale,
William Strode.
Pool,
Sir John James,
John Morton.
Pontefract,
Sir John Dawney,
William Lowther.
Portsmouth,
John Bunkly,
Richard Norton.
Preston,
Edward Rigby,
Jeffery Rushton.
Queenborough,
James Herbert,
Edward Hales.
Radnor County,
Sir Richard Lloyd.
Radnor Town,
Sir Edward Harley.
Reading,
Sir Thomas Doleman,

Richard Aldworth.
Retford,
Wm. Hickman,
Thomas Fitz-Gerrard.
Richmond,
Sir John York,
John Craddock.
Rippon,
Edmund Jennings,
John Lambert.
Rochester,
Sir Francis Clark,
Sir Wm. Battin.
Rumney,
Sir Charles Barclay,
Sir John Norton,
Rutlandshire,
Edward Noell,
Philip Sherrard.
Rye,
Henry Morley,
Wm. Hay.
Ryegate,
Roger James,
Edward Thurland.
Salop County,
Sir F. Rawleigh,
Sir Richard Okeley.
Salop Town,
Samuel and Thomas Jones.
Saltash,
Francis Bulwar,
John Butler.
Sandwich,
Edward Montague,
James Thurbane.
Sarum, New,
Francis Swanton,
Edward Tooker.
Sarum, Old,
John Norden,
Algernoon Cecil.
Scarborough,
Sir John Crosland,
Wm. Thompson.
Seaford,
Sir Thomas Dyke,
George Parker.
Shaftsbury,
Henry Whitaker,
Thomas Low.
Shoreham,
Sir Henry Springcott,
Edward Blaker.
Somersetshire,
Sir John Howel,
Edward Philips.
Southamptonshire,
Lord St. John,
Sir John Norton.
Southampton Town,
Wm. Stanley,
Robert Richbell.
Southwark,
John Moore,
Thomas Bludworth.
Staffordshire,
Sir Thomas Leigh,
Sir Randolph Egerton.
Stafford Town,
Robert Millard,
Wm. Chetwynd.
Stamford,
Wm. Stafford,
Wm. Montague.
Steyning,
Henry Goring,
John Fagg.
Stockbridge,
Sir Robert Howard,
Robert Philips.
Sudbury,
Isaac Apleton,
Thomas Waldegrave.
Suffolk County,
Sir Henry Felton,
Sir Henry North.
Surry County,
Adam Brown,
Sir Edward Bowyer.
Sussex County,
John Ashburnham,
Sir John Pelham.
Tamworth,
Lord Clifford,
John Swinfen.
Tavistock,
Wm. Russel,
George Howard.
Taunton,
Sir Wm. Portman,
Wm. Wyndham.
Tewkesbury,
Sir Henry Capel,
Richard Dowdeswell.
Thetford,
Sir Allen Apsley,
Sir Charles Gaudy.
Thirsk,
Henry Boucher,
Wm. Stanley.
Tiverton,
Sir Thomas Stewkley,
Sir Thomas Carew.
Totness,
Thomas Chase,
Thomas Clifford.
Tregony,
Hugh Boscawen,
Thomas Herl.
Truro,
John Arundel,
Thomas Boscawen.
Wallingford,
George Fane,
Richard Packer.
Warwickshire,
Sir Robert Holt,
Sir Henry Pickering.
Warwick Town,
Sir Clement Throgmorton,
Hen. Puckering.
Wareham,
George Pitt,
Robert Culliford.
Wells,
Lord Boteler,
Sir Maurice Berkley.
Wendover,
Robert Crook,
Richard Hampden.
Wenlock,
Sir Francis Lawley,
Thomas Whitmore.
Wrobly,
Thomas Tomkins,
John Barnaby.
Westbury,
Richard Lewis,
Wm. Brunker.
Westlow,
Sir Henry Vernon,
John Trelawney.
Westminster,
Sir Philip Warwick,
Sir Rich. Everick.
Westmorland County,
Sir Philip Musgrave,
Sir Thomas Strickland.
Weymouth,
Sir John Strangeways,
Winston Churchhill.
Whitchurch,
Henry Wallop,
Giles Hungerford.
Winchelsea,
Sir Nicholas Crisp,
William Howard.
Winchester,
Richard Goddard,
Laurence Hyde.
Windsor,
Sir Richard Bream,
Francis Higgins.
Wilton,
John Nicholas,
Thomas Mompesson.
Wiltshire,
Henry Hyde,
Charles Seymour.
Woodstock,
Sir Wm. Fleetwood,
Sir Tho. Spencer.
Wooton Basset,
Sir Walter St. John,
John Pleydell.
Wygan,
Lord Antrim,
Jeffrey Shackerly.
Worcestershire,
Sir John Packington,
Samuel Sandys.
Worcester City,
Sir Rowland Barclay,
Thomas Street.
Yarmouth (Norfolk)
Wm. Coventry,
Sir Wm. Doyley.
Yarmouth (Hants)
Richard Lucy,
Edward Smith.
Yorkshire,
Sir John Guthrie,
Conyers Darcy.
York City,
Sir Metcalf Robinson,
Thomas Osborn.
Speakers in this Parliament.
Sir Edward Turner,
Sir Job Charlton,
Edward Seymour, esq.

The Speaker's Speech to the King.] May 16. The king being again set in his royal throne, in his regal robes, the lords being also in their robes, the commons presented unto his majesty sir Edward Turner, knight, solicitor to the duke of York,* for their Speaker; who, being brought to the bar, with great reverence began his speech in this manner:

"May it please your most excellent majesty;—The knights, citizens, and burgesses of the commons house of parliament, being there assembled by virtue of your majesty's most gracious writ, have been pleased (I dare not say to choose, but) to name me their Speaker.—It is an undoubted privilege of every member in that house, to be heard speak, much more when he speaks for or against himself. But, sir, whether more out of favour to me or injury to themselves I cannot tell, they were not pleased to hear, at least they would not accept, my just apology and excuse from this service.—Therefore, from this their judgment, if I must so call it, I do most humbly appeal to your sovereign justice; beseeching your ma-

* And afterwards to the king.

jesty, for the errors that are too visible and apparent in their proceedings, that you will review and reverse the same. My inexperience in the Customs and Orders of the house, my inability to collect their sense, and state the questions rising upon long and arduous debates, do justly render me unfit, and therefore unworthy, of this weighty employment.—Your majesty well knows, when a ship puts forth to sea, she should be provided with mariners of all sorts. In case a storm doth rise, some must trim and lower the sails, some must watch aloft the decks, some must work at the pump; but he had need be a very good seaman that is the pilot. Sir, I hope I may be useful to this your sovereign vessel in some of these inferior places; but I dare not undertake to be their steersman.—I do most humbly therefore beseech your majesty, that you will not take us at our first word; our second thoughts are best. Pray, therefore, be pleased to command the members of the house of commons to return into their house, to recollect themselves, and to present your majesty with a better choice."

This being said, the Lord Chancellor, having first conferred with his majesty, answered as followeth:

"Mr. Speaker; You have not discredited yourself enough to persuade the king to dissent from his house of commons in the election they have made. If he had never seen you before, you have now spoke too well against yourself, for his majesty to suspect you are no good Speaker: but you have the honour to be well known to the king; have spoken very often before him; and his majesty well knows that you are not without any of those parts; of knowing the Orders of the house, where you have sat long; or collecting and stating and putting the Questions aptly, which must constitute a right good Speaker. Therefore his majesty is so far from thinking the house hath made an ill choice, that he believes they could not have made a better; or from admitting your excuse, that he confirms their election, and thanks them very heartily for making it; and requires you to submit to it, and to betake yourself with all alacrity to the service."

His majesty having thus denied Mr. Speaker's Excuse, and approved of the Commons choice of him; Mr. Speaker proceeded, and said,

"He that knows his master's will, and doth it not, is worthy to be beaten with many stripes. I shall therefore humbly and chearfully, to the best of my poor skill and knowledge, apply myself to the performance of my duty; not doubting therein to obtain your majesty's gracious pardon for all involuntary transgressions; for it is a rule in law, and in conscience too, 'Actus non facit reum, nisi mens sit rea.'—And, since I have found this favour in the sight of my lord the king, pray let me beg your majesty's patience for a while, to make a stand, and from this place to look about me. Sir, a weak head is soon giddy; but the strongest brain may here be turned: the presence of this glory, and the glory of this presence, do transport me. Whilst I contemplate the incomparable beauty of this body politic, and the goodly order of this high court of parliament, where at once I behold all the glory of this nation, I am almost in the condition of St. Paul, when he was taken up into the third heaven. All he could say upon his return was, 'he saw things unutterable.'—God, that made all things for the use of man, and made him governor over all his works, thought it not fit to leave him to himself, nor to live without a law and government. The forms and species of governments are various; monarchical, aristocratical, and democratical: but the first is certainly the best, as being nearest to divinity itself. Aristocracy is subject to degenerate, and run into faction; but democracy naturally runs into confusion. Then every man becomes a tyrant over his neighbour; 'Homo homini lupus, homo homini dæmon.'—This famous island, historians tell us, was first inhabited by the Britains, then by the Romans, then by the Saxons, then by the Danes, then by the Normans; and during all these successions of ages, and variety of changes, though there was sometimes 'Divisum imperium,' yet every division was happy under a monarchical government.—Since the entrance of the Norman race, 25 kings and queens, famous in their generations, from whom your sacred majesty is lineally descended, have swayed the royal sceptre of this nation.—The Children of Israel, when they were in the Wilderness, though they were fed with God's own hand, and eat the food of angels, yet they surfeited, and murmured, and rebelled against Moses. The same unthankful spirit dwelt in this nation for divers years last past. The men of that age were weary of the government, though it was refined to the wonder and envy of all other nations; they quarrelled with our Moses, because he was the Lord's anointed. 'Nolumus hunc regnare,' was their first quarrel; but leveling, parity, and confusion followed; then tyranny and usurpation was the conclusion. We read of the emperor Adrian, when he lay a dying, he complained that many physicians had destroyed him; meaning, that their contrary conceits and different directions for his recovery had hastened his death. So it is with us: we were sick of reformation; our reformers were of all ages, sexes, and degrees; of all professions and trades. The very cobler went beyond his last. These new statesmen took upon them to regulate and govern our governors: this was the sickness and plague of the nation. Their new laws were all written in bloody letters; the cruelty of their tribunals made the judgment-seat little differ from a slaughter-house: the rich man was made an offender for a word; poor men were sold for slaves, as the Turks sell heads, twenty for an asper: yet for all this villainy there was at length found a Protector.—No amendment at length would serve these reformers turns; no concessions, though the most gracious that could be imagined, would satisfy these usurpers; but root and branch, all must go. Our late sovereign lord, of blessed memory, must be offered up a sacrifice to their lust; your sacred person (great sir) proscribed, and all the royal family exiled. Monarchy itself was voted burdensome, and therefore they must try a Commonwealth; and, the better to digest it, the people were intoxicated with a belief that they should all, like themselves, be princes in their turns.—Amongst the Persians, after the death of their governor there was used to be, *ἀνομία πέντε ἡμερῶν*, 'a five days lawlessness,' in which time every man might do what he listed: during those five days there was such killing, and robbing, and destroying one another, that, before they were ended, the people longed again for their old government.—After the death of your majesty's most royal father, here was the like licentiousness; but, alas! is continued more than twice five years: liberty they called it; but it was 'Libertas quidlibet audendi.' Your loyal subjects were a prey to wolves and tygers; and to the most cruel of all beasts, unreasonable men. Every man did what seemed good in his own eyes; for in those days there was no king in our Israel.—But, as the former spirit of reformation at first brought us into this misery; so the spirit of giddiness, which God sent amongst our reformers, at length cured us. The Brazen Serpent was the best cure for those that were bitten by the Fiery Serpent. The divisions and subdivisions of those that exercised dominion over us, weakened their own power, and stirred up the hearts, and strengthened the hands, of your loyal subjects, to restore our ancient government, and to bring your sacred majesty back to your royal throne in peace, as, to the joy of all our hearts, we see it this day. This was the work of God, and it is admirable in our eyes. And as we have cause at all times to bless God, that he hath thus brought your majesty to your people; so we have just cause at this time to return our hearty thanks unto your majesty that you have thus brought your people to yourself. The sun exhales the vapours from the earth, and sends them down again in showers of plenty. So we, to our great joy, do find that our obedience and affection to your majesty are returned upon our heads, in plenty, peace, and protection.—The last meeting here in parliament was happy, in healing the bleeding wounds of this nation. They were blessed also, even for their works sake. Your sacred majesty did bless them; and therefore they shall be blessed to all posterity. But, sir, we hope you have a blessing left for us too. That was your parliament by adoption, but this is yours by birth-right. This parliament is free born. I hope this honour will beget in us an emulation to exceed the actions of our predecessors; and not only to meet your majesty as our sovereign with the duty of subjects, but with the love of sons to a most indulgent father.—Next to the glory of your majesty's royal throne, I cannot but observe the brightness of this second orb. This firmament is richly deckt with stars of several magnitudes; each star appears like the morning star, and yet each star differs from another in glory. You cannot want Commanders, either by sea or land, to manage your designs, whilst all these sons of Mars stand candidate to serve you in the wars. You cannot want Counsellors, to advise you in the great affairs of the nation, whilst all these statesmen, senators, each fit to be a consul, contend who shall most ease you in the thorny cares of the government.—Amidst these noble English Barons are placed the Reverend Judges of the land, the sages of the law; men so learned and expert in the customs and statutes of this land, that if Wat Tyler, or Jack Cade, or the new fanatics of this latter age, had burned our books, they were able to restore our laws in purity and perfection.—And next to these, though in a lower orb, appear the worthy knights, the prudent citizens and burgesses, of the house of commons, being the third estate of parliament.—When the fame of Solomon's wisdom had filled the neighbour nations, the queen of Sheba could not contain herself at home; but, with many camels, laded with spices, with gold, and precious stones in abundance, she comes to Solomon, to commune with him of all that was in her heart.—Great sir, Whilst this your native country was unworthy of you, foreign nations were made happy in the knowledge of your person, your piety, and your wisdom. And now the Lord our God hath brought you home, and set you on your throne, your subjects long to see you. What striving and rejoicing was there, at your first landing, to see our rising sun! What striving was there, at your Coronation, to see the imperial crown set upon your royal head! What striving hath here lately been, in all the counties, cities, and boroughs of this nation, who should be sent up to hear your wisdom, and confer with you in parliament!—Royal sir, these chosen worthy messengers are not come empty-handed; they are laden, they are sent up to you heavy laden, from their several counties, cities, and boroughs. If the affections of all Englishmen can make you happy; if the riches of this nation can make you great; if the strength of this warlike people can make you considerable at home and abroad; be assured, you are the greatest monarch in the world. Give me leave, I beseech you, to double my words, and say it again, I wish my voice could reach to Spain and to the Indies too, You are the greatest monarch in the world.—I fear your royal patience may be tired. I will therefore speak no more my own words; but, in the name of the commons of England humbly present unto your majesty their accustomed Petitions when first they are assembled in parliament, and so conclude: 1. I do beseech your majesty, That, for our better attendance on the important service of the house, ourselves and our necessary servants may be free, in our persons and estates, from all arrests and troubles. 2. That, debate and disputes being necessary to the disquisition of many matters in the house, your majesty will be pleased to vouchsafe us liberty and freedom of speech; which, I doubt not, we shall use with loyalty and sobriety. 3. That, if the great affairs require it, your majesty, upon our humble suit, will vouchsafe us access to your royal person. 4. That the proceedings of the house may receive a benign interpretation, and be free at all times from misconstructions."

The Lord Chancellor's Speech.] The Speaker's Speech being ended, the Lord Chancellor again conferred with his majesty; and answered,

"Mr. Speaker; The King is well pleased with your obedience, and that you have so chearfully submitted to undergo that province the house of commons hath designed you to: he promises himself and the kingdom as great fruit and benefit from your joint services, as ever any of his progenitors received from a Speaker and a house of commons. The king did his part, by publishing the very day he intended the parliament should meet, a good time before the writs were sealed; by sending out the writs much longer than was necessary before the day of meeting, that the country might not be surprized in their elections, but that they might send up such, as he might make a clear view and prospect of the affections and desires of his people; and he is persuaded that the commons of England were never more exactly represented than they are at present, in you, the knights, citizens, and burgesses. And yet I have a very particular command from his majesty to tell you, which in truth he meant to have said to you himself the other day, and which he hopes you will not take ill in point of privilege, that his majesty takes notice, indeed he cannot choose but take notice, of one ill circumstance in many elections, which he imputes rather to the vice of the times, a vice worthy your severity, than to any corrupt intention; that is, Excess of Drinking,* which produceth that other scandalous excess in the expence. His majesty doth very heartily recommend it to your wisdom, for the honour and dignity of parliaments, that you will take some course to prevent this inconvenience for the future; and if you think fit to call for any help from him towards it, you will be sure to have it.—You have made, Mr. Speaker, a very lively description of the extravagancy of that confusion which this poor nation groaned under, when they would throw off a government they had lived and prospered under so many ages, indeed from the time of being a nation, and which is as natural to them as their food or their raiment, to model a new one for themselves, which they knew no more how to do, than the naked Indians know how to dress themselves in the French fashion; when (as you say) all ages, sexes, and degrees, all professions and trades, would become reformers, when the common people of England would represent the commons of England; and abject men, who could neither write nor read, would make laws for the government of the most heroic and the most learned nation in the world; for sure none of our neighbours will deny it to have a full excellency and perfection both in arms and letters. And it was the grossest and most ridiculous pageant that great impostor ever exposed to public view, when he gave up the nation to be disposed of by a handful of poor mechanic persons, who, finding they knew not what to do with it, would (he was sure) give it back to him again, as they shortly did, which makes his title compleat to the government he meant to exercise. No man undervalues the common people of England, who are in truth the best and the honestest, aye, and the wisest common people in the world, when he says they are not fit to model the government they are to live under, or to make the laws they are to obey. Solomon tells us, 'there is a time when one man rules over another to his own hurt;' we have had abundant instances of such a time. It is the privilege, if you please the prerogative (and it is a great one), of the common people of England, to be represented by the greatest, and learnedest, and wealthiest, and wisest persons, that can be chose out of the nation; and the confounding the commons of England, which is a noble representative, with the common people of England, was the first ingredient into that accursed dose, which intoxicated the brains of men with that imagination of a commonwealth; a commonwealth, Mr. Speaker, a government as impossible for the spirit and temper and genius of the English nation to submit to, as it is to persuade them to give their cattle and their corn to other men, and to live upon roots and herbs themselves. I wish heartily that they who have been most delighted with that imagination knew in truth the great benefit under the government. There is not a commonwealth in Europe, where every man that is worth 100*l.* doth not pay more to the government than a man of 1000*l.* a year did ever to the crown here before these troubles. And I am persuaded that monster Commonwealth cost this nation more, in the few years she was begot, born, and brought up, and in her funeral (which was the best expence of all), than the monarchy hath done these 600 years.—You

* "With the Restoration of the king a spirit of extravagant joy spread over the nation, that brought on with it the throwing off the very professions of virtue and piety. All ended in entertainments and drunkenness, which over-run the three kingdoms to such a degree, that it very much corrupted all their morals. Under the colour of drinking the king's health, there were great disorders and much riot every where." Burnet, vol. i. p. 93.

have well done, Mr. Speaker, in taking notice of the great esteem the king hath of the memory of the last parliament. He takes all occasions himself to do it; and it deserved it at his hands: but, as the wisest father takes joy in the hopes his heir will be wiser than he, and the greatest monarch in the hopes that his successor will be greater than he; and if the souls departed feel any joy upon what is done in this world, it is in the case of such an heir, such a successor; so, you may be confident, the ghost of the deceased parliament will be much delighted, much exalted, to see your actions excel theirs, and your fame exceed theirs. It was a blessed parliament; but there are other and greater blessings reserved for you. They began many things which you may have the happiness to finish; they had not time, nor opportunity, to begin many things which you may have the honour to begin and finish. They invited his majesty home, restored him to his throne, and monarchy to the nation. It will be your glory so to establish him in his power and greatness, so as to annex monarchy to the nation, that he and his posterity shall be never again forced to be abroad, that they be invited home, nor in danger to be restored; so to rivet monarchy to the hearts, and to the understandings of all men, that no man may ever presume to conspire against it. Let it not suffice that we have our king again, and our laws again, and parliaments again; but let us so provide, that neither king, nor laws, nor parliament, may be so used again. Let not our monarchy be undermined by a Fifth Monarchy, nor men suffered to have the protection of a government they profess to hate. Root out all anti-monarchical principles; at least, let not the same stratagems prevail against us. Let us remember how we were deceived; and let not the same artifices over-reach us again. Let king, and church, and country, receive more and greater advantages, by the wisdom and industry of this parliament. Let trade abroad and at home be encouraged and enlarged, all vices and excesses be restrained and abolished, by new laws and provisions; let profitable arts and industry find so great encouragement, that all thriving inventions may be brought from all parts of the world to enrich this kingdom, and that the inventors may grow rich in this kingdom. And upon this argument of encouraging industry, I have a command from the king, to recommend to you the encouragement or preservation of a great work of industry, in which the honour and interest of the nation is more concerned than in any work this age hath brought out, it may be in any nation; and that is, all the Drainings in England, which have given us new countries upon our own continent, and brought an inestimable benefit to the king and people, by an act of creation making earth, and mending air by wit and industry. Let no waywardness in particular persons, or consideration of private and particular advantage, give disturbance to works of so public a nature, much less destroy such works; but provide out of hand for the upholding and supporting them by some good law, in which due care may be taken for all particular interests, when the public is out of danger.—I have but one desire more, Mr. Speaker, to make to you from the king, to which the season of the year, as well as your inclinations to gratify him, will dispose you; and that is, that you will use such expedition in your councils of most importance, that the rest may be left to a recess in the winter, after an adjournment; that his majesty may have a time to bestow himself upon his subjects in a Progress, which he would be glad to begin before the end of July. I have leave to tell you the Progress he intends; that he desires again to see his good city of Worcester, and to thank God for his deliverance there, and to thank God even in those cottages, and barns, and haylofts, in which he was sheltered, and feasted, and preserved; and in the close of that progress he hopes he shall find his queen in his arms, and so return to meet you here in the beginning of winter.—Mr. Speaker, All your Petitions are very grateful to the king. You and your servants, in your persons and estates, are free from all arrests or molestations. Your liberty and freedom of speech is very willingly granted to you. When you would repair to his majesty, you shall be welcome. And his majesty will be so far from jealousy of your actions, that he believes it is impossible for him to be jealous of you, or you of him; and, if you please, he will make it penal to nourish that unwholesome weed in any part of the kingdom."

The Thanks of both Houses given to his Majesty.] These ceremonies being over, the Parliament proceeded to the great affairs of the kingdom; and within three days both houses came to a Vote and Resolution concerning the King's intended Marriage, and accordingly attended his majesty at Whitehall with their humble Acknowledgment and Thanks "for the free and gracious communication of his resolution to marry with the infanta of Portugal; which they conceived to be of so high a concernment to this nation, that they received it with great joy and satisfaction, and did with all earnestness beg a blessing upon, and a speedy accomplishment of it; and they could not but express their own unanimous Resolutions, which they were confident would have a general influence upon the hearts of all his subjects: that they should upon all occasions be ready to assist his majesty in the pursuance of these his intentions against all oppositions whatsoever." To which the King returned his particular thanks, declaring, "That he did, in the matter of the intended Marriage, as much study their good, as his own."

The Commons oblige themselves to take the Sacrament, and order the Solemn League and Covenant to be burnt.] While this was transacting, the commons, first, ordered all their

Members to take the Sacrament according to the prescribed Liturgy, on pain of expulsion; and then, in conjunction with the lords, on the 20th of May, ordered that the instrument of writing, that had caused so much mischief, called, 'The solemn League and Covenant,' should be burnt by the hand of the common hangman, in the Palace-Yard at Westminster, in Cheapside, and before the Old-Exchange, on the 22d of May; and be forthwith taken off the Record in the house of Peers, and all other courts and places where the same is recorded; and that all copies thereof be taken down out of all churches, chapels, and all other public places in England and Wales.—On the 28th they likewise ordered, the Act for erecting a High Court of Justice for Trying and Judging Charles Stuart, the Act for Subscribing the Engagement against a king and house of Peers; the Act for declaring the people of England to be a Commonwealth and Free-State; the Act for Renouncing the Title of Charles Stuart, and also the Act for the Security of the Lord Protector's Person, to be burnt by the hands of the common hangman, in the midst of Westminster-Hall, while the courts were sitting.

The King's Letter for confirming the Act of Indemnity.] June 22. Mr. Secretary Morrice delivered to the Speaker a Letter from his majesty: which was read as follows:

"Trusty and well beloved, we greet you well: At the opening our parliament you were told, That we had a great desire this summer to make a Progress through some parts of our kingdom, which we resolve to begin in devotion to our city of Worcester, that we may pour out our thanks to God for our deliverance there: and the season of the year quickens us in that inclination, as we presume it disposes you to a desire to withdraw from this city, and to visit your countries. But you may remember we told you then, That we had caused some Bills to be prepared for you, for confirmation of what we enacted in our last meeting; and we said all we could to you of the value we set upon the Act of Indemnity (as we have great reason to do) and if we could have used stronger expressions to have conjured you speedily to have dispatched it, we assure you we would have done it. And we did think what we said would have made an impression on all who profess a desire to serve us; and therefore we expected every day, that the same Bill would have been presented to us for another assent. We must confess, we hear you have shewed great affection to us, since your coming together, and that you have already prepared and passed some very good bills (for which we heartily thank you) that are ready for the royal assent: yet we cannot but tell you, That though we are enough concerned to expedite those Bills, we have no mind to pass them till the Act of Indemnity be likewise presented to us, upon which, if you take our word, most of our quiet and good depends, and in which we are sure our honour is concerned. Therefore we must again, and as earnestly as is possible, conjure you to use all possible expedition in passing that Act in the same terms we already passed it (to which we take ourself obliged) and that you will for the present lay aside all private business, that so betaking yourselves only to the public, you may be ready to adjourn by the middle of the next month, which will best suit with all our occasions."

The Act of Oblivion passed.] This Letter did not fail of being received with due respect, and the house resolved to bring in a Bill accordingly; but, as a new instance of their loyalty and duty, proceeded, first, to settle the Revenue on such a footing as might more effectually maintain the splendor and grandeur of the kingly office. Accordingly, this capital point was referred to the consideration of a committee, of which sir Philip Warwick was chairman; who reported, "That on a thorough examination, there was a deficiency of full 265,000*l.* on the different funds, already appointed to answer that end: upon which it was ordered, That forthwith be provided a plentiful Supply for his majesty's present unavoidable great occasions, as well as a Settlement of a constant, and standing Revenue:" and accordingly, a Bill was brought in, 'To enable his majesty to send out commissions to receive the free and voluntary Contributions of his people, towards the present supply of his majesty's affairs, &c.'

The Speaker's Speech to the King on presenting the Act of Oblivion.] July 8. The commons having completed the above bill, and the bill for Confirmation of the Act of Oblivion and Indemnity, this day the king came to the house of peers, where being seated on his throne, the Speaker of the house of commons spoke thus to his majesty:

"May it please your most excellent majesty; The writ of summons, whereby your majesty was pleased to call together the knights, citizens, and burgesses, of the commons house of parliament, gave us to understand, "That your majesty had divers weighty and urgent matters to communicate to us; such as did concern your royal person, your state and dignity, the defence of the kingdom, and the church of England;" and in the same method propounded to us by your majesty, we have applied ourselves to offer you our best counsel and advice.—We found your majesty miraculously preserved, by the hand of God, from the hands of your enemies; we found you peaceably seated in the throne of your ancestors; we found the hereditary imperial crown of these nations auspiciously set upon your royal head: and all this after a sharp and a bloody Civil War.—We held it our duties, in the first place, to endeavour the Safety and Preservation of your majesty's Person and Government; and to that purpose have prepared a Bill.—Next to the safety of your majesty, we took into consideration the state and power that is necessary for so great a prince;

and do hope ere long to settle your Militia so, that, by the blessing of God, you need not fear storms from abroad, or earthquakes here at home.—Your majesty was pleased, at the opening of the parliament, to recommend unto us two Bills; one, for confirming of public acts; another, for the private acts that passed the last parliament. They were so many in number, and great in weight, that hitherto we could not consider of them all: but some we have perused; the Act for Confirmation of Judicial Proceedings; for taking away the Court of Wards and Liveries, and Purveyances; and also all those that do relate to your majesty's Customs and Excise.—And, that we might with some chearfulness see your majesty's face, we have brought our brother Benjamin with us? I mean, your Act of Oblivion; I take the boldness to call it Yours, for so it is by many titles; your majesty first conceived it at Breda; you helped to contrive and form it here in England; and, we must all bear you witness, you laboured and travailed till it was brought forth: and since it had a being, some question being made of its legitimation, your royal heart is not at 'ease until it be confirmed. And now, sir, give me leave to say, by the suffrage of a full, a free, and legal parliament, it is presented to your majesty to be naturalized. Your majesty's desires are fully answered by all the representatives of the people: and their hearty prayer to God is, that all your subjects may be truly thankful to you; and that your majesty may long live to enjoy the fruits of this unparalleled mercy.—Your majesty was pleased to intimate to us on Saturday last, 'That you so valued the quiet and satisfaction of your people, and the keeping of your royal word with them, that, although divers other Bills were made ready for you, you would vouchsafe the honour to this Bill alone, your favourite, to come and pass it.' Sir, hereby you have made this a great holiday; and we shall observe it with joy and thanksgiving. Upon such solemn festivals, there useth to be a second service, an anthem, and a collect, or at least an offering. My anthem shall be, 'Quid tibi retribuam, Domine?' And my collect, a short report of your Revenue. We know, great sir, that money is both the sinews of war, and bond of peace. We have, therefore, taken care of your majesty's Revenue; and do desire to make it in some good proportion suitable both to your grandeur and your merit.—We do believe, the state of our king is the honour of our state; and the best way to preserve our peace, is to be well provided for war. Our time hath not permitted us to finish this work: but, as an earnest of our good affections, we desire your majesty to accept an offering from us.—We cannot enough admire your majesty's patience, providence, and frugality abroad. You did not bring home a debt for us to pay, great as a prince's ransom. And since your return, you have not, with king Edw. III. after his wars in France, or Henry IV. Henry VII. or Henry VIII. desired new and great Aids and heavy Subsidies from your people for your supplies.—No, sir; you have been so far from asking, that part of the Money which was given you last parliament for your household provision, you have issued out towards payment of our debts; you have robbed your own table (I had almost said given the meat out of your own belly), to feed the hungry seamen.—Dear sir, these things have a just influence upon the people; they fill our hearts with joy and affection to your majesty. I do not pretend much to physiognomy: but, if I mistake not greatly, the faces of the people do promise great frankness and chearfulness in your present supplies. What would not your majesty's friends have given, within these 18 months, to have seen your majesty thus happily settled? And what can be too much for those to return, who have received all they enjoy from your majesty's mercy? Great sir, To conclude this solemn service: the commons of England do, by me their servant, humbly present you with this Bill, intituled, 'An Act for a free and voluntary Present,' and wish it a success answerable to your royal heart's desire."

The King's Speech on passing the Act of Oblivion.] After passing the above two Bills, his majesty spoke as follows:

"My Lords and Gentlemen; It is a good time since I heard of your passing this Bill for Money; and I am sure you would have presented it to me sooner, if you had thought I had desired it: but the truth is, though I have need enough of it, I had no mind to receive it from you, till I might at the same time give my assent to this other very good Bill that accompanies it, for which I longed very impatiently. I thank you for both with all my heart; and though there are other good bills ready, with which you will easily believe I am very well pleased, and in which I am indeed enough concerned, yet I chuse rather to pass these two bills together, and to pass them by themselves without any other, that you may all see, and in you the whole kingdom, that I am at least equally concerned for you and them, as for myself: and in truth it will be want of judgment in me, if I ever desire any thing for myself, that is not equally good for you and them. I am confident, you all believe that my well-being is of some use and benefit to you; and I am sure your well-being, and being well-pleased, is the greatest comfort and blessing I can receive in this world.—I hope you will be ready within a few days to dispatch those other Public Bills which are still depending before you, that I may come hither and pass all together, and then adjourn till winter, when what remains may be provided for: and I would be very glad that you would be ready by the 20th of this month, or thereabouts, for the adjournment: which methinks you might easily be, if you suspended all private business till the recess. The last parliament, by God's blessing, laid the foundation of the happiness we all enjoy; and therefore I thought it but justice to the memory of it, to send you Bills for the confirmation of what was enacted then; and I cannot doubt but you will dispatch what remains of that kind with all convenient speed; and that you will think, that what was then thought necessary or fit for the public peace to be enacted, ought not to be shaken now, or any good man less secure of what he possesses, than he was when you came together. It is to put myself in mind as well as you, that I so often (I think as often as I come to you) mention to you my Declaration from Breda: and let me put you in mind of another Declaration, published by yourselves about the same time, and which, I am persuaded, made mine the more effectual; an honest, generous, and Christian Declaration, signed by the most eminent persons, who had been the most eminent sufferers, in which you renounced all former animosities, all memory of former unkindnesses, vowed all imaginable good-will to, and all confidence in, each other.—"My Lords and Gentlemen; Let it be in no man's power to charge me or you with breach of our word or promise, which can never be a good ingredient to our future security. Let us look forward, and not backward; and never think of what is past, except men put us in mind of it, by repeating faults we had forgot; and then let us remember no more than what concerns those very persons.—God hath wrought a wonderful miracle in settling us as he hath done. I pray let us do all we can to get the reputation at home and abroad of being well settled. We have enemies and enviers enough, who labour to have it thought otherwise; and if we would indeed have our enemies fear us, and our neighbours love and respect us, and fear us enough to love us, let us take all the ways we can, that, as the world cannot but take notice of your extraordinary affection to me, and of the comfort I take in that affection, so that it may likewise take notice of your affection to and confidence in each other; which will disappoint all designs against the public peace, and fully establish our joint security."

Protest against the Bill to vacate sir E. Powell's Fines.] July 17. An Act for making void divers Fines unduely procured to be levied by sir Edw. Powell, and dame Mary his wife: The question being put, whether this bill with the proviso shall pass for a law? It was resolved in the affirmative. Upon which the following Protest was entered on the Journals: "Whereas before the question was put for passing the said bill, leave was desired for entering protestations of divers lords, in case the vote should be carried for passing the said bill; we whose names are underwritten do protest against the said bill for these reasons following; 1. That Fines are the foundations upon which most titles of this realm do depend, and therefore ought not to be shaken, for the great inconvenience that is likely to follow thereupon. 2. Such proceeding is contrary to the statute of 25 Edw. 1, now in force, which saith, 'Forasmuch as fines levied in our court ought and do make an end of all matters: and therefore principally are called fines.' 3. And to another statute made in the 5th Edw. 3, where it is enacted, 'That no man shall be forejudged of lands or tenements, goods or chattels, contrary to the term of the great charter. 4. And to another statute made in the 28th Edw. 3, where it is enacted, That no man, of what estate or condition that he be, shall be put out of land or tenement, nor disherited, without being brought in to answer by due process of law. 5. This proceeding by bill, as we conceive, is contrary to a statute made in the 4th of Hen. 4, wherein it is declared, That in pleas real and personal, after judgment given in the courts of our lord the king, the parties be made to come in upon grievous pains, sometimes before the king himself, sometimes before the king's council, and sometimes to the parliament, to answer thereof anew, to the great impoverishing of the parties, and in the subversion of the common law; it is ordained, that after judgment given in the courts of our lord the king, the parties and their heirs shall be thereof in peace until the judgment be undone by attaint or by error, if there be errors, as hath been used by the laws in the times of the king's progenitors. 6. The proceedings upon this bill have been, as we conceive, directly against the statutes aforesaid, by calling persons to answer of judgments anew, given in the common pleas, and vacating the same without either attaint or error, and calling persons to answer without the due and ancient process of law, and forejudging the tenants of the lands in question, without ever hearing of them. 7. For that there hath not occurred to us one precedent wherein any fine hath been vacated by act of parliament without consent of parties, the law looking upon fines as always transacted by consent, and with that reverence, that neither lunacy, ideotism, nor any other averment whatsoever shall be admitted against fines when perfected. 8. We conceive, to vacate assurances by a future law, good by the present law, is unreasonable and of dangerous consequence, both in respect of what such a precedent may produce upon the like pretences, as also rendering men's minds so doubtful, that not only the rude and ignorant, but the learned, may be at a loss how to make or receive a good title. 9. For that it is averred in the said bill, that all the lady Powell's servants were removed; whereas it appeared by depositions in Chancery, that Antonia Christiana, one who had lived with the lady Powell many years, was not removed. 10. That Dr. Goddard a physician, and Foucaut an apothecary, examined in the said cause, did testify they saw no fear in, or force upon, the lady Powell; and had there been any, we conceive it impossible for a woman to hide the passion of fear from a physician, which is not easily dissembled from a vulgar eye: and Foucaut the apothecary deposed, that he was twice a day with the said lady Powell for one month together immediately preceding her death.—W. Roberts, Campden, Stafford, T. Willoughby, Brecknock, Will. Petre, Montague, Portland, Albemarle, Chr. Hatton."

A Bill passed for restoring Bishops to their Seats in Parliament.] Before the session was concluded, a Bill was passed for the Repeal of that act of parliament, by which the Bishops were excluded from sitting there. "It was first proposed," says lord Clarendon,* "in the commons by a gentleman, who had been always taken to be of a Presbyterian family: and in that house it found less opposition than was looked for; all men knowing, that besides the justice of it, and the prudence to wipe out the memory of so infamous an Act, as the Exclusion of them with all the circumstances was known to be, it would be grateful to the king. But when it came into the house of peers, where all men expected it would find a general concurrence, it met with some obstruction; which made a discovery of an intrigue, that had not been suspected. For though there were many lords present, who had industriously laboured the passing the former Bill for the Exclusion, yet they had likewise been guilty of so many other ill things, of which they were ashamed, that it was believed that they would not willingly revive the memory of the whole, by persevering in such an odious particular. Nor in truth did they. But when they saw that it would unavoidably pass (for the number of that party was not considerable), they either gave their consents, as many of them did, or gave their negative without noise. The obstruction came not from thence. The Catholicks less owned the contradiction, nor were guilty of it, though they suffered in it. But the truth is, it proceeded from the mercurial brain of the earl of Bristol, who much affected to be looked upon as the head of the Catholicks; which they did so little desire that he should be thought, that they very rarely concurred with him. He well knew that the king desired (which his majesty never dissembled) to give the Roman Catholicks ease from all the sanguinary laws; and that he did not desire that they should be liable to the other penalties which the law had made them subject to, whilst they should in all other respects behave themselves like good subjects. Nor had they since his majesty's return sustained the least prejudice by their religion, but enjoyed as much liberty at court and in the country, as any other men; and with which the wisest of them were abundantly satisfied, and did abhor the activity of those of their own party, whom they did believe more like to deprive them of the liberty they enjoyed, than to enlarge it to them.—When the earl of Bristol saw this Bill brought into the house for restoring the Bishops to their seats, he went to the king, and informed his majesty, "that if this Bill should speedily pass, it would absolutely deprive the Catholicks of all those graces and indulgence which he intended to them: for that the Bishops, when they should sit in the house, whatever their own opinions or inclinations were, would find themselves obliged, that they might preserve their reputation with the people, to contradict and suppose whatsoever should look like favour or connivance towards the Catholicks: and therefore, if his majesty continued his former gracious inclination towards the Roman Catholicks, he must put some stop (even for the Bishops own sakes) to the passing that Bill, till the other should be more advanced, which he supposed might shortly be done;" there having been already some overtures made to that purpose, and a committee appointed in the house of lords to take a view of all the sanguinary laws in matters of Religion, and to present them to the house that it might consider farther of them. The king, surprised with the discourse from a man who had often told him the necessity of the restoring the Bishops, and that it could not be a perfect parliament without their presence, thought his reason for the delay to have weight in it, and that the delay for a few days could be attended with no prejudice to the matter itself; and thereupon was willing the Bill should not be called for, and that when it should be under commitment, it should be detained there for some time: and that he might, the better to produce this delay, tell some of his friends, 'that the king would be well pleased, that there should not be overmuch haste in the presenting that Bill for his royal assent."—This grew quickly to be taken notice of in the house that after the first reading of that Bill, it had been put off for a second reading longer than was usual when the house was at so much leisure; and that now it was under commitment, it was obstructed there, notwithstanding all the endeavours, some lords of the committee could use for the dispatch; the Bill containing very few words, being only for the repeal of a former Act, and the expressions admitting, that is, giving little cause for any debate. The chancellor desired to know how this came to pass, and was informed by one of the lords of the committee, 'that they were assured that 'the king would have a stop put to it, till 'another Bill should be provided which his 'majesty looked for." Hereupon the chancellor spake with his majesty, who told him all the conference which the earl of Bristol had held with him, and what he had consented should be done. To which the other replied, 'that he was sorry that his majesty had been 'prevailed with to give any obstruction to a 'Bill, which every body knew his majesty's 'heart was so much set upon for dispatch; 'and that if the reason were known, it would 'quickly put an end to all the pretences of the 'Catholicks; to which his majesty knew he 'was no enemy.' The king presently concluded that the reason was not sufficient, and wished 'that the Bill might be dispatched as 'soon as possible, that he might pass it that

* Lord Clarendon's Life, p. 138.

'session;' which he had appointed to make an end of within few days: and so the next day the report was called for and made, and the Bill ordered to be engrossed against the next morning; the earl not being at that time in the house. But the next morning, when the chancellor had the bill engrossed in his hand to present to the house to be read the third time, the earl came to him to the woolsack, and with great displeasure and wrath in his countenance told him, 'that if that bill were 'read that day, he would speak against it;' to which the chancellor gave him an answer that did not please him: and the bill was passed that day. And from that time the earl of Bristol was a more avowed and declared enemy to him, than he had before professed to be; though the friendship that had been between them had been discontinued or broken from the time the earl had changed his religion."

Act for the Security of the King's Person and Government.] An Act was likewise passed, for the 'Security of the King's Person and Government,' by which it was made capital treason to devise the king's death, or imprisonment, or bodily harm, or to deprive and depose him from his kingly name, &c. It enacted likewise, that whoever affirmed the king to be an Heretic, or a Papist, or should by writing, printing, preaching, or other speaking, stir up the people to hatred or dislike of his majesty, or the established government, should be rendered incapable of holding any employment in Church or State. It also declared the Long Parliament to be dissolved, the Solemn League and Covenant to be illegal; and that there was no legislative power in either, or both houses of parliament, without the king; and whoever asserted the contrary, were made liable to the penalty of a Premunire.

Act to limit the Number of Petitioners.] Recollecting further the Abuse of Petitioning, in the preceding reign, they prepared a Bill, by which it was enacted, that no more than 20 hands should be subscribed to any Petition or Remonstrance, unless with the sanction of 3 justices, or the major part of the grand jury; and that such Petition should not be presented to the king, or either house, by above ten persons, on the penalty of 100*l.* and 3 months imprisonment.*

Proceedings against the Regicides.] As the king seemed on one hand to make it a point to perfect the Act of Indemnity, the commons, on the other, appeared as zealous to offer up victims to the memory of his father. Accordingly, they proceeded to the Confiscation of the estates of 21 Regicides deceased. They likewise ordered the lord Mounson, sir Henry Mildmay, and Mr. Robert Wallop, to be brought to the bar of the house of commons; where confessing their crimes, a Bill was ordered to be brought in to confiscate their estates, as also those of sir J. Harrington and John Phelps, not yet apprehended: and it was further ordered, "That the lord Mounson, sir J. Harrington, and sir H. Mildmay should be degraded of their several honours and titles; and that those now in custody, and the other two, when apprehended, should all be drawn upon sledges with ropes about their necks, from the Tower of London to, and under the gallows at Tyburn, and thence conveyed back to the Tower, there to remain prisoners during their lives. Which sentences were solemnly executed upon the 30th of Jan. following.

The Speaker's Speech to the King at the Adjournment.] July 30. This day his majesty came to the house of peers; and, sitting in his throne, arrayed with his royal robes, the peers likewise sitting in their robes, the king gave command to the gentleman usher of the black rod, to give notice to the house of commons, that they attend his majesty forthwith. And accordingly they came up with their Speaker, who made this Speech following:

"May it please your most excellent majesty; The Wise Man tells us, 'There is a 'time to sow, and a time to reap.' Since your majesty did convene the knights, citizens, and burgesses of the commons house of parliament, they have with unwearied labour consulted for the service of your majesty and the good of this nation; and now the fields grow white to harvest. In the great field of nature, all fruits do not grow ripe together; but some in one month, some in another: one time affords your majesty primroses and violets; another time presents you with July flowers. So it is in the course of our proceedings: some of our fruits are in the blossom, when others are in the bud; some are near ripe, and others fit to be presented to your majesty. Amongst the number of our choicest ripe fruits, we first present you with a Bill for the Safety and Preservation of your majesty's royal person and government.—Your predecessor queen Elizabeth, of famous memory, in the 13th year of her reign, by Pius Quintus, then bishop of Rome, was excommunicated and anathematized. John Felton posted up a Bull at the bishop of London's palace, whereby she was declared to be deprived of her title to the kingdom, and all the people of this realm absolved from their allegiance to her; the queen of Scots was then a prisoner in England; and the duke of Norfolk, for many designs against our queen, committed to the Tower. Historians tell us, the times were very troublesome, full of suspicions and conspiracies. But, sir, what then was only feared, hath in our time been put in execution. No age hath known, no history makes mention of, such sad tragedies. It therefore now becomes your people, after this glorious Restitution, to endeavour all just ways of preservation.—The queen, in her time of trouble and danger, summoned a parliament; and such was the love of the people to her and her government, that they forthwith made a law for her Security. According to which precedent, we your loyal commons also, who have before them no less cause of fear, but more

* See Ralph, vol. i. p. 47.

obligations and affection to your majesty, do humbly tender you a Bill, wherein we desire it may be enacted, "That if any person shall compass, imagine, or design, your majesty's death, destruction or bodily harm, to imprison or restrain your royal person, or depose you, or shall levy war against your majesty within or without your realm, or stir up any foreign power to invade you, and shall express or declare such his wicked intention by printing, writing, preaching, or malicious and advised speaking, being thereof legally convicted, shall be adjudged a traitor."—And, because much of our late misery took its rise from seditious Pamphlets, and Speeches from the pulpits, it is provided, "That if any man shall maliciously and advisedly publish or affirm your majesty to be an Heretic, or a Papist, or that you endeavour to introduce Popery, or shall stir up the people to hatred or dislike of your royal person or government, then every such person shall be made incapable of any office or employment either in Church or State; and if any man shall maliciously and advisedly affirm, that the parliament begun at Westm. the 3rd of Nov. 1640, is yet in being; or that any Covenant or engagement since that time imposed upon the people doth oblige them to endeavour a change of the government either in church or state; or that either or both houses of parliament have a legislative power without your majesty; then every such offender, being thereof legally convicted, shall incur the penalties of a Premunire, mentioned in the statute made 16 Rd. II."—In the next place, sir, give me leave, I beseech you (without any violence to the Act of Oblivion), to remember a sad effect of the distempers in the last age. When the fever began to seize upon the people, they were impatient till they lost some blood. The lords spiritual, who in all ages had enjoyed a place in parliament, were by an act of parliament excluded. Your majesty's royal grandfather was often wont to say, "No Bishop, No King." We found his words true; for, after they were put out, the fever still increasing, in another fit the temporal lords followed, and then the king himself. Nor did the humour rest there; but, in the round, the house of commons was first garbled, and then turned out of doors. It is no wonder, when a sword is put into a madman's hand, to see him cut off limb by limb, and then to kill himself. When there is a great breach of the sea upon the low grounds, by the violence of the torrent, the rivers of sweet waters are often turned aside, and the salt waters make themselves a channel; but when the breach is made up, good husbands drain their lands again, and restore the ancient sewers.—Thanks be to God, the flood is gone off the face of this Island. Our turtle dove hath found good footing. Your majesty is happily restored to the government; the temporal lords and commons are restored to sit in parliament. And shall the Church alone now suffer? 'Sit Ecclesia Anglicana libera, et habeat Libertates suas illæsas.' In order to this great work, the commons have prepared a Bill to repeal that law which was made in 17 Car. whereby the Bishops were excluded this house: these noble lords have all agreed; and now we beg your majesty will give it life. Speak but the word, great sir; and your servants yet shall live.—We cannot well forget the method, how our late miseries, like waves of the sea, came in upon us: First, The people were invited to petition, to give colour to some illegal demands. Then they must remonstrate, then they must protest, then they must covenant, then they must associate, then they must engage against our lawful government, and for the maintenance of the most horrid tyranny that ever was invented. For the prevention of this practice for the future, we do humbly tender unto your majesty a Bill, intituled, "An Act against Tumults and Disorders, upon pretence of preparing or presenting public Petitions, or Addresses, to your majesty or the parliament."—In the next place, we held it our duty to undeceive the people, who have been poisoned with an opinion, that the Militia of this nation was in themselves, or in their representatives in parliament; and, according to the ancient known laws, we have declared the sole right of the Militia to be in your majesty. And forasmuch as our time hath not permitted us to finish a Bill intended for the future ordering of the same; we shall present you with a temporary Bill, for the present managing and disposing of the Land Forces; and likewise another Bill for establishing certain Articles and Orders for the Regulation and Government of your majesty's Navies and Forces by sea.—According to your majesty's commands, we have examined many of the Public and Private Bills which passed last parliament; and have prepared some Bills of Confirmation. We have also ascertained the Pains and Penalties to be imposed upon the persons or estates of those miscreants who had a hand in the murder of your royal father of blessed memory, and were therefore excepted in your majesty's Act of Oblivion; wherein we have declared to all the world, how just an indignation we had against that horrid regicide.—We have likewise prepared a Bill for the Collection of great Arrears of the Duty of Excise; which I do here, in the name of the commons, humbly present unto your majesty. The reason, we conceive, why it was not formerly paid, was because the people disliked the authority whereby it was imposed. But, understanding that it is now given to your majesty, it will come in with as great freedom; aliquisque malo erit usus in illo.—Your majesty was pleased, at the opening of the parliament, to tell us, 'That you intended this summer to take a Progress, and see your people, and at your return did hope to bring a queen home with you.' Sir, this welcome news hath made us cast about all ways for your accommodation. And therefore, that no conveniences might be wanting, either for your majesty, your queen, or your attendants, we have prepared a Bill, intituled, 'An Act for providing necessary Carriages, in all your royal Progresses and Removals.'—Your majesty was likewise pleased, at our first meeting, to say, 'You would not tire us with hard duty and hot service; and therefore about this time intended a Recess.' That royal favour will now be very seasonable; and we hope advantageous both to your majesty and ourselves: we know, in our absence, your princely heart and head will not be free from cares and thoughts of our protection; and when we leave our hive, like the industrious bee, we shall but fly about the several countries of the nation to gather honey; and, when your majesty shall be pleased to name the time, return with loaded thighs unto our house again."

The King's Speech at the Adjournment.] After giving his royal assent to the said Bills, the King made the following speech:

"My Lords and Gentlemen; I perceive, by the thin appearance of the members of both houses this day, that it is high time to adjourn. In truth, the season of the year as well as your particular affairs require it; and therefore I do willingly consent to it.—I thank you for the many good Bills you have presented me with this day; of which, I hope, the benefit will redound to the whole kingdom. I thank you for the care you have taken for the safety of my person; which, trust me, is the more valuable to me, for the consequence I think it is of to you. And, upon my conscience, there is nobody wishes ill to me, but they who would quickly revenge themselves of you if they could.—I thank you for the care you have taken of yourselves, of your own safety and honour, in the Act against Tumults and Disorders upon pretence of Petitions; to which license we owe much of the calamities we have undergone: But I thank you with all my heart, indeed as much as I can do for any thing, for the repeal of that Act which excluded the Bishops from sitting in parliament. It was an unhappy act, in an unhappy time, passed with many unhappy circumstances, and attended with miserable events; and therefore I do again thank you for repealing it. You have thereby restored parliaments to their primitive institutions. And I hope, my lords and gentlemen, you will in a short time restore them to the primitive order, and gravity of debates and determinations, which the license of the late distempered times had so much corrupted; which is the only way to restore parliaments to their primitive veneration with the people, which I heartily wish they should always have.—My Lords and Genlemen; You are now going to your several countries; where you cannot but be very welcome, for the services you have performed here. I do very earnestly recommend the good government and peace of your countries to your care, and your counsel, and your vigilancy. There are distempered spirits enough, which lie in wait to do mischief, by laying reproaches upon the court, upon the government, reproaches upon me, and reproaches upon you. Your wisdoms and reputation and authority will, I doubt not, weigh down their light credit; and the old and new good laws will, I hope, prevent any mischief they intend. However, you have done very well (and I do very heartily thank you for it) in declaring my sole right over the Militia; the questioning of which was the fountain from which all our bitter waters flowed. I pray make haste to put the whole kingdom into such posture, that evil men, who will not be converted, may yet choose to be quiet, because they find that they shall not be able to do the harm they desire to do.—I know you have begun many Bills in both houses which cannot be finished till your meeting again: And, that they may be finished then, I forbear to make a sessions now; but am contented that you adjourn till the 20th of Nov. when I hope, by God's blessing, we shall come happily together again.—In a word, my lords and gentlemen, I thank you for what you have done; and am confident, that what you have left undone you will dispatch with all alacrity, and to all our satisfactions, at our next meeting. And so you may adjourn till the 20th of November."

The King's Speech at the Meeting of Parliament.] Nov. 20. The parliament met persuant to adjournment, the Bishops being restored to their seats in the house of peers. Upon which occasion the King was pleased to declare his mind to both houses in the speech following:

"My Lords and Gentlemen of the House of Commons: I know the visit I make you this day is not necessary, is not of course: yet, if there were no more in it, it would not be strange that I come to see, what you and I have so long desired to see, the Lords Spiritual and Temporal and the Commons of England met together to consult for the peace and safety of Church and State, by which parliaments are restored to their primitive lustre and integrity: I do heartily congratulate with you for this day. But, my lords and gentlemen, as my coming hither at this time is somewhat extraordinary; so the truth is, the occasion of my coming is more extraordinary. It is to say something to you on my own behalf, to ask somewhat of you for myself; which is more than I have done of you or of those who met here before you, since my coming into England. I needed not have done it then; and, upon my conscience, I need not do it now. They did, and you do, upon all occasions, express so great an affection and care of all that concerns me, that I may very well refer both the matter and manner of your doing any thing for me, to your own wisdoms and kindness. And indeed, if I did think that what I am to say to you now did alone or did most concern myself; if the uneasy condition I am in, if the streights and necessities I am to struggle with, did not manifestly relate to the public peace and safety, more than to my own particular otherwise than as I am concerned in the public, I should not give you this trouble this day.

I can bear my necessities which merely relate to myself with patience enough.—Mr. Speaker and you Gentlemen of the house of Commons: I do not now importune you to make more haste in the settling the constant Revenue of the crown, than is agreeable to the method you propose to yourselves; to desire you seriously to consider the insupportable weight that lies upon it, the obligation it lies under, to provide for the interest, honour and security of the nation, in another proportion than in any former times it hath been obliged to: But I come to put you in mind of the crying Debts which do every day call upon me; of some necessary provisions which are to be made without delay for the very safety of the kingdom; of the great sum of money that should be ready to discharge the several fleets when they come home; and for the necessary preparations that are to be made for the setting out new fleets to sea against the spring, that revenue being already anticipated upon as important services which should be assigned to those preparations. These are the pressing occasions which I am forced to recommend to you with all possible earnestness, and to conjure you to provide for as speedily as is possible, and in such a manner as may give a security at home, and some reputation abroad. I make this discourse to you with some confidence, because I am very willing and desirous that you should thoroughly examine whether these necessities I mention be real or imaginary, or whether they are fallen upon us by my fault, my own ill managery, or excesses, and provide for them accordingly. I am very willing that you make a full inspection into my Revenue, as well the disbursements as receipts; and if you find it hath been ill-managed by any corruption in the officers I trust, or by my own unthriftiness, I shall take the information and advice you shall give me very kindly; I say, if you find it; for I would not have you believe any loose discourses, how confidently soever urged, of giving away four score thousand pounds in a morning, and many other extravagancies of that kind. I have much more reason to be sorry that I have not to reward those who have ever faithfully served the king my father and myself, than ashamed of any bounty I have exercised towards any man*. My Lords and Gentlemen; I am sorry to find that the general temper and affections of the nation are not so well composed as I hoped they would have been, after so signal blessings from God Almighty upon us all, and after so great indulgence and condescensions from me towards all interests. There are many wicked instruments, still as active as ever, who labour night and day to disturb the public peace, and to make all people jealous of each other. It will be worthy of your care and vigilance, to provide proper remedies for the diseases of that kind; and if you find new diseases, you must study new remedies. Let us not be discouraged: If we help one another we shall, with God's blessing, master all our difficulties. Those which concern matters of Religion, I confess to you are too hard for me; and therefore I do commend them to your care and deliberation, which can best provide for them.—I shall not need to recommend, or put you in mind of, the good correspondence that ought to be kept between you, for the good of yourselves and me, and the whole kingdom; and I may tell you, it is very necessary for us all. You will find, whoever doth not love me, doth not love you? and they who have no reverence for you have little kindness for me. Therefore, I pray, let us adhere fast to each other; and then we shall with the help of God, in a short time persuade or oblige all men to that submission and obedience to the law, as may constitute a full measure of happiness to prince and people, and persuade our neighbours to that esteem and value they have formerly had for us."

Information given to the House of a Presbyterian Plot.] The commons were no sooner returned to their house, than sir John Packington, member for Worcester, gave Information of a dangerous Presbyterian Plot on foot; and that many of the chief of the conspirators were in prison at Worcester: the members also who served for Oxfordshire, Hertfordshire, Staffordshire, and several other counties, gave in the like Informations.

Nov 21. The lords received a Message from the commons by Mr. Secretary Morrice to let them know, "That the house of commons have intelligence that divers Malecontents, Fanatics, Cashiered and Disbanded Officers and Soldiers, and others, have some Design amongst them, tending to the breach

* "Let no man wonder," says lord Clarendon, "that within so little time as a year and a half, or very little more, after the king's return, that is, from May to November in the next year, and after so great sums of money raised by acts of parliament upon the people, his majesty's Debts could be so crying and importunate, as to disturb him to that degree as he expressed. It was never enough understood, that in all that time he never received from the parliament more than the 70,000*l.* towards his Coronation; nor were the Debts which were now so grievous to him contracted by himself (though it cannot be supposed but that he had contracted debts himself in that time): all the money that had been given and had been applied to the payment of the Land and Sea forces, and had done neither. Parliaments do seldom make their computations right, but reckon what they give to be much more than is ever received, and what they are to pay to be as much less than in truth they owe; so that when all the money that was collected was paid, there remained still very much due to the soldiers, and much more to the seamen; and the clamour from both reached the king's ears, as if they had been levied by his warrant

of the peace of this kingdom; therefore they desire their lordships would join with them, to move his majesty that he would please to issue out a Proclamation, that all suspicious and loose persons may be forthwith sent out of these towns of London and Westminster, and the liberties thereof for some time."

This day, the commons, to shew their readiness to assist the king in his wants, voted "That the sum of 1,200,000*l.* be speedily paid and raised for the Supply of the king's majesty's present occasions;" and so proceeded accordingly. For which the king soon after returned his hearty Thanks, and particularly express'd, how exceeding much he was beholden to the commons for their great gift, and the manner of it, in giving so freely. After which, he declared by a Message to the commons, signifying, "That, making the good of his people the subject of his thoughts, and considering that the calling in the Money, called the Commonwealth's Money, by the last of this month, might be prejudicial to his people, and hazard the exportation of a great part thereof, he was graciously pleased, by the advice of his privy council, to direct a Proclamation to be issued, signifying his majesty's pleasure to accept of the said Money in any payment to be made to him till the 25th of March next."

Proceedings against the Regicides renewed.] Nov. 25. The first parliament having respited the punishments of several of the Regicides, as well those that lay under condemnation, as others not so flagrantly guilty of that crime, the houses resumed the matter, and this day those Regicides that came in upon Proclamation were brought to the bar of the house of lords, to answer what they could say for themselves, why judgment should not be executed against them. They severally alledged, 'That, upon his majesty's gracious Declaration from Breda, and the Votes of Parliament, and his majesty's Proclamation, published by the advice of the lords and commons then assembled in parliament, they did render themselves, being advised that they should thereby secure their lives; and humbly craved the benefit thereof, and the mercy of the houses, and their mediation to his majesty in their behalfs.' Harry Marten briskly added, 'That he had 'never obeyed any Proclamation before this, 'and hoped that he should not be hanged for 'taking of the king's word now.' New debates arose about them, and a Bill was brought in for their execution, which was read twice, but afterwards dropt; and so they were all sent to their several prisons, and but little more heard of them. The difficulty had like to have been the heavier upon them, by reason of several seditious pamphlets published about this time; and likewise by reason of a Message from the King, delivered by the Lord Chancellor in a conference between both houses.†

The Lord Chancellor's Declaration concerning a Plot in agitation.] Dec. 19. The Lord Chancellor acquainted the lords, "That he had a Message to deliver from the King; which was, to let them know, that besides the Apprehensions and Fears that are generally abroad, his majesty hath received Letters from

---

and for his service. And his majesty understood too well, by the experience of the ill husbandry of the last year, when both the army and the ships were so long continued in pay, for want of money to disband and pay them off, what the trouble and charge would be, if the several Fleets should return before money was provided to discharge the seamen; and for that the clamour would be only upon him.—But there was an expense that he had been engaged in from the time of his return, and by which he had contracted a great Debt, of which very few men could take notice; nor could the king think fit to discover it, till he had first provided against the mischief which might have attended the discovery. It will hardly be believed, that in so warlike an age, and when the armies and fleets of England had made more noise in the world for 20 years, had fought more battles at land and sea, than all the world had done besides, or any one people had done in any age before; and when at his majesty's return there remained a 100 ships at sea, and an Army of near threescore thousand men at land; there should not be in the Tower of London, and in all the stores belonging to the crown, Fire-Arms enough, nor indeed of any other kind, to arm three thousand men; nor powder and naval provisions enough to set out five ships of war.—From the death of Cromwell, no care had been taken for supplies of any of the stores. And the changes which ensued in the government, and putting out and in new officers; the expeditions of Lambert against sir George Booth, and afterwards into the North; and other preparations for those factions and parties which succeeded each other; and the continual opportunities which the officers had for embezzlement; and lastly, the setting out that fleet which was sent to attend upon the king for his return; had so totally drained the stores of all kinds, that the magazines were no better replenished than is mentioned before: which as soon as his majesty knew, as he could not be long ignorant of it, the first care he took was to conceal it, that it might not be known abroad or at home, in how ill a posture he was to defend himself against an enemy. And then he committed the care of that province to a noble person, whom he knew he could not trust too much, and made sir Wm. Compton master of the Ordnance, and made all the shifts he could devise for monies, that the work might be begun. And hereby insensibly he had contracted a great Debt: and these were part of the crying debts, and the necessary provisions which were to be made without delay for the very safety of the kingdom, which he told the parliament." Life, p. 145.

† Echard, p. 795.

several parts of the kingdom, and also by intercepted letters it does appear, that divers discontented persons are endeavouring to raise new troubles, to the disturbance of the peace of the kingdom, as in many particulars was instanced: which matter being of so great consequence, his majesty's desire is, That the house of commons may be made acquainted with it, that so his majesty may receive the advice and counsel of both houses of parliament, what is fit to be done herein; and to think of some proper remedy to secure the peace of the kingdom."—Upon this, a joint committee of both houses was appointed to sit, notwithstanding the usual recess at Christmas, in order to make discoveries, and prepare a Report against the next meeting; the substance of which, as delivered by the lord chancellor Clarendon, was as follows:—"That there was found with Salmon a List of 160 Officers of the late Army: that it was further discovered that there should have been a meeting in London about the 10th of Dec. and that they intended about the end of Jan. to have made sure of Shrewsbury, Coventry, and Bristol, and that they should rise in several parts at once: that where they were prevalent they should begin with Assassination, which moved one of them to relate, 'That some of the late king's Judges were entertained in France, Holland and Germany, and held constant correspondence with those, and were fomented by some foreign Princes.' That many arms were brought in order to this design, and that they bragged, 'If they once got footing, they should not want means to carry on their work.' That they were discovered by one of their party, and his relation confirmed by such intelligence from abroad, as never failed." He further told them, "That at Huntington many there met under the name of Quakers, that were not so, and rode there in multitudes by night, to the great terror of his majesty's good subjects. That it might be wondered at, that some proposals were not made to remedy this impending evil: but the king had advised with the duke of Albemarle, now present at this committee, and has put two troops into Shrewsbury, and as many into Coventry; who, by the way, have broken a great knot of thieves, and taken twenty. That a rumour was spread, that the appointing of this Committee was only a Plot to govern by an Army; but the committee was very sensible of the real danger, and hoped the houses would be so too; and that since all their adversaries were united to destroy them, so they should unite to preserve themselves."

Corporation Act passed.] Dec. 19. The Act for regulating Corporations was passed. It made a great noise, and met with some struggles in the house. It proved indeed a severe mortification and a blow to one party, and made a mighty alternation in several places, which the court was pleased to look upon as nests of sedition. Part of the Preamble very well shews the design of the Act, namely, That the Succession in such Corporations may be most properly perpetuated in the hands of persons well affected to his majesty, and the established government; it being too well known, that notwithstanding all his majesty's endeavours, and unparalleled indulgence, in pardoning all that is past, nevertheless many evil spirits are still working: therefore, for this, every mayor, alderman, common-councilman, or any other officer in a Corporation, was obliged, besides the common Oath of Allegiance and Supremacy, and a particular Declaration against the Solemn League and Covenant, to take an Oath, declaring, 'That it was not lawful, upon any pretence whatsoever, to take Arms against the king; and that he did abhor that traiterous position of taking arms by his authority against his person, or against those commissioned by him.' And, to put this in execution, the king was authorized to grant a commission to such persons as he thought fit, to last above two years, with sufficient power to answer the ends of the act.

The Speaker's Speech to the King on presenting the Money Bill, and the Corporation Act.] Dec. 20. The Money Bill, the Corporation Act, and two other bills, being ready for the royal assent, the king came to the house of peers. The commons being sent for, came with their Speaker; who made the following Speech:

"May it please your most excellent majesty; The last time the knights, citizens, and burgesses of the commons house of parliament, had the honour to wait upon you in this place, your majesty was graciously pleased to congratulate with them, for the glorious meeting of the lords spiritual and temporal and commons of England, in this your full, free, and legal parliament.—Great sir, it is our present comfort, and will be our future glory, that God hath made us instrumental for the repairs of those breaches which the worst of times had made upon the best of governments. The late great eclipse in our horizon, occasioned by the interposition of the earth, is now vanished; the stars in our firmament are now full of light; the light of our moon is become like the light of the sun; and the light of our sun is sevenfold.—A man that sees the river of Thames at a high water, and observes how much it sinks in a few hours, would think it running quite away; but, by the secret providence of God, we see that when the ebb is at the lowest, the tide of a rising water is nearest the return.—Your majesty was likewise graciously pleased to speak something to us on your own behalf; and did vouchsafe to say, you would ask something for yourself; withal declaring some uneasiness in your condition, by reason of some crying Debts which daily called for satisfaction.—Great sir, I am not able to express, at the bearing of those words, with what a sympathy the whole body of the parliament was presently affected. The circulation of the blood, of which our naturalists do tell us, was never so sensibly demonstrated as by this experiment. Before your majesty's words were all fallen from your lips, you might have seen us blush: all our blood came into our faces; from thence it hasted down without obstruction to every part of the body; and, after a due consulting of the several parts, it was found necessary to breathe a vein.—We cannot forget how much our treasure hath been exhausted; but we remember also it was by usurping and tyrannical powers; and therefore we are easily persuaded to be at some more expence to keep them out. The merchant tells us, it is good policy, in a troubled sea, to lose some part of our cargo, thereby to save the rest.—With your majesty's leave, we have been bold to look into the present state of affairs; and find those great sums that have been heretofore advanced upon us were raised most of them in bad times, and for ill purposes, to keep your majesty out of this your native kingdom; and when your majesty returned home from your long banishment, you found the naval storehouse unfurnished, which will not easily be supplied. The unsettled humours, and unquiet spirits, that are amongst us, do necessitate a costly guard for your royal person: the honourable accessions of Dunkirk, Tangier, and Jamaica, do at present require a great Supply; but, we have reason to believe, in time to come, will repay this nation their principal with good interest.—Your majesty hath sent a royal fleet upon a happy errand, to bring your royal consort hither: and is there any Englishman will stick to pay the wages of those mariners, whose ships do bring so good a freight?—Upon all these considerations, your loyal commons were in pain, until, like prudent and good husbands, they had redeemed the nation from all its public Debts. And that your majesty may at once have a full measure of their duty and affection to yourself, and that your neighbours abroad, as well as the discontented Commonwealth's men with all their complicated interests here at home, may see the happy correspondence that is between our head and all the members of this body politic; we have cheerfully and unanimously given your majesty twelve hundred and three score thousand pounds; which sum we desire may be levied in 18 months, by six quarterly payments, after the rate of 70,000*l.* per mensem, to begin the 25th of this present Dec.; in order whereunto, we humbly pray your majesty's royal assent unto this bill."

The King's Speech thereon.] After passing the said Bills, his majesty was pleased to make this short Speech:

"Mr. Speaker, and you Gentlemen of the House of Commons; You have made me this day a very great and a very noble present; a present that I have received benefit from already, before you presented it: for, trust me, the benefit is not small, which I and you both have already, from the reputation of this present, from the alacrity and affection you have so unanimously expressed in this affair.—My Lords and Gentlemen; I do thank you with all my heart for it; and I will not enlarge those thanks further, than by telling you, that I do not come more willingly this day to pass this Bill, than I will do to pass any other bills which you shall provide for the ease, benefit, and security of my people; and I do verily believe that you and I shall never be deceived or disappointed in the expectation we have of each other." The parliament was then adjourned to the 7th of January.

Message from the King to the Commons relative to the Money Bill.] Feb. 18. Mr. Secretary Morrice informed the commons, "That he had directions from his majesty to desire the house, that they would put a Supersedeas to any further debate upon the Bill for permission to such persons as should advance Money for his majesty's present occasions, to take interest at 10 per cent. That his majesty, finding the Bill might have some ungrateful relish in it, resolved to put himself upon the greatest streights, rather than adventure upon any course that might in the least seem to disgust this house, or prejudice his good subjects; and therefore would endeavour to find some other means to supply his present urgent occasions, and desired the Bill might be laid aside." This Message affected them so much, that they immediately returned their humble Thanks to the king for his tenderness to his people, and ordered, "That his majesty be made acquainted, that this house would leave no means unattempted to advance his majesty's Revenue, and supply his present urgent occasions."

The King's Speech to the Commons in the Banquetting House, concerning his Necessities.] March 1. The King finding his necessities to increase, ordered the commons to attend him at Whitehall, in a body by themselves: which was accordingly done this day; when his majesty addressed them as follows:

"Mr. Speaker, and Gentlemen of the House of Commons; Finding it necessary to say somewhat to you, I thought once of doing it by a Message, which hath been the most usual way; but when I considered, that speaking to you myself with that plainness and freedom I use to do, hath more of kindness in it; and with what affection you use to receive what I say to you, I resolved to deliver my Message to you myself; and have therefore sent for you hither, which hath been frequently done heretofore, though it be the first time I have done so.—I do speak my heart to you, when I tell you, that I do believe, that, from the first institutions of parliaments to this hour, there was never a house of commons fuller of affection and duty to their king, than you are to me; never any that was more desirous and solicitous to gratify their king, than you are to oblige me; never a house of commons in which there were fewer persons without a full measure of zeal for the honour and welfare of the king and country, than there are in this.—The wonderful alacrity that you shewed at your first coming together, in giving me so liberal a Supply, was an unquestionable instance of this; and, I assure you, made our neighbours abroad look upon me, and you with much the more respect and esteem; and I am persuaded, even broke the heart of some desperate and seditious designs at home: in a word, I know most of your faces and names, and can never hope to find better men in your places.—You will wonder now, after I have willingly made this just acknowledgment to you, that I should lament, and even complain, that I, and you, and the kingdom, are yet without that present fruit and advantage which we might reasonably promise ourselves from such a harmony of affections, and a unity in resolutions, to advance the public service, and to provide for the Peace and Security of the kingdom; that you do not expedite those good counsels which are necessary for both. I know not how it comes to pass, but for these many weeks past, even since your last adjournment, private and particular business have almost thrust the consideration of the public out of doors; and, in truth, I do not know, that you are nearer settling my Revenue, than you were at Christmas: I am sure I have communicated my condition to you, without reserve; what I have coming in, and what my necessary disbursements are: and I am exceedingly deceived, if whatsoever you give me, be any otherwise given to me, than to be issued out for your own use and benefit.—Trust me, it shall be so; and, if you consider it well, you will find, that you are the richer by what you give; since it is all to be laid out, that you may enjoy the rest in Peace and Security.—Gentlemen, I need not put you in mind of the miserable effects which have attended the Wants and Necessities of the crown: I need not tell you that there is a Republican party still in the kingdom, which have the courage to promise themselves another Revolution: and, methinks, I should as little need to tell you, that the only way, with God's blessing, to disappoint their hopes, and indeed to reduce them from those extravagant hopes and desires, is, to let them see, that you have so provided for the crown, that it hath wherewithal to support itself, and to secure you; which, I am sure, is all I desire, and desire only for your preservation.—Therefore I do conjure you, by all the professions of affection you have made to me, by all the kindness I know you have for me, after all your deliberations, betake yourselves to some speedy resolutions; and settle such a real and substantial Revenue upon me, as may hold some proportion with the necessary expences I am at, for the peace, and benefit, and honour of the kingdom; that they who look for troubles at home, may despair of their wishes; and that our neighbours abroad, by seeing that all is well at home, may have that esteem and value of us, as may secure the interest and honour of the nation, and make the happiness of this kingdom, and of this city, once more the admiration and envy of the world.—Gentlemen, I hear you are very zealous for the Church, and very solicitous, and even jealous that there is not expedition enough used in that affair: I thank you for it, since, I presume, it proceeds from a good root of piety and devotion: but I must tell you, I have the worst luck in the world, if, after all the reproaches of being a papist, whilst I was abroad, I am suspected of being a Presbyterian now I am come home.—I know you will not take it unkindly, if I tell you, that I am as zealous for the Church of England, as any of you can be; and am enough acquainted with the enemies of it, on all sides; that I am as much in love with the Book of Common Prayer as you can wish, and have prejudice enough to those that do not love it; who, I hope, in time will be better informed, and change their minds: and you may be confident, I do as much desire to see a Uniformity settled, as any amongst you: I pray, trust me, in that affair I promise you to hasten the dispatch of it, with all convenient speed; you may rely upon me in it.—I have transmitted the Book of Common Prayer, with those Alterations and Additions which have been presented to me by the Convocation, to the house of peers, with my approbation, that the Act of Uniformity may relate to it: so that I presume it will be shortly dispatched there; and when we have done all we can, the well settling that affair will require great prudence and discretion, and the absence of all passion and precipitation.—I will conclude with putting you in mind, that the season of the year; the convenience of your being in the country, in many respects for the good and welfare of it (for you will find much tares have been sowed there, in your absence); the arrival of my Wife, who I expect some time this month; and the necessity of my own being out of town to meet her, and to stay some time before she comes hither; makes it very necessary, that the parliament be adjourned before Easter, to meet again in the winter: and that it may do so, I pray lay aside private business, that you may, in that time, dispatch the publick: and there are few things I reckon more public, than your providing for the security of the Fen-Lands, which I have so often recommended to you; and do it now, very earnestly. I pray let no private animosities or contests endanger a work of so great a benefit and honour to the nation; but first provide for the support of the work, and then let justice be done for determination of particular interests.—The mention of my Wife's arrival puts me in mind to desire you to put that compliment upon her, that her entrance into the town may be with more decency than the ways will now suffer it to be: and, to that purpose, I pray you would quickly pass such laws as are before you, in order to the mending those ways; and that she may not find Whitehall surrounded with water.—I will detain you no longer, but do promise myself great fruits of this conversation with you; and that you will justify the confidence I have in your affection, by letting the world see, that you take my concernments to heart, and are ready to do whatsoever I desire for the peace and welfare of the kingdom."

Hearth-Money Bill.] These assurances of his majesty, had their desired effect. A Bill to lay a duty upon every Chimney Hearth, in each house of above two shillings a year, for ever, was forthwith agreed upon; and his majesty was moreover enabled to raise, for the 3 next ensuing months, one month's tax in each year, after the rate of 70,000*l.* a month, if necessity should so require.

The Press put into the hands of a Licenser.] Nor, says Ralph, did they rest here: the Press had offended as well as the pulpit; the parliament had been treated with the same freedom as the king, and both seemed more disposed to silence clamours, than remove the cause. As therefore the pulpit was to be purged by the Uniformity Act, care was taken to bridle the Press, and put the reins into the hands of a Licenser; who was generally so careful to seal the lips of falshood and abuse, that even truth and justice could rarely obtain a hearing.

To convince his majesty yet farther, how extremely desirous they were, that the republican spirit should be entirely subdued, they took the affair of the Militia again into consideration, and prepared that Bill, which has put the power of the sword in the king's hand.

The Quakers' Bill passed.] There was yet another Bill, continues the above writer, which had hung in the house of Lords ever since last session, and which was now to be passed into a law: and this was the Bill to oblige the Quakers to take the Oaths. Favourable as the crisis was to every rigorous and penal measure, the lords, as we have already remarked, had not stomachs strong enough to digest quite so fast, as the commons furnished them with this sort of food. Thus, with regard to the Bill now before us, finding the Title had relation only to the Quakers, and that in the body of it, a provision was made for extending the penalties to 'others,' they started exceptions, treated it as an inconsistency at least, and ordered, That it should be limited to the Quakers 'only.' A free conference ensued between the two houses, the commons adhered to the letter of their Bill, and upon the report thereof, their lordships so qualified their Alterations, that all objections were removed, and the bill was passed by commission on the 2d of May.* (Ralph, vol. i. p. 69.)

* "In the late Debates upon the Quakers Bill, &c. reference was made to the horrid impulses of what they called 'the Spirit,' not only dictating the most extravagant opinions, but driving to the most abominable practices. Many of that party had their brains dislocated and displaced. Some whereof have taken their children, and gone and sacrificed them, pretending a particular command, like that God gave to Abraham; as a woman of Dover cut off her child's head, and alledged this Scripture. Others have shut themselves up with a Bible, and resolved to eat nothing, because it is written, that 'Man shall not live by bread 'alone, but by every word that proceedeth 'out of the mouth of God.' Some have killed their cat, because she had taken a mouse on Sunday, but deferred the execution till Monday. Evach ap Evan, near Shrewsbury, killed his own mother and brother in cold blood; having no other quarrel against them but that they loved the Liturgy," &c. Hist. of the English and Scotch Presbyterians.

Petition of the distressed Royalists.] During this session, the distressed Royalists set forth their miserable case in the following remarkable Paper; which drew an Aid in their favour of 60,000*l.*

"An humble Representation of the sad condition of many of the King's Party; who, since his majesty's happy Restoration, have no Relief, and but languishing hopes. Together with Proposals how some of them may be speedily relieved, and others assured thereof, within a reasonable time.

"What miseries and persecutions we Roya-

On the other hand, to discountenance these strange stories, we find the following affecting Petition in G. Fox's Journal: "There being very many Friends in prison in the nation, Richard Hubberthorn, and I George Fox, drew up a paper concerning them, and got it delivered to the King, that he might understand how we were dealt with by his officers. It was thus directed: "For the KING.

"Friend, who art the chief ruler of these dominions, here is a list of some of the Sufferings of the people of God, in scorn called Quakers, that have suffered under the changeable powers before thee, by whom there have been imprisoned, and under whom there have suffered for good conscience sake, and for bearing testimony to the truth as it is in Jesus, 3173 persons: and there lye yet in prison in the name of the Commonwealth 73 persons that we know of. And there have died in prison in the time of the Commonwealth, and of Oliver and Richard the Protectors, through cruel and hard imprisonments upon nasty straw and in dungeons, 32 persons. There have been also imprisoned in thy name, since thy arrival, by such as thought to ingratiate themselves thereby to thee, 3068 persons. Besides this, our meetings are daily broken up by men with clubs and arms (though we meet peaceably, according to the practice of God's people in the primitive times) and our friends are thrown into waters, and trod upon, until the very blood gusheth out of them: the number of which abuses can hardly be uttered. Now this we would have of thee, to set them at liberty, that lye in prison in the names of the Commonwealth, and of the two Protectors, and them that lye in thy own name, for speaking the truth, and for a good conscience, &c." G. Fox's Journal, p. 589.

lists have suffered, for 19 years past, no one, we presume, is a stranger to, that could see, or hear. The war began with the plunder of our goods and seizure of our rents, and it ended with the sale of our estates, or, at best, a composition, which engaged us in debts; the burthen whereof, where the parties were either indebted before, or had families to provide for, could not but be ruinous to them: such of us as had no lands, but lived by their honest endeavours, were not only thrust out of their proper employments, but made incapable of any other that could afford them a tolerable subsistence, so as many, the most deserving of their country, have been forced to part with their inheritances to buy them bread: others, of free and generous minds, have languished in tedious imprisonments: few, in comparison of the rest, by singular providence and frugality, have preserved themselves.—With what courage and constancy of affection we have owned our cause, and party, even then, when but to name them civilly was treason, and worse, if worse could be; with what faith and perseverance we have expected our King's return; with what invisible comforts we have supported our feeble hopes, at their lowest ebbs of outward possibility, whilst all the politicians derided us as fond and credulous persons, who, with the purgatory of wise men, purchased only the Paradise of Fools; a kind of Alchymists, or Jews, who looked for a Messiah that would come; and this confidence (grounded chiefly on our integrity), how it engaged us in attempts, which, perhaps, were more honest than prudent, by opposing Plots to Councils, and tumults to the best armies; will not, I trust, be forgotten by English men in our days.—Let it not be once objected, that our endeavours were not successful; rather, let it be construed to our advantage, that though our valour was at first unfortunate, yet (through God's blessing) our cheerful patience hath at length, fulfilled our hopes, by degrees inclining the hearts of the most obstinate to a relenting; wherein as our trials were, so our triumphs are now the greater; for to prevail by loyal sufferings, is the prerogative of true desert. —We joyfully, indeed, partake in the glory of his majesty's Restitution, the peace of our country, the security of laws, and the prospect of future Settlements, which are most pleasant to us: but, alas, we are still exposed to the same necessities, nay, many of us are in worse condition, as to livelihood, than ever, partly by exhausting ourselves with unusual expences, that we might appear (like ourselves) concerned in his majesty's welcome, and coronation; partly, by prosecuting honest, but fruitless, pretences, chiefly by the fate of poverty, which seldom continues without increasing, and, for the accomplishment of our misery, hope, which hitherto alone befriended and supported, hath now forsaken us.—Were our pressures moderate, or common, we should never mention them, but wait yet further upon Providence; for we reckon our martyrdom so honourable, and our cause so dear, that none but extreme exigents would be sensible on that behalf, such poverty being (we are sure) without reproach; had we complied with any of the late usurpers, otherwise than as prisoners must comply with goalers, we should not have dared to look backward, nor presumed to look forward: but innocency and extremity together imbolden, or rather compel us to utter our complaints, where we think we may challenge, at least, a favourable audience.—For, since the cause, we so earnestly contended for, was indeed least of all, our own (who might easily have saved our stakes, as many others of the same persuasion did), and but in part the king's; principally our countries, whose liberty, and even its being was at stake; it may seem a hard piece of justice, that the price of public freedom (when restored) should be the ruin only of such, as with their utmost perils chiefly asserted it; and the nation will appear (at least equally with his majesty) concerned in an expedient, lest if the martyrs and champions of their country be now by it forsaken, (they being disabled by their sufferings, and others by their ill success discouraged) hereafter, in the like exigent, which God prevent, our liberties should find neither champions, nor martyrs.—It grieves us, in all serious companies, to meet with these and the like reflections; how will it discourage our tender plants of loyalty, to be the spectators of its ruin? How will it multiply neuters, to observe noble families extirpated, and their estates possessed, as many will be apt enough to collect, by wiser men? viz. such as took the strongest side. And may not the next generation, from such premises, draw this conclusion, 'He loves danger too well, that loves it for its own sake?'—Certainly, it were too much ignorance in us to suppose, that his majesty is able to contribute, in any proportion, to our relief; rather, we are sensible, that, should he impoverish himself, to gratify us, he would soon be in a condition, neither to support us nor himself; besides, we are satisfied of his kindness towards us: but our recourse is (properly) to the parliament, who (being equally concerned) can relieve us more powerfully, and with less exception, wherein, we doubt not of his majesty's gracious concurrence, and furtherance.—Wherefore, not to importune his majesty, (who, no doubt, hath a real and tender sympathy for us) we do (with much freedom, but with all submission) declare to our representatives, as to good Englishmen, That as we on our part, shall for public good, as cheerfully subscribe to the general Indemnity (when by their wisdoms confirmed) as any that have benefit thereby; so if they, on their part, shall by confirming it, intercept those Remedies, which the law, our great birth-right, would afford us; we conceive, they oblige themselves to study somewhat of recompence, lest they give us subject of complaint, That, in such an Oblivion, they did but too well remember our enemies and only forget us.—And in truth, we hope, that the people in general, whose peace is thereby established, our friends in particular, whose honour is thereby asserted; but especially our late adversaries, whose interests are thereby redeemed at our expence, will frankly approve of such moderate satisfaction to us, as the parliament, in their wisdoms shall think reasonable.—The rather, for that the Arrears of the late Army and Navy, though contracted most of them in times of usurpation, being in effect discharged; those of his majesty's party in Ireland, provided for by special allotments in his majesty's late Declaration concerning that kingdom; the Purchasers of Crown and Church Lands, protected by his majesty's commission in their favour; the Clergy, not only restored to the improved possessions, but to fines of 20 years growth; many private persons rewarded with great gifts, offices, and honours; we only seem abandoned as worthy of nothing but pity from those that will vouchsafe it, unless our condition may be considered by our country in this parliament.—Wherein, for their encouragement, we assure them, our pretences are not lofty, we covet not to engross the plenty of the nation, by purchasing palaces and parks with our debentures: no; the sum of our misfortune is, that in this estate, we are not only burdensome to ourselves and friends, but useless to our king and country; alas, we have too long conversed with ruin, to conceive vast hopes; and if, upon serious scrutiny, greater difficulties should appear, than we imagine, it is our known fundamental to acquiesce in the judgment of our superiors; only we beg, that our case may be judged, to deserve some public consideration; for however, it will much enliven us, to find ourselves not wholly despised, but that expedients to relieve us are, at last, debated, for which we humbly offer these our Proposals. 1. That the greatest services may be most rewarded, but the greatest necessities first relieved. 2. That his majesty would be graciously pleased to take an Account of all his Gifts and Grants, and suspend the conferring of any more, till persons of the highest sufferings and deserts be, in some sort, accommodated. 3. That the sufferings, wants, and merits of pretenders may be examined by select committees, and certified to his maj. and that his maj. would accordingly provide for their relief, by giving express orders for their admittance to such vacant employments as they are capable of, without referring them to subordinate officers, whereby they may be wearied with attendance, and his majesty's grace unto them frustrated. 4. In case Vacancies be not found competent, that then Reversions may be assured to others. 5. That such as have plentiful estates, or have already obtained any considerable grant from the king's bounty, may be postponed, in his majesty's, and the parliament's consideration. 6. That such as shall appear to have unworthily betrayed, or any ways deserted his majesty's party, may be, from thence, wholly excluded. 7. That deserving tenants of Bishops, Deans and Chapters, &c. may be generally, and effectually recommended to the Church's favour, in their great plenty, to accept of moderate Fines from them. 8. That the like public recommendation may be made to all his majesty's chief ministers, officers and commanders, for the employing, countenancing, and encouraging, (by all lawful means) such as have eminently deserved, or suffered for his majesty. 9. That for such Soldiers and Sufferers of his majesty's party, as are old, maimed, without callings, or stocks to exercise them, provision may be made, according to their conditions, viz. for some of them good hospitals, the founders whereof, doubtless, could they speak out of their graves, would so direct; for others reasonable sums, or small annuities, but duly paid, that they may no more depend on private alms, which many cannot find, and some cannot seek; this we suppose, will prove rather matter of care, than much charge. 10. That the parliament would lay some public Assessment, such as they shall think reasonable, our country's poverty being considered as well as ours, to be distributed by his majesty's direction, amongst the surviving officers and soldiers of his majesty's armies, and those of the late king of blessed memory, who never received any recompence of their service, whose number being much contracted by time and other accidents, the bulk will not prove so great as perhaps it seems. 11. That the children of such as have been sacrificed, or died in the bed of honour, or done any memorable action for his majesty, (whose catalogue is easily known) may, in due time, reap the fruits of their father's martyrdom, and, for the present, receive some character of signal favour from their country to be transmitted to posterity, for the encouragement of them and theirs, to follow the footsteps of their noble progenitors, to stir up in others an emulation of such loyalty and virtue, and leave the justice of his majesty's arms sufficiently vindicated to future ages."

Proceedings in both Houses relative to the Act of Uniformity.] The Act of Uniformity depended long, and took up much debate in both houses. "In the house of peers," says lord Clarendon,* where the Act first began, there were many things inserted, which had not been contained in the former Act of Uniformity, and so seemed to carry somewhat of novelty in them. It admitted 'no person to 'have any cure of souls or any ecclesiastical 'dignity in the Church of England, but such 'who had been or should be ordained priest or 'deacon by some bishop, that is, who had not 'episcopal ordination; excepting only the ministers or pastors of the French and Dutch 'Churches in London and other places, allowed 'by the king, who should enjoy the privileges 'they had.' This was new; for there had

* Lord Clarendon's Life, p. 152.

been many, and at present there were some, who possessed benefices with cure of souls, and other ecclesiastical promotions, who had never received orders but in France or in Holland; and these men must now receive new ordination, which had been always held unlawful in the Church, or by this act of parliament must be deprived of their livelihood, which they enjoyed in the most flourishing and peaceable time of the Church. And therefore it was said, 'That this had not been the opinion of 'the Church of England; and that it would 'lay a great reproach upon all other Protest'ant churches who had no bishops, as if they 'had no ministers, and consequently were no 'churches: for that it was well known the 'Church of England did not allow reordina'tion, as the ancient Church never admitted 'it; insomuch as if any Priest of the Church 'of Rome renounces the communion thereof, 'his ordination is not questioned, but he is 'as capable of any preferment in this church, 'as if he had been ordained in it. And there'fore the not admitting the ministers of other 'Protestants to have the same privilege, can 'proceed from no other ground, than that they 'looked not upon them as ministers, having 'no ordination; which is a judgment the 'Church of England had not ever owned: and 'that it would be very imprudent to do it 'now.' To this it was answered, 'That the 'Church of England judged none but her own 'children, nor did determine that other Pro'testant churches were without ordination. It 'is a thing without her cognizance: and most 'of the learned men of those churches had 'made necessity the chief pillar to support 'that ordination of theirs. That necessity 'cannot be pleaded here, where ordination is 'given according to the unquestionable prac'tice of the church of Christ: if they who pre'tend foreign ordination are his majesty's sub'jects, they have no excuse of necessity, for 'they might in all times have received episco'pal ordination, and so they did upon the mat'ter renounce their own church; if they are 'strangers, and pretend to preferment in this 'church, they ought to conform and to be sub'ject to the laws of the kingdom, which concern 'only those who desire to live under the pro'tection thereof. For the argument of reor'dination, there is no such thing required. 'Rebaptization is not allowed in or by any 'church: yet in all churches where it is doubt'ed, as it may be often with very good reason, 'whether the person hath been baptized or no, 'or if it hath been baptized by a midwife or 'lay person; without determining the validity 'or invalidity of such baptism, there is an hy'pothetical form, 'If thou hast not been al'ready baptized, I do baptize,' &c. So in this 'case of ordination, the form may be the same, 'If thou hast not been already ordained, then 'I do ordain, &c.' If his former ordination 'were good, this is void; if the other was in'valid or defective, he hath reason to be glad 'that it be thus supplied.' After much debate, that Clause remained still in the Act: and very many, who had received Presbyterian orders in the late times, came very willingly to be ordained in the manner aforesaid by a Bishop; and very few chose to quit or lose a parsonage or vicarage of any value upon that scruple.

"There was another Clause in the bill, that made very much more noise afterwards, though for the present it took not up so much time, and in truth was little taken notice of: that is, a Form of Subscription that every man was to make, who had received, or before he received, any Benefice or Preferment in the Church; which comprehended all the governors, superiors, and fellows, in all the colleges and halls of either University, and all schoolmasters and the like, who are subservient towards learning. Every such person was to declare 'his 'unfeigned Assent and Consent to all and 'every thing contained and prescribed in and 'by the Book, entitled 'The Book of Com'mon Prayer,' &c. The subscription was generally thought so reasonable, that it scarce met with any opposition in either house. But when it came abroad, and was to be submitted to, all the dissenting brethren cried out, 'that it was a snare to catch them, to say that which could not consist with their consciences.' They took great pains to distinguish and to make great difference between Assent and Consent: 'they could be content to read the 'Book in the manner they were obliged to do, 'which shewed their Consent; but declaring 'their unfeigned Assent to every thing con'tained and prescribed therein would imply, 'that they were so fully convinced in their 'judgments, as to think that it was so perfect, 'that nothing therein could be amended, 'which for their part they thought there might. 'That there were many expressions in the 'Rubrick, which they were not bound to read; 'yet by this Assent they declared their ap'probation thereof.' But after many tedious discourses of this tyrannical imposition, they grew by degrees ashamed of it; and were persuaded to think, that Assent and Consent had so near the same signification, that they could hardly consent to do what they did not assent to: so that the chiefest amongst them, to avoid a very little inconvenience, subscribed the same.

"But there was shortly after another Clause added, that gave them trouble indeed. When the Bill had passed the lords house, it was sent of course to the commons; where though all the factions in religion had too many friends, for the most contrary and opposite one to another always were united and reconciled against the Church, yet they who were zealous for the government, and who hated all the other factions at least enough, were very much superior in number and in reputation. And the Bill was no sooner read there, than every man according to his passion thought of adding somewhat to it, that might make it more grievous to somebody whom he did not love;

which made the discourses tedious and vehement, and full of animosity. And at last they agreed upon a Clause, which contained another Subscription and Declaration which every man was to make before he could be admitted into any Benefice or Ecclesiastical promotion, or to be a Governor or Fellow in either of the Universities. He must first declare, 'That it 'is not lawful, upon any pretence whatsoever, 'to take Arms against the king; and that he 'doth abhor that traiterous position of taking 'Arms by his authority against his person, or 'against those that are commissioned by him; 'and that he will conform to the Liturgy of the 'Church of England, as it is now by law established." And he doth declare, 'That he 'doth hold there lies no obligation upon him, 'or any other person, from the Oath commonly called The Solemn League and Covenant, to endeavour any change or alteration 'of government, either in Church or State; 'and that the same was in itself an unlawful 'Oath, and imposed upon the subjects of this 'realm, against the known laws and liberties 'of the kingdom;' with some other Clauses, which need not be mentioned because they were afterwards left out. And with this Addition, and some other Alterations, they returned the Bill again to the lords for their approbation.

"The framing and forming this Clause had taken up very much time, and raised no less passion in the house of commons: and now it came among the lords, it was not less troublesome. It added to the displeasure and jealousy against the Bishops, by whom it was thought to be prepared, and commended to their party in the lower house. Many lords, who had taken the Covenant, were not so much concerned that the clergy (for whom only this Act was prepared) should be obliged to make this Declaration; but apprehended more, that when such a Clause should be once passed in one act of parliament, it could not after be disputed, and so would be inserted into all other acts which related to the function of any other offices, and so would in a short time be required of themselves. And therefore they opposed it warmly 'as a thing unnecessary, and which would widen the breach, 'instead of closing up the wounds that had 'been made; which the king had made it his 'business to do, and the parliament had hitherto concurred with his majesty in that endeavour. That many men would believe or 'fear (which in such a case is the same), that 'this Clause might prove a breach of the Act 'of Indemnity, which had not only provided 'against indictments and suits at law and penalties, but against reproaches for what was 'past, which this Clause would be understood 'to give new life to. For what concerned the 'conformity to the Liturgy of the Church as 'it is now established, it is provided for as 'fully in the former subscription in this act, 'and therefore is impertinent in this place. 'That the Covenant contained many good 'things in it, as defending the king's person, 'and maintaining the Protestant religion: and 'therefore to say that there lies no obligation 'from it, would neither be for the service of 'the king or the interest of the Church; especially since it was well known, that it had 'wrought upon the conscience of many to serve 'the king in the late Revolution, from which 'his majesty had received great advantage.' However it was now dead, all men were absolved from taking it, nor could it be imposed or offered to any man without punishment; and they, who had in the ill times been forced to take it, did now inviolably and cheerfully perform all the duties of allegiance and fidelity to his majesty. If it had at any time produced any good, that was an excuse for the irregularity of it: it could do no mischief for the future; and therefore that it was time to bury it in oblivion."—Many men believed, that though they insisted principally on that part which related to the Covenant, They were in truth more afflicted with the first part; in which it was declared, 'that it was not lawful, upon any pretence whatsoever, to take 'Arms against the king; and that he doth 'abhor that traiterous position of taking Arms 'by his authority against his person:' which conclusions had been the principles which supported their rebellion, and by which they had imposed upon the people, and got their concurrence. They durst not oppose this, because the parliament had already by a former Act declared the law to be so in those particulars: yet this went much nearer to them, that by their own particular Declaration (for they looked upon it as that which in a short time must be their own), they should upon the matter confess themselves to have been traitors, which they had not yet been declared to have been; and no man could now justify the calling them so.

"They who were most solicitous that the house should concur with the commons in this Addition, had field room enough to expatiate upon the gross iniquity of the Covenant. They made themselves very merry with the allegation, 'that the king's Safety and the Interest 'of the Church were provided for by the Covenant, when it had been therefore entered 'into, to fight against the king and to destroy 'the church. That there was no one lawful 'or honest clause in the Covenant, that was 'not destroyed or made of no signification by 'the next that succeeded; and if it were 'not, the same obligation was better provided for by some other oaths, which the 'same men had or ought to have taken, 'and which ought to have restrained them 'from taking the Covenant; and therefore it 'may justly be pronounced, that there is no 'obligation upon any man from thence. That 'there was no breach of the Act of Indemnity, 'nor any reproach upon any man for having 'taken it, except what would result from his 'own conscience. But that it was most absolutely necessary for the Safety of the king's 'person, and the peace of the kingdom, that 'they who had taken it should declare, that 'they do not believe themselves to be bound 'by it: otherwise, they may still think, that 'they may fight against the king, and must 'conspire the destruction of the Church. And 'they cannot take too much care, or use too 'much diligence, to discover who are of that 'opinion; that they may be strictly looked 'unto, and restrained from doing that which 'they take themselves obliged to do. That the 'Covenant is not dead, as was alleged, but 'still retains great vigour; was still the idol 'to which the Presbyterians sacrificed: and 'that there must and would always be a ge'neral jealousy of all those who had taken it, 'until they had declared that it did not bind 'them; especially of the Clergy, who had so 'often enlarged in their pulpits, how abso'lutely and indispensably all men were obliged 'to prosecute the end of it, which is to de'stroy the Church, whatever danger it brings 'the King's Person to. And therefore they 'of all men ought to be glad of this opportu'nity, that was offered, to vindicate their loy'alty and obedience; and if they were not 'ready to do so, they were not fit to be trusted 'with the charge and care of the souls of the 'king's subjects."—And in truth there were not any more importunate for the enjoining this Declaration, than many who had taken the Covenant. Many who had never taken it, and had always detested it, and paid soundly for being known to do so, were yet very sorry that it was inserted at this time and in this place; for they foresaw it would make divisions, and keep up the several factions, which would have been much weakened, and in a short time brought to nothing, if the Presbyterians had been separated from the rest, who did perfectly hate and were as perfectly hated by all the rest. But since it was brought upon the stage, and it had been the subject of so much debate, they believed the house of lords could not now refuse to concur with the commons, without undergoing some reproach and scandal of not having an ill opinion enough of the Covenant; of which as they were in no degree guilty, so they thought it to be of mischievous consequence to be suspected to be so. And therefore, after they had expunged some other parts of that Subscription which had been annexed to it, and mended some other expressions in other places, which might rather irritate than compose those humours which already boiled too much, they returned the bill to the commons; which submitted to all that they had done: and so it was presented to the king, who could not well refuse his royal assent, nor did in his own judgment or inclination dislike what was offered to him.—By this Act of Uniformity there was an end put to all the liberty and license, which had been practised in all churches from the time of his majesty's return, and by his Declaration that he had emitted afterwards. The Common Prayer must now be constantly read in all churches, and no other form admitted: and what clergyman soever did not fully conform to whatsoever was contained in that Book, or enjoined by the Act of Uniformity, by or before St. Bartholomew-Day, which was about three months after the Act was published; he was, ipso facto, deprived of his benefice, or any other spiritual promotion of which he stood possessed, and the patron was to present another in his place, as if he were dead: so that it was not in the king's power to give any dispensation to any man, that could preserve him against the penalty in the Act of Uniformity."

The Speaker's Speech to the King at the end of the Session.] The Act of Uniformity, and several other Acts, being now ready for the royal assent, the king came this day to the house of peers, and having sent for the commons, he was addressed by their Speaker as follows:

"May it please your most excellent majesty; The glorious body of the sun doth exhilarate the soul of man with its light, and fructify the earth by its heat. In like manner, we, the knights, citizens, and burgesses of the commons house of parliament, do with all humility and thankfulness acknowledge, these frequent accessions to your royal presence do both comfort our hearts, and influence our actions.—Geographers do tell us, the Land of Egypt is a dry soil, but made fertile by the overflowing of the river Nilus; and, according to the degrees of the flood, the inhabitants do prognosticate the fruitfulness of the ensuing year. If it flows to 12 degrees, it presages a good harvest; if to 13, then more plentiful; but if to 14 degrees, their hopes are raised to an expectation of an abundant increase.—Great Sir; Your return into this nation in the 12th year of your reign resembles the flowing of the river Nilus in the 12th degree; that year was crowned with the enjoyment of your royal person. The last year, being the 13th year of your majesty's reign, we were made happy in your Coronation, and by your sanction of many good and useful laws, both for the Church and State. And now our river Nilus begins to flow 14 degrees, we are, by the mercies of God, in an humble expectation of a great jubilee. Our gracious Queen is now happily landed; who, we do hope, and daily pray, may prove a suitable companion to your royal person, and, ere long, a nursing mother in this nation.—If your majesty but please to cast your eyes upon the table, and behold the great number of Bills that there present themselves before you, like so many sheaves of corn bound up and ready to be housed; and will vouchsafe to see how both my hands are filled with no light presents from your loyal commons; and if your royal majesty, the great Lord of the Harvest, shall vouchsafe to crown this day by your gracious concessions to our desires; the world will then see how great a duty your people cheerfully pay both to your royal person and your government; and likewise how great a zeal your majesty hath, by the faithful advice of the lords spiritual and temporal and commons assembled in parliament, to settle the Church in her ancient glory, and to restore the happy people of this nation to their ancient rights and privileges.—Some foreign writers, that envy the happiness of our government, injuriously asperse this nation with a reproachful saying, 'That the crown of England is only maintained by the Benevolence of the people; which never is granted, but in exchange of some royal prerogative.'—Great Sir; We know, the strongest building must fall, if the coupling pins be pulled out: therefore our care hath been, to prepare such constitutions, that the prerogative of the crown and the propriety of the people may, like squared stones, in a well-built arch, each support the other, and grow the closer and stronger for any weight or force that shall be laid upon them. —We cannot forget the late disputing age, wherein most persons took a liberty, and some men made it their delight, to trample upon the discipline and government of the Church. The hedge being trod down, the foxes and the wolves did enter; the swine and other unclean beasts defiled the temple. At length it was discerned, the Smectymnian Plot did not only bend itself to reform Ceremonies, but sought to erect a popular authority of Elders, and to root out Episcopal Jurisdiction. In order to this work, Church Ornaments were first taken away; then the means whereby distinction, or inequality might be upheld amongst ecclesiastical governors; then the Forms of Common Prayer, which as members of the public body of Christ's Church were enjoined us, were decried as superstitious, and in lieu thereof nothing, or worse than nothing, introduced.—Your majesty having already restored the governors and government of the Church, the patrimony and privileges of our churchmen; we held it now our duty, for the reformation of all Abuses in the Public Worship of God, humbly to present unto your majesty, a Bill for the Uniformity of public Prayers and Administration of Sacraments.—We hope the God of Order and Unity will conform the hearts of all the people in this nation, to serve him in this Order and Uniformity.—Next to the Worship and Service of God, we applied ourselves to the settling our great concern, the Militia. We have already, according to our duties and the laws, declared the sole right of the Militia to be in your majesty: and now, with your permission, we humbly tender your majesty a Bill for the better Regulation and Ordering the Standing Forces of this nation; wherein we have taken care to make all things so certain, that your majesty's lieutenants and their deputies may know what to command, and all the people learn how to obey.—And because our late wounds are yet but green, and possibly, before the body politic be well purged, may incline to break out again, whereby your majesty may be forced to draw your sword before your treasury be supplied with Money; we have consented that your majesty may raise, for the 3 next ensuing years, one month's tax in each year, after the rate of 70,000*l.* per mensem, if necessity shall so require.—In the next place, according to your majesty's commands, we have surveyed the wasted Revenue of the Crown; and, in pursuance of our promises, do humbly propound unto your majesty a fair addition. We considered, that great part of your majesty's Revenue is but for life: and both that, and also part of the rest, depends upon the peace, the trade, and traffic of the nation, and therefore may be much impaired by wars with foreign nations. This put us upon the search of something that might arise within our own walls, and not to be subject to such contingencies. We pitched our thoughts at last upon those places where we enjoy our greatest comforts and securities, our dwelling-houses; and, considering even that security is secured unto us by your majesty's vigilance and care in the government; we have prepared a Bill, whereby we desire it may be enacted, That all houses in this kingdom, which are worth in yearly value above 20s. and not inhabited by almsmen, may pay unto your majesty, your heirs and successors, 2s. yearly for every Chimney Hearth in each house for ever.—When the great Ahitophels of our latter age had by force ravished the venerable laws of this nation (and Absurdo dato, sequuntur mille); then every petty artist in his way, yea, even the very common beggars, had the confidence to offer violence to their chastity. We have therefore been constrained to prepare several Bills for the Regulation of Trade, our Cloathing Trade, our Fishing Trade, our Trade for Stuffs, our Trade for Silks; and, for the better maintenance of intercourse in Trade, to reinforce our former laws for maintaining the Highways, with some additions for decency and pleasure of travellers.—God, in his providence, hath determined that Poor we must have always with us: some are made so by the immediate hand of God; others by their loyalty, duty, and service of your royal person and your blessed father; others by their own wickedness and idleness. We have taken care to relieve the first, to encourage the second, and to reform the last.—Nor hath the case of any private person been unwelcome to us. Those many Private Bills that lie before your majesty do enough confirm this truth, that where we found it just and honourable, we have denied our helping hand to none that prayed it.—And now, Great Sir, after these many months most painful and faithful service of your majesty and our countries, we hope we shall have leave to go home, to visit our relations, to tell our neighbours what great things your majesty hath done for us; what great things (absit invidia verbo) we have done for your majesty; and what great things God hath done for us all; and so pray Almighty God for his mercy to this nation, in the continuance of your majesty's long and happy reign over us."

The King's Speech at the end of the Session.]

The King having given his royal assent to 31 Public, and 39 Private Bills, made this gracious Speech following:

"My Lords, and you Gentlemen of the House of Commons; I think there have been very few sessions of parliament in which there have been so many Bills as I have passed this day. I am confident, never so many Private Bills; which I hope you will not draw into example. It is true, these late ill times have driven men into great straits, and may have obliged them to make conveyances colourably, to avoid inconveniences, and yet not afterwards to be avoided. And men have gotten estates by new and greater frauds than have been heretofore practised; and therefore, in this conjuncture, extraordinary remedies may be necessary, which hath induced me to comply with your advice, in passing these bills. But I pray let this be very rarely done hereafter. The good old rules of the law are the best security. And let not men have too much cause to fear that the settlements they make of their estates shall be too easily unsettled when they are dead, by the power of parliaments.—My Lords and Gentlemen; You have so much obliged me, not only in the matter of those Bills which concern my Revenue, but in the manner of passing them with so great affection and kindness to me, that I know not how to thank you enough. I do assure you, and I pray assure your friends in the country, that I will apply all you have given me to the utmost improvement of the peace and happiness of the kingdom, and will, with the best advice and good husbandry, I can, bring my expences within a narrower compass.—Now I am speaking to you of my own good husbandry, I must tell you, that will not be enough: I cannot but observe to you, that the whole nation seems to me a little corrupted in their excess of living. Sure all men spend much more, in their cloaths, in their diet, in all their expences, than they have used to do. I hope it hath only been the excess of joy, after so long sufferings, that hath transported us to these other excesses. But let us take heed, that the continuance of them doth not indeed corrupt our natures. I do believe I have been faulty that way myself: I promise you, I will reform: and if you will join with me in your several capacities, we shall by our examples do more good, both in city and country, than any new laws would do. I tell you again, I will do my part; and I will tell some of you, if you do not yours. I hope the laws I have passed this day will produce some reformation with reference to the multitude of Beggars and poor people which infest the kingdom. Great severity must be used to those who love idleness, and refuse to work; and great care and charity towards those who are willing to work. I do very heartily recommend the execution of those good laws to your utmost diligence; and I am sure I need not put you in mind so to settle the Militia, that all seditious Insurrections may not only be prevented, to which the minds of too many are inclined, but that the people may be without reasonable apprehension of such insecurity.—You will easily believe, that it is very necessary for the public justice of the kingdom, and even for the preservation of the reverence due to parliaments, that I make this a session. And it will be worthy of your wisdoms, when you come together again, to provide that there be not so great clamour against the multitude of Protections. I will say no more; but renew my hearty thanks to you all, and refer the rest to the Chancellor."

The Lord Chancellor's Speech at the end of the Session.] The King's Speech being ended, the Lord Chancellor Clarendon came from his place, and kneeled to the king, and, having received directions, returned to his place, and made this ensuing Speech:

"My lords; and you, the knights, citizens, and burgesses of the house of commons; It is now little more than a year that the king first called you to attend him here, at the opening of the parliament: then, you may remember, he told you, 'That he thought there were not many of you, who were not particularly known to him; that there were very few of whom he had not heard so much good, that he was (he said) as sure as he could be of any thing that was to come, that you would all concur with him, and that he should concur with you, in all things which might advance the peace, plenty, and prosperity of the nation.' His majesty said, He should be exceedingly deceived else.—It was a princely declaration, and a rare confidence, which could flow from no other fountain but the sincerity and purity of his own conscience, which, admitting no other designs or thoughts into his royal breast, but such as must tend to the unquestionable prosperity and greatness of his people, could not but be assured of your full concurrence and co-operation with him. It was a happy and a blessed omen, which at the instant struck a terror into the hearts of those who promised themselves some advantages from the differences and divisions in your counsels, and hoped from thence to create new troubles and molestations in the kingdom. And, God be thanked! the king hath been so far from being exceedingly deceived, that he doth acknowledge he hath been exceedingly complied with, exceedingly gratified in all he hath desired; and he hopes, he hath not in the least degree disappointed your expectation.

"Mr. Speaker, and you Gentlemen of the House of Commons; You have, like the richest and the noblest soil, a soil manured and enriched by the bountiful hearts of the best subjects in the world, yielded the king two full harvests in one year; and therefore it is but good husbandry to lie fallow for some time. You have not only supplied the crown to a good degree, for discharging many debts and pressures under which it even groaned, and enabled it to struggle with the present straits and necessities; debts not contracted, and necessities not run into, by improvidence and excess; you may, when you please, receive such an accompt, as will clear all such reproaches: but you wisely, very wisely, provided such a constant growing revenue, as may with God's blessing preserve the crown from those scandalous wants and necessities as have heretofore exposed it and the kingdom to those dismal miseries, from which they are but even now buoyed up; for, whatsoever other human causes may be assigned, according to the several fancies and imaginations of men, of our late miserable distractions, they cannot be so reasonably imputed to any one cause, as to the extreme poverty of the crown: the want of power could never have appeared, if it had not been for the want of money.—You have, my lords and gentlemen, worthily provided for the vindication and manifestation of the one, by the bill of the Militia; and for the Supply of the other, by the act for the additional Revenue: and I am confident, both the present and succeeding ages will bless God, and celebrate your memories, for those two Bills, as the foundation of their peace, quiet, and security, how froward and indisposed soever many are at present, who, finding such obstructions laid in their way to mutiny and sedition, use all the artifice they can to persuade the people, that you have not been solicitous enough for their liberty, nor tenacious enough for their profit; and wickedly labour to lessen that reverence towards you, which sure was never more due to any parliament.—It was a very natural and an ingenious animadversion and reflection, which the late incomparable lord viscount of St. Albans made upon that old Fable of the Giants, who were first overthrown in the war against the Gods, when the earth, their mother, in revenge thereof, brought forth Fame: which, he said, is the same when princes and monarchs have suppressed actual and open rebellion, then the malignity of the people, the mother of rebellion, doth bring forth libels, slanders, and taxation of the state; which, he says, is of the same kind with rebellion, but more feminine. And without doubt this seditious daughter of the earth, this spirit of libelling, was never more pregnant than it is now; nor king, nor parliament, nor church, nor state, ever more exposed to those *flagella linguæ*, those strokes of the tongue, from which God Almighty can only preserve the most innocent and most excellent persons; as if repining and murmuring were the peculiar exercise of the nation, to keep it in health; as if England had so much of the merchant, 'Nunquam habendi fructu felix, semper autem quærendi cupiditate miserrima.'—Men are in no degree disposed to imitate or remember the general excellent temper of the time of queen Elizabeth; the blessed condescension and resignation of the people then to the crown, the awful reverence they then had to the government, and to the governors both in church and state. This good and happy spirit was in a time beyond our memory; but they remember, as if it were but yesterday, how few Subsidies parliaments then gave to that queen, how small supplies the crown then had from the people; and wonder that the same measures should not still fill the coffers, and give the same reputation, and make the same noise in Christendom.—But, my Lords and Gentlemen, how bold soever some unquiet spirits are with you, upon this argument, you are much superior to those reproaches. You know well, and you can make others know, without breaking the Act of Indemnity, how the crown hath been since used; how our sovereign lord the king found it at his blessed return to it. You can tell the world, that as soon as he came hither, besides the infinite that he forgave, he gave more, more money to the people, than he hath since received from them; that at least two parts of three, that they have since given him, have issued for the disbanding Armies never raised by him, and for paying of Fleets never sent out by him, and of debts never incurred by him. You will put them in mind of the vast disparity between the former times and these in which we live; and consequently of the disproportion in the expence the crown is now at for the protection and benefit of the subject to what it formerly underwent: how great a difference there is in the present greatness and power of the two crowns, and what they were then possessed of, is evident to all men; and if the greatness and power of the crown of England be not in some proportion improved too, it may be liable to inconveniencies it will not undergo alone. How our neighbours and our rivals, who court one and the same mistress, trade and commerce, with all the world, are advanced in shipping, power, and an immoderate desire to engross the whole traffic of the universe, is notorious enough; and this unruly appetite will not be restrained or disappointed, nor the trade of this nation supported and maintained, with the same fleets and forces which were maintained in the happy times of queen Elizabeth. Not to speak of the naval power of the Turks, who, instead of sculking abroad in poor single ships as they were wont to do, domineer now on the ocean in strong fleets, make naval fights, and have brought some Christians to a better correspondence, and another kind of commerce and traffic with them, than was expected; insomuch as they apprehend no enemy upon the sea, but what they find in the king of England's ships, which hath indeed brought no small damage upon them, with no small charge to the king, but a great reputation to the nation.—My Lords and Gentlemen; You may with a very good conscience assure yourselves, and your friends and neighbours, that the Charge the crown is now at, by sea and land, for the peace and security and wealth and honour of the nation, amounts to no less than 800,000*l.* a year, all which did not cost the Crown before these troubles fourscore thousand pounds the year; and therefore they will never blame you for any Supply you have given, or addition you have made to the Revenue of the crown. And whosoever unskilfully murmurs at the expence of Dunkirk, and the other new acquisitions, which ought to be looked upon as jewels of an immense magnitude in the royal diadem, do not enough remember what we have lost by Dunkirk, and should always do if it were in an enemy's hands; nor duly consider the vast advantages those other dominions are like, by God's blessing, in a short time, to bring to the trade, navigation, wealth, and honour of the king and kingdom. His majesty hath enough expressed his desire to live in a perfect peace and amity with all his neighbours; nor is it an ill ingredient towards the firmness and stability of that peace and amity, which his royal ancestors have held and maintained with them, that he hath some advantages in case of a war, which they were without.—It was a right ground of confidence, such an one as seldom deceives men, that the great law-maker, the wise Solon, had, when he concluded that reverence and obedience would be yielded to his laws, because he had taken the pains to make his citizens know, and understand, that it was more for their profit to obey law and justice, than to contemn and break it. The extravagant times of license, which I hope we have almost out-lived, have so far corrupted the minds, and even the nature of too many, that they do not return with that alacrity they ought to do, into the road and paths of order and government, from which they have so long been led astray; nor, it may be, is there pains enough taken to make them understand the profit, benefit, and ease, which always attends a chearful obedience and submission to laws and government. I am persuaded, a little pains and kindness, and condescension, in the wise towards the weak, half the diligence and dexterity in conversation and example which hath been used to corrupt the people in their loyalty and understanding, will quickly reduce them to their primitive temper; which is, to be the best neighbours, and the best friends, and the best subjects of the world: and I make no question, but the great piety and devotion, the moderation, wisdom, charity, and hospitality, of my lords the Bishops, in their several dioceses, will in a short time recover the poor misled people. And though the frowardness and pride of some of their teachers may not be yet enough subdued, though some of the clergy still repeat their old errors, for which they have been glad to receive pardon, and do in truth discredit all their other doctrine with the absence of any visible repentance for what mischief they have formerly done; yet I hope the laity will soon return into the bosom of their dear mother the Church, and easily discern the fraud and imposture of their seducers; and that all diligence and dexterity will be used, seriously and heartily to reconcile both clergy and laity, by all means which may prove effectual.—You have, my Lords and Gentlemen, likewise patriots. Upon your observation, that the most signal indulgence and condescensions, the temporary suspension of the rigour of former laws, hath not produced that effect which was expected; that the humours and spirits of men are too rough and boisterous for those soft remedies; you have prepared sharper laws and penalties, to contend with those refractory persons, and to break that stubbornness which will not bend to gentler applications; and it is great reason, that they upon whom clemency cannot prevail, should feel that severity they have provoked. You have done your parts like good physicians, made wholesome prescription for the constitution of your patients; well knowing, that the application of these remedies, the execution of these sharp laws, depends upon the wisdom of the most discerning, generous, and merciful prince, who, having had more experience of the nature and humour of mankind, than any prince living, can best distinguish between the tenderness of conscience and the pride of conscience, between the real effects of conscience and the wicked pretences to conscience, who having 'fought with Beasts at Ephesus,' knows how to guard himself and the kingdom from the assaults and violence of a strong, malicious, corrupted understanding and will, and how to secure himself and the kingdom from the feeble traps and nets of deluded fancies and imaginations: In a word, a prince of so excellent a nature and tender a conscience himself, that he hath the highest compassion for all errors of that kind, and will never suffer the weak to undergo the punishment ordained for the wicked, and knows and understands better than any man that excellent rule of Quintilian, 'Est aliquid quod non oportet, etiamsi licet, et aliud est jura spectare, aliud justitiam.'—My Lords and Gentlemen; Machiavel, who, they say, is an author much studied of late in this kingdom, to extol his own excellent judgment and insight in history, in which indeed he was a master, would persuade men to believe that, the true reason why so many unexpected accidents and mischiefs fall out to the destruction of states and empires is, because their governors have not observed the same mischiefs heretofore in story, and from whence they proceeded, and what progress they made; which, he says, if they had done, they might easily have preserved themselves from ruin, and prevented the inconveniencies which have fallen out. I am sure, you are all good historians, and need only to resort to the records of your own memories. Remember how your peace hath been formerly disturbed, by what contrivance and artifices the people have been alarmed with unreasonable and unnatural Fears and Jealousies, and what dismal effects those fears and jealousies have produced. Remember how near monarchy hath been dissolved, and the law subverted, under pretence of reforming and supporting government, law, and justice. And remember how many honest persons were misled by not discerning consequences, who would as soon have renounced their part in

Heaven as have concurred in the first unwarrantable action if they had suspected what did follow. And if we suffer the same enemy to break in upon us at the same avenues, if we suffer our peace to be blown up by the same trains and machinations, we shall be held very ill historians, and worse politicians.—There is an enemy amongst us, of whom I doubt we are not jealous enough, and towards whom we cannot be too vigilant, and, in truth, in comparison of whom we may reasonably under-value all other enemies; that is the Republicans and Commonwealth's Men, who are every day calling in aid of the law, that they may overthrow and abolish the law, which they know to be their irreconcileable enemy. Indeed, my lords and gentlemen, there is a very great party of those men in every faction of religion, who truly have no religion but as the pretence serves to advance that faction. You cannot be too solicitous, too inquisitive after these men, who are restless in their councils, and wonderfully punctual and industrious in their correspondencies, which they maintain abroad as well as at home; and you cannot doubt they have encouragement enough from abroad. Few of our neighbours love us so exceeding well, but that they would be glad to see us entangled in domestic broils. These men are worthy of your care and diligence, in your speedy settling the Militia which the king hath even now so particularly recommended unto you. I shall conclude with only putting you in mind, that there was scarce ever a more dangerous sedition in the Republic of Rome, than in a time of full peace: when the citizens were sullen, when there was no noise but in whispers, when men neglected their trades, and stayed idle in their own houses, as if they cared not which way the world went; from whence alone their neighbours the Etrurians were encouraged to make a war upon them. 'Novum seditionis genus' says Livy, 'silentium otiumque inter cives.' Never any nation under Heaven has less cause of sullenness than we, never more of joy and thanksgiving. We all know that God Almighty loves a chearful giver, and we may as well know that he loves a chearful receiver. Besides all other stupendous blessings conferred upon us, he hath given us the most chearful giver that ever people hath been blest withal; a king that hath with all imaginable chearfulness given us all we have asked of him, all he hath to give; who would not take or retain any thing we give to him, but for our own sakes; that by receiving and retaining it, he may give it to us again in more abundance in abundance of peace and plenty, and honour, and all the comforts which can make a nation happy.—This time hath made a glorious addition to our happiness, which ought proportionably to increase our chearfulness. We wanted only one blessing, the Arrival of our Queen, whom God hath now safely brought to us; a queen of such a rare perfection in body and mind, of such endowments of wisdom, virtue and piety, that we may reasonably promise ourselves from her all the happiness we are capable of, and a succession of princes to govern us till the end of the world: and there cannot be a more transcendent instance of the king's love and passion for his people, than that he hath staid these four days to take his leave of you; and that he might give you this day's work, all these good laws, hath denied himself so long the enjoying the greatest comfort he is assured of in this world.—If there be not the most universal joy in the reception of these blessings, if there be not an universal contentedness, and satisfaction in the hearts of all men, and if that contentedness and satisfaction do not break out, and is not visible, in the looks, and thoughts, and words, and actions of the whole nation, to the inflaming the hearts of the other nations under his majesty's obedience by our example; we are guilty of an ingratitude that is worthy to deprive us of all we enjoy, and to disappoint us of all we pray for. And therefore I do most humbly beseech you, my lords and gentlemen, that, as there is a most noble chearfulness and alacrity visible in you, and hath shed itself over all your countenances, so that you will think it worthy of your pains, to infuse the same good spirit into city and country, that they may all express that joy and delight in the blessings they are possessed of, and chearfully endeavour to improve those blessings by their chearful enjoying them, that God may continue those blessings to us, and the king's comfort may be increased, by the comfort he sees we have in him, and in what he hath done for us; and as all princes may take a pattern from him to govern, and make their subjects happy, so that all subjects may learn from us how to obey, by an eminent and innocent alacrity in their acknowledgment.—I am, by the king's express command, to add one particular, which his majesty meant, but forgot to say himself: you cannot but observe, that his majesty hath not passed the Bill that concerns the earl of Derby; which you cannot imagine proceeds from his majesty's want of care of, and kindness to, that noble family, which hath served him so faithfully, and suffered so much for so doing; but all parties having referred the matter to his majesty, he doubts not but to make a better end for that noble earl, than he would attain if the Bill had passed.—I shall only add the king's commands for the Prorogation of this parliament till the 18th day of Feb. And this parliament is prorogued till the 18th day of Feb. next."

Occurrences during the Recess.] As a short account of what took place during the recess of parliament may not be unacceptable to the reader, we shall present him with the following extract from Mr. Hume. "On the 21st of May was concluded, seemingly with universal consent, the inauspicious marriage with Catherine, a princess of virtue, but who was never able, either by the graces of her person or humour, to make herself agreeable to the king. The report, however, of her natural incapacity to have children, seems to have been groundless; since she was twice declared to be pregnant.—The festivity of these espousals was clouded by the trial and execution of criminals. Berkstead, Cobbet, and Okey, three regicides, had escaped beyond sea; and after wandering some time concealed in Germany, came privately to Delft, having appointed their families to meet them in that place. They were discovered by Downing, the king's resident in Holland, who had formerly served the Protector and Commonwealth in the same station, and who once had even been chaplain to Okey's regiment. He applied for a warrant to arrest them. It had been usual for the States to grant these warrants; though, at the same time, they had ever been careful secretly to advertise the persons, that they might be enabled to make their escape. This precaution was eluded by the vigilance and dispatch of Downing. He quickly seized the criminals, hurried them on board a frigate which lay off the coast, and sent them to England. These three men behaved with more moderation and submission than any of the other regicides, who had suffered. Okey in particular, at the place of execution, prayed for the king, and expressed his intention, had he lived, of submitting peaceably to the established government. He had risen during the wars from being a chandler in London to a high rank in the army; and in all his conduct appeared to be a man of humanity and honour. In consideration of his good character and of his dutiful behaviour, his body was given to his friends to be buried.—The attention of the public was much engaged by the trial of two distinguished criminals, Lambert and Vane. These men, though none of the late king's judges, had been excepted from the general indemnity, and committed to prison. The convention parliament, however, was so favourable to them, as to petition the king, if they should be found guilty, to suspend their execution: but this new parliament, more zealous for monarchy, applied for their trial and condemnation. Not to revive disputes, which were better buried in oblivion, the indictment of Vane did not comprehend any of his actions during the war between the king and parliament: it extended only to his behaviour after the late king's death, as member of the council of state, and secretary of the navy, where fidelity to the trust reposed in him required his opposition to monarchy.—However odious Vane and Lambert were to the presbyterians, that party had no leisure to rejoice at their condemnation. The fatal St. Bartholomew approached; the day, when the clergy were obliged by the Act of Uniformity, either to relinquish their livings, or to sign the articles required of them. A combination had been entered into by the most zealous of the presbyterian ecclesiastics to refuse the subscription; in hopes that the bishops would not venture at once to expel so great a number of the most popular preachers. The catholic party at court, who desired a great rent among the protestants, encouraged them in this obstinacy, and gave them hopes that the king would protect them in their refusal. The king himself, by his irresolute conduct, contributed, either from design or accident, to increase this opinion. Above all, the terms of subscription had been made strict and rigid, on purpose to disgust all the zealous and scrupulous among the presbyterians, and deprive them of their livings. About 2000 of the clergy, in one day, relinquished their cures; and to the astonishment of the court, sacrificed their interest to their religious tenets. Fortified by society in their sufferings, they were resolved to undergo any hardships, rather than openly renounce those principles, which, on other occasions, they were so apt, from interest, to warp or elude. The church enjoyed the pleasure of retaliation; and even pushed, as usual, the vengeance farther than the offence. During the dominion of the parliamentary party, a fifth of each living had been left to the ejected clergyman: but this indulgence, though at first insisted on by the house of peers, was now refused to the presbyterians. However difficult to conciliate peace among theologians, it was hoped by many, that some relaxation in the terms of communion might have kept the presbyterians united to the church, and have cured those ecclesiastical factions, which had been so fatal, and were still so dangerous. Bishoprics were offered to Calamy, Baxter, and Reynolds, leaders among the presbyterians; the last only could be prevailed on to accept. Deaneries and other preferments were refused by many.—The next measure of the king has not had the good fortune to be justified by any party; but is often considered, on what grounds I shall not determine, as one of the greatest mistakes, if not blemishes, of his reign. It is the Sale of Dunkirk to the French. The parsimonious maxims of the parliament, and the liberal, or rather careless disposition of Charles, were ill suited to each other; and notwithstanding the supplies voted him, his treasury was still very empty and very much indebted. He had secretly received the sum of 200,000 crowns from France for the support of Portugal; but the forces sent over to that country, and the fleets maintained in order to defend it, had already cost the king that sum; and together with it, near double the money, which had been payed as the queen's portion. The time fixed for payment of his sister's portion to the duke of Orleans was approaching. Tangiers, a fortress from which great benefit was expected, was become an additional burden to the crown; and Rutherford, who now commanded in Dunkirk, had increased the charge of that garrison to 120,000*l.* a year. These considerations had such influence, not only on the king, but even on Clarendon, that this uncorrupt minister was the most forward to advise accepting a sum of money in lieu of a place which he thought the king, from the narrow state of his revenue, was no longer able to retain. By the treaty with Portugal it was stipulated that Dunkirk should never be yielded to the Spaniards: France was therefore the only purchaser that remained. D'Estrades was invited over by a letter from the chancellor himself in order to conclude the bargain: 900,000*l.* were demanded: 100,000*l.* were offered. The English by degrees lowered their demand: the French raised their offer: and the bargain was concluded at 400,000*l.* The artillery and stores were valued at a fifth of the sum. The importance of this sale was not, at that time, sufficiently known, either abroad or at home. The French monarch himself, so fond of acquisitions, and so good a judge of his own interests, thought that he had made a hard bargain; and this sum, in appearance so small, was the utmost which he would allow his ambassador to offer.—A new incident discovered such a glimpse of the king's character and principles as, at first, the nation was somewhat at a loss how to interpret, but such as subsequent events, by degrees, rendered sufficiently plain and manifest. He issued a Declaration (26th Dec.) on pretence of mitigating the rigours contained in the Act of Uniformity. After expressing his firm resolution to observe the general indemnity, and to trust entirely to the affections of his subjects, not to any military power, for the support of his throne, he mentioned the promises of liberty of conscience, contained in his Declaration of Breda. And he subjoined, that, 'as in the first place he had been zealous to settle the Uniformity of the church of England, in discipline, ceremony, and government, and shall ever constantly maintain it: so as for what concerns the penalties upon those who, living peaceably, do not conform themselves thereunto, through scruple and tenderness of misguided conscience, but modestly and without scandal perform their devotions in their own way, he should make it his special care, so far as in him lay, without invading the freedom of parliament, to incline their wisdom next approaching sessions to concur with him in making some such act for that purpose, as may enable him to exercise, with a more universal satisfaction, that power of dispensing which he conceived to be inherent in him.' Here a most important prerogative was exercised by the king; but under such artful reserves and limitations as might prevent the full discussion of the claim, and obviate a breach between him and his parliament. The foundation of this measure lay much deeper, and was of the utmost consequence.—The king, during his exile, had imbibed strong prejudices in favour of the catholic religion; and according to the most probable accounts, had already been secretly reconciled in form to the church of Rome. The great zeal, expressed by the parliamentary party against all papists, had always, from a spirit of opposition, inclined the court, and all the royalists, to adopt more favourable sentiments towards that sect, which through the whole course of the civil wars, had strenuously supported the rights of the sovereign. The rigour too, which the king, during his abode in Scotland, had experienced from the presbyterians, disposed him to run into the other extreme, and to bear a kindness to the party most opposite in its genius to the severity of those religionists. The solicitations and importunities of the queen-mother, the contagion of the company which he frequented, the view of a more splendid and courtly mode of worship, the hopes of indulgence in pleasure; all these causes operated powerfully on a young prince, whose careless and dissolute temper made him incapable of adhering closely to the principles of his early education. But if the thoughtless humour of Charles rendered him an easy convert to popery, the same disposition ever prevented the theological tenets of that sect from taking any fast hold of him. During his vigorous state of health, while his blood was warm and his spirits high; a contempt and disregard to all religion held possession of his mind; and he might more properly be denominated a deist than a catholic. But in those revolutions of temper, when the love of raillery gave place to reflection, and his penetrating, but negligent, understanding was clouded with fears and apprehensions, he had starts of more sincere conviction; and a sect, which always possessed his inclination, was then master of his judgment and opinion.—But though the king thus fluctuated, during his whole reign, between irreligion, which he more openly professed, and popery, to which he retained a secret propensity, his brother, the duke of York, had zealously adopted all the principles of that theological party. His eager temper and narrow understanding made him a thorough convert, without any reserve from interest, or doubts from reasoning and inquiry. By his application to business he had acquired a great ascendant over the king, who, though possessed of more discernment, was glad to throw the burden of affairs on the duke, of whom he entertained little jealousy. On pretence of easing the protestant dissenters, they agreed upon a plan for introducing a general toleration, and giving the catholics the free exercise of their religion; at least, the exercise of it in private houses. The two brothers saw with pleasure so numerous and popular a body of the clergy refuse conformity; and it was hoped that, under shelter of their name, the small and hated sect of the catholics might meet with favour and protection."

SECOND SESSION OF THE SECOND PARLIAMENT.

The King's Speech on opening the Session.] Feb. 18, 1662-3. This day parliament met after a recess of nine months; upon which occasion his majesty made the following Speech to both houses:

"My Lords and Gentlemen; I am very glad to meet you here again; having thought the time long since we parted, and often wished you had been together, to help me in some occasions which have fallen out: I need not repeat them unto you; you have all had the noise of them in your several countries, and (God be thanked!) they were but noise, without any worse effects.—To cure the distempers and compose the differing minds that are yet among us, I set forth my Declaration* of the 26th of Dec. in which you may see I am willing to set bounds to the hopes of some, and to the fears of others; of which when you shall have examined well the grounds, I doubt not but I shall have your concurrence therein: The truth is, I am in my nature an enemy to all severity for Religion and Conscience, how mistaken soever it be, when it extends to capital and sanguinary punishments, which I am told were begun in Popish times: Therefore, when I say this, I hope I shall not need to warn any here not to infer from thence, that I mean to favour Popery. I must confess to you there are many of that profession, who having served my father and myself very well, may fairly hope for some part in that indulgence I would willingly afford to others, who dissent from us. But let me explain myself, lest some mistake me herein, as I hear they did in my Declaration: I am far from meaning by this, a toleration or qualifying them thereby to hold any offices or places of trust in the government; nay, further, I desire some laws may be made, to hinder the growth and progress of their doctrine.—I hope you have all so good an opinion of my zeal for the Protestant Religion, as I need not tell you, I will not yield to any therein, not to the bishops themselves, nor in my liking the uniformity of it as it is now established; which, being the Standard of our Religion, must be kept pure and uncorrupted, free from all other mixtures: And yet, if the Dissenters will demean themselves peaceably and modestly under the government, I could heartily wish I had such a power of indulgence, to use upon occasions, as might not needlessly force them out of the kingdom, or, staying here, give them cause to conspire against the peace of it.—My Lords and Gentlemen, It would look like flattery in me, to tell you to what degree I am confident of your wisdom and affection in all things that relate to the greatness and prosperity of the kingdom: If you consider well what is best for us all, I dare say, we shall not disagree. I have no more to say to you at present, but once again to bid you heartily welcome."*

Address of the Commons to the King, relative to the Indulgence to Dissenters from the Act of Uniformity.] The commons being withdrawn, appointed the 25th for taking into consideration, both his majesty's Speech and the Declaration mentioned therein: at which time they unanimously resolved, That the Thanks of the house should be returned to the king for all that was contained in the Declaration, except what related to the Indulgence; with regard to which, they appointed a Committee (who chose sir Heneage Finch † the king's solicitor, for their chairman) to draw up an Address, which, after several amendments and additions, was presented to his majesty, by the Speaker on the 27th: It was as follows:

"May it please your most excellent majesty; We your majesty's most dutiful and loyal subjects, the knights, citizens, and burgesses of the house of commons, in parliament assembled, having, with all fidelity and obedience, considered of the several matters comprised in your majesty's late gracious Declaration of the 26th of Dec. last; and your most gracious Speech at the beginning of this present session; do, in the first place, for ourselves, and in the names of all the commons of England,

* The said Declaration consisted of the following particulars, viz. That it had been alledged against him, 1. That he intended nothing less than the observation of the Act of Indemnity. 2. That upon the pretence of Plots, he intended to introduce a Military Way of government. 3. That, notwithstanding his promise from Breda, and Declaration for Liberty of Conscience, he had fetter'd the scrupulous by the Act of Uniformity; and 4. That he was indulgent to Papists to such a degree, as might endanger the Protestant Religion. To all these he gave particular and direct answers; but as to the Act of Uniformity, he declared his own firm adherence to it; only, for the sake of others he was ready and willing to dispense with some matters in it. In the conclusion he promised, 1. To punish by severe Laws that Licentiousness and Impiety, which since the dissolution of the government, had overspread the nation. 2. As well by Sumptuary Laws, as his own example of frugality, to restrain the Excess in men's expences, which was grown so general and exorbitant, beyond all bounds, either of their qualities or fortunes. 3. So to retrench all his own ordinary and extraordinary charges, as to bring them within the compass of his settled Revenue, that thereby his subjects might have little cause to fear his frequent pressing them for new assistances. And lastly, so to improve the good consequences of these three particulars to the advancement of Trade, that all his subjects finding the advantage of them in that prime foundation of plenty, they might all with minds happily compos'd by his indulgence, apply themselves comfortably to their several vocations, in such a manner as the private interest of every one might encourage him to contribute to the general prosperity. Echard, p. 805.

* About this time a very remarkable piece was published under the whimsical title of 'A Speech visibly spoken in the presence of 'the Lords and Commons assembled in parliament, by a Ghost in a white sheet of paper, &c.' It will be found in the Appendix No. IV.

† Afterwards attorney-general, lord-chancellor, and created earl of Nottingham.

tender to your sacred majesty the tribute of our most hearty thanks, for that infinite grace and goodness, wherewith your majesty hath been pleased to publish your royal intentions of adhering to your Act of Indemnity and Oblivion, by a constant and religious observance of it: and our hearts are further inlarged in these returns of thanksgiving, when we consider your majesty's most princely and heroick professions, of relying upon the affections of your people, and abhorring all sort of military and arbitrary rule. But, above all, we can never enough remember, to the honour of your majesty's piety, and our own unspeakable comfort, those solemn and most endearing invitations of us your majesty's subjects, to prepare laws, to be presented to your majesty, against the Growth and Increase of Popery; and, withal, to provide more laws against Licentiousness and Impiety; at the same time declaring your own resolutions, for maintaining the Act of Uniformity. And it becomes us always to acknowledge and admire your majesty's wisdom, in this your Declaration; whereby your majesty is pleased to resolve, not only by Sumptuary Laws, but by your own royal example of frugality, to restrain that excess in men's expences, which is grown so general, and so exorbitant; and to direct our endeavours to find out fit and proper laws for advancement of Trade and Commerce.—After all this, we most humbly beseech your majesty to believe, that it is with extreme unwillingness and reluctancy of heart, that we are brought to differ from any thing, which your majesty hath thought fit to propose: and, though we do no way doubt, but that the unreasonable distempers of men's spirits, and the many mutinies and conspiracies, which were carried on during the late intervals of parliament, did reasonably incline your majesty to endeavour by your Declaration, to give some allay to those ill humours, till the parliament assembled; and the hopes of an Indulgence, if the parliament should consent to it; especially seeing the pretenders to this Indulgence did seem to make some title to it, by virtue of your majesty's Declaration from Breda; nevertheless, we your majesty's most dutiful and loyal subjects, who are now returned to serve in parliament from those several parts and places of your kingdom, for which we were chosen, do humbly offer it to your majesty's great wisdom; that it is in no sort adviseable, that there be any Indulgence to such persons, who presume to dissent from the Act of Uniformity, and Religion established; for these reasons:—We have considered the nature of your majesty's Declaration from Breda; and are humbly of opinion, That your majesty ought not to be pressed with it any further; because, it is not a promise in itself, but only a gracious Declaration of your majesty's intentions, to do what in you lay, and what a parliament should advise your majesty to do: and no such advice was ever given, or thought fit to be offered: nor could it be otherwise understood; because there were laws of Uniformity then in being, which could not be dispensed with, but by act of parliament.—They, who do pretend a right to that supposed promise, put their right into the hands of their representatives, whom they chose to serve for them in this parliament: who have passed, and your majesty consented to the Act of Uniformity.—If any shall presume to say, That a right to the benefit of this Declaration doth still remain, after this Act passed; it tends to dissolve the very bonds of government; and to suppose a disability in your majesty, and your houses of parliament, to make a law contrary to any part of your majesty's Declaration, though both houses should advise your majesty to it.—We have also considered the nature of the Indulgence proposed, with reference to those consequences which must necessarily attend it. It will establish schism by a law; and make the whole government of the Church precarious, and the censures of it of no moment or consideration at all. It will no way become the gravity or wisdom of a parliament, to pass a law at one session for Uniformity; and, at the next session (the reasons for Uniformity continuing still the same), to pass another law, to frustrate or weaken the execution of it.—It will expose your majesty to the restless importunity of every sect or opinion; and of every single person also, that shall presume to dissent from the Church of England. It will be a cause of increasing sects and sectaries: whose numbers will weaken the true Protestant profession so far, that it will, at least, become difficult for it to defend itself against them: and, which is yet further considerable, those numbers, which, by being troublesome to the government, find they can arrive to an Indulgence, will, as their numbers increase, be yet more troublesome, that so, at length, they may arrive to a general Toleration, which your majesty hath declared against; and, in time, some prevalent sect will, at last, contend for an establishment; which, for aught can be foreseen, may end in Popery. It is a thing altogether without precedent; and will take away all means of convicting recusants, and be inconsistent with the methods and proceedings of the laws of England.—Lastly, it is humbly conceived, that the Indulgence proposed will be so far from tending to the peace of the kingdom, that it is likely rather to occasion great disturbance: and, on the contrary, that the asserting of the laws, and the religion established, according to the Act of Uniformity, is the most probable means to produce a settled peace and obedience through the kingdom; because the variety of professions in religion, when openly indulged, both directly distinguish men into parties, and withal, gives them opportunity to count their numbers; which considering the animosities that, out of a religious pride, will be kept on foot by the several factions, doth tend, directly and inevitably, to open disturbance: nor can your majesty have any security, that the doctrine or worship of the several factions, which are all governed by a several rule, shall be consistent with the peace of your kingdom.—And, if any person shall presume to disturb the peace of the kingdom, we do, in all humility, declare, That we will for ever, and upon all occasions, be ready, with our uttermost endeavours and assistance, to adhere to, and serve your majesty, according to our bounden duty and allegiance."

The King's Answer.] To this Address, his majesty gave this gracious Answer: "That he gave them hearty thanks for their many thanks; that never any king was so happy in a house of commons, as he in this; that the Paper and Reasons were long, and therefore he would take time to consider of them, and send them a Message; that they could never differ but in judgment, and that must be when he did not rightly express himself, or they did not rightly understand him; but their interest was so far linked together, that they could never disagree." According to this promise, on the 16th of March, he sent this Message to the house of commons: "That he was unwilling to enlarge upon the Address lately made to him by his house of commons, or to reply to the Reasons, though he found what he said not much understood; but he renewed his hearty thanks to them, for their expressions of so great duty and affection, and for their free declaration, That if any person shall presume to disturb the peace of the kingdom, they will for ever, and upon all occasions, be ready with their utmost endeavours and assistance, to adhere to, and serve his majesty; and did very heartily desire them so to enable him, and to put the kingdom into such a posture of defence, as that if any disturbance or seditious designs arose, they might be easily suppressed."—To all which the commons returned their particular thanks and promises.

Petition of both Houses to the King, against Jesuits and Priests.] March 31. The house having thus manifested their zeal against Dissenters, proceeded next, in conjunction with the lords, to draw up an humble Representation to the king, concerning Romish Priests and Jesuits; which was as follows:

"The humble Representation and Petition of the Lords and Commons sheweth;

"That notwithstanding your majesty's unquestionable affection and zeal for the true Protestant Religion, manifested in your constant profession and practice, against all temptations whatsoever: yet, by the great resort of Jesuits and Romish Priests into this kingdom, your good subjects are generally much affected with jealousy and apprehension, That the Popish Religion may much increase in this kingdom, which your majesty hath most piously desired may be prevented; and so the peace both in church and state may be insensibly disturbed, to the great danger of both. Your two houses of parliament are therefore humble suitors to your majesty, to issue out your Proclamation to command all Jesuits, and all English, Irish, and Scottish Popish Priests, and all such other Priests as have taken orders from the see of Rome, or by authority thereof, (except such Foreign Jesuits or Priests, as by contract of marriage are to attend the persons of either of the Queens, or by the law of nations to attend Foreign ambassadors) to depart this kingdom by a day, under pain of having the penalties of the law inflicted upon them."

The King's Answer.] This Petition having been read to his majesty, he immediately made the following Speech:

"My Lords, and Gentlemen; You do not expect that I should give you an Answer, presently to your Petition, yet I tell you, that I will speedily send you an Answer, which I am confident will be to your satisfaction. It may be the general jealousy of the nation hath made this address necessary; and indeed I believe nothing hath more contributed to that jealousy than my own confidence, That it was impossible there should be any such jealousy, and the effects of that confidence; but I shall give you satisfaction, and then I am sure you will easily satisfy and compose the minds of the nation. I confess, my lords and gentlemen, I have heard of one jealousy, which I will never forgive the authors of, That I had a jealousy of your affections; that I was offended with the parliament to that degree that I intended to dissolve it. They say men are naturally most angry with those reports which reflect upon their understanding, which make them thought weak men: truly, I should appear a very weak man, if I should have any such passion, any such purpose. No, my lords and gentlemen, I will not part with you upon those terms. Never king was so much beholden to a parliament as I am to you, and if my kindness to you and my confidence in you be not proportionable, I am behind-hand with you; which, God-willing, I will not be.—Mr. Speaker, and you Gentlemen of the House of Commons, I am willing to take this occasion to give you my particular thanks for your great kindness in taking hold upon an easy intimation, rather than an invitation from me, to enter upon the consideration of my Revenue: It was kindly done, and I shall never forget it. I have given order, that you may be fully informed of the true State of it, and then I know you will do that which is good for me and you: and I pray pursue your good resolution, in putting the kingdom into such a posture, that we may prevent, at least not fear, any desperate insurrection."

The King's Second Answer.] The king, according to his promise, the very next day sent an Answer to the Petition in writing to the house of lords, which, in a conference between both houses, was likewise delivered to the commons, and was as follows:

"His majesty having seriously considered and weighed the humble Representation and Petition of his lords and commons assembled in parliament, and the great affection and duty with which the same was presented to him; and after having made some reflections on himself and his own actions, is not a little troubled, that his lenity and condescensions towards many of the Popish persuasion (which were but natural effects of his generosity and good-nature, after having lived so many years in the dominions of Roman-Catholic princes; and out of a just memory of what many of them had done and suffered in the service of his royal father of blessed memory, and of some eminent services performed by others of them, towards his majesty himself in the time of his greatest affliction) have been made so ill use of, and so ill deserved, that the resort of Jesuits and Priests into this kingdom hath been thereby increased; with which his majesty is, and hath long been highly offended. And therefore his majesty readily concurs with the advice of his two houses of parliament, and hath given order for the preparing and issuing out such a Proclamation as is desired, with the same Clause referring to the Treaty of Marriage, as was in the Proclamation; which, upon the like occasion, was issued out upon the advice of both houses of parliament in the year 1640. And his majesty will take further care, that the same shall be effectual, at least to a greater degree than any Proclamation of this kind hath ever been. And his majesty further declares and assures both his houses of parliament, and all his loving subjects of all his dominions, that as his affection and zeal for the Protestant Religion and the Church of England hath not been concealed, or untaken notice of in the world; so he is not, nor ever will be so solicitous for the settling his own Revenue, or providing any other expedients for the peace and tranquillity of the kingdom, as for the advancement and improvement of the Religion established, and for the using and applying all proper and effectual Remedies to hinder the growth of Popery; both which he doth in truth look upon as the best expedient to establish the peace and prosperity of all his kingdoms."

State of the King's Revenue.] The commons proceeded next to take the State of the King's Revenue into consideration; and found upon enquiry, that the whole did not amount to quite 1,100,000*l.* That is to say, according to the following Estimate, which was made the preceding year, and is called, as high and true an Estimate as can be made of the King's Revenues:*

RECEIPTS.	£.
Customs,	450,000
Excise,	400,000
Crown Lands	100,000
Post-Office in Farm	21,500
Wine Licences	15,000
First Fruits and Tenths	18,811
Coals	8,000
Dean Forest	1,000
Alienation	3,000
Hanaper	4,000
Post-Fines	1,000
Green-Wax	1,000
Issues of Jurors	1,000
Aulnage	1,000
Butlerage	500
Faculties	300
Ballast-Office	600
Coinage and Preemption	12,000
	1,038,711
Hearth-Money	162,882
	1,201,593

ISSUES.	£.
Navy with Stores and Ordnance	600,000
Guards	120,000
Home Garrisons	80,000
Dunkirk	113,000
Tangier, Jamaica, and East Indies	100,000
Houshold and Stables	150,000
Treasurer of the Chamber	30,000
Band of Pensioners	6,000
Robes	6,000
Works	10,000
Embassadors and their Intelligence	30,000
Privy-Purse	10,000
Duke of York	40,000
Presents to Embassadors	10,000
Judges and Justices	12,000
Secretaries of State and Intelligence	4,000
Angel-Gold (for the King's Evil)	5,000
Pensions and Fees for Servants	20,000
Queen Mother	35,000
Queen Consort	40,000
Queen of Bohemia	12,000
Prince Rupert	4,000
	1,437,000

The King's Speech to the Commons at the Banquetting House, concerning his Revenue.] June 12. But while they were thus employed, his majesty, by a Message, demanded their attendance at Whitehall, where he received them with the following Speech:

"Mr. Speaker, and you Gentlemen of the House of Commons; I have sent for you this day to communicate with you, as good friends ought to do, when they discover the least jealousy growing, which may lessen their confidence in each other. It is a freedom very necessary to be used between me and you: and you may all remember, that when there was lately a little jealousy amongst you, upon somewhat I had said or done, I made all the haste I could to give you satisfaction; for which you all returned me your hearty thanks, and were, I think, satisfied. Gentlemen, it is in no man's power, no, not in your own power, to make me suspect, or in the least degree imagine it possible, that your af-

* This Estimate is taken from the noble collection of MSS. in 22 volumes in folio, relating to the Revenue and Exchequer, compiled by Charles Montagu, lord Hallifax, first lord of the treasury, and chancellor of the Exchequer, in the reign of William III. See Ralph, vol. i. p. 88.

fection or kindness is lessened or diminished towards me. I know very well, that the people did never in any age use that vigilance and circumspection in the election of persons of known and try'd affections to the crown, of your good principles and unquestionable inclinations to the peace of the Church and the State, for their representatives in parliament as they did when they chose you. You are the very same men, who at your first coming together, gave such signal testimonies of your affection and friendship to my person, of your zeal for the honour and dignity of the crown, and liberal support of the government, and of your horror and detestation of those men, whose principles you discerned keep them awake to take all occasions to disturb the peace of the kingdom, and to embroil us in a new civil war; which is as much their endeavour now as ever, and it may be not enough abhorred by others, whose principles and ends are very different from them. You are the same men, who, at your first meeting, by a wonderful and chearful harmony and concurrence in whatsoever I could wish, gave me reputation abroad and security at home, made our neighbours solicitous for our friendship, and set a just value upon it. And, trust me, such a reputation is of such a vast importance, as made my evil subjects even despair of bringing their wicked purposes to pass, And is it possible that the same persons can continue the same together, without the same affection for me? I am sure it is impossible.—And yet, I must tell you, the reputation I had from your concurrence and tenderness towards me, is not at all improved since the beginning of this session; indeed it is much lessened. And I am sure I never stood in more need of that reputation than at present, to carry me through the many difficulties, in which the public is at least concerned, as much as myself. Let me and you think never so well of ourselves, if all the world knows or believes that we are poor, that we are in extremity of want, if our friends think we can do them no good, or our enemies believe we can do them no harm, our condition is far from being prosperous. You cannot take it amiss, (you shall use as much freedom with me) that I tell you there hath not appeared that warmth in you of late in the consideration of my Revenue, as I expected, as well from some of your Messages, as my own confidence in your care and kindness. It hath been said to myself, that it is usual for the parliament to give the crown extraordinary Supplies upon emergent occasions, but not to improve the constant Revenue of the crown. I wish, and so do you, that nothing had lately been done in and by parliaments but what is usual: but if ill parliaments contrive the ruin and disinherison of the crown, God forbid but good parliaments should repair it, how unusual soever it is. If you yourselves had not in an extraordinary manner improved my Revenue, the government could not have been supported; and if it be not yet improved to the proportion you have designed, I cannot doubt but you will proceed in it with your old alacrity. I am very well contented that you proceed in your inspection; I know it will be to my advantage, and that you will neither find my receipts so great, nor my expences so exorbitant, as you imagine; and for an evidence of the last, I will give you an Account of the Issues of the twelve hundred thousand pounds you so liberally gave me: one penny whereof was not disposed but upon full deliberation with myself, and by my own order, and I think you will all say for the public service. But, gentlemen, this inquisition cannot be finished in the short time we can now conveniently stay together: and yet, if you do not provide before we part, for the better paying and collecting what you have already given me, you can hardly presume what it will amount to: and if you do not support what you have already given me by some addition, you will quickly see lawful ways found to lessen the Revenue more than you imagine: and therefore I cannot but expect your wisdoms will seasonably and speedily provide a remedy for that growing mischief. Believe me, gentlemen, the most disaffected subjects in England are not more unwilling to pay any tax or imposition you lay upon them, than I am to receive it; God knows, I do not long more for any blessing in this world, than that I may live to call a parliament, and not ask or receive any money from them; I will do all I can to see that happy day. I know the vast burdens the kingdom hath borne these last 20 years and more; that it is exceedingly impoverished: but, alas! what will that which is left do them good, if the government cannot be supported; if I am not able to defray the Charge that is necessary for their peace and security? I must deal plainly with you, (and I do but discharge my conscience in that plainness) if you do not, besides the improving my Revenue in the manner I have recommended to you, give me some present Supply of Money to enable me to struggle with those difficulties I am pressed with, I shall have a very melancholic summer, and shall much apprehend the public quiet.—You have heard, I presume, of the late design in Ireland for the Surprize of the Castle of Dublin, which was spread all over that kingdom, and many parliament-men were engaged in it. There is an absolute necessity that I forthwith send over a sum of money thither, for the payment of the Army, and putting the Garrisons there in good order. You will not doubt but that those seditious persons there, had a correspondence with their friends here: and I pray let us not be too careless of them. I assure you, I have so great occasion for Money here, which my Revenue cannot supply me with, that I every day omit the doing somewhat that is very necessary for the public benefit. These sure are just motives to persuade you to give me a Supply, as ever moved a house of commons. And therefore I conjure you to go chearfully about it, and let me not be disappointed in my confidence of your affections: and I pray remember the season of the year, and how necessary it is that we make a recess at or about midsummer. I have enlarged much more to you upon this occasion than I have used to do; and you may perceive it hath not been very easy to me: but I was willing that you should understand from myself what I desire and expect from you: and the rather, because I hear some men have confidently undertaken to know my mind, who have had no authority from me, and to drive on designs very contrary to my desires. I do pray heartily that the effect of this day's conversation may be the renewing of our confidence in each other, and raising our joint reputation, which will be our strongest security, with God's blessing, the kingdom can have for its peace, plenty, and full prosperity: and upon my word, you shall have great comfort in what you shall do for me, upon this very earnest and hearty recommendation."

Four Subsidies voted.] This Speech did not fail of its desired effect, for, shortly after, the house voted his majesty four Subsidies.

Sir Rd. Temple accused of sending a Message to the King by the Earl of Bristol, undertaking for the Compliance of the House, in case a Supply should be demanded.] June 13. Upon information given to the commons, by Mr. Coventry, That his maj. had commanded him to impart to the house that a Message was delivered to his maj. by a person of quality, from sir Rd. Temple, to the effect following; viz. 'That 'sir Richard was sorry his majesty was offended 'with him that he could not go along with 'them that had undertaken his business in the 'house of commons: but, if his majesty would 'take his advice, and intrust him and his 'friends, he would undertake his business 'should be effected, and Revenue settled, better 'than he could desire; if the courtiers did not 'hinder it:' It was ordered, That a committee be appointed to examine the said matter, and report it to the house.

June 20. It was resolved, That the king be humbly desired, that he would be graciously pleased to name the person that did deliver the Message to his majesty from sir Rd. Temple: and that his majesty's two principal secretaries of state, Mr. Treasurer, and sir William Compton, do attend his majesty, and acquaint him with the desires of this house.

June 26. Mr. Secretary Morrice acquainted the house, That he had received command from his majesty to declare to the house, That the earl of Bristol was the person that did deliver the Message from sir Rd. Temple to his majesty. Upon which it was resolved, That a copy of the first Message sent by his majesty, against sir Rd. Temple, be sent to the earl of Bristol: and he be made acquainted, That the king hath sent word to this house, That he brought the Message to him, from sir Richard; and his Answer desired, Whether sir Richard did desire him so to do: and that Mr. Vaughan and Mr. Garraway do attend the earl with this Message.

June 27. Mr. Vaughan reported, "That he and Mr. Garraway had attended the earl of Bristol; and had acquainted him with the order of this house; and with the transcript of so much of his majesty's Message, as did relate to the Message which he did receive from sir Rd. Temple: and that his lordship did render his most humble and hearty thanks to this house, That, in such an important matter, and so much concerning his honour, they did signify their desires to him in so obliging a manner: but, in regard the thing was of so great consequence, partly relating to his majesty, and also concerning his own honour, and the reputation of a member of this house, he could not intrust any other person to deliver his Answer, for fear of mistakes which might thereby happen; and because he might probably if present clear any matter which might further accrue: and, therefore, that he might give full satisfaction to so illustrious a representative of his country, he desired a day might be prefixed, when he might be admitted to give an account to the house, in person, concerning this matter: and that he would make his address to the lords, that he might be permitted so to do." Upon this, it was resolved, That Wednesday next be appointed for the earl of Bristol personally to give in his Answer to the house.

The Earl of Bristol's Speech, before the Commons, thereon.] July 1. The house having received information, that the earl of Bristol was at the door, and did pray admittance into the house, to give an account, in person, of the matter concerning sir Rd. Temple, his lordship was, by direction of the house, placed in a chair, set for him on purpose, on the left side of the house, within the bar: and Mr. Speaker did open unto him his majesty's Message, and the votes and proceedings of the house thereupon, concerning sir Richard Temple. This being done,

The Earl of *Bristol* rose and addressed the house as follows:—"Mr. Speaker; Were I to be wrought upon by the arts and menaces of my enemies, or by the alarms of my friends in my behalf, contrary to the firmness and assurance which a clean heart and a good conscience does always uphold in a man of honour, I should have appeared in this place with such fear and trembling, as could not chuse but disorder any man's reason and elocution: the niceness of the subject upon which I am brought hither, were enough to discompose one; but over and above that, I am not ignorant what personal prejudices I am under, and how industriously they have been improved among you. But when I look round this illustrious assembly, and see three parts of it composed of men who wear, as I do, a sword by their sides, and who have drawn it so often for the king's service, gentlemen of birth, integrity, fortune, all apprehensions vanish from a man, who hath served and suffered for the king as I have done. Mr. Speaker, I know the time of this house, upon whose prudent deliberations the happiness of the king and kingdom depends, is too precious to have any part of it spent in vindication of me: but, since not only the reputation and innocence of one of your members depends upon what I shall say, but even his majesty's honour may in some sort be concerned in the right apprehension of it, I hope it will be thought no presumption in me to beg of you, as I do, in all humility, one quarter of an hour's patience and attention.—Mr. Speaker, I am here exposed as the Bearer of a Message to his majesty from sir Richard Temple, which he hath thought worthy to be complained of to this house, and which sir Rd. Temple affirms he never sent. Lay your hands upon your hearts, gentlemen, and say truly, does not your innate candour pity my condition, brought into a streight, in all appearance so inextricable? For, on the one side, if I avow to have carried from sir Rd. Temple the Message, which his maj. has been pleased to make so high and so unusual an expression of his being offended at, and which sir Rd. Temple denies to have sent; how can men of honour forgive me so ungentlemanly a proceeding towards a person who hath trusted me, as a friend, to do him (as he thought) a good office with his majesty? On the other side, Mr. Speaker, should I disavow the having delivered the Message from sir Rd. Temple, which his majesty hath thought fit to affirm, that he received from him and by me, what subject can be strong enough not to sink for ever under the weight of such a contradiction to his sovereign? I ask you again, gentlemen, does not the condition you see me brought into, by the arts of my enemies, move you at the same time to pity and indignation? Mr. Speaker, when David was put to his choice of one of the three calamities, he made election of the plague. And why? that he might fall into the hands of God, and not of men. In like manner, Mr. Speaker, if one of the two extremes, with which I am threatened, be, as it appears, unavoidable, let me fall into the hands of God's vice-gerent the king: the world will never pardon me an unworthy action; his goodness, I am sure, would in time pardon a generous fault. But when you have heard me out, gentlemen, I am confident you will find, that I shall need neither the world's pardon nor the king's, but only yours. In the first place, Mr. Speaker, I am bound to clear sir Richard Temple, which I here do upon my honour, that he never sent by me a Message to the king, that had in it the least tincture of an undertaking of his; which I conceive could be the only part that could give offence to his majesty, or be a ground for the Complaint made against him.—In the next place, if the king, who, the law says, can do no wrong, hath thought fit to affirm, that I brought him that undertaking Message from sir Rd. Temple, it must needs be true, and I do with all submission avow whatever his majesty is pleased to affirm of me; but, having discharged that duty towards my sovereign, I hope I may be allowed to lay the fault home upon myself, and to tell you, that my tongue, I know not by what distemper, delivered that which, I protest to God, was never in my thoughts; I was so far from thinking to deliver such a Message from sir Rd. Temple, that I did not think myself charged with any thing by way Message. It is true, Mr. Speaker, that, being full of indignation at ill offices done him, I made a warm address to his majesty in sir Rd. Temple's behalf, wherein I expressed his grief, that his majesty should be offended with him, and having joined thereunto some reasonings of his to justify his conduct, in relation to his majesty's service, very agreeable to my own sentiments, I pursued his expressions with such of my own, as (all circumstances considered) the most unattentive person, and the most biassed with passion against sir Richard Temple, might have easily understood it to be no undertaking of his, but only a warm discourse, and confident undertaking of my own.—Sir Rd. Temple being thus cleared, without the least contradiction to his majesty, if to undertake for you, gentlemen, be a guilt, it is only I that stand guilty before you. But you are too noble, I am sure, and too just, to condemn me in your judgments, before you have heard the nature and circumstances of my undertaking; which, with your leave, I shall declare to the full, taking the matter (as I must needs, to be rightly understood) from an higher original. Mr. Speaker, having had the honour heretofore of discharging, with approbation, a place of so high trust, as that of Secretary of State to his majesty's father of blessed memory, and to himself: and since my quitting that place, being admitted so frequently to the happiness of his princely conversation, you cannot imagine, but that sometimes he vouchsafed to speak to me of business, especially of parliaments, where I have the honour at present to be a peer, and have heretofore been as much versed, as some of my contemporaries, in the proceedings of the honourable house of commons. I confess, that, before this last assembling, he did it more than once, and the opinion I most constantly delivered concerning this house was, that never king was so happy in a house of commons, as he was in you; a house composed of so many gentlemen of birth and fortune, eminent in their faithfulness to him, and such as could never be suspected of any sinister designs, or of any other dependance, but upon the crown, and upon the care of those that chose them, and such as in the last sessions had manifested their affections to him by such large Aids and Supplies; adding, that nothing could be more important to his service, than to make and preserve you still popular with those that sent you. To which end I took the liberty to tell him, that if the necessity of his affairs, (of which I, having no part in his council, was no good judge) could admit of it, he ought not in prudence to let you give him any Money this sitting, but rather to oblige you wholly to apply yourselves to the making of such laws as might endear both him and you to the people; by which means, at another meeting, he would be master of the hearts and purses of his subjects. But in case his necessities should urge him to press you, before the rising, for a new Supply, that he ought, by all means, to let it be accompanied, if not preceded, by some eminent Acts for the Reformation of former Abuses, and for the securing his subjects from the like for the future.—I persisted, Mr. Speaker, in pressing, upon all occasions, this advice to his majesty, till within some few weeks after their meeting; when finding myself (I know not by what misfortune) fallen under some prejudice, I thought that a total forbearance from speaking to him of any business, would be the best way of my serving him. And I protest unto you, gentlemen, with all sincerity, that from that time, until that of his majesty's expressing to me some displeasure against sir Rd. Temple, I never once opened my lips to him of any public affair whatsoever: it is true, Mr. Speaker, that a ground being given me to enter again with his majesty, upon a subject which my heart was still full of, I laid hold on the occasion, and in pursuance of what I had said in behalf of sir Rd. Temple, told his majesty, perhaps with more freedom and fervour than did become me, that I found his courtiers gave him wrong measures, both of the temper of the house of commons, and of the means to attain from them any new Supplies, whether by way of present, gift, or of such establishments in his revenues, as might indeed put him out of necessity; since there could be no reasonable hopes of obtaining from them any such assistance, but by a committance, if not a precedence of such Acts, as might be grateful and beneficial to his subjects, and secure them, that what shall be given hereafter should be better managed for his majesty's service, than those vast sums that had been formerly granted: that if his majesty, in his princely wisdom, should think fit to drive on his business upon solid grounds, and not upon the false and self-interested measures of some courtiers, he had a house of commons composed of members so full of affection to his person, and zeal for his prosperity and glory, that not only sir Rd. Temple, but the most unprejudiced and wisest men of the kingdom, as well as myself, durst undertake for them. See here, gentlemen, the bold undertaking that such a house of commons would never let him want such present Supplies, as the true necessity of his affairs should require, nor such an established Revenue, as is fit to support the greatness and honour of his crown. If this was a criminal undertaking, you have, before you, gentlemen, confitentem reum; but whilst I am endeavouring to clear sir Rd. Temple, and to vindicate or arraign myself, according as you shall be pleased to understand it, by telling you what passed from me to his majesty, I must not omit to give him the honour due to him for the kingly Reply he made to me upon this occasion, which was, 'That he had a true 'sense of the merit of the house of commons 'towards him, even far beyond what I had 'expressed, and this was the reason why, 'relying so entirely as he did, upon the affections of that whole body, he was, and ever 'should be offended at any proposition to 'carry on his business there by officious undertakings and cabals, either of his courtiers or 'others.' An expression fit to be written with the rays of the sun, that all the world may read it; an expression which cannot chuse but inflame the affections of all this noble assembly that hear me, and carry you to make good these happy impressions of you, which are so deeply stampt in his royal breast: such as I should think it a crime to doubt, but that all suspicions being now vanished of his majesty's owning the Supply desired, to any acts or contrivances of others, your own zeal for his service will, even in the proportion and timeliness of that, exceed the vain proposals of all pick-thank undertakers.—Mr. Speaker, I should have here put a period to your trouble of hearing me, did I not think I might incur the imputation of much weakness and supineness in my own highest concernments, if, valuing, as I do, above all earthly concernments, the favour and the esteem of my country, of which you are the illustrious representatives; and knowing what industry has been used to blast me with you, I should not lay hold on this just occasion to remove from me some unjust prejudices under which I have laboured. And this Mr. Speaker, I humbly beg leave to do in very few words. I appeal, gentlemen, to numbers of you, that hear me, whether I have not been represented unto you for the giver of advice of a far different tenor from what you have heard upon this occasion; whether I have not been painted out unto you for an inflamer of his majesty against his parliament; for an enemy of the Church of England, and for a dangerous driver on of the Papistical interest. It is true, Mr. Speaker, I am a Catholic of the Church of Rome, but not of the Court of Rome; no Negotiator there of Cardinal's Caps for his majesty's subjects and domestics, a true Roman Catholic as to the other world, but a true Englishman as to this: such a one, as had we a king inclined to that profession (as on the contrary, we have one the most firm and constant to the Protestant Religion, that ever sat upon the throne) I would tell him as freely as the Duke of Sully, being a Protestant, told his grandfather Henry IV. That if he meant to be a king he must be a constant professor and maintainer of the Religion established in his dominions. Believe me, gentlemen, Roman Catholic as I am, there is no man amongst you all, more throughly persuaded than I am, that the true pillars, that can uphold this monarchy, must ever be the maintenance of the subjects just rights and liberties, and the careful preservation of that State Ecclesiastical, whereof his majesty is the supreme governor; and I do clearly profess, that should the Pope himself invade that Ecclesiastical right of his, I should as readily draw my sword against him as against the late usurper. Mr. Speaker, one prejudice more I am under, which ought to have great weight indeed with this honourable house, if there were a real ground for it; and that is, that the earl of Bristol is one of those, who by the vast Grants that he hath got of the king, hath, in part, contributed to the groans of the people, to find their king still in such necessity, after such unexampled charges laid upon the subjects for his Supplies. It is true, Mr. Speaker, that though I have neither offices to keep, nor offices to sell, his majesty's gifts to me have been great, in proportion to my merit, which is none: for in serving and suffering for him with faithfulness, I did but my duty, which carries a reward with itself, enough to raise a comfort to me, from the very ruin of my fortune. It is also true, I have had the satisfaction from his majesty, that he never refused me any thing I asked him for myself. But I hope I shall make it appear also, that I have not only been a very modest asker, but also a most careful one, to ask nothing considerable, but what carried advantage with it, as well to his majesty's interest as my own. I know well, Mr. Speaker, that, with so kind and so generous a nature as our king is, an ill proportion of bounty to merit, and consequently the largeness and kindness of his royal heart that way, may have contributed much to the present streights he is in. Happy is the nation that hath nothing to fear for the public, but from the virtues of their prince. It is your proper work, gentlemen, to reduce the effects of them to a right temperament, by your prudent inspection; and may you begin it with all my concernments, which I most readily lay at your feet, humbly begging of you to appoint a time, when I may display them all faithfully before you; in hopes that no man, who hath been a partaker of his majesty's bounty, will prove himself so unworthy of it, as not to follow the example. Mr. Speaker, If having thus poured out my soul before you, I have been so happy as to have begot in this honourable house a right persuasion of the sincerity of my heart, I expect and implore two gracious effects of it. The first, that you will be pleased to grant me your pardon, if the same zeal for his majesty's service, and the good of my country, which made me presume (being no counsellor) to press upon his majesty my opinion in matters of such importance, has transported me also, at this time, in some sort, so as to become your adviser. You have heard, gentlemen, of the dumb man, whose tongue was set free by the imminent danger of his father's life; wonder not then, gentlemen, that such a lover of his king and country as I am, having seen them, within these three years in a prospect of such glory and happiness, both at home and abroad, and finding to what a sad condition things are now reduced, (by what means it is more proper for you to enquire, and may Heaven bless your inspection;) wonder not, I say, gentlemen, that a man so affected as I am, should, by some eruptions of heart, let you see, that *periculum patriæ* ought to have a more powerful effect upon a man of public soul, than *periculum patris*, and is capable, if I were a mute, to make me become a counsellor. The next is, Mr. Speaker, that if (as I said before, I have been so happy in what I expressed, as to have raised in you some more favourable thoughts concerning me, you would vouchsafe me some demonstration of it, whereby I may no more be made, by my enemies, such a bugbear as I am: as if a gracious look of his majesty upon me, were enough to ruin all his affairs with you. I shall then continue the way I am in with comfort; but if I be so unfortunate, as that there still remains in this incomparable representative of my country, any umbrage of danger to it by my access to his majesty; as dear as the conversation of the amiablest prince that ever breathed is to me, I shall banish myself for ever from his sight, into the obscurest part of his dominions, rather than continue upon me the jealousy of those on whom his prosperity depends; or if this be not enough, I shall once more try my fortune abroad, where, I trust, this sword, this head, and this heart shall make me live as heretofore, in spite of my enemies, with lustre to myself and some honour to my nation."

After the earl had finished his speech he withdrew; the house then proceeded in the debate of the matter and came to the following Resolutions: "That this house is satisfied,' that sir R. Temple hath not broke any privilege of this house, in the matter in question concerning him. That this return be made from the house, to the Answer of the earl of Bristol: viz. That the earl of Bristol, in the account which he hath given this house, in the matter concerning sir R. Temple, hath carried himself with all dutifulness towards his majesty; hath cleared the member of this house; and that the house is well satisfied with his respect to them."—His lordship was again called in: and Mr. Speaker acquainted him with the return of the house.—Ordered, That such members of the house, as are of his majesty's privy-council, do acquaint his maj. with the said Vote: That sir Rd. Temple have the leave of this house, to petition his majesty for his favour; and to give him satisfaction, as to the other informations mentioned in his majesty's Message.

Articles of High Treason, exhibited by the earl of Bristol against Lord Clarendon.] July 10. This day the earl of Bristol exhibited into the house of lords, the following

ARTICLES of HIGH TREASON, and other heinous Misdemeanors, against Edw. earl of Clarendon, lord Chancellor of England.

"That, being in place of highest trust and

confidence with his majesty, and having arrogated to himself a supreme direction in all his majesty's affairs both at home and abroad, he hath wickedly and maliciously, and with a traiterous intent to draw scandal and contempt upon his majesty's person, and to alienate from him the affections of his subjects, abused the said trust in manner following:—That he hath traiterously and maliciously endeavoured to alienate the hearts of his majesty's subjects from him, by words of his own, and by artificial insinuations of his creatures and dependents, "That his majesty was inclined to Popery, and had a design to alter the Religion established in this kingdom." That in pursuance of that traiterous intent, he hath, to several persons of his majesty's privy council, held discourses to this effect: 'That his majesty 'was dangerously corrupted in his Religion, 'and inclined to Popery; that persons of that 'Religion had such access and such credit with 'him, that, unless there were a careful eye had 'unto it, the Protestant Religion would be 'overthrown in this kingdom.' And, in pursuance of the said wicked and traiterous intent, upon his majesty's admitting sir Henry Bennet to be Principal Secretary of State in the place of Mr. Secretary Nicholas, he hath said these words, or words to this effect, 'That his majesty had given 10,000*l.* to remove a zealous 'Protestant, that he might bring into that 'place of high trust a concealed Papist;' notwithstanding that the said sir Henry Bennet is known to have ever been, both in his profession and practice, constant to the Protestant Religion.—That, in pursuance of the same traiterous design, several near friends and known dependents of his have said aloud, 'That, were it not for my lord chancellor's 'standing in the gap, Popery would be intro-'duced into this kingdom;' or words to that effect.—That in pursuance of the aforesaid traiterous design, he hath not only advised and persuaded the king to do such things, contrary to his own reason and resolutions, as might confirm and increase the scandal which he had endeavoured to raise upon his majesty as aforesaid, of his favour to Popery; but more particularly to allow his name to be used to the Pope and several Cardinals, in the solicitation of a Cardinal's Cap for the lord Aubigny, one of his own subjects and great almoner at present to his royal consort the queen.—That, in pursuance of the same wicked and traiterous design, he had recommended to be employed to the Pope one of his own domestics, Mr. Rd. Beling, a person, though an avowed Papist, known to be trusted and employed by him in dispatches and negotiations concerning affairs of greatest concernment to the nation.—That, in pursuance of the said traiterous design, he, being chief minister of state, did himself write, by the said Mr. Rd. Beling, letters to several cardinals, pressing them in the king's name to induce the Pope to confer a Cardinal's Cap on the said lord Aubigny; promising, in case it should be obtained, exemption to the Roman Catholics of England from the penal laws in force against them: by which address unto the Pope for that ecclesiastical dignity for one of his majesty's subjects and domestics, he hath, as far as from one action can be inferred, traiterously acknowledged the Pope's ecclesiastical sovereignty, contrary to the known laws of this kingdom. That, in pursuance of the same traiterous design, he hath called unto him several Priests and Jesuits, whom he knew to be Superiors of Orders here in England, and desired them to write to their generals at Rome, to give their help, for the obtaining from the Pope the Cardinal's Cap for the lord Aubigny as aforesaid; promising great favour to Papists here, in case it should be effected for him.—That he hath promised unto several Papists, that he would do his endeavour; and said, he hoped to compass the taking away all the penal laws against them, which he did in pursuance of the traiterous design aforesaid, to the end they might presume and grow vain upon his patronage, and, by the publishing their hopes of a toleration, increase the scandal endeavoured by him and by his emissaries to be raised upon his majesty throughout the kingdom.—That, in pursuance of the same traiterous design, being intrusted with the Treaty of the Marriage betwixt his majesty and his royal consort the queen, he concluded it upon Articles scandalous and dangerous to the Protestant Religion.—That, in pursuance of the same traiterous design he concluded the said Marriage, and brought the king and queen together, without any settled Agreement in what manner the rites of marriage should be performed; whereby, the queen refusing to be married by a Protestant bishop or priest, in case of her being with child, either the succession should be made uncertain for want of the due rites of matrimony, or else his majesty be exposed to a suspicion of having been married in his own dominions by a Romish priest, whereby all the former scandals endeavoured to be raised upon his majesty by the said earl as to point of Popery might be confirmed and heightened.—That, having thus traiterously endeavoured to alienate the affections of his majesty's subjects from him upon the score of Religion, he hath endeavoured to make use of all the malicious scandals and jealousies which he and his emissaries had raised in his majesty's subjects, to raise from them unto himself the popular applause of being the zealous upholder of the Protestant Religion, and a promoter of new severities against Papists.—That he hath traiterously endeavoured to alienate the affections of his majesty's subjects from him, by venting in his own discourses, and by the speeches of his nearest relations and emissaries, opprobrious scandals against his majesty's person and course of life; such as are not fit to be mentioned, unless necessity in the way of proof shall require it.—That he hath traiterously endeavoured to alienate the affections of his highness the duke of

York from his majesty, by suggesting unto him jealousies as far as in him lay, and publishing abroad by his emissaries, That his majesty intended to legitimate the duke of Monmouth.' 'That he hath wickedly and maliciously, contrary to the duty of a privy counsellor of England, and contrary to the perpetual and most important interest of this nation, persuaded his majesty against the advice of the lord general to withdraw the English garrisons out of Scotland, and to demolish all the forts built there at so vast a charge to this kingdom.—That, his majesty having been graciously pleased to communicate the desires of the parliament of Scotland, for the remove of the said garrisons, to his parliament of England, and to ask their advice therein, the said earl of Clarendon not only persuaded his majesty actually to remove those garrisons, without expecting the advice of his parliament of England concerning it, but did, by menaces of his majesty's displeasure, deter several members of parliament from moving the houses, as they intended, to enter upon consideration of that matter,—That he hath traiterously and maliciously endeavoured to alienate his majesty's affections and esteem from this his parliament; by telling his majesty, 'That there never was 'so weak nor so inconsiderable a house of 'lords, nor never so weak nor so heady a 'house of commons,' or words to that effect; and particularly, 'That it was better to 'sell Dunkirk, than to be at their mercy for 'want of money,' or words to that effect.—That he hath wickedly and maliciously, contrary to his duty of a counsellor, and to a known law made the last sessions, by which money was given and particularly applied for the maintaining of Dunkirk, advised and effected the Sale of the same to the French king.—That he hath maliciously and contrary to law enriched himself and his creatures by the Sale of Offices.—That, contrary to his duty, he hath wickedly and corruptly converted to his own use great and vast sums of public money raised in Ireland, by way of subsidy, private and public benevolences, and otherwise, given and intended to defray the charge of government in that kingdom; by which means a supernumerary and disaffected army hath been kept up there, for want of money to pay them off; and their want of pay, so occasioned, seems to be the cause of the late and present distempers in that kingdom. That, having arrogated to himself a supreme direction of all his majesty's affairs, he hath with a malicious and corrupt intention prevailed to have his majesty's Customs farmed at a far lower rate than others did offer, and that by persons with some of whom he goes a share in that and other parts of monies resulting from his majesty's Revenue. BRISTOL."

"In pursuance of this Charge, it is desired, That the person of the earl of Clarendon may be secured, That his majesty's counsel learned in the law be appointed to draw up a Charge in form, according to these Heads and such others as the earl of Bristol shall exhibit, and to prosecute in the king's behalf. That there be a liberty granted of additional Charges, according as the earl of Bristol shall be enabled to make out proofs of new matter. That Commissions be granted for examination of divers witnesses, both in Scotland and Ireland, according to the List the earl of Bristol shall give in. That order be taken, that the lord Aubigny and Mr. Rd. Beling, two most important witnesses, depart not the kingdom, till they have answered fully to the interrogatories which are to be proposed unto them.

"BRISTOL."

To which Articles the Lord Chancellor * made a short speech extempore to some of the particulars, and declared his innocence.

---

* Lord Clarendon's own account of this transaction is as follows: "The earl of Bristol came one morning to the house of peers with a Paper in his hand; and told the lords, 'that 'he could not but observe, that after so glorious a return with which God had blessed 'the king and the nation, so that all the world 'had expected, that the prosperity of the 'kingdom would have far exceeded the misery 'and adversity that it had for many years endured; and after the parliament had contributed more towards it, than ever parliament 'had done: notwithstanding all which, it was 'evident to all men, and lamented by those who 'wished well to his majesty, that his affairs 'grew every day worse and worse; the king 'himself lost much of his honour, and the affection he had in the hearts of the people. 'That for his part he looked upon it with as 'much sadness as any man, and had made enquiry as well as he could from whence this 'great misfortune, which every body was sensible of, could proceed; and that he was 'satisfied in his own conscience, that it proceeded principally from the power and credit 'and sole credit of the Chancellor: and therefore he was resolved, for the good of his 'country, to accuse the Lord Chancellor of 'High Treason; which he had done in the 'Paper which he desired might be read, all 'written with his own hand, to which he subscribed his name.'—The Paper contained many Articles, which he called Articles of High Treason and other Misdemeanors; amongst which one was, 'that he had persuaded the king to send a gentleman (a creature of his own) to Rome, with letters to the Pope, to give a Cardinal's Cap to the lord Aubigny, who was almoner to the queen.' The rest contained 'his assuming to himself the government of all public affairs, which he had administered unskilfully, corruptly and traiterously; which he was ready to prove.'—The Chancellor, without any trouble in his countenance, told the lords, 'That he had 'had the honour heretofore to have so much 'the good opinion and friendship of that lord, 'that he durst appeal to his own conscience, 'that he did not himself believe one of those 'Articles to be true, and knew the contrary of 'most of them. And he was glad to find

Then the house ordered, "That a Copy of the aforesaid Articles should be prepared, and delivered to the king, that so he might be made acquainted with them.—And the Lord Chancellor is to have a Copy of them; and another Copy is to be made, and delivered to the Judges."—And this ensuing Order was also made; viz. "Ordered, by the lords spiritual and temporal in parliament assembled, That a Copy of the Articles of High Treason exhibited this day, by the earl of Bristol, against the Lord Chancellor, be delivered to the lord chief justice, who with all the rest of the Judges, are to consider, whether the said Charge hath been brought in regularly and legally? and whether it may be proceeded in? and how? and whether there be any Treason in it, or no? and to make report thereof to this house on Monday next, if they can, or else as soon after as possibly they can."

Opinion of the Judges upon the said Articles.] July 13. This day being appointed for the Judges to deliver their Opinion upon the Articles of High Treason exhibited by the earl of Bristol against the Lord Chancellor; the lord chief justice Bridgman, by the agreement, and

---

'that he thought it so high a crime to send to 'Rome, and to desire a Cardinal's Cap for a 'Catholick lord, who had been always bred 'from his cradle in that faith: but he did assure them, that that gentleman was only sent 'by the queen to the pope, upon an affair 'that she thought herself obliged to comply 'with him in, and in hope to do some good 'office to Portugal; and that the king had 'neither writ to the Pope, nor to any other 'person in Rome.' He spake at large to most of the Articles, to shew the impossibility of their being true, and that they reflected more upon the king's honour than upon his; and concluded, 'That he was sorry that lord had 'not been better advised, for he did believe 'that though all that was alledged in the Ar'ticles should be true, they would not all 'amount to High Treason, upon which he de'sired the Judges might be required to deliver 'their opinion;' the which the lords ordered the Judges to do. It was moved by one of the lords, 'That the Copy of the Articles might be sent to the king, because he was mentioned so presumptuously in them;' which was likewise agreed; and the Articles were delivered to the lord chamberlain to present to the king. —The Chancellor had promised that day to dine in Whitehall, but would not presume to go thither till he had sent to the king, not thinking it fit to go into his court, whilst he lay under an accusation of High Treason, without his leave. His majesty sent him word, "That he should dine where he had appointed, and as soon as he had dined that he should attend him.' Then his majesty told him and the lord treasurer all that had passed between the earl of Bristol and him in the presence of the lord Aubigny; and in the relation of it expressed great indignation, and was angry with himself 'that he had not immediately sent him to the Tower,' which he said 'he would do as soon as he could apprehend him.' He used the Chancellor with much grace and told him, 'that the earl of Bristol had not treated him so ill as he had done his majesty; and that his Articles were more to his dishonour, and reflected more upon him, for which he would have justice.'—his majesty commanded the lord chamberlain to return his thanks to the house 'For the respect they had shewed to him, in sending those Articles to him: and to let them know, 'that he looked upon them as a libel against himself more than a charge against the chancellor, who upon his knowledge was innocent in all the particulars charged upon him;' which report the lord chamberlain made the next morning to the house: and at the same time the Judges declared their Opinion unanimously, 'that the whole Charge contained nothing of treason though it were all true.' Upon which the earl of Bristol, especially upon what the lord chamberlain had reported from the king, appeared in great confusion, and lamented his condition, 'That he, for endeavouring to serve 'his country upon the impulsion of his consci'ence, was discountenanced, and threatened 'with the anger and displeasure of his prince; 'whilst his adversary kept his place in the 'house and had the Judges so much at his de'votion that they would not certify against 'him.' The Chancellor moved the house, 'that 'a short day might be given to the earl, to 'bring in his evidence to prove the several 'matters of his Charge; otherwise that he 'might have such reparation, as was in their 'judgments proportionable to the indignity;' The earl said, 'He should not fail to pro'duce witnesses to prove all he had alleged, 'and more: but that he could not appoint a 'time when he could be ready for a hearing, 'because many of his most important wit'nesses were beyond the seas, some at Paris, 'and others in other places; and that he must 'examine the duke of Ormond who was lieu'tenant in Ireland, and the earl of Lauther'dale who was then in Scotland, and must 'desire commissioners to that purpose.'—But from that day he made no farther instance: and understanding that the king had given warrants to a sergeant at arms to apprehend him, he concealed himself in several places for the space of near two years; sending sometimes letters and petitions by his wife to the king, who would not receive them. But in the end his majesty was prevailed with by the lady and sir Harry Bennet to see him in private; but would not admit him to come to the court, nor repeal his warrants for his apprehension: so that he appeared not publicly till the Chancellor's misfortune; and then he came to the court and to the parliament in great triumph, and shewed a more impotent malice than was expected from his generosity and understanding." Life, p. 209.

in the name, of all the rest, delivered in this unanimous Answer following; viz. 1. "We conceive, That a Charge of High Treason cannot by the laws and statutes of this realm be originally exhibited by any one peer against another unto the house of peers; and that therefore the Charge of High Treason by the earl of Bristol against the lord chancellor hath not been regularly and legally brought in. 2. And if the matters alledged in the said Charge were admitted to be true (although alleged to be traiterously done), yet there is not any treason in it."

The King's Message thereon.] July 13. The Lord Chamberlain presented to the house the following Message for the king: "His majesty, having received from his house of peers a Copy of the Writing which the earl of Bristol had delivered in, containing Articles of supposed High Treason and other Misdemeanors against the Chancellor of England, doth give your lordships very many thanks for your great care and regard in transmitting the same to him; upon view of which, his majesty finds several matters of fact charged, which upon his own certain knowledge are untrue. And his majesty cannot but take notice of the many scandalous reflections in that Paper upon himself and his relations, which he looks upon as a libel against his person and government; for which, and other things, his majesty will in due time take such course against him as shall be agreeable to justice."

Resolutions of the Lords concerning the said Articles.] July 18. The lords resumed the debate, upon the above opinion of the Judges, and the question being put "whether this house doth concur with the opinion of the Judges herein," it was resolved in the affirmative, nem. con *.

Protest against the Bill for Encouragement of Trade.] July 21. A Bill entitled, 'An Act for the Encouragement of Trade,' being this day read the third time, and ready to be put to the question for passing into a law; it was moved, and granted by the house, that if the question passed in the affirmative, such peers as were against the Bill might enter their Protestation; and accordingly we whose names are subscribed do protest against the said Bill being made a law, for the reasons following: 1. Because, in the free liberty given for transporting of money and bullion, this Bill crosseth the wisdom and care of our ancestors in all ages, who by many laws and penalties, upon excellent and approved grounds, have restrained such exportation, and thereby preserved trade in a flourishing condition; 2. There appearing already great want of Money in his majesty's dominions, and almost all the gold of his majesty's stamp gone, notwithstanding the restraint made by law, and the importation of foreign commodities (which are grown to so great an esteem and use amongst us) being much greater than the export of our native and simple commodities, it must necessarily follow, by this free exportation, that our silver will also be carried away into foreign parts, and all trade fail for want of money, which is the measure of it. 3. It will make all our native commodities lie upon our hands, when, rather than stay for gross goods, which pay custom, the merchant, in a quarter of an hour, when his wind and tide serve, freights his ship with silver. 4. It trencheth highly upon the king's prerogative, he being by the law the only exchanger of money, and his interest equal to command that, as to command the Militia of the kingdom, which cannot subsist without it; and it is dangerous to the

"* The earl of Bristol's friendship with Clarendon, which had subsisted with great intimacy during their exile and the distresses of the royal party, had been considerably impaired since the restoration, by the chancellor's refusing his assent to some grants, which Bristol had applied for to a court lady: and a little after, the latter nobleman, agreeably to the impetuosity and indiscretion of his temper, broke out against the minister in the most outrageous manner. He even entered a charge of treason against him before the house of peers; but had concerted his measures so imprudently, that the judges, when consulted, declared, that, neither for its matter nor its form, could the charge be legally received. The articles indeed resemble more the incoherent altercations of a passionate enemy, than a serious accusation, fit to be discussed by a court of judicature; and Bristol himself was so ashamed of his conduct and defeat, that he absconded during some time.—Notwithstanding his fine talents, his eloquence, his spirit, and his courage, he could never regain the character which he lost by this hasty and precipitate measure. But though Clarendon was able to elude this rash assault, his credit at court was sensibly declining; and in proportion as the king found himself established on the throne, he began to alienate himself from a minister, whose character was so little suited to his own. Charles's favour for the catholics was always opposed by Clarendon, public liberty was secured against all attempts of the over-zealous royalists, prodigal grants of the king were checked or refused, and the dignity of his own character was so much consulted by the chancellor, that he made it an inviolable rule, as did also his friend Southampton, never to enter into any connexion with the royal mistresses. The king's favourite was Mrs. Palmer, afterwards created duchess of Cleveland; a woman prodigal, rapacious, dissolute, violent, revengeful. She failed not in her turn to undermine Clarendon's credit with his master; and her success was at this time made apparent to the whole world. Secretary Nicholas, the chancellor's great friend, was removed from his place; and sir Harry Bennet, his avowed enemy, was advanced to that office. Bennet was soon after created lord Arlington." Hume.

peace of the kingdom, when it shall be in the power of half a dozen or half a score rich, discontented, or factious persons, to make a Bank of our coin and bullion beyond the seas for any mischief, and leave us in want of money; and it shall not be in the king's power to prevent it, the liberty being given by a law; nor to keep his mint going, because money will yield more from than at the Mint. 5. Because a law of so great change, and threatening so much danger, is made perpetual, and not probationary. 6. Because, in the restraint laid on Importation of Irish Cattle, common right and the subjects liberty is invaded; whilst they, being by law native Englishmen, are debarred the English markets, which seems also to monopolize the sale of cattle to some of his majesty's English subjects, to the destruction of others. 7. It will, we conceive, increase the king's charge of Ireland, by calling for revenue from England, if that, which is almost the only Trade of Ireland, shall be prohibited, as in effect it is; and so the people, we conceive, disabled to pay the king's dues, or grant subsidies in Ireland. 8. It threatens danger to the peace of the kingdom of Ireland, by universal poverty; which may have an unhappy influence upon the rest of his majesty's dominions. 9. The restraint upon Importation of Irish and Scotch cattle will, we conceive, be decay of two of his majesty's cities of England, Carlisle and Chester, make a dearth in London, and discommode many other parts of England. Other reasons are forborne, which time will produce. ANGLESEY."

A Bill for the better Observation of the Sabbath, lost off the Table of the House of Lords.] July 27. The house being informed, by the clerk of the parliaments, That the Bill for the better Observation of the Lord's-Day hath been, during the sitting of the house, taken from the table, and is not now to be found, the lords thought fit, in a business of this high concernment (the like being never known or heard of to have been done before), that every lord and assistant to this house should declare himself, whether he hath it or not, or can tell what is become of it. To that end, the clerk of the parliaments and the clerk assistant had their oaths given them; who, upon the said oaths, did aver that the said Bill now missing was upon the table, in a bag, this morning, amongst the other bills which were to be presented to the king for his royal assent this day. And being commanded by the house to tell, 'Whether any lords were at the table, meddling with any of the said bills, this morning:' They did depose, 'That divers lords were at the table this morning, and did take the Bills out of the said bag, and scattered them upon the table: whereupon the clerk of the parliaments, taking the said bills into his custody, telling the number of them, found one to be wanting; and immediately examining the titles by the list, found the said Bill for the better Observation of the Lord's-day wanting.'—Upon this, every lord was called by name; and those present did make their purgation; and the assistants likewise did particularly clear themselves. But, in regard some lords were now absent who were present this morning, the house did order, That if any member or assistant of this house hath taken the said Bill away, and doth not bring it again time enough to have it pass the royal assent this day, this house will proceed against them severely for the same.

The Speaker's Speech to the King at the Prorogation.] This day the king came down to the house of peers, and gave command to the gentleman usher of the Black rod, to signify his pleasure to the house of commons, That they should presently come up, with their Speaker, to attend his majesty. Who accordingly being come, the Speaker made this Speech following:

"May it please your most Excellent Majesty; The knights, citizens, and burgesses of the commons house of parliament, have, since their last meeting, in many weighty and arduous affairs, presented your majesty with their humble advice, which, with all thankfulness they acknowledge, never wanted a most gracious reception. Never any prince did so freely commune with his people; and never any people did with more joy and duty commemorate their happiness.—The last session of parliament, our care was chiefly to secure the being of this nation under our ancient, happy monarchical government. This session, we have endeavoured to advance the peace and well-being both of Church and State.—Material structures are best secured by deep foundations in the earth; but the foundations of true happiness are from above. We have therefore, in the first place, perused the laws which do enjoin the Observation of the Lord's-day; and where we found any defect, either in rules or penalties, we have with great care supplied them; well knowing that he who doth not remember on the first day of the week to observe a Christian Sabbath, will hazard before the week comes round to forget he is a Christian.—We read in the story of Lewis the 9th of France, when he took his voyage into the Eastern empire to assist the distressed Christians, the fame of his holiness moved the king of Tartary to send his ambassadors, to offer him friendship, and to acquaint him he had a desire to become a Christian; whereupon Lewis sent him preachers, to instruct him in the Christian religion. But the Tartarians observing the lives of the Christians were not answerable to their profession, they returned with the shame of their own ill lives upon them, whose doctrines were so famous.—That which in those days was the reproach of those Christians, is much more at this day the shame of this nation; we know more, but practice less, than they did: we generally love a sceptical rather than a practical religion; and are contended to spend that time in study of curious deceitful notions, which ought to be employed in the practice of known truths. Too many amongst us are of the sect of the gnostics, hunting after novelties and phantasms, till variety of notions makes them mad. Hence do arise all those sects and schisms in the Church, which, being nursed up in pride, refuse to conform to any laws, and make religion itself the cloak of all their separations; whereas true religion is the band of society, the sinews that hold fast the joints of the body politic. If these be broken, the body must be dismembered; if they be but sprained, the whole body is in pain, and the members made unuseful.—At the opening of this session, your majesty was most graciously pleased to call upon us to prepare some laws for the prevention of the Growth of Popery; and we have heartily laboured therein, both to prevent the Growth of Popery and all sorts of Sectaries and Non-Conformists. But, as the rankest corn and the fullest ears are aptest to be laid, so fares it in this matter: these fruits are not yet ready for the harvest. But we are confident, by the wisdom of your majesty's government, and the readiness of your faithful subjects to support it by the just and due execution of the laws (especially if such persons be intrusted with the execution of the laws as do love them), these persons will either be persuaded to conformity, or forced into a peaceably and orderly conversation.—To this purpose, I am commanded, by the knights, citizens, and burgesses of the commons house of parliament, humbly in their name to beseech your majesty, that you will be pleased to issue out your Proclamation, for the putting those laws which now are in force, against the Popish Recusants, Sectaries, and Non-conformists, in effectual execution.—I am likewise commanded to desire your majesty, that you will be pleased to issue out another Proclamation, for the Prevention of that Prophaneness, Debauchery, and Licentiousness, which, to the high displeasure of Almighty God, the dishonour of your majesty's government, and the grief of all good men, is now practised amongst us: and, for the better securing the peace of the nation against the united counsels of all the Dissenters to our Religion and established discipline, we have prepared an additional Bill for the ordering the Forces of the kingdom, whereby your majesty's lieutenants and their deputy lieutenants will be enabled to train, discipline, and keep together, such a party as will be able to prevent disorders, and sufficient to check any insurrections, till the great body of the Militia can come in to their assistance.—During the late unhappy wars in this nation, our neighbours eyes were open, to spy out all advantages of spoiling our Trade, and to advance their own; but, by the several good bills made ready for your majesty's royal assent, we hope, we shall restore and increase the flourishing Trade of this nation.—Great Sir, I have but one word more; and that is by command from your majesty's loyal and dutiful subjects the commons of England. They have duly considered the present unsettled condition of this nation, and the great expence which must attend such distractions; and do humbly beseech your majesty to accept an Aid from them, consisting of four entire Subsidies; two of which are to be paid by the 1st of Nov. next, and the other two by the 1st of May next following."

The King's Speech at the Prorogation.] After giving the royal assent to 14 public and 12 private Bills his majesty made the following Speech:

"My lords and gentlemen; I thank you for the present you have made me this day; and I hope your countries will thank you when you come home for having done it. I am not conscious of having brought the streights and necessities I am in upon myself, by any improvidence or ill husbandry of my own: I know the contrary; and, I assure you, I would not have desired or received the Supply you have now given me, if it were not absolutely necessary for your peace and quiet as well as mine. And, I must tell you, it will do me very little good, if I do not improve it by very good husbandry of my own, and by retrenching those very expences which in many respects may be thought necessary enough. But you shall see, I will much rather impose upon myself than upon my subjects; and if all men will follow my example in retrenching their expences, which (it may be) they may do with much more convenience than I can do mine, the kingdom will in a very short time gain what you have given me this day.—I am very glad you are now going into your several countries, where your presence will do much good? and I hope your vigilance and authority will prevent those disturbances which the restless spirits of ill and unquiet men will be always contriving, and of which, I do assure you, they promise themselves some effects this summer.—There have been more pains and unusual ways taken to kindle the old fatal fears and jealousies than I thought I should ever have lived to have seen, at least to have seen so countenanced.—I do desire you and conjure you, my lords and gentlemen, to watch this evil spirit and temper with your utmost care and prudence, and secure the persons of those whom you find are possessed with it, that the peace of the kingdom be not sacrificed to their pride, humour and madness.—I did expect to have had some Bills presented to me against the several Distempers in Religion, against seditious Conventicles, and against the Growth of Popery: but, it may be, you have been in some fear of reconciling those contradictions in religion, in some conspiracy against the public peace, to which, I doubt, men of the most contrary motives in conscience are inclinable enough, I do promise you to lay this business, and the mischiefs which may flow from the licenses, to heart. And if I live to meet with you again, as I hope I shall, I will myself take care to present two Bills to you to that end. And, as I have already given it in charge to the Judges, in their several circuits, to use their utmost endeavours to prevent and punish the scandalous and seditious Meetings of Sectaries, and to convict the Papists; so I will be as watchful, and take all the pains I can, that neither the one or the other shall disturb the peace of the kingdom.—I shall not need to desire you to use all diligence in levying and collecting the Subsidies you have given me; and heartily wish the distribution may be made with all equality and justice, and without any animosity or faction, or remembering any thing that hath been done in the late ill times, which, you know, we are all obliged to forget, as well as to forgive. And indeed, till we have done so, we can never be in perfect peace; and therefore I can never put you too much in mind of it.—I think it necessary to make this a session, that so the current of justice may run the two next terms without any obstruction by privilege of parliament; and therefore I shall prorogue you till the 16th day of March, when I doubt not, by God's blessing, we shall meet again to our joint satisfaction, and that you shall have cause to thank me for what I do in the interval."

His majesty, having ended his aforesaid Speech, called unto him the Lord Privy Seal, who was Speaker this day, and gave him directions what to say further; who returning to his place pronounced these words: "My lords and gentlemen; The king doth prorogue this parliament until the 16th day of March next. And accordingly this parliament is prorogued until the 16th day March next, 1663."

THIRD SESSION OF THE SECOND PARLIAMENT.

The King's Speech on opening the Session.] March 16, 1663-4. This day both houses met, and on the 21st, the king opened the Session with a Speech from the throne, as follows:

"My Lords and Gentlemen; You see, God be thanked, you have met together again at the time appointed: and I do assure you, I have been so far from ever intending it should be otherwise, that I do not know one person who ever wished it should be otherwise. Think, therefore, I pray, what good meaning those men could have, who, from the time of the prorogation to the day of your meeting, have continually whispered, and industriously infused into the minds of the people, that the parliament should meet no more; that it should be presently dissolved; or so continued by prorogation, that they should be kept without a parliament. I pray, watch these whisperers all you can, as men who use their utmost endeavours to sow jealousies between you and me. And I do promise you, they shall not prevail with me; and I do promise myself, they shall not prevail with you. And the truth is, we are both concerned they should not; and we shall then, with God's blessing, prevent all the mischief they intend.—You may judge by the late Treason in the North, for which so many men have been executed, how active the spirits of many of our old enemies still are, notwithstanding all our mercy. I do assure you, we are not yet at the bottom of that business. This much appears manifestly, that this conspiracy was but a branch of that which I discovered as well as I could to you about two years since, and had been then executed nearer-hand, if I had not, by God's goodness, come to the knowledge of some of the principal contrivers, and so secured them from doing the mischief they intended. And if I had not by the like providence, had timely notice of the very hour and several places of their rendezvous in the North, and provided for them accordingly, by sending some of my own troops, as well as by drawing the trained bands together, their conjunction would have been in greater numbers than had been convenient.—You will wonder, but I tell true, they are now even in those parts, and at this time, when they see their friends under trial and execution, still pursuing the same consultations. And it is evident they have correspondence with desperate persons in most counties, and a standing council in this town, from which they receive their directions, and by whom they were advised to defer their last intended insurrection; but those orders served only to distract them, and came too late to prevent their destruction. I know more of their intrigues than they think I do, and hope I shall shortly discover the bottom; in the mean time, I pray, let us all be as watchful to prevent, as they are to contrive, their mischief. —I cannot omit, upon this occasion, to tell you, that these desperate men in their counsels (as appears by several examinations) have not been all of one mind in the ways of carrying on their wicked resolutions. Some would still insist upon the authority of the Long Parliament, of which, they say, they have members enough willing to meet; others have fancied to themselves, by some computation of their own upon some clause in the Triennial Bill, that this present parliament was at an end some months since; and that, for want of new writs, they may assemble themselves and choose members of parliament; and that this is the best expedient to bring themselves together for their other purposes.—For the Long Parliament, you and I can do no more than we have done, to inform and compose the minds of all men. Let them proceed upon their peril. But methinks there is nothing done to disabuse them in respect of the Triennial Bill. I confess to you my lords and gentlemen, I have often myself read over that bill: and though there is no colour for the fancy of the determination of this parliament, yet I will not deny to you, that I have always expected that you would, and even wondered that you have not considered the wonderful clauses in that bill, which passed in a time very uncareful for the dignity of the crown, or the security of the people.—I pray, Mr. Speaker, and you gentlemen of the house of commons, give that Triennial Bill once a reading in your house; and then, in God's same, do what you think fit for me, and yourselves and the whole kingdom. I need not tell you how much I love parliaments. Never king was so much beholden to parliaments as I have been; nor do I think the crown can ever be happy without frequent parliaments. But, assure yourselves, if I should think otherwise, I would never suffer a parliament to come together by the means prescribed by that Bill.—My Lords and Gentlemen; I must renew my thanks to you, for the free Supply you gave me this last session, of 4 subsidies: yet I cannot but tell you, that that supply is fallen much short of what I expected, or you intended. It will hardly be believed, yet you know it to be true, that very many persons, who have estates of 3 or 4000*l.* a year, do not pay for those 4 subsidies 16*l.* so that, whereas you intended and declared that they should be collected according to former precedents, they do not now arise to half the proportion they did in the time of queen Elizabeth; and yet sure the crown wants more now than it did then, and the subject is at least as well able to give.—The truth is, by the license of the late ill time, and ill-humour of this, too many of the people, and even of those who make fair professions, believe it to be no sin to defraud the crown of any thing that is due to it. You no sooner give me Tonnage and Poundage, than men are devising all the ways they can to steal custom; nor can the farmers be so vigilant for the collection, as others are to steal the duties.—You give me the Excise, which all people abroad believe to be the most insensible imposition that can be laid upon a people. What conspiracies and combinations are entered into against it by the brewers, who, I am sure, bear not that burden themselves, even to bring that revenue to nothing, you will hear in Westminster hall.—You have given me the chimney-money, which you have reason to believe is a growing revenue, for men build at least fast enough; and you will therefore wonder that it is already declined, and that this half year brings in less than the former did. I pray, therefore, review that bill; and since I am sure you would have me receive whatsoever you give, let me have the collecting and husbanding of it by my own officers; and then I doubt not but to improve that receipt, and will be cozened of as little as I can.—I will conclude with desiring and conjuring you, my lords and gentlemen, to keep a very good correspondence together, that it may not be in the power of any seditious or factious spirits to make you jealous of me, till you see me pretend one thing and do another, which I am sure you never have yet done. Trust me, it shall be in nobody's power to make me jealous of you.—I pray, contrive any good short bills which may improve the industry of the nation. And, since the season of the year will invite us all shortly to take the country air, I desire you would be ready for a session within two months or thereabouts; and we will meet next earlier in the year. And so God bless your councils."

The King's Speech upon repealing the Triennial Act.] April 5. In compliance with these instructions from the throne, the house immediately set about repealing the obnoxious Triennial Bill, which they stigmatized as derogatory to the prerogative of the crown, and, as a short compensation, prepared another short one, which provided that parliaments should not be intermitted above three years. This was no sooner ready, than his majesty went to the house on purpose to give the royal assent to it: which he accompanied with the ensuing Speech:

"My Lords and Gentlemen; You will easily believe that I have come very willing to give my assent to this bill. I do thank you very heartily for your so unanimous concurrence in it, and for your desiring me speedily to finish it. And if I understand any thing that concerns the peace and security of the kingdom, and the welfare of my subjects (all which I study more than my prerogative, and indeed I consider my prerogative in order only to preserving the other) every good Englishman will thank you for it: for the Act you have repealed could only serve to discredit parliaments, and to make the crown jealous of parliaments, and parliaments of the crown, and persuade neighbour princes that England was not governed under a monarch. It could never have been the occasion of frequent parliaments. I do promise you, I will not be an hour the less without one for this act of repeal, nor I am sure will you be the less kind to me in parliament. I do again thank you for your excellent temper and respect to me, and desire you so to proceed, that the session may be within the time I proposed to you last. And I do assure you upon my word, and I pray believe me, that I will have no other thoughts or designs in my heart, but to make you all happy in the support of the religion and laws established: and if my own wants and necessities are at any time grievous to me, it is only as I apprehend I may not be able sufficiently to provide for those, and for the peace and security of the kingdom. And therefore I am confident, that you and I, who agree in the end, shall never differ in the way."

Resolution of both Houses against the Dutch.] April 22. The following Resolution passed both houses, viz. "That the wrongs, dishonours, and indignities done to his majesty by the subjects of the United Provinces, by invading his rights in India, Africa, and elsewhere; and the damages, affronts, and injuries done by them to our merchants, are the greatest obstructions of our foreign Trade: and that the same be humbly and speedily presented to his majesty: and that he be most humbly moved to take some speedy and effectual course for redress thereof, and all other of the like nature, and for prevention of the like in future: and in prosecution thereof, they will, with their lives and fortunes, assist his majesty against all oppositions whatsoever."

The King's Answer thereto.] April 27. Upon this occasion both houses waited upon his majesty at the Banquetting-House, and the next day received the following Answer in writing:

"His majesty, having considered the Address made to him by his two houses of parliament, is very well pleased with the great zeal they have expressed for the advancement of the Trade of this kingdom, and removing all obstructions which may hinder the same; being wholly convinced, that it is that which contributes most to the honour and glory of the nation, and the prosperity of his people: and therefore his majesty will examine and peruse the particular Complaints which have been represented to his parliament; and thereupon, according to their advice, appoint his minister at the Hague to demand speedy justice and reparation from the States-General, and also use his utmost endeavours to secure his subjects from the like violences for the future: in the prosecution of which, or upon the denials of justice, he depends upon the promises of both houses to stand by him, and returns them his hearty thanks for their frank declaration therein."

Mr. Prynne censured for altering the Draught of a Bill.] May 13. Mr. Prynne, having taken the liberty to alter the draught of a Bill relating to Public-Houses, having urged in his excuse, 'That he did not do it out of any ill intent, but to rectify some matters mistaken in it, and to make the Bill agree with the sense of the house;' the house ordered him to withdraw, and after debate, being again called in, the Speaker acquainted him, 'That the house was very sensible of this great mistake in so ancient and knowing a member as he was, to break so material and essential an order of the house, as to alter, amend, or interline a bill after commitment: but the house had considered of his Answer and Submission, and were content at this time, in respect thereof, to remit the offence.'

The Speaker's Speech to the King at the Prorogation.] May 17. The business of the Session being now brought to a period, the king came to the house of peers, and being seated on the throne, the Speaker made the following Speech to his majesty:

"May it please your most exc. majesty; At the opening this session, your maj. was pleased to recommend several things to the care of your two houses of parliament; the which we have deliberately considered, and unanimously presented our humble advice thereupon.—The first thing we took into consideration was, the Act made in the 16th year of the late king of glorious memory, for Triennial Parliaments: when we had given it a reading, we found it derogatory to the essential prerogative of the crown, of calling, holding, and dissolving parliaments; we found it unpracticable, and only useful to learn the people how to rebel: therefore we melted it down, extracted the pure metal from counterfeit and drossy alloys, and then presented it to your majesty, to be new stamped, and made current coin, for the use of the nation. We do return our most humble thanks to your maj. that you were pleased to accept our advice, and to pass our Bill; but more especially for those gracious expressions your maj. was pleased to use at that solemnity, whereby we are assured, not only of your personal affection to parliaments, but of your judgment also, that the happiness of the crown consists in the frequency of parliaments.—In the next place, we reviewed the Act for Chimney-money, which we intended a great branch of your majesty's Revenue, although by some mistakes it is fallen short: and, in hopes your maj. may improve that receipt, we have prepared a Bill for the collecting that duty by such officers as your maj. and your successors shall from time to time think fit to appoint.—Whilst we were intent upon these weighty affairs, we were often interrupted by petitions, and letters, and motions, representing the unsettled condition of some countries, by reason of Fanatics, Sectaries, and Non-conformists. They differ in their shapes and species, and accordingly are more or less dangerous: but in this they all agree, they are no friends to the established government either in Church or State; and if the old rule hold true, 'Qui Ecclesiæ contradicit non est pacificus,' we have great reason to prevent their growth, and to punish their practice. To this purpose, we have prepared a Bill against their frequenting of Conventicles, the seed-plots and nurseries of their opinions, under pretence of religious worship. The first offence we have made punishable only with a small fine of 5*l.* or three months imprisonment, and 10*l.* for a peer. The second offence with 10*l.* or 6 months imprisonment, and 20*l.* for a peer. But for the third offence, after a trial by a jury at the general quarter sessions or assizes, and the trial of a peer by his peers, the party convicted shall be transported to some of your majesty's foreign plantations, unless he redeem himself by laying down 100*l.*: 'Immedicabile vulnus ense rescindendum, ne pars sincera trahatur.'—We have had much thought how to improve the industry of the nation, and prevent that idleness and licentiousness which too fast grows upon us, especially by excessive and disorderly Gaming. Men are not contented to sport away their precious time, and play away their ready money; but to lose or pawn their houses and lands, their manors, and their honours also. For the prevention of the growth of this disease, we have prepared a bill, to make all Securities for Money won at play, whether real or personal, to be void.—We have examined also the reasons of the Decay of Trade. In the first place, we found our merchants are undermined by fraud and practice, and sometimes beaten out, in the East and West Indies, in Turkey and in Africa, by our neighbours the Dutch, who, besides the unsufferable indignities offered to your royal maj. have in a few years spoiled your subjects to the value of 7 or 800,000*l.*: for remedy whereof, we have made our humble Address to your majesty, and received a gracious Answer; and have no cause to fear but a short time will produce a just and honourable satisfaction.—The next Obstruction to our Trade hath been, a base and dangerous practice of some seamen, who are willing to be robbed by pirates, that they may share in the prize. We have therefore prepared a bill for the punishment of such treacherous actions, and for the just reward of those honest seamen that shall preserve their owners goods, and manfully maintain the honour of our English nation.—Some other discoveries we have made, which may be the subject matter of future bills; but, in respect of your majesty's intimation of a short session, we were not willing to attempt more than we could reasonably dispatch.—And now, great sir, give me leave with joy to remember that unparalleled unanimity that hath this session attended our counsels. Our constancy and resolution hath been tried beyond the precedent of former parliaments, or any other session of this parliament.—The heathens were wont to observe, and envy the Christians, for their unity and love of one another: 'Ecce ut invicem se diligunt Christiani!' and may this happy correspondence between your royal majesty and your two houses of parliament increase, and grow to be the envy of the world, till all your majesty's enemies are forced to cry, 'Ecce ut invicem se diligunt Anglicani!"

The King's Speech at the Prorogation.] After passing the said Bills, the king made the following Speech:

"My Lords and Gentlemen; I did desire and conjure you, at the opening of this session, that you would keep a very good correspondence together, that it might not be in the power of any seditious or factious spirits to make you jealous of each other, or either of you jealous of me; and I desired you to be ready for a session within two months or thereabouts. I must confess to you, you have complied very fully with me, for which I can never thank you enough: you have performed those good respects towards me, and kept so very good correspondence towards each other, that you have exceedingly disappointed those ill men, who both at home and abroad had raised great hopes and expectation of new troubles and confusions; you have gratified me in all I desired, and are now ready for a session within the time proposed. This harmony will (with God's blessing) make us all esteemed abroad, and secure at home; and these obligations cannot but make me think the time long till we meet again. The season of the year and your own affairs will invite you into the country; and your presence there is of great importance to my service, and to the public peace. You will watch those unquiet spirits, which are still lurking and ready to embrace all opportunities to involve the nation in new distractions, under what specious pretences soever; and you will carefully inform the people, how much it is in their own power to be as happy as they can wish to be: indeed, if they are truly sensible of their present happiness, it will quickly be improved. I will add no more, but that I thank you all and every one of you; and if God bless us till Nov. we will meet here again: I name Nov. to you, because, if nothing extraordinary fall out, I resolve not to meet till then: but, because somewhat extraordinary may fall out, you shall be at present prorogued but till August; and before that day you shall have seasonable notice, by proclamation, not to give your attendance, except there be occasion; and then Nov. will be the time."

FOURTH SESSION OF THE SECOND PARLIAMENT.

The King's Speech at the opening of the Session.] Nov. 24. This day the parliament met, and the session was opened by his majesty, in a Speech from the throne, as follows:

"My Lords and Gentlemen; When we parted last in this place, I told you that I did not think we should meet here again till Nov. though I prorogued you but to a day in August. But I must now tell you, that if I could have suspected, or reasonably have imagined, that our neighbours would have dealt so unneighbourly with me, and have forced me to make such preparations as they have done for my defence, at so vast an expence; I say, if I could have foreseen in Aug. that they would have treated me thus, I should not have prevented your coming together then. Yet truly I have reason even to be glad that it hath been deferred thus long. You have had leisure to attend your own conveniencies in the country, and the public service there; and I have been able to let our neighbours see, that I can defend myself and my subjects, against their insolence, upon the stock of my own credit and reputation; and that, when I find it necessary for the good of my people, I can set out a fleet to sea, which will not decline meeting with all their naval power, even before the parliament comes together; which, I am persuaded, if they had believed possible, they would not so importunately have prest me to it. I will not deny to you, I have done more than I thought I could have done; which I impute to the credit your vote gave me, and to the opinion all men have, that I did what you wished I should do. By borrowing very liberally from myself out of my own stores, and by the kind and chearful assistance the city of London hath given me, I have a fleet now at sea worthy of the English nation, and (to say no more) not inferior to any that hath been set out in any age, and which (that I may use all freedom with you) to discharge to-morrow, and replenish all my stores, I am persuaded, would cost me little less than 800,000*l.*—What hath passed between me and the Dutch, and by what degrees, accidents, and provocations, I have been necessitated to the preparation and expence I have made, you shall be told when I have done. I shall only tell you, that if I had proceeded more slowly, I should have exposed my own honour and the honour of the nation, and should have seemed not confident of your affections, and the assurance you gave me to stand by me in this occasion.—That which I am now very earnestly to desire, and indeed expect from you, is, that you will use all possible expedition in your resolutions; lest that, by unnecessary formalities, the world should think that I have not your full concurrence in what is done, and that you are not forward enough in the support of it; which I am sure you will be, and that, in raising the Supplies, you take such sure order, that when the expence is obvious and certain, the Supplies be as real and substantial, not imaginary as the last Subsidies were, which you all well enough understand.—Master Speaker, and you Gentlemen of the House of Commons; I know not whether it be worth my pains to endeavour to remove a vile jealousy, which some ill men scatter abroad, and which I am sure will never sink into the breast of any man who is worthy to sit upon your benches, that, when you have given me a noble and proportionable Supply for the support of a war, I may be induced by some evil counsellors (for they will be thought to think very respectfully of my own person) to make a sudden peace, and get all that money for my own private occasions. I am sure, you all think it an unworthy jealousy, and not to deserve an answer. I would not be thought to have so brutish an inclination, as to love war for war-sake. God knows, I desire no blessing in this world so much, as that I may live to see a firm peace between all Christian princes and states: but let me tell you, and you may be most confident of it, that when I am compelled to enter into a war, for the protection, honour, and benefit of my subjects, I will (God willing) not make a peace but upon the obtaining and securing those ends for which the war is entered into; and when that can be done, no good man will be sorry for the determination of it.—To conclude: my lords and gentlemen, I conjure you all, in your several stations, to use all possible expedition, that our friends and our enemies may see that I am possessed of your hearts, and that we move with one soul; and I am sure you will not deceive my expectation."

The King's Narrative concerning the Dutch Affairs.] After this, his majesty delivered a Narrative; which was read, as followeth:

A brief NARRATIVE of the late Passages between His Majesty and the Dutch, and His Majesty's Preparations thereupon.

"C. R. His maj. doth not doubt but that his two houses of parliament do well remember the Address they made to his maj. about the end of April last, upon the general representations which had been made to them of the great injuries and oppressions the subjects of this nation sustained in the East and West Indies, and in other places, from the Dutch, and the universal obstruction they brought upon the Trade of this kingdom; and the warm and vigorous Vote they then presented his maj. with, if he could not otherwise remove that mischief. The Answer they received from his maj. was so full of candour, as if he thought his good allies the States General would never put him to use extreme remedies, but would meet the complaints of his subjects with just and proportionable satisfaction; and that he did really believe, as well as wish, that they would do so, is manifest, by his having provided for that season a much less guard of ships than he had set out ever since his happy restoration, intending, by the saving that unnecessary expence (as he then thought) to have plentifully supplied his magazines and stores, which is a treasure he hath always laboured to have still in readiness by him.—His maj. took this occasion to require his minister at the Hague to press the States General very earnestly for expedition in doing that justice which for above a year he had in vain pressed them to do, and in which, he told them, the oppressions his subjects underwent could not bear longer delay. Instead of returning any Answer to his maj. which for some months they deferred to do, they with great passion and noise sent orders to their several admiralties, to prepare and equip a great number of ships of war, the number whereof they increased every 10 or 12 days; with unusual orders, that no time should be lost in making the preparations, but that they should work night and day, as well the Sundays as the other part of the week; and great numbers of landmen were likewise appointed to be raised for their expedition.—This strange kind of treatment, together with many rude pamphlets and insolent expressions, which can hardly be prevented in popular governments, prevailed with his maj. (although he yet believed himself secure in the wisdom of the States General against any rash attempt in the violation of the peace) to take speedy course for the putting 10 or 12 ships into a readiness (which yet he meant should be no further than rigging), if they should pursue their present distempers.—In August, they received news that capt. Holmes, who, with one of his majesty's ships, had convoyed some merchants of the royal company to the coast of Guiney, had by assault taken and possessed himself of a fort near Cape de Verte, belonging to their West Indian Company; whereupon the States General sent a wonderful brisk Message to the king, at once complaining of the injury, and requiring, in very peremptory terms, that his majesty would forthwith give order for the re-delivery of the said fort to them. The king assured the ambassador, upon his princely word, 'That he had given no commission or order to capt. Holmes for that purpose, nor did know upon what grounds he had proceeded to that act of hostility; that he expected him shortly at home; and that he would then proceed in a very strict examination of his proceedings, and would cause exemplary justice to be done, as well in the re-delivering the fort, as in punishing the person if his carriage and demeanor deserved it.' This Answer had no better luck than the former Message: new orders for more ships, for raising of money, for raising of men, publishing in their prints, that what was done by capt. Holmes was by his majesty's warrant and authority; and within a very short time after they had the confidence to demand of his maj. in express terms, that he would give it under his royal hand to them, that he would cause the fort to be delivered within such a time.—His maj. did not yet, after all these provocations, lay aside all hope of awakening the States General to a more temperate consideration of what had passed. He desired them, in an Answer which he made to some of their propositions, and which he transmitted to them under his own hand by their ambassador, to reflect a little upon the method of their proceeding with him, and the course he had observed towards them: not to mention those loud affronts, indignities, and injuries, he had put into oblivion in his late Treaty with them, he put them in mind that, since that treaty, he had given them redress upon their complaints, in many particular cases, with that expedition, that he had not put them to the formalities even of courts of justice; that, instead of any return in this kind from them, his minister at the Hague had importuned these 18 months for about 20 ships taken from his subjects upon the coast of Guinea, and very great affronts and damages sustained by others in the East Indies, without any other shadow of right, but being the stronger, and able to oppress. And yet, since the Treaty required such formalities in the demand of reparations, how slow soever their justice was, he had thus long forborne to be his own carver. He wished them to consider, whether their order of proceeding towards them had been pursuant to the Treaty, or agreeable to the respect that was due to him: that, upon the first information of an act of violence committed by the captain of one of his ships upon their subjects, disowned and disavowed by his maj. himself, and justice and reparation being promised, they have upon the point declared war against his maj. in resolving to recover by force of arms what they could not expect by the course of justice. He conjured the States General to remember the obligations of their own sovereignty, by which they entered into alliances with their neighbour princes: that, if they suffered their particular societies of merchants to involve them in a war with their neighbour nations for their particular interest and benefit, and to support their furious and extravagant assuming a dominion against the law of nations, (putting them in mind, of what he had often demanded justice for, of the Declarations published by their commanders both in the East and West Indies, interdicting all trade and commerce to all other nations, to the natives of those countries, because they call them their subjects,) they would make themselves insupportable to their neighbours, and their friendship inconsistent with the liberty of all the world but themselves.—And, upon this occasion, his maj. thinks fit that his two houses of parliament should know the very compendious way these States have found out to make themselves monarchs of the sole trade of the whole East and West Indies. They have, it is very true, by their very commendable industry, and by other acts of horrible injustice and cruelty, planted themselves in stronger factories than any prince in Europe hath done, especially in the East Indies, where their naval power is very great. When they find the natives inclined to traffic with other nations, as they do generally desire to do, being in truth universally weary of the yoke the Dutch lay upon them, some Dutch ships are sent to lie before those ports, and then declare that they are in war with this or that prince or that city, and thereupon inhibit all other nations to have any traffic or commerce with them; and, by this new reason of state, they inhibited and restrained the English ships, under the command of the earl of Marlborough, 2 years since, to go to Porcatt, and to take in a great cargason of goods provided there by the East Indian company here, and forced his majesty's ships to return empty home: and being exalted with this success in the East, they have published the same Declaration in the West Indies, and not only hindered the English boats and other vessels from going on shore to traffic with the natives, but have very frankly sent to some of the factories, requiring them to remove from the places they are in, because they are resolved they shall not live so near them: and, after all this, to shew how good neighbours they would be at any distance, they hired the king of Fantine, at the price of a great sum of money, arms and ammunition, to surprize his majesty's fort at Cormantine, which he endeavoured to do, by two strong assaults; but, being driven off with loss, he confessed, with sorrow and shame for his own infidelity, being in terms of friendship with the English, that he had been corrupted by the Dutch to that undertaking: his majesty's garrison having had the good fortune to surprize a good part of the arms, ammunition, and grenadoes, which the Dutch sent to the natives. When the king complained to them of this infamous and treacherous proceeding of their chief officers in those parts, of which he hath as full evidence as he can have that there are English and Dutch ships on that coast, or that he hath a Fort called Cormantine, they do assure him, 'That his maj. is misinformed, and desire him not to give any credit to it; for that they have received letters from their commanders there, which mention no such thing, and which informs them that the king of Fantine had taken a particular exception to the English governor;' taking no notice that the king had likewise charged them, that their ships came at the same time, and lay before the Fort, kept several of the English vessels and boats from landing, and took the boats, and kept the men prisoners, till they found the enterprize had miscarried.—To conclude: his maj. used all the arguments he could, to decline these hostile preparations, and to betake themselves to those ways for the preservation of the public peace as were prescribed by the Treaty; assuring them, that as he expected reparation for the damages his subjects had sustained, and security for the future against the like excesses, so he was as ready to give them all the satisfaction for any injuries done to them, which justice could require.—The Answer they gave his maj. to his expostulation for their so sudden giving direction for the provision of so many ships of war, only upon his demanding justice for injuries done, and damages sustained, ought to be made known to you. They answered, 'It was easy to judge how much they were troubled and surprized by the tricks and devices of those that forestalled the parliament of England, and had obliged them by evil informations to carry such sharp complaints against them and their country to his maj.; and therefore it was not strange that, in the unquietness and disturbance which the animosity of the parliament did give them, they had prepared an extraordinary equipage, to be upon their guard.'—When the king found that his moderate way of proceeding was so far from abating any of their preparation, that it did but render them the more confident and exalted; and the ambassador himself had told his majesty, 'That they had given instructions to the admiral of their fleet, that was then going for Guiney, to take their Fort near Cape de Verte by force, and to take any English which had had a hand in doing them injury;' his maj. gave speedy directions for the setting out those ships to sea, towards which he had before only made some light preparations; and declared that he would send his cousin prince Rupert admiral of that fleet, to protect his subjects upon the coast of Guiney. This was no sooner known and published amongst them, than in truth their choler somewhat seemed abated, though their preparations were not diminished: and they then sent, 'That they had a wonderful desire to preserve the peace between the two nations, and to prevent the effusion of Christian blood, which would probably happen, if, in a conjuncture of so much jealousy, two such fleets as were now prepared for Guiney should meet in those seas;' and thereupon proposed, that the fleets on either side might be detained within the harbours, and not suffered to put to sea; and that some expedients might be found out by Treaty for each other's satisfaction, they having, at the same time when they made this plausible overture, sent orders to their fleet in the Streights, under the command of De Royter, to make all possible haste to Guiney, to execute all those Instructions which they had given to their fleet here, which they seemed to be contented, upon those motives of charity, should remain in their ports; and it is now about 2 months since De Ruyter left the Streights upon that expedition, since which time they have done all within their power to make their other fleets ready to convoy each other through the Channel, and which, by the blessing of God, in the cross winds, they have been hitherto restrained from doing; and now his maj. is very willing they should attempt it.—It is a very unpleasant circumstance to his maj. in these proceedings, to find that it hath been in the power of the Dutch West Indian Company to involve their own and this country in a war, without the consent or privity of the States General, whose alone security his maj. hath for the preservation of the peace between the two nations. And his maj. is well assured, that the States General have given no order for this expedition of De Ruyter, though their subjects in general are like to be sufferers in the war thus made by them; for it cannot be imagined but that his maj. will take all the ways he can, that he may have wherewithal in his hands to satisfy his good subjects for the damages he expects to hear, after this denunciation of a war, they have sustained by De Ruyter on the coast of Guiney and other places; and another damage and indignity which, there is too much cause to fear, we shall shortly hear of concerning Polaroone; for, though his maj. cannot expressly say that the delivery of it up is denied to that ship which is gone to receive it, yet, by the carriage of the governor of Batavia to that ship and the officers thereof in its passage to Polaroone, and upon the discourse of that subject, there is too great a presumption that it is not yet delivered up, and in truth that the East India Company in Holland never intended it should be. The States General having likewise begun, without colour of right, by an embargo of ships bound for this kingdom, and driven into their ports by the foulness of the weather, as particularly a Swedish ship laden with masts and cordage bound for London, upon the account of several English merchants here.—This being the true state of what hath passed in this affair; and his maj. having been, by these furious proceedings, and, in truth, denunciation of a war against him, forced to put himself into the posture he is now in, for the defence of his subjects, at so vast an expence, doth not in the least degree doubt but that his two houses of parliament will chearfully enable him to prosecute the war with the same vigour he hath prepared for it, by giving him Supplies proportionable to the charge thereof. C. R."

Thanks to the King for making Preparations against the Dutch.] Nov. 25. Both houses came to the following Resolutions: 1. "That the humble Thanks of both houses be presented to his majesty for his most gracious Speech and Narrative, to his two houses of parliament, and his great care of the preservation of the honour and safety, and trade of the nation, by his Preparations for the defence thereof against the Dutch; and that his maj. would give leave that his Speech may be printed: 2. That the Thanks of both houses be given to the city of London for their forwardness in assisting his majesty; and in particular by furnishing him with several great sums of money towards his Preparations for the bonour, safety, and trade of this nation."

Lord Clarendon's Account of a Meeting of some Lords and principal Commoners, to concert Measures to dispose Parliament to grant a Supply for a Dutch War.] The following curious Account of what took place at a meeting of some lords and principal commoners, to concert measures to dispose parliament to grant a Supply for the carrying on of a Dutch war, is given by the then lord chancellor Clarendon:* "The parliament still promised fairly, and entered upon consultation how and what money to raise. And now the king commanded the chancellor and the treasurer to meet with those members of the house of commons, with whom they had used to consult, and to whom the king had joined others upon whom he was told he might more depend, and to adjust together what sum should be proposed, and how and in what manner to propose and conduct it. The meeting of those persons the king appointed was at Worcester-house, where the chancellor and treasurer (who were known to be averse from the war) told the rest, 'that there was no more debate now to be, war or no war: it was come upon us, and we were now only to contrive the best way of carrying it on with success; which could only be done by raising a great present sum of money, that the enemy might see that we were prepared to continue it as well as to begin.' They who were most desirous of the war, as sir Harry Bennet and Mr. Coventry (who were in truth the men who brought it upon the nation), with their friends, were of the opinion, 'that there should not be a great sum demanded at present, but only so much as might carry out the fleet in the spring, and that sufficient provisions might be made for the summer service: and then, when the war was once thoroughly entered into, another and a better Supply might be gotten about Michaelmas, when there was reason to hope, that some good success would dispose all men to a frank prosecution of the war.' Whereas these gentlemen had hitherto inflamed the king with an assurance, 'that he could not ask more money of the parliament than they would readily give him, if he would be engaged in this war which the whole kingdom so much desired.'—The chancellor and the treasurer were of opinion, 'That the house of commons could never be in a better disposition to give, than they were at present; that hereafter they might grow weary, and apt to find fault with the conduct, especially when they found the country not so well pleased with the war as they were now conceived to be: whereas, now the war was begun, and the king engaged in it as much as he could be after ten battles, and all upon their desire and their promise; they could not refuse to give any thing proposed within the compass of that reason, which all understanding men might examine and judge of. That it was evident enough, that the true ground of all the confidence the Dutch had was from their opinion of the king's necessities and want of money, and their belief that the parliament would supply him very sparingly, and not long to continue such an expence, as they very well knew that a war at sea would require: and they would be much confirmed in this their imagination, if at the beginning they should see the parliament give him such a sum of money, as seemed to be implied by what had been said. That they therefore thought it absolutely necessary, that the king should propose as much, that is, that his friends should move for such a sum, as might upon a reasonable computation, which every man would be ready to make, and of which wise men upon experience would easily make an estimate, carry on the war for a full year; that is, for the setting out the present fleet and paying it off upon its return, and for the setting out another fleet the next spring. If this were now done, his majesty would not be involved in importunate necessities the next winter; but he might calmly and deliberately consult upon such farther supplies, as the experience of what would be then past should suggest to be necessary: and that this would give his majesty such a reputation with all his neighbours, and such terror to his enemies, that it would probably dispose them to peace.' They concluded, 'that a less sum than two millions and a half ought not to be proposed, and being once proposed ought to be insisted on and pursued without consenting to any diminution; for nobody could conceive that it would do more than maintain the war one year, which the parliament could not refuse to provide for in the beginning, as there was so much in truth of it already expended in the preparations and expedition the duke had made in November, when he went to sea upon the fame of the Dutch fleet's intention to convoy their Guinea ships through the channel.'—There was not a man in the company, who did not heartily wish that that sum or a greater might be proposed and granted: but they all, though they agreed in few other things, protested, 'that they could not advise that so prodigious a sum should be as much as named; and that they did not know any one man, since it could not be thought fit that any man who had relation to the king's service should move it, who had the courage to attempt it or would be persuaded to it.'—The two lords continued very obstinate, 'that a less sum should not be named for the reasons they had given,' which the other confessed to be just; and they acknowledged too, 'that the proposition ought not to be made by any man who was related to the court, or was thought to be in any

* Life, p. 228.

grace there that might dispose him, nor yet by any gentleman, how well soever thought of, who was of a small estate, and so to pay little of so great a sum he was so liberal to give.' They therefore desired them to name some of those members, who were honest worthy men, and looked upon as lovers of their country, and of great fortunes, unsuspected to have any designs at court; and if they were not enough acquainted with them, the lords would find some way by themselves or others to move them to it.' Whereupon they named five or six persons very well known, of whom the house had a very good esteem, but without any hope that any of them would be prevailed with to undertake it. The lords said, 'they would try what might be done, and give them notice the next day, that if it were possible it might be the business of the following day.'—The Chancellor and the Treasurer chose three Norfolk gentlemen of those who had been named, because they were good friends and grateful to each other, and desired them the next day 'that they might confer together.' They told them, 'that they knew well the state of affairs; the parliament had engaged the king in a war, that could not be carried on without a vast expence: and therefore if at the entrance into it there should be a small or an ordinary Supply given, it would blast all their hopes, and startle all other princes from joining, with whom the Dutch were not in favour, and who would be inclined to the king, if they saw such a provision for the war as would be sufficient to continue it for some time. And therefore they desired to confer with them, who upon all occasions manifested good affections to the king, and whose advice had a great influence upon the house, upon the whole matter how it might be conducted.' They all consented to what had been said, and promised their own concurrence and utmost endeavours to compass what the king should desire. The lords said, 'They promised themselves more from them, and that they would not only concur, but propose what should be necessary to be granted.' And thereupon they enlarged upon the charge which was already in view, and upon what was to be expected, and concluded, 'that two millions and a half were necessary to be insisted on;' and desired, 'that when the debate should be entered upon, which they hoped might be the next day, one of them would propose this sum and the other would second it.'—They looked long one upon another, as if they were surprised with the sum. At last one of them said, 'that the reasons were unanswerable for a liberal Supply; yet he did not expect that so prodigious a sum, which he believed had never yet been mentioned in parliament to be granted at one time, would be proposed: however he did not think it too much, and that he would do the best he could to answer any objections which should be made against it, as he doubted many would; but he confessed he durst not propose it.' Another was of the same mind, and with many good professions desired to be excused as to the first proposing it. The third, who was sir Robert Paston, a person of a much greater estate than both the other, who had yet very good fortunes, and a gentleman of a very antient extraction by his father (and his mother was daughter to the earl of Lindsey), declared very frankly, 'That he was satisfied in his conscience, that it would be very good for the kingdom as well as for the king that such a sum should be granted; and therefore if they thought him fit to do it, he would propose it the next morning, let other men think what they would of him for it.'"

Sir Robert Paston moves for a Supply of 2,500,000l.: which is agreed to by the House.] "The lords gave him the thanks they ought to do, and said what was necessary to confirm him, and to thank the other gentlemen for their promise to second him, and gave notice to the rest of the resolution, that they might call for the debate the next day; which was entered into with a general cheerfulness, every man acknowledging the necessity and the engagement of the house, but no man adventuring to name the proportion that should be given. When the house was in a deep silence expecting that motion, sir Robert Paston, who was no frequent speaker, but delivered what he had a mind to say very clearly, stood up, mentioned shortly the obligation, the charge of the war, and 'that the present Supply ought to be such as might as well terrify the enemy as assist the king; and therefore he proposed that they might give his majesty two millions and a half, which would amount to five and twenty hundred thousand pounds.' The silence of the house was not broken; they sat as in amazement, until a gentleman, who was believed to wish well to the king, without taking notice of what had been proposed, stood up, and moved that they might give the king a much less proportion. But then the two others, who had promised to second, renewed the motion one after the other; which seemed to be entertained with a consent of many, and was contradicted by none: so that, after a short pause, no man who had relation to the court speaking a word, the Speaker put it to the question, 'Whether they would give the king five and twenty hundred thousand pounds for carrying on the War against the Dutch;' and the affirmative made a good sound, and very few gave their negative aloud, and it was notorious very many sat silent. So the Vote was presently drawn up into an Order; and the house resolved the next day to be in a committee, to agree upon the way that should be taken for the raising this vast sum, the proportion whereof could no more be brought into debate."*

* Mr. Secretary Bennet, in a letter to lord Hollis at Paris, alludes to the above debates in the following words: "My last told your excellency of the opening of the parliament by his majesty's Speech, and the next day, to jus-

The Speaker's Speech on presenting the Money Bill to the King.] Feb. 9, The grand Money bill being ready for the royal assent, the king came this day to the house of peers, where the Speaker of the house of commons presented his majesty with the said bill, and made the speech following:

"May it please your most excellent majesty; The last session of this parliament, the lords and commons did humbly represent unto your maj. the many wrongs and indignities that were done to your maj. and the many injuries done to your merchants, by the subjects of the United Provinces: and did most humbly beseech your maj. that some effectual course might be taken for redress thereof.—Your maj. at the opening of this session, was graciously pleased to acquaint your two houses, that, in pursuance of their desires, you had, by your agent, required satisfaction; but that way proved ineffectual, and many fresh provocations were offered, whereby your maj. was necessitated to a warlike preparation; by the speedy Dispatch whereof, you had let your neighbours see, that you could defend yourself and your subjects against their insolence, upon the stock of your own credit, before your parliament came together.—And now, sir, give me leave to say, your neighbours may see how a great king is made greater by his parliament. Your loyal commons, after they convened, did not suffer full four and twenty hours to pass, before they most chearfully gave your maj. more than four and twenty hundred thousand pounds.—Historians tell us, that in Biscay, a signiory of Spain, when the king entereth into the frontiers of the country, the lords and gentlemen there dwelling proffer him some few brass pieces, called Maravedis, in a leather bag hanged at the end of a lance: but withal they tell him, that he must not take them.—Great sir; Your lords and commons will not only yield obedience to you with their bodies, but with their purses also: in token whereof, I do, in the name of all the commons of England, present unto your maj. this Bill, whereby we have given unto your maj. a royal aid of 2,477,500*l.* to be paid in 3 years, by 12 quarterly payments, to begin from the 25th of Dec. last. And we do humbly beseech your maj. to accept it, as a pregnant demonstration of our most unfeigned duty and thankfulness to your majesty."

The King's Speech.] After passing the Bill, his majesty made the following short Speech: "Mr. Speaker, and you Gentlemen of the house of Commons; You have given me a very noble present, worthy of yourselves, and worthy of the Vote you passed on the 22d of April last; for which I thank you as much as is possible for me to do. I hope that your liberality herein will appear to be good husbandry. And I assure you that the monies shall be employed as you yourselves would wish. My Lords and Gentlemen; I perceive by the Bill, that you have put an engagement upon yourselves to be suddenly in the country; and therefore I desire you to hasten your councils, that so I may put an end to this session as soon as is possible. I have no more to add, but again to give you my hearty thanks."

The King's Declaration of War against the States of Holland.] Feb. 22. The parl. having thus shewn the sense of the people by this royal aid, and the hearts of the trading part of the nation being now entirely turned against the Dutch, the king ordered the drawing up of a formal Declaration of War, signed and approved this day, and is as follows:

"Whereas upon complaint of the several injuries, affronts, and spoils done by the East and West India Companies, and other the subjects of the United Provinces, unto and upon the ships, goods, and persons of our subjects, to their grievous damages, and amounting to vast sums: instead of reparation and satisfaction, which hath been by us frequently demanded, we found that orders had been given to De Ruyter, not only to abandon the consortship against the pyrates of the Mediterranean seas, to which the States-General had invited us, but also to use all acts of depredation and hostility against our subjects in Africa. We therefore gave order for the detaining the ships belonging to the states of the United Provinces, their subjects and inhabitants: yet, notwithstanding we did not give any commission for Letters of Mart, nor were there any proceedings against the ships detained, until we had a clear and undeniable evidence that De Ruyter had put the said orders in execution by seizing several of our subjects ships and goods. But now finding by these fresh injuries and actings of theirs, and the intelligence we have had of their great preparations for war, and their granting of Letters of Mart against our people, that both our forbearance, and the other remedies we have used to bring them to a compliance with us, have proved ineffectual, and that they are resolved what they

---

tify all the fair hopes we had of their supporting cheerfully this war, the house of commons voted the raising to his majesty, in 3 years, two millions five hundred thousand pounds sterling: but coming the next day to debate the manner of raising it, they did not agree so well, but parted late in the evening with great heat: notwithstanding which, they have this day concluded very peaceably, that the committee of the whole house do proceed to consider of the raising of the 2,500,000*l.* in a regulated, subsidiary way, reducing the same to a certainty in all counties, so as no person for his real or personal estate be exempted. The great strife hath been between subsidies and land-tax: the first will make a great noise, and one of uncertain value; the last was the child of these ill times, hath been renounced since the king came home, and, at the best, is unequally laid upon all the counties; so that your excellency must not be surprised, if you hear some days have been spent in making the manner effective, since all agree in the quantum."

have done by wrong, to maintain by arms and war against us:—We have therefore thought fit, by and with the advice of our privy-council, to declare, and do hereby declare to all the world, That the said states are the aggressors, and that they ought in justice to be so looked upon by all men: so that as well our fleets and ships, as all other ships and vessels that shall be commissionated by Letters of Mart from our dear brother the duke of York, lord high admiral of England, shall and may lawfully fight with, subdue, seize, and take all ships, vessels, and goods belonging to the States of the United Provinces, or any of their subjects or inhabitants within any of their territories. And we do hereby command as well all our own subjects, as advertise all other persons of what nation soever, not to transport or carry any soldiers, arms, powder, ammunition, or any other contraband goods, to any of the territories, lands, plantations, or countries of the said States of the United Provinces; Declaring, That whatsoever ship or vessel shall be met withal, transporting or carrying any soldiers, arms, powder, ammunition, or other contraband goods to any of the territories, lands, plantations, or countries of the said States of the United Provinces, the same being taken, shall be condemned as good and lawful prize. And we do farther declare, That whatsoever ship or vessel, of what nation soever, shall be met withal, having any goods, merchandizes, or any number of persons in her belonging to the said States of the United Provinces, or any of their subjects or inhabitants, the whole being taken, shall be adjudged as good and lawful prize. As likewise all goods and merchandizes, of what nation soever, whether of our own or of foreigners, that shall be laden aboard any ship or vessel that shall belong to the States of the United Provinces, or any of their subjects, or any inhabiting with them, and shall be taken, the whole shall be condemned as good and lawful prize; except the said ship or vessel hath ours, or our dear brother's Letters of Safe Conduct granted to them. And to the end that due intimation and publication of this our Declaration may be made, and public notice thereof be taken, it is our will and pleasure that this our present Declaration be published in due and usual form*."

Account of the Act for taxing the Clergy in Parliament.] During this session there began, says archdeacon Echard, a very extraordinary change in the liberties and properties of the Clergy of England, by altering the way of taxing themselves as formerly, and being taxed in common with the people in parliament. It is to be observed, that by the original constitution of the nation, the lords spiritual and prelates and Clergy were esteemed one of the three estates of the realm, and therefore met in Convocation on the civil account of giving their own Money, and securing their own secular rights and liberties. This right of taxing themselves, and of not being taxed by parliaments, had been inviolably observed before, as well as after the Reformation; only with this small difference, that, after the Reformation, their grants of subsidy, for the more certainty of collecting of them, were usually confirmed by acts of parliament; and yet they gave Benevolences as formerly, to be levied and paid according to rules and constitutions of their own making. The Rebellion in the late reign, and the following usurpations, were the first that broke in upon this peculiar privilege: for the ministers of those times, either out of voluntary compliance, affectation of popularity, or for want of proxies to represent their body, had their benefices taxed with the laity, in the pretended parliaments then held. But at the king's Restoration, this antient right of the Church was recovered with him; and thus the matter continued for the first 4 years. But now, as it appeared, some of the bishops and clergy fell into sentiments very different from those of their predecessors. They began to think this customary method of taxing themselves somewhat burthensome: they probably thought the expectations of the court might be set too high upon them this way; and that the commons were often discontented, unless they over-charged themselves, and swelled their Subsidies beyond a reasonable proportion. We shall not examine how well these jealousies were founded; but it is said, that the apprehension of these and other inconveniences, brought abp. Sheldon, and some other leading prelates, into a concert with chancellor Clarendon, treasurer Southampton, and some others of the ministry. And now, at a consultation, it was concluded, that the Clergy should silently wave the ancient custom of taxing their own body, and suffer themselves to be included in the Money-Bills prepared by the commons: and to encourage their assent to this cession, two of their 4 Subsidies, they had granted last year, were to be remitted; and over and above they had the promise of a clause for saving their ancient rights.—This being complied with, the security was accordingly given, and a very clear comprehensive Proviso inserted in the 'Act for granting a Royal Aid unto the King's majesty,' which ought not to be forgot. It stands thus: 'Provided always, and be it enacted by the authority aforesaid, That all spiritual promotions, and all lands, possessions or revenues annexed to, and all goods and chattels growing, or renewed upon the same or elsewhere, appertaining to the owners of the said spiritual promotions, or any of them, which are or shall be charged, or made contributing to this act towards the payment aforesaid, during the time therein appointed, (which

* It is observable that though this Declaration was approved of by no less than 22 of the privy-council, whose names are placed in the front, yet we find that neither the chancellor Clarendon, nor the treasurer Southampton, were, or would be concerned in this great and difficult affair. Echard, p. 817.

was to be raised, levied, and paid in the space of 3 years) shall be absolutely freed and discharged from the two last of the 4 Subsidies granted by the Clergy to his maj. his heirs and successors, by an Act made in the former session of this present parliament, entitled 'An Act for confirming of 4 Subsidies, granted by the Clergy,' any clause or thing in the said act to the contrary notwithstanding. Provided always, That nothing herein contained shall be drawn into example, to the prejudice of the ancient rights belonging unto the lords spiritual and temporal, or clergy of this realm, or unto either of the said universities, or unto any colleges, schools, alms-houses, hospitals, or cinque ports.' Notwithstanding this saving Proviso, which has expressly secured all rights, the Clergy seemed to have acquiesced for the future, and never after resumed their great claim; and from this time, during the whole reign, the Convocation met principally for form sake. The parochial Clergy however gained one privilege, which they had not before, which was their voting for members of the house of commons: but whether they were gainers or losers in the whole, has been a matter of some dispute; yet we think a very little consideration will determine whether the gaining of the latter privilege be a full compensation for the waving, if not the losing the former.*

Proceedings in the H. of Lords, relative to a Bill for granting Indulgences for Liberty of Conscience.] The following curious account of the Proceedings relative to a Bill for granting of Indulgences for Liberty of Conscience is given by the lord chancellor Clarendon †.

"In the former session of the parliament,' says his lordship, 'the lord Ashley out of his indifferency in matters of Religion, and the lord Arlington out of his good-will to the Roman Catholicks, had drawn in the lord Privy Seal, whose interest was most in the Presbyterians, to propose to the king an Indulgence for Liberty of Conscience: for which they offered two motives; the one the probability of a war with the Dutch, though it was not then declared; and in that case, the prosecution of people at home for their several opinions in Religion would be very inconvenient, and might prove mischievous.' The other was, 'That the fright men were in by reason of the late Bill against Conventicles, and the warmth the Parliament expressed with reference to the Church, had so prepared all sorts of Non-Conformists, that they would gladly compound for liberty at any reasonable rates: and by this means a good yearly revenue might be raised to the king, and a firm concord and tranquillity be established in the kingdom, if power were granted by the parliament to the king to grant Dispensations to such whom he knew to be peaceably affected, for their exercise of that religion which was agreeable to their conscience, without undergoing the penalty of the laws.' And they had prepared a schedule, in which they computed what every Roman Catholick would be willing to pay yearly for the exercise of his religion, and so of every other sect; which upon the estimate they made, would indeed have amounted to a very great sum of money yearly.—The king liked the arguments and the project very well, and wished them to prepare such a Bill; which was done quickly, very short, and without any mention of other advantage to grow from it, than 'the 'peace and quiet of the kingdom, and an entire 'reference to the king's own judgment and dis'cretion in dispensing his dispensations.' This was equally approved: and though hitherto it had been managed with great secrecy, that it might not come to the knowledge of the chancellor and the Treasurer, who they well knew would never consent to it; yet the king resolved to impart it to them. And the Chancellor being then afflicted with the gout, the committee that used to be called was appointed to meet at Worcester-House: and thither likewise came the Privy Seal and the lord Ashley, who had never before been present in those meetings.—The king informed them of the occasion of their conference, and caused the draught for the Bill to be read to them; which was done, and such reasons given by those who promoted it, as they thought fit; the chief of which was, 'That there could be no danger in trusting the king, whose zeal to the Protestant Religion was so well known that nobody would doubt that he would use this power, when granted to him, otherwise than should be for the good and benefit of the church and state.' The Chancellor and the Treasurer, as had been presaged, were very warm against it, and used many arguments to dissuade the king from prosecuting it, 'as a thing that could never find the concurrence of either or both houses, and which would raise a jealousy in both, and in the people generally of his affection to the Papists, which would not be good for either, and every body knew that he had no favour for either of the other factions.' But what the others said, who were of another opinion, prevailed more; and his majesty declared, 'That the Bill should be presented to the house of peers as from him, and in his name; and that he hoped none of his servants, who knew his mind as well as every body there did, would oppose it, but either be absent or silent:' To which both the lords answered, 'That they should not be absent purposely, and if they were present, they hoped his majesty would excuse them if they spake according to their conscience and judgment, which they could not forbear to do;' with which his maj. seemed unsatisfied, though the lords of the combination were better pleased than they would have been with their concurrence.—Within few days after, the Chancellor remaining still in his chamber without being able to go, the Bill was presented in the house of peers by the Lord Privy Seal, as by the king's direction and approbation, and thereupon had the first reading: and as soon as it was read, the Lord Treasurer spake against it,

* Echard, p. 818. † Life, p. 245.

'as unfit to be received and to have the countenance of another reading in the house, being a design against the Protestant Religion and in favour of the Papists,' with many sharp reflections upon those who had spoken for it; and many of the Bishops spake to the same purpose, and urged many weighty arguments against it. However it was moved, 'That since it was averred that it was with the king's privity, it would be a thing unheard of to deny it a second reading:' and that there might be no danger of a surprisal by its being read in a thin house, it was ordered 'that it should be read the 2nd time upon a day named,' with which all were satisfied. In the mean time great pains were taken to persuade particular men to approve it: and some of the Bishops were sharply reprehended for opposing the king's prerogative, with some intimation, 'that if they continued in that obstinacy they would repent it;' to which they made such answers as in honesty and wisdom they ought to do, without being shaken in their resolution. It was rather insinuated than declared, 'That the Bill had been perused,' some said 'drawn, by the Chancellor,' and averred that he was not against it: which being confidently reported, and believed or not believed as he was more or less known to the persons present, he thought himself obliged to make his own sense known. And so on the day appointed for the 2nd reading, with pain and difficulty he was in his place in the house: and so after the 2nd reading of the bill, he was of course to propose the commitment of it. Many of the Bishops and others spake fiercely against it, as a way to undermine religion; and the Lord Treasurer with his usual weight of words shewed the ill consequence that must attend it, and 'that in the bottom it was a project to get Money at the price of Religion; which he believed was not intended or known to the king, but only to those who had projected it, and it may be imposed upon others who meant well.'—The Lord Privy Seal, either upon the observation of the countenance of the house or advertisement of his friends, or unwilling to venture his reputation in the enterprise, had given over the game the first day, and now spake not at all: but the lord Ashley adhered firmly to his point, spake often and with great sharpness of wit, and had a cadence in his words and pronunciation that drew attention. He said, 'it was the king's misfortune that a matter of so great concernment to him, and such a prerogative as it may be would be found to be inherent in him without any declaration of parliament, should be supported only by such weak men as himself, who served his maj. at a distance, whilst the great officers of the crown thought fit to oppose it; which he more wondered at, because nobody knew more than they the king's unshakeable firmness in his religion, that had resisted and vanquished so many great temptations: and therefore he could not be thought unworthy of a greater trust with reference to it, than he would have by this bill.' —The Chancellor having not been present at the former debate upon the first day, thought it fit to sit silent in this, till he found the house in some expectation to hear his opinion: and then he stood up and said, 'That no man could say more, if it were necessary or pertinent, of the king's constancy in his religion, and of his understanding the constitution and foundation of the Church of England, than he; no man had been witness to more assaults which he had sustained than he had been, and of many victories; and therefore if the question were how far he might be trusted in that point, he should make no scruple in declaring, that he thought him more worthy to be trusted than any man alive. But there was nothing in that Bill that could make that the question, which had confounded all notions of religion, and erected a chaos of policy to overthrow all religion and government: so that the question was not, whether the king were worthy of that trust, but whether that trust were worthy of the king. That it had been no new thing for kings to divest themselves of many particular rights and powers, because they were thereby exposed to more trouble and vexation, and so deputed that authority to others qualified by them: and he thought it a very unreasonable and unjust thing to commit such a trust to the king, which nobody could suppose he could execute himself, and yet must subject him to daily and hourly importunities, which must be so much the more uneasy to a nature of so great bounty and generosity, that nothing is so ungrateful to him as to be obliged to deny.'—In the vehemence of this debate, the lord Ashley having used some language that he knew reflected upon him, the Chancellor let fall some unwary expressions which were turned to his reproach, and remembered long after. When he insisted upon the wildness and illimitedness in the Bill, he said, 'it was Ship-Money in Religion, that nobody could know the end of, or where it would rest; that if it were passed, Dr. Goffe or any other apostate from the Church of England might be made a bishop or abp. here, all oaths and statutes and subscriptions being dispensed with:' which were thought two envious instances, and gave his enemies opportunities to make glosses and reflections upon to his disadvantage. In this debate it fell out that the duke of York appeared very much against the Bill; which was imputed to the Chancellor, and served to heap coals of fire upon his head. In the end, very few having spoken for it, though there were many who would have consented to it, besides the Catholick lords, it was agreed that there should be no question put for the commitment; which was the most civil way of rejecting it, and left it to be no more called for.—The king was infinitely troubled at the ill success of this Bill, which he had been assured would pass notwithstanding the opposition that was expected; and it had produced one effect that was foreseen though not believed, in renewing the bitterness against the Roman Catholicks. And they, who watch-ed all occasions to perform those offices, had now a large field to express their malice against the Chancellor and the Treasurer, 'whose pride only had disposed them to shew their power and credit in diverting the house from gratifying the king, to which they had been inclined;' and his majesty heard all that could be said against them without any dislike. After 2 or 3 days he sent for them both together into his closet, which made it generally believed in the court, that he resolved to take both their offices from them, and they did in truth believe and expect it: but there was never any cause appeared after to think that it was in his purpose. He spake to them of other business, without taking the least notice of the other matter, and dismissed them with a countenance less open than he used to have towards them, and made it evident that he had not the same thoughts of them he had formerly.—And when the next day the Chancellor went to him alone, and was admitted into his cabinet, and began to take notice 'that he seemed to have dissatisfaction in his looks towards him;' the king, in more choler than he had ever before seen him, told him, 'his looks were such as they ought to be; that he was very much unsatisfied with him, and thought he had used him very ill; that he had deserved better of him, and did not expect that he would have carried himself in that manner as he had done in the house of peers, having known his majesty's own opinion from himself, which it seemed was of no authority with him if it differed from his judgment, to which he would not submit against his reason.' The other, with the confidence of an honest man, entered upon the discourse of the matter, assured him 'the very proposing it had done his maj. much prejudice, and that they who were best affected to his service in both houses were much troubled and afflicted with it: and of those who advised him to it, one knew nothing of the constitution of England, and was not thought to wish well to the Religion of it; and the other was so well known to him, that nothing was more wonderful than that his maj. should take him for a safe counsellor.' He had recourse then again to the matter, and used some arguments against it which had not been urged before, and which seemed to make impression. He heard all he said with patience, but seemed not to change his mind, and answered no more than 'That it was no time to speak to the matter, which was now passed; and if it had been unseasonably urged, he might still have carried himself otherwise than he had done;' and so spake of somewhat else."

The Speaker's Speech to the King at the Prorogation.] March 2. The Bills being ready for the royal assent, and a prorogation being resolved on, the king came this day to the house of peers, where the Speaker of the commons addressed his majesty as follows:

"May it please your most excellent majesty; The knights, citizens, and burgesses of the commons house of parliament, having in the beginning of this session applied themselves to the aiding your majesty in your naval preparations, have of late considered of some Bills that may be most grateful to the people, either in redressing things that are grievous to them, or in advancing their trade and commerce, which are the soul and life of the nation.—Evil manners produce good laws; but the best laws in time may grow obsolete: and such is the wicked nature of man, that when he cannot by force break through a law, he will by fraud and tricks endeavour to evade it.—I may with great truth affirm, the Common Law of England is the best municipal law in the world; and yet, if the legislative power were not ready to countermine the works, and make up the breaches that are daily made upon it, the sons of Zeruiah would be too strong for us.—We have now presented your maj. with several Bills for the Regulation of the Law, which will serve to prune some exuberant branches, and to pull away the ivy that robbed this tree of her just nourishment: and if your majesty now be pleased graciously to shine upon her, she will yield her fruit in great abundance, to the content of your majesty and all your people.—Cosmographers do agree, that this Island is incomparably furnished with pleasant rivers, like veins in the natural body, which conveys the blood into all the parts, whereby the whole is nourished, and made useful; but the poet tells us, he acts best, 'qui miscuit utile dulci:' therefore we have prepared some Bills for making small Rivers navigable; a thing that in other countries hath been more experienced, and hath been found very advantageous: it easeth the people of the great charge of land carriages; preserves the highways, which are daily worn out with waggons carrying excessive burdens; it breeds up a nursery of watermen, which, upon occasion, will prove good seamen; and with much facility maintain intercourse and communion between cities and countries.—We have been much affected with the cries and wants of the poor this hard season, especially those about this town, who are ready to starve for want of fuel, the price of coals being so unreasonably enhanced by the extorting engrossers. We have, therefore, for their present and future ease, prepared a Bill authorizing the lord mayor and the court of aldermen in the city of London, and 3 justices of peace in the country, whereof one to be of the quorum, from time to time, to set the prices of Coals, having regard to the price paid to the importer, and other emergent charges.—And now, great sir, having finished our present councils, we hope your majesty will give us leave to return for a time into our countries, where, in our several spheres, we shall be ready to serve you with our persons and our purses, and also with our prayers to the great God of Hosts, that he will be pleased to strengthen your hands in the day of battle, and make your majesty victorious over all your enemies both at home and abroad."

The King's Speech at the Prorogation.] After passing the Bills, his majesty made a short Speech, the effect of it was: "He told the lords and commons, he had very little to say more than again to renew his thanks to them for the present they made him when he met them last here.—He desired the gentlemen of the house of commons, that, when they are returned into their countries, they would take care for the equal rating the Taxes laid upon the people.--His majesty told the commons, He had been at some charge himself, that no counties might be over-rated: and he persuaded himself, that if the members of the house of commons and the rest of the commissioners will take care that it might be equally taxed in the several countries, it will be the more readily and chearfully paid in. And his majesty desired those that were lieutenants and deputy lieutenants, that they would take care to preserve the peace of the kingdom; for, his maj. did assure them, the republican party have still their councils on foot, and are yet in hopes to make some advantage to themselves, upon the score of the present war. But his maj. did not doubt but, by God's blessing upon his and their endeavours, their expectations would be frustrated.—His maj. said, his intentions were, that the houses should not meet here again till this time 12 months. But, lest there should be any occasion of his needing their assistance sooner, he did intend the prorogation shall be only till June next; before which, he should by a timely proclamation give notice of the next meeting, if it hold not at that time."

Both houses were then prorogued to the 21st of June; afterwards to the 1st of Aug. and lastly to the 9th of October.

FIFTH SESSION OF THE SECOND PARLIAMENT. HELD AT OXFORD.

The King's Speech on opening the Session.] Oct. 9, 1665. The Plague raging in London and Westminster, the parliament met this day at Oxford, where the University-Schools were prepared for the reception of both houses: notwithstanding which, the king commanded both houses to attend him in the Great Hall at Christ-Church, and, on the 10th, opened the session with the following Speech:

"My Lords and Gentlemen; I am confident you all believe, that if it had not been absolutely necessary to consult with you, I would not have called you together at this time, when the Contagion hath so spread itself over so many parts of the kingdom. I take it for a good omen to see so good an appearance this day; and I doubt not but every day will add to your number; and I give you all my thanks for your compliance so far with my desires.—The truth is, as I entered upon this War by your advice and encouragement, so I desire that you may, as frequently as is possible, receive information of the conduct and effects of it; and that I may have the continuance of your chearful Supply for the carrying it on. I will not deny to you, that it hath proved more chargeable than I could imagine it would have been: the addition they still made to their Fleets beyond their first purpose, made it unavoidably necessary for me to make proportionable preparations, which God hath hitherto blessed with success in all encounters. And as the enemies have used their utmost endeavours, by calumnies and false suggestions, to make themselves friends, and to persuade others to assist them against us; so I have not been wanting to encourage those princes who have been wronged by the Dutch, to recover their own by force; and, in order thereunto, have assisted the bishop of Munster with a very great sum of ready money, and am to continue a Supply to him, who is now in the bowels of their country with a powerful army. These issues, which I may tell you have been made with very good conduct and husbandry (nor indeed do I know that any thing hath been spent that could have been well and safely saved); I say, this expence will not suffer you to wonder, that the great Supply which you gave me for this war in so bountiful a proportion is upon the matter already spent, so that I must not only expect an assistance from you to carry on this war, but such an assistance as may enable me to defend myself and you against a more powerful neighbour, if he shall prefer the friendship of the Dutch before mine.—I told you, when I entered upon this war, that I had not such a brutal appetite, as to make war for war-sake. I am still of the same mind; I have been ready to receive any propositions that France hath thought fit to offer to that end; but hitherto nothing hath been offered worthy my acceptance: nor is the Dutch less insolent; though I know no advantage they have, but the continuance of the contagion. God Almighty, I hope, will shortly deprive them of that encouragement. The Chancellor will inform you of all the particulars."

The Lord Chancellor (Clarendon's) Speech, detailing the State of Public Affairs.] The Lord Chancellor then rose and spoke as followeth:

"My lords; and you the knights, citizens, and burgesses, of the house of commons; The king is not content, you see, to leave you to yourselves, to make a state of the war, and the success that hath attended it, by your own observation, and the general communication of all that hath fallen out, which in truth have left few men ignorant of any thing, who have had any curiosity to inform themselves; but takes care that you be informed by himself, that you may know all that he knows, that so you may be able to give him your counsel upon the clearest evidence.—In order to this, it will not, I hope, be unreasonable or ungrateful to you, to refresh your memory, by looking some years backwards, even to the time of his majesty's happy restoration, that we may take the better prospect of the posture we are now in, and how we have come into it. What inclinations his maj. brought home with him to live in amity with his neighbours of Holland, though he had received indignities enough from them, and in truth had been little less proscribed there than he had been in England, needs no other manifestation, than that he chose that place to embark himself in, when he was pressed by the two neighbour kings, from whom he had received more civilities, to have made use of their ports.—It cannot be denied but that his reception in Holland was with great civility and lustre, and a sufficient evidence that they had a full sense of the high honour his maj. had vouchsafed to them, and the departure from thence was with equal and mutual satisfaction in each other; which made many men the more wonder, that, albeit the ambassadors who were to follow had been nominated before the king left the Hague, there was so long an interval before their arrival here, that the two neighbour kings and many other princes had finished their embassies of congratulations, before we had heard any more from the United Provinces.—You all remember how long it was before the armies were disbanded, and the fleets paid off; during which time his maj. lived upon his credit, and easily contracted a great debt, for the mere support of himself and his household, which was not so easily discharged afterwards. There was one thing that exceedingly surprized him, when he found (which will be incredible to posterity) that a triumphant nation, that had made itself terrible to Christendom, by having fought more battles that all the neighbour kingdoms and states together had ever done in so few years, and seemed to be in a posture ready to fight them over again, that had so long reigned over the ocean in formidable fleets, should, at the time of his majesty's happy return, as if on the sudden all their arms had been turned into plough-shares, and their swords into pruning-hooks, not have in all the magazines, in all the stores, arms enough to be put into the hands of 5000 men, nor provision enough to set out ten new ships to sea; which his maj. did not desire should be known to his best neighbours, how little soever he suspected their affections, nor did indeed so much as make it known to his parliament; but made it his first care, without the least noise, and with all imaginable shifts, to provide for the full supply of those important magazines and stores, which have been ever since replenished as they ought to be.—He had not the least imagination, that any of his neighbours would wantonly affect to interrupt the happy calm that he and themselves enjoyed; and therefore resolved to retrench the vast expence of the Navy, under which he found the nation even to groan, and out of that good husbandry to provide for more necessary disbursements. Yet, that the world might not think that he had abandoned the Ocean, and that the memory of the glorious actions the English had so lately performed upon it might not vanish in an instant, after he had provided such a guard as the Narrow Seas never ought to be without, in the Spring he sent a strong fleet against the pirates of Argiers and Tripoli (who had grown to that strength and boldness that they interrupted the whole trade of Christendom), as the only enemies he would choose to have.—It was a design of great glory and equal expence, crowned in the end by God Almighty with the success we could wish, and with an entire submission to the English flag, and as great security to all his majesty's subjects in their trade as the engagement and honour of infidels can give; and this agreement ratified with all formality (the like whereof had never been before) by the Great Turk himself.—Hereupon the king again renewed his resolution for a further retrenchment of his naval expence, even to the lessening the guard in the narrow seas, his merchants in all places receiving less interruption in their trade than they had in any former time undergone, until he received intelligence from the Straights, that the faithless people of Argiers, who had so lately submitted to him, had committed new insolencies upon some of his subjects, or rather upon foreign persons taken by his subjects into their protections, and which the Turks pretended they might do without violation of the Treaty. But his maj. resolving to admit none of those elucidations, lost no time in sending a new strong fleet into the Mediterranean Sea, to chastise those perfidious pirates; and after a chargeable war made upon them for near or full 12 months, and after having taken several of their ships from them, and upon the matter blocking them up in their harbours, he received a second submission from them, with better and more advantageous conditions than the former.—I must not omit one circumstance, that about this time the Dutch, who received much more prejudice and damage from the Turks than the English had done, besought his maj. that he would once more send a fleet into those seas against those pirates, and that it might upon all occasions join with one they were likewise ready to send out to the same Christian end, and for the extirpation of those sea robbers; and within a very short time after the English Fleet was gone, they likewise sent De Ruyter with a good fleet thither, which was so far from any conjunction with us, that when our ships chaced any Argier men near them, they never offered to obstruct their flight, but quickly made it manifest that they rather brought money with them to buy a dishonourable and disadvantageous peace, than to make a war upon them.—Matters standing thus, the king's fleet being gone into the Streights against the Turkish pirates, and there remaining few ships in the Narrow Seas, we began every day to hear of depredations by the Dutch upon our merchants in all parts. Instead of delivering up the Island of Poleroone in the East Indies, as by the Treaty they ought to have done, they, by their naval power in those parts, hindered our ships to take in their lading of such merchandize as the factors had provided and made ready for their freight, upon pretence that those ports where the merchandize was ready to be embarked were in the dominions of some princes who they had declared to be their enemies, and so they would not suffer any traffic to be maintained with them; and they published the like declaration, and challenged the same sovereignty, in Africa, and by virtue thereof would not suffer our ships to trade upon that coast, where we had a trade long before the Dutch had any footing in those parts.—These insolencies made that noise in the world, that the English merchants felt the effects of it in all places, till it reached the ears of the parliament, which in April was 12 months presented the same to his maj. and besought him that he would take some speedy and effectual course for the redress of those wrongs, dishonours, and indignities, which were the greatest obstructions of our Trade; and declared, that, in the prosecution thereof, they would with their lives and fortunes assist his maj. against all opposition whatsoever.—My Lords and Gentlemen; You very well remember, that though his maj. was very well pleased with the great zeal you shewed for the Advancement of Trade, he was far from resolving to make a war upon the warmth of that Declaration; but told you, that he would examine and peruse the particular complaints which had been represented to his parliament, and would thereupon demand justice and reparation from the States General; which demand he appointed his minister residing there to make in a short time after. What effect that candid way of proceeding found, is enough known to the world: instead of other application, they declared themselves wonderfully offended with the declaration of the parliament, with many insolent expressions, suitable to the manners of a Commonwealth. They gave present order for equipping a very great fleet, and the raising many land soldiers, making greater preparations for war than they had done in many years before. They had made a complaint to his maj. that a captain of one of the ships which his maj. had lent to the royal company had, in his voyage thither, taken a Fort belonging to them, near Cape Verte, for which they demanded satisfaction. The king assured them, that he had not the least commission or authority from him for so doing: that he expected him home very speedily; and then he should be sure to undergo that punishment which the nature of his offence required, when the matter should be examined; and they should be sure to receive full reparation. This satisfied them not; but, in a great fury, they resolved to send forth a strong fleet to Guinea, and granted a commission (which they took care to publish) to the commander in chief, to make war upon the English in those parts, and to do them all the mischief they could.—The king found himself now obliged, in what straight soever, to provide for the protection of his subjects in those parts, and for the support of that trade, which, I doubt, is not enough taken to heart, and the value thereof not enough understood; and, in order thereunto, with great speed, caused a fleet to be made ready for that expedition, under the command of his highness prince Rupert, who was under sail for the voyage, when his maj. found it necessary to stop the prince's further prosecution of it, upon good intelligence that the Dutch had appointed their admiral, with a fleet of 50 sail, to convoy the other fleet designed for Guinea, through the Channel, in contempt of his maj. who had a very small fleet in readiness; and that De Ruyter was likewise sent out of the Straights from prosecuting the Turks, to make war upon the English in Guinea, when at the same time they had earnestly pressed the king, upon many professions of desire to prevent a war, that prince Rupert's fleet might stay in harbour, as theirs should do, till some means might be found for an accommodation of all differences; and, in truth, this very difficult stratagem, of pretending one thing and intending another, of promising with all solemnity and never resolving to perform, of swearing this day not to do a thing when they had served their turn by having done it yesterday, that nobody could know, is the highest pinnacle of their wisdom of state, by which they govern their affairs, and delude their neighbours.—The winds were not favourable to this triumphant design. And now the king found the value of the Vote and Declaration of his parliament; it was a rich and a massy vote, which in a short time he coined into 200,000*l.* ready money, in the Chamber of the city of London, with which he gave order forthwith to make ready more ships: and the duke going himself to the fleet, by his indefatigable industry, with incredible expedition, added so many good ships to those under the command of prince Rupert, that in Nov. he put himself on board the fleet, resolving to stop the Dutch, if the wind gave them leave to pursue their former resolution, which, from the time the duke was known to be at sea, they fairly declined, and were content rather to be safe in their own harbours, than to look to the security of their merchants. It was high time now to seize upon as many of their ships as came in our way, to satisfy the damages we had reason to believe we should sustain from De Ruyter's expedition into Guinea with the commission mentioned before; but there was not the lading of one ship sold, or disposed of, till his maj. received full information of De Ruyter's having begun the war upon the coast of Africa, by seizing upon our ships, taking our forts, and committing all the acts of hostility which his commission directed him unto; his maj. likewise at the same time receiving new advertisement of their refusal to deliver up the Island of Poleroone to him, which they were bound to by their Treaty. And will you not wonder, after all this, at the confidence of these men; and more, that any neighbour prince should have that confidence in them, as to declare, that the king our master is the aggressor, that he first began the war?—From this time the war began to be more in earnest, and to be carried on at another expence. Though his royal highness ventured himself in Nov. in a fleet consisting of little more than fifty ships, to stop the Dutch from passing through the Channel; yet, in April (which was within few days after your prorogation at the end of your last session), he went again to sea, with a much stronger fleet, and more proportionate to the great preparations the enemy had made; and even after he was gone to sea, upon great additions of strength every day made by the Dutch, more good ships were sent to reinforce the Fleet; insomuch as, upon that glorious 3rd of June, when they had the courage to visit our coasts, after the duke had in vain called upon them at their own doors, and took many of their merchants ships in their sight, the English fleet consisted of very few less than 100 sail. The action and blessing of that day hath been celebrated in all the churches in England, and in the hearty devotions of all true Englishmen; and therefore I shall say no more of it here, save only, that whether the public joy then, even upon the solemn Thanksgiving-day, was superior to the universal consternation that spread itself over the nation before, I appeal to the breasts of all here present. We, who had the honour to be near the king at that time, observed him to be in that agony that cannot be expressed, an agony himself could not have long endured, even when, by all the intelligence he received hourly from the coast, he had reason to assure himself of the victory. In that great action, we sunk, burned, and took, 18 good ships of war, whereof half were the best they had, with the loss of one single small ship of ours, but of many noble and gallant persons, of too much value to be ventured (if there had not been a greater venture) against such trash, and whose memories ought ever to be preserved, and extolled, and made precious to posterity. No diligence was omitted, but all imaginable expedition used in refreshing, repairing, and setting out the fleet again; in order to which the king himself made a journey thither, and stayed till he saw all ready, and fit to sail; but then, no intreaty, no importunity, could prevail with him to venture his brother again, though his family and all preparations for the voyage were still on board. His maj. too well remembered, and still felt, the impressions he had undergone the 3d of June; and having got his brother into his arms again, he would not return without him, committing the charge of the fleet to the earl of Sandwich, who had acted so good a part in it.—Within few days after, the beginning of July, the earl of Sandwich went again to the coast of Holland, with a fleet in no degree inferior with the former, and rode before the Texel, to invite the Dutch to a new engagement, they having used all the arts at home to conceal the loss and dishonour they had undergone, and pretended to be very ready and solicitous for another battle, when there was no appearance of their purpose to come out: and upon sure intelligence that the East India fleet was coming about by the north, he received orders to go for Norway, upon such encouragement as was not made good, so that he was disappointed of the expectation he had very reasonably carried with him thither, and at a season when that climate gives little encouragement to abide in those seas. I am not yet to enlarge upon that matter, till we hear a better account from some of our friends; however, though he could not meet with their whole fleet as he endeavoured to do, yet he hath had the good fortune, in two encounters, to take 8 of their great ships of war, 2 of their best East India ships, and about 20 of their merchant ships, all under the protection of their fleet, or ought to have been; and was then, by tempest, and other reasons which no wisdom of his could prevent, obliged to put into our own harbours.—I do not mention the great number of prisoners we have taken, an army of prisoners, who in truth do us more harm at land than ever they did at sea: and are a charge that never fell under our estimate and computation. I would not be understood that we had entered upon a war and never thought of prisoners, and sick and wounded men; but that the prisoners and wounded men should bring upon us so prodigious an expence, and of which we can yet see no bottom, insomuch as in one place, I think Colchester, that charge comes to 1200*l.* the week; I say, such an expence never came into our computation.—The king tells you, He hath enabled the prince and bishop of Munster to demand justice from those who have so notoriously oppressed him with such outrageous circumstances of insolence and scorn as are enough known to the world; and he hath demanded it bravely, in such an equipage as hath not been made for little money, in which he can take as well as ask satisfaction.—After all this, since there is a justice due to the worst enemies, we must do them this right, that they do not at all seem weary of the war, they do not discover the least inclination to peace.—It is true, the French king hath offered his mediation; and truly, if he intends no more than a mediation, it is an office very worthy the most Christian king. I wish with all my heart that (as a mediator) he would make equal propositions, or that he would not so importunately press his maj. to consent to those he makes, upon an instance and argument that he holds himself engaged by a former Treaty (of which we never heard till since the beginning of this war, and had some reason to have presumed the contrary) to assist the Dutch with men and money if his maj. doth not consent.—His maj. tells you, that he hath not an appetite to make war for war-sake, but will be always ready to make such a peace as may be for his honour and the interest of his subjects; and no doubt it will be a great trouble and grief to him, to find so great a prince, towards whom he hath manifested so great an affection, in conjunction with his enemies. Yet even the apprehension of such a war will not terrify him to purchase a peace by such concessions as he would be ashamed to make you acquainted with; of which nature you will easily believe the propositions hitherto made to be, when you know that the release of Puleroone in the East Indies, and the demolishing the fort of Cabo Corso upon the coast of Guinea, are two, which would be, upon the matter, to be content with a very vile trade in the East Indies, under their controul, and with none in Guinea; and yet those are not propositions unreasonable enough to please the Dutch, who reproach France for interposing for peace, instead of assisting them in the war, boldly insisting upon the advantage the contagion in London and some other parts of the kingdom gives them, by which, they confidently say, the king will be no longer able to maintain a fleet against them at sea, and as if God Almighty had sent this heavy visitation upon the kingdom on their behalf, and to expose it to their malice and insolence.—They load us with such reproaches as the civility of no other language will admit the relation. The truth is, they have a dialect of rudeness so peculiar to their language and their people, that it is high time for all kings and princes to oblige them to some reformation, if they intend to hold correspondence or commerce with them.—My Lords and Gentlemen: You see in what posture we stand with reference to our neighbours abroad, who are our declared enemies. Their malice and activity to make others declare themselves so too, the great preparations they make, and even declarations that they will have another battle, towards which they have in readiness an equal number of new, greater, and better ships to those they have lost, furnished with larger and greater artillery, so that if they were to be manned with any other nation than their own, they might be worthy our apprehension. What preparations are to be made on our part, you can best judge.—I have fully obeyed the command that was laid upon me, in making you this plain, clear, true Narrative of what hath passed. I have no order to make reflection upon it, nor any deduction from it. The king himself hath told you, that the noble unparalleled Supply you have already given him is upon the manner spent: spent with all the animadversions of good husbandry that the nature of the affair will bear. What is more to be done, he leaves entirely to your own generous understandings: being not more assured of any thing that is to come in this world, than that the same noble indignation for the honour of the king and the nation, that first provoked you to inflame the king himself, will continue the same passion still boiling in your loyal breasts, that all the world may see, which they hoped never to have seen, that never prince and people were so entirely united in their affections, for their true, joint, inseparable honour, as the only, sure, infallible expedient to preserve their distinct several interests.—My Lords and Gentlemen: Having yet only presented you a short view of your foreign enemies, it may not be altogether unseasonable that you take a little prospect of those at home; those unquiet and restless spirits in your own bowels, upon whose infidelity, I doubt, your enemies abroad have more dependence than upon their own fleets. I must appeal to every one of your observations, whether the countenances of these men have not appeared to you more erected, more insolent, in all places, since the beginning of this war, than they were before. In what readiness they were, if any misfortune had befallen the king's fleet (which they promised themselves), to have brought the calamity into your fields and into your houses, is notoriously known.—The horrid murderers of our late royal master have been received into the most secret counsels in Holland; and other infamous prostituted persons of our nation are admitted to a share in the conduct of their affairs, and maintain their correspondence here, upon liberal allowances and pensions. Too many of his majesty's subjects, who were lent by this crown to assist and defend this ungrateful state against their enemies, have been miserably wrought upon, for the keeping a vile mean subsistence, rather than livelihood, to renounce their allegiance, and become enemies to their native country; some of whom have wantonly put themselves on board the enemy's fleet, without command or office, purely out of appetite, and delight to rebel against their king, and to worry their country. It is great pity these men should not be taught, by some exemplary brand, that their allegiance is not circumscribed within the four seas; but that they have obligations upon them of duty and loyalty towards the king, in what part soever of the world they shall inhabit.—Their friends at home, impatient of long delays for the successes they had promised themselves, and for the succours which others had promised to send to them, made no doubt of doing the business themselves, if they could appoint but a lucky day to begin the work; and you had heard of them in all places upon the 3rd of the last month (their so much celebrated 3rd of Sept.), if the great vigilance and indefatigable industry of the good general, who is always active for the king's safety and the peace of the kingdom, had not two days before apprehended the seditious leaders, and given advertisements for the securing others in most parts of the kingdom; by the confessions of many of whom, their wicked design is enough manifested, and ready for justice; yet some of the principal persons are not yet taken, and some others got themselves rescued after they were apprehended.—My Lords and Gentlemen: Let it not, I beseech you, be said of us, what was heretofore said of the senate of Rome, when they were prosperous enough, and when they had obtained greater victories over their enemies abroad than we have done,

'Excellentibus ingeniis citiùs defuit ars, quâ 'civem regant, quàm quâ hostem perdant.' Let not those scorpions be kept warm in our bosoms till they sting us to death: let not those who hate the government, would destroy the government be sheltered under the shadow and protection of the government.—It is possible, and God knows it is but possible, that some men, who are not friends to this or that part of the government (for you are not to believe that they always discover what in truth they are most angry with), who would not buy those alterations they most desire at the price of a civil war they would bring it fairly about, wait for a godly parliament, and do all by their consent: yet those persons must not take it ill that we cannot desire they should ever have it in their power to bring those alterations to pass, by these means they now seem to abhor: and I do heartily wish, I am sure they will not be the worse men nor the worse subjects for it, that they would a little reflect upon what is past, remember how much they have outdone, more than they intended to have done; nay, what they heartily abhorred the thought of doing; and they will then find the only way to preserve themselves innocent is to keep their minds from being vitiated by the first impressions, by jealousies, murmurings, and repinings, and above all, by their conversations with those men, or indulgence towards them, who would sacrifice the peace of the kingdom to their own ambition, pride, and even to their humour.—If you carefully provide for the suppressing your enemies at home, which will put you to little other expence than of courage, constancy, and circumspection, you will find your enemies abroad less exalted, and in a short time more inclined to live in amity with you than to make war upon you, especially when they see you do 'in bello pacis gerere negotium;' and that you take the carrying on the war to heart, as the best and the only expedient to produce a happy and an honest peace."

A Supply of 1,250,000l. voted.] In consequence of the above Speeches, the commons with great unanimity came to these two Resolutions: 1. "That the humble and hearty Thanks of this house be returned to his majesty for his care and conduct in the preservation of his people, and the honour of this nation: and that this house will assist his majesty with their Lives and Fortunes against the Dutch, or any other that shall assist them in opposition to his majesty. 2. That the humble Thanks of this house be returned to his majesty for the care he hath had of the person of h. r. h. the duke of York." To both which Votes the lords gave their chearful concurrence.—The commons, to make good their promise, voted a new Supply of 1,250,000l. to be raised by a proportionable Addition to the Monthly Assessment to begin at Christmas next; all which [illegible]y soon turned into a Bill. After which they [illegible]ght in another Bill for a Month's further [illegible]ment of 120,000l. to commence from the expiration of the former Assessment, to be granted to his majesty, with a desire to his majesty to dispose of it to h. r. h. the duke of York.

The famous Five Mile Act passed.] During this short Session the famous Five Mile Act was passed, which gave occasion to such grievous complaints. By this Act it was enacted, "That no Non-conforming Teacher, under what denomination soever, shall dwell, or come, unless upon the road, within five miles of any corporation, or any other place where they had been Ministers, or had preached after the Act of Oblivion, unless they first took the following Non-resisting Oath: 'I, A. B. do 'swear, that it is not lawful, under any pre'tence whatever, to take up Arms against the 'king, and that I do abhor the traiterous posi'tion of taking Arms by his authority against 'his person, or against those that are commis'sioned by him, in pursuance of such commis'sions; and that I will not at any time endea'vour any Alteration of government either in 'Church or State.' The penalty was 40l. and 6 months imprisonment, unless they took the said Oath before their commitment.—The reason of this severity given in the Act is, That these Teachers had settled themselves in divers Corporations, sometimes three or more in a place, and took opportunity to distil the poisoned principles of schism and rebellion, to the great danger of the church and kingdom.

An Attempt to impose the Non-Resisting Oaths on the whole Nation, frustrated.] In the house of peers, however, the above Act met with some opposition; and that not only from the lords Ashley and Wharton, who were more than half Non-conformists themselves; but even from the lord treasurer Southampton. But neither the authority of the one, nor the arguments of the other, had any weight: on the contrary, a hint was taken, from those very arguments, to bring in another Bill in the house of commons, by which the said Oath, and Declaration, were to have been imposed on the whole nation. But, on the question, it was rejected by 3 voices; "who had the merit," says Mr. Ralph, "of saving their country from the greatest ignominy which could have befallen it; that of riveting as well as forging its own chains."*

Thanks of the Commons to the University.] Oct. 31. The Commons resolved, "That the Thanks of this house be given to the Chancellor,

* "The providence by which it was thrown out was very remarkable: for Mr. Peregrine Bertie, being newly chosen, was that morning introduced into the house by his brother, the now earl of Lindsey, and sir Thomas Osborne, now lord treasurer, who all three gave their votes against the Bill; and the numbers were so even upon that division, that their three voices carried the question against it." See Mr. Locke's Letter from a Person of Quality, in the Appendix to the present Volume. No. V. p. xl.

Scholars, and Fellows of the famous University of Oxford, for their eminent loyalty to his maj. and his father of ever-blessed memory during the late Rebellion; especially for their unparalleled zeal and courage in refusing to submit to be visited by the usurped powers, and to subscribe the Solemn League and Covenant, and for those excellent Reasons they published to the world to justify their refusal, and to assert his majesty's righteous cause."

The Speaker's Speech to the King, at the Prorogation.] This day, the king came to the house of peers, in order to pass the several Bills, and to make a prorogation: at which time, the commons being sent for, their Speaker, in presenting the Bills, delivered himself thus:

"May it please your most excellent majesty; The knights, citizens, and burgesses of the commons house of parliament, in obedience to your majesty's writ of adjournment, came chearfully to this city of Oxford, to receive your royal commands. And when your maj. was pleased to speak to them, and acquaint them with your great Expences this summer, and the continuing insolencies of the Dutch, they were so inflamed with an affection and zeal for your majesty's service, that they could not suffer the least puncto of time to pass, before they had made a return suitable to their engagements, that they would assist your majesty with their lives and fortunes against the Dutch, or any others that should assist them, in opposition of your majesty, 'Tibi nos, tibi nostra supellex, ruraque servierint.'—The Englishman useth to speak as he writes, and the English parliament to speak as they think. No security upon earth can be greater than the engagement of your two houses of parliament. 'Sed quid verba audiam, dum facta videam?' As a demonstration of their fidelity, I am commanded to present unto your majesty this Bill, whereby they have given you, for a present Supply, 1,250,000*l.* to be levied in 2 years, to begin from Christmas next, by quarterly payments, added to the former royal aid.—And, to the end your majesty's occasions may be supplied with ready money before this additional aid can be raised, we have by this Bill prepared an undoubted security for all such persons as shall bring their money into the public Bank of your exchequer: as the rivers do naturally empty themselves into the sea, so we hope the veins of gold and silver in this nation will plentifully run into this ocean, for the maintenance of your majesty's just Sovereignty on the Seas.—Great Sir; When first we besought your maj. to correct the insolencies, and to repair your subjects against the rapines of the Dutch, we did reasonably suppose, that the justice of your majesty's demands, would at least have had a fair and ingenuous reception: but the Dutch resolved, with Machiavil, to keep by force what they had got by wrong, and to return their answer by the thundering voice of their cannon. The Great God of Hosts, to whom vengeance belongs, hath eminently appeared in your majesty's quarrel, and sharply rebuked the insolence of that proud people, whose heart is hardened, even to destruction. —'Tis true, our sins do cry aloud, as well as theirs; but God is pleased in mercy to correct us himself, whilst by our hands he doth punish them, and make them fly before us. I hope this mercy will invite us to a national repentance: and 'if God be with us, who then can be against us?'—We cannot but take notice of the sordid defection of some English Fugitives, who have traiterously joined with the Dutch, both in their councils and actions, against your majesty and this their native country. We therefore have prepared a Bill, whereby they are enjoined to return by a day, and answer to the law; or else they shall be attainted and be subject to the pains and penalties of condemned traitors.—It hath been an old observation, "That scandalous Livings make scandalous Ministers;" and this most frequently falls out in cities and corporate towns, where are little or no predial tythes; and therefore the preachers, for mere want, are forced to chant such tunes as may best please the rich men in their parishes: for prevention of this for the future, there is a Bill prepared, for the uniting of small Churches and Chapels in cities and towns corporate by the consent of the patron, reserving all other parochial rites distinct as they were before.—This being a time wherein your maj. needs great Supplies, we held it our duty to ease the people in some unnecessary expences; and therefore we have prepared a Bill for the more effectual proceeding upon Distresses and Avowries for Rents; another to avoid Circuity of Actions; and a third to lessen the Charge of unnecessary Suits in Law: there is an ancient Fee received in your majesty's courts of law, called Damage Clear, or Damna Clericorum, which is the tenth penny of such damages as are there recovered in many actions. This was first introduced for the encouragement of clerks, to employ themselves to the study of drawing special pleadings, which are grown so familiar by the disuse of real actions, that the fee now is looked upon as a grievance, especially when the plaintiff is forced to pay it upon the signing of his judgment, and perhaps the defendant is not able to answer any part of the execution: therefore we have prepared a Bill for the regulating of this for the present, and after 7 years to take it quite away.—Tacitus hath a saying, 'Such as are false in their love, are true in their hate:' and this rule we find verified in our Non-conformists. Whilst they were in the bosom of the Church of England, they were like inward vapours and inward bleedings, always oppressing and strangling the body of the Church; and now they are ejected and excluded from their ministerial function, they have more malice, and no less opportunity to propagate their principles, than they had before. Some of them are objects of pity. They submitted their reason to their leaders of a higher classis, who failed them in their hopes, and left them to the rigour of the law. These poor creatures have seen their error, and feel the smart, and would live peaceably; but their Jesuitical leaders keep up their spirits, and herd with them in cities and corporate towns, where, by pretence of persecution and self-denial, they move the pity of good-natured people, and with their charity keep up their party, lessen the maintenance of conforming ministers, and spread their contagion amongst the youth of the nation: for the prevention of this growing mischief, we have prepared a Shiboleth, a Test to distinguish amongst them, who will be peaceable and give hopes of future Conformity, and who of malice and evil disposition remain obdurate. The one we shall keep amongst us with all love and charity; the other we shall exclude from cities and corporate towns, like those that have an infectious disease upon them.—It is not unusual for the commons, at the close of a session of parliament, by their Speaker, to present a Petition to their sovereign; and, with your majesty's leave, I am now commanded that service.—We do, with all humble thankfulness to God, acknowledge our great happiness, that we are governed by a prince, whose prudence in counsel, whose valour in action, and whose fatherly care in protection of his people, is eminent through all the world: and it is not the least mercy, both to your maj. and your people, that God hath blessed you with a Brother so like yourself.—The name of his royal highness is already enrolled amongst the heroes of other nations: but this his native country had not so great experience of him, till your maj. was pleased in this summer's Expedition to trust him with the conduct of the most royal fleet that ever sailed upon the British seas, wherein he shewed that prowess, and that prudence; and, by the blessing of Almighty God, was crowned with that success against the Dutch, that we cannot pass it by in silence; and yet we are at a loss how to express our thanks both to your maj. and to him. I am commanded, therefore, to beseech your maj. that you will vouchsafe to let us make a present to you, of a Month's Tax, to come in the rear, after the 24 months of your majesty's royal aid; and that your maj. will be pleased to bestow it upon his royal highness.—And now, Great Sir, I have no more, but to beseech Almighty God, who hath so miraculously preserved your royal person and your two houses of parliament from all sickness and contagion, during this session, that he will be pleased to send health throughout the nation; that he will crown all your designs against your enemies with victory and success, and give your majesty a long and happy reign over us."

The King's Speech at the Prorogation.] After passing the Bills, the King made a short Speech to this effect:

"His majesty told his two houses of parliament, That he did not compliment with them, when he should tell them, that they had done for him all that he could wish they should have done; and therefore thanked them heartily. —His maj. further said, That he believed that no one there would imagine that he would have called them hither at this time, if there had not been an absolute necessity for it. He thanked them with all his heart for their affections shewed to him in this present Supply; which though it is not to be supposed that it can last till the end of the time in which it is to be raised (if the war should so long continue), yet his maj. said, He could not expect that his two houses should do more than they had done at this meeting, considering the deadness of trade through the whole nation, by reason of the Contagion, which addeth to the many streights they have to struggle with. And his maj. said, That for their kindness to his Brother, he thanked them no less than if what they had done for his brother had been done for himself; he having deserved so well of himself and the whole nation.—His maj. told them, that it is probable they should not meet till April next; but yet, lest he might have occasion for their assistance sooner, he had given order for the proroguing this parliament but till Feb. next; and if there should be no occasion of coming together then, he would, by a proclamation, give timely notice thereof."

SIXTH SESSION OF THE SECOND PARLIAMENT.

The King's Speech on opening the Session.] September 21, 1666. This day, the parliament, after several prorogations, and a long recess of ten months and three weeks, met again at Westminster, where his majesty from the throne thus declared himself to both houses:

"My Lords and Gentlemen; I am very glad to meet so many of you together again; and God be thanked for our meeting together in this place! Little time hath passed, since we were almost in despair of having this place left us to meet in: you see the dismal ruins the Fire hath made; and nothing but a miracle of God's mercy could have preserved what is left from the same destruction. I need make no excuse to you for dispensing with your attendance in April. I am confident you all thanked me for it. The truth is, I desire to put you to as little trouble as I can; and I can tell you truly, I desire to put you to as little cost as is possible. I wish with all my heart, that I could bear the whole charge of this war myself, and that my subjects should reap the benefit of it to themselves. But we have two very great and powerful enemies, who use all the means they can, fair and foul, to make all the world to concur with them; and the war is more chargeable (by that conjunction) than any body thought it would have been. I need not tell you the success of this Summer, in which God hath given us great success, and no question the enemy hath undergone great losses. And if it had pleased God to have withheld his late judgment by Fire, we had been in no ill condition.—You have given me very large Supplies for the carrying on the war. And yet I must tell you, if I had not, by anticipating my own revenue, raised a very great sum of money, I had not been able to have set out the Fleet this last spring: and I have some hopes, upon the same credit, to be able to pay off the great ships as they come in. You will consider what is to be done next, when you are well-informed of the expence. And I must leave it to your wisdoms, to find out the best expedients for the carrying on this war with as little burden to the people as is possible. I shall add no more, than to put you in mind that our enemies are very insolent; and if they were able this last year to persuade their miserable people, whom they mislead, that the contagion had so wasted the nation, and impoverished us, that we would not be able to set out any fleet, how will they be exalted with this last impoverishment of this city, and contemn all reasonable conditions of peace!* And therefore I cannot doubt but you will provide accordingly."

* The King did not till now understand the damage he had sustained by the Plague, much less what he must sustain from the Fire. Monies neither could be collected nor borrowed where the Plague had prevailed, which was over all the city and over a great part of the country; the collectors durst not go to require it or receive it. Yet the fountains yet remained clear, and the waters would run again: but this late Conflagration had dried up or so stopped the very fountains, that there was no prospect when they would flow again. The two great branches of the Revenue, the Customs and Excise, which was the great and almost inexhaustible security to borrow money upon, were now bankrupt, and would neither bring in money nor supply credit: all the measures by which computations had been made were so broken, that they could not be brought to meet again. By a medium of the constant receipts it had been depended upon, that what had been borrowed upon that fund would by this time have been fully satisfied with all the interest, whereby the money would have been replaced in the hands to which it was due, which would have been glad to have laid it out again; and the security would have remained still in vigour to be applied to any other urgent occasions: but now the Plague had routed all those receipts, especially in London, where the great conduits of those receipts still ran. The Plague and the war had so totally broken and distracted those receipts, that the farmers of either had not received enough to discharge the constant burden of the officers, and were so far from paying any part of the principal that was secured upon it, that it left the interest unpaid to swell the principal. And now this Deluge by Fire had dissipated the persons, and destroyed the houses, which were liable to the reimbursement of all arrears; and the very stocks were consumed which should carry on and revive the trade." Lord Clarendon's Life, p. 366.

A Committee appointed to receive Informations of the Insolence of Priests and Jesuits.] About this time, a Committee was appointed to receive and certify Informations of the Insolence of Popish Priests and Jesuits, and of the Increase of Popery. Of this Committee, Mr. Hungerford was chairman: they sat till the latter end of Oct. examined a cloud of witnesses, delivered in a variety of informations, and, at last agreed upon a Resolution, which had the approbation of the house, as follows: "Resolved, That, in order to the suppressing the Insolency of the Papists, his majesty be humbly desired forthwith to issue out his royal Proclamation, for the Banishment of all Priests and Jesuits out of this kingdom, within 30 days to be therein limited, other than such (not being his majesty's natural born subjects) who are obliged to attend upon the queen-consort, or the queen-mother: and that, if any Priest or Jesuit shall happen to be taken in England, after the said days, that the laws be put in due execution against them." The house moreover resolved, "That, in the said Proclamation, proper orders should be given for the putting the laws in execution against popish Recusants, and such as were suspected of being so: That his majesty be humbly moved, that, considering the present juncture of affairs, all popish Recusants, and such as, being suspected so to be, shall refuse to take the Oaths of Supremacy and Allegiance, being tendered to them, may be forthwith so disarmed, as to remove all apprehensions from the people, of their possibilities to disturb the public peace of the nation: and that all officers, military and civil, and soldiers, as shall not within 20 days take the Oaths of Allegiance and Supremacy, may be disbanded and displaced:'—That the Commissaries of the Musters be commanded and enjoined, upon penalty of losing their places, not to permit any officer or soldier to be mustered in the service and pay of his majesty, till he or they shall have taken the Oaths of Supremacy and Allegiance, and received the Sacrament of the Lord's Supper, according to the laws and usage of the Church of England.' Also, That his maj. be humbly desired to issue out a new commission, for tendering and administering the Oaths of Allegiance and Supremacy to the members of both houses."

Discontents in the House of Commons.] Lord Clarendon tells us,* that, "When the numbers of the members increased, the parliament appeared much more chagrined than it had hitherto done; and though they made the same professions of affection and duty to the king they had ever done, they did not conceal the very ill opinion they had of the court and the continual riotings there: and the very idle discourses of some (who were much countenanced) upon the miserable event of the Fire made them even believe, that the former jealousies of the city, when they saw their houses burning at such a distance from each other, were not without some foundation, nor without just up-

* Life, p. 367.

prehension of a conspiracy, and that it had not been diligently enough examined; and therefore they appointed a Committee, with large authority to send for and examine all persons who could give any information concerning it. When any mention was made of the declaration the commons had so lately passed, for giving the king a Supply and 'that it was high time to dispatch it, that all necessary provisions might be made for the setting out a fleet against the spring;' it was answered with passion, 'that the king's wants must be made first to appear before any Supply must be discoursed of: that there were already such vast sums of money given to the king, that there was none left in the country; nor could any commodities there, upon which they should raise wherewith to pay their taxes, be sold for want of money, which was all brought to London in specie, and none left to carry on the commerce and trade in the country, where they could not sell their corn or their cattle or their wool for half the value.'—They who had not sate in the parliament at Oxford were exceedingly vexed, that there had been so much given there, so soon after the two millions and a half had been granted; and said, 'if the king wanted again already, that he must have been abominably cheated, which was fit to be examined. That the number of the ships, which had been set out by the king in several fleets since the beginning of this war, was no secret; and that there are men enough who are acquainted with the charge of setting out and manning and victualling ships, and can make thereby a reasonable computation what this vast expense can amount to: and that they cannot but conclude, that if his maj. hath been honestly dealt with, there must remain still a very great proportion of money to carry on the war, without need of imposing more upon the people, till they are better able to bear it. And therefore that it was absolutely necessary, that all those, through whose hands the money had passed, should first give an exact Account of what they had received, and what and how they had disbursed it: and when that should appear, it would be seasonable to demand an addition of Supply, which would be cheerfully granted."*

A Bill brought in for inspecting the Publick Accounts.] And for the better expedition of this, continues the noble historian, it was proposed, 'That forthwith a Bill should be prepared, which should pass into an act of parliament, in which such commissioners should be appointed as the houses should think fit, to examine all Accounts of those who had received or issued out any Monies for this War; and where they found any persons faulty, and who had broken their trust, they should be liable to such punishment as the parliament should think fit:' and a Committee was presently named to prepare such a Bill accordingly. This proposition found such a concurrence in the house, that none of the court thought fit to oppose it; and others who knew the method to be new, and liable to just exceptions, thought it to as little purpose to endeavour to divert it: and so all motions for present Supply were to be laid aside till a more favourable conjuncture; and the overture had been contrived and put on by many who seemed not to like it, which is an artifice not unusual in courts or parliaments. The persons who were principally aimed at were sir George Carteret the Treasurer of the Navy, through whom all that expense had passed, who had many enemies upon the opinion that his office was too great, and the more by the ill offices sir Wm. Coventry was always ready to do him; and the lord Ashley, who was Treasurer of all the money that had been raised upon Prizes, which could not but be a great proportion. The former was a punctual officer and a good accomptant, and had already passed his Account in the exchequer for 2 years, upon which he had his *quietus est*; which was the only lawful way known and practised by all accomptants to the crown, who can receive a good discharge no other way: and he was ready to make another year's account. But what method commissioners extraordinary by act of parliament would put it into, he could not imagine, nor be well satisfied with. The other, the lord Ashley, had more reason to be troubled, for he was by his commission exempted from giving any other Account but to the king himself, which exemption was the only reason that made him so solicitous for the office; and he well knew that there were great sums issued, which could not be put into any publick account: so that his perplexity in several respects was not small. And they both applied themselves to the king for his protection in the point.—His majesty was no less troubled, knowing that both had issued out many sums upon his warrants, which he would not suffer to be produced; and called that committee of the privy council with which he used to advise, and complained of this unusual way of proceeding in the house of commons, which would terrify all men from serving his maj. in any receipts; to which employment men submitted because they knew what they were to do, and what they were to suffer. If they made their account according to the known rules of the exchequer, their discharge could not be denied; and if they failed, they knew what process would be awarded against them. But to account by such orders as the parliament should prescribe, and to be liable to such punishment as the parliament would inflict, was such an uncertainty as would deprive them of all rest and quiet of mind; and was in itself so unjust that his maj declared 'that he would never suffer it: that he hoped it would never find a consent in the house of commons; if it should, that the house of peers would reject it; but if it should be brought to him, he was resolved never to give his royal assent.' There was no man present, who did not seem fully to concur

* Life, p. 368.

with his maj. that he should never consent to it: 'however that the best care and diligence should be used, that it might never be presented to him, but stopped in the houses; and to that purpose that the members should be prepared by giving them notice of his pleasure.' —The Chancellor upon this argument, in which he discerned no opposition, enlarged himself upon what he had often before put his majesty in mind of; 'that he could not be too indulgent in the defence of the privileges of parliament; that he hoped he would never violate any of them;' But he desired him 'to be equally solicitous to prevent the excesses in parliament, and not to suffer them to extend their jurisdiction to cases they have nothing to do with; and that to restrain them within their proper bounds and limits is as necessary, as it is to preserve them from being invaded. That this was such a new encroachment as had no bottom; and the scars were yet too fresh and green of those wounds which had been inflicted upon the kingdom from such usurpation.' And therefore he desired his majesty to be firm in the resolution he had taken, and not to depart from it; and if such a Bill should be brought up to the house of peers, he would not fail in doing his duty, and speaking freely his opinion against such innovations, how many soever it might offend.' All which discourse of his was in a short time after communicated to those who would not fail to make use of it to his disadvantage.

A Bill brought into the House of Commons against the Importation of Irish Cattle.] There had been for many months a great murmur, rather than complaint, 'of the great damage the kingdom in general sustained by the Importation of such great quantities of Irish Cattle, which were bred there for nothing, and transported for little, that they might well undersell all the cattle here; and from hence the breed of cattle in the kingdom was totally given over, and thereby the land would yield no rent proportionably to what it had ever done: and that this was a principal cause of the want of money in the country, which could only be remedied by a very strict act of parliament to forbid the Importation of any sort of Cattle out of Ireland into this kingdom.' And some of them who had most thought of the matter had prepared a Bill, and brought it into the commons, where it was read. At first it underwent very calm and reasonable debates. Very many members of several counties desired, 'that their counties might not undergo any damage for the benefit of other individual places.' They professed 'that their counties had no land bad enough to breed: but that their great traffic consisted in buying lean cattle, and making them fat, and upon this they paid their rent; and if the bringing over Irish cattle should be restrained, their counties must be undone.' And this appeared to be the case of very many counties in England. And the complaint was of so new a nature, that it had never been heard of in England till some few months before this meeting in parliament; only it had been mentioned in the parliament at Oxford, as a grievance to the Northern counties, which complained no less of the Scots than of the Irish Cattle; and the Bill that was at this time brought into the Commons provided as well against the one as the other. The bill was carried with great difficulty, and long opposition given to it by those members of several counties, which professed, 'that the bringing over the Irish Cattle was so much for their benefit, that they could not live well without it,' and were exceedingly perplexed that it should pass; which yet they hoped would be prevented in the house of peers: and so the Bill was in great triumph, and by all the members (as in cases they much delight in is usual), presented to the house of peers.*

The Bill for inspecting Public Accounts passed by the Commons.] The commons no sooner repaired to their own house, than they assumed the debate upon the Public Accounts, with the same fervour they had pursued the other bill of Ireland, and with the same declaration, 'That they would not enter upon the subject of Money, till they saw what success that bill would likewise have; and appearing every day more out of humour, expressed less reverence towards the court. And some expressions were frequently used, which seemed to glance at the license and disorders and extravagant expence of that place, not without some reflections which aimed at the lady, and at the exorbitant power exercised by her. And this imperious way of proceeding confirmed those in their wariness, who had no mind to oppose or contradict the party that they would and meant should prevail: but they the more endeavoured to render themselves gracious to the leaders, as being willing to administer fewel to the fire the others intended to kindle; and, so they might preserve themselves, were very willing to expose other ministers to the jealousy of them, who they thought would not be quiet without some sacrifice. And thus they alarmed the king with the new apprehensions, 'that the house, which had yet dutiful intentions, if they were crossed in what they designed for his service, might be provoked to be bolder with his majesty than they had been yet, and to mention the prevalence of the lady,' which every body knew the duke of Buckingham would have been glad to have contributed to.† And with these continued

* Life, p. 371.

† "There was a correspondence by this time begun and warmly pursued between some discontented members of the house of peers, who thought their parts not enough valued (and the duke of Buckingham was at the head of them), and some members of the house of commons, who made themselves remarkable by opposing all things which were proposed in that house for the king's service, or which were like to be grateful to him, as sir Rd. Temple, Mr. Sey-

representations, but especially with their old argument of casting it out by the house of peers, where his power could not be doubted, they at last prevailed with the king to leave all men to themselves in the business of the Accounts, as he had done in the Irish Bill: and, so that bill likewise was transmitted to the lords.*

Great Animosities in the H. of Lords upon the Bill against Irish Cattle.] Oct. 16. The house of peers was no sooner possessed of the Bill against Irish Cattle, but it was read, and a marvellous keen resolution appeared in many to use all expedition in the passing it; though if the matter itself had been without exception, there were so many clauses and provisos in it so derogatory to the king's honour and prerogative, that many thought it a high disrespect to his majesty to admit them into debate. The duke of Buckingham appeared in the head of those who favoured the Bill, with a marvellous concernment: and at the times appointed for the debate of it, contrary to his custom of coming into the house, indeed of not rising till 11 of the clock, and seldom staying above a quarter of an hour, except upon some affair which he concerned himself in, he was now always present with the first in a morning, and stayed till the last at night; for the debate often held from the morning till 4 in the afternoon, and sometimes till candles were brought in. And it grew quickly evident, that there were other reasons which caused so earnest a prosecution of it, above the encouragement of the breed of Cattle in England: insomuch as the lord Ashley, who next the duke appeared the most violent supporter of the Bill, could not forbear to urge it as an argument for the prosecuting it, 'that if this Bill did not pass, all the rents in Ireland would rise in a vast proportion, and those in England fall as much; so that in a year or two the duke of Ormond would have a greater revenue than the earl of Northumberland;' which made a visible impression in many, as a thing not to be endured. Whereas the duke had indeed at least four times the proportion of land in Ireland that descended to him from his ancestors, that the earl had in England; and the revenue of it before the Rebellion was not inferior to the others. But nothing was more manifest, than that the warmth of that prosecution in the house of peers in many lords did proceed from the envy they had of the duke's station in one kingdom, and of his fortune in the other.—And the whole debate upon the bill was so disorderly and unparliamentary, that the like had never been known: no rules or orders of the house for the course and method of debate were observed. And there being, amongst those who advanced the Bill, fewer speakers than there were of those who were against it, those few took upon them to speak oftener than they ought to do, and to

---

mour, and Mr. Garraway, and sir Rob. Howard; who were all bold speakers, and meant to make themselves considerable by saying, upon all occasions, what wiser men would not, whatever they thought. The duke of Buckingham took more pains than was agreeable to his constitution to get an interest in all such persons, invited them to his table, pretended to have a great esteem of their parts, asked counsel of them, lamented the king's neglecting his business, and committing it to other people who were not fit for it; and then reported all the license and debauchery of the court in the most lively colours, being himself a frequent eye and earwitness of it. He had a mortal quarrel with the lady, and was at this time so much in the king's displeasure (as he was very frequently), that he forbore going to the court, and revenged himself upon it by all the merry tales he could tell of what was done there.—It cannot be imagined, considering the loose life he led (which was a life more by night than by day) in all the liberties that nature could desire or wit invent, how great an interest he had in both houses of parliament; that is, how many in both would follow his advice, and concur in what he proposed. His quality and condescensions, the pleasantness of his humour and conversation, the extravagance and sharpness of his wit, unrestrained by any modesty or religion, drew persons of all affections and inclinations to like his company; and to believe that the levities and the vanities would be wrought off by age, and there would enough of good be left to become a great man, and make him useful to his country, for which he pretended to have a wonderful affection and reverence; and that all his displeasure against the court proceeded from their declared malignity against the liberty of the subject, and their desire that the king should govern by the example of France. He had always held intelligence with the principal persons of the Levelling party, and professed to desire that liberty of conscience might be granted to all; and exercised his wit with most license against the church, the law, and the court. The king had constant intelligence of all his behaviour, and the liberty he took in his discourses of him, for which he had indignation enough: but of this new stratagem to make himself great in parliament, and to have a faction there to disturb his business, his majesty had no apprehension, believing it impossible for the duke to keep his mind long bent upon any particular design, or to keep and observe those hours and orders of sleeping and eating, as men who pretend to business are obliged to; and that it was more impossible for him to make and preserve a friendship with any serious persons, whom he could never restrain himself from abusing and making ridiculous, as soon as he was out of their company. Yet with all these infirmities and vices he found a respect and concurrence from men of different tempers and talents, and had an incredible opinion with the people." Lord Clarendon's Life, p. 369.

* Life, p. 374.

reply to every man who declared himself to be of another opinion: and when they were put in mind, of the rule of the house, 'that no man should speak above once upon the same question,' they called presently to have the house resolved into a committee, which any single member may require, and then every man may speak as often as he please; and so the time was spent unprofitably without the business being advanced. In the mean time the commons proceeded as irregularly, in sending frequent Messages to hasten the dispatch of the Bill, when they knew well the debate of every day: and it was frequently urged as an argument, 'that the commons was the fittest judge of the necessities and grievances of the people; and they having passed this Bill, the lords ought to conform to their opinion.' In fine, there grew so great a license of words in this debate, and so many personal reflections, that every day some quarrels arose, to the great scandal and dishonour of a court that was the supreme judicatory of the kingdom.*

The Lord Ossory challenges the Duke of Buckingham.] The duke of Buckingham, who assumed a liberty of speaking when and what he would in a dialect unusual and ungrave, his similes and other expressions giving occasion of much mirth and laughter, one day said in the debate, 'that whoever was against the above Bill had either an Irish interest or an Irish understanding;' which so much offended the lord Ossory, who was eldest son to the duke of Ormond, that meeting him afterwards in the court, he desired the Duke that he would walk into the next room with him, and there told him, that he had taken the liberty to use many loose and unworthy expressions which reflected upon the whole Irish nation, and which he himself resented so much that he expected satisfaction, and to find him with his sword in his hand: which the duke endeavoured to avoid by all the fair words and shifts he could use, but was so far pressed by the other, whose courage was never doubted, that he could not avoid appointing a place where they would presently meet, which he found the other would exact to prevent discovery, and therefore had chosen rather to urge it himself, than to send a message to him. And so he named a known place in Chelsea Fields, and to be there within less than an hour.—The lord Ossory made haste thither, and expected him much beyond the time; and then seeing some persons come out of the way towards the place where he was, and concluding they were sent out to prevent any action between them, he avoided speaking with them, but got to the place where his horse was, and so retired to London. The duke was found by himself in another place on the other side of the water, which was never known by the name of Chelsea Fields, which he said was the place he had appointed to meet.

The Duke of Buckingham informs the House of the Affair.] Finding that night that the lord Ossory was not in custody, and so he was sure he should quickly hear from him, and upon conference with his friends that the mistake of the place would be imputed to him, he took a strange resolution, that every body wondered at, and his friends dissuaded him from. And the next morning, as soon as the house was sate, the lord Ossory being likewise present that he might find some opportunity to speak with him, the duke told the house, "that he must inform them of somewhat that concerned himself; and being sure that it would come to their notice some other way, he had therefore chose to acquaint them with it himself:" and thereupon related "how the lord Ossory had the day before found him in the court, and desired him to walk into the next room, where he charged him with many particulars which he had spoken in that place, and in few words told him he should fight with him; which though he did not hold himself obliged to do in maintenance of any thing he had said or done in the parliament, yet that it being suitable and agreeable to his nature, to fight with any man who had a mind to fight with him, (upon which he enlarged with a little vanity, as if duelling were his daily exercise and inclination), he appointed the place in Chelsea Fields, which he understood to be the fields over against Chelsea; whither, having only gone to his lodging to change his sword, he hastened, by presently crossing the water in a pair of oars, and stayed there in expectation of the lord Ossory, until such gentlemen, whom he named, found him there, and said, 'They were sent to prevent his and the lord Ossory's meeting, whom others were likewise 'sent to find for the same prevention.' Whereupon, concluding that for the present there would be no meeting together, he returned with those gentlemen to his lodging, being always ready to give any gentleman satisfaction that should require it of him."—Every body was exceedingly surprized with the oddness and unseasonableness of the discourse, which consisted, with some confusion, between aggravating the presumption of the lord Ossory, and making the offence as heinous as the violating all the privileges of parliament could amount unto; and magnifying his own courage and readiness to fight upon any opportunity, when it was clear enough that he had declined it by a gross shift: and it was wondered at, that he had not chosen rather that some other person might inform the house of a Quarrel between two members, that it might be examined and the mischief prevented. But he believed that way would not so well represent and manifest the lustre of his courage, and might leave him under an examination that would not be so advantageous to him as his own information: and therefore no persuasion and importunity of his friends could prevail with him to decline that method.—The lord Ossory seemed out of countenance, and

---

* Ibid. p. 375.

troubled that the contest was like to be only in that place, and cared not to deny any thing that the duke had accused him of; only wondered, that he should say he had challenged him for words spoken in the house, when he had expressly declared to him, when his grace insisted much upon the privilege of parliament to decline giving him any satisfaction, 'that 'he did not question him for any words spoken 'in parliament, but for words spoken in other 'places, and for affronts, which he had at other 'times chosen to bear rather than to disturb 'the company.' He confessed, 'He had attended in the very place where the duke had done him the honour to promise to meet him;' and mentioned some expressions which he had used in designing it, which left the certainty of it not to be doubted.—When they had said as much as they had a mind to, they were both required, as is the custom, to withdraw to several rooms near the house: and then the lords entered upon debate of the transgression; many insisting upon the magnitude of the offence, which concerned the honour and safety of the highest tribunal in the kingdom, and the liberty and security of every member of the house. That if in any debate any lord exceeded the modest limits prescribed, in any offensive expressions, the house had the power and the practice to restrain and reprehend and imprison the person, according to the quality and degree of the offence; and that no other remedy or examination could be applied to it, even by the king himself. But if it should be in any private man to take exceptions against any words which the house finds no fault with, and to require men to justify with their swords all that they say in discharge of their conscience, and for the good and benefit of their country; there is an end of the privilege of parliament and the freedom of speech: and, therefore, that there could not be too great a punishment inflicted upon this notorious and monstrous offence of the lord Ossory, which concerned every lord in particular, as much as it did the duke of Buckingham; who had carried himself as well as the ill custom and iniquity of the age would admit, and had given no offence to the house, towards which he had always paid all possible respect and reverence.'—They who considered the honour and dignity only of the house, and the ill consequence of such violations as these, which way soever their affections were inclined with reference to their persons, were all of the opinion, 'That their offences were so near equal that their punishment ought to be equal: for that besides the lord Ossory's denial that he had made any reflection upon any words spoken in parliament, which was the aggravation of his offence, there was some testimony given to the house by some lords present, that the lord Ossory had complained of the duke's comportment towards him before those words used in the house by him, 'of the Irish inter-'est or Irish understanding,' and resolved to expostulate with him upon it; so that those words could not be the ground of the quarrel. And it was evident by the duke's own confession and declaration, that he was as ready to fight, and went to the place appointed by himself for encounter; which made the offence equal.' And therefore they moved, that they might be both brought to the bar, and upon their knees receive the sentence of the house for their commitment, the lord Ossory to the Tower, and the Duke to the custody of the Usher of the Black Rod. Which was done accordingly on the 29th of Oct. On the 31st both were brought before the house and released."*

Quarrel between the D. of Buckingham and the Marq. of Dorchester at a Conference.] Dec. 19. Those two lords were no sooner at liberty, but another more untoward outrage happened, that continued the same disturbance. It happened that upon the debate of the same affair, the Irish Bill, there was a Conference appointed with the commons, in which the duke of Buckingham was a manager; and as they were sitting down in the Painted Chamber, which is seldom done in good order, it chanced that the marquis of Dorchester sat next the Duke, between whom there was no good correspondence. The one changing his posture for his own ease, which made the station of the other the more uneasy, they first endeavoured by justling to recover what they had dispossessed each other of, and afterwards fell to direct blows; in which the marquis, who was the lower of the two in stature, and was less active in his limbs, lost his perriwig, and received some rudeness, which nobody imputed to his want of courage, which was ever less questioned than that of the other. The misdemeanor, greater than had ever happened in that place and upon such an occasion, in any age when the least reverence to government was preserved, could not be concealed; but as soon as the Conference was ended, was reported to the house, and both parties heard, who both confessed enough to make them undergo the censure of the house. The duke's friends would fain have justified him, as being provoked by the other; and it was evident their mutual undervaluing each other always disposed them to affect any opportunity to manifest it. But the house sent them both to the Tower; from whence after a few days they were again released together, and such a reconciliation made as after such rencounters is usual, where either party thinks himself beforehand with the other, as the marquis had much of the duke's hair in his hands to recompence for his pulling off of his perriwig, which he could not reach high enough to do to the other.†

Arguments urged against the Irish Cattle Bill, in the House of Peers.] When all things were thus far quieted, the bill was again entered upon with no less passion for the stock that had been wasted. The arguments which were urged against the Bill for the

* Life, p. 376. † p. 378.

injustice of it were, 'That they should, without any cause or demerit on their part, or any visible evidence of a benefit that would accrue from it to this kingdom, deprive his majesty's two other kingdoms of a privilege they had ever been possessed of. That they might as reasonably take away the trade from any one county in England, because it produced some inconvenience to another county more in their favour. That the large counties of Norfolk, Suffolk, Kent, and other provinces, would lose as much by the passing of this act, as the northern and any other counties would gain by it. That those two kingdoms might with the same justice press his majesty's concurrence, that they might have no trade with England, which would bring more Damage to England by much, than it would gain by this act of restraint: and that it was against all the maxims of prudence, to run the danger of a present mischief and damage, as this would produce in Ireland by the testimony of the lord lieutenant and council of that kingdom, only upon the speculation of a future benefit that might accrue, though it were yet only in speculation.'—These, and many other arguments of this kind, which for the most part were offered by men who had not the least relation to Ireland, made no other impression, than that they were content to leave Scotland out of the Bill; which increased their party against Ireland, and gave little satisfaction to the other, who did not so much value the commerce with the other Kingdom. And this alteration the commons likewise consented to, but with great opposition, since in truth that concession destroyed the foundation upon which the whole fabrick of the Bill was supported.—Then the debate fell upon some derogatory Clauses, and Provisos very contrary to his majesty's just prerogative and power (for they made his majesty's own license and warrant of no effect or authority, but liable to be controlled by a constable; nor would permit the Importation of 3000 beeves, which, by an act of parliament in Ireland, were every year to be delivered at Chester and another port for the provision of the king's house); which in many respects the house generally disliked, and desired, 'That it might have no other style than had been accustomed in all the penal acts of parliament which were in force, it being to be presumed, that the king would never dispence with any violation of it, except in such cases as the benefit and good of the kingdom required it; which might naturally fall out, if there should happen such a murrain amongst the beasts of that species, as had been these late years amongst horses, which had destroyed so many thousand, that good horses were now hard to be procured. And if the same or the like destruction should fall upon the other cattle, we should have then more cause to complain of the scarcity and the dearness of meat, than we have now of the plenty and cheapness, which was the only grievance now felt, and which kingdom seldom complained of: and in such a case it would be very great pity, that the king should not have power enough to provide for the supply of his subjects, and to prevent a common dearth.'—But this was again opposed with as much passion and violence as had fallen out in any part of the debate; and such rude arguments used against such a power in the king, as if the question were upon reposing some new trust in him, whereas it was upon divesting him of a trust that was inherent in him from all antiquity: and 'That it was the same thing to be without the Bill, and not to provide against the king's dispensing with the not obeying it, whose inclinations were well known in this particular; and therefore the effect of them, and of the importunity of the courtiers, must be provided against.' And throughout this discourse there was such a liberty of language made use of, as reflected more upon the king's honour, and indeed upon his whole council and court, than had been heard in that house, but in a time of rebellion, without very severe reprehension: and it so much offended the house now, that, notwithstanding all the sturdy opposition, it was resolved that those Clauses and Provisos should be amended in some places, and totally left out in others. And with these Alterations and Amendments it was sent down to the commons.*

The Commons adhere to their Bill.] When the Bill was sent to the commons with those Alterations and Amendments, they rejected them all, and voted, 'That they would adhere to their own Bill without departing from a word of it, except with reference to Scotland,' from which they had receded. And if upon this very unusual return the house of peers had likewise voted, 'that they too would adhere,' which they might regularly have done, and would have been consented to by the major part of the house if the question had been then put; there had been an end of that Bill. But that must not be suffered: the party that cherished it was too much concerned to let it expire in a deep silence, and were numerous enough to obstruct and defer what they liked not, though not to establish what they desired. Some of them, that is, some who desired that the Bill should pass, though uncorrupted by their passions, did not like the obstinacy of the commons in not departing from some unusual clauses and pretences; yet were not willing to have the like vote for adhering to pass in that house, which it might do when all other remedies should fail; and therefore moved, That a conference might be required in which such reasons might be given as might satisfy them.' Many conferences, and free conferences, were held, in which the commons still maintained their adherence with a wonderful petulance: and those members, who were appointed to manage the conferences, took the liberty to use all those arguments, and the very expressions, which had been used in the

* Life, p. 379.

house of peers, against leaving any power in the king to dispense; and added such other of their own as more reflected on his majesty's honour; and yet concluded as if they could say more if they were provoked, upon which every man might make what glosses he pleased, and the king himself was left to his own imaginations.

The Bill at length consented to by the Lords.] But there was nothing gotten in all those Conferences, but the discovery of new jealousies of the king and the court, and new insinuations of the discontents and murmurs in the country, that this Bill was so long obstructed. Which being still represented to the king with the most ghastly aspects towards what effects it might produce, his majesty in the end was prevailed upon, notwithstanding very earnest advice to the contrary, not only to be willing to give his royal assent when it should be offered to him, but to take very great pains to remove those obstructions which hindered it from being offered to him, and to solicit particularly very many lords to depart from their own sense, and to conform to what he thought convenient to his service; which gave those who loved him not great argument of triumph, and to those who loved him very passionately much matter of mortification. Yet after all this, and when his majesty had changed some mens resolutions, and prevailed with others to withdraw and to be absent when the Bill should come again to be discussed, it was carried with great difficulty and with great opposition, and against the Protestation of many of the lords.*

Articles of Impeachment against Lord Mordaunt.] January 3, 1666-7. This day, the earl of Anglesey reported the matter of the conference with the commons on the 29th of Dec. last, concerning the Impeachment of John viscount Mordaunt: 'That Mr. Seymour said, he would not trouble their lordships with a large induction, or preface; but deliver the Articles against John visc. Mordaunt, Constable of the Castle of Windsor; which Articles would speak for themselves.' Then the particular Articles of Impeachment being read by Mr. Seymour, he said, The crimes are so fully expressed, that he had little to add; he expressed, that here is an illegal dispossession and arbitrary imprisonment of Wm. Tayleur, esq. by the lord accused, because Mr. Tayleur's daughter would not prostitute herself to his lust. He said, That all the commons of England are wounded through the said Mr. Tayleur: for what the lord viscount Mordaunt hath done arbitrarily against one, he may by his power do against as many others as he please; and then concluded, that the commons would be ready to make good the charge, and attend the prosecution in such ways and time as their lordships shall according to the course of parliament appoint.'—Then the lords commanded the said Impeachment to be read, as followeth:

* Life, p. 382.

ARTICLES OF IMPEACHMENT, by the Commons assembled, in the name of themselves and of all the commons of England, against John lord visc. Mordaunt, Constable of the Castle of Windsor, for several High Crimes and Misdemeanors committed by him.

"I. That the said lord visc. Mordaunt, being a peer of this realm, and constable of the Castle of Windsor and commander of the Garrison soldiers there; understanding that one Wm Tayleur esq. (who had faithfully served his late majesty king Charles I. in his wars, and being a great sufferer for his loyalty to him during the time of the usurpation, and by his majesty king Charles II. since his most happy Restoration by letters patents under his great seal of England, promoted to several offices of trust within the said Castle and Honour of Windsor, and in actual possession of certain lodgings with the said Castle, claimed by him as appertaining to his said offices or one of them), did intend to stand for the election of one of the burgesses of the borough of Windsor, to serve in this present parliament (for which writs of summons were issued); in the month of March, 1660 (some weeks before the time of the election), to disparage and prevent the free election of the said Wm. Tayleur, and strike a terror into those of the said borough which should give their voices for him, and deprive them of the freedom of their voices at the election, by colour of a warrant from his maj. on or about the 17th of the said month of March, did, by soldiers, forcibly eject the said Wm. Tayleur, together with his wife (then great with child), family, and goods, out of the said lodgings and Castle, the rude carriage of which soldiers then frightened a young child of the said Mr. Tayleur out of its wits, whereof it soon after died; and moreover, on the 23rd of the same month, the said lord M. did command and cause the said Wm. Tayleur to be forcibly, illegally, and arbitrarily seized upon, by soldiers, in the prison of the said borough, out of the precincts of the said Castle, which soldiers broke open the said prison doors where the said Wm. Tayleur was then prisoner under an arrest for debt, and carried him out of the said prison into the said Castle, without any warrant but their swords, or any lawful cause, and there detained him prisoner, by the said lord M.'s command, from two in the afternoon, till near one the next morning, in a cold low room, some steps under ground, refusing to accept of 2000*l*. bail, then proffered for his enlargement.

II. That the said lord M. at the time of Mr. Tayleur's imprisonment, when 2,000*l*. bail was proffered for his release, being told that the said Mr. T. was the king's servant, and had the king's Great Seal for his place as well as he the said lord M. had for his, in high contempt of his majesty's royal authority and Great Seal, replied, "He would dispose of the said Mr. Tayleur's places, and break the Great Seal, and justify it when he had done.'

III. That the said lord M. in March 1664, by letters and otherwise, made sundry uncivil addresses to the daughter of the said William Tayleur; which she rejecting, and threatening to make the said viscount's lady acquainted with them, the said viscount swore, by a most dreadful oath and imprecation, he would persecute her and her family to all eternity.

IV. That on the 23d of Nov. 1665, by order of the said viscount Mordaunt, the said Wm. Tayleur was forcibly and illegally dispossessed, by soldiers, of certain rooms in the Timber-yard belonging to the said Castle, without the walls thereof, claimed by the said Wm. Tayleur as belonging to his offices of pay-master and surveyor of the said Castle.

V. That a warrant, obtained from his majesty by untrue suggestions and misinformations, dated Nov. 30, 1665, but not produced till some months after, upon a Pluries Habeas Corpus, for the restraining of the said Wm. Tayleur from going out of the said Castle, was directed to the said lord M. who, by virtue of his own warrant, not mentioning the said Warrant of his majesty, about the 9th of Dec. following, caused the said Mr. Tayleur to be again forcibly and illegally apprehended and taken into custody, in the said borough of Windsor, without the precincts of the said Castle, by one Rd. Voyle, then marshal of the said Castle, assisted with a file of musketeers, who, by command from the said lord M. carried him prisoner into the said Castle, and there continued and illegally detained him prisoner, during the space of 20 weeks, and 5 thereof a close prisoner, not admitting him to go to church though he desired it; and, locking him up every night, refused to take bail for him, when offered, soon after his imprisonment, whereas his majesty's Warrant was only to restrain him within the Castle; at which time Henry Marten, a traitor, one of the late regicides, then a prisoner there, had liberty to go abroad out of the said Castle without a keeper.

VI. That the said lord M. during the said Wm. Tayleur's imprisonment, illegally refused to return and obey an Habeas Corpus brought by the said Mr. Tayleur for his enlargement; and being afterwards served with an Habeas Corpus by Simondson, servant to the said Mr. Tayleur, for his enlargement, the said lord M. in high contempt of his majesty's authority and laws of this realm, gave the said servant reproachful language, calling him 'rogue' for delivering the said writ; and saying, that was all the answer he would give to it,' directly refusing to obey the same: and continued the said Mr. Tayleur divers weeks after a prisoner till set at liberty upon a Pluries Habeas Corpus, by his majesty's Court of King's Bench.

VII. That the said Mr. Tayleur, soon after his enlargement, hearing and fearing that he should be again illegally imprisoned by the said lord M. did hereupon make application to his lordship, by his friends, for a reconciliation; who answered them, 'he would never be reconciled to him;' and threatened to imprison him again; and then, if he brought another Habeas Corpus, he would imprison him again and again, and keep him prisoner as long as he lived, and likewise turn him out of all his employments and offices, and dispose of them to others as he pleased;' by reason of which threats and menaces, the said Mr. Tayleur was enforced to desert his wife, family, and employments, at the said borough of Windsor, and to obscure himself elsewhere, till this present session of parliament, to prevent future illegal imprisonments by the said viscount.—All and every of which proceedings are contrary to the Great Charter, and other laws and statutes of this realm, and the rights and liberties of all the Commons and Freemen of England; and of dangerous consequence and example, if unredressed. And the said commons by protestation, saving to themselves the liberty of exhibiting at any time hereafter any other Accusation or Impeachment against the said viscount, and also of replying to the Answer to the said Articles, or any of them, or of offering proof of the premises, or any other Impeachment or Accusations that shall be exhibited by them, as the case shall (according to the course of parliaments) require, do pray, That the said viscount M. may be called to answer the said several Crimes and Misdemeanors, and receive such condign punishment as the same shall deserve; and that such further proceedings may be upon every of them had and used against him as is agreeable to law and justice."

Lord Mordaunt's Answer to the said Articles.] Jan. 17. The lord Mordaunt gave the house humble thanks, for giving him so long time to advise for the putting in his Answer to the Impeachment of the house of commons against him; and, in obedience to their lordships command, now presented his Answer in writing, with a desire that the same may be communicated to the House of Commons. Then the said Answer was read as followeth:

The Humble ANSWER of John lord visc. Mordaunt, constable of his majesty's Castle and Honour of Windsor, to certain ARTICLES OF IMPEACHMENT, exhibited against him by the Commons assembled in Parliament, for several High Crimes and Misdemeanors supposed to be committed by him.

"The lord visc. Mordaunt, not being conscious to himself of any malice or purpose of evil to any man alive, nor having had other displeasure against Wm. Tayleur, in the said Articles named, than what arose from his insolent and provoking deportment towards his majesty, in disobeying his warrants and his lordship in the execution of his office (under whose immediate government he is by the offices he holds in Windsor Castle), and from the variety of complaints which have been reiterated to his ldp. by the country against him for his oppression in those offices, and from the manifest abuses by him committed, in mispending the revenue of the said Castle, and defrauding the artificers, as also clandestinely and fraudulently endeavouring to pass Accompts without controul, which matters are now depending in the courts below at Westminster Hall, accounts it a singular unhappiness, that so worthy a body as the hon. house of commons, for whom his ldp. hath ever had so great respect, should think themselves concerned in that one man's person to accuse him, in their names, and in the names of all the commons of England: and he did well hope that it being offered to that hon. house on his behalf, that he would (with leave from your lordships) be ready to answer Mr. Tayleur in any action at law, and wave his privilege, they would have spared themselves and your lordships the trouble of this examination, and him the misfortune of being accused by them: therefore, praying your lordships that no informality in this his Answer, nor any mistaken word or expression, may be construed to his disadvantage, and saving to himself all privileges and rights belonging to him as a peer of this realm, and all advantages of exceptions to the insufficiency and informality of the said Impeachment, humbly answers,

'To the 1st Article, Which concerns the dispossession of Wm. Tayleur of certain rooms in Windsor Castle, the said lord visc. M. answereth, That he was very ignorant of those faithful services Mr. T. had done to the late king of ever-blessed memory, or of any sufferings upon the account of his loyalty to him; which had he known, they would have obliged him to a due consideration of him; and doth affirm he is yet as great a stranger to his merits, as he was at that time to his person; and heartily wishes his obedience and integrity to his maj. that now reigns could have justified that character of him: but, to satisfy your lordships how ill he deserved from his maj. and the lord M. in the matters of this Article, saith, That, in the year 1660, when his maj. was pleased, on his grace and favour, to confer upon him that important trust of Constable and Governor of the Castle of Windsor, he found Mr. T. in possession of that house which belongs to the Chancellor of the Garter; that, the first installation being presently to be solemnized, his maj. was pleased, by his immediate warrant of the 24th Feb. 1660, to command, that within 20 days the possession of that house, in habitable condition, should be delivered to the Chancellor of the Garter; with which Warrant Mr. T. being acquainted, and having perused it, positively refused to remove upon that warrant; but he was advised by the lord M. to consider better of it: however, he afterwards returned the same answer, with somewhat more stubbornness; and his wife being importuned by his ldp. to persuade her husband to yield obedience, she said, she would acquaint her husband with it: all those fair ways being essayed, and finding no obedience, rather than suffer his majesty's commands to be disputed by his servant, and contumaciously disobeyed in his own house, his ldp. found it necessary, in observance to the said Warrant, to command a serjeant of the garrison, with some few soldiers, to remove his goods and family, yet with all civility imaginable; which they punctually observed, and assisted them in carrying out their goods.' As to the affrightment of the child out of its wits, his ldp. cannot think the sight of soldiers in Windsor Castle should have such effect, the child having been seen playing and well after that time of removal, and, as his ldp. is informed, was sick of the worms, and this affrightment never spoken of till this occasion.—The dispossession was indeed by soldiers; the king's commands not being otherwise to be executed there, no sheriff or other civil officer being permitted to come into the king's house and garrison, by order of the place: and these were the only causes of this dispossession, and not any concernment in his election to parliament, which is most evident, in that he did stand for burgess, wherein the election was free, and was elected by the commonalty of the town; but his election afterwards was avoided by the house of commons. As to the seizing Mr. T. by soldiers out of the precincts of the Castle, and carrying him into the Castle, without warrant or any lawful cause, his ldp. saith, That the time of his securing was 3 weeks before his election; and that the place where Mr. T. was apprehended, was within the jurisdiction of the Castle (as he taketh it), for that the courts were there held by the said Wm. T. as clerk to the Constable of the Castle, who, being a counsellor at law, would not have kept courts there as his lordship's deputy, if the same had been out of the Jurisdiction of the said Castle. And his ldp. saith, That be being informed and assured that the said Mr. T. was not a prisoner for debt; and the said Mr. T. having insolently disobeyed his majesty's commands concerning his own house, and spoken several scandalous and opprobrious words against his ldp. and his family, his ldp. did command an officer and some few soldiers to carry him to the guard, where he was detained some few hours, and after set at liberty; and his ldp. denies that any bail was tendered to him for his enlargement: and his ldp. being constable and governor of the said Castle (it being then a garrison for the king), and believing that it might be a great encouragement to others to disobey commands, if this insolence were not taken notice of and punished; these were the true causes of his being sent for; and hopes it will not be imputed to him as done arbitrarily, or in contempt of the law, to which he hath always shewn ready obedience, and hath asserted its authority in the worst of times, with the hazard of his life.

'To the 2nd Article, he saith, That, as Constable of the said Castle, his ldp. claims to have the disposition of several of those offices in possession of Wm. T. by colour of his patent: but denies any contemptuous words spoken of the king's Great Seal, or otherwise than to the effect and purpose to vacate his patent, which his ldp. was informed by his Counsel to be void in law.

'To the 3rd Article, His ldp. denies any uncivil addresses to Wm. T.'s daughter, or of any threats of ruin to her family.

'To the 4th, he saith, That there were several rooms in the Timber Yard in the possession of the said Wm. T. all which (except such as he claimed to belong to him as surveyor of the said Castle) did belong to several artificers, to some by patent, and to others by constant usage and enjoyment; and that, by his majesty's order under his majesty's privy signet of the 28th Feb. 1664, the rooms belonging to the artificers of the said Castle are commanded to be restored to them; and, that his ldp. might be sure to do no man injury, he desired several gentlemen of the neighbourhood, who had been well acquainted with the offices and usage of the said Castle (whereof the said Wm. T. was one), to make enquiry, and certify concerning the said rooms; which all of them (except Mr. T.) accordingly returned, 'That the Rooms possessed by the said Wm. T. belonged to divers artificers;' whereof Mr. T. having notice left at his house, his wife and family there refused to deliver possession according to his majesty's commands, but instead thereof returned reviling language; and at this time when he was removed from the said rooms, the said Wm. T. was suspended from the place of Receiver by an order of his maj. and council, and Mr. Dudley Rouse placed in the said office, the said rooms claimed to belong to the said office were delivered to the said person that was placed in the said office, and the rest to the artificers to whom they belonged; but the rooms as surveyor are still in his possession, without any disturbance.

'To the 5th Article, he saith, That the suggestions in his majesty's Warrant of the 30th Nov. 1665, for restraining Wm. T. from going out of the said Castle, are true; and that he was taken by the marshal and brought into the Castle without any soldiers, and during his restraint there he was not a close prisoner by his lordship's directions as by his lordship's warrant will appear; neither did he at any time refuse bail for him, for none was tendered. And as for Henry Marten's liberty, his lordship saith, it was not done with his privity or consent; but saith, he hath since enquired thereinto, and finds the fact to be, that the lord Lovelace, being lord lieut. of the county, coming to Windsor, sent to the officer, to desire leave for Henry Marten (his brother-in-law) to dine with him, who accordingly gave him leave, and sent the marshal with him, who brought him back again.

'To the 6th, he saith, That the first Habeas Corpus was returnable immediate, and was delivered in his lordship's absence, he being then attending his maj. at Oxford, and did not know of the same till after the return thereof. The 2nd Habeas Corpus was not delivered to his ldp. till Saturday afternoon at Windsor, and the term ended on Monday following; so as, by reason of the shortness of the time, he could not make return thereof; and his ldp. doth deny that he called the person that delivered the said writ, 'rogue;' or used any reviling or reproachful language against him for the Delivery of the said writ; and upon the Pluries Habeas Corpus, his ldp. made a return thereof in due time, and the court of king's bench saw cause to hold him bound by recognizance to appear the last day of the term, to answer any information that should be exhibited against him for the matters in the Warrant.

'To the 7th he saith, That he knows not what Mr. T. might hear concerning his future imprisonment, nor what his guilt might make him apprehend; but that his lordship had not the least thought of it himself. He assured a noble peer of this house, who writ to him on Mr. T.'s behalf, that he would not imprison him; neither was he afterwards imprisoned by his ldp. or did any warrant or command from his ldp. issue to that purpose. And as to the allegation, that he hath been enforced to leave his wife and family, it is surely a great mistake; for he oftentimes since kept courts publicly at Windsor, without interruption, or cause of fear.—Having thus most plainly expressed to your lordships the truth of his proceedings, he humbly submits the same to your lordships judgment."

The said Answer was communicated to the commons, but it does not appear from the Journals that they made any replication thereto.

Disagreement between the two Houses.] Soon after this Impeachment, a difference ensued between the lords and commons, concerning a Poll-Bill, and the Bill for taking the Public Accounts; the former were for doing it by commission from the king, and not by Bill, as was proposed by the commons. The consequence of which was, that the latter in some heat resolved, "That this proceeding of the lords in going by Petition to the king for a Commission for taking the Public Accounts, while there was a bill sent up by this house, and depending before them, for taking the Accounts another way, is unparliamentary, and of dangerous consequence." A few days after, they likewise declared, "That, according to the right and settled course of parliament upon Bills, neither a bill, nor any part thereof is to be communicated to his majesty by either house, until the whole be agreed unto by both houses." As to the Poll-Bill, the lords in a free Conference insisted, among other things, upon adding some names to the commissioners. To which the commons disagreed; but without the least asserting their peculiar rights as to Money-Bills: they only gave this reason for their non-compliance, "That it hath been observed, that in all Acts of Subsidies and of Poll-Money, the greater the number of commissioners, the less money hath been raised; for many commissioners incumber one another, and rather procure the ease of themselves, and their many friends, than the advance of the king's service, and the public benefit."

The Speaker's Speech to the King, on presenting the Poll-Bill.] Jan. 18. The king came to the house of peers, and commanded the attendance of the commons; who being come, their Speaker addressed his majesty as follows:

"May it please your most excellent majesty; Since the two houses of parliament, by your majesty's command, were last convened, they have with great care inspected the state of the kingdom: they find your majesty engaged in a sharp and costly war, opposed by mighty princes and states, that are in conjunction against us. They see with sorrow the greatest part of your metropolitan city buried in ashes. These are 'Ardua Regni' indeed, and fit only for the advice of a loyal parliament. But, sir, looking narrowly into things, we found our body politic entering into a consumption; our treasures, that are the sinews of war and the bond of peace, as much exhausted; the great aids which are given to your majesty for the maintenance of the war are but like the blood in its circulation, which will return again, and nourish all the parts: but a great deal is yearly transported in specie into France, to bring home apes and peacocks; and the best returns are but superfluities and vanities: we have therefore unanimously besought your majesty to stop this issue of blood; and we hope your majesty's most seasonable and gracious Proclamation will prevent the future expiration of these spirits.—We have likewise been alarmed from all parts of the kingdom, by the Insolencies of Popish Priests and Jesuits, who, by their great numbers and bold writings, declare to all the world, they are in expectation of a plentiful harvest here in England: but your majesty, by your gracious Answer to the desire of both your houses, your command for all officers and soldiers in your majesty's pay to take the oaths of allegiance and supremacy, and your Proclamation for the Departure of Priests and Jesuits out of this nation, have in a great measure secured us against those fears.—When your majesty was pleased, at the opening of this session, to speak to us, you commanded us to find out the best expedients we could, for carrying on the war with as little burden to the people as was possible.—The knights, citizens, and burgesses of the commons house of parliament, have industriously applied themselves to the consideration of this matter. They quickly resolved of a Supply for your majesty, suitable to your occasions, of 1,800,000*l.*: but it hath taken up much of their time, so to lay this aid, that it may not seem a burden. A little weight lying always upon one shoulder will at length become uneasy; but being shifted sometimes to the other shoulder, there will be some refreshment.—The greatest part of the taxes that have been raised these 26 years were laid upon our lands, which made us desire to give them some rest: we have therefore prepared a Poll Bill; whereby we have brought in all sorts of persons, professions, and personal estates, to give their assistance to your majesty, and to ease the land-tax: 'Multorum manibus grande levatur onus.' This Bill, we hope, will speedily bring in a considerable sum of ready money for your majesty's present use. We have likewise taken care for supplying the remainder by another Bill remaining with us, which in a short time will be ready to be presented to your majesty.—The better to enable your majesty's good subjects to pay these several Aids, and with chearfulness to supply your majesty's future occasions; we thought it necessary to remove a nuisance out of their way. The infinite number of Foreign Cattle that were daily imported did glut our markets, and bring down the prices both of our home-bred cattle and our lands; therefore we have prepared a Bill for the prohibiting of any Foreign Cattle for 7 years.—We find your majesty's Mint is not so well employed as formerly; and the reason is, because the fees and wages of the officers and workmen is in part paid out of the bullion that is brought to be coined, and what is wanting is made up by your majesty. We have, therefore, for the ease of your majesty and those that shall bring in any plate or bullion to be coined there, made another provision, by an imposition upon wines, brandy, and cyder, imported from any foreign nations.—Having given your majesty this short account at present, we shall, with your leave, return to perfect those bills that still remain with us; and we hope so to finish them to your majesty's satisfaction, that all your majesty's enemies both at home and abroad may see and feel the effects of this blessed correspondence between our gracious king and his loyal parliament."

The King's Speech, on passing the Poll Bill.] After passing the said Bill, his majesty made the following Speech:

"My Lords and Gentlemen; I have now passed your Bills; and I was in good hope to have had other bills ready to pass too. I cannot forget, that within few days after your coming together in Sept. both houses presented me with their Vote and Declaration, that they would give me a Supply proportionable to my occasions: and the confidence of this made me anticipate that small part of my Revenue which was unanticipated for the payment of the seamen: and my credit hath gone farther than I had reason to think it would; but it is now at an end.—This is the first day I have heard of any money towards a Supply, being the 18th of Jan. and what this will amount to, God knows; and what time I have to make such preparations as are necessary to meet three such enemies as I have, you can well enough judge: and I must tell you, what discourses soever are abroad, I am not in any treaty; but, by the grace of God, I will not give over myself and you, but will do what is in my power for the defence of myself and you. It is high time for you to make good your promise; and it is high time for you to be in the country, as well for the raising of money, as that the lords lieutenants and deputy lieutenants may watch those seditious spirits which are at work to disturb the public peace; and therefore I am resolved to put an end to this session on Monday next come sevennight, before which time, I pray, let all things be made ready that I am to dispatch. I am not willing to complain you have dealt unkindly with me in a Bill I have now passed, in which you have manifested a greater distrust of me than I have deserved. I do not pretend to be without infirmities: but I have never broken my word with you; and, if I do not flatter myself, the nation never had less cause to complain of grievances, or the least injustice or oppression, than it hath had in these 7 years it hath pleased God to restore me to you. I would be used accordingly."

Notwithstanding this intimidating speech, the commons proceeded with the affairs before them; especially the Impeachment of lord Mordaunt, which had likewise given his majesty some offence. Serj. Maynard, sir R. Atkins, Mr. Wm. Prynne, &c. were appointed to manage the evidence at the hearing: and on the 26th of Jan. read the Articles before the house of lords: but with dissatisfaction observed, that, during the reading of them, the lord Mordaunt was within the bar of the house. Of this the commons complained, and moved, 'That, according to former precedents in such proceedings, his ldp. might stand without the bar of the house.' And when one appeared as council for him, was beginning to plead in this matter, they thought fit to interrupt him, acquainting the peers, 'That his ldp. ought not to have any council assigned him to plead for him in matter of fact upon the Impeachment.' This caused a conference, and, indeed, a difference between the two houses: The lords insisted upon their rights and privileges, and on the 4th of Feb. confirmed their Order for the lord Mordaunt's sitting within the bar at his trial, produced two precedents for it, and declared themselves ready for the trial the next morning. The commons upon this were still more dissatisfied, and desired a free conference; in which matters were carried so high, that the lords declared, 'That they desired this conference to preserve a right understanding between both houses; but insisted upon it, that they might deny a free conference with the commons, citing a precedent, 12th Jac. where a free conference was denied the commons in point of one imposition; and that in point of judicature (which the lords insisted on to be only in the king and themselves) they might deny the commons a free conference.

The Speaker's Speech to the King at the Prorogation.] Feb. 8. But all these disputes were ended this day by the appearance of the king in the house of peers, who sent for the commons in order to a prorogation. Their Speaker sir Edw. Turner, having several Bills ready, presented them with this following Speech to his majesty;

"May it please your most excellent majesty; Nothing conduceth more to the happiness of a nation than a right understanding between the prince and the people: and nothing more advanceth this correspondence than frequent meetings in common council. By the wisdom of our fore-fathers, the security of our lives, our liberties, and our properties, is lodged in our English parliaments; and so gracious have your majesty's predecessors been, that, for the satisfaction of their people, they have made several laws, some for Triennial, some for Annual parliaments. Your majesty, by their example, upon the humble suit of your lords and commons, hath in a former session of this parliament, passed an act for Triennial meetings in parliaments; but in this your maj. hath exceeded all your predecessors, that, as your happy Restoration was in a Convention of parliament, so of your own accord, for the public good, and as a demonstration of your extraordinary love to parliaments, you have vouchsafed, ever since your return, to converse with your people in parliament; this being the 6th year, and the 6th session, of this present parliament.—The last time your maj. was pleased to speak to us, you commanded us to make ready all things you were to dispatch this session. In obedience thereunto, we have with all industry imaginable endeavoured so to prepare those matters that were before us, that your maj. and the whole nation may receive satisfaction in our dispatches.—First, it concerned us to keep our words with your majesty, in finishing that Supply which we promised you for the carrying on the war. In order whereunto, I do here present unto your maj. this Bill of 11 Months Assessment upon our lands, to take place in a post-charge after the additional royal aid now current is expired. This act, together with the Poll Bill lately passed, we conceive, will fully make up the 1,800,000*l.* we promised to your majesty.—We must for ever with humility acknowledge the justice of God, in punishing this whole nation by the late dreadful Conflagration of London. We know they were not the greatest sinners on whom the Tower of Syloe fell; and doubtless all our sins did contribute to the filling up that measure, which, being full, drew down the wrath of God upon that city. But it very much reviveth us to behold the miraculous blessing of God upon your majesty's endeavours for the preservation of that part of the city which is left: 'Et fas est resurgere mœnia Trojæ.' We hope God will direct your royal heart, and fortunate hand, in a few days, to lay a foundation stone in the rebuilding that royal city; the beauty and praise whereof shall fill the whole earth.—For the encouragement of this noble work, we have prepared several Bills: one, for the establishing a Judicatory, for the speedy determining all actions, and causes of action, that have or may arise between landlords and tenants, upon this sad accident. Though, I persuade myself, no Englishman would be exempted from making some offering to carry on this pious undertaking, yet the exemplary charity of your majesty's 12 reverend Judges is fit with honour to be mentioned before your majesty: they are willing to spend all their sand that doth not run out in your majesty's immediate service, of dispensing justice in their several courts to your people, in hearing and determining those controversies that may arise upon old agreements, and making new rules between owners and tenants, for their mutual encouragement in this glorious action. We have likewise prepared a Bill for the Regularity of the new Buildings, that they may be raised with more conveniency, beauty, and security, than they had before. Some streets we have ordered to be opened and enlarged, and many obstructions to be removed; but all with your majesty's approbation. This we conceive cannot be done with justice, unless a compensation be given to those that shall be losers: we have therefore laid an Imposition of 12 pence upon every chalder, and 12 p. upon every ton of coals, that shall be brought into the port of London, for 10 years, the better to enable the lord mayor and aldermen to recompense those persons whose grounds shall be taken from them.—Rome was not built in a day; nor can we, in the close of this session, finish the rules for the dividing of Parishes, rebuilding of the churches, and the ornamental parts of the city. These things must rest that we intended, till another session. But we know your maj. in the mean time will take them into your princely consideration, and make it your care that the houses of God and your own royal chamber be decently and conveniently restored.—And now, great sir, having thus happily finished the business of this session, we beg your majesty's leave that we may return to our own homes, there to put in execution the good laws which you have made, and to defend our several countries against all designs to disturb the peace of the nation. And we beseech Almighty God, who hath hitherto wonderfully preserved your majesty's person, and made you glorious in all your achievements, still to prosper your forces both at sea and land, till he hath made your maj. an asylum for all your friends, and a terror to your enemies both at home and abroad.'

The King's Speech at the Prorogation.] After passing the said Bills his majesty made the following Speech;

"My Lords and Gentlemen; I thank you for this other bill of Supply which you have given me; and I assure you, the money shall be laid out for the ends it is given. I hope we shall live to have bills of this nature in the old stile, with fewer provisos. I looked to have had somewhat offered to me concerning the Accompts of the Money that hath been already raised since the war; which since you have not done, I will take care (after so much noise) that the same be not stifled, but will issue out my commission in the manner I formerly promised the house of peers: and the commissioners shall have very much to answer, if they do not discover all matters of fraud and cozenage.—The season of the year is very far spent, in which our enemies have got great advantages over us; but, by the grace of God, I will make all the preparations I can, and as fast as I can. And yet I must tell you, that if any good overtures be made for an honourable peace, I will not reject them; and I believe all sober men will be glad to see it brought to pass.—I shall now prorogue you till towards winter, that you may in your several places intend the peace and security of your several countries, were there are unquiet spirits enough working. And I do pray you, and I do expect it from you, that you will use your utmost endeavours to remove all those false imaginations in the hearts of the people, which the malice of ill men have industriously infused into them, of I know not what jealousies and grievances; for I must tell you again, and I am sure I am in the right, that the people had never so little cause to complain of oppression and grievances as they have had since my return to you. If the taxes and impositions are heavy upon them, you will put them in mind, that a war with such powerful enemies cannot be maintained without taxes: and I am sure that the money raised thereby comes not into my purse.—I shall add no more, but that I promise myself all good effects from your affections and wisdoms, where-ever you are. And I hope we shall meet again of one mind, for my honour, and the good of the kingdom. And now, my lord privy seal, do as I have directed you." Whereupon the Lord Privy Seal declared the parliament to be prorogued to the 10th of October.

Principal Occurrences during the Recess.] The following is a short account of the principal Occurrences which took place during the recess. "Charles began to be sensible, that all the ends, for which the war had been undertaken, were likely to prove entirely abortive. The Dutch, even when single, had defended themselves with vigour, and were every day improving in their military skill and preparations. Though their trade had suffered extremely, their extensive credit enabled them to levy great sums; and while the seamen of England loudly complained for want of pay, the Dutch navy was regularly supplied with money and every thing requisite for its subsistence. As two powerful kings now supported them, every place, from the extremity of Norway to the coasts of Bayonne, was become hostile to the English. And Charles, neither fond of action, nor stimulated by any violent ambition, earnestly sought for means of restoring tranquillity to his people, disgusted with a war, which, being joined with the plague and fire, had proved so fruitless and destructive. The first advances towards an accommodation were made by England. When the king sent for the body of sir Wm. Berkeley, he insinuated to the states his desire of peace on reasonable terms; and their answer corresponded in the same amicable intentions.

Charles, however, to maintain the appearance of superiority, still insisted that the States should treat at London; and they agreed to make him this compliment so far as concerned themselves: but being engaged in alliance with two crowned heads, they could not, they said prevail with these to depart in that respect from their dignity. On a sudden, the king went so far on the other side as to offer the sending of ambassadors to the Hague; but this proposal, which seemed honourable to the Dutch, was meant only to divide and distract them, by affording the English an opportunity to carry on cabals with the disaffected party. The offer was therefore rejected; and conferences were secretly held in the queen-mother's apartments at Paris, where the pretensions of both parties were discussed. The Dutch made equitable proposals; either that all things should be restored to the same condition in which they stood before the war; or that both parties should continue in possession of their present acquisitions. Charles accepted of the latter proposal; and almost every thing was adjusted, except the disputes with regard to the Isle of Pelerone. This island lies in the East Indies, and was formerly valuable for its produce of spices. The English had been masters of it; but were dispossessed at the time when the violences were committed against them at Amboyna. Cromwel had stipulated to have it restored; and the Hollanders, having first entirely destroyed all the spice trees, maintained, that they had executed the treaty, but that the English had been anew expelled during the course of the war. Charles renewed his pretensions to this island; and as the reasons on both sides began to multiply, and seemed to require a long discussion, it was agreed to transfer the treaty to some other place; and Charles made choice of Breda.—Lord Hollis and Henry Coventry were the English ambassadors. They immediately desired, that a suspension of arms should be agreed to, till the several claims could be adjusted: but this proposal, seemingly so natural, was rejected by the credit of de Wit. That penetrating and active minister, thoroughly acquainted with the characters of princes and the situation of affairs, had discovered an opportunity of striking a blow, which might at once restore to the Dutch the honour lost during the war, and severely revenge those injuries, which he ascribed to the wanton ambition and injustice of the English.—Whatever projects might have been formed by Charles for secreting the money granted him by parliament, he had hitherto failed in his intention. The expences of such vast armaments had exhausted all the supplies; and even a great debt was contracted to the seamen. The king therefore was resolved to save, as far as possible, the last supply of 1,800,000*l.* and to employ it for payment of his debts, as well those which had been occasioned by the war, as those which he had formerly contracted. He observed, that the Dutch had been with great reluctance forced into the war, and that the events of it were not such as to inspire them with great desire of its continuance. The French, he knew, had been engaged into hostilities by no other motive than that of supporting their ally; and were now more desirous than ever of putting an end to the quarrel. The differences between the parties were so inconsiderable, that the conclusion of peace appeared infallible; and nothing but forms, at least some vain points of honour, seemed to remain for the ambassadors at Breda to discuss. In this situation, Charles, moved by an ill-timed frugality, remitted his preparations, and exposed England to one of the greatest affronts which it has ever received. Two small squadrons alone were equipped; and during a war with such potent and martial enemies, every thing was left almost in the same situation as in times of the most profound tranquillity.—De Wit protracted the negotiation at Breda and hastened the naval preparations. The Dutch fleet appeared in the Thames under the command of de Ruyter, and threw the English into the utmost consternation. A chain had been drawn across the river Medway; some fortifications had been added to Sheerness and Upnore-castle: but all these precautions were unequal to the present necessity. Sheerness was soon taken; nor could it be saved by the valour of sir Edward Sprague, who defended it. Having the advantage of a spring tide and an easterly wind, the Dutch pressed on, and broke the chain, though fortified by some ships, which had been there sunk by orders of the duke of Albemarle, (10th June). They burned the three ships which lay to guard the chain, the Matthias, the Unity, and the Charles the fifth. After damaging several vessels, and possessing themselves of the hull of the royal Charles, which the English had burned, they advanced with six men of war and five fire-ships, as far as Upnore-castle, where they burned the Royal Oak, the Loyal London, and the Great James. Captain Douglas, who commanded on board the Royal Oak, perished in the flames, though he had an easy opportunity of escaping. 'Never was it known,' he said, 'that a Douglas had left his post without orders.' The Hollanders fell down the Medway without receiving any considerable damage; and it was apprehended, that they might next tide sail up the Thames, and extend their hostilities even to the bridge of London. Nine ships were sunk at Woolwich, four at Blackwall; platforms were raised in many places, furnished with artillery: the trained bands were called out; and every place was in a violent agitation. The Dutch sailed next to Portsmouth, where they made a fruitless attempt: they met with no better success at Plymouth: they insulted Harwich: they sailed again upon the Thames as far as Tilbury, where they were repulsed. The whole coast was in alarm; and had the French thought proper at this time to join the Dutch fleet, and to invade England, consequences the most fatal might justly be apprehended. But Lewis had no intention to push the victory to such extremities. His interest required that a balance should be kept between the two maritime powers; not that an uncontrouled superiority should be given to either.—Great indignation prevailed among the English to see an enemy, whom they regarded as inferior, whom they had expected totally to subdue, and over whom they had gained many honourable advantages, now of a sudden ride undisputed masters of the ocean, burn their ships in their very harbours, fill every place with confusion, and strike a terror into the capital itself. But though the cause of all these disasters could be ascribed neither to bad fortune, to the misconduct of admirals, nor to the ill behaviour of seamen, but solely to the avarice, at least to the improvidence, of the government; no dangerous symptoms of discontent appeared, and no attempt for an insurrection was made by any of those numerous sectaries, who had been so openly branded for their rebellious principles, and who upon that supposition had been treated with such severity.—In the present distress, two expedients were embraced: an army of 12,000 men was suddenly levied: and the parliament, though it lay under prorogation, was summoned to meet.*"

SIXTH SESSION OF THE SECOND PARLIAMENT.

July 25, 1667. His majesty having prorogued the parliament to the 10th of October,† and being advised, that the weighty affairs of the kingdom might require a sooner day of their meeting; he therefore, by his proclamation, having summoned them to meet on this day; both houses met accordingly, when the commons were proceeding to business, the Speaker informed them, that his majesty had commanded him to let them know, that, conceiving the house might not be full at their first meeting, he had deferred his coming to acquaint them with what he had to say, till Monday next: and that the house should adjourn till that day. "Whether, says Mr. Ralph, "the house was disgusted with this usage, or met in an ill humour from the ill situation of the public affairs, or wanted to make their own advantage of the public calamities, they did not obey his majesty's injunction, till they had first come to a Resolution nem. con. "That his maj. be humbly desired, by such members as are his privy counsel, that when a peace is concluded, the new-raised Forces be disbanded."

The King's Speech.] July 29. This day his majesty came to the house of peers and made a short Speech to both houses to this effect:

"He conceived, he could not give his houses of parliament a greater testimony of his affections to them, than by sending for them when he was in such straits as were superior to any other counsels; which now being over, he was confident, he could not better please them, than to dismiss them again to their several countries at such a time as this is. His maj. said, The Peace being now concluded, the Articles would be made public within a few days, which he supposed would seem reasonable to them, and all Christendom as much rejoice at the peace as they were disturbed by the war. His maj. further told his houses, That their own affairs now require their presence elsewhere; and he did hope they would use all industry and severity (for both were necessary) to reduce the people to a better temper than they have been in of late. His maj. further said, He wondered what one thing he had done since his coming into England, to persuade any sober person that he did intend to govern by a Standing Army; he said he was more an Englishman than so. He desired, for as much as concerned him, to preserve the laws; and if others will pay that due respect they owe to the laws, there would be no fear of any such thing. His maj. said, The last year he raised some troops, which he disbanded as soon as the season would permit; and he was certain, he deferred raising forces long enough this year, in that he gave not one commission till the enemy was landed; and he was sure, that the persons now in commission are such as will be as desirous to be out of the employment as to continue in it. He further said, he would say no more, but that he hoped his two houses of parliament should meet here in Oct. next, and that they would then come with such inclinations as may restore the kingdom to as good a condition as it were ever in; and he did assure them he should not be wanting on his part."—The parliament was then prorogued to the 10th of October.

Principal Occurrences during the Recess—Fall of the lord Chancellor Clarendon.] "The signing of the Treaty at Breda," says Mr. Hume,* "extricated the king from his present difficulties. The English ambassadors received orders to recede from those demands, which however frivolous in themselves, could not now be relinquished, without acknowledging a superiority in the enemy. Polerone remained with the Dutch; satisfaction for the ships Bonaventure and Good-hope, the pretended grounds of the quarrel, was no longer insisted on: Acadie was yielded to the French. The acquisition of New-York, a settlement so important by its situation, was the chief advantage

* Hume, vol. vii. p. 427.

† It being a current opinion, or rather an unquestioned certainty, that upon a prorogation a parliament cannot be convened before the day, though upon an adjournment it may; Mr. Prynne had been brought privately to the King to satisfy him, that upon an extraordinary occasion he might do it: and his judgment, which in all other cases he did enough undervalue, very much confirmed him in what he had a mind to." Lord Clarendon's Life, p. 423.

* Hume Vol. vii. p. 431.

which the English reaped from a war, in which the national character of bravery had shone out with lustre, but where the misconduct of the government, especially in the conclusion, had been no less apparent.—To appease the people by some sacrifice seemed requisite before the meeting of parliament; and the prejudices of the nation pointed out the victim. The Chancellor was at this time much exposed to the hatred of the public, and of every party which divided the nation. All the numerous sectaries regarded him as their determined enemy; and ascribed to his advice and influence those persecuting laws, to which they had lately been exposed. The catholics knew, that while he retained any authority, all their credit with the king and the duke would be entirely useless to them, nor must they ever expect any favour or indulgence. Even the royalists, disappointed in their sanguine hopes of preferment, threw a great load of envy on Clarendon, into whose hands the king seemed at first to have resigned the whole power of government. The sale of Dunkirk, the bad payment of the seamen, the disgrace at Chatham, the unsuccessful conclusion of the war; all these misfortunes were charged on the chancellor, who, though he had ever opposed the rupture with Holland, thought it still his duty to justify what he could not prevent. A building, likewise, of more expence and magnificence than his slender fortune could afford, being unwarily undertaken by him, much exposed him to public reproach, as if he had acquired great riches by corruption. The populace gave it commonly the appellation of Dunkirk house.—The king himself, who had always more revered than loved the chancellor, was now totally estranged from him. Amidst the dissolute manners of the court, that minister still maintained an inflexible dignity, and would not submit to any condescensions, which he deemed unworthy of his age and character. Buckingham, a man of profligate morals, happy in his talent for ridicule, but exposed in his own conduct to all the ridicule which he threw on others, still made him the object of his raillery, and gradually lessened in the king that regard which he bore to his minister. When any difficulties arose, either for want of power or money, the blame was still thrown on him, who, it was believed, had carefully at the restoration checked all lavish concessions to the king. And what perhaps touched Charles more nearly, he found in Clarendon, it is said, obstacles to his pleasures as well as to his ambition.—The king, disgusted with the homely person of his consort, and desirous of having children, had hearkened to proposals of obtaining a divorce, on pretence either of her being pre-engaged to another, or of having made a vow of chastity before her marriage. He was farther stimulated by his passion for Mrs. Stuart, daughter of a Scotch gentleman; a lady of great beauty, and whose virtue he had hitherto found impregnable: but Clarendon, apprehensive of the consequences attending a disputed title, and perhaps anxious for the succession of his own grandchildren, engaged the duke of Richmond to marry Mrs. Stuart, and thereby put an end to the king's hopes. It is pretended that Charles never forgave this disappointment.—When politics, therefore, and inclination both concurred to make the king sacrifice Clarendon to popular prejudices, the memory of his past services was not able any longer to delay his fall. The great seal was taken from him, and given to sir Orlando Bridgeman, by the title of lord keeper. Southampton, the treasurer, was now dead, who had persevered to the utmost in his attachments to the chancellor. The last time he appeared at the council-table, he exerted his friendship with a vigour which neither age nor infirmities could abate. "This man," said he, speaking of Clarendon, "is a true protestant, and an honest Englishman; and while he enjoys power, we are secure of our laws, liberties, and religion. I dread the consequences of his removal."—But the fall of the Chancellor was not sufficient to gratify the malice of his enemies: his total ruin was resolved on. The duke of York in vain exerted his interest in behalf of his father-in-law. Both prince and people united in promoting that violent measure; and no means were thought so proper for ingratiating the court with a parliament, which had so long been governed by that very minister, who was now to be the victim of their prejudices."

SEVENTH SESSION OF THE SECOND PARLIAMENT.

The King's Speech at the opening of the Session.] Oct. 10. This day both houses met: his majesty opened the Session with the following short Speech:

"My Lords and Gentlemen; When we last met here, about 11 weeks ago, I thought fit to prorogue the parliament till this day, resolving that there should be a session now, and to give myself time to do some things I have since done, which I hope will not be unwelcome to you, but a foundation for a greater confidence between us for the future. The other reasons of that prorogation, and some other matters with which I would acquaint you, I have commanded my Lord Keeper to declare unto you."

The Lord Keeper Bridgman's Speech.] Then the Lord Keeper* spake as followeth:

* "Sir Orlando Bridgman was a man of good natural parts, which he very carefully improved by study and application. He was, soon after the Restoration, made lord chief baron of the exchequer; whence he was, in a few months, removed to the common pleas. While he presided in this court, his reputation was at the height: then his moderation and equity were such, that he seemed to carry a chancery in his breast. Upon his receiving the great seal, his reputation began to decline: he was timid and irresolute, and this timidity was still increasing with his years. His judgment was

"My lords; and you knights, citizens, and burgesses of the house of commons; This parliament (after many good and wholesome laws made with your advice in several sessions, many great Supplies and Aids given to his majesty, and for the maintenance of the wars, and many other signal testimonies of your affection and duty to him, for which he again and again renews unto you his most hearty thanks) was, as you very well know, prorogued from Feb. last, till this 10th day of Oct.; his majesty having then reason to believe, that there would be no cause of your re-assembling in the mean time.—But, in this interval, the Dutch (who, since the war begun, were strengthened by the union of France and Denmark, having a great fleet) actually invaded the land; and the French at the same time had a royal army in the field, not far from the sea coast, the conjunction of which with the others, in some design against England, or some other of his majesty's dominions, we had then cause to suspect.—In this strait his maj. (who in lesser difficulties had frequent recourse unto his parliament, as his great and faithful council, and therefore hath every year once, often twice, re-assembled you) thought it necessary to anticipate the time, and issued out proclamations for your meeting on the 25th of July last past.—This (though unusual) was done by the advice of his privy council; public necessity and exigencies allowing, or at least dispensing with, many things, which (except in such cases) were not to be allowed, or dispensed withal.—Before that 25th of July, there was a prospect and daily expectation, and (within 3 days following) an assurance of a Peace, concluded with, and ratified, by our three potent adversaries. The storm which threatened us being thus blown over, and succeeded by so great a serenity, it was raised as a doubt by grave and wise men, whether or no, the necessities and difficulties which caused so early a summons being removed, you could sit or act as a parliament before the 10th of Oct. being the fixed time to which you were formerly prorogued. For this cause, together with those others mentioned by his majesty, he, in his princely wisdom, held it necessary, in a matter of so great consequence, again to fix upon this day for your meeting in parliament, about which there can be no dispute; which being thus twice prefixed, and you meeting here upon a double call, his maj. hopes it is a happy omen, that this session of parliament (which in law is but one day, all acts of this session referring to it unless otherwise specially provided) will be happy and prosperous to his majesty, to you and to the whole kingdom.—My Lords and Gentlemen; His maj. supposes that no man would expect, that during your recess he should have refused overtures of Peace; the vicinity, as well as potency, of his united enemies, the great expences of the war, carried on with much disadvantage, by reason of the Plague and dismal Fire in London, the consideration of the posture of affairs abroad (besides many other motives obvious unto you), induced him to embrace the opportunity of concluding a peace.—But you well know, that though the war be at an end, all the effects thereof are not yet ended: it will require time, and your good advice, to remove those obstructions which hinders the current of trade, both at home and abroad; and in this particular, his maj. thinks fit to recommend it to your wisdom, to settle such a balance of Trade between his subjects of this kingdom and those of Scotland, as that we may not be prejudiced, by the import of their commodities hither, nor yet they so discouraged as to leave off trading here, and find out another vent abroad, more dangerous to us. This he finds too hard for him without your assistance, though (upon your recommending it to him) he hath used some endeavours therein.—His maj. formerly promised that you should have an Accompt of the Monies given towards the war, which his maj. hath commanded his officers to make ready; and since that way of commission (wherein he had put the examination of them) hath been ineffectual, he is willing you should follow your own method, examine them in what way and as strictly as you please. He doth assure you, he will leave every one concerned to stand or fall, according to his own innocence or guilt.—His maj. hath reason to believe, that some disaffected persons (taking advantage of the public necessities) have spread abroad discourses and rumours reflecting upon the government, intending thereby to beget a dissatisfaction in his good subjects. And it is an easy thing to take exceptions, 'cum neque culpam humana infirmitas, neque calumniam regnandi difficultas, evitet.' But his maj. promises himself, from your good affections, that every one of you, in your several places, will endeavour to preserve a good understanding between him and his people; and if any just grievances shall have happened, his maj. will be as willing and ready to redress them for the future, as you to have them represented unto him.—And his maj. doubts not but you will give healing and moderate counsels, and imprint that known truth into the hearts of his subjects, that there is no distinct interest between the king and his people; but the good of the one is the good of both."

Address of both Houses to the King.] Oct. 15. Immediately after, the house of commons took

not equal to all the difficulties of his office. In nice points he was too much inclined to decide in favour of both parties; and to divide what each claimant looked upon as his absolute property. His lady, a woman of cunning and intrigue, was too apt to interfere in chancery suits; and his sons, who practised under him, did not bear the fairest characters. He is said to have been removed from his office for refusing to affix the seal to the king's Declaration for Liberty of Conscience." Granger, vol. iii. p. 361. See also North's Life of the Lord Keeper Guilford, p. 88.

into consideration what had been said to them, and resolved upon an Address of thanks to his majesty, in which they desired and obtained the concurrence of the lords. Accordingly, this day the two houses in a body, with their Speakers, attended the king in the Banqueting House at Whitehall; where the Lord Keeper, as Speaker of the house of peers, in the name of both houses, repeated this following Address to his majesty:

"We your majesty's loyal and faithful subjects, the lords and commons in parliament assembled, having taken into our serious consideration your majesty's gracious Speech, wherein you were pleased to let us know, that your majesty thought fit to prorogue this parliament till the 10th of Oct. that you might give yourself time to do something which would not be unwelcome, but a foundation for a greater confidence between your majesty and your people; we find ourselves bound in duty to return your majesty our humble and hearty Thanks for the gracious Declaration of your royal intentions in that your majesty's gracious Speech, and in that delivered by your majesty's command by the Lord Keeper. And particularly, 'that your majesty hath been pleased to disband the late raised Forces; and to dismiss the Papists from out your guards, and other military employments: for your maj.'s care in quickening the execution of the Act for restraining the Importation of foreign cattle: for causing the Canary Patent to be surrendered and vacated: and, more especially, that your majesty hath been pleased to displace the late Lord Chancellor, and remove him from the exercise of public trust and employment in affairs of state.' To which Address his maj. was pleased to make this return; 'I thank you for your Thanks; I am glad the things I have done have given you so good satisfaction: and for the earl of Clarendon, I assure you I will never employ him again in any public affairs whatsoever.'" *

PROCEEDINGS RELATIVE TO THE IMPEACHMENT OF THE EARL OF CLARENDON.

Oct. 26. The commons took into examination the conduct of the earl of Clarendon, to

* "When the house of commons came together, one Tomkins, a man of very contemptible parts and of worse manners (who used to be encouraged by men of design to set some motion on foot, which they thought not fit to appear in themselves till they discerned how it would take), moved the house 'that they might send a Message of Thanks to the king for his gracious expressions, and for the many good things which he had done, and particularly for his removing the Chancellor;' which was seconded by two or three, but rejected by the house as a thing unreasonable for them who knew not the motives which had disposed his majesty: and so a committee was appointed to prepare such a Message as might be fit for them to send. And the lords the same day sent to the king, without consulting with the commons, to give his majesty Thanks for the Speech he had made to them in the morning, which commonly used to be done. The king declared himself very much offended that the proposition in the house of commons for returning Thanks to him had not succeeded, and more that it had been opposed by many of his own servants; and commanded them 'to press and renew the motion: that his honour was concerned in it; and therefore he would expect Thanks, and would take it very ill of any of his own servants who refused to concur in it.'—Hereupon it was again moved: but notwithstanding all the labour that had been used contrary to all custom and privilege of parliament, the question held six hours debate, very many speaking against the injustice and irregularity of it; they on the other side urging the king's expectation of it. In the end the question being put, it was believed the Noes were the greater number: but the division of the house was not urged for many reasons; and so the Vote was sent to the lords, who were desired to concur with them.—But it had there a greater contradiction. They had already returned their Thanks to the king; and now to send again, and to add any particular to it, would be very incongruous and without any precedent: and therefore they would not concur in it. This obstinacy very much displeased the king: and he was persuaded by those who had hitherto prevailed with him, to believe that this contradiction, if he did not master it, would run through all his business that should be brought into that house. Whereupon his maj. reproached many of the lords for presuming to oppose and cross what was so absolutely necessary for his service: and sent to the abp. of Canterbury, 'that he should in his majesty's name command all the Bishops bench to concur in it; and if they should refuse it, he would make them repent it;' with many other very severe reprehensions and animadversions. This being done in so extraordinary a manner, the duke of York told his majesty, 'how much it was spoken of and wondered at:' to which his maj. replied, 'that his honour was engaged, and that he would not be satisfied if Thanks were not returned to him by both houses; and that it should go the worse for the Chancellor if his friends opposed it.' And he commanded h. r. h. that he should not cross it, but was contented to dispense with his attendance, and gave him leave to be absent from the debate; which liberty many others likewise took: and so when it was again moved, though it still was confidently opposed, it was carried by a major part, many being absent.—And so both houses attended the king and gave him Thanks, which his majesty graciously received as a boon he looked for, and said somewhat that implied that he was much displeased with the Chancellor; of which some men thought they were to make the best use they could. And therefore, after the king's Answer was reported to the house of peers, as of course what-

whose charge Mr. Edward Seymour* then laid many great and heinous crimes. Upon which there arose a debate in the house how they should proceed upon it, some moving he should be impeached in the name of the commons, till Articles should be formed against him; others urged, that witnesses should be first examined, to see how the Charge might be made good, lest, in case of failure, it might reflect on the honour of the house. After a long debate, a committee was appointed to search records for parliamentary proceedings in the like cases; from which Mr. Vaughan making report on the 29th, that they had found various proceedings in several parliaments, there arose another long debate, which was maintained with great warmth.

Sir *Thomas Littleton* said, that in cases criminal, they find proceedings to have been, sometimes by Articles, sometimes by word of mouth; but in capital crimes no proceedings appear till the earl of Strafford's case, against whom the house carried up a general Impeachment; the reason whereof seems to be this: some votes were made in the house at which the king takes offence, as if they would proceed upon common fame; whereupon they vindicate their proceedings as done in a parliamentary way, and appoint a committee to withdraw for about half an hour to consider the matter for a conference with the lords about the Charge, and upon their report a general Charge is carried up to the lords' bar; the principal Charge then was for advising to bring over the Irish Army, and the single proof was sir Henry Vane, so the Impeachment went up for High-Treason, though no member would positively say he would make the Charge good. So for the bishop of Canterbury there was no Impeachment, but a Charge in general. And if you take not the same course now, but insist upon examining witnesses first, the difficulties will be unanswerable; for is it like that men before they shall see you in earnest will have their names produced against the earl of Clarendon? If this be your proceeding, we must never expect to impeach a great man more. If you think there is nothing in the Charge leave it, but if you think it is worth your while take heed of making such a dangerous precedent as by neglecting it to wound your liberties; but proceed in the usual way with a general Impeachment.

Serjeant *Maynard*.† I stand not up to give advice, but to speak to matter of fact in the business of Strafford and Canterbury. I attended that business from the beginning: sir J. Clotworthy informed something against Strafford to be direct treason, that he had assumed an arbitrary power in Ireland, and dispossessed one Savage by force of arms, and undertook to prove it. Sir H. Vane also told them that he had a note taken out of his father's cabinet, containing the advice which Strafford gave the king in that case. Namely, the king wanting money, and the question being how

soever the king says upon any Message is always reported, it was proposed, 'That the king's Answer might be entered into the Journal-Book;' which was rejected, as not usual, even when the king himself spoke to both houses; nor was what he now said entered in the house of commons. However, when they had consulted together, finding that they had not yet so particular a record of the displeasure against the Chancellor, as what he had said upon this Message did amount unto, they moved the house again, 'that it might be entered in the Book:' and it was again rejected. All which would not serve the turn; but the duke of Buckingham a third time moved it, as a thing the king expected: and thereupon it was entered." Clarendon's Life, p. 443.

* Afterwards sir Edward, Speaker of the House of Commons, a Commissioner of the Admiralty, and Treasurer of the Navy.—"The ablest man of his party was Seymour, who was the first Speaker of the house of commons, that was not bred to the law. He was a man of great birth, being the elder branch of the Seymour family; and was a graceful man, bold and quick. He was violent against the court, till he forced himself into good posts. He knew the house and every man in it so well, that by looking about he could tell the fate of any question." Burnet.

"From being a wild spark about town, he came early into the court, and was of that gang that routed the lord chancellor. His entrance was through the parliament; for, being buoyed upon the Western alliance, he was considerable in the house of commons. He served as Speaker there eleven years; and, as such, was called to the privy council. He was ambitious and proud in the highest degree; and was supposed to decline no means that tended to his advancement. When he was of the privy council, he scorned to speak at the lower end, where his place was, but commonly walked up near the king, and standing behind the chairs of the chancellor, or other great lords, spoke to the king. And, as his nature, so his speeches were often arrogant and disrespectful. Once, at the council, he said to the king, 'Sir, how long will your majesty prevaricate with yourself?' The king muttering, repeated the word 'prevaricate' divers times, but made no reply. This, probably, joined with other like tempered speeches, lost him the king's favour." North's Life of the Lord Keeper Guilford, p. 228.

† Of this celebrated lawyer, who lived till after the Revolution, this remarkable story is told by bishop Burnet. He came with the men of the law to wait on the prince of Orange, being then 90 years old, and yet said the liveliest thing that was heard of on that occasion. The prince took notice of his great age, and said that he had outlived all the men of the law of his time. He answered, he had like to have outlived the law itself, if his highness had not come over.

he should supply it, he replied, 'That if the parliament was refractory and would not, you stand loosed and absolved from rules of government; you have an army in Ireland which you may employ to reduce them.'

Then there was a debate, Whether they should accuse him of Treason. And,

Sir *Edw. Herbert* (the Attorney) said, if you are persuaded the truth is, as is pretended, you may, and so it was; but when the close committee had examined the business, they moved the house, that some lawyers might be added to them, and had they gone, when they said they were ready, they had not touched one hair of Strafford's head. Then it was considered what was fit to be done: To accuse him of Treason would be a dangerous precedent, as if out of many other crimes a Treason could be drawn, thereupon it was Resolved not to demand judgment from the lords, because some Articles were not Treason. Then it was propounded not to state what his offences were, lest it should give advantage to inferior courts so to proceed; but said he deserved to be accused of Treason, and in conclusion a proviso was added, not to make that case a precedent. For the bishop of Canterbury, the 4 Articles were general, and he was long in prison without any proceeding against him; but after long time be demurred, then new Articles were framed, on which he died.

Mr. *John Vaughan.** You have had a charge opened of a strange nature, and I know not what part of it can be proved, but the reputation of this house is at stake, and of the king too; for, where a Charge is brought in by some of your members, whereof one Article is, That he should say such words of the king, as by a statute made by you is a præmunire, and to give council to levy war upon the kingdom; is it agreeable to our duty to the king and kingdom to let it die? For the person concerned, I know not which way his honour can be whole without his giving an Answer to his Charge; for mark the consequence, if the king should take him to favour again, before cleared, will not the world say, a person is received to favour again who gave the king council against the kingdom, and traduced the king, and how can he be whole in his honour this way; *Obj.* But it will be said, we must have ground to put him to Answer. *Ans.* Whether you have ground enough to prove I know not, but you have ground enough to make him Answer to clear himself. Suppose those two Articles had been charged on a member of this house, what would it have become that member to do; should he sit still and say, 'I will make no Answer, but see whether the house will make more proof;' if he should do so, the not making an Answer is reason enough to charge him. I can give you instances of persons charged in parliament, who, though not nominated, yet being (as it were) pointed at, petitioned that they might Answer, and so would any man; but when this is bruited up and down, will not the world say, You never ask the party whether guilty?—The Duke of Suffolk was charged upon common fame, and if that were a ground for a charge then (which I do not say it was) so it is in this case: but he moved that he might be heard, and though it was desired he might be committed, yet it was justly rejected till he had answered: then for the nature of the Charge, if it be true, it is very high, but whether it be Treason is another matter, it is brought to you under no name, when you make the charge, it becomes you to say what it is; therefore choose a Committee to reduce the accusation into Heads, and bring them to you, without which you cannot right yourselves, nor him, if innocent.—For the way of it, it cannot be thought fit to publish your witnesses and the matter before-hand; if in private causes the defendant and plaintiff should have a publication before hand, no cause would be rightly judged, much less when you have publication of all which concerns the one, but nothing of the other. Again, if a witness be examined concerning matters in his own knowledge, if he gives evidence, where he is not brought judicially to give it, if he hath testified any thing which brings him within the statute of false news, how can he avoid the penalty? For it is not enough for him to say he knows it, but he must have others to justify it.—As for the persons who bring the Charge, they are your own members, which the writs return for honest and discreet men, and if you are satisfied of that, how can you reject their complaint, though grounded upon Common Fame, as all accusations are, seeing they tell you, they can bring proof of what they say?—Then for Common Fame, if a man spends largely, and hath no visible way to get an estate, no man accuseth him to have gotten it unlawfully; yet he may be put to clear himself from what Common Fame chargeth him with. Upon suspicion of felony, I may bring a man before a magistrate to clear himself, so in the course of Indictments, and Presentments, a Charge is given of what things are to be presented; then a proclamation is made, That if any one can give evidence, he may be sworn, but if no evidence appear, yet they may indict.—Then it will be said, the oath is a material thing, but we are proceeding without an oath. To this I answer, What this house shall charge is of more authority than the oaths of ordinary witnesses; peers though not upon oath are supposed to do right, so are we upon the reputation of our honesty and discretion.

Mr. *Laurence Hyde.** I am sensible, the

* Afterwards Chief Justice of the Common Pleas.

* The earl of Clarendon's second son. "He is a man of far greater parts than the eldest. He has a very good pen, but speaks not gracefully. He was thought the smoothest man in the court; and during all the disputes concerning his father, he made his court so dextrously, that no resentment ever appeared on that head." Burnet.

house may think me partial, but I shall endeavour to shew myself not so much a son of the earl of Clarendon as a member of this house; and I assure you that if he shall be found Guilty, no man shall appear more against him than I; if not, I hope every one will be for him as much as I: let every man upon his conscience think what of this Charge is true, for I believe that if one Article be proved, he will own himself guilty of all.

Sir *Heneage Finch*.* An Impeachment there must be, if there be Cause; such accusations are not to be passed over in silence. I believe not one truth in the law more than this proposition, that there is no such thing as treason by common-law, or by equity, and we hold our lives by that law; before the 25th of Edw. III. a man could scarce speak any thing but it was treason in parliament or out, but no man ought to die as a traitor, who hath not literally offended that law, or some other made since: there is indeed in that law a proviso about the parliaments declaring what is treason, but note the danger of taking declaratory powers, which I fear hath brought us into a reckoning of blood, which we have not yet paid for. The power of parliaments is double, legislative, which hath no bounds, declaratory, by pronouncing judgments. And though I know not what the legislative power of a parliament cannot do, yet it is not in the power of the parliament, king, lords, nor commons, to declare any thing to be treason which is not in the common-law felony before. The proviso in Strafford's case was (it is true) made for inferior courts; but I hope we shall not so proceed as must needs draw after it a 'ne trahatur in exemplum,' and your own act this parliament shews, that all done by Strafford, a part, or together, was not treason: and it behoves us to take heed we thwart not our own argument. —For the manner then, consider how you should proceed if it were out of parliament, and how the bringing of it into the house alters it. If it were out of parliament, without doubt the accusation should be proved before hand, and those who discover it are guilty of felony. This provides for the subject, that the witnesses must be two, and for the king, that none shall discover the evidence.—But suppose the Charge be for misdemeanors, the trial then is not to be by the lords, but by the commons; for the lords are his peers only in cases capital. How then doth the bringing it into parliament alter the case? If the parliament set aside laws in this case, we should be happy to see law declaring what is the power of parliaments. There is no precedent produced which is singly of weight to guide you, therefore if you proceed, let it be as near as possible by the good old laws; namely, That there be an Accusation founded upon an oath and the evidence kept secret, I propose th[is] way for the very reason that others oppose [it,] viz. The Accusation goes over the kingdo[m,] and it will bring dishonour to the house, t[he] king, and the earl; for the honour of t[he] house, it will be hard to say, the Charge w[as] brought in upon misinformation; a pers[on] accused for advising to bring in arbitrary g[o]vernment, &c. And for saying the king is n[ot] fit to govern; if this be true, though it [is] not treason in the formality of the law, it deserves no less punishment then if it were; if not found guilty, consider the case. If [I] say, A. killed a man and it is not so, must he give reparation? We have an accusati[on] upon hear-say, but if it be not made good, t[he] blackest scandal which hell can invent, lies [at] our door.—Then sir Tho. Meares moving [to] refer it to the Committee of Grievances,

Mr. *Vaughan*. You should have put t[he] first question before another had been mov[ed;] the earl of Middlesex (Cranfield's Case) w[ill] not hold parallel; he was accused of bribe[ry,] which might be proved by their own boo[ks,] but this is for scandalizing the king, &c. A[nd] where shall the committee of grievances enqu[ire] about it? You say let them hear the persons. But suppose they be of the lords house, can you send for them? Or if you do, will they come and say it? The matter of this accusation is such, that if it lies in the knowledge of a single person, if he delivers it extrajudicially (which he doth, if not upon oath) he may be undone by it, and hazard his person too: at the committee of grievances the persons must be known, and what they can say, and then we may conclude what will follow: besides, their quality may be such as they cannot be brought, or their discretion such as they will not answer.

Sir *Rd. Temple*. Tell but the lords that a man in public place hath misbehaved himself, and they will sentence him, if he purge not himself; never yet were witnesses examined before the trial in case of treason or felony, for then, if there be two witnesses, a way may be found by poison, or some other way, to take away one. Let not this son of Zeruiah be too strong for king and parliament.

Mr. *Marvell** would have the faults hunt the

* "Finch was a man of probity, and well versed in the laws. He was long much admired for his eloquence; but it was laboured and affected." Burnet.

* "This was the famous Andrew Marvell, who was representative for the town of Kingston upon Hull. He discharged this trust with strict integrity and fidelity; and was highly esteemed by his constituents, to whom he constantly sent a particular account of every proceeding in the house, with his own opinion thereupon: a conduct so diligently respectful, together with his general obliging deportment towards them, did not fail to endear him perfectly to their affection; and they were not wanting on their side to testify their grateful sense of it, by allowing him an honourable pension the whole time he represented them." Marvell's Life, prefixed to his works, p. 9, 10 He died in 1678. See Note to p. 106.

persons: would not have a sudden impeachment by reason of the greatness of the person or danger of escape, lord Clarendon not being likely to ride away post.

Sir *Tho. Clifford.** It will make an end of all impeachments here, to have witnesses examined.

Serj. *Maynard.* No man can do what is just, but he must have what is true before him; where life is concerned you ought to have a moral certainty of the thing, and every one be able to say upon this proof 'In my conscience this man is guilty.' Common fame is no ground to accuse a man where matter of fact is not clear; to say an evil is done, therefore this man hath done it, is strange in morality, more in logic.

Upon the whole debate it was voted, "That the Committee do reduce the Accusation to Heads and present them to this house."

Articles of Impeachment against the Earl of Clarendon.] Nov. 6. Sir Tho. Littleton reported from the Committee appointed to draw up the Heads of Accusation against the earl of Clarendon, certain Articles, which he read in his place, and afterwards delivered the same in at the clerk's table, which are as followeth, viz:

I. "That the earl of Clarendon hath designed a Standing Army to be raised, and to govern the kingdom thereby, and advised the king to dissolve this present parliament, to lay aside all thoughts of parliaments for the future, to govern by a military power, and to maintain the same by Free Quarter and Contribution.

II. That he hath, in the hearing of the king's subjects, falsely and seditiously said, That the king was in his heart a Papist,—Popishly affected, or words to that effect.

III. That he hath received great sums of Money for the procuring of the Canary Patent, and other illegal Patents, and granted illegal Injunctions to stop proceedings at law against them, and other illegal Patents formerly granted.

IV. That he hath advised and procured divers of his majesty's subjects to be imprisoned against law, in remote islands, garrisons, and other places, thereby to prevent them from the benefit of the law, and to produce precedents for the imprisoning any other of his majesty's subjects in like manner.

V. That he hath corruptly sold several Offices, contrary to law.

VI. That he procured his majesty's Customs to be farmed at under rates, knowing the same; and great pretended Debts to be paid by his majesty, to the payment of which his maj. was not in strictness bound; and hath received great sums of money for procuring the same.

VII. That he received great sums of money from the Company of Vintners, or some of them, or their agents, for enhancing the prices of Wines; and for freeing of them from the payments of legal Penalties, which they had incurred.

VIII. That he hath, in short time, gained to himself a greater estate than can be imagined to be lawfully gained in so short a time; and, contrary to his oath, hath procured several Grants, under the great seal, from his majesty, to himself, and his relations, of several of his majesty's lands, hereditaments, and leases; to the disprofit of his majesty.

IX. That he introduced an arbitrary government in his majesty's Plantations; and hath caused such as complained thereof before his majesty and council, to be long imprisoned for so doing.

X. That he did reject and frustrate a Proposal and Undertaking, approved by his majesty, for the preservation of Nevis and St. Christopher's, and reducing the French Plantations to his majesty's obedience, after the commissions were drawn up for that purpose; which was the occasion of our great losses and damages in those parts.

XI. That he advised and effected the Sale of Dunkirk to the French king, being part of his majesty's dominions; together with the ammunition, artillery, and all sorts of stores there; and for no greater value, than the said ammunition, artillery, and stores, were worth.

XII. That the said earl did unduly cause his majesty's letters patents, under the great seal, to one Dr. Croucher, to be altered, and the enrollment thereof to be unduly razed.

XIII. That he hath, in an arbitrary way, examined, and drawn into question, divers of his majesty's subjects, concerning their lands, tenements, goods and chattels, and properties; determined thereof at the council-table; and stopped proceedings at law, by order of the council-table; and threatened some that pleaded the Statutes of 17 Car. I.

XIV. That he hath caused Quo Warrantos to be issued out against most of the corporations of England, immediately after their charters were confirmed by act of parliament; to the intent he might receive great sums of money from them, for renewing their charters; which when they complied withal, he caused the said Quo Warrantos to be discharged, or prosecution thereupon to cease.

XV. That he procured the Bills of Settlement for Ireland, and received great sums of money for the same, in most corrupt and unlawful manner.

XVI. That he hath deluded and betrayed his majesty, and the nation, in foreign treaties and negotiations, relating to the late war; and discovered and betrayed his secret counsels to his enemies.

* "Clifford began (in 1665) to make a great figure in the house of commons. He was the son of a clergyman, born to a small fortune: but was a man of great vivacity. He was reconciled to the church of Rome before the Restoration. He struck in with the enemies of the earl of Clarendon." Burnet.—He was afterwards advanced to a peerage, was made Lord Treasurer, and was one of the CABAL.

XVII. That he was a principal Author of the fatal Counsel of dividing the Fleet about June 1666."

Mr. *Edw. Seymour*, after having charged the lord chancellor, in general, thus expressed himself: He makes the earth groan by his Building* (the monument of his greatness) as we have done under his oppression: and speaking of the king's being a Papist, said, As if the ills he had done must be supported by greater†.

Sir *Tho. Littleton.* [On presenting the Articles.] If he did not the crimes alledged, he is able to clear it upon others; he whined after a peace. At the beginning of the war he had no preparations. The wind was wonderfully in a corner, that the Dutch could not come out. He gave perpetual assurance that the French would not come out, he made plots, and a committee of lords and commons were appointed to enquire; but all came to no effect; nothing discovered. He made those plots as a ground to raise an army. The commons do of course send to the lords. The course is, that the lords do desire him to be secured.

Lord *Cornbury*‡. If any one article in this charge be proved, lord Clarendon will submit to the rest.

Another particular touching the dividing the Fleet, being delivered in, was added to the rest; and the heads again read at the table; on which a debate arose, whether the heads of the accusations brought in against the earl of Clarendon should be referred to a committee to take the proofs.

Mr. *Dowdswell* moves to have the Heads committed to enquire the truth, and argues that common fame is not sufficient to bring him upon the stage.

Sir *F. Goodrick* seconds it, because new matter was now added to what was formerly charged *viva voce* in the house.

Sir *R. Howard.* Suppose the earl innocent, and yet charged and imprisoned (which is the worst of the case) he afterwards appears innocent and is discharged, receiving no more hurt than other subjects have done; namely, one great man lately, (the Duke of Buckingham.) *Object.* But why should you commit him? *Answ.* For proof, whether the Articles be true or not: suppose men for self-preservation will not venture to come, not knowing how they may trust themselves, and so you have no proof, he very guilty, and you not able to proceed; is the inconveniency greater for an innocent person if he prove so, to suffer a few days, than for you to loose your reputation for ever. If this man be not brought to his trial, it may force him to fly to that which he councelled, that is, that we may never have parliament more.

Sir *John Goodrick* would have the gentleman make his own case. Moves that the impeachment may not go out of the house, till recommended to a grand committee.

Col. *Birch** said that sir W. Pennyman, as evidence against lord Strafford, was checked for not offering to give his evidence.

Mr. *Vaughan.* You admit the accusation to be matter for a charge, if the committee find proof; if you intend to make this a distinct case I leave it to you; but if this be to settle the course of the proceedings of the house, I am against it; for this is ordering a way of proceeding in the earl's case, which shall not be a general rule. Though I cannot say one of the articles to be true, yet I know them to be a full charge if made good, and you are prescribing a course neither proper, nor ever practised. A witness who speaks without oath, is subject to damage; not so upon oath, because the law compels him: and whereas it hath been said, if witnesses attest before the house of commons, what judges dare meddle in it; I answer such judges are meddled in the case of sir John Elliot, &c. and the ship money.

---

* "The king had granted lord Clarendon a large piece of ground near St. James's, to build a house on. He intended a good ordinary house: but not understanding these matters, he was run into a vast charge of 50,000l. Some called it Dunkirk-House, intimating that it was built by his share of the price of Dunkirk. Others called it Holland-House, because he was thought to be no friend to the war." Burnet.—Lord Clarendon says himself, that he was not so much ashamed of any one thing he had done, as he was of the vast expence he had made in the building of his house, which had more contributed to that gust of envy that had so violently shaken him, than any misdemeanor that he was thought to have been guilty of. He adds, that it cost a third part more than he intended. Life, p. 512.

† "After many days spent in close contrivances and combinations, Mr. Seymour, a young man of great confidence and boldness, stood up in the house of commons, and spoke long and with great bitterness against the Chancellor, and of his great corruption, &c. Clarendon's Life, p. 445.

‡ The Earl of Clarendon's eldest son. "He was so provoked at the ill usage his father met with, that he struck in violently with the party that opposed the court." Burnet.—On king James's accession he was made Lord Privy Seal, and died in 1709.

* "Col. Birch was a man of a peculiar character. He had been a carrier at first, and retained still, even to an affectation, the clownishness of his education. He got up in the progress of the war to be a colonel, and to be concerned in the excise. And at the restoration he was found to be so useful in managing the excise, that he was put in a good post. He was the roughest and boldest speaker in the house, and talked in the language and phrases of a carrier; but with a beauty and eloquence that was always acceptable. He spoke always with much life and heat; but judgment was not his talent." Burnet.

Sir *John Holland.* No man impeached in the house of commons but blasted for ever after; therefore we should be wary how we proceed. If any person will undertake to make it good, as sir Henry Vane did lord Strafford's impeachment, he is for an impeachment.

Mr. *Seymour*, speaking of precedents, said, that precedents in the church by the fathers are rather to facilitate assent, than impose belief—fitter for lower courts than a parliament. As soon as their own matter is accorded, treason is done away, as in the late precedents. One argument of the earl's guilt is, that he has not put himself upon his trial all this while. We are now disputing whether we shall ever impeach any person. Of his own knowledge many persons have been menaced in case they give evidence. 'Serpens qui serpentem devorat fit draco.' Lord Clarendon has reserved to himself the monopoly of bribes. He says, he has a moral assurance of the proof of all his charge.

Sir *R. Howard.* If we proceed only by the common law, we may be censured at some of the bars below; we must do it to satisfy, and then not satisfy by doing it. Though common law has its proper sphere, 'tis not in this place, we are in a higher sphere. If impeachments of this nature be not allowed, we have no way left of impeaching a great person. M. de la Pole so charged, and lord chancellor, who then governed all, and probably in the fault then.

Sir *Henry North* says, the amends he can make for any impertinency is not to hold them long. Understands the charge upon common fame only. Being without evidence, moves to have the articles argued head by head, what they amount unto.

Sir *Rob. Atkins.* We have things at the third hand; persons without doors say they know it by information. Urges the shame of accusing an innocent person; and credulous persons will retain some of the accusations, though false.

Sir *W. Lowther.* In parliament 1 Car. common fame was a good ground of proceeding in any accusation from the house of commons. Resolved then upon the question in Dr. Turner's case against the duke of Buckingham.

Sir *Tho. Strickland.* Lord Strafford complained of nothing done before his trial, but at his trial, and put it home to the lords as their own case in accumulative treason. The hardship he rejects, but the easy one in proceeding he would have. Never knew a child named before born, and so would not have the impeachment.

Mr. *Waller* *. The door was locked in the debate of lord Strafford's and the abp. of Canterbury's case. The reason, because of the greatness of the men. The king might dissolve the parliament before the impeachment.

Sir *R. Temple.* In several impeachments no witness but from impeachments without doors. Grand juries present upon their own knowledge, and if the fact known by any, bound to present. M. de la Pole was impeached for common fame. When voted impeached, then time to inform a committee for accusations.

Sir *John Holland.* In lord Strafford's case information was to the committee of grievances by sir John Clotworthy—He moves for particular charge before impeached—Torches a-far off make a greater show than near at hand. From lord Bacon.

Sir *Ch. Wheeler.* Charges him with countenancing the Non-conformists. He charges the clergy with drunkenness in the proclamation, forgetting gluttony, himself so guilty of, he made many a poor gentleman believe at Paris, that he came from his Embassy in Spain, full of money—he sent prince Rupert into Germany—engrosses all money and counsels—corresponds with Cromwell, and had money from him—oppressed the duke of York, till his alliance with his daughter.

The question being then put, that the Heads of the Accusation be referred to a committee to take the proofs, and report; it passed in the negative 194 to 128. The house then proceeded on the Heads of the Accusation.

Nov. 7. The house resumed the farther consideration of the Heads of the Accusation delivered in against the earl of Clarendon.

Sir *Tho. Osborne* *. The king ready to change his religion!—no money remaining—no person in employment, but who can buy it—we are upon our last legs—no one man ever had more employments—threatens any man that gave advice—no vessel to swim without his hand at the rudder—no money issued out of the treasury without his approbation.—Sir Wm. Coventry brought orders out of the chancellor's closet, when the king was with him—if any other men had the thoughts, they had not the power—he has no pique against him, but as he is one of the 400 † (of the house of commons) thought by the chancellor useless and inconsiderable.

The First Article read.—Sir *Rob. Howard*

* "Waller was the delight of the house: And even at 80 he said the liveliest things of any among them. He was only concerned to say that which should make him be applauded. He deserves the character of being one of the great refiners of our language, and poetry: He was for near 60 years one of the best of our writers that way." Burnet.

* Sir Tho. Osborne was a very plausible Speaker, but too copious, and could not easily make an end of his discourse. He had been always among the high cavaliers, and missing preferment, he had opposed the court much, and was one of lord Clarendon's bitterest enemies." Burnet.—He was afterwards made lord Treasurer and earl of Danby, and at last duke of Leeds.

† This expression (said by lord Clarendon himself to have been laid to his charge by Mr. Seymour) was, "That 400 country gentlemen were only fit to give money, and did not know how an invasion was to be resisted." Life, p. 445.

heard from persons of quality, That it would be proved.

The Second Article was read.—Lord *St. John*, persons of great quality have assured him to make it good, and if they perform not, he will acquaint the house who they are.

The Third Article read.—Mr. *Rd. Seymour.* Sufficient persons will make it good, with this addition, when he received the money, he said, 'so long as the king is king, and I lord chancellor, the patent will stand.'

The Fourth and Fifth Articles read.—Sir *R. Temple.* Divers have undertaken to make them good; if they do not I will name them.

About the receiving Money of Vintners.—Sir *Rob. Car.* That he knows who will prove it.

About his getting a great Estate so suddenly. Mr. *Seymour.* I suppose you need no proof the sun shines at noon day.—Sir *T. Littleton.* The matter of fact in the Article is easily made out, for his place as chancellor could not be worth above 4 or 5000*l.* per ann.

About introducing an Arbitrary Government in the Plantations.—Sir T. Littleton and sir T. Osborn alledged, that one Farmer and others came from the Barbadoes to complain of it, and lodged their petition in this house, but were imprisoned that they might not be heard.

About frustrating Proposals for preserving Nevis, &c.—Sir *Ch. Wheeler.* The war, fire, and plague, not so great a loss as Nevis and St. Christopher's; Nevis worth 20,000*l.* per ann. to the king, and he receives not a shilling of it.

About the sale of Dunkirk.—Sir *T. Osborne* said, a great lord told him that the earl had made a bargain for Dunkirk three quarters of a year before it was known.

Mr. *Waller.* Paying for Dunkirk would entitle it to the crown, and us to the keeping it. The king might as well sell the Isle of Wight.

Mr. *H. Coventry.* It is as much treason to part with Dunkirk, as disband the guards; both being mentioned in the preamble of the act for supplying the king.

Sir *R. Howard,* thinks it was treason to sell the guards, if any enemy was in being. It is the way to confirm somebody else in the sale of Tangier too. A great man has said, if it could not be kept, it might be sold. He has heard the king of France should say, he hoped his next purchase should be London.

Mr. *Prynne* never heard that the selling a place with the king's consent, and the king had the money, was treason; but delivering a fort before reduced to extremity, is treason.

Mr. *Vaughan.* Dunkirk was an acquisition by arms, and therefore not alienable: Tangier, a portion with his wife, and therefore he might dispose of it. Dunkirk as much the king's dominion as Scotland or Ireland, and to sell it is treason by the law.

Sir *Edw. Harley* *. The king, apprehending that the Spanish ambassador might importune him for it, bid him prepare an act for annexing it to the crown of England. The Act of 1,500,000*l.* does, he conceives, declare it to be part of the king's dominions. He left there, in ready money, as appears, 9,640*l.* according to the settlement of 600*l.* a week. A place of extraordinary relief to us.

Mr. *Swynfin,* in the charge of corresponding with Cromwell, alledges the act of indemnity.

Mr. *Vaughan.* The chancellor might, in his defence, plead that or any other pardon, from the king.

Sir *R. Howard* would have him plead to it, that they may know the king's enemies from his friends.

Mr. *Dodswell* let slip a word, viz. 'violent stream against the chancellor;' called to the bar by many; at last put to explain himself: he professed no reflective intention, and humbly craved the pardon of the house.

Mr. *Hampden** spoke to that part of the act of indemnity, wherein the person grieved should have his treble damages in any court.

Sir *Jon. Denham* † The lord chancellor could not be out-lawed; but he is not clear in equity. —This Article was accordingly left out.

Mr. *Thomas* will make good, when it is convenient, the article of council-table-orders, against law.

Sir *Edw. Masters* asserts the article of Quo Warrantos for the corporation of Canterbury.

The 16th Article was then read.

Sir *R. Howard.* No man can deny that corresponding with the king's enemies is treason. If it be not, treason has neither name nor definition.

Sir *T. Littleton.* Deluding his maj. in all foreign treaties relating to the late war. Setting out no navy, in expectation of peace, and his undertaking that the French would not engage against us, this last summer, when we expected a peace in April, and had it not till August.

Mr. *Waller.* He might hold correspondence with the king's enemies, and not betray him to his enemies.‡

---

* He was governor of Dunkirk when that town was sold, he strenuously opposed the sale of Dunkirk, and by his interest in the house of commons procured a bill to be brought in, at the Restoration, for annexing it inseparably to the crown. But it was laid aside after being once read.

* Eldest son of the famous patriot. He had before been chosen one of the five Knights of the shire for Bucks, by the Protector in his parliament 1656, who also about the same time created him a lord, or a member of his upper house. Ath. Oxon. vol. ii.

† The celebrated author of Cooper's Hill.

‡ "This was no sooner said than a young confident man, the lord Vaughan, son to the earl of Carbery, a person of as ill a face as fame, his looks and his manner both extreme bad, asked for the paper that had been presented from the committee, and with his own hand entered these words, 'That being a privy counsellor, he had betrayed the king's secrets to the enemy.'" Lord Clarendon's Life.

Lord *Vaughan* desires that betraying his secret counsels may be put into the Article; it will be made out by a person of honour, that he would have discovered his secret counsels to his enemies. He spoke thrice to this.

Sir *John Holland* moves that it may be declared by the members who gave the inducement for this head, whether they received information from a foreigner or not.

Mr. *Henry Coventry*. Possibly a foreign ambassador, and no oath can be given him.

Mr. *Vaughan*. Achilles was said to be shot-free, and some would have the king to be treason-free. Positively says, it must be from a foreigner, or no way.

Lord *Vaughan*. Tied upon his honour not to discover the persons. At last, after some time, brings this answer in writing to the table, 'That lord Clarendon hath deluded his maj. and the nation in foreign treaties and negotiations relating to the late war, and discovered his majesty's secret counsels to his enemies.'

The question being propounded, that it may be declared, by the members that gave the inducement for this Head, whether they received information from a foreigner, or not; and the question being put, that the question be put, it passed in the negative. It was then resolved that these words, 'and discovered and betrayed his secret counsels to his enemies,' be added to that head.—The 16th Article being then read, as amended, and the question being put, that the earl of Clarendon, upon this head, be impeached of treason, it passed in the affirmative 161 to 89.

Mr. *Marvell* charged Mr. Seymour with saying in his accusation, That the king was insufficient for government, which is now omitted in the Charge, and desires he may declare where he had it.

Mr. *Seymour*. The party that told me at first, differed something afterwards, therefore I rather withdrew it than to trouble you with uncertainties; but a gentleman in the house can give you farther satisfaction on it.

Sir *John Denham*. A peer of the land heard the earl say in a coach, That the king was an unactive person and indisposed for government: this will be made good.—After further debate, the house resolved, "That an Impeachment of Treason and other Crimes and Misdemeanours be carried up to the lords against the earl of Clarendon."

Nov. 12. It was resolved, That Mr. Seymour do carry up the Impeachment to the lords. Accordingly, he went up; where at the bar of the lords house, the lord-keeper Bridgman being come to the bar to meet him, he delivered himself to this purpose:* "The commons, assembled in parliament, having received information of divers traiterous practices and designs of a great peer of this house, Edward earl of Clarendon, have commanded me to impeach the said earl of Clarendon of treason, and other high crimes and misdemeanors: and I do here, in their names, and in the names of all the commons of England, impeach Edward earl of Clarendon of treason, and other high crimes and misdemeanors. I am farther commanded, by the house of commons, to desire your lordships, that the earl of Clarendon may be sequestered from parliament, and forthwith committed to safe custody. They have farther commanded me to acquaint your lordships, that they will, within a convenient time, exhibit to your lordships the articles of the charge against him."

Nov. 15. The lords sent down to desire a Conference in the Painted Chamber: at which the earl of Oxford delivered a Paper in writing (without any debate) the contents whereof were as follows: "Resolved, upon the question, that the lords have not complied with the desires of the house of commons, concerning the commitment of the earl of Clarendon, and sequestring him from parliament; because the house of commons have only accused him of treason in general; and have not assigned or specified any particular treason."

Upon this there arose a warm debate, in which Mr. Garraway, said, 'I had rather the house should lose the punishment of this man, though a great offender, than that this house should lose its privilege; for if this house may at no time impeach a lord without giving in particular Articles, it may fall out to be at a time (as in the duke of Buckingham's case) where a great man by his interest with the king procured the dissolution of the parliament, and then the accusation falls.'—The debate ended in a Resolution to appoint a Committee to draw up Reasons of the present proceedings against the earl of Clarendon.

Nov. 18. Sir Tho. Littleton reported from the said Committee the Reasons agreed by the committee: which were severally agreed to; viz. 1—"That what can or ought to be done by either house of parliament, is best known by the custom and proceeding of parliament in former times; and that it doth appear by example, that, by the course of parliament, the lords have committed such persons, as have been generally charged by the house of commons for High Treason, to safe custody, though the particular treason hath not been specified at the time of such charge. 2. That a commitment for High Treason in general is a legal commitment; and, if the party so committed bring his Habeas Corpus, and the cause of his commitment thereupon be returned to be for high treason, generally; he may be lawfully remanded to prison, by the judges, upon that return. 3. If, before securing the person, the special matter of the treason should be alleged; it would be a ready course, that all complices in the treason might make their es-

* "By a mistake, instead of the earl of Clarendon's impeachment, the earl of Strafford's, which lay on the table, was put into Mr. Seymour's hands, and he was obliged to trust to his memory when he came to the lords bar; but he afterwards delivered a paper of the impeachment to the clerk." Grey's Debates.

cape; or quicken the execution of the treason intended, to secure themselves the better thereby. 4. If the house of peers should require the particular treason to be assigned, before the party charged be secured, they leave the commons uncertain and doubtful (and that from time to time) how particular they must make their charge, to their lordships satisfaction, before the offender be put under any restraint. 5. The commons conceive, that, if they should desire the lords to secure a stranger, or native commoner, upon suspicion of treason, which the commoners had of him; and which was by them under examination, to be evidenced to their lordships in due time; their lordships, in justice, for the safety of the king and people, would secure such person or persons upon the desire of the commons: and, in such case, there will be no difference, in the consequent, between a lord, and a commoner, so desired to be secured. 6. The proceeding of inferior courts between the king and the subject, or subject and subject, and the discretion of judges in such courts, is bounded and limited by the discretion of the parliament which trusts them; and it is not left to the discretion of judges in ordinary jurisdiction, to give the king, or take from him, inconvenient power for the subject; nor to dispense the law partially between subject and subject, for malice and affection: but the discretion of the parliament, which is the whole public, comprehending the king, lord, and commons, (for the king's presence is supposed in the lords house) is, and ought to be, confined for the safety and preservation of the whole, which is itself. It cannot be malicious to a part of itself, nor affect more power, than already it hath; which is absolute over itself, and parts; and may therefore do, for preservation of itself, whatsoever is not repugnant to natural justice."—Resolved, That a conference be desired with the lords, and the Reasons carried up.

Nov. 21. The lords desired another Conference, to which the commons replied by messengers of their own, giving an account of their proceedings, and intimating that they expected the lords would have desired a free Conference.

Nov. 23. The lords desired a present Conference; at which a Vote of their lordships was communicated, signifying that the commons denial of the late Conference was contrary to the course of parliamentary proceedings; as likewise, their lordships Reasons why it was not yet time for a free conference.

Nov. 25. The commons having agreed to the conference, the committees of both houses met, and the lords declared that they had considered of the Precedents and Reasons formerly sent them by the commons, but were not satisfied to secure the earl of Clarendon, or to sequester him from parliament until some special Treason be assigned.

Report of the Conference about committing the E. of Clarendon on a general Charge.] Nov. 28. The Lord Chamberlain and the other lords appointed to manage the free Conference with the commons yesterday, reported the substance and effect of the said free Conference, as followeth:

"This Conference was managed, on the house of commons part, by sir Robert Howard, Mr. Vaughan, Mr. Swinfin, and Mr. Waller. The introduction was made by my lord chamberlain; who told the commons, That this free conference was desired by them; and though that house had lately declined giving the lords a conference when desired, yet the house of peers upon this occasion had dispensed with some forms, to keep a good correspondency with the house of commons, and were willing to confer freely with them, and ready to hear what they had to say.—Sir R. Howard was the first that opened the business. He said, this conference was not upon particular account of any person, but in relation to public justice.—The lords closed in the same, and were very glad it was so understood; for they had no particular regard to the earl of Clarendon in what they had resolved, but to the justice of the kingdom; in the administration whereof in this particular, nothing was ordered in the case of the peer now impeached which they should not have insisted upon in the case of any commoner.—Then sir R. Howard and the rest of the commons proceeded; and made the subject-matter of this free conference to be some of the Reasons formerly given by the commons, which they enforced what they could; and the proceedings of the earl of Strafford's case, the abp. of Canterbury, lord keeper Finch, and sir G. Ratcliff's. But the precedent chiefly pressed, was the earl of Strafford's; on which by large discourse (which intimated their insisting mainly on that) they urged that precedents did shew best the course of parliaments, which was the law of parliaments; and that the precedents they had vouched, especially that of the earl of Strafford's, were clear in the point: that the end of the act of repeal was to repeal the act of attainder, and the proceedings relating thereunto; that the manner of impeachment and commitment, and other proceedings thereupon, were still in force; and that the latest and newest precedents were the best. They descanted long upon the words of the act of repeal, to evince what they had said; and distinguished the first year of the Long Parliament for gravity and wisdom, from the rest, which was disorderly and unquiet; and said, That their precedents were made in the first year; and that proceedings in times of peace, when the courts of Westminster were open, were always allowed for good; and concluded, that the lords ought to commit upon every general impeachment of the commons for Treason: and this grew to be the question stated at this conference: which the commons affirmed, and the lords denied. Some things were also said by the commons, of the credit that was to be given to all the commons of England, which they represented; and that they could not be supposed to intend any thing herein but public justice and safety, &c.—The lords answered, and argued from the very same act for reversing the earl of Strafford's attainder, as followeth: That this precedent was not allowable, being in an ill time, and branded by an act of repeal, by which it was clear, this very parliament intended it should never be made use of; for besides that the act of attainder recites the very impeachment particularly, and other proceedings thereupon, and stands absolutely and totally repealed, which is enough to condemn the whole, yet they were so careful that this precedent which led on the other three should never rise in judgment again, that they further enacted in express words, That all records and proceedings of parliament relating to the said attainder be wholly concealed and taken off the file, or otherwise defaced and obliterated, to the intent the same may not be visible in after-ages, or brought into example to the prejudice of any person whatsoever; in which general words, every circumstance and passage of that precedent must needs be included, none being excepted, so that this left the course of parliament for accusations and trials for treasons as it was before. And there were no other proceedings previous to the said Attainder, but the said impeachment upon trial, and proceedings thereupon. The lords said, They could not allow all for good that was done in parliament whilst the courts of Westminster sat; nor would the commons, if they reviewed the transactions of the Long Parliament. They absolutely denied the newest precedent to be the best. Antiquity was always venerable; laws, and old precedents, with a constant course of them, were most to be esteemed. They had both for them in this controversy. The lords gave these further Reasons in Answer to the commons, and to shew why they ought not upon every general accusation of treason by the commons to commit to custody the person or persons accused: That there could be no precedent of commitment produced upon a general accusation of treason before the earl of Strafford's case; which must necessarily have been, to make it the course of parliament. The last drops of a river make not a stream or course, but the constant current. So a new precedent, but of yesterday as it were, and within the sad memory of us all, could not be called the course of parliament. It seems contrary to natural justice and reason, that a person accused should be punished before he knows his crime; and though the imprisonment may be said to be for custody, yet there is no person that knows not his fault, but takes it for a punishment; and it is really so, if he come after to be acquitted. It is not suitable to the dignity or trust of judges in inferior courts, much less in parliament, the highest court, that they should be kept ignorant of the crimes, whilst they are pressed to commit to prison upon a general mention of them, or that the prosecutors should conceal what they know from the judges, or have ground to ask what they will, and not let the judges have ground to proceed upon. If the lords ought to commit upon the commons impeachment, they seem rather to be executors of process or orders, than judges; which ever implies a power to consider, and do as they shall be satisfied in judgment. The precedents are contrary; as 14 E. 2. M. 7. abp. of Arundell's case, 21 R. 2. the lord Stanley's case, 38 H. 6.; and W. de la Pole duke of Suffolk's case; as the commons themselves, in the argument at the free conference upon the Petition of Right, by sir Edw. Cooke, acknowledged, and urged strongly, as being in the very point; This was 28 H. 6. No. 16, &c. Such a course of proceeding would not leave it in the power of the house of peers to preserve Magna Charta and the Petition of Right (which favour liberty) from invasion; and herein the lords insist not only for themselves, but for all the commons. Though this be a house of commons excellently composed; yet the admitting this claim of theirs just or warrantable, if ever there should be a house of commons ill disposed or engaged in faction, as such have been, they might by pretence thereof make dangerous inroads upon the justice and ancient government of the kingdom, terrify and discompose the highest judicature, and invade that freedom which ought to be in parliament, and indeed bring the house of lords to as small a number as they please to leave unaccused. Judges in inferior courts may bail for treason specified; à majore, may the house of lords refuse to commit till specification, or bail after. There are no real mischiefs or inconveniences the other way, but many appear by committing before the judges be satisfied in the crimes. The practice of all judges and justices, in favour of liberty, and to prevent oppression, is to examine upon oath the particular crimes before commitment, that the ground may appear to them for commitment, or else they are of duty to bail where the offence is bailable, though the accusation may be laid to be treason? much more should the parliament be careful herein, who gives examples and precedents of justice to all other courts. If the king and his counsel are not to imprison without special crime, as the commons now argue, and did so before in the conference for the Petition of Right, to which the lords agreed, and yet the king is 'caput parliamenti;' whence comes this power of the house of commons by vote to enforce a commitment? And how dangerous is it to the subject! The Petition of Right having concluded, That no man ought to be imprisoned or detained without being charged with something to which they might make answer according to law; how will it stand with that to commit upon generals, to which no man can make answer or defend himself? There were no new Reasons offered by the commons; and therefore the lords told them, That having considered of those they had given, and over-ruled them, after a rule twice given by the highest court, it is not to be disputed but the parties must submit; or, as they resolved last session, there could be no proceedings or dispatch in causes. At this conference, Mr. Vaughan said, The commons do think the judicature so well and safely lodged in the lords, that the commons do not wish any part of it. The commons would not agree, that the case of Wm. de la Pole was upon the Impeachment of the commons; and said, That the case of abp. Arundell was repealed 1 H. IV. But the first . the lords evinced clearly, by the record which was present; and the repeal of Arundell's case did not weaken, but strengthen it as a precedent in this case, being in the repeal it was in the least impeached in the point the lords vouched it for. And the chief ground of not repealing the acts of that parliament was, for the hard measure it shewed to the house of York, for maintenance of whose title the said archbishop was a chief instrument. Some members of the house of commons urged their former third Reason before, That if, before securing the person, the special matter of treason should be alledged, it would be a ready course that all complices in the Treason might make their escape, or quicken the execution of the treason intended, to secure themselves the better thereby. To which the lords made Answer, That it would be very hard with the subject, if they should be committed when neither the judge nor the accuser did know the crime; and if, in this case, the house of commons, who were the accuser, did know it, they might safely impart it to the lords, for though in 500 counsellors, there may be allowed to be wisdom, yet there is not to be expected secresy."—The lords took this Report into consideration; and after a long debate, the question being put, "Whether, upon the Report of the last Free Conference given the house of commons, and upon the whole matter, their lordships are satisfied to commit the earl of Clarendon, and sequester him from parliament, before particular treason specified or assigned?" It was resolved in the negative.

The Lords refuse to commit the Earl.] Dec. 2. The lords confirmed their proceedings, and sent down a Message to the commons to this effect: "That upon the report made to them of the last free Conference, they are not satisfied to commit or sequester from parliament the earl of Clarendon, without the particular treason be mentioned or assigned." This threw the commons into a great ferment, and occasioned several warm speeches.

Mr. *Waller* said, The lords are a noble estate, but whatever the matter is, they have of late some advice given them, which makes them proceed as they never did yet; for scarce any thing happens, but they encroach upon us. The Militia is now as burthensome to the 50*l.* man in the country, almost as all other taxes, and the lords have gotten this advantage on us, that they touch not the burthen of it with their finger: so in the time of the Plague, the commons must be shut up, but not they; insomuch that a good act provided to that purpose passed not. We impeached the lord Mordaunt, and could not bring him to the bar, though formerly I have known an earl and a lord brought thither; you desired a free conference about it, but could not obtain one to this day. Rome was at first modest, and only meddled with spirituals, but afterwards concerned themselves so much with other matters, that every thing was made to be 'in ordine ad spiritualia,' and many kingdoms thereupon broke from them. The lords now insist upon one thing, because they say it is in order to their judicature; perhaps hereafter they will tell us we must come to them on our knees, because it is in order to their judgment. Consider therefore whether there be any hope of giving them satisfaction.

Mr. *Vaughan* was long about precedents and law, upon the latter of which the lords had insisted; and he said, That in the free conference there was much discourse about the Great Charter, and of the Statute of the 28th Edw. 3. but not applied: so that I thought law in a lord's mouth was like a sword in a lady's hand; the sword might be there, but when it comes to cut, it would be aukward and useless. The conclusion must be, that no impeachment by the commons must go on, unless it be by presentment; and so there is an end of all that for which the parliament is principally called; unless we are part of 'those 400 contemptible ones, who are only fit to give money:' that may be reserved for us, but nothing else.

Mr. *Coleman* argued in favour of the lords: The lords say, that committing upon a general Impeachment was against law, and he thought would appear so: he denied not, but a mittimus without special cause might be legal, and grounded upon the Petition of Right; the reason of which was to secure men against commitment by a special warrant, and a judge ought not to discharge where treason was alleged: but in this case it was different, the judges could not discharge a man committed after examination, but the lords ought not to commit a man, except there were particular treason. That if he came before a justice of peace, and said, I accuse this man of treason, would any wise man commit him? He made his warrant indeed, but he that accused must go farther, and make it more particular, and the special matter must appear before he commits; and this was the present case. The common law was, That no man ought to be committed without particular cause; because no man could commit in capital matters, without taking examination before-hand, otherwise no man could justify a commitment; therefore he was not satisfied, that the lords had not reason to deny it. That the commons were in the nature of a grand jury to present, but the lords were the judges: that commitment was not the judgment, but in order to it; and the lords had a discretionary power in the case: they said not that they would nót commit, but that they were not satisfied to do it without special matter, therefore the commons ought to send it up.—After a long debate, the house came to this Resolution, "That the Lords having not complied with the desires of the commons for the commitment of the earl of Clarendon, and sequestering him from parliament, upon the Impeachment from that house, is an obstruction to the public justice of the kingdom, and a precedent of evil and dangerous consequence." They appointed a committee to draw up a Declaration to vindicate their proceedings.

The Earl of Clarendon withdraws, and leaves a remarkable Apology.] About this time the earl of Clarendon thought proper to withdraw, and having left an Apology for his conduct, addressed to the lords, that house, upon receiving this Address, on the 3d of Dec. sent a Message to the commons, signifying, "That they had received a large Petition from the earl of Clarendon, which intimated that he was withdrawn;* and soon after desired a present conference with them. At which conference, the duke of Buckingham, who was plainly aimed at in the Petition, delivered it to the commons, and with his usual way of insult and ridicule said, "The lords have commanded me to deliver to you this scandalous and seditious Paper sent from the earl of Clarendon: they bid me to present it to you, and desire you in convenient time to send it to them again; for it has a style which they are in love with, and therefore desire to keep it."

The Earl of Clarendon's Apology.] The said Paper was then read, and is as follows:

To the right hon. the lords spiritual and temporal, in parliament assembled: The humble PETITION and ADDRESS of Edward earl of Clarendon.

"May it please your lordships; I cannot express the insupportable trouble and grief of mind I sustain, under the apprehension of being misrepresented to your lordships, and when I hear how much of your lordships time has been spent upon the mention of me, as it is attended with more public consequences, and of the differences in opinion, which have already, or may probably arise between your lordships, and the hon. house of commons; whereby the great and weighty affairs of the kingdom may be obstructed in a time of so general a dissatisfaction. I am very unfortunate to find myself to suffer so much under two very disadvantageous reflections, which are in no degree applicable to me.—The 1st, from the greatness of my estate and fortune, collected and made in so few years; which, if it be proportionable to what is reported, may very reasonably cause my integrity to be suspected.—The 2nd, that I have been the sole manager, and chief minister, in all the transactions of state, since the king's return into England, to Aug. last; and therefore that all miscarriages and misfortunes ought to be imputed to me, and to my counsels.—Concerning my estate, your lordships will not believe, that, after malice and envy hath been so inquisitive and so sharp-sighted, I will offer any thing to your ldp.'s, but what is exactly true; and I do assure your ldp.'s, in the first place, that, excepting from the king's bounty, I have never received nor taken one penny, but what was generally understood to be the just and lawful perquisites of my office, by the constant practice of the best times; which I did, in my own judgment, conceive to be that of my lord Coventry, and my lord Elsmore: the practice of which I constantly observed, although the office, in both their times, was lawfully worth double to what it was to me, and, I believe, now is.—That all the courtesies and favours which I have been able to obtain from the king for other persons in church and state, or in Westminster-Hall, have never been worth to me five pounds: so that your lordships may be confident I am as innocent from corruption, as from any disloyal thought; which, after near 30 years service of the crown, in some difficulties and distresses, I did never expect, would have been objected to me in my age.—And I do assure your lordships, and shall make it very manifest, that the several sums of money, and some parcels of land, which his maj. hath bountifully bestowed upon me since his return into England, are worth more than all I have amounts unto: so far I am from advancing my estate by any indirect means. And though this bounty of his maj. hath very far exceeded my merit, or my expectation, yet some others hath been as fortunate at least in the same bounty, who had as small pretences to it, and have no great reason to envy my condition.—Concerning the other imputation, of the credit and power of being chief minister; and so causing all to be done, that I had a mind to; I have no more to say, than that I had the good fortune to serve a master of a very great judgment and understanding; and to be always joined with persons of great ability and experience; without whose advice and concurrence, never any thing hath been done.—Before his majesty's coming into England, he was constantly attended by the then marq. of Ormond, the late lord Culpeper, and

* "When the chancellor found it necessary to withdraw himself, he thought it as necessary to leave some address to the house of peers, and to make as good an excuse as he could for his absence without asking their leave; which should be delivered to them by some member of their body (there being many of them ready to perform that civil office for him) when his absence should be known, or some evidence that he was safely arrived on the other side of the sea: and that time being come (for the packet-boat was ready to depart when the Chancellor landed at Calais,) the earl of Denbigh said, He had an Address to the house from the earl of Clarendon, which he desired might be read." Lord Clarendon's Life, p. 458.

Mr. Sec. Nicholas; who were equally trusted with myself; and without whose joint advice and concurrence, when they were all present, (as some of them always were) I never gave any counsel. As soon as it pleased God to bring his maj. into England, he established his privy-council; and shortly, out of them, a number of honourable persons, of great reputation, who, for the most part, are alive, as a committee for foreign affairs, and consideration of such things, as, in the nature of them, required much secrecy; and with these persons he vouchsafed to join me: and I am confident this committee never transacted any thing of moment, (his maj. being always present) without presenting the same first to the council board: and I must appeal to them, concerning my carriage; and whether we were not all of one mind, in all matters of importance.—For more than two years I never knew any difference in the counsels, or that there were any complaints in the kingdom; which I wholly impute to his maj.'s great wisdom, and the entire concurrence of his counsellors; without the vanity of assuming any thing to myself. And therefore I hope I shall not be singly charged with any thing that hath since fallen out amiss. But from the time that Mr. Sec. Nicholas was removed from his place, there were great alterations: and whosoever knew any thing of the court or councils, knew well how my credit hath, since that time, been diminished; though his maj. graciously vouchsafed still to hear my advice in most of his affairs: nor hath there been, from that time to this, above one or two persons brought to the council, or preferred to any considerable office in the court, who have been of my intimate acquaintance, or suspected to have any kindness for me; and most of them notoriously known to have been, very long, my enemies; and of different judgments and principles from me, both in church and state; and who have taken all opportunities to lessen my credit with the king, and with all other persons, by misrepresenting and misreporting all that I said or did; and persuading men, that I had done them some prejudice with his majesty, or crossed them in some of their pretensions; though his majesty's goodness and justice was such, that it made little impression upon him.—In my humble opinion, the great misfortunes of the kingdom have proceeded from the war; to which it is notoriously known that I was always most averse; and may, without vanity, say, I did not only foresee, but did declare, the mischiefs we should run into by entering into a war, before any alliances made with the neighbour princes: and, that, it may not be imputed to his majesty's want of care, or the negligence of his counsellors, that no such alliances were entered into, I must take the boldness to say, that his maj. left nothing unattempted, in order thereunto: and, knowing very well, that France resolved to begin a war upon Spain, as soon as his Catholic maj. should depart this world; which being much sooner expected by them, they had, in the two winters before, been a great charge in providing plentiful magazines of all provisions upon the frontiers that they might be ready for the war; his maj. used all possible means to prepare and dispose the Spaniard with that apprehension; offering his friendship to that degree, as might be for the security and benefit of both crowns: but Spain flattering itself that France would not break with them, at least, that they would not give them any cause, by administering matter of jealousy to them, never made any real approach towards a friendship with his majesty; but, both by their ambassador here, and to his majesty's ambassador at Madrid, always insisted, as preliminaries, upon the giving up Dunkirk, Tangier, and Jamaica.—Though France had an ambassador here, to whom a project for a Treaty was offered, and the lord Hollis, his majesty's ambassador at Paris, used all endeavours to pursue and prosecute the said Treaty, yet it was quickly discerned, that the principal design of France was to draw his maj. into such a near alliance, as might advance their design; without which they had no mind to enter into the treaty proposed.—And this was the State of Affairs when the war was entered into with the Dutch: from which time, neither crown much considered the making of an alliance with England.—As I did, from my soul, abhor the entering into this war; so I never presumed to give any advice or counsel for the way of managing it, but by opposing many propositions, which seemed to the late lord treasurer, and myself, to be unreasonable; as, the payment of the seamen by tickets: and many other particulars, which added to the expence.—My enemies took all occasions to inveigh against me: and, making friendship with others out of the council, of more licentious principles, and who knew well enough, how much I disliked and complained of the liberty they took to themselves, of reviling all councils and counsellors, and turning all things serious and sacred into ridicule; they took all ways imaginable, to render me ungrateful to all sorts of men (whom I shall be compelled to name in my defence); persuading those, that miscarried in any of their designs, that it was the chancellor's doings: whereof I never knew any thing. However, they could not withdraw the king's favour from me; who was still pleased to use my service with others; nor was there ever any thing done, but upon the joint advice of, at least, the major part of those who were consulted with.—And, as his majesty commanded my service in the late Treaties, so I never gave the least advice in private; nor wrote one letter to any person in either of those negotiations, but upon the advice of the council, and after it was read in council, or, at least, by the king himself, and some other: and, if I prepared any Instructions, or Memorials, it was by the king's command, and the request of the secretaries, who desired my assistance: nor was it any wish of my own, that any ambassador should give me any account of the transactions, but to the secretaries, with whom I was always ready to advise: nor am I conscious to myself of having ever given advice, that hath proved mischievous or inconvenient to his majesty: and I have been so far from being the sole manager of affairs, that I have not, in the whole last year, been above twice with his maj. in any room alone, and very seldom in the 2 or 3 years preceding: and, since the parliament at Oxford, it hath been very visible, that my credit hath been very little; and that very few things have been hearkened to, which have been proposed by me, but contradicted, *eo nomine*, because proposed by me.—I most humbly beseech your lordships to memember the office and trust I had for 7 years, in which, in discharge of my duty, I was obliged to stop and obstruct many mens pretences, and to refuse to set the seal to many pardons, and other grants, which would have been profitable to those who procured them; and many whereof, upon my representation to his majesty, were for ever stopt; which naturally have raised many enemies to me: and my frequent concurring, upon the desires of the late Lord Treasurer (with whom I had the honour to have a long and a fast friendship, to his death) in representing several excesses and exorbitances, the yearly issue so far exceeding the Revenue, provoked in many persons concerned, of great power and credit, to do me all the ill offices they could. And yet I may faithfully say, that I never meddled with any part of the Revenue, or the administration of it, but when I was desired by the late lord treasurer to give him my assistance and advice (having had the honour formerly to serve the crown, as chancellor of the exchequer); which was, for the most part, in his majesty's presence. Nor have I ever been, in the least degree, concerned, in point of profit, in the letting any part of his majesty's revenue; nor have ever treated or debated it, but in his majesty's presence; in which my opinion concurred always with the major of the counsellors, who were present.—All which, upon examination, will be made manifest to your lordships, how much soever my intregity is blasted by the malice of those, who, I am confident, do not believe themselves: nor have I, in my life, upon all the Treaties, or otherwise, received the value of one shilling from all the kings and princes in the world (except the Books of the Louvre print, sent me by the chancellor of France, by that king's direction) but from my own master, to whose entire service, and to the good and welfare of my country, no man's heart was ever more devoted.—This being my present condition, I do most humbly beseech your lordships to retain a favourable opinion of me, and to believe me innocent from those foul aspersions, until the contrary shall be proved; which, I am sure, can never be by any men, worthy to be believed. And since the distempers of the times and the differences between the two houses in the present debate, with the power and malice of my enemies, who give out, that they shall prevail with his majesty to prorogue or dissolve this parliament in displeasure, and threaten to expose me to the rage and fury of the people, may make me looked upon as the cause which obstructs the king's service, and the unity and peace of the kingdom; I most humbly beseech your lordships, that I may not forfeit your lordships favour and protection, by withdrawing myself from so powerful a prosecution, in hope that I may be able, by such withdrawing, hereafter to appear, and make my defence, when his majesty's justice, to which I shall always submit, may not be obstructed or controuled by the power and malice of those, who have sworn my destruction.

CLARENDON."

When the earl's Apology was read by the commons, it occasioned a new turn, and a new warmth in the debates of that house. Mr. Vaughan among other things said, 'It is the first time that ever I heard an innocent man run away under the greatest charge, with hopes to return again and vindicate himself. Mark one expression; he says, he is as far from corruption, as he is from disloyalty: if he had said he was guilty of neither, he had said something, but by that expression he may be guilty of both. So insolent a paper I never met with in this kingdom, nor have I ever heard the like in any other: so inconsiderable a part of the nation as he is, to lay it upon the nation, who, if innocent, might defend himself; if guilty, why does he charge the nation with persecuting? Therefore, without troubling ourselves with it, do as the lords have done, who, delivered it to us as a scandalous and seditious Paper; it has malice in it, and is the greatest reproach upon the king and the whole nation, that ever was given by man.'—Therefore, in conclusion he put the question, Whether the Paper should be voted scandalous and malicious, and a reproach to the justice of the nation? Which was carried in the affirmative.—Sir R. Howard moved that it should be burnt by the common-hangman; but that was opposed, because the lords desired the Paper to be returned; yet still at last that was carried also in the affirmative.*

* "This Address was no sooner read, in the house of lords, but they who had contributed most to the absenting himself, and were privy to all the promises which had invited him to it, seemed much troubled that he had escaped their justice, and moved, 'That orders might be forthwith sent to stop the ports, that so he might be apprehended;' when they well knew that he was landed at Calais. Others took exceptions to some expressions, 'which,' they, said, 'reflected upon the king's honour and justice.' Others moved, That it might be entered in their Journal Book, to the end that they might farther consider of it when they should think fit;' and this was ordered. The Address was no sooner read in the other house,

A Bill passed for the Banishment of the Earl.] Dec. 13. A Bill was sent down from the lords for the Banishment of the earl of Clarendon. Upon the reading of which, several objections were made; and it being alledged, That it was an abuse put upon the commons by the lords, and that a Bill of Attainder being proposed, after some debate the house passed this vote; "Resolved, That, this house taking notice of the Flight of the earl of Clarendon, being under an Impeachment of High-Treason by this house, the king's majesty be humbly desired to issue out his Proclamation for summoning the said earl to appear by a day, and to apprehend him in order to his trial: and that the lords be sent to for their concurrence in this vote." But the lords would not concur: and on the following day delivered their Reasons, and particularly declared, "That their lordships upon consideration of the whole state of affairs, and of the kingdom, have, upon grounds of prudence and justice, thought fit, for security of king and kingdom, to proceed in a legislative way against the said earl; and have to that end passed and sent down a Bill of Banishment and Incapacity against him; with which their vote was inconsistent." This brought on a debate concerning the Bill of Banishment, which some thought too little for the crimes alleged; and others too great for the cause in hand. Mr. Swinfen said, 'The lords will neither secure nor summon him, but will condemn him unheard; and thus they put you upon, which is against honour and justice, especially to do it upon reason of state. The power of parliaments is indeed great; it hath no bounds but the integrity and justice of parliaments. If reason of state be a motive of parliament to banish one man, so it may be for many. If you go in this legislative way, you bring upon yourselves all the dishonour of the business; but the lords will have some excuse, which you cannot; for they looked upon the charge so slight, as not to imprison him. The party is gone, apprehending, he says, the fear of the multitude, not of his trial: so the lords not giving credit to your charge against him, he says, He flies not from justice. Now, if upon this bill you should banish him, it would be said, you could not make good your charge, and therefore laid this sentence upon him. The precedent is also dangerous, if, having gone so far in a judicial way, you should now go in a legislative. If, upon reason of state, lords might be banished, it may be by dozens: as you proceed justly, so you will be justified.'—After several speeches on the 18th, the bill was read a third time and passed, there being 65 for it, and 42 against it.*

but they who had industriously promoted the former resolution were inflamed, as if this very instrument would contribute enough to any thing that was wanting; and they severally arraigned it, and inveighed against the person who had sent it, with all imaginable bitterness and insolence. Whilst others, who could not, in the hearing it read, observe that malignity that it was accused of, sat still and silent as if they suspected that somewhat had escaped their observations and discovery, that so much transported other men; or, because they were well pleased that a person, against whom there was so much fury and malice professed, was got out of their reach. In conclusion, after long debate it was concluded, 'That the paper, containing much untruth and scandal and sedition in it, should be publicly burned by the hand of the hangman.' which vote they presently sent to the lords for their concurrence, who, though they had not observed any such guilt in it before, would maintain no farther contests with them, and so concurred in the sentence. And the poor paper was accordingly with solemnity executed by the appointed officer." Lord Clarendon's Life, p. 464.

* "Lord Clarendon survived his banishment six years; and employed his leisure chiefly in reducing into order the history of the civil wars, for which he had before collected materials. The performance does honour to his memory; and except Whitlocke's memorials, is the most candid account of those times, composed by any contemporary author.—Clarendon was always a friend to the liberty and constitution of his country. At the commencement of the civil wars, he had entered into the late king's service, and was honoured with a great share in the esteem and friendship of that monarch: he was pursued with unrelenting animosity by the long parliament: he had shared all the fortunes, and directed all the counsels of the present king during his exile: he had been advanced to the highest trust and offices after the restoration: yet all these circumstances, which might naturally operate with such force, either on resentment, gratitude, or ambition, had no influence on his uncorrupted mind. It is said, that when he first engaged in the study of the law his father exhorted him with great earnestness to shun the practice too common in that profession, of straining every point in favour of prerogative, and perverting so useful a science to the oppression of liberty: and in the midst of these rational and virtuous counsels, which he reiterated, he was suddenly seized with an apoplexy, and expired in his son's presence. This circumstance gave additional weight to the principles which he inculcated. The combination of king and subject to oppress so good a minister affords, to men of opposite dispositions, an equal occasion of inveighing against the ingratitude of princes, or ignorance of the people. Charles seems never to have mitigated his resentment against Clarendon; and the national prejudices pursued him to his retreat in France. A company of English soldiers, being quartered near him, assaulted his house, broke open the doors, gave him a dangerous wound on the head, and would have proceeded to the last extremities, had not their officers hearing of the violence, happily interposed." Hume.

Protests relating to the Proceedings against the Earl of Clarendon.] Nov. 20. The house took into consideration the Report of the Conference with the commons yesterday, concerning the Proceedings against the earl of Clarendon; in order thereunto the Reasons of the commons were read, and then these precedents mentioned by the commons were read: 1. The precedent of the Impeachment against the earl of Strafford, the 11th Nov. 1640. 2. The Impeachment against Wm. Laud, abp. of Canterbury, the 18th Dec. 1640. 3. The Impeachment against the lord Finch, lord keeper, the 22nd of Dec. 1640. 4. The Impeachment against sir Geo. Radcliffe, the 29th Dec. 1640. And, after a long debate on the first Reason, and the aforesaid precedents, the 2nd, 3rd, 4th, 5th and 6th Reasons were again read. And, after a serious debate thereof, the question being put, Whether, upon these Precedents and Reasons of the commons, and the whole debate thereupon, their lordships are satisfied to comply with the desires of the commons for sequestering from this house, and committing the earl without any particular Treason assigned or specified? It was resolved in the negative.

"We whose names are underwritten do according to the antient right and usage of all the peers of the realm assembled in parliament, enter and record our Protestation and particular Dissents as follow, and for these Reasons: 1. That we are satisfied, in agreement with so much of the Reasons of the commons alledged to that purpose, as upon a very long and solemn debate in this house did concur with our sense, that the earl of C. should be committed to custody, without assigning of special matter, until the particular Impeachment shall be exhibited against him by the commons before the lords in parliament; or else, how shall any great officer of the crown, and his accomplices, be prevented from evading to be brought to a fair and speedy trial? 2. We do conceive, that the four precedents urged by the commons for his commitment as aforesaid, and to justify the way of their proceedings by general Impeachment only, are valid, and full to the point of this case; and that the precedent of Wm. de la Pole, duke of Suffolk, in the 28th of Hen. 6, is no precedent at all to the contrary, in regard that it was no judgment nor appeal in parliament, but rather an appeal to the king from the judicature of the parliament, whilst the parliament was sitting, which is not according to the known privilege and customs of this house. 3. The earl of C.'s power and influence in the absolute management of all the great affairs of the realm hath been so notorious, ever since his majesty's happy return into England, until the great seal was taken from him, that whilst he is at liberty few or none of the witnesses will, probably, dare to declare in evidence, all that they know against him; for defect whereof the safety of the king's person, and the peace of the whole kingdom, may be very much endangered. 4. We conceive, that, in cases of treason and traiterous practices, the commons have an inherent right in them to impeach any peer of the realm; or other subject of England, without assigning of special matter, because treason either against the king's person, or the government established, which are indivisible, is such a speciality in itself alone, that it needs no further specification as to the matter of safe custody; nor can it be suspected, that so honourable a body as the house of commons would have accused a peer of the realm, of the earl of C.'s eminency and condition, without very good cause.—Buckingham, Albemarle, Teynham, W. St. David's, T. Lucas, Cha. Gerrard, Berkshire, Paulett, Howard of Charlton, Pembroke and Montgomery, Rochester, Jo. Duresme, W. Sandys, Jo. Berkeley, Northampton, Kent, Carlisle, Dover, Norwich, Vaughan, Hen. Hereford, Byron, Bathe, Bristol, Arlington, Say and Seale, Powis."

Nov. 21. A message was sent to the commons by sir Wm. Childe and sir John Cole, to desire a present conference, concerning the matter of the last conference touching the earl of Clarendon. The messengers sent to the commons returned with this Answer: That the commons are now in debate of matters of great consequence, and will return an answer presently by messengers of their own.—A message was brought from the commons by sir R. Howard and others, to desire a conference upon the last Message. The question being put, Whether to give the commons a present conference upon the last message? It was resolved in the Affirmative.—"Memorandum. That before the putting of the above question, these lords following desired leave to enter their dissents, if it were carried in the affirmative; which being granted, they do accordingly enter their Dissents, by subscribing their names to the Reasons following: 1. Because the lords having first desired a conference, the commons did not give it. 2. Because there is no precedent, that they can find, of any such proceeding in parliament before this. 3. Because the commons could not tell what was to be offered at the conference desired by the lords. 4. Because, for ought they knew, the lords at the conference intended to agree with the Reasons, or give reasons against them. 5. Because there were no precedents of free conferences (nor can they, as we conceive, be) in points relating to judicature, which is entirely the lords, whose work is to consider the Reasons offered by the commons, and give the rule. Anglesey, Chandos, J. Bridgewater."

Dec. 12. An Act for banishing and disenabling the earl of Clarendon, was read a 3rd time. The question being put, whether this Bill shall pass; It was resolved in the affirmative. "I whose name is underwritten do, according to the ancient right and usage of all the peers of the realm assembled in parliament, after due leave demanded from the house in the usual manner and form, as the Journal Book doth shew, enter and record my Protestation and dissent as follows: 1. That without having ever been in prison, or imprisonment appointed, or any legal charge brought, it seems unjust to punish the earl of Clarendon for only withdrawing himself; it not being at all certain to the house, that he is gone out of the kingdom; and if it were known to the lords that he were fled beyond the seas, though the fault would be very great in a person who hath lately been in such trust, yet perpetual exile, and being for ever disabled from bearing any office, and the penalties in the Bill, seem too severe a censure. 2. That it may, perhaps, give some occasion for the scandal to have it believed, that the house of commons, and others, by standing so long upon pretence of a privilege to require commitment before special matter of treason assigned, were in doubt, that no proof of treason could be made out against the party accused; and that they had therefore designed, through terror, to make him fly and fear, lest he should yet return to be tried, in case they should bring in special matter of treason, as they ought to do, whensoever they accuse. 3. That by this Bill, power being taken from the king to pardon, it appeareth to be a great entrenchment upon his majesty's royal prerogative. 4. That there can be no such case, as have been pretended, ever to cause a necessity in the house of commons not to acquaint the lords with the particulars openly made known to them, by which they were first satisfied to find ground to accuse. 5. That the commons, so far judging any article to be treason, as to insist upon commitment, without imparting the particulars to the lords, do seem therein to usurp that first part of judicature from the lords, who are the highest court of justice in the kingdom. 6. That to require such commitment seems to be contrary to the Petition of Right and Magna Charta, and the rights not only of the peers and great persons of this kingdom, but the birth right even of the meanest subjects; and therefore those proceedings not having been according to law and the ancient rules of parliament, hath given opportunity to the earl of C. to absent himself. 7. The commitment upon a general Impeachment hath been heretofore, and may be again, of most evil and dangerous consequence; and as is conceived, the lords have yet no way for them so well to justify their fair and upright proceedings in the earl of Clarendon's business, and the true regard that they have had herein to the king and kingdom, as to decline this Bill of Banishment, and to expect a particular accusation of the said earl; and thereupon according to law and justice to appoint him a day for appearance, which if he observe not, without farther process, sentence might lawfully be pronounced against him. Strafford."

"We having this day given our negatives to the passing of a Bill for banishing and disenabling the earl Clarendon; and having asked leave of the house to enter our Dissents, to the end that it may appear to posterity that we did not give our consents to that Bill, we do now take liberty to enter our Dissents, by subscribing our names. Berkeley of Berkeley, Holles, Ro. Lexington, T. Culpeper."

Dec. 19. The king by commission passed the above and four other bills. Immediately after, Mr. Secretary Morrice delivered this Message from the king to the house of commons; "His majesty having by a former Message acquainted you, that he intended an Adjournment to the beginning of Feb.; he doth now conceive, that Thursday the 6th of Feb. is a convenient day to which such an Adjournment may be made: and his majesty is willing to adjourn to that time." Accordingly, the Parliament broke up, after it had sat a little above two months, and without any prorogation had now a recess of above seven weeks.

[*The King's Speech to both Houses.*] Feb. 10, 1667-8.—Both houses met again, when his majesty made the following Speech from the throne:

"My lords and gentlemen, I am glad to see your here again, to tell you what I have done in this interval, which I am confident you will be pleas'd with, since it is so much for the honour and security of this nation. I have made a League defensive with the States-General of the United Provinces, and likewise a League for an efficacious Mediation of Peace between the two crowns of France and Spain; into which league, that of Sweden, by its Ambassador, hath offer'd to enter as a principal. I did not at our last meeting move you for any Aid, though I lie under great Debts contracted in the last war; but now the posture of our neighbours abroad, and the consequence of the new alliance, will oblige me, for our security, to set out a considerable fleet to sea this summer; and because I must build more great ships, and it is as necessary, that I do something in order to the fortifying some of our forts: I have begun something myself in order to these ends; but if I have not your speedy assistance, I shall not be able to go through with it. Wherefore I do earnestly desire you to take it into your speedy consideration; for the loss of a little time now may beget a prejudice not to be repaired. And for the settling a firm Peace, as well at home as abroad, one thing more I hold myself obliged to recommend to you, at this present; which is, That you would seriously think of some course to beget a better union and composure in the minds of my Protestant Subjects in matters of Religion; whereby they may be induced not only to submit quietly to the government, but also cheerfully give their assistance for the support of it."

[*The Duke of Albemarle's Narrative of the Miscarriages of the late War.*] The commons deferred the consideration of this Speech till after the Committee appointed to enquire into the Miscarriages of the late War, had given in their Reports. In order to which the duke of Albemarle, prince Rupert, and even the duke of York himself, laid each his own Account before them. That of the duke of Albemarle being as follows:

"I went early on Tuesday, the 11th of June to Chatham, where I found scarce 12 of 800 men, which were then in the king's pay, in his majesty's yards; and those so distracted with fear, that I could have little or no service from them. I had heard of 30 boats, which were provided by his royal highness; but they were all, except 5 or 6, taken away by those of the yards, who went themselves with them, and sent and took them away by the example of commissioner Pett, who had the chief command there, and sent away his own goods in some of them. I found no ammunition there, but what was in the Monmouth; so that I presently sent to Gravesend for the train to be sent to me, which got thither about 2 the next day. After I had dispatched this order, I went to visit the Chain, which was the next thing to be fortified for the security of the River; where I found no works for the defence of it. I then immediately set soldiers to work for the raising of two batteries, for there were no other men to be got; and when I employed them in it, I found it very difficult to get tools; for commissioner Pett would not furnish us with above 30, till by breaking open the stores we found more. I then directed timber and thick planks to be sent to the batteries and guns also, that they might be ready to be planted as soon as the batteries were made; and in the next place I sent capt. Wintour with his company to Upnore-Castle, which I took to be a place very fit to hinder the enemy from coming forwards, if they should force the chain: and upon further consideration, though I had horse near the fort, lest the enemy should land there, I commanded sir Edw. Scot, with his company, for a further strength of the place; and gave him the charge of it, with orders to let me know what he wanted for the security thereof.—Having thus provided for Upnore, I considered where to sink ships without the Chain, next to the enemy, as a further security to it. I found 5 fire-ships, and the Unity upon the place; and advising with commissioner Pett, and the master of attendance, and the pilot, how to do it; Pett told me, It was their opinion, that if 3 ships were sunk at the narrow passage by the Muscle-Bank, the Dutch Fleet could not be able to come up: and I, relying upon their experience who best knew the River, gave orders accordingly for the doing of it. But when this was done, they said they wanted two ships more, which I directed them to take and sink. After this, I ordered sir Edw. Spragg to take a boat and sound whether the sinking of those would sufficiently secure the Passage (which the pilot and master of attendance had not before observed) that was deep enough for great ships to come in; I thereupon resolved to sink some ships within the chain, and provide some against there should be occasion. I went then to look after the other ships and batteries, and to see the men and all things ready; but I found the guns, which I had before ordered to be there, nor yet come down; and instead of thick, oaken planks, (of which there was good store in the yards, as it afterwards appeared) the commissioner would only send planks of deal, saying, he had no other; which proved very prejudicial in the use of them: for they were so weak, that at every shot the wheels sunk through the boards, which put us to a continual trouble to get them out.—About noon, before the batteries were quite raised, the enemy came on to the place where our first ships were sunk: I went on board the Monmouth with 50 volunteers, and appointed soldiers in other ships to make the best defence we could, if they had proceeded; but they were so incumbered before they could clear the way through the sunk ships, and find another passage, that the tide was spent, and therefore they made no further advance that day; whereby we had time to consider what to do against the next attempt. There were two ships ordered to lie within the chain, to be ready to sink, if occasion should be: and wanting one ship more to sink in the middle between these two ships, I that night ordered the Sancta Maria, a great Dutch prize, to be sunk in the deepest place between the two aforesaid ships; and I judged it so necessary to be done, that I charged Pett, and the master of attendance, on peril of their lives, to do it by morning; they having time enough before the tide served to provide things to carry her down. Pett, who had received orders from h. r. h. on the 26th of March to remove the Royal Charles above the Dock, had, for about 9 or 10 weeks, neglected those orders: and, when I was getting all the boats I could (for I wanted many) for carrying materials for the batteries, and ammunition and soldiers for the defence of all our places, he came and told me, He would carry her up that tide, if he might have boats, which I could not then spare; for if they were gone, all our batteries must have been neglected, and I could not transport the timber, powder and shot, and men to them, to resist the enemy the next day. And beside, it was advised that instant, if the Dutch should have landed in the marsh by the crane, she might have been useful and have hindered them, having guns on board. Nevertheless, having notice shortly after, that there was neither sponge, ladle, powder nor shot in her, I sent capt. Millet, commander of the Matthias, about ten in the morning with orders to Pett to carry her up as he could the next tide; who pretended he could not then do it because there was but one pilot that would undertake it, and he was employed about sinking of ships. And seeing she was not removed in the morning, I myself spoke to Pett in the evening, in the presence of col. Mac-Noughton and cap. Mainsfield, to fetch her off that tide; but notwithstanding these orders, the ship was not removed, but lay there till the enemy took her. On the same morning, by break of day, I went to see what was done about the Sancta Maria, and found men towing her along to the place intended, and they had time enough to do their business: but soon after I had dispersed my orders to the ships, I looked and saw the Sancta Maria, by the carelessness of the pilots and masters of attendance, was run on ground, at which I was much troubled: for if that ship had been sunk in the place where I appointed, the Dutch Ships could not have got beyond those of ours sunk within the chain, and thereby none of the king's ships within could have been destroyed, in regard that our guard-ships within our batteries would have hindered them from removing our sunk ships.—About ten o'clock on Wednesday, the enemy came on with part of their fleet, and two men of war, 5 or 6 fireships, and some other men of war seconding them. They first attempted the Unity, which was placed on the right-hand close without the Chain to defend it; and they took her; and one of their fireships struck upon the chain, but it stopped it. Then came another great fireship, and with the weight of the two the chain gave way; and then the ships came on in that very passage where the Sancta Maria should have been sunk. They burnt the two guard-ships, and took off the Royal Charles, wherein the gunners and boat-swain did not do their duty in firing her, though they say they attempted it twice, but the fire did not take. This was all that I observed of the enemies action on Wednesday. Our next care was to provide against the tide which served the next day: I enquired what had been done by sir Edw. Scott at Upnore, and sent him as many of those things he needed as I could get boats to carry them to him, and sent likewise a company more than was formerly ordered, to reinforce the place in case of landing; and then directed 3 batteries to be made in the king's Yard; but could not get a carpenter, but two that were running away. I also planted that night about 50 cannon in several places, besides those that came with the train of artillery, which were also planted; I staid all night in the place with the men, and having no money to pay them, all I could do or say was little enough for their encouragement: for I had no assistance from commissioner Pett, nor no gunners or men to draw on the guns, except the two masters of attendance.—On Thursday morning betimes, Upnore was in a pretty good condition, and our batteries ready: I got some captains of ships and other officers, sea-volunteers, and others that came to me, to ply the guns; and other land-volunteers did assist them to draw them on the batteries. About noon the enemy came on again with two men of war, and two fireships, and some more men of war following them: the first two anchored before Upnore, and played upon it whilst the fireships passed up to the Great James, the Royal Oak, and the Loyal London: The two first fireships burnt without any effect; but the rest went up and burnt the three ships mentioned: and if we had had but 5 or 6 boats to cut off the boats of the fireships, we had prevented the burning of those ships; but those being burnt, as soon as the tide turned, they went back, and made no further attempt. I had, in the morning before this action, received his majesty's command to return to London; but I thought it most for his service to stay till the attempt was over: and then, having left upon the place the earl of Carlisle, and the earl of Middleton to command there till further order, I came away about 8 in the evening, and by two in the morning arrived at London."

Some Miscarriages in the late War voted.] From this and other Examinations, the commons discovered and voted several Miscarriages in the late War, and particularly in the Expedition at Berghen; in the plundering the East-India ships while the Dutch passed by; in the not setting out a sufficient Fleet last year; in the separation of those that were out, so that they became useless: in the want of provision and ammunition in the fleet, and in the forts; in payment of the seamen by tickets; in the want of intelligence, and dividing the fleets in the second year of the war; in the business of Chatham, &c. And they particularly resolved, "That, notwithstanding his majesty had 18,000 men in pay, in dispersed ships in the year 1667, there was not a sufficient number of ships left to secure the Rivers Medway and Thames." They strictly examined into one Miscarriage as to the first Battle against the Dutch, in which it appeared, 'That if the orders of the duke of York had been strictly observed, as they ought, in that Engagement, the whole fleet of the enemy had probably been destroyed.' For this, Mr. Brunkard, a member of the house, was accused of giving false orders to sir John Harman to slacken sail, while the duke was reposing himself, and when they were pursuing the enemy with the utmost advantage; for which Mr. Brunkard * was both expelled the house, and ordered to be impeached.

Impeachment of Commissioner Pett.] The Miscarriage at Chatham was so conspicuous, that the house thought they could do no less than impeach Commissioner Pett for so great a delinquency in that affair: accordingly, they drew up Articles against him to this effect:

I. "That the said Peter Pett, being a commissioner especially authorized and entrusted with the care of his majesty's yards, stores and provisions of the Royal Navy at Chatham, and having received orders from the duke of York about the 26th of March last, requiring him to bring up and moor his majesty's ship, the

* "Mr. Brunkard's ill course of life, and his abominable nature, rendered him so odious, that this affair of slacking sail was taken notice of in parliament, and upon examination found to be true; upon which he was expelled the house of commons, as an infamous person, though his friend Coventry adhered to him, and used many indirect arts to have protected him." Lord Clarendon's Life, p. 270.

Royal Charles, and other ships, did wilfully neglect and refuse so to do; whereby the said ships were lost, and became a prey to the enemy. II. That his majesty having upon the 11th of June last appointed the duke of Albemarle to repair to Chatham, to secure all things against the invasion of the Dutch; he the said duke found the Royal Charles not brought up, but lying below in a place of danger; and having given orders to the said Pett to cause the said ship to be brought up as high as could be into a place of safety, the said Pett neglected the doing thereof. III. That capt. Brooks, one of his majesty's attendants at Chatham, knowing that the duke had given express orders to cause the Royal Charles to be brought up, did prepare anchors and other tackling ready for the same; and desired the said Pett to give orders for his so doing, which be refused to do. IV. That the duke of York having given orders to the said Pett to provide 30 boats for the defence of the River and Navy, he did not only himself misemploy some of the said boats for the removing some of his particular goods, but suffered the rest to be likewise misemployed, and did also seize a boat belonging to sir Edw. Spragg; so, for want of these boats, many of his majesty's ships were lost, and the security of the rest hindered. V. That the commissioners of his majesty's Navy, having signified to him on the 4th of June, that the Dutch were out, and given him special charge to command all captains on land, to their ships, and to be vigilant in the rest of the charge committed to him; he was so negligent, that of eight hundred persons, which were under his care and command, when the duke of Albemarle repaired thither, there were not above ten ready upon the invasion of the enemy. VI. That the said duke, having appointed soldiers to raise batteries for the defence of the Navy, he to obstruct the service, refused to give them the number of tools required, notwithstanding he had a sufficient quantity in his majesty's stores, as it appeared when those stores were broke open. VII. That the said lord general having sent orders to him to send out of his majesty's yards some oaken planks for his platforms and batteries, he sent only deal boards, which were prejudicial to the service, notwithstanding that there were in his majesty's yards several oaken planks fit for that service.—For all which Crimes and Misdemeanors they demanded justice and condign punishment, &c. at the bar of the lords."

Impeachment of Sir W. Penn.] Not satisfied with this Impeachment, by means of some Discoveries and Informations, the commons found and singled out sir W. Penn,* another of his majesty's commissioners, and drew up Articles against him to this purpose: "1. Whereas in Sept. 1665, the Golden Phœnix, and the Slothany, two Dutch Ships, were taken at sea as prize by his majesty's fleet under the earl of Sandwich, in which the said sir W. Penn was then vice-admiral; he the said sir Wm. contrary to his duty, &c. did conspire with several persons to open the holds of the said ships, before judgment pass'd in the admiralty-court, and from thence embezzled great quantities of rich goods, whereby his majesty was defrauded of above 115,000*l*. 2. The said sir Wm. in pursuance of the conspiracy, did about the same time repair on board the Prize-Ship the Slothany, with sir Wm. Berkley, vice-admiral under his command, and did therefore give orders to Capt. Waerden, to whose charge the said ship was committed, to follow the directions of sir Wm. Berkley; who thereupon broke open the hold of the said ship, and took out several rich goods of great value, after it was closed and sealed up, and by the assistance of sir Wm. Penn, who sent several men on board for that purpose. 3. He the said sir Wm. got a considerable part of the goods into his possession, and shortly after did sell divers parcels of the said goods, and further warranted the sale thereof. IV. The better to colour the said fraud and embezzlement, orders were obtained from the earl of Sandwich for distributing some part of the said goods among several officers, whereof sir Wm. was chief, to be submitted, as was pretended, to his majesty's further pleasure, though sir Wm. well knew the orders of the earl of Sandwich were void in every respect; And afterwards a warrant for distributing the goods was duly procured from his majesty; whereas the said sir Wm. had, before that, possessed himself of divers of the goods; and, over and above did dispose of a further quantity of goods than was contained in the orders of the earl of Sandwich, or his majesty's warrant, to the value of above 2000*l*. For all which Crimes and Misdemeanors the commons likewise demanded judgment, &c. of the lords."

A Bill for the frequent holding of Parliaments withdrawn.] Feb. 18. Sir *Rd. Temple* brought in a Bill for the frequent holding of parliaments. He said, in Edw. 3rd's time a statute was made for annual parliaments; but they were too frequent, and therefore laid aside.

Sir *Hugh Wyndham*. This bill is brought in, I had almost said with impudence: [which expression was taken ill by many, and some said, 'that his words were impudently brought in:' but his words being asserted, no farther debate arose about them, and he explained not.]

* Sir W. Penn was Vice-Admiral of England, and father of the founder of Pensylvania, "From a common man he had grown up, under Cromwell, to the highest command, and was in great favour with him till he failed in the action of St. Domingo, when he went admiral at sea, as Venables was general at land, for which they were both imprisoned in the Tower by Cromwell, nor ever employed by him afterwards." Lord Clarendon's Life, p. 239. He died in 1670, aged 49.

Mr. *Steward.* This bill reproaches the very fundamental laws of England; for without the king's consent it gives the lord chancellor a power greater than the king; viz. That if in three years the king calls not a parliament, the chancellor for the time being, for such default, has power to issue out writs without him.

Sir *R. Temple.* The king has established all courts by law, which formerly followed his own court wherever it removed, but that was found inconvenient. This bill is no more for the highest court. He said he had forgot his breviate, which the Speaker should have had with the bill.

The *Speaker** excepted against it, as likewise that the bill was blotched and interlined, which ought not to be when first presented.—With much difficulty a first reading was obtained: but from that time the gentleman that brought it in did not increase his interest in the house.

Sir *John Birkenhead.* This bill bottoms itself upon the statute of Edward 3d. for annual parliaments; but there was never any annual parliament. There have been two in a year, and may be one or more in a year, if need be. The question is, if the bill be not felo-de se, of itself. The plague may alter the time, it being limited to so long time, and no longer impossible to be performed.

Mr. *Mallet.* Never any king prospered better both at home and abroad, by reason of frequency of parliaments.

Sir *T. Littleton.* By prorogations the effect of the triennial law is not eluded; which, by the former bill, might be. He knows not a more modest way of compelling the king by law. [Some said 'thing by law,' in excuse of him, for great exception was taken at the expression; but what he said was plainly and organically 'King.']

Sir *T. Meres.* In regard that leave was not asked, he wonders at the tendering the bill. That it may not put a slur on the former law, would have it laid aside.

Mr. *Milward.* This bill assures the calling of future parliaments; and an oath to the lord keeper, to issue out the writs. Let us trust the king with this, as we have done his predecessors. This bill does not: so the trust is here transferred, which is upon oath—that makes a difference.

Sir *Robt. Howard.* If this bill be a 'compelling' the king, all laws do so. Should the people see this bill thrown out, what would they say who have given so much money?

Sir *T. Clifford.* This is a bill of ill consequence, breeding jealousy betwixt the king and his people. All persons are indicted in the king's name; but this writ the lord keeper is to issue out, quite puts it out. A lion put into an iron cage never leaves roaring.—This bill is contrary to monarchy. Corruption of manners causes laws. Is this proper for this house, who has repealed that act? Is this proper for the king, who has declared so much affection to the parliament? In another country, (Sweden) there is a calling of a parliament by officers; but it is only in the minority of the king.

Sir *Rob. Brooke.* The bill being interlined, it ought to be laid aside; but would not have it thrown out, lest apprehensions should be in the minds of the people.

Sir *Lan. Lake.* This bill necessitates the lord keeper to be a traitor. If he does issue out his writ he is a traitor, if he does not he is a traitor. This will make him, as in times of usurpation, a keeper of the liberties of England.

Mr. Solicitor *Finch* would have the bill withdrawn, only because not orderly brought in. This is a bill to bring in a bill of repeal without leave. No bill, of good manners, is to be brought in, though of money, without leave. That the king may have no negative, would have it withdrawn till leave be obtained of the house.

Sir *Tho Clifford.* If the person be voted to have leave to withdraw it, and the person that brought it in will not, then are you possessed of it, it having been read.

Sir R. Temple was then ordered to withdraw the Bill; and it was ordered, That no Bill of this nature should be tendered to the house without leave and order.

The King's Messages to the Commons to hasten the Supply.] Meanwhile, the king believing that these proceedings and impeachments retarded the Supplies he had demanded, sent no less than three Messages, to bring back the stream of business to his favourite channel; the first of which was in these words: "His majesty hath been unwilling hitherto to interrupt you in your proceedings; but considering the posture in which his neighbours now are, and that the spring is already so far advanced, and that his allies (as they have great cause) pressed his majesty to hasten his preparations, he holds it absolutely necessary, in respect of the safety as well as the honour of the nation, that a fleet be set forth with all speed, and that course be taken for fortifying his ports, and building more ships: And therefore he doth again earnestly recommend it to you, forthwith to provide for such a Supply as these occasions

* Sir Edw. Turner, who had held that post from the beginning of this parliament in 1661, and continued in it till 1672, when, according to Mr. North, "it having been discovered that he had taken a small present from the East India company, it so far lessened him in the opinion of the house, and lost him so much of his credit and authority, that it was thought advisable to remove him; which was done by making him lord Chief Baron of the Exchequer." Life of lord Keeper Guildford, p. 52. Oldmixon says, "that he was infinitely fond of speaking, but was so pedantic, so trifling, so full of gingle, and other old fashions, that his harrangues are by no means worthy remembrance." Critical History of England, p. 255.

shall require: And because you have not yet had satisfaction upon the Bill of Accounts of the former Supply, his majesty is very willing that this be collected and issued for those purposes, by such persons only as you shall think fit." The second and the third Message were only to enforce this: but in the last he let them know that he designed to put a period to this session on the 4th of May. But finding this design not so well relished, he sent a fourth Message to them on the 24th of April, in these word: "His majesty by his former message thought fit to acquaint you, that he intended the present session of parliament should determine on the 4th of May; but, finding the proceedings in many important businesses, now under agitation, would be lost, if there should be a session; and that many things not yet foreseen may happen to induce him to call you together again before winter, hath now thought fit to acquaint you, that he intends only an adjournment for three months; and desires you therefore to perfect the bills for Supplies, and such others as may be made ready by the said 4th of May, so that he may then give his royal assent to them before the adjournment."

[*The Commons petition the King for a Proclamation against Conventicles.*] The house notwithstanding proceeded with the business that lay before them; and especially the Informations they received from some counties, particularly Staffordshire, of the insolent carriage and Abuses committed by persons in several places, in interrupting and disturbing of Ministers in their Churches, and holding Meetings contrary to law. In consequence of which, after a solemn debate and resolution, they made and presented an humble Petition to his majesty, "That he would issue out his Proclamation for enforcing the laws against Conventicles; and that care might be taken for the preservation of the peace against all unlawful Assemblies of Papists and Nonconformists." The king thought himself obliged to comply with his commons, and accordingly gave this Answer; "I will issue forth my Proclamation according to your desire; and I do not doubt but you will take the second part of my Speech into consideration, according to the Vote."

[*Debate on the latter Part of the King's Speech, concerning the Union of his Protestant Subjects.*] March 11. The commons resumed the consideration of the latter part of the King's Speech, about uniting his majesty's Protestant subjects.

Sir *John Goodrick* moved that the Convocation might take this business into their consideration.

Sir *T. Meres.* It may be his majesty's Proclamation may reconcile them, finding no countenance from hence.

Sir *R. Holt* would know what the Nonconformists desire, declared by somebody; if their arguments are not convincing, then to adhere to our former vote.

Col. *Sandys* never knew a Toleration, without an army to keep all quiet. Let persons concerned propose what they would have.

Sir *Humphry Winch.* What they will ask, and what they will take is vastly different: thinks we need not give an indulgence, nor make the laws severer. Heresies commonly take root from the innocency of their authors, which has made them increase here. An army is as dangerous to establish by being too strait-laced, as by giving toleration. He had rather new model the Sectaries, than that they should have an interest in future parliaments to model us.

Sir *John Earnly* would have the Ecclesiastical Courts reformed, which are so obnoxious.

Sir *Wm. Hickman.* The bishop has little power in the Church but Ordination. The Ecclesiastical Courts are complained of by the bishops as mysterious and troublesome to the people.

Mr. *Swynfin.* Education in another way has been a great cause of separation. Proposes one question concerning the thing itself, That some condescension from the laws in being may be had, to unite his majesty's Protestant subjects.

Sir *Philip Warwick.* If we could so relax the law, as not to lose the law, he would willingly condescend to some indulgence, that neither the agenda nor the credenda may be violated. If I prove that a man needs not scruple any thing in the Church, why should he be farther indulged?—Would have care taken, that, after indulgence, they get not a footing to destroy the whole—It is an unreasonable thing to pass a vote, that some condescension may be, before we know what.

Mr. *Ratcliffe.* Would have the Act of Uniformity revised, to discover what, in that act, is too strict, as renouncing the Covenant, Assent and Consent—Moves that a conference may be allowed, of both persuasions, and to recommend that, in which they all agree, to your consideration; and that if any thing should be established for a law, that an eye may be had to real tender consciences—That Ecclesiastical Courts may be regulated.

Sir *Walter Yonge.* The case of the Clergy of England with the king, is as a master of a family that has quarrelsome servants; one will not stay unless the other goes away. No good to be had by conference, or the convocation.

Sir *Ch. Wheeler.* Has a great kindness for the Presbyterians, being assistant in their prayers and endeavours in the restoration of his majesty; but could wish their penitence had been as public as their first offences were, as the custom of the Church ever was—But for the Independents, which are Anabaptists, &c. many of them are not Christians, some Arians, and some Socinians; but the Presbyterians are right as to matters of the first Four Councils, which are indisputable—But when they scruple that of the chancellors in the Church, and other novelties, not above 500 years standing, and if no other thing than reducing things to the first four General Councils, be the case, would have a committee appointed by us and the lords, to consult with both houses of Convocation, and hopes by that to bring in many Papists also.

Sir *T. Littleton.* Let us do what is fit for ourselves to do; and if we do what is reasonble, and that gives them not satisfaction, it rests not at our door—The kingdom of Poland has the greatest toleration in the world, and no standing army, but upon occasion of war—Their militia is their only standing army, which is made up of all opinions, and they have never had any wars upon religious accounts; and in their civil wars upon temporal affairs, persons of all opinions have mixed—Barnevelt, in Holland, only offered at a disturbance, and was taken off—The only party there was Arminian, which he could wish was not so much received amongst our clergy—Predestination and free-will, in our 39 Articles, have occasioned all our disputes in the Church of England—The Calvinist way has a loop-hole to let Arminianism into our articles—All along queen Eliz.'s, king James's, and king Charles's time, whenever any of these points were disputed, at degree of doctor, all the points were regulated by the Convocation, and then the current of the Church of England ran the Calvinist way—Besides at the synod of Dort—So long as the Church was true to itself, the Nonconformist never hurt the Church; but as soon as innovation and alteration came in by the churchmen, and they favourites with the crown, the Church declined—In Ceremonies we have much alteration; the Communion-table set Altar-manner, whereas it ought to be in the body of the Church, that the guests might come to the table, and the second service might be the better heard—No canon for the bowing at the altar, or, if any, quite laid aside—Now, if new ceremonies have been made, besides putting the tapers (on the Communion-table,) if private persons have dared to intrude these things against law, what will be the end? and none but such as will comply with this innovation shall have any preferment; and as this way has once ruined the Church, he hopes the parliament will not countenance the doing of it again—King Edw. and queen Eliz. prepared all things before they came to the parliament—Would have the king applied to, to give us some subject-matter to work upon.

Sir *John Cotton.* The Presbyterian tenets are most destructive to our government.—'That the king is but minister Bonorum:' 'he is greater than any one man, but less than the people:' 'Salus populi suprema lex,' and many more such.

Sir *John Birkenhead.* Theodosius, the emperor, so enjoined the sanctions of the councils, that no man, unconformable to them, could administer the sacraments—Socinus's opinions crept into the sects of Poland, which made the Cossacks always enquire, when they made any inroads, what the sectaries did—Religion in Holland is subservient to trade—They reproved Mr. Price, the English minister, and sent him away, for preaching against their Sunday markets.—Queen Elizabeth's council advised her to keep Edw. 6th's liturgy, in which she made little alteration, and enjoined conformity; and king James in his acts of indemnity, excepts Nonconformists—Queen Eliz. would never suffer Nonconformity, though the earl of Essex would have given security for the peaceableness of the persons—King James let them have a conference at Hampton Court; he would abate nothing: at last Dr. Reynolds came in and conformed—Queen Eliz. was favourable to Papists, but made severe laws against priests; and when the people had no mass they came to Church—The Articles of the Church of England were drawn so, that both parties might subscribe—The convocation was a very mixed assembly of both persuasions—No canon nor sanction enjoins bowing at the altar—Bishop Morton never did it; it is left at liberty—In Judaism, Paganism, Mahometanism, and Christianity, in none of them a toleration is suffered—The pope may suffer Milan to have St. Ambrose's litany, and Bohemia to administer the sacrament in both kinds; this he may do in one Church, but not several customs in one Church—He would never advise his prince to do what has destroyed his father—He would not have the odium of this business lie upon the king—He would have no application made to him in it—Let there be no conventicles, and Church will be fuller—Must their mother, the Church of England, bow to a few novices? and for the old ones, they have falsified their former oaths and subscriptions—For benefices, no man has three, as is alleged; if any man has three, they are, ipso facto, by law forfeited—Conference has been already at the Savoy—It has done no good—He would have the convocation sent to.

Mr. *Coventry.* Here is one side against bishops, and other against the silenced ministers; between them both, I fear, we shall have no religion—The king bids us, in his Speech, do it, and we send to the king to do it—Would have the Committee for Religion revived, to receive what shall be proposed.

Mr. *Boscawen.* The civil wars in England come upon various occasions—Though the occasion of the last was much upon this account, yet it is not probable there will be any more—Many other occasions may bring them.

Mr. *Seymour.* Will rather veil the infirmities of his mother, the Church, then proclaim, them in Gath and Askalon—He is for comprehension—Two or three of the most eminent presbyters may be made bishops, and so an end of Nonconformity—Would have a liberty, but no farther than whether to wear a plain garment, a fringed or embroidered one, that these persons may be useful to the support of the government—He is for no middle way—If a man finds not his account in the government he lives under, he will never labour to support it—The effects of the Act of Uniformity have been much for the good of Holland, in point of trade—Mischiefs having outgrown politic remedies, they must have gentle remedies—He would have an address to his majesty, to give them some liberty that might not endanger the public peace.

Sir *R. Atkins* * would have his majesty name some persons, such as he shall think fit; not of both persuasions, but persons of prudence.

Sir *R. Carr* fears that his maj. is possessed that the h. of commons is fond of toleration, and that we are possessed that his majesty is fond of it.—The farther debate was ordered to be re-assumed on the 8th of April.

March 13. Upon some proffers of a debate about the latter part of the King's Speech, which the Bill against Conventicles seemed to cross,

Sir *Tho. Littleton* said, it is dangerous to make laws too big to be executed, although some over-forward men may execute them—The Churchmen are arrived to that pass, as to bring in what ceremonies they please, though they lie under suspicion of popery; and that others must conform to these innovations—What hope can we have of their doing any good from those that should be men of mercy, and carry things with the greatest severity?

Sir *Giles Strangeways.* When such formidable mushrooms should start up in a night that are too great for the law, no prudent state will suffer their laws to be flown upon—It is a trouble to him to hear the Church of England arraigned—It was upon the suspicion of popery that abp. Laud's head was cut off; and what will they have popery 7 years hence, when asking blessing is now popery?—Is this the way to make union, for every man to be tolerated his profession?—Would have ourselves in this house reformed—He is sorry to hear any thing of toleration countenanced here—No man can blame him for being zealous in his religion, as they are in theirs—Must a father yield his authority to his son?—Leave was given to bring in a Bill for continuance of the former Act against Conventicles.

April 8. The debate was resumed.

Sir *Fretchv. Holles* moves, after many discourses of decay of trade, That his maj. may be desired by this house to call together what number he pleases, and whom, of Dissenters, as he thinks fit, to hear them.

Sir *John Northcote* moves to have it referred to the consideration of the Convocation now sitting.

Mr. *Progers* would have it referred to the Committee of Religion.

Col. *Birch* says he knows no sect, unless Quakers, that will not subscribe the 36 Articles; three of them not concerning doctrine but discipline—The dissenters are either enemies, or we shall make them so—if so, there must be something to keep them quiet—he much doubts whether it be lawful amongst Christians to use any other weapons than what our master used—much more easy to govern persons of several opinions than one, by setting them up one against another—The dissenters doubt their condition, and secure a good part of their money beyond sea, as a more secure place—for dissenters, the Church will be stronger the fewer it has—this principle of liberty the Pope admits not of, to read the Scriptures—the Turks suffer no learning, and the papists pray in an unknown tongue, lest the people should send their own prayers to Heaven, as we do—some would have the Cross, some not; some the surplice, some not—he ever acknowledged prayers to be a convenient thing in the church—he is not against them, but would have us consider of Assent and Consent, and so proceed upon the rest, and the fittest for us only to do.

Sir *Walter Yonge* is for taking off Assent and Consent, and could wish that Birch was as orthodox in the rest of his discourses.

Mr. *Steward* expected some proposals from dissenting persons, but for us to be *felo de se* of our own act, is a strange weakness; and so scan our government, piece by piece—would make a bridge of gold for them if they would come over, but never upon such terms as he hears discoursed of—it is to be frighted out of our government with bugbears—he lives in a county (Norfolk) of much trade; he knows not of a family removed, nor trade altered, and in the country a general conformity, which grows daily upon the people—in Norwich are 20,000 persons, and not 20 dissenters—he believes an interruption of trade, but merely out of design, which he hopes will not take here—the king can call persons of all persuasions without our desires; it was once done when the king came in, but without effect—but when they propose, if any thing be *Scandalum datum*, or *acceptum*, he would have it seriously weighed; but not to be *felo de se* in arrainging our own act.

Mr. *Waller* stands up to prevent the heat that always attends debates concerning Religion—if proposals be made to the house, they will hinder the king's business, now we are ready to part—for the Convocation to consider of it, not proper for them, but absolutely exclusive; for when they altered the book of Common Prayer from what came from us, we allowed it not—Their business is *in puris spiritualibus*; it is our business to fence about and wall religion, not theirs—so the question is, whether to continue these laws, which were made *in terrorem*—The king proposed it at Breda, when we were not a people; at the Convocation also, when we were not a people—he

* "Knight of the Bath, and afterwards lord chief-justice of the Common-pleas: but in 1679, from a foresight of very troublesome times, he thought fit to resign and retire into the country. Having been zealous for the revolution, he was made by king William lord chief baron of the Exchequer, and died in 1711, aged 88." Biogr. Brit.

wished then he had listened to this business, and is of the same mind still—The sheriffs oath against Lollards is mended since sir Edw. Coke refused that oath—he repents not his being against severe laws—the Quakers, a people abused—he hoped that would have abolished them; but since the severity of the law against them, they begin to be respected—the vulgar ever admire such sufferers as do it almost above nature—he hears the proclamation is not executed—the people of England are a generous people, and pity sufferers—The Justice of the Peace fears the offender will leave his wife and children upon the parish—as our church resembles the primitive church in doctrine, so it does in believers also; amongst us some know not so much as a Holy Ghost; and our clergymen, by their laziness, whip people out of the church—he would have all the opinions address themselves to his majesty—he presumes they will but differ in opinion, and so nothing will be granted, and they kept different—he would not have the Church of England, like the elder brother of the Ottoman family, strangle all the younger brothers—Empson and Dudley were hanged after the death of Hen. 7, not for transgressing the law, but for pressing too much the penal laws, which was the great blemish of that prince.

Mr. *Vaughan*. It is not proper for us to return this upon the king who proposed it to us—if it goes to the king, we may be apprehended not to deal candidly; and what we are subjected to in this case, the king is the same; and should the king chuse persons that may persuade him, is it likely that we should acquiesce in that persuasion? No.

Mr. *Swynfin* would have his maj. moved to call some persons to consult with him; it will prepare the business the readier for us—the dissenters increase, and the severity of the law increasing too, is never the way to unite us.

Sir *Rob. Howard* would have nothing have a tacit fate, but come clearly to you, whether it be fit to do something or no.

Sir *Tho. Clifford*. The question of going to the king being carried in the negative, is, in effect, a negative to the whole—it may terrify any person from advising the king.

Sir *Tho. Meres*. Those little things, so called, are nothing less than Ordination, and many other alterations in the government besides, and Toleration at the last—his maj. did acquiesce in our reasons against the Toleration; all the rest of the conference was spent in bitter railing, and invectives, and reflections upon the ecclesiastical government, as in 1640, and so will be again upon conference—the Dissenting party did not generally rest satisfied with the king's Declaration.

Sir *Walter Yonge*. The address is fit to be made to his majesty; he best knowing the temper of persons; they may be so best consulted with—there has been good use of colloquies, though no good of that at Hampton-Court, nor when the king came in; but in queen Eliz.'s time, and Edw. the 6th's time, very successful.

Sir *John Goodrick*. These persons would have a superstructure without a foundation: they propose nothing—though at Hampton-Court conference the authority of truth stopped some mens mouths, yet the rest were never satisfied—The Synod at Dort, and the conference in Scotland, as fruitless.

Sir *Tho. Littleton* sees no reason for apprehending terrifying of counsellors, for addresses of this nature have been formerly done—they take no privilege from the parliament—the king has so large a prerogative, that he apprehends the king may do more than is now desired.

Sir *Adam Browne*. Suppose they should persuade the king not to put the laws in execution against Conventicles, what a rock do we put the king upon!

Sir *Rob. Atkins*. Many are of opinion in the house that something should be done, who will be precluded by the negative, if no Address to his majesty; and so a prejudice to them who are friends to the end, but not to the means, by addressing his majesty.

Mr. *Hampden*. It will be said abroad, Why no proposals from the Nonconformists? Says one, if we grant something, you will have more and more, will you make the law already *felo de se?* So let what will be proposed, here is a negative in effect—The envy will not come upon his majesty, but upon the last persons that it rests upon, which is the house—this is a thing which has, in all ages, been done, and this Address is most suitable to the occasion.

Sir *Tho. Lee* moves that the oaths may be taken off, many having fallen from the church since they were imposed, it is probable, if taken away, they may return. They cannot meet without being thought tumultuous, so that we are to grant them, what, in our judgment, we think fit.

Sir *Tho. Meres* would, before any thing be farther proceeded in, have a vote pass that we shall have no Toleration.

Sir *Tho. Littleton* would have a toleration of some things; how could people else bow to the Altar, a thing not enjoined in the Rubrick? It is a question of a large extent.

Mr. *Vaughan*. As long as persons conform outwardly to the law, we have no inquisition into opinion, and a toleration will go a great way in that; but if you generally give it, it is to all Dissenters in point of conscience—he takes Arius and Nestorius to be with Mahometans and Jews, the same reason for all as for one: he would never do it, to introduce anarchy: thinks no man so impudent as to desire it: laws arise from within us, or without us: new laws, or repeal of laws, must be either by petition, or leave asked to bring in a bill: nothing of the toleration being within us, or without us, we mispend our time to no purpose: consider what offence it is to dissuade the people from obedience to the law: it is, in law, to disturb the government, and execution of the law; and then, how far will our interests lead us to it, or rather, a greater word, our obligation!

Mr. *Swynfin.* It was never thought that the law for Conventicles extended to any other persons than such as were out of all communion with us in doctrine, and hold no salvation in our church: it was never till now construed a Conventicle, the Dissenters being a people in communion with us in doctrine, though different in ceremonies.

Sir *Ch. Wheeler.* Condescension is as wide as the ocean: tender conscience is primitiæ gratiæ, which, when the devil has done with, he puts a man upon spiritual pride.

Mr. *Vaughan.* To the one kind of Dissenters, would have the Bill of Conventicles gone on with; for the inconvenience is as great from many others, as from the Dissenters mentioned.

Mr. *Coventry.* If a bill be brought in, he would not have it countenance the taking away the oath about the Covenant; and he that brings it in, at his peril: but yet would have an oath to alter nothing either in Church or State —by way of tacit consent, not by order of the house, to bring in such a bill.

The question being propounded, That his majesty be desired to send for such persons as he should think fit, to make Proposals to him, in order to the uniting of his Protestant Subjects, it passed in the Negative, 176 to 70.

Debate on the Bill for suppressing Seditious Conventicles.] April 28. An ingrossed Bill, for continuance of a former Act, to prevent and suppress Seditious Conventicles, was read.

Mr. Secretary *Morrice.* The fire of zeal for suppression of Conventicles may be so hot, that it may burn those that cast them in, as well as those that are cast in.

Mr. *Waller.* School divines cannot unite them with us: we have united them; what? against both State and Church—make the fire in the chimney, and not in the middle of the room—let the zeal be in the Church—we have seen the fruits of this formerly: let them alone, and they will preach one against another: by this bill they will incorporate, as being all under one calamity.

Mr. *Vaughan.* To be against this bill, is to cure a disease by doing things against it. Though this be but an adjournment, yet there may be reasons why we shall not meet again; therefore this may be a sufficient reason for passing it. Liberty has been given for any man to bring in a bill for union; no such thing has been done. In my own judgment, I am for indulging the people; the harm is not to be feared from the people: but if persons must be suffered to subvert the laws by seditious teaching, judge the consequence, and prevent it, by passing the bill at this time.

Some words fell from Sir Trevor Williams to this effect, 'That if the Proviso, concerning making the Roman Catholics part of this Bill of Conventicles, be not admitted of, he desires liberty to bring in a Bill to tolerate Popery;' which discourse gave great offence, and he narrowly escaped calling to the bar; but at length was permitted to explain, which he did, 'expressing much trouble for the offence he had given the house, and that he had no ill meaning in what he had said.'

Mr. *Vaughan.* The statute of queen Eliz. has given liberty to the lords to sit in parliament, without test of their religion; the commons not: therefore, if a man should say, the lords would not pass the Bill with the proviso of the Papists, because a great party amongst them are so, it is no reflection upon the lords: it would be otherwise to the commons, they having a test upon them.—The Bill was then passed, 144 to 78.

Great Misunderstanding between the two Houses, in Skinner's Case.] About this time, a Difference happened between the lords and commons, occasioned by Mr. Skinner, a considerable merchant of London, who, having received great damages from the East-India Company, had brought the matter by Petition into the house of lords originally, by whom he was relieved in 5000*l.* cost.* The commons hearing of this, after a debate, came to these Votes and Resolves on the 2d of May: 1. "That the lords taking cognizance of the matter set forth and contained in the Petition of Thomas Skinner, merchant, against the Governor and Company of Merchants trading to the East-Indies, concerning the taking away the petitioner's ship and goods, and assaulting his person, and their lordships over-ruling the plea of the said Governor and Company, the said cause coming before their house originally, only upon the Complaint of the said Skinner, being a Common-Plea, is not agreeable to the law of the land; and tending to deprive the subject of his right, ease and benefit due to him by the said laws. 2. That the lords taking cognizance of the right and title of the island in the Petition mentioned, and giving damages thereupon against the said Governor and Company, is not warranted by the laws of this king-

* "The case was this: Skinner, the plaintiff, was a considerable merchant of London; the defendants were the East India Company, and, in their right, sir Samuel Barnardiston, as their governor. The matter of complaint was, That the said Company had seized a ship and cargo of Skinner's, and assaulted his person. Skinner, instead of commencing his suit in Westminster-hall, has recourse at once to the house of lords, who give him a hearing, and allot him 5000*l.* damages. Sir Samuel and the Company, on the other hand, knowing no balance for the power of one house, but that of the other, appeal to the commons, who vote Skinner's Complaint, and the lords proceedings thereon, illegal. The lords did the same by the Company's Appeal. The commons order Skinner into the custody of the Serjeant at Arms; and the lords did the same by sir Samuel, as likewise sir Andrew Riccard, Mr. Rowl. Gwynn, and Mr. Christopher Boone." Ralph.

dom. 3. That the said Tho. Skinner, in commencing and prosecuting a suit by Petition in the house of lords against the Company of Merchants trading to the East-Indies (wherein several members of this house are parties concerned with the said Company, in particular interests and estates) and in procuring judgment therein, with directions to be served upon the Governor, being a member of this house; or upon the Deputy-Governor of the said Company, is a Breach of the Privilege of this house." In conclusion, they ordered the said Mr. Skinner, for so acting, to be taken into custody of the serjeant at arms.

Votes of the Commons upon it.] The East-India Company having petitioned the commons, as well as Mr. Skinner the lords, the commons after their three Votes, further resolved, "That the Petition of the Merchants trading to the East-Indies, and the two first Votes of this house now passed, relating to the jurisdiction of the lords, be delivered by a Message to the lords' bar, with reasons for enforcing the said Votes."

The Duke of Buckingham's Speech thereupon, at a Conference with the Commons.] This occasioned two or three Conferences with the peers; in one of which,

The duke of *Buckingham* delivered the following speech:—" Gentlemen of the house of commons; I am commanded by the house of peers, to open to you the matter of this Conference; which is a task I could wish their lordships had been pleased to lay upon any body else, both for their own sakes and mine: having observed, in that little experience I have made in the world, there can be nothing of greater difficulty, than to unite men in their opinions, whose interests seem to disagree.—This, gentlemen, I fear is at present our case; but yet I hope when we have a little better considered of it, we shall find that a greater interest does oblige us, at this time, rather to join in the preservation of both our Privileges, than to differ about the violation of either.—We acknowledge it is our interest to defend the right of the commons, for should we suffer them to be oppressed, it would not be long before it might come to be our own case; and I humbly conceive it will also appear to be the interest of the commons to uphold the privilege of the lords, that so we may be in a condition to stand by and support them.—All that their lordships desire of you upon this occasion, is, That you will proceed with them as usually friends do, when they are in dispute one with another; that you will not be impatient of hearing arguments urged against your opinions, but examine the weight of what is said, and then impartially consider which of us two are the likeliest to be in the wrong.—If we are in the wrong, we and our predecessors have been so for these many hundreds of years, and not only our predecessors, but yours too: this being the first time that ever an Appeal was made, in point of Judicature, from the lords house to the house of commons. Nay, these very commons, which turned the lords out of this house, though they took from them many other of their Privileges, yet left the constant practice of this till the very last day of their sitting; and this will be made appear by several precedents these noble lords will lay before you, much better than I can pretend to do.—Since this business has been in agitation, their lordships have been a little more curious than ordinary, to inform themselves of the true nature of these matters now in question before us; which I shall endeavour to explain to you as far as my small ability, and my aversion to hard words, will give me leave: for howsoever the law, to make it a mystery and a trade, may be wrapt up in terms of art, yet it is founded in reason and is obvious to common sense.—The power of Judicature does naturally descend, and not ascend; that is, no inferior court can have any power which is not derived to it from some power above it. The king is by the laws of this land, supreme judge in all causes ecclesiastical and civil. And so there is no court, high or low, can act but in subordination to him; and though they do not all issue out their writs in the king's name, yet they can issue out none but by virtue of some power they have received from him. Now every particular court has such particular power as the king has given it, and for that reason has its bounds: But the highest court in which the king can possibly sit, that is, his supreme court of lords in parliament, has in it all his judicial power, and consequently no bounds, I mean no bounds of jurisdiction; for the highest court is to govern according to the laws as well as the lowest. I suppose none will make a question, but that every man and every cause is to be tried according to Magna Charta; that is, by his peers, or according to the laws of the land. And he that is tried by the Ecclesiastical Courts, the Court of Admiralty, or the high Court of Lords in parliament, is tried as much by the laws of the land, as he that is tried by the King's-Bench, or Common-Pleas. When these inferior courts happen to wrangle among themselves, which they must often do by reason of their being bound up to particular causes, and their having all equally and earnestly a desire to try all causes themselves, then the supreme court is forced to hear their complaints, because there is no other way of deciding them. And this, under favour, is an original cause of courts though not of men. Now, these original causes of courts, must also of necessity induce men, for saving of charges, and dispatch sake, to bring their causes originally before the supreme court. But then the court is not obliged to receive them, but proceeds by rules of prudence, in either retaining or dismissing them as they think fit. This is, under favour, the sum of all that your precedents can show us, which is nothing but what we practise every day; that is, that very often, because we would not be molested with hearing too many particular causes, we refer them back to other courts; and all the argument you can possibly draw from this, will not, in any kind, lessen our power, but only show an unwillingness we have to trouble ourselves often with matters of this nature. Nor will this appear strange, if you consider the constitution of our house, it being made up partly of such whose employments will not give them leisure to attend the hearing of private causes, and entirely of those that can receive no profit by it. And the truth is, the dispute at present is not between the house of lords and the house of commons, but between us, and Westminster-Hall. For as we desire to have few or no causes brought before us, because we get nothing by them, so they desire to have all causes brought before them for a reason a little of the contrary nature. For this very reason, it is their business to invent new ways of drawing causes to their courts, which ought not to be pleaded there. As for example, this very cause of Skinner that is now before us (and I do not speak this by rote, for I have the opinion of a reverend judge in the case, who informed us of it the other day in the house) they have no way of bringing this cause into Westminster-Hall but by this form; the reason and sense of which I leave you to judge of. The form is this, that instead of speaking as we ordinary men do that have no art, that Mr. Skinner lost a ship in the East-Indies: to bring this into their courts, they must say, that Mr. Skinner lost a ship in the East-Indies, in the parish of Islington, in the county of Middlesex. Now some of us lords, that did not understand the refinedness of this style, began to examine what the reasons of this should be; and so we found, that, since they ought not by right to try such causes, they are resolved to make bold, not only with our privileges, but the very sense and language of the whole nation. This I thought fit to mention, only to let you see that this whole cause, as well as many others, could not be tried properly in any place but at our bar; except Mr. Skinner would have taken a fancy to try the right of jurisdictions between Westminster-Hall and the Court of Admiralty, instead of seeking relief for the injuries he had received, in the place only where it was to be given him. One thing I hear is much insisted upon, which is the trial without juries: to which I could answer, that such trials are allowed of in the chancery and other courts, and that when there is occasion for them we make use of juries too, both by directing them in the King's-Bench, and having them brought up to our bar. But I shall only crave leave to put you in mind, that if you do not allow us in some cases to try without juries, you will then absolutely take away the use of Impeachments, which I humbly conceive you will not think proper to have done at this time."

In the close of this Conference, the lords declaring the Company's Petition to the other house scandalous, &c. this raised such a ferment there, as produced the following new Votes and Resolves; as, 1. "That the Petition of the East India Company to this house, touching the proceedings of the house of lords, in the case of Tho. Skinner, is not scandalous. 2. That the delivery of the said Petition of the East-India Company to the house, and the entertainment thereof, and the Proceedings and Votes of this house thereupon, was no Breach of the Privilege or encroachment upon the Jurisdiction of the h. of lords; but very proper and fit for this house, without breach of the fair correspondence, which ought to be between the two houses. 3. That a Message be sent to the lords to acquaint them, That this house doth take notice of the desire of the lords at the last Conference, for a good union to be kept between both houses: And it is the opinion of this house, that the best expedient to preserve such an union is, That all proceedings be forborn upon the Sentence and Judgment of the lords in the case of Tho. Skinner against the East India Company; and that sir Andrew Riccard, sir Samuel Barnardiston, Mr. Rowland Gwyn, and Mr. Christ. Boone be set at liberty; this house being unsatisfied with their lordships Reasons offered at the last Conference." Last of all, after a long debate, they resolved, "That whosoever shall be aiding or assisting in putting in execution the Order or Sentence of the house of lords, in the case of Tho. Skinner against the East-India Company, shall be deemed a betrayer of the rights and liberties of the commons of England, and an infringer of the privileges of this house."*

The King's Speech, at the Adjournment.] May 8. They had no sooner finished this Vote, but the king, by the usher of the black-rod, sent for them to the house of peers, where, after passing several Acts, his majesty made a short Speech as follows:

"My lords and gentlemen; I came hither purposely to pass some Acts which are now ready, and to thank you for the Supply you have now given me; which I hope will be sufficient, our neighbours being now agreed upon articles of peace. I cannot chuse but take notice of what I hear abroad, of some differences between both houses, touching the East India Company. I am as sensible of the privileges of the h. of peers (wherein I am concerned) as I am of the liberty of the h. of commons. But I hope, in this recess, there may be some means found out for an accommodation therein. I am willing you should adjourn to the 11th of Aug. next; and if there be no pressing occasion of your meeting then, I will give you timely notice by proclamation."

On the 11th of Aug. both houses adjourned

* "These proceedings, in regard to Skinner and the East India Company, occasioned a remarkable quarrel between the two houses; and, in order to reconcile them, the king recommended to them to strike out all proceedings relating thereto from their journals." Grey.

to the 10th of Nov. On the 10th of Nov. they again met, and adjourned to the 1st of March 1668-9. Upon which day they met and were prorogued by his majesty to the 19th of Oct. 1669.

New Regulation of the Civil List.] The duke of Buckingham, says Mr. Ralph,* was now as much out of love with the parliament, as his royal master. In order, therefore, that their meeting might be deferred the longer, the Civil List was put under a new Regulation according to the following thrifty Scheme:

"At the Court of Whitehall 22d July, 1668, present, the king's most excellent majesty, h. r. h. d. of York, lord abp. of Canterbury, lord privy seal, d. of Buckingham, d. of Albemarle, d. of Dorchester, lord chamberlain, e. of Anglesey, e. of Bath, e. of Craven, e. of Carlisle, e. of Lauderdale, e. of Carbery, e. of Orrery, lord Holles, Mr. Treasurer, Mr. Vice-chamberlain, Mr. Sec. Morrice, sir John Duncombe.—Upon reading this day at the Board the annexed Report of the right hon. the lords appointed to consider of the several branches of his majesty's Expences and Issues, and what proportions of each may best and most conveniently be retrenched and spared for the future; his maj. taking the same into consideration, and well approving thereof, did order that the right hon. the lords commissioners of the Treasury be, and they are hereby, authorized and required to cause all the particulars of the said Report to be put in execution."

The King's Revenue.

	£
Customs	400,000
Excise	340,000
Chimney-Money	170,000
Small Branches	120,000
	1,030,000

Proposal for the Retrenchment of the Expence within the Revenue.

The Navy Orders	200,000
Army and Garrisons	182,000
City of Tangier	55,500
Houshold	90,000
Buildings and Repairs	8,000
Privy Purse	12,000
Intelligence	4,000
Treasury Chamber	20,000
Great Wardrobe	16,000
Pensioners	5,000
Jewel-House	2,000
Office of the Ordinance, ordinary and extraordinary	30,000
Queen-Consort	23,000
Queen-Mother	40,000
Embassadors, Agents, &c.	20,000
Foreign Embassadors	10,000
The Twelve Judges	12,000
Courts of Ludlow, and Masters of Chancery and Requests	2,500
Angel Gold, for healing	1,200
Master of the Horse, for Horses	2,000
Master of the Studd-Horses	500
Creation-Money	1,500
Lord Privy Seal's Diet	1,400
Liberates of the Exchequer	1,500
Dormant Privy Seals	300
Chief Officers of the Falconry Besides an Allowance of keeping Two Casts of Hawks.	4,000
Harriers	700
Tents	500
Tower Expences	768
Game-keepers, and Keepers of the Forests	108
Interest paid yearly	150,000
Deductions upon Farms, and for other Accidents and Contingencies	100,000
Total	996,476
Remains	33,525

"The remain of 33,525*l.* to be employed (after all the ordinary Charge before-mentioned, with interest and deduction, in manner and order following, as his maj. shall direct) for the payment of pensions: 1. To those who had a hand in the King's Escape from Worcester, &c. 2. To the Coldstreamers. 3. To those who have Pensions or Salaries for present service. 4. To those who have Grants, on valuable consideration. 5. For past-services. 6. For Grants, on mere grace.

Rules for regulating of the Revenue, and easing of the Charge.

All Pensions and Payments hereafter shall be removed from other funds or branches of the Revenue, and made payable only in the exchequer, that the king may have the view of his whole Expence in one place.—A new Establishment to be made of the Expence of the Houshold, in one book.—The Impost of Ambassadors from Michaelmas 1668, to be as in the time of his late maj. Ch. I.—The Papers to be looked out, and new orders to be settled for the establishing and clothing the Yeomen of the Guard.—All that by office or otherwise have houses or lodgings of the king's out of the court, or his houses of residence, to be obliged to keep them, at their own charge, in repair; and the surveyor is to look to it."*

The court itself, likewise, in this long interval, underwent some alterations. Sir Tho. Clifford was made treasurer of the houshold, in the room of lord Fitzharding deceased, being succeeded by lord Newport, as comptroller, and sir John Trevor, secretary of state in the room of sir Wm. Morrice, who had a donative of 10,000*l.* to dispose him to resign.†

EIGHTH SESSION OF THE SECOND PARLIAMENT.

The King's Speech on opening the Session.] Oct. 19, 1669. This day the parliament met, after a long recess of one year, five months and

* Ralph, vol. i. p. 175.

* From lord Hallifax's Collection of MSS. vol. i. † Sir W. Temple's Letters.

ten days. His majesty opened the Session, with the following Speech from the throne:

"My Lords and Gentlemen; I am very glad to see you here at this time, and I hope this will be a happy meeting; for I have had great experience of your affection and loyalty to me, and am very confident of your continuance of it. It is now almost a year and a half since your last sitting; and though my Debts have pressed me very much, yet I was unwilling to call for your assistance till this time.—What you gave me last, was wholly applied to the Navy, and that extraordinary Fleet for which it was intended. I desire that you will now take my Debts effectually into your considerations. Something I have to propose to you of great importance, concerning the Uniting of England and Scotland; but it will require some length; and I have left that, and some other things, to my Lord Keeper, to open them fully to you."

The Lord Keeper Bridgman's Speech.] Then the Lord Keeper spake as follows:

"My lords; and you knights, citizens, and burgesses of the h. of commons; His majesty, in his most gracious Speech, hath expressed his great satisfaction in seeing you here at this time, and his hopes of a happy issue of this meeting: to obtain this, nothing can conduce more than a good correspondency and union among yourselves.—He hath reason to believe that you all come with the same common affections for the general good, and therefore persuades himself there will be no differences between the two houses: but if there should be any such, he earnestly recommends it to you, that, by your moderation and wisdoms, such expedients may be found out as may compose them, and that thereby no delay or obstruction be to your other proceedings.—His maj. has also desired you to take his Debts effectually into consideration: I need not mention to you the uneasiness of his condition with that burden; nor the inconveniences or mischiefs which might fall out if he should continue under it.—It is not unknown to you, that his maj. hath been a happy instrument, by the Treaty at Aix and by the Triple Alliance, to procure peace between the two neighbouring crowns; the securing of that peace (wherein our own peace is concerned), and his majesty's reputation abroad, will also much depend upon your kindness to him; and therefore he hopes that you will consider of how great an importance it is, at this time, that his maj. be enabled to bear such a part in the affairs of Europe, as may contribute most to his own honour, and the safety, benefit, and glory, of this nation.—My Lords and Gentlemen; You may remember that, upon his majesty's recommendation, an Act was lately made, for settling freedom and intercourse of Trade between England and Scotland, which was occasioned upon complaints of new duties imposed in each kingdom upon divers commodities of the growth, production, or manufacture, of the other.—According to this act, commissioners were appointed by his maj. for both kingdoms, to treat upon that affair; and they had several meetings, which produced no effect, unless it were a conviction of the difficulty, if not impossibility, of settling it in any other way than by a nearer and more complete Union of the two kingdoms.—His maj. is fully persuaded, that nothing can tend more to the good and security of both nations, than such an Union; and finds that his royal grandfather king James of blessed memory, went so far on towards this good work, that by act of parliament in the first year of his reign, commissioners were authorized to treat and consult with commissioners from Scotland concerning it.—And, in pursuance of their treating, in the 4th year of his reign, an Act was made for the repeal of hostile laws, and the abolition of the memory of hostility between the two nations; and, after the end of that session, about the 7th year of his reign, it was (by the judges of all the courts at Westminster Hall) solemnly adjudged, in the case of the Post Nati, that those who (after the descent of the crown to king James) were born in Scotland were no aliens in England, and consequently were capable, not only of lands, but all other immunities, as if they had been born here.—By these steps, so great an advance hath been made towards this Union, that his maj. well hopes, that what is yet wanting to the perfecting it may be now accomplished; the continuance under the same obedience and subjection for near threescore and seven years having begotten the same common friends and common enemies to both nations, and taken off a great part of those difficulties which at the first stood in the way.—And therefore his maj. doth most heartily recommend it unto you, that Commissioners may be nominated, to treat and consult with commissioners from Scotland, concerning this Union. His maj. hath given directions to the earl of Lauderdale, his commissioner for Scotland, to make the like proposal to the parliament which is now sitting there; and doubts not but, upon the meeting of such commissioners of both kingdoms, those things will be offered to your considerations, in order to the Union, as shall tend to the honour of his majesty and the common good of all his subjects."

Sir George Carteret expelled.] Instead of taking these speeches into consideration, the commons enquired into the points of Privilege, with relation to the two houses, and were strict in the Examination of the Accounts of the Monies expended by the public; in the passing of which, they found sir George Carteret, the vice chamberlain, who had the keeping of some of the books, so blameable, that they expelled him the house. But, being much obliged with the king's last Proclamation, they soon resolved, "That the humble and hearty Thanks of this house be returned to the king's majesty for issuing out his Proclamation for putting in execution the laws against Nonconformists, and for suppressing

Conventicles, with the humble desire of this house for his majesty's continuance of the same care for suppressing of them for the future." The concurrence of the lords being desired, and readily obtained, on the 6th of Nov. both houses, in pursuance of this Vote, attended his majesty in the Banquetting-House in Whitehall, where the lord-chief-justice Vaughan, supplying the room of the Lord-Keeper then indisposed, in the name of both houses returned his majesty the fore-mentioned Thanks: for which he returned them this particular Answer, "My lords and gentlemen; I thank you for this mark of your affection to me: I doubt not of the continuance and concurrence of it in other things, as well as in this of my Proclamation: I recommend to you, that you would well weigh all that I say and desire in it towards the welfare and peace of the nation; in order to which, as I shall always be ready to contribute my utmost endeavours, so I hope you will never be failing in yours to enable me to do it." After which, the commons appointed a committee to enquire into the behaviour of the Dissenters, who reported, "That there were divers Conventicles and other seditious meetings near the parliament, where great numbers of evil-affected persons frequently meet; which they conceived, was not only an affront to the present government, but also of imminent danger to both houses of parliament, and the peace of the kingdom." Upon which, the whole house made this Declaration and Resolution, "That they will adhere to his majesty in the maintenance of the government of the Church and State, as it is now established, against all enemies whatsoever." Shortly after, information was given to the house from the Lord General, "Of the great resort of dangerous and disaffected persons to this town, and of their meetings and endeavours to disturb the public peace; and that he had, and would take care what he could to prevent their attempts." Upon which the commons immediately resolved, "That the thanks of the house be returned to the Lord-General, for his care in preserving the peace of the kingdom." So that the suppressing or restraining of Conventicles was now looked upon not so much a matter of Religion, as of necessity and safety to the government.

Sir S. Bernardiston's Narrative to the House.] As to the point of Privilege, the commons, not having satisfaction in the last session, revived the debate of the Difference between the two Houses, as it stood upon the Case of the East-India Company, and Skinner the merchant; and, understanding that sir Samuel Bernardiston was a particular sufferer by the lords in this case, they examined him in the matter, who, at the bar of the house, gave them this short account: "Mr. Speaker, as soon as the commons, according to his majesty's command, had adjourned themselves on the 8th of May, 1668, I was presently called as a delinquent upon my knees to the bar of the lords house, and demanded, What I had to say for myself why the judgment of that house should not pass upon me, for having a hand in, and being one of the contrivers of a scandalous Libel against that house: to which my reply was, That I knew not myself to be concerned in any scandalous libel; but true it was, I did deliver a Petition to the house of commons, in behalf of the East-India Company by their order, being Deputy-Governor; and I did it out of no other design, than to preserve the Company's interest and estate, according to my oath and duty of my place. Then I was commanded to withdraw, and others were called in: soon after some of the lords came to me in their lobby, and told me, the house was highly incensed against me; that I should presently be called in again, and if I did not then submit myself, and own my fault I must expect the indignation of the house of peers to fall upon me. And being called in again the second time, it was demanded, What further had I to say for myself, before judgment should pass against me. When repeating my former discourse, adding, That I had no design to create any difference between the two houses, but to preserve the Company's estate: yet if I had offended their lordships, I humbly begged their pardon. Being then commanded to withdraw again, I was afterwards called in: and, being upon my knees, sentence was pronounced against me, to pay 300*l.* fine to his majesty, and to lie in custody of the black-rod till the money was paid. And accordingly, sir John Eyton, usher of the black-rod, kept me in his custody till the 10th of Aug. following, when, at 9 at night, he came to me and said, sir Samuel, I am come to discharge you from your imprisonment, and you may go when, and where you please. I then demanded how this unexpected releasement came to pass, and to whom I was beholden for the same. He replied, You are discharged upon honourable terms, but pray ask me no questions, for I must make you no answer: yet if I see you to-morrow, after the house is adjourned, I will tell you more; there is a mystery, but I have sufficient authority for what I do."

Resolutions of the Commons thereupon.] Upon hearing of this, the house fell into a warm debate about some expedients for settling the Difference in point of Privilege and Jurisdiction of the two houses, which could not be ended that night; and after that they resolved to bring in a Bill for that purpose. This appeared to be a matter of too great nicety and difficulty to be effected in a short time. However, after conferences with the house of lords, they came to these Resolutions. "I. That it is an inherent right of every commoner of England to prepare and present Petitions to the house of commons in case of grievance, and the house of commons to receive the same: in evidence whereof, it is one of the first works that is done by the commons, to appoint a grand committee to receive Petitions and Informations of Grievances. II. That it is the undoubted right and privilege of the commons to judge and determine concerning the nature and matter of such Petitions, how far they are fit or unfit to be received; and that in no age they found any person presenting a Grievance by way of Petition to the house of commons, and received by them, that was ever censured by the lords, without complaint by the commons. III. That no court whatsoever hath power to judge or censure any Petition presented to the house of commons, and received by them, unless transmitted from thence, or the matter complained of by them: and that no suitors for justice in any inferior court in law or equity, are therefore punishable criminally, though untrue, or suable by way of action in any other court; but are only subject to a moderate fine or amercement by that court, unless in some cases specially provided by act of parliament, as appeals, or the like. In case men should be punishable in other courts for presenting Petitions to the house of commons, it may deter his majesty's subjects from seeking redress of their grievances, and frustrate the principal end for which parliaments were ordained. IV. Whereas a Petition from the East-India Company was presented to the house by sir Samuel Bernardiston and others, complaining of Grievances therein, which the lords have censured under the notion of a Scandalous Paper or Libel: the said censure, and proceeding of the lords against the said sir Samuel, are contrary to, and a subversion of the rights and privileges of the house of commons, and liberties of the commons of England; and further, no Petition, or any matter depending in the house of commons, can be taken notice of by the lords, without breach of privilege, unless permitted by the house of commons. V. That the continuance upon record of the Judgment given by the lords, and complained of by the commons, in the last session of this parliament, in the case of Tho. Skinner and the East-India Company, is prejudicial to the rights of the commons of England." In conclusion they added this further Allegation, "That the house of peers, as well as all other courts, are in all their judicial proceedings to be guided and governed by law: but if they shall give a wrongful Sentence contrary to law, and the party grieved might not seek redress thereof in full parliament, and for that end repair to the house of commons, (who are part of the legislative power); that either they may interpose with their lordships for the reversal of such Sentence, or prepare a Bill for that purpose, and for the preventing the like Grievances for the time to come; the consequence thereof would plainly be, That their lordships judicature is boundless and above law, and that the party grieved shall be without remedy." Therefore, as a present Remedy, they resolved upon these two following Propositions to be presented to their lordships: "1. That the lords be desired to vacate the Judgment against sir Samuel Bernardiston, given the last session of this present parliament. 2. That the lords be also desired to vacate the Judgment against the East-India Company, given by them the last session of this parliament."

PROCEEDINGS RELATIVE TO THE IMPEACHMENT OF THE EARL OF ORRERY.

Nov. 25. A Petition of Sir Edw. Fitzharris, bart. and Philip Alder, gent. against the earl of Orrery * was read, containing in substance, raising of moneys, by his own authority, upon his majesty's subjects; defrauding the king's subjects of their estates. The money raised was for bribing hungry courtiers to come to his ends, and if the king would not, he had 50,000 swords to compel him.

Mr. *Garroway* moves to have the point of time asserted when these things were done: if the petitioners had concealed it long, then his majesty was in danger. The Petitioners were then called in, and affirmed the words spo e and things done, since the Act of Indemnity.

Colonel *Sandys* moved it to be taken into consideration; and attributed our misfortunes to moneys so disposed of.

Sir *R. Carr* moves that the treasonable words may be read, and the gentlemen of the long robe may give their judgments what they amount unto.

Serj. *Maynard.* The charge is general, treason and misdemeanor. He thinks the words are treason. 25 Edw. 3d, is the measure of treason.

Sir *Fr. Goodrick.* Words make not a treason, but this is by act 25 Edw. 3d.

Mr. *Edw. Seymour.* We have found that a charge of high treason in the house of commons, is a remedy for the gout. Wonders that the words have been called in question, 'reflecting on the duke of Ormond.' This had never been brought in question, if those had been silenced—Would have him summoned; but if he cannot come, would have his charge sent him.

Colonel *Sandys.* Would know who the persons are Seymour mentions.

Sir *R. Howard.* No discourses of well or ill men should come before us, when a person is accused. It is a hard thing these words should have been concealed thus long; no man can make this treason by 25 Edw. 3d.

Lord *Cavendish* takes him down to the Orders. Not proper to launch into any thing that is not in the business before us.

Mr. *Edw. Seymour.* The charge had not been brought against lord Orrery, if one had been brought against the duke of Ormond.

Sir *R. Howard.* The earl of Meath came to acquaint him with his business, which he will tell you more of hereafter—Moves that the business may be prosecuted, and that if lord Orrery cannot come he may be brought in a chaise. What way would you go, pray resolve on presently on 25 Edw. 3d: he cannot

* Third son of the first, commonly called the great, earl of Cork, and equally distinguished as a general, a statesman, and a poet.

be accused; if on 13 Car. II. it lies at their doors that so long have concealed it.

Sir *Tho. Lee.* Common fame has made these two great lords enemies. He hopes, by their falling out, the king and his subjects may be the better for it.

Sir *R. Temple* thinks the words are a misprision of the king's government: words though not treason, may be evidence of treason; if they do design to perpetrate some treason, they are treason: Would have the Petitioners called in, to know whether they have two witnesses to prove these words. By too long silence, they might have time to execute their treason. If you conclude it treason, the person must hear his charge read in his place, and his answer, and then withdraw.

Sir *Job Charlton* cites Pine's case, 'that the king was a fool, and unfit to govern.' The Irish Friar at Lisbon, who said, 'he would come over to kill king James,' was guilty of treason.

Mr. *Swynfin* would be informed how you will proceed, in order to information where he may be tried, the treasonable words being said to be spoken in Ireland. He must first be heard, and witnesses must be examined. The words may be treason, or not treason, according to circumstance: Thinks it a parliamentary way to appoint some short time for examination of witnesses, and then call it what you will, and draw up the charge.

Mr. *Garroway* would not have him committed, but heard in the house: would have the petitioners give security to prosecute, and the member likewise be secured to appear.

Sir *R. Howard.* If they be trucking witnesses, to keep this in the dark so long, they deserve a rebuke, and at least to give security to prosecute. Lord Orrery will undergo any torture rather than the torture of not answering his charge.—On a division it was resolved, that Treasonable Matter was contained in this Charge, 182 to 144.

Sir *Winston Churchill* knew not how we could proceed against lord Orrery, being a privy counsellor. But it was averred he had no Privilege in that case. It was then Resolved, "That lord Orrery be sent for in custody of the serjeant at arms." It was also ordered, That a copy of the Articles against lord Orrery be sent him by the serjeant at arms, and his attendance required, to give his Answer to them; if he be not able to come, then that the serjeant is to leave a keeper with him, to attend him till he is*.

The Earl's Defence.] Dec. 1. The earl of Orrery, in his seat near the bar, answers his Charge. Because of his indisposition of the gout ** sir Robert Howard asked leave that he might sit, which was granted.—The earl began with acknowledging, with all humbleness, the justice and favour of the house, in having the ten Articles sent him. The Articles bring no less than his life and estate, and, what should be more than both, his loyalty, in question; but he has innocence, without which he durst not appear before the house. He should be unworthy to serve his country in this place, should he fly your justice. In some places the Articles are dark, in some places intricate and immethodical. If, by reason of some months sickness, and a spirit wounded with such a charge, he mis-express himself, he hopes he shall be pardoned.—Art. I. He thinks rather a Narrative than a Charge. The Charge says not that those he corresponded with were traitors or rebels. It is no crime to hold correspondence with the militia, for if they had power to do ill, they had power to keep from ill; they were the interest the king took care of. Should he say, 'England lies a bleeding, now London is burning,' these were words to stir up compassion rather than rebellion. They (the petitioners) accuse him of no bad intention in what he did, and no ill consequence followed upon it.—To Art. II. That he gained to his own use great sums of money, to raise up sedition, and told the purchasers, that unless money was raised to feed the hungry courtiers, nothing would be done; and levied 13,750*l.* to obtain his ends by corrupt means, which moneys were converted to his own use:" Answers, It is not his custom to use uncivil language to any, much less to a courtier. The king will find those who exhibited the Articles more apt to rebel than the Irish interest. There were voluntary subscriptions of one penny per acre towards the charge of getting an Act of Settlement. Is it a likely thing that he should put them into rebellion, and not head them; cheat them of their money, and think to have an interest in them? If this Article were true, he was fitter to be sent to Bed-

* During the Debate no member was suffered to go out, without leave asked, and when obtained, was enjoined by the Speaker not to communicate any thing that passed in the House.—"It was the sentiment of a great and dangerous minister, sir Tho. Clifford, that he should be able to do nothing in Ireland, while Orrery was president of Munster; and this is the secret of bringing the impeachment against him into parliament. The earl having had timely notice of the design of his enemies, came over, and took his seat in the English house of commons, but being seized with a violent fit of the gout, that opportunity was taken by his adversaries to bring on his affair, and to get him committed." Love's Memoirs of the earl of Orrery.

** "As the earl of Orrery, being scarce half recovered from his gout, was going up the stairs leading from Westminster-hall to the Court of Requests, one of his friends observing to him that he ascended the steps with great difficulty and pain, 'Yes,' said he 'my feet are weak, but if my heels will serve to carry me up, I promise you my head shall bring me safe down again." Morrice's Memoirs of the earl of Orrery, chap. 6. His lordship prophesied right.

lam than to answer it here: he protests he lost 300*l.* by that business: desires that he who received the money, may certify what he received. It is as ordinary to take subscriptions of this nature, as for the fens. This has been these 9 years, and no complaint made: denies the black list: it is strange that 700*l.* raised voluntarily in 1661, should beget a rebellion in 1663: another penny per acre was raised by Act of Parliament: it is not likely he should refuse what is given him by act of parliament.—To Art. III. Imprisoning of people for bringing Certioraries:' Answers, If any were punished it was for some insolence done, not for bringing certioraries. Denies letters for non-appearance. He has granted many Petitions: denies incroaching upon any man's freehold, unless in forcible detainers. His court of precedency never meddles with it; but they have power to quiet possessions, after 3 years quiet possession. Fitzgerald * was a person who forfeited his estate by rebellion. There was a letter from a high sheriff, directed to the lord president of Munster, and, in his absence, to the vice-president, complaining of Fitzgerald's forcible detaining a castle, and resisting the sheriff's power; defying his power in open words, as if running into rebellion. The lord chief justice of Ireland said to him, 'he was obliged to assist the sheriff, and his forces to be subservient to the sheriff,' and this in a time when we feared invasion from the French, and a strong place, and the best port in Ireland. Never heard complaint against any man, nor ever hindered due prosecution of law.—To Art. IV. The Article before was of protecting English, now of an Irish murderer †, 'that he should get him bailed, and so he escapes.' If the justice, upon his letter, do bail a man not bailable by law, it was his fault; he knows not for what the man was committed.—To Art. V ‡. Has witness to clear this. Sir John Broderick and sir Rd. Osborne will prove the action to be voluntary; that land in his possession, and had set it for 99 years.—To Art. VI §. Denies any trust from either soldiers or adventurers, but as a friend to both, and a privy-counsellor of England and Ireland.—To Art. VII. † Denies any creatures of his own to have taken to farm the King's revenue. The revenue is openly set at the council-board in Ireland: never saw the lord lieutenant, nor any counsellor, refuse the larger offer. Only the Excise beginning in 1663 and ending 1664, it was not valued at above 20,000*l.* But the aldermen of Dublin proffered, if he would take it, they would give 30,000*l.* rent, and if they might take it, they would secure the rent to Lord Kingston and him. The Article mentions not in what kingdom, It is obscure, as if it meant more than it does express. By this they got but 150*l.* a-piece. They had a warrant after a full hearing to set it for 36,000*l.* and they gave 39,000*l.*—To Art. VIII. ‡ Answers, He paid arrears to the army, according to the king's Declaration at Breda: knows not to have done it either to those out of the army, or to such as opposed the king's Restoration: only one gentleman of quality turned out of the army, for being an Anabaptist, a little before the king's Restoration. This was the man that came eightscore miles to discover the plot at Dublin, to whom he gave 100*l.* which he looked upon with contempt, and protested he would never serve any farther, if rewards were offered him: denies the 'employing the Halberdiers that were the guard at the king's murder.' He turned out a nephew of his own, who had married a daughter of one of the king's judges. To Art. IX *. Denies the selling of a foot of land to any Irish rebels: Denies the buying of any lands of any Irish Papist, except 15 acres near Dublin, for which he paid 400*l.* for the convenience of his horses; had the seller of it been judged nocent, he had lost his title: One acre of land in Limerick is valued at eight in Kerry, and his lot happened to be in Kerry, and so his troop after that rate were satisfied in Kerry, according to the claim; but they have lost both their time and money, for want of due claim by the Act.—To Art. X. and last †. This Article, if true, would

* The charge was, 'That he, by a paper-order, dispossessed one Edmund Fitzgerald of a house, and 2000 acres of land; slew one of Fitzgerald's servants, and mortally wounded others, &c.'

† This was one John Mac Davey Mulcahill, who, being committed by the governor of Waterford for treason, murder, &c. was bailed by a justice of peace (as the Article recites) 'at the earl's direction.'

‡ Art. V. This was 'for compelling one Thomas Walsh, of Pilltown, esq. to convey to him lands of inheritance to the yearly value of 600*l.* under pretence of procuring witnesses to prove him guilty of the late rebellion.'

§ Art. VI. This was 'for prejudicing the adventurers and soldiers, to whom the marquis of Antrim's lands were allotted, by granting a lease of a part of them to col. Talbot, who married his sister.'—† Art. VII. This was 'for causing some of his own creatures to take and farm several branches of the revenue, at far lower rates than others had offered.'—‡ Art. VIII. This was 'for converting several sums of his majesty's treasury in Munster to his own use, for ordering payment of arrears for service done for the late usurpers, and for employing some of the guard of halberdiers, who assisted at the late king's murder.'

* Art. IX. This was 'for purchasing lands, before trial, of persons pretending to innocence, and then concealing and withdrawing the evidence against them: and for procuring lands to be assigned to himself and his troop, for service done to the usurped powers.'

† Art. X. This was 'for committing several breaches of trust to his majesty, and tempting the officers of the Treasury by bribes; and evidencing a great ambition and scorn to his majesty's power, by threatening, 'that if his

strike him dumb with its weight. The charge is general, and he denies it. All these look rather like aspersions than accusations, and so this general Article he must answer generally, No. He, being one of the council, advises one way for the farming of the king's rents; another, another way. He had nothing to do with what the king would do in mercy; they are only to do what law enjoins them. It is not crime, but difference of opinion, he is charged with. The great point is of 'compelling the king with 50,000 swords;' had it entered into his heart, he durst not have appeared here; and he wishes those 50,000 swords in his heart, if he said the words: hopes that his judges will consider the accusers, and the accused. At least it is not a probable thing he should utter such words in 1659; they had then such tumblings and tossings as were in England. He had then sent a letter to his brother, lord Shannon, then with the king, viz. 'That if your majesty will be pleased to transport yourself into Ireland, to your protestant subjects, we will receive you, and do our best to restore you to the rest of your dominions.' This was as early as any. If doubted, the king will clear it. If this be true, and whilst uncompelled by necessity, and out of choice and duty, is it likely that when the king was actually restored he should say these words? Fitter for Bedlam, if ever he said them, than to be here, and is it likely that in six or seven years he should put nothing in action? 50,000 swords must surely be meant English. He has done several services since the words, but no overt act since the saying them. That a man, at the head of an army seven years, should not do some overt act, is strange. That these words should lie seven years concealed is a misprison of treason. Not accused of any overt act, since only men say it. What he can say in point of law will be ridiculous; yet though the words that were asserted, the judges declared formerly not treason, yet he trusts more in the judgment of the house. 'Concealing his majesty's affairs, and advancing his private fortune,' are generals: Humbly desires no more to be done for him than your justice will put you upon; and so beseeches God to direct the house, and withdraws*.

'majesty did not confirm the estates of a party, 'at that time headed by the said earl, that his 'majesty should be compelled to do it with '50,000 swords;' and for exercising high oppressions and extortions; and also for giving his maj. false informations and suggestions."

* "Lord Orrery defended himself so well, that this Charge produced no effect, except opening the eyes of such of his old friends as had differed from him, and who now saw, with how small reason they had taken this step, and how far he was from endeavouring to return it, restraining himself, on the contrary, within the strict bounds of a direct defence, as the answers to the charge show." Biogr. Brit.

The Accusation left to be prosecuted at Law.] Sir *Wm. Lewis* moved to have the Accusation remitted to the King's Bench.

Sir *Tho. Clifford.* Would not have the sword of this house of Impeachments be blunted upon offences of this nature: stars, in their courses do not amaze us; but comets give us apprehensions. Would have impeachments of this nature upon great and considerable occasions.

Serj. *Maynard,* considering the time, and the thing, if ever it was, and the petitioners must go into Ireland for their witnesses, and this noble lord's reputation suffer in the mean time, would have it referred to the law. One of the king's council once under the gallery, he remembers, desired, in another case, this might be the question, If any man in his conscience thinks this to be treason, let him say, Aye.

Mr. Solicitor *Finch.* There is little foundation in lord Orrery's Answer made, to build upon. We may say by his Answer, that the greatest part is not probable, and some things impossible to be true. He affirms words may be treason, or not, according to circumstance; and in a case of blood infinitely to be considered before acted—To say, 'I will kill the king,' ever was treason. By a statute of Hen. 8. it was felony to scatter papers that such and such a man has spoken treason. The words to be treason must be within such a time; for the words should be after the Settlement in Ireland; and what need 'compelling,' when the thing is done, and all the acts concomitant and subsequent have been for quiet and settlement? Let every man lay his hand upon his heart. It is an accusation to this house, and from this house; will you imprison upon out-doors accusation? You may have the house, at this rate, garbled when you please. Would have the accusations transmitted to the lord lieutenant in Ireland, where the offences charged were done, and so represent it to the king.

The question being propounded, That a day be appointed for the accusers to produce witnesses to make good the Charge, the previous question for putting it was carried, 116 to 111. After which the main question passed in the negative, 121 to 118. It was then resolved, "That this accusation against the earl of Orrery be left to be prosecuted at law."

Dec. 10. Sir *Robert Carr,* moves that witnesses may be sent for by order, there being, he hears, strict proceedings against persons who come over out of Ireland, without leave, by loss of command: would not have the business lie at our doors.

Col. *Sandys.* The lord lieutenant of Ireland is so strict upon our members, that, if they come over to do their duty here, others must be put into their commands. Moves that some directions may be given to prosecute lord Orrery; for his being quit of his Charge will be the greatest honour that ever came to him.

Mr. *Wild* said, that when sir John Morley was accused of high treason, he was to answer it at the bar, and it was referred to the law, but no particular direction given in it.

Sir *Tho. Meres.* The lawyers, unâ voce, said, That the charge was Treason; but that question was not in lord Orrery, who was used very civilly; but would not have us lose our justice in our civility.

Col. *Birch,* would not have the thing reached into but in a straight line.—It was then resolved to address the king, that Witnesses may have liberty to come over from Ireland*.

The Parliament prorogued.] Dec. 11. The king, by commission, suddenly put a stop to all proceedings, by proroguing both houses to the 14th of Feb. next. Thus ended the eighth Session of the Second Parliament, without passing one Act, although a Supply of 400,000*l.* had been voted for his maj.'s special occasions.

NINTH SESSION OF THE SECOND PARLIAMENT.

The King's Speech on opening the Session.] Feb. 14, 1669-70. This day the parliament met again, when his majesty, having been attended to the house with the additional pomp of his new guards,† made the following speech from the throne:

"My Lords and Gentlemen; I sent forth my proclamation, that there might be a good appearance at this meeting; having most confidence in full houses, where the well-being of the Church, and all other interests of the crown and nation, are best secured. When we met last, I asked you a Supply; and I ask it now again with greater instance. The uneasiness and straightness of my affairs cannot continue without very ill effects to the whole kingdom. Consider this seriously and speedily. It is yours and the kingdom's interest, as well as mine; and the ill consequence of a want of an effectual Supply must not lie at my door: and that no misapprehensions or mistakes touching the expences of the last war may remain with you, I think fit to let you know, that I have fully informed myself in that matter; and do affirm to you, that no part of those Monies that you gave me for that war have been diverted to other uses; but, on the contrary, besides all those Supplies, a very great sum hath been raised out of my standing revenue and credit, and a very great debt contracted; and all for the war.—One thing I must earnestly recommend to the prudence of both houses: that you will not suffer any occasion of Difference between yourselves to be revived, since nothing but the unity of your minds and counsels can make this meeting happy, either to me or to the nation.—I did recommend to you, at our last meeting, the Union of the two kingdoms, and I did the same to my parliament in Scotland: they have made a great step towards it, and I do again seriously recommend that matter to you. I have directed my lord keeper to speak more at large to you."

The Lord Keeper Bridgman's Speech.] Then the Lord Keeper spake as followeth:

"My lords; and you knights, citizens, and burgesses of the house of commons; At your last meeting, his majesty did acquaint you with the great occasions he had for a Supply; and that he had forborn to ask it sooner, more in consideration of giving some time for the ease of the people, after the burthen of the war, than that the condition of his affairs could so long have wanted it: and his majesty hath commanded me now to speak more fully and plainly upon this subject.—His majesty hath not only by his ministers, but in his own royal person, examined the Accounts touching the Expences of the last War; and hath thought himself concerned to let you know, that all the Supplies which you gave him for the war have been by him applied to the war, and no part of them to any other uses: nay, so far from it, that if the preparations towards the war shall be taken to be for the use of the war, as they must be, a great part of his own revenue, to many hundred thousands of pounds, hath been employed also, and swallowed up in the charges of the war, and what did necessarily relate to it: to which may be added, the great debts contracted by his majesty in the war, and the great charge in the repairs of the hulls of his ships, and putting his navy into such a condition as it was before.—Besides his majesty thinks it ought to be considered, that when the Charges of the War were at the highest, the inevitable effects of it, and those other calamities which it pleased God (at that

---

* "Though the managers of this affair had interest enough to procure a vote for bringing over witnesses, yet they had more wit than to trust the house, or his lordship, with the examination of those witnesses, and so the matter fell." Biogr. Brit.

"Thus ended this affair. No witnesses ever came, no prosecution was caried on at law, nor was any farther attempt ever made against lord Orrery. Had he continued still president of Munster, it is more than probable, that the name of sir Edw. Fitzharris and master Philip Alder had not been entered, on any occasion, in the Journals of parliament. But when the lion has lost his strength, the wild asses, and all the unclean animals of the wood, trot forth from their lurking-places, and cowardly spurn at him." Preface to the Earl of Orrery's State Papers, published by his great grandson.

† "On the 14th of Feb. the king, not in the guise of difficulty and distress, but with unusual pomp and state, being attended to the house by his new guards (which is the first instance we meet with in history, of the sovereign's entering upon the exercise of his legislative power, under the awe and influence of the sword) opened the session with a Speech, which had more the air of the master, than the servant of the Commonwealth. The lord keeper bore his under-part as usual: but though he spoke much longer, added nothing to the purpose, except by asserting, "That the loss which the king had sustained in the Customs, Excise, and Hearth-money, by the war, plague, and fire, amounted to 600,000*l.*" Ralph.

time) to bring upon us, did make so great a diminution in his Revenues, that (besides all other accidents and disadvantages) the loss that he sustained in three branches of his Revenues, in his Customs, Excise, and Hearth-money, by reason of the war, the plague, and the fire, did amount to little less than 600,000*l.* Thus you see, that though your Supplies have been great, yet the charges occasioned by the war, and the calamities which accompanied it, have been greater; and that the Debt which is left upon his majesty, and which he complains of, hath been contracted by the war, and not by the diversion of the monies designed for it.—His majesty hath commanded me to say one thing more to you upon this subject: that he did not enter into this war upon any private inclination or appetite of his own. The first step he made towards it did arise from your advice and the promises of your assistance; but if the charges and accidents of the war have outgone all your Supplies, and left him under the burthen of this Debt, he thinks that, as well the justice to your promise, as the duty and loyalty you have always shewed him, will oblige you to relieve him from it; and the rather, when you shall seriously consider, how uneasy this burthen must be to him, and what ill consequence the continuance under it must draw upon all his affairs. In which particular, you, and every person you represent in this nation, will be concerned as well as himself.—His maj. doth therefore command me, in his name, to desire you once more, and to conjure you, by that constant duty and loyalty which you have always expressed to him, and by all the concernment you have for the support of the honour and safety of his government, to provide such a Supply for him at this time as may bear proportion to the pressing occasions that he hath, and to the state of his affairs at home and abroad; and so speedily and so effectually, as may answer the ends for which he hath desired it.—His majesty hath further commanded me to put you in mind of what was at your last meeting proposed to you concerning an Union between the two kingdoms; and to let you know, that the parliament of Scotland hath since declared to his majesty, that such commissioners as his majesty shall name shall be authorised on their part to treat with commissioners for this kingdom upon the grounds and conditions of the Union. His majesty therefore thought fit now again to recommend it to you, to take that matter effectually into your consideration."

The King's Proposal to both Houses, in the Case of Skinner.] Feb. 22. During this short session, which lasted but about seven weeks, four things were chiefly in debate and agitation, namely the unhappy Difference between the two houses, the Prosecution of the Dissenters, the Union of the two kingdoms, and the Supplies for his majesty's service. The first being revived to such a degree as might hazard the success of the last, the king himself thought fit to interpose, and to make a Proposition of an expedient; which he did to both houses summoned to Whitehall, in the following short Speech:

"My Lords and Gentlemen; I did very earnestly recommend to you the other day, that you would not suffer any Differences between yourselves to be revived; and I think it of so great importance, that I have sent for you again upon the same subject. I remember very well, that the Case of Skinner was first sent by me to the lords. I have therefore thought myself concerned to offer to you what I judge the best and safest way to put an end to the Differences: I will myself give present Order to raze all Records and Entries of this matter in the Council Books, and in the Exchequer, and to desire you to do the like in both houses, that no memory may remain of this Dispute between you; and then I hope all future apprehensions will be secured."

This had such an effect upon the commons who thought themselves the only persons aggrieved, that they immediately resolved, 'That in obedience to his majesty's command in his speech, a razure or vacate be made in the Journal of the house of all the matters therein contained, relating to the business of the East India Company and Skinner.' Which was not only done, but they further resolved, 'That the humble Thanks of this house be returned to his majesty, in the name of this house, and of all the commons of England, for his majesty's gracious Speech, and favour therein expressed to this house, and the commons of England.'*

Bill for suppressing Conventicles.] March 2. The bill for suppressing and preventing Conventicles † was read the second time.

* "At coming down from the king's presence, a pretty ridiculous thing! (says Marvel) sir James Clifford carried Speaker and Mace, and all members there, into the king's cellar to drink his health."

† Marvell calls this Act 'the price of money,' adding, 'the king told some eminent citizens, who applied to him against it, 'That they must address themselves to the houses; that he must not disoblige his friends; and if it had been in the power of the lords, he had gone without money.' The substance of this act was, that if any persons, upwards of sixteen, should be present at any Assembly, Conventicle, or Meeting, under colour or pretence of any exercise of religion, in any other manner than according to the liturgy and practice of the church of England, where there were five persons, or more, besides those of the said household; in such cases, the offenders were to pay 5*s.* for the first offence, and 10*s.* for the second; and the preachers and teachers in any such meetings were to forfeit 20*l.* for the first, and 40*l.* for the second offence. And, lastly, those who knowingly suffered any such Conventicle in their houses, barns, yards, &c. were likewise to forfeit 20*l.*

Mr. *Waller.* This bill looks more like a levying of money than a punishment; if one be poor, another must pay it. It may be of great scandal and hindrance to the Church, to make it more penal than that of the papists. Here is a general distrust of the whole nation, in effect; jealousy upon every officer, from the highest to the lowest. The people have a kindness for persecuted people, ever since Hen. 8. and queen Mary. These people are like children's tops; whip them, and they stand up, let them alone and they fall. The lords would not trust trial per pares with the judges. In this bill one justice of peace weighs down all. This is a strange requital for the trust the people have put in us. Should the people be to trust again, it is not likely it should be us, they being not tried by themselves as the papists are. The people naturally have a distrust of those that distrust them. The people of Rome, in their best times, would not be confined to chuse Patricians, but would chuse Plebeians, if they pleased, for officers. When Clodius saw it conduce to his ends to get the Tribuneship (of which he was incapable, because a Patrician) he suffered himself to be adopted. But against this adoption, two exceptions were found; one that he was adopted by a man of a lower rank, a Plebeian, which was unnatural, and by a younger man than himself, which took away the reputation of a father. But the people never did chuse any; no more will the people ever quit any of these men. When people are trusted, they chuse well; when not, it is ever ill; therefore let these men have the same trial as the papists have.

Sir *Tho. Meres.* The gentleman would have the same penalty upon the conventiclers as upon the papists, which is just none at all.

Sir *John Birkenhead.* Anciently Juries never had any thing to do with Conventicles; but the ecclesiastical power is so enervated, that it can do nothing without the secular power. Edw. I. put out five Proclamations against such Conventicles as are with us now.

Sir *Ch. Wheeler.* Persecution and punishment are different; the pagans and heathens persecute Christians. No man is compelled to come to Church. This bill is rather a toleration.

Mr. *Henry Coventry.* The rules of our law are drawn from the civil law, as the more ancient. A man in a riot, and one killed, all are principals. In the militia, men are punished without jury; challenges any man to show what government ever gave leave to all meetings. In effect, it is a government without religion at all.

Sir *R. Temple.* This promiscuous toleration is more hurtful to the Church than a general one. The French king has reduced his from a mountain to a mole-hill, by allowing them set and limited places for the exercise of religion.

Col. *Birch.* Would have it considered whether it be your interest, or not, to pass this bill. A man that has no preaching near him, will take it where he can. You want only this bill to make you more miserable than you are, in wanting people. Is it reasonable to punish men when they must go four or five miles for a sermon? This driving it into corners, looks more like toleration, than publickly allowing them churches. The trading part of England is as the soul to the body. To whip them, and not to be able to tell them why you do so, is unreasonable, they having no churches in many places to go to.

Sir *Rob. Howard.* A general toleration is a spot in any government. Queen Elizabeth's greatest power was her indulgence; though the Protestants broke faith with her at Newhaven, yet she kept up all by indulgence. All do conclude that the king of Spain's decay was the expulsion of the Moors by the inquisition, and the duke of Alva in Flanders. The French and Dutch Churches, here, are Conventicles by the king's power; and is it not strange that the king should have this power over strangers, and not on his own subjects? Would have a short act to punish them that the king does not indulge, according to his own wisdom. He thinks the king uses every thing well, and would have him given this.—The Bill was ordered to be committed.

March 8. The commons resolved, "That the Thanks of this house be returned to his majesty, for his care in giving Order to bring the Offenders to justice; and that his majesty would be pleased to consider the danger of Conventicles in and near London and Westminster, from the nature of those further offenders, and to give Order for the speedy suppressing them: and, likewise, that his majesty would give Order to put the laws in execution against Popish Recusants; and that leave be given to bring in a Bill for the more easy and speedy Conviction of Popish Recusants." In this Vote the lords unanimously joined; and accordingly, on the 11th of March, they attended the king in the Banquetting-House with the said Vote and Desire, who was pleased to declare, "That effectual course should be taken in both cases."

Several Bills being now got ready, his majesty came to the house of peers; and after passing the said Bills his majesty declared that it was his pleasure that the parliament should be only adjourned, and that to the 24th of October.

March 28. The commons entered into the consideration of the lords Amendments, Provisos, and Clauses, to be added to the Bill for suppressing Conventicles.—First Proviso, "That no peer of the realm shall have his house searched, but by immediate warrant from his majesty, under his sign manual, or in the presence of the lord lieutenant of the county."—Second Proviso. "Provided always, and be it farther enacted, by the authority aforesaid, that neither this act, nor any thing therein contained, shall extend to invalidate or avoid his majesty's Supremacy in ecclesiastical affairs, [or to destroy any of his majesty's rights, powers, or prerogatives, belonging to the imperial crown of this realm, or at any time exercised or enjoyed by himself, or any of his majesty's royal predecessors, kings or queens of England]; but that his majesty, his heirs and successors, may, from time to time, and at all times hereafter, exercise and enjoy all such powers and authorities aforesaid, as fully and as amply as himself, or any of his predecessors, have or might have done the same; any thing in this act, [or any other law, statute, or usage to the contrary] notwithstanding.*—The words in brackets were rejected by the commons, 122 to 68.

The King attends the Debates on Lord Roos's Bill.] As long, says Mr. Ralph, as the king was in the hands of Buckingham, and the rest of his motly cabal, he was upon ill terms with his brother; and made no difficulty to hearken to projects, to disappoint him of the Succession. Lauderdale or Buckingham, it is uncertain which, one while recommended the legitimating of the duke of Monmouth; and then a divorce; that his majesty might have unquestionable heirs of his own. The last of these projects seems to have been relished most; and, in order to reconcile the public to it, the Bill which lord Roos had brought in against his wife, for adultery, was forwarded by the king, with as much zeal as if the case was his own: the duke, on the other hand, opposed it as violently, having all the Popish lords, and all the bishops except Cosins, Reynolds, and Wilkins, on his side. When it was first read, the debate lasted till 10 o'clock at night: when a question for a second reading being put, it appeared, there were 42 sitting members and 6 proxies against it, and 41 sitting members and 15 proxies for it. Marvell affirms, that lord Arlington had a power in his pocket to annul the Proxies, if there had been a necessity for it. The duke and his party, however, entered their Protests.—On the second reading it was carried for a committee, by a round dozen. The king, afterwards, by the advice of Lauderdale, attended the debates in person, to the great surprize of the house, and dismay of the duke of York, who could not conceal his sense of it. Having seated himself on the throne, he told them it was a privilege he had from his ancestors, to be present at their deliberations; and, therefore, directed to proceed and be covered. This, at some periods, would have been thought a flagrant breach of privilege, as tending to overawe the house, but now it was interpreted into an honour; and the lords with White Staves were ordered to wait upon him with the thanks of the house for it. This kind reception induced him to make his attendance there his daily practice; and he declared, 'it was better than going to a Play.'—But though the Bill was finally carried by a few voices, and the king had said publicly, That he knew no reason why a woman should not be as well divorced for barrenness, as a man for impotency, he made no use of the precedent. Bishop Burnet, indeed, says, 'That Mr. Baptist May, of the privy purse, had told him, that a day was appointed for making the motion in the house of commons, that the king had engaged himself far in the laying of the thing, and in managing those who were to undertake the debates. But then we are assured, by the same authority, that his majesty had given directions to the said Mr. May, to cause that matter to be let alone, for it would not do.

The Speaker's Speech to the King at the Adjournment.] April 11. This day, the king came to the house of peers, in order to pass the several bills, and to make an adjournment: at which time the commons being sent for, their Speaker, in presenting the Bills, delivered himself thus:

"May it please your most excellent majesty; At the opening of this session of parliament, your majesty was pleased to speak to your two houses, and recommended three things especially to us; Unity amongst ourselves, the Union of your majesty's two kingdoms of England and Scotland, and the Supply of your majesty's present and urgent occasions: in obedience to your majesty's commands, we have industriously applied ourselves to the consideration of these matters. By the blessing of God, all Differences are buried in oblivion. Your majesty's happy Expedient hath, like a strong gale of wind, blown up the rolling sands, and filled up all impressions; Vestigia nulla retrorsum. And as your people will universally enjoy the fruit of this happy Union, so our united prayers to God shall be, that your majesty may be crowned with the promised blessing, 'beati pacifici.' In order to the Union of your majesty's two kingdoms, both your houses of parliament have humbly besought your majesty to name commissioners for this your kingdom of England; and we have prepared a Bill to authorise them to treat with commissioners to be appointed for your kingdom of Scotland, upon such grounds as shall be thought conducing to that end, and to report them to your majesty, and to both houses of parliament of this your kingdom of England, reserving always to your maj. and the two houses of parliament, the entire consideration of the whole, and the allowing or disallowing thereof, or any part thereof, as they shall think fit. We have also considered of a Supply for your majesty's occasions: and I am commanded, by the knights, citizens, and burgesses of the house of commons, to present your maj.

* "In this Session," says Mr. Marvell, in his Letters, "the Lords sent us down a Proviso for the king, that would have restored him to all civil and ecclesiastical prerogatives, which his ancestors had enjoyed at any time since the conquest. There never was so compendious a piece of absolute, universal tyranny. But the commons made them ashamed of it, and retrenched it." He adds notwithstanding, "The Parliament was never so embarrassed beyond recovery. *We are all venal cowards, except some few.*"

with this bill whereby we have given to your majesty an Imposition upon all Wines and Vinegar imported, after the rate of 8*l.* per tun for all French wines and vinegar, and 12*l.* per tun for all other wines; and have granted this unto your majesty for eight years, to commence from Midsummer next. And I am further commanded to acquaint your majesty, that we apprehended the Revenue arising by the power of granting Wine Licences, settled upon his r. h: by act of parliament, hath been prejudiced by the last imposition upon wines, and will be much more impaired by this present imposition: we therefore added the last year to this bill of Supply with this Vote, 'That your maj. be humbly desired therewith to recompence h. r. h. the duke of York for the damage he hath received, and shall receive, in his revenue of Wine Licences, by this and the last imposition.' Having thus in the first place with all dutifulness obeyed your majesty's commands, we held it necessary to remember those that sent us hither, and to present unto your maj. some Bills that will be of public use for all the people of this nation. There is, first, a Bill for the preventing of seditious Conventicles, whereby no man is hindered the use of his own judgment in the exercise of religion, by himself or in his own family, or in the presence of four strangers: but, because the peace of the nation may be endangered by more populous meetings, contrary to the liturgy and practice of the church of England, we have imposed a penalty of 5s. for the first offence, and 10s. for the second and every other offence, upon all such offenders, to be levied by distress and sale of the offender's goods. We are informed, that your maj. suffers much by the stealing and embezzling of your ordnance, ammunition, sail cloths, and stores; and likewise your good people are much damnified by a wicked sort of people, who make it their practice, in the night time, to steal woollen cloths and stuffs from off the racks: and they are much encouraged in this their wickedness, by reason they have their clergy: We have therefore prepared a Bill for the taking away the Benefit of Clergy, upon the conviction of all such offenders. We have likewise prepared an additional Bill for the rebuilding the city of London, wherein we have revived the judicatory of your majesty's 12 Judges, empowering them to hear and determine the remainder of causes and controversies, which have not already received a settlement by them; we have also made provision for the widening of many more streets than were mentioned in the former act, and to enable the lord mayor and aldermen of the city of London to give satisfaction to those whose grounds shall be taken from them; and also for laying the foundation at least of the famous Cathedral of St. Paul, and towards the rebuilding of 51 parish churches, we have added an imposition of two shillings for every chaldron of coals that shall be brought into the port of London for the space of 17 years yet to come. 'We have likewise prepared a bill for the ascertaining the measures of corn and salt, and provided that one measure shall be used in all the market towns of this kingdom. We have found great inconveniencies by the want of due repairing the Highways of this kingdom; and have therefore taken care for time to come, both to amend them, and to prevent the spoiling of them again, by carrying excessive loads, and drawing them with extraordinary number of horses and other cattle.—Experience tells us, when the consumption of foreign commodities exceeds the use and exportation of our native commodities, the nation must insensibly grow poor, and our treasure will be exhausted: we have therefore prepared a Bill for the Encouragement of Tillage, by permitting the exporting of corn; and also for the encouragement of other sorts of good husbandry, by exporting of horses, swine, and other cattle, and of butter and cheese; and have made them all free merchandize, paying certain duties to your majesty upon the exportation.—Having given your majesty this account of our proceedings since our last meeting in this our short, but happy, session; it is evident we have not mispent our time: but, with the good servant in the gospel, have gained many talents, so that we may with comfort and satisfaction return to our houses; and we hope we shall carry our masters blessing with us."

The King's Speech at the Adjournment.] After giving the royal assent to the several Bills, his majesty made a short Speech, to this effect:

"My Lords and Gentlemen; I am unwilling to let you go away without telling you, that I am very well satisfied with the success of this meeting, and that you have so well complied with my desires, both in the correspondence between the two houses, and in the progress you have made towards an Union between the two kingdoms. I heartily thank you for the Supply you have given me; and I assure you I will make it go as far I can towards the satisfying of my debts. And because you have been long from home, I am content you adjourn yourselves till the 24th of Oct. next."—The Lord Keeper accordingly declared the parliament to be adjourned to the 24th day of October.

Principal Occurrences during the Recess—Character of the CABAL*—Secret Alliance with France.*] The following interesting account of the leading Occurrences that took place during the Recess, we shall give in the words of Mr. Hume: "We now come to a period, when the king's counsels, which had hitherto, in the main, been good, though negligent and fluctuating, became, during sometime, remarkably bad, or even criminal; and breeding incurable jealousies in all men, were followed by such consequences as had almost terminated in the ruin both of prince and people. Happily, the same negligence still attended him; and, as it had lessened the influence of the good, it also diminished the effect of the bad measures, which he embraced.—It was remarked, that the Committee of Council, established for foreign affairs, was entirely changed; and that prince Rupert, the duke of Ormond, secretary Trevor, and lord keeper Bridgman, men in whose honour the nation had great confidence, were never called to any deliberations. The whole secret was intrusted to five persons, Clifford, Ashley, Buckingham, Arlington, and Lauderdale. These men were known by the appellation of the CABAL, a word which the initial letters of their names happened to compose. Never was there a more dangerous ministry in England, nor one more noted for pernicious counsels.—Lord Ashley, soon after known by the name of earl of Shaftesbury, was one of the most remarkable characters of the age, and the chief spring of all the succeeding movements. During his early youth, he had engaged in the late king's party; but being disgusted with some measures of prince Maurice, he soon deserted to the parliament. He insinuated himself into the confidence of Cromwell; and as he had great influence with the Presbyterians, he was serviceable in supporting, with his party, the authority of that usurper. He employed the same credit in promoting the restoration; and on that account both deserved and acquired favour with the king. In all his changes, he still maintained the character of never betraying those friends whom he deserted; and which ever party he joined, his great capacity and singular talents soon gained him their confidence, and enabled him to take the lead among them. No station could satisfy his ambition, no fatigues were insuperable to his industry. Well acquainted with the blind attachment of faction, he surmounted all sense of shame: and relying on the subtilty of his contrivances, he was not startled with enterprises the most hazardous and most criminal. His talents, both of public speaking and private insinuation, shone out in an eminent degree; and amidst all his furious passions, he possessed a sound judgment of business, and still more of men. Though fitted by nature for beginning and pushing the greatest undertakings, he was never able to conduct any to a happy period; and his eminent abilities, by reason of his insatiable desires, were equally dangerous to himself, to the prince, and to the people.—The duke of Buckingham possessed all the advantages, which a graceful person, a high rank, a splendid fortune, and a lively wit could bestow; but by his wild conduct, unrestrained either by prudence or principle, he found means to render himself in the end odious and even insignificant. The least interest could make him abandon his honour; the smallest pleasure could seduce him from his interest; the most frivolous caprice was sufficient to counter-balance his pleasure. By his want of secrecy and constancy, he destroyed his character in public life; by his contempt of order and œconomy, he dissipated his private fortune; by riot and debauchery, he ruined his health; and he remained at last as incapable of doing hurt, as he had ever been little desirous of doing good, to mankind.—The earl, soon after created duke of Lauderdale, was not defective in natural, and still less in acquired, talents: but neither was his address graceful, nor his understanding just. His principles, or more properly speaking his prejudices, were obstinate, but unable to restrain his ambition: his ambition was still less dangerous than the tyranny and violence of his temper. An implacable enemy, but a lukewarm friend; insolent to his inferiors, but abject to his superiors; though in his whole character and deportment, he was almost diametrically opposite to the king, he had the fortune, beyond any other minister, to maintain, during the greater part of his reign, an ascendant over him.—The talents of parliamentary eloquence and intrigue had raised sir Tho. Clifford; and his daring impetuous spirit gave him weight in the king's councils. Of the whole Cabal, Arlington was the least dangerous, either by his vices or his talents. His judgment was sound, though his capacity was but moderate; and his intentions were good, though he wanted courage and integrity to persevere in them. Together with Temple and Bridgeman, he had been a great promoter of the triple league; but he threw himself, with equal alacrity, into opposite measures, when he found them agreeable to his master. Clifford and he were secretly catholics: Shaftesbury, though addicted to astrology, was reckoned a deist: Buckingham had too little reflection to embrace any steady principles: Lauderdale had long been a bigoted and furious presbyterian; and the opinions of that sect still kept possession of his mind, how little soever they appeared in his conduct.—The dark counsels of the Cabal, though from the first they gave anxiety to all men of reflection, were not thoroughly known but by the event. Such seem to have been the views which they, in concurrence with some catholic courtiers, who had the ear of their sovereign, suggested to the king and the duke, and which these princes too greedily embraced. They said, that the parliament, though the spirit of party, for the present, attached them to the crown, were still more attached to those powers and privileges which their predecessors had usurped from the sovereign: that after the first flow of kindness was spent, they had discovered evident symptoms of discontent; and would be sure to turn against the king all the authority which they yet retained, and still more those pretensions which it was easy for them in a moment to revive: that they not only kept the king in dependence by means of his precarious revenue, but had never discovered a suitable generosity, even in those temporary supplies which they granted him: that it was high time for the prince to rouse himself from his lethargy, and to recover that authority which his predecessors, during so many ages, had peaceably enjoyed: that the great error or misfortune of his father was the not having formed any close connexion with foreign princes, who, on the breaking out of the rebellion, might have found their interest in supporting him: that the present alliances, being entered into with so many weaker potentates, who themselves stood in need of the king's protection, could never serve to maintain, much less augment, the royal authority: that the French monarch alone, so generous a prince, and by blood so nearly allied to the king, would be found both able and willing, if gratified in his ambition, to defend the common cause of kings against usurping subjects: that a war, undertaken against Holland by the united force of two such mighty potentates, would prove an easy enterprise, and would serve all the purposes which were aimed at: that, under pretence of that war, it would not be difficult to levy a military force, without which, during the prevalence of republican principles among his subjects, the king would vainly expect to defend his prerogative: that his naval power might be maintained, partly by the supplies, which, on other pretences, would previously be obtained from parliament; partly by subsidies from France; partly by captures, which might easily be made on that opulent republic: that in such a situation, attempts to recover the lost authority of the crown would be attended with success; nor would any malcontents dare to resist a prince, fortified by so powerful an alliance; or if they did, they would only draw more certain ruin on themselves and on their cause: and that, by subduing the states, a great step would be made towards a reformation of the government; since it was apparent, that that republic, by its fame and grandeur, fortified, in his factious subjects, their attachment to what they vainly termed their civil and religious liberties.—These suggestions happened fatally to concur with all the inclinations and prejudices of the king; his desire of more extensive authority, his propensity to the catholic religion, his avidity for money. He seems likewise, from the very beginning of his reign, to have entertained great jealousy of his own subjects, and, on that account, a desire of fortifying himself by an intimate alliance with France. So early as 1664, he had offered the French monarch to allow him, without opposition, to conquer Flanders, provided that prince would engage to furnish him with ten thousand infantry, and a suitable number of cavalry, in case of any rebellion in England. As no dangerous symptom at that time appeared, we are left to conjecture, from this incident, what opinion Charles had conceived of the factious disposition of his people.—Even during the time when the triple alliance was the most zealously cultivated, the king never seems to have been entirely cordial in those salutary measures, but still to have cast a longing eye towards the French alliance. Clifford, who had much of his confidence, said imprudently. 'Notwithstanding all this joy, we must have a second war with Holland.' The accession of the emperor to that alliance had been refused by England on frivolous pretences. And many unfriendly Cavils were raised against the states with regard to Surinam and the conduct of the East-India Company. But about April 1669, the strongest symptoms appeared of those fatal measures, which were afterwards more openly pursued.—De Wit, at that time, came to Temple, and told him, that he paid him a visit as a friend, not as a minister. The occasion was, to acquaint him with a conversation which he had lately had with Puffendorf the Swedish agent, who had passed by the Hague in the way from Paris to his own country. The French ministers, Puffendorf said, had taken much pains to persuade him, that the Swedes would very ill find their account in those measures which they had lately embraced: that Spain would fail them in all her promises of subsidies; nor would Holland alone be able to support them: that England would certainly fail them, and had already adopted counsels directly opposite to those which by the Triple League she had bound herself to pursue: and that the resolution was not the less fixed and certain, because the secret was as yet communicated to very few, either in the French or English court. When Puffendorf seemed incredulous, Turenne showed him a letter from Colbert de Crossy, the French minister at London; in which, after mentioning the success of his negociations, and the favourable disposition of the chief ministers there, he added. 'And I have at last made them sensible of the full extent of his majesty's bounty.' From this incident it appears, that the infamous practice of selling themselves to foreign princes, a practice which, notwithstanding the malignity of the vulgar, is certainly rare among men in high office, had not been scrupled by Charles's ministers, who even obtained their master's consent to this dishonourable corruption.—But while all men of penetration, both abroad and at home, were alarmed with these incidents, the visit which the king received from his sister, the dutchess of Orleans, was the foundation of still stronger suspicions. Lewis, knowing the address and insinuation of that amiable princess, and the great influence which she had gained over her brother, had engaged her to employ all her good offices, in order to detach Charles from the Triple League, which, he knew, had fixed such unsurmountable barriers to his ambition; and he now sent her to put the last hand to the plan of their conjunct operations. That he might the better covert his negociation, he pretended to visit his frontiers, particularly the great works which he had undertaken at Dunkirk; and he carried the queen and the whole court along with him. While he remained on the opposite shore, the dutchess of Orleans went over to England (16th May;) and Charles met her at Dover, where they passed ten days together in great mirth and festivity. By her artifices and caresses, she prevailed on Charles to relinquish the most settled maxims of honour and policy, and to finish his engagements with Lewis for the destruction of Holland; as well as for the subsequent change of religion in England.—But Lewis well knew Charles's character, and the usual fluctuation of his counsels. In order to fix him in the French interests, he resolved to bind him by the ties of pleasure, the only ones which with him were irresistible; and he made him a present of a French mistress, by whose means he hoped, for the future, to govern him. The duchess of Orleans brought with her a young lady of the name of Querouaille, whom the king carried to London, and soon after created dutchess of Portsmouth. He was extremely attached to her during the whole course of his life; and she proved a great means of supporting his connexions with her native country. The satisfaction which Charles reaped from his new alliance, received a great check by the death of his sister, and still more by those melancholy circumstances which attended it. Her death was sudden, after a few days illness; and she was seized with the malady upon drinking a glass of succory water. Strong suspicions of poison arose in the court of France, and were spread all over Europe; and as her husband had discovered many symptoms of jealousy and discontent on account of her conduct, he was universally believed to be the author of the crime. Charles himself, during some time, was entirely convinced of his guilt; but upon receiving the attestation of physicians, who, on opening her body, found no foundation for the general rumour, he was, or pretended to be, satisfied. The duke of Orleans indeed did never, in any other circumstance of his life, betray such dispositions as might lead him to so criminal an action; and a lady, it is said, drank the remains of the same glass, without feeling any inconvenience. The sudden death of princes is commonly accompanied with these dismal surmises; and therefore less weight is in this case to be laid on the suspicions of the public.—Charles, instead of breaking with France upon this incident, took advantage of it to send over Buckingham, under pretence of condoling with the duke of Orleans, but in reality to concert farther measures for the projected war. Never ambassador received greater caresses. The more destructive the present measures were to the interests of England, the more natural was it for Lewis to load with civilities, and even with favours, those whom he could engage to promote them.—The journey of Buckingham augmented the suspicions in Holland, which every circumstance tended still farther to confirm. Lewis made a sudden interruption into Lorraine; and though he missed seizing the duke himself, who had no surmise of the danger, and who narrowly escaped, he was soon able, without resistance, to make himself master of the whole country. The French monarch was so far unhappy, that, though the most tempting opportunities offered themselves, he had not commonly so much as the pretence of equity and justice to cover his ambitious measures. This acquisition of Lorraine ought to have excited the jealousy of the contracting powers in the Triple League, as much as an invasion of Flanders itself; yet did Charles turn a deaf ear to all remonstrances made him upon that subject.—But what tended chiefly to open the eyes of de Wit and the States, with regard to the measures of England, was the sudden recall of sir Wm. Temple. This minister had so firmly established his character of honour and integrity, that he was believed incapable even of obeying his master's commands, in promoting measures which he esteemed pernicious to his country; and so long as he remained in employment, de Wit thought himself assured of the fidelity of England. Charles was so sensible of this prepossession, that he ordered Temple to leave his family at the Hague, and pretended, that that minister would immediately return, after having conferred with the king about some business, where his negociation had met with obstructions. De Wit made the Dutch resident inform the English court, that he should consider the recall of Temple as an express declaration of a change of measures in England; and should even know what interpretation to put upon any delay of his return."

The King's Speech at the Meeting of Parliament.] Oct. 24, 1670. While these measures were secretly in agitation, the parliament met according to adjournment, when the king made the following short Speech:

"My Lords and Gentlemen; My principal design being the good of the kingdom, and believing that will be best provided for when the houses are fullest, I thought fit by my proclamation to summon you all to be here. My Lord Keeper will open at large the Particulars I have to recommend to you at this present; and what you do, I would have dispatched before Christmas, that you may then have leisure to return home, and that your own domestic affairs may not suffer by the care you take of me and the public. You have given me so many great testimonies of your zeal and affection, that it were to do you an injury to suspect your want of kindness at a time when there is so much need of it; and if you could possibly make any question of the value and love I have for you, I should think myself unhappy, since I have nothing more in my heart than to give evidences of it to the whole world."

The Lord Keeper Bridgeman's Narrative of the State of Public Affairs.] Then the Lord Keeper spake as follows:

"My lords; and you knights, citizens, and burgesses, of the house of commons; When the two houses were last adjourned, this day as you well know, was prefixed for your meeting again. The proclamation, since issued, requiring all your attendances at the same time, shews, not only his majesty's belief that his business will thrive best when the houses are fullest, but the importance also of the affairs for which you are so called; and important they are.—You cannot be ignorant of the great forces, both for land and sea service, which our neighbours of France and the Low Countries have raised, and have now in actual pay; nor of the great preparations which they continue to make, in levying of men, building of ships, filling their magazines and stores with immense quantities of all sorts of warlike provisions.—Since the beginning of the last Dutch War, the French have increased the number and greatness of their ships so much, that their strength by sea is thrice as much as it was before; and since the end of it, the Dutch have been very diligent also in augmenting their fleets.—In this conjuncture, whilst our neighbours arm so potently, even common prudence requires that his maj. should make some suitable preparations, that he may at least keep pace with his neighbours (if not outgo them) in the number and strength of his shipping; for, this being an island, both our safety and our trade, our being and our well-being, depend upon our force at sea.—His majesty, therefore, of his princely care for the good of his people, hath given order for the fitting out of 50 sail of his greatest ships against the spring (besides those which are to be for security of our merchants in the Mediterranean); as foreseeing that, if he should not have a considerable fleet whilst his neighbours have such forces both at land and sea, temptation might be given, even to those who now seem not to intend it, to give us an affront, at least, if not to do us a mischief.—To which may be added, that his maj. by the Leagues which he hath made for the common peace of Christendom and the good of his kingdoms, is obliged to a certain number of forces, in case of infraction thereof, as also for the assistance of some of his neighbours in case of invasion: and his majesty would be in a very ill condition to perform his part in the Leagues, if, whilst the clouds are gathering so thick about us, he should, in hopes that the wind would disperse them, omit to provide against the storm.—My Lords and Gentlemen; having named the Leagues made by his majesty, I think it necessary to put you in mind, that, since the close of the last war, his majesty hath made several Leagues, to his own great honour, and of infinite advantage to the nation: one, known by the name of the Triple Alliance, wherein his majesty, the crown of Sweden, and the States of the United Provinces, are engaged to preserve the Treaty at Aix la Chapelle, concerning a Peace between the two then warring princes; which League produced that effect, that it quenched the fire which was ready to have set all Christendom on a flame; and, beside other great benefits by it which she still enjoys, gave opportunity to transmit those forces against the Infidels, which would, otherwise, have been embrued in Christian blood.—Another, between his majesty and the said States, for a mutual assistance, with a certain number of men and ships, in case of invasion by any others.—Another, between his majesty and the duke of Savoy, establishing a free Trade for his majesty's subjects at Villa Franca, a port of his upon the Mediterranean, and through the dominions of that prince, and thereby opening a passage towards a rich part of Italy and part of Germany, which will be of very great advantage, for the vending of cloth and other our home commodities, and bringing back silk and other materials for manufactures here. Another, between his maj. and the king of Denmark, whereby those impositions which were lately laid upon our trade there are taken off, and as great privileges are granted to our merchants as ever they had in former times, or as the subjects of any other prince or state do now enjoy. And another League upon a Treaty of Commerce with the crown of Spain, whereby there is (not only) a cession, and giving up to his maj. of all their pretensions to Jamaica, and other the islands and countries in the West Indies, in the possession of his maj. or his subjects; but withal, free liberty is given for his majesty's subjects to enter their ports, for victuals and water, and safety of harbour; and return, if storms or other accidents bring them thither: privileges which were never before granted by them, either to the English or any others. Not to mention the Leagues formerly made with Sweden and Portugal, and the advantages which we enjoy thereby; nor those Treaties now depending between his maj. and France, or his maj. and the States of the United Provinces, touching Commerce, wherein his maj. will have a singular regard to the honour of the nation, and also to the trade of it, which was never greater than now it is. In a word, almost all the princes of Europe do seek his majesty's friendship, as acknowledging they cannot secure, much less improve, their present condition without it. His majesty is confident that you will not be content to see him deprived of all the advantages which he might procure hereby to his own kingdoms, nay even to all Christendom, in the repose and quiet of it; that you will not be content abroad to see your neighbours strengthening themselves in shipping so much more than they were before, and at home to see the government struggling every year with difficulties, and not able to keep up our navies equal with theirs. He finds, by his Accompts, that from 1660, to the late war, the ordinary Charge of the Fleet, communibus annis, came to about 500,000*l.* a year, and it cannot be supported with less: If that particular alone takes up so much, add to it the other constant Charges of the government, and the Revenue (although the Commissioners of the Treasury have managed it with all imaginable thrift) will in no degree suffice to take off the debts due upon interest, much less give him a fund for the setting out this Fleet, which, by estimate thereof, cannot cost less than 800,000*l.* His maj. in his most gracious Speech, hath expressed the great sense he hath of your zeal and affection for him: and as he will ever retain a grateful memory of your former readiness to supply him in all his exigencies, so he doth with particular thanks acknowledge your frank and cheerful gift of the new Duty upon Wines, at your last meeting: but the same is like to fall very short in value of what it was conceived to be worth; and should it have answered expectation, yet far too short to ease or help him upon these occasions. And therefore, such a Supply as may enable him to take off his debts upon interest, and set out this Fleet against the next spring, is that which he desires from you, and recommends it to you as that which concerns the honour and support of the government, and the welfare and safety of yourselves and the whole kingdom. My Lords and Gentlemen; You may perceive, by what his maj. hath already said, that he holds it requisite that an end be put to this meeting before Christmas: It is so, not only in reference to the preparation for his Fleet, which must be in a readiness in the spring, but also to the season of the year: it is a time when you would be willing to be in your countries, and your neighbours would be glad to see you there, and partake of your hospitality and charity; and you thereby endear yourselves unto them, and keep up that interest and power amongst them which is necessary for the service of your king and country. And a recess at that time (leaving your business unfinished till your return) cannot be either convenient for you, or suitable to the condition of his majesty's affairs, which requires your speedy, as well as affectionate consideration."

Several Money Bills in Agitation.] This Speech produced a Vote from the house, "That his majesty should be supplied proportionably to his present occasions." Accordingly, they went upon ways and means of all sorts, and in a short time began to form three several Money Bills; the first was for raising 800,000*l.* by way of Subsidies upon real and personal estates: the second was an additional Excise upon Beer, Ale, &c. for six years; and the last was for laying Impositions on Proceedings at Law, which was to continue nine years. While these things were in agitation, sir Samuel Sterling, the late lord mayor, sir Joseph Sheldon, sir Andrew King, and others of the lieutenancy, having committed Mr. Hayes, and Mr. Jekell, for attempting to bribe the magistrates in case of the act against Conventicles; the matter was brought before the house of commons, and being debated, it was thus resolved; "That this house doth give approbation to what was done by the late lord mayor, sir Samuel Sterling, and the lieutenancy of London, in committing Mr. Hayes and Mr. Jekell; and that it was done in order to the preservation of the king, and peace of the kingdom." Notwithstanding this Vote, Mr. Jekell soon after ventured to sue sir Andrew King at law; of which information being given to the commons, they fell into a heat, and resolved, "That Mr. Jekell be sent for in the custody of the serjeant at arms, to answer his contempt in prosecuting his suit at law against sir Andrew King, after the Vote of this house, whereby it was declared, That the commitment of the said Mr. Jekell was in order to the preservation of the king, and peace of the kingdom." And further, they ordered Mr. Burton, counsel for Mr. Jekell, and Mr. Ogden his attorney, to be likewise sent for in custody of the serjeant at arms, for their contempt in moving and acting for Mr. Jekell, after the fore-mentioned Vote: but were afterwards on their submission discharged.

Proceedings relative to the Assault upon sir John Coventry.] While the house of commons was in a committee on Ways and Means, a motion was made, "That towards the Supply, every one that resorts to any of the Play-houses who sits in the box, shall pay 1*s.* every one who sits in the pit, shall pay 6*d.* and every other person, 3*d.*:" the house disagreed. This motion was opposed by the courtiers, who gave for a reason, 'That the Players were the 'king's servants, and a part of his pleasure.' To this sir John Coventry, by way of reply, asked, 'If the king's pleasure lay among the 'men or women Players?' This was reported at court, where it was so highly resented, that a resolution was taken to set a mark on sir John, to deter others from taking the like liberties for the future. Accordingly, the house adjourning till after Christmas, on the very night of the adjournment, 25 of the duke of Monmouth's troop, and some few foot, lay in wait from ten at night till two in the morning, by Suffolk-street, and as he returned from the tavern where he supped, to his own house, they threw him down, and, with a knife, cut the end of his nose almost off; but company coming made them fearful to finish it; so they made off. Sir Tho. Sands, lieutenant of the troop, commanded the party; and Obrian, the earl of Inchequin's son, was a principal actor. The court hereupon sometimes thought to carry it with an high hand, to question sir John for his words, and maintain the action. Sometimes again they flagged in their counsels. One while the king commanded sir Thomas Clarges and sir Wm. Pulteney to release Wroth and Lake, who were two of the actors, and taken; but, the night before the house met, surrendered them again.*

Jan. 9. The house being called over, according to former order, upon calling the name of sir John Coventry, information being given of an Assault made upon him, on the same night of that day the house did rise before Christmas, by a number of about 15 persons armed, horse and foot, who did assassinate and wound the said sir John Coventry; and that he continues still so ill of his wounds, that he is not in a condition to attend; resolved, That the matter of Breach of Privilege committed, and assault made, upon sir John Coventry, a member of this house, be taken into consideration the first business to-morrow morning.

* Ralph, vol. 1. p. 193.

The Coventry or Maiming Act brought in.] Jan. 10. Sir Tho. Clarges, one of the Justices of the Peace who took the Examination of the business, gave a Narrative to the house thereof.

Sir *Edm. Wyndham*, knight-marshal, desires to know whether you will proceed in it here, now it is prosecuted at law; and how far your proceedings may hinder the legal prosecution.

Sir *John Hotham* questions whether the king himself, and we, shall not be under proscriptions, as in Sylla and Marius's time: moves that we may right ourselves in this business, which deserves our vengeance.

Earl of *Ancram** knows not how we can have greater vengeance than the law can inflict: if any of these be hanged by law, you have justice sufficient.

Sir *Rob. Holt* agrees not with lord Ancram: it is the greatest breach that ever was since the first constitution of parliaments. In Charles I. time, remembers what noise the business of the Five Members made: his majesty has a place here when he commands or does justice: if these persons are of his guards, they that will not fear God, will never honour the king. guards have been the betrayers of the empire; the Prætorians did it: thinks the king should have his guards; and amongst them are many worthy persons: would have his maj. moved to inspect his guards; lords noses are as ours are, unless they be of steel: it concerns the lords as well as us, as in lord Ormond's case: this wounds all the commons of England: in a plot, you had a committee of lords and commons, and they sat all Christmas: we may do so too: we know not what a petty jury may do in it: that will not right our privilege: you cannot, Mr. Speaker, at this rate, go home with your mace.

Sir *John Monson* has been lately in the country, and never saw a greater concern for a business: they fear we shall come under the government of France, to be governed by an army: moves for a Bill for these 16 that assaulted one man, to render themselves by a day, or be banished for ever.

Mr. *Hale.* Notice has been taken of this horrid fact here, but was not at the relation of it, but hears it in every street. If a man must thus be assaulted by ruffianly fellows, we must go to bed by sun-set, like the birds: the danger of post facto is not in this business: would have them hanged, if they could be caught: seconds the motion of Monson.

Sir *Rob. Howard.* He that likes this fact would do it; he that extenuates it, would be persuaded to do it: if any condition be to be pitied, it is the gentlemen that did capitulate the business: is sorry any English gentleman should wear a sword to do such a business: is persuaded that no gentleman in England but desires their room more than their company: the guards were fairly delivered to justice: in all companies there may be ill men, as well as in the guards: you may extend your enquiry to those whom the law cannot meet with.

Mr. *Garroway* would have something added: he would pity the gentlemen accessaries who were under command.* In this Bill of yours would have a gate opened for safety for these gentlemen now committed. If they should declare their knowledge of the whole matter, they should plead this bill for their pardon: but will you pardon men who shall persist in a concealing? Would have them pardoned, if they will give an account to the lord chief justice of the thing, provided they were not actors in the assassination.

Sir *Rob. Atkins.* Until you can discover names, it will be too soon to bring in a Bill: would have you know upon what colour these persons did this assassination upon your member: would have your member heard himself; or, if he be not able, would have some persons sent to him; and you may do more or less, according to the aggravations: would not have any matter proceeded in till this business be over.

Sir *Wm. Coventry.* Has asked sir John Coventry if he could recollect what moved this misfortune upon him, but he remembers nothing they said that might point out the cause: knows nothing that may come of it, but delay, by farther speaking with him, it being felony, and all involved: it was a great good fortune to have any by-standers; and without some such expedient as Garroway proposed, you cannot possibly find out more.

Mr. *H. Coventry.* He is bound in point of modesty not to say much; but his relation prompts him to say somewhat: seconds the motion for a Bill.

Sir *R. Temple.* In Chedder's case, a Bill was brought in for the person that beat him on the highway, and a day was set for his appearance: cannot see how these persons can be witnesses, when attainted.

Lord *Richardson*,† looks upon these persons as capable of being witnesses, being not yet attainted; the Bill being found only by the grand jury.

Sir *Nich. Carew* would have something added for the security of your members for the future; and not to proceed in any other business till this Bill be finished: his reason is, that we

* Afterwards created, by king William, marquis of Lothian, and made justice-general of Scotland. Burnet says, "that he had no principles either as to religion or virtue;" yet adds, "that he had studied the most divinity of any man of quality he ever knew."

* "That matter was executed by orders from the duke of Monmouth; for which he was severely censured, because he lived then in professions of friendship with Coventry; so that his subjection to the king was not thought an excuse for directing so vile an attempt on his friend, without sending him secret notice of what was designed." Burnet.

† A Peer of Scotland. The title is now extinct.

may have freedom of speech till this Bill be done: without a better guard than Coventry had, he cannot speak freely to any thing else: perhaps this may be a new way of frightening people, that they may be alarmed and afraid: hopes you will add more *to maim*, and let some general law be included in this particular occasion, for our safety for the future.

Sir *Fr. Goodrick.* To kill a judge in the execution of his office is treason: that of killing a privy counsellor, is repealed: Stroude's case is a general law: if the judges shall not take notice in their courts of any thing said here, you will not suffer 12 red coats to do it: there is as much due to you as to the judges: would have it Treason and Felony for the time to come.

Mr. *Jones.* It is the way to make your money come in the better, to punish this horrid un-English act, when there is a sense in the minds of the people of this horrid abuse; that by privilege of parliament being broken, the people are wounded: his soul trembles at the sad consequences: it is a greater thing than he has ever seen here: it concerns the person, justice, and honour of the king, council, and house of commons: great sums have been given, and great sums must be given; there are many malecontents: every ill humour goes to the place hurt: the people say, that the house has met these several years for nothing but to give money; and raising money to that high degree as we have done, they may be displeased: moves that by this Act they may right themselves. By this precedent, upon some of the guards, would have the world know you are in earnest: would have been silent, but the weight of the matter charms him: and that the king's business may not wait, would be at this, day and night; and proceed no farther in any business, till this be over.

Sir *Job. Charlton.* What hath been done for the people these 9 years? When this is over, he will give his vote for money as soon as any man.

Sir *R. Temple.* If he was jealous that all the Money-Bills should pass before this bill, would have this precede; but this may go with them.

Mr *Garrowny.* Those Bills are so many snares, and sacrifice us to the fury of the people: suspects we shall have nothing, when this of money is passed, and therefore presses it.

Sir *John Duncombe.** Whilst we are angry at this Bill, why should we hurt ourselves? knows not what effect the hastening of the bill may have, but the obstruction of the king's business: if the Bill was ready, would have it read now: read it twice in a day; make what haste you will; consents to it.

Sir *Winston Churchill.* Not to be for this bill, would be to upbraid the house: those persons who sit quiet in their sovereign's blood, wonder this thing should be so pressed: it seems to him a cutting the king over the face. [The words gave offence.] Explains himself, that he said it by way of simile: not only our own affairs, but of Christendom, are upon their crisis; and the king put into a capacity to defend the kingdom: moves that we may, de die in diem, proceed on this bill, which will certainly have a preference to the other: would have these two bills go *simul & semel.*

Sir *Tho. Meres.* The Bill doubtless has been in our thoughts ever since the fact was done: it will take up no time, and it is so far from prejudicing the king's affairs, that it will advance them: wherever your members are intimidated, your laws may be questioned: the lords are included in your privileges: they have adjourned several weeks, we would have but three days for this bill: if we lose this question, we lose all, and begs your leave we may be gone.

Sir *Rob. Howard.* With what boldness can any man speak here, that must be pulled by the ears at night for what he says? The people say in the country, that unless you right yourselves in this business, your money is not given, but taken away.

Mr. *Seymour* has found none that speak with the indignation the thing deserves. But because injury has been done us abroad, therefore must we hurt ourselves? Hire some persons to assault some members of this house, and Supply may be hindered at any time: suppose this bill do not pass, must no other business be proceeded upon? Desires other business may not stand still.

Sir *John Ernly.* Nothing will make the people give more cheerfully than doing ourselves right in this business; and would sit morning and afternoon till it be done.

Mr. *Cheney* wonders that a thing of common justice, as this is, should be so obstructed: there was some suspension of justice: the lord chief justice was spoke with, and the secretaries, before justice was done; and some by that means escaped: necessity of the nation is at our doors, to take off that arbitrary power upon us.

Mr. Secretary *Trevor* concurs heartily with what has been done this day; but this deferring will be thought a jealousy, where he hopes there is none.

Mr. *Waller* has seen a stop in all business till members have been vindicated, and released out of prison: has seen the Petition of Right passed before Supply, but no vote passed in it: should it be said that the Supply depends upon passing another bill not in the power of us? When the Greeks and Romans had slaves disfigured and marked, it was a dishonour to the master; but that a free man, an ambas-

* "Duncombe was a judicious man, but very haughty, and apt to raise enemies against himself. He was an able parliament-man; but could not go into all the designs of the court; for he had a sense of religion, and a zeal for the liberty of his country." Burnet. He was at this time a Commissioner of the Ordnance.

sador of the people, should be thus marked, is much more horrible. These actions have sometimes wrought reformation; sometimes good effects, and sometimes ill, as the government is affected: we got the Petition of Right by discreet handling the business: the business of the Five Members was so ill handled, that great disorder happened: God brings light out of darkness: must give his No to this question.

Mr. Attorney *Finch.* The security of your satisfaction is not the question; what then should be the reason of this addition? He thinks you are satisfying the nation in our resentment: this satisfaction is a higher satisfaction than ever was known: 11 Hen. iv, "Any man assaulting a Member going or coming to parliament, if he render not himself to the King's Bench in such a time, they would proceed to fine; and if he do come, and be found guilty by inquest, by examination, or otherwise, he shall pay his double damages found by the inquest, or be taxed by the discretion of the judges, and make fine and ransom at the king's will." Lord Cromwell, 28 Hen. vi, was assaulted in the palace-yard; the offender imprisoned in the Tower for a year: we go about to do more than ever was, or attempted to be, done before: we put, by this vote, a stand to the government: no man can think this question can pass, and all other things stand still: why you should, for an imaginary opinion of the people, set a stop to all things, he knows not.

Mr. *Vaughan.* Persons argue for giving the king money, and yet would hinder it: you must, in nature, have a father, before you can have a son: if we act not with the same liberty and freedom as our ancestors, we trust as a person would an arbitrator that his adversary has a power upon: the people will tell us that we serve the king, not by law, but contrary to law.

Col. *Titus.* This has been a thing without precedent, and hopes you will prevent it for the future from being so: would not have you revenged upon yourselves. Whatever urgent accidents shall happen, not to be relieved until this Bill pass.

Mr. *Hen. Coventry.* Should be an unnatural man to his relation, and undutiful to the house, if he did not resent this; and would rather have all his wounds than hinder the prosecution: it is objected, 'that men may put clogs into a Bill that it shall not pass, and by consequence all business stands;' which he cannot well answer: would have it that this bill shall have a preference to all other bills; and, when it is ready, be read before all bills: would not have the nation believe that any persons that have a share in the government do in any wise countenance this business.

Col. *Birch* thinks you cannot do too much in this business: for the same reasons that many are against it, he is for it: nothing can be a greater mischief than a division upon this question; and he looks upon these bills of Supply to have their fate accordingly: cannot believe that any in the government had a share in this business, because they would have timed it better: would have the people think you act freely and speak freely: on my word, they think not so now: will say nothing of the nature of the thing: former precedents will not reach us: we must have the people have a good opinion of us (I would they had!): if this bill pass not, we know now to make it (with respect spoken): the other bills will pass this.

It was at length resolved, "That a Bill be brought in for banishment of sir Tho. Sandys, Ch. Obrian, esq. Simon Parry and Miles Reeves, actors in assaulting and wounding sir John Coventry, if they do not render themselves to justice by a day; and that no other business be proceeded in, whilst the Bill is passing."—On the 11th and 12th the Bill was read a first and second time.—Ordered, That it be referred to the committee formerly appointed to bring in the Bill for the banishing sir Tho. Sandys, and others, &c. to prepare and bring in a Clause against to-morrow morning, for preventing mischiefs of the like nature for the future.

Jan. 13. The house went into a grand committee on the Bill to prevent Malicious Maiming and Wounding *. Mr. Coleman in the Chair.

Mr. Attorney *Finch.* It is against the thing to make it felony: that former law of Hen. iv † gave such a terror that the thing was never done since: laws that look like the products and effects of passion, may not meet with the same passion, at the lords: why not forfeiture of goods, and imprisonment for life? Sir Hen. Spelman tells us of the penalty of cutting off hands and legs, leaving nothing but a living trunk; *lex justior nulla, &c.* the first fate of that law was upon him that made it.

Mr. *Vaughan.* The statute of queen Mary says, 'She holds herself safer in the hearts of her subjects than in the severity of law:' would have distinction of offences a hurt a surgeon may cure; dismembering he cannot. You ought to adapt it to this particular case, which gives the occasion of it.

Sir *Tho. Lee* would not have it go less than to an abjuration of the realm: would have the penalty changed, but the thing continued: were you a perpetual legislature, it were another case: would have those preserved that sent us hither, that we represent: agrees to abjuration.

Sir *Wm. Coventry.* If foreigners shall do it by being hired, what is the penalty for them to be abjured the realm? We are now more acquainted with them, than when the former statute was made.

Sir *Rob. Howard.* You will set up men to swear premeditation, and make felony, for every disturbance in the street; the reason of the thing is only applicable to your member; and he would fix it there.

* This was in regard to the Clause ordered the day before, and which probably occasioned the title of the Bill to be altered as above.

† Cutting out of tongues.

Sir *Rd. Temple.* If you apply a less penalty than felony to this case it will not reach: it is felony now, but by clergy, which is much more than abjuring: they are burnt in the hand, and forfeit their goods: would have it thus put in, 'by surprize, and at unawares;' by day these things are not so commonly done.

Mr. Secretary *Trevor.* What consideration this will have abroad, he always reflects: the parliament upon this occasion makes a general law upon particular occasions, but knows no reason why it should be for people in general: as parliament-men are now liable to greater hardships than formerly, so would have distinction: when prorogation comes, we are as other men, and lie under hardships for what we say here: soldiers of fortune may live in another country as well as here: would not have it banishment.

Sir *Tho. Clarges.* Few were saved in Hen. iv's time by clergy, for few could read; so it was severer than now.

Mr. Serj. *Maynard.* You have precedents of a special occasion for a general law, as Chedder's case: thinks that proper and prudent; and has no inconvenience against making it death: would have it more than abjuration, because to aliens, and such as desire to be abroad—but he must approve; and if he return felony: would have it perpetual banishment, but not death.

Sir *Wm. Coventry.* For the case of a parliament-man, thinks abjuration proper, but for all people would have it felony.

Mr. Serj. *Maynard.* Clergy is now a matter of nothing; Clergy at common law was not an absolution from the offence; he then had a writ declared of restoration upon his purgation.

Sir *Tho. Clifford.* Much more to be said in the bill of lord Clarendon than this, in point of pardon: the second precedent entails things upon you: would not have the people out of power of pardon. It is the first time you have totally put a thing out of the king's pardon.

Sir *Rob. Holt.* Several crimes as this, of robbing and murder, the king cannot pardon, only respite execution: if they come by a day, would not have power of pardon taken away.

Sir *Nich. Carew.* If the action be without precedent, why should not the prosecution? This was done by the guards; if they should be pardoned, knows not what they may do to the king, and moves it for his majesty's ease and advantage.

Col. *Kirby.* A greater offence than this we petitioned the king to pardon, which was his father's murder.

Sir *Tho. Meres.* This house twice petitioned for execution, and it rested with the lords: therefore that is a mistake.

Mr. Attorney *Finch*, objects against the bill, that you convict them by the bill: would have it thus, 'in which assault a supposed robbery was done, which they are not yet convicted of.' The things may have been lost. As for pardoning, it is the same thing to pardon and not to execute, which is never done, unless the king's attorney sends the warrant, and that he will not do without command, this clause is a jealousy, and without effect of our ends: it is an indecent thing to shut up mercy: he who advised the emperor to shut up the sanctuary, fled to the horns of the altar, and could not lay hold of it.

Sir *Wm. Coventry*, would not have the nature of the fact otherwise than it is: 'lost,' instead of 'robbed:' he will have no other thoughts than what the house has of it. What fell from Mr. Attorney, is a reason for confirmation of the clause. He is never desirous of any man's blood; and if you continue this clause, it will reach the end of the member injured, without blood. Let every man consult his heart, whether his blood would not be higher than any philosopher can conquer; for it may put your member upon unchristianly revenge; and appeals to any gentleman what he would do, if he should see such a person walk the streets that had so injured him. Whatever we do here is petition; and it is a greater thing to petition to pardon than not to pardon: for the safety of all Englishmen lies in doing of justice. It is no new thing to find pardons interceding for persons: 51 Ed. iii. the Speaker had order to move the lords for Peirce, &c. It is not new for you, in case of an honourable member. In lord St. John's case, you went yourself with the house, in a body, to ask his pardon: for desire against pardon, 21 Edw. iii.: murders, &c. were frequent, by reason of pardon.

Sir *Tho. Clifford.* Coventry's precedents were before Henry vth's time. He has read them, and been told, that before Henry vth's time, the king put the sceptre upon one clause of a bill that he approved of, and left out another. Now the king passes all, or passes none: these ancient precedents have not the force that is urged by Coventry: moderate it so, that you tie no shackles on his majesty.

Dr. *Arras* made an extravagant motion for a Bill to be brought in, to punish any man that should speak any reflective thing on the king. By some he was called to the bar; but his explanation and excuse were admitted of. He said, 'He was the only physician of the house, and, *humanum est errare:* he hoped he should be pardoned.'

Sir *Tho. Clifford.* Your Chair has not been infallible. Do you know what Martin said, the impunity whereof was a great cause of what followed; and if the majority will not punish seditious expressions, thinks such a bill for the honour of the house.

Sir *Tho. Lee*, would not have that pass for doctrine, that, because once the majority of the commons have rebelled, hereafter they will do so; and if that be taken for granted, we pass a high reflection on ourselves.

Mr. *Hen. Coventry.* There was a violence; and should only the person that takes the money, and not they that stand armed to assist the other, be guilty, it would be strange.

Mr. *Vaughan.* Sandys consented to the assassination, but not to the robbery; it is *alterius generis.* But here every one is principal, though of one kind, and they present when cutting is committed: lord Dacre's case, when his men went a deer-stealing.

Sir *Rob. Howard.* Here is more in the case; for these persons were present, and might have prevented; if you will have all accessaries incapable of pardon, it will reach many. If he had struck only, and not taken away, &c.

Mr. Attorney *Finch.* The fear that there should be a general pardon from the king, which you cannot mend, nor add exceptions to, is objected. Answers, he hopes to see such a pardon, but is in no prospect of such a pardon; and this jealousy may hinder such an intention: this is grafting one jealousy upon another: this is *primæ inventionis*, ingeniously rolled in gentlemen's thoughts; and if ever any such thing was done, will sit down.

Sir *Rob. Howard.* The king may pardon all but such as actually wounded, maimed, struck, or took away: he would have him named, if he does get his pardon, that mankind may know.

Sir *Tho. Meres.* Is it imaginable that such persons, so infamous, should hinder an act of grace? Would have added 'unless such persons shall be particularly named in the act.'

Sir *John Duncombe.* Is not for that clause: knows not but he himself may want an act of grace as much as any man; and knows not whether this clause may not stop it: does not remember, in an act of this nature before, any such thing was mentioned.

Mr. *Cheney* is persuaded, that if such an act be intended, these words will not hinder it; and therefore would have the persons named.

Mr. *Milward* would not, to remedy a single person, insnare all the commons of England' 'wound, maim, or bruise,' it may be done by mistake: upon a bare proclamation, if the person appeared not, a member should have judgment and double damages: this our ancestors thought a fair distinction of a parliament-man, from another man.

Sir *Tho. Higgins.* It was never death to strike a senator of Rome, nor now to strike a senator of Venice, out of the senate. Would not have us take more upon us than our ancestors did.

Sir *Rd. Temple.* The two particular cases beget a general law, of double damages. Would you have any man for double damages venture to beat a member of parliament? Would have a general law, to prevent making more, for the future: the law implies malice, when there is no act of provocation.

Mr. *Vaughan.* Is against making a bare trespass felony; would have it farther considered.

Sir *Rob. Carr* would have the law secure those we represent, as well as ourselves; therefore would have another bill brought in.

Sir *Tho. Lee.* Times and manners are altered, and men are: time was, when none should go armed in parliament-time. What penalty have you now more for a member than another person? We come to provide for the commons of England, as well as for a particular member: we are, upon occasion of speaking, exposed to that which other men are not.

Col. *Stroude.* We shall, by this, give other provocation, and they not dare to provoke us.

Sir *John Birkenhead.* Swinnerton quarrelled with Ipstock, and killed him; it was but as killing another man; parliament-men will be afraid of one another: riding armed, forbidden in three several parliaments, 'within the liberties of Westminster, unless his majesty's officer's,' an integral part in that proclamation.

Mr. *Hen. Coventry* would not only have it felony upon the member, but upon any man: if he may not have a privilege against bastinadoes, cares not for having it against hurts: would have it against cudgels as well as swords.

Mr. *Vaughan.* We have privileges that other persons have not, from arrests: why should we not have it in other things?

Col. *Birch.* If we have a greater guard than other men, we shall be less regarded: desires we should be no more distinguished than other men; but to have our noses cut, should be deferred—is against it—if we were a people that went not to plays nor taverns, another thing; but at this rate, no man will play with us.

Sir *Job. Charlton.* It is not felony if he 'wounds' a man that is chancellor, or judge, executing his office; 'killing' is treason: this making it felony upon one of the house is unreasonable, that it should be more than upon those that represent his majesty's person.

Sir *Adam Brown* would have care taken to prevent combinations: would not have the clause disjoined from the bill, which occasioned the penning of the bill.

Sir *Tho. Clifford.* Is for the clause of a general assassinating; and it is not proper to make ourselves, who are not judges born, as the lords are: we are 500 to day, and 500 new men a month hence: there can be no notoriety to the people: would have some gentlemen accommodate this to the bill.

The Bill, with the amendments, was ordered to be ingrossed; and on the 14th, it was resolved, That the Bill do pass, and that the title be, "An act to prevent malicious Maiming and Wounding."

Debate on a Clause in the Subsidy Bill, for doubly assessing Members, defaulters in Attendance.] Feb. 16. A Clause for doubly assessing the Members, defaulters in attendance, in the Bill of Subsidies, was moved.

Mr. Attorney *Finch.* Whoever is so unfortunate as to be in this black list, to be upon record, had better quite be thrown out of the house. What will be the consequence? Suppose they will justify themselves by reasonable cause, will you allow them to deny that which you have voted to be true? If not heard, they are condemned unreasonably. Will the lords pass it without scanning? And do you let them in to examine what are the weighty affairs of this house, and judge it? You have other ways; you have power to fine them; and that you appoint a day to pay it, upon penalty of expulsion from the house. You may do it, but would not have such a clause to stand on record, to the disgrace of so many families.

Sir *Tho. Lee.* It is no more than an additional penalty to the statute of 5 Hen. viii. for that loss of wages was as notorious as this additional penalty. Mr. Attorney has told you, that after session you have no power to fine them; therefore, this way you take, you have as much judgment in this as the peers, for they had your assistance by that statute to fine their own members, and no man can imagine the peers thought it our judging them. A gentleman born petitioned to be discharged his employment, but could not obtain it: the inconvenience and burthen is now ten years parliament, but that must not be a pretence for absence; but when you come to a division of eightscore, rarely 300, this shews the world that you take it to be your interest to have a full house; and this will carry on the weighty affairs of the kingdom, which are not frivolous, and so the lords can take no exceptions at your preamble.

Sir *T. Clifford* would have the debate kept to one point. He agrees that the honour of the nation is a full house; see whether this way be a proper way. This way will intimate you have no other way. Can you punish them no other way but to go to the lords for it? Suppose the commons had a vote in the lords punishment; you pretend to have the sole power of punishing your members, and yet you will subject your opinion to the lords: every body for a full house: for a rod and terror, set a day a month hence, and if you are not satisfied in their excuse for their absence, send out new writs. In Edw. ii's time it was so. If you did resolve to punish them, would you do it by this bill? Bills of Supply never stick with the lords, usually not three days time, without conferences. Suppose they petition the lords, as supreme judicature of the nation, that 'such a mulct is put upon us, we desire you to strike us out, and let the bill be amended;' surely you would send him to the Tower that should do it. By this you do not let a man have the freedom of helping himself. As long as the other bills are not passed, you have the rod still, and may punish them by fines, or sending out new writs. If the lords should see you mix Judicature with Subsidy, what will the lords say, the preamble mentioning nothing of it? Here will you punish men that give to the king.

Mr. *Garroway.* You are told, it agrees not with the preamble of the bill, but thinks those gentlemen would still stay at home, though the French were landed at Dover; as for turning out of the house, so it be without reproach, thinks it an advantage, and would be out himself. The Lords have only their consent, as in other things. Some are half undone by being here, and should they be exempted, weigh it: is it a little thing that summons after summons has been given by the sheriff, and other ways, and they contemn your service?

Sir *Rd. Temple.* It never came before the commons, such names as should be fined, as is now intended in ours; but they returned their names to the exchequer. Thinks no member would submit Judicature to the lords: it is a mistake that the house cannot fine; they have fined persons 200*l.* and that levied: they have committed a person for printing a scandalous book, and fined him, and he stood committed after the session, until he has recanted his book, and submitted: if you send it to the lords, they will not pass it blindly, without examining things, to be assured of the fact; would have you fine them, and the monies to be distributed in the boroughs or counties they serve for.

Sir *Tho. Meres.* The great argument is the disadvantage we subject ourselves to. Distinguish the legislative capacity, and we can take nothing ill from the lords. All our proceedings are to the legislature. The greatest evil in the world is a thin house; the very noise of this Clause has sent people up.

Sir *Rob. Howard.* Not above 40 of 500 are wanting.

Mr. *Vaughan.* Whoever is elected, is in as great a trust as a man can be capable of; either by his absence he indulges his own private affairs, or neglects your service; and they deserve a mark not to be chosen for the future: they that absent themselves from your judgment, deserve to have your judgment passed upon them. As to those who say, the lords are judges in this case; was not lord Clarendon judged legislatively? The pecuniary punishment is but gentle, and if not inflicted, you may have yet an emptier house next session.

Sir *Henry Herbert.* Meres said, 'he was cold when the house was empty;' he may be too hot when it is full: doubts whether in punishing these members, we punish not ourselves: privileges of parliament are *non so che*, as the Italian says, neither described nor circumscribed. Whenever this Clause passes in this bill, you condemn people unheard; you expose your privilege to reference and examination of the lords; and suppose the lords refuse this clause? Offers an expedient—all of a mind to punish nocent persons: from 1621, has observed that this power has not been thus exercised: would have the members sent for in custody.

Mr. *Henry Coventry.* Generally people say it is of the sharpest: you have been well offered for a Bill to be brought in: it was your fault in not committing your members formerly to the Tower, and fining them. What great charge do gentlemen come at here, by being chosen knights of the shire? Shall not a gentleman go home, and look after his estate, now lands are thrown up? If your rigour be so great, and your session so long, you will have none but such as have nothing else to do: unless you build your house bigger, it will not hold us. Would have enquiry into your members that have not been here for two or three years together. There are many now that miss you but a week, upon some extraordinary occasion; will you make them equal with those that contemn you?

Mr. *Waller.* Consider what good you have by it; you have had the best effects already in a full house; some afterwards will be gone, and those fined will not come up. If you go to the lords, you do in effect acknowledge you cannot punish without the lords. If we say we cannot punish, do we not invite other courts to do it? For offences must be punished somewhere. He has seen 40 in a morning turned out. Seldon said we could not do it without the lords, and we have had ill consequences of it: would have them sent for, and called to the bar, or sent to the Tower, or what we shall judge fit.

Sir *Edward Dering* would have the blanks filled up, before the question be put, to make it part of the bill.

Sir *John Duncombe.* You will punish six, and excuse 250; what justice is there in this? You will put them upon appeals to the lords, and they will have justice there: do you want power to punish, when you can send them to the Tower, and fine them?—The Clause was then rejected, 115 to 98.

Lord Lucas's celebrated Speech on the Subsidy Bill.] Feb. 22. On the second reading of the Subsidy Bill in the house of lords,

The Lord *Lucas,* * made the following noble speech, his majesty being present:

"My Lords; When, by the providence of Almighty God, this nation recalled his majesty to the exercise of the regal power, it was the hope of all good men, that we should not only be restored to his majesty's royal presence, and the divine laws, but that we should be free from those heavy burthens under which we had lain so long oppressed; we did believe that from thenceforth every every man should sit under his own vine, enjoying the fruits of peace and plenty; and that Astrea herself, long since for the sins of men fled up to Heaven, should have been invited, by his majesty's most gracious and happy reign, to return hither and dwell with us, and converse amongst mortals again.—But alas, we are all fallen very short of our expectations, and our burthens are so far from being made lighter to us, that they are heavier than ever they were; and as our burthens are increased, so our strength is also diminished, and we are less able to support them.—In the times of the late usurping powers, although great Taxes were exacted from us, we had then means to pay them, we could sell our lands our corn and cattle, and there was plenty of money throughout the nation; now there is nothing of this; brick is required of us, and no straw allowed to make it with. For that our lands are thrown up, and corn and cattle are of little value, is notorious to all the world.—And it is as evident there is a scarcity of Money; for all that money called 'Breeches' (as fit for the coin of the Rump) is wholly vanished; the king's Proclamation and the Dutch have swept it all away; and of his now majesty's Coin, there appears but very little; so that, in effect, we have none left for common use, but a little, old, lean, coined money of the three former princes; and what supply is preparing for it, my lords? I hear of none, unless it be of Copper Farthings*; and this is the metal that is to vindicate; according to the Inscription on it, 'the Dominion of the four Seas.'† And yet, if amidst this scarcity, the vast sums given were all employed for the king and kingdom, it would not so much trouble us; but we cannot, without infinite regret of heart, see so great a part of it pounded up in the purses of other private men; and see them flourish in estates, who, in the time of his majesty's most happy Restoration, were worth very little or nothing: and now the same men purchase lands, and keep their coach and six horses, their pages and their lacqueys; while, in the mean time, those that have faithfully served the king are exposed to penury and want, and have scarce sufficient left to buy them bread.—And is this, my lords, the reward of our services? Have we for this borne the heat of the day, been imprisoned, sequestered, and ventured our lives and our families, our estates and our fortunes? And must we, after all this, sacrifice so much of our poor remainder to the will of a few particular men, and the maintenance of their vanities?—But suppose all the money given were employed for the use of his majesty, and his majesty were not cozened (as without doubt he is) is there no bounds to, or moderation in giving? Will you say, that if we shall not plentifully supply his majesty, he will not be able to defend us, or maintain the Triple League? And we shall thereby run the hazard of being conquered.—It is true, my lords, that this may be a reason for giving

* "This Speech was burnt by the hangman," says an Address to the Reader "to the great grief and astonishment of all true Englishmen, to whom my lord Lucas's loyalty to his prince, and inviolable love to his country was abundantly manifested."—Mr. Marvell in his Letters writes thus: 'Dear Will; I think I have not 'told you, that on our Bill of Subsidy, the lord 'Lucas made a fervent, bold speech against our 'prodigality in giving, and the weak looseness 'of the government, the king being present. 'Copies going about every where, one of them 'was brought into the lord's house, and lord 'Lucas was asked whether it was his: he said, ''part was,' and 'part was not.' Thereupon 'they took advantage, and said it was a libel 'even against Lucas himself. On this they 'voted it a libel, and to be burned by the hang-'man, which was done; but the sport was, the 'hangman burned the lords Order with it."

* Called the Lucas-Farthing to this day.

† Quatuor Maria vindico.

something; but it is so far from being an argument for giving so much, that it may be clearly made out to your lordships, that it is the direct and ready way to be conquered by a foreigner. And it may be the policy of the French king, by those often alarms of armies and fleets, to induce us to consume our treasure in vain preparations against him: and after he has by this means made us poor and weak enough, he may then come upon us and destroy us.—It is not, my lords, the giving of a great deal, but the well managing of the money given, that must keep us safe from our enemies; your lordships may be pleased to call to mind the story of Sampson; while he preserved his hair, wherein his strength lay, he was still victor over his enemies; but when, by the enticement of his Dalilah, his hair was cut off, the Philistines came upon him, and overcame him: and so, my lords, if we shall preserve and husband well our treasure, wherein our strength and the sinews of war lie, and apply it to the right uses, we shall still be superior to all our enemies; but if we shall vainly and imprudently mispend it, we shall become an easy prey to them.—Besides, my lords, what is this but *ne moriare mori*, and for fear of being conquered by a foreigner, put ourselves in a condition almost as bad; pardon me, my lords, if I say in some respects a great deal worse; for when we are under the power of the victor, we know we can fall no lower; and the certainties of our miseries are some kind of dimunution of them: but in this wild way we have no certainty at all; for if you give thus much to-day, you may give as much more to-morrow, and never leave giving till we have given all that ever we have away; and the anxiety of mind which arises from this doubtful estate is an high addition to our afflictions.—All that I beg, my lords, is, that we may be able to make some estimate of ourselves: would his majesty be pleased to have a quarter of our estates? For my part, he shall have it: would his maj. be pleased to have half? for my part, upon a good occasion, he shall have it: but, I beseech your lordships, then, that we may have some assurance of the quiet enjoyment of the remainder, and know what we have to trust to.—My lords, the commons have here sent us up a Bill for giving his majesty the 20th part of our Estates, at the full extended value; and I hear there are other bills for Money also preparing; which together, according to the best computation, will amount to little less than 3 millions of money; a prodigious sum, and such, that if your lordships shall not afford relief, we must of necessity sink under the weight of so heavy a pressure.—My lords, the Scriptures tells us, that God Almighty sets bounds unto the Ocean, and says unto it, 'Hither shall thy proud waves come, and no farther.' And so I hope your lordships, in imitation of the divinity, will set some bounds, some limits, to this over-liberal humour of the commons, and say to them, 'Hither shall your profuseness come, and no farther.'—My. lords, either your lordships can deny, or moderate a bill for Money coming from the commons; and if you cannot, all your great estates are wholly at their disposal, and your lordships have nothing that you can properly call your own, and then let us pass this Bill without farther examination; but if you can deny or moderate (as without question you can) your lordships never had, nor possibly will have such a fair occasion to shew it.—My lords, upon the whole matter, I must humbly propose to your lordships, that your lordships will be pleased to reduce the 12*d* in the pound to 8*d*.: and truly, my lords, I have reason to hope, that if your lordships will truly reflect upon it, ye will find it do accordingly; for in the first place, it will be so far from being a disservice to his majesty, that your lordships will do his maj. in it the highest service in the world; for although ye shall thereby take from his majesty a part of the sum, you will give him a great deal more in the love and hearts of his subjects; and there his majesty must reign, if he will be great and glorious.—And next, your lordships will acquire to yourselves eternal honour; ye shall thereby endear yourselves to the whole nation, who for the future will look upon you as the Antients did upon their Tutelar Gods; nor shall the House of Commons, but the House of Peers, be hereafter precious in their sight.—My lords, give me leave to mind your lordships, that noble acts are the steps whereby the great men of the world ascend to the Throne of Glory; and can there be a nobler act than to release a distressed kingdom, which lies languishing under so many hard oppressions, and about to be so much more oppressed? I detain your lordships too long, and therefore shall say no more; but must beg your lordships pardon, and submit all to your better judgments."

About this time, the king sent a Message to the commons to acquaint them, "That his majesty was informed, that there had some Bills passed both houses, and that there were others depending near their dispatch, which he desired them to hasten, especially those for his Supply: and lest they should not be ready for his assent by the 22d of this instant Feb. he had given order for the adjourning of the session until the 10th of March next."

Petition of both Houses against the Growth of Popery.] March 10. But notwithstanding this Message, the commons proceeded to other matters as well as the supplies, and in particular drew up the following remarkable Petition against Popery, in which the lords afterwards joined:

"May it please your most excellent majesty; We your majesty's most humble and loyal subjects, the lords spiritual and temporal and commons in this present parliament assembled, being sensible of your majesty's constancy to the Protestant Religion both at home and abroad, hold ourselves bound in conscience and duty to represent to your most sacred maj. the Causes of the dangerous Growth of Popery in these your majesty's dominions, the ill consequences whereof we heartily desire may be prevented; and therefore what we humbly conceive to be some present Remedies for the said growing mischiefs, we have hereunto added, in our most humble Petitions."

"*Causes of the Growth of Popery:*

"1. That there are great numbers of Priests and Jesuits frequenting the cities of London and Westminster, and most of the counties of this kingdom, more than formerly, seducing your majesty's good subjects. 2. That there are several chapels and places used for saying of mass, in the great towns and many other parts of this kingdom, besides those in ambassadors houses, whither great numbers of your majesty's subjects constantly resort and repair without controul, and especially in the cities of London and Westminster, contrary to the established laws. 3. That there are Fraternities or Convents of English Popish Priests and Jesuits, at St. James's, and at the Combe in Herefordshire, and others in other parts of the kingdom; besides, several schools are kept in divers parts of this kingdom, for the corrupt educating of youth in the principles of popery. 4. The common and public selling of Popish Catechisms, and other seditious Popish Books, even in the time of parliament. 5. The general remisness of the magistrates, and other officers, or clerks of assize and clerks of the peace, in not convicting of Papists according to law. 6. That suspected Recusants are free from all offices chargeable and troublesome; and do enjoy the advantages of offices and places beneficial, executed either by themselves, or by persons intrusted for them. 7. That the Advowsons of churches and presentations to livings are disposed of by Popish recusants, or by others intrusted by them, as they direct, whereby most of those livings and benefices are filled with scandalous and unfit ministers. 8. That many persons take the liberty to send their children beyond the seas, to be educated in the Popish religion; and that several young persons are sent beyond seas, upon the notion of their better education, under tutors or guardians, who are not put to take the oaths of allegiance and supremacy, and usually corrupt the youths under their tuition into popery. 9. That there have been few Exchequer process issued forth since the Act of Oblivion against the Popish Recusants convict, though many have been certified thither. 10. The great insolencies of the Papists in Ireland, where do publicly appear archbishops and bishops, reputed to be made such by the Pope, in opposition unto those made under your majesty's authority, according to the religion established in England and Ireland; and the open exercise of mass in Dublin, and other parts of that kingdom, is a further great Cause of the present Growth of Popery; and that Peter Talbot, the reputed abp. of Dublin, was publicly consecrated so at Antwerp with great and public solemnity, from whence he came to London, where he exercised his function, and was all along his journey to Chester treated with the character of his grace, by the Popish Recusants whom he visited; and at his landing in Dublin, he was received with very great solemnity by those of the Popish Religion there; where also he exercised his function publicly, great multitudes then flocking to him, and still continues to do the same. His present residence is within three miles of Dublin, at his brother's col. Rd. Talbot, who is now here, soliciting your maj. as public agent on the behalf of the Irish Papists of that kingdom.

The Remedies against these growing Mischiefs.

We, the lords spiritual and temporal and commons in this present parliament assembled, do in all humility represent to your sacred majesty in these Petitions following. 1. That your majesty, by your Proclamation, would be most graciously pleased to command, That all popish priests and jesuits do depart this realm, and all other your majesty's dominions, on or before a short day to be prefixed, at their perils (excepting only such foreign priests as attend her majesty's person by the contract of marriage, and ambassadors according to the law of nations); and that all judges and justices of the peace, and all other ministers and officers of justice, do cause the laws now in force against popish recusants to be put in due execution, and, in the first place, for the speedy conviction of such popish recusants; and that all judges and justices aforesaid do strictly give the said laws in charge unto the juries, at all assizes and sessions, under the penalty of incurring your majesty's highest displeasure. 2. That you would be graciously pleased to restrain and hinder the great concourse of your native subjects, from hearing of mass, and other exercises of the Romish religion, in the houses of foreign ambassadors or agents, and in all other chapels and places of this kingdom. 3. That your maj. would be most graciously pleased, out of your most princely wisdom and pious consideration, to take care, and cause, that no office or employment of public authority, trust, or command, in civil or military affairs, be committed to, or continued in the hands of any person being a popish recusant, or justly suspected to be so. 4. That your maj. would be graciously pleased to take notice of all fraternities and convents of English and other popish priests, jesuits, and friars, and schools for the educating of youth in the principles of popery, erected within your majesty's dominions; and to cause the same to be abolished, and the said priests, jesuits, friars and shoolmasters, to be duly punished for such their insolencies. 5. That your maj. would be graciously pleased, from time to time, to require and cause, that all the officers of or relating to the exchequer, according to their several duties, do proceed in, and issue forth, the exchequer process effectually upon popish recusants convict, certified thither; and that every such officer as shall refuse or neglect to do his duty as aforesaid, be severely punished for such his failure. 6. That your maj. would be graciously pleased to give order for apprehending, and bringing over into England, one Plunkett, who goes under the name of primate of Ireland, and one Peter Talbott, who takes on him the name of abp. of Dublin; to answer such matters as shall be objected against them. To these our most humble Petitions, proceeding from our duty and zeal for the glory of God, and good care of your sacred majesty, and from the care incumbent on us for the safety and peace of these your majesty's kingdoms; we do in all humility beseech your maj. to vouchsafe a gracious Answer. And we, your majesty's most loyal and obedient subjects, shall ever pray for your long and happy reign over us; and, as in conscience we are obliged, shall constantly adhere to, and assist your majesty, in the maintenance and defence of your majesty's Supremacy, and the true Protestant religion now established in your majesty's dominions, in opposition to all foreign powers and popish pretensions whatsoever."

The King's Answer to the above Petition.] To the above Petition his majesty made this most gracious Answer to them; "My Lords and gentlemen; I will take care of all these things; I will cause a Proclamation to be issued out against the Priests; I will cause the judges, and all other officers to put the laws against Papists in execution, and all other things that may conduce to the Prevention of the Growth of Popery. But I suppose no man will wonder, if I make a difference between those that have newly changed their Religion and those that were bred up in that religion, and served my father and me faithfully in the late wars."

The King's Proclamation against Papists.] The houses returned their Thanks for this Answer, and the king accordingly issued out his Proclamation; the substance of which was, "Whereas the lords and commons in parliament assembled, have by their Petition presented to his majesty their fears and apprehensions of the Growth of Popery, together with the Causes thereof, and also such Remedies as they conceive most proper to prevent such mischiefs: which Petition his majesty having seriously considered, and with much contentment approving the great care of the said lords and commons, for the preservation of the true Religion established; to which his majesty declares, as he hath always adhered against all temptations whatsoever, so he will still employ his utmost care and zeal in the maintenance and defence of it. And therefore strictly commands all jesuits and Romish priests to depart out of England before the 1st of May, upon pain of having the penalties of the laws of this realm inflicted upon them. And his majesty commands all judges, &c. forthwith to put the laws in execution against all Popish Recusants, and such as are suspected to be so, in order to their speedy conviction, and due process upon such conviction. And because there may be some priests imprisoned in this realm, unknown to his majesty; all sheriffs, &c. are within 20 days to advertise some of the lords of the privy-council of their names, and for what cause they were committed, to the end orders may be given for their transportation."

After this, the commons proceeded with all vigour upon the king's Supplies, the Subsidy-Bill, the Excise-Bill, and the Law-Bill; to which three they afterwards added a fourth bill for Impositions on Foreign Commodities.

The great Controversy between the Lords and Commons concerning the Lords making Amendments to Money Bills.] Two Money-Bills remained to be passed, the one 'for Impositions on Proceedings at law,' and the other, for an 'Additional Imposition on several Foreign Commodities:' which the merchants esteeming a Grievance, they petitioned the house of lords for relief, who thought their Reasons of such weight, that they demanded a Conference with the commons upon the case in dispute; and this being complied with, a committee from both houses were appointed. The earl of Anglesea was Speaker for the lords, and sir Heneage Finch, attorney-general, for the commons. The particulars of the Conference were as follows:

First Conference between the two Houses, on the Bill for Additional Impositions on Foreign Commodities.] April 17. The earl of Anglesea, and the rest of the lords that managed the Conference with the commons on Saturday last, concerning the Amendments in the bill, intituled, 'An additional Imposition on several Foreign Commodities, and for the Encouragement of several Commodities and Manufactures of this kingdom,' reported the effect of the said conference: viz.

"He said, Mr. Attorney General was the first man who spake; and told their lordships, That the commons had desired this conference upon the subject-matter of the last conference, which was concerning the Act of Imposition, intitled, 'An additional Imposition on several Foreign Commodities,' &c. He said, in the end of it, your lordships communicated the Form of an Address to his majesty, against the use of, and to discountenance those that do use, foreign manufactures in prejudice of our own; which they chearfully concur in, and humbly thank your lordships for: they differ so much in the rest, that he fears this is the only thing they agree in; but hope for a good agreement in conclusion, the commons having done as much as they can, to narrow the differences.—He said, In several clauses, we had varied the rates, in sums, in the species, and in the time.—They desire nothing that is not the subject-matter may come into debate between us (that is, concerning the right of laying Impositions on the subject in general); the present question being concerning rates and impositions on merchandize only. And in this there is a fundamental right in the house of commons, both as to the matter and the measure, and the time, unalterable, and which they cannot part with. He told us, we have formerly agreed a Book of Rates without so much as seeing it, signed by the Speaker sir Harbottle Grimston, 12 Carolus ii. confirmed 13 of king Charles, which they sent not up, lest your Speaker might sign it too, whereas never Book of Rates was read in the lords house.—The title they have to the giving Aids, is the only poor thing the commons can value themselves upon to their prince. If there be any fault in this bill, it is that they mentioned any rates at all in particular. If they had sent up a Bill of six lines, referring to a Book of Rates, there could be no reason why your lordships should not have agreed to that, with the same difference to the h. of commons, as you did for the other. Book of Rates 12 Car. ii. We desire we may not dispute what is not the question. The Rates upon Goods and Merchandize is that before us. They sent it this way, to shew their duty to the king, and respects to the lords; and never supposed it would be made a handle of difference to obstruct the gift for ever, as if it were too great to get through.—Your lordships begin a new thing. We find ourselves possessed of it in all ages, and find not one grant of Tonnage and Poundage that is not barely the gift of the commons. They hope your lordships will not now go about to assume this; a right so fundamentally settled in the commons, that I cannot give a reason for it, for that would be a weakening of the commons right and privilege, which we can never depart from, being affirmatively possessed of it in all ages, and negatively as to the lords. But, out of respect to your lordships, we have called ourselves to account upon the Reasons of our proceedings in this Bill; and do find that nothing that we have done in it is against the interest of trade; but no syllable of the variations made by your lordships but is prejudicial to the balance of trade. Some intrusted therewith will present your lordships the Reasons we shall offer; and though the expressions should be somewhat harsh in the maintaining the Right and Privilege of the h. of commons, we desire all may be received with candour and patience, and you would give it a fair interpretation.

"The next that spoke was sir Robert Howard, for the particular Amendments. [Here follow the several Amendments.] He concluded by saying, "your lordships cannot believe we, in the same barque with your lordships, should desire storms: we give freely, to prevent them. We are commanded also to say, we should not pursue our own interest, if we did not labour for accommodation. We have done all we can, to invite the lords to a happy concurrence.'—Then sir Rd. Temple said, 'I am commanded to back all with some observations on your lordships precedents: under favour to your precedents, I find at the same time you sent down for a Conference, March 13, 1580, which was reported in the house of commons, and they justified it by the Entry; the issue was, you did proceed on the new bill. The second precedent, 29th Eliz. It was in a private bill, which we have no entry of. I shall now observe, in the year 1660, Dec. 6, 'An Act against planting Tobacco in England,' an office and fees was erected in it: we laid it aside, and sent a new one, which the lords passed. It hath been observed to your lordships, the irregularity of sending us down a Bill for Prohibition turned into a Bill for an Imposition; trenching hereby on the right of the h. of commons, in beginning an imposition. The substance is the same in both, we differ only in the way; so that we hope you will agree. Mr. Attorney concluded: 'My lords; Aids were never more necessary; and this is no common present, a grant for nine years, and cannot miscarry but upon difference between the two houses. We desire that in no place, upon no occasion they may be made wider. There are two differences upon it: 1. Difference in judgment and opinion; we hope we have satisfied you therein fully. 2. In interest and privilege: this is in a narrow compass, we stand upon this; rates on merchandize you never did impose, never diminish. Books of rates have been kept from you, lest you should enquire into them. Nothing so dangerous as differences, nothing so unparliamentary. My lords, pray let nothing be done unparliamentary."'—Upon the report of this Conference and consideration had thereupon: It was resolved, upon the question, by the lords, nem. con. "That the power exercised by the house of peers, in making Amendments and Abatements in the Bill, entitled, 'An Act for an additional Imposition on several Foreign Commodities, &c.' both as to the matter, measure, and time, concerning the Rates and Impositions on Merchandize, is a fundamental, inherent, and undoubted right of the house of peers, from which they cannot depart."

Second Conference.] April 19. This second conference was desired by their lordships upon the subject-matter of the last Conference, concerning the Bill for Impositions on Merchandize, &c. wherein the commons communicated to the lords, as their Resolution, "That there is a fundamental right in that house alone, in Bills of Rates and Impositions on Merchandize, as to the matter, the measure, and time." And though their lordships had neither Reason nor Precedent offered by the commons to back that resolution, but were told 'That this was a right so fundamentally settled in the commons, that they could not give Reasons for it, for that would be a weakening of the commons right and privilege;' yet the lords in parliament, upon full consideration thereof, and of that whole conference, are come to this Resolution, nem. con.: "That the power exercised by the house of peers, in making the Amendments and Abatements in the Bill, entitled, 'An Act for an additional Imposition on several Foreign Commodities, &c.' both as to the matter, measure, and time, concerning the Rates and

Impositions on Merchandize, is a fundamental, inherent, and undoubted right of the house of peers, from which they cannot depart:"

Reasons of the Peers.

1. "The great happiness of the govt. of this kingdom is, that nothing can be done in order to the legislature, but what is considered by both houses before the king's sanction be given unto it; and the greatest security to all the subjects of this kingdom is, that the houses, by their constitution, do not only give assistance, but are mutual checks, to each other. 2. Consult the writs of summons to parliament; and you will find the lords are excluded from none of the great and arduous affairs of the kingdom and church of England, but are called to treat and give their counsel upon them all without exception. 3. We find no footsteps in record or history for this new claim of the house of commons; we would see that charter or contract produced, by which the lords divested themselves of this right, and appropriated it to the commons, with an exclusion of themselves: till then we cannot consent to shake or remove foundations, in the laying whereof it will not be denied that the lords and grands of the kingdom had the greatest hand. 4. If this right should be denied, the lords have not a negative voice allowed them in bills of this nature; for if the lords, who have the power of treating, advising, giving counsel, and applying remedies, cannot amend, abate, or refuse a bill in part, by what consequence of reason can they enjoy a liberty to reject the whole? When the commons shall think fit to question it, they may pretend the same grounds for it. 5. In any case of judicature, which is undoubtedly and indisputably the peculiar right and privilege of the house of lords, if their lordships send down a bill to the commons for giving judgment in a legislative way, they allow and acknowledge the same right in the commons to amend, change, and alter such bills, as the lords have exercised in this Bill of Impositions sent up by the commons. 6. By this new maxim of the house of commons, a hard and ignoble choice is left to the lords, either to refuse the crown supplies when they are most necessary, or to consent to ways and proportions of aid, which neither their own judgment or interest, nor the good of the government and people, can admit. 7. If positive assertion can introduce a right, what security have the lords, that the house of commons shall not in other bills (pretended to be for the general good of the commons, whereof they will conceive themselves the fittest judges) claim the same peculiar privileges in exclusion of any deliberation or alteration of the lords, when they shall judge it necessary or expedient. 8. And whereas you say, 'This is the only poor thing which you can value yourselves upon to the king!' their lordships have commanded us to tell you, that they rather desire to increase, than any ways to diminish, the value and esteem of the house of commons, not only with his majesty, but with the whole kingdom; but they cannot give way that it should be raised by the undervaluing of the house of peers, and an endeavour to render that house unuseful to the king and kingdom, by denying unto it those just powers which the constitution of this government and the law of the land hath lodged in it, for the service and benefit of both. 9. You did at the conference tell us, 'That we did agree a Book of Rates, without so much as seeing it; and that never Book of Rates was read in the lords house; and that the said Book of Rates was signed by sir Harbottle Grimston, then Speaker of the house of commons, and not sent up, lest the lords' Speaker might sign it too.' The Book of Rates instanced in by the house of commons was made in a way different from all former books of rates, and by an assembly called without the king's writs, and which wanted so much the authority of parliament, that the act they made was no act till confirmed by this parliament: Though the work which happily succeeded in their hands, for restoration of the ancient government of the kingdom, will ever be mentioned to their honour, yet no measure for parliamentary proceedings is to be taken from this one instance, to the prejudice of the right of the crown in making Books of Rates, and of the lords in having their due consideration thereof when they shall be enacted in parliament: which was so far from being according to former usage, that the lords considering the necessity and condition of that time, and there being no complaint, passed that Bill upon three readings in one day, without so much as a commitment, little imagining the forwardness of their zeal to the king's service in such a time would have created an argument in the future against their power; and if the lords never did read books of rates in their house, it is as true that the house of commons do not pretend, nor did shew, ever any was read there but this."

Next, the precedents were reported: thus,

"Though, where a Right is so clear, and Reasons so irrefragable, it is not to be required of those who are possessed of the right, to give Precedents to confirm it, but those who dispute the right ought to shew precedents or judgments to the contrary (not passed sub silentio, but) upon the point controverted; yet the lords have commanded us to offer and leave with you these following Precedents:—" By Records both ancient and modern it doth appear, 1. That the lords and commons have consulted together, and conferred one with another, upon the subject of Supply to the king, and of the manner how the same may be levied; as 14 E. iii. N. 5. 'Apres grand trete & parleance entre les grands et les ditz chivaliers et autres des communes esteans en dit parliament, est accordes et assentus par tous les grandz & communes, &c.' That they grant to the king the ninth of corn and wool.—29 E. iii. N. 11. 51 E. iii. N. 18. certain lords there named, from time to time, to confer with the commons, for their better help in consulting for the raising of Money; and this sometimes by the king's command, as, 22 E. iii. N. 3; sometimes by motion and appointment of the lords, as 5 E. iii. N. 8. and in the case of the great Contract for Tenures and Purveyances, 7 Jac. 14 Feb. 1609; sometimes by the desire of the commons; as, 47 E. iii. N. 6. and 4 R. ii. N. 10, 11, 12, 13, 14, 15, upon a great sum demanded for the king, the commons come to the lords, and desire a moderation of the sum, and their consideration how it should be levied; and hereupon was granted, by lords and commons, 12*d.* of every man, &c. It is observable that N. 13, it is said, The lords sent for the commons several times before them, and proposed to them the manner of levying the money; and afterwards it was given.' And again 6 R. ii. N. 14. And in the case of the great Contract before mentioned, 7 Jac. 18 June, 1610, the commons, at a conference, desire to know what project their lordships will propound for levying that which shall be given, other than upon land. And afterwards, at another conference, by the commons, answer was made to the lords proposal; agreed, that the manner of levying it may be in the most easeful and contentful sort that by both houses can be devised. See the whole proceedings of this intended contract, which doth in several remarkable instances shew that the house of commons themselves did allow the house of peers their part in treating and debating on the subject of Money to be levied for his majesty.—2. That, in Aids and Subsidies, the lords have anciently been expressly joined with the commons in the gift; as in the first we can meet with in our statutes, that in the body of Magna Charta, cap. 37, 'The archbishops, bishops, abbots, priors, earls, barons, knights, freeholders, and other our subjects, have given unto us the 15th part of all their moveables,' (which must include Merchandizes). This style the ancient grants of Subsidies and the modern ones too do retain (the troublesome time of the wars between the houses of York and Lancaster only excepted, and even then it was, 'The commons, by advice and assent of the lords, do give and grant)' till the beginning of king Charles 1st. By the words, 'We your majesty's loyal subjects in parliament assembled,' implicitly; or by the words, 'We the lords spiritual and temporal and commons in parliament assembled,' expressly; the lords are joined in the grant, as by perusal of the statutes will appear.—3. That, in Subsidies of this nature, viz. Customs, the lords have joined with the commons in the grant of them; and that at the very beginning of these Impositions, as when 40*s.* on every sack of wool (a home native commodity) was granted to E. 1st. in the 3d of his reign, to him and his heirs, the grant is, 'Magnates prelati, & tota communitas concesserunt.' See Parl. Roll. 3 E. i. M. 1. N. 1. And other ancient rolls do also shew that the lords joined with the commons in the gift of Monies; as, Close Roll, 3. E. i. M. 12. in Dorso 3. Grant of a 15th, and Pat. Roll. 3 E. i. M. 6.—4. And more particularly in Impositions of this very species, tonnage and poundage, the lords were even at the first beginning joined with the commons in the grant, as the Parl. Roll in the 47 E. iii. N. 10. the first establishment of it by act doth declare, where it is expressly, 'The lords and commons do grant.' And this stile did continue in acts of this nature till the end of R. ii. After which, in those troublesome times, the stile was various till Hen. viii's time; and then the stile of acts of Tonnage and Poundage, was, 'We the commons, by advice and consent of the lords spiritual and temporal, do give and grant." This form of gift in Tonnage and Poundage lasted E. vi. Mary, Eliz. and king James's time, as the statutes themselves do declare.—5. And to prove most undeniably that the lords have their share in the Gift of Aids and Supplies to the king, see the act of 9 H. iv. commonly called, 'The Indemnity of the lords and commons;' which provides, 'That the lords shall commune apart by themselves, and the commons by themselves:' and at the latter end enacts expressly, 'That the king shall thank both the lords and commons for Subsidies given to him.'—6. That the lords may make Amendments and Alterations in Bills which grant Tonnage and Poundage (the very question now between us), appears in an eminent Book, case 33 H. vi. fol. 17. (which was a consultation of all the Judges of England, and the master of the rolls and clerk of the parliament, called to inform them of the manner of proceedings of bills in parliament), where it is said, 'That if the commons grant 'Tonnage and Poundage to endure for 4 years, 'and the lords grant it but for two years, it 'shall not be carried back to the commons, 'because it may stand with their grant, but 'must be so enrolled.' And that the lords have made Amendments and Alterations in bills granting Tonnage and Poundage, appears by the stat. of 1 E. vi. and 1 Eliz. even in the very point now in dispute, such Amendments as do lessen the sum to the king, as the 1st of Hen. viii. &c."—The Proviso itself was read at the Conference.

"We have seriously consulted our judgments and Reasons, to find objections, if it were possible, against this power of the lords; and are so far from finding any, that we are fixed in opinion that the want of it would be destructive to the government and peace of the kingdom, and the right of the crown, in the balancing and regulating of trade, and the making and preserving leagues and treaties with foreign princes and states; and the exercise of it cannot but be for the security of all, and for the ease, benefit, and satisfaction of the subject.—Their lordships are very far from desiring to obstruct this gift, no not for a moment of time, much less for ever, as was hinted to them at the last conference: and therefore they desire the house of commons to lay it to heart, and consider, if it should so happen (which they heartily wish it may not) that there should be an obstruction upon occasion of this difference, at whose door it must lie; those that assume to themselves more than belongs to them, to the prejudice and diminution of the others right, or theirs that do only exercise that just and lawful power which by the very nature and constant practice of parliament is, and for many ages hath been, vested in both houses.—Their lordships had under their consideration and debate the desiring a free conference with your house, upon the Reasons of the Amendments in difference between the houses; but when they found that you had interwoven your general position with every Reason you had offered upon particulars, it seemed to them that your judgments were prepossessed; and they hold it vain and below the wisdom of parliament to reason or argue against fixed resolutions, and upon terms of impossibility to persuade; and have therefore applied themselves only to that point which yet remains an impediment in the way of free and parliamentary debates and conferences, which must necessarily be first removed, that so we may come to a free conference upon the Bill itself, and part with a fair correspondence between the two houses."

Third Conference.] April 22. The earl of Anglesey began the Report of this Conference; who said, That Mr. Attorney (sir Heneage Finch), told them, That, because the matter is of moment, the h. of commons have trusted none to give their words but themselves; therefore have ordered it to be in writing, as followeth: "The commons have desired this Conference, to preserve a good correspondence with the h. of peers, and to prevent the ill consequences of those misunderstandings which may possibly interrupt the happy conclusion of this session, and of all future parliaments too, if they be not very speedily removed: wherein the commons are not without hopes of giving your lordships full satisfaction in the point in question, and that without shaking any foundations, unless it be such as no man should lay, much less build upon, the foundations of a perpetual dissention between the two houses. Three things did surprize the commons at the former conference concerning the Bill for an additional Imposition on several Foreign Commodities: 1. That where they expected a discourse upon some Amendments to that bill, they met with nothing but a debate of the liberties of their house, in the matter, measure, and time, of rates upon merchandize, with a kind of a demand, that these liberties might be delivered up to your lordships by our public acknowledgement before there should be any further discourse upon that bill. 2. That your lordships should declare so fixed and settled a Resolution in this point, before you had so much as heard what could be replied in defence of the commons. 3. That your lordships should be so easily induced to take this Resolution, if there be no other motives for it than those Precedents and Reasons which your lordships have been pleased to impart to us.—The commons confess, that the best rule for deciding questions of Right between the two houses, is the law, and usage of parliament; and that the best evidences of that usage and custom of parliament are, the most frequent and authentic Precedents: therefore the commons will first examine the Precedents your lordships seem to rely upon; then they will produce those by which their right is asserted; and in the last place, they will consider the Reasons upon which your lordships ground yourselves.—By the nature of the Precedents which your lordships produce, there is an evident departure from the question as the former conference left it. There the doubt was narrowed to this single point, Whether your lordships could retrench or abate any part of the Rates which the commons had granted upon merchandize? Here the precedents do go to a joint power of imposing and beginning of taxes, which is a point we have not yet heard your lordships to pretend to, though this present difference prepares way for it: therefore, either these precedents prove too much, by proving a power of imposing; or they prove nothing at all, by not proving a power of lessening. And yet they do not prove a power of imposing neither; for those words 'the lords and commons grant,' must either be understood reddendo singula, singulis; that is, the lords grant for themselves, and the commons grant for the counties, cities, and boroughs, whom they represent; or else the word 'grant' must be understood only of the lords assent to what the commons grant, because the form of law requires, that both join in one bill to give it the force of a law.—This answers the statute of Magna Charta, c. 37, and those few instances wherein it is said, 'The lords and commons grant;' viz. the 47 E. iii. N. 10. 4 R. ii. N. 10, 11, 12, 13, 14. 6 R. ii. N. 14. But what answer can be given to those ancient and modern precedents and acts, where the grant moves, and is acknowledged to come from the commons alone; of which a multitude shall be hereinafter mentioned? The case of the 14 E. iii. N. 5, 'Apres grand trete et parlance 'entre lez grantz et chevaliers et communs, 'fuit assentus,' &c. is no grant of the 9th sheaf, as your lordships cited it to be; but an agreement that the nones granted in a former parliament should now be sold, because the money came not in fast enough.—22 E. iii. N. 3, which your lordships cite to prove that the king did sometimes command the lords to consult with the commons about raising Money, proves little of that; but it proves expressly, that the commons granted 3 fifteenths; and as the grant runs wholly in their name, so the record is full of many reasons why they could grant no more, and upon what conditions they granted so much.—And yet all these records, wherein the lords advised with the commons about raising money, though they seem to make a shew in your lordships paper, yet they prove two things of great importance to the commons: 1. That all Aids must begin with the commons; else the lords needed not to have conferred about the aids, but might have sent down a bill. 2. That when they are begun, the lords can neither add nor diminish; else it was in vain to adjust the matter by private conference beforehand, if the lords could have reformed it afterwards; which shews how little service the records of 29 E. iii. N. 11, 51 E. iii. N. 18, can do your lordships in the present question.—From the time of R. ii. your lordships come to 7 Jac. to tell us of the Treaty between the lords and commons touching the Contract for Tenures in capite, wherein, the lords and commons being to be purchasers, it was less subject to objection, to confer both of the method and manner how the price agreed might be paid for the satisfaction of the king: but this matter hath so little affinity with the present question of lessening Rates upon Merchandizes, given by the commons, that nothing but a scarcity of precedents could ever have persuaded your lordships to make use of this instance.—As for the precedent of 3 E. i, cited by your lordships, the commons have most reason to rely upon that case.—Your lordships say, in the beginning of impositions, when 40*s.* upon a sack of wool was granted to E. i. and his heirs, the lords joined in the grant; for the words are, 'Magnates, 'prelati, et tota communitas concesserunt,' wherein there are these mistakes: first, that record was not a grant of 40*s.* upon the sack of wool, as your lordships suppose, but a reducing of 40*s.* upon a sack, which E. i. took before Magna Charta was confirmed, to half a mark, viz. 6*s.* per sack; and it was at the prayer of the commons, as some books say, and cite for it 3 E. i. M. 24. Secondly, the record which your lordships cite is twice printed, once in the 2d part of the Institutes, p. 531, and again in the 4th part of the Institutes, p. 29; and by both those places it is evident that the 'concesserunt' is to be applied only to the 'tota communitas,' and not to the 'Magnates;' for this was a grant of the commons only, and not a grant of the lords; and, to demonstrate this beyond all possibility of scruple, the printed books do refer us to the Statute of 25 E. i. c. 7, called 'Confirmationes Chartarum,' wherein it is expressly so declared by act of parliament; for, by the last statute, it appears that the Maletot of 40*s.* upon a sack was again demanded by E. i. and was therefore now abrogated, saving to the king and his heirs the demi-mark upon a sack of wool granted by the commonalty, which is the very same grant of 3 E. i. cited by your lordships in the present question; but this is also a convincing evidence that those words 'The lords and commons grant' are words of form, and made use of in such cases where the grant did certainly proceed from the commons alone. And to clear this point yet more fully by a modern precedent, we pray your lordships to take notice of the statute of the 2d and 3d of Ed. vi. c. 36, where a relief is given to the king by parliament; and the title of the act, as also in the body of it, it is still called all along 'The grant of the lords and commons;' yet in 3 & 4 Ed. vi. c. 23, this former act is recited, and there it is acknowledged to be only a grant of the commons.—And as for the case of 9 H. iv, called 'The Indemnity of the lords and commons,' these things are evidently proved by it; 1. That it was a grievance to the commons, and a breach to their liberties, for the lords to demand a committee to confer with about aids. 2. That the lords ought to consider by themselves apart. 3. That no report should be made to the king of what the commons had granted, and the lords assented to, till the matter be perfected; so that a plain declaration is made, that the commons grant, and the lords assent. 4. That the gift ought to be presented by the Speaker of the commons. The Book Case of 33 H. vi. 17, is the weakest of all; for the words are, 'Si les com-m'es grant Tonage p' 4 ann. and s'n'rs grant mes pur deux anns, ceo ne sera reliver aux commoners; mes via versâ, si co'ones grant p' 2 ans et s'n'rs p' 4. ceo sera reliver.' Now, 1. This was no opinion of any judge, but only of Kirkby, cl. de parliament. 2. This was a case put by the bye, and not pertinent to the matter in hand. 3. It is impossible to be law, being against the constant practice and usage of parliament; for then your lordships may not only lessen the rates and time, but you may choose whether you will send us the bill or no back again, with amendment, which was never heard of; and if that may be, why was it not done so now? 4. That clerk says, your lordships may increase impositions too, which part of the case you thought not fit to cite, because you pretend not to it. 5. Brooke, parliament, 7, puts a query upon the case, as it deserved. But if the law books are to be heard in this matter, 30 H. viii. Dyer 43, is a judicial authority, where Subsidy is defined to be, a tax, 'assess par parliament, et grant al roy par les co'ones durant vyde chesc. roy, tantum pour le defence des merchants sur le mere.'—The provisos in the bill of 1 H. viii. which your lordships seem mainly to rely upon, we conceive to be of no force at all, unless it be against your lordships; for, by your lordships Journals, the case was this: the Bill itself did not pass till the 3d of Hen. viii.; and upon the 43d day of parliament, the lords assented to it. Afterwards, upon the 45th day, two provisos came in touching the merchants of the Hans Towns, another touching the merchants of the Staple of Calais; both were signed by the king; and the chancellor and bp. of Winchester did declare that the signing of those provisos by the king's own hand was enough, without the consent of either house; so that the addition of those provisos prove nothing for which your lordships cited them; because, 1. They were signed by the king: 2. They were brought in, against all course of parliament, after the bill passed;

3. The provisos were nothing but a saving of former rights, usually considered in former acts of that nature: 4. Your lordships Journal declares, that the king without these provisos, might have done the same thing by his prerogative. Only this may be fit to be observed by the way, that as the bill was a grant of the commons alone, so the thanks for that bill was given to the commons alone; and so appears upon the indorsement of that record. The Precedents for the commons, which on the sudden we find, for we have had but few hours to search, are all these following: 11 E. i. Walsingham 471, 'Populus dedit regi tricesimam partem bonorum.' 25 E. i. Walsingham 486, 'Populus dedit regi denarium novum.' 7 H. iv. Walsingham 566, 'postquam milites parliamentares diu distulissent, concedere regi subsidium in fine tamem fracti concessere.' 6 H. iv. Walsingham 564, 'Subsidium denegatum fuit proceribus remittentibus.' So hitherto when granted, the commons give it; when denied, the whole bill rejected, never abated. 1 E. iii. stat. 2, c. 6, The commons grieved, that when they granted an aid, and paid it, the taxes were reviewed. 18 E. iii. c. 1, stat. at large, The commons grant two fifteenths; the great men grant nothing, but to go in person with the king. 36 E. iii. c. 11, the king having regard to the grant made by the commons for three years of wool and leather, grants that no Aid be levied, but by consent of parliament. 21 R ii. N. 75, is the first grant of Tonnage and Poundage for life; and it was given by the commons alone. 2 H. vi. N. 14, The commons grant tonnage and poundage for two years. 31 H. vi. N. 7, 8, 9, 10, The commons grant Tonnage, &c. for life. 8 E. iv. N. 30, The commons grant two tenths and two fifteenths. 12 E. iv. c. 3, The grant for Tonnage and Poundage for life is recited to be by the commons, and most of the rates mentioned in the bill. The wars of York and Lancaster are so from weakening these precedents, it strengthens them rather; for no man can think the lords were then in less power, or less careful of their rights, than your lordships are now; wherefore, if in those days those forms were approved by those mighty men, it is a sign the right is clear. 1 H. vii. The commons, by assent of the lords, grant Tonnage. 15 H. vii. In Ireland was the first grant of Tonnage and Poundage; but it is said, at the prayer of the commons it is enacted: which in a kingdom where they are not tied to forms, shews the clear right. 1 E. vi. c. 13, 1 M. c. 8, 1 Eliz. c. 19, 'We your poor commons by advice, &c. grant: And also avers the right, time out of mind, to be in the commons in like manner. This statute of the 1st of Eliz. c. 19, gives us occasion to put your lordships in mind of another precedent which appears in your own Journals; for, while this bill was passing, the inhabitants of Cheshire and Wales petition the lords, upon the second reading, That forasmuch as they were subject to pay the queen a certain duty called Mises, that therefore they might be excused of the subsidy, and abated their parts of it. The lords, who then knew they had no power to diminish any part of the Aid granted by the commons, did therefore address themselves to the queen in their behalfs. The queen commands an entry to be made in the Journal of the house of lords, That she was pleased that the Cheshire men and the Welch men should be respited the Mises when they pay subsidies, and respited the subsidies when they pay Mises; which is a strong proof, that as the commons alone grant, so nobody can diminish their grant; else what need had the lords to apply themselves to the queen for it? 17 Car. i. Tonnage and Poundage was granted once for a month, then again for three months; but still the grant was by the commons: in those days, how tumultuous soever, the commons did not rise against the lords. they agreed well enough. And the preamble of this very bill now in question. All grants of the commons; yet none of these bills were ever varied by your lordships or your predecessors; which, if there had been such a right, would some time or other have been exercised, though in very small values, purposely to preserve that right. Thus an uninterrupted possession of this Privilege ever since 9 H. iv. confirmed by a multitude of precedents both before and after, not shaken by one precedent for these 300 years, is now required to be delivered up, or an end put to all further discourse; which opinion, if it be adhered to, is, as much as in your lordships lies, to put an end to all further transactions between the houses in matter of Money, which we pray your lordships to consider."

The Reasons offered by the House of Commons were these:—"Because it appears not to the commons, any colour from the Precedents cited by your lordships, why your opinions should be so fixed in this point. We suppose the main defence is in the Reasons that have been given for it. That Paper begins with an observation, 'That your lordships have neither 'Reason nor Precedent offered by the com'mons to back their Resolution;' and yet concludes with an Answer to a precedent then cited by the h. of commons, viz. the Act of Tonnage and Poundage now in force. And if your lordships heard, but one precedent then, you have now a great number, besides those of 3 Ed. i. and 1 H. viii. and 9 H. iv. and divers others your lordships furnished us with.—Before the commons answer to your lordships Reasons in particular, they desire to say, first, in general, That it is a very unsafe thing in any settled government, to argue the Reasons of the fundamental constitutions; for that can tend to nothing that is profitable for the whole. And this will more sensibly appear to your lordships, if the grounds and foundations of judicature be examined; for there are several precedents in the parliament, and some in Book Cases, which prove that the judicature is not to be exercised by all the lords, but only such as the king is pleased to appoint. So is the Book Case of 22. E. iii. 3. a. b. and so is the Parliament Roll, 25 E. iii. N. 4.—Several other Precedents, where the commons by the king's good pleasure have been let into a share of the very judicature, are 42 E. iii. N. 20, 21. 31 H. vi. N. 10, 8 E. iv. Hugh Brice's Case in the Rolls of parliament.—Some precedents there are, where it was assigned for error in the house of peers, 'That the lords gave judgment 'without Petition or Assent of the commons.' So is the 2 H. v. N. 13.—Would your lordships think it safe, that a dispute should now be made of the very rights of judicature, because we have such precedents? If usage for so long a time have silenced all disputes touching your lordships judicature, shall that usage be of no force to preserve the privileges of the commons from all further question? Also, there is a precedent of an act of parliament passed by the king and commons alone, without the lords, viz. 1 E. vi. C. 5, and that twice approved, viz. 1 Eliz. C. 7, and 5 Eliz. C. 19, which both allow and commend this act. Shall we therefore argue the foundations of the legislature, because we have such precedents? —But to come to particulars: Your lordships first Reason is, from the happiness of the constitution, That the two houses are mutual checks upon each other. *Answ.* So they are still; for your lordships have a negative to the whole. But, on the other side, it would be a double check upon his majesty's affairs, if the king may not rely upon the quantum, when once his people have given it; therefore the privilege now contended for by your lordships is not of use to the crown, but much the contrary. 2. Your lordships Reason, drawn from the Writ of Summons, is as little concluding; for, though the writ do not exclude you from any affairs, yet it is only 'de quibusdam arduis negotiis,' and must be understood of such as by course of parliament are proper, else the commons upon the like ground may entitle themselves to judicature; for they are also called to treat 'de quibusdam arduis.' 3. Your lordships proceed to demand, 'Where is that record or contract in parliament to be found, where the lords appropriate this right to the commons in exclusion of themselves?' *Answ.* To this rhetorical question the commons pray they may answer by another question; 'Where is that record or contract, by which the commons submitted that judicature should be appropriated to the lords in exclusion of themselves?' Wherever your lordships find the last record, they will shew the first endorsed upon the back of the same roll. Truth is, precedents there are where both sides do exercise these several rights, but none how either side came by them. 4. If the lords may deny the whole, why not a part? Else the commons may at last pretend against the lords negative voice. *Answ.* The king must deny the whole of every bill, or pass it; yet this takes not away his negative voice: the lords and commons must accept the whole general pardon, or deny it; yet this takes not away their negative. The clergy have a right to tax themselves, and it is a part of the privilege of their estate: doth the upper convocation house alter what the lower grant? or do the lords or commons ever abate any part of their gift? Yet they have a power to reject the whole. But, if abatement should be made, it would insensibly go to a raising, and deprive the clergy of their ancient right to tax themselves.—5. Your lordships say, 'Judicature is undoubtedly ours; yet in bills of judicature we allow the commons to amend and alter: why should not the commons allow to us the same privilege in bills of money?' *Answ.* If contracts were now to be made for privileges, the offer might seem fair: but yet the commons should profit little by it; for your lordships do now industriously avoid all bills of that nature, and choose to do many things by your own power, which ought to be done by the legislative; of which we forbear the instances, because your lordships, we hope, will reform them; and we desire not to create new differences, but to compose the old.—6. Your lordships say, You are put to an ignoble choice, either to refuse the king's Supplies when they are most necessary, or to consent to such ways and proportions which neither your own judgment nor good of the government or people can admit.—*Answ.* We pray your lordships to observe, That this reason, first, makes your lordships judgment to be the measure of the welfare of the commons of England. 2. It gives you power to raise and increase taxes, as well as to abate, for it may sometimes, in your lordships judgments, be for interest of trade to raise and increase a rate; and then still you are brought to the same ignoble choice, unless you may raise the tax.—But it is a very ignoble choice put upon the king and his people, That either his maj. must demand, and the commons give, so small an aid as can never be diminished, or else run the hazard of your lordships re-examination of the rates, whose proportions in all taxes, in comparison to what the commonalty pay, is very inconsiderable.—7. If positive assertions can introduce right, the lords have no security; but the commons may extend their rights, as they judge it necessary or expedient. *Answ.* We hope no assertions or denials, though never so positive, shall give or take away a right; but we rely upon usage of our side, and non-usage on your lordships part, as the best evidences by which your lordships or we can claim any privilege.—8. Your lordships profess a desire to raise our esteem with his maj. and the whole kingdom, but not by the under-valuation of the house of peers. *Answ.* We have great confidence in his maj.'s goodness, that nothing can lessen his esteem of our dutiful affections to him; and we hope we have deserved so well of our country, by our deportment towards his majesty, that we shall not need your lordships recommendations to any who wish well to his maj. or the present government. But we are so far from wishing to raise an esteem by any diminution of your lordships honour or privileges, that there never was any house of commons who had a more just and true respect of that noble constitution of a house of peers; of which your lordships have had frequent instances, by our consenting to several clauses in Bills for securing and improving your lordships privileges.—We are sorry to see your lordships undervalue the precedent of this last Act of Tonnage and Poundage; because, though it were an act of the last Convention, it was confirmed in this. And because the right of the commons there asserted was pursuant to a former precedent in 1642, and possibly had not passed so, if the younger members of that Convention had not learned from some of these great and noble lords who now manage the conference for your lordships, and were then commoners, that this was the undoubted right of the commons.—To conclude: The commons have examined themselves and their proceedings, and find no cause why your lordships should put them in mind of that modesty by which their ancestors shewed a great deference to the wisdom of the lords; for they resolve ever to observe the modesty of their ancestors, and doubt not but your lordships will also follow the wisdom of yours."

To these the Lords proceeded to make some Replies: and, particularly, "as to their having no power to alter the Subsidies of the Clergy, nor an Act for a general Pardon; they said, these were things eccentric to parliaments, and had their motion in another sphere: the Convocation gave one, and the king of his free grace bestowed the other; and the parliament only gave them the force of law, and might chuse whether they would do it or not; and consequently this was no ways to the case in dispute. But to read the commons Money-Bill three times in their house, and to commit it, without any power of debating upon it, was a solemn piece of pageantry, beneath the dignity of a parliament. As to the point of Judicature, they alledged, it belonged to the peers before the very being of a house of commons, rather as the grand council of the nation, than as part of the parliament; and being vested in the king, as well as themselves, might possibly exist without the sitting of a parliament. As to Precedents they alledged, we have several for us; but it were enough for our justification, if there be none against us; and there could be but one of these kinds, either that we have of ourselves disclaimed such a power, or that it hath been denied them when they have claimed it, and whosoever sheweth one of either, 'Erit nobis magnus Apollo.'"

The Speaker's Speech to the King, at the Prorogation.] April 22. But before a period could be put to this great Controversy, his majesty came to the house of peers in order to a prorogation. The commons being come, the Speaker addressed his maj. to this effect:

"That his majesty was pleased in Oct. last (when the parliament then met), to acquaint them how his Revenue was clogged with Debts; and that the commons, taking the same into consideration, resolved to supply his maj. accordingly; and that, on the 6th of March last, he presented his majesty, from the house of commons, with the Subsidy and Excise bills; and now, by their command, he presented his maj. with the bill for laying Impositions on Proceedings at Law: that he was commanded humbly to beseech his majesty, that the Revenue thereof might be effectually applied to the payment of his debts: and that he had further in command from them, to let his maj. know, That they had enlarged the time for the Impositions on Proceedings at Law to 9 years, that thereby his maj. might be the better enabled to satisfy his Debt owing to the prince of Orange; he begged his pardon, that he called it his Debt, it being contracted for Supplies afforded to his royal father and himself in their unhappy necessities, and therefore not to be forgotten. He said, that geographers write of some Islands called 'Insulæ Fortunatæ,' whose harvest is said to be in March and April; he hoped, that England might be accounted one of those Islands, having afforded his maj. such a crop in March last and this April, which he humbly besought his maj. to accept as a pledge of their dutiful affection to him."

The King's Speech.] After passing several Bills his majesty spake thus:

"My Lords and Gentlemen; I give you very hearty thanks, for the Supply you have now given me."—His majesty also proceeded further to thank them for what they had further intended him; and assured them, "That what they had given him should be employed toward the payment of his Debts, and his expences for this year: that it was now time for them to go into their countries; and he desired them to take care that in the laying and collecting of the Subsidy they had given him, it might be improved to what they intended. He said further, That he intended the parliament should be prorogued, not to meet again for almost a year; but hoped that when they did meet, they would come again with the same affections to his service as formerly; and what he had further to say to them, they should understand by the Lord Keeper."

Then the Lord Keeper spake to this effect:

"My Lords and Gentlemen; His maj. hath told you with how great satisfaction he hath accepted your Supplies, as real testimonies of the constancy of your good affections." His lordship further told them, "That many of them being commissioners in the country for the new Subsidy; his maj. desired them to use their endeavours to make it effectual, and suitable to their intentions; and wished them to assure their neighbours, that he would employ the monies entirely towards the payment of his debts."—He then prorogued the parliament to the 16th of April next.*

* The state of the nation, at and about this time, is thus summed up by Marvell, in his

April 16, 1672. Both houses met on the day appointed. The commons, with the clerk of the house, went up to the house of lords, where the Lord Keeper declared his majesty's pleasure for the proroguing, and did prorogue the parliament to the 30th of Oct. next.

Oct. 30. Both houses met accordingly, when the Lord Keeper declared his majesty's pleasure for a further prorogation to the 4th of Feb. next.†

Principal Occurrences during the Recess—The Exchequer shut—Attack of the Smyrna Fleet—Dutch War.] "Long and frequent prorogations," says Mr. Hume, "were made of the parliament; lest the houses should declare themselves with vigour against counsels, so opposite to the inclination as well as interests of the public. These long prorogations, if they freed the king from the importunate remonstrances of that assembly, were, however, attended with this inconvenience, that no Money could be procured to carry on the military preparations against Holland. Under pretence of maintaining the Triple League, which at that very time he had firmly resolved to break, Charles had obtained a large supply from the commons; but this money was soon exhausted by debts and expences. France had stipulated to pay 200,000*l.* a year during the war; but the supply was inconsiderable, compared to the immense charge of the English navy. It seemed as yet premature to venture on levying money, without consent of parliament; since the power of taxing themselves was the privilege, of which the English were, with reason, particularly jealous. Some other resource must be fallen on. The king had declared, that the staff of Treasurer was ready for any one that could find an expedient for supplying the present necessities. Shaftesbury dropped a hint to Clifford, which the latter immediately seized, and carried to the king, who granted him the promised reward, together with a peerage. This expedient was the shutting up of the Exchequer (2d Jan.), and the retaining of all the payments which should be made into it.—It had been usual for the bankers to carry their money to the Exchequer, and to advance it upon security of the funds, by which they were afterwards reimbursed, when the money was levied on the public. The bankers, by this traffic, got 8, sometimes 10, per cent. for sums which either had been consigned to them without interest, or which they had borrowed at six per cent.: profits, which they dearly paid for by this egregous breach of public faith. The measure was so suddenly taken, that none had warning of the danger. A general confusion prevailed in the city, followed by the ruin of many. The bankers stopped payment; the merchants could answer no bills; distrust took place every where, with a stagnation of commerce, by which the public was universally affected. And men full of dismal apprehensions, asked each other, what must be the scope of those mysterious counsels, whence the parliament and all men of honour were excluded, and which commenced by the forfeiture of public credit, and an open violation of the most solemn engagements, both foreign and domestic. Another measure of the court contains something laudable, when considered in itself; but if we reflect on the motive whence it proceeded, as well as the time when it was embraced, it will furnish a strong proof of the arbitrary and dangerous counsels pursued at that time by the king and his ministry. Charles resolved to make use of his supreme power in ecclesiastical matters; a power, he said, which was not only inherent in him, but which had been recognized by several acts of parliament. By virtue of this authority, he issued a Proclamation; suspending the penal laws enacted against all non conformists or recusants whatsoever: and granting to the protestant dissenters the public exercise of their religion, to the catholics the exercise of it in private houses. A fruitless experiment of this kind, opposed by the parliament, and retracted by the king, had already been made a few years after the Restoration; but Charles expected, that the parliament, when ever it should meet, would now be tamed to greater submission, and would no longer dare to control his measures. Meanwhile, the dissenters, the most inveterate enemies of the court, were mollified by these indulgent maxims: and the catholics, under their shelter, enjoyed more liberty than the laws had hitherto allowed them.—At the same time the Act of Navigation was suspended by royal will and pleasure: a measure, which though a stretch of prerogative, seemed useful to commerce, while all the seamen were employed on board the royal navy. A like suspension had been

Letters: "The court is at the highest pitch of want and luxury; and the house of commons are grown extremely chargeable to the king, and odious to the people, who are full of discontent."

† They were to have met Oct. 30, but just before the time, when men's minds began to be filled with hopes or fears, a Proclamation came out for a further prorogation; of which the earl of Arlington gives the following account in a Letter to sir Bernard Gascoyn, then resident at Vienna: "The last week his majesty resolved in council on a further prorogation of the parliament to the 4th of Feb. next, by which a great measure of the Hollanders is broken, having fancied to themselves, that they should prevail with many of the members of it, to make them clamorous upon his majesty for a separate Treaty upon easy terms, and with exclusion to France; so that they seeing this trust broken, and finding no great ease to their present calamity from the auxiliary forces of Germany, we persuade ourselves we shall find them very reasonable in a short time; and in Feb. his majesty bringing into parliament a determinate resolution either of peace or war, will much more easily obtain all the ends there."

granted, during the first Dutch war, and was not much remarked; because men had, at that time, entertained less jealousy of the crown. A Proclamation was also issued, containing rigorous clauses in favour of pressing: another full of menaces against those who presumed to speak undutifully of his majesty's measures, and even against those who heard such discourse, unless they informed in due time against the offenders: another against importing or vending any sort of painted earthen ware, "except those of China, upon pain of being grievously fined, and suffering the utmost punishment which might be lawfully inflicted upon contemners of his majesty's royal authority." An army had been levied; and it was found, that discipline could not be enforced without the exercise of martial law, which was therefore established by order of council, though contrary to the petition of right. All these acts of power, how little important soever in themselves, savoured strongly of arbitrary government, and were no-wise suitable to that legal administration, which the parliament, after such violent convulsions and civil wars, had hoped to have established in the kingdom.—It may be worth remarking, that the lord-keeper refused to affix the great seal to the Declaration for suspending the Penal Laws; and was for that reason, though under other pretences, removed from his office. Shaftesbury was made chancellor in his place; and thus another member of the CABAL received the reward of his counsels.—Foreign transactions kept pace with these domestic occurrences. An attempt, before the declaration of war, was made on the Dutch Smyrna fleet by sir Robert Holmes. This fleet consisted of 70 sail, valued at a million and a half: and the hopes of seizing so rich a prey had been a great motive for engaging Charles in the present war, and he had considered that capture as a principal resource for supporting his military enterprises. Holmes, with nine frigates and three yachts, had orders to go on this command; and he passed Sprague in the channel, who was returning with a squadron from a cruize in the Mediterranean. Sprague informed him of the near approach of the Hollanders; and had not Holmes, from a desire of engrossing the honour and profit of the enterprize, kept the secret of his orders, the conjunction of these squadrons had rendered the success infallible. When Holmes approached the Dutch (March 13), he put on an amicable appearance, and invited the admiral, Van Ness, who commanded the convoy, to come on board of him: one of his captains gave a like insidious invitation to the rear-admiral. But these officers were on their guard. They had received an intimation of the hostile intentions of the English, and had already put all the ships of war and merchantmen in an excellent posture of defence. Three times were they valiantly assailed by the English; and as often did they valiantly defend themselves. In the third attack one of the Dutch ships of war was taken: and three or four of their most inconsiderable merchantmen fell into the enemies hands. The rest, fighting with skill and courage, continued their course; and, favoured by a mist, got safe into their own harbours. This attempt is denominated perfidious and piratical by the Dutch writers, and even by many of the English. It merits at least the appellation of irregular; and as it had been attended with bad success, it brought double shame upon the contrivers. The English ministry endeavoured to apologize for the action, by pretending that it was a casual renconter, arising from the obstinacy of the Dutch, in refusing the honours of the flag: but the contrary was so well known, that even Holmes himself had not the assurance to persist in this asseveration.—Till this incident the States, notwithstanding all the menaces and preparations of the English, never believed them thoroughly in earnest; and had always expected that the affair would terminate, either in some demands of money, or in some proposals for the advancement of the prince of Orange. The French themselves had never much reckoned on assistance from England; and scarcely could believe that their ambitious projects would, contrary to every maxim of honour and policy, be forwarded by that power which was most interested, and most able to oppose them. But Charles was too far advanced to retreat. He immediately issued a Declaration of war against the Dutch (March 17); and surely reasons more false and frivolous never were employed to justify a flagrant violation of treaty. Some complaints are there made of injuries done to the East-India company, which yet that company disavowed: the detention of some English in Surinam is mentioned; though it appears that these persons had voluntarily remained there: the refusal of a Dutch fleet, on their own coasts, to strike to an English yacht, is much aggravated: and to piece up all these pretensions, some abusive pictures are mentioned, and represented as a ground of quarrel. The Dutch were long at a loss what to make of this article; till it was discovered, that a portrait of Cornelius de Wit, brother to the pensionary, painted by order of certain magistrates of Dort, and hung up in a chamber of the town-house, had given occasion to the complaint. In the perspective of this portrait, the painter had drawn some ships on fire in a harbour. This was construed to be Chatham, where de Wit had really distinguished himself, and had acquired honour; but little did he imagine, that, while the insult itself, committed in open war, had so long been forgiven, the picture of it should draw such severe vengeance upon his country. The conclusion of this manifesto, where the king still professed his resolution of adhering to the Triple Alliance, was of a piece with the rest of it.—There was no ally on whom the Dutch more relied for assistance than the parliament of England, which the king's necessities at last obliged him to assemble."

TENTH SESSION OF THE SECOND PARLIAMENT.

Sir Job Charleton chosen Speaker.] Feb. 4. 1672-3. This day both houses met, and sir Edw. Turner, the last Speaker of the house of commons, having been made lord chief-baron of the exchequer, the first thing they did was to choose a new Speaker; to this end, sir Job Charleton, serjeant at law, was recommended to them, and unanimously elected. Who, being presented to the king, made the following excuse:

"Most gracious sovereign, The knights, citizens, and burgesses of your house of commons, in obedience to your royal command, have proceeded to the choice of a Speaker. They have among them many worthy persons eminently qualified for so great a trust; yet, with too favourable an eye, have cast it upon me, who am really conscious to myself of many infirmities rendering me much unfit for so great an employment. And although my endeavours of excusing myself before them have not been successful, yet they have been so indulgent as to permit me to continue my endeavours therein before your majesty's most piercing and discerning judgment. The veneration due to your majesty, which lodgeth in every loyal breast, makes it not an easy matter to speak before your maj. at any time, or in any capacity. But to speak before your maj. in your exaltation, thus gloriously supported and attended, and that as Speaker of your house of commons, requires greater abilities than I can pretend to own. I am not also without fear that the public affairs, wherein your maj. and your kingdom in this juncture of time are so highly concerned, may receive detriment through my weakness. I therefore, with a plain humble heart, prostrate at your royal feet, beseech that you will command them to review what they have done, and to proceed to another election."

Then the Lord Chancellor, (Shaftsbury) by directions from his maj. returned this Answer:

"Mr. Serjeant Charleton, The king hath very attentively heard your discreet and handsome discourse, whereby you endeavour to excuse and disable yourself for the place of Speaker: In answer whereof, his majesty hath commanded me to say to you, that he doth in no sort admit of the same; for his majesty hath had long experience of your abilities, good affection, integrity, and resolution, in several employments of great trust and weight. He knows you have been long a parliament man, and therefore every way fitted and qualified for the employment. Besides, he cannot disapprove the election of this house of commons, especially when they have expressed so much duty in choosing one worthy and acceptable to him. And therefore the king doth allow of the election, and admits you for Speaker."

Whereupon Mr. Speaker made this Reply:

"Great Sir. Since it is your gracious pleasure, not to accept of my humble excuse, but by your royal approbation to fix me under this great though honourable weight, and to think me fit to be invested with a trust of so high a nature as this is; I take it, in the first place, to be incumbent upon me, that I render your maj. all possible thanks; which I now humbly do, with a heart full of all duty, and affected with a deeper sense of gratitude than I can find words to express. Next, from your royal determination in this affair, whereby you have imprinted a new character upon me, I take courage against my own diffidence, and cheerfully bend myself, with such strength and abilities as God shall give, to the service so graciously assigned me; no way doubting that your majesty will please to pardon my frailities, to accept of my faithful endeavours, and always to look favourably upon the work of your own hands. And now, sir, my first entrance upon this service obliges me to make a few necessary, but humble petitions, on behalf of your most loyal and dutiful house of commons: 1. That, for our better attendance on the public service, we and our servants may be free, in our persons and estates, from arrests and other disturbances. 2. That, in our debates, liberty and freedom of speech be allowed us. 3. That, as occasions shall require, your majesty, upon our humble suit, and at such times as your majesty shall judge seasonable, will vouchsafe us access to your royal person. 4. That all our proceedings may receive a favourable construction. That God who hath brought you back to the throne of your fathers, and with you all our comforts, grant you a long and prosperous reign, and send you victory over all your enemies; and every good man's heart will say, Amen."

Upon which, by his majesty's further direction, the Lord Chancellor said as followeth:

"Master Speaker, The king's maj. hath heard, and well weighed, your short and eloquent oration; and in the first place, much approves that you have with so much advantage introduced a shorter way of speaking upon this occasion. His maj. doth well accept of all those dutiful and affectionate expressions, in which you have delivered your submission to his royal pleasure; and looks upon it as a good omen to his affairs, and as an evidence that the house of commons have still the same heart, that have chosen such a mouth. The conjuncture of time, and the king and kingdom's affairs, require such a house of commons, such a Speaker; for, with reverence to the holy scripture, upon this occasion the king may say, 'He that is not with me, is against me;' for he that doth not now put his hand and heart to support the king in the common cause of this kingdom, can hardly ever hope for such another opportunity, or find a time to make satisfaction for the omission of this."

The King's Speech on opening the Session.] Then his majesty spake as followeth:

"My Lords and Gentlemen; I am glad to see you here this day. I would have called you sooner together, but that I was willing to ease you and the country till there were an absolute necessity. Since you were last here, I have been forced to a most important, necessary, and expensive war; and I make no doubt but you will give me suitable and effectual assistance to go through with it. I refer you to my Declaration for the Causes, and indeed the Necessity of this War; and shall now only tell you, that I might have digested the indignities to my own person, rather than have brought it to this extremity, if the interest as well as the honour of the whole kingdom had not been at stake: and if I had omitted this conjuncture, perhaps I had not again ever met with the like advantage.—You will find, that the last Supply you gave me did not answer expectation for the ends you gave it, the payment of my Debts: therefore I must, in the next place, recommend them again to your especial care.—Some few days before I declared the War, I put forth my Declaration for Indulgence to Dissenters, and have hitherto found a good effect of it, by securing peace at home when I had war abroad. There is one part in it that hath been subject to misconstructions, which is that concerning the Papists; as if more liberty were granted them than to the other Recusants, when it is plain there is less; for the others have public places allowed them, and I never intended that they should have any, but only have the freedom of their religion in their own houses, without any concourse of others. And I could not grant them less than this, when I had extended so much more grace to others, most of them having been loyal, and in the service of me and of the king my father; and in the whole course of this indulgence, I do not intend that it shall any way prejudice the Church, but I will support its rights, and it in its full power. Having said this, I shall take it very ill to receive contradiction in what I have done. And, I will deal plainly with you, I am resolved to stick to my Declaration.—There is one jealousy more, that is maliciously spread abroad, and yet so weak and frivolous that I once thought it not of moment enough to mention, but it may have gotten some ground with some well-minded people; and that is, that the forces I have raised in this war were designed to controul law and property. I wish I had more forces the last summer; the want of them then, convinces me I must raise more against this next spring; and I do not doubt but you will consider the charge of them in your Supplies. —I will conclude with this assurance to you, That I will preserve the true Reformed Protestant Religion and the Church as it is now established in this kingdom, and that no man's property or liberty shall ever be invaded. I leave the rest to the Chancellor."

The Lord Chancellor Shaftsbury's Speech.] Then the Lord Chancellor spake as follows:

"My lords; and you the knights, citizens, and burgesses of the house of commons; The king hath spoken so fully, so excellently well, and so like himself, that you are not to expect much from me. There is not a word in his speech that hath not its full weight, and, I dare with assurance say, will have its effect with you. His maj. had called you sooner, and his affairs required it, but that he was resolved to give you all the ease and vacancy to your own private concerns, and the people as much respite from payments and taxes, as the necessity of his business, or their preservation, would permit. And yet (which I cannot but here mention to you), by the crafty insinuations of some ill-affected persons, there have been spread strange and desperate rumours, which your meeting together this day hath sufficiently proved both malicious and false.—His maj. hath told you, that he is now engaged in an important, very expensive, and indeed a war absolutely necessary and unavoidable. He hath referred you to his Declaration, where you will find the personal indignities by pictures and medals, and other public affronts, his maj. hath received from the States; their breach of Treaties both in the Surinam and East India business; and at last they came to that height of insolence, as to deny the honour and right of the Flag, though an undoubted jewel of this crown, never to be parted with, and by them particularly owned in the late Treaty of Breda, and never contested in any age. And whilst the king first long expected, and then solemnly demanded satisfaction, they disputed his title to it in all the courts of Christendom; and made great offers to the French king, if he would stand by them against us. But the most Christian king too well remembered what they did at Munster, contrary to so many treaties and solemn engagements, and how dangerous a neighbour they were to all crowned heads.—The king and his ministers had here a hard time, and lay every day under new obloquies: sometimes they were represented as selling all to France, for money to make this war; Portsmouth, Plymouth, and Hull, were to be given into the French hands for caution. The next day news came, that France and Holland were agreed. Then the obloquy was turned from treachery to folly. The ministers were now fools, that some days before were villains. And indeed the coffee-houses were not to be blamed for their last apprehensions, since, if that conjunction had taken effect, then England had been in a far worse case than now it is, and the war had been turned upon us. But both kings, knowing their interest, resolved to join against them, who were the common enemies to all monarchies, and I may say, especially to ours, their only competitor for trade and power at sea, and who only stand in their way to an universal empire as great as Rome. This the States understood so well, and had swallowed so deep, that, under all their present distress and danger, they are so intoxicated with that vast ambition, that they slight a Treaty, and refuse a Cessation.—All this you and the whole nation saw before the last war; but it could not then be so well timed, or our alliances so well made. But you judged aright that at any rate 'delenda est Carthago,' that government was to be brought down; and therefore the king may well say to you, It is your war. He took his measures from you, and they were just and right ones, and he expects a suitable assistance to so necessary and expensive an action, which he hath hitherto maintained at his own charge, and was unwilling either to trouble you, or burthen the country, until it came to an inevitable necessity. And his majesty commands me to tell you, that unless it be a certain sum, and speedily raised, it can never answer the occasion.—My Lords and Gentlemen; Reputation is the great support of war or peace. This war had never begun, nor had the States ever slighted the king, or ever refused him satisfaction, neither had this war continued to this day, or subsisted now, but that the States were deceived in their measures, and apprehended his majesty in that great want of money, that he must sit down under any affronts; and was not able to begin or carry on a war. Nay, at this day the States support themselves amongst their people by this only falsehood, 'That they are assured of 'the temper of England, and of the parliament, and that you will not supply the king 'in this war; and that if they can hold out till 'your meeting, they will have new life, and 'may take new measures.' There are lately taken two of their principal agents, with their credentials and instructions to this purpose, who are now in the Tower, and shall be proceeded against according to the law of nations. But the king is sufficiently assured of his people; knows you better; and can never doubt his parliament. This had not been mentioned, but to shew you of what importance the frankness and seasonableness of this Supply is, as well as the fulness of it. Let me say, the king hath brought the States to that condition, that your hearty conjunction at this time, in supplying his majesty, will make them never more formidable to kings, or dangerous to England. And if, after this, you suffer them to get up, let this be remembered; The States of Holland are England's eternal enemy, both by interest and inclination.—In the next place to the Supply for the carrying on of the war, his maj. recommends to you the taking care of his Debts. What you gave the last session, did not near answer your own expectation. Besides, another considerable Aid you designed his maj. was unfortunately lost in the birth; so that the king was forced, for the carrying on of his affairs, much against his will, to put a stop to the payments out of the exchequer. He saw the pressures upon himself, and growing inconveniences to his people, by great interest: and the difference, through all his business, between ready money and orders. This gave the king the necessity of that proceeding, to make use of his own revenue, which hath been of so great effect in this war. But, though he hath put a stop to the trade and gain of the Bankers, yet he would be unwilling to ruin them, and oppress so many families as are concerned in those Debts. Besides, it were too disproportionable a burthen upon many of his good subjects. But neither the bankers nor they have reason to complain, if you now take them into your care, and they have paid them what was due to them when the stop was made, with 6 per cent interest from that time. The king is very much concerned both in honour and interest to see this done: and yet he desires you not to mis-time it, but that it may have only the second place; and that you will first settle what you intend about the Supply.—His maj. hath so fully vindicated his Declaration from that calumny concerning the Papists, that no reasonable scruple can be made by any good man. He hath sufficiently justified it by the time it was published in, and the effects he hath had from it; and might have done it more, from the agreeableness of it to his own natural disposition, which no good Englishman can wish other than it is. He loves not blood, nor rigorous severities; but where mild or gentle ways may be used by a wise prince, he is certain to choose them. The church of England and all good Protestants have reason to rejoice in such a head, and such a defender. His maj. doth declare his care and concerns for the church, and will maintain them in all their rights and privileges, equal if not beyond any of his predecessors. He was born and bred up in it; it was that his father died for: we all know how great temptations and offers he resisted abroad, when he was in his lowest condition; and he thinks it the honour of his reign, that he hath been the restorer of the Church: it is that he will ever maintain, and hopes to leave to posterity in greater lustre, and upon surer grounds, that our ancestors ever saw it. But his maj. is not convinced that violent ways are the interest of Religion, or of the Church.—There is one thing more that I am commanded to speak to you of, which is, the Jealousy that hath been foolishly spread abroad, of the forces the king hath raised in this war; wherein the king hath opened himself freely to you, and confessed the fault on the other hand: for, if this last summer had not proved a miracle of storms and tempests, such as secured their East India fleet, and protected their sea coasts from a descent, nothing but the true reason (want of money) could have justified the defect in the number of our forces. It is that his maj. is providing for against the next spring, having given out orders for the raising of 7 or 8 regiments more of foot, under the command of persons of the greatest fortunes and quality. And I am earnestly to recommend to you, that in your Supplies you will take into your consideration this necessary addition of charge.—And after his majesty's conclusion of his speech, let me conclude, nay let us all conclude, with blessing God and the king: let us bless God, that he hath given us such a king, to be 'the Repairer of our Breaches' both in church and State, and 'the Restorer of our Paths to dwell in;' that, in the midst of war and misery, which rages in our neighbour countries, our garners are full, and there is no complaining in our streets; and a man can hardly know there is a war: let us bless God, that hath given this king signally the hearts of his people, and most particularly of this parliament, who, in their affection and loyalty to their prince have exceeded all their predecessors; a parliament with whom the king hath many years lived with all the caresses of a happy marriage. Has the king had a concern? You have wedded it. Has his maj. wanted Supplies? You have readily, chearfully, and fully provided for them. You have relied upon the wisdom and conduct of his maj. in all his affairs, so that you have never attempted to exceed your bounds, or to impose upon him: whilst the king on the other hand, hath made your counsels the foundations of all his proceedings; and hath been so tender of you, that he hath upon his own revenue and credit endeavoured to support even foreign wars, that he might be least uneasy to you, or burthensome to his people. And let me say, That though this marriage be according to Moses' law, where the husband can give a bill of divorce, put her away, and take another, yet I can assure you, it is as impossible for the king to part with this parliament, as it is for you to depart from that loyalty, affection, and dutiful behaviour, you have hitherto shewed towards him.—Let us bless the king, for taking away all our Fears and leaving no room for Jealousies; for those assurances and promises he hath made us. Let us bless God and the king, that our Religion is safe; that the Church of England is the care of our prince; that Parliaments are safe; that our Properties and Liberties are safe. What more hath a good Englishman to ask, but that this king may long reign; and that this Triple Alliance of king, parliament and people, may never be dissolved."

The King's second Speech.] After this, his majesty spake to this effect:

"One thing I forgot to mention to you, which happened during this prorogation: I did give order that some writs might issue out, for the election of members instead of those that are dead, to the end the house might be full at their meeting; and I am mistaken if this be not done according to former precedents: but I desire you that you fall not to any other business till you have examined that particular; and I doubt not but precedents will justify what is done. I am as careful of all your privileges as of my own prerogative."

Debate on the Lord Chancellor's issuing Writs and making Elections and Returns, without Order or Warrant from the House.] Feb. 6. The house of commons went into a debate on the matter of issuing Writs, and making Elections and Returns, without Order or Warrant from the house, by the Lord Chancellor, the parliament not sitting.*

Sir *John Birkenhead.* If you tie up the hands of the lord chancellor, how will you be supplied with members when you come to sit?

Sir *John Knight.* The king's prerogative is not judged at all, by annulling these writs: you are to take notice of the thing; and therefore moves that these writs may be suspended.

Sir *Tho. Littleton.* Though some writs were not issued out, it was for want of notice; though

* "The new Lord Chancellor blundered at the threshold, and his first use of the Seal was for a trick, which, as tricks use, ended in disappointment and shame. There had been a long vacancy of parliament, in which interval divers members of the house of commons were dead, and some taken into the nobility. His lordship had a mind to fill these vacancies, especially such as were in the county of Dorset (where his own estate and interest lay) with creatures of his own. But there he had been formerly opposed by the noble col. Strangways, one of a mighty estate and interest in the west, and, (which was worst of all) an inexpugnable loyalist; who, for his eminent fidelity, was afterwards called to serve the king as a privy counsellor. His lordship thought that now, having power, he might manage the matter so as to get the better of him. And, for that end, he caused the writs, for the new elections, to issue, without staying for the meeting of the parliament and having the Speaker's Warrant, as the use, especially, of late, hath been: for that had given notice of the elections: but so his lordship's men, having the carriage of the writ, and, dodging with it, by surprise, (as was said) carried all against the interest of the loyal colonel, which put him into a great rage. This device was no sooner communicated and understood by the western gentlemen, with the colonel's sentiment of it, but they all determined to join, and get all these elections set aside; and, with that resolution, they came up, and the noble colonel at the head of them. At the first meeting of the house, when the usual forms were over, a member stood up, and looking about, said he observed divers new faces in the house, and did not remember that, before their last rising, the house had been moved for the filling of so many places; so he doubted the regularity of the sitting of those persons, and moved their titles might be examined. Another member, seconding, said he supposed those gentlemen would have the modesty to withdraw, whilst their case was in debate, and not attend the order of the house. So this whole set of new elects, (although mostly loyalists) filed out, and came in no more upon that choice. For, although it was shewed such writs had formerly issued during such prorogations, enough to have served the turn in *causa favorabili*, yet the late practice being otherwise, and the current strong that way, and the court party not able to hinder, all the elections, on that foot, were voted null, and new writs ordered to go." North's Examen. p. 56.

it happened now, it is not possible to be so again. It is confessed, on all hands, that no members were chosen so since the Long Parliament; there are precedents before; there are many precedents that the chancellor did issue out writs.

Mr. Secretary *Coventry*. Conveniency, or inconveniency, is not the question, but right; whether the chancellor has done legally or not—divers precedents even to the Long Parliament: Moves that the several opinions do lay their precedents on the board; if it be with law, we must have a law to take away the inconveniency.

Col. *Strangways*. Has not had time to search precedents, but here is an usage for many years. It is strange, that, the same week of attendance, the writs should be sent out; both right and crown must subsist together: we are in possession of the thing, and would have gentlemen take the same care that are against it, on one side, as well as the other; let the thing be done clearly.

Mr. *Cheney*. Mr. Attorney said, 'That the chancellor had precedents,' and he would have a committee to examine those precedents.

Mr. Attorney *Finch*. Will any man think that this is an universal proposition, that either warrant from the Speaker, or writs from the Chancellor, is an error? Notification from the Speaker to the chancellor is the course if a vacancy be: If there be sent to supply the places of sick persons, or beyond the sea, you may question them: If in prorogation, for a member that is dead, that sat here by a questionable election, that writ is questionable; but sitting by unquestionable right, this writ is not only lawful, but expedient. There never was any age, wherein members were questioned for default of a lord steward [to give the oath of allegiance and supremacy, &c.] persons elected in queen Eliz. by the chancellor's writ, came not in, but when sworn by the lord steward Lincoln, who was absent, admitted. The 7th of James is an authority both ways. No less than 34 now dead, and as many chosen during vacation of parliament. The writs were issued out by lord Ellesmere; some were cases of barons removed, and persons dead, &c. and then voted where members are dead in prorogation, and no contrary usage after, and writs then went out. But six parliaments since king James's time, and will the precedents of six parliaments question those of sixty parliaments? No precedents in 1618 to the contrary. There was a writ in prorogation for Hertford, but not executed. When the parliament met, sir Rd. Wynne kept it in his pocket. A supersedeas may be before, but not after, the execution of the writ; if not executed, no injury done to the borough, or member. Though there was a then supersedeas (Hertford,) yet here we have persons chosen in the room of such whose elections were never questioned. It would be wonderfully hard now to declare a new privilege that was practised before. These privileges, thus, introduced, are particular respects to this great assembly, that signification might come to the Speaker. It is a necessity to the public that things might not be carried in a thin house: a peer may knock at the door, and call for his writ to the chancellor. In privilege-time we ought not to be at the chancellor's pleasure, to send or not send, out writs. If use be made of the ceremony beyond the civil intention, it is burdensome: your displeasure is too great for any man to bear: If any ingredient of displeasure be in your vote, it will lessen the authority of the vote: If precedents in the thing be disputable, would have a committee to inspect and report in time certain, that the world may see you delay not the business.

Sir *Tho. Meres*. No great man, be he as great as he will, desires to contend with the house of commons for privilege; no man that considers the merits of this house of commons, who have given more than all the parliaments since the Conquest: Many kindnesses we have done, and if privilege be a kindness from the king, we have not the least reason to lose it: We are now upon perfect point of right; have we nothing of right? Must all be prudence and convenience? If you resolve for the same privilege, why should you lose it now more than in the former Speaker's time? Mr. Attorney has granted 'that the writs not executed are superseded,' and those writs, moved for, he would have go out: notification was not the word formerly, nor certificate, but the Speaker, in 1603, sent his warrant to the clerk of the crown.

Mr. Secretary *Coventry*. In the time of lord chancellor Clarendon, the writs went by way of certificate, not warrant.

Mr. *Powle* speaks to the merits of the cause: issuing out of writs, the parliament not sitting: it is against reason that an inferior court should judge of the defects of a superior: the inferior courts at Westminster cannot judge the defects of chancery; the chancellor cannot judge of returns. If he issues out writs, he makes himself judge of returns: he must judge that the member is dead, and that the person returned has a right to the place, and so becomes a judge of things done in this house. Formerly the king never chose a Speaker till the house informed him of a defect, much less can he take notice of defects of members. The chancellor does more; he judges of removes out of this house into the lords house—31 Hen. vi. a baron of the exchequer sat then, and now the house thinks it not fit.* Attorney-generals have been discharged the house: and shall the lord chancellor take out of our house so learned a gentleman as Mr. Attorney? Judge Popham was sent for out of the house of lords, when reported to be there. Until 7 Hen. iv. all writs were returned to the clerk of parliament: the King's-bench judges of returns of writs, though issued out of chancery; and though in Hen. iv's time, writs were returned to chancery, yet that

* In the Speaker's case. See p. 501.

alters not the jurisdiction of this house: if you admit the writs, you admit the chancellor judge of returns—23 Eliz. writs issued out, and members were discharged, so returned; and ordered, That during the sitting of this house, no warrants should be issued out, but according to ancient usage: sitting is in common acceptation from first day of sitting, though in a restrained sense, to the time of parliament actually being here, restrainedly whilst it sits, but in common sense from the first day. They in parliament farther agree, That issuing shall not be at any time without a warrant from the Speaker—3 James, nothing done against it—Hertford writ for election suspended—1 Jam. sir Francis Goodwin was chosen, though sir John Fortescue was recommended, for the county of Buckingham; Goodwin was clearly elected, and not Fortescue; when it came to the council, both writs were voided, and a new election.* Great inconveniences by it—admit the chancellor to judge of these returns, and by consequence he will judge all your returns. The right of judging returns was, in Goodwin's case, pretended to be in chancery, but judged against it here. By this means the chancellor may chuse whom he will, and so no great person ever be called to an account here—There is no time set in these writs, when the member died; no time of death, nor remove to the lords house. And the gentleman that vouched the precedent of queen Eliz. might have done as many in this parliament, if they would serve his turn: the calling of a member into the lords house, must be by our consent.

Mr. Secretary *Coventry*. If such writs are rightfully issued out, you can put no question upon the superseding them.

Mr. *Hampden*. The meaning of your order is, to issue out writs for places void here represented.

Mr. *Swynfin*. Whether such elections are good or no, without referring the matter to a committee, is the question: has not heard one precedent offered where such elections have been allowed of, if notice taken of them; it is but of late usage the moving of the Speaker: how does it appear that the writs, urged as precedents, were not issued out by the Speaker's warrant, the house sitting? These elections out of sitting. The main concern is, he takes the book of this house to be a record. The Statute 6 Hen. viii. makes any person departed the house, recorded in your books, to lose his wages. In any thing that concerns this house, all courts must take your books for a record, and whether a member be or not, your book must testify: how can any court say such a member is dead? They can say he was returned; but that he was a member, your book must be sought: a man may sit here a year, and die, and yet not have been duly elected. If the chancellor has power to send out, he has power to deny, a writ. Now the question is, whether you will search records? Your book must still decide it.

Sir *Tho. Strickland*. The chancellor has the king's command to issue out writs.

Sir *Tho. Clarges*. The question is not whether the king has power to issue out writs, but whether the chancellor, or the h. of commons, are to judge of vacancies. A member cannot be arrested, and yet the king's authority is preserved: we should not be able to serve our king or country, if our privilege be not preserved: if scrupled, wonders that the reasons are not answered.

Mr. Attorney *Finch*. On the question of security and satisfaction, you have done it by voiding the elections already passed. You have done it, and outdone all parliaments: it is questioned, How a chancellor can know a member? Answers, by return. He knows he is dead by record, by executors and administrators. If they died since last session of parliament, no warrant could be had from the Speaker. If, instead of 30 or 40, 150 members should be dead, if writs may not go out, the parliament must be dissolved for want of number. Until you have made the thing unlawful, and say so, it is lawful to do so.

Sir *Tho. Meres*. No government but is subject to objections of all sorts relating to mankind. If such an extraordinary thing should happen once in a thousand years, the king may then, if he please, call a new parliament. Precedents are muddy, not clear, on the best side: the king is as much king of this court as chancery, and those arguments to the contrary are disobliging arguments.

Mr. Secretary *Coventry*. In committees of privileges, you first send for the mayor or bailiff that returns the election, before you condemn him: will not you hear precedents for the chancellor? All that we have to do is to induce the king to be of our opinion: do you believe the chancellor will acknowledge he has done wrong, by submitting to your supersedeas;

It was at length resolved, "That all Elections upon the Writs issued by the Chancellor since the last Session, are void; and that Mr. Speaker do issue out warrants to the clerk of the crown to make out new Writs for those places."

Declaration of War against Holland.] The Declaration against Holland alluded to in his majesty's Speech was as follows:

"We have been always so zealous for the quiet of Christendom, and so careful not to invade any other kingdom or state, that we hope the world will do us the justice to believe, that it is nothing but inevitable necessity forceth us to the resolution of taking up arms. Immediately upon our Restoration to our crowns, the first work we undertook, was the establishing of peace, and the settling a good correspondence between us and our neighbours: and in particular, our care was to conclude a strict League with the States-General of the United Provinces, upon such equal terms, as would certainly not have been

* See the Case between sir Francis Godwin and Mr. John Fortescue at length, in vol. i. p. 998.

broken, if any obligations could have kept them within the bounds of friendship and justice. This League was maintained inviolable on our part: but in 1664, we were stirred up by the complaints of our people, and the unanimous Vote of both houses in parliament, finding it a vain attempt to endeavour the prosperity of our kingdoms by peaceable ways at home, while our subjects were still exposed to the injuries and oppressions of the States abroad. That whole summer was spent in negotiations and endeavours on our side, to bring them to reasonable terms, which, notwithstanding all we could do, proved at length ineffectual: for the more we pursued them with friendly propositions, the more obstinately they kept off from agreeing with us. Upon this ensued the war in 1665, and continued till 1667; in all which time our victories and their losses were memorable enough to put them in mind of being more faithful to their Leagues for the future. But instead of that, the peace was no sooner made, but they returned to their usual custom of breaking articles, and supplanting our trade. For instance, the States were particularly engaged in an article of the Treaty of Breda, to send commissioners to us at London, about the regulation of our Trade in the East-Indies; but they were so far from doing it upon that obligation, that when we sent over our ambassador to put them in mind of it, he could not in three years time get from them any satisfaction in the material points, nor a forbearance of the wrongs which our subjects received in those parts.—In the West-Indies they went a little farther, for by an Article in the same Treaty, we were to restore Surinam into their hands; and by Articles upon the place confirmed by that Treaty, they were to give liberty to all our subjects in that colony, to transport themselves and estates into any other of our plantations. In pursuance of this agreement, we delivered up the place, and yet they detained all our men in it; only major Banister they sent away prisoner, for but desiring to remove according to the Articles. Our ambassador complaining of this behaviour, after two years solicitation, obtained an order for the performance of those Articles: but when we sent Commissioners, and two ships to bring our men away, the Hollanders (according to their former practice in the business of Poleroon for above 40 years together) sent private orders contrary to those they owned to us in public: and so the only effect of our commissioner's journey thither, was to bring away some few of the poorest of our subjects, and the prayers and cries of the most considerable and wealthiest of them, for relief out of that captivity. After this, we made our complaints by our Letters in August last to the States-General, wherein we desired an Order to their governors there, for the full observance of those Articles; yet to this time we could never receive one word of answer or satisfaction. But it is no wonder that they venture at these outrages upon our subjects in remote parts, when they dare be so bold with our royal person, and the honour of the nation, so near us as in their own country, there being scarce a town within their territories that is not filled with abusive pictures, and false, historical medals and pillars; some of which have been exposed to view by command of the States themselves, and in the very time when we were joined with them in united councils for the support of the Triple League, and the peace of Christendom. This alone were cause sufficient for our displeasure, and the resentment of all our subjects. But we are urged to it by considerations yet nearer to us, than what only relates to ourself; the safety of our Trade, upon which the wealth and prosperity of our people depends, the preservation of them abroad from violence and oppression, and the Hollanders daring to affront us almost within our very ports, are the things which move our just indignation against them.—The Right of the Flag is so ancient, that it was one of the first prerogatives of our royal predecessors, and ought to be the last from which this kingdom should ever depart. It was never questioned, and it was expressly acknowledged in the Treaty of Breda; and yet this last summer it was not only violated by their commanders at sea, and that violation afterwards justified at the Hague, but it was also represented by them in most courts of Christendom, as ridiculous for us to demand. An ungrateful insolence! That they should contend with us about the dominion of these seas, who, even in the reign of our royal father (in the years 1635-6, and 7) thought it an obligation to be permitted to fish in them, by taking of Licences and for a Tribute; and who owe their being now in a condition of making this dispute, to the protection of our ancestors, and the valour and blood of their subjects. Notwithstanding all these provocations, we patiently expected satisfaction, not being willing to expose the peace of Christendom for our particular resentments, while they ceased not on their parts to endeavour to provoke the most Christian king against us: of which they thought themselves so secure, that for above these 12 months their ministers here have threatened us with it. At length, hearing nothing from them, we sent another ambassador to them, who after several pressing Memorials in our name, could receive no answer, till after he had declared his revocation. Then they offered a Paper to this effect, 'That, in this conjuncture, they 'would condescend to strike to us, if we would 'assist them against the French; but upon 'condition, that it should never be taken for a 'precedent hereafter to their prejudice.' Since the return of our said ambassador, they have sent an extraordinary one to us, who, in a most extraordinary manner, hath given us to understand, 'That he can offer us no satisfaction, till he hath sent back to his masters.' Wherefore, despairing now of any good effect of a further Treaty, we are compelled to take up arms in defence of the ancient prerogative of our crowns, and the glory and safety of our kingdoms: and we put our trust in God, that he will give us his assistance in this our just undertaking, since we had no way left to defend our people from the artifice of that nation in peace, but by the valour of our subjects in war."—The rest of the Declaration was only form, and therefore unnecessary to be inserted; only the conclusion must not be omitted, which was more strange and surprising to some than all the rest. It runs in these words: "And whereas we are engaged by a Treaty to support the Peace made at Aix la-Chapelle, we do finally declare, 'That notwithstanding the prosecution of this war, we will maintain the true intent and scope of the said Treaty, and that in all the alliances which we have or shall make in the progress of this war, we have and will take care to preserve the ends thereof inviolable, unless provoked to the contrary.'"

Declaration of Indulgence.] The Declaration of Indulgence referred to in his majesty's Speech, was in substance as follows: "Our care and endeavours for the preservation of the rights and interests of the church, have been sufficiently manifested to the world, by the whole course of our government, since our happy Restoration, and by the many and frequent ways of coercion that we have used for reducing all erring or dissenting persons, and for composing the unhappy differences in matters of religion, which we found among our subjects upon our return: But it being evident by the sad experience of twelve years, that there is very little fruit of all those forcible courses, we think ourselves obliged to make use of that supreme power in ecclesiastical matters, which is not only inherent in us, but hath been declared and recognized to be so by several statutes and acts of parliament: And therefore we do now accordingly issue out this our royal Declaration, as well for the quieting the minds of our good subjects in these points, for inviting strangers in this conjuncture to come and live under us, and for the better encouragement of all to a chearful following of their trades and callings, from whence we hope, by the blessing of God, to have many good and happy advantages to our government; as also for preventing for the future the danger that might otherwise arise from private meetings, and seditious conventicles. And in the first place, we declare our express resolution, meaning, and intention to be, That the Church of England be preserved, and remain entire in its doctrine, discipline and government, as now it stands establish'd by law: And that this be taken to be, as it is, the basis, rule and standard of the general and public worship of God, and that the orthodox conformable clergy do receive and enjoy the revenues belonging thereunto; and that no person, though of different opinion and persuasion, shall be exempt from paying his tythes, or other dues whatsoever. And further, we declare, That no person shall be capable of holding any benefice, living, or ecclesiastical dignity or preferment of any kind in this kingdom of England, who is not exactly conformable. We do in the next place declare our will and pleasure to be, That the execution of all and all manner of penal laws in matters ecclesiastical, against whatsoever sort of non-conformists, or recusants, be immediately suspended, and they are hereby suspended. And all judges of assize and gaol-delivery, sheriffs, justices of the peace, mayors, bailiffs, and other officers whatsoever, whether ecclesiastical or civil, are to take notice of it, and pay due obedience thereunto. And that there may be no pretence for any of our subjects to continue their illegal meetings and conventicles, we do declare, That we shall from time to time allow a sufficient number of places, as shall be desired, in all parts of this our kingdom, for the use of such as do not conform to the Church of England, to meet and assemble in, in order to their public worship and devotion; which places shall be open and free to all persons. But to prevent such disorders and inconveniencies as may happen by this our indulgence, if not duly regulated, and that they may be the better protected by the civil magistrate, our express will and pleasure is, That none of our subjects do presume to meet in any place, until such place be allowed, and the teacher of that Congregation be approved by us. And lest any should apprehend, that this restriction should make our said allowance and approbation difficult to be obtained, We do further declare, That this our indulgence, as to the allowance of public places of worship, and approbation of teachers, shall extend to all sorts of non-conformists and recusants, except the recusants of the Roman catholic religion, to whom we shall no ways allow in public places of worship, but only indulge them their share in the common exemption from the executing the penal laws, and the exercise of their worship in their private houses only. And if after this our clemency and indulgence, any of our subjects shall presume to abuse this liberty, and shall preach seditiously, or to the derogation of the doctrine, discipline, or government of the established church, or shall meet in places not allowed by us; we do hereby give them warning, and declare, we will proceed against them with all imaginable severity: And we will let them see, we can be as severe to punish such offenders, when so justly provoked, as we are indulgent to truly tender consciences."

A Supply Voted.] Feb. 7. The house, in a grand committee, resolved, "That a Supply be given to his majesty of eighteen months assessment, according to the proportion of the last royal Aid, not exceeding 70,000*l.* a month."*

* Amounting in the whole to 1,260,000*l.* On this matter of the Supply, bishop Burnet writes as follows: "The court desired at least 1,200,000*l.* for that sum was necessary to the carrying on the war. The great body of those who opposed the court had resolved to give

Debates on the King's Declaration for Indulgence to Dissenters.] Feb. 8. A debate arose on that part of the king's Speech, which related to his Declaration for Indulgences to Dissenters.

Sir *Rd. Temple* said, the end of this declaration was to invite people into the nation, and is not against a bill of general naturalization—the king of France has naturalized almost all nations, except Spaniards and English—we want people, and this will bring them in.

Mr. *Garroway.* If we have a general liberty, we may have good as well as bad people amongst us: knows not yet what religion we have ourselves: moves that those who would be naturalized, may be named in several bills, as many as they please at a time, paying 20s. a piece only for the charge: some have come in, but very few, upon that declaration, though used very civilly.

Sir *Rd. Ford* moves for a committee to enquire into the Declaration, to offer you such an expedient as may be for the good of the nation.

Col. *Birch.* We hear the Dutch go to Embden, and other places, but few to us; unless you do something of this nature the nation cannot subsist. The staple commodity is corn and wool, and if the people cannot get by it, they will come up by the carriers, as we see daily they do, as if they were guards to them, and so to the plantations, where they may do better: when the bill comes in, then it will be a time to talk to you of their religion.

Sir *Lancelot Lake* remembers a complaint of Irish cattle coming in, and an imposition on them. Would have an imposition on the Dutch beasts also.

Col. *Titus.* We want nothing but persons to eat and work, be they of what religion they will. The improvement of lands is a mischief to us. Fullness of markets and few to eat: Old Rome grew rich, by naturalizing all people, and we have naturalized Wales and Scotland. Our workmen are few, and dear, and so wool and other things are cheaper thereby: 5s. for a pair of shoes, that the land-owner gets not 1s. by, there is but such a number of good journeymen about the town, and they will work, or not work, as they please themselves: Would have alien duties free for native commodities.

Mr. *Garroway* moves to consider the Declaration, that we may the better remove the ill constructions which other persons put upon it, and keep law and prerogative from interfering, which he hopes will be done with that modesty that becomes us. He is far from oppressing tender consciences, but would have the thing settled.

Mr. Secretary *Coventry.* The king intends not to violate your laws; but the question is, Whether the king be mistaken in his Declaration, or no?—The farther debate was adjourned to

Feb. 10. Lord *Cavendish* moves, that the Votes of the house in 1662 and 1663 may be read, and the reasons against Toleration; read; which were accordingly.

Sir *Tho. Meres,* after a silence some time, said, In this affair we are like waters, the deeper the silenter; it is of great weight: he would have us leave the laws as we find them, to our posterity: in the country, upon the first putting out the Declaration, he has conferred with books, and learned persons in the laws, and finds that a general suspension of the penal statutes is against law; if we are mistaken, let us hear it clearly proved.

Mr. *Waller.* When the state is rightly put, you will find it otherwise: the king says, 'he will stick to his Declaration, and likewise will not invade our rights and liberties.' Something there was of this at his first being in parliament in king James's time; the parliament desired him to put the penal laws in execution against Recusants; not a word then of property. They proceeded to the Petition of Right when property was touched: in the business of Ship-Money, they went to the lords to have the judges punished: opinion of this house clear, no prerogative: our ancestors knew that kings can do no wrong, and, for point of safety, the most unbounded monarchy in the world: the king beats his drum for war, when no man can: Henry vii's proclamations were heard farther than his guns: has observed formerly too much pressing of penal laws: lord Coke says (who was no great friend to prerogative) 'that kings have, and ought to have, power in these things:' Empson and Dudley never broke any law, but advised only the setting penal laws on foot; whenever the legal prerogative may supersede: has often heard that the king allows the French churches, for good of trade, as at Venice the Greek churches. Shall the king dispense for trade, and not for peace? Because he is an Englishman, must he not have the benefit of the indulgence by the king's power? has heard it from lawyers, that no prerogative that is legal can be taken away by inferences of state. No branch of the common law must be taken away but in express words; *in conceptis verbis.* To take away flowers of the crown, we bring stones on our heads. The king pardons trai-

only 600,000*l.* which was enough to procure a peace, but not continue the war. Garroway and Lee had led the opposition to the court all this session in the house of commons." [The Supply was granted the third day of the session, and these gentlemen had been at the head of the opposition long before.] "So they were thought the properest to name the sum. Above eighty of the chief of that party had met over night, and had agreed to name 600,000*l.* But Garroway named 1,200,000*l.* and was seconded in it by Lee; so this surprize gained that great sum, which enabled the court to carry on the war. They had good reward from the court, and yet continued acting on the other side."

tors, who are as bad as Dissenters. 'Armis ornatum et legibus armatum,' says Justin. He believes that the Dissenters repent of what they have done; but that Dissenters should at every session have all hope taken away, can you imagine greater persecution? You will find they will affect your rents, and your trade. In this the king innovates nothing; the Church is part of the state, but the state no part of the Church: Theodosius and Constantine made edicts, and he that disputed them was put into a sack, and thrown into a river: bishops were not as some are now; they were humble and godly men. The ignorant zeal was then as now: the emperors without that power could not keep all quiet. The more supreme power resembles divine, the better it is. God uses menaces as to Nineveh, but does not always destroy: the Petition of Right shall never be altered: must the king beat his subjects with one hand, and Amsterdam with another? You had no mind to take the king's power from him, because your vote in the act of Conventicles does not say so: moves not to strike at a power so near the king, and necessary for the people, and peace.

Mr. *Powle* would comply with the king, to do in a legal way, as now the Declaration does in an illegal: would know the king's power in temporal laws. He does conceive, if the king can dispense with all penal laws, he may dispense with all laws, with a *non obstante.* Special cases may so happen, that cannot be executed, but in others the king cannot dispense, but may pardon the offender. In the great case in the Exchequer now about Wine-Licences, a general suspension of law amounts to an abrogation, which none can do but parliament. This being so, by the words of the Declaration, 40 acts of parliaments are suspended, some treason, some felony, banishment, mulcts, and the king cannot dispense them. By the Declaration the king intended no imposing upon his Protestant subjects; but it is clearly so upon the judges and justices of the peace, who are sworn to execute the laws: does not this impose upon causes ecclesiastical and temporal? You make the king equal in ecclesiastical matters to temporal, and no more. Ecclesiastical matters anciently were committed to such persons as the temporal magistrates: no appeals to Rome, no legate, or nuncio, to come into England, without leave of the king: when the Pope and Hen. viii, differed, he resumed his ancient right, by being declared supreme head of the Church, in the convocation, by instrument, which was nothing but the ancient common law restored, which was clearly expressed: 1. Eliz. all causes ecclesiastical restored to her, as well as temporal; no more power in the one than in the other. The Proviso in the Conventicle-Bill might as well have exempted in that bill, and as well put in, in the Bill of the Irish cattle: the king cannot command, but by matter of record: the officers are to pass seals against law at their perils: this is only a paper order (the Declaration) under no seal; how can the Justices take notice of it? Their commission is under seal. The consequence of this is direful; the king by this may change religion as he pleases; we are confident of him, but knows not what succession may be: something of this nature was in the Spanish match. Bishop Abbot said, 'No toleration could be but by act of parliament;' Williams, the lord-keeper, excepted against it. When the king was rightly informed, in his speech in parliament, he disclaimed it: look into the nation, and you will find nothing ever raised such doubts as this Declaration: if it be found to have these inconveniences, hopes the king will be moved to recal it.

Mr. *Seymour.* It has not been very unusual that this house has stopped the current of his majesty's grace and favour. To Mr. Powle's argument 'of the magistrates oaths.' By 25 H. viii. which regulates Dispensations, the Judges have declared the right is not taken from the king, in the case of Port and Love: in lord Hubbard: in Hen. iv. dispensation for a bastard to be a priest, against the Pope's jurisdiction; the king had the right then: capital laws cannot be suspended, but punishment pardoned. It may be the penal laws are so lodged in the crown: that of the subject is so mixed with the king in the penalty, the king may dispense with his own part, the subject's part he cannot: the Irish Cattle hic et nunc: 2 Eliz. felony to export money *malum prohibitum*: laws that relate to government the king cannot part with, and è contra—Sir A. Ingram's case was an office bought, and void, because against law; but in this case here has been no man's property invaded: will you think that this shall have royal assent to bind up the king's hands? If an act restrain the power of the king, these acts are void: if our liberties are invaded, would have an Address to the king, and doubts not of a redress from him.

Col. *Strangways.* Will lay down some postulata of our government: in all kingdoms there must be a legislative power, and in ours not without consent of both houses of parliament; the judges, in doubt, to explain the king's laws. Laws, when first made, were necessary, and in process of time useless, and may be repealed, but still by law. Must not the judges execute the law according to their oaths; and if they do not, are they not responsible? We own the king's power to dispense with the punishment, by pardon; but the king cannot dispense with a man to be a Papist, or Nonconformist: values not ceremonies, but that they are by the magistrate's authority. You grant that indulgence to persons that do not allow that power, in all lawful and honest things. What are we sent for here, if this be not 'arduum negotium?' If justices of the peace have difficulties, they advise with the judges; and those that have the honour to serve the king, might have advised this business with the parliament: no country in the world where there is this indulgence, but there is a standing army. If the sheriff shall, without occasion, summon the posse comitatus of the county, upon complaint made, he ought to be punished. The king's ministers have done wrong, and by colour of the king's command to justify them!—Would never have the king deprived of the advice of both houses, composed of so many persons of worth and loyalty to be trusted: he counsels the king best, who does it to maintain his laws: an usurper has as much power as a king that breaks his laws. If no settled course be taken, we cannot expect any thing but confusion: it is the law of England that condemns treasons against him, and preserves his person; let us maintain it for his interest: it was his misfortune to sit here when negative voice was denied, and hopes he will not deny us.

Mr. Secretary *Coventry*. Thinks a positive declaration in this business dangerous; what will become of us all in emergencies, if, in fire, we are restrained from breaking open houses, or, in war, from marching over men's grounds? Would not have us enquire into the just extent of the king's power, but address ourselves to his majesty about it: the master of a ship has power to throw goods overboard in a storm, though it is not consequential in a calm; though all laws are not of the same importance, yet all are of the same authority. This house has made Addresses to the king for a Dispensation for Lent; it is no ecclesiastical thing, but to preserve cattle. You would not move him to an illegal and bad thing: to take away a liberty, and to give, are both alike in power: you desired the king to issue out his Proclamation to forbid bringing in of Wines, that none should be landed after such a time: would tread in those ways we always have done, that when we have any thing that offends us, we may address ourselves to the king to redress it, be it religion, or treaty, or property; but to say that we shall irritate the king to all the penal laws of the kingdom, which if they must be the king's duty, Empson and Dudley were wrongfully taken away: either the king must have the liberty of dispensing, or else is always obliged to put the penal laws in execution.

Sir *George Downing*. The king says, 'the power is inherent in him;' but if the question must be of the power of the king, be will be tender in it. Gentlemen that make account of their loyalty may give their voices freely in it; he, that has done otherwise*, cannot be so free: we are now modelling the government: in 1641, nothing but calm questions; nothing but securing property. But what followed at last? Monarchy came in, without conditions. Laws are in words; but that government that shall be in words, is destroyed. The Speaker said, "We have been taught by his predecessor, that privilege, whether 20 or 40 days, is not to be put in writing to be circumscribed." —Can government be without arbitrary power? The courts of justice make rules by the judges and chancellors, according to equity, conscience, and circumstances. If every bond put in suit, and loss of evidence, be not relieved, where are we? And yet all this is arbitrary, you must at last go to the lords, and be well armed, to make it out with them.

Sir *Philip Warwick*. The gentlemen of the long robe have left the dispute to us, being loth to disturb what they have most advantage by.

Sir *Tho. Lee*. The judges have not changed their charges, in their circuits, upon this Declaration: moves that as pardons are made void by circumstances (many are not) how far a power by dispensation may dispense the law, may be declared: doubts whether, if judges had been consulted in the Declaration, it had passed, or no. Transporting silver, without leave, felony. Laws may be useful to-day, and not to-morrow; but would have the judgment here: would not meddle with prerogative, any more than with your privileges: could something happen that no mortal man could foresee and the king raise money; were necessity so great that all men may see it, no parliament would question it. It is not the first time the king has been deceived in prerogative: hopes that, in this, he will be advised by the two houses of parliament.

Mr. Attorney *Finch*. The long robe he perceives blamed for being backward in declaring themselves in this business. What is incumbent on him he will discharge. He has been unhappy that his mistakes have been represented to his prejudice, rather than his good meaning to his advantage. There is no question of the king's power of dispensation, where the forfeiture is his own. The penalty, in popular laws, is moiety to the informer; the king may inform for the whole, and dispense for the whole: monopoly nor licence good in many cases: it is no question that the king may not repeal by prerogative. In this case the king does not repeal; undoubtedly the king is not more absolute in ecclesiastical affairs than in temporal: by common law the king grants leave to hold livings *in commendam*, and unite parishes; and the same power the pope had, the king is restored to by the statute of Hen. viii.; the law is not changed at all. The king by that statute is head; that no foreign power can pretend to; and therefore it was ever the interest of the nation to take a temporal pope for a spiritual one: the canons not to contradict the law of England: necessity cogent that this Declaration should be made for quiet, there was so universal a connivance with an indulging recusants got from their neighbours; and now they may thank the crown. Now the question is, Whether the king cannot dispense with the laws, in order to the preservation of the kingdom, (and we are all miserable if he cannot do it.) There

* Alluding to his having been in the interest and service of Cromwell.

is an impossibility of foreseeing all inconveniences: some laws can never be executed, as the law about cart-wheels, suspended by Proclamation; no complaint made of: planting hemp in Ireland: we have allowed the thing, but differ *de modo*: would have it laid aside, because the king desires it, and his enemies do not desire it; let us do it with all reverence to the crown: would have us show more affection than learning in it: a mathematical security we cannot have; a moral one we have from the king. The king cannot dispense with common law; religion cannot be changed without act of parliament. You may secure what you would have, without making so hard a vote as is proposed. Some would have a Bill for it; that is hard. Will you tie the king to indulge those consciences whether he will, or no? Now tender, hereafter may not be so: there is a great necessity to keep a bone from betwixt the king and parliament, and hopes you will propose nothing but what the king may well grant.

Mr. *Vaughan.* When the king may dispense with any law, it must be manifestly for the good of the subject; if it does injury to the subject, it is illegal; if not, it is otherwise; no man is bound to a law, where there is not a punishment; and if this Declaration signifies any thing, the Church of England signifies nothing. He argued the dispensation with Merchant-strangers. You cannot hinder them, by law of nations; if they come for gain to the kingdom, it implies toleration. The king may pardon murder, or treason, but not give licence to do them. If not dispensable to violate the Sabbath; if the king cannot dispense with the law of man, à fortiori, not with the law of God: all sorts and manners of people are dispensed with by this Declaration, Turks, Jews, &c. This Declaration is a repeal of 40 acts of parliament, no way repealable but by the same authority that made them: this Declaration does repeal 14 statutes of this king: those who will take no oaths at all, and so justice cease. It voids all testimony, and takes away my liberty, or estate. It is point-blank opposite to his laws; they and this cannot consist. If monarchs were as lasting as their kingdoms, there could be no danger in this Declaration: we, that are magistrates, lie under the king's censure for our oaths, but in a perpetual danger, in all places, from God. As liberty of the subject consists in his right, so would have it measured by law. This prerogative is illegal, and our vote will say no more than the Declaration does in effect.

Sir *Rob. Howard.* We are told 'that all is swept away by this Declaration;' but what is the Church, if you come not to the observation of all its ceremonies, church-wardens, visiting, and presenting, &c.? Is it an argument that the Church of England is unsupported, unless every man be compelled to every thing in it? But the Church of England is not concerned in this Declaration. Things are come to that height, we cannot pull them down again: he has expected to hear where property has been concerned; life, liberty, and estate is property; now, would you know how any of these is invaded? You have seen dispensations here, and have not thought them grievances. The abp. of Canterbury, Laud, found fault with the French and Dutch churches. Will you set up another government? The Long Parliament inserted this into one of its Articles; see how parliaments change: an unhappy time was that, and some took unhappy parts in it: nothing can gratify the Pope more than to say the king has no such jurisdiction. It is said, 'what shall the judges and justices of the peace do?' They receive an indulgence, the king has power to grant. It is a strange question to dispute what prerogative is, when all statutes make it so sacred a thing. The king says, 'it is legal, and he will stick to it;' and we say, 'it is not legal, and he shall not.' Is the Black Rod at the door? Shall we so hastily fall into such a vote? If you think your civil rights are in danger, you make the Declaration 'probabilis causa litigandi. Do papists make ill use of it, or any other cause? Then address the king, but vote it not illegal: proceed not this way to the king, else the Hollanders will rejoice.

Sir *Wm. Coventry.* This is a point tenderly to be handled, and hopes to propose something towards a close of the business: will wave all arguments from an universal claim of prerogative to be universally exercised. Our ancestors never did draw a line to circumscribe prerogative and liberty. He hears no man urge this prerogative more than when the king cannot have a parliament: but when a parliament does come, something, you say, must of necessity be done, else you say it is legal, and that allows it. It has been moved for an Address, but no man says upon what subject-matter: this vote of the subject-matter of great difficulty: but since you may enter into debates you would avoid, he proffers you words not his own, but yours, upon the Declaration of Breda. It says, 'Laws then in being, that could not be dispensed with but by act of parliament.'

Sir *Thomas Meres.* We may, at that time, come nearer his majesty than ever, for now the house of commons having seen how little good force will do, it may be, the reason of the thing will oblige us in a fair legal way of doing what the king has been designing these 12 years. This may prevent those heats that have been, more or less, about ecclesiastical affairs, almost every session this parliament.

Sir *Philip Musgrave* believes that his maj. had gracious intentions in this Declaration, but it did make disturbances in most loyal hearts: moves to take that way that may have the least reflection on the king: has seen sad effects of it: moves for an humble Address of this house to his majesty, to preserve the Act of Uniformity.

Serj. *Maynard.* Dispensation of the penal laws to be illegal, is more than you intend to vote. It is agreed on all hands, that the king cannot suspend so as to repeal; else why do we make any law? He may make them as well in ecclesiastical matters: Whether universal dispensation, not limited, does repeal a law, or no, he will not enter into dispute: would distinguish, in the question, 'Popish recusants,' but whether 'legal or illegal,' is too harsh. Rather for an humble Address to the king to remove our fears in the business.

Sir *Rob. Carr.* When we consider what ways have been taken to quiet people, the thing was dispensed with by justices of the peace, and the people ought not to owe that to the justices, which should be to the king: hears not one instance against property: would have a committee to pen the Address in such words as we may not repent when we have done.

Sir *John Birkenhead.* Recusants were tolerated ten years in the beginning of queen Eliz. and no laws were made against them, until she was sure she could make them good. The Oath of Supremacy not exacted in the lords house; but the commons got them in, by incapacitating them for offices until they had taken that oath: conformity a thing much in option.

Col. *Titus.* On both sides gentlemen have acquitted themselves well: Coventry's motion was to alter the words of voting; the Declaration illegal is not the matter: moves for an Address to the king, "That penal Laws in Ecclesiastical matters, may not have their force till the parliament shall declare some act in the business."

Sir *Edw. Dering.* Is no advocate for the legality of Declarations; we need not look farther back than 3 Charles, liberty infringed; some sent abroad, Hammond and Glanville; banishment, martial law; then an Address was made to the king, that the thing might be redressed: we rather now speak what we fear, than what we feel. The king has given you liberty of Address in all difficult cases, and moves for a committee now for an address to the king.

Col. *Birch.* If ever men were to answer for a trust, it is this: can laws be any ways suspended but here? Desires, unless some will make it out, that we may pass it by; we must do it; if dispensation cannot be made out, then put the question.

Serj. *Seys.* The carrying out wool, and bringing in Gascon wines, and transporting bell-metal out of England, were particular things and not at all invading the rights of the subject. From the dispensing with cart wheels to jump to that of conscience, is *à parvis ad magnum*, that makes us have reason to fear. Patents are judged unlawful every day in Westminster, and voided by scire facias. The laws are no ways to be suspended but by act of parliament.

Sir *Tho. Osborne* does not wonder that the king expresses these things to be in his inherent right, when his own council thinks so, and his counsel at law: moves that the Address may be referred to a committee.

Mr. *Harwood* hopes the king will hear the counsel of this house; his great council, as well as his other council.

Sir *Tho. Lee.* What is the use of his great council of parliament, but to inform the king he has been misled and mistaken by his privy-council? It is our duty to the people, and the king calls you to declare your opinion. It plainly appears to be a mistake in the crown, and you must inform him of it.

Sir *Robt. Howard.* If a noli pros. be entered by the king's attorney-general, is not this a suspension, and will you hinder that?

Mr. Attorney *Finch* knows not one of the king's counsel learned in the law, that ever saw this Declaration otherwise than in print, and he never made any other inferences from it than you have done. The king, by his supremacy, may discharge any cause in ecclesiastical courts, they being his. Why do you put an universal term upon a thing particular? Moves that we may humbly petition the king that it may be so no more.

Mr. *Cheney* would not have it thought abroad that there is such a necessity of this Declaration as is implied, the king having his militia to protect him: would address the king to suspend his Declaration, and form it into a law.

Sir *Cha. Harbord.* Laws must be altered by the same authority they were ordained by. It has done him more hurt among his father's friends, than good to those indulged: support the prerogative by the affections of the people; they are twins. Is against the question.

Mr. *Waller.* Words that sound true, and are parliamentary, are better than those that are not. It has been good doctrine, that an Ordinance has had the power of an Act by the king's consent.

Col. *Strangways* thinks it worth enquiry, whether the late lord-keeper did not refuse the seal; the judges never consented: would not have those that are not lawyers, nor divines, prescribe out of their profession: does not find them consulted: In point of law, would have the king advised by those that profess the law.

Mr Attorney *Finch.* Some Canons, 1 of king James, the king may dispense with. Is it your intention that the king shall not dispense with them?

Mr. *Powle.* Those Canons were not passed by act of parliament, nor ever confirmed, and so not within your vote.

It was then resolved, "That Penal Statutes, in matters Ecclesiastical, cannot be suspended but by Act of Parliament, 168 to 116; and a Petition and Address were ordered to be drawn up to be presented to his majesty.

The Commons' Address to the King, against the Declaration for Indulgence.] Feb. 14. Mr. Powle reported the Petition and Address to the king upon the above vote, as follows:

"Most gracious sovereign; We your maj.'s most loyal and faithful subjects, the commons assembled in parliament, do, in the first place, as in all duty bound, return your majesty our most humble and hearty thanks for the many gracious promises and assurances which your maj. hath, several times, during this present parliament, given to us, that your maj. would secure and maintain unto us the true reformed Protestant Religion, our liberties and properties; which most gracious assurances your maj. hath, out of your great goodness, been pleased to renew unto us more particularly, at the opening of this present session of parliament.—And farther we crave leave humbly to represent, that we have, with all duty and expedition, taken into our consideration several parts of your majesty's last Speech to us, and withal the Declaration therein mentioned, for indulgence to Dissenters; and we find ourselves bound in duty to inform your majesty, that penal statutes, in matters Ecclesiastical, cannot be suspended but by act of parliament. —We, therefore, do most humbly beseech your majesty, that the said laws may have their free force, until it shall be otherwise provided for by act of parliament; and that your majesty would graciously be pleased to give such directions herein, that no apprehensions or jealousies may remain in the hearts of your majesty's good and faithful subjects."

Debate on the above Address.] Sir *Tho. Littleton.* Several motions were made at the committee for an Address to the king 'for ease of tender consciences.' When we say this vote, we ought to do the other; but the committee would not agree to it: moves now for a committee to draw such a Bill, and that the Address may be re-committed.

Mr. *Swynfin* thinks you rightly moved by Littleton. Your sense was to go no farther than to secure the law, and preserve the true strength of the statute-law. Nay, farther, it seemed to all men's sense, that some consideration should be had of the indulgence; great reasons were given for the matter of it, as the war, trade, &c. as far as might be for the safety of religion; but the committee could not originally express it, having no authority from you, therefore no haste, it being to be sent to the lords: we have had so ill experience of those laws, that he hopes we shall consider them: if the kings of France and Spain should draw their subjects to prison, and persecute them, they could not preserve unity: sees nothing in the Declaration but you may well dispense with, but the preservation of the laws. If you shall go so far as a law for the Declaration, it will be no difference, only the Declaration turned into a law, and so you have your end in it: moves to appoint a committee to prepare a Bill to that end, which cannot but appear well, both to king and people.

Sir *Tho. Meres* is one of those that think 'ease fit for tender consciences,' in the words of Breda Declaration, 'for union of the Protestant subjects;' but how shall we proceed? No committee can do it, that is numerous: three men of a committee better to draw a bill, than 12 upon the subject-matter of a vote: would appoint to-morrow for this end, that no jealousy may be objected: knows how matters will go when money is passed: would not have this debate stop the Address to the king.

Mr. *Cheney.* Would have persons withdraw, to add a few words to the Address, of uniting his majesty's Protestant subjects.

Sir *John Monson* thinks it not proper to add any thing to the Address, until we have passed this address by vote: moves for to-morrow, to take this business into consideration.

Mr. *Crouch.* The question is, 'Agree, or not, with the committee;' adding to the Address is but to distract things; and if you agree not with the committee, then it is irregular to debate adding.

Mr. *Garroway.* It would have looked so like bargaining, if the committee had put it in, that they waved adding any thing to it.

Sir *Rd. Temple.* The committee left out the addition, because they expected some previous vote from you. Though the manner was not concluded in your debate, yet every man agreed to the matter of the Declaration: will it not be an abrupt Address to the king to find fault with the Declaration, and not say any way you would have the thing remedied in the matter? What difficulty do you put upon the king? Would it not be proper for you now to speak it, that you have it under consideration to provide for relief of dissenting brethren? Would have a vote passed, to take Dissenters into consideration, and have it put into your Address.

Sir *Tho. Lee* would have you informed by the chairman of the committee, whether ever it was debated to have it part of your Address.

Mr. *Powle.* No sense of your committee that it should be part of your Address.

Mr. *Vaughan* denies that it was the sense of the committee: they thought it unparliamentary to inform the king of any such thing, and they had no ground for it; for until you had voted the thing, they could add nothing to it.

Sir *Rob. Howard.* You must first put the question of 'agreeing with the committee' before you can add any thing.

Col. *Birch* does not agree with those gentlemen. It is not parliamentary to add (if you intend it) after having voted the thing. The thing moved to be added, could not appear to be true at the committee: would always have the king thanked by Dissenters. The committee could not do it, the house having not voted the thing of Indulgence: desires it for the honour of the king, that you make a vote for taking the thing into consideration, and then vote your Address.

It was then resolved, "That this house doth agree with the committee in the Petition and Address."

Sir *Tho. Meres.* What will you do with this Address? The Address must go to the king, and it is usual to send to the king to know when he will command us to wait on him, by some of the lords of the council of our house.

Mr. *Garroway* has seen many laws passed, with much zeal, against Nonconformists and Dissenters in this house, and much hardship upon the people, but without effect: would have all things done with sobriety and tenderness, and for that end would have a vote from this house, that you will declare so much to his majesty in this Message; we can make no other promise, but that we have such a thing under consideration, though we cannot see the effect upon debate.

Sir *C. Harbord.* Usually the lords concurrence is asked, and hopes they will agree with you.

Mr. *Crouch* would know what this Bill should be brought in for, upon what heads, what you would add, or repeal? Seconds the motion for the lords concurrence.

Mr. *Seymour.* Never thought it fit to persecute or prosecute any person, that believes not as he believes; it may have the power of the sword, but not the power of godliness: when this Address is presented to the king, would have it declared to the king, that this house has it under consideration.

Sir *Wm. Coventry* is the same man in this to day, as he was the other day at the debate of the Declaration. That thing was knocked on the head at the committee, because no order from you; and the committee thought it not fit to promise that which we were not certain to effect, and that was the great reason at the committee. If we promise, we must perform, though to our detriment: the committee must have heads to work upon: some are for indulging Protestant subjects only, and some for extending it to Catholic subjects. It may be, those great promissory words may amount to more than either you or the king means: would have Monday set apart for the matter of Dissenters to be taken into consideration, though he believes men are, by the discourse of the thing, prepared in their opinions, though not in their judgments.

Sir *Tho. Lee* thinks it necessary that now you do something, because possibly something in your Address to the king may startle those kind of people, the Dissenters: to pass a general vote may be so construed, that it may perhaps be too general; such a vote, perhaps, never passed here before: moves for a Bill for Uniting Protestant subjects. Here is ground for you, though he would be glad to see a man so happy as to comprehend all your senses in that bill: pass the vote, and I hope something may be done this day.

Mr. Secretary *Coventry.* Though the thing be of as great importance and large extent as may be, if you intend to thrive in the Address to the king, you must prepare something of such a vote, as is mentioned, to the king: would have no Bill admitted, but upon your vote, and reasons for it.

Sir *Nich. Carew.* 'Tender conscience' is of large extent; Turks, Jews, &c. have consciences: would have 'uniting Protestant subjects' added to the question.

Sir *Rob. Howard.* As you would confirm the minds of some, so you would give terror to others. You must do something to indulge as well as unite; it is not fair to bind it up thus.

Sir *Rob. Carr* is pleased with Carew's motion. For aught he thinks, he that pretends to be one thing, may be a Turk in his heart, and therefore would have it general.

Sir *Tho. Meres* does believe the word 'ease' is the business which is disputable, whether toleration or comprehension. The words of his majesty's Speech are, 'ease of Protestant subjects in matters of Religion.'

Col. *Birch.* If you will give indulgence in an act of parliament, your question must be 'for ease of Protestant Subjects.' Moves for it.

Sir *G. Downing.* You intend this vote to be presented to the king; he should be loth you tell the king what we shall not be able to do: would, on Monday, have the house in a grand committee, and stop the Address in the mean time.

Sir *John Duncombe.* Upon this debate of tender consciences, every man is for himself, and excluding others. He speaks of a tender conscience-man, such as has been born in his religion, and lives peaceably in it: do what is agreeable to charity; lay not your foundation too narrow; let all have the benefit of indulgence. Not an universal ease, but you must qualify it. They all are alike to him. He would consider none of them for indulgence as opposite to the Church of England. The last session, the motion for indulgence was diverted: thinks no peace now without it: would have the debate be 'for ease of tender consciences.'

Sir *C. Harbord.* The king, in this business, is most troubled of all men. Something must be done, we shall else put the king upon some great necessity: would have a bill 'for ease of tender consciences in matters of Religion,' and that will be capacious enough: has regard to the church, as built upon the state, the monarchy.

Mr. *Harwood* sees something at the brink of men's lips that will not come out; our aim is to bring all dissenting men into the Protestant Church, and he that is not willing to come into the Church should not have ease. Many of these persons differ not but in discipline, not in doctrine: would have the question 'for Dissenters of the Protestant subjects only.'

Mr. *Milward* is for debating this business in a grand committee, that persons may reply one upon another. They may be seemingly Protestants, yet not truly so: he has a great tenderness for such as have been brought up in their religion: would have a difference between monarchical dissenters and antimonarchical.

Sir *Lancelot Lake* would spare tender consciences, because so few make any consciences of their ways: before we proceed, would have us agree in the definition of a tender conscience.'

Mr. *Garroway.* In plain English, would not put Romanists in the Bill: would give them some ease, but would have them publicly in all their robes; and if you might see them in all their frippery, believes you would not have so many of them. If the Papists had arrived at their end, you had not sat here now: would have them favoured, but not as trees to bear fruit, only as pillars to be seen, they giving no such liberty in any place of the world, they having inquisitions and persecutions.

Col. *Strangways* conceives that the Declaration, issued out in the war, was to have peace at home: would not have it in any man's power to hurt the Church; first consider the Protestant interest, and put that to the question.

Mr. Secretary *Coventry* hopes you will provide something that men may not be outlawed: a preliminary vote cannot be brought in, for you are not resolved whether comprehension or toleration: thinks it a thing of the greatest consequence in the world to bind up yourselves, and not hear reasons first.

Sir *Tho. Clarges.* It was an insinuation from ill people, that the late king had an inclination to Popery. After Edgehill fight he did declare, 'that the Papists in the parliament's army were equal, if not more, in number, than in his own.' He blamed much the remissness of the Papists in that battle, that they did not their duty: will say nothing to their estates, but to be part of this Bill will destroy all our religion: until 11 Eliz. no difference in Religion; all went to Church, until Pius vth's Bull came forth, dissolving all allegiance of her subjects to her. No acts were made against the Papists until 22 Eliz. In king James's time, the jealousies of that religion were much the cause of what followed: the duke of Ormond made a treaty with that army in Ireland, to the end he might preserve the king's person, then in danger in England, and they were, by those articles, to have liberty of open profession of their religion, and equal numbers of officers in the army there. They fell from this, and declared for the Pope, and so they showed their loyalty; but the parliament army, when they were better informed, laid their arms at the king's feet, under general Monk—Molinos, Zuares, and many other Jesuits, held it lawful to depose kings. One has written a book at Paris, which he is ready to publish when called for, that proves the Jesuits were the authors of the king's death. These people, out of an excellent good intention, commit high treason every day, going to jails to convert people condemned; they get into our houses, perverting people every day; surely his majesty's good intentions are abused.

Mr. *Waller.* Whether general words of inclusion? thinks rather general words, because he would not have an act of despair on Papists. There are but two ways of changing religion, by act of parliament, or by force; by parliament impossible, none coming in here amongst us. If we were to make new laws against them again, we could not do it: has a sense of kindness for any persons that suffer. Our Saviour had some for him that suffered with him: hopes the Papists may be capable of some favour, as well as other dissenters.

Sir *Tho. Littleton.* We ought not to make the Address partial as to Dissenters: in the king's Speech the Papists are not spoken of. It is better to reduce the Papist to something, for he is now always in fear, and yet, always escapes: would have a full answer to the king's Declaration.

Sir *Tho. Meres.* What is it that makes us now so zealous in this question, but our fears of Popery? And he hoped never to have occasion to speak to it here: let us take care that, whilst we dispute the indulging the Protestant subjects, the third dog does not take the bone from us both.

Mr. Attorney *Finch.* You are labouring to put a question in terms exclusive. It is an unnatural way to exclude case of persons: at a committee you have lately voted, an Address to the king. The king may believe that the manner, and not the matter, does displease you. Your thinking his Declaration illegal cannot be grateful to him. Vulgarly speaking, a Protestant is a negative, viz. not a Papist, but, affirmatively, what, is difficult to define. If a Protestant, according to the Church of England, you exclude all persons that differ but in one article. We cannot consider religion in parliament, but as part of the civil government; its doctrine, God forbid we should: does any man hope ever to see the time that there shall be never a Papist in England? He may hope never to see an error, and yet the Scripture says, 'there must be errors, that they that are approved may be made perfect.' In all times there were Roman Catholics, though the Bull of Pius v. in queen Eliz.'s time, and the Powder Treason in king James's time, fired every man with indignation. Priests there will ever be. Queen Eliz. employed lord Clanrickard, a papist, in highest trust. They may do good, when impossibility is taken from them of doing harm: when you go and tell the king he is mistaken, and that no temperament or relaxation, believes it will have no vote: we are masters of our vote, but not of the interpretation of standers-by. Hopes it will suit with all the ends of piety and Christianity, if the vote be general, and it is for your honour to have it so.

Sir *Wm. Coventry.* It has been said, the word 'Protestant' excludes the Papists: would have have the word 'Protestant' to stand, that they may know you use some other manner of kindness, than to the Papists. The king has restrained his favours to them; I would have you do so too. Believes it is the intention of no man here to equalize them in his thoughts. [Here he stopped a while, and desired leave a little for recollection, and then proceeded.] He supposes the Declaration was to quiet persons in consideration of their numbers, so that the Papists have no claim, if few, then not considerable. If so few as we apprehend and hope, they are not considerable in the war; if many, it is time to look after them, and hinder the growth, and would not mingle them therefore, but retain the word 'Protestant' in the question.

Sir *Rob. Carr* likes neither the papists nor dissenters, but the papists have fought for the king, the others have not; therefore would have more kindness for them.

Mr. *Powle* never thought of extirpating the Papists, but would not have them equal to us. Their insolence is the complaint in every street. This has filled the minds of the people with apprehensions. They have abused the king's favour. There are some good and some bad among them. Would have the nation secured of our own religion, especially seeing that some of them have crept into commands and employments: would have the word 'Protestant' in the question.

Sir *Henry Herbert* is not for enlarging the question, for the Papists at this time enjoy liberties beyond us. They are neither sheriffs, constables, nor tything-men, nor are any laws put in execution against them. Knows very well that at Edgehill battle, the late king complained that they did not their duty, and during the war they lay couchant at Worcester. Religion is to be preferred before all considerations. The best foundation of the state is religion; it makes men more peaceable and better subjects. The Quaker and Anabaptist have no foundation. He has greater apprehensions of the Papists than of any others. Superfetations of religion are horrible. Has travelled, and (he thanks God) came home a better Protestant than he went. Their wine is the better in France by being brought into England, but our gentry worse by going into France. The Papists are wholly excluded out of the question; for they are not quiet and peaceable men, as others are.

It was then resolved, nem. con. "That a Bill be brought in for the Ease of his majesty's Protestant subjects that are Dissenters in matters of Religion from the Church of England."

Debate on desiring the Concurrence of the Lords to the Address.] The question being put, That the Concurrence of the Lords be desired, to the Petition and Address to the King,

Mr. *Swynfin* said, If you had voted, upon a single vote, what laws to be suspended, and what not, you must have gone to the lords; but now it is involved with other things, you cannot; your Message must have been singly upon the vote. It is a matter in which the lords cannot agree with you, viz. You say you have taken the matter of the Speech into consideration; if the lords have not, they cannot agree with you. For a single judgment uninvolved, you must go to them, and for an opinion in law.

Sir *Rd. Temple*. No precedent that ever we went single to the king in things of this nature without the lords. You went to the king and offered him reasons for what you could not concur with in his Speech. About relaxation in the Petition of Right, you went to the lords to join with you in petitioning the king, that the laws might have their free course. This Address is to the same effect. We never went alone in a public concern of the kingdom to the king. The matter of your Petition is a judgment in law. Hopes not for a good success if you go without the lords. If you take this course, the lords may justly object, that you declare law without them.; the king may possibly say, he will have the advice of the lords before he gives an answer, and will think it unreasonable to do it, without consulting the lords and the judges.

Mr. Attorney *Finch*. The former going without the lords, about the Declaration of Breda, was no judgment of law. Did you ever desire a Proclamation against the Papists, but by both Speakers, hand in hand? Do you think this matter of less consequence? He granted this indulgence to peers as well as commons. If they shall differ from you, it lies at their doors, and you have discharged yourselves. Will not you acquaint the lords in an universal judgment of law? The king may deny it because not parliamentary. To send it to the lords, is the way to make it more easily pass, and it is for your honour to do so.

Sir *Wm. Coventry*. When you asked liberty of access to the king's person, it was for yourselves, not the lords. In the Petition of Right there was more need than in this, for that had the force of a law. We usually go to the lords when things are in doubt; but may we not by ourselves claim our laws, and that they may have a free course? Some among the lords may be distasted with your vote. It may be, the lords will have conferences to delay. In all the debates we have avoided disputes of prerogative and liberties; the committee would not touch reasons for fear of offence. Will you go from your former precedents, and put hazard of conferences, which will put us upon arguing what we would not argue here, and put ourselves upon that rock we would avoid?

Mr. *Milward*. In your vote you have declared the law, and now you would avoid the judgment of the highest judicature. The Petition of Right is *de jure* to be granted, and therefore the lords to be consulted. Before the lords come to Addresses they will consider, and conferences are natural, and can never be avoided in any transaction with the lords.—The Question being put that the concurrence of the lords be desired, &c. it passed in the negative, 125 to 110.

Sir Job Charlton quits the Chair, and Mr. Seymour chosen in his place.] Feb. 15. The Speaker, Sir Job Charlton, being much indisposed*, the house adjourned to Tuesday, Feb. 18; when being met, and the Speaker's in-

* "Some insinuated that the Speaker was sick of his post." Grey.

disposition growing still more upon him, that he was not able to attend the service of the house, and having, by letters, desired leave of his majesty and the house to resign the place of Speaker, and retire into the country, Mr. Edward Seymour, eldest son of sir Edw. Seymour, bart. being nominated and recommended, by Mr. Secretary Coventry, as a fit person, both in respect of his ability and experience, as also of his constitution and health of body, for the Speaker; he was accordingly chosen, presented, and approved of by his maj.

Debate on the Bill for granting Ease to Protestant Dissenters.] Feb. 19. The house resolved into a committee, to take into consideration the subject-matter of a Bill for Ease to his maj.'s Protestant subjects, who are Dissenters, in matters of Religion, from the Church of England.

Sir *Lancelot Lake*, citing a passage in St. John of those who called themselves Jews and were not, moved to have the 39 Articles read, and would have that the test.

Mr. *Hale* moved to know what the gentlemen concerned in the king's Declaration would move you in, for redress of their grievances.

Sir *Tho. Lee.* Our debate is from the late vote, who you would have 'eased.' Would have the question to 'Subscribers to the Articles of the Church of England,' and thinks that a good test.

Sir *Nich. Carew* would have the Church of England as strong as you can against the Church of Rome. Would be loth to ask toleration of them. Would take in 'those that dissent not in matters of doctrine.'

Sir *John Birkenhead.* The leveller will not have the minister have two livings, nor the gentleman two manors, no emperor, no king. Are such as these the men you would ease? Before you consider what ease to give them, know from them what they would have, for one thing will not please them all; but says one, Who represents them? By licences granted since the Declaration you may know who represents them. And made a large discourse of our Religion settled by act of parliament.

Mr. *Garroway.* We are all beholden to Birkenhead for telling us that the parliament makes Religion, and the Articles, valid. Consider your vote and your Address. Dissenters are many, and not one vote can comprehend them all: would make your first steps to bring in the better sort, and if you find the door too strait, make it wider to bring in more, Moves, for the least, so many 'as will agree to the 39 Articles, or as many of them as relate to the doctrine of the Church of England.' We have people that would come in: the Papists are under an anathema, and cannot come in under pain of excommunication.

Mr. Secretary *Coventry.* It is a good motion, made to see what those out of the Church do desire. A man would give something to get something, but would not give something to get nothing. We confess that things of ceremony are in themselves indifferent, and therefore they keep out, and may have the same arguments with the Papists of salvation in their Church, and not in ours, &c. It is confessed that never any Liturgy was like our Common Prayer. We may suppose that all people here are for the Common Prayer, because said in the house every day. What do we mean by 'taking in?' It may be to be bishops, and bring the Covenant upon their backs. If we take them so in, we leave ourselves out.

Mr. *Vaughan.* If any one asks, Who are these Dissenters' representatives? We are their representatives, as for other people, and we must judge what is fit for them. Put some test upon them, and then we may know what to be relaxed.

Mr. *Crouch.* 'Ease' implies a burden of some weight. Would any physician advise with a patient, without knowing what he ails? Would know what it is would satisfy these people, before we proceed any farther.

Sir *Wm. Coventry.* It is reasonable that you consider them to whom you would 'give ease.' Did not know that the levellers, as many others, were religious, before Birkenhead called them so. And another sort he mentioned, those who believed Christianity because settled by act of parliament, knows not where that sort is. Moves that the persons we shall take care of, may be those that will subscribe to the doctrine of the Church of England, and will take the oaths of Allegiance and Supremacy.

Sir *Tho. Doleman* would not have it extend to such, as allow a Dispensation for such as take the Oaths of Allegiance and Supremacy.

Sir *Wm. Coventry* does not rise to controvert what Birkenhead said, but to rectify an error. Does doubt that it may be apprehended that 'such as will take the Oaths of Allegiance and Supremacy' shall be capable of preferment in the Church of England. The test that must be put upon persons to make them capable of preferment, must be a farther thing.

Resolved, at the committee, "That ease shall be given to his majesty's Protestant subjects that will subscribe to the doctrine of the Church of England, and take the oaths of allegiance and supremacy."

Sir *Philip Warwick.* That you may be able to do something, moves that the Convocation may have the business to consider of it.

Sir *Tho. Lee.* Thinks this 'ease,' in order to taking them into the Church, may be 'a great ease to them.' By this vote, they may comfortably follow their trades. Ceremonies are necessary for your house, and for the church, as your cloaths are for your person. Would next have it taken into consideration what shall make them capable of Preferment in the Church.

Mr. *Love.*[*] What would satisfy them, is a

[*] This gentleman, who was an alderman of the City of London, was himself a Dissenter. See p. 538. Note.

question no man here can answer, but for once desires leave to personate these people. Hopes that all, that shall reap the fruits of this bill, will demonstrate their gratitude to the king and this house, by their quiet deportment. He confesses he has no kindness for them that desire so immodest a thing as Preferment in the Church, unless they are conformable to the laws. Nor do they desire to be exempted from all chargeable offices, paying of tythes, to the poor or church, one office excepted, viz. that of church-warden only, and not without being willing to pay a fine for the contempt. They desire that, after the test, you will permit those that are preachers to preach, but not without the magistrates leave, the doors open and in the public churches, when no divine service is there. [This latter motion he retracted, being generally decried.] He said he mentioned 'in the Church' because they could not be thought to plot in such a place. This is the sense of most of the Dissenters, and will please them, and, he hopes, this committee also.

Colonel *Strangways.* Whatever the parliament shall make to unite, he shall be for it, but never to set up altar against altar. One sort of Dissenters you hope to gain, another you never hope. Does value those Churches that have charity, and damn not all opinions different from them. Would do this business as if he were immediately to answer it to God. If they were things commanded, or forbidden by God, would not alter them. He puts no value upon ceremonies, which are alterable, according to time and prudence. Would consider what you ordain, that things may be obeyed. We may remember what principles brought the king to the block. Those principles were never grounded upon the Church of England. Do what becomes good Christians and moderate men. Would not have these laws of ease made perpetual; would see how they behave themselves upon it.

Sir *John Duncombe* hopes this house will well consider what they are about, before they make a law. This may sway the very government so as to overbalance it. Will never think it fit that those men should have 'ease,' that, when the Church says, you must suffer or die; and they say you must fight. Invite them to you, but never form them into bodies; lose nothing yourselves. Their principles are not consistent with honest people; let them not set up a government by themselves, for the Presbyterian will ever be for a Commonwealth. Would have trial of them for a year, by some law, and no longer.

Sir *Tho. Lee.* In 35 Eliz. there was something of this nature. Would have the act to be upon revival, not perpetual, but to try them during this war.

Mr. Secretary *Coventry* desires that those, that are in the Church, may be clear in the Church. Is for a temporary toleration. In Holland they have no leave for any public religion but that of Calvin. The law favours none else; the rest are by connivance. Would have the indulgence here temporary.

Mr. *Powle.* To repeal all laws from queen Eliz.'s time against Dissenters would be very dangerous. Would only have the indulgence temporary. To the end of the next session of parliament would have freedom from all penal laws, ecclesiastical or temporal, and then consider of qualifications for preferment.

Sir *R. Howard.* No laws can be suspended, unless named particularly. They bind not else. It will be a strange thing, at one blow to execute all the laws since queen Eliz.'s time.

Col. *Birch.* Their argument of things indifferent in ceremonies, we cannot well answer them. Till you have some experience in the thing, would not have one stone taken out of the building. If we must enumerate the laws in this, why not in every thing else? We may say 'any law, statute, &c. to the contrary, notwithstanding."

Feb. 18. p. m. The Speaker reported, that he had, according to their direction, presented their humble Petition and Address to his majesty, who was pleased to return this answer, 'That it was of importance, and he would take it into his consideration.'

Feb. 20. In a grand committee for preparing a Bill for granting Ease to his majesty's Protestant Dissenting subjects, &c.*

Sir *Lionel Jenkins.*† As to receiving the

---

* "Great pains were taken by the court to divert the Popery Bill. They proposed that some regard might be had to Protestant Dissenters, and that their meetings might be allowed. By this means they hoped to have set them and the Church party into new heats; for now all were united against Popery. Love, who served for the city of London, and was himself a Dissenter, saw what ill effects any such quarrels might have: so he moved, 'That an effectual security might be found against Popery, and that nothing might interpose till that was done. When that was over, then they would try to deserve some favour: but at present, they were willing to lie under the severity of the laws, rather than clog a more necessary work with their concerns.' So a vote passed to bring in a Bill in favour of the Protestant Dissenters, though there was not time enough, nor unanimity enough, to finish one this session. But this prudent behaviour of theirs softened the Church party." Burnet.

† "Jenkins was a man of exemplary life and considerably learned: but he was dull and slow. He was suspected of leaning to Popery, though very unjustly. But he was set on every punctilio of the Church of England to superstition, and was a great asserter of the Divine Right of monarchy, and was for carrying the prerogative too high. He neither spoke nor writ well; but being so eminent for the most courtly qualifications, other matters were the more easily dispensed with. All his speeches and arguments against the Exclusion were heard with indignation." Burnett.

Communion twice a year in the parish churches for both lewd persons and sectaries, some persons are of no religion at all, and may be known by being kept from the communion till they amend. Humbly moves that, whatever you would do for these persons, you will support the Church; that a new Altar may not be erected for these persons, and that no new law may erect them any new Churches for public worship.*

Sir *Wm. Coventry* offers to consideration what we may do to keep persons in the Church, and to bring in such as are out; for when all is done, the preservation of religion must be in the Church of England established by law, and we must strengthen that, wherein our main defence does lie, against popery and policy. Whereas now the Dissenters have the disadvantage of their labours, for want of Preferment, by coming in they may have the benefit of them. Moves that what has been laid on them, without the convocations, may be taken off, as those things laid on since the king came in, by Act of Parliament, as Covenant, Assent and Consent, &c.

Mr. Secretary *Coventry*. As for removing the Covenant, if we are to increase our garrison, would not do it with those that have the plague. It was a brave vote the burning the Covenant, and by dispensing with the renunciation of the Covenant, you may burn your vote with the Covenant. This is a calling in other men in triumph over the Church of England.

Mr. *Vaughan*. If the Covenant be a false oath, there is no need of renunciation; taking the Oath of Allegiance and Supremacy voids all that. If we say 'no man shall or can be, of the Church of England, that comes not up to all the strictness of the Ceremonies,' it is to make ours as infallible as the Church of Rome makes hers.

Mr. Secretary *Coventry*. You have condemned the Covenant to be burnt, and will you bring it in again? Shall we be more merciful than God is, to bring in men without repenting?

Mr. *Garroway*. The case is altered now; we are providing that the Church of England shall not be devoured by the Papist. If we answer not our vote by an Act, wonders not that now we must fence off the thing. Things are not so clear: we are not at the end of the war; let us reconcile persons. Shall we leave the people in confusion? Now we will neither let them out, nor in. Shall we put them out of the nation? It may be, we shall leave few in. Though our medicine may seem empirical, yet, in the danger we are in, we must make use of it. Moves to take off the Oath of Assent and Consent, and the renunciation of the Covenant.

Mr. Secretary *Coventry*. Will you have them make subscription to what they neither 'assent' nor 'consent' to? Let one of them be taken in, either 'Assent' or 'Consent.'

Sir *Lionel Jenkins* does not know what the Dissenters mean by taking away the Oath of 'Assent and Consent.' Who are these contended for? Not the laymen; their ministers only. If they conform, they need not subscribe; if not, they need not contend for it.

Sir *John Duncombe*. If we knew what would ease them, would willingly hear them; we know not what pains them, and therefore not what will ease them. Does to thus much agree, that he would leave the thing as you found it. If we believed that the Covenant was the only clog, would take that away, but would have the Declaration what it is.

Sir *Philip Warwick* moves to have the words 'other persons' in the renunciation of the Covenant left, and believes most of the Dissenters will not scruple the rest.

Mr. Secretary *Coventry*. Many will say they are not obliged by it, because they have not taken it. Thinks we are not to buy those persons off (that think themselves obliged by the Covenant, that have taken it) at so dear a rate.

Mr. *Harwood*. We are not buying these persons, but you are making an experiment but for twelve months: The Covenant will expire of itself in nine years, in regard it is but temporary. Would have the question put.

Sir *Rd. Temple*. He that does come into the Church does materially renounce the Covenant. Men will not make forcible confessions; it is voluntary that is required. Many have said 'that by renouncing the Covenant they shall lose their interest with all men.' It is a branch not essential to the Church; it is against the nature of a renunciation to be forced. A man would ask forgiveness for an injury done if not forced to it.

Col. *Strangways*. We argue the thing now, as a civil consideration, among men of true reputation, not to do an unjust thing. Would have no man come in that does not renounce, with his tongue and heart, this odious Covenant.

Sir *Tho. Osborne*. Would have as many Dissenters brought in as may be: Does think this most unreasonable, and cannot consent to it; it is both to the king and this house: to the king, because we should seem to encourage the wickedness of those men; to the house, because of the vote, &c. No man, he thinks, will ever come in, and he would exclude them. It is a great scandal to bring them in by special act of parliament. The nation groans under

* "Sir Lionel Jenkins was, at the time of this debate, judge of the admiralty, judge of the prerogative court of Canterbury, and principal of Jesus college, Oxford, which last he resigned in 1673, when he was sent plenipotentiary to the treaty of Cologn, as he was also to that of Nimeguen, in 1678. In 1679, he succeeded Mr. Coventry in the place of Secretary of State, which he resigned for a valuable consideration in 1684, and died the year after." See Biog. Brit. Mr. North calls him "the most faithful drudge of a Secretary that ever the court had." Life of Lord Keeper Guilford, p. 229.

it, and he thinks they would return into rebellion.

Mr. *Street.* Those that are still fond of the Covenant, suppose you intend them not. He supposes persons will not renounce it for their reputation's sake. This k. James calls, in conference at Hampton-court, 'a Scottish argument.' There were then in England but 49 Dissenters. You will now gratify but a few in dispensing with it. At the Savoy Debate they agreed not what they would have; in the time of the war they made use of it as a snare to such as had not taken it. They that are fond of this idol, let them keep it, but never let it come into the Church.

Sir *Wm. Coventry* thinks that dispensing with the Covenant will strengthen you against such as will not take the Oath of Allegiance and Supremacy, who hold any thing lawful that the Pope commands, but would not press it under the notion of a thing that may be of scandal. They desire to speak and to swear only for themselves, and not for others; therefore would have them accept it to themselves, and not to others.

Mr. Secretary *Coventry.* These persons did take the Oath of Allegiance and Supremacy. In keeping out the fox from the flock, shall I let in the wolf?

Mr. *Vaughan.* This which stands in your Act is a reproach to them that they have been traitors; if it has authority, the Declaration does lessen it already. Desires the distinction only may be removed.

Col. *Birch* rises up, because some persons here were not old enough to see what was done formerly. After he had the honour to come into this house, some intentions were to renew the Covenant. Cromwell, Ireton, and the rest, would not have it done. He said then, that these men would alter the government, and the house then would have sent them to the tower: he never saw such mettle in this house; he had forty notes sent him, "Stick to the Covenant and you shall die." This was his greatest inducement to stick to it: Not one of these men could be brought to change the government. Love lost his life for it; the Presbyterian party declared against the king's murder. To the Restoration of the king all agreed. Had he not engaged for the king, by the Covenant, he had prevented himself twenty-one imprisonments he has suffered. When the king was restored, these were the men we only durst trust: he had never gone to the king at Worcester, but with sincere intentions. For the Engagement, he cannot find any of that persuasion that took it. It is a harder matter to make a man renounce, repent, and confess publicly, which is so much done in private confession.

Sir *Rob. Carr.* At the same time that the Covenant was pressed in the house, damnable heresy was coupled with the hierarchy—reflecting on col. Birch.

Sir *Tho. Lee* is loth, as they were then coupled, that now any protestant should be joined with Popery. But wonders, in all the arguments, that reputation should be "a Scotch argument" and not an English one. The house was of opinion, when the Act of Uniformity passed, that it was a prejudice to the kingdom that the renunciation of the Covenant should be perpetual. It is but for a few years to come.

Sir *Tho. Osborne.* If there be any one that thinks himself under the obligation of this Covenant, he is no good man. Mr. Calamy discoursed and pressed the bringing in the king on conditions, when he came to him that commanded next under gen. Monk.

Mr. *Garroway.* Uses this as a counter-poison, and no otherwise, against those that renounce the Oath of Allegiance and Supremacy. A great many persons are not concerned in the Covenant—a few old gentlemen. Says nothing of former things, but moves for the present pacification of England.

Mr. *Love* did hope to see yesterday some good issue. Some men may possibly think what principles he is of, which he is not ashamed to own and justify. Must give his vote, that such as will renounce the Covenant, as to their own obligation to it, without reference to others, shall be left out of the exception? but this will amount to little or no general Ease. Moves for a general Indulgence, by way of comprehension.

Debate on a Motion, to desire an Answer from the King to the Message.] Feb. 22. Sir *John Hotham.* Moves for "a desire to his maj. for a speedy Answer to the last Address of this house."

Mr. *Palmes* seconds the motion, for some of the lords of the Council of this house to move his majesty in it.

Sir *Wm. Coventry.* It is but a few days since we made the Address; and his maj. has taken time to consider of it.

Sir *Rob. Dillington.* Possibly his maj. may have forgotten our address; and desires he may be minded of it, in all humbleness, for a gracious Answer.

Sir *John Hotham,* he thought 'a speedy Answer' would be a 'gracious' one, and meant no otherwise by the word 'speedy' without any intention of unmannerliness.

Sir *John Duncombe.* Will you precipitate an Answer from the king? He has not seen such a thing in the house the twelve years we have sat: why so hasty? No man, in common conversation, is pressed at this rate: Is troubled he must speak against it. Do not let these things interrupt you: Lay these things by; and let the Speaker leave the chair.

Sir *Nich. Carew.* We sit not again till Tuesday, and it is some time for an answer, Whether Declaration can be a law, or parliament-law, a law? This is only to enable us to pay our money the more cheerfully.

Col. *Birch.* The house has declared their opinion of the Declaration: thinks that this business to day will not go well without the Message. Dissenters will think, by your vote the other day, they shall have no benefit of this day. This day will prepare you the better for that motion to the king; therefore would not have it made till after to-day.

Sir *Philip Musgrave* doubts not of an Answer from the king to our satisfaction: thinks the Message too quick: those of the lords of the council hearing your desires, will, he supposes, mind the king of an Answer: is against the question.

The *Speaker* remembers no precedent of this nature, but towards the latter end of a session.

Mr. *Hopkins.* In the case of lord Arundel the lords made a much quicker message than this; and hopes we have the same privilege.

Sir *Rob. Howard.* The king sees our information; and hopes an act of parliament, now towards, will remedy all; which is the only proper means and remedy. Consider what cause you have a-new to make another Address to king: he may possibly hear something of this debate; and possibly of that something may come, of its own nature, much more than your Address may produce: moves to wave it: possibly you may have a good success of your Bill to prevent all fears: doubts not of a fair success without a Message.

Mr. *Vaughan* stands up in order to the king's service. The slackness of the Money Bill, yesterday, possibly was from the delay of the king's Answer: we have either done too much, or too little, in this business: to contend with the king, during these distractions abroad, if our arguments are not warrantable, will be the destruction of us and the crown itself. If this be the case, we shall be thought persons rather pragmatical than to have right on our sides. If we do not renew our Address, how can we discharge our trust? If properties be not safe, we shall not know what to give, nor to whom to give.

Sir *John Trevor.* Since this so much concerns our allegiance, and the property of the subject, is moved to speak: differs from Vaughan: the question is not, whether the laws and our liberties are safe; but whether we shall importune the king so unseasonably at this time? Would fain see any gentleman (which he must say according to his profession) bring a precedent that any Answer has been so suddenly pressed: has read Petitions and Answers, 2 and 6 Hen. iv. The king is not obliged to answer but at his own time: jealousies presently whispered abroad, and would not have such a motion chopped in, but to the business of the day.

Sir *John Mallet.* We have formerly addressed about the Papists, and disbanding the Army: the same day the king gave a gracious Answer; and hopes we shall have so of this.

Sir *Wm. Coventry.* Is against the question, as thinking it too early; not above 3 days since you carried the Address; and the Answer may possibly be the same again, if you send so soon: the privy counsellors of the house will be tender to acquaint the king of your debates, without your order; but they may, as of themselves, inform the king how time slips away, and prevent the impatience of the house of commons.

Sir *Tho. Lee.* Our laws and liberties are concerned, and wonders at so great arguing against the thing: what was your Petition? That the laws might have their free course: in order to a legislative Address, money and grievances ever went together: would be glad of an effect of this debate, in all the cool manner imaginable; but money now begins sooner than ordinary; formerly, it was last debated, and last ended. The motion not so 'chopped in' as was said: it is most necessary, considering the fears of the people, their laws being at stake. Moves to have it adjourned to Tuesday, if thought too sudden.

Mr. *Garroway.* It is not so much our fears, as the account we are to give the people. There is no ill-intention in the motion; but with all candour moves to adjourn the debate.

Sir *Rob. Carr.* It has always been the wisdom of this house to do things with all decency; and if this last motion did do so, would not be against it: no man can find a precedent, and he would not have the debate adjourned.

Mr. *Harwood.* Has not heard of this in our forefathers time; but, it seems, we are come here to learn manners. It does not look well. It is confessed, but a few days since, we attended the king; therefore would respite the debate till Tuesday, without a farther question.

Sir *Tho. Meres* speaks to Tuesday: hopes gentlemen are convinced how necessary that vote was: whatever we ask here of the king, is the right we were born to; no new thing: if this be a new Address, the Declaration is as new; and one new thing begets another. No man can show such a Declaration by any counsel learned. The Judges soon going out of town to their circuits; now is the time to advise with them, or they will be gone. It is a great while since our Vote; and it is known about the town. It will be two days till we shall sit, and we, poor country-fellows, may be rude and unmannerly; but we have as good hearts as the finest of them all; we mean as well as the best of them. If we have too much heat (he means zeal for our laws) if we contend for nothing else, shall we fall flat without a question? It may be we shall never have an Answer, because a few plain country gentlemen move for it: it will look like a desertion of the thing, not to have a question for it: if this Declaration be still in force, what signifies your debate? Your hearts are dead like a rotten oak. How can you make any law that you have no assurance of the execution of? Should not the debate be adjourned, the most unhappy thing in the world.

Sir *John Duncombe.* If the word 'unmannerliness' has offended, the word 'bold expression' was as much from Meres: how can the gentlemen know, but that some of the Judges are absent, that the king would ask the question of, or some of his council that he would trust? In common conversation, would you refuse a man two or three days time consideration? Much less the king: this adjournment signifies something of indecency. He says it again, if the king has a reason for his delay, doubtless he hears of your impatience. It is not becoming this house: would have the things that gentlemen desire, but moderate courses in it: if by Tuesday you have not an Answer, consider it then.

Lord *St. John* would pass this Money bill as soon as may be, the time of the year coming on: would, in the mean time, satisfy the minds of men, and is for Tuesday.

Mr. Sec. *Coventry*. Meres has used the terms of 'side and side' of the house; it is not parliamentary: both Country Gentlemen and Courtiers have been loyal; both very good and very bad: desires the gentlemen would leave these reflections: he is as loyal as he or any man; and many have made applications at court* that have missed their ends; and he that will say, 'No Courtier,' may as well say, 'No King.'

Sir *Tho. Lee*. Is sorry to hear a distinction made from Coventry: no man, that he knows, ever made the distinction before him.

Mr. *Garroway*. The word Courtier was not made use of, only 'fine man:' would not have the house Hectored by any man.

Sir *Tho. Lee*. There was nothing said of 'Gentlemen living about town.' Country Gentlemen may live about town: desires no reflection may be made; and that Coventry may explain.

Sir *Rob. Carr*. The words were 'fine gentlemen about the town:' never heard more sharpness here than by Meres: but let us leave off reflections, and go about the business.

Col. *Samuel Sandys* is not ashamed that he has received the king's bounty: he never begged any thing: he shall serve his country as chearfully as any man: moves that these things may be laid aside.

Col. *Titus*. Whatever becomes of the debate of the Address, would have this debate adjourned: believes that many Courtiers would be Country Gentlemen, and many Country Gentlemen would be Courtiers: knows that we would not only not be guilty, but not be liable to the suspicion of ill manners: if this was towards the end of a session, the more reason.

Col. *Strangways* is troubled at the clashings of the house: would have every man have freedom of speech: those that have fought for the king may be pardoned in their expressions; though not bred at inns of Court and Universities, to furnish their expressions with elegancies: hopes the Message is honest; the Judges are sworn to do things indifferently to king, court, and relative to the subject: would ask any gentleman, Whether he would have the Act of Indemnity voided? Which may be, if the king has power of suspending the laws by his Declaration. The king can do no hurt; those that advise him may do hurt both to king and people: happiness of both king and country depends upon one another: those that crucified our Saviour, and lay in wait for St. Paul, were zealous men; but zeal must be in a good matter, and hopes our zeal is so for this: moves for Tuesday.

Mr. *Waller*. Consider the occasion of all this debate, and your Address, and consider what reputation your brave Vote for Supply gave his majesty, and that a debate should put this day by: put all in the balance: the Declaration is a year old, and pretended to have done much good: deferring this debate, is pulling down your walls, the ships. See what is at stake. The state is no stronger than they are that defend it: the king is at an end of his credit, and money, without your aid. Let nothing jostle out this bill: avoid this debate for Tuesday.

Mr. *Powle*. All your Supplies will go on heavily without this; and if laws may be suspended, we have nothing we can call our own. Let any man examine, whether this Declaration has not caused more discontent than has been since the king's happy Restoration: neither Judge, nor any counsel of Westminster Hall, but is of our minds. Lord Arundel's case puts him in mind of sir Dudley Diggs's case of imprisonment. If the king pleases to send us a satisfactory Answer, we may go on chearfully.

Ordered, That this debate be adjourned to Tuesday the 25th.

The King's Answer to the Address.] Feb. 24. The king's Answer to the preceding Petition and Address was delivered to the house by Mr. Secretary Coventry, and is as follows:

"C. R. His majesty hath received an Address from you, and he hath seriously considered of it, and returneth you this Answer: That he is very much troubled that that Declaration, which he put out for ends so necessary to the quiet of his kingdom, and especially in that conjuncture, should prove the cause of disquiet in his house of commons, and give occasion to the questioning of his power in Ecclesiasticks: which he finds not done in the reigns of any of his ancestors. He is sure he never had thoughts of using it otherwise than as it hath been intrusted in him, to the peace and establishment of the Church of England, and the ease of all his subjects in general. Neither doth he pretend to the right of suspending any laws, wherein the properties, rights, or liberties of any of his subjects are concerned; nor to alter any thing in the established doctrine or discipline of the Church of England: but his only design in this was, to take off the penalties the statutes inflicted upon the Dissenters; and which, he believes, when well considered of, you yourselves would not wish executed, according to the rigour and letter of the law. Neither hath he done this with any thought of avoiding, or precluding, the advice of his parliament; and if any Bill shall be offered him,

* "Reflecting upon Meres." Grey.

which shall appear more proper to attain the aforesaid ends, and secure the peace of the church and kingdom, when tendered in due manner to him, he will show how readily he will concur in all ways that shall appear good for the kingdom.—Given at the Court at Whitehall, Feb. 24, 1672-3."

Debate thereon.] Sir *Philip Warwick.* Is very glad that the king's Answer is come in so soon: it answers all your ends; and he would have it recorded, and the king thanked.

Col. *Birch.* The thing, if well looked into, is as much as we can desire, and he would have the king thanked for it.

Sir *Tho Lee* would have the Answer considered, it consisting of many branches: though in one part he would be very ample in our thanks, yet, in such a general Answer, we contradict our vote of the king's power in ecclesiastical matters: it seems to him that our vote will be of great consequence and weight: would be loth to make hard inferences from the thing; therefore would have a due Answer, and no sudden vote.

Sir *Rob. Howard.* We have now a probable cause of our happiness, but no *probabilem causam litigandi.* We have that plainly which we have long hoped for: appeals to any man whether he had not a diffidence of mind, from the time of your Message till now: the Answer, in its own nature, is perfectly kind, as the nature of the prince it comes from: "That power you desire is called for by your prince: would have your thanks ordered without a question.

Sir *Tho. Meres.* To speak on a sudden to this thing is an unreasonable hardship; It seems here is a distinction made in the king's power in 'ecclesiastical' and 'temporal' matters. Those of the long robe did declare they knew no such difference. Our Address only mentioned ecclesiastical matters, because it referred to the Declaration: knows that in the king's Message this is implied; he will not do it in 'temporal' but that he may do it; and we say it is not to be done: would have some time to consider it; and they are the words of the king: if we answer it in haste, it will look rash; if we give general thanks, being contradictory to our vote, it will look like levity.

Sir *Joseph Tradenham* thinks this debate a mistaken one; thinks the jealousy vain; for if the king will dispense with what belongs to himself, we cannot be against it.

Sir *Wm. Coventry.* The objection lies in two points; the king says, 'He is sorry you should question what never was questioned in the reigns of any of his ancestors.' The king may complain, and it is a misfortune to him that he is sensible, and we ought to be so too: appeals, if our business be not at an end today. If you will have the penal statutes put in execution, the king tells you what he is willing to do in signing a Bill, and moves you to give the king thanks.

Col. *Strangways.* The Message consists of several parts, and they are of great moment: many things involved in it, and it being a point of great tenderness, moves to have it considered to-morrow morning, and would have the thing weighed as it deserves to be weighed.

Sir *Rd. Temple.* It seems to him fraught with so much condescension as never yet came from a king, and sees no reason to retard the thanks, especially at such a time as this: the king tells you, 'he designed nothing but taking off penalties, not dispensing with laws, and that if you will pass an Act, he is willing to it; and therefore now the king has given no occasion to delay your thanks, an hesitation in this thing will look like an endeavour to take an exception: moves for thanks.

Sir *Wm. Coventry* moves not for giving thanks; that is indecent; it implies that either you must give reasons, and present them, or humbly ask his majesty's pardon for what we have done: sees no difficulty on our parts to thank the king for preserving our properties, and no more.

Mr. *Powle.* The Message does seem to charge us with undutifulness in 'questioning the king's power, never done before.' It is true, too, the occasion was never given before: moves to thank the king for preserving our properties and assurance of them, and 'that we will take the matter of his Message into consideration.'

Mr. *Harwood.* No man, in decency and good manners, can deny giving thanks; but the suddenness of the thing would be thought indecent: when he considers the trust reposed in him, cannot agree to a sudden Answer.

Mr. *Garroway* is glad we have this gracious Answer, therefore moves for a committee to pen it, that we may not commit yet a greater error (if it be one) than our vote.

Sir *John Duncombe.* Could the king say a more kind thing than his Message? Thinks he desires nothing but peace: the thing troubles the king, and troubles the whole nation: how could the king keep all things quiet but by suspending these laws? Is sorry, that any thing should look like a doubt of giving him thanks.

Mr. Attorney *Finch* supposes that no new addition shall substract what was proposed in the former question: would have your address with all gratitude imaginable. It is a mistake that an Answer of thanks excludes farther grace: why should we refuse thanks for this degree his maj. has given us of Answer, when he might have refused us this gracious answer, or any farther answer?

Sir *Tho. Lee* would have the house understand, that the fear is, whether a power is not asserted in our Answer, whether by priests preaching in English, and mass being said in several places, the laws are not so suspended as taken off by the Declaration: agrees for giving the king thanks, but would be secured that penal laws cannot be suspended but by act of parliament. If he makes too harsh an inference, begs the pardon of the house: it is the greatest question that ever was in parliament, and may shut the door to all Addresses for the future: in our thanks let us not lose our rights and liberties, lest we say, 'we thank your maj. for suspending the laws.' If this be the consequence, let every man lay his hand on his heart, and say, How shall any penal laws be made? Or else your vote signifies nothing.

Sir *Lionel Jenkins.* The king says, 'He was under a necessity of dispensing;' and having the power of peace and war by his prerogative, he has power of doing things in order thereunto; but 'when a Bill shall be preferred,' his maj. says, 'he will pass it;' he therefore conceives thanks to his majesty requisite and proper.

Mr. *Vaughan* wonders at Jenkins's inference, 'that power of peace and war, is power of repealing laws;' as much as to say, if power of war, power to determine whether law or no law: would have such thanks, as we may have no occasion of giving more upon this account: as the question is proposed, we thank him for the particulars afterwards: if we thank our king so, we condemn ourselves: would have such an Answer as we may thank him for preservation of us and himself: moves for a committee to consider the Answer and Reasons.

Sir *Edw. Dering* thinks this Bill of Religion under an ill planet: one day, appointed for it, lost in the king's Answer, and another in our desires for that Answer: would not have such a question determined with incogitancy: no man does think that such a thing, not intended in the question, ought to be crowded in obliquy: moves for the question.

Mr. *Waller.* Whether the word 'gracious' shall be applied to the whole Answer, or to part of it, is the question: the danger to the whole is contradicting our Address. Says the king, 'it was never in the time of my ancestors questioned,' which is not an assertion of the king's: is not this a gracious thing? And the word 'gracious' may be applied to the whole Answer, for the king not asserting it, is a gracious Answer.

Sir *Tho. Meres.* In the king's Answer, the power in ecclesiastical matters is plainly asserted. The Message says, 'he only designs to take off that penalty of the statutes;' if any will say, that so taking off penalties be not to suspend laws, what you have voted is not right. If you will thank him for suspending, it is a levity he hopes this house will never be guilty of.

Mr. Secretary *Coventry* avers there is no assertion in the Message, nor distinction; it joins both our liberties and ecclesiastical matters. In the words of the Message, the king 'never had thoughts of using it otherwise, than for the good of his subjects;' not to properties, nor to alter any thing established by law in church or state.

Mr. *Powle.* Jenkins said, 'there was a necessity of the Declaration.' The violation of our laws has been necessity. The States of Normandy desired the king of France not to raise any more taxes but by their consent; his answer was, 'he would not do it but upon necessity:' and that necessity has been ever since, and he has raised money without them: Shall we rest in a doubtful and ambiguous Answer, where our rights and liberties are concerned? Would have the Answer of Thanks and Complaint go together, and how you can do it without a committee, a wiser man than he must tell you.

It was then resolved, "That the Thanks of this house be presented to his maj. for his gracious Assurances and Promises in his Answer to the Address presented by this house."

Feb. 25. Sir *Wm. Coventry.* It concerns us to proceed with all duty to his maj. for preservation of our laws and liberties: Finds no way more expedient for this business, than going into a grand committee: hopes it may be done substantially, and answer all the ends of the house, and heats avoided: We have always referred Reasons for things to be prepared by a committee, and the house to approve of them; and he thinks it now most expedient to your purpose.

Mr. *Powle.* Before you refer it to a committee, would open the exceptions we have to his majesty's Answer. It is apparent, that those persons that advised his maj. to this Declaration, still inform him that it is his right. 'Not questioned in the reigns of any of his ancestors,' will seem to imply, an unquestionable right without parliament—3 James, Petition of Grievances; some wholly relating to ecclesiastical matters—The jurisdiction of the High Commissioned Court abused, in pursuance of their citations and excommunications; all ecclesiastical matters—In the next session, complaint of the Canons of 1 James, without consent of parliament, which were then protested against, and complained of. In the next session, complaint that the ecclesiastical laws were not put in execution against non-residents and recusants—The king then, it seems, has been strangely misinformed of his power in ecclesiastical maters: the law gives penalties, not by way of profit or revenue, but for punishment of offenders: If the king can remit penalties, always complained of in parliament, and redressed there, it tends to the overthrow of all things; and hopes this assertion will be waved: taking the co-herence all together, that the king may, for peace, suspend laws, the pretence of necessity may never be wanting—The saying 'a Bill may be more proper,' implies suspension to be proper: These things have extremely weighed with him: and doubts not but, upon our informing the king, he will be graciously pleased to satisfy us; else the consequence will be an endless dispute betwixt the king and this house.

Sir *Tho. Lee* hopes that care will be taken, for the future, that there shall be no occasion of this nature. thinks this business too great for a committee.

Sir *Tho. Meres* would have the committee so far empowered, as plainly to show that the power is not in the king: If not so instructed, time will be lost, and new debates again.

Resolved, "That it be referred to a Committe, to consider what Answer to return to his majesty's last message, and to make report thereof."

The Commons' second Address to the King.] Feb. 26. Mr. Powle reports the following Answer agreed by the committee:

"Most Gracious Sovereign, We your maj.'s most humble and loyal subjects, the knights, citizens, and burgesses, in this present parliament assembled, do render to your sacred maj. our most dutiful Thanks, for that, to our unspeakable comfort, your maj. hath been pleased so often to reiterate unto us those gracious promises and assurances of maintaining the Religion now established, and the Liberties and Properties of your people: And we do not in the least measure doubt, but that your maj. had the same gracious intentions in giving satisfaction to your subjects, by your Answer to our late Petition and Address; yet upon a serious consideration thereof, we find, that the said Answer is not sufficient to clear the apprehensions that may justly remain in the minds of your people, by your majesty's having claimed a power to suspend penal Statutes, in matters Ecclesiastical, and which your maj. does still seem to assert, in the said Answer, to be 'intrusted in the crown, and never questioned in the reigns of any of your ancestors;' wherein, we humbly conceive, your maj. hath been very much mis-informed; since no such power was ever claimed, or exercised, by any of your maj.'s predecessors; and, if it should be admitted, might tend to the interrupting of the free course of the laws, and altering of the legislative power, which hath always been acknowledged to reside in your majesty, and your two houses of parliament. We do therefore, with an unanimous consent, become again most humble suitors unto your sacred majesty, that you would be pleased to give us a full and satisfactory Answer to our said Petion and Address: and that your maj. would take such effectual order, that the proceedings in this matter may not, for the future, be drawn into consequence or example."

After debate, it was resolved, "That the whole Address be agreed to, as it was brought in by the committee; and that it be presented to his majesty."

Further Debate on the Bill of Ease to Protestant Dissenters.] Feb. 27. In a grand committee on the Bill of Ease to his majesty's Protestant Dissenting subjects,

Mr. *Powle* said, it was the advice of St. Paul, to 'bear with those that were weak in faith:' Those that are of the same belief with us desire 'Ease,' which must relate to burdens. By the law of queen Eliz. no man was punished that did not teach heretical or erroneous opinions. Now before the last law of Conventicles, no law reached them. Here we have a sort of people that teach nothing but the truth, and knows not why we should deny these people liberty, that have it in all places but where the inquisition is.

Mr. *Garroway* would confirm to the Dissenters such houses as are already granted them.

Sir *Adam Browne.* Every sectary will say he is a Protestant and no Papist: You must take care for the other parties as well as the Presbyterians.

Sir *Tho. Clarges* agrees not to the places already appointed: would have great caution as well to places as to the religion established: would have it penned 'for such places as shall be appointed by act of parliament.'

Sir *Wm. Hickman*, thinks it not reasonable they should have their meeting-houses out of town; the Act being temporary, they will not build houses.

Mr. *Swynfin.* You have great expectations upon you, and you have partly intended them the thing under consideration. If then something must be done, consider, that some think it far greater than it is: the Test for subscription of qualifying persons is as much as was in queen Eliz.'s time: compare the Church then and now; there were many professed enemies then, all the opposition the Church of Rome could make, and other dissenters: hopes that this may bring a small number of the Church to be a greater: 'Meeting' must import some place, but how to describe the place? either 'left to their own choice,' and that possibly may have two great a latitude, and then you cannot find them to have the Test: if 'by certificate to the sessions,' then such places as are already allowed by licence; but thinks that gives too much countenance to the Declaration.

Sir *Tho. Lee.* If at this day they meet at any house without Bible, or religious worship, they are not within your act: these sort of people having a design to do mischief, may meet together, and you cannot punish them: if you find them tumultuous, you need not continue the Bill, but would have the liberty with the largest.

Mr. *Crouch.* The question is, what place they shall have? Cambridge, the place he serves for, desires that they may not be there.

Sir *Wm. Coventry*, hoped Crouch did more that they might have been in Cambridge: would have them in the universities, that they may convert them.

Mr. *Crouch.* They will be disturbed by the youths there with disputing: would not have them there.

Colonel *Strangways.* Public places are, in our religion, for divine worship, that people may find them; and that no disturbance be made, and no ill doctrine preached: indulgences that were to itinerant preachers 'per totum Angliam,' those disturbed most.

It was then voted, "In such places only as by this Act shall be appointed."

It was next proposed "That the Bill continue but for one year, and from thence to the end of the next session of parliament."

Sir *John Duncombe.* Would have it stop at one year; you will in that time find inconvenience sufficient both to church and state.

Sir *Ch. Harbord*. Will you put them into a snare for a year? better let it alone totally. Let them fully in, and they will be concerned for their good behaviour, and you may do good with them.

Sir *Wm. Coventry*. Would not have them bear offices, nor have the benefit by not bearing offices; but would have them contribute to the charge.

Mr. *Crouch*, would not have them churchwardens that care not for the Church, and would let it fall: would have them not capable, but fine for it.

Sir *Wm. Coventry* If he does not execute his office as he should, he will fall into the bishop's hands; and his courts will handle him sufficiently. It is said 'that the bishops cannot handle them;' but you do not take the penalties off any more than in not coming to the Church, and be will have a writ *de excom. capiendo*, which is not by this Act voided.

Mr. *Crouch*. This writ will cost 3*l*. to the person that takes it out; and no sooner in the jail but let loose; and no remedy but what is worse than the disease.

Sir *Tho. Lee*. The ecclesiastical courts in some things have too much power, and in others too little, and the bishops usually the least: this bill has no relation to offices: and if you debate this, you must also the regulating the ecclesiastical power.

Sir *John Duncombe*. If you let them in to be church-wardens, or overseers of the poor, you will be sure to have all of their opinion well fed, and the rest starved.

Sir *Tho. Lee*. One church-warden is named by the parson, and the other by the parish, so you are sure that one will be a churchman; and as for the overseers of the poor, chosen by the parish, and allowed of at the justices monthly meeting, there is seldom any distinction in distributing the money; and if there is, the justices may remedy it.

Sir Thomas Meres reported the Heads of a Bill for the ease of Dissenters.—The following are the said Heads, as abridged from the Journal." "To subscribe to the Articles of the Doctrine of the Church of England: to take the Oaths of Allegiance and Supremacy: 'Assent and Consent' taken away: pains for meeting taken away: Teachers to subscribe and take the Oaths at quarter sessions: before two Justices of the Peace, out of sessions, to teach till next sessions, doors open: to continue for a year, and from thence to the end of the next session of parliament."

Debate on removing Papists from Public Employments.] Feb. 28. Mr. *Sacheverell*, moves for removing all popish recusants out of military office or command.

Mr. *Tho. Lee* complained of divers who were got into command lately.

Sir *Rob. Carr*. Neither Lee, nor any man else, knows that any considerable papists are in arms: if one papist be qualified with 40 or 50 Protestants, there is no danger: if any more be, they are likely to go beyond sea, and not trouble you here.

Mr. *Vaughan*. Drums beat about the streets; there are many Irish popish officers; and in the coffee-houses they say 'some of us are to be hanged, when the parliament rises:' when these men are once raised, we shall not know how to get them suppressed: therefore moves for a vote for an Address to the king, for removing them.

Sir *Tho. Osborne*. The king was pleased to have the commissions searched, and there were not 16, before these new forces were raised: he considered not their religion, but that they were soldiers and good officers: the king knew them to be good officers, but not Catholics: you will not, he hopes, expect that those of the fleet (so considerable) should be excluded the service.

Earl of *Ogle**. He must chuse some Roman Catholics, or he cannot raise the king a good regiment: he must do them this justice, that many of them have been killed, and lost their estates, for the king's service: he has but two officers papists in his whole regiment, and one was put upon him: it does not become us to think of so great danger of Popery.

Sir *Rob. Howard*. What you are to do now, is to appoint some members to draw a Bill, to exempt them from this trust: he is no great affecter of their religion, but would not have the swords of gallant men taken from them.

Mr. *Garroway*. Has no man in particular to charge. Yet common fame makes them lavish, in saying, they are only able to serve the king: is sorry to have it said here, that we have no persons capable of service, but papists: the greater is the danger of them: we have many young gentlemen, protestants, who may learn, and in time be put in employment: the king, in his speech, has formerly thought them incapable; and therefore he does. As for facilitating the king's business, which gave this day's interruption, when the people shall see we have not forgot them in their fears of Popery, the money will be given with the better will, and their spirits quieted.

Earl of *Ogle*. Says he is lieutenant of Northumberland, which county is divided betwixt papists and such as have fought against the king: he is the son of a father that has fought for him, and so are they also; therefore it cannot be thought amiss to employ them.

Col. *Strangways*, is sorry that those of the Church of England are dead, and those alive that have not served the king: many that have served the king cannot get employment: would have lord Ogle carry those abroad that have disserved the king: let us do that which becomes prudent men: he has a kindness for their persons, but would not have power in their hands to do mischief: but will nothing satisfy them but to be in competition with you: would have none of that.

* Son of the famous marquis and duke of Newcastle, whom he succeeded in those titles in 1676, and died without issue male in 1691.

Mr. *Powle*, would distinguish between old and new converts: putting them in employment looks like a reward of their apostacy: lord Ogle said, 'he had but two, and one put upon him.' He is sorry they have such interest: another said, 'there were not above 15 or 16.' All agree, that amongst the new-raised men, there are many: it may be said, many have served the king: desires not the rigour of execution of the laws; but when such have arms in their hands, knows not but they may make use of them to establish their own power.

Mr. *Harbord*. Unless you do something more than a vote, you will be under the same power the Presbyterians were in the Long Parliament, awed by the Independents, who had arms in their hands: would have a law for it: there was great rejoicing at Rome, by the Cardinal Protector of the English, for the king's murder: and to these they durst speak their minds to they said, 'they could not prevail upon him for his religion.' Now in this he takes the liberty rather to displease his king than undo him. [The words gave offence.] He explains himself upon the Declaration, that it would unde the king and the subject.

Sir *Tho. Meres*. The words gave no offence; every man ought to say so, if he be persuaded in his heart 'for what is not of faith, is sin' that it will undo the king.

Sir *John Duncombe* takes things of this nature with as much humanity, as he would have other men do of him: Harboard knows he has great respect for him: but though the king gives us freedom of speech, yet he never heard the like before here.

Sir *Tho. Osborne* hopes the words were not as he apprehends them, but would have them asserted.

Col. *Strangways* thinks the words may be justified, and no hurt in them, take them in the true meaning.

Mr. Attorney *Finch*. The reason of law why we have liberty of speech, is, that whatever ill is said of us without doors, we may be censured here only for it: supposes the gentleman does sufficiently correct himself for what he has said.

Mr. *Garroway* desires for the sake of your member, that the words may be asserted, that the things may not be reported without doors which were not said within.

Sir *John Duncombe*. A man would be troubled for the very approaches of offending this house: it would grieve him to the soul to do it.

Mr. *Harbord* explains: not at all satisfied with the Declaration; he intended no reflection on the king, and would submit to all the severity in the world rather than be thought such a one.

Sir *Tho. Meres* could have wished the thing had been better worded, but the sense was good.—[So it passed over, and the debate was resumed.]

Sir *Tho. Lee*. If the word 'popish' be without 'suspected,' you have not one 'convicted recusant' in England.

Col. *Birch*. Men will be more able to pay the tax, by the clause of corn, more willing, by recalling the Declaration, and out of fear for the future, by this vote of Popery. Ireland for 50 years, in queen Eliz's. time, had no rebellion in it, and good trade; but when the Papists once got into office there cheek-by-jowl with the Protestants, then they rebelled. If you put not a stop to this, all will be ineffectual: when he considers at the first Reformation in Henry viiith's time, how few we were, and what a swing it had when once got in fashion,—let men apply it: a great many that took the Oaths of Allegiance and Supremacy rebelled: what has been done may be done: would have the king and you assured in the business, and that is all he aims at.

Sir *John Duncombe*. The servant that had so much forgiven him, and took his fellow servant by the throat for a small debt, such people must be looked to. Let men carry humanity about them when they run so into religion. Men that have been locked up in their own walls (as the Romish Fryars) know not how to use their tongues in company, and some are indiscreet through zeal; for zeal and love never were discreet.

Resolved, "That all persons who shall refuse to take the Oaths of Allegiance and Supremacy, and to receive the Sacrament according to the Rites of the Church of England, shall be incapable of all public employments, military or civil."

The King's Speech, complaining of Addresses received from the Commons.] March 1. The king came this day to the house of lords, and made a short Speech as follows:

"My lords; you know that, at the opening of this session, I spake here to your satisfaction: it hath notwithstanding begotten a greater disquiet in the h. of commons than I could have imagined. I received an Address from them which I looked not for; I made them an Answer that ought to have contented them: but on the contrary, they have made me a reply, of such a nature, that I cannot think fit to proceed any further in this matter without your advice. I have commanded the Chancellor to acquaint you with all the transaction, wherein you will find both me and yourselves highly concerned. I am sensible for what relates to me; and I assure you, my lords I am not less so for your privileges and the honour of this house."

Debate thereon.] This Speech was taken into consideration, and both his maj. and the duke chose to continue in the house, in expectation of the event.—Of the debate which ensued, there is no regular account remaining, though it was one of the most important in our annals. Bishop Burnet has, indeed, made a shift to glean up some particulars concerning it, which he has favoured the public with, as also of the intrigue which followed; and quotes for his vouchers, the duke of York, the duke of Lauderdale, and col. Titus.—According to him, lord Clifford was the hero for the Declaration, and had not only shewed the heads of his Speech to the king, but received hints from him. "He began the debate with rough words. He called the Vote of the commons '*monstrum, horrendum, ingens*' and ran on in a very high strain. He said all that could be said, with great heat, and many indecent expressions. When he had done, the earl of Shaftsbury, to the amazement of the whole house, said, He must differ from the lord who spoke last *toto cœlo*.* He said, while those matters were debated out of doors, he might think with others, that the Supremacy, asserted as it was by law, did warrant the Declaration. But now that such a house of commons, so loyal and affectionate to the king, were of another mind, he submitted his reason to them: they were the king's great council: they must both advise and support him: they had done it, and would do so still, if their laws and religion were secure to them."—The bishop adds: the king was all in fury to be thus forsaken by his chancellor, and told Clifford how well he was pleased with his speech, and how highly he was offended with the other. The debate went on; and upon a division, the court had the majority. But against that Vote about 30 of the most considerable of the house protested. So the court saw, they had gained nothing in carrying on a Vote that drew after it such a protestation. The issue of all was, that, the same day, they waited upon his majesty with the following Address:

"We the lords spiritual and temporal in parliament assembled, do unanimously present your sacred majesty our humble thanks, for having pleased to communicate unto us, what hath passed between your majesty and the h. of commons; whereby your maj. hath graciously offered the means of shewing our duty to your majesty, and of asserting the antient, just rights and privileges of the house of peers."

Whereunto the King returned this Answer:

"My lords; I take this Address of yours very kindly, and will always be affectionate to you; and I expect that you shall stand by me, as I will always by you."

And now from this alliance offensive and defensive, between the king and lords, against the commons, what was not to be feared? No doubt, all who were acquainted with the proceedings of that day dreaded the next: and yet, instead of a storm, which was gathering overnight, it produced an unexpected calm, the lords voting, "That the king's Answer to the house of commons, in referring the points now controverted to a parliamentary way, by Bill, is good and gracious; that being a good and natural course for satisfaction therein."

"To account," says Mr. Ralph,* "for this sudden and surprising reverse, we must have recourse again to bishop Burnet; for no other author pretends to be enough in the secret to say any thing to the purpose upon it. Lord Arlington possessed Colbert, the French ambassador here, with such an apprehension of the madness of violent councils; and that the least of the ill effects they might have would be, the leaving the war wholly upon the French king; and that it would be impossible to carry it on, if the king should run to such extremities, as some were driving him to at home; that he gained him both to press the king and his brother to comply with the parliament; and to send an express to his own master, representing the whole matter in the light in which lord Arlington had set it before him.—In the afternoon of the day, in which the matter had been agreed in the house of lords, the earls of Shaftsbury and Arlington got all those members of the h. of commons on whom they had any influence (and who had money from the king and were his spies, but had leave to vote with the party against the court, for procuring them the more credit) to go privately to him, and to tell him, that, upon lord Clifford's Speech, the house was in such fury, that probably they would have gone to some high votes and impeachments: but the lord Shaftsbury, speaking on the other side, restrained them; they believed he spoke the king's sense, as the other did the duke's: this calmed them: so they made the king apprehend, that the lord Chancellor's Speech, with which he had been so much offended, was really a great service done him; and they persuaded him farther, that he might now save himself, and obtain an indemnity for his ministers, if he would part with the Declaration, and pass the bill (for a Test). This was so dextrously managed by lord Arlington, who got a great number of the members, to go, one after another, to the king, who, by concert, spoke all the same language, that, before night, the king was quite changed, and said to his brother, That lord Clifford had undone himself, and spoilt their business, by his mad speech; and that though lord Shaftsbury had spoke like a rogue, yet that he had stopt a fury, which the indiscretion of the other had kindled to such a degree, that he could serve him no longer. He gave him leave to let him know all this. The duke was struck with all this; and imputed it wholly to lord Arlington's management. In the evening, he told lord Clifford what the king said. The lord Clifford, who was naturally a vehement man, went upon that to the king, who scarce knew how to look him in the face. Lord

* "While he was speaking, the duke of York, enraged at him, whispered the king, 'What a rogue have you of a lord chancellor!' The king briskly replied, 'Cod's Fish; what a fool have you of a lord-treasurer!' The debate ended in a ruffle, and the lord Clifford narrowly escaped being sent to the Tower; and finding himself thus given up by the king, like his new opponent, he declared, 'he would serve no prince in the world who had not courage to avow his principles and support his ministers in the execution of his demands." Echard.

* Vol. i. p. 226.

Clifford said, he knew how many enemies he must needs make to himself, by his Speech in the house of lords: but he hoped, that, in it, he both served and pleased the king; and was therefore the less concerned in every thing else: but he was surprized to find by the duke, that the king was now of another mind. The king was in some confusion: he owned all he said was right in itself; but he said, that he, who had sat so long in the h. of commons, should have considered better what they would bear, and what the necessity of his affairs required. Lord Clifford, in his first heat, was inclined to have laid down his staff, and to have expostulated roundly with the king: but a cooler thought stopped him. He reckoned he must now retire; and, therefore, he had a mind to take some care of his family in the way of doing it: so he restrained himself, and said he was sorry, that his best-meant services were so ill understood. Soon after this, letters came from the French king, pressing the king to do all that was necessary to procure money of the parliament; since he could not bear the charge of the war alone. He also wrote to the duke and excused the advice he gave, upon the necessity of affairs; but promised faithfully, to espouse his concerns, as soon as he got out of the war; and that he would never be easy, till he recovered that which he was now forced to let go."

Address of both Houses against the Growth of Popery.] March 7. Both houses agreed to the following Address to his majesty:

"Most gracious sovereign; We, your majesty's most loyal subjects, the lords spiritual and temporal, and commons, in this present parliament assembled, being very sensible of the great dangers and mischiefs that may arise within this your majesty's realm, by the increase of Popish Recusants amongst us; and considering the great resort of Priests and Jesuits into this kingdom, who daily endeavour to seduce your majesty's subjects from their religion and allegiance; and how desirous your loyal subjects are, that no Popish Recusants be admitted into employments of trust and profit, and especially into military commands over the forces now in your majesty's service; and having a tender regard to the preservation of your majesty's person, and the peace and tranquillity of this kingdom, do in all humility desire: 1. That your maj. would be pleased to issue out your royal Proclamation, to command all Priests and Jesuits (other than such as, not being natural-born subjects to your majesty, are obliged to attend upon your royal consort the queen) to depart within 30 days out of this your majesty's kingdom; and that if any Priest or Jesuit shall happen to be taken in England after the expiration of the said time, that the laws be put in due execution against them; and that your maj. would please, in the said Proclamation, to command all judges, justices of the peace, mayors, bailiffs, and other officers, to put the said laws in execution accordingly. 2. That your maj. would likewise be pleased, that the lord chancellor of England shall, on or before the 25th of March inst. issue out commissions of Dedimus Potestatem to the Judge Advocate and Commissaries of the Musters, and such other persons as he shall think fit (not being officers commanding soldiers, to tender the Oaths of Allegiance and Supremacy to all officers and soldiers now in your majesty's service and pay; and that such as refuse the said oaths may be immediately disbanded, and not allowed or continued in any pay or pension; and that the chancellor shall require due returns to be made thereof within some convenient time after the issuing out of the said commissions. 3. That the said Commissaries of the Musters be commanded and enjoined, by your majesty's warrant, upon the penalty of losing their places, not to permit any officer to be mustered in the service and pay of your majesty, till he shall have taken the Oaths of Allegiance and Supremacy; and received the Sacrament of the Lord's Supper according to the laws and usage of the Church of England; and that every soldier serving at land shall take the said Oaths before his first muster, and receive the Sacrament in such manner before his second muster.—And this we present in all dutifulness to your majesty's princely wisdom and consideration, as the best means for the satisfying and composing the minds of your loyal subjects; humbly desiring your maj. graciously to accept of this our petition as proceeding from hearts and affections entirely devoted to your majesty's service, and to give it your royal approbation."

The King's Speech to both Houses.] March 8. This day the king went to the house of lords, and, sending for the commons, made the following Speech:

"My lords and gentlemen; Yesterday you presented me an Address, as the best means for the satisfying and composing the minds of my subjects; to which I freely and readily agreed: and I shall take care to see it performed accordingly. I hope, on the other side, you, gentlemen of the h. of commons, will do your part; for I must put you in mind, it is near 5 weeks since I demanded a Supply; and what you voted unanimously upon it, did both give life to my affairs at home, and disheartened my enemies abroad: but the seeming delay it hath met withal since, hath made them take new courage; and they are now preparing for this next summer a greater fleet (as they say) than ever they had yet; so that, if the Supply be not very speedily dispatched, it will be altogether ineffectual; and the safety, honour, and interest of England, must of necessity be exposed. Pray lay this to heart; and let not the fears and jealousies of some draw an inevitable ruin upon us all.—My Lords and Gentlemen; If there be any Scruple remain with you concerning the Suspension of Penal Laws, I here faithfully promise you, that what hath been done in that particular shall not for the future be drawn either into consequence or example; and as I daily expect from you a bill for my Supply, so, I assure you, I shall as willingly receive and pass any other you shall offer me, that may tend to the giving you satisfaction in all your just grievances."

The King's Answer to the Address.] March 8. The lord chancellor reported, That both houses waited upon the king yesterday, and presented him with the Address against the Growth of Popery; and his maj. hath been pleased to return this Answer:

"My lords and gentlemen; I do heartily agree with you in your Address, and shall give speedy order to have it put in execution: there is one part to which I believe it is not your intention that it should extend; for I can scarce say those are in my pay that are presently to be employed abroad; but as for all the other parts, I shall take care it shall be done as you desire."

The King cancels the Declaration of Indulgence.] "There was another particular," the lord chancellor said, "he thought fit to acquaint them with; which, though it was by his majesty's leave, yet it was not by his command: however, he thought it his duty to acquaint the house with it (Mr. Secretary Coventry intending to acquaint the h. of commons with the same): That his maj. had the last night, in pursuance of what he then intended, and declared this morning, concerning the Suspension of Penal Laws not being for the future drawn either into consequence or example, caused the original Declaration under the great seal to be cancelled in his presence; whereof himself and several other lords of the council were witnesses."

All this was so satisfactory to the parliament, that both houses joined in the following vote, 'Resolved nem. con. That the humble and hearty Thanks of these houses be returned to his majesty, for his gracious full and satisfactory Answer this day given to their humble Petitions and Addresses.' This was declared to the king in the Banquetting-House, by the mouth of the lord chancellor at the head of both houses: to which his majesty made this Answer, "My lords and gentlemen, I hope there never will be any difference amongst us; I assure you there shall never be any occasion on my part."

Debate on the Bill to prevent the Growth of Popery; commonly called the Test Act.] March 12. A Bill to prevent the growth of Popery was read a third time in the house of commons.

Mr. *Harwood* tendered a Proviso 'for renouncing the doctrine of Transubstantiation, for a farther Test to persons bearing office.

Mr. Secretary *Coventry*. After Consubstantiation, now Transubstantion. Will you not have God there? Will you exclude him?

Sir *John Birkenhead*. In queen Mary's time, persons were never put to swear it. Though there are distinctions of 'realiter, et verè et corporaliter,' would not have a scholastical oath: we say God is there, and the difference is de modo: great charge on the Synod of Dort, who would impose swearing controversial points: as the words are now penned, people are put to swear they know not what; and for the dangerousness thereof, would lay it aside.

Mr. *Harwood* has discoursed this point with able men. Doubts not, but they must make more of the bread and wine in the Sacrament, than bread and wine; what by faith is one thing, and this tends no farther.

Col. *Titus* thinks the thing of dangerous consequence. If this proviso is to make a Test, you have your end. They hold, that, after Consecration, the elements are turned into the body and blood of Jesus Christ; but we hold, that, after Consecration, nothing remains but bread and wine; and he would have the Proviso no more.

Sir *Tho. Higgins*. If you intend it as a Test, no Papist, after taking the Oaths of Allegiance and Supremacy, but will swallow this. Why do not you put renouncing all the rest of the Romish points?

Sir *Wm. Coventry*. Higgins says, 'the Test is unnecessary, because evaded.' Has studied controversy little: if he errs in the matter, asks pardon: thinks a farther Test requisite. The Sacrament they will take, and the Oath of Allegiance, but not that of Supremacy; certain bulls forbidding them, and the Pope may dispense with his own bulls. This doctrine of Transubstantiation is part of their faith, and the Pope cannot dispense with it; therefore there is need of a farther Test, and this the Pope cannot take away: it would be ill resented abroad to refuse a better and farther Test than the Oath of Allegiance and Supremacy, and he would have this received.

Mr. *Vaughan*. The Church of England holds, that our Saviour spoke the words, 'This is my Body,' figuratively: no remembrance but of things absent: the church of Rome says, we hold Christ is mystically there; they, that Christ is as much present then, as when crucified. Cannot but hold, that Christ was but once crucified—[He reads the passage in the Common Prayer Book, of no corporal presence.]

Sir *Tho. Clarges* is afraid of this proviso: swearing doctrinal points will give offence to the Lutherans: the Papists say, Christ is really there after consecration; and therefore adoration. The Lutherans believe Transubstantiation, but only at the instant when delivered, and communicated: you are told, 'It is matter of faith, and the Pope cannot dispense.' If the Pope can dispense with one thing, he may do it with another. He never heard the Oath of Supremacy dispensed with: in the troops, some few years since here, few soldiers would take the Oaths of Supremacy; they would rather lose their places: in the late times there was an Oath like this Test, which many that now go to mass would take.

Mr. Solicitor *North** would have no swearing: he was for the Covenant Test, as a seditious

* Afterwards successively attorney general,

thing; but as this is no way tending to it, but only as to doctrinal points, is against such an oath.

Mr. *Waller*. The word, 'merely bread and wine,' in the proviso, he excepts against: believes the doctrine of the Sacraments well expressed in the 39 Articles: the thing is of great consequence, and no Clergy here present; we believe the very body, and therefore the word 'merely' is not reconcileable: would have the subscription in the very words of the Articles, which will take off the objection of swearing scholastically.

Sir *Rob. Holt*. Pope Pius V. offered a dispensation to the emperor Maximilian, as well as to queen Eliz.; you are to renounce all the Articles of the Council of Trent, as well as this: thinks the thing secure enough by the Oaths of Allegiance and Supremacy, but if you will go farther, would have the bishops consulted with.

Earl of *Ancram*. The Lutherans opinion, as Clarges said, is not Transubstantiation; the Papists say, one body goeth, and another cometh in the place: consubstantiation, which the Lutherans hold, is grammatically 'with it,' and not 'changed into it.'

Sir *Rd. Temple*. If we so scruple the wording it here, it will be much more scrupled in the nation: in Henry viii th's time, the five Articles were to be subscribed, under the penalty of treason: knows not that the Pope ever gave indulgence for taking the Oath of Supremacy, but believes he grants absolution after the thing is done: besides this Test, would make subscribing the 39 Articles, but pray leave these Oaths of Abjuration in matters so mystical.

Sir *Eliab Harvey* observes one thing in this Ease: we have been told, we have no Test upon the Papists; if there be none for the Papists, this is none for the Protestants, in the bill of Ease.

Sir *John Duncombe* fears it will have this effect, that some will let religion and all go, if preferment lies in the way, and so it will make men Atheists.

Sir *John Birkenhead*. Did ever any Church impose swearing doctrinal points? No Church, either Greek or Latin, ever did it; never was such an oath before.

Col. *Strangways*. Though great disputes are between us and the Papists, yet all Protestants hold against it: if once we deny our senses, we lose our senses; for every new shift of the Pope, would have another shift from us: you are now making distinction betwixt Protestant and Papist: a criterion you must have; the Pope will never dispense with doctrinal points; with human laws of the Church he can: thinks that this Test will puzzle all Priests and Jesuits.

The Bill with the Amendments passed; the title was, "An Act for preventing dangers that may happen by Popish Recusants."*

The Earl of Bristol's Speech in favour of the Test-Act.] March 15. When the Bill came to be debated in the house of peers, in the presence of the king himself, the earl of Bristol, though a professed Roman Catholic, unexpectedly stood up for the Bill in general, and spoke remarkably upon it; of which some account shall be given to shew the temper of the times, as well as the ingenuity of the speaker. —Towards the beginning of his speech he declared himself 'a Catholic of the Church of Rome, not a Catholic of the Court of Rome; a distinction he thought worthy of memory and reflection, whenever any severe proceedings against those they called Papists should come in question, since those of the court of Rome did only deserve that name.' Therefore he insisted, 'That they should not speak here as Roman Catholics, but as faithful members of a Protestant parliament.' Coming to the Bill itself he proceeded thus: "In the first place, my lords, I beseech you to consider, that this bill

lord chief justice of the common pleas, and lord keeper, and, in 1683, created lord Guilford. We are told by his nephew Mr. North, "that he was not an orator, as commonly understood, that is, not a flourisher, but all his speech was fluent, easy, and familiar, and he never used a word for ornament, but for intelligence only." Life, p. 332.

* "The Popish party had rendered themselves formidable by their obtaining many places of honour, profit, and trust; but now a Bill was depending that would certainly throw them out of all, and secure all places to those of the Church of England alone. This was called the Test-Act, which was particularly promoted, if not invented by the earl of Shaftsbury, who resolved to strike directly at the duke of York and his friends; though the act reached all sorts of Dissenters. This bill gave a great alarm to many persons, who used all means to oppose it; but it soon passed the house of commons, whose apprehensions of Popery daily increased. By this Act, it was provided, 'That all persons bearing any office, or place of trust, or profit, should take the Oaths of Supremacy and Allegiance in public and open Court, and should also receive the Sacrament of the Lord's-Supper, according to the usage of the Church of England, in some parish church, on some lord's day immediately after divine service and sermon, and deliver a certificate of having so received the Sacrament, under the hands of the respective minister and church-wardens, proved by two credible witnesses upon oath, and put upon record in court: and that all persons taking the said Oaths of Supremacy and Allegiance, should likewise make and subscribe this following Declaration: 'I, A. B. do declare, that I do believe there is not any Transubstantiation in 'the Sacrament of the Lord's-Supper, at, or 'after the Consecration thereof, by any person 'whatsoever.' This Act, and Test therein prescribed, has been generally accounted a great Bulwark to the Established Church of England." Echard.

for securing of general fears; is brought up to you from the house of commons, the great representative of the people, and consequently the best judges of the true temper of the nation: A house of commons surpassing all that ever have been, in the illustrious marks of their duty, loyalty and affection to the sovereign, both in his person and government; such a house of commons as his majesty ought to consider, and cherish always, with such a kind of love as is due to a wife, never to be parted with unkindly, and not as a mistress to be turned off when our turn is served by her. My Lords, this casual mention of a wife, suggests to my thoughts a pursuance of the comparison. I have observed in the course of my life, that men who have wives somewhat coquets, that is a little subject to gallantries, live easier lives with them, and freer from troublesome contentions, than those who have wives of exact rigid virtue; and the reason is clear: for the more gamesome ladies being conscious of the failings in that essential part, are careful to disguise, and repair them by kind and tender compliances with their husband's humour in all other things; whereas wives severely punctual and exact in the chief matrimonial duty, expect and even exact far greater compliances from their husbands, and think themselves as it were privileged by the rigidness of their virtue to be sometimes troublesome in domestic affairs; especially if there be any jealousy in the case. In like manner, my lords, it is not to be much wondered at, if this incomparable house of commons, transcending all that ever were in the grand essentials of duty, loyalty, and affection to their king, should at sometimes be a little troublesome to him in lesser occurrences; especially when once fears and jealousies are on wing. My lords, I shall not pretend to determine whether there have been any just grounds given by any violent men, or by the unseasonable ambition of any Roman Catholics for such fears, and jealousies; it suffices to exact the necessity of a timely remedy, since they have indeed most violently seized, and distempered the minds of the major part of his majesty's Protestant subjects, which certainly no man conversant in the world can deny. Now, my lords, in popular fears and apprehensions, those usually prove most dangerous that are raised upon grounds not well understood, and may rightly be resembled to the fatal effects of panic fears in armies, where I have seldom seen great disorder arise from intelligences brought in by parties and scouts, or by advertisements to generals; but from alarms upon groundless and capricious fears of danger, taken up we know not either how, or why: This no man of moderate experience in military affairs but hath found the dangerous effects of one time or other, in giving a stop to which mischiefs the skill of great commanders is best seen. In like manner, my lords, this great and judicious assembly of the h. of commons, rightly sensible of the dangerous effects which so general a disturbance of mens minds in the concernments of Religion (how groundless soever) might produce, have applied their care to obviate them by this Bill: A bill, in my opinion, as full of moderation towards Catholicks, as of prudence, and security towards the religion of the state. In this bill, my lords, notwithstanding all the alarms of the Encrease of Popery, and Designs of Papists, here is no mention of barring them from private, and modest exercise of their religion; no banishing them to such a distance from court, no putting in execution of penal laws in force against them; all their precautions are reduced to this one intent, natural to all societies of men, of hindering a lesser opposite party from growing too strong for the greater and more considerable one: And in this just way of prevention, is not the moderation of the house of commons to be admired, that they have restrained it to this sole point, of debarring their adversaries from Offices and Places, and from accessions of wealth by favour of the sovereign? And after all, my lords, how few do these sharp trials, and Tests of this act regard? only a few such Roman Catholics as would fain hold offices, and places at the price of hypocrisy, and dissimulation of their true sentiments in religion. My lords, I am none of those, none of those wherry men in religion, who look one way, and row another. Upon the whole matter, my lords, however the sentiments of a Catholic of the Church of Rome (I still say, not of the Court of Rome) may oblige me, upon scruple of conscience, in some particulars of this bill to give my negative to it, when it comes to passing; yet as a member of a Protestant parliament my advice prudentially cannot but go along with the main scope of it; the present circumstances of time, and affairs considered, and the necessity of composing the disturbed minds of the people."

Debate on ingrossing the Bill for the Supply.] March 15. Mr. Sec. *Coventry.* Hears that the Dutch call in their privateers, and will be speedily out: Remember Chatham business: Whenever the king neglects execution of the laws, he fails of his duty; and when you neglect to supply him you do not your duty; the king has done his part to the full: moves for a shorter day, for reading the ingrossed Bill.

Captain *Legge** gives an account of many

* Created lord Dartmouth in 1682. He was afterwards Master of the Horse to James ii, Governor of the Tower, &c. and at the time of the Revolution, he was Admiral and Commander in Chief of the English fleet, which was detained in the Thames by the same wind that brought the Prince of Orange over. In 1691, he was committed to the Tower, where he died of an apoplexy, three months after. Burnet says, "He was one of the worthiest men of king James's court. He loved him, and had been long in his service and in his confidence: But he was much against all the conduct of his affairs; yet he resolved to stick to him at all hazards." † Echard.

men deserting his ship, (the Royal Catherine) upon the rumour that the parliament would give the king no money.

Sir *Tho. Meres.* There was such a time as seamen's deserting us, (within a fortnight) and then there was reason for it; but now, blessed be God! the reason is removed: The motion is good, in relation to the king's affairs: Remembers with what unanimous consent the money was given, intended for his best service; and remembers then who moved for it. The bill may have its due execution, within its time, if delayed a little: As to the affairs of this house, businesses cannot go fairly up to the lords' house, now upon our hands: As to the lords, he denies not but things do yet go fairly on. Would not have this bill sent up to hinder them, to make the parenthesis in a business there to interrupt them; he offers the lords leisure, but imposes nothing on them: If any man would have the Money Bill pass in the lords house the next week, concludes that the rest of the bills cannot go with this.

Sir *Tho. Osborne,* is sorry to hear a day named so far off, you hear the approach of the Holland fleet: and is sorry to have occasion so often to tell you of the backwardness of ours.

Mr. *Vaughan.* The giving this Bill so speedily out of our hands may call us a kind and bountiful parliament, but never a wise one: The not passing the other bill will expose us to right of conquest again: A greater matter than any thing else: When the king has hearts, he has purses also, and can never want seamen: 'There is that scatters and yet increases; and there is that with-holdeth more than is meet, and it tendeth to poverty.'

Sir *Rob. Howard.* After Chatham business, the king had a greater opportunity to impose than he has now: It looks hard, that after the king has granted so much, you should be jealous: the king has not left any thing to do to us; and must we stop Supply, because other persons (the lords) have not done what you would have them? This bill cannot be ingrossed suddenly: It would look ugly in any man to do it: no man can write the Bill fairly till Tuesday: hopes the thing will be as full of good intentions as ever; but that those intentions, with delay, will be defeated.

Mr. *Garroway,* hopes in time we shall have an answer from the king, as to the impositions; and possibly some persons, that advised that with the Declaration, may have apprehensions upon them: he forgives them and prays God that he would: hopes for a general pardon, that they may have the benefit of it.

Mr. *Powle,* conceives it the right of parliament not to enter into debates, so much as of Supply, till redress of grievances; and it seems a tacit obligation upon the king, to redress the grievances, because it smooths the way the better for money: no man can think that we have no more grievances than already complained of: would not delay the bill till all the grievances be redressed, but would till they are stated to the king: sees by authority, a printed paper of imposition on commodities, not imposed by act of parliament: It is said, 'that, by stopping the bill, we shall put a violence on the lords;' but we put none upon them: if this issue with them answers not our ends, we may think of something else: all arguments he hears spoken of, for the hastening this bill, are the tragical fates of necessity; but still asks, Who occasioned this necessity: when it might have been prevented by the parliament's being called in Oct. last; and thinks them guilty of a great crime that were the authors of the advice of prolonging it till now; and hopes to have that, and some other grievances, redressed; your clerk, he hears, sat up all night to ingross part of the Money Bill, and it cannot be retarded by a few days.

Mr. *Thomas.* We have exposed the person of the king, by answering our grievances of Popery; and thinks the king not safe without removing some persons; and names lord Arúndel of Wardour, col. Rd. Talbot, and father Patrick.

Sir *John Duncombe,* is much surprized at the motions he has heard to day; very unreasonable, and untimely brought forth: no prince ever made such an answer as the king has made; he has done what lies in him: is sorry to see still new clouds rise: nothing is gone from you yet, but the Bill of Popery, and the first moment read in the house of lords, and they are now sitting upon it: why is this? He never heard a question, that after this bill is perfected, it should not be ingrossed: your fears are taken away; if ingrossed, you may stop it still. Is ashamed to tell you of the lowness of the exchequer *; but those arguments are stopped by money: appeals to gentlemen concerned in the revenue and navy-office, if things are not at a stop for want of money: the thing is not graceful, it has not a good countenance; it is so methodical, so easy and decent, the question for ingrossing, that he wonders any man can press against it: no man can take any thing from us: the bill, after being ingrossed, may lie upon the table, and you may call for it as you shall see occasion.

Col. *Strangways.* Consider the nature of the thing; we owe the removal of our jealousies to the king, who has graciously done it: was it not a great point, the redressing our laws, when attempted to be destroyed at one blow? every man knows, that these Money Bills are ingrossed to your hands: when we follow the steps of our ancestors, we shall do as wise things as they did. 'Let the Bill be ingrossed, and lie upon your table,' say some; but what calling will there be for it then? fears nothing but surprizes: would not force the lords, but would have them pressed by some arguments we use here: is for Friday.

Sir *Tho. Lee.* If one great and extraordinary grievance be, and that redressed, shall

* He was at this time chancellor of the exchequer.

that be an argument for the king to redress us no more? When no more grievances are mentioned, it will be thought we have no more: not to mention other things, besides that of Ireland, the great growth of Popery, and our neighbour's house on fire: hopes that persons concerned will acquaint you with it farther. He loves his ease in the country, and would be there, but would not have the king ignorant of many things: with that of the Order of Council imposing a rate upon coals: hopes, in due time, to have a redress of these things and others.

Col. *Birch.* Is far from thinking that the king has the least jealousy of the Money Bill, but that we intend his honour and safety, any thing of great or rich he has came from us; when we could not tell who was master when we came hither, thanks God we know now, and hopes no more clouds will be stirring. Impositions against law, the people pressed, and that of Ireland, and should be loth that if any thing farther should be offered of grievances, any man should say, Why have you left these things unrepresented, and the king so gracious, in granting what you have asked? Bills are much more slippery in parchment than in paper: what he moves, is for the king's honour and safety: was the enemy here now, would say nothing of it; but why were we not here in Oct. last? No man can say there has been the least backwardness in this parliament: would have the paper Bill lie on the table till Friday.

Sir *Trevor Williams.* What he has heard makes his heart bleed; and therefore moves for Monday, to consider redress of Grievances.

Sir *Edw. Dering.* We all tend to the same end, and let us go the same way: after Friday but a few days to Easter: the Bill of Supply will take up a whole day reading, and some unforeseen delays may stop it: therefore moves for Friday.

Sir *Wm. Coventry.* The clerk is ingrossing the Bill without order; and you were told another shrewd thing, that a great deal of the Bill was slipped in the ingrossing: would not have any thing doubted hereafter; you are judges of it here, and others, when you have done: would have what is written already, cancelled, and not brought to you.

Mr. *Waller.* Ingrossing without order! It may be copied in parchment for some gentleman's use, as well as in paper; sometimes we were in such great haste, that the Act of Oblivion, in its confirmation, was not read at all: when a question has been of not putting the question now, has known that question never put at all: if that question should be now, no man can speak to the ingrossing the bill afterwards: are not necessity and speed acknowledged by the house? Are not our grievances redressed, and have not our forefathers taken care to keep Papists out of authority, and we greater? In the late times, this house had a passionate suspicion, and we would have removed Papists, and it was afterwards, by that passion, done much worse; 'never was doubt of a Bill once voted but passed,' it is said: but we may remember, but last session, that a dispute with the lords about heightening and lowering rates, damned our bill of foreign commodities*; our Votes since have lost their credit: is against Popery, and we have both leges et mores against them, law and inclination of the people against them: will you neither trust them, the king, nor God, but trust an enemy in retarding this bill? Would you have them come out to sea, before our Act comes out in print! If you find out a way, there will be 'viam inveniam aut faciam' necessity stamps all things with a face of justice: would have Friday ordered for ingrossing the bill.

Sir *Tho. Littleton.* Sir Henry Vane was the first that ever proposed putting a question, "whether the Question should be now put,'† and since, it has been always the forerunner of putting the thing in question quite out: therefore would not have that question put now.

Sir *Wm. Coventry.* There is great difference between, 'whether the Question shall be put,' and 'now put.' It is no new thing to put that question in point of adjournment; and if it passed in the negative, it never was, but that the house was afterwards adjourned.

Mr. *Garroway.* It is certainly agreed by us all, that that question of the Bill shall be put; though the question of the day be as is proposed.

Mr. Secretary *Coventry.* Can any man tell that the Hollanders are not strong enough to come out, or that they, by their confederates, may not invade us? An enemy that can invade us and will not, no man can say: when you shall give it, and the enemy come and gather it, you will put the king upon his necessity: the shew-bread was eaten by David; it was not forbid, but told us for precedent.

Col. *Strangways* is sorry to hear of these necessities: bring us the men that have been the occasion of these necessities, and he will tell you what to say to them: he that does the necessity is not the judge of it: was not 'salus populi periclitatur' the occasion the Ship-Money was called for? Knows not what belongs to these little bye tricks: great necessity is to be argued in the lords house, not here: those arguments, if used, let them be there; let us hear no more of these arguments; and let us not be reproached with these arguments of necessity, that were not the occasion of it, but let them be laid on persons that occasioned it.

Mr. *Garroway.* If those gentlemen will join issue on the argument of necessity, let the causers of it be accountable for it.

Mr. Secretary *Coventry* is not afraid of our's, nor any man's hearing what counsel he gave the king: desires that whoever is faulty, be it

* See p. 480.

† Now usually called 'The previous Question.'

any man, he may answer it: when a man has been debauched by another, and falls into a distemper, your first business is to cure the man, and then blame him that debauched him: if there be such men, that have been the occasion of this advice, let them answer it.

Sir *Tho. Meres.* This thing of 'necessity' was an ill argument at first, and would not have Waller (who proffered to speak again) speak twice to it, to inflame it more.

The *Speaker.* No man can find any precedent of sir Henry Vane's Question: by that question we can never come to an end of any business: the question in being may be the next day put, and so you usher in an impossibility of bringing things to a period.

Sir *Rob. Howard.* This Question is like the image of the inventor, a perpetual disturbance.

Mr. *Garroway.* If you can find out an expedient, that may carry off the heat, is for it.

Col. *Titus.* Some gentlemen believe the bill already ingrossed; if so, it is more haste than could be wished: the desire of some is to get a competent time to get grievances redressed; others, that the necessity of the king and kingdom require a dispatch: a competent time is agreed on both sides; he thinks Friday so; and then to bring in our Grievances remaining.

Sir *Tho. Osborne* would know the cause why the rest of our grievances are not alledged: as for the Declaration and Religion, he appeals, whether, when there was a stop of the Money bill, those two things were not the cause then: all that the king could do, he has done: does believe that by Friday we shall have an Answer from the lords: it is necessary, either in this house or out of it, for subjects to give the king time, and a right representation of things: should be sorry that any of the privy counsellors endeavours should be so blasted in this house, that they do not their part, till the king give you farther cause to apprehend so: there needs no jealousy on our parts now; how shall we have assurance, that the king has satisfaction in our intentions? Why should not the marks from this house be undeniable? If this be your case, then to put a question that has dangerous construction in it: Is not for putting it.

Mr. *Vaughan.* The king has no fault, the law says he has none, and hopes that none say so in this house. Grievances have come before Supply, in right course of parliament, if now they come after, it is an example of great affection, and in few parliaments: if we are content to part with that right, and let it be for the present overlooked, hopes it shall not for the future be urged as as precedent.

Ordered, "That the Money Bill be ingrossed, and brought in on Friday."

Further Debate on the Bill for granting Ease to Dissenters.] March 17. On the motion that the Bill be ingrossed,

Sir *John Duncombe.* Is against all the Bill: as far as it is for Union, is for it, and the bringing men into the Church: as to 'assent and consent,' would have it taken away; but that will give men an impunity for not coming to Church; they will never come to Church: offers it to consideration, whether mankind will not generally live after this law: the parliament have overcome themselves, and they make this law 'for a year and to the end of the next session of parliament:' if you should read over and examine your reasons to the king formerly, against Toleration, they would fly upon you: you have provided against Popery, and this is a great party; ambitious men will rise with them, and will support them to your posterity: what will the young men say at the Universities? 'Let us turn our parts to preach sedition and new lights, and return to the Church, as to an hospital, when we are old; which, by subscription, they may get into. No preferment in dull logic.' This will be the effect; they will support one another by marriages and interests; it will be past your power to revoke it with all the interest you have: you are to have an eye over them, and watch them: dreads the consequence of this part of the bill: it will work upon all your concerns and interests: leaves it to God and you.

Sir *John Bramstone* supposes you would have every man to be of some religion, and to be master of his servants; and have the teacher and his congregation deliver their names to the parson of the parish.

Mr. Sec. *Coventry.* You are not making a bill to destroy the Church, he hopes: you are not only doing a new thing in the kingdom, but in all the world: here are no limitations in it to churches, no limitations to congregations; it has been no where so, wherever he has been: it is said, 'they are the wiser and richer part of the nation;' the more is the danger. You do a thing never tried before, and you put it out of your power to remedy the inconveniences of it: they, in intermission of parliament, may put the kingdom in an uproar, and in great danger, before you can provide any remedy by parliament.

Sir *Ch. Harbord.* The severity of the Churchmen has driven 80 families out of town; that has done us irreparable hurt in our manufactures of wool: since the Declaration they have met *Pompi Gratia*, and yet reduced from two to one; restrain them and you increase them: a bishop, in the northern parts, has told him, that, since the Declaration, many have come into the Church; this Bill is for that end.—The Bill was ordered to be ingrossed.

March 19. The Bill was read a third time.

Mr. *Waller* said, Usury, during the time of Popery, was unlawful, as supposed to be against the law of God. We know not the will of God but by his two Books, the law of God and the law of nature: a man gives away all he has, for his liberty, to summa potestas: he may do and take what he will from his body, but his mind cannot be given or taken; he may command me not to speak my mind, and not to do my mind, and, in a word, to be hypocritical: though this be a violence in general, it will be a violence but upon a few: in the inquisition of Spain, a few shall suffer rather than many. Tacitus calls it 'a good government for a man to do what he will, and speak what he thinks.' Restraint is against the genius and whole complexion of the nation: let these Dissenters alone, and people will despise them; punish them, and the people will have compassion for them: the quakers suffered bravely, and were the more esteemed; the persecuted party ever gets uppermost: in queen Mary's time those of the reformed religion were persecuted, and they soon got uppermost. In queen Eliz.'s time, in our times, 'Prelacy and Popery' were coupled together, and people flocked to Mr. Gunning's congregation: neither sons of cavaliers nor cavaliers were admitted into the Convention, and yet they brought in the king, because that was then the persecuted party: if you believe the king, this liberty has kept peace, and you have had proof of it: this Bill is according to the law of God, law of nations, and complexion of the nation, and he would pass it.

Sir *John Duncombe*. Appeals, if ever any thing in England of persecution to Dissenters: Waller had liberty in his own house, and his friends, by former acts: nothing now persecuted but Popery, and therefore, by his argument, popery must thrive and be uppermost: this Bill is quite different from the law of God: where are the persons that must visit these congregations, and examine and inspect what doctrine they teach? This is not according to the law of God; smiths, shoemakers, and coblers preach. If this be according to the law of God, he must read the Bible again: would have gentlemen tell him, that are so much for this Bill in what part of the world the Church has no power to enquire what men preach? By this consequence, you will leave them to say what they will: law after law, reason after reason; has been against them these 12 years, and is against the Bill now.

Sir *Ch. Harbord*. Josephus, notoriously known, tells us, 'that the two sects of the Jews, the Saduces and the Pharisees, held, the one spirits, and the other no spirits, nothing more contrary; but they never divided, they were all united as to the public government'—A book, lately published, "Of the Rise and Progress of the Netherlands,"* tells you, that mighty things have been done there by what you intend in this act; the severity of Spain, and their Plantations, have ruined them, and will us, if we look not to it: in our maritime towns we have not the sixth part of the people: the populous places of Brabant, by this persecution, have been dispeopled, and Holland has got sufficiently by it, and so did we: he confesses that he has communicated with them in Holland, and will do it again: he has had as good advice, and as learned upon it, as any man can give him, which held it lawful: hopes this people that have ease by the bill will occasion you to continue it.

Sir *Philip Warwick*. You have the genius of the nation, God, and the complexion of the people, spoken to: as to the genius of the nation, till Popery made us all afraid, he has endeavoured to make the foundation of the Church so full as to abide a good superstructure: look upon the Jewish story of the sects, and they were never there till the time of captivity, and never here till our Rebellion, till the Temple was shaken. Morality is not so planted in man, but that customs and constitutions destroy all that; Cain and Abel owed duty to Adam—*Libera mens* overthrows all Christianity. Christians at first were but a body of men, and they planted the Church, and Excommunication in the Church; and he was no Christian that was out of it: never were men, by nature, either Jews or Christians. By this liberty you will lose all Registers, Marriages, and Genealogies. Let not great words make a noise; you give them liberty, and not barely indemnity: he is perfectly against the bill.

Col. *Birch* doubts not but the people will be sheep, quiet and peaceable; and had it been only to mark them in the forehead, he is not against it: doubts not but in a short time we shall see that the enforcing laws upon these people, and crying out against the infallibility of the Pope, are not consistent: you would not have the Papists govern you, and that is not a persecution of them.

Dr. *Burwell*. They grow numerous: if you pass this act, you give away the peace of the nation: a Puritan was ever a rebel; begin with Calvin: these Dissenters made up the whole army against the king; the destruction of the Church was then aimed at: pray God it be not so now!

Sir *John Birkenhead*. There was not a Pharisee till the fall of the Persian monarchy; the dispensations then were to the Proselytes of the Gate, viz. Strangers; that is the true case of the Jews: subscription of the Clergy is 'omnibus his articulis;' by this Subscription in the Bill, they will have 26 of the 39 Articles left out, subscribing only the doctrines; you have not in the Creed ten Articles of it, nor ever thought so. Had you a list of these men you ease, the king might have apprized you of some; now you will have preachers that have had their hands in his father's blood: here are 2000 of these preachers already, and there may be 10,000 more: shall the old officers of the army count numbers and know persons? They may come like Venner, the Fifth Monarchy-man, with their arms.*

Sir *Rob. Howard*. Will not trouble you with the rabbinical law, nor history; but offers to consider, that one time you were

* Written by sir William Temple.

* See p. 186.

against this, and now are changed, thinking it more fitted and calculated for the nation: the parliament must do something at all times: they are not such enemies as is said; the Act of Oblivion has made a grave for that: will you now crush the expectation of the nation in this thing? Thoughts are active in mens minds, when they have hope for something: should have thought of making the king's Declaration a law for a time; but that being not to be done, will you not compose people's minds at home, when all abroad is in distraction? If this bill be too much, or too little; if matters be too short in it you may lengthen them; if inconvenient, you may alter them; you will leave, by laying the Bill aside, as much disorder in the imaginations of the people, as in the thing itself; therefore would pass the bill.

Mr. Secretary *Coventry*. In the main, we may fling out this Bill, or keep it, and not offend the law of God: there is some inconvenience as to toleration; indifferent without limit: does think the honour of the house engaged by voting and acting he hopes it may be mended in the lords house, and with that hope sends it up.—The Bill was then passed.

Debate on the Bill of Supply.] March 21. The Bill of Supply was brought in, ingrossed, and laid on the table.

Mr. *Garroway* desires that the Money-Bill may not be read till Tuesday next, because you have the Bill of Popery, with Amendments,* returned from the lords, where he hears we have been strangely represented: we are all concerned to see this Bill of Popery dispatched, and to clear the reputation of this house: therefore would have the Money-Bill for the present, laid aside.

Mr. Sec. *Coventry*. It is very reasonable that the fears and jealousies of Popery should be removed, but would not defer the Tax-Bill so long: would go upon the Bill of Popery today, and would not have the king think we take any thing ill from him, who has promoted this Bill so much in the house of lords, by his countenancing it.

Sir *John Coventry* hopes in time we may make this Bill of Popery a good one: this bill has had hard passage hither again: if we believe common fame, it nearly miscarried in the lords house: many more Grievances may come betwixt this and Tuesday, and would have that day for the Tax-Bill.

Sir *Tho. Osborne*. 'Common fame' came never from nobody, but by somebody; the gentleman ought to tell you by whom it came: we cannot take notice of what is done in the lords house.

Mr. *Powle* hopes that our zeal for this Bill is not looked upon as an offence to the king, but acceptable to him—' Common fame!' No man can nominate on the sudden, who—This discourse cannot be without some fire; in time it may come out, and those gentlemen will tell you, when they can, where they had it: moves for Tuesday, and hopes no ill intentions can be made out of it.

Sir *John Duncombe* would have you look at the end you would be at: go upon this Bill from the lords; you are master of your Orders: go and ask satisfaction of the king for your Grievances, and he is sure you will have it.

Sir *Rob. Carr* finds no difference among gentlemen in the thing. 'Till we read the Amendments the lords have sent down, we cannot tell whether satisfactory or not; we may possibly agree at a conference. Why will you do things that may look like dislike, when it is not? Would not have a blemish on the Supply; do the one and not the other.

Col. *Birch* hears much said of 'common fame:' it seems to be now the lord keeper, bishop Williams's case, in 1614, or 1616—' common fame from the house of lords!' Would go with safe steps for the king and kingdom; one thing is before you, that the king may not think we stop his business: would have this Tax Bill for Tuesday, and hopes by that time we shall give such advice, as may secure the king and kingdom: stands up to remind you that this is a parliamentary way of 'common fame.'

Sir *Courtney Poole* thinks we are upon such a point that we have reason to think it will startle the king: 'Common fame' is not a right way for the lords or the king, therefore would not insist upon it.

Sir *Tho. Meres* tells the Speaker that he turns the question to another thing: he would have the question for the Bill of Popery, and the other question, for Tuesday, firsted and seconded: demands whether he will be pleased to own that to be the question; and demands whether he can deny that that question was firsted, seconded and thirded?

Mr. *Cheney*. There has been something on your hands these two or three days, which is to be ready with the Tax, 'the Grievances:' would not put a certain day for the Tax, and doubts not of redress of Grievances in due time.

Mr. *Powle* gives an account of the 'Address about Grievances,' which cannot be finished till the committee can see the inspection into the affairs of Ireland, the secretary not having been attended, and could not be dispatched—This is not for the service of the king, his satisfaction, and good of the nation, and therefore we cannot in conscience part with the Money-Bill, till that business of Ireland be determined; but he has reason to take hold of things of 'common fame,' when some great officers have told the king, 'that, if the Money Bill passed not, the king may be supplied otherwise.'

Lord *Cavendish* thinks those Bills now depending, to quiet the minds of the king's subjects, as necessary as any whatsoever: there are Grievances of an high nature, besides what are already depending; some are the root of all those grievances, the authors of these dis-

* It was returned from the lords, with some Amendments and Provisos, a little before this debate.

turbances, and those are evil counsellors: because other grievances are not named, hopes people will not think there are not more, therefore moves for Thursday for 'Grievancies.'

Lord *St. John.* Should 'common fame' have weight, you would have much to do; therefore would lay it aside: as to the Bill of Popery before you, he has so great love and tenderness for the king's person, that without this bill, neither the king nor we can be safe: would have a little time to consider these things, and would have Tuesday.

Sir *Rob. Howard.* Are you afraid of any trick being put by the Money Bill? You are masters of every day, and of what is fit to be done.

Sir *Tho. Meres.* Does any body imagine no other business but this Bill? If there was none, it could not be before Monday: would have this debate on Monday.

The Debate was adjourned to Monday by consent.

The King's Message respecting a Recess.] March 24. Mr. Secretary Coventry delivered the following Message from the king:

"C. R. I am commanded by his majesty, in pursuance of his late Message, to acquaint you that his majesty intends you shall rise before Easter, and therefore expects an expedition of such Bills as are of most importance; the bill of Popery, and that of Supply particularly: and for such other bills as concern either the public or particular, and cannot be so soon ready, that they may may not receive a disappointment, his maj. resolves to make this an Adjournment till the beginning of Oct. when you may continue their prosecution; in the mean time his maj. will take such care of the Protestant Religion, that you shall have no cause to complain."

Debate on the Bill of General Naturalization.] March 24. The Bill of General Naturalization was read a second time.

Sir *Rd. Ford.* This bill exposes the great immunities of Corporations to be prostituted.

Mr Sec. *Coventry* supposes you do not intend, by this Bill, that every gentleman shall set up what trade he pleases when he comes over: it is said, that Papists may come in by this bill; you may, to prevent that, put in 'transubstantiation' for a Test: the king has been at great charge this war: it was looked upon, at the beginning of the war, to invite the Dutch; and should this bill be thrown out, you will discourage them here and send them to the French: he shall not by this bill be entertained in a town as a poor man: a Hollander told him, 'if we were certain of a peace, he could bring over 4000 men, much to the advantage of your cloth and other manufactures trade.'

Sir *George Downing.* Most of our manufactures came from Holland: he is against their being freemen in corporations: if a native must come through the difficulties of 7 years apprenticeship, would not have a town filled with foreigners: but to trades you want would give them encouragements by freedoms; as packers of fish, gold and silver-workers, dyers and copper-makers, and would have such reserved from the penalties of 1 Eliz. of being indicted for not serving 7 years to a trade: many Hollanders get themselves naturalized, or denisoned, and trade here all summer, and then in winter go to Amsterdam, with what they get here: would have great care taken of that in the bill.

Mr. *Boscawen.* They that come in will be merchants and monied men, who will be willing to get an Act for naturalization: you have more merchants already than you have trade; you want them not for more shop-keepers: you have so many natives, they eat out one another: for artisans, they may be useful to you; the greatest want of all is of them, and would have the bill for the encouragement of them.

Sir *John Duncombe* thinks it a good bill, but to be committed, with care to be taken, if, after naturalization and the oaths, they go not away back from you, and stay neither here, nor in the Plantations: would have them taken care for to stay; if they go away, to lose their naturalization.

Sir *Lancelot Lake.* Anciently, in matters of great weight, we went home to our country to advise with them: he would have that now done.

Mr. Attorney *Finch.* Before commitment of the bill, would well consider, whether possibly a good bill may come out of this: naturalization makes any man equal in privilege to original birth, in the kingdom of England: it is not here as in the Roman state, when admitted a long time to the first degree, and some good distance of time before they were capable of offices: you at one blow beget so many foreigners to be Englishmen: this Bill admits any Protestant born under any prince or potentate; in this you make all the world merchants of England; you grow an opulent nation; that supplies your industry and luxury: lead, wool, and tin, you give them an opportunity to export: by this bill, all your Turkey trade is destroyed in a moment: he that brings salt, is immediately entitled, by that little commodity, to trade and export your commodity; he may live cheaper than you, and truckle with the French consul in Turkey, and you shall be but factors, and stay at home: wonders that now we are naturalizing all the world, no part of the world naturalizes us: you aliens every where, and they naturalized here: if once they are at home here, where will be the distinction between the English and Dutch manufacture? Your lead, wool, and tin, are your Indies; no imposition upon them to stay here with a family; not one line to fix them, neither Oaths nor Tests: it makes them natural subjects, and, unless you otherwise provide, free of Corporations: your ancestors, in queen Elizabeth's time, knew two-thirds of England destroyed by the plague, and yet they had no thoughts of naturalization: you will find them suck your blood: they destroy common and statute law: you make them gentry and nobility: you bring people not to make you rich, but to starve the poor: how comes it to pass, that you think fit now to change your government, and all your municipal laws, and all at the charge of your estates and understandings? would have many years to consider of this bill.

Col. *Birch.* It is not fully expressed, but intended, in the bill, that they should reside here: that which he admires, is, that many Turkey merchants are in the house, and they say nothing in this business; they cannot speak so well as the attorney; but he would take it ill, if they should speak in his trade as he does in theirs: we had all our arms first from Germany; fustians and silks all came from abroad, ninety parts out of an hundred: but if we must stick to our forefathers opinion, he is outdone: if the Scriptures be true, that 'a multitude of subjects is the glory of a king,' this is a good bill.

Mr. *Waller* spoke to their coming in poor upon our poor. King James desired an union with Scotland; the parliament denied him nothing, but granted him not that; but the lawyers found out a way of the *post nati*: they are an *alterius nos*: there was no danger then; now they must either come in with stocks, or go to the house of correction: we have had plague and war, and civil war, and have peopled Ireland with 100,000 souls: 40*s.* a year, when he was a boy, was a good servant's wages; now in Buckinghamshire, 8*l.* a year, and are forced to send 30 miles for reapers, and fellers of wood: we labour under a paucity of people certainly: no man was ever denied naturalization here, paying his fees: that which was said by the Ancients, of the 'vivacity of youth and wisdom of age,' [complimenting the Speaker] is in you; you want not the Fees of Naturalization bills in your fortunes, and would have a mark of honour upon you, whilst you are Speaker, for doing it.*

Mr. *Vaughan* remembers not the reason of the *post nati*, but thinks it because under our allegiance: is against reading the bill again; the most destructive thing in the world to your interest and government.

The Bill was committed, in the afternoon, 208 to 61.

The Commons' Address on Grievances in Ireland.] March 25, p. m. Mr. Powle reported from the Committee the Address to the King concerning the Irish Grievances, which was agreed to, and is as follows:

"We your majesty's most loyal subjects, the commons in this present parliament assembled, taking into consideration the great calamities which have formerly befallen your majesty's kingdom of Ireland, from the Popish Recusants there, who, for the most part, are professed enemies to the Protestant religion and the English interest; and how they, making ill use of your majesty's gracious disposition and clemency, are, at this time, grown more insolent and presumptuous than formerly, to the apparent danger of that kingdom and your majesty's Protestant subjects there; the consequence whereof may likewise prove very fatal to this your kingdom of England, if not timely prevented; and having seriously weighed what remedies may be most properly applied to these growing distempers, do, in all humility, present your majesty with these our Petitions: —That, for establishing and quieting the possessions of your majesty's subjects in that kingdom, your maj. would be pleased to maintain the Act of Settlement, and the explanatory Act thereupon; and to recall the Commission of Enquiry into Irish affairs, bearing date the 17th of Jan. last, as containing many new and extraordinary powers, not only to the prejudice of particular persons, whose estates and titles are thereby made liable to be questioned, but in a manner to the overthrow of the said Acts of Settlement; and, if pursued, may be the occasion of great charge and attendance to many of your subjects in Ireland, and shake the peace and security of the whole kingdom: —That your maj. would give order, that no Papist be either continued or admitted to be a Commander or Soldier in that kingdom; and, because the Irish Papists have furnished themselves with great quantities of arms, that your maj. would please to give directions so to disarm them, that they may not be dangerous to the government there, and that their arms be brought into the public magazines:—That the like order may be given, that no Papist be either continued, or hereafter admitted to be judges, justices of the peace, sheriffs, coroners, mayors, sovereigns, or portreves in that kingdom:—That the titular popish abps. bishops, vicars-general, abbots, and all others exercising ecclesiastical jurisdiction, by the Pope's authority, and, in particular, Peter Talbot, pretended abp. of Dublin, for his notorious disloyalty to your majesty, and disobedience and contempt of your laws, may be commanded, by proclamation, forthwith to depart out of Ireland, and all other your majesty's dominions, or otherwise to be prosecuted according to law; and that all convents, seminaries, and public Popish schools, may be dissolved and suppressed, and the regular priests commanded to depart, under the like penalty: —That no Irish Papists be admitted to inhabit in any corporation of that kingdom, unless duly licensed, according to the aforesaid Acts of Settlement; and that your maj. would be pleased to recall your Letters of the 26th of Feb. 1671, and your Proclamation thereupon, whereby general licence is given to such Papists to inhabit in Corporations there.—That your majesty's Letter of the 28th of Sept. 1672, and the Order of Council thereupon, whereby your majesty's subjects are required not to prosecute any actions against the Irish, for any

* "Alluding to the Speaker's giving all his Fees of private Bills to the Poor of St. Giles's parish, in which he lived." Grey.

wrongs or injuries committed during the late Rebellion, may likewise be recalled.—That col. R. Talbot, who hath notoriously assumed to himself the title of Agent of the Roman Catholics in Ireland, be immediately dismissed out of all command, either civil or military, and forbid an access to your majesty's court.—That your maj. would be pleased, from time to time, out of your princely wisdom, to give such farther orders and directions to your lord lieutenant, or other chief governor of Ireland for the time being, as may best conduce to the encouragement of the English Planters, and Protestant interest there, and the suppression of the insolencies and disorders of the Irish Papists.—These our humble Desires we present to your majesty, as the best means to preserve the peace and safety of that your kingdom, which hath been so much of late endangered by the practices of the said Irish Papists, and, particularly, of the said Rd. and Peter Talbot; and we doubt not but your maj. will find the happy effects thereof, to the great satisfaction and security of your majesty's person and government, which, of all earthly things, is most dear to us, your majesty's most loyal and obedient subjects."

The Commons Address on Grievances in England.] Mr. Powle also reported the following Address to the King, about Grievances in England; which was also agreed to:

"We your majesty's most loyal subjects, the commons in this present parliament assembled, conceiving ourselves bound in necessary duty to your majesty, and in discharge of the trust reposed in us, truly to inform your maj. of the estate of this your kingdom; and, though we are abundantly satisfied, that it hath always been your royal will and pleasure, that your subjects should be governed according to the laws and customs of this realm; yet finding, that, contrary to your majesty's gracious intentions, some Grievances and abuses are crept in; we crave leave humbly to represent to your majesty's knowledge, and to desire,—That the imposition of 12d. per chaldron upon coals, for the providing of convoys, by virtue of an Order of Council, dated the 15th of May, 1672, may be recalled, and all bonds, taken by virtue thereof, cancelled.—That your majesty's Proclamation of the 4th of Dec. 1672, for prevention of disorders which may be committed by soldiers; and whereby the soldiers, now in your majesty's service, are, in a manner, exempted from the ordinary course of justice, may likewise be recalled. And whereas great complaints have been made, out of several parts of this kingdom, of divers abuses committed in quartering of soldiers, That your maj. would be pleased to give order to redress those abuses, and, in particular, that no soldiers be hereafter quartered upon any private houses; and that due satisfaction may be given to the innkeepers and victuallers where they lie, before they remove. And, since the continuance of soldiers in this realm will necessarily produce many inconveniences to your majesty's subjects, we do humbly present it, as our Petition and Advice, that, when this present war is ended, all the soldiers which have been raised since the last session of parliament may be disbanded.—That your maj. would likewise be pleased to consider of the irregularities and abuses of pressing soldiers, and to give order for the prevention thereof for the future. And although it hath been the course of former parliaments to desire redress in their Grievances, before they proceeded to give a Supply, yet we have so full assurance of your majesty's tenderness and compassion towards your people, that we humbly prostrate ourselves at your majesty's feet with these our Petitions; desiring your majesty to take them into your princely consideration, and to give such order for relief of the subjects, and the removing these pressures, as shall seem best to your royal wisdom *."

Resolved, "That the Addresses be presented to his majesty; and that those members of the council that are of the house, be desired to know his majesty's pleasure, when this house shall attend him with the Addresses concerning Grievances."

The King's Answer.] March 26. His majesty's Answer to the Address of Grievances, was reported by the Speaker:

"That he observed the Address did consist of many different parts; and therefore it could not be expected there should be a present Answer; but for the several particular things contained in it, he would, before the next meeting, take such care, that no man should have reason to complain."

Ordered, "That the Thanks of this house be returned to his majesty, for the often accesses they have been admitted to his majesty's person, and for his most gracious Answer to the several Addresses of this house; and,

* "It is worthy observation, that the grand points of 'the irregular Writs,' 'the War,' 'the Alliance with France;' and 'the shutting up of the Exchequer instead of applying for the advice and assistance of parliament,' are not so much as mentioned in this Address: and that in the introduction to these articles are many tender expressions. Now, supposing it was necessary, for decency's sake, to presume, that the king was ignorant of measures transacted in his own name, and well disposed to govern as he ought, it could not be presumed that these measures had no author nor adviser; and that these abuses and grievances had crept in by chance: notwithstanding which, instead of tracing the evil to its source, and making a wholesome example of the wicked ministers, who had so notoriously misled his majesty, and aggrieved and endangered his people, they suffered 'An Act of Grace,' (which was so worded, as to contain an absolute pardon of every offence against the state before the 25th of March, 1673) to be brought in, and passed; which put them out of the reach of justice for ever." Ralph.

particularly, for his last gracious Message, and, for the care he hath declared he will take of the Protestant Religion."

Debate on printing the Addresses on Grievances.] March 29. Mr. *Thomas* moved to have the Addresses concerning Grievances, and the king's Answer, printed.

Sir *John Mallet.* Divers Grievances have been by soldiers since the Address, and it is fit the people should have notice of it.

Mr. Sec. *Coventry.* You will show your complaints to the king of Grievances, but not his Answer, for the king has not yet published any thing relating to it: you have no power to print it.

Sir *Tho. Meres.* He will not say you have power to print the king's Speech, but we have power to print our own Address; there are many instances this parliament, and it may be of great use.

Mr. Sec. *Coventry.* By the act of printing, you cannot print.

Sir *Tho Meres.* Since that act, sir Edward Turner, late Speaker, has appointed things to be printed several times.

Sir *Tho. Clarges* will not dispute whether we have power or no; it is a kind of appeal to the people; but printing this will much heighten and increase the love of the people to the king: would have the privy counsellors of the house desire his maj. to cause them to be printed.

Mr. *Harwood* stands up to second the motion. Some inconveniences have lately been by soldiers: you have had a member lately robbed (Mr. Wharton) by persons like soldiers, armed and horsed; his motion is no more than to keep the people quiet: thinks it a reasonable motion, and would have the king moved in it.

Sir *R. Temple.* You would not let your transactions be printed in news-books; you have decried this printing, begun in the Long Parliament, as of ill consequence; let these things, like appeals to the people, be avoided.

Sir *Tho. Lee.* The motion is far from an appeal to the people; this is only, that the king having given us a gracious Answer, you publish it. To what intent? It will be a means to prevent farther mischief; the people may address the king for remedy for the future.

Mr. Sec. *Coventry.* To print this, as if it were a statute or a law, will look like remonstrating; the Long Parliament was condemned for it.

Col. *Birch.* The question is not your directing it to be printed, but desiring the king to cause it to be printed. If this were printed, it would end many disputes in the country about quartering of soldiers.

Sir *Rob. Carr.* What can this printing be but a mistrust of the king, that he will not do what he has promised? No doubt but the king will do it as effectually as he has promised.

Mr. *Vaughan.* These are good objections, if the house was to order it to be printed; but we do no more appeal to the people by this than by publishing a law: it is to publish his majesty's gracious favour to his people.

Mr. *Cheney.* For the ill consequence that hath been made of it, and may be of this, would not have it printed.

Sir *Rob. Howard.* The first motion is out of doors by the Act of printing: as for the next motion, printed things are always the best speakers to the people: to what end should the people think you do this?

Mr. *Swynfn.* It has been debated long, and you cannot rise without a question; as he cannot think the Address improper, or the king's Answer such as you cannot rest upon as satisfactory, therefore he is clear for moving the king to have it printed: it is said 'this is but an Address of this house to the king.' Your usual course is, when your Grievances are not redressed, to have recourse to the lords for a law: in regard you have waved all other ways, and taken this, it is most reasonable to have it printed, that a countryman may have something to show.

Sir *Tho. Lee.* If you will adjourn now, adjourn the debate likewise to the next session, and let it be upon your books.

The House divided even upon the Question, 105 to 105: the Speaker had the casting voice, and gave it for adjourning.*

Adjournment.] March 29. p. m. Sir Tho. Meres reported, from the Conference had with the lords, upon the Amendments of this house, to the amendments and provisoes by them sent to the Bill for Ease of his majesty's subjects Dissenters from the Church of England; those Amendments which the lords insist on; of those sent from them; and those they do agree in; with the Amendments from this house: which he read; and delivered in at the table.—The Lords insisting on their first Amendment, the question being put for candles, upon division of the house 75 were for candles, and 136 against candles. Those that were for candles, were for prolonging the debate, that the black rod might call them up to the house of lords before they had voted, 'adhere;' and though divers motions were made for adjourning the debate till next session, yet no question could be put, the black rod knocking at the door. After passing several Bills, the king made the following short Speech:

"My lords and gentlemen; I thank you very kindly for the Supply you have given me; and, that you may see how kindly I take it, I have given to my subjects a General Pardon, which I have made as large as ever was granted by any of my predecessors. What you have now left undone, I hope you will finish at your next meeting; and so you may adjourn yourselves to the 20th day of Oct. next."—The house was then adjourned by his majesty's de-

* And jestingly said "He would have his reason for his judgment recorded, viz. because he was very hungry." Grey.

sire to Oct. 20.* And so ended this session, on Easter Eve, at 9 of the clock at night.

The Parliament prorogued.] Oct. 20, 1673. The parliament met according to adjournment, and immediately voted "That an Address be made to his majesty, by such members of the house as are of his majesty's privy council, to acquaint his majesty, that it is the humble desire of this house, that the intended Marriage of his royal highness with the princess of Modena be not consummated; and that he may not be married to any person but of the Protestant Religion."†—Upon which, the king immediately prorogued the parliament to the 27th.

* The king came to the house of lords, before the Bill for Ease of Dissenters, and some others, could be fixed, and, besides the Money-Bill (which passed under the title of 'A Supply of his majesty's extraordinary Occasions') and the Popery Bill commonly called 'The Test Act,' passed 8 public Acts. "Thus ended," says Burnet, "this memorable Session. It was, indeed, much the best session of that Long Parliament. The Church Party showed a noble zeal for their religion; and the dissenters got great reputation by their silent deportment."—In consequence of the Test Act, the duke of York himself, who was lord high admiral of England, and the lord treasurer Clifford, both laid down their places. The latter is said to have been so much disgusted at the king's passing that Bill, and some other condescensions, that he retired, and died in privacy and discontent, in Devonshire. Sir Tho. Osborne succeeded him as Treasurer, being created lord visc. Dumblain and Earl of Danby, &c.

† "In the former session it was known, that the duke was treating a Marriage with the archduchess of Inspruck; but the empress happening to die at that time, the emperor himself married her, and yet no Address was made to the king to hinder his marrying a Papist. His honour was not then engaged; so it had been seasonable and to good purpose, to have moved in it then: but now he was married by proxy, and lord Peterborough had brought the lady to Paris. Yet the house of commons resolved to make an Address to the king, to stop the princess of Modena's coming to England, till she should change her religion. Upon this, the duke moved the king to prorogue the parliament for a week, and a commission was ordered for it. The duke went to the house on that day, to press the calling up the commons, before they could have time to go on to business. Some peers were to be brought in: the duke pressed lord Shaftesbury to put that off, and to prorogue the parliament. He said coldly to him, 'there was no haste:' but the commons made more haste; for they quickly came to a Vote for stopping the Marriage, and by this means they were engaged (having put such an affront on the duke) to proceed farther." Burnet.

ELEVENTH SESSION OF THE SECOND PARLIAMENT.

The King's Speech on opening the Session.] Oct. 29. The king opened the Session with the following Speech to both houses:

"My Lords and Gentlemen; I thought this day to have welcomed you with an honourable Peace; my preparations for the War and condescensions at the Treaty gave me great reason to believe so: but the Dutch have disappointed me in that expectation, and have treated my ambassadors at Cologne with the contempt of conquerors, and not as might be expected from men in their condition. They have other thoughts than peace.—This obligeth me to move you again for a Supply, the safety and honour of the nation necessarily requiring it: it must be one proportionable to the occasion; and I must tell you besides, that if I have it not speedily, the mischief will be irreparable in my preparations for the next spring. The great experience I have had of you, gentlemen of the h. of commons, will not suffer me to believe, that the artifices of our enemies can possibly divert you from giving me this Supply, or that you can fail of adjusting the proportion of it.—I hope I need not use many words to persuade you that I am steady in maintaining all the professions and promises I have made you concerning Religion and Property; and I shall be very ready to give you fresh instances of my zeal for preserving the Established Religion and laws, as often as any occasion shall require.—In the last place, I am highly concerned to commend to your consideration and care the Debt I owe the Goldsmiths, in which very many other of my good subjects are involved. I heartily recommend their condition to you, and desire your assistance for their relief. There is more that I would have you informed of, which I leave to the Chancellor."*

The Lord Chancellor Shaftsbury's Speech.] Then the Lord Chancellor, going to his majesty, received directions from him, and made the Speech following:

"My lords; and you the knights, citizens, and burgesses of the house of commons; His maj. had reason to expect that he should have met you with the olive branch of Peace: his naval preparations, greater than in any former years, together with the land forces he had

* "When the week of the prorogation was ended, the session was opened by a Speech of the king's: which had such various strains in it, that it was plain it was made by different persons. The duke told me, that lord Clarendon during his favour had penned all the king's Speeches; but that now, they were composed in the cabinet, one minister putting in one period, while another made another, so that all was not of a piece.' He told me, 'lord Arlington was almost dead with fear; but lord Shaftesbury reckoned himself gone at court, and acted more roundly." Burnet.

ready for any occasion, gave him assurance to obtain it before this time; and the rather, because his aims were not conquest, unless by obstinacy enforced: but his condescensions at the Treaty have been so great, that the very mediators have declared, they were not reasonably to be refused: he could not be king of Great Britain without securing the Dominion and Property of his own Seas; the first, by an Article clear, and not elusory, of the Flag; the other, by an Article that preserved the Right of the Fishing, but gave the Dutch permission, as tenants, under a small rent, to enjoy and continue that gainful trade upon his coasts. The king was obliged, for the security of a lasting peace, as also by the laws of gratitude and relation, to see the house of Orange settled, and the Lovesteine* that Carthagenian party† brought down; neither in this did the king insist beyond what was moderate and agreeable to their government, and what the prince's ancestors enjoyed amongst them. Besides these, there was necessary to the trade of England, that there should be a fair adjustment of commerce in the East-Indies, where the king's demands were reasonable, and according to the law of nations; and their practice of late years hath been exorbitant and oppressive, suitable only to their power and interest, and destructive, if continued, to our East India Company. These were all of any moment the king insisted on, as judging aright, that that peace, that was reasonable, just and fair to both parties, would be sacred and durable; and that by this means he should depress the interest and reputation of that Lovesteine party ‡ amongst them, who sucked in with their milk an inveterate hatred to England, and transmit it to their posterity as a distinguishing character, wherein they place their loyalty to their country. In return to this candid and fair proceeding on the king's part, his majesty assures you, he hath received nothing but the most scornful and contemptuous treatment imaginable; papers delivered in to the mediators owned by them to be stuffed with so unhandsome language that they were ashamed and refused to shew them; never agreeing to any article about the Flag, that was clear or plain; refusing any article of the Fishery, but such a one as might sell them the right of inheritance for an inconsiderable sum of money, though it be royalty so inherent in the crown of England, that I may say (with his majesty's pardon for the expression) he cannot sell it. The article of the prince of Orange, and the adjustment of the East India trade, had neither of them any better success; and, to make all of a piece, they have this last week sent a trumpeter, with an address to his majesty, being a deduction of their several offers of peace, as they call them, and their desires for it now; but it is, both in the penning and the timing of it, plainly an appeal to his majesty's people against himself. And the king hath commanded me to tell you, He is resolved to join issue with them, and print both their Address and his Answer, that his people, and the world may see how notorious falshoods and slights they endeavour to put upon him. In a word, in England, and in all other places, and to all other persons of the world, they declare they offer all things to obtain a peace from the king of England; but to himself, his ministers, the mediators, or his plenipotentiaries, it may with confidence and truth be affirmed, that to this day, nay, even in this last address, they have offered nothing. They desire the king's subjects would believe they beg for peace; whilst their true request is, only to be permitted to be once masters of the Seas, which they hope, if they can subsist at land, length of time may give them, and if once got, is never to be lost, nor can it be bought by any state or emperor at too great a rate; and what security their agreement with us in religion will afford, when they shall have the power, former instances may give demonstration of. Joint interests have often secured the peace of differing religions; but agreeing professions have hardly an example of preserving peace of different interests. This being the true and natural state of things, his maj. doth with great assurance throw himself into the arms of you his parliament, for a Supply suitable to the great affairs he is engaged in. When you consider we are an island, it is not riches nor greatness we contend for, yet those must attend the success; but it is our very beings are in question; we fight *pro aris et focis* in this war. We are no longer freemen, being islanders and neighbours, if they master us at sea. There is not so lawful or commendable a jealousy in the world, as an Englishman's of the growing greatness of any prince at sea. If you permit the sea, our British wife, to be ravished, an eternal mark of infamy will stick upon us: therefore I am commanded earnestly to recommend to you, not only the proportion, but the time of the Supply; for, unless you think of it early, it will not be serviceable to the chief end, of setting out a fleet the next spring. As for the next part of the king's Speech, I can add nothing to what his majesty hath said; for, as to Religion and Property, his heart is with your heart, perfectly with your heart. He hath not yet learned to deny you any thing; and he believes your wisdom and moderation is such, he never shall: He asks of you to be at peace in him, as he is in you; and he shall never deceive you. There is one word more I am commanded to say, concerning the debt that is owing to the Goldsmiths;

* The party in Holland against a Stadtholder; so called from the Castle of Lovestein, where the father of the prince of Orange had imprisoned certain of the States, when he had entertained designs on the liberties of his country.

† "This expression made the Chancellor as ridiculous as the other had made him odious." Burnet.

the king holds himself in honour and conscience obliged to see them satisfied: besides you all know, how many widows, orphans, and particular persons, the public calamity hath overtaken, and how hard it is that so disproportionable a burden should fall upon them, even to their utter ruin. The whole case is so well and generally known, that I need say no more: your great wisdoms hath not done it at the first, peradventure, that the trade of Bankers might be suppressed, which end is now attained; so that now your great goodness may restore to those poor people, and the many innocent ones that are concerned with them, some life and assurance of payment in a competent time.—My Lords and Gentlemen; I have no more in command; and therefore shall conclude, with my own hearty prayers, that this session may equal, nay exceed, the honour of the last; that it may perfect what the last begun for the safety of the king and kingdom; that it may be ever famous for having establised upon a durable foundation our religion, laws and properties; that we may not be tossed with boisterous winds, nor overtaken by a sudden dead calm; but that a fair gale may carry you, in a steady, even, and resolved way, into the ports of wisdom and security."

Debate concerning the Speaker.] Oct. 27. Sir *Tho. Littleton.* Many exceptions were taken against your service, when you was last called to the chair: excepts that you are a privy counsellor; hardly a precedent, at least not since the Reformation: Speakers, in queen Mary's time, were chosen for the re-establishment of the Roman religion: you might be made a privy counsellor afterwards, as a reward of your service, but not whilst you are Speaker: other offices you hold inconsistent with that chair, and have admittance to the most secret councils, and how improper is that, we having no man to present our Grievances but you! You are too big for that Chair, and for us; and you, that are one of the governors of the world, to be our servant, is incongruous: and as Carteret, treasurer of the navy, in that place which you hold, took up the main business of a session; by way of supposition, if that should happen again, were it proper for you to be in the chair? For who then will be so much concerned?—Moves for a Speaker, pro tempore, and it is very incongruous you should sit when so immediately concerned.

Sir *Tho. Clarges* thinks what has been said so rational, that he cannot think that any man can be against it: we entrust you with all our secrets; and in your predecessors times, no Speaker had liberty to go to court, without leave: it is the Order, 'that when any reflection is upon a member, he stands up and speaks his defence, and retires,' and would have it so now.

Sir *Wm. Portman.* What we say here can be no secret among 400 men; persons in the Hall know what we do: craves leave, that some precedents, out of Hackwell's book, of Speakers being privy counsellors, may be read.

Sir *Joseph Tredenham.* Former ages have known none more fit for Speakers than privy counsellors: sir John Bushell, who was favourite to Rd. ii. was Speaker of all the parliaments in his time: sir Tho More, in 14 Hen. viii. In 4 Mary, Cordell, a privy counsellor: has it ever been objected that a privy counsellor cannot be a parliament-man? We have often made use of privy counsellors to send messages by to the king: the eyes of all the kingdom are upon our actions; it is a mark of the king's favour, that you are in the chair: would have it referred to a committee, but not you to quit the chair, that being a yielding of the question.

Sir *John Birkenhead.* Never was it an exception against any man before in your chair, that he was a privy counsellor; if any precedent can be of it, then turn me out of the house: the making him Speaker, is the king's and your joint act: if any complaint be against you, answer it, but for *causa inaudita*, it was never heard of: it is clear that the first Speaker, Hungerford, was of the privy council, and he was *ex concilio Domini Regis*: Froisard, the Historian, was another, no gown-man: sir Tho. Gargrave, of the queen's honourable council [many may say of the Council of the North] a Speaker, in Henry viii th's time, and a great instrument of the Reformation; this will reflect upon the king's making you a privy counsellor: never any Speaker quitted the chair upon that account.

Mr. *Powle* is not envious at your promotion, but thinks it an improper thing for you to be in the chair, and both inconvenient to the king and this house; the king's welfare consists in the freedom of this house. When you a privy counsellor, and so near the king, your frowns may be a terror to any man that shall speak how the council have misled the king, and given him counsel to overtop us; you are a public accomptant of the king's revenue, and vast sums must go through your hands, and can we make complaint to you of your own misdemeanors? Or take measures from any person but from the intention of this house? Believes that the precedents will fail; at this time, most especially, would not have it; for, if allowed once, it may be always so by precedent: the precedent of the Speaker, in Rd. ii d's time, an ill one; that Speaker was a minion of the king, but no counsellor, as the Record says; he was greatly the occasion of the misfortunes of those times—1st and 2d of Philip and Mary, unprosperous times; in two parliaments they could do nothing; but when Highems was Speaker, the obedience to the Pope was confirmed: he was not sworn counsellor till ten months after, and Cordell was not counsellor till some time after.

Mr. *Wm. Harbord.* You expose the honour of the house in resorting to Gaming-houses, with foreigners as well as Englishmen, and ill places; I take this to be a great misdemeanor: as for your being a privy counsellor, I think that no exception, but I am sorry to see the honour of the house exposed. I think you to be an unfit person to be Speaker, by your way of living.

Col. *Strangeways.* What he has heard to day weighs not with him; exceptions against the Speaker, as a privy counsellor, will be a garbling the house: you are charged here for being a Gamester: wishes men were guilty of no greater crime: the judges may as well be excepted against.

The *Speaker* rose up and complimented the house to this effect, "That he held no employment a greater honour to him than that which he had in their service," &c.

The question being propounded, That Mr. Speaker do leave the Chair, and a Speaker, pro tempore, be appointed: The question being put, That that Question be now put; it passed in the negative.

Debate on Sir Paul Neale's sitting in the House.] Oct. 30. Mr. *Sacheverell.* Sees a person [sir Paul Neale] sit in the house, whom he knows not to be a Member; desires to know by what right he sits there?

Sir *Paul Neale* proffered to speak, but was not suffered; "because if admitted to speak in his place, you allow him to be a member:" by divers he was called to the bar, and explained, "not as criminal, but only as not being allowed a member, as lord Bristol, lord chief justice Keeling, and others have been, not members."

Earl of *Ogle.* Desired to inform the house by what right sir Paul Neale sat there; viz. as being returned a burgess for Newark with Mr. Savile, by virtue of the king's charter granted to that borough.

Mr. *Sacheverell.* He is informed that that charter has taken in many towns which were not in the former charter, to their great prejudice, and would have it considered.

Sir Paul Neale did at last withdraw, and the thing was proceeded no farther in.

The King's Answer to the Address against the Duke's Match.] Mr. Secretary Coventry delivered the following Message concerning the intended Marriage of the Duke with the Princess of Modena:

"C. *R.* His majesty having received an Address from the house of commons presenting their humble desire, that the intended Marriage between his royal highness and the princess of Modena be not consummated, commandeth this Answer to be returned: That he perceiveth the h. of commons have wanted a full information of this matter, the marriage being not barely intended, but completed, according to the forms used amongst princes, and by his royal consent and authority: nor could he in the least suppose it disagreeable to his h. of commons, his highness having been, in the view of the world, for several months, engaged in a treaty of Marriage with another Catholic princess, and yet a parliament held during that time, and not the least exception taken at it."

Upon the Question, "Whether an Address should be prepared to be presented to his majesty, concerning the Match between his royal highness and the princess of Modena," it passed in the affirmative, 184 to 88, and a committee was appointed to prepare an Address accordingly.

Debate on the Test in the Popery Act.] Mr. *Cheney,* moved for declaring the opinion of the house about the Test, in the Act of Popery, how far it does reach to your own members.

Mr. *Garroway.* Is against the form of the motion, though not against the matter: would have a Bill, that every member may take the Test here; and would have it go higher, into the lords house, that those that have a share in the law-making, should be of the same religion.

Sir *Rob. Howard.* Without a thorough care, we shall be in a worse condition for Religion than before: the destiny of a heretic determines what they will do with us: would have have such a Test fitted for nothing but what the Papists may reject; it is necessary, that where any fountain is, it may be pure; and he would have the Protestant Religion pull up the very roots of Popery, wherever they grow; would have it reach all under the notion of Protestants, and be caculated for Popery only.

Mr. *Cheney* thinks that his motion is well improved; he would have former laws for Popery inspected.

Sir *Nich. Carew* thinks it will be too great a clogging the bill, but would have it so as to clear the house of lords, and the court, of Papists.

Resolved, "That a Bill be prepared for a General Test, to distinguish between Protestants and Papists: and those that shall refuse to take it, be incapable to enjoy any office, military or civil; or to sit in either house of parliament; or to come within five miles of the court."

Debate on refusing a Supply.] Oct. 31. Mr. *Boscawen.* In the king's Speech there is 'money' in the first place, and 'money' in the last; all 'money:' therefore would have it debated in a grand committee.

Mr. *Cheney.* Has heard that the Dutch have some thoughts that we might come into the peace immediately; then there can be no necessity for money: moves, that if the Dutch do not, in some time, agree to an honourable peace, that we may supply the king: it is in vain to give money, if not applied to the purpose we intend it: before any thing of money be, moves that we may come to this vote, 'that if, in two months time, the Dutch come not to an honourable peace, we may assist his majesty as becomes us."

Mr. *Sacheverell* has ever understood, that giving of money ought to be debated at a committee of the whole house, where we may lay open our grievances, which are very many, with the more freedom.

Sir *John Duncombe.* It has not been usual to go into a committee, without directions from the whole house: for Religion you have proceeded very prudently in: cannot but advise you to make peace at home; people will quiet their passions best with calming all at home, if men could be satisfied, and not afraid of their own good: would now go into this business of Religion: that burns in every man's heart, and he sees every man's face full of it, and that is the beginning of the king's Speech.

Sir *Tho. Meres.* There are Orders remaining upon your books, and practice: says, upon search of ancient orders, that the king's Speech was ever debated in a grand committee: agrees with Duncombe, if we may not be surprized with rash votes, that the house may rectify what surprize we may have upon us.

Sir *John Monson.* In the French Gazette the Pope approves of the progress of the French arms; the last fight was, as if the English and Dutch had been the gladiators for the French spectators *: if the prince had been well seconded, there had been an end of the war, and the Dutch must have begged a peace of us: we gave two millions to set out but part of a navy for a summer: what greater encouragement can be given to the Dutch? Our native commodities give no price; want of coals make us want fire, and floods have destroyed grass and hay: fire and water against us! We have want of people; many are sent away, and he will say nothing of the end for which they are sent; therefore moves against a Supply.

Mr. Sec. *Coventry.* If the king had wasted his treasure for magnificent buildings, or palaces, would be against giving money; but if, for not paying some few taxes the nation may be lost, would have gentlemen consider of it: avers that the Dutch have not made any proposition, only a piece of one, 'for the Flag;' and 'if we will quit the king of France, they will then tell us more, and they are allied with the king of Spain, and Lorrain, and cannot agree without them.' You yourself, sir Cha. Harbord, have been obliged by the Hollanders; he has served there under them in their army, and honours the Orange family before any, next to that of his own prince, and loves the country; but consider they have provided a great fleet against the summer, and you will give no money, and so have no fleet; which way will you secure the plantations and Tangier? If you think they will give peace, it will be such a one then as to a people they contemn: if you come upon a vote of 'no money,' it will be as fatal as that of the Long Parliament, of 'no farther Addresses to the king." Were a man jealous of his wife, would he make her poor and naked, and force her to put herself into the arms of another man? Concludes this vote to be the most fatal blow you can give the nation.

Lord *Cavendish.* Here is money asked of us to carry on a war we were never advised about, and what we have given is turned to raising of families, and not paying the king's debts: there is so little fruit of the Addresses of the last session, that we now find greater Grievances, as articles of war and martial law: the nation's interest is laid aside for private interest: supposes that what we gave the last session may be a sufficient Supply for the war, and moves for a negative 'against Money.'

Col. *Strangways.* It is a sad condition we are reduced to, and who have reduced us to it is a secret not yet come to his knowledge, and in due time may be considered: if you shall pass negative votes, what advantage do you give your enemies in such a vote? Are you sure you shall have peace? Would never have the king hold his crown of the king of France: desires we may not depend for our security either upon France or Holland: the Hollanders are a trading and a subtle people, and would have a fleet set out: he aims at this; begin with Grievances and your liberty: France has entangled us; the public articles are ill enough; what are then the private articles? We are to provide 60 ships, and the French 30: if the house does not assist the king, then the French come upon us for breach of articles: in a parliamentary way consider first 'Grievances,' and then 'Money.' The house of commons keeps the purse; and never put the question for 'Money,' before you know what you shall have for it: but is against a negative question.

Sir *Tho. Lee.* When you gave away so much money, then began the alliance with France, and no debts paid, though money given for it: the Dutch were not the aggressors in the last war, when we were weary of fighting alone; now the French are weary of us, and will fight alone; when we gave money for a fleet and had peace without it! Now we are the support of the crown of France, England may be as necessary to France as other countries, and so they may conquer us: the kingdom is ever safe when money is in our purses; we may have occasion to use it perhaps, to defend us against France: must we give 5 millions more to have what we might have had without it? Must money be given both in war and peace? Concurrent aids were never before heard of, money having been the foundation of our Grievances to raise a Standing Army; the marine regiments paid to this day; now, instead of five-pence, they take six-pence for their quarters: France once would invade us, and now is our friend. Still more men are raised; so many in a company are, indeed, disbanded, but the officers remain. This is your Standing Army, and it is Money still that maintains this army: 50 per cent. upon our goods in France, and yet the war with Holland upon account of trade: money for league, and no league, war and peace: moves to have the kingdom once free from taxes.

Sir *Rob. Howard* is sorry to hear this ques-

* A desperate engagement had happened with the Dutch, on the 11th of August, in which the brave sir Edw. Spragg lost his life; while the French remained quiet spectators, disobeying, or pretending not to understand, prince Rupert's orders.

tion moved for in the negative; this will utterly shiver all our hopes in this Vote: consider the arguments; 'to maintain an ill Alliance:' we have brought about the French alliance to us, whilst united to Holland, and both navies were against us: religion is not the case, but interest: if money be ill managed, any body may see it; he (as Secretary to the Treasury) will give an account of it, and ask no time to do it, registers being all in order; the money all gone out to public uses: you must have the nation poor if we have peace, if we give no money: what will the Dutch say to this negative? Will you shake the king in it? You say the Papists have power; by this you give more way yet to have it; they have their counsels to give the king by such a Vote: we are going now to make a purchase, and before we get our religion and properties by this purchase, we throw away all by this vote: he must be a God that can say, 'there shall be no enemies, and we shall have peace;' and yet we do so by this negative: let not the word of king and people be lost now—'Seek ye first the kingdom of Heaven,' settle Religion, 'and all things will be added:' Go in a parliamentary way for Grievances and Religion, and think of this vote last.

Mr. *Sacheverell.* Is one of those that think giving of Money one of the greatest Grievances: it seems to him, that those villainous counsellors, that persuaded the king to make this war, have deceived him in this speech; do not they know of the unpaid taxes granted the last session, with the prizes and the customs? It seems to him like the first design: these gentlemen would have only a Bank, that they may carry on their design, and use you no more: he abhors it: it was said before, 'Give money, and Grievances shall be redressed:' this army is so insolent, that they may turn you out of doors: if redress of Grievances be an argument for 'Money,' you will never want 'Grievances:' will you not heighten France, by giving more money, and make him more friends, that he may at last have Dominion at Sea, which we now contend for? And, by this negative, we may deliver ourselves both from France and Rome.

Sir *Eliab Harvey.* Giving of money now is certainly to ruin king and kingdom: give money, and you destroy the revenue of the nation, wool: you are letting the king of France be the merchant of the whole world: by falling out with Spain, we spoil the best trade we have: he has kept 100 men at work upon the woollen manufacture, and now cannot keep one: will you set the woollen manufacture up in France? Lose the Straits trade, and you must land all your commodities at Marseilles, and bring them over land, and so France and Holland will out-trade you, by the great expence we must be at by inland carriage.

Mr. *Bennet.* Both at home and abroad people would be glad of this negative: he has much to do in the world, and knows the poverty of the nation; but would not have it thought that we are unable to raise the king money.

Sir *Wm. Coventry* is as unwilling to give money for the maintenance of this alliance as any man, it being destructive both to trade and religion: what probability is there, if we beat the Hollander, that we shall get all trade? But it is industry and parsimony, and by underselling us: suppose we beat them, what think you they will be beaten hither? The last summer but one we beat them low enough, but with all the invitation that could be given them, few of them came hither; you may beat them into France, Sweden, or Denmark; any where but here; who will come to us, thus divided, as we are, in jealousies, and fears of Popery? He that knows least, has most fears: a stranger knows not what you have in your heart: we all know that we shall not stay if Popery prevail: pray God they will let us go away alive, considering the Inquisition! He has said enough to give reason for his negative for 'Money.' The Hollanders, in all reason, had better have no quarrels. But upon the king of France's account, if we leave him, his difficulties will increase: it is strange that we and Holland should be divided by one, whose interest is destructive to us both: when we go by ourselves, we may have a fair peace in all probability, going upon a pure national account: would not have it out of the house's power to assist the king: he is not so confident of the Hollanders good-nature in a peace, but doubts not, but upon Money granted upon good grounds, we may be sure of a peace; yet for all this he is not for money.

Sir *Henry Capel.** If this war was for the maintenance of the crown and nation, would venture all he has, life and fortune, for it: he is descended from one that lost his life for maintaining of both: would know how we came into this war, before we give money to it; is not for giving money for the war, but not for a negative 'no Money;' and doubts not but the king will redress our Grievances.

Sir *Rob Carr* moves to proceed in a parliamentary way: proceed to your 'Grievances,' (if you have any) and the king will give you redress. [Laughed at.]

Lord *Cornbury.* Here is now a question proposed, and he agrees with Coventry's question: it will be wondered that he should be against money: some men have been under prejudice for giving votes, and that may possibly be a Grievance: all he has is from the king, and he would willingly give it again, if he calls for it; he has begged for the king, and wanted for him, and would willingly do so again: Carr says 'if there are any Grievances;' he wonders at it, when so many have been opened to you: the last tax could not be anticipated;

* Second son of lord Capel, (who was beheaded for his loyalty to Charles I, in 1648) and brother to the earl of Essex. He was created lord Capel, of Tewkesbury, in 1692, and died lord lieutenant of Ireland, in 1696.

besides the customs, excise, and the prizes: some cannot get their money due to them, glad to be content with half; those that have interest get all: would vote, 'that Money be not considered till Grievances are redressed.'

Mr. *Garroway*. Ruin of trade, loss of religion, no Grievance! Papists threnten us in the very lobby, to our faces; soldiers raising money; a war; the French king broke the Pyrenean league, conquered Lorrain, the king of Spain's country, en passant, and this a good Alliance! And now the question, whether money or no Money to maintain this League, and no enquiry made into what remains of what we have already given—Lands turned into our hands, (as it is his good fortune) and no Grievances neither! As to our sea war, the French give us money, and they come to see how we fight for it: one clapped up in the 'Bastile for fighting:* where will there be an end of the French conquests? If any fleet be to be set out, we may do it time enough: moves, 'That till this tax be expired,' (which will be August first) 'we may give no Money;' and then, if occasion be, would give, but till then, would not.

Sir *John Hotham* comes from a place so impoverished, [Beverly] that it is impossible to raise money there, and that place is much impoverished by soldiers already; they quarter there in private houses, and one person was fined, because he would not render his house and bed to the soldiers: you have now an army, and it is grown a principle amongst them, (an ill nursery for young men) that parliaments are roots of rebellion, and Magna Charta sprung out of them: money is the way to continue these persons, and no money, to disband them; therefore is against money.

Mr. Attorney *Finch*, is of opinion that there are grievances, and never expects such a healthful constitution in the body politic, that shall be so equally poised, as to be without them: 'not to give money' is at this time a grievance not to be redressed in many ages: this is an English war, and no other: they are not afraid, in Flanders, of the Protestant religion, because joined with a Protestant army: would treat this matter with more temperament; surely, for the honour of our prince, we must not treat crowned heads here, in alliance with us, as if they were our enemies: if we have but good trade, the Dutch presently make war with that prince, in alliance with us, that we may have no trade with their enemy; commends much the piety of this, but sees not the policy: you are now in war, and you carry the purse: supposing it such, and the alliance, as is said, yet in the condition we are in, it is absolutely necessary to support the war to the utmost of our power, the king being engaged with a prince who has punctually observed articles: suppose us weary of the war, yet the king of France is actually engaged with us, and has remitted many articles that would have obliged the king to much expence: the war we cannot get out of with a prince loving his honour above his life; you may make it an unprosperous and a ruinous war, but you cannot make it cease to be a war; you may dishearten all the soldiers that are to go over, but if you make the chariot wheels drive heavily, yet they must drive on, if the king please to command it: if that war was now to be made, the discourse would be most seasonable; but now will be ruinous, and wiser men than he think so: the king may engage in a war, but when his people shall storm him out of it, the hour will come that his enemies wish for; for the Dutch will now be upon greater terms, having ever desired such a storm as the king could not allay: it is all one to the king whether his designs be checked at home or abroad: is this agreeable to this house, wherein there is scarce a man that has not bled for the crown? moves, that whatever is grievous, either in church or state, we may go upon, with all calmness and temper, and to do the king that honour (if with submission he may say it) that one day may be for 'Grievances,' and the other for 'Supply,' hand in hand, that the world may see you neither neglect the king nor yourselves.

Mr. *Powle*. We see priests daily admitted into the king's presence, and our Address (as he is informed) is but lately sent into Ireland: a Papist major general acting in disguise: has not one told you (sir James Smith) that he sat in a council of war when the military articles were agreed to? pressing against so many statutes, may reach your members, and the peers themselves: and this army has done nothing but the famous expedition from Blackheath to Yarmouth*: shall never think that privilege of parliament is not violated as long as a privy counseller sits in the Chair†: members represented to the king in an ill sense for what they have said here: he that was the contriver of the Declaration‡, made lord privy seal, the third office in the kingdom, and another‖, as much concerned, made chief governor of Scotland: this is to bring in Popery in triumph: would be glad to see promises made in parliament, once kept in intermissions of parliament: he cannot go so far in the question proposed, as not to give any farther Supply till ten months; but at this time cannot give his consent to supply.

---

* In the sea fight of the 11th of August, the French rear admiral Martel, who was not in the secret, fought in earnest; for which, at his return to Paris, he was committed to the Bastile, and the relation of the battle, which he had prepared, was suppressed.

* "Part of the summer about 6000 troops were encamped at Yarmouth, under the command of count Schomberg; from whence it was understood that they might easily be wafted over to Zealand, as soon as the allied fleet had cleared the sea of the enemy." Ralph.

† Reflecting again on the Speaker. See the Debate on that subject, p. 589.

‡ Earl of Anglesea.

‖ Duke of Lauderdale.

Sir *Thos Meres.* With the length and expatiating on an argument oftentimes the edge of a thing is lost: you will be sure to have Grievances, if that be doctrine, that money must be given when grievances are redressed: if that money, twice given in a session, be not unparliamentary, yet there are 1,200,000*l.* granted in a year: has seen so often Grievances pressed, and so seldom redressed, that he now has little hopes of having it; but it may be answered, we will be redressed first; but have we not seen people's spirits are a little wearied with long sitting, and that a few redressed pleases us? in short we are the best-natured house of commons that ever sat: consider what we do about Popery, in the lords house, by putting out popish lords, a matter of inheritance, which will have conference upon conference, and we under great disadvantages: it was said, that Popery was but the handle for the ambitious and covetous, in 1641, to raise sedition: when we speak of a Standing Army, we are answered, 'cannot the king raise what men he pleases?' and to the French league, 'cannot the king make leagues?' Yet the gentleman said, 'the king cannot have Money without the house of commons: what war can the king make, when the house of commons shall storm him out of it?' To which thus he answers: In such great wars as this, and in most wars, the kings of England have advised with their parliaments; believes that it might be the king's intention to do so, however advised to the contrary; we owned not the war in the last tax: the king may make war, but the house of commons may or may not give money: other Grievances there are, as Evil Counsellors; to which it will be said, 'cannot the king chuse his own servants?' And that is plausible. Should these things be amended, he would give money.

Mr. *Stockdale.* If we were able, as we are not, it is not now a time to give at all: the question is a single question, 'Whether money or no money, till this tax be out?'

Sir *Tho. Lee.* This question is for the king's service now, more than ever: has great reason to believe, that the king needs it not; because one has told you (Mr. Attorney) 'that the king of France has released several chargeable articles in the treaty:' as for the carrying on the war, we look upon it as a Grievance. 'The parliament may talk, say the people, but still you give money: fears not proroguing for not giving; but if you show yourselves willing to give no money, the king will be restored to the affections of his people, when they shall see that grievances are redressed without giving of money.

Mr. Secretary *Coventry.* Nothing is so wise nor so obligatory to the king, as to redress Grievances without giving money; but as far as he is master of his own life, he had rather lose it, than you should pass this negative vote.

Mr. *Garroway.* Coventry tells you how the French have conquered; but now the case is altered, it might have been wished the Tripartite League * had stood: Is sorry for the Attorney's expression, of being 'stormed out of a League:' The prince of Orange will be a good advocate to keep the Hollanders in war with the French, that he may be continued general; but would never have such a peace as the French shall assign us: We are more put to the blush about redress of Grievances, than for any other thing; those that have been the promisers have been the opposers: The proroguing will do us as much good as it did us a prejudice, and, if need be, we may be suddenly sent for again: Is for the question.

Mr. *Howe* † is dissatisfied with the person that is to have the money in his hands, the Speaker.

Sir *Tho. Clarges* cannot apprehend such an imminent necessity of giving, as Solicitor North says there is: The remaining taxes, the customs, the revenue, and prizes, and for one reason above all, viz. 400,000*l.* given away in donatives: Does not repine at the king's bounty, but apprehends no necessity of giving by it: Thinks that the counsels, now prevalent, design the ruin of the king, the duke, and the kingdom; the Irish Grievances not sent away above ten days ago; priests and the lord almoner at court; 1500 and 2000 guineas given to officers disbanded; 13, 14, 20 Popish officers taken in, and the French regiments filled with them, and some ordered not to muster, to prevent discovery: Acts of parliament can do nothing; as these men have, notwithstanding, taken up arms: It looks like treason in levying war without commission: When he was at Paris, the Holland ambassador told him, "You have broken your faith with the Bankers; France an absolute monarchy, and you a limited one; no help nor advantage by your alliance:" The Chancellor is keeper of the king's conscience, and the treasurer, of his word: the Bankers broken, and Exchequer shut up, in Jan. and we to meet in March: they have persuaded the king to ask to pay the Bankers, and they are already paid, by the sale of the free-farm rents, 600,000*l.*—Subsidy, excise, law-bill by this—Where shall we find treasure to supply these exorbitances: these evil counsellors intercept all the king's goodness; no good is to be hoped for till they be removed: it was insinuated that the last Supply would give us peace in a few months; we

* "The Triple Alliance between England, Holland, and Sweden, was formed in 1668. The design of it was to support the Spanish monarchy, restrain the exorbitant power of France, and prevent a dreadful war, in which all Europe would probably have been involved. It was therefore generally applauded, and seemed to be, in all respects, the wisest measure that was taken in England during the whole reign of Charles ii." Smollet.

† Brother to sir Scroope Howe, and Paymaster General in the reign of queen Anne. He died in 1721.

then considered not the war, nor the alliance: our duty to the king overcame all those enquiries; and since there appears no want of money, put the question at the largest extent, as first moved.

Sir *Tho. Littleton* cannot imagine that such consequences as are alledged will attend the putting the question, as penned, with the words retained in: is persuaded that, if an effectual course be taken, as things change, men's minds will change, and is not so terribly afraid of it: nor so dismal a vote but as happy.

Sir *Edw. Dering.* By whose hands are we tied but by our own? Should we be tied by any other, we cannot go back with honour, nor forward with safety.

Mr. *Boscawen* would make no other use of the Vote but in order to peace: the great grievances have been by pretence of the war, the rest but trivial: the war, at the first, was against the advice of the whole body of the merchants, only some particular men that had losses: thinks the peace a good peace, and the Triple League much for the satisfaction of the nation: some trifling injuries were done to the merchants at Surinam; as if a man, with a flea on his forehead, would strike it off with a beetle: would make use of that Vote, that we might have a peace: it is better to deny an aid to the war than to meddle with a peace: we never deny money when there is a just occasion for it; it were to deny self-preservation.

Sir *Wm. Coventry* hears it said, 'that the king cannot go off with honour from his alliance with France;' and what then shall we say of the Triple Alliance, that the peace of Christendom was so much concerned in, so solemn, as to be sworn to by the king of France, and registered in the parliament of Paris by that king's command, but yet renounced by him, because not consistent with the good of his people: Munster made a war with our money; it was not for the good of his subjects, it seems, and he made peace with Holland: the same did Brandenburgh: the king of France, by the Pyrenean treaty, was not to assist the king of Portugal; it was not for the good of his people, and he broke that treaty; Princes have ever done it for the good of their people, and if we live by another rule than they do, we shall have the worst of it; Now has the king of France kept treaty with us, as is said? Knows not what the private articles were, but surely they were made unfortunately, that we should have no share in this conquest; has he kept his word with us? He was to send 30 ships for our 60; had that conjunction been as it should be, they would have fought; has heard but of two captains killed in the French fleet, and one died of an unfortunate disease (the Pox); thinks we had no advantage by their company. One unfortunate gentleman did fight (Martel) and because that gentleman said, (as he has heard) 'That the French did not their duty,' he is clapped up into the Bastile. 'His own squadron,' he said, 'deserted him;' his captains said, 'upon secret orders, which they had*.' D'Estrees sent positive orders not to fight, unless by word of mouth, or by writing; and if that man that brought them, had been knocked on the head, no orders could have been had; 'no regard to be had to prince Rupert's signals,' (which is the custom at sea) 'D'Estrees must, by a council of war, know whether the prince's orders were good orders or no;' could a fleet coming with such orders, ever be serviceable to us? Thinks it better we had no fleet; thinks not so highly of the Dutch, nor meanly of ourselves, but that we may do well without the king of France: an indifferent casuist will say, having been so used, that we are absolved from an alliance so ill maintained; the interest of the king of England is to keep France from being too great on the continent, and the French interest is to keep us from being masters of the sea; the French have pursued that interest well; moves to insert in the Question, 'unless it shall appear that the obstinacy of the Dutch shall make a supply necessary.'

Mr. *Garroway.* Spain says, 'have peace with England, and war with all the world:' we lost 1600 ships in the last Spanish war, great and small: as for Duncombe's argument of building ships futurely, money may be had; the East-India Company had it at 4 per cent. for the prizes; you may have a short Bill for the remainder of the last Supply, which is not at all engaged to any other use.

Sir *Tho. Littleton* doubts not but redress of Grievances will alarm the Dutch more than any Supply we can give.

The Commons refuse a Supply.] It was then resolved, "That this house, considering the present condition of the nation, will not take into any farther debate, or consideration, any Aid, or Supply, or Charge upon the subject, before the times of payment of the 18 months Assessment, &c. granted last session, be expired: unless it shall appear, that the obstinacy of the Dutch shall render it necessary; nor before this kingdom be effectually secured from the dangers of Popery, and popish counsels and counsellors, and the other present Grievances be redressed."

The Commons Second Address against the Duke's Match.] Mr. Powle reported from the Committee the Address to be presented to his

* Dr. Campbell, in his Lives of the Admirals, has preserved the conclusion of Martel's relation of the battle; which, it seems, had found its way to England, and was published in a piece called, 'An exact Relation of the Actions of the Fleet under Prince Rupert, printed anno 1673,' and was to this effect; "That if count D'Estrees would have fallen in with a fair wind upon De Ruyter and Bankert, at their first engaging, when in numbers they much exceeded the Prince, they must of necessity have been inclosed between his Highness and D'Estrees; and so the enemy would have been entirely defeated."

majesty, concerning the Match between his royal highness the duke of York, and the princess of Modena; which was agreed to by the house, and is as follows:

"We your majesty's most humble and loyal subjects, the commons, in this present parliaments assembled, being full of an assurance of your majesty's gracious intentions to provide for the establishment of Religion, and the preservation of your people in peace and security; and foreseeing the dangerous consequences which may follow the marriage of his r. h. the duke of York with the princess of Modena, or any other person of the popish religion, do hold ourselves bound in conscience and duty to represent the same to your sacred majesty; (not doubting but those constant testimonies that we have given your majesty of our true and loyal affections to your sacred person, will easily gain a belief, that these our humble desires proceed from hearts still full of the same affections towards your sacred majesty, and with intentions to establish your royal government upon those true supports of the Protestant religion, and the hearts of your people) with all humility, desiring your majesty to take the same into your princely consideration, and to relieve your subjects from those fears and apprehensions which at present they lie under from the progress that has been made in that Treaty.—We do therefore humbly beseech your maj. to consider, That if this Marriage do proceed, it will be a means to disquiet the minds of your Protestant subjects at home, and to fill them with endless jealousies and discontents, and will bring your majesty into such alliances abroad, as may prove highly prejudicial, if not destructive, to the interest of the very Protestant Religion itself.—That we find, by sad experience, that such Marriages have increased and encouraged Popery in this kingdom, and given opportunity to priests and jesuits to propagate their opinions, and seduce great number of your Protestant subjects.—And we do already observe, how much that party are animated with the hopes of this Match, which were lately discouraged by your majesty's gracious concessions in the last meeting of this parliament.—That we greatly fear, this may be an occasion to lessen the affections of the people to his r. h. who is nearly related to the crown, and whose honour and esteem we desire may be always entirely preserved.—That, for another age, at least, this kingdom will be under continual apprehensions of the growth of Popery, and the danger of the Protestant religion.—Lastly, we consider, That this princess, having so near a relation and kindred to many eminent persons of the court of Rome, may give them great opportunities to promote their designs, and carry on their practices amongst us; and, by the same means, penetrate into your majesty's most secret councils, and more easily discover the state of the whole kingdom.—And finding that, by the opinions of very many learned men, it is generally admitted, that such treaties and contracts by proxy are dissolvable, of which there are several instances to be produced, we do, in all humbleness, beseech your majesty to put a stop to the consummation of this intended Marriage.—And this we do the more importunately desire, because we have not, as yet, the happiness to see any issue of your majesty's that may succeed in the government of these kingdoms; which blessing we most heartily pray Almighty God, in his due time, to bestow upon your maj. and these kingdoms, to the unspeakable joy and comfort of all your loyal subjects, who desire nothing more than to continue under the reigns of your majesty, and your royal posterity for ever."

Resolved, "That this Address be presented to his majesty, and that the lords of the privy council, members of this house, be desired to attend his majesty, to know his pleasure when he will be attended therewith."

A Standing Army voted a Grievance.] Nov. 3. In a debate upon Grievances,

Sir *T. Meres* said, several Grievances were enumerated the other day: the next Grievance he thinks fit to propose is that of a 'Standing Army.' Some said it was to land to beat the Dutch; but it turned off, it seems, to take Harwich, as you have been told. He has been informed that they are of no service; the king's treasure is wasted by them, so that aids are asked twice in one year: loves not to be the first man that moves a thing, but would now form you a question, 'That this Standing Army is a Grievance.' The reasons for it: it brings in the billetting of soldiers, against the Petition of Right: the last session they took 5d. from persons to be exempted from quartering soldiers, and now it is raised to 6d. not only in inns, and alehouses, but in private houses (a man's house is his castle) contrary to the privileges of the English subjects: you are told also of Martial Law, made for the governing these men, against all the laws of England. Martial law has arbitrary principles and arbitrary power: we like not these arbitrary principles in any councils: this army has the youth of the nation; it debauches them, and fills them with such principles, that towns by them are debauched; common violences they commit. Besides the French League and 'Evil Counsellors,' this is still a terror in our fears of Popery: if any one of these are left out, it will help to set up the other three: asks, at last, That this may be voted 'a Grievance;' the others are 'grievances,' but the army is 'a Legion:' and, to follow the metaphor, hopes they shall not 'be choaked in the sea,' nor cast away beyond sea, to support this alliance, but disbanded.

Sir *Eliab Harvey* knows of abundance of petitions that will be presented you against these men: if you send them abroad, they must be turned Catholics, and so many sent us back again: hopes you will vote it 'a grievance.'

Mr. Sec. *Coventry*, would have you agree

upon terms, what is 'an Army,' and what 'a Standing Army,' knows not why they are called 'Legions,' for among the Romans a legion was a band of 2000 men: he is unwilling that his country should be exposed; but now you are in a war, thinks not that you intend that the king should fall down, and beg a peace of Holland: they know what your trained bands are, since the business of Landguard point: for the king to raise troops is not against law, but for those troops to be disorderly is against law; but if such a captain, or company, has done ill without order, it is no general grievance: two vintners killed two gentlemen; shall vintners therefore be a grievance? Some merchants robbed upon the highway; must all merchants therefore be a grievance? The gentleman is not well informed about martial law; it is as it ever was: in lord Strafford's command, and the earl of Holland's, when he disbanded the Northern army, and those of lord Essex's army (we may learn of our enemies) these were compared with all articles, and the best were extracted, and you will find them no French articles: hopes you will not say, it is not in the king's power to raise men, but let gentlemen show you any disorders owned by authority, and it is another case: but how will you vote this 'grievance,' when there is no illegality in it, only exorbitances of particular persons? Hopes you will not vote it a Grievance.

Sir *Tho. Lee* thought, that, though the practice of accumulative treason against lord Strafford was condemned, yet his setting up Martial Law was justly disapproved then: The oaths in the articles, he is sure, are not legal: But you are told of vintners and merchants, and that these exorbitances are not allowed; but if we have no grievances till they are allowed by authority, we shall never have any: but they are to have another sort of trial than other men, and that makes them a terror: You have been told this morning, 'that upon their marches they have been quartered in private houses in Hampshire, and that they made people bring out their provisions, or they would take them by force in their marches.' They are taught to believe that they may do it; and should you make this Address to the king, he would find it 'a grievance' as well as you: you are now arming the king; nothing disarms him more than these exorbitances: But must these dragoons ride over the sea? We have no wooden horses to carry them, and by this you give the Dutch great advantage: We had success by the militia in 1588; you had no army but them at that time: It has ever been the custom, that when men have been thus raised they have been complained of as a grievance, especially we wanting hands and mouths now in the nation; and would now have it voted a grievance.

Sir *Rob. Howard.* If there be not an intention of 'a standing army,' which we know not, it is too hasty a vote: would not have any distrust betwixt the king and us, and would give no argument to the king to apprehend it: Present only, 'an army now in being and no occasion for:' lay only your duty before his majesty, 'that it may be a terror to the people, as you apprehend,' and tread in the easier steps to him.

Sir *Henry Capel.* You have been told how difficult it is for armies and properties to stand together: Is not of that opinion that they are a security to us at home; knows nothing of affairs abroad: Our security is the militia; that will defend us and never conquer us: our defence abroad is our ships; the seaman's pay, and peas, and his coarse diet, well given him: Moves to vote this army 'a grievance.'

Lord *St. John.* In the former king's time, a much less thing than this was voted a Grievance; and now an army in our bowels all this summer and no employment for them, and for the county he serves, [Hampshire] he is particularly obliged to represent it as a Grievance.

Sir *Tho. Clarges* will not say it is fit now to disband them all; but at the conclusion of the last war some were made standing regiments, and fears now, after the war, it will be the same again: but the king is not minded of his promises by those that should do it; he is persuaded that the king would do it, but forgets it: but the raising money, and 15 or 16 to quarter in a poor alehouse, full of children, is a Grievance.

Mr. *Harwood.* The king has many things laid upon him that he has not done: the king raised not these men but his counsellors, who have got by these things: How many Addresses against Popery, and yet papists put into command! He that commands our men in chief is a stranger*, and he next in command a Papist†: Cannot wonder at those persons that have spoke against these things as Grievances. Were he as they, possibly he should say so too; but they cannot think so. We are come to that pass, that no law can restrain these people; houses taken from us, our lives in danger; he cannot say one has suffered death by them, but some have been soundly swinged: would vote it a Grievance.

Sir *Rob. Carr.* No man can say, that a Standing Army in a time of peace, was ever attempted: most of the forces were about Norfolk and Suffolk, where the Dutch have attempted landing; Your Addresses formerly were 'to disband them, when the war should be ended,' and will you now do it 'the war in being?' It is not for your service.

Sir *Rd. Temple.* The practice of these men is a Grievance. He knows no law that can empower them to raise money; the continuance of them will be more a grievance, and what is an oppression, is a grievance.

Mr. *Powle* answers Mr. Sec. Coventry—Whatever body of men are raised for no use,

* Count (afterwards duke) Schomberg, killed at the battle of the Boyne, in 1690.

† Earl of Feversham, a Frenchman by birth, and nephew to Marshal Turenne.

are 'a Grievance;' he thinks 'the raising them a Grievance'—These forces were not raised for the war, but the war made for raising these people: He is no soldier, but has conversed with such as are, and they hold a descent into Zealand impossible; for the enemy might, at any time, get betwixt them and the land with their fleet, and, if landed, hinder recruits: They are glad that the militia may be useless, and the gentlemen that serve in it are put upon chargeable employments, but in Chatham business were not thought fit to command them: which has been such a discouragement, that many have laid down their commissions: When money or honour was to be got, then they were put out of command: As for the fleet, we are in a naval war, at least we are told so, and hopes it so, but the money is all spent upon land soldiers: You know that in your office [the Speaker's] the seamen are not paid; the money being diverted to pay those landmen. Part of those men are drawn out of Ireland, and the Papists, last session, were grown formidable there: why are they not sent back thither? We desire them not here, and they want them there: our laws to be thus awed! The law of England will protect the king: knows not what these men will do; but the veteran bands, at last, chopped, and changed, and sold the Roman empire: the king himself may be no longer king, but at the choice of this army: let the soldiers be paid, and you may have them again when you will: quartering of soldiers, or buying them off, is an intolerable oppression: why should an ale-house-keeper, a subject, buy off his oppressions? Soldiers to present their muskets in the face of a court! Would have it voted 'a grievance.'

Col. *Kirby*. Hears it said, 'that these men were raised to no purpose.' Had you not had landmen, you would have had none to man your guns, and they would have been much put to it; but for our regiment, you might have had no fleet: before you move the king for disbanding, consider how you will maintain the war.

Col. *Birch*. Kirby has given you the greatest reason imaginable for disbanding these men; he calls the men aboard a ship, 'our regiment;' and he commands none of the new raised men: he has ever told you, that this war was against the grain of the people, and then against their interest, and we were prorogued on, till the war was so far entered into that we could not come out of it: no people can be governed but by perfect love, or perfect fear: we are asked, 'why this army is a grievance now, and not when we were here last? We saw not then what we see now. He saw them at Blackheath with their swords drawn; it terrified him then, but, thank God, he is pretty well recovered since he came into the house: If this vote makes the Dutch insolent, 'giving money' will be the consequence, and then all is well: the great river of Babylon was cut into small rivulets, and that destroyed the city, when nothing else could; so has our money been diverted, he fears. Would have the Standing-Army voted 'a Grievance.'

Resolved, "That the Standing-Army is a Grievance."

Sir Tho. Meres moved that some gentlemen may draw up an Address to the king, showing in what manner this army is a Grievance. A Committee was appointed accordingly.

Nov. 3. p. m. Mr. Speaker reported, That in pursuance of their commands, he had read, and presented to his majesty, the Address of the house, concerning his royal highness's Match with the princess of Modena; and that his maj. was pleased to declare, "that it was a matter that he would take into his present consideration, and return a speedy Answer."

The Parliament suddenly prorogued.] Nov. 4. After the Speaker, who came not to the house till 10 o'clock, though the house was the day before adjourned to eight, had been called to the Chair by a great voice, he at last took the chair; and then sir Robert Thomas moved to take into consideration the business of 'evil counsellors,' as 'a grievance,' hinted the other day, and would name one, 'the duke of Lauderdale*.' The word was no sooner out of his

* "The duke of Lauderdale had been for many years a zealous Covenanter: but in 1647 he turned to the king's interest; and had continued a prisoner all the while after Worcester fight, where he was taken. He was kept for some years in the Tower of London, in Portland Castle, and in other prisons, till he was set at liberty by those who called home the king. He was very learned, not only in Latin, in which he was a master, but in Greek and Hebrew. He was a man, (as the duke of Buckingham called him to me) of a blundering understanding. He was haughty beyond expression, abject to those he saw he must stoop to, but imperious to all others. He had a violence of passion, which carried him often to fits like madness, in which he had no temper. He was the coldest friend, and the violentest enemy I ever knew. He at first seemed to despise wealth; but he delivered himself up afterwards to luxury and sensuality. He was in his principles much against Popery and arbitrary government; and yet, by a fatal train of passions and interests, he made way for the former, and had almost established the latter; and whereas some, by a smooth deportment, made the first beginnings of tyranny less discernible and unacceptable: he, by the fury of his behaviour, heightened the severity of his ministry, which was liker the cruelty of an inquisition than the legality of justice. With all this, he was a Presbyterian, and retained his aversion to king Charles i, and his party, to his death [which happened in 1682.]" Burnet.—Many years after his death there was published a translation by him of Virgil's Æneid, which had been shewn in MS. to Dryden, and from which he has borrowed many lines.

mouth but the usher of the black rod knocked at the door, and the serjeant gave notice of it to the Speaker, who forbade sir Robert proceeding any farther.*

The King's Speech.] The king made a short Speech to both houses as follows:

"My lords and gentlemen; I need not tell you how unwillingly I call you hither at this time, being enough sensible what advantage my enemies both abroad and at home will reap by the least appearance of a difference betwixt me and my parliament; nay, being assured they expect more success from such a breach (could they procure it) than from their arms.—This, I say, shall, whilst I live, be my chief endeavour to prevent; and for that reason I think it necessary to make a short recess, that all good men may recollect themselves against the next meeting, and consider whether the present posture of affairs will not rather require their applications to matters of Religion, and support against our only competitors at sea than to things of less importance; and in the mean while, I will not be wanting to let all my subjects see, that no care can be greater than my own, in the effectual suppressing of Popery; and it shall be your faults if, in your several countries, the laws be not effectually executed against the growth of it.—I will not be idle neither in some other things which may add to your satisfaction; and then I shall expect a suitable return from you. And so I shall give order to the Lord Chancellor to prorogue you to the 7th Jan. next."*

* "The Address (agreed to the day before) was to have been presented this afternoon; but the king disappointed all by coming unexpectedly to the house of lords, and ordering the commons to attend him. It happened that the Speaker and the usher both met at the door of the house of commons, and the Speaker being got within the house, some of the members suddenly shut the door, and cried out 'To the Chair! To the Chair!' while others cried, 'The Black Rod is at the door.' The Speaker was immediately hurried to the chair, and then it was moved, 1. 'That our Alliance with France was a Grievance. 2. That the Evil Counsellors about the king were a Grievance. And 3. That the duke of Lauderdale was a Grievance, and not fit to be trusted or employed in any office or place of trust. Upon which there was a general cry, 'To the Question! To the Question!' But the Black Rod knocking earnestly at the door, the Speaker leaped out of the chair, and the house rose in great confusion." Echard.

"What a dreadful picture have we here of the disorders of these times! Though there was sufficient cause for a close enquiry into the state of the nation, and a firm opposition to the favourite views of the court: and though the alliance with France, and the ruin of Holland, were equally inconsistent with the interest and safety of England; yet surely such violence and fury, without any previous remonstrances or endeavours to bring the court to reason, more resembled the turbulence of a faction, than the regularity and decorum of a Senate." Ralph.

Next day a sermon was to have been preached before them by Dr. Stillingfleet. And Oldmixon asserts, "That some time this session, a *wooden shoe*, such as the peasants wear in France, with the arms of England drawn at one end of it, and those of France at the other with these words in the interval, *Utrum horum mavis accipe*, was laid in the house, near the Speaker's Chair."

* "During the interval, Shaftsbury, whose intrigues with the mal-content party were now become notorious, was dismissed from the office of Chancellor; and the great seal was given to sir Heneage Finch, by the title of Lord Keeper. The Test had incapacitated Clifford, and the white staff was conferred on sir Tho. Osborne, soon after created earl of Danby, a minister of great abilities, who had risen by his parliamentary talents. Clifford retired into the country and soon after died." Hume.

According to archdeacon Echard, Shaftsbury was dismissed in the following remarkable manner: "The earl was sent for on Sunday morning to court, as was also sir Heneage Finch, attorney general, to whom the Seals were promised. As soon as the earl came, he retired with the king into the closet, while the prevailing party waited in triumph to see him return without the purse. His lordship being alone with the king, said, 'Sir, I know you 'intend to give the Seals to the attorney general; but I am sure your maj. never designed to dismiss me with contempt.' The king, who could not do an ill-natured thing, replied, 'Cod's-fish, my lord, I will not do it 'with any circumstance as may look like an 'affront.' 'Then Sir,' said the earl, 'I desire 'your maj. will permit me to carry the Seals 'before you to chapel, and send for them afterwards from my own house.' To which his maj. readily complied; and the earl entertained the king with news, and other diverting stories, till the very minute he was to go to chapel, purposely to amuse the courtiers and his successor, who he believed was upon the rack for fear he should prevail upon the king to change his mind. The king and the still chancellor came out of the closet talking together and smiling, and went together to chapel, which extremely surprized them all, who could have have no opportunity to inform themselves what was to be expected; and some ran immediately to tell the duke of York all their measures were broken, and the attorney general was said to be inconsolable. After sermon the earl went home with the Seals, and that evening the king gave them to the attorney-general, a man of great parts and abilities, with the title of Lord-Keeper. And thus ended the reign of the great earl of Shaftsbury, the prevalency of which had continued above

3 years, but the grandeur of it, in which he had no equal, lasted, a few days less than one year."

TWELFTH SESSION OF THE SECOND PARLIAMENT.

The King's Speech at the opening of the Session.] Jan. 7, 1673-4, Both houses met according to the prorogation; and the session was opened with the following Speech from the throne:

"My Lords and Gentlemen; When I parted with you last, it was but for a little time, and with a resolution of meeting suddenly again. That alone was enough to satisfy my friends that they need not fear, and my enemies that they could not hope for, a breach between us. I then told you, that the time of this short recess should be employed in doing such things as might add to your satisfaction: I hope I have done my part towards it; and if there be any thing else which you think wanting to secure Religion or Propriety, there is nothing which you shall reasonably propose, but I shall be ready to receive it. I do now expect you should do your parts too; for our enemies make vigorous preparations for war; and yet their chief hopes are to disunite us at home: it is their common discourse, and they reckon upon it as their best relief.—My Lords and Gentlemen; It is not possible for me to doubt your affections at any time, much less at such a time as this, when the evidences of your affection are become so necessary to us all. I desire you to consider that as the war cannot be well made without a Supply, so neither can a good peace be had without being in a posture of war. I am very far from being in love with war for war's sake; but, if I saw any likelihood of peace, without dishonour to myself and damage to you, I would soon embrace it: but no proposals of peace have yet been offered, which can be imagined with intent to conclude, but only to amuse. Therefore the way to a good peace is, to set out a good fleet; which we have time enough to do very effectually, if the Supply be not delayed: If, after this, a Peace should follow, yet the Supply would be well given; for whatever remains of it, I am willing it should be appropriated for building more ships.—To conclude: A speedy, a proportionable, and above all a chearful Aid, is now more necessary than ever; and I rely upon you for it. I lately put you in mind of my Debt to the Goldsmiths: I hope a fit time will come, to take that into consideration.—I cannot conclude without shewing the entire confidence I have in you. I know you have heard much of my alliance with France; and I believe it hath been very strangely misrepresented to you, as if there were certain secret Articles of dangerous consequence; but I will make no difficulty of letting the Treaties and all the Articles of them, without any the least reserve, to be seen by a small committee of both houses, who may report to you the true scope of them; and, I assure you, there is no other Treaty with France, either before or since, not already printed, which shall not be made known. And having thus freely trusted you, I do not doubt but you will have a care of my honour, and the good of the kingdom.—The rest I refer to my Lord Keeper."

The Lord Keeper Finch's Speech.] Then the Lord Keeper came from his place where he stood, and kneeling received his majesty's direction; and returning again to his said place, made this Speech:

"My lords; and you the knights, citizens, and burgesses of the house of commons; The king hath already in part told you what he hath done for you since the last recess, what he is still ready to do, and what it is he doth now expect from you; and this in terms so full and so obliging, so generous and so satisfactory, that he whose affections are not raised by that discourse, he who cannot acquiesce in the fulness of this assurance, he whose heart is not established by it in such a belief as may entirely dispose him to the service of the crown, will hardly be recovered to a better disposition by any other expedient: for indeed what better way can be found to undeceive those who have been abused? The king refers you to the time past, not to his promises, but to his performances; gives men leave to judge by what they see of what they hear, by what hath been done since the last session of what is offered you now, and what is likely to be done for the time to come. And doth not every man see that the king hath given new life and motion to such laws as were long dead, or fast asleep; that he hath once more repaired the hedge about our vineyard, and made it a fence indeed, against all those who are enemies to the planting of it, who would be glad to see it trodden down or rooted up, and study how to sap and undermine our very foundations?—Do we not see that the king hath made it his care and his business to do all that is possible to preserve us in our civil rights too; that he makes the laws of his kingdom the measures, not only of his power, but his prudence; that he suffers no man to be wiser than the law; that he thinks he cannot judge of the health or sickness of his state by any better indication than the current of his laws, and suffers nothing to remain that may in the least measure hinder justice from flowing in its due and proper channels?—A very few instances, of many that might be used, will serve to demonstrate it: If the Conviction of all Recusants, and bringing them under the Penal Laws, can suppress Popery; If, without staying for the forms of law in points of conviction, the present forbidding all papists, or reputed papists, to come to court, and the extending this prohibition to his royal palace at St. James's, be enough to discountenance them; If the not extending his prerogative beyond its due limits can secure your liberties; If his majesty's lessening and reducing all his land forces, and maintaining so few extraordinary, that they will scarce be enough to help to man his fleet this summer, can extinguish the fears of a Standing Army; If a rigorous and severe prosecution at law, of all the officers and soldiers in his majesty's ordinary guards, when they misbehave themselves towards the meanest subject, can secure your properties; If the abrogation of all the privileges from arrests, which were claimed by his majesty's servants extraordinary, who are very numerous, can prevent the delays and obstructions of justice: Then surely his maj. hath reason to believe that nothing is wanting which can lawfully be done, or modestly be wished, either for your satisfaction or your security.—These are not single and transient acts, but such acts as flow from habits; these are not leaves and blossoms, but true, solid, and lasting fruits. Long! long! may that royal tree live and flourish, upon which these fruits do grow!—And yet his majesty's Indulgence to you rests not here: he gives you leave to study and contrive your own assurance; and if you think you want any further security, if any thing have escaped his majesty's care, who meditates nothing more than your preservation, you see you have free leave to make any reasonable proposition, and his gracious promise that he will receive it.—This is a satisfaction equal to all your wishes: now, if ever, your joys are full. There wants no more to the improvement of this happiness, but the wisdom of the parliament to use these advantages with a due moderation.—If, therefore, upon enquiry, you shall think it needful to apply any other Remedies, it is extremely to be wished that those remedies may be few, and withal, that they may be gentle and easy too: for they that are sick perish as often by too many remedies, as by none at all; but none fall so fatally and so finally, as they who, being entered into some degrees of convalescence, resolve to recover in an instant, and had rather make some great effort, or try some bold experiment upon themselves, than observe the methods, or attend those gradual progressions, which are necessary to perfect that health, and compleat that recovery.—I must not omit one instance more of his majesty's care for you; and that is, the great industry and application of mind which his maj. hath used all along, in hopes to have obtained by this time, if it had been possible, an honourable and a just peace.—A very few words will serve to give you the whole deduction of it, from the first original to this present moment. Much time was spent in agreeing the place of Treaty, wherein the Dutch were gratified in their desires, and the city of Cologne is accepted for the place.—When his majesty's ambassadors arrived there, the very first meeting with those from the States General made it evident, that their plenipotentiaries came not with any intention to enter upon a serious Treaty, but only to draw the matter out into length, until their affairs might meet with a better and more pleasing conjuncture: for their very credentials or plenipotencies were so penned, that there were no less than four gross equivocations in the body of them; which was so manifest, and without all reply, that they were fain to send to their masters at the Hague, to get them amended.—But that which gave greatest offence of all, and was purposely done for that end, was the Preamble, wherein they take upon them to beg the question, to decide the justice of the cause, and to affirm such matters of fact, as they had reason to believe would never be admitted.—No arguments of our ambassadors, no instances of the mediators, though never so importunate, could prevail then, or yet can prevail, to have it altered.—The Treaty should naturally have stopt here, but that his maj. was resolved to give a beginning to it, and (which was all that could be done) suffered his ambassadors to enter upon it with a protestation. Our demands are no sooner given in, but presently two of the Dutch ambassadors go away to the Hague on pretence to consult their masters, where they staid a full month, without any kind of Answer given, or exceptions taken to his majesty's demands, or any the least step made in this negotiation.—When they came back, their Answer was a Remonstrance rather than an answer, and such a remonstrance as was fitter for a rupture than a treaty: there was scarce one period in it which did not rather give occasion of new offence, than any satisfaction for what was passed.—Their very conversation from that time forward wanted much of its former civility. They waited for the conclusion of a Treaty with Spain; wherein one Article was, That as soon as Spain had broke with France, they would presently break off the Treaty at Cologne. And now this Article is in effect performed; for two of their principal ambassadors are actually gone away from Cologne, as they long threatened they would do, leaving only two other for form sake, who in all probability either must not, or will not, conclude without their collengues.—His majesty, notwithstanding, hath not suffered himself to be diverted from using all the ways and means that were possible, to facilitate a peace. To this end, he directed his ambassadors, from time to time, to moderate their demands in such particulars as were capable of it; and wholly relaxes some points which were of highest importance to the Dutch to gain, and very considerable abatements of his majesty's just satisfaction; a condescension well received and esteemed by the mediators, though it have not yet found any suitable reception from the Dutch ministers, or their superior lords.—By this time they began to hope that the subjects of England would grow weary of the war, and that they should be able to profit themselves very much by our impatience. To increase this as much as was possible, they prepare a Letter, which they send by a trumpeter, sitting the parliament, or very near it, and cause it to be given out that nothing more could be desired than they had offered.—His maj. quickly made that Letter, and his Answer to it, public; and for that time defeated the design of this Paper Stratagem.—Their next recourse was, to such Proposals as they could procure the Spanish ambassador to deliver on their behalfs; wherein, besides the demands of Restitution of Prizes, which was wholly impracticable, there was a total omission of any regulation of trade in the Indies; no mention made of releasing his majesty's subjects at Surinam, where they remain in a state of bondage; no recompence offered in, or so much as leave asked for, the liberty of Fishing upon our coasts: and yet the Right of our sole Fishing is so clear, that we find in our ancient Rolls of Parliament, in the time of Rd. ii. a Tax laid upon all strangers who fish in our seas; and this not by way of custom when they come into our ports, but by way of Tribute for Fishing in our Seas; and this evidence of his majesty's Dominion within his own Seas hath been in all ages downward preserved in some measure, until the time of the late Usurper, who for private reasons first abandoned it.—As for that satisfaction in the Matter of the Flag which the Proposals mention, it is but reasonable to understand it in that sense wherein they sometimes used to express themselves at Cologne; that is, the thing shall be done, whole fleets shall strike their sails to single ships, and they shall do it out of his majesty's Seas too; but that of Right they ought so to do, will never be acknowledged.—So they desire to change the ancient inheritance of the crown into a new purchase, and to turn that purchase into a matter of civility, which they may equally pay to all crowned heads, and equally resume, according to their good pleasure and occasions.—Now, though these Proposals have been backed with some kind of intimation of a war with Spain in case of a refusal; yet his majesty, who knows the Articles of Peace between himself and that king, and his own care to preserve them, who knows the usefulness of his alliance to that king, and the many good offices he hath been always ready to do for him, and withal considers the great wisdom and prudence of that council, and how carefully they use to deliberate before they come to great and important resolutions, will not easily believe it possible for that king to proceed to such extremities; the rather, because the Dutch themselves have since departed from those very Proposals which they procured the Spanish ambassador so earnestly to recommend; for they afterward sent the ambassador a Reply to his majesty's Answer to their Letter, wherein they abate much of what the ambassador had offered, and seek to reduce things to the state they were in at Breda. So that it is hard to know by what kind of Proposals they intend to be bound; but it is most reasonable to believe they intend those made by themselves, rather than those made for them.—And yet this Reply, besides the disrespect it carried to Spain, whose Proposals it shrunk from, was so offensive to his majesty, that the ambassador, like a wise and great minister, that is, like himself, thought it became him to send it back again, without offering to present it.—Nevertheless this Paper hath since stolen into the press, and is printed at the Hague as a Letter delivered, and hath been sent hither under covers to several members of the house of commons, of that house of commons whom they libeled in the former war for their zeal, and now pretend to reverence for their deliberation; and all this in hopes you will not think them obstinate, who refuse to treat at the place of their own appointment, or to be well understood any where else.—How is it possible to understand these proceedings to be real, and with a true desire of peace? and if they should yet send during this session any new proposal (for who knows the designs of an enemy?), what form soever those overtures may be dressed in, we may justly suspect that their end is, if, they cannot divide us, at least to amuse us, and lessen our care in providing for the war. Perhaps it is more than an honourable war doth allow, to go about to raise sedition, though in the country of an enemy; but surely the artifice of appealing in a manner to the people, and making them the judges of peace and war, is a little too plain and open to take any effect here.—I have done with these few instances of his majesty's Care. Those of his Kindness are infinite; that which you have heard this morning is of a transcendent, and indeed a very surprising nature; it is an act of so entire a confidence on his majesty's part, that it can never be repaid by any other tribute on your part, but that of a true and humble affiance in him.—I must now proceed to put you in mind that there are some other things, which his maj. with great justice and great assurance doth expect from you again.—The first is, a speedy and a proportionable Supply; and this is of absolute necessity both for war and peace. His maj. is well assured, his fleet is in such a forwardness, that, if the Supply come in any reasonable time, you will find no time hath been lost in preparation; and it was no small matter to bring it to that pass, that we may be as forward as our enemies if we please, or very near it. If the Supply be at all delayed, it will have as ill effect almost as if it were denied; for we may chance to be found, like Archimedes, drawing lines in the dust, while the enemy is entering into our ports. And if the further progress of this fleet be stopt for want of your concurrence, make account all hopes of peace are stopt too; for, though the fruit of war be peace, yet it is such a fruit as we must not hope to gather without our arms in our hands.—It is not the way to have a brave peace, to shew ourselves weary of the war. Who ever trusted to the good-nature of their enemies? It is a vigorous assistance of the crown, that must make not only your arms considerable, but your treaties too.—On the other side, if the putting of yourselves into a good posture of war should produce a peace, as possibly it may do, yet you will have the best account of your Supply your hearts can wish; for his maj. is content it be appropriated to the building of more ships. Therefore, if the discourse upon this subject be a little more pressing than ordinary, you may be sure the occasion is so too.—There cannot be a higher gratification of your enemies, than to be backward in this point. The very opinion they have that you would be so, hath already done us so much harm, that perhaps it is one great cause of the continuance of the war. Had the enemy despaired of any division here, it is likely his proceedings had been more sincere, and our peace had not been so far off as now it seems to be.—There is one thing more the king hath mentioned, and only mentioned to you; that is the consideration of the Goldsmiths, which involves so many persons and families, that the concern is little less than national: it is an affair the king lays very much to heart, and hopes a proper time will come when a favourable regard may be had of it.—My Lords and Gentlemen; The king doth not only assure himself of your affections to him at this time; but, *from* such affections so known and so tried as yours, he doth yet expect far greater things than these.—He doth expect that you should do your endeavours to restore and improve the mutual confidence between him and his people, and that you should do it to such a degree, that it may recover its full strength, and quite extinguish all their Fears and Jealousies; for the king takes notice, that the malice of his enemies hath been very active, in sowing so many tares as are almost enough to spoil that harvest of love and duty which his maj. may justly expect to reap from the good seed which he himself had sown.—Among the many venomous insinuations which have been made use of, the Fears and Jealousies of Religion and Liberty are of the worst sort, and the most dangerous impressions. Certainly malice was never more busy than it hath been in these reports, and it hath been assisted by a great deal of invention. But it is to be hoped that no man's judgment or affections will be either misled or disturbed by such reports: for calumnies and slanders of this nature are like comets in the air; they may seem perhaps, especially to the fearful, to be ill prognostics, and the direst forerunners of mischief; but in themselves they are vain apparitions, and have no kind of solidity, no permanence or duration at all; for after a little while, the vapour spends itself, and then the base exhalation quickly falls back again into that earth from whence it came.—Religion and Liberty stand secured by the most sacred ties that are; nay, the king hath a greater interest in the preservation of both than you yourselves; for, as Religion, the Protestant religion, commands your indispensable obedience, so it is a just and lawful Liberty which sweetens that command, and endears it to you. Let other princes therefore glory in the most resigned obedience of their vassals. His maj. values himself upon the hearts and affections of his people, and thinks his throne, when seated there, better established than the most exalted sovereignty of those who tread upon the necks of them that rise up against them. Since the world stood, never any king had so great a cause to rest upon this security. They were your hearts that mourned in secret for the absence of the king. They were your hearts and affections to the king, which tired out all the late usurpations, by your invincible patience and fortitude. It was you that taught our English world to see and know, that no government could be settled here, but upon the true foundations of honour and allegiance. This, this alone, made way for all the happy changes which have followed. And yet posterity will have cause to doubt, which was the greater felicity of the two, that Providence which restored the crown, or that which sent us such a parliament to preserve it when it was restored. What may not the king now hope from you? what may not you assure yourselves from him? Can any thing be difficult to hearts so united, to interests so twisted and interwoven together, as the king's and yours are? Doubtless the king will surpass himself at this time, in endeavouring to procure the good of the kingdom. Do you but excel yourselves too, in the continued evidences of your affections; and then the glory of reviving this state will be entirely due to this session. Then they who wait for the languishing and the declination of the present government will be amazed to see so happy a crisis, so blest a revolution; and ages to come will find cause to celebrate your memories, as the truest physicians, the wisest counsellors, the noblest patriots, and the best session of the best parliament, that ever king or kingdom met with."

Address of both Houses for a Fast.] Notwithstanding these Speeches, both houses soon manifested their discontent at the continuance of the War with Holland, at the exorbitant power of France, the prevalence of Popish Counsels, &c. which they took care to signify, by joining in an Address to his majesty for a General Fast, using these very words: "We your majesty's most loyal and obedient subjects, &c. being passionately sensible of the calamitous condition of this kingdom, not only by reason of the war wherein it is at present involved, but many other intestine differences and divisions amongst us, which are chiefly occasioned by the undermining contrivances of Popish Recusants, whose numbers and insolencies are greatly of late increased, and whose restless practices threaten a subversion both of Church and State; all which our sins have justly deserved; and being now assembled in parliament as the great council of this your kingdom to consult on such means as we shall think fittest to redress the present evils, wherewith we are surrounded; we do, in the first place, humbly beseech your majesty, that, by your special command, one or more days be solemnly set apart, wherein both ourselves and this your kingdom may, by Fasting and Prayer, seek a reconciliation at the hands of Almighty God;

and with humble and penitent hearts beseech him to heal our breaches; to remove the evils we lie under; and to avert those miseries wherewith we are threatened; to continue the mercies we yet enjoy; and that he will be graciously pleased to bestow his abundant blessing upon your maj. and this present parliament, that all our councils and consultations may tend to his glory, and the honour, safety, and prosperity of your majesty, and all your people."—To which the king readily replied, and the 4th of Feb. was appointed.

Debate on pressing Men for Soldiers.] Jan. 22. Mr. *Sacheverell* complains of pressing for soldiers men of quality, against Magna Charta, and persons put to death against law: articles of war were complained of in the last session, to set up martial law: you have made particular laws about burning of houses, and yet by those articles they may burn houses and stacks of corn, and death to any soldier that shall disobey: soldiers sent beyond sea, which would stay here, for our safety: therefore it is to no end to proceed to particular business till these things are remedied: he has told you his thoughts, and hopes that other gentlemen will do the like.

Mr. Sec. *Coventry.* It will not be found out that men have been sent out of England against their wills: in queen Eliz.'s time, she succoured France, and sent men into Ireland, and no act of parliament for doing it then: never heard of any complaint of injuries done by the soldiers, but it was remedied; but the complaint should be, that such things have been done 'by authority:' avers that no such things have been done by the king's authority: the Articles were the same as in lord Essex's army, and lord Strafford's, the best of them extracted, and only to be executed when the army is beyond sea: when you find a fault, then lay it there: let not the disorders of particular men be thought general: the king has told you what he is willing to do, and pray proceed to the king's Speech.

Mr. *Sacheverell.* The Articles were published by the king's authority.

Mr. Sec. *Coventry.* The king's name may be used, but you will find them by prince Rupert's authority: they determine with his commission.

Sir *John Monson.* As to the pressing of men in queen Eliz.'s, and Edw. 6th's time, the 16th of Cha. 1. declared it illegal, and an act was then particular for the pressing of men for Ireland: it is said, we have had redress, when complained of, but we cannot but reflect, with what applause the Triple League was entertained, (that was too great a happiness to enjoy) but what we have had since, let every man judge: dates the design from the great persons going into France, and the consequence, shutting up the Exchequer, and the Declaration, which struck at all our laws, temporal and ecclesiastical, and all to countenance Popery: the parliament then was by the same hand prorogued, that we might not consider other things: the forces sent out of Ireland, little to be spared there; the joy of the Papists; but an army was the foundation of their joy, which they flocked to, and had commands in: we have had invasion of property; and till grievances are redressed, we cannot proceed any farther: hopes we shall have time to give those persons thanks who had a hand in the prorogation, declaration, &c. and hopes we shall be rid of popery and popish counsellors.

Mr. Sec. *Coventry* does say he did not exempt Grievances, when he moved for the consideration of the king's speech.

Mr. *Russel.* You have had so exact an account, that he has little farther to say of our deplorable condition: with an ill prince we must pray and suffer, but when God has blessed us with so good a king, and yet property, religion, and all invaded, we ought to find out the authors of our misfortunes, the ill ministers about the king, that prorogued the parliament; stopped the proceedings of the courts of justice; broke Articles, in that attack of the Smyrna fleet; shut up the Exchequer: have Pensions from France, and accuse us of being Pensioners to Holland: desires not their ruin but the security of our lives and fortunes for the future.

Debate on Mr. Mallet's reading his Speech.] Mr. Mallet read a long speech.

Sir *Cha. Harbord* takes him down to order. The precedent of reading a speech is dangerous: the attorney, now Lord Keeper, reprehended him once only for making use of heads in a paper; pray never let speeches be read in parliament.

Sir *Tho. Lee.* Mallet was irregularly interrupted: if his memory be not so good as others, he may be indulged to make use of his paper, and would have people write what they intend to speak.

Mr. *Garroway.* It may be Mr. Mallet cannot contract his notions as other men can do, and he would have him read his speech: you may but wink and it is the same thing.

Sir *Rob. Howard.* Reading all and reading some is the same thing, and he believes he has almost done, as he observes, by the paper in his hand.

Sir *Wm. Lewis.* The best reason he has yet heard for his going on, is 'that he has almost done:' it may be without doors ill reported, not to let him make an end; though he is not for reading of entire speeches, yet short notes are always commendable; he may go on for this time, but hopes you will not admit it for the future.

Debate on Grievances.] Col. *Birch.* Is glad to see how merrily we begin, and hopes we shall continue so; it is the great part of an orator to persuade, but hopes, as paper speeches may be laid aside here, they may also be in other places (the pulpits): we have leave to debate our own security by the king's and the lord keeper's speech, and therefore will open our present condition; doubts not but the king will at last find, that they who advise him to follow the parliament's counsel are his best subjects; the Grievances, as to law, have been opened very well, and the remedy, in some part; but thinks all is vain, if, by any means, we are incited to carry on this league with France, and war with Holland; and because of the second article of the treaty with France, 'the setting up the Catholic religion in every conquered town in Holland,' if we must go on in that union, leaves it to every man's conscience in the consequence: would not do by day, what he shall be ashamed of at night, that his conscience shall give him the lie: how we entered into this war he remembers: the Triple Alliance we thanked the king heartily for; how we came out of it, the Instructions will give you an account: the greatest princes have called parliaments to advise in peace and war; but he is still doubting that this parliament was prorogued by strong persuasion: what is under the Great Seal is a man's freehold. We have not had a smile, since the French alliance began, and the second article of that alliance is to set up the Pope; and now we are invited to carry on that war, he cannot consent to it: the consequence would have been, if the French king had continued in his greatness by conquests, we had not been doing here what we do now: either France or Holland must be bigger: if France, we may purchase what we fear; if Holland, they may be too big to grant: would be far from doing any thing derogatory to the king; but when the League is not honourable nor safe for the king, he cannot find arguments to part with our Money for the support of it.

Mr. Sec. *Coventry* would know what it is he should speak to; several things relating to the war [then he paused—was bid go on.] As to the business of the war, he was ordered to tell Sweden, where he was ambassador, 'that if the king of France invaded any of the Spanish dominions, our king would defend the Triple League: the proposition was, 'in every town the French should have rendered to them, they should have a Papist Church as we would have a Protestant.' Every man must answer in his turn for his actions, as he must do for his; but would not give an opinion to continue a war against the genius of the nation: but you have no peace, nor likelihood of any, but what must come from the conduct of this house, which a good Vote will certainly do, he believes: tell the king your Grievances, but so supply him that the navy may go on, which, you know, needs it: and if you put the king into these straits and desperation, what will be the consequence? Now for the Declaration against the French Treaty; being so deserted, Holland will have no need of you. Can any man have the impudence to say, that because you have a treaty with France, you are obliged to fight to the last man? Secure things in the treaty how you please, that the money may not be attached, and that it may be for shipping (which, under favour, the navy must have): moves that you will propose Grievances, and in the mean time that the kingdom may be secured.

Mr. *Garroway.* Secretary Coventry desires 'that you would not press the king:' wonders at it: when we were prorogued two months, those that advised it 'pressed the king,' and we must postpone all considerations, without consideration of Religion, Property, or Trade: nothing, but we must carry on a war we know not how long; let those good counsellors that advised it look after it: did our ambassadors give Holland no security by the Triple League and Breda, that we would not fall on them? We are told, 'that our war will ruin our plantations;' since March last we have laid out 300,000*l.* in freight to strangers; our corn vessels, passing from port to port, taken; some of our great ships swept away by the Dutch; our men pressed for sea and land; the gentleman said, the last session 'he would warrant a peace with a vote for money,' but now he says otherwise: Londoners are at a tax upon the collier, and in the country we pay five and six pounds per chaldron: the ploughman finds his wants: it is 300,000*l.* tax to London by proportion, and this is one of the benefits you have by the war, and the effects are upon the counties about London, decay of manufacture! War is a subtle thing; lose a correspondence in trade, and you know not how to get it again; the making bays, a great trade, you have lost by this war; if France can supply Spain with commodities, as they left you in the war so they will do in trade; we employ all foreigners for shipping, and if the war continues, your Act of Navigation will will be of no use; pressing of seamen! By the last fatal war you saw that the courage of your nation, when deserted by the French, brought you off; the French may serve you so by land; a war at sea will never make an end of the war; grass grew in Middleburgh streets, now grown rich by depredations this war; is one of those that are for peace, and hopes it is no crime to offer things with modesty; would not depend upon the Spanish ambassador, but upon a war upon the English interest, and never saw want of money or help; cleanse the house at home; know those that have intrigued you; he would not sweep away gentlemen by general Votes; would reach them according to law, and go upon things: the Keeper says in his speech, 'the fleet is in good readiness;' money remains not paid in of the last tax, prizes, and the advance upon the excise farm; therefore would have full enquiry into the state of the kingdom, but not like empirics, to give a catholicon for all diseases; but let gentlemen propose the State of Affairs, and go upon that.

Sir *Tho. Clarges.* If we had gone on, the last prorogation, things might not have been at this pass; but as those evil Counsellors about the king persuaded him then, they do still exasperate him, that our best counsels will be perverted; this is the great grievance: if it be apparent that any sort of men do design the ruin of the kingdom, so as to prostitute the king's word; and if any new treason be enacted, would have that made one: it is of consequence never to be recovered: no example that ever any war of this nature began without parliament. Instances Edw. i, Edw. iii, and Hen. v, the miracle of men, that (unless our king) never any of more honour and gallantry since Julius Cæsar's time. Hen. viii. as ambitious, perhaps, as any, young, and though his coffers were full, advised, in the 3d year of his reign, with his parliament, about making of war: the best thing to rivet the king and his people, is mutual confidence. 43 Edw. iii, when he was to make peace with Scotland with David Bruce, he advised with his parliament: Rd. ii. would not make peace without subjecting his articles to the parliament: hopes, if so now, we shall do it for the king's honour. We may date a great deal of our misfortunes from the Million Act: submits to all gentlemens opinions here, the universal hatred against this French alliance: we were so jealous formerly of our ports, that no foreigners scarce with a packet-boat were suffered to enter them without leave, but now whole shoals of them: but it occurs to him, that the alliance with France is broken; all alliances are understood as to circumstances of things when made; it is strange that we should consent to the 'Popish Article:' moves to adjourn the house till tomorrow, that we may enumerate our Grievances before we enter upon the debate of Supply: would have the Test law against Popery revived, and some things added to it, and all to take it that are in the king's counsels, and something for the security of the king's person; and would have Religion, after the king's death, secured, and the Statute of Suggestions, for men to undergo a penalty if they make not accusations out; but the first thing to enter upon, would have 'the Counsellors;' we have always gracious Answers from the king, but they are still intercepted: Proclamation against papists, and yet priests are walking in Whitehall in defiance of it; Popish commanders at the head of companies; no minister sent with our companies into France to comfort the sick, and to do other spiritual offices, but exposed to Popery: one man has had 7 pardons for treason and murder; shall we not put such out of the reach of pardon? the general pardon would not suffice, but special ones must be obtained since that pardon: would go first upon 'evil Counsellors.'

Lord *Cavendish.* When we consider the prorogation, and the other misfortunes of the nation, fears we shall have the same advice as long as such 'Counsellors' are about the king: moves in the first place, that we proceed to secure the nation by removing them.

Sir *John Monson.* When 'Counsellors' have pardons in their pockets, from murder to petty larceny, what security can the kingdom have? Therefore agrees with the motions made before.

Sir *Cha. Wheeler,* should be glad that the king might have some prospect, through this vote, that, when our Grievances are redressed, we may take his Supply into consideration: we carry on all things for the interest of the nation, and assist him upon the public interest of the nation, and no farther.

Sir *Rob. Howard* was sorry for the prorogation when it was, but as the king has now invited and trusted you, make him not jealous of us: the eyes of all the world are upon us now, and should we not do things as amicably as possible, the censures of the people will lie as heavy upon us, as in any other thing: winds up all in this motion, 'To order an Address to the king to give him thanks for his trust and invitation, and to tell him there remains something as to our 'security:' no doubt we want many things, but shall we slip by the king in his invitations? Knows it not in your hearts, and if 'Evil Counsellors' be one thing, and all other things are considered one by one, then you are in a method.

Sir *Tho. Lee.* The expression of Howard's of 'passing by the king,' is harsh; the war so long debated is not a 'passing by the king.'

Mr. *Jones,* would always be tender in reflective expressions; he has neither preparation, nor intention, to offer Grievances, but from the greatness of the debate, and the place he serves for, (London) something is expected he should say about their Grievances; he has sufficiently expressed his loyalty in the worst times, but being not a man of trade, knows no more than those that walk the streets speak of: the imposition upon Coals is hard upon the rich, but destructive to the poor: thousands had died for the want of them, but for the favourableness of the weather: he has known London these 45 years, and never knew that impudence in meetings that the Papists have now; they are so in most parts about; a great aggravation of their insolence and increase, that they attempt meeting where it never was: protections from the lords house, and this, ruin trade, together with shutting up the Exchequer; how can we be secure, that the Exchequer be not stopped to-morrow again? If ruin were at the door, and the nation ready to sink, who will send 100*l.* thither? Still the Goldsmiths are postponed; was it their personal concern, would not regard it, but thousands are concerned in it.

The Question being propounded, That the Thanks of the house be returned to his majesty, for his gracious Speech; and the question being put, That the house do now proceed in the debate of that question, it passed in the affirmative, 191 to 139.

Resolved. "1. That this house will proceed, in the first place, to have Grievances effectually redressed, the Protestant Religion, Liberties, and Properties, effectually secured, to suppress Popery, and to remove persons, and Counsellors, popishly affected, or otherwise obnoxious, or dangerous, to the government." 2. "That the humble and hearty Thanks of this house be returned to his majesty for his gracious Promises and Assurances in his last Speech, and for those Acts which he has done since the last prorogation, towards the suppressing and discountenancing of Popery; and that he would please to give order for the Militia of London, Westminster, and Middlesex, to be ready at an hour's warning, and the other Militia of the kingdom at a day's warning, for the suppressing any tumultuous meeting of Papists, or other malecontent persons whatsoever; and that the house will go with this Address to his majesty in a body."

PROCEEDINGS AGAINST THE DUKE OF LAUDERDALE.

Jan. 13. Mr. *Stockdale*. Many Grievances have been represented; the way is now, how you will redress your grievances? the last session produced many good votes as to that, but we were prorogued; and to the intent that that may not happen again, consider that the same Counsellors are interposing, and interpreting our intentions may procure the same prorogation; therefore moves to begin with the last part of the vote first, viz. 'Evil Counsellors.' You cannot have Grievances effectually redressed, without removing those that have advised these things, and, when that is done, he perhaps will name one.

Sir *Rob. Thomas*. We have a great many Grievances; hazard of Religion, Counsellors advising the king to take away religion and properties: must name one; (by the bye, the Black Rod being called in by you, Mr. Speaker, the last session, before he knocked *, he could not do it then) a person that has contributed as much to our misfortunes as any man; the duke of Lauderdale—You will have proofs of his advice by four of your members; viz. '† Your majesty is bound in honour to justify your Edicts: I wonder at the confidence of any person to deny your majesty's Edicts, and those persons that do, I think, deserve to be most severely punished ‡.' The act of the Militia in Scotland, 'which forces are to be in a readiness to be called to march into England or Ireland, upon any service where the honour, authority, or greatness of the king shall be concerned.' Other gentlemen know more: he has great forces in readiness and pay, and for no other end, he believes, than to awe us.

Sir *Nich. Carew*. We should never have Grievances, but by such 'Counsellors:' the duke is at the head of a great army in Scotland; desires that we may move the king, that he may keep there and return no more into England.

Sir *Tho. Littleton*. The words are ready, and desires you will order the gentlemen that heard them, to declare them.

Sir *Rob. Thomas* names sir Scroope Howe,* Mr. Man, and Mr. Rob. Pierpoint †, who heard the words, and lord St. John.

Lord *St. John*. The last session, Feb. he was called to do it, but then refused, because there was a dispute then betwixt the duke of Lauderdale and himself; Mr. Howe, then sick, being concerned for Mr. Whalley, desired him to go hear the business at the Council, where Mr. Whalley (a justice of peace in Nottinghamshire) was summoned, who had committed a preacher, contrary to the Declaration. Whalley was to answer the contempt, the parson had no licence to preach, but entry was made of it in the Secretary's Book; a law bound Whalley, and a Declaration did not bind him. Lauderdale then spoke the words mentioned by sir Rob. Thomas, that he wondered at the words and said, 'Lauderdale may be questioned in parliament.' Some members being present, Lauderdale spoke as before, none else of the Council spoke, and all were bid to withdraw.

Sir Scroope Howe averred the words as before; Mr. Pierpoint, and Mr. Man likewise.

Sir *Tho. Littleton*. Now you are possessed of this, he shall offer his sense: the last session, we were cut off in the beginning: in Scotland, an army is raised by this great duke; though by act of parliament, yet his power is great, and the army under his power: it is in vain to act here, without converting our thoughts to Scotland. Pray God! this be not elsewhere: a man, so principled and arbitrary! You had need look about you; needs say nothing to aggravate, the bare thing aggravates itself: a cloud hangs over us, and it is high time it was scattered; it has made Counsellors in England so much the bolder: moves 'to address the king to exclude the duke of Lauderdale from his Counsels in England:' keep him from counsels here, and you may shake his authority in Scotland; he is in all respects a commoner ‡, and so we cannot clash with the lords in point of trial: there are 20,000 foot, and 2000 horse, ready in Scotland, and no colour for it: a man of such principles is not fit to be trusted with such an army, nor with

* See p. 609.

† The expressions mentioned in the Journal are, "Your majesty's Edicts ought to be obeyed; for your majesty's Edicts are equal with the laws, and ought to be observed in the first place."

‡ "A gentleman, there present, informed me, that the king should say to Mr. Penyston Whalley (the person then before the council) 'I wonder that you should withstand my Declaration. I would have you know, that I will be obeyed according to my interpretation of the law, and not yours; and if you will not I shall put in those that will.'" Grey.

* "Created lord viscount Howe in 1701. In 1688 the earl of Devonshire concerted with him the means for inviting the prince of Orange into England." Kennet's Memoirs of the family of Cavendish. He died in 1711.

† Nephew to the Marquis of Dorchester.

‡ The Duke was at this time only a Peer of Scotland. But in June following he was created an English peer, by the title of earl of Guilford.

our counsels, and, without any more ceremony, would address the king, as he is a commoner.

Sir *Ch. Harbord* has a double charge against him, that of the army in Scotland, and his words at the Council here. You may miss of trial, but an Act may reach him.

Mr. *Dalmahoy* has heard the duke of Lauderdale deny the words: he was not in Scotland when the Act about the Militia was made: he knows not who was then commissioner.

Mr. *Powle* supposes that every man is sensible of a pernicious design to alter the government, and these Counsellors have brought us to the brink of destruction: we have a gracious prince, but the great design was, first to abuse the king, and then to oppress the people, fearing his good disposition to us: the Triple League was made to check a great prince: to ruin the Protestant religion was the design, and, without Money, that was not to be carried on, which money was given for the maintaining the Triple Alliance; and then more money was got, by stopping the Exchequer, to the undoing of many hundreds of persons—Then a Declaration for the ease of tender consciences, and, under pretence of Toleration, suspending by it all ecclesiastical laws, and, in consequence, laying all laws aside: upon the declaration of war against Holland, armies were raised, and popish officers at the head of them, and in places of civil authorities, honours, and dignities; then Popish officers are sent over into Ireland, Papists put into trust and office there; then in Scotland, an army is raised to march into England, &c. or for any other cause wherein 'the king's honour or greatness may be concerned;' but the greatness of the king consists in governing a free people: the parliament supplied and brought him from banishment, and, because the king would hearken to their advice, they must be prorogued, the juncture of their time not being fit for the fleet against Holland; they suppose we would give, and, if not, the necessity must justify raising of money: what benefit had we but fruitless battles at sea, and engaging us, by the French, with his allies? The king was persuaded that the parliament would not assist his interest, but doubts not but time will demonstrate the contrary: when we would have reached these men, we were prorogued, and now there is a necessity of giving money: the king's credit lost, the people poor, jealousies great, and all might have been remedied by our meeting—Lauderdale asserted 'Edicts superior to law,' and it was spoken in the presence of the king and council; no greater argument, though some, he doubts not, have done it privately, but he publicly: Hamilton's book asserts the king's authority of raising Money without Parliament, and it was countenanced by Lauderdale in 1667. When lord Rothes was commissioner, then was the foundation of this army, but it came not to maturity till 1669, when Lauderdale was commissioner; it was then kept on foot, and boasted of: it is not unknown at what vast greatness this person has lived, thereby bringing the king into necessity, and disobliging the house, that we should not supply: Lauderdale sued out the king's pardon; a new trick our great men have gotten, fearing our enquiry, and would arm themselves against us with the king's pardon; let this be considered and weighed well: less crimes than these have brought men to the scaffold, but the temper of this house is not desirous of blood. The 5th Rd. ii. counsellors were removed without cause; the people only spoke ill of them. 11 Rd. ii. the duke of Ireland, and sir John Crosby were impeached; the people spoke ill of them. 20 Hen. vi. the lord Dudley, for the same cause: It may be the case of peers of England, and this upon no other article but merely the people speaking ill of them. 3d Ch. i. remonstrance against the duke of Bucks, bishop Neale, and abp. Laud, to be removed, as evil counsellors: moves, "That this great person, the duke of Lauderdale, may for ever be removed from the king's presence."

Mr. Sec. *Coventry*. To condemn a man, without hearing, he never knew the precedent before in this house.

Mr. *Stockdale*. If for taking away blood, witnesses must be sworn; but to remove this man you have testimony sufficient to ground an Address to the king; so notorious a man!

Sir *Rob. Carr*. A person was accused, and you gave a day: moves to consider of it.

Col. *Birch*. It is true, there was a person had a day, but he had no pardon, and he would have Lauderdale sent where 'Edicts' are in fashion.

Sir *John Duncombe*. It is hard to condemn a man without being heard; 'removed from the king's presence' is as hard a judgment as a man can have: thinks it worthy consideration to give him a day.

Sir *John Trevor*. If you proceed merely to suspend him from the king's 'Counsels,' you may do it, but if from the king's 'presence' where no manner of proof is taken, you ought to give him a day: by way of confiscation, or attainder, you give time, but as to 'removal from counsels,' you need give none.

Mr. *Howe*. He was the most active person to bring the late king to his murder: he was solicitor from Scotland to bring the late king to the block, and to destroy this king by giving ill advice to him.

Mr. *Garroway* has often heard that this man brought the Declaration from Scotland to bring the late king to the block, and those people had a horror for the fact: would have him come and answer it here, and all that are concerned with him: he has heard of one Murray, kept in the Tower, by the instigation of Lauderdale, for complaining against him; these are violences, when no writs of Habeas Corpus can be had; and would send to the Gatehouse, where he now stands committed, for the Mittimus: you will find it of his own making, and illegal: agrees to the Address for removing him;' and would have a Bill to make it treason if ever he return hither again.

Mr. Sec. *Coventry.* If he be guilty of this horrid crime alleged, will not defend him; neither will he condemn him without proof.

Sir *John Birkenhead.* The duke of Ireland, Oxford, and Somerset, had a day assigned them—No man has been banished the king's presence on this formality, though you cannot have greater evidence; it may be he may confess it: many things are law in Scotland, and not so here; would not have a precedent to reach every body: assign him a day, and you will tread more safely, and do him right, and no man wrong.

Sir *Tho. Littleton,* has heard a great man in the Rump, and a counsellor then, say, 'That Lauderdale did solicit that bloody Kirk-Declaration against the king;' does not name the person, because desired not do it: would have him removed from the king's person and counsels for ever. This thing is not so hard, he at a great distance, and great affairs in Scotland to attend, and so he may excuse himself from coming, and perhaps when come we may not be sitting, and if he will come, at any time, he may be tried by parliament.

Col. *Sandys.* Since he has heard that Lauderdale had some part in the king's murder, that has raised him; and would have him as much sequestered from the world, as from the King, and would have 'a Bill of Attainder against him.'

Mr. *Sacheverell* fears that this lord has not lost his old evil principles, but improved them; the Scotch Act of Militia plainly shows it: It puts the king in power plainly to alter any thing in Church or State, and so, by this army, Popery may be set up: not content to keep their law in Scotland, but printed here by authority: it was done this time twelvemonth, when the question was, whether all your laws must be set aside; and therefore is for secluding him for ever from the king's presence, and an Act of banishment.

Col. *Strangways* would have the words 'obnoxious and dangerous' retained in the Vote: our Saviour pardoned them that persecuted him, but where a man, by after-actions, has done ill, his righteousness shall be forgotten, when transgressing *de novo:* he abhors the crime; but consider your case; 'sequestering him from the king's presence and the kingdom:' common fame from this house is a greater ground for accusation than thought to be.

Sir *R. Temple* does not remember that, by any of the precedents, men were sent for, and time given them to answer; this vote is with that moderation, 'to remove' only: would add something, that it may have more strength, viz 'as a man found by this house to be dangerous.' Has heard of his being no less arbitrary in Scotland than here; to have made himself a perpetual commissioner there.

Sir *John Monson* hears it said, 'that every subject has right to come into the king's presence;' therefore to prevent that, when we are up, would have a Bill, as well as an Address now.

Sir *Eliab Harvey* would have a Bill ordered to make it treason for him to return to England.

Mr. *Waller* thinks as bad of this case as any man here: If so much had been against lord Strafford, would not have then been against his Impeachment.

Sir *Wm. Coventry.* The bill as proposed, is contradictory to what you have spoken of 'removing him from the king's presence.' The king may remove him, by his own power, 'from his presence,' at the request of any private man, and when it is done, it is well done: every subject has a right of petitioning the king, though he be not of his bed-chamber or council; but it is not so easy a thing to exclude any man out 'of the kingdom.' To make a precedent to exclude a man 'the kingdom,' without hearing him, cannot agree to it.

Mr. *Boscawen* desires that lord Clarendon's Bill of banishment may not be a precedent: that was done somewhat hastily.

Sir *Tho. Clarges* would have a Bill 'to forbid him coming within 12 miles of the court, wherever the king shall be:' will consent to that, and no farther.

Resolved nem. con. "That an Address be presented to his majesty to remove the duke of Lauderdale from all his employments, and from his presence and councils, for ever; being a person obnoxious and dangerous to the government."

PROCEEDINGS AGAINST THE DUKE OF BUCKINGHAM.

A Letter being brought in to the Speaker, signed "Buckingham," on his offering to read it,

Mr. *Stockdale* said, He would not have the Letter now read, he having something to offer against the duke of Buckingham.* Whatever

* "The duke of Buckingham was a man of a noble presence. He had a great liveliness of wit, and a peculiar faculty of turning all things into ridicule with bold figures and natural descriptions. He had no sort of literature; only he was drawn into chemistry; and for some years he thought he was very near finding the Philosopher's Stone. He had no principles of religion, virtue, or friendship; pleasure, frolic, or extravagant diversion, was all that he laid to heart. He was true to nothing, for he was not true to himself. He had no steadiness, nor conduct. He could never fix his thoughts, nor govern his estate, though then the greatest in England. He was bred about the king, and for many years he had a great ascendant over him; but he spoke of him to all persons with that contempt, that at last he drew a lasting disgrace upon himself; and he at length ruined both body and mind, fortune and reputation, equally. The madness of vice appeared in his person in many instances; since at last he became contemptible and poor, sickly, and sunk in his parts, as well as in all other respects; so that his conversation was as much avoided as ever it had been courted. The

that Letter contains, he has a charge against the person, of as high a nature as the Letter can be: says, it is irregular for the Speaker to bring us a new business; the Letter—He was interrupted by

Sir *Ch. Wheeler.* To Order of proceedings, in reference to your Vote, after what manner! Would have some previous consideration, that one man may not prevent another.

Mr. *Stockdale.* Would have all men concerned, named; and you are possessed of one against whom he has a charge, the duke of Buckingham; that, if encouraging or practising, and, he supposes, establishing Popery; if taking money from the subject, and breaking the Triple Alliance, and engaging us in this French alliance be a Charge, he has a Charge against the duke of Buckingham: the proofs are not so ready as the last, but the particulars will all be proved: offers not an Impeachment: though the crimes may be proved, impeachments take up a long time; it may be longer than we have to sit: his own letters show corresponding with Peter Talbot, the pretended archbishop. When Ireland was in great danger by Popery, he advised the army to be drawn out of that kingdom, and headed his own regiment with Popish officers. At Knaresborough, Whitsuntide last (the Standing Army was then forming) this duke came into Yorkshire to raise men; a poor man, being pressed, came to the overseers of the poor, and told them, 'You must provide for my wife and children, I am pressed away and cannot maintain them.' The duke sent for the overseer, and beat him for not doing it, and sent a warrant to the marshal of the West Riding of Yorkshire, to keep him, till farther order from him; the man applied to the duke, and, after 3 days imprisonment, was delivered by the marshal (Wainman) who demanded 30*l.* fees, and got 5*l.* for three days: this was done, when there was a prospect of arbitrary power, and this was the first action of martial law, committed by a martial-man. The next is the duke's taking of money, 2*s.* 6*d.* upon every horse exported at Dover, by virtue of his place of Master of the Horse, against law: breaking of the Triple Alliance: the duke was sent into France, and what treaty he made there we know by the effect; the Triple Alliance broken: lord Bellasis was sent to Dunkirk, and the duke, though he had no business, yet would go to see the king of France, and has heard what presents he had there, and believes it will be proved: his endeavours to take away the affections of the king's good subjects, by saying, 'that the king was an arrant knave, and unfit to govern;' Dr. Williams can prove it: he has defrauded the king's servants of their wages, so disadvantageous to his service; this is public: now, there is a Petition against him in the house of lords of a strange nature; killing the earl of Shrewsbury,* and living scandalously with his widow. Not only that, but he has attempted a horrid sin not to be named; not to be named at Rome, where their other practices are horrid: moves, 'That a person so dangerous to the government, and of so ill a life and conversation, may be removed from the king's presence and from all his employments; and for 'an Act of Banishment' against him, as against the duke of Lauderdale.

Sir *John Coventry.* This man has made it his business to sow dissension betwixt the king and this house, but he is not a man to put things in execution when much danger is in the case: when the king had his ministers in France, the duke of B. put many of his servants, incognito, to treat with the ministers of that state, Papists and persons ill affected to our government: it is a sad condition we are in, to have a man so near the king's person that contemns his person: this duke has given night and lanthorn counsels, not to be owned by the rest of the counsellors. He corresponds with a traytor, Peter Talbot; the letter was burned in the king's bed-chamber, and part remains: some say the duke is not ashamed of that profession; it is known to you all, that these people have been protected by him: it may be said, that the officers of his regiment are Protestants, but we may thank the commons of England for it: if these things be proved, he desires the duke may be removed from the king's person for ever.

Mr. *Howe.* Besides all this, when the king was at Windsor, because he would not stay so long as the duke would have him,† he took the bridle from the king's horse, to the great danger of the king's person, and the duke was then Master of his Horse.

Sir *Winston Churchill.* He that would answer this charge of the duke's may do himself

main blame of the king's ill principles, and bad morals, was owing to the duke of Buckingham." Burnet.

Dryden's character of him (under that of Zimri) in his Absalom and Achitophel, and Pope's description of the last scene of his life, which was closed at an alehouse at Helmsley in Yorkshire, in the year 1687, are well known and justly admired.

* This was in a duel, March 16, 1667. "The Countess is said to have held the duke's horse, disguised like a page, during the combat; to reward his prowess in which, she went to bed to him in the shirt stained with her husband's blood. The loves of this tender pair are recorded by Pope,

> Gallant and gay in Clifden's proud Alcove,
> The Bower of wanton Shrewsbury and Love.

Walpole's Noble Authors, vol. ii. p. 82, 3.

Of this intrigue, Marvell, in one of his Letters, makes the following mention: "Buckingham runs out of all with Lady Shrewsbury; by whom he believes he had a son, to whom the king stood godfather: it died young, earl of Coventry."

† It was whispered "at a drinking-bout." Grey.

more wrong than the duke has. Wishes the particulars as easily proved as charged: the business of Windsor he knows: the duke is not far from you, and supposes, if the letter be not of importance, the duke has forfeited his understanding, as the charge makes him forfeit his reputation: men of his quality will not inform you of trifles: the letter may be of concernment; it may discover something you know not (as that in the lords house about a plot) therefore would read it.

Lord *Cavendish*. Should the artifice of the man put it out of our power to proceed, it would be of ill consequence: would have him removed from offices and councils about the king and suspended his presence till farther proceeded against.

Sir *Tho. Clarges* would first put the question for 'the Address,' and then read the letter. No great need of particular proof; but all you desire, is, that he may not be near the king's person to pursue these dangerous counsels: in Scotland, did he not correspond with Argyle and ransack the king's close-stool for papers? There were shrewd suspicions of him in the rebellion in the north, and soon after he got his pardon. Is it no crime to kill the husband, and prostitute the wife? He accuses him not, for it may be pardoned; but for us to countenance such things, will bring God's judgments upon us: after so great an accusation, to come so familiarly amongst the lords, his judges, and to do his offices about the king, argues a strange boldness: there are seven persons that have had five Pardons since the Restoration of the king; two by act of parliament, and three under the great seal, for murder, treason, &c. so that you can never lay hold of him: since March last he has got another Pardon, and, as the docket says, 'for all treasons, insurrections, murders, misprisions, manslaughters, &c. committed or done before the 14th of Nov. last.' This is in some sort a confession of the guilt of so many crimes as are enumerated in the pardon: you must give it, by Vote, for the safety of witnesses, and he to be 'removed from the king's person.' Men are awed; and at the reading of the Petition against him, in the house of lords, there was a great silence: he has not common bowels of mercy; he beat an old gentleman for desiring him not to ride over his corn, till the blood ran down his hoary head. At Barnet he beat a poor soldier in bonds about the unfortunate killing lady Shrewsbury's coachman: moves as before.

Sir *Edm. Jennings*. The Letter may be of consequence. The paper of discovery was read in the lords house, and he would have the duke's Letter read.—The duke's Letter was then read, as follows:

'Mr. Speaker; I desire you to do me the 'favour to get leave of the hon. house of com'mons, that I may inform them, in person, of 'some truths relating to the public; by which 'you will much oblige, &c. BUCKINGHAM. 'Jan. 13, 1673.'

Mr. *Sacheverell*. You ought to hear the Duke, because the matter, he pretends, is public, and you may be concerned.

Mr. *Garroway* hopes you will do justice to all men. If you pass your vote against him, of what validity will any thing be that he can say? Moves that that right may be done to the duke, which you will not deny to the meanest commoner: lord chief justice Keeling, and the earl of Bristol, had a chair set for them: you heard them speak, and Bristol cleared your member, sir Rd. Temple*: would now hear the duke.

Sir *Tho. Clarges*. This man has done his impieties in the face of the sun; he prevented our meeting in Oct. last. Has he not perverted the king's word? Would only now have him removed from the king's council. My lord of Bristol's coming hither was a voluntary desire, and nothing against him here: is not against his coming in, but would first remove him from the king's person.

Col. *Birch*. Such things as the duke has done, cannot be without company: would have him come in, and hear him what he can say.

Mr. *Sawyer*. Your vote may discourage him, that he may say little to you, and possibly he may reveal something in compensation, by way of discovery: would hear him.

Col. *Strangways*. Hear him what he can say: some vices of the man may not take away a man's testimony.

The Duke of Buckingham was ordered to be called in,† and a chair was set for him on the left hand of the bar, the serjeant standing with his mace on his right hand. Then the duke saluted the house round.

Ordered, "That the Speaker ask him, Whether he owned the Letter he sent him, and what he has to communicate to the house, of concernment?"

The Duke sat a short space, covered; then the Speaker asked him, &c. and showed him the Letter, which the Duke owned. The Speaker then said, "The house is ready to hear what your grace has to say, relating to the public service."

The Duke's Speech to the House of Commons.] The Duke, standing, then said, "I have written something," [fumbling a Paper in his hand] "but will trust to my own present thoughts. I give this hon. house humble thanks for the honour done me, in admitting me to come and speak here. I have always made it my business to get the good opinion of this house; I desire that my actions may be examined, and I will stand, or fall, by the censure and judgment of this house: the business against me, I understand, is the breaking of the Triple Alliance; I had as great a hand in making it as

* See p. 270.

† Burnet says, "That the Duke, the first day of his being before the house, fell into such a disorder, that he pretended he was taken ill, and desired to be admitted again. But that next day he was more composed."

any man: my going to Holland was to hinder De Witt's conjunction with France, and I did no ill service in it, and the more the thing is examined, the more my innocence will appear. I was not of the opinion of a war, and France to take all, and give us nothing; if my advice had been followed, there would have been better effects: it is not my practice to accuse, but it is hard if a man may not clear himself. I have been in as much danger, for my respect to this house, as any man; have been turned out of all my places at court; proclaimed traitor; witnesses hired to swear against me, and confessed so; no man can be exempted from malicious accusations, and all for favouring Bills from this house; and, after the proclaiming me traitor, I had a Letter from a sister of mine, which was alledged one from Dr. Haven, a conjurer, but through his name any man might see Richmond and Lenox.* I was not afraid of my enemies in the house of commons, but afraid of being tried for my life, before you met. There have been great desires of having me removed from the king. I can hunt the hare with a pack of hounds, but not with a pack of lobsters.† If this house desires it, I will remove from the king, and go beyond sea; no man ought to serve the king, whom the nation has no good opinion of. I have spent an estate in the king's service, when others have got thousands. Beggars that run away with the bags, when a robbery is done, you stop; but a fine gentleman, riding upon the highway, you let go. I desire to be removed from my place, and to have leave to sell it. Persons are vehement upon me, and would ruin me. I submit myself, and actions, to the good construction of the hon. house."—He then withdrew.

Debate thereon.] Mr. *Stockdale* desires, that, seeing the duke is of your mind, you may join issue with him, and let him go beyond sea.

Lord *Buckhurst*.* The duke has informed you of nothing concerning 'public affairs,' and why will you put him out of all capacity? Though his relation to him were ever so near, or obligations ever so great, would have him answer his accusations: but hear him first.

Mr. Sec. *Coventry*. This duke's is not the same case with the duke of Lauderdale's. The king may turn any man out of his service, and especially on your desires; but when it shall be upon record, that the duke has uttered such words against the king, if a man asks whether such words are treason, it may be represented, that he said the words, 'of the king's being a knave, and unfit to govern.'

Mr. *Boscawen* has no kindness nor relation to the duke, but we ought to hear him. Your judgment will not be thought just, though it is so in truth, by persons that understand not the reasons: would have him acquainted with what is against him, and then you may proceed.

Col. *Birch*. The duke has not spoken one word of 'public' in what he has offered, but all 'private.' It seems to him, that he would be drawn to accuse, but in modesty would not do it of himself: would adjourn now, and let him know, if he has any 'public' thing to say, we are ready to hear him.

Mr. *Garroway* would make no false steps in the business; would adjourn the debate, but would have nothing said to the duke. He

---

* "There was a poor fellow, who had a poorer lodging about Tower Hill, to whom the duke often repaired, in disguise, in the night; and lord Arlington had caused that fellow to be apprehended, and his pockets and chamber to be searched; where were found several letters to the duke of Buckingham, and one original letter from the duke to him, in all which there were many unusual expressions, which were capable of very ill interpretations, and could not bear a good one. This man and some others, were sent close prisoners to the Tower, and a warrant being issued, under the king's sign manual, to apprehend the duke, he at last surrendered himself, and, on his examination at the council board, the letter being produced, as soon as he cast his eyes upon it, he said, 'It was not his hand, but his sister's 'the dutchess of Richmond's, with whom, he 'said, it was known he had no correspondence.' Whereupon the king called for the letter, and having looked upon it, he said, 'He had been mistaken,' and confessed, 'that it was the dutchess's hand;' and seemed much out of countenance at the mistake: though the letter gave still as much cause of suspicion, for it was as strange that she should write to such a fellow, in a style very obliging, and in answer to a letter; so that it seemed very reasonable still to believe, that she might have written it upon his desire and dictating." Earl of Clarendon's Life, p. 430-434.

† "The duke justified his own designs, laying all the ill counsels upon others, chiefly on lord Arlington; intimating plainly, that the root of all errors was in the king and the duke of York. He said, 'Hunting was a good diversion, but if a man would hunt with a brace of lobsters, he would have but ill sport.' He had used that figure to myself; but had then applied it to prince Rupert and lord Arlington. It was now understood to go higher." Burnet.

seemed discomposed, and fumbled with a pa-

* "Son of the earl of Dorset, to which title he succeeded in 1677, having been created earl of Middlesex, 1675. He was a volunteer in the first Dutch war, in 1665, and the night before the engagement, composed the famous Song, 'To all you Ladies now at land,' &c. At the Revolution he was early engaged in the interest of the prince of Orange, and was pitched upon to convey the princess (afterwards queen) Anne, out of the reach of her father's displeasure. He was a great patron of men of letters, who have not been ungrateful in transmitting his name with lustre to posterity. He died in 1705." Biog. Brit.

per, and would 'sell his place,' and could hunt 'with hounds and not with lobsters;' but if any man desires he may be heard on any 'public occasion,' would have him heard, but not any thing 'private' from him.

Lord *Cornbury* observes that the duke has good intelligence of what we do here; for he began his discourse with the great business of France: if you accuse him, he is pardoned, and has the king's pardon; being so secured, there is no justice to proceed upon these crimes: but suppose he should acquit himself of all the great matters relating to the king, yet here is a crime in the face of the sun, a murder, and his living with that miserable woman in that perpetual adultery. He never was tried for killing her husband, and would be satisfied how you may try him; but how will you reach him? He must be tried by the lords. Every body knows the great friendship that you, Mr. Speaker, have for him; and would not have you write or speak to him: but if he has any thing more to say, you may hear him to-morrow.

Sir *Rob. Howard* moves to adjourn the debate till to-morrow.

Mr. *Powle.* In Impeachments, 'by way of justice,' is another way of proceeding, but, 'in point of fame,' every man must lay his hand upon his heart, in his judgment of him.

Sir *John Monson* has attended this noble lord's speech, but wonders that he should interpret the weighty affairs of this house to be his own private affairs, and believes, that his mind changed from what he had to say at first, upon our debate.

The debate was adjourned till the next day.

The Speaker reminded the house, That it is against Order, that members should salute messengers from the lord's house, as if this house was the School of Compliments: the Speaker only ought to do respect for the whole house.

The Speaker reported, "That he had presented the Addresses to his majesty, who was pleased to return Answer to this effect: "That he was always ready to preserve them in their Liberties and Properties, and to secure the Protestant Religion; and would take care the Militia should be in readiness upon all occasions, to secure the Government,"

Jan. 14. Sir *John Monson* would know whether the Speaker has any more letters, or intimations, from the duke; and that, if he had, he would produce them.

Sir *Eliab Harvey* moves to state the question, upon the matter of the debate adjourned yesterday; the question, 'to remove the duke of Buckingham from his majesty's person, and employments, for ever,' to be the Address to the king.

Sir *Cs. Wheeler* would do things so like an honest man, that, if informed of any other matter, he may not repent him of his vote. The debate arises fairly from the first vote, 'all Papists, and persons obnoxious, to be removed from the king.' That he will stick close to. If the house will add 'all others guilty of murder' &c. and have all scandalous livers removed, he is content: many others may be as perplexed in the vote, and entangled as he is; therefore would come to a fair debate. If any person, be it who it will, is 'so obnoxious,' would fairly give his vote to have him removed: would a man be content that every duke in England that has killed a man, or lived in adultery, should be comprehended in your vote as dangerous to the government? Whether 'seizing on money,' 'popishly affected' or 'has made a league,' let all these come fairly before us: How carefully did we proceed in the duke of Lauderdale's vote? The duke said 'he was not a man to be an accuser, but, if examined, he would throw himself upon the judgment of the house;' if he did not make the League (French Alliance) he may know who did it: shall we lose such an opportunity, as this offer of the duke's? Though not expressed, yet it is fairly implied, that he can tell you: would set the saddle upon the right horse, and send for him, if he will come.

The *Speaker.* Dr. Williams addressed himself to him thus: 'that his name, he has heard, was made use of in the house, about what he should hear the duke say of the king; protests he never heard the words, nor said he heard them *.'

Mr. *Rob. Philips.* Dr. Williams told him, 'That the words were not only spoken once, but frequently, by the duke.'

Sir *John Coventry* has no malice against the duke, but could not be silent when a worthy member, col. Titus, can tell you as much.

Col. *Titus* rises up very unwillingly to speak in the matter, for he has been under a misfortune from this person: will not do a public good for a private revenge: he has heard the same things from Dr. Williams.

Mr. *Sacheverell.* We are not going to hang the duke, nor try him for his life; we only desire to remove him from the king. The question might have been yesterday, but he being too foul, we would not touch him: Wheeler said, 'affairs are not mended since lord Clarendon's banishment;' but the house is a judge of that, not he; but if this person is not removed, will never move to have any removed more.

Sir *Tho. Clarges.* The duke told you, 'he had no hand in the French Alliance,' and at the same time that, 'he would have had no ships, but towns:' Averse from the war, and yet would have towns and no ships! When he told you, 'he was not for breaking the Triple Alliance,' a thing of great honour! but 'for putting most of the towns into the French hands,' it was one of the elegancies of speech which men call a Bull: 'would have leave to sell his place:' he has, under the signet, 2,400*l.* a year, in compensation of what he has given for the place of Master of the Horse; and yet he affirms 'he has nothing from the crown:'

* See p. 632.

the method we take is by common fame here; the wisest parliaments have taken it before us. Hen. iv. in the case of the Abbot of ——, his Confessor, removed him for no other reason but for not being loved by the people, though the king knew nothing against him: many more have been removed at the instance of the commons: would not have a hair of his head touched, but a learned judge (Atkins) said here, in lord Clarendon's case (about removing him) 'Was he a young gentleman, and came to town with money in his pocket, and gave it to a gamester to improve it for him by play, and he lost it, believes he should not put another bag into such unlucky hands to play for him:' would have the question, 'That he is not a man fit to be about the king.' Whom will you impute your Grievances to? No man will say, to the king; but if such a man's crimes must be alleviated, he is for the king and the common-wealth: would, perhaps, move you, that no member for the future, whilst parliaments sit, should have the temptation of offices: moves for the single question, as before.

Col. *Sandys* has met with a servant of the duke's, who informs him, 'that the duke desires to be heard here again; being under a surprize yesterday, he has something farther to say.'

Sir *Joseph Tredenham* says the same.

Mr. *Russell* has no malice against the duke, but would have this question 'for removing him' passed; fearing the danger the king and the nation are in,' from a knot of persons that meet at the duke's, who have neither morality nor Christianity, who turn our Saviour and parliaments into ridicule, and contrive prorogations; and would have such persons removed.

Col. *Sandys* remembers that my Lord Keeper Finch* desired to be heard, and was heard, but ran away; but the duke has no reason to do so; you have dealt favourably with him: but would hear him; you cannot, it may be, have notice of things without hearing him.

Sir *Tho. Lee* knows nothing of what the duke intends, but he has been at the head of councils, and knows much: the kingdom is in misery, a little knowledge of affairs may bring you to more, and you may at last know the end: he has no design, nor hopes, but to keep his property in the country: pardons, it seems, in parliament have not served the turn: would call in any man that can inform the house.

Lord *St. John* is a friend to no man that gives ill counsels: any in the private Cabal that advised against the house of commons, 'to force the house of commons to pass Bills, and, if any refused, to take off their heads†: would have these things enquired into: he has been told it by one of the Cabal*.

Mr. *Sawyer* did not expect, yesterday, excuses, from the duke, of his own actions, but discoveries of matters of concernment to the nation, relating to the public; but would not call him in to do the same thing again, only would have light into those causes that have produced such ill effects. He was called in only for discovery: the house proceeds not by fame of vulgar persons, but upon things as plain as the sun. This new light, a thing called wit, is little less than fanaticism, one degree below madness: of Democritus's family, he laughs always at all religion and true wisdom: we come here to take away examples of such things; such as this duke, as great as any. This kind of wit's best ornament is most horrid blasphemy, oaths, and imprecations, which have done more hurt, in a few years, than all the Convents and Jesuits could do in a 100 years: prays, that the duke may not be heard to 'matters of excuse,' to acquaint you with that which all the world is satisfied in; but confined only to matters of discovery.

Mr. *Garroway* fears not any thing the duke can say, in 'excuse' of himself; he had little advantage upon us by it yesterday. 'Sequestering him only from his employments, and the king's presence,' is a gentle way, and would have it done in as gentle words as possible: it is likely he may have been as ill an instrument as any; you have Grievances, but will you not have the causes discovered? would call him in, and hear him at large: would have lord St. John's question asked the duke, or any other delivered you.

Mr. Sec. *Coventry*. Lord St. John said, 'one of the Cabal told him, &c.' would know what the meaning of the Cabal is.

Mr. *Garroway*. That is so great a mystery, that he would know it above all things.

Mr. Sec. *Coventry*. We do things, not voluntarily, but by law; the king's privy counsellors! and it is perjury for us to reveal: as for the committee of foreign affairs (of which he is the only man of this house) wishes (he protests to God) that you knew what opinion he has ever given of affairs.

Sir *Wm. Lewis*. The way is to hear him at large, and then propose your questions, and he has time by it to ask the king's leave to answer: that has been anciently done in these cases.

Mr. *Powle* commends secretary Coventry for his secrecy. This house has liberty to examine any man, not being a peer, and what he discovers is no breach of his oath; but if this house must take no notice of things, and persons are rescued from punishment, we may be

---

* See vol. ii. p. 693.

† Burnet says, "That sir Ellis Leighton assured him, that the duke of Buckingham, and lord Berkeley, offered to the king, if he would bring the army to town, that they would take out of both houses the members that made the opposition to the Declaration."

* The Cabal (so called from the initial letters of their titles) consisted originally of Clifford, Arlington, Buckingham, Ashley, (afterwards Shaftesbury) and Lauderdale. Of these, three only, who were now attacked by the commons, remained; Clifford being dead, and Shaftesbury having made his peace.—See p. 451.

all destroyed. A privy counsellor may do it safely, without breach of his oath: in lord Strafford's case, examination was upon oath of what was done at the council-table, and no exception was then taken against it: Cabal is a new word, and what is said there is not said in council, any more than in the bed-chamber; and those few men of the Cabal to encroach upon royal power, as the duke of Ireland did! would have that question 'of the Cabal' proposed to the duke.

Sir *Tho. Meres*. 'Cabal' and 'Council' are different, but we have power over both.

Sir *John Birkenhead*. In lord Strafford's case, the attorney general, when he was examined here, said, 'he would answer, when he had his master's leave:' it is perjury in any privy counsellor to answer without it.

Sir *Cha. Harbord*. To give counsel to the king 'to take away privilege of parliament!' no council can protect him.

Serj. *Maynard*. Supposed this 'of the parliament-men's heads' [said in the king's council] 'to be set upon the house;' will not meddle with that: knows not how the question propounded about the CABAL is understood.

Mr. *Sacheverell*. The duke said, '3, 4, or 5,000*l.* a year some had got;' would have him asked to every one of them.

The *Speaker*. The things proposed to be asked the duke he will state; 'the private Cabal to destroy the privileges of this house' 'altering the government, where and by whom?' 'What meant by 4, 5, or 6,000*l.* a year gotten?' 'Who got it? and by what means the Triple Alliance was broke?' 'The Smyrna fleet set upon?' 'The parliament prorogued?'

Sir *Rob. Holmes*. He was commanded to fall upon the Smyrna fleet, and has his orders to show from the lord high admiral to do it*.

Sir *Nich. Carew*. 'By whose advice a Frenchman was made general of an army, when here raised,' another question.

Mr. Sec. *Coventry*. Count Schomberg is far from a Frenchman; his mother was an Englishwoman, and his father a German. He first commanded the Scots under the duke; and, would he have been a Papist, might long ago have been Marshal of France.† Though Germany be one country, they are not of one mind in this war; divers princes are now arming in Germany, that will neither obey the emperor, nor the king of France: he came first to marshal Turenne, when he was a Protestant.

Sir *Wm. Coventry*. What was said from the bar, of M. Schomberg, needs not his confirmation. This gentleman might be abler than another man, it may be reasonably supposed, for the king's service, having served long in Holland, and knows the condition of that country: would lay no more weight on this than will be borne: I wish this was our greatest Grievance; the gentleman came only for the command of the army, when intended for foreign service, and when that intention was laid aside, he went away.

Sir *Tho. Lee* is for avoiding all things that give any umbrage or jealousy: it may be thought as necessary to have 'a foreign army,' as to have 'a foreign general;' they may both give umbrage or jealousy, and therefore would avoid them.

Sir *Ch. Wheeler* does not believe that an English general would serve for such purposes; but a 'foreigner' has given us great jealousies and would have that one of the questions.

Mr. *Love* would have it another Question, who advised that the army should be appointed to draw up towards London, to awe this house, to make us vote what they please?'

The Duke's Second Speech to the House of Commons.] The Duke of Buckingham was then called in, as before, and spoke thus:

"In the first place, I return this hon. house humble thanks for the honour of twice admitting me; especially when I consider, how ill I expressed myself yesterday: consider the condition I am in; in danger to pass for a vicious person, and a betrayer of my country, all the world over. I have the misfortune to bear the blame of other men's faults. I know that it is laid against me the 'revealing the king's counsels,' 'correspondency with the enemy, in time of war,' and 'having hindered what the Council would have done.' I hope I shall have pardon, if I speak truth for myself. I told you, that, if the Triple Alliance had advantage in it, I had the honour to have as great a hand in it (I speak it without vanity) as any man: then upon the French ambassador's and other intelligence, I had orders to compliment upon the sad subject of Madame*. I thought it for the service of the king, that the French ought not to endeavour to be considerable at sea; we were jealous of them, that the Dutch should make their peace with them, because they had power to conquer. When I

* "This perfidious and piratical attempt on the Smyrna fleet, though performed with the utmost bravery and resolution by sir Robert Holmes, and the earl of Ossory, miscarried. Though the Dutch defended themselves with amazing obstinacy, they could not have escaped, (as they did) if sir Rob. Holmes had condescended to impart his design to sir Edw. Spragge, (whom he met at sea) and desired his assistance. But though sir Robert applied to him for intelligence concerning the game he sought, he kept the secret, that he might engross the whole honour and profit to himself, and thereby fell into the disgrace of undertaking a bad thing, without having the glitter of good success to gild it over." Ralph.

† He was made Marshal in 1676.

* King Charles's sister, the dutchess of Orleans, who, in 1671, soon after her return from an interview with her brother at Dover, was poisoned at Paris, (as was supposed) by the direction of her husband. The duke of Buckingham was sent over, on that occasion, with compliments of condolence.

returned, I had all the demonstrations imaginable that the French had no such thoughts, but that the king of England should be master at sea. I pretend not to judge, whether I, or another, was in the right, but leave the house to judge. At that time, I, and lord Shaftsbury, were of opinion not to begin a war, without advice of the parliament, and the affections of the people, that the parliament might join in it; and I believe the king, at the head of his parliament, the greatest prince in the world: this was Shaftsbury's opinion and mine, but not lord Arlington's. Then I was of opinion not to make use of the French ships? but to have half the value of them in money, for English ships, which would have been of more service; the French ships of no use to us, because of no experience, and the use of our seas, learned by them, of great danger to us: lord Arlington was of a contrary opinion. I was sent to Dunkirk to the king of France, Arlington to Utrecht. I endeavoured to have money, instead of ships; at my first audience, the French king was willing to comply with it, but, after some time, by letters and returns from hence, it was altered. I make no reflections, but declare matter of fact. Then lord Shaftsbury and I were of opinion to order the war so, that the French were to deliver towns into our hands; an useful precedent! lord Arlington was of opinion to have no towns at all delivered, for one year, and here is the cause of the condition of affairs, with that of the fleet, and the French army let go on to conquer; they get all, and we nothing, and agree for none neither; consider who it was locked up with the French ambassador †; my spirit moves me to tell you. When we are to consider what to do we must advise with the French ambassador: I will not trouble you with reports. Look not upon me as a peer, but as an honest English gentlemen, who have suffered much for my love to my country. I had a regiment given me, which was sir Edw. Scott's: and, not knowing the law of England, I gave him 1,500*l.* for it; no Papists, nor Irish in the regiment. I will say nothing of my extraordinary gains. I have lost as much estate as some have got, and that is a big word. I am honest, and when I shall be found otherwise, desire to die. A man that has not gotten by all this. I leave it to you. If I am a Grievance, I am the cheapest Grievance, after all this, that ever this house had: and so humbly ask pardon of the house for the trouble I have given it."

Questions put to the Duke: with his Answers.]

† Reflecting on lord Arlington. The French ambassador, here mentioned, was M. Rouvigny, a Protestant, whose son was created earl of Galway, by king William, and commanded the British forces in Portugal, in the reign of queen Anne. Burnet says, "he had the appointment of an ambassador, but would not take the character, that he might not have a chapel, and mass said in it."

Then the Speaker told the duke, 'That he was commanded, by the house, to ask his grace some Questions, if he pleased to make answer to them.' The duke answered, 'he was willing.'

Question 1. "Whether any persons have, at any time, declared to him any of their advices, or ill purposes, against the liberty of this house, or propounded any ways to him for altering our government; and if they did, what was that advice, and by whom? *Answ.* It is an old proverb, 'over shoes, over boots.' This reflects upon one now not living [lord Clifford] and I would have pardon for not naming him, and fear it will be thought a malicious invention of mine. I have said nothing yet but what I can justify; but this not.—2. What his grace meant by this expression yesterday 'that he had gotten nothing, and that others had gotten 3, 4, and 5,000*l.*;' who they were that had gotten it, and by what means? *Answ.* I cannot acquaint you how they got it, because not well acquainted myself with the means of getting money. What the duke of Ormond has got is upon record. Lord Arlington has not got so much, but a great deal.—3. By whose advice the army was raised, and Papists set to officer them, and M. Schomberg to be their general? *Answ.* I cannot say 'by whose advice,' but, on my honour, not by my advice; but was told by a man that is dead, 'that lord Arlington sent for him,' and it will be easily proved.—4. Whether he knows, that any have advised to make use of the army to awe the debates and resolutions of this house? *Answ.* This is the same question of a discourse from a man that is dead to a man that is living. If I had desired it, I might have had the command of the army that M. Schomberg had: but I have been told, that lord Arlington would have the government by an army.—5. By whose counsel and ministry the Triple League was made? *Answ.* Lord Arlington and I were only employed to treat, and finding the danger that we were in of being cheated, pressed the ambassadors to sign before they had power. It was an odd request to the ambassadors, yet they did sign.—6. Who made the first Treaty with France, by which the Triple League was broken, and the Articles thereof? *Answ.* I made no Treaty.—7. Who advised the shutting up the Exchequer, whereby the orders of assignment and credit of the exchequer were broken and destroyed? *Answ.* I was not the adviser. I lost 3,000*l.* by it.—8. And the Declaration about matters of Religion made? *Answ.* I do not disown that I advised it, but no farther only than what might be done by the Declaration by law.—9. And the Smyrna fleet fallen upon, before war was declared? *Answ.* It was lord Arlington's advice; I was against it; so much against it (as careful of the honour of the nation) that I incurred some anger from the king. Lord Arlington principally moved it: and I might say more.—10. And the second Treaty with the French king at Utrecht, and the Articles thereof? *Answ.* Lord Arlington and I were sent over to Utrecht, and found in the common people of Holland, in our journey thither, the greatest consternation imaginable: like burning the Rump in England, crying, 'God bless the king of England!' and 'cursing the States;' and had we then gone over and landed our men, we might have conquered the country; the prince of Orange would have had peace with France; but what share should we have had? Though he was the king's nephew, yet the king must be kind to his own country. If peace had been then, we had been in worse condition than we were before: at last, the prince of Orange hoped for a good peace; but I was not for France to have all, and England nothing. The consequence would have been, Holland must depend on France, if France had conquered near Germany. I think it a wise Article, that France should not make peace without us.—11. By whose counsels the war was made, without advice of parliament; and the parliament thereupon prorogued? *Answ.* Lord Shaftsbury and I were for 'the advice of parliament for the war.' I can say nothing to 'the prorogation' I believe the parliament will never be against a war for the good of England; and so desire the pardon of the house: I know not how words may have slipped me, and lay myself at the feet of the house, as an English gentleman."—The Duke then saluted the house, as before, and withdrew.

Debate on the Duke's Answers.] Colonel *Birch.* What the duke has told us are personal discourses of one that 'is dead.' He may inform us, if he pleases, of one of those 'living:' Would have him declare them, and have him called in again.

Mr. *Sawyer.* What came from a dead man can be of no use imaginable; but here is no answer made to 'setting upon the Smyrna fleet.' Probably he is less guilty as to state affairs, but for public scandal, would have the Question put 'for his removal.'

Sir *Nich. Carew* hoped for great light from the duke, but he gives no light as to persons of a contrary opinion to him.

Sir *Courtney Poole,* thinks us not so much in the dark: thinks this noble lord will satisfy you farther to-morrow: he named but one about the army, he may tell you more.

Sir *Tho. Lee.* All he has said terminates in one man; but he believes no man so big as he represents him: it was in his power to have given larger answers if he would: he cannot believe that some one person, without help, could carry counsels against two or three; not one evil against two good: by the same right, you may send for him, as he came before; and if not, you may send to the house of peers for their leave.

Mr. Sec. *Coventry.* We have little light from the duke without explaining: no oath of secrecy does bind a man to promote an ill act; but as for promoting, or not promoting a league, it is no sin: in one of the Answers, the duke makes lord Arlington instrumental in breaking the Triple Alliance; but it is not the duke's saying it, that makes him so: nor lord Arlington's saying it that makes the duke so: otherwise, happy is the first accuser: would be equal on both sides, but would ask, Whether any man believes that lord Arlington would own all this? You are to have farther light from the duke. Send to him to come again, if he be willing, or, if not, to the house of lords, for leave for him.

Col. *Birch* would send out two gentlemen to know, whether the duke has any thing farther to say: that is parliamentary.

Sir *Rob. Howard.* Some things came from the duke that require us to proceed more carefully, than we are are about to do; but the question that is pressed is like hearing him after, and condemning him first. Upon the whole, you cannot but think the time of the day, and the thing, great enough to put us upon considering it till to-morrow.

Mr. *Russel.* If the debate be adjourned, the duke, by his power, may prorogue us again, as he has done formerly.

Mr. *Sawyer* pities the duke's condition here, and the loss of his estate; but would have you proceed in it.

Sir *Nich. Pedley.* The duke may have patents for life. The serjeant of your mace has a patent for his place, for life, and it is a freehold in him. You cannot take away the duke's office without legal proceedings against him: by rule of law, there must be a *scire facias:* you cannot put a man from his freehold; and he would not have the question.

Sir *Tho. Lee* sees not such danger in this, as is alleged: by impeachments, the lords are judges. By the Address we make to the king, the king cannot grant against law more than is in his power: would clear it to the house. It may fall out to have the same case before you again, and would not have any person out of the power of the house of commons.

Mr. *Waller* moves, not for the duke's sake, but for his own. You take away from him more than you leave him: common fame against one of the lords is the same thing here: you go with an humble desire to the king to have our judgment put in execution: because you have not liked men, they have been removed: some say, he never said the word alleged against him; others say, others said them—no proof—witnesses may be corrupted: not many men are hanged for want of their pardon, if recorded: never any man was hanged, with his pardon in his hand: this is a great convulsion of state, a peer to come down to your house. If times are so corrupt, I must piece out my innocence with a pardon: if this nation be ever preserved, it must be in this place; and where so great a power is, if not as exact a justice with it, we are not safe: God has given us great power, and thank God for it.

Mr. Sec. *Coventry.* The duke's office is a patent, and a freehold: the duke may have a recompence for his office.

Sir *Cha. Harbord.* The duke's office cost him a great sum of money, and it may be any man's case: pray be tender in what you cannot put the king upon, in point of law.

Sir *Wm. Lewis.* We have cause to be tender in the things offered, and 'to desire that the king would be pleased to give him leave to sell his place.'

Lord *Cavendish*, should not be for the latter part of the question, if it 'took his place' from him, for the king may 'give him leave to sell it.'

Lord *Cornbury* is not for taking away the duke's life. Would have things rightly understood: it concerns not his freehold; he holds it only during the king's pleasure. Is not against his 'leave to sell it:' do you intend to leave 'employment' wholly out of the question? He has a patent for gentleman of the bedchamber, and a pension for it, and his lieutenancy of Yorkshire; and, on the other side, would not recommend him to the king, and not think him fit to be about his person.

Sir *John Duncombe* has a great compassion for this honourable person's misfortunes: what comfort can a man have, after shuch a charge, without some compensation for his place: which he moves for.

Mr. *Harwood* has had great honour for this person, but now must lay all aside here! with what face can you make such an Address to the king? you do nothing to take away the king's charity, in compensation of his places, and doubts not but the king will do it: it is a burden greater than he could wish he had, but would not put it upon the king by our Address.

Sir *Wm. Coventry.* 'To remove him' is the general sense, but would not wound other men, by destroying his patent, nor wound his freehold, nor take away his blood: would have added to the Question, 'reserving to him the profits of such places, as of right, he has by any inheritance, or freehold.'

Mr. *Powle* would have him removed out of offices that are granted him at his majesty's pleasure.

Mr. *Swynfin.* Be the offender ever so great, or the offence, you may err in the manner of proceeding: would have you proceed by such rules as agree with justice: in the duke of Lauderdale's case, persons did prove things against him (your members): looks for judicial proof before you; information has been but remembers no proof: it has been, the course that great ministers of state do take out those pardons, sometimes one or two in a year: as to impeachment, this way was well; for then all evidence on both sides is heard: does not think 'removal from the king's presence' a light thing. Put the case, you had this upon your own members—would you have freeholds taken away without proof? Thinks it an ill precedent: let the case be this, lords or whose it will, we have nothing but justice for our own preservation: whoever shall judge a man, and not hear him to the point, though his judgment be just, he is unjust in judging.

Col. *Strangways.* There is no freehold in a grant 'at the king's pleasure:' will you make 'Lex et consuetudo parliamenti' nothing? We do as a grand jury does, persuaded in conscience that the thing is so—'Neither fornicator, nor adulterer, &c. shall enter into the kingdom of Heaven'—Hopes that virtue will be countenanced here: this vote is only 'to remove such a Counsellor,' to restore the king, and honour and integrity unto the kingdom: no sanguinary law: not for taking away his freehold, but only what he holds at the king's pleasure: hopes that men of sobriety and honesty will be near the king, and would have the duke removed.

Sir *Tho. Meres.* 'Removing from the king's person' is, in consequence, removing from places and employments: it is also said, 'we are heard as a grand jury, in impeachments;' but, as you proceed now, there are objections; you now give your last judgment, whatever the king will do. Says another gentleman, 'you have heard no proofs;' but these shall not go without an answer: this house had great power in judgment by common fame, as every one of us is told without doors. Lex Parliamentaria. Thirty persons, in Mr. Prynne's books, were desired to be removed from former kings, because the people spoke ill of them; some of them, though not all, were removed: the duke is a fine person, and taking with us, and we have a tenderness; but it does not become this house to countenance selling of places: though common fame is the great prerogative of this house, yet would use it very sparingly.

Sir *John Birkenhead* is against clancular and clandestine proceedings: in the common law, if the Christian neighbourhood say, 'one keeps another man's wife,' yet upon his oath he may clear himself: lord Bacon calls common fame 'a common liar;' and the precedents cited, of removals, were in ill times: is against the latter part of the question.

Mr. *Powle.* Birkenhead said, 'the precedents, cited, were of ill times;'—11 Ed. ii. a great while before his deposing: that was done in the 22d. The effects of those censures then kept things quiet, till his deposing: the duke of Ireland was then removed, for encroaching upon royal power: wishes we might ever use this power moderately, and that we had no occasion of using it now:

Col. *Birch* is one of those who desired no resolution of this matter till another day; and did it then for another reason, not for favour to the duke: it is the custom, that the Speaker call for a clear account, and wishes it had been now from the duke: but cannot a gentleman give a clear opinion in the question? Would not call for it: when once the debate was, in the Convention, of recommending Counsellors to the king, it was answered, 'all the awe you have upon the king's Council hereafter is, if they be such as the people have an ill opinion of, you may remove them;' and it is better for us then to name them, for we must be responsible for them: shall you depart from this, and call for direct proof of persons only, and not things? You have great prejudice by it: you cannot take his freehold from him by your vote, and he is therefore for the question.

Sir *Tho. Littleton* fears, that you may clash with the lords upon another thing: when the point was of removal from the king's presence, 29 Hen. vi. as now, the king answered, 'he is content to remove them from his presence, except they be lords, unless they approve.' Whether any clear precedent, the commons originally to go to the king to remove, in case of peers, is not satisfied: it is not the case of the duke of Lauderdale, who is no peer.

Lord *Cornbury*. Littleton is mistaken in the precedent of 29 Hen. vi. The duke of Somerset, and the bishop of Winchester, were removed: the words of the accusation were, 'the people spake ill of them:' the king grants the request of the commons, unless to some few persons that were lords, who are necessary about him: the lords concurrence will beget another debate, but the king is still at the same freedom.

Resolution against the Duke.] At length it was resolved, "That an Address be presented to his majesty, to remove the duke of Buckingham from all his Employments that are held during his majesty's pleasure, and from his Presence and Councils for ever."

The above proceedings induced the lords, on the 15th, to refer it to the committee of privileges to search the Journals, what hath been formerly the practice in such cases. On the 20th the committee reported "That their lordships have searched and perused several precedents; and thereupon conceive that it may deeply intrench into the privileges of this house, for any lord of this house to answer an Accusation in the house of commons, either in person, or by sending his Answer in writing, or by his counsel there:" Upon serious consideration had thereof, and perusal of the said Precedents in this house, it is Ordered, "That, for the future, no lord shall either go down to the house of commons, or send his Answer in writing or appear by counsel, to answer any accusation there, upon the penalty of being committed to the Black Rod, or to the Tower during the pleasure of this house." And it is further Ordered, "That this Order be added to the Standing Orders of this house, that the lords may the better take notice of the same."

PROCEEDINGS AGAINST THE EARL OF ARLINGTON.

Jan. 15. Sir *Gilbert Gerrard.* Has a complaint against a great minister of state, the earl of Arlington [*] all great affairs and transactions go through his hands: he has been the great treasurer; the management of that must pass by him: he has no prejudice to him, or disobligation from him, but it is a duty he owes the king and nation: it was just upon your heels the taking away your liberties, contrary to the laws of the kingdom; and, to back this, an army was raised of dangerous men, unfit to command: nothing has passed for some years but through his hands; the army, the Declaration; he the great conduit-pipe; this instance many within these walls know, and abroad he is reported a Papist, and reconciled to the Church of Rome: in the Journal you may find the Act for suppressing of Conventicles; upon his majesty's power to suspend Laws in the Proviso; upon the division of the house, Arlington staid in for it with not above 30: every thing passed through his hands; all Licences, according to the Declaration.

Articles of Impeachment against him.] The Articles he has to exhibit against lord Arlington are these:

ARTICLES of treasonable and other Crimes of High Misdemeanor against the Earl of Arlington, principal Secretary of State.

I. "That the said earl hath been a constant, and most vehement promoter of Popery and Popish Counsels; 1. By procuring Commissions for all the Papists lately in command, and who made their application to him, as a known favourer of that faction; there being not one commission signed by the other secretary; many of which commissions were procured and signed by him, since the several Addresses of the two houses of parliament to his majesty and the passing the late Act against Popery: 2. By procuring his majesty's Letter, commanding Irish papists and rebels to be let into corporations, and admitted into the commissions of the peace, and other offices of trust military and civil, contrary to the established laws and constitutions of that realm, to the great terror of the king's protestant subjects there: 3. By not only setting up and supporting the aforesaid Papists there, but bringing the most violent and fiercest of them to command companies and regiments of the king's English subjects here to the great dishonour and danger of this kingdom: 4. By openly and avowedly entertaining and lodging in his family a Popish priest, contrary to the known laws of the land; which said priest was

[*] "Bennet, advanced afterwards to be earl of Arlington, was made secretary of State, by the interest of the Popish party, [in 1662.] He was a proud man. His parts were solid, but not quick. He had the art of observing the king's temper, and managing it beyond all the men of that time. He was believed a Papist. He had once professed it, and when he died, he again reconciled himself to that church. Yet in the whole course of his ministry, he seemed to have made it a maxim, that the king ought to show no favour to Popery, but that all his affairs would be spoiled, if ever he turned that way; which made the Papists become his mortal enemies, and accuse him as an apostate, and a betrayer of their interests." Burnet.—He died in 1685, leaving an only daughter, married to king Charles's favourite son, the duke of Grafton.

a noted solicitor and promoter of the Popish faction, and has since fled out of this kingdom: 5. By procuring pensions, in other mens names, for Papist officers, contrary to, and in illusion of the late act of parliament: 6. By obtaining several grants of considerable sums of money, to be charged upon the revenue of Ireland, for the most violent and pernicious papists there; particularly 2000*l.* for one col. Fits Patrick, a notorious Irish rebel, whose mother was hanged in the late war, for murdering several English, and making candles of their fat; this grant being procured for the said Fits Patrick at a time when he was accused to the lord Arlington of high crimes, by the now lord lieut. of Ireland: 7. By procuring his maj. to release several Irish papists (some whereof deeply engaged in the horrid rebellion of that kingdom) the chiefries or head rents reserved to the crown, out of the forfeited estates of Papists there, being a principal part of his majesty's revenue in that kingdom:—II. That the said earl hath been guilty of many and undue practices to promote his own greatness; and hath embezzled and wasted the treasure of this nation; 1. By procuring vast and exorbitant grants for himself, both in England and Ireland, breaking into the Settlement of that kingdom, and dispossessing several English adventurers and Soldiers of their properties and freeholds, in which they were duly and legally stated, without any colour of reason, or suggestion of right: 2. By charging excessive and almost incredible sums for false and deceitful intelligence: 3. By procuring his majesty's hand for the giving away, between his first entrance into his office, the value of 3 millions of sterling money, at the least; the several grants whereof are extant, countersigned by him, and by him only. 4. That the said earl, presuming to trample upon all estates and degrees of the subjects of this realm, the better to subdue them to his will and pleasure, hath causelessly and illegally imprisoned many of his majesty's subjects. 5. That he did procure a principal peer of this realm to be unjustly imprisoned, and to be proclaimed traytor, without any legal proceed or trial; and did maliciously suborn false witness, with money, to take away his life, upon pretence of treasonable words.—III. That the said earl hath falsely and traiterously betrayed the great trust reposed in him, by his majesty, as counsellor and principal secretary of state; 1. By entertaining a more than usual intimacy with the French ambassador; not only lodging him in his house, but letting him into the king's most secret counsels. 2. By altering in private, and singly by himself, several solemn determinations of his majesty's councils. 3. By procuring a stranger to have the chief command of the late raised army, for invasion of Holland, to the great dishonour and discouragement of all the loyal nobility and gentry of this nation. 4. By advising his maj. to admit of a squadron of French ships to be joined with our English fleet; the sad consequence whereof we have since felt, notwithstanding the king of France had agreed to send a supply of money, in order to the having the fleet wholly English. 5. Whereas the king was advised by several of his council to press the French king to desist from making any further progress in his conquest of the inland towns of Holland, whereof England was to have no benefit, and to turn his arms upon those maritime towns that were by the Treaty to have been ours, his ldp. gave the king counsel to desist; whereby that part of our expectation was wholly frustrate. 6. Whereas the king was advised, by several of his council, not to enter into this war, till his maj. was out of debt, and had advised with his parliament, his ldp. was of opinion to the contrary, and gave his advice accordingly. 7. When the French ships were dispersed after the late Fight at sea, and had lost all their anchors and cables, by reason of the foul weather that then ensued, he persuaded his maj. to send them fourscore cables and anchors; although it was then objected, and he knew it to be true, That his maj. had not, at that present time, any more in his stores than would supply his own ships, in case of the like necessity. 8. He hath traiterously corresponded with the king's enemies, beyond the seas, and contrary to the trust reposed in him, hath given intelligence to them."

Debate thereon.] Sir *Rob. Carr* assures the house that he does not oppose the bringing in the Articles, or any thing objected against lord Arlington; but he has a letter to the Speaker to be communicated to the house.

Lord *Obrien* knows not but what has been said yesterday may have been the occasion of this Letter, and would have it read.

The Earl's Letter to the House of Commons.] The Speaker moves that he may read lord Arlington's Letter. The Letter was read accordingly, as follows:

'Mr. Speaker; Hearing that the hon. house 'of commons are informing themselves of pub'lic affairs, wherein, I humbly conceive, what I 'can say may be of use and satisfaction to them, 'I beseech you to do me the favour, by the 'means of this house, to obtain leave for me to 'be heard by the hon. house. ARLINGTON.'

Mr. *Tho. Lee* moves that lord Arlington may be asked the same questions with the duke of Buckingham, excepting that of M. Schomberg, being one of the Articles lord Arlington is accused of.

Mr. Sec. *Coventry* hopes that the house will not vote that we shall examine him: no member of the lords house can answer us.

Sir *Wm. Lewis.* He is at his own pleasure for answering our Questions: he, by his Letter, offers information only.

Sir *Tho. Lee.* He is judge of his own discretion; you may ask him what you please.

Sir *Rob. Carr* believes, that any question this house will ask this noble lord, he will answer.

The *Speaker* reminded the house of making

a noise yesterday, and that we ought not particularly to salute any man, because the respects of the house are paid by the Chair; an irregular motion when performed by any else.

Sir *Edm. Jennings.* If you lose the opportunity of asking him questions here, perhaps you will not see him again.

Col. *Birch.* Can any thing be more natural than asking of questions? and the Speaker has drawn questions this way and that way, till you have come to the bottom: if he gives full Answers, you need go no farther: it was not so managed yesterday.

Sir *Cha. Harbord.* If, upon the relation he makes, you find no cause, then would have no Questions asked: you cannot examine a peer nor can you send for him again.

Mr. *Sacheverell* would have no questions asked him to accuse himself: five of the Questions concern him, and he would have all these laid aside.

The Earl's Speech to the House of Commons.] The Earl of *Arlington* was admitted into the house, in the same manner, in all respects, with the duke of Buckingham. He then spoke to this effect:

"I acknowledge the honour the house has done me in admitting me to speak here: In private conversation, and at dinners, I have met with a paper of Articles against me, in the nature of an Impeachment, though upon uncertain grounds: had I as much memory as innocence, I assure myself of all favour from this house: I have a bad memory, and so must make use of papers. I reduce the accusations to three heads. 1. Matter of Religion. 2. Matter of War and Treaties. 3. Particular Fortune and Acquisitions I have got since the king's Restoration. 1st, For Religion. I never did one act to derogate from the Protestant religion, neither have I heard mass, nor made any reconciliation to the Church of Rome. I hope you will not rest upon aspersions, unless any hon. member will aver it on his knowledge, and, if so, I am content it should pass for a conviction. I am accused of 'having a part in composing the Declaration for Liberty of Conscience.' I was present in council when it was resolved, that, in time of war, it might be of great advantage to do any temporary thing, till the parliament might consider of it; but, as soon as I was convinced that it was contrary to law, I was the first man that advised to desist from what was not tenable by law: as for what concerns the Papists (Roman Catholics) I suppose, that, according to the function of my place, I might pen it, but it was brought to me changed to what was resolved in council: to the charge of being 'a favourer of Papists,' I answer, In particular I have favoured those of the Church of England; but I have promiscuously obliged men of merit, without distinction of religion.—To the 2nd. 'That I have promoted Irish Papists and Rebels, to be let into corporations and commissions of the peace, offices of trust, military and civil, &c.' This is so ill imputed to me, that I was not at London, at the council, but at my country house, when the order was made. Any gentleman here, that knows the forms in this matter, can tell, that these letters are by the king's particular direction.—3. 'Bringing the most violent Papists into command of companies and regiments of the king's English subjects, &c. and though they refused the oaths by the act enjoined, procuring them new commissions.' It was affirmed to me, that col. Panton would take the Oaths and Test, and by his looks seemed to accept his commission accordingly. I dare pronounce that not one commission was signed by me, but for such as went into foreign parts, and were not likely to return.—4. 'That I stopped prosecution of the piracy in Ireland, of one Fitzpatrick.' My hand is no way seen in it, but in an order for his prosecution. A letter was sent me from the lord lieutenant of Ireland; but I gave no interruption, directly nor indirectly, to his prosecution.—5. 'Entertaining and lodging in my house a Priest, contrary to the known laws, a noted solicitor of the Popish faction, &c.' I know of none, except father Patrick, that ever frequented my house, unless by chance, upon some sudden emmergency.—6. 'That I was the adviser to begin the war, without consent of parliament.' Whatever others may have done, few had a more positive share in hindering it than myself. There was no such thing as 'constraining the ambassadors to sign,' as was alleged *. What was done was on the other side of the water, and I was sensible of all approaches of violation of the league; in this I can scarce vindicate myself without reflection on others: I cannot affirm, but will lay before you my presumptions and others in this business. France, to bring the duke of Buckingham on their side, contrived his going over to Paris, on pretence of some easy coaches for the king, which he had leave for. The king warned him by no means to meddle with affairs. The king of France used him well, and gave him a jewel. He counselled me about it; to requite him, I told him in what state matters lay: 'I see you fast to the Spanish interest, if you will procure me a pension from the Spanish ambassador;' the duke took the pleasure of telling the tale, and, upon my honour, I appeal if many have not heard the duke say, with oaths, 'Arlington is to be turned out, and he would furnish the king with a better secretary;' which he might easily have done. The first time the duke discovered himself, he desired to go with a compliment into France, which might have been done by a more ordinary man. He had authority to sound that court, and brought word of the French resolutions for war, and so magnified that king and his ministers, that all wondered at it. He brought accounts of resolutions of France for our interest, but no particulars; sometimes seriously, sometimes pleasantly. The

* See the duke of Buckingham's Speech.

king told me the reports. I answered, 'Examine the thing, and be not guided by particular partiality.' I have leave from the king for my coming hither, for the purgation of myself. I am taxed with having spoiled the treaty with France. Many, that I can name, present in council, have heard the duke say, 'I am persuaded, what lord Arlington says is with reflection. Either I did, or did not say, he changed the Treaty.' I fear the duke has forgot the Treaty. This French treaty confirmed the Triple Alliance; the king established it in the treaty. It is true, the progress of the war has begotten some disturbance; as the business of Charleroy. If France disturbs, this Treaty is violated: France was thus warned. The king of France asked leave for some forces to pass through Flanders; Monteri gave him a civil denial; which being resented by the king, on the behalf of France, diverted the French king from marching. As for 'the delivery of towns to us,' it is so silly a thing, that it deserves not an answer. We have ever pressed France for money instead of ships. France had stores, but could not spare money. The king sent to compliment the king of France at Dunkirk; Buckingham offered himself, and treated of things unknown to me; he hoped satisfaction to wait upon so great a king, so obliging, when we approached so near the war. Ambassador Montagu, under the king's own hand, was commanded not to speak to the ministers, but to the king of France himself; 6000 men for the king to maintain. I pressed the king that Montague might desist from that proposition. Buckingham was the head of them, and his officers. As to my charge of 'being privately shut up with the French ambassador;' my doors were not shut to him, nor the Spanish ambassador; but as for 'pensions,' those that wrote the paper of Articles should have had the good manners to have told mine. As for 'M. Schomberg's being general of the English;' his mother was an English-woman, and he commanded the king's troops in Portugal. If he would have changed his religion, he might have been marshal of France. It was not strange he should be sent for to command, when a descent was intended into Holland, in which country he had long commanded. Though Buckingham is a man of wit and parts, yet his experience is little or none at all in military affairs. Buckingham proposed that he might go to Utrecht, and I be joined with him, to temper him with my slow pace. Hard by, the king of France staid in his camp ten days, expecting the Holland Deputies; neither prince was to treat without the other. I and Halifax were for moderate courses; Buckingham was for exorbitant. As to 'the parliament's not being acquainted with the war by my means;' it was represented, that the king had money to carry it on; it was never moved, nor urged, by any, that the war should come to the parliament. And as for our 'having towns,' what should we have done with them, if the king of France had given us half his conquests? To 'the falling upon the Smyrna fleet before war was declared against Holland,' I remember that my opinion was not prevalent, for I never pretended to maritime affairs; neither do I remember, that I had more concernment in it than others. 'That we should be governed by a Standing Army.' None in this house, nor out of it, abominate it more than I. I think it impossible to awe it with 20,000 men. I never heard the thing said, no, not by the duke of Buckingham. It was never in debate, and we never had it in our mouths. As for 'my having had extraordinary Grants from the king, &c.' had I presumed to beg of the king, as others have done, I might have had more; but if I have to maintain half the dignity of my employment, I am the falsest man that lives. I never begged any thing in England, but 'I have had 10,000*l.* out of Ireland.' I have lord Bense's estate, in Ireland, given me, (which I begged) which he forfeited in the Rebellion; worth 1000*l.* per ann. I proved I was never in rebellion, and so I claimed his estates myself. 'Engrossing all affairs into my hands.' I should think myself the happiest man in the world, if I might retire from the management of affairs. Any gentleman of honour or parts, that hath had any business with the king, I have gone with and assisted. I beg pardon for tiring the house with this abrupt paper. I doubt not but to be found an innocent man. If what I have said is applicable to any thing the house desires to be informed of, I will serve the house: I think myself safe in your hands, and lay myself at your feet."

Questions put to the Earl: with his Answers.] Then the Speaker desired to know, 'Whether he was pleased to make answer to some Questions he had in command from the house to ask his lordship?' Who answered, 'he was willing.'

Question 1. "Whether any persons have, at any time, declared to him any of their advices or ill purposes against the liberties of this house, or propounded any ways to him for altering the government; and if they did, what was that advice, and by whom? *Answ.* I cannot apply this to any discourse I have heard, either public or private.—2. By whose advice the army was raised, and Papists set to officer them? *Answ.* On account of the war there was a necessity of good officers, and the Papist officers, many of them, were represented more skilful; but cannot apply the advice to any person.—3. And that army to awe the debates of this house? *Answ.* I can say nothing to it. —4. By whose counsel and ministry the Triple League was made? *Answ.* It has been suggested by me. Sir Wm. Temple was the fortunate man that dispatched it.—5. Who advised the first treaty with France? *Answ.* The making that League was the concurrent opinion of us all. I did not expect the French in earnest, if some blots had not happened.—6. By whose advice the Exchequer was shut up? *Answ.*

You may easily believe I was passive in it. I can say but suspicions only: many things were proposed, but I have nothing to do with the Treasury.—7. By whose advice the Declaration for Liberty was made and published? *Answ.* It was a concurrent opinion, and, we thought, upon good grounds, and advisable by law; but when found contrary to law, I detested it.—8. By whose advice the Smyrna fleet was fallen upon? *Answ.* It was a concurrent advice, and I cannot apply it to any man's particular advice.—9. By whose advice the war was undertaken without advice of parliament? *Answ.* There was all probability of peace imaginable, and it was ill to show our adversaries any ill distempers, and it was a concurrent opinion.—10. And the parliament prorogued upon it, in Nov. last? *Answ.* It is a hard matter to say who was the adviser. I protest, I know not the author of it. I may wrong persons. I have presumptions, but no evidence."—Then his lordship, after saluting the house, withdrew.*

Resolution against the Earl.] After several long debates upon the above Articles, the question being put, "That an Address be presented to his majesty to remove the earl of Arlington from all his employments that are held during his majesty's pleasure, and from his majesty's presence and councils for ever;" it passed in the negative, 166 to 127.

It was then resolved, "That the Articles be referred to a committee, and that they report what matter is therein contained, and can be proved, that is fit for an Impeachment." †

* "Lord Arlington spoke much better than was expected: he excused himself, but without blaming the king: and this had so good an effect, that though he, as secretary of state, was more exposed than any other, by the many warrants and orders he had signed, yet he was acquitted, though by a small majority. But the care he took to preserve himself, and his success in it, lost him his high favour with the king, as the duke was out of measure offended at him. So he quitted his post, and was made lord chamberlain." Burnet.

The Author of his Life, in the Biographia, says, "That it was neither his speech, nor his cause, that brought him off, but the personal friendship of a noble person nearly allied to him, viz. the earl of Ossory, eldest son to the duke of Ormond, and then the most popular man of his quality in England, who stood for five days, that the debate lasted, in the lobby of the house of commons, and solicited the members in his favour as they entered the house."

† Nothing further appears to have been done in this Accusation. "No greater mistake," says Ralph, "can be made by the prosecutors of a bad minister, than to charge him with any one Article which they cannot support with undeniable proofs. If he has it in his power to loosen any one link of the chain, he infallibly makes his escape; and, instead of being punished himself, renders odious his accusers. This was the circumstance in the case before us: these gentlemen had suffered their Charge to outrun their evidence, by dealing in presumptions instead of proofs: lord Arlington saw the opening, and improved it with all the address imaginable: for, being admitted to be heard by the house, in his turn, he so far exploded, or evaded, all that the duke had said the day before, and set so plausible a gloss on his own actions, that the Impeachment died away, and he escaped, even without the least censure: he had been charged in particular with corresponding with the king's enemies beyond the seas: his friends, who had taken heart on seeing him come off so triumphantly, called upon sir Gilbert Gerrard for his vouchers: he was unprovided, would have withdrawn that Article, was not allowed, had recourse to the wretched expedient of desiring time; and, at last, took refuge in saying, that this treacherous correspondence was carried on during the last Dutch war."

Debate on Regulating of Elections.] Jan 22. Sir *R. Howard.* The expences of Elections are grown so vast, that it goes beyond all bounds, the charges considered in the country and here.

Mr. *Garroway.* It is dangerous for a man to be thrown out for his hospitality in the country: these charges arise commonly from competitors that live in another country: they must be undone by out-doing him that comes from another country, with indirect intentions.

Mr. *Swynfin.* Some carry elections by awe and force, and some by ability to expend. Unless you do it to some effect, it takes up your time, and the thing will never be practicable: by the effect he observes of sumptuary laws, he believes you will have the same effect of this,—none at all, but for an informer to get by it, and no man else. The examples of the king and court would have more effect than any law you can make, and when you find elections carried thus, and quash them here, that may remedy something. You having as good a law now, which does no good, therefore would forbear a helpless law as this is.

Serj. *Seys.* The penalty of a sheriff, for a false return, is but 100*l.*; and in the spending 1500*l.* the sheriff may be well gratified, by the party returned, for his fine.

Mr. *Boscawen.* The person elected ought to be resident in the borough or county for which he is chosen, by the statute, but that is antiquated and out of practice; but if you restrain it to persons resident in the county, to be chosen in boroughs, or that have estates in that county, you may do well; though the old statute is really a law, but out of practice: and this may cure all the evils.

Mr. *Waller.* Let us mend our proceedings here, and we shall mend elections: times are much changed now. Formerly the neighbourhood desired him to serve; there was a dinner, and so an end; but now it is a kind of an empire. Some hundred years ago some boroughs sent not; they could get none to serve; but, now it is in fashion and a fine thing, they are revived. Some bishops and lords for their poverty have been excused: it comes by custom; there is no appeal from us, and we judge elections with impunity, and what we should take most care of we take least.

Resolved, "That a committee be appointed to bring in one or more Bill or Bills for the Regulating of Elections of members to serve in parliament; and for the better ascertaining of the returns of members to be elected; and for the better attendance of such as are elected and returned; and upon the other debates of the house."

Debate on a Bill for restraining Buildings near London.] Jan. 23. Sir *Wm. Coventry* moves that there may be a restraint of Buildings here; it will better the houses in the city, and those here: would have a committee appointed to consider what is fit to be done in this business.

Serj. *Maynard.* This building is the ruin of the gentry, and ruin of religion, having so many thousand people without Churches to go to: this enlarging of London makes it filled with lacqueys and pages; therefore in the Bill would prevent the design of enlarging either the city or places adjacent, which else will ruin the nation.

Sir *Wm. Coventry* would not have a beauty and uniformity in the city, and a deformity in the king's court. He has no houses, nor intends to build any; (it is not his interest:) he finds that parenthesis sometimes very necessary in this house. The great houses of the bishops and nobility, and all are put into small tenements. That which is your aim is, to suppress the great number of small houses for private profit, there being scarce any new built for a nobleman's or ambassador's use. Such a thing may be by restraining the roofs to so many feet high, which will not turn to account for tradesmen to inhabit, and may be useful for the nobility and ambassadors.

Sir *Tho. Littleton.* An address to the king, 'That no Licences be granted,' may comprehend all gentlemen's opinions.

Sir *John Duncombe.* At this end of the town whole fields go into buildings, and are turned into alehouses filled with necessitous people; and should a sickness come, all the gentry would go away and they would be left a burden to the parish: the Council sends forbiddances, and the man has laid his foundation, and where is the law to restrain it? The lords of the Council cannot remedy it. To stop this, confine them to build such an height, 12 feet high, and 4 rooms on a floor: refer it to a Committee, and let them judge what places are fit to build in, and so proportioned, and that will stop the increase of buildings.

Sir *Tho. Clarges.* They may build in ancient boroughs, by the Law.—27 Eliz. it is prohibited 'within ten Miles of the city of London, and not converting great houses into tenements, and for building of great houses;' but that act was to last but 7 years.

Mr. Garroway. It is worth the honour of the house to have these immense buildings suppressed. The country wants tenants, and here are 400 soldiers that keep alehouses, and take them of the brewers, and now they are come to be Prætorian guards: that Churches have not been proportionable to houses, has occasioned the growth of Popery and Atheism, and put true religion out of the land: the city of London would not admit rare artists, as painters and carvers, into freedom; and it is their own fault that they have driven trade out of London into this end of the town, and filled the great houses with shops.

Mr. *Sawyer.* Recommend these buildings to the committee, and you must make it a nuisance.

It was then referred to a committee to bring in a Bill for restraining any farther new Buildings in all places within the Bills of Mortality, except the city of London and liberties thereof.

The King's Speech concerning certain Proposals for a Peace.] Jan. 24. The king came to the house of peers, and sending for the commons made the following Speech:

"My Lords and Gentlemen; At the beginning of this session, I told you, as I thought I had reason to do, that the States General had not yet made me any Proposals which could be imagined with intent to conclude, but only to amuse. To avoid this imputation, they have now sent me a Letter by the Spanish ambassador, offering me some terms of peace, upon conditions formally drawn up, and in a more decent stile than before. It is upon this that I desire your speedy advice; for, if you shall find the terms such as may be embraced, your advice will have great weight with me; and if you find them defective, I hope you will give me your advice and assistance how to get better terms. Upon the whole matter, I doubt not but you will have a care of my honour, and the honour and safety of the nation, which are now so deeply concerned."

With this Speech, the king delivered to the two houses copies of the Memorial from the Spanish ambassador, together with Proposals from the Dutch in order to a Treaty. Upon the reading of which, and the Dutch Proposals in the house of commons, they voted their humble and hearty Thanks to be returned to his maj. for his most gracious Speech; and immediately after they resolved, "That, upon consideration had upon his majesty's said gracious Speech, and the Proposals of the States-General of the United-Provinces, this house is of opinion, That his maj. be humbly advised to proceed in a Treaty with the States-General, in order to a speedy Peace." The lords also joining in the same Resolution of Advice, it was solemnly presented to his majesty, who returned this Answer; "My lords and gentlemen, I cannot better thank you for your Advice than by following it; which I shall endeavour, and doubt not of your assistance to enable me to perform it."

Debate on the First Reading of the Habeas Corpus Bill.] Jan. 27. A Bill to prevent the Imprisoning of the Subjects in illegal Prisons:

or sending them to Prisons beyond the Seas, was read the first time.

Mr. Attorney *North.* This bill is of great consequence, and would have it read the second time in a full house.

Sir *Tho. Lee.* Though it is not your method, yet, that we may be sure of that gentleman's company (the Attorney) desires a day may be appointed for reading the bill.—The 29th was appointed.

Debate on the Second Reading of the Habeas Corpus Bill.] Jan. 29. The Habeas Corpus Bill was read a second time.

Mr. Attorney *North.* The penalties in this bill are like those in the Act of Popery; but those are remedied by conformity, but here is a perpetual disability of conforming, and loss of office, &c. 'Legal and known prisons;' no imprisonment in law in order to examination or punishment—If a man commits a murder in Ireland, or Jersey, &c. by this bill there is no law to try him here: if a man is committed to York jail, and lies by the way, that is a prison where he lies. Knows no need of such a law, and mischiefs make a general law. As the law is, no man can be imprisoned, but in a legal prison, nor sent abroad, but in order to trial.

Sir *Rd. Temple.* Custody, in order to examination, is not a prison: if we have value for our liberties, we would secure them by law. Several have been sent to Tangier, and the islands, since the king came in: thinks your provisions against it, in this bill, not strong enough: reached by actions and indictments; some people may be too great to be reached by actions, and the king may enter a *noli pros.* upon an indictment, and hopes, upon commitment of the bill, that may be remedied.

Sir *Tho. Lee.* No penalty is too great or heavy for unlawful prisons. For murder committed beyond the sea, there is a remedy; for treasons, there is a special act of parliament for trial in England: formerly objected against the Bill: less mischief to the English nation, that those men should go unpunished in the place where the offence is done (and few escaping there) than that Englishmen should be sent abroad for offences done here.

Sir *Ch. Wheeler.* 'Legal and known prisons:' knows not how 'legal' a prison is, when there is a garrison, by the king's commission, where no sheriff can come.

Sir *Nich. Carew* hopes you will give power for the sheriff, if he has it not already: the Green-Cloth messengers imprison in their houses; they are 'unlawful prisons,' and would have these considered at the committee.

Mr. *Powle.* Imprisonment to custody is no part of punishment, and so would have excessive jailors fees of prisons stinted and settled.

Sir *John Duncombe.* It often falls out in the Treasury, that men are taken into custody, for fear of losing the king's money: sending a man to jail, and he meeting ill company there, may ruin him, therefore better for the subject.

Mr. Sec. *Coventry.* The bill is tender in many places; if not committed close prisoner, very inconvenient in some cases, a man informs, that ships are to be burnt at Chatham, or the town to be fired, or a murder; if the party be not kept close, he may be tampered with by his accomplices. Such business cannot be done without it: when the bill is committed, would have such regard had to it, that may make it possible to be practised.

Mr. *Waller.* 'Common prison'—Sometimes the plague comes into it; sometimes a man is kept in an house, in favour of the prisoner: the Guards is no prison: tells this story: in the Usurpation, some gentlemen of good quality were sent to the Guards, at St. James's. They would have made their escape, and killed the soldier that guarded them: but they would not kill them again, for fear of retaliation in the king's quarters at Oxford. When they were indicted, some counsel told them, they were in no legal prison, and it was not murder, being prisoners of war. There was a brave jury upon them, (he speaks it for their honour) who found them not guilty: would take care that no courts of guards be prisons.

Col. *Birch.* Consider where our mischief in this has been. It has been very common to commit by the king's or some great minister's warrant: he has heard in this house, that the king cannot commit a man to prison; it is not reasonable he should be both party and judge: knows the king is uneasy by it. A man is first committed by a privy counsellor, and a day after the king's hand to it. Does not like it, that all things should resort to the king's command. If so, all your provisions against it signify nothing. Knows not by what causes and counsels, but put upon the king. The doctrine he has always heard here is, 'the king can do no wrong.' It was told you, 'a person may burn the ships.' Can tell you of many committed, but where is any one proceeded against? When he has nothing left, then turn him out of prison, and no man knows what is become of him (the Herefordshire Priest) no man is committed but cause is shown, and a person found by the lord keeper to prosecute.

Sir *T. Byde.* A year and a half ago he was sent for by a messenger, and brought to the Green-Cloth, with 4 of his servants. He desired a copy of his accusation. They threatened to lay him by the heels, if he sued the messenger. He paid 5*l.* for Mile-money. The term was not in being, and he could not have his Habeas Corpus, nor any remedy, and he fears it again: sir Wm. Boreman, of the Green-Cloth, told him, 'you must not tell us of statute-law; neither lawyer nor you understand compting-house law, which is our law.' So he paid his fees for being in custody.

Sir *Tho. Clarges.* More warrants to the Tower under the king's hand now, than in 200 years before. Would have those that subsign these warrants be answerable for them.—To proceed on the 7th of February.

Debate on an Address for the Removal of the Dukes of Buckingham and Lauderdale.] Sir

Wm. Coventry moves for an Address to the king for the removal of the dukes of Lauderdale and Buckingham.

Lord *Cornbury* is against an Address, especially at this time. If you have no more Counsellors to remove, nor other Grievances to redress, then you may now do it: concerning one of these dukes, for removal there is no reason; would have gentlemen, therefore, to consider whether they have any other persons to remove, and then resolve, &c.

Sir *Nich. Carew* differs from Cornbury. Two lords in one Address is enough. Like rods, too many in a bundle, are not easily broken: would take two or three at a time, and hopes at last to remove all the ill ones.

Mr. *Sacheverell* would not have them both in an Address; it is proper for Lauderdale now for 'maintaining the king's Edicts,' &c. You cannot sit here on these terms: would assign that for a cause.

Sir *Tho. Lee* would deliver the vote by the Speaker, without any variations or alterations.

Sir *Tho. Clarges* would have the concurrence of the peers, either at a conference, with reasons, or at their bar; appoint a committee to consider of the manner to begin a thing of this moment. Would not make ill precedents now.

Sir *Tho. Meres* would have a difference betwixt Lauderdale a commoner, and Buckingham a peer. A precedent, in case of a commoner, was that of sir John Griffith, who commanded Gravesend blockhouses; the commons went to the king, and he displaced him.

Mr. *Cheney*. You have given yet no reasons for your vote.

Mr. *Garroway*. To subvert all laws, and to say, 'none shall be, but verbal laws, for the future!'—You cannot be too severe; the king may do what he pleases with him in Scotland; you think him not fit to govern here.

Sir *Winston Churchill*. Though we are satisfied, yet the king knows none of our reasons, and therefore would mention them.

Col. *Strangways*. If the king requires you hereafter to give reasons, and thinks your vote unreasonable, you may then present them.

Ordered, "That the privy counsellors of the house do attend the king, to know when this house shall attend him with the vote relating to the duke of Lauderdale."

Sir *Nich. Carew* would go to the king with this Vote now, and to the lords with the other vote.

Mr. *Stockdale* is indifferent whether we go to the lords or not, with the Address concerning the duke of Buckingham; you have a great privilege to address the king by common fame; his ill life, &c. Are you ever like to carry this charge of common fame to reach this man?

Sir *Tho. Lee*. Unless you make this as a Vote of favour, you may go to the lords with Impeachment; you may demand it of justice, and not precariously.

Sir *Tho. Meres*. In 3d Charles, there was a debate about common fame, and your book tells you of what validity it was; would lose no privilege we have a right to, nor exceed that right; would adjourn the debate for two days.

Debate on Members taking Bribes.] Sir *Nich. Carew*. We went not on suddenly after the Vote, and in a few days 5000 guineas were dispersed to adjourn it longer. It may be, so many days more may cost so many guineas, and so make guineas dearer yet.

Col. *Strangways*. If Carew knows any members that have received these guineas, he should name them; and would have a Test upon us: if any man be suspected of guineas or pension, let him purge himself.

Sir *Tho. Lee* was told that one Masters, of Lincoln's Inn, had reported, 'That this session a Member had said, that he hoped to get 5000 guineas.'

Mr. *Harwood*. Both giver and taker manage their business very ill that will discover giver or taker; if any man's condition here be so that he cannot live without a salary, let him have it from the place that sends him; here is common fame in the case, but since the great men were talked of here, many thousand guineas have been paid out in Lombard-street, which you may enquire into; would have a Test to acquit every gentleman of any thing so unworthy.

Lord *Cavendish*. Many are accused of being Pensioners to the court, for giving money here, and from the States General, for their interest.

Col. *Birch* has heard such reports, both in town and country. Observe the case, and what need there is to bring you off: how will this reflect upon the king, that it is thought by the people that the king should give us money to do any thing contrary to the interest of the kingdom! You hear one named; if an extraordinary thing, there is an extraordinary occasion for ways to clear themselves; present member by member, and in the presence of God and the house let them clear themself, as you once did about the Libel: refer it to a committee to examine this Masters, for the honour of the king, and vindication of the kingdom.

Sir *Wm. Coventry*. So much has been said in it that it is for the honour of the house to have it thoroughly examined; let a committee consider the way, and let Masters be examined at the committee, and not at the bar; that admitting not so thorough a disquisition, the mace being upon the table, and the Speaker not quick enough to ask questions; as Masters may retire, and recollect himself, whilst you are preparing new questions, how to evade your questions for discovery; a Committee is more likely to come to the quick and bottom of the matter.

It was referred to a Committee to examine this matter, and to consider what is fit farther to be done to vindicate the honour of the Members of this house. The Committee soon after met, and Masters was examined as to the words, and, after much unwillingness to discover who said the words, at last said, 'that being at Mr. John Howe's house in Gloucestershire, where he was very civilly entertained several days, (and therefore did give this account with great unwillingness, begging to be excused) he did hear Mr. Howe say, 'That he hoped this session might be worth 5000 guineas to him;' but whether in relation to the Irish Cattle coming in again, or what was precedent or subsequent in the discourse does not at all remember.

The Habeas Corpus Bill passes the Commons.] Feb. 7. The Habeas Corpus Bill was read a third time, passed, and was entitled, "An Act to prevent the illegal Imprisonment of the Subject."*

Resolved, "That the continuing of any Standing Forces in this nation other than the Militia, is a great Grievance and vexation to the people; and that this house do humbly petition his majesty to cause immediately to be disbanded that part of them that were raised since Jan. 1, 1663.

The Speaker reported, That he had attended his majesty with the Vote relating to the duke of Buckingham, and that his majesty had returned this Answer, "That he would take it into his consideration."

The King's Speech, on concluding a Peace with Holland.] Feb. 11. The king came to the house of peers, and sending for the commons made the following Speech to both houses;

"My Lords and Gentlemen; I have pursued your advice, and am come hither to tell you, that, according to your desires, I have made a speedy, honourable, and, I hope, a lasting Peace, signed already.—Mr. Speaker, and you Gentlemen of the house of commons; I told you yesterday in the Banqueting house, that I would give you a speedy Answer to your Address about disbanding the Forces therein mentioned; and I do assure you, that before you made your Address, I had given orders for the doing of it, as soon as I should be sure of the peace; and I shall reduce them to a less number than they were in the year 1663, and shall give direction for the march of those who are to return to Ireland, who were brought from thence. And as our forces are lessened at land, it will be necessary to build more great ships; for we shall not be safe, unless we equal the strength of our neighbours at sea: therefore I shall recommend it to your care to give me means for the effectual doing thereof. And this is all I have to say to you at this time."

This Speech produced an immediate Resolution; "That humble and hearty Thanks be returned to his maj. for his making a speedy Peace, and for his gracious Answers to the Addresses concerning the Standing Forces."

The King's Speech at the Prorogation.] Feb. 24. The king came to the house of peers, where, sending for the commons, he made a short Speech, to this effect:

"That when his majesty was here last, he told them, that the Peace was signed: he was come now to tell them, that it is ratified; and his majesty hopes it will be a happy and a lasting Peace to both nations. This, and the Spring coming on so fast, his maj. said, He knows they will all desire to be at home in their several countries, where they may do their own business and his majesty's also. His maj. therefore thinks it fit to make a recess at this time; the winter being more fit for business and consultation here. In the mean while, his maj. will do his endeavour to satisfy the world of his stedfastness to the Protestant Religion as it is now established; and of his desire for the securing of their properties. And so, his maj. said, he hath given order to the Lord Keeper to prorogue the parliament to the 10th of Nov. next."*

Principal Occurrences during the Recess—Scheme of the Cabal—Campaign of 1674.] Both houses met on the 10th of Nov. and were farther prorogued to the 13th of April 1675. For the following brief account of the principal Occurrences during this long recess, we are indebted to Mr. Hume. "Four days after the parliament was prorogued, the Peace was proclaimed in London, to the great joy of the people. Spain had declared that she could no longer remain neuter, if hostilities were con-

* "This gave rise to the famous Habeas Corpus Bill, which was calculated to set bounds to the arbitrary proceedings of ministers, and preserve those who fell under their displeasure from being sent into banishment, or otherwise imprisoned, without cause, measure, or relief. But though this invaluable Bill was now perfected by the commons, and sent up to the lords, it did not receive the royal assent till some years after." Ralph.

* "We cannot take leave of this remarkable session, without observing, that if the leaders of the commons had no other motives for their measures, than the necessity of espousing the cause of religion, of making an abandoned court feel the weight and efficacy of parliament, and providing for the security of the subject; it ought to be acknowledged, that they had done their best to answer all those valuable ends: and if, on the other hand, they began to entertain any thoughts of making reprisals on the court, for their ill designs on them, that they had approved themselves to be as thorough politicians in the one case, as patriots in the other: for, by the separate peace with the Dutch, they had reason to think they had effectually divided England from France; by withholding the Supply, and breaking the Army in England, and laying a foundation for doing the same in Scotland, they disabled the king from making use of force; and the Habeas Corpus Bill was both a wise and popular expedient to put the liberty of the subject out of the power of the crown." Ralph.

tinued against Holland; and a sensible decay of trade was foreseen, in case a rupture should ensue with that kingdom. The prospect of this loss contributed very much to increase the national aversion to the present war, and to enliven the joy for its conclusion. There was in the French service a great body of English, to the number of ten thousand men, who had acquired honour in every action, and had greatly contributed to the successes of Lewis. These troops, Charles said, he was bound by treaty not to recal; but he obliged himself to the States by a secret article not to allow them to be recruited. His partiality to France* prevented a strict execution of this engagement.—If we consider the projects of the famous Cabal, it will appear hard to determine whether the end which those ministers pursued were more blameable and pernicious, or the means by which they were to effect it, more impolitic and imprudent. Though they might talk only of recovering or fixing the king's authority; their intention could be no other than that of making him absolute: since it was not possible to regain or maintain, in opposition to the people, any of those powers of the crown abolished by late law or custom, without subduing the people, and rendering the royal prerogative entirely uncontrollable. Against such a scheme, they might foresee, that every part of the nation would declare themselves, not only the old parliamentary faction, which, though they kept not in a body, were still numerous; but even the greatest royalists, who were indeed attached to monarchy, but desired to see it limited and restrained by law. It had appeared, that the present parliament, though elected during the greatest prevalence of the royal party, was yet tenacious of popular privileges, and retained a considerable jealousy of the crown, even before they had received any just ground of suspicion. The guards, therefore, together with a small army, new levied, and undisciplined, and composed too of Englishmen, were almost the only domestic resources which the king could depend on in the prosecution of these dangerous counsels.—The assistance of the French king was, no doubt, deemed by the Cabal, a considerable support in the schemes which they were forming; but it is not easily conceived, that they should imagine themselves capable of directing and employing an associate of so domineering a character. They ought justly to have suspected that it would be the sole intention of Lewis, as it evidently was his interest, to raise incurable jealousies between the king and his people; and that he saw how much a steady uniform government in this island, whether free or absolute, would form invincible barriers to his ambition. Should his assistance be demanded; if he sent a small supply, it would serve only to enrage the people, and render the breach altogether irreparable; if he furnished a great force, sufficient to subdue the nation, there was little reason to trust his generosity, with regard to the use which he would make of this advantage.—In all its other parts the plan of the Cabal, it must be confessed, appears equally absurd and incongruous. If the war with Holland were attended with great success, and involved the subjection of the republic; such an accession of force must fall to Lewis, not to Charles: and what hopes afterwards of resisting by the greatest unanimity so mighty a monarch? How dangerous, or rather how ruinous, to depend upon his assistance against domestic discontents? If the Dutch by their own vigour, and the assistance of allies, were able to defend themselves, and could bring the war to an equality, the French arms would be so employed abroad, that no considerable reinforcement could thence be expected to second the king's enterprises in England. And might not the project of over-awing or subduing the people be esteemed, of itself, sufficiently odious, without the aggravation of sacrificing that state, which they regarded as their best ally, and with which, on many accounts, they were desirous of maintaining the greatest concord and strictest confederacy? Whatever views likewise might be entertained of promoting by these measures the catholic religion, they could only tend to render all the other schemes abortive, and make them fall with inevitable ruin upon the projectors. The catholic religion, indeed, where it is established, is better fitted than the protestant for supporting an absolute monarchy; but would any man have thought of it as the means of acquiring arbitrary authority in England, where it was more detested than even slavery itself?—It must be allowed, that the difficulties, and even inconsistencies, attending the schemes of the Cabal, are so numerous and obvious, that one feels at first an inclination to deny the reality of those schemes, and to suppose them entirely the chimeras of calumny and faction. But the utter impossibility of accounting, by any other hypothesis, for those strange measures embraced by the court, as well as for the numerous circumstances which accompanied them, obliges us to acknowledge (though there remains no direct evidence of it) that a formal plan was laid for changing the religion, and subverting the constitution, of England, and that the king and the ministry were in reality conspirators against the people. What is most probable in human affairs, is not always true; and a very minute circumstance, overlooked in our speculations, serves often to explain events, which may seem the most surprising and unaccountable. Though the king possessed penetration and a sound judgment, his capacity was chiefly fitted for smaller matters, and the ordinary occurrences of life; nor had he application enough to carry his view to distant consequences, or to digest and adjust any plan

* In the Appendix to the present volume, No. XI. will be found a curious document, taken from lord Somers' Tracts, intitled "A Scheme of the Trade between England and France," at this period.

of political operations. As he scarcely ever thought twice on any one subject, every appearance of advantage was apt to seduce him; and when he found his way obstructed by unlooked for difficulties, he readily turned aside into the first path, where he expected more to gratify the natural indolence of his disposition. To this versitality or pliancy of genius, he himself was inclined to trust; and he thought, that after trying an experiment of enlarging his authority, and altering the national religion, he could easily, if it failed, return into the ordinary channel of government. But the suspicions of the people, though they burst not forth at once, were by this attempt rendered altogether incurable; and the more they reflected on the circumstances attending it, the more resentment and jealousy were they apt to entertain. They observed, that the king never had any favourite; that he was never governed by his ministers, scarcely even by his mistresses; and that he himself was the chief spring of all public counsels. Whatever appearance, therefore, of a change might be assumed, they still suspected, that the same project was secretly in agitation; and they deemed no precaution too great to secure them against the pernicious consequences of such measures. —The king, sensible of this jealousy, was inclined thenceforth not to trust his people, of whom he had even before entertained a great diffidence; and, though obliged to make a separate peace, he still kept up connexions with the French monarch. He apologized for deserting his ally, by representing to him all the real undissembled difficulties under which he laboured; and Lewis, with the greatest complaisance and good humour, admitted the validity of his excuses. The duke likewise, conscious that his principles and conduct had rendered him still more obnoxious to the people, maintained on his own account a separate correspondence with the French court, and entered into particular connexions with Lewis, which these princes dignified with the name of friendship. The duke had only in view to secure his succession, and favour the catholics: and it must be acknowledged to his praise, that, though his schemes were, in some particulars, dangerous to the people, they gave the king no just ground of jealousy. A dutiful subject, and an affectionate brother, he knew no other rule of conduct than obedience; and the same unlimitted submission which afterwards, when king, he exacted of his people, he was ever willing, before he ascended the throne, to pay to his sovereign.—As the king was at peace with all the world, and almost the only prince in Europe placed in that agreeable situation, he thought proper to offer his mediation to the contending powers, in order to compose their differences. France, willing to negotiate under so favourable a mediator, readily accepted of Charles's offer; but it was apprehended, that, for a like reason, the allies would be inclined to refuse it. In order to give a sanction to his new measures, the king invited Temple from his retreat, and appointed him ambassador to the States. That wise minister, reflecting on the unhappy issue of his former undertakings, and the fatal turn of counsels which had occasioned it, resolved, before he embarked anew, to acquaint himself, as far as possible, with the real intentions of the king, in those popular measures which he seemed again to have adopted. After blaming the dangerous schemes of the Cabal, which Charles was desirous to excuse, he told his majesty very plainly, that he would find it extremely difficult, if not absolutely impossible, to introduce into England the same system of government and religion which was established in France: that the universal bent of the nation was against both; and it required ages to change the genius and sentiments of a people: that many, who were at bottom indifferent in matters of religion, would yet oppose all alterations on that head; because they considered, that nothing but force of arms could subdue the reluctance of the people against Popery; after which, they knew, there could be no security for civil liberty: that in France every circumstance had long been adjusted to that system of government, and tended to its establishment and support: that the commonalty, being poor and dispirited, were of no account; the nobility, engaged by the prospect or possession of numerous offices, civil and military, were entirely attached to the court; the ecclesiastics, retained by like motives, added the sanction of religion to the principles of civil policy: that in England a great part of the landed property belonged either to the yeomanry or middling gentry; the king had few offices to bestow; and could not himself even subsist, much less maintain an army, except by the voluntary supplies of his parliament: that if he had an army on foot, yet if composed of Englishmen, they would never be prevailed on to promote ends which the people so much feared and hated: that the Roman Catholics in England were not the hundredth part of the nation, and in Scotland not the two hundredth; and it seemed against all common sense to hope, by one part, to govern ninety-nine, who were of contrary sentiments and dispositions: and that foreign troops, if few, would tend only to inflame hatred and discontent; and how to raise and bring over at once, or to maintain many, it was very difficult to imagine. To these reasonings Temple added the authority of Gourville, a Frenchman, for whom he knew the king had entertained a great esteem: "A king of England," said Gourville, "who will be 'the man of his people,' is the greatest king in the world: but if he will be any thing more, he is nothing at all." The king heard, at first, this discourse with some impatience; but being a dextrous dissembler, he seemed moved at last, and, laying his hand on Temple's, said, with an appearing cordiality, "And I will be the man of my people."—Temple, when he went abroad, soon found that the scheme of meditating a peace was likely to prove abortive. The allies, besides their jealousy of the king's mediation, expressed a great ardour for the continuance of war. Holland had stipulated with Spain never to come to an accommodation, till all things in Flanders were restored to the condition in which they had been left by the Pyrenean treaty. The emperor had high pretensions in Alsace; and as the greater part of the empire joined in the alliance, it was hoped that France, so much overmatched in force, would soon be obliged to submit to the terms demanded of her. The Dutch, indeed, oppressed by heavy taxes, as well as checked in their commerce, were desirous of peace; and had few or no claims of their own to retard it: but they could not in gratitude, or even in good policy, abandon allies, to whose protection they had so lately been indebted for their safety. The prince of Orange likewise, who had great influence in their councils, was all on fire for military fame, and was well pleased to be at the head of armies, from which such mighty successes were expected. Under various pretences, he eluded, during the whole campaign, the meeting with Temple; and after the troops were sent into winter quarters, he told that minister, in his first audience, that till greater impression were made on France, reasonable terms could not be hoped for; and it were therefore vain to negociate.—The success of the campaign had not answered expectation. The prince of Orange, with a superior army, was opposed in Flanders to the prince of Condé, and had hoped to penetrate into France by that quarter, where the frontier was then very feeble. After long endeavouring, though in vain, to bring Condé to a battle, he rashly exposed, at Seneffe, a wing of his army; and that active prince failed not at once to see and to seize the advantage. But this imprudence of the prince of Orange was amply compensated by his behaviour in that obstinate and bloody action which ensued. He rallied his dismayed troops; he led them to the charge; he pushed the veteran and martial troops of France; and he obliged the prince of Condé, notwithstanding his age and character, to exert greater efforts, and to risque his person more than in any action, where, even during the heat of youth, he had ever commanded. After sun-set, the action was continued by the light of the moon; and it was darkness at last, not the weariness of the combatants, which put an end to the contest, and left the victory undecided. "The prince of Orange," said Condé, with candour and generosity, "has acted, in every thing, like an old captain, except venturing his life too like a young soldier." Oudenarde was afterwards invested by the prince of Orange; but he was obliged, by the Imperial and Spanish generals, to raise the siege on the approach of the enemy. He afterwards besieged and took Grave; and at the beginning of winter, the allied armies broke up, with great discontents and complaints on all sides.—The allies were not more successful in other places. Lewis, in a few weeks, reconquered Franche-comté. In Alsace, Turenne displayed, against a much superior enemy, all that military skill, which had long rendered him the most renowned captain of his age and nation. By a sudden and forced march, he attacked and beat at Sintzheim the duke of Lorrain and Caprara, general of the Imperialists. Seventy thousand Germans poured into Alsace, and took up their quarters in that province. Turenne, who had retired in Lorrain, returned unexpectedly upon them. He attacked and defeated a body of the enemy at Mulhausen. He chased from Colmar the elector of Brandenburgh, who commanded the German troops. He gained a new advantage at Turkheim. And having dislodged all the allies, he obliged them to repass the Rhine, full of shame for their multiplied defeats, and still more, of anger and complaints against each other.—In England, all these events were considered by the people with great anxiety and concern; though the king and his ministers affected great indifference with regard to them. Considerable alterations were about this time made in the English ministry. Buckingham was dismissed, who had long, by his wit and entertaining humour, possessed the king's favour. Arlington, now chamberlain, and Danby the treasurer, possessed chiefly the king's confidence. Great hatred and jealousy took place between these ministers; and public affairs were somewhat disturbed by their quarrels. But Danby daily gained ground with his master: and Arlington declined in the same proportion. Danby was a frugal minister; and, by his application and industry, he brought the revenue into tolerable order. He endeavoured so to conduct himself as to give offence to no party; and the consequence was, that he was able entirely to please none. He was a declared enemy to the French alliance; but never possessed authority enough to overcome the prepossessions which the duke retained towards it. It must be ascribed to the prevalence of that interest, aided by money remitted from Paris, that the parliament was assembled so late this year; lest they should attempt to engage the king in measures against France, during the ensuing campaign. They met not till the 13th of April 1675."

THIRTEENTH SESSION OF THE SECOND PARLIAMENT.

The King's Speech on opening the Session.] April 13, 1675. This day both houses met, after a recess of nearly fourteen months; when the king opened the session with the following Speech to both houses:

"My Lords and Gentlemen; The principal end of my calling you now is, to know what you think may be yet wanting to the securing of Religion and Property, and to give myself the satisfaction of having used the uttermost of my endeavours to procure and settle a right and lasting understanding between us; for, I must tell you, I find the contrary so much laboured, and that the pernicious designs of ill men have taken so much place under specious pretences, that it is high time to be watchful in preventing their contrivances; of which it is not the least, that they would, by all the means they can devise, make it unpracticable any longer to continue this present parliament: for that reason, I confess, I cannot think such have any good meaning to me; and therefore, when I consider how much the greatest part of this parliament has, either themselves, or fathers, given me testimony of their affections and loyalty, I should be extreme loath to oblige those enemies, by parting with such friends; and they may be assured, that none shall be able to recommend themselves to me by any other way than their good services.—I have done as much as on my part was possible, to extinguish the Fears and Jealousies of Popery, and will leave nothing undone that may shew the world my zeal for the Protestant Religion as it is established in the Church of England, from which I will never depart.—I must needs recommend to you the condition of the Fleet, which I am not able to put into that state it ought to be; and which will require so much time to repair and build, that I should be sorry to see this summer (and consequently a whole year) lost, without providing for it.—The season of the year will not admit any long session; nor would I have called you now, but in hopes to do something that may give content to all my subjects, and lay before you the consideration of the Fleet; for I intend to meet you again at winter.—In the mean time, I earnestly recommend to you all such a temper and moderation in your proceedings, as may tend to unite us all in counsel and affection, and disappoint the expectation of those who hope only by violent and irregular motions to prevent the bringing of this session to a happy conclusion. The rest I leave to the Lord Keeper."

The Lord Keeper Finch's Speech.] Then the Lord Keeper spake as followeth:

"My lords; and you the knights, citizens, and burgesses of the house of commons; The solemnity of this day's appearance is equal to the weight and importance of the occasion. The matters to be treated of deserve no less than an assembly of the three estates, and a full concourse of all the wise and excellent persons who bear a part in this great council, and do constitute and complete this high and honourable court.—The king hath called you, at this time, to examine and concur with him in the best expedients for the preservation of the Protestant Religion, for securing the establishment of it by a due execution of the laws, for providing for the safety of the kingdom, and for the improvement of its honour and reputation; and withal, in order to these ends, and above all the rest, to unite the hearts of his parliament and people to himself, by all the emanations of grace and goodness that from a great and generous prince can be expected.—To all which the king is pleased to add, the consideration of your Liberties and Properties; and while he does so, you may be sure, that he who is so careful of your rights will be mindful of his own too; for he that does justice to all, can never be wanting to himself.—These points are such, as though they be but mentioned by the king, though they are but only touched, as I may say, by his golden sceptre, yet this royal declaration of himself, joined to what he hath already done, doth not only raise all our hopes, but carries in itself so evident an assurance, and is stampt by so sacred an authority, that there remains no place for doubting, nothing can be added to the efficacy of it.—His maj. begins with the consideration of Religion. He sees it is the first thing in all your thoughts; and you cannot but see that it hath been, and still is, the first and principal part of his care.—His maj. hath considered Religion, first, in general, as it is Protestant, and stands in opposition to Popery; and upon this account it is that he hath awakened all the laws against the papists: there is not one statute extant in all the volume of our laws, but his maj. hath now put in a way of taking its full course against them; and upon this account also it is, that, in a League lately renewed with a Protestant crown, his maj. hath made it one article of that League, That there shall be a mutual defence of the Protestant Religion.—His maj. hath considered Religion again more particularly, as it is the Protestant religion established by law in the Church of England: he sees, that as such, it is not only best suited to the monarchy, and most likely to defend it, but most able to defend itself against the enemies of all reformation; and therefore upon this account it is, that his majesty, with equal and impartial justice, hath revived all the laws against Dissenters and Non-conformists, but not with equal severity; for the laws against the Papists are edged, and the execution of them quickened, by new rewards proposed to the informers; those against Dissenters are left to that strength which they have already. Both these, and all other laws whatsoever, are always understood to be subject to the pleasure of a parliament, which may alter, amend, or explain themselves, as they see cause, and according unto public convenience.—For, when we consider Religion in Parliament, we are supposed to consider it as a parliament should do, and as parliaments in all ages have done; that is, as it is a part of our laws, a part, and a necessary part, of our government: for, as it works upon the conscience, as it is an inward principle of the Divine Life by which good men do govern all their actions, the state hath nothing to do with it, it is a thing which belongs to another kind of commission than that by which we sit here.—Now, as it relates to Government, it is somewhat an unpleasant observation, to see how slow many inferior magistrates are in the discharge of this part of their duty, which refers to the safety of the Church against the enemies on both sides of it, the Papists and the Dissenters: for this is that which opens mens mouths to object against the laws themselves; this is that which encourages offenders to dispute that authority which they should obey, and to judge those laws by which they ought to be judged. They have found a way to make even justice itself criminal, by giving it a hard name, and calling it persecution.—To what a strange kind of perplexity do men labour to reduce this government: if the law against Recusants be not executed, the Church of England is abandoned; if they be, all sorts of recusants complain of persecution, as if the abandoning of the Church of England were not in some sense a persecution too.—Let us suppose that possible, which the piety and goodness of the king hath made next to impossible: but let it be for once supposed, that the Church of England were forsaken, her authority made insignificant, her government precarious; suppose her disarmed of all those laws by which she is guarded, denied all aid from the civil magistrate, and that none were obliged to obey her commands but those that have a mind to it! Would not this turn a national church into nothing else but a tolerated sect or party in the nation? would it not take away all appearance of Establishment from it? would it not drive the Church into the wilderness again, where she should be sure to find herself encompassed with all sorts of enemies, if at least she could find herself, at all, in the midst of so many tolerations?—Seeing then no way can be taken, but one side or other will either call or think it persecution, the choice is not difficult; it is better to have a strict rule than none at all, better to make the law that rule than to leave every man to be a law and a rule unto himself.—Happy is that government when men complain of the strict execution of the laws, especially when a parliament is sitting which can take the truest measures, and where the wisdom of the nation is to judge of the interest of it.—In the next place, the king hath thought fit to direct your considerations upon the safety and honour of the state; both which are then best provided for, when we keep up the strength and reputation of our Fleet.—So the Roman state thought, when (as the orator tells us) they decreed, 'Non solum præsidii, sed etiam ornandi imperii causa navigandum esse.'—It is not altogether the natural decay of Shipping, no, nor the accidents of war, that have lessened our Fleet, though something may be attributed to both these; but our fleet seems rather to be weakened for the present, by being out grown, and out-built by our neighbours.—Now, as the times of youth and health are best employed in providing against the incommodities and inconveniences of sickness and old age; so there cannot be a better use made of times of peace, than to provide for times of war; there cannot be a greater security against your enemies, than to be always in a posture ready to receive them.—Fleets may secure you abroad, but good laws are necessary to preserve you at home. Nothing recommends the present age unto posterity so much as the wisdom and the temper of the laws that are made in it; for all succeeding ages judge of our laws, as we do of our ancestors, by the true and unerring rule of experience.—In making of laws, therefore, it will import us to consider, That too many laws are a snare, too few are a weakness in the government; too gentle are seldom obeyed, too severe are as seldom executed; and sanguinary laws are, for the most part, either the cause or the effect of a distemper in the state.—To establish this state, there seems not to need many new laws: some will always be wanting; and though all that is wanting should not now be finished, yet whatever shall remain unfinished, may be perfected in winter, at which time, we have a gracious intimation from his majesty, that we shall meet again.—But, lest your greater and weightier affairs should make you pass by things of lesser moment, it may not be amiss to put you in mind to provide against the Excess of new Buildings near London and Westminster: it is a growing mischief, which nothing but a new law can put a stop to; a mischief which for a long time hath depopulated the country, and now begins to depopulate the city too, by leaving a great part of it uninhabited.—Yet, that you may not only entertain yourselves with careful and provident thoughts for the future, be pleased a little to consider and rejoice in the happiness of our present estate.—If we look upon the state of things abroad, we shall find ourselves in such circumstances, that it were great impiety not to acknowledge those mercies which, by a rare felicity, have distinguished us from our now miserable neighbours.—Wars and confusions cover the face of the rest of the Christian world; while we have no other part in all these afflictions but that of a Christian compassion. We are newly gotten out of an expensive war, and gotten out of it upon terms more honourable than ever. The whole world is now in peace with us, all ports are open to us, and we exercise a free and uninterrupted traffic through the Ocean; and we are reaping the fruits of all this peace, by a daily improvement of our Trade, and in the increase of our Shipping and Navigation. Our constitution seems to be so vigorous and so strong, that nothing can disorder it but ourselves. No influences of the stars, no configurations of the heavens, are to be feared, so long as these two houses stand in a good disposition to each other, and both of them in a happy conjunction with their lord and sovereign. Why should we doubt it? Never was discord more unseasonable. A difference in matters of the Church would gratify the enemies of our religion, and do them more service than the best of their auxiliaries. A difference in matters of state would gratify our enemies too, the enemies of our peace, the enemies of this parliament; even all those, both at home and abroad, that hope to see, and practise to bring about, new changes and revolutions in the government.—They understand well enough that the best health may be destroyed by too much care of it; an anxious scrupulous care, a care that is always tampering, a care that labours so long to purge all ill humours out of the body, that at last it leaves neither good blood nor spirits behind. In like manner, there are two symptoms which are dangerous in every state, and of which the historian hath long since given us warning. One is, when men do '*Quieta movere*,' when they stir those things or questions which are and ought to be in peace; and, like unskilful architects, think to mend the building by removing all the materials which are not placed as they would have them.—Another is, 'Cum res parvæ magnis motibus aguntur,' when things that are not of the greatest moment are agitated with the greatest heat, and so much weight is laid upon a new, and not always very necessary proposition, as if the whole sum of affairs depended upon it.—Who doth not see that there are in all governments difficulties more than enough, though they meet with no intestine divisions; difficulties of such a nature, that the united endeavours of the state can hardly struggle with? But, after all is done that can be, they will still remain insuperable.—This is that which makes the crowns of princes, when they are worn by the clearest and the noblest title, and supported with the mightiest aids, yet at the best but wreaths of glorious thorns. He that would go about to add to the cares and solicitudes of his prince, does what in him lies to make those thorns pierce deeper and sit closer to the royal diadem than ever they did before.—No zeal can excuse it; for, as there may be a religious zeal, a zeal for God which is not according to knowledge, so there may be a state zeal, a zeal for the public which is not according to prudence, at least not according to the degree of prudence which the same men have when they are not under the transport of such a fervent passion.—Hath it not been a strange mistake in some general councils, and a mistake which is fatal at this day to the peace of the Christian Church, that in most of their canons and sanctions they have more considered whom they should oppose, than what they should establish? And may it not prove a piece of as ill conduct in any secular assembly, to pursue good ends by violent means, and, in the heat of that pursuit, to choose rather to lose that good they might have compassed, than to fall short of any of those good ends which they have once proposed unto themselves?—My Lords and Gentlemen; The king is far, infinitely far, from fearing any excess of this kind here. He knows too well the wisdom, the honour, and the loyalty, of this great assembly, to apprehend any kind of error, either in your judgments or your affections. He does not only find himself safe, but he thinks himself armed too, while he is attended with such a nobility, such a gentry, as this. You that were able to raise the king's affairs when they were in their lowest and most deplored condition, will surely be able to keep them from any relapse. You that were able to make this government take root again, will surely be able to preserve it in a growing and a flourishing estate. Such pilots need not fear a storm. If you could, this consideration alone were enough to support you, 'That you carry Cæsar and his fortunes:' you serve a prince, in whose preservation miracles are become familiar; a prince, in whose style *Dei Gratia* seems not to be written by a vulgar pen, but by the arm of Omnipotence itself.—Raise up then, by your example, the hearts and hopes of all those whom ill men have wrought upon to such a degree, as to cast them into a sadness, and into a despondency, which is most unseasonable. What the Romans scorned to do after the Battle of Cannæ, what the Venetians never did when they had lost all their terra firma, that men are now taught to think a virtue, and the sign of a wise and good man, *desperare de Republica*; and all this in a time of as much justice and peace at home, as good laws for the security of religion and liberty, as good execution of these laws, as great plenty of trade and commerce abroad, and as likely a conjuncture of affairs for the continuance of these blessings to us, as ever nation prospered under. Confirm the faith then of those that are made weak, by shewing them the stedfastness of your belief. Give the king the hearts of all his subjects, by making him a present of yours. Then will the king esteem himself a richer prince than if he were possessed of all the treasures of the east. Then, though this session should close in a few weeks, yet it may be perpetual, for the fruit it shall produce, and for the commemoration that will follow it. Then will this year be a true year of jubilee; and we shall have nothing left to wish or pray for in this world, but the blessed continuance of his majesty's long and happy reign over us."

The first step the house took after this, was to vote; 'Their humble and hearty Thanks to his majesty for his gracious promises and assurances, explained in his said Speech, to preserve and maintain us in the Established Religion, and our Properties according to law, and for calling us together at this time for that purpose.' Which being presented to the king in a full body in the Banquetting-House; his majesty returned this gracious Answer, 'That he had a great confidence in his house of commons; and that the said house may be confident that he would always preserve them in the Established Religion, and in their Liberties and Properties.'

April 10. Resolved, "That an humble Address be presented to his majesty for the speedy re-calling of all his subjects home out of the French king's service, and for hindering any more from going over into that service, for the future."

Debate on the Bill for restraint of Building near London.] April 20. A Bill for restraint of Building, [illegible] and Inclosures, near to the cities of London and Westminster, was read the first time.

Mr. *Waller*. The law favours buildings. If you build with another man's brick or timber, the law gives you damage for it, but not the brick and timber. Again, it is said 'that these buildings make poverty.' We are undone in the country, without building—And yet not build at all. The relief of the poor ruins the nation—By the late Act they are hunted like foxes out of parishes, and whither must they go but where there are houses? We shall shortly have no lands to live upon, to relieve them, the charge of many parishes in the country is so great.

Mr. *Sawyer*. The Act for settlement of the poor, does, indeed, thrust all people out of the country to London. This Bill remedies the matter: by this increase of building, in a while the people will come into such disorder as to destroy the buildings themselves.

Mr. *Child*.* Sixty years experience has made it evident, in fact, that rents have increased the more for building houses. London has more inhabitants than before the Fire: the circumference must be subservient to the center.

Mr. *Jones*. If increase of buildings makes the houses in London of better value, it is a great paradox. Where is the demonstration? Is it because rents fall every day? but if this bill be so much against law as to give right away, is against it.

Sir *Nich. Pedley*. It is said that the buildings are not a nuisance at common law. In Q. Eliz.'s time, they were judged a nuisance, and in king James's time. Not by statute. But when a thing grows too big and inconvenient, it is a nuisance. The builders have been pardoned by Act, but for the future would prevent it.

Resolved, "That this Bill be withdrawn, and that a Committee be appointed to prepare and bring in a new Bill, upon the debates of the house, to restrain the farther increase of building near the cities of London and Westminster, and to remedy the inconveniencies occasioned thereby."

Debate on sir John Prettyman's Case: he being a Member and detained Prisoner in the King's Bench.] Sir John Prettyman's Case, he being a member, and detained prisoner in the King's Bench, upon execution, was reported by sir Thomas Meres.

Mr. *Sawyer*. Whether this case be of the nature of privilege, or upon being outlawed before his election, is the question. To the law of parliament the case of privileging belongs. But as to reason, no prescriptions show that ever it was done. Prorogations are of the nature of several parliaments, and privilege commences as if it were a new parliament, 13 Hen. viii. And in Plowden's Commentaries 79, being of the same nature with those cases of judgment and execution in time of prorogation. No injury can, by privilege, be done to an innocent person; your subsequent privilege cannot do wrong to another, a third person. Should it do so, the inconveniencies were great. In effect, by allowing privilege in this case, you make 'privilege of prorogation' equal to 'privilege of adjournment.' If you deliver a man in execution, it is against what the law has vested the party in, and he loses also all the charges he has been at. There are judgments in the Case—31 Hen. vi. The Speaker* was then taken in execution, in time of prorogation. It was debated and referred to the judges, and reported by them to be according to law of parliament, judged in the house of lords. It was then ruled that the Speaker should not be discharged; and the commons thereupon chose a new Speaker. It may be objected, That this was a judgment given by the lords: but it is answered; the lords were then the proper judges of it, but the judgment was confirmed by the commons. Many cases that may be instanced, were in the time of privilege, when wrong was done by the aggressor. To what purpose has the house, at any time, debated limitation of time of privilege, if out of the time you deliver the party? Martin's case 28 Eliz. There was then a case when a member was taken within '14 days' on a prorogation, which was then the time of privilege. But about '20 days,' upon report of Ferrer's case, it divided the house in opinion, whether a time should be asserted, or not, for privilege, or defined. The first question was, Whether the house would assert a time? It was resolved 'No; but a convenient time.' The next question was, Whether Martin was taken in that convenient time? 'Yea.' But whether the party should be punished, because the case was doubtful, was the great objection. There is the same reason for the one as the other, that the member might attend the house without disturbance. Before any person sits, he has privilege. The true reason why the person in execution should not be delivered, as the case is stated, is that the party should not be left remedyless. 1 K. James, sir Robert Shirley was in execution in the fleet four days. There was a Habeas Corpus granted to bring him to the bar. It was then declared there should be a bill, for the jailors and sheriff's indemnity. It provides that he may be taken again, after the session is over, 'after parliament.' No punishment for procuring such an arrest as that is.

Sir *John Birkenhead* would know whether Prettyman is in execution for a debt owing to any of your members. That may alter something of his case.

Mr. Sec. *Coventry*. In case of a peer's eldest son arrested in execution for debt, if his father should die, and he become a peer, he shall not come out of prison. And will you set up your privileges higher than where privilege is born with a man, and yet he cannot be taken out of execution? Take heed what ye do,

* Afterwards Sir Josiah.

* Thorpe. See vol. i. p. 391.

Sir *Rd. Temple.* All the ancient precedents, before the statute of 1st. James, will not be of any great use in this business. Formerly the house had power of punishing the prosecutor that put the party in prison, but had no power to release the party. Thorpe's case was a distinction between a debt to the king, and one to the subject, and yet has been over-ruled since. All precedents before 1 k. James, are out of the case. The preamble of the act is general and universal. Sawyer mistakes the case, for by this statute 'when privilege shall cease, the party shall be in execution again, all proceedings remaining as they were before,' and so persons concerned not be put to any new trouble of process. Would have one instance, let a member's taking be when it will, that ever he was detained, the parliament sitting. It is said, the party has an interest in the prisoner; so has the public likewise, and before the party had any, and you will not send a new writ, to chuse another in his stead. The case is of great weight, and he would not subject the keepers of prisons to any action of escape, but believes that persons taken in prorogation have been delivered out. The reason is the same whether the party is attached, the parliament sitting, or not.

Col. *Strangways.* We grant privilege in an adjournment. This case is privilege in prorogation. The privilege continues while he is a parliament-man. Upon delivering him, the parliament sitting, the sheriff is cleared by the statute of 1 k. James. By suffering him to be detained, you deprive a county, or a borough, of a representative.

Sir *Wm. Coventry.* It is a tender argument to speak against the privilege of this house. Parliaments now are of longer continuance than formerly: and therefore it is an argument not to extend them more than formerly. The member's (Prettyman) council quoted no precedents in the case to the committee. But something so applicable from the bar of the 'case of a peer's son' that he thinks we have no reason to extend our privileges more than they do. No man will doubt but that there is such a sleeping of privilege in prorogation, which, if awaked, must have power, not only to stop, but to reverse the course of law, or the next step to it, if it rises. If a member be enlarged by privilege, it is restrained to those cases where, by that privilege, he might be before the statute. You may say, that he may serve the execution again when the parliament is dismissed: but can the party catch him? He that took him before was innocent, and he must catch him. It may be he has nothing responsible for the debt, neither goods, nor lands, and nothing but his person to be had, and this privilege is during the whole parliament. What may be the consequence of this? You would have often remedied buying of places in elections; this privilege will be a temptation to do it still, all debts being paid by privilege. This may tend to sending hither the most unfit men in England, and to put men upon breaking to be here. Let us not give occasion to people abroad to say we are rather extending than straitening our privileges, and never explaining them. Considering especially, that men, by death of witnesses, (our privileges being longer now than formerly) may lose their lands, as well as their debts, and therefore would not agree with the committee to send for Prettyman out of custody.

Mr. *Swynfin* agrees with the latter part of Coventry's speech, 'That titles and estates may be lost by death of witnesses, when privilege continues long,' and 'that it may be an invitation to bad men to come into parliament.' So that if any act of compassion to the subject could be made, to suspend privilege in some cases, would be glad of it: but in this case of Prettyman's, believes it a right, and that when a member is chosen, the town and the house have a right to that privilege. It is granted that any member, during sitting, has privilege; but here is the question, Whether a member taken in execution out of privilege has the same right of being released out of prison, as in privilege? If it be allowed, how will it be answered upon an original writ out of time? If you make precedents in one case, you must do it in another. The objection of 'a peer's son,' spoken of, is not this case; his father living when he was in execution, he had no title to the peerage, but this man has. The lords cannot make him a new title. The reason of privilege is the public service of the house and place he serves for, But one objection.—'Privilege is just such a thing as is found by precedent, and we have but one precedent that gives light, and that is Thorpe's case, the Speaker.' If this precedent had been since that statute of 1 k. James, no answer could be given to it; but it was before. But how appears it that there were no more precedents in the case? The reports are short; it appears not plainly that such as have been imprisoned were in time of privilege, but clear that they were delivered, the parliament sitting, which then sat not long, and this case before us could not then arise. For as to the proviso in that act to save the officers harmless, it may be out of privilege as well as in.

Mr. *Sacheverell* thinks not this case so different from Thorpe's case as is imagined, nor that of a peer's son so different: a peer serves for himself. If this releasing the person to attend here were to debar a man of his debt, would be against it. If his estate be not capable to make restitution, and he have neither land nor goods, it seems an act of malice to keep him from hence.

Sir *Thos. Meres.* If a man must be detained upon execution, though not mere process, 10, 20, 30 useful members may be taken out, to the destruction of parliaments.

Sir *Rob. Howard* finds that we have nothing to resort unto in this business as a clear precedent.

Mr. Serj. *Crook.* Did he think that this was 'lex et consuetudo parliamenti,' would not speak against it. He thought this case of Thorpe a settled and quiet case long. He was Speaker, and taken in execution, and a new one was chosen, before the statute of 1 k. James. If once a member taken in execution, were let out, or escaped, he was never to be taken again upon the same execution. It is urged that the kingdom loses a member; you will allow breach of the peace above any privilege of parliament: the keeping the peace, the very being of the kingdom; there is no supersedeas against execution, the very life of the law. Not 'morando, eundo, redeundo, lex Parliamenti,' being the usage of parliament. In so great a case as this, he doubts himself, in what he delivers, this place being the best school, and must learn here. Before 1 k. James, the person in execution being delivered, the sheriff brought his action against the jailor, and it was a crime and incapacity to take him again. Would not agree with the committee.

Col. *Titus.* It is no argument that you should take away this privilege, because it is inconvenient. Are there not greater conveniences that balance the inconveniences? You may be deprived of many members of parliament. Men may be clapped up that are against a bill to be presented here. Better far a mischief on particulars, than an inconvenience in general.

Resolved, on a division 143 to 67, "That sir John Prettyman be delivered out of the custody of the Marshal of the King's Bench, by sending the Serjeant at Arms attending on this house, with the mace, to bring him to the service of this house."

Dr. Burnet's Examination respecting the Duke of Lauderdale, reported.] April 21. Mr. Powle reports Dr. Burnet's* Examination at the Committee appointed for the Address about the Duke of Lauderderdale's removal: viz. "On the 27th *** last, Dr. Burnet was, by Mr. Secretary Coventry, ordered, in the king's name, to go 12 miles out of town. The occasion was from some words Burnet should say to a peer, which were by him denied; whereupon Burnet petitioned the king, but was, by the secretary, ordered 12 miles† out of town; speaking with the secretary again, he told him 'that the king's pleasure was changed from the 12 miles, to forbid him the Court.' Since, the duke of Lauderdale, in company of the archbishop of St Andrews, and the bishop of Salisbury, said 'he would push the punishment farther.' That, in 1672, he attended the duke of Lauderdale, at Holy-rood House, to intercede for some conventiclers, his kindred, and told him 'he feared if the security was great against them now in the Dutch war, there might be rebellion.' The duke of Lauderdale replied 'he could wish that those rogues would rebel, that he might send for some Irish Papists to suppress them.' As to the matter of the Scotch army, he is free to speak of what others were present at, as well as himself; but what passed between the Duke of Lauderdale and himself, desired to be excused till the utmost extremity."

* Afterwards bishop of Salisbury.

† Burnet, himself, says it was 'twenty.'

Address for the Removal of the Duke of Lauderdale.] April 23. The commons agreed upon the following Address to the king, for the removal of the Duke of Lauderdale:

"We your majesty's most dutiful and loyal subjects, the commons in this present parliament assembled, do, with humble thankfulness, acknowledge your majesty's care for the safety of your people, in calling us together at this time to consult of the best means for the preservation of our religion and properties; and though we have great cause to rest assured of the continuance of your majesty's gracious disposition towards us, yet we find, upon a serious examination of the state of this kingdom, that there are great jealousies risen from some late proceedings, in the hearts of your subjects, that some persons, in great employment under your majesty, have fomented designs contrary to the interest both of your maj. and your people, intending to deprive us of our ancient rights and liberties, that thereby they might the more easily introduce the Popish religion, and an arbitrary form of government over us, to the ruin and destruction of the whole kingdom.—Amongst those who are at present employed under your majesty, we have just reason to accuse, for a promoter of such designs, the duke of Lauderdale, lately created earl of Guilford; because we have had it testified in our house, by several of our members, that in the hearing before the council, of the case of Mr. Peuystone Whalley, who had committed Mr. John James, contrary to your majesty's Declaration of the 15th of March, 1671, he, the said duke did openly affirm, in the presence of your maj. sitting in council, and before divers of your subjects then attending there, 'That your majesty's Edicts ought to 'be obeyed, for your majesty's Edicts are equal with laws, and ought to be observed in the first place,' thereby, as much as in him lay, justifying the said Declaration, and the proceedings thereupon, and declaring his inclination to arbitrary counsels in terror of your good people.—And we are farther confirmed in this opinion by two late Acts of parliament, of a very strange and dangerous nature, which we have observed amongst the printed statutes of the kingdom of Scotland; the first whereof was in the third session of the first parliament, held there under your majesty, c. 25. And the other in your majesty's 2nd parliament, c. 2. The like whereof have never passed since the union of the crowns, and are directly contrary to the intention of an Act passed here in the 4th of king James, for the better abolition of all memory of hostility, and the dependencies between England and Scotland, and for the repressing of occasions of discords and disorders in time to come; and of a like Act, passed about the same time in the kingdom of Scotland, by force of which said late acts there is a Militia settled in that kingdom of 20,000 foot, and 2000 horse, who are obliged to be in readiness to march into any part of this kingdom for any service 'wherein your majesty's honour, authority, and greatness, may be concerned, and are to obey such orders and directions as they shall from time to time receive from the privy council there.' By colour of which general words we conceive this realm may be liable to be invaded, under any pretence whatsoever. And this hath been done, as we apprehend, principally by the procurement of the said duke, he having, all the time of those transactions, been principally secretary of the said kingdom, and chiefly entrusted with the administration of affairs of state there; and himself commissioner for holding the parliament at the time of passing the latter of the said acts, whereby the providing of the said horse and foot is effectually imposed upon the said kingdom, and this extraordinary power vested in the privy council there: and we conceive we have just reason to apprehend the ill consequences of so great and unusual a power, especially while the affairs of that kingdom are managed by the said duke, who hath manifested himself a person of such pernicious principles.—We do therefore, in all humility, implore your sacred majesty, considering how universal a fame and clamour of the said misdemeanours runneth openly through all your realm, That for the ease of the hearts of your people, who are possessed with extreme grief and sorrow to seen your maj. thus abused, and the kingdom endangered, that your maj. would graciously be pleased to remove the said duke from all his employments, and from your majesty's presence and councils for ever; as being a person obnoxious and dangerous to the government."

Dr. Burnet's Examination respecting the Duke.] Lord Carendish informed the house of one Hamilton who held a Thesis at Leyden, of a strange nature, against the present government, 'De Ærario publicæ necessitatis,' for which the duke of Lauderdale procured him to be knighted, and he was presented with 500*l.* for it; and had an office given him of secretary of the inspections in Ireland: would have Dr. Burnet called in, who is at the door, and interrogated about it.

Sir *Nich. Carew.* An arbitrary duke may cause Dr. Burnet to be hanged, drawn, and quartered, when we are up, for informing us: therefore, as we may punish Dr. Burnet, if he refuses to speak his knowledge of what we shall ask him, so desires the house may protect him, if he rightly informs them.

Mr. *Vaughan.* Dr. Burnet comes under as high an obligation before us, next an oath, that can be: you cannot indeed extort a question from him, but you may punish him for refusing to answer what you shall interrogate him.

Sir *Nich. Carew* would have him told the power you have.

Sir *Tho. Lee* moves that you mention the words that fell from him at the committee who drew the Address for Removal of the duke of Lauderdale, which are the occasion of his being sent for hither.

Dr. Burnet was brought to the bar. Then the Speaker admonished him, That he was sent for to speak his knowledge to what he should be interrogated. He then was asked about the words which fell from him at the committee, and told the power the house had to punish him, if he refused to answer, or prevaricated.

Dr. Burnet then said 'That when he was sent for to the committee he told them, what others knew as well as himself he would declare, but humbly begged pardon if he did not inform the committee what passed in private discourse betwixt himself and the duke; there having been some difference between him and the duke, it might be thought done in revenge:' would willingly prevent ill things: but, with all humbleness in the world, begs pardon of the house for his silence, and submits it to the sense of the house.'—Then the Speaker asked his knowledge about sir Robert Hamilton's Thesis at Leyden, 'De Ærario publicæ necessitatis.' Burnet said, 'he had not read it till within these eight days.' And withdrew.

Sir *Nich. Carew.* You have heard Burnet's answer, and desires the opinion of the house to his declaring the discourse betwixt him and the duke of Lauderdale: he believes it to be something of a high nature: would call him in to declare what he knows, which, if he refuses, would send him to the Tower.

Sir *John Hanmer.* It is an ill precedent for a man to be put upon declaring private discourse: would not have him sent for in.

Sir *Wm. Hickman.* This is not a private matter: it concerns the public, and would have him sent for in.

Mr. *Sacheverell* fears that Burnet comes a fishing to know whether you will have any from him. If the matter he knows be dangerous, he ought to reveal it; if not, he is in no danger, and of which you are to judge.

Mr. *Vaughan.* The common safety is the cause. Counsellors reveal their secrets in their closets, not in the streets. 'That it is not for Burnet's honour to say what he knows,' is no argument, when he seemed to insinuate something more he had to say: for the danger of the discourse betwixt him and the duke he is no judge of.

Dr. Burnet then was again called in. And the Speaker told him, 'That the house was not at all satisfied with his answer, but believes he knows something important that fell from this lord, which, if he concealed, he must expect to be proceeded against accordingly.'

Dr. Burnet then said, "He shall always pay obedience to the authority of this house, as becomes him. He never heard the duke of Lauderdale say 'That he intended to bring the Scotch army into England,' but the duke once asked him, 'Whether he thought Scotland would assist the king, if he needed them, about supporting the Declaration?' To which he indefinitely answered, 'He thought they would not.' The duke replied, 'He thought they would, and that they would bring a great many with them.' This discourse passed betwixt them the first Saturday in Sept. 1673, in the duke's dressing room, at the Gatehouse, in Whitehall."—He withdrew.

Sir *Tho. Littleton.* Burnet tells us, this was the substance of his discourse with the duke; but would have him called in to inform them the circumstances likewise, which will much enlighten the thing.

Mr. *Vaughan* would know whether he came casually to the duke, or was sent for by him.

Col. *Strangways* would have him asked, what Declaration he means?

Sir *Eliab Harvey* would have him asked, what he does know as to other matters?

Mr. *Garroway.* About that time he came over out of Scotland, you were about the Declaration: if you have a mind to the thread of all the counsellors that advised this Declaration, possibly he may give you some light: would know of him whether he was sent for, or whether this was an accidental discourse.

Sir *Rob. Howard* would have repeated to him what he has already said, that he may explain himself farther.

The Clerk, who was ordered to form what Dr. Burnet had given an account of at the bar, did read it to him, which Burnet did avow, and is as follows: "That coming into England, out of Scotland, the first Saturday in Sept. 1673, he went to visit the duke of Lauderdale, at his lodgings over the Gatehouse in Whitehall, where the duke and he discoursed of the affairs of this nation, and of Scotland, and particularly concerning the proceedings of parliament touching the Declaration for suspending penal laws, in matters ecclesiastical, and being afterwards asked, 'Whether if Scotland being called in to assist the king in supporting the said declaration, they would assist him or not?' he answered 'He thought they would not.' But the duke replied, 'He believed that they would, and that their coming into England would bring a great many.' That the duke asking him of the affairs of Scotland, he answered, 'The people of Scotland, that were at such a distance, could not imagine what to think of the king's Speech, and what was afterwards done concerning the Declaration.' Whereto the duke replied 'They have all forsaken the king except myself and lord Clifford." *

PROCEEDINGS RELATIVE TO THE IMPEACHMENT OF THE LORD TREASURER DANBY.

April 26. Mr. *Russel* said, He was glad to hear, on Saturday last, an account that the

* The Bishop's own account of this affair is as follows: "The house of commons fell upon duke Lauderdale, and those who knew what had passed between him and me, moved that I should be examined before a committee. I was brought before them. I told them how I had been commanded out of town. But though that was illegal, yet since it had been let fall, it was not insisted on. I was next examined concerning his design of arming the Irish Papists. I said, 'I, as well as others, had heard him say, He wished the Presbyterians in Scotland would rebel, that he might bring over the Irish Papists to cut their throats.' I was next examined concerning the design of bringing a Scottish army into England. I desired to be excused as to what had passed in private discourse, to which I thought I was not bound to answer, unless it were high treason. They pressed me long; and I would give them no other answer; so they all concluded that I knew great matters; and reported this specially to the house. Upon that I was sent for, and brought before the house. I stood upon it as I had done at the committee, 'That I was not bound to answer; that nothing had passed that was high treason, and as to all other things, I did not think myself bound to discover them.' I said farther, I knew duke Lauderdale was apt to say things in a heat, which he did not intend to do; and since he had used myself so ill, I thought myself the more obliged not to say any thing that looked like revenge for what I had met with from him.' I was brought four times to the bar. At last I was told, the house thought they had a right to examine into every thing that concerned the safety of the nation, as well as into matters of treason: and they looked on me as bound to satisfy them. Otherwise they would make me feel the weight of their heavy displeasure, as one who concealed what they thought was necessary to be known.' Upon this I yielded, and gave an account of the discourse formerly mentioned†. They laid great weight on this, and renewed their address against duke Lauderdale."

† At vol. i. p. 355 of his History, where it is thus related, "At my coming to court, duke Lauderdale took me into his closet, and asked me the state of Scotland. I upon that gave a very punctual and true account of it. He seemed to think that I aggravated matters, and asked me, 'If the king should need an army from Scotland to tame those in England, whether that might be depended on?' I told him 'certainly not.' The commons in the southern parts were all presbyterians, and the nobility thought they had been ill used and were generally discontented, and only waited for an occasion to show it.' He said 'he was of another mind: the hope of the spoil of England would fetch them all in.' I answered, 'The king was ruined if ever he trusted to that.' And I added, 'That with relation to other more indifferent persons, who might be otherwise ready enough to push their fortunes without any anxious enquiries into the grounds they went on, yet even these would not trust the king, since he had so lately said, he would stick to his Declaration, and yet had so soon after given it up.' He said 'Hinc illæ lachrymæ: but the king was forsaken in that matter, for none stuck to him but lord Clifford and himself.' And then he set himself into a fit of railing at lord Shaftsbury."

Navy was in so good a condition; but thinks all we give is too little when the Treasury is managed to set up private men and their heirs. The earl of Danby has acted in it in a high and arbitrary manner, and disposed of the treasure as he pleased: and has publicly declared at the Treasury 'that a new proclamation is as good as an old law,' moves, 'that he may be removed from the king and his employments,' and that an Impeachment be drawn against him.

Sir *S. Barnardiston* has no malice against this lord, but if the king be well served, he cares not by whom. He has Articles to present the house against him for his ill management of the treasury, and his arbitrary proceedings in it.

The *Speaker.* The nature of the Articles must be first opened, before delivered by the orders of the house.

Sir *S. Barnardiston* opens them. They contain many mscarriages in the management of the Treasury. And that he should there say, 'that a new proclamation is better than an old law,' causing a person to be banished that prosecuted, &c. And his arbitrary proceedings in the marriage of his second son to Mrs. Hyde.

Mr. *Powle* always had, and still has, an unwillingness to accuse great men, it looking like faction; they being more exposed in their actions than other men, are thereby more liable to exception; what he does is out of discharge of his duty here: is not for removing of one man to mend the prospect of another: all things are managed in the Exchequer by him by colourable and fictitious practices: the Exchequer constitutions are very excellent; all things managed there must be by persons sworn, and are equally liable to the king's debts, as if persons that acknowledged a statute staple: the checks and controuls there are perpetual evidence of what is done, no money being paid or received, but a record is kept of it: but this Lord Treasurer has removed the money into other hands, that thereby no record may be kept of it: by this means the money is got into private hands, without record for it in the Exchequer: by this means, no enquiry, either for the king or the subject, can be made, what becomes of the money. Formerly the trade crept in by small sums, which made way for greater; but now by whole sums, tallies by anticipation entered; but he has gone farther: such a patent he has obtained for his office as no age yet ever saw, and hopes no future age ever will see. There is a patent granted for the customs, but he passes it to another to keep it in his hands, till his order for disposing of it, the better to invest himself in them. The patent for the excise makes the account to be passed in the Exchequer, or else where. In the preamble of that patent it is said to be done by the advice of the Chancellor of the Exchequer (sir John Duncombe, (who at present is not here) but doubts not he will truly acquaint you whether by his advice. The taking these two great branches of the revenue, is like a steward who takes all the domains into his own hands, and leaves the lord of the manor a few tenements: by this way of farming, he takes all he can into his hands, and disposes of it how he pleases. Here have been extraordinary advances upon these farms, besides the ordinary revenue spent: but is the fleet repaired, or debts paid, or stores laid in? All this spent without applying any thing to that use: the patents are on record, and may be seen by any body: the punishment of one great officer of state, in such cases as these, is better than any laws you can make: first, let us settle the king at home, and then let us look abroad: and he will undertake the proof of these Articles himself rather than they shall go without.

Mr. *Garroway* sees the Charge against the Lord Treasurer wherein he is concerned in several things, viz. 'The precharging the revenue of the customs with sums of money,' but he that sees what is transmitted to the Exchequer from thence, will not find that Article against the Lord Treasurer so considerable: except some pensions, does not know any thing charged on the Exchequer account, viz. prince Rupert's pension, the bed-chamber men's, and the allowance to the commissioners of the customs. On his cognizance, knows no more: but whether the house will take cognizance of proceedings in the Exchequer, where the Lord Treasurer of England is so trusted, and when he has consulted with the king's counsel in the drawing his patent; will you let no man sit easily in his employments? When you consider his power, he has a vast one by law: and he would see the patents, before you make his actions crimes: when you come to see whether this patent was surreptitiously gotten, and whether sir John Duncombe knows of this patent, then you will be better informed to give your judgments. For that charge of the Lord Treasurer's saying, 'a new proclamation is better than an old law,' remembers the charge against lord chief justice Keeling about Magna Charta. If interlocutory discourses may be wrested, there is an end of all conversation. For the charge about 'banishing the man mentioned,' he knows the Lord Treasurer's tenderness so much in his actions, that when the commissioners of the customs had turned out a man that had an office in the customs, for misdemeanour, they were to justify it before the Lord Treasurer. For the charge 'of the marriage of his second son to Mrs Hyde,' he has heard discourses, but knows nothing of it. If there be any thing in it, it is cognizable at law, and why should we take up the cudgels for another man, without that man's petitioning us about it? If he can have no redress at law, let him come hither: would have the patents seen here, before you proceed any farther.

Sir *Rd. Temple.* In all cases, he has observed the Treasurer to take the best advice he could, and has made the law his rule in all things within his observation. The customs were never so little charged as in this Lord Treasurer's time. For the other charges against him, which are not public, we do not the nation service in charging these little things, which have more sound than substance: would appoint another day for viewing the patent, and farther examination of the matter.

Sir *Nich. Carew.* Agrees not with Temple's motion for another day, he would not have any criminal made innocent here, nor innocent, criminal: would have the Articles read, one by one, and so receive them or reject them, as they shall be made out.

Sir *John Coventry* has an honour for this great lord, but has it for no man that would alter the government: the Articles are new to him, but doubts not but in due time they will be made good, and that some members will make them every one good. If you find matter in them, punish him, if not, clear him.

Lord *Cavendish* hears few say that the Articles are not a ground of Impeachment against this lord: it may be the first article is doubtful in law.

Mr. *Vaughan.* At the first sight, these Articles are of a high nature: he thinks the persons that have undertaken them, have a hard part to manage, and it has been ill fortune to accuse men in this house, since to accuse is to strengthen court parties: for the Articles read, men must give their opinions of them with their judgments, and must come with all their judgments.

Mr. *King* would take time to consider of these Articles, and not proceed hastily upon them: he has known great good the Lord Treasurer has done: he has paid off the navy and army: these Articles are high, and should be well considered of.

Earl of *Ogle* moves to put off the debate for two or three days: is sure that no such thing as is alleged the Lord Treasurer should say about the proclamation, was ever said in the council.

Sir *Tho. Meres.* Here are Articles brought you, and men undertake to prove them. This was thought sufficient to impeach in lord Clarendon's case: but now people are disproving them before they are proved: at this rate, every man will be acquitted that shall be accused: joins with Vaughan's motion, 'That whoever is next bring the Articles as these are,' and he will go to the lords bar with them: putting the thing off to another day, is but a bye way to lose time, to destroy it: let the patents be brought hither to-morrow.

Sir *Courtney Poole* speaks to the method of proceeding. This is a great crime, and a great man: supposes that those gentlemen that brought them in, know how to prove them, and are prepared to do it; and that others that are not, may have time to consider of them: moves it.

Mr. *Powle.* He has no intention to engage you in a hasty vote; but he thought these alleged, great crimes: would have a day appointed to consider, and the patents brought, and let the officers of the exchequer compare them with former grants: if they be found legal, shall comply as much as any man

Mr. Sec. *Coventry.* Many things must go to the making a man so criminal as fit for notice in this house; they ought to be great. Sometimes a minister of state, in favour, carries things higher than other men have done in their place: would not have the house engaged in that which they may not go fairly off from.

Sir *Tho. Lee.* There must be divers questions before you come to impeachment. He would do nothing to draw an ill precedent upon this house, for any man's sake. All agree that the impeachment when passed, must be carried to the lords bar, and you are at your liberty for your method of proceeding: members undertake the proof of the Articles, and will not you accept them? Then comes the whole question, Whether upon the proofs you have matter to proceed to impeachment? This way you must go, and have always done, unless you will lose all method of proceeding: the man is equal to him, in all respects.

Sir *Cha. Harbord.* If there be no such thing as these Articles, you give a wrong judgment: he has had the honour to serve the king under seven or eight Lord Treasurers, and by the duty of his place he is to advise with all things relating to the revenue: he has endeavoured all his time to save the Treasury, but sees he cannot do it: so far as he has been acquainted with the Lord Treasurer he has not found his understanding defective in it; and has wondered at it, that a young man, and a country gentleman, should understand it so soon. In this business would go as faithfully and as truly as any man: as he has charity for the gentleman that brought in these Articles, so he knows many of these things to be otherwise: would have you view the state of the revenue first, and, if proper, then would enter into the merits of the cause: he can disprove many of these things alleged.

Mr. *Garroway.* He thinks it for the interest of the Treasurer that you should proceed in the articles: but would wave that article 'of the Treasury,' till the patents are viewed, and would have that done to-morrow.

Mr. Sec. *Williamson.* You cannot do a greater right to the Treasurer and your own justice than to proceed: he cannot give his judgment that any of the Articles are criminal, though proved: the proceedings of the Treasury must be compared with former times: you are not ripe for the thing now; therefore moves for Friday.

Sir *Cha. Wheeler* doubts not but as common fame leads this matter, it will be considered on the right hand as well as on the left; he believes the Treasury will appear as well to-morrow as the navy did the other day: would lose no time: he hears it said 'that things come to be disproved before they are proved;' when one side says, 'money is paid,' the other 'not paid,'. no wonder; he believes there is not one penny paid out of the Exchequer, but by order: if commissions have ran, legally and fairly, higher than formerly, if one Lord Treasurer by commission has more power given him by his patent than ordinary, it is not illegal.

Sir *Edmund Jennings* would have no time lost, and is confident that if the noble lord concerned was here present, he would be of that mind: would postpone that first Article, and proceed to the rest, and doubts not but the lord, upon examination of the whole matter, will rather deserve the thanks of the house for his good management of the Treasury, than their accusation.

Col. *Titus*. If the Treasurer has offended, it must be in the male-administration of his place in the revenue, and until you inspect that, would defer the consideration of the Articles.

Col. *Birch*. If any thing had been done amiss in the excise, would have been so faithful a servant to the Treasurer as to have told him of it before he told the house: that the Treasury is gone is certain, but as to the Treasurer's being in fault, hopes he will come out purified like gold: if the Treasurer was here present, believes he would not have this business go over: remembers that in lord Clarendon's case, before he gave his consent to impeach him, he would have the Articles proved; and if they are not so now, he will be of the same mind he was of then: would have them read, head by head, and would have some light into them presently.

Mr. *Sacheverell* moves, as to the method of your proceeding: you must first judge whether these Articles are criminal, abstractedly proved, and, though so judged, you must consider, whether they are such as you will proceed upon.

Sir *Robert Howard*. You must consider whether the thing done be that, or no, and those, crimes, or no: then your time is to give judgment, whether the things done are these crimes, or no.

Mr. Attorney *Montagu*. Strange that he should be so conversant in the Exchequer, and yet know not the least of this charge: for the patents, they must be seen, and for the charge of the proclamation, &c. no man walks by rule of law in his place more than this lord Treasurer: would have some short time appointed for the proof of the Articles.—After further debate, the house agreed to proceed in the business to-morrow.

Articles of Impeachment against the Earl of Danby.] April 27. The Articles against the Lord Treasurer Danby, were this day delivered, more fully drawn up, by sir S. Barnardiston, and were as follows:

A Charge or Impeachment against Thomas earl of Danby, Lord High Treasurer of England; containing several Offences, Crimes, and Misdemeanors of a very high nature.

I. "That the said earl hath overthrown and violated the ancient course and constitution of the Exchequer, by perverting the method of receipts, payments, and accounts, contrary to law; whereby the king's revenue is put into confusion, and a wasteful way of expence; to the destruction of his majesty's credit; and exposing his majesty's treasure and revenue to private bargains and corruptions; and hath ingrossed into his own hands, the sole power of disposing almost all the king's revenue; laying aside the chancellor and under-treasurer of the Exchequer, and other officers: whereby the usual and safe government of his majesty's affairs relating to his revenue, and all checks and comptrolls are avoided.—II. That, a suit of law being intended about the Marriage of the daughter of sir Tho. Hyde, the said earl caused one Mr. Brandly, a principal witness in the said case, to be arrested by an extraordinary warrant from one of the secretaries of state; and to be kept for some time in close custody; during which time the agents of the said earl did labour the said Mr. B. by threatenings and promises of reward, not to declare the truth: and at midnight he was brought, and examined before his majesty, upon oath; where the said earl was present, and assisting: whereupon the said Mr. B. did, by the means aforesaid, deliver in a testimony, contrary to his own knowledge, and against his conscience; he being then in duress: by which illegal practices his maj. was highly abused, the parties concerned in the said law suit greatly prejudiced, and the truth suppressed, to the manifest obstruction of justice: and all this was done with an intent to procure the said heiress to be married to the second son of the said earl.—III. That the earl hath received very great sums of money, besides the ordinary revenue, which have been wastefully spent, and far greater sums than ever issued for secret service, without account; the king's debts remaining unpaid, the stores unfurnished, and the navy unrepaired, to the discredit and hazard of the king and kingdom.—IV. That the said earl hath violated the rights and properties of the people, by stopping without authority, their legal payments, due in the exchequer.—V. That though the office of Lord High Treasurer of England is always very full of great and necessary employments, yet the said earl hath also assumed to himself the management of the Irish affairs, which were in precedent times dispatched always by the secretaries, and passed in council; thereby interrupting the said secretary's office; and neglecting his own; and subtily enabling himself, the better to convert a very great sum of money out of the Irish revenues, to his own private advantage.—VI. That the said earl hath procured great gifts and grants from the crown, whilst under great debts, by warrants countersigned by himself—VII. That about the 4th of Dec. 1674, at the hearing of a cause in the Treasury-Chamber, some Acts of parliament, now in force, were urged against a Proclamation, and contrary to what his lordship aimed at; whereupon the said earl, in contempt of the law, uttered this arbitrary expression, 'That a new Proclamation is better than an old Act;' several of his majesty's subjects being present: and, upon his lordship's report to the privy council, the person in question, being a foreigner, and not obeying such proclamation, but pursuing his right at law, was banished the kingdom."

Resolved, &c. "That as to the Charge presented against Thomas earl of Danby lord high treasurer of England, this house will proceed head by head; and hear such proofs, instances, and circumstances relating to each Article, as are requisite to an Impeachment."

The Impeachment dropped.] On the 27th and 30th of this month, and the 3rd of May, the house heard severally Evidence and examined Witnesses; and, upon the question put on each Article, "Whether any fit matter doth appear in the Examination of this Article to impeach the Lord Treasurer?" They were all passed in the negative. *

Debate on the Bill to incapacitate Parliament-men from taking Places.] April 29. A Bill was read the second time to incapacitate persons from taking any Offices of benefit, who are Parliament men, during parliament, and if any such persons be chosen, that election to be void. But the borough, or county, may chuse the same person again, and that election stand good.

Sir *Cha. Wheeler.* He supposes 100 persons in this house that would lay down their lives for their country. It may be, some few persons in this house are prisoners in the King's Bench. But this is an extraordinary case: persons that have been with the king in banishment, and they, at the king's return, for want, could not buy places of advantage, whilst other men that staid at home grew rich: would have posts come upon particular men, and let it be laid on every man's door, but rather would have it got upon honour: this Bill is a great reflection upon us all, and, without cause, it creates a perfect incapacity in a man to serve his prince, and country, at one time. After all the inconveniencies he has had these 30 years, thinks he should be highly tempted if he take an office: that gentlemen should have places of 4 or 5,000*l.* per. ann. and those that have been ruined have none! Why should not those have offices that have suffered, as well as others? Consider the temptations of being disloyal in the late times. The king may be willing to give a man an office (and he is a great man that would refuse it)—A man that has done ill, that the king might not remove that office to a Parliament man, that has done well, and deserves it: strange that the king should be so confined! No age wherein men were of greater loyalty than this, and now, for a few Parliament men that have offices, to cast a reflection upon the whole assembly!

Sir *Rob. Holt.* This Bill is in direct terms, that no man that serves the king shall be capable of being a Parliament man.

Sir *Tho. Lee* is a great enemy to garbling the house, as he has heard some say this Bill is. It only leaves it to a man's choice, to stay here, or go home, and that when he has an office. There are many changes in 10 or 12 years, when a parliament sits so long. Men are altered in some capacity or other. This Bill relates to no man's office now in being: knows not but that Parliament-men may be compelled to be sheriffs; though, indeed, in time of privilege it is true we may not go into the county to attend, yet knows not when in prorogation you may not be compelled to it. For the reason he has heard from Wheeler, this Bill will make the king look that popular names may not be an inducement to chuse officers from hence, and so may not be deceived.

Sir *Courtney Poole.* This Bill is a garbling the parliament, and a new modelling the government, from a monarchy into a commonwealth.

Col. *Strangways* observes that few are in office, that formerly have served the king: neutral persons most. The guards are mercenary, and therefore dangerous. He that has endured all the heat of the day, would have him receive his penny too, but is for no more. Would not have those shut the door after them that have offices. Never was poor prince, nor kingdom, abused as ours is. No mariners paid, and yet those that bought their debentures at 4 and 5*s.* per pound, presently paid. For the danger he incurs and his service, he deserves an office. (For office of profit he desires none.) As for the office of sheriff, no man will desire it, unless for Yorkshire. Would have all that have offices leave them, and be chosen to them again; and the king have liberty to remove them, and take them again: as that of Parliament-man in this Bill.

Mr. Sec. *Coventry* would willingly quit his office, if it hinders him from serving the king and his country here. Justices of the peace, and the office of deputy-lieutenants require attendance in the country, though those offices are excepted in the Bill. Would not for any office, or place whatsoever, but discharge his conscience here. Some hardships will arise in this Bill upon men: Dimmock, Champion to the king by descent, must not be chosen a parliament man. That any thing should force a man to a new election, that forfeits it not, is very hard; whereas, by parity of reason, if his office incapacitates a man once, it should incapacitate him again. Any man may enter

* "Whether the Charge against the Lord Treasurer was held frivolous or malicious, whether sufficient proof was wanting to make it good, or whether he had more friends in the house than his royal master, on examining the foundation, the whole building fell to the ground. It must be owned our lights fail us in this matter. Bp. Burnet contents himself with saying, 'The majority were for him.' Marvell is express, 'That he got off by *high bribing.*' Nothing is easier to be said, nothing is harder to be proved." Ralph.

into a bond to his corporation, of 1,000*l.* when he takes an office, after being chosen Parliament-man, to be forfeited. Is not your mace frequently sent for the gentlemen of the long robe, into the Hall to attend your service? You are pleased to make use of the privy counsellors to carry your messages to the king. Formerly they had cushions to sit on, but were thrown out of doors, and must they be thrown out of doors too? This Bill is not consistent with the government, and he would lay it by.

Mr. *Vaughan.* Though we are loyal, yet there have been parties in the parliaments, court, and country; and, in many things, have desired to advise with their country, before they give consent. Men have varied in their principles, and it is natural for men to do so. Where an office is inconsistent with the service of the country in the person that has it, it is reasonable that place should chuse another person, and where that place has no jealousy to think they shall not be well served, it is for the honour of the person to be chosen again. Moves for commitment of the bill.

Serj. *Maynard.* If you make a law against such bribes as are given to come into a place to serve here, you would do full as much as by this bill.

Col. *Titus.* Never had any place at court, but what he has had these 25 years. Weighing all circumstances, he is against commitment of the bill: there are reasons against the right of the subject: no reason why any man, but a fool or a knave, should be incapacitated to sit here. This is some invasion of the king's prerogative. If the king thinks a man qualified for an office, that is as much as to say 'You will not trust him that the country trusts.' You may hereby put the king upon a necessity of putting unfit men into offices. Suppose an admiral at sea, either this man must not go to sea, or you turn him out for serving his country. These splendid and extraordinary things never yet did good. After the Long Parliament had passed the Self-denying Ordinance, they never did deny themselves any thing.

Sir *Wm. Coventry* differs from sir Thomas Meres in his motion for adjourning the debate. The hand that did it (himself) will stand, with all submission, to the judgment of the house in its determination, with the same heart he brought it in with. The Bill does not provide that great officers shall not serve the king. Those that have offices may be the safer in them, and those that have no places shall not get them from them that have. The old way was, men were chosen into parliament, after they had been privy counsellors, and hopes so still, to be the better able to serve the country, and place they are chosen for. You are told 'it is hard for an admiral;' and 'that the Bill is not large enough for the militia officers,' which may be answered: and all the others are no objections for throwing out the bill. We have served here a great while, and, it may be, his corporation would not chuse him again because he has no office, that another may serve them better: consider what may be the consequence. If qualifications change—and not only absence may make us ignorant of the affairs of the place we serve for, but our presence here may do it to the office also. Edicts may meet with a stop in the parliament of Paris, in their verification, but seldom a defeat. This case, without this bill, may be so here. In 13 Edw. iii, a writ was prayed that none of that parliament should be viscount, (sheriff) or other minister, and so it went out. Here is no injury to the person by this bill; if he have no mind to the penalty of being chosen again, if he have an office, he may chuse what he will do. Whatsoever fate you give the bill, he does highly acquiesce in your judgment, and believes, if the bill does not pass, it may revive in future parliaments.

Sir *Henry Ford.* We find, by experience, that offices may be hurtful in parliament-time, but we find that popularity has done much more hurt.

Mr. *Finch.* Those, possibly, may speak to the sense, though not the acceptation of the house: the consequence of this bill is, that the service of the crown is incompatible with that here; when you consider a man so that he has betrayed one trust, to accept of another, he will come to his corporation, to be chosen again with an ill grace. We are not to pull feathers thus from the king. There was a time when we had wages for our service in parliament. If no suspicion upon a man then, why must an officer be suspected now that he gets by it? If thought necessary that he should have an estate that is chosen a parliament-man, by increasing it he is the better qualified; having the better stake, and the more reason to support his property. In that writ mentioned of Edw. iii. there is a clause, 'that no lawyer should be chosen a parliament man.' The character of that parliament was, 'Indoctum Parliamentum.' And lord Coke observes, 'that not one good law was made in that parliament.' And if we should now say no lawyer, nor officer, should be a parliament-man, it is in effect to say, no person that understands the business of the nation shall be. For business of the country, gentlemen may have experience, but for affairs of state they must be informed from officers of state—Self-denial, is not so plausible an argument for this bill. If the king knows not able men here, where shall he send, hue and cry, after them in the country? The consequence will be, you must have all officers of State out of the Lords house.

Sir *Wm. Coventry* sees that the sense of the house is against the Bill; and whether 'rejected' or 'not ingrossed' be the question, is indifferent; but the country would think better of it, if the question were 'not ingrossed' than 'rejected.'—The Bill on a division was rejected, 145 to 113.

May 5. Resolved, "That an Address be

presented to his majesty that he would be pleased to issue forth his Proclamation for the speedy Recalling those his subjects that are now in the service of the French king, and for the preventing any more from going over into that service."

Resolved, "That a farther Address be presented to his majesty concerning the duke of Lauderdale:" (the question for adjourning being carried in the negative,) 119 to 99.

The King's Answer to the Address against the Duke of Lauderdale.] May 7. Mr. Secretary Williamson* acquainted the house, That, having received their commands, to know his majesty's pleasure when he would be attended with a further Address concerning the duke of Lauderdale; that his maj. had been acquainted with it: but before that he received the order of the house to know his majesty's pleasure, his majesty had given direction for an Answer to the first Address, which he delivered in writing, and the same was read as follows:

"C. R. His maj. has considered of the Address against the duke of Lauderdale, and the Reasons accompanying it. As to the acts of parliament, mentioned to have been passed in Scotland, his maj. observes, that the first of those acts was in the year 1663; which was long before the duke of Lauderdale was his majesty's commissioner in that kingdom: the latter was in pursuance of the former. As to the words, by the time of Mr. Penistone Whaleye's case, his maj. perceives, that if they had been spoken, they must have been spoken before the last act of General Pardon: and his maj. being sensible how great a satisfaction and security the inviolable preservation of the former act of indemnity and oblivion has been to all his subjects, cannot but apprehend the dangerous consequences of inquiring into any thing that has been pardoned by an act of General Pardon, lest the example of that might give men cause to fear their security under the first Act of Oblivion."

The King's Answer to the Address for recalling the English Forces.] May 8. Mr. Secretary Coventry delivered the King's Answer to the Address about recalling the English Forces out of France; which was as follows:

"C. R. His majesty having received an Address from the house of commons, concerning the Recalling such of his subjects as are soldiers in the French king's service, hath thought fit to return this Answer: That such troops of his subjects as were in the most Christian king's service, before the last treaty made with the States General of the United Provinces, and were not, by that, to be recalled, as they are at present become inconsiderable in their numbers, so his majesty conceiveth that they cannot be recalled without derogation to his honour and dignity, and prejudice to the peace he now enjoyeth, and hath publicly professed to maintain with all his neighbours. But as to the prohibiting the going over of any more, his maj. will renew his Proclamation, and use all other effectual means both to forbid and hinder it."

The farther consideration of his majesty's Answer was adjourned to the 10th.

Debate on the King's Answer.] May 10. The house proceeded to take the above Answer into consideration.

Sir *Tho. Littleton.* Here is an Answer from the king: desires that what is said upon it may not be thought to reflect upon the king, but on the authors of this Answer. He thinks it a very ill one; so highly prejudicial to the people, and destructive to the king! Would clear the matter of fact: the Answer is, 'Such of his subjects in the most Christian king's service.' It is no unusual thing to call him 'the French king' in parliament; but he rests not upon that. Would be informed, whether by the late peace we made with Holland, the king is left free, and at full liberty, to keep these men actually in that king's service. How contrary would it be to his honour, if against no treaty, nor article (fettered) to recal them! Under that Proclamation mentioned, all this mischief is grown. The number of English forces there is now great; 8000 men at least. The duke of Monmouth's regiment, and the Irish, go a great way in the number, besides the Scotch. Great numbers going into France is no breach of the treaty; but into Holland, is a breach. Would have that cleared. If we thank the king for this Message, we do it for sending men over into France.

Mr. Sec. *Coventry.* That treaty does not command the forces to stay; but it is enough to tell you, that by that treaty the king is not obliged to recal those troops. It is no error to call the k. of France 'the most Christian King,' as all the world besides call him. He tells you, on his reputation, by all he knows, there are not above 2000 of these forces in all. The king, besides, tells you of his Proclamation, and 'will use all other effectual means to prevent more going over.' Is this such an abuse to the nation, and such a horrid thing? This is an advice to the king, in a thing he is entrusted with. This is not to be murmured at, but thanked for, to give you such an Answer, against his prerogative. Do you believe that the king, in making peace with Holland, did

* "In a letter from sir Wm. Temple to his father, dated March 27, 1674, notice is taken of a bargain, which had been made between lord Arlington and sir Joseph Williamson, for the Secretary's place: the latter was to give 6000*l.* for it, and the former was to resign it, as soon as lord St. Albans should be willing to part with the Chamberlain's Staff, for which lord Arlington had agreed to pay him 10,000*l.* On the 1st of Sept. this bargain was executed; and on the 14th, the public was informed by the Gazette (No. 420.) that those two removes were made 'in recompence of the long and faithful services of sir Joseph Williamson, as a clerk of the council; and of lord Arlington, as secretary of state." Ralph.

write no respectful letter to the king of France? And just at that hour of the king's mediation of peace, and ambassadors for it, to do such a partial act as to recal these men! Shall he be considerable neither on one side, nor the other, nor in mediatorship? Suppose the king was resolved to do it; it is not proper now. Cannot he keep a word, or a promise? What, if the king make a promise, and the h. of commons break it, of what value will it be for the future? If you desire a farther explanation of this Answer, you may. But he thinks it a great condescension in the king, as it is already.

Mr. *Garroway* observes many things to be debated, peace and war. The thing is lodged and he will not break into it, nor meddle with it. We are not ready yet for a conclusion of our opinions to this Answer. If we open the matter of fact, see how we contribute to France's greatness. The king's honour, crown, and dignity are concerned in it. If the Low Countries and Flanders should be conquered, knows not what our condition will be. We know of no obligation to the numbers of men in France, and so can say nothing to the recal of them. Moves to have the king's Answer debated in a Grand Committee.

Sir *Tho. Littleton* seconds the motion, to come the better to the right understanding of the matter. Coventry has yielded the matter, that no treaty does impose the staying of these forces on the king. If any thing falls from him, out of zeal to his country, desires pardon; but if we let those things go, we give the greatest blow both to our country and the confederates imaginable.

Mr. Sec. *Coventry*. What he said was, 'the Treaty of Holland obliged it not.'

Sir *Tho. Clarges* conceives, that where the king is dishonoured, and there is a contempt of his Proclamation, and a violation of his honour, we are concerned. The Message tells you, that 'the king has sent out his Proclamation to forbid all;' but, by letters from the ports, we are informed that recruits go frequently over into France, 3 James, ch. 31. 'No officer can go into any foreign service without taking the oaths of allegiance.' At Dover that has not been done; they go over as if they were to be instructed in the Popish religion, to our destruction; and by that law mentioned, 'bonds are to be entered into, and oaths (and all returned into the Exchequer) to practise nothing against that oath.' This going over is to the dishonour of the king, and danger of religion.

Col. *Birch* sees many that speak, crave grains of allowance: he has most need of any, and hopes he shall not be denied them: is for a Grand Committee: if this thing be well done hardly any thing else can be ill done. He agrees that war and peace are in the king's hand; but he thinks that in this business of the peace with Holland, the king asked the advice of this house. You are embarked in it, and the miscarriage will be the fault of this house: would not quarrel with any of our neighbours, but especially not with the great prince on the other side the water; but better now than at another time: while the people are under dissatisfactions, he knows no other way to satisfy them but in this house, and no way here, but in a Grand Committee.

Mr. Sec. *Coventry*. A peace there was advised in this house, but not this peace: the terms the king made himself, and he would not have Birch tell you what the articles are, or should be.

Sir *Ch. Wheeler* observes, that great things are brought into this house, and still prove but matter of enquiry. For the term of 'the French king' spoken of, when we have wars we say so of him, and what have we got by it? In all foreign affairs they come up to the title of 'the British king' with us. Of these men in the French service, he looks upon the Scotch guards as a thing particular to their nation, who have been in France sixty years at least in that capacity; the rest are the duke of Monmouth's regiment, and sir George Hamilton's; col. Churchill's regiment being reformed into the duke of Monmouth's (sometimes we are forced to be quit of the Irish, and now we must recal them.) He cannot inform himself, any way, of above 1000 horse: when you have made all these means to prevent their going over, idle fellows will go. [He was taken down to Order.]

The *Speaker*. It is disorderly to take a man down, before you know what he will say,

Sir *Ch. Wheeler* goes on. You can stop them no more than you can the exportation of wool: here came over German and French gentlemen of the horse, to buy horses; and there goes over, at least, a man to three horses; and so, many men under that pretence steal over. If there be not above 8000, how is the honour of the nation exposed! He fears the honour of the nation as much as another, but would have a reason for his fears.

Lord *Cavendish*. It is said 'there are not above 2000 English and Irish.' It is strange there should be no more. They won two battles for the French, the last summer, by their own confession, and are a number to do the like this summer: would go into a grand committee.

Sir *Edw. Jennings*. The king tells you, 'he will use all effectual means for preventing the going over of more men into France.' If that be so good an Answer, return thanks for that part of the Answer; and, when that is done, go into a grand committee to consider the rest.

Sir *Tho. Meres*. What part of the king's Answer will require a farther Address to the king, will be the subject-matter of the grand committee's debate. It may be, Thanks to his maj. will be a part; we know not: sees it contended, 'that the forces in France, before the Treaty, are not obliged to be recalled;' but the objection must be thoroughly understood at the committee. No man can say that there is any thing in our Address contrary to any treaty.

Mr. *Waller.* He has formerly seen how dear our meddling with peace and war has proved to us. We have no light nor measure at all, in such things. All that comes to the king is from his own and foreign ambassadors. These enquiries have been very fatal and costly to us. The house, in the last Treaty with Holland, gave advice; and the king asked it. Now it falls out properly, to see how that advice has been infringed; followed, or not followed. It is the nation's glory to have the king the mediator of peace, and Christian commisseration requires it. The thing is of great weight, and would go into a grand committee.

Sir *John Ernly.* Since you have had a question firsted, and seconded, 'for Thanks for that part of the king's Speech, of his effectual care to prevent the going over of more forces,' you ought to put it.

Mr. Sec. *Williamson.* Here are two questions; one, the main question, about Thanks, &c. and the other, for going into a Grand Committee. If the matter be opened, doubts not but the whole Answer will require your Thanks. Supposes the thing may be done in the house, as well as in the Grand Committee. He is but young in it, and leaves that question as you please.

Mr. *Powle.* To the first part of your Address you have a denial; to the second you have no Answer at all. There are several forces gone over since the Address: but men being sent away, and the thing depending, would therefore have it go to a grand committee.

Mr. Sec. *Coventry.* He has heard the king say, 'Have not the ports a standing order, to stop persons? Must he send them one every week?'

Mr. *Hale.* There are few in number, indeed, of these forces left, because they are most killed: he knows he saw upon the road 80 in a company: They land at Boulogne, and will not land at Calais, because in view of the packet-boats: the duke of Monmouth's regiment is recruited by these men, and Turenne's army had been lost without them; and it is said in France, 'they set the crown upon the king of France's head.' He has lately had opportunity to know it in France.

Mr. *Vaughan.* Your vote cannot make that to be, which naturally is not, viz. 'Thanks for the Answer, and that it is *satisfactory.*' Possibly there may be a league in the case, and the king's honour concerned; and when we come freely to debate it, in a Grand Committee, we lay aside all these considerations.

The House then resolved into a Grand Committee; sir Charles Harbord in the Chair.

Mr. *Garroway.* This is one of the seriousest businesses that ever was in the house: would do nothing in it, to involve the nation in a war; but it staggers him to hear the king's obligation named; but yet what that obligation is, not spoken of. Whether it be a treaty, or no; for what time, or on what condition, if declared, we may avoid that rock of a war. All we have told us is but a penny-worth of news in the Gazette every week. Sometimes we know things that they do not tell us. Let them set us up some marks whereby we shall not touch upon the king's honour, and they will be good guides to us for our debate. The king of France is ready to overrun us all, if his conquests go on.

Sir *Rd. Temple.* If the Proclamation recalls not these forces, he would go as far in a Bill in it as may be. Proposes a farther Address to the king, 'to recal all persons gone over since the Holland peace.'

Mr. Sec. *Williamson.* How difficult is it to meddle, or come to any resolutions, in things where the facts are not known? He is not to answer for the king France's violences and oppressions. It is said he took Treves for his convenience only, and on intercession of letters, to break the neutrality of that place, he took that town himself into his possession. As soon as that spark fell upon the Palatinate, the king offered a mediation at Cologne.* Some matters are such in these affairs as cannot be laid open unto you. He thinks that the king will do more than he says. It is our great interest to balance the matter with Holland. He is as jealous of the successes of France as any man; and if this alliance be made with Holland and Denmark, and they strengthened by sea and land, we ought to think of that balance. When the peace shall be made, it is our interest to have it go through the king's hands. You were told of an exception, at Vienna, against our mediation; but he hears no such thing. Give this matter the best end you can, it will hazard our mediation. France has paid Sweden, though but a stander-by, and neutral; and whilst we show such a partiality as this recalling the forces will be, it will put the French king upon providing for himself, as not trusting our mediation. He fears that declaring ourselves so generally as is proposed in the recalling these forces, and being not obliged to it by the treaty of Holland, may be a just exception against our mediation, and may encourage France forsaking us in the general treaty of peace; they discovering we are declaring partialities, and so will reject us.

Sir *Tho. Littleton.* The second sort of men are gone into France, since the Holland peace. the first are wholly omitted in the Answer. doubts that the last part of the king's Answer is intricate. It is a general prohibition, but that is no part of our Address. The king tells you, 'He will take any farther way to prevent their going over.' If taken in a general sense, he is not satisfied that it is an Answer to our Address. As to that of the old men there, he says that there was no Article to the contrary,

* Sir Joseph Williamson himself was one of the Plenipotentiaries.

but that the king might recal them: easy to know a secret article—No man to go into France or Holland—But the going into France is so public, the private article is now as public. How know we what promises have passed from the king about these forces? he knows of none, nor is willing to believe any; being only spoken of by way of supposition: Williamson said, 'We, not knowing the intimacy of things, might be deceived.' But it is as certain, that the French king has taken Treves for his convenience, as that he has made this war for his glory. And farther, he tells you, 'That the business of the Palatinate happened through the neglect of the interposition of the king of England.' Is sorry to hear the authority of the king of England was employed to hinder the elector: he might not have been so overrun—It is said, 'this recalling, &c. would prejudice our mediation.' Is one of those who understands not how the mediation can stand to the good of England. He apprehends that the king, without the assistance of the parliament, could not carry a war on against Holland: and is afraid that the authority and figure the king has in his neutrality would be made use of for the French advantage; therefore desires the king may now be put out of that capacity of mediation, to make the king of France a terror to all Christendom. To continue France in all these acquisitions, and secured in all, or the greatest part. The confederates wasted, and the French army maintained in the bowels of the confederates country, scarce reparable in this age. If the confederacy be dissolved before the French be reduced back to France again, the most ruinous thing in the world! when once the confederates dissolve, and France in this high posture, fears that the confederacy is never to be renewed to the end of the world. He speaks like an ordinary man; you have his good will. It is a plain thing; he sees no good we can have when the confederates are broken, and we strive to put the French king into that formidable condition, that we should be afraid to anger him now, what will it be to anger him then, when the confederates are broken? he must have Dover, because he is angry with us, and over-run us at last, as he has done others. [Exceptions being taken by Mr. Sec. Coventry at what fell from him, thus explains himself.] The king not to be in such a mediation as to leave the king of France a terror to all the world.

Mr. *Garroway.* If we were off from France, all the world would put us upon being mediators.

Col. *Birch.* Littleton's words were, 'such mediation as may make the king of France a terror to all Christendom.'

Sir *Tho. Lee.* The words are to be written down, that to eternity the world may know what the opinion of this house was.

Col. *Titus.* It belongs to the gentleman to explain himself. 'As if the king should be so inconsiderable as not to be mediator.' If any interpret the words so, the gentleman must explain himself; and he has done it, and sees no reason why the words should be set down.

Sir *Wm. Coventry* begs leave to pass by what has passed, as a parenthesis, and proceed to the business. It is good news to him that the balance of France was so near being made by these forces. When France first made an inroad into Holland, how long was it before there was any thing to look her in the face! France sees, by that, the danger of letting the confederates come together. When disunited and peace, no such thing as balance. That no predominant power be a terror to the rest, is our true balance between France and Spain. He wishes that the dust was a little shaken from the balance in the matter. He has not heard that mediations have been of such a value as to leave out the aid of a kingdom for them. He does not think that this withdrawing the forces would make us improper for being mediator, for some times mediations may help to obstruct peace as well as make peace. Many others are admitted for mediators as well as we. He has heard of the state of Venice, and the pope, and respects are seldom refused when offered as mediation: fears that the prevalency of France will spoil our markets more than any thing. When she has got peace, we are like to have a hard market. We can buy our wines but of one chapman then, but if France be brought low, you have choice of chapmen for any wares she can carry to market. Will offer something to the matter of recalling these forces. Does not conceive it possible to have these forces back, or prevent others going over, unless it be before Holland have peace with France. It was intended by the king and his ministers, that no more should go over; yet they do. As long as regiments and officers are there, it is his interest to have them recruited, to keep the troops up to such a degree. The root will draw nourishment as long as it grows in your garden, and to destroy it you must pluck it up. When the thing is rightly considered, hopes the king will have other thoughts. There appears no treaty between France and Holland, and is confident that there is none. We have no treaty yet finished with Holland to establish commerce, and believes we would not send subjects to assist the king of France, to make him greater, until that be settled. It is a probability, that after France has made peace, and ever shall be in a condition to reckon with us, they will do it, for making peace without them, as well as for withdrawing men away now. It is not ordinary for princes to be bound up thus; the honour of a prince, at home, is the maintenance of his subjects; and, abroad, not mistaking his interest. Did the king intimate he was to send no more forces? if the French king has used means to draw men over, he has cancelled all obligations to the contrary; therefore he hopes, that there is nothing in the whole matter but what we may have a gracious Answer to; and is for the Address for recall of the forces.

Mr. Sec. *Coventry.* All the long discourses here have been, 'Whether we shall go to war with France, or no.' As to the comparison of the 'plant in a garden,' the best answer to experience is experience. There is not one English pair of colours in Holland, and yet more men gone over into Holland, by thrice the number, than into France. These are things that cannot be avoided. A man of honour breaks not his word with any man, but much less where he is most obliged. If there should be any such agreement of no more acceptance of our troops, 'the eagles will go where the carcass is,' where money is. More of our men have come over to Holland from the French army than we have sent into France. Should the world take notice of any unanimity betwixt you and the king, let all men lay their hands upon their hearts, and declare, whether the king can recal these forces with his honour.

Col. *Birch.* England is of that spirit, rather to desire to know the worst of a danger, than stay till to-morrow for it. You are told of 'secret engagements that may prostrate the honour of the king.' In this case here is an end of your debate. Either we must debate thus, or consider how the interest of the nation is. The king cannot miscarry when he goes into this bottom. There are 90 in a 100 against France, all England over. You may make war with France with the money he overbalances you in your trade, which you get, like bees, by industry: remembers that if you had not only made peace with the Dutch, but told the king of France why you did it, you had not now debated this matter here. If you will not adjourn the debate, put the question.

Mr. *Sawyer.* Whenever you demand right you stick to it. As on the imprisonment of one of your members, there is either cause shown for it, or else you deliver him. You have made Address upon Address for him, and if not released you adjourn, as in lord Arundel's case, in the lords house.* Where an Address for a thing is matter of advice only, and not of right, you have always acquiesced in the king's Answer. If it be a demand of right, he is for adhering; but it being pure matter of advice, and the king tells you positively, 'he cannot do it with his honour,' where will it end if the king should deny you? And you cannot force the matter upon him, but leave him at his liberty: he appeals to precedents in this kind.

Mr. *Vaughan* finds now the whole stress of the business to be 'the king's honour.' 'If all national contracts are broken, no nation will trust us.' It is so amongst common men: but after you find leagues have been destructive, it has been the prudence of princes, (who may err like other men) to recall such leagues. When a peace shall be made, you expose these men to be knocked on the head; and when wounded, they have been knocked on the head to make room for the French. If you allow them to be there, you may be put to pay them before long: therefore would recall them.

Mr. Sec. *Coventry.* Inspect records, and you will find whenever a king has told you, 'he could not concede a thing with his honour,' that you never have farther pressed him to it.

Sir *Edw. Dering* would, in this great affair, take the deliberation of one whole night to consider of it, and would now adjourn the debate.

Disorder on the Division.] The question being put, "Whether a farther Address should be made to the king for Recall of his subjects now in the service of the French king," the grand committee thereupon divided; and the tellers, viz. sir Trevor Williams, and sir John Hanmer, appointed by the chairman, sir Charles Harbord, differing in their account of the Yeas and Noes, some called, 'Tell again,' others, 'Report;' on which great disorder began; gentlemen rising from their places and mingling in the pit; hot and provoking discourses and gestures passed on both sides, especially betwixt lord Cavendish and sir John Hanmer. Some said, that lord Cavendish's sword was half drawn out, but prevented by Mr. Russel, who kept close to him. Others said, that lord Cavendish spit in sir John Hanmer's face, but that was only eagerness of speech, and so some might accidentally fly from him. But it was visible to all that sir James Smith, setting his arms on his side, did, in a rude manner, make through the crowd, and jostled several, and came up to the table, where yet more hot discourses passed between him and lord Cavendish, Mr. Stockdale, Mr. Sacheverell, and several others; Mr. Stockdale and some others, setting their feet upon the mace, which lay below the table, in the usual place at grand committees. This disorder continued near half an hour, the standers by, on the upper benches, expecting very fatal consequences, especially when the young gallants, as Mr. Thynne, Mr. Newport, and several others, leaped over the seats to join lord Cavendish. But the Speaker, very opportunely and prudently, rising from his seat near the bar, in a resolute and slow pace, made his three respects through the crowd, and took

* See vol. ii. p. 125. This was in 1626, when the earl of Arundel was committed to the Tower for being too severe in language on lord Spencer, concerning the marriage of his eldest son, Henry, lord Maltravers, to the lady Eliz. Stuart, eldest daughter to the duke of Lenox; which, it was alleged, was done contrary to the king's consent and knowledge, he having designed her for lord Lorn. When the parliament met, the lords, being discontented, presented several petitions to the king, to preserve the privilege of parliament, and, no cause of his commitment being expressed, at length refused to sit, until he was restored to them; which was ordered accordingly, in about three months. See Collins's Peerage, vol. i. p. 139.

the chair. The mace was still retained by the said gentlemen, but, at last, being forcibly laid upon the table, all the disorder ceased, and the gentlemen went to their places. The Speaker, being sat, spoke to this purpose, "That to bring the house into order again, he took the Chair, though not according to Order." Some gentlemen, as Mr. Sacheverell, and others, excepted against his coming into the Chair, but the doing it was generally approved, as the only expedient to suppress the disorder *.—Then

Sir *Tho. Lee*, approving of the Speaker's taking the Chair, though not according to Order, moved, That there might be an engagement passed upon the honour of every member, standing up in his place, to proceed no farther in any thing that had happened in the unfortunate disorder at the Grand Committee, fearing that, as soon as the house had risen, the thing might be recriminated, and ill consequences ensue thereupon.—Which was seconded by several, and agreed to. So every member, standing up in his place, did consent accordingly; then particularly,

Col. *Somerset Fox* declared that some warm expressions had passed between him and sir Rob. Thomas, but, upon command of the house, he would give his honour to proceed no farther thereupon.—Sir John Hanmer did the same, but named nobody. So the house adjourned to the next day.

May 11. The house resumed the further consideration of his majesty's Answer. The question being propounded, that a further Address be presented to his majesty, for Recalling all his subjects that are in the service of the French king; the question being put, that the word 'all' do stand in the question:

The house divided. For the yeas, 172; for the noes, 173. And so it passed in the negative.—The question being put, That a further Address be presented to his majesty; It was resolved in the affirmative.

Debate on receiving no more Bills.] May 17. Mr. *Eyre* wishes the digestive faculty of this house answerable to the hands that feed it, that we might dispatch what business now may be brought before us; but because we have much upon our hands, and the time we are to sit probably not very long, moves 'That no other Bills may be received, but what are already before us, or which may come from the lords.'

Sir *John Coventry*. We have yet neither removed Privy Counsellor, nor broken the French league, since we sat. Would have members stay here, and attend their duty, and not go down these holydays; and seconds Eyre's motion.

Sir *Tho. Lee* thirds the motion.

Sir *Joseph Tredenham* would never tie up our hands from other business. He never knew a precedent of it. He being interrupted by many saying 'No, No,' said, He would be answered by reason, and not by noise.

Sir *Nich. Carew* has known this, that is now moved for, done almost every session, and would have it so now; especially because the business of religion may not be interrupted.

Sir *Rob. Carr* has known when no private business might be brought in, to interrupt the public; but he never knew such an order made as is moved for. It is very extraordinary to exclude public business, which may be of dangerous consequence: would, therefore, exclude private business only.

Sir *Tho. Meres*. Anciently this motion was parliamentary, when parliaments sat a shorter time than now: no new petitions were to be brought in. You cannot have a more advantageous thing to the bills before you. Let such as will go down see what is before you that no new matter may be started.

Sir *Henry Ford* is glad to see the house so unanimous for Bills in your hands, but is not for this question: will you preclude yourselves from taking any more bills? What occasion can you tell but you must have more bills? You were told, not long since, your being depends on the Address about the French forces; and will you shut up your hands against all possible cases whatsoever?

Mr. *Vaughan*. We are but passing a vote, not making a law for it. If we were, would then be of Ford's opinion: constantly parliaments have set a time for receiving petitions, when parliaments were shorter than they are now. The king has pointed out to us Religion, and Property, and Safety. We have let others in, and that out, by new business; and is the more for it, by what he has heard abroad of our sudden recess. Therefore moves, 'that all Bills we are not already possessed of, or may come from the lords, may be excluded.'

Sir *Ch. Wheeler* should not have been against the motion, had you said, 'till the Bills before you were finished, no new bills should be brought in.' If the king adjourns us not yet, or we sit six months, will you sit still, and do nothing? The precedents of 1641 and 1642, may be brought up an 100 years hence, like the 19 Propositions: are we not masters of our own sense and resolutions? The vote is altogether needless.

* Grey.—There is no mention of this disturbance in the Journal; all that is there said is, 'Mr. Speaker resumed the Chair.' But a writer, who was, probably, present at it, gives us the following account. "One day upon a dispute of telling the numbers upon a division, both parties grew so hot, that all order was lost; the members ran in confusion up to the table, grievously affronted one by the other, every man's hand upon his hilt, and all ready to decide the question by the sword. But when the tumult was loudest, the Speaker had the honour to restore the peace, by maintaining the dignity of the Chair, after that of the house was gone, and obliging every man to stand up in his place and engage his honour not to resent any thing of that day's proceedings." Marvell.

Sir *Tho. Lee* moves to order. After the motion firsted, and seconded, to tell you of 'adjourning,' and 'the 19 Propositions in 1641 and 1642!' Would have no resolutions.

Sir *Tho. Meres.* We abominate the actions of 1641 and 1642, as much as Wheeler; though he is not so old as Wheeler, our ancestors have suffered as well as he; abominates 'the 19 Propositions' as much as he, or any man.

Mr. Sec. *Coventry.* To say, positively, not to receive any thing from the king, we know not how such a thing may be. He has no foresight of any thing that may come from the king. The thing is too much unprecedented, and, whenever done, it ought to be with great deliberation. Pray God, our difference with the lords may be happily composed! He should hate himself, if he did not desire it. It is not easy to see an accommodation with the lords, but by a Bill, and possibly more natural for us. We are not yet prepared for matter for so good a bill, but the long robe may adjust your privileges and is sure it would be prejudicial to your reputation, should such a bill come from the lords. Why should our hands be bound? We are in a profound and safe peace, by God's providence: who knows but there may be a necessity of the very safety of the government, by loss of battles abroad, and other contingencies? Would not presume upon God's providence, so much as this vote will.

Mr. *Swynfin.* The motion is, 'That no new Bill be received, other than what shall come from the lords.' What is moved hinders no bills from the lords. If any thing should be extraordinary, as the miscarriage of a battle, mentioned, you are secured by the Vote not excluding Bills from the lords, and you are free: but here is your danger, a custom of receiving new bills almost every morning. So many bills make your committees diverted; and scarce a new bill, but the committee is called from the attendance of the former bills. He has observed of this parliament, that there were never more explanatory bills. This motion is not to tie up your hands, but not to stretch them so, that business may fall from you by grasping more; having already several bills, that cannot pass this session, of great importance, and like to have long debates. There may be an emergency, and it is supposed only. If you take more bills upon you, you cannot pass many before you. It is a reasonable motion.

Sir *Francis Drake.* If this difference between the lords and us be accommodated by Bill, Westminster-Hall must judge our privileges, which, he hopes, he shall never see. They say abroad, that the king of France will not go into the field till this parliament be up, and for that reason he would not lengthen the session.

Sir *Tho. Clarges.* It is a necessary motion, not to exclude any thing from the lords, and is for the motion.

Col. *Titus.* It is reason, that the bills before you should not be obstructed, till they shall have their doom; possibly something as necessary may happen as any thing already before you: It is answered, 'it may then come from the lords.' Supposing the lords have such notice, they may make such a vote likewise. It may be of dangerous consequence.

Mr. *Hale.* Considering the time of the year, and the little yet done, must leave other gentlemen to find a reason for it, he cannot hope to do it, how to be dispatched. He fears a thin house, this festival calling people out of town; and if a motion should be for a million of money, here would be few to maintain the battle.

Sir *John Birkenhead.* Suppose the king should send us an Act of Indemnity, he should be loth to lose his share of it: will you tie your hands against receiving it? A gentleman said, 'he heard the king of France will not take the field till we rise;' therefore he would sit on. The thing has an ill aspect: he would have precedents for it.

Sir *John Talbot.* You are offered arguments for this motion, which are strong reasons against it, 'Members going out of town.' Is, therefore, against the motion, because it will keep members here: but would have the word 'private' added to 'Bill.'

Sir *Edw. Dering.* This is an unusual vote proposed; would see one such vote that ever passed: remembers only something like it, when our days were numbered. He usually gives his negative to what he understands not: would willingly have some consideration of it. If it be a good vote, it is a good one two days hence; and would adjourn the debate to Wednesday.

Mr. *Powle.* This vote proposed does not so oblige, but, that, if any extraordinary thing come to pass, we may revoke it. Had we put Popery, Property, and the Fleet, in any way, we might have come to such a vote, in obedience to the king's Speech. What can be done by bills is already before us; to admit more, is but to incumber those. This seems to him to be perfectly the state of the question, whether we shall do any thing, or no? Therefore he concurs with the motion.

Mr. *Pepys.* The little he has to say, is, to join with Powle about the Navy. How far Religion and Property are secured, he knows not, because he has not seen the bills. In his humble apprehensions, the navy is not provided for. He takes his rise from the bill for appropriating the Customs; if what he said the other day be true and he can make it out, that there is yet no provision made out for it. If 400,000*l.* be no superfluity, to make this fleet of yours equal to what it should be with your neighbours—plainly, in view, it is necessary, indispensibly: to the value of the bill, then, have you complied with the king's Speech? For all this is but necessary to keep the fleet as it is.

Mr. *Harwood* is sorry the crown of England has gone so far backward, as France has gone forward. We hear of the ill condition of the navy, but not of the good. If we ought to be afraid of the French, by sea, or land, why do we suffer our men to stay there? As to the navy, so considerable to us, when our wooden walls are down, every one may come at us. The French having so admirable navies, and we so poor ones—Which might have been otherwise, if all the money given to that purpose had been so spent. If that which you have appropriated to the navy will not do, you may think farther of it, when you meet again. He concurs with the motion.

Mr. *Sawyer*. Here is a great debate. For fear of confusion on one side, and surprize on the other, moves to have no more bills brought in, after the first day of the next term. It is for the interest of the king to finish those before you; and he would have a convenient time set, for bringing in any more. The surprize of the passing the bill for the Fee-Farm Rent—great defect followed. A convenient time set to limit the bringing in of Bills would salve the doubts on both sides.

Mr. *Finch* *. We ought not to put the question, to prejudice any other business; we have not yet proceeded sufficiently for that. We are not to exclude Property, by petitions from private persons, that cannot have remedy in another place. He has received many particular papers; he calls them so, because delivered to him by particular men. Trade respects property. The motion about trade, for planting flax in England, is public, because it saves 800,000*l.* a year for coarse cloth, brought from beyond the sea. Religion ought to have the first place in your thoughts; but he moves that last, to rest it in your thoughts the better. The last session, you considered of Indulgence; and because we are safe on the shore, shall we have no consideration for them who struggle with the tide? Whatever the case be, it is charity and prudence to think on them, so considerable a part of the nation; and would not have them in despair.

Mr. Sec. *Coventry* would have this word added to the question, not foreseeing what great occasions might come; for extraordinary occasions alter all orders; therefore would have the words, 'unless upon extraordinary occasion,' added to the question.

Sir *Tho. Meres*. Writing the question is the best service for the house; they are the very words proposed by the first man that moved it.

Mr. *Swynfin* rises to speak to the words, 'extraordinary occasion,' proposed to be added to the question. 'If the extraordinary occasion be from abroad or at home,' must be meant, which this house has no prospect of now. It will be private interpretation in this case; it will occasion, no man knows how many motions and interpretations, a man's own way, and give interruptions to your business, and he is therefore against the words being added to the question. Of two inconveniences, the greatest is to be avoided: if any man thinks that, by it, he has excluded all extraordinary things, the house is the judge of that only.

Sir *Rd. Temple* thinks you sufficiently armed against these 'extraordinary occasions.' Your vote itself will give you liberty sufficient. It is only a trial, whether any man will offer you any thing extraordinary, or not.

Mr. *Hopkins* remembers that the last tax was, 'for the king's extraordinary occasions.'

Sir *Wm. Coventry*. He has the less to say, because his sense is already expressed: the word 'extraordinary' is not only useless but dangerous; as if the house, without those words, was not masters of their own orders. Should be loth that it binded us up so as not to alter it, either on some great victory obtained, or new occurrences.

Sir *Tho. Meres*. Whenever a necessity comes, that is for our advantage, or the nation's, it will over-rule all orders: believes that no-body that urged the question intended those words.

Mr. Sec. *Coventry*. The word 'necessity' is always avoided in this house; and would have it so now.

The word 'extraordinary' in the question, was then rejected, 169 to 121. And the main question "That no Bill be brought in, or received, but such as are already ordered to be brought in, or shall be sent down from the lords, until after the recess mentioned in his majesty's Speech," was passed.

The famous Non-Resisting Test brought into the House of Lords *.] While the commons were thus employed "the grand push" says Mr. Ralph † "was made in the house of lords, to disarm disaffection and republicanism, according to the royalists; or, according to the patriots, to extinguish the last spark of English

* Son to the Lord Keeper. He succeeded to the earldom of Nottingham on his father's death in 1682, as he did to that of Winchelsea in 1729, a few months before he died. In the reigns of king William and queen Anne he was Secretary of State, and in king George the 1st's, Lord President of the Council. Burnet, speaking of his conduct at the Revolution, says, "That he had great credit with the whole church party, for he was a man possessed with their notions, and was grave and virtuous in the course of his life. He had some knowledge of the law, and of the records of parliament, and was a copious speaker."

* After the session broke up, a Pamphlet, entitled, "A Letter from a person of Quality 'to his Friend in the Country, giving an account of the Debates and Resolutions in the 'House of Lords, in April and May 1675, 'concerning a bill entitled, 'A Bill to prevent 'the dangers which may arise from persons 'disaffected to the Government," was published by the celebrated Mr. Locke, who drew it up at the desire of the earl of Shaftsbury. It will be found at length in the Appendix to the present volume, No. V. † Vol. i. p. 170.

liberty. The expedient which was to facilitate this mighty event, and which was the joint product of all the subtilty that the schools, the bar, or the court, could furnish, was contained in the following oath: 'I A.B, do declare, that it is not lawful, upon any pretence 'whatsoever, to take up Arms against the 'king; and that I do abhor that traiterous 'position, of taking up arms, by his authority, 'against his person, or against those that are 'commissioned by him, in pursuance of such 'commission: and I do swear, that I will not, 'at any time, endeavour the alteration of the 'government, either in Church or State. So 'help me God.'—The person who had the honour of being the first mover for the court, upon this great occasion, was the earl of Lindsey, lord great chamberlain. One party, who had for their mouth the Lord Keeper, called it 'a moderate Security to the Church and Crown.' The other declared, 'That no conveyance could ever, in more compendious or binding terms, have drawn a dissettlement of the whole birthright of England.'—The penalty which the peers became liable to, on refusing this Oath, being incapacity to sit and vote in their own house, the first stage of opposition to it arose from the peculiar rights of the peerage; and all objections on that head being over-ruled by the major vote, 24 lords entered their protest; in which they gave it as their opinion, that the privilege they had of sitting and voting in parliament was an honour they had by birth, and a right so inherent in them, and inseparable from them, as that nothing could take it away, but what, by the law of the land, must, withal, take away their lives and corrupt their blood.—After five days debate, the Bill was committed; but not without another Protest; in which it was urged, that the bill struck at the very root of government, since it took away all freedom of votes and debates: for he that swore never to 'alter' parted with all his legislative power at once, and became perjured by endeavouring to 'amend.'—The majority were so incensed at this second Protest, that some thoughts were entertained of sending the 12 peers who signed it to the Tower: but the lord Holles desiring leave of the house to add his name to it, that he might have the honour to suffer with them, they did not think proper to carry their resentment so far, but contented themselves with voting, That the Reasons given in the said Protest did reflect upon the honour of the house, and were of dangerous consequence: which Vote was also protested against by 21 of their lordships, as a great discountenancing of the very liberty of protesting.—To take off the edge of so fierce an opposition, the penalty of forfeiting their seats in parliament, by refusing the Oath, was taken off by order of the house; and, by another order, a Proviso was added, to secure the freedom of parliamentary proceedings: but the house still persisting to subject every member to the first enacting-clause of the Bill, whereby an oath was to be imposed on them, as members of either house, and at the same time refusing to admit of a proviso inserted in a late Act for 'preventing Dangers that might happen from Popish Recusants;' whereby the privilege of every peer, and all their privileges, would be as fully secured from this act, as the other; a fourth Protestation was entered, which was signed by 16 peers, who thought these latter proceedings of the house inconsistent with their two former orders.—During the course of the debate on the privileges of parliament, the earl of Bolingbroke observing, that, though the proviso left the business within doors free, the Oath took away all private converse without, on matters of state, even with one another; the lord keeper, the lord treasurer, and the duke of Lauderdale, told the committee, in plain terms, That they intended to prevent caballing, and conspiracies against the government; and they knew no reason why any of the king's officers should consult with parliament-men, about parliament-business; and particularly mentioned those of the army, treasury, and navy: and when the marquis of Winchester proposed an additional Oath, That every man should swear to vote according to his opinion and conscience, independent of threats, or promises, rewards or expectations, the lord keeper made no scruple to declare, in a very fine speech, that it was an useless oath; for all gifts, places, and offices, were likeliest to come from the king: and no member of parliament, in either house, could do too much for the king, or he too much on his side: and that men might, lawfully and worthily, have in their prospect such offices and benefits from him.—Proceeding to those extravagant words in the Oath, 'or against those commissioned by him,' the house fell into yet greater heats; the opposing lords making no difficulty to declare, That if whatever is by the king's commission be not opposed by the king's authority, then a standing army is law, whenever the king pleases. This was illustrated in the following free manner: if, in suit with a great favourite, a man recovers house and land, and by course of law, be put into possession by the sheriff, and afterwards a warrant is obtained, by the interest of the person, to command some soldiers of the standing army to take the possession, and deliver it back; in such case, the man in possession may justify the defending himself, and killing those who shall violently endeavour to enter the house; yet the party whose house is invaded takes up arms by the king's authority against those who are commissioned by him. And it is the same case, if the soldiers had been commissioned to defend the house against the sheriff, when he first endeavoured to take the possession according to law; neither could any order or commission of the king put a stop to the sheriff, if he had done his duty, in raising the whole force of that county to put the law in execution; neither can the court, from whom that order proceeds, (if they observe their oath and duty) put any stop to the execution of the law in such a case, by any command or commission from the king whatsoever; nay, all the Guards* and Standing-Forces in England cannot be secured by any commission from being a direct riot, and unlawful assembly, unless in time of open war and rebellion. And it is not out of the way to suppose, that if any king hereafter, contrary to the Petition of Right, demand and levy money by privy seal, or otherwise, and cause soldiers to enter and distrain for such-like illegal Taxes, that, in such a case, any man may by law defend his house against them; and yet this is of the same nature with the former, and against the words of the Declaration. And these being called 'remote' instances by the Lord Keeper, the earl of Salisbury replied, That they would not hereafter prove so, when this Declaration had made the practice of them justifiable.—The next thing in course was the Oath itself: against which the following objection lay so plain and so strong, at the very entrance, viz. That there was no care taken of the doctrine, but only of the Discipline, of the Church; or, in other words, of its power and dominion. No papist would scruple to take an oath for the maintenance of episcopacy: and though, by the re-establishment of the Popish religion, the king would lose his supremacy, the bishops would be secure of their mitres, and all the trappings of wealth and power they were enriched and adorned with. This consideration, which was urged in its full force, compelled the advocates for the Oath to give it a new bias: and, accordingly, the next day, it was introduced again in these words: 'I do swear, that I will not endeavour 'to alter the Protestant religion, or the government of either Church or State.' By this the ministers, and their godfathers the bishops, thought, they had salved all; and now began to call their Oath a security for the Protestant Religion, and the only good preservative against Popery, in case the throne should be filled by a Popish prince: in which their confidence was not a little wondered at, since it was notorious, that till now they had no such point in view; that they had been shamed into this addition, by the debates of the preceding day; and that some of the bishops had made their court to some of the Catholic lords† by saying, 'That care had 'been taken it might be such an Oath as 'might not bear upon them.'—When the Clause relating to the Church came under deliberation, it was observed, That it was not agreeable to the king's crown and dignity to have his subjects sworn to the government of the Church equally as to himself: that it was necessary to understand thoroughly what this ecclesiastic system was, which the subject was to swear allegiance to: and the bishops alledging, That the priesthood, and its powers, were derived from Christ, but the licence to exercise those powers from the civil magistrate, it was replied, That it was a dangerous thing to secure, by oath or act of parl. those in the exercise of an authority and power in the king's country, and over his subjects, which being received, as they urged, from Christ himself, could not be altered nor limited by the king's laws: that this was directly to set the mitre above the crown: and that this Oath was the greatest attempt that had been made against the king's Supremacy since the Restoration.—And as to swearing not to make any Alterations in the state, it was said, That such an Oath overthrew all parliaments, and left them capable of nothing but giving money: For the very business of parliaments was Alterations, either by adding or taking away some part of the executive power in church or state. Besides, it was well asked, What kind of government must that be, which men must swear not to endeavour to alter, upon any alteration of times, emergency of affairs, nor variations of human things whatever? Would it not be requisite, that such a government should be communicated by God himself, visibly appearing, or denouncing his immediate presence, by an exertion of all the wonders of omnipotence?—The Penalty of the Bill was considered in the last place; and was made different, according to the different qualifications of the persons: all that were, or should be, privy counsellors, justices of the peace, or possessors of any beneficial office, ecclesiastical, civil, or military, were to take the Oath when summoned, upon pain of forfeiting 500*l.* and being made incapable of bearing office: and though the members of either house were not subject to incapacity, they were to the 500*l.* penalty: nay, it was moved, that those who did not come up and sit as members should be obliged to take the oath, or liable to the penalty till they did so: and it was at last carried, that every (sitting) member should either swear, or pay 500*l.* every parliament: the opposing lords however took up several hours in shewing the many hardships of this Clause; especially as it affected all the members of the house of commons, and all the acting justices in England; the first of whom had it not in their power to be unchosen; nor the last, to be left out of the commission, before the act came in force (which was to have been the 1st of Sept. following) and both thereby became subject to an imposition that neither of them thought of, when they undertook their respective services: they likewise remonstrated, that the lords

* An Army had, as yet, received no sanction from the legislature.

† These lords in a body joined the opposition on this occasion; which, according to Mr. North, they were induced to do by the earl of Shaftsbury's dinning in their ears; "That the Test tended to deprive peers of their right of sitting and voting in the house of lords; which was a right so sacrosanct, and radically inherent in the peerage, as was not to be temerated on any account whatsoever; and that, if this Act passed, the next would be to turn them out of the house."

themselves were subjected by it to the meanest condition of mankind, if they could not enjoy their birthright, without being enforced to swear to every fancy of the present times, which appeared to be the most variable in our story; since, but 3 years before this, all was liberty and indulgence; and now nothing would serve but rigid conformity. To all this no reply was made, nor attempted to be made: numbers were made to sanctify what reason could not be made to countenance; and, on putting the question, it appeared, that Magna Charta itself was of no force against a majority."

The Test carried by the Lords.] "Thus, after 16 or 17 days debates, it appeared, that it was not the fault of minister or bishop, that the people of England were not 'declared' into a new government, more absolute and arbitrary than the Oath of Allegiance, or the old law, knew; and then 'sworn' to obey, what they had been compelled to set up. In contracts where both parties are to be gainers, there is no fear of nonperformance of either side: the king admitted the bishops to share with him in the allegiance of his people; and the bishops, by way of consideration, gave them up to the will and pleasure of the king. Nothing can be urged in excuse of a scheme, at once so treacherous, and so wicked as this, but the apprehensions of the court, that the opposite faction were forming designs upon the constitution, as ruinous in the opposite extreme: but these were at that time, apprehensions only; at least, not one fact had been proved to justify them: and if the case had been otherwise, why should the iniquities of the fathers be visited on their children? Why should a whole nation be enslaved, because a few malignants turmoiled the public for their own private advantage?—The laws in being were very sufficient to guard the crown against any violence from the people, as long as they were suffered to operate equally between the people and the crown; but they would not authorize oppression, which was the thing in pursuit: now, it is only in case of oppression, when law itself is set aside, that the right of resistance has been contended for, as the last resort of a free people: and we shall find in the course of this history, even the very bishops themselves refusing to express their *Abhorrence* of an open invasion, when they found their own possessions in danger. Fundamentals ought to be held sacred on both sides: but if a government sets aside the laws, the governed may do the same: let the subject, however, always remember, that if he draws his sword under whatever provocations, even at a time of day when the doctrine of *Passive Obedience* has been ever so long and so effectually exploded, by deeds as well as words, it must be at his own peril; and that he will find the great statute of treasons has more power to condemn, than Magna Charta to absolve him.—To return: We left the court-party in possession of their darling Test, though somewhat purged by the fiery trial it had undergone: for now it was conceived as follows: 'I, A. B. do declare, 'that it is not lawful, on any pretence whatsoever, to take up Arms against the king: 'and I do abhor the traiterous position of 'taking Arms by his authority against his person, 'or against those that are commissioned by him, 'according to law, in time of rebellion and 'war, and acting in pursuance of such commission. I, A. B. do swear, that I will not 'endeavour any Alteration of the Protestant 'religion, now established by law in the church 'of England; nor will I endeavour any Altera'tion in the government in church or state, 'as it is by law established.'—Nothing therefore remained, but to send it down to the commons, and to prepare it a favourable reception, and speedy passage.* According to the seeming temper of that house, the business before them, and their manifest distrust of the court, this appeared to be no easy task: and it might be rather presumed, that they would have rejected it at the first reading, than inclined to strengthen such a king and such a ministry, with such a law. But according to sir John Reresby, who took his † seat as a member this session, the two parties were so equal, that neither durst stand the issue of a question: we have evidence left us, that they had their relentings in the case of the lord treasurer: and in any affair where the Church was concerned, there was great reason to fear they would make no difficulty to abandon the people. It is therefore reasonable to conclude, that lord Shaftsbury, and those who were deepest in the secrets of the Opposition,

* Andrew Marvell in his "Growth of Popery," speaking of this remarkable contest, says, "It was, I think, the greatest, which had perhaps ever been in parliament; wherein those lords that were against this Oath, being assured of their own loyalty and merit, stood up now for the English liberties, with the same genius, virtue, and courage, that their noble ancestors had formerly defended the Great Charter of England, but with so much greater commendation, in that they had here a fairer field, and the more civil way of decision: they fought it out, under all the disadvantages imaginable: they were overlaid by numbers: the noise of the house, like the wind was against them; and, if not the Sun, the Fire-side (the king generally stood there) was always in their faces: nor being so few, could they, as their adversaries, withdraw to refresh themselves in a whole day's engagement: yet never was there a clearer demonstration, how dull a thing is human eloquence, and greatness how little, when the bright truth discovers all things in their proper colours and dimensions, and, shining, shoots its beams through all their fallacies."

† On the country interest, it may be presumed; for he gives us to understand, that he was introduced by the lords Russel and Cavendish.

thought it more advisable to prevent its finding its way into that house, than to run the risque of its passing through." A quarrel, however, which ensued between the two houses, prevented the passing of all the Bills during the present session.

PROCEEDINGS IN THE HOUSE OF COMMONS, ON AN APPEAL BEING BROUGHT IN THE HOUSE OF LORDS, BY DR. SHIRLEY, AGAINST SIR JOHN FAGG, AND OTHERS THEIR MEMBERS.*

Sir John Fagg's Complaint.] May 4. Sir John Fagg, bart. this day informing the house, that he was summoned to appear to a Petition in the house of lords, a Committee was thereupon appointed to search for Precedents to that purpose.

May 5. Resolved, 'That a Message be sent to the lords to acquaint them that this house hath received information, that there is a Petition of Appeal depending before them, at the suit of Thomas Shirley esq. against sir John Fagg, a member of this house; to which Petition he is, by order of the house of lords, directed to answer on Friday next: and to desire the lords to have a regard to the privileges of this house: and that sir Trevor Williams do go up with the Message to the lords."

Sir Trevor Williams reports, That he had attended the lords with the Message of this house, concerning sir John Fagg; and the lords will return an Answer by messengers of their own.

May 7. A Message from the lords by sir Wm. Beversham and sir Samuel Clarke.—"Mr. Speaker, the lords have considered of the Message received from the house of commons, concerning Privilege in the Case of sir John Fagg, and do return this Answer, That the house of commons need not doubt, but that the lords will have a regard to the privilege of the house of commons, as they have of their own."

May 8. A Committee was appointed to inspect the Lords Journals, to see what Entries are therein made against sir John Fagg, a member of this house, and to report the same.

May 12. Resolved, That Dr. Tho. Shirley be sent for in custody, to answer his Breach of the Privileges of this house, in prosecuting a suit by Petition of Appeal in the lords house, against sir John Fagg, a member of this house, during the session and privilege of parliament.—And a Committee is also to inspect the Lords Journals, to see what hath been done in like cases; and the said sir John Fagg is ordered not to proceed, or make any Answer to the said Appeal, without the licence of this house.

Sir T. Lee's Report from the Lords Journals.] May 14. Sir Tho. Lee reports from the Committee appointed to inspect the Journals of the house of lords, and the Entries therein, in the Case between Dr. Tho. Shirley and sir John Fagg, a member of this house, that the committee had perused the Journals of the lords house, and found the Entries to be as follow: "April, the 30th. Tho. Shirley, esq. presented a Petition to the lords.' Ordered, 'That the said sir John Fagg may have a copy of the said Petition and put in his Answer thereunto in writing, on the 7th of May next, if he thinks fit.'—May, the 5th. 'The Commons send a Message by sir Trevor Williams: The knights, citizens, and burgesses of the house of commons, in parliament assembled, have been informed, that there is a Petition of Appeal depending before their lordships, at the suit of Tho. Shirley esq. against sir John Fagg a member of their house; to which Petition he is, by their lordships order, directed to answer, on Friday next, and desire their lordships to take care of their privileges.'—Answer. 'That this house have considered of their Message, and will send an Answer by messengers of their own.'—Ordered, 'That the Committee for Privileges do meet this afternoon to consider of the Messages received from the house of commons this day, concerning Tho. Shirley esq. and sir John Fagg, a member of the house, and search precedents in the case, and report to the house to-morrow morning.'—May 6th. The earl of Berks reported, 'That the Committee of Privileges having met and considered of what was referred to them, in the Case be-

* "A quarrel which ensued between the two houses, prevented the passing of every bill projected during the present session. One Dr. Shirley, being cast in a law-suit before chancery against sir John Fagg, a member of the house of commons, preferred a petition of appeal to the house of peers. The lords received it, and summoned Fagg to appear before them. He complained to the lower house, who espoused his cause. They not only maintained, that no member of their house could be summoned before the peers: they also asserted, that the upper house could receive no appeals from any court of equity; a pretension which extremely retrenched the jurisdiction of the peers, and which was contrary to the practice that had prevailed during this whole century. The commons send Shirley to prison; the lords assert their powers. Conferences are tried; but no accommodation ensues. Four lawyers are sent to the Tower by the commons, for transgressing the orders of the house, and pleading in this cause before the peers. The peers denominate this arbitrary commitment a breach of the great charter, and order the lieutenant of the Tower to release the prisoners: he declines obedience: they apply to the king, and desire him to punish the lieutenant for his contempt. The king summons both houses; exhorts them to unanimity: and informs them, that the present quarrel had arisen from the contrivance of his and their enemies, who expected by that means to force a dissolution of the parliament. His advice has no effect: the commons continue as violent as ever; and the king, finding that no business could be finished, at last prorogued the parliament." Hume.

tween Tho. Shirley esq. and sir John Fagg, a member of the house of commons, and a Message from the house of commons thereupon; have ordered him to report, that the Committee have found that the house did refer the business of Mr. Hale and Mr. Slingsby, upon the like Message of the house of commons, to the Committee of Privileges; who did report to the house, that it is the undoubted Right of the lords in judicature, to receive and determine in time of parliament, Appeals from inferior courts, though a member of either house be concerned, that there may be no failure of justice in the land; and the house did agree with the committee therein: and thereupon the Committee do humbly offer to their lordships, upon this occasion, to take the same course, and to insist upon their just Rights in this particular, which their lordships will be pleased to signify to the house of commons, in such manner as they shall think fit.'—The house agreed with the Committee in this Declaration, and ordered the same to be entered into the Journal-Book of this house as their Declaration, viz. 'That it is the undoubted Right of the lords in judicature, to receive and determine in time of parliament, Appeals from inferior courts, though a member of either house be concerned, that there may be no failure of justice in the land.'—Then it was moved that the former Answer sent to the house of commons in the Case of Mr. Slingsby and Mr. Hale, might be given now to the house of commons, in this Case of sir John Fagg; and that the Declaration and Report, agreed to this day, might be added to it.—The Declaration aforesaid was read, and the question being put, Whether this shall be as a part of the Answer to be given to the house of commons? It was resolved in the negative.—The Answer returned formerly to the house of commons, in the Case of Mr. Slingsby, and Mr. Hale, was in these words: 'That the house of commons need not doubt but that their lordships will have a regard to the Privileges of the house of commons, as they have of their own.'—The question being put, Whether this Answer shall be now returned to the Message from the house of commons? It was resolved in the affirmative.—May 7th, it was sent accordingly.—May 7. 'Whereas this day was appointed for sir John Fagg to put in an Answer to the Petition and Appeal of Tho. Shirley, esq. depending in this house, if he thought fit; the said sir John Fagg appearing personally this day at the bar, and desiring longer time to put in an Answer thereunto: It is thereupon ordered that the said sir John Fagg hath hereby further time given him for putting in his Answer, till the 12th day of this instant May."—Sir John Fagg put in his Answer to the Petition of Mr. Shirley.

Resolution thereon.] A debate arising thereupon, touching the Privilege of their house,

Resolved, &c. "That the Appeal, brought by Dr. Shirley in the house of lords against sir John Fagg, a member of this house, and the proceedings thereupon, is a Breach of the undoubted Rights and Privileges of this house."

The house being informed, that the Warrant of this house for taking of the said Dr. Shirley into custody, was forcibly taken away and detained from the serjeant at arms his deputy, attending this house, by the lord Mohun: and the serjeant's deputy being called in and examined as to the matter of fact, gave this testimony: "That he found Dr. Shirley in the inner lobby of the house of lords, and that he came to him and desired to speak with him, and acquainted him, that he had a Warrant from the house of commons to apprehend him, and desired to know whether he could shew him any reason to excuse him, that he might not serve the warrant on him: and that he likewise told him, that he would not execute the warrant on him in that place, but desired of him that he would go along with him freely; and that in case he would not, he would take his opportunity in another place. And that the said lord Mohun coming in, in the mean time, required him to shew his warrant; which he producing, the lord Mohun laid hands on it, and held it so fast, that it was in danger of being torn; and that therefore he was forced to part with it, and desiring to have it again, the lord Mohun refused it, but carried the warrant into the house of lords. That Dr. Shirley afterwards refused to go along with him, saying, that he was not then his prisoner; and that, several persons interposing, the doctor escaped from him;" and a debate arising thereupon,

Resolved, "That a Message be sent to the lords to complain of lord Mohun, for forcibly taking away and detaining the Warrant of this house, from the deputy serjeant at arms, for taking of Dr. Shirley in custody; and to demand the justice of the lords house against the said lord Mohun. And that the lord Antram do go up to the lords with the Message."

Dr. Shirley ordered into Custody.] Ordered, "That Mr. Speaker do issue forth a new warrant to the serjeant at arms attending this house, for apprehending Dr. Tho. Shirley, to answer his Breach of Privilege, for prosecuting a suit by Petition of Appeal in the lords house against sir John Fagg, a member of this house, during the session and privilege of parliament."

Lord Antram's Report from the Lords.] May 15. The Lord Antram reports from the lords, that he had, in obedience to the commands of this house, attended the lords, and delivered the Message concerning the lord Mohun's taking away, and detaining the Warrant for apprehending Dr. Shirley, and that the lords had returned this Answer: "Gentlemen of the house of commons, The lords have considered of your Message, and of the Complaint therein; and they return you this Answer, that they find the lord Mohun hath done nothing but what is according to his duty."

Dr. Shirley's Appeal voted a Breach of Privilege.] The house then resumed the debate of the matter concerning the Privileges of this house; and the matter being debated; Resolved, "That the Appeal, brought by Dr. Shirley in the house of lords against sir John Fagg, a member of this house, and the proceedings thereupon, is a breach of the undoubted rights and privileges of the house of commons; and therefore the commons desire, that there be no farther proceedings in that cause before their lordships."

Ordered, That, a conference be desired with the lords concerning the Privileges of this house, in the Case of sir John Fagg; and that sir Tho. Lee do go up to the Lords to desire a Conference.

A Message from the lords by sir Mondeford Bramston, and sir Wm. Glascock. "Mr. Speaker, We are commanded to let this house know that the lords spiritual and temporal, assembled in parliament, having received a warrant, signed Edw. Seymour, which they have appointed us to shew you and desire to know whether it be a Warrant ordered by this house."—The matter of the Message being debated, the question being put, that the word 'unparliamentary' be part of the Answer to the lords Message, it passed in the negative.

Resolved, That the messengers be called in, and that this answer be returned, 'that this house will consider of the message.' The messengers being called in, Mr. Speaker does acquaint them, that the house will consider of the Message.

Resolved, "That the Message last received from the house of lords, is an unparliamentary message. That a Conference be desired to be had with the lords, upon the subject matter of the last Message: That it be referred to Mr. Garraway, &c. to draw up Reasons to be offered at the said Conference."

Then the house being informed that there is a cause upon an Appeal brought up by sir Nich. Stoughton, against Mr. Onslow, a member of this house, appointed to be heard at the bar of the lords house; Resolved, "That a Message be sent to the lords to acquaint them, that this house has received information, that there is a Cause upon an Appeal brought by sir Nich. Stoughton against Mr. Onslow a member of this house, appointed to be heard at the bar of the house, on Monday next; and to desire their lordships to have regard to the privileges of this house, and that sir Rd. Temple do go up with the Message to the lords."—Ordered, "That Mr. Onslow do not appear any farther in the prosecution of the Appeal brought against him by sir Nich. Stoughton, in the house of lords: That sir Nich. Stoughton be sent for in custody of the serjeant at arms attending this house, to answer his Breach of Privilege in prosecuting a suit in the house of lords against Arthur Onslow, esq; a member of this house, during the session and privilege of parliament."

Resolved, "That whosoever shall appear at the bar of the house of lords, to prosecute any suit against any member of this house, shall be deemed a breaker and infringer of the Rights and Privileges of this house."

Sir Tho. Lee's report from the Committee.] May 17. Sir Tho. Lee reports, from the Committee appointed to draw up Reasons for the Conference to be had with the lords, Reasons agreed by the committee; which are as follow, viz. "For that the Message is by way of interrogatory upon the proceedings of the house of commons in a Case concerning the Privilege of a member of that house, of which they are proper judges. For that the matter of the Message carries in it an undue reflection upon the Speaker of the house of commons. For that the matter of the Message doth highly reflect upon the whole house of commons, in their lordships questioning that house concerning their own orders; which they have the more reason to apprehend, because, the day before this Message was brought to them, the warrant was owned by the complaint of the house of commons to their lordships that the same was taken and detained from a servant of theirs, by a peer; which imports, that the question in that Message could not be for information only, and so tends to interrupt that mutual good correspondency, which ought to be preserved inviolably between the two houses of parliament."

May 18. Sir Rd. Temple reports from the lords, that he had attended their lordships, according to the command of this house, with the Message in the Case of Mr. Onslow, to which the lords returned an Answer, which being in writing, was delivered at the clerks table, and read, as followeth: "The lords do declare, That it is the undoubted Right of the lords in judicature, to receive and determine in time of parliament, Appeals from inferior courts, though a member of either house be concerned, that there may be no failure of justice in the land: and from this Right, and the exercise thereof, their lordships will not depart."

The matter of the lords Answer being debated, Resolved, "That it is the undoubted privilege of this house, that none of their members be summoned to attend the house of lords, during the sitting or privilege of parliament. That a Conference be desired with the lords, upon the privileges of this house, contained in the lords Answer to the message of this house, in the Case of Mr. Onslow.

Reasons to be offer'd to the Lords at the Conference.] May 20. Sir Tho, Lee reports, from the committee appointed to draw up Reasons to be offered at the Conference to be had with the lords upon the Privileges of this house, contained in the lords Answer to the last Message of this house, in the case of Mr. Onslow; which Reasons were twice read, and, with some alterations at the clerk's table, agreed to, as follow: 1. "That, by the laws and usage of parliament, Privilege of Parliament belongs to every member of the house of commons, in all cases except treason, felony, and breach of the peace; which hath often been declared in parliament, without any exception of Appeals before the lords. 2. That the reason of that Privilege is, that the members of the house of commons may freely attend the public affairs of that house, without disturbance or interruption, which doth extend as well to Appeals before the house of peers, as to proceedings in other courts. 3. That, by the constant course and usage of parliament, no member of the house of commons can attend the house of lords, without the especial leave of that house first obtained, much less be summoned or compelled so to do. 4. If the lords shall proceed to hear and determine any Appeal, where the party neither can, nor ought to attend, such proceedings would be contrary to the rules of justice. 5. That the not determining of an Appeal against a member of the house of commons, is not a failure of justice, but only a suspension of proceedings in a particular case, during the continuance of that parliament which is but temporary. 6. That in case it were a failure of justice, it is not to be remedied by the house of lords alone, but it may be by act of parliament."

The Lords Reasons.] Mr. Powle reports, from the Conference had with the lords upon the subject matter of the former Conference, concerning the Warrant for apprehending Dr. Shirley, That the lords had returned an Answer to the Reasons of this house, delivered at the former Conference, and are as follows: "The lords have appointed this Conference, upon the subject matter of the last conference, and have commanded us to give these Answers to the Reasons and other matters then delivered by the house of commons. To the first question, the lords conceive that the most natural way of being informed, is by way of question; and seeing a Paper here, which did reflect upon the privileges of the lords house, their lordships would not proceed upon it, till they were assured it was owned by the house of commons: but the lords had no occasion at that time, nor do they now think fit, to enter into the debate of the house of commons being, or not being proper judges in the case concerning the Privilege of a member of that house; their lordships necessary consideration, upon sight of that paper, being only how far the h. of commons ordering (if that paper were theirs) the apprehension of Dr. Shirley, for prosecuting his Appeal before the lords, did entrench upon their lordships both privilege and undoubted right of judicature, in the consequence of it, excepting all the members of both houses from the judicature of this the highest court of the kingdom; which would cause a failure of that supreme justice, not administrable in any other court, and which their lordships will never admit. As to the 2nd Reason, the lords answer, That they do not apprehend how the matter of this Message is any reflection upon the Speaker of the house of commons. To the 3d Reason, The lords cannot imagine how it can be apprehended in the least to reflect upon the h. of commons, for the h. of peers, upon a Paper produced to their lordships, in form of a Warrant of that house, whereof doubt was made among the lords, whether any such thing had been ordered by that house, to enquire of the commons whether such warrant was ordered there or no? And, without such liberty used by the lords, it will be very hard for their lordships to be rightly informed, so as to preserve a good correspondence between the two houses, which their lordships shall endeavour; or to know when warrants, in the name of that house, are true or pretended: and it is so ungrounded an apprehension, that their lordships intended any reflection in asking that question, and not taking notice in their Message of the Complaint of the h. of commons owning that warrant, that the lords had sent their Message concerning that Paper, to the h. of commons, before the lords had received the said commons complaint.—But their lordships have great cause to except against the unjust and strained reflection of that house upon their lordships, in asserting that the question in the lords Message could not be for information, as we affirm, but tending to interrupt the mutual correspondence between the two houses; which we deny, and had not the least thought of.—The lords have farther commanded us to say, that they doubt not but the h. of commons, when they have received what we have delivered at this conference, will be sensible of their error, in calling our Message strange, unusual, or unparliamentary. Though we cannot but take notice, that their Answer to our Message, that they would consider it, was the first of that kind that we can find to have come from that house."

The Lords Reasons voted unsatisfactory.] The question being put, Whether the house be satisfied with the Reasons delivered by the lords at the last Conference? it passed in the negative.—Resolved, That a free conference be desired with the lords upon the matter delivered at the last Conference; and that the former managers do attend, and manage the free conference.

Sir T. Lee's Report from the Committee.] May 28. Sir Tho. Lee reports, from the committee to whom it was referred to draw up Reasons to be offered at a Conference to be had with the lords, upon the subject matter of their Answer to the last Message of this house, in the Case of Mr. Onslow, several Reasons agreed by the said committee: which were severally agreed unto, and are as follow; "For that the commons desired a Conference upon their Privileges concerned by the lords Answer to a Message sent to the lords the 18th of May, in the Case of Mr. Onslow; their lordships have not agreed to any conference in the case of Mr. Onslow, but have only agreed to a conference concerning their Privileges in general, without reference to the Case of the said Mr. Onslow; which was the only subject matter of the desired conference.—The limitation in the lords agreement to a conference, with proviso that nothing be offered at the conference that may any way concern their lordships judicature, is in effect a denial of any conference at all, upon the subject on which it was desired: which ought not to be; the judicature which their lordships claim in Appeals against a member of the h. of commons, and the privilege of that house, being in that case so involved, that there can be no conference upon the latter, without some way touching upon the former. That this manner of agreeing to a conference with any limitation or proviso, is against the course of proceedings betwixt the two houses of parliament, in coming to conference, and doth seem to place a power in the managers of such conferences to judge whether such provisos be broken or not, and accordingly to proceed, or break off the conference upon their own judgments."

May 31. A Message from the lords by sir Mondeford Brampston, and sir Wm. Beversham: "Mr. Speaker, The lords have commanded us to acquaint you, that they desire a Conference presently in the Painted-Chamber, with the h. of commons, upon their not coming to the Conference desired by them, on Thursday last, and by the lords appointed to be at ten o'clock in the Painted-Chamber, on Friday the 28th inst."—The messengers being withdrawn, and the Message debated, a present conference upon the question was agreed.

Sir John Trevor reports, from the Conference, that the lords had declared the intent of this conference, to the effect following, viz. "That the lords have appointed this conference, out of that constant desire and resolution they have to continue a fair correspondence between the two houses; which is of the essence of parliamentary proceedings. For this end their lordships have commanded us to tell you, that they cannot but take notice of the h. of commons failing to be, on Friday last, at a conference desired by themselves and appointed by the lords at 10 o'clock in the Painted-Chamber. That they conceive it tends to an interruption of all parliamentary Proceedings, and to evade the right of the lords to appoint time and place for a conference."

Ordered, That it be referred to the former committee, who are appointed to draw up Reasons, to be offered at a Conference to be had with the lords upon the subject matter of their Answer, to the Message of this house, in the Case of Mr. Onslow, to consider of the matter delivered by the lords at the last conference; and to prepare and draw up farther Reasons, to be offered at another conference. And Mr. Serjeant Maynard, and Mr. Sawyer, are to take notice to attend the same.

June 1. Sir Tho. Lee reports, from the Committee appointed to inspect the Journals of the house of lords, and to see what proceedings have been entered, in the Case of Mr. Dalmahoy, and Mr. Onslow, that they had inspected the Lords Journals as to the Case of Mr. Dalmahoy, and collected what proceedings had been in that Case; but had no opportunity or time yet to do it in the Case of Mr. Onslow: which proceedings being reported, were read, and delivered in at the Clerk's-table; and are as follow, viz. "April 19, 1675;

"The Appeal brought by Crispe and Crispe, complaining against a decree in chancery made, wherein Mr. Dalmahoy is recited to be one of the petitioners; Cranbourne and Bowyer are ordered to put in an Answer, and Dalmahoy if he please.—May 12. Ordered, That this house will hear counsel at the bar, upon the Petition and Appeal of sir Nich. Crispe, and others, against the lady viscountess Cranbourne, the lady Anne Bowyer, and Thomas Dalmahoy, esq. and their Answer thereunto, depending in this house on Wednesday the 19th inst. whereof the petitioners are to cause timely notice to be given to the said defendants, or their agents in the said case, for that purpose.—May 19. Whereas sir Nich. Crispe, bart. having an Appeal depending in this house, against the lady Cranbourne, lady Bowyer, and Tho. Dalmahoy, esq. a member of the house of commons; hath prayed that counsel may be assigned him to plead his cause upon the said Appeal, and hath named counsel for that purpose: it is ordered that sir John Churchill, serj. Peck, serj. Pemberton, and Mr. Porter, named by the said sir Nich. Cripse, be, and are hereby appointed to open, and manage the said cause, on the part and behalf of the said sir Nich. Crispe; on the 27th of this instant May; and at such other times, as it shall be depending in this house.—Upon reading the Petition of sir Nich. Crispe, bart. Tho. Crispe, and John Crispe, esqrs. shewing; that having an Appeal depending in this house against Tho. Dalmahoy, esq. a member of the house of commons, and others; they are in danger of being arrested by an Order of the h. of commons; and therefore pray the protection of this house, that they may have liberty to prosecute their said Appeal with freedom: it is thereupon ordered, that sir Nicholas Crispe, &c. or any of them, their or any of their counsel, agents or solicitors, or such other person or persons as they shall employ, in prosecuting the said Appeal before this house, be, and are hereby privileged, and protected accordingly by this house, until the matter upon the Appeal be determined by their lordships. And all persons whatsoever are hereby prohibited from arresting, imprisoning, or otherwise molesting, the said sir Nich. Crispe, &c. upon any pretence whatsoever, during the time prefixed, as they or such of them will answer the contrary to this house.—May 26. The Cause between sir Nich. Crispe, &c. plaintiffs, and Tho. Dalmahoy, esq. defendant, appointed to be heard the 27th, was ordered to be heard the 28th.—May 27. Upon reading the Petition of sir Nich. Cripse, complaining, that the counsel assigned him by this house, to plead his cause at the bar, wherein Mr. Dalmahoy is one of the defendants, do refuse to plead for him in this case, in regard of a Vote of the house of commons; sir Nich. Crispe was called in, and testified, that he shewed the Order of this house to serjeant Peck, serjeant Pemberton, sir John Churchill, and Mr. Porter. Whereupon it is Ordered, That, whereas sir John Churchill, serj. Peck, serj. Pemberton, and Mr. Porter, were, by order of this house, dated on the 19th inst. assigned to be of counsel for sir Nicholas Crispe, John Crispe, and Tho. Crispe, in their Cause depending in this house, against Tho. Dalmahoy, esq. a member of the h. of commons, and other defendants, at such time as the said Cause shall be appointed to be pleaded at the bar of this house; and having appointed to hear the said cause, by counsel on both sides, to-morrow at three in the afternoon; It is this day Ordered, That the said sir John Churchill, serj. Peck, serj. Pemberton, and Mr. Porter, be, and are hereby required, to appear at the bar of this house, to-morrow, at three in the afternoon, as counsel to plead in said Cause, on the behalf of the said sir Nich. Crispe, John Crispe, and Tho. Crispe, as they will answer the contrary to this house.—May 28. Counsel heard at the bar on both parts, upon the Petition and Appeal of sir Nicholas Crispe, &c. and the Answer of Diana viscountess Cranbourne, &c. and Tho. Dalmahoy, esq. put in thereunto concerning a decree in chancery: Resolved, That the Petition and Decree be dismissed."

"The same day, the house heard the counsel of sir Nich. Crispe, John Crispe, and Thomas Crispe, upon their Petition and Appeal depending in this house; and also the counsel of the lady Bowyer, and Mr. Dalmahoy, upon their Answer thereunto; and, after a serious consideration thereof, the question being put, whether this Petition and Appeal shall be dismissed this house? It was resolved in the affirmative.

Proceedings against several Barristers for pleading before the Lords in Breach of an Order of the Commons.] June 1. Mr. serj. Pemberton, sir John Churchill, Mr. Serj. Peck, and Mr. Porter, attending at the door, in obedience to the order of the house of commons; and being severally called in, Mr. Speaker did severally acquaint them, that they were summoned to give an account to the house, of their appearing as Council at the bar of the house of lords, in the prosecution of a Cause depending upon an Appeal, wherein Mr. Dalmahoy, a member of this house, is concerned, in the manifest Breach of the Order of this house; and giving up, as much as in them lies, the rights and privileges of the commons of England: and they having answered and made their excuses to the effect following: "That they had no notice of the Order or Vote of this house, but what they had heard in common discourse abroad; and because they conceived Mr. Dalmahoy, a member of this house, might be concerned, they refused several times to appear as council, or to accept their fees; but being assigned of council for sir Nicholas Crispe, and an Order of the house of lords being served on them to attend at their peril, and that then attending, and Mr. Dalmahoy having put in his Answer in the lords house, and not insisting on his privilege afterwards, and the council for lady Bowyer, who was the principal party concerned, denying to be of council for Mr. Dalmahoy, they conceived they might safely appear as council without breach of the Order, or invading the rights and privileges of this house, which was not intended by them; and sir John Churchill, by way of farther excuse for himself, said, that he had witnesses ready to prove that Mr. Dalmahoy was willing and desirous to have the business go forward.

They are ordered into Custody.] And the said Mr. serj. Pemberton, sir John Churchill, Mr. serj. Peck, and Mr. Porter, did all of them humbly submit themselves to the pleasure of the house, if they had in any thing misbehaved themselves; and being withdrawn, and the matter debated, the question being put, That serj. Pemberton be taken into custody of the serjeant at arms attending this house. It was resolved in the affirmative. Ordered, That serj. Pemberton, sir John Churchill, Mr. serj. Peck, and Cha. Porter, esq. be taken into custody of the serjeant at arms attending this house*.

Other Reasons to be offered to the Lords.] June 2. Ordered, That sir Rd. Temple, Mr. Vaughan, and sir Thomas Lee do withdraw, and attend the Reasons upon the debates of the house: which was done and the Reasons agreed to are as follow: "The house of commons do agree with the lords, that conferences between the two houses, are essential to parliamentary proceedings, when they are agreed in the usual and parliamentary way; but the manner of the lords agreement to the Conference, to have been on Friday the 28th of May, in the Painted-Chamber, with limitation and proviso, did necessitate the house of commons to forbear to meet at that conference, and gave the first interruption to parliamentary proceedings, in conferences between the two houses.—For that the Conference desired by the commons, was upon their Privileges, concerned in the Answer of the lords to a Message of the house of commons, sent to the lords the 17th of May, in the Case of Mr. Onslow; to the which the lords did not agree, but did only agree to a conference concerning their Privileges in general, without reference to the case of the said Mr. Onslow;

* "During the debate upon this Resolution, some ladies were in the gallery, peeping over the gentlemen's shoulders. The Speaker spying them, called out, 'What Borough do those ladies serve for?' to which Mr. Wm. Coventry replied, 'They serve for the Speaker's Chamber!' Sir Tho. Littleton said, 'The Speaker might mistake them for gentlemen with fine sleeves, dressed like ladies:' Says the Speaker, 'I am sure I saw petticoats.'" Grey.

which was the only subject matter of the desired conference. The limitation in the lords agreement to a conference, with proviso that nothing be offered at the conference that may any ways concern the lords judicature, is in effect a denial of any conference at all, upon the subject upon which it was desired; which ought not to be. The judicature which the lords claim in appeals against a member of the house of commons, and the privilege of that house in that case, is so involved, that no conference can be upon the matter, without some way touching the former. That this manner of agreeing to a conference, with any limitation or proviso, is against the course of proceedings between the two houses, in coming to conferences; and both seem to place a power in the managers of such conferences, to judge whether such provisos be broken or not, and accordingly to proceed or break off the conference upon their own judgments.—The house of commons doubt not, but that, when the lords have considered of what is delivered at this Conference, the good correspondence which the lords express they desire to continue between the two houses (which the commons are also no less careful to maintain) will induce them to remove the present interruption of coming to conferences; and therefore to agree to the conference, as it was desired by the house of commons, upon the privileges of their house, concerned in the lords Answer to the Message of the house of commons, in the Case of Mr. Onslow: That the particular limitation, that nothing be offered at the Conference, that may any way concern the judicature of the lords, appears unreasonable; for that their lordships judicature in parliament is circumscribed by the laws of the land, as to their proceedings and judgments; and is, as well as all other courts, subjected to parliament."

The Lords Replies.] June 3. Mr. Vaughan reports, That the lord privy seal did manage the Conference, and had delivered the intent and occasion of the Conference; which Mr. Vaughan did report to the house, to the effect following: "The lords to take notice of the house of commons their ordering into custody of their serjeant, Mr. serj. Peck, sir John Churchill, Mr. serj. Pemberton, and Mr. serj. Porter, counsellors at law; assigned by their lordships to be of counsel in an Appeal heard at their lordships bar, in the case of sir Nich. Crispe, against the lady Bowyer, Mr. Dalmahoy, and others; the lords in parliament, where his majesty is highest in his royal estate, and where the last resort of judging upon writs of error, and appeals in equity, in all causes and over all persons, is undoubtedly fixed, and permanently lodged. It is an unexampled usurpation and breach of privilege against the house of peers, that their orders or judgments should be disputed, or endeavoured to be controlled, or the execution thereof obstructed by the lower house of parliament; who are no court, nor have authority to administer an oath, or give any judgment.—It is a transcendent invasion on the right and liberty of the subject, and against Magna Charta, the Petition of Right, and many other laws, which have provided, that no freeman shall be imprisoned or otherwise restrained of his liberty, but by due process of law.—This tends to the subversion of the government of the kingdom, and to the introducing of arbitrariness and disorder.—Because it is the nature of an injunction from the lower house, (who have no authority or power of judicature over inferior subjects, much less over the king and lords) against the orders and judgments of the supreme court.—We are farther commanded to acquaint you, that the lords have, therefore, out of that justice which they are dispensers of against oppression and breach of laws, by judgment of this court, set at liberty, by the gentleman usher of the black rod, all the said serjeants and counsellors; and prohibited the lieutenant of the tower, and all other keepers of prisons and goalers, and all persons whatsoever, from arresting and imprisoning, detaining, or otherwise molesting, or charging the said gentlemen, or any of them in this case: and if any person, of what degree soever, shall presume to the contrary, their lordships will exercise the authority with them entrusted for putting the laws in execution. And we are farther commanded to read to you a roll of parliament in the 1st year of the reign of king Hen. ivth, whereof we have brought the original with us."

And a debate arising thereupon; resolved, That a Conference be desired with the lords upon the subject matter of the last Conference; and that these members following be appointed to prepare and draw up Reasons upon the debates of the house, to be offered at the conference.—Ordered, That the officer, in whose custody is the Record of the 1st of Hen. ivth, mentioned at the conference with the lords, do attend the committee appointed to draw up Reasons for another conference this afternoon.

Ordered, That no member of this house do attend the lords house, upon any summons from the lords, without leave of the house.

The Thanks of the House given to the Speaker for causing serj. Pemberton to be seized in Westminster-hall.] June 4. Ordered, "That the Thanks of the house be returned to Mr. Speaker, for causing Mr. Serj. Pemberton, formerly committed by order of this house to the custody of the serjeant at arms attending this house, for Breach of Privilege, to be seized and taken into custody in Westminster-hall, for his breach of privilege."

The four Barristers seized and sent to the Tower.] The house being informed, that sir John Churchill, Mr. Serjeant Peck, and Mr. C. Porter, who were ordered to be taken into custody of the serj. at arms attending this house, are now in Westminster-hall; Ordered, That the serjeant at arms now attending this house, do go with his mace into Westminster-hall, and do execute the Order of this house and the Warrant of Mr. Speaker thereupon, for seizing and bringing in custody Mr. serj. Peck, sir John Churchill and Mr. Ch. Porter, for their breach of the privilege of this house.—The serjeant returning, gave an account, that he had executed the Order of this house and Mr. Speaker's Warrant thereupon, and had brought the said Mr. serj. Peck, sir John Churchill and Mr. Ch. Porter, in custody, into the Speaker's Chamber.—The question being put that sir John Churchill, Mr. serj. Peck, Mr. serj. Pemberton, and Mr. Ch. Porter be sent to the Tower, for their breach of privilege and contempt of the authority of this house? It was resolved in the affirmative.

Ordered, That John Popham, esq. the now serjeant at arms attending this house, be protected against all persons that shall any ways molest or hinder him from executing his office.

Other Reasons to be offered the Lords.] Sir Tho. Lee reports from the Committee, the Reasons agreed to be offered at the Conference to be had with the lords, upon the matters delivered at the last conference, which were twice read, and agreed to, as follows: "Your lordships having desired the last Conference, upon matters of high importance, concerning the dignity of the king, and the safety of the government, the commons did not expect to hear from your lordships at that conference, things so contrary to, and inconsistent with, the matter upon which the said conference was desired, as were then delivered by your lordships. It was much below the expectation of the commons, that, after a representation of your lordships Message, of matters of so high importance, the particular upon which the conference was grounded, should be only the commitment of four lawyers to the custody of their own serjeant at arms, for a manifest violation of the privileges of their house. But the commons were much more surprized, when your lordships had introduced the conference with an assurance, that it was in order to a good correspondency between the two houses, that your lordships should immediately assume a power to judge the orders of the h. of commons for imprisonment of Mr. serj. Pemberton, Mr. serj. Peck, sir John Churchill, and Mr. Ch. Porter to be illegal and arbitrary: and the execution thereof a great indignity to the king's majesty; with many other high reflections upon the h. of commons, throughout the whole conference: whereby your lordships have condemned the whole h. of commons as criminal, which is without precedent or example, or any ground or reason so to do.—It is not against the king's dignity for the h. of commons to punish by imprisonment, a commoner that is guilty of violating their privileges, that being according to the known laws and customs of parliament, and the right of their privileges declared by the king's royal predecessors in former parliaments, and by himself in this.—But your ldps. claiming to be the supréme court, and that his maj. is highest in his royal estate in the court of judicature there, is a diminution of the dignity of the king, who is highest in his royal estate in full parliament; and is derogatory to the authority of the whole parliament, by appropriating it to yourselves. The commons did not by this imprisonment infringe any privileges of the h. of peers, but only defend and maintain their own: on the other side, your lordships do highly intrench upon the rights and privileges of the h. of commons, by denying them to be a court or to have any authority or power of judicature; which, if admitted, will leave them without any power or authority to preserve themselves.—As to what your lordships call a transcendent invasion of the rights and liberties of the subject, and against Magna Charta, the Petition of Right, and many other laws; the h. of commons presume that your lordships know that neither the Great Charta, Petition of Right, or any other laws, do take away the law and custom of parliament, or of either house of parliament, or else your lordships have very much forgotten the Great Charter, and those other laws, in the several judgments your lordships have passed upon the king's subjects in cases of privilege. But the commons cannot find by Magna Charta, or by any law or ancient custom of parliament, that your lordships have any jurisdiction in cases of Appeal from the courts of equity.—We are farther commanded to acquaint you, that the enlargment of those persons in prison by order of the h. of commons, by the gentleman-usher of the black rod, and the prohibition which threatens all officers and other persons whatsoever, not to receive or detain them; is an apparent breach of the rights and privileges of the h. of commons: and they have, therefore, caused them to be retaken into the custody of the serjeant at arms attending this house, and have committed them to the Tower.—As for the Parliament-Roll of the 1st Hen. ivth, caused to be read by your lordships at the last Conference, but not applied; the commons apprehend it doth not concern the case in question: for that this record was made upon occasion of judgments given by the lords, to depose and imprison their lawful king; to which the commons were not willing to be made parties. And therefore the commons conceive it will not be for the honour of your lordships to make farther use of that Record.—But we are commanded to read your lordships the Parliament-Roll of 4 Edw. iii. N. 6, which if your lordships please to consider, they doubt not but your lordships will find occasion to apply it to the present purpose."

Ordered, That the Thanks of the house be given to the Speaker, for his care in issuing the Warrant for retaking the persons committed yesterday into custody.

The Serjeant at Arms was then ordered to be sent to the Tower; and the other serjeant at arms attending, was ordered to apprehend him for betraying his trust, in not executing his office, in bringing the persons committed yesterday to his custody, to the bar of the house.—An address was ordered to be prepared to be presented to his majesty, to desire a new Serjeant at Arms to attend the house.

June 5. Mr. Sec. Coventry acquainted the house, that it was his majesty's desire, that the house would adjourn till 4 in the afternoon, and that both houses should at that time attend him in the banqueting-house at Whitehall.—A debate arising touching the Removal of John Popham esq. serjeant at arms in ordinary, attending the house yesterday, the farther debate thereof was adjourned till 5 o'clock in the afternoon, and then the house adjourned till 4 in the afternoon.

The King's Speech to both Houses at the Banqueting House] June 5. p. m. The commons met, and went in a body to his majesty at White-hall; and the house of lords being also present, his majesty made the following Speech:

"My Lords and Gentlemen; You may remember, that, at the meeting of this session, I told you no endeavour would be wanting to make the continuance of this parliament unpracticable. I am sorry that experience hath so quickly shewed you the truth of what I then said; but I hope you are well convinced, that the intent of all these contrivances is only to procure a Dissolution. I confess, I look upon it as a most malicious design of those who are enemies to me and the Church of England; and, were the contrivers known, I should not doubt but the dislike of their practices would alone be a means of bringing the houses to a good understanding; * but, since I cannot prescribe any way how to arrive to the discovery of it, I must tell you plainly my opinion, that the means to come to any composure between yourselves, cannot be without admitting of such free Conferences, as may convince one another by the Reasons then offered; or enable me to judge rightly of the differences, when all hath been said on both sides which the matter will afford: for I am not to suffer these differences to grow to disorders in the whole kingdom, if I can prevent it; and I am sure my judgment shall always be impartial between my two houses of parliament. But I must let you know, that whilst you are in debate about your Privileges, I will not suffer my own to be invaded. I have nothing more to say to you at this time, but to desire, as I did when we met first, that you would yet consider, and not suffer ill men's designs to hinder the sessions from a happy conclusion."

The house of lords presented an Address to his majesty, to remove the lieutenant of the Tower; whereupon the lord treasurer reported his majesty's Answer, viz. "That his majesty hath considered the circumstances of the matter, and is not satisfied how with justice he can remove him."

The commons then took into consideration his majesty's Speech, and resolved, nem con, That the humble Thanks of this house be returned to his majesty, for the gracious expressions in his Speech this day made to both houses of parliament; and such members of this house as are of his majesty's privy council are desired to present the humble thanks of this house to his majesty.

Resolved, "That it doth not appear to this house, that any member thereof hath either contrived or promoted the Difference between the two houses of parliament; or, in asserting the Rights of the commons of England, and the Privileges of this house, hath done any thing inconsistent with his duty, or the trust reposed in him." And then adjourned to June 7.

June 7. The house resolved, That what serj. Popham did in retaking the four lawyers into his custody, and conducting them to the Tower of London, was in pursuance of his duty, and by the order of the house; and the farther debate concerning the said serjeant at arms was adjourned till Wednesday.

A copy of an Order from the house of lords for the hearing counsel in the Case of sir John Fagg, a member of this house, to-morrow morning, was then read and debated: and resolved, That as to the Case of Appeal brought against sir John Fagg in the house of lords, he shall have the protection and assistance of this house.

Resolved, nem con, "That if any person or persons shall be aiding or assisting in putting in execution any Sentence or Judgment that shall be given by the house of lords, upon the Appeal brought by Dr. Shirley against sir John Fagg, a member of this house, such person or persons shall be adjudged and taken to be betrayers of the rights and liberties of the commons of England, and the privileges of this house, and shall be proceeded against accordingly."

Ordered, That these Votes be made public, by setting them up in Westminster-hall, and in the lobby of this house, and the clerk of the house to take care to see it done.

June 7, p. m. The commons proceeded in the farther consideration of effectual means for the preservation of their Rights and Privileges, and resolved, 1. "That no person, committed by Order or Warrant of this house, for breach of the Privileges or contempt of the authority of the house, ought to be discharged during this session of parliament, without the Order or Warrant of this house. 2. That the Lieutenant of the Tower of London, in receiving and detaining in custody sir John Churchill, serj. Peck, serj. Pemberton, and Mr. Porter, hath performed his duty according to law; and for his so doing he shall have the

* Burnet affirms, "That lord Shaftsbury acknowledged himself to be the 'contriver,' but that others assured him, the thing happened of course." Marvell acknowledging, very candidly, the lords supremacy, in point of judicature, gives it as his opinion, "That the commons did not embark in earnest in that affair, but that some crafty members blew the coals, to prevent the Test's coming amongst them."

assistance and protection of this house. 3. That the Lieutenant of the Tower, in case he hath, or shall receive any writ, warrant, order, or command, to remove or deliver any person or persons committed to his charge, for breach of the privileges, or contempt of the authority of the h. of commons, by order or warrant of the house, shall not make any return thereof, or yield any obedience thereto, before he hath first acquainted the house therewith, and received their order and direction how to proceed therein."—Ordered, That these Resolutions be immediately sent to the Lieutenant of the Tower, and then the house adjourned.

June 8. A Message was sent to the lords to remind them of the last conference; upon the subject matter delivered by the lords at the last conference.

Sir John Robinson informing the house, that he had received the four lawyers committed to his custody by this house, and denied to deliver them to the gentleman-usher of the black-rod; and that he was served last night with four writs of Habeas Corpus, to bring the said four lawyers before the king and his parliament at Westminster this morning, and craved the advice of the house what to do therein: Ordered, That the Thanks of the house do be given to the said sir John Robinson for his behaviour therein, and Mr. Speaker intimated to him, that he should forbear to return the said Writs of Habeas Corpus, which were read and debated; and the farther debate thereof was adjourned till to-morrow morning, and a committee appointed to search the Lords Journals, to see what hath been done in the case of the four lawyers, the Writs of Habeas Corpus, and Mr. serjeant Popham, and to search for Precedents on the Writs of Habeas Corpus; and adjourned.

June 9. Sir Tho. Clarges reports, from the Committee to whom it was referred to search for Precedents touching Writs of Habeas Corpus, returnable in parliament; That the committee had found several precedents of Writs of Habeas Corpus returnable in parliament, and had considered of them: and that the Committee thereupon had agreed upon four Resolves to be presented to the house, which were severally agreed to, as follow: Resolved, nem. con. 1. "That no commoners of England committed by the Order or Warrant of the house of commons, for Breach of Privilege or contempt of the authority of the said house, ought, without order of the house, to be, by any Writ of Habeas Corpus, or any other authority whatsoever, made to appear and answer, or receive any determination in the house of peers, during that session of parliament wherein such persons were so committed. 2. That the Order of the house of peers, for the issuing out the Writs of Habeas Corpus concerning Mr. serj. Pemberton, Mr. serj. Peck, sir John Churchill, and Mr. Ch. Porter, is insufficient and illegal; for that it is general, and expresses no particular cause of privilege, and commands the king's great seal to be put to writs not returnable before the said house of peers. 3. That the Lord-Keeper be acquainted with these Resolutions, to the end that the said Writs of Habeas Corpus be superseded, as contrary to law and the privileges of this house. 4. That a Message be sent to the lords, to acquaint their lordships, that Mr. serj. Peck, sir John Churchill, Mr. serj. Pemberton, and Mr. Ch. Porter, were committed by order and warrant of this house, for manifest breach of privilege, and contempt of the authority of this house."

Ordered, That col. Birch do go up to the lords with a message, that a Conference is desired upon the subject matter of the last Conference.

The King's Speech at the Prorogation.] June 9. The king came to the house of peers, and made the following Speech to both houses:

"My Lords and Gentlemen; I think I have given sufficient evidence to the world, that I have not been wanting on my part, in my endeavours to procure the full satisfaction of all my subjects, in the matters both of Religion and Property: I have not only invited you to those considerations at our first meeting, but I have been careful through this whole session, that no concern of my own should divert you from them.—Besides, as I had only designed the matter of it to be the procuring of good laws, so for the gaining of them, I have already waited much longer than I intended; and should have been contented still to have continued my expectation, had there any hopes remained of a good conclusion. But I must confess, the ill designs of our enemies have been too prevalent against those good ones I had proposed to myself, in behalf of my people; and those unhappy differences between my two houses are grown to such a height, that I find no possible means of putting an end to them but by a prorogation. It is with great unwillingness that I make use of this expedient, having always intended an adjournment, for the preservation of such Bills as were unfinished. But my hopes are, that, by this means, the present occasion of differences being taken away, you will be so careful hereafter of the public as not to seek new ones, nor to revive the old. I intend to meet you here again in winter, and have directed my Lord-Keeper to prorogue you till the 13th day of October next."

FOURTEENTH SESSION OF THE SECOND PARLIAMENT.

The King's Speech on Opening the Session.] Oct. 13. Both houses met, according to prorogation*; and the king opened the session with the following Speech:

* In the APPENDIX to the present volume, No. VI. will be found a Tract intitled "A Letter from a Parliament-man to his Friend, concerning the Proceedings of the House of Commons, this last Session, begun the 13th of Oct. 1675," written by the earl of Shaftsbury.

"My lords and gentlemen; I meet you now with more than usual concern for the event of this session; and I know it is but what may reasonably be expected from that care I owe to the preservation of the government. The causes of the last prorogation, as I, for my part, do not desire to remember, so I hope no man else will, unless it be to learn from thence, how to avoid the like occasions for the future: and I pray consider how fatal the consequence may be, and how little benefit is like to redound to the people by it. However, if any thing of that kind shall arise, I desire you would defer those debates, till you have brought such public Bills to perfection as may conduce to the good and safety of the kingdom; and particularly I recommend to you, whatever may tend to the security of the Protestant Religion, as it is now established in the Church of England.—I must likewise desire your assistance in some Supplies, as well to take off the anticipations which are upon my Revenue, as for building of ships; and though the war has been the great cause of these anticipations, yet I find, by a late account I have taken of my expences, that I have not been altogether so good a husband, as I might have been, and as I resolve to be for the future: although, at the same time, I have had the satisfaction to find, that I have been far from such an extravagancy in my own expence, as some would have the world believe. I am not ignorant, that there are many who would prevent the kindness of my parliament to me at this time; but I as well know that your affections have never failed me: and you may remember, it is now above three years since I have asked you any thing for my own use. The rest I refer to my Lord Keeper."

The Lord Keeper Finch's Speech.] Then the Lord Keeper made the following Speech:

"My lords, and you the knights, citizens, and burgesses of the house of commons. The causes of this present assembly, and the reasons which have moved his majesty to command your attendance upon him at this time, are of the highest importance. The king resolves to enter into terms of the strictest correspondence and endearment with his parliament, to take your counsel in his most weighty affairs: to impart all his cares to you; to acquaint you with all his wants and necessities: to offer you all that can be yet wanting to make you enjoy yourselves; to establish a right understanding between himself and his three estates, and between the estates themselves; to redress all your just complaints, and to put all his subjects at ease, as far as in him lies, and can consist with the honour and safety of the government. And, having made all these advances, he doubts not but you will behave yourselves like those that deserve to be called the king's friends, and that you will put him at ease too. There is no cause why any fears of religion or liberty should divert you: for his maj. hath so often recommended to you the considerations of Religion, so very often desired you to assist him in his care and protection of it, That the Defender of the Faith is become the advocate of it too, and hath left all those without excuse who still remain under any kind of doubts or fears. Again, the care of your Civil Rights and Liberties hath been so much his majesty's, that the more you reflect upon these concerns, the more you will find yourselves obliged to acknowledge his majesty's tenderness of you, and indulgence to you. Search your own annals, the annals of those times you account most happy, you will scarce find one year without an example of something more severe, and more extraordinary, than a whole reign hath yet produced. Peruse the histories of foreign nations, and you shall find statues and altars to have been erected to the memories of those princes, whose best virtues never arrived to half that moderation, which we live to see and enjoy. No king did ever meet a parliament with juster cause of confidence in their affections: and therefore his maj. will not suffer himself to doubt, but relies firmly upon it, that you never will forsake him, when he is under any kind of difficulties. He doth assure himself that you will now think fit to provide for his honour and your own safety, by helping him to pay some part of his Debts, and to make his Navy as great and as considerable, as it ought to be. For the greatness of the king, is the greatness and safety of his people. The springs and rivers which pay tribute to the ocean, do not lessen, but preserve themselves by that contribution. It is impossible that those affections that piety and allegiance first planted, which persecution could not abate, which the gracious influences of his majesty's happy government have hitherto increased, should now appear to wither and decay: but then the best indication of the heart is by the hand. And because it is of infinite moment to the king's affairs that there should be a chearful concurrence to his Supplies, there let hand and heart both join in the oblation, for that will make it a sacrifice well pleasing indeed.—My Lords and Gentlemen; The happiness of this present age, and the fate and fortune of the next too, is very much in your hands, and at this time; all that you would desire to settle and improve; all that you would wish to secure and transmit to your posterities, may now be accomplished. Would you raise the due estimation and reverence of the Church of England to its just height? Would you provide for the safety and establishment of it? Do there want any laws to secure the peace and quiet of the state? Would you enrich and adorn this kingdom, by providing for the extent and improvement of Trade, by introducing new and useful Manufactures, and by encouraging those we have already? Would you prevent all frauds and perjuries, all delays and abuses in the administration of justice? Would you preserve a famous city from being depopulated by the suburbs? Would you restrain the excess of those new Buildings which begin to swarm with inhabitants unknown? All your Petitions of this kind will be grateful to the king; and you may with ease effect all these and much more which your great wisdoms will suggest to you. A little time will serve to make many excellent laws, and to give you the honour to be the Repairers of all our Breaches; so as that time be wholly employed upon the public, and not taken up by such considerations as are less meritorious. If therefore there be any, without doors, that labour to disunite your counsels, or to render them ineffectual; if they can hope that the occasions for this may arise from some Differences within yourselves, or hope by those differences to disguise their own dissatisfactions to your good proceedings; it is in your power to defeat those hopes, to pull off this disguise, and to secure a happy conclusion of this meeting, by studying to preserve a good correspondence, and by a careful avoiding all such questions as are apt to engender strife. And, if ever there were a time, when the gravity of the council, the wisdom, and good temper of a parliament, were necessary to support that government which only can support these assemblies, certainly this is the hour. You see with what zeal the king hath recommended to you a good Agreement between yourselves, and that he doth it with all the care and compassion, all the earnestness and importunity, fit for so great a prince to express, who would be very sorry that any such misfortune as your disagreement should either deprive him of your advice and assistance, or his people of those good laws which he is ready to grant you. There is no other way our enemies can think of, by which it is possible for this session to miscarry; for Fears and Jealousies cannot enter here, calumnies and slanders will find no place amongst wise and good men. They that use these arts abroad, will quickly be discredited, when the world shall see the generous effects of your confidence. Men will despair of attempting any disturbance in the state, when they see every step that tends that way, serves only to give you fresh occasions to testify your loyalty and your zeal. You have all the reason in the world to make men see this; for you have the same monarchy to assert, the same church to defend, the same interests of nobility and gentry to maintain, the same excellent king to contend for, and the same enemies to contend against.—And now, my Lords and Gentlemen, since the whole session of parliament is, in the judgment and construction of our law, but as one day, let us all endeavour that the morning of it, the first entrance upon it, may be with such fair and auspicious circumstances as may give the whole kingdom an assurance of a bright and chearful day. Let no ill humours gather into clouds to darken or obscure it, for this day is a critical day, and more depends upon that judgment of our affairs which will be made by it, than can easily be imagined. It imports us therefore to take care that no part of this time be lost; let every precious minute of this day be spent in receiving such acts of grace and goodness as are ready to flow from the king, and in making such retributions for them as may become the grateful hearts of the best of subjects to the best of kings. So shall this day become a day of disappointment and discomfort to our enemies, but to us and all good men a glorious day, a day of triumph and deliverance, a memorable and joyful day to this present, and to all future generations."

Debate on the King's Speech.] The king's and lord keeper's Speeches being ended, the house of commons came down, and sat some time, looking on one another in a profound silence, till at length sir Thomas Meres broke silence and said, 'He was sorry to see the house, as it were, in an amazement, and was afraid it might prove ominous, and therefore prayed the Speaker to acquaint the house with the substance of the king's speech.'—The Speaker excused himself for that, not daring to rely so much upon his memory. It was then moved, that some Bill might be read, and sir Tho. Littleton desired it might be that of the last session, 'for appropriating the Customs to the use of the fleet.' But the Speaker objected against that, because it was indorsed on the backside, and not fair written, and he had no brief of it. Upon which sir Nich. Carew told him, he had a Bill which was not indorsed, but fair written, of which he had a brief. It was a Bill, to incapacitate any Papist to sit in either house of parliament, without taking the Test in the late Act against Popery, &c.' It was read accordingly, and ordered a 2nd reading sine die. After this, Mr. Sec. Williamson brought in the king's Speech, which was read, and thereupon a motion was made, 'That Thanks might be given to his majesty for his gracious care of the Protestant religion.' To which Mr. Secretary Coventry answered, 'That it would not be decent to separate one part of the king's Speech from the other.' Upon which some disputes did arise for a time, till it was moved, that the consideration of the Speech might be adjourned till Monday, which was agreed to, provided the house might be adjourned till that time, which was accorded; each party hoping for strong recruits.*

Mr. Howard's Letter found in St. James's Park.] Before the house adjourned, there happened a passage, which requires something to be said antecedently to make it the better understood.—In one of the actions between the Germans and the French, after Turenne's death, col. John Howard, brother to the earl of Carlisle, amongst many Englishmen, was killed, which being told for news in St. James's Park, it was reported, that lord Cavendish, and sir T. Meres, being together, when they heard it, should say, 'That they were well enough served, and that they wished that never any Englishman might fare better, who was to serve abroad against a vote of parliament.' Upon which, a paper, that called lord Caven-

* Grey.

dish and sir Tho. Meres, 'incendiaries,' with other such language, was given about, subscribed 'Thomas Howard, of Richmond and Carlisle.' This paper was brought into the house by sir Trevor Williams, who informed the house, 'that it was found the night before in St. James's Park, by his servant, and given unto him, who finding two honourable members shamefully traduced in it, could not but acquaint them with it,' and having no opportunity before this morning, showed it to the members concerned in the house. Upon which lord Cavendish, seeming much surprized at it, went out of the house in heat, which was the beginning of the thing. Mr. Russel then acquainted the house, 'that he saw some disorder in that lord, and, being afraid of the consequence, desired he might be commanded not to go out.' Sir Trevor then told the aforesaid story, and the paper was read, viz.:

"Sir; The last severity upon Roman Catholics having forbid me the ambition to any place or pretension at court, and the severe usage of the gout making me unfit to appear in any company, but where I am well acquainted; besides a most sensible loss of my poor brother John, killed at Strasbourg, I resolved not only to retire in person, but thought, from all temptations this world could give me, and to spend the rest of my days with such domestic and private content, as a man of those principles, and some sense, might hope for, in an honourable retreat. But it happens by a certain, though unjust and malicious accident, that I am awakened from the quiet and repose I hoped for, and find myself engaged by the nearest ties of friendship and honour, (obligations I have always esteemed dearer than my life) to let some unworthy and base people see that I am yet alive. Not long since, in St. James's Park, lord Cavendish and sir Thomas Meres, two bold and busy members, upon the news of the French retreat over the Rhine, where many English were reported to be killed, (which, amongst all honest men, was much regretted) these barbarous incendiaries, with a most plausible temper of such worthy patriots, openly declared, 'that it was but a just end for such as went against any vote of parliament.' With all respect to that hon. house, that cankered and malicious saying will neither deserve the thanks of that house, (it being false as to my brother, who went by his majesty's command, at the head of his company, before that vote was in force) nor the approbation of any man out of it. I will not trouble myself, nor others, to let you see, by any exact character, how these two worthy and unbiassed Senators ought to be credited. Next October will produce such effects of their care and capacities of securing property and religion in a Christian and humane way, that I believe I shall be called to the bar, to answer their slanders, as I presume they will call them; yet I doubt they will not, for though an ill orator, I shall most certainly prove what I write. As for any other way of revenge, I do not anyway apprehend it; for men that are given to spit blood, seldom draw it. Sir, I have troubled you too long with my just resentments, but knowing the share you have always taken in my concerns, I must beg of you, that you will in St. James's Park, at the Mall, disperse these copies, it being all the way that is left to do right to the dead; and, to assure you, that I will not do you the ill office of dispersing a libel, I will sign the copies with all my titles. T. HOWARD, of Richmond and Carlisle." From Ashtead in Surry, Aug. 30, 1675.

Lord Cavendish and sir Tho. Meres were enjoined not to prosecute any quarrel against Mr. Howard, or to send or accept any challenge in order thereto, without acquainting the house.

Oct. 18. Resolved, "That sir Trevor Williams, sir Anth. Irby, sir Tho. Littleton, sir Ch. Harbord, and Mr. Crouch, be appointed to go to Mr. Howard, who, by reason of his indisposition of the gout, could not attend the house, to know of him whether he will own the aforesaid paper."

Debate on the King's Debts; Anticipations of the Revenue, and Supply.] Sir *Philip Musgrave* moves to proceed in the matter of Supply and Religion, mentioned in the king's Speech, and to appoint a day for each of them.

Sir *Edw. Dering* seconds the motion, and hopes for as full a concurrence from every gentleman, as from him. Religion is the honour of the nation, and has always been the care of this house. Little progress was made the last session, by reason of the Difference with the lords; but would begin now early, that we may ripen things to perfection before we rise. Another thing, as properly under our cognizance as Popery, is, regulating mens manners, very worthy of our consideration. Under that notion of religion, it may be done. We want *censores morum*, as well as inquisitors of faith: thinks, that else we cannot see Religion prosper. Our dominion of the sea is *magni nominis umbra*, without strength there—It is not prudent to trust the nation long to the French army's going into winter quarters.

Sir *John Holland.* The king is pleased to desire a Supply; we are all here to speak our minds freely, and hopes we shall with that modesty which becomes us, and desires to be heard out with patience and favour. He is no honest man, that loves not the king, the government, and the nation. If we consider, that, after such supplies, never given before, (Edw. iii. who reigned above 50 years, never had near this king's Supply,) now to have every branch of the Revenue anticipated; and not only that, but Debts so great, to the ruin of the people; and, besides, the king's wants so great, as to be forced to break the credit of the Exchequer, to the ruin of widows, orphans, and numerous other people, as it puts so great a damage upon our English manufactures: he will go no farther, for instance, than his own county, the city of Norwich—These are necessary to the king's sovereignty, and preservation of trade—The fleet neglected, and his nearest and most powerful neighbours so armed—The French, by over-balance of our trade—When you were told, the last meeting, that the French commodities imported, over-balance to the value of 900,000*l.* and though London is not very sensible of this, yet the country, from whence supply must come, is impoverished by it. The Chimney-money and Excise, brought hither, and the nobility's expences, increase the consumption here, and hither the money will come. By this means, the country, in some places, is drained of money, and, by reason of the cheapness of all commodities, farms are cast into gentlemens hands, and no hopes of remedy on their parts; and the farmers come here, and set up taverns, and alehouses, and keep lodgings, and there are no hopes of their return back into the country. The humour of the yeomanry is changed; the youth are not bred up as they used to be. This, in short, is our condition; and yet, for the king's necessity, as well as our safety, the king must have supply; else the people cannot be protected; but, if the charge of the government be greater than the people can bear, the government cannot stand, though supported by arms. But, should it be so endeavoured, it cannot be long endured by the temper of the English nation. Would to God he could say, this was not our condition! There is a necessity that it must be said. He cannot but think himself bound in conscience to take this opportunity to say, that the charge of the government is greater than the nation can bear—Cannot but say, the expences of the Court may be reduced; especially the matters of the Treasury may be better managed. The truth is, the prodigal and excessive way of living now, was unknown to our forefathers, who kept hospitality. It is a leprosy that has almost overspread the nation. Hears an unusual discontent, and want will put men upon desperate resolutions, and from that arose those unhappy times we had.—This may bring us again into the unhappy hands we were in; and we shall be an easy prey and conquest to whoever will over-run us—Was, am, and ever will be, for the due rights of this house, and against the peers encroachments; would not give, and, he hopes, the house will not be ready to take, new occasion of difference. Upon the whole, moves to enter into a present consideration of an humble Petition to the king, with the lords concurrence, in which, in all dutiful, modest, and loyal manner we may represent to him 'the present poverty of the nation, together with the mischiefs of unseasonable prorogations; and that we be continued without prorogation, until we have dispatched Bills for the security of Religion and Property; and then declare, that we will give Supply to provide shipping and stores, to be equal, if not stronger than our neighbours.'

Sir *Tho. Lee.* When he considers the old course of parliament, what has been moved is not the usual way: upon your books, a motion being made for a Supply, the house went into a Grand Committee; therefore moves for it to-morrow.

Sir *Rob. Carr* seconds the motion for to-morrow, to consider Anticipations and Supply.

Sir *Tho. Meres* would have that ancient Order, which Lee mentioned, read. When that Order is lost, the house of commons is lost. If there be occasion for Supply, let us see it at a grand committee.

Mr. *Neale* has heard, that the Lord Treasurer has brought the State of the Revenue into the Council.* Would see that here, to be your guide the better, in what you are to do; and moves, that all the money may be employed to the use we give it, on penalty of treason.

The Order mentioned was read, viz. "That a motion being made for a Supply, is not presently to be entered upon, in the house, but the consideration referred to a committee of the whole house."

Mr. *Sacheverell* is willing to take Anticipations upon the Customs, and the King's Debts, into consideration, as soon as may be: to be plain, he believes there is no need of a Supply, when things shall be well considered.

Sir *Tho. Meres* sees there is no occasion of a Supply as plain as the sun that shines, and believes he can make it out: no man has yet made a direct motion but Holland, which is a conditional one, and a very good one; so that a committee cannot go upon it, without being first moved by some-body.

Mr. Secretary *Coventry* moved it.

Sir *John Ernly* must inform the house, that we want a squadron of ships, and 30 at least, of 1st, 2nd, and 3rd rates; therefore seconds Coventry, for Supply for building of Ships.

* "All this time, the principal business at Whitehall had been to inspect the Revenue, and to put the Disbursements on such a footing, that the growing frugality of the house of commons might the less affect both king and minister for the time to come. By a Paper of the Lord Treasurer's dated Sept. 29, 1675, and presented to the Council Oct. 8, it appears, that the annual Disbursements amounted to 1,387,770*l.* the Revenue to 1,358,000*l.* which was clogged with Anticipations, to the value of 866,954*l.*; and yet by a general Account of all the Receipts and Issues in the Exchequer, it farther appears, that between the 20th of June 1673, and the 25th of June 1675, 4,529,649*l.* &c. had been received, and 4,526,945*l.* 3*s.* 3*d.* discharged. This scrutiny gave rise to a Scheme of Retrenchments, by which an annual saving was to be made of 250,000*l.* On the other hand, all imaginable expedients were put in practice, to make the Exchequer rise higher than ever; insomuch, that even the smallest branches were not forgotten: and particular orders were sent from the Lord Treasurer to the several officers, to know exactly what their yearly value was; how the same arose; how charged; how accounted for; and how far it was improveable." Ralph.

Resolved, "That this house will to-morrow, resolve into a Grand Committee, to take into consideration that part of his majesty's Speech, which relates to a Supply for taking off Anticipations upon his majesty's Revenue, and building more ships."

Mr. Howard's Answer to the Committee reported.] Oct. 19. Sir T. Littleton, and the rest of the gentlemen mentioned, who were sent to Mr. Howard, reported, That, in obedience to the order of the house, they went to Mr. Howard, to demand of him, whether he signed, or owned, the Paper then produced to him?' Who replied, 'Gentlemen, being informed of some displeasure of the house of commons (for whom I always had, and ever shall have, a most dutiful regard) I doubt, that, if I should give any Answer to your Message, being a person unexperienced in such affairs, I might give occasion of their displeasure; and therefore I must beg your pardon; and I must answer only to what can be proved against me; and, in the mean time, I do now again, as I did, before Mr. Collingwood, to the Speaker, promise, upon my word and honour, not to question any person for any thing relating thereunto."

Debate thereon.] Mr. *Sacheverell* moves to have him committed to the Tower.

Mr. *Powle.* For a private gentleman to vilify your members with the terms of 'unworthy, biassed senators, barbarous incendiaries, busy members!' If men without doors may do this it takes away liberty of speech. Former times have had nothing like it; only in queen Eliz.'s time, Arthur Hall, who was a member, (this gentleman none) for publishing a libellous book, called 'Opera Tenebrarum,' was called to the bar, and giving no satisfactory answer, was committed to the Tower, and fined 500*l*. and not to return thence until he had given satisfaction; and hopes this gentleman will be so punished.

Mr. *Mallet* would put the thing in a way of proof, since Howard puts it upon you: there is another precedent, of Withers the poet, which, if true, does us justice: he requires it, and would vindicate the members reflected on.

The *Speaker* knows not when you have sent for a man in custody, upon no other ground than what is before you.

Mr. Sec. *Williamson.* If the gentleman refused to appear, and you had the proofs before you, then it would be proper to send for him in custody. He would have a better answer than is yet given; but sending for in custody is a kind of punishment before proof.

Sir *Ch. Harbord.* The offence is yet neither proved nor confessed: would have a day's time; and if he cannot come, he may be brought hither, before you commit him.

Sir *Tho. Littleton.* Knows the gentleman, and has a value for him; but nobody will deny this to be a breach of privilege. To the purpose: a man, you suppose, has broken your privilege, and he keeps his bed, and you send to him, and he will not tell you whether he has broken your privilege or no. You send for men, upon presumption of breach of privilege. If the gentleman cannot come to attend you, he may remain in custody of the serjeant. It has been a hundred times done in breach of privilege only.

Sir *John Ernly* looks upon committing Howard as a pre-judging him, it not appearing to be his act: sending for him in custody is a punishing him: would you have a man confess a thing against himself? Go in the common way; send for him, but not in custody.

Sir *Rob. Howard* is as much for the honour of the house as any man, although related to this gentleman. When you send for him, and he appears, and you censure him, he will abide by that censure.

Sir *John Birkenhead.* You send for people in custody, when afraid of an escape. He is a prisoner before you send for him, by his lameness of the gout: when a felon is upon his trial, he must speak with his shackles off, at as much ease as may be. The loss of his brother, whom he loved more than his own life, might make him utter, it may be, something he should not.

Lord *Cavendish.* The words, the paper says, he should say of col. John Howard (whom he knew not) are, 'That it was a just judgment he was killed;' which was a foolish thing; and he will not own saying of a foolish thing. But possibly he might say, 'He was sorry this gentleman should die fighting against the interest of his country.' If he said it not then, he does now say it.

Sir *Tho. Meres.* As to saying, 'he was sorry that an Englishman should die in that cause,' he *is* sorry for it; and it was always the thought of his heart, and is still so.

Sir *Tho. Lee* had always a respect for this gentleman; but it is not what respect you show the gentleman, but how this matter will stand upon your Journal to posterity. Every paper, read by order in the house, must be entered; and for sending an answer not direct to a paper of so great reflection, what will appear upon your books but sending a committee of yours? (which, by the way, was a mistake to a man that has offended you.) For your honour, you must send for him; and nothing else moves him to speak in it.

Sir *Ch. Wheeler.* Whenever a mistake arises amongst persons of honour, all quarrels cease. This here arises upon such a thing; and no question but Howard will retract what is grounded upon a mistake. If this be so, an end may be put to this matter. He is persuaded that Howard had not the least intent to reflect on the house; because, when gentlemen fall out, they invent and take up names and words provoking, though not true; therefore would have Howard asked, whether he had the least thought of reflection on the house.

Mr. *Stockdale* would not have Howard forejudged, but let him have a day for notice to appear.

Sir *Nick. Carew* is sensible of the gentleman's infirmity, the gout; it is his own. Has known him long to be an honourable person; and hopes, as to this matter, he will be innocent: would have a day appointed for his appearance.

Ordered, "That Mr. Howard be sent to, to attend this house on this day seven-night."

Sir *Nick. Carew.* Be the Paper whose it will, it is a scandalous paper; and moves to have it burnt.

Sir *Tho. Littleton.* If the Paper be burnt, we shall not have it here to prove it. Would not have it burnt till the whole thing be over.

Mr. *Garroway.* Until you declare it a breach of privilege, what will you send for Howard for? Therefore moves to have it voted a scandalous paper, and a breach of privilege.

Col. *Birch.* The Paper might be read, before you put the question; but not upon an adjourned debate.

The *Speaker.* The Paper was once read, and needs not be read again.—The Letter was then read as above.

Sir *Tho Meres.* If he speaks not, he may be thought to yield to the report of the letter. He has had papers, long before this, thrown into his house, and has been so far from giving you the trouble, that he has not so much as spoken of them; but, as to this Paper, it was handed to him in the house, and he showed it to lord Cavendish.

Further Debate on the King's Debts, Anticipations of the Revenue, and Supply.] The house went into a grand committee on the king's Speech: sir Cha. Harbord in the chair.

Sir *Tho. Meres.* Your first business is, taking the Anticipations upon the Customs into consideration. Pray let us see what they are.

Mr. *Sacheverell.* If there be such Anticipations, they are either occasioned by the war, or voluntarily. If voluntarily, he believes, nobody will take them off. Birch said once, '4*l.* per head, per month, might defray the navy charge;' and Pepys said, 'it cost not so much.' Suppose the fleet consisted of 100 sail, and 49 ships of attendance, and, according to Pepy's list, 30,000 men, it will not come, for 4 months, to 800,000*l.* We all know the tax-prices, &c. and we in peace, 1,700,000 or 1,800,000*l.* And if this cannot defray the charge of 1,900,000*l.* leaves you to judge. Now, let the managers of the Navy show how they have expended 1,700,000*l.* and they say something.

Mr. *Walter.* Hears something said, that makes him stand up, for the honour of king and people. There is no other trust in the government than where the law makes it. The king has it; and if we supply, or not supply, we have our trust. Sees there is much stress laid upon that part of the king's Speech relating to Anticipations. The king says, "There has been ill husbandry, besides what fell out in the war.' And the king must take it upon him. But Bracton says, 'the king cannot err'—'Ill management!' between the wisdom of the king, and direction of the law, you may know where the fault is. We believed, when the king was called back, that the law was come again. Pray let not the Standing Army be brought under that consideration of Anticipations. The king speaks of the government; he owns his care of it; and no government can be more advantageous to him than this. It is a monarchy. The king governs by law. Let us look back to the evils we had, in order to prevent more. There was Loan, and Ship-money, and extremes begat extremes. The house would then give no money. Let the king rely upon the parliament; we have settled the crown and the government. It is strange that we have sat so many years, and given so much money, and are still called upon for Supply. The lords may give Supply with their own money, but we give the peoples; we are their proxies. The king takes his measures, by the parliament, and he doubt not but that all the commons will supply for the government; but giving at this rate that we have done: we shall be 'a branch of the revenue.' They will 'anticipate' us too. But, let the officers say what they will, we will not make these mismanagements the king's error. It is better it should fall upon us than the king. We give public money, and must see that it goes to public use. Tell your money, fix it to public ends, and take order against occasions of this nature for the future. We cannot live at the expence of Spain, that has the Indies; or France, who has so many millions of revenue. Let us look to our government, fleet, and trade. It is the advice that the oldest parliament-man among you can give you; and so, God bless you!"

Sir *Tho. Lee* expected to have known what occasion there is for asking money for these Anticipations, or what they would ask. If gentlemen knew, they would have told us before now. He expects it.

Sir *Rob. Howard.* If it be expected that he should give you an account of what belongs to his office, he is ready to do it. As to former Anticipations, he shall wave them, but shall tell you how late Anticipations have been struck upon money growing out of the revenue. If you please to know this, you shall. He believes; in tallies, not satisfied, there is not much exceeding, 800,000*l.* value; some of this charge, about 80,000*l.* is growing out. Tallies, not satisfied, 800,000*l.* value; some other charges to the bankers, as a year's interest; with that prospect, the whole may be a million; by which charge the Excise is wholly taken up; not above 5 or 6,000*l.* will remain, at the most. He has nothing to tell you, but the king's condition, and will make all this appear indisputably, if you please, in writing; and if he does not now explain himself, he will do it fully.

Sir *Tho. Meres.* Expences, we see, are more and more, and things worse and worse; and no occasion of Supply. There is no end in giving, to take off these Anticipations, and we cannot in conscience do it. Our ancestors gave not their money so away, because they would be bountiful. The people give us no such authority. The defray of all public charges, and the king's living, may be made out sufficiently by the revenue. But the charge of the government is not supportable, at this rate.

Lord Cavendish. If this be admitted a supposition, then we must satisfy all debts. The people have trusted us with their money, and Magna Charta is not to be given up, with their money, and liberty, into a bottomless pit. Moves for the question, 'Whether an Aid shall be granted for taking off these Anticipations from the king's revenue.'

Sir *John Duncombe.* It is hard to calculate the charge of an expensive war, till the end of it. Howard has told you all the particulars of Anticipations, clearly and faithfully, and with the most, he believes the sum to be between 7 and 800,000*l.* You know the constitution of the government; when it has war, it comes to you for aid. The king tells you he was engaged in a war, and over-run his measures in it: he is so much in debt, that he knows not whither to go but to you; he knows it is hard to come by, and you have been often asked; but if the king be at ease, you are all at ease. If the crown be in debt, it is a misfortune to the creditors, and many people besides. It has not cost so much money, in any three kings reigns, as this war has been: this is the king's condition, as it appears to him: would not put extremities to work, as it is a dangerous thing.

Mr. *Sacheverell* would have Duncombe explain what he means by 'putting extremities to work.'

Sir *John Duncombe.* Means, by 'putting extremities to work,' making the crown, and them that depend upon it, uneasy.

Mr. *Powle* is sorry to hear any thing laid upon the king in this business; he thinks him to have the least part in it. Had he those counsellors and officers constantly to represent to him the state of his Revenue, it would not be thus. But some officers may find private advantages out of public necessities. The war was carried on before without any Anticipations; and, since that, many great sums have been received; as the prize-money, French and Dutch money, and advances on the excise, and hearth-money, and now two years of peace, and then three fourths of this tax to come in. No fleet, and hardly necessary repairs upon the ships in harbour, and the debt yet more, not less. Is not this a sum to astonish every body, in time of peace? What will become of us in a foreign war, if this expence be in peace? fears that the Church-revenue may go in time of war. He believes the Revenue so great already, that, in a short time, these Anticipations may wear off. Supply is, in this case, but to increase 'ill husbandry.' As to the Navy, believes that due consideration, in time, may be had of it; and, when we are free of these Anticipations, we may go on more cheerfully with the other.

Mr. Sec. *Coventry.* A considerable charge of the Revenue is left out; the foot army, the ten regiments. He, as in a double capacity, as servant to the king, and member of the house, has informed himself, as well as he can, in these things. Redressing of Grievances, and giving Supply, is the business both of court and country. The point before us is, whether we shall first go upon Supply, or enquire into Mismanagements. It is easier for the king to redress a Grievance, than for the people to give a tax. It is necessary now to lay open the state of the kingdom; it will be too late to think on it on Monday, if you pass your vote against taking off the Anticipations to-day. By the last intelligence, the French had 55 sail of ships at sea, and we 7, and so far out of repair, as not in 2 or 3 months to be reparable. The trade and peace of Europe is ours now; and a short time may show that we are upon the precipice of the most inevitable ruin that ever was. It is an unsafe condition we are in, when no longer safe than whilst our neighbour pleases. Suppose Articles concluded at Nimeguen,—that hour peace is made with France there, marshal Montmorency, an old, and considerably experienced officer, may land 30,000 men in England. He may draw them out of Maestricht, and the rest of the garrisons of Flanders, being all full, and may march with what army he pleases, 40,000 men hither, if he pleases. If you cannot oppose him at sea, our condition is desperate. If men be faulty, let them answer it that manage it, and consider, whether time else will not be lost, for consideration of the Navy. When you have done this, for the present, agree with the king for a certain revenue for the Navy, for the future. Let us not make our faith so much upon what may be showed us, as upon what is already showed us. If it be not meant to maintain ships, when you have them, and whenever God shall bless you and the king with a right understanding, and leave all you would have, without a navy—Your vote can furnish the king with credit; but, without it, neither your hearts nor your prayers can build ships. Suppose a town on fire, and a man steal the buckets, he deserves to be hanged, but believes the magistrates will not resolve, therefore, never to buy more buckets.

Sir *Tho. Meres.* Be the Anticipations what they will, he shall give his vote to pay none. Has observed, that if once we begin to tumble papers over, we are wearied out, and give money, and leave the question. It is said, 'do not make councils desperate; therefore give money; but, he says, therefore give no money. At Christmas 1671, such desperate councils followed giving money, that he has no mind to mention them, repeal of no less than 30 laws by the Declaration, a standing Army, the Exchequer stopped up, and a War without advice of parliament, and the Triple League broken, and a League with France made; and, if you give no more money, you will have no more desperate councils; for these were upon your giving money; therefore now would give none.

Mr. *Sawyer*. When we gave formerly, our judgments governed our wills. As for the desperate counsellors, they were those who were protected by your pardons. Some were laid aside, and some are laid in the dust. Shall we say, desperate counsellors contracted these debts? and shall we leave things desperate? now, whether the king, by his good husbandry, can pay off these debts? if the government be not maintained, it must drop, one time or another. Would farther enquire, whether possibly there is a way to take these Anticipations off. Would have these matters first inspected, before the question.

Sir *Wm. Coventry* will apply himself singly to matters of Anticipation. This is the first time any thing has been asked for this matter. The last time we met, it was not big enough for an aid. It must be nursed up to be big enough to be paid; but it is free for us all to speak here. He can never concur, that this debt, contracted by a war, against the opinion of this house, should be preferred before that which widows and orphans call for. We passed once assignments, especially to pay debts; and were there nothing but this in it, can never prefer this of Anticipations, until the house think themselves rich enough. These men that lent upon the customs, &c. had warning enough, by the Bankers precaution, and let them take it, in God's name. This has had the provision of the house already, but it is diverted and gone. Remembers what Clifford said; 'you shall have a fleet; you shall have no more of debts.' Nothing was said then, that the revenue was not able to bear the charge of the government. But it was improper to call for the account; and had it been proper for you, it would have been brought, and they would have been armed for it, over and over. There is something mentioned, as to the peace abroad (God preserve our own!) which would be the greatest misfortune that could befal us. It is happy for us, that they abroad spend their strength upon one another, if it be so great as is said. But this should not make him give up the game: believes that our neighbours are not so stupid as to give France leave to over-run us. But when we compare kingdom with kingdom, and nation with nation, they have no bowels, and are to have no bowels. Friendship has failed, and always will fail: and it is not the interest of Holland to let France be master of England. France, who has long made love to Flanders, comes only to see Dunkirk, and to fortify it. That king sees that the Dutch have a great fleet, and, believes, not to defend the Hague: but then it is the interest of Holland to support Flanders: says France, 'England is engaged, I will break the Triple League;' and for this they have hazarded their all. This digression is only to show you, that, if peace was made, we need not give up the game; and the rest of the princes would think it their interest to hinder such an accession as England to the crown of France. But this business of Anticipations seems to have influence on that very thing: if apprehensions that the Confederates are weak, it may induce a peace. What we do here can be no secret; they know our votes, and see we incline more to them than the French; but the Confederates apprehend the king's ministers more inclined to the French. Does England judge amiss of this? The Confederates will so; they hear the king is clearing his revenue, and we fear he will declare against us, having more men, in the armies against us, than for us. Therefore he is against taking off the Anticipations by a Supply.

Sir *John Duncombe* proffers a state of the expences, and the incomes of the revenue. —But they would not be received.

Col. *Birch*. Whenever the house has been upon matters of money, he has been thought to be too forward. It may be, he thinks so too. Could never have believed to have heard that these Anticipations have risen from a war, which this house had no opinion of. Not only without the consent of the house begun at first, but even against the opinion of our ancestors, We are now not only out of the Triple League, but out of all league. In one session, Thanks were given to the king for this League; and, in another, we were to give money to pay for the breaking it. If 90 of a 100, nay, 99, should hear him say, that, to pay these Anticipations, is for the interest of the country (and he is acquainted in three or four counties) they would call him he knows not what. Therefore is against Supply.

Mr. *Vaughan*. When you have passed your Vote, the counsel will prove good counsel, and the war a good war. When so many millions have been given, he lies in amazement how money can be called for: and now that we are forced to pay Subsidies, at our doors, to poor families ruined by the Exchequer, stands in amazement at the motion.

Sir *Tho. Meres* will not say, at the rate of vain expences, how to make the revenue good, notwithstanding the payment of these Anticipations, but believes it may be done.

Sir *Edw. Dering* takes the Anticipations, at least, to be 700,000*l.* and yet finds we are going into a Vote against taking them off. Is of opinion there were dangerous counsels; he never stood up to defend any of them, nor ever will. Those counsels and counsellors are laid aside. As for danger of Popery, the Protestant Religion was never more protected. Let us shut our hands until we open our eyes. A voluntary engagement of the Revenue may be justifiable; the officers will subject the Revenue to enquiry. Would have the paper that Duncombe offered, received; and adjourn the farther debate to Thursday.

Sir *Tho. Littleton*. We are not told how much of these Anticipations is for service to come, or what is already paid; so believes it not such a bug-bear as it is represented. As for the great stop of the Exchequer, though done in time of war, no reason why in time of peace. Now the continuation is without privy seal, or order of the privy council; though formerly it was otherwise. As for Popery, there was a Proclamation, but sees not that matter at all mended. At this time, few men doubt the intention to make peace, to fetch off the French with flying colours, and to dissolve the present confederacy. These are the present counsels, and if they be desperate, would not make the last counsels worse than the first.

The Commons refuse a Supply for the taking off the Anticipations upon the Revenue.] The house having resumed, sir Ch. Harbord reported from the committee of the whole house, That they had taken that part of his majesty's Speech into consideration, which relates to a Supply for taking off the Anticipations upon his Revenue; and had agreed (172 to 165) a Vote to be reported to the house; and humbly moved from the said committee, that the house would again resolve into a committee of the whole house on Friday next, to consider the other part of his maj.'s Speech relating to a Supply for building more ships. Which Vote of the committee was as followeth; viz. "That it is the opinion of the committee, not to grant his majesty any Supply for the taking off the Anticipations upon his majesty's Revenue."—Resolved, "That this house doth agree with the committee, that it is the opinion of this house, not to grant his majesty any Supply for the taking off the Anticipations upon his majesty's Revenue."*

Debate on Lord Cavendish's posting Mr. Howard.] Oct. 20. Information was given the house, that lord Cavendish had caused a Paper to be posted up at Whitehall-Gate, and Westminster-hall, by his footman, to this effect "That Thomas Howard who subscribed the Letter, was a coward." It was said, that the occasion of this was from some reports that lord Cavendish had heard, that Mr. Howard should say, "That his lordship knew of the Letter some time before the parliament met, and did not call Mr. Howard to an account for it."

Mr. *Sacheverell* complained on lord Cavendish's behalf, but the compiler* could not well hear him.

Mr. Secretary *Williamson* gave this account. He was commanded by the king to cause the earl marshal to enquire into the business. Mr. Frowde, son to sir Philip Frowde, was said to have taken down the said posted-up Paper, who was not to be found. He came to him, and he asked him, whether he had any quarrel with lord Cavendish? He confessed the taking down the paper, but denied the words he should say of lord Cavendish, &c. Then Williamson told him, he was commanded by the king, not to farther engage lord Cavendish. Frowde said, 'he had no quarrel with lord Cavendish, and what he did was out of respect to him.'

Sir *Tho. Lee.* If this gentleman had no quarrel with lord Cavendish, perhaps that lord may have with him. In this kind of paper-war, he fears family quarrels; therefore would have some gentlemen propose a way to extricate you out of the thing.

Mr. *Swynfin.* The honour of the house is to be preferred before any particular member.

* "When the king's Speech came under consideration, a demand was made on one side, and allowed as reasonable on the other, of a scrutiny into those Debts and Charges, which the people were called upon to make good: the result of which was, that it appeared, the expence of the late two years war with the Dutch amounted, in the whole, to 2,040,000*l.* and that the money given by parliament; what arose from the Customs, which ought to have been appropriated; what was gained by prizes; and the 800,000 Patacoons given by the Dutch; at least amounted to 3,040,000*l.* Whence it was inferred, that, instead of the king's being run almost a million in debt by the war, as those who took upon them to answer for the court alledged, he might have been a million in pocket. It was, upon these principles, farther observed, that, by the illegal stop of the Exchequer payments, the whole of the Revenue, as well as the Customs before-mentioned, came clear into the exchequer, and was more than sufficient to answer all the reasonable expences of the crown; those of the government not much exceeding 700,000*l.* per ann. whereas the clear income of the Revenue amounted to at least 1,600,000*l.* From the whole it was more than insinuated, that the Debts of the crown arose rather from the extravagancies of the court, than the necessities of the government: and some undertook to demonstrate, that, by an honest and careful management, both his majesty's Expences might be sufficiently supplied, and his Debts discharged, out of his present Revenue, in the course of a few years: adding, that no parliament was obliged to pay the king's debts, by taxing the subject: that such precedents were dangerous, and might be fatal: for if once a house of commons grew over-prodigal, and a court but moderately frugal, the parliaments of England would become as insignificant as those of France. Either these facts and considerations had such weight with the house, or the majority, contrary to the opinion that is generally entertained of them, were so little under the influence of the court, that they resolved not to grant any Supply to his majesty for the taking off the Anticipations of his Revenue. In comparison with the lavishness and extravagancies of later times, these things have all the air of patriotism and public spirit; but if Mr. North, and all the other writers on the side of the prerogative deserve any credit, we are to conclude, that this excess of many do not arise from any tenderness to the public, but a settled resolution to distress the king." Ralph.

* Mr. Grey.

When quarrels may arise from persons to families, knows no way to prevent it, but by laying hands on them both. In the mean time, would have an engagement of no farther proceeding in the matter from this noble lord.

Mr. *Vaughan*. In this case, it is regular to send to the lord keeper, to take security of them both for quiet deportment.

Mr. *Garroway*. You have declared the Paper to be scandalous, and fears it a little too hasty to put the thing to another way of decision. Moves, that, though you have appointed a day for Mr. Howard's appearance, it may be a shorter day, lest it should reflect, in consequence, on every individual man in the house, and the whole house.

Sir *Ch. Harbord* thinks that what Frowde did was a very safe thing, and he not to blame. Believes that no man dares attack a member: Frowde has engaged, and Howard also, who will be here to-morrow. If you will have him come, he will, though he should die at the door.

The *Speaker*. All will bear him witness how tender he is of the honour of the house. The best way to secure your members is, not to suffer them to do injuries; and he must acquaint you with what he knows. He knows that lord Cavendish posted Mr. Howard for a coward.

Col. *Birch*. By how much the more lord Cavendish is esteemed here, you cannot do a better thing than showing justice. To come rightly to the bottom, the house must know what the Paper contains. Do right within doors, and you will stop wrong the better without doors.

Sir. *Philip Warwick*, notwithstanding his great respect to lord Cavendish, yet would not have you adjourn, till some order be taken in it.

Mr. *Cheney*. Would confine lord Cavendish, in the mean time.

Mr. *Bertue* would send for Frowde, to see the Paper, and then would know whether lord Cavendish owns it, before you proceed; as you did with Mr. Howard.

Mr. *Stockdale*. Perhaps neither Howard nor Cavendish owns the Papers.

Mr. *Swynfin*. It is as plain as any thing can be; you need not put the question to lord Cavendish; but the matter is, what you should do for your own honour to prevent quarrels.

Col. *Birch*. Is of opinion that lord C. has done a great fault, being enjoined by the house to do nothing of tendency to farther quarrel.

Sir *Edw. Baynton*. Lord Cavendish has heard the debate. Would have the Speaker ask him, whether he has any thing to say to it, and then withdraw.

Mr. *Garroway* would preserve your privilege to the loss of his hand. Would have it understood that this commitment is not in order to lord C.'s coming to the bar on his knees.

Mr. *Powle*. The commitment of your member is not for his confinement, but security, therefore would have him confined till farther order.

Mr. *Vaughan*. Commitment is not for his security, but punishment.

Mr. *Garroway*. His commitment then must be solely for breach of Privilege, and on no other account.

Mr. *Boscawen*. You may proceed without asking lord Cavendish, whether he has any thing to say. He may possibly say something to his own prejudice.

Col. *Titus*. Any man that knows his conversation, knows his obligations to lord C.'s family. He believes if lord C. had any thing to say, he would have done it before now, being present at the debate. Having said nothing in his own justification, and having proceeded in what he did after your order, therefore would have him committed.

Sir *Tho. Lee*. The foundations of the house you are not masters of, to dispense with, as reading of a bill three times. You must ask lord C. what he has to say for himself.

Mr. *Garroway*. He is not obliged to make any answer, if you ask him. But, in voting him to commitment, without asking him, you take away the greatest liberty you have.

Sir *Rob. Carr*. Since lord C. has been present at the debate, you have broken your order, as much as you can already; therefore would not ask him any quetions.

Mr. *Sawyer*. In all this debate, you are upon matter of enquiry only, and then the member may be present to give you information of fact, but when you give an opinion, he must withdraw. Some members have told you of a Paper, but none that lord C. wrote it.

Sir *John Ernly*. Your member is at liberty to answer, or not. Possibly his answer may be as much as his life may be worth.

The *Speaker* then said to lord Cavendish, "The house has been informed that you have broken the privilege of the house, and would know what you have to say before you withdraw."

Lord *Cavendish*. He shall ever have great respect to the privilege of this house, and shall be satisfied with what the house shall determine concerning him.—And withdrew.

Col. *Birch*. If any man has any thing to say, why this lord should not be secured, let him speak; and, in the next place, Where? He moves for the Tower.

Mr. *Garroway*. In Howard's case you sent to him, to know whether he owned the paper, or no; who returned you a dissatisfactory answer; in the mean time, you obliged this lord not to proceed in the business. You are informed that he has set up a Paper; you have asked him what he has to say; he has given you no answer; therefore for that would send him to the Tower.

Mr. *Sawyer*. Sir John Fagg was sent to the Tower, for proceeding in the lords house, after this house had possessed themselves of his business. And for lord C. to proceed, whilst the matter was depending in this house, is a breach of Privilege.

Sir *Eliab Harvey*. Lord C. has not broken promise, for that lasted not till Monday, but the matter being under the house's cognizance is the thing.

Sir *Tho. Meres*. Breach of order is of large sense in privilege, but it is a less word than breach of privilege, and would have it run so in the commitment.

Mr. *Sacheverell*. Would have the commitment 'for being charged with the Paper, and giving the house no satisfactory answer.'

The Order was read, viz. "That lord Cavendish and sir Tho. Meres be enjoined not to prosecute any quarrel against Mr. Howard, or to send, or accept, any challenge in order thereto, without acquainting the house."

Col. *Titus*. Lord C. in having said nothing for himself, satisfies him, that he put up the Paper, and in that he has broken the Order of the house, and for that would have him committed to the Tower.

Ordered, "That lord Cavendish be sent to the Tower for his breach of the privilege of this house in prosecuting a quarrel against Mr. Howard, whilst the matter was depending before the house; and that the Speaker do issue out his warrant to the serjeant to convey lord Cavendish to the Tower, and deliver him to the lieutenant, there to remain till farther orders."

Oct. 22. In a grand committee on the building more Ships; sir Ch. Harboard in the chair. Resolved, "That it is the opinion of the committee, that 20 Ships of the 1st, 2nd and 3rd Rate, shall be built with all convenient speed," which was agreed to by the house.

This day, Lord Cavendish having sent a Petition to the house, acknowledging his Breach of Privilege, and craving pardon, was ordered to be discharged from his imprisonment in the Tower.

Oct. 23. Resolved, 1. "That it is the opinion of the committee, that all the Forces that are, or shall be, in the service of the French king, contrary to his majesty's late Proclamation, shall be taken to be contemners of his majesty's royal authority, and opposers of the interest of their country 2. That the lords concurrence be desired to this Vote. 3. That a Bill be brought in to enforce the Proclamation with penalties."

Debate on lord Cavendish's being challenged.] Oct. 25. Mr. *Howe* complains, that whilst we are about the nation's business, we should be subjected to Challenges. He hears that lord Cavendish has been challenged.

Mr. *Russel* gives an account of his suspicion of some such thing, by Mr. Francis Newport's coming to lord Cavendish's house, on Sunday morning last; which occasioned him to find out lord C. and not to leave him till he had acquainted the duke of Ormond with it, who told the king of it, and Mr. Newport was secured.

Sir *John Coventry*. It seems, there is great encouragement from great persons to affront this lord. The quarrel is not against lord C. but the whole house. Some course must be taken, or we shall be hectored by every life-guard-man, and be obliged to fight him. Is informed that a lawyer of the Temple should say, 'It is a pretty story this of lord C. and Mr. Howard; the lord had the Paper 3 weeks before the sitting of the parliament, and complained only at the opening of the parliament, to hinder the king's business.' (And named him,) Mr. Sawyer, of this house, who said it, in a coffee house, to sir Tho. Eastcourt, a member, in the hearing of one Mr. Bradbury, a lawyer, and Philips, a stationer near Temple-Bar.

Mr. *Sawyer* finds that he is the person that, you are informed, should have said something of lord C. He was asked by lord C. about it, and told him he said no such words: but some accidental discourse, he said, was rumoured about town, that the Paper was abroad a month before the parliament sat. He never said the words alleged: but will tell you something: since that some persons have been abroad, to enquire and raise an accusation against him. As for that 'of hindering the king's business,' he never said it; nor could it be the consequence of any thing he said.

Sir *Philip Harcourt* desires that Mr. Bradbury may be summoned, to hear what he can say.

Sir *Tho. Lee* would not have you enquire into coffee-house discourse. Your member plainly denies it, and you can have no advantage by farther enquiry. But if any such thing as a Challenge be, it is fit for your enquiry, and the person that did it should be made a severe example of. The king and you have made enquiry, and any body that dares to concern himself is worthy your farther enquiry. Yourselves are more concerned than lord C. and would have severe enquiry into it.

The *Speaker*. Has not yet heard that the house has been informed that there was a challenge. Mr. Russel only told you of the presumption of a quarrel.

Lord *Cavendish*. Mr. Newport was with him on Sunday morning, but cannot say he brought him a challenge.

Mr. *Howe*. The king sent to secure Mr. Newport, and no question but there was a challenge.

Mr. *Hale*. Lord C. is not forward, nor willing, to tell you of a challenge. His own inclination possibly may induce him that way.

The *Speaker* would have it referred to the committee of privileges.

Sir *Rd. Temple*. It is hard to put it upon lord C. whether he had a challenge sent him, or not.

Sir *Tho. Littleton* moves that, by reason Mr. Howard is to be here to-morrow, you would have Mr. Newport here also.

Sir *Nich. Carew* is not for delays. More challenges may be sent us at this rate.

Sir *Scroope Howe* would have Mr. Atkins sent for also, who is concerned in the challenge.

Ordered, "That Mr. Newport and Mr. Atkins be summoned forthwith to attend the house."

Col. *Birch.* Calling any thing in question that the house has done, is calling the honour and dignity of the house in question. When the house punished lord Cavendish—and any man to question what you have done, is high presumption, and would consider it.

Sir *Tho. Lee* expected that Birch would have concluded his premises, with some remedy for these things. Desires he would tell you.

Col. *Birch.* Though some body else is more fit for it than he, yet he shall move, 'That whoever shall call in question what this house does, shall be punished as disturbers of the peace of the nation, and privilege of parliament.'

Mr. *Garroway.* The laws already are severe, and he would be upon even terms with such kind of men as life-guard-men, that if we defend ourselves against such as have no estates, we may not forfeit ours that have.

Sir *Tho. Clarges.* As it is proposed, it is too general. Lord C. having done something in breach of privilege of this house, and been punished for it, we ought to do equally with the rest.. We are trustees for the people of England; their honour and fortune are in our hands; and for persons to undertake to censure us, would have their punishment more particular.

Mr. *Waller.* They that will fight against king, lords, and commons, (against law) will fight with any of us. In France there are edicts against Duels, but that will stand with arbitrary government only. Would have a committee named to prevent this present mischief.

Mr. *Swynfin.* What the Speaker repeated was not to the question proposed. It is a vain thing to put a question, that any man without doors shall not speak against what we do. It is out of question. No man doubts it. But what you are to do in the matter before you, betwixt lord C. and Mr. Howard, to prevent farther quarrels, in this business, highly reflective upon the house. As yet you have had no answer from Mr. Howard, and in the interval you hear every day of Challenges. You are to do all you can to put a stop to these things.

Mr. *Williams.* There being an assault made upon a member, it is necessary that some provision should be made against promotion of such assaults. Sees no law more for members than other men. In such provocations as these, would have one.

Some members retired to draw up an Order according to the debate, which was posted up at Westminster-hallgate, and the Inns of Court, and was as follows: "Forasmuch as this house, being informed of certain Papers, containing provoking language, posted up by the lord Cavendish, a member of this house, did inflict a punishment upon him, by committing him to the Tower; and whereas they are informed, that, notwithstanding such their care and justice, some persons have presumed to call the said business in question; and, from occasion or pretence of those papers, to give out threatening words, or send Challenges, or provoking papers, to the said members of this house, or others, to be communicated to him; this house doth declare, that if any person whatsoever shall begin or prosecute any quarrel upon that account, or upon any matter or thing any way relating thereunto, he shall be esteemed a disturber of the public peace, and a contemner of the justice and privilege of this house; and shall be proceeded against accordingly."

Mr. *Williams* proposes, that if any person fight a Duel, he be reckoned incapable of pardon.

Sir *Wm. Coventry.* A gentleman said, 'That the king had taken notice of it, and the persons were under confinement.' Finds lord C. here: would know what engagement he has made to the king.

Mr. *Howe.* The message from the king to lord C. was, 'That he should not send nor receive any challenge from Mr. Howard, nor any man else.'

Sir *Wm. Coventry.* If this came from the king, believes it will not fail of its success. What he rises for, was to prevent what he hopes is prevented, and if so, the king to have thanks from you for his care of our member, and to implore his farther protection.

Sir *Rd. Temple.* The great occasion of Duels is, that the law gives not remedy proportionable to injuries received. In France a strict course is taken to repair men in their honour, wherein the law is defective: as it is in some things men highly esteem, as affrontive words.

Ordered, "That a Bill be brought in to prevent Duels, and provocations to Duels."

Debate on the State of the Nation—A Dissolution proposed.] In a grand committee on the State of the Nation, sir John Trevor in the chair:

Sir *Tho. Meres* would have you consider the impiety and corruption of manners, and the protestant religion established by law. Next, rents falling. This is not new matter, but records extant; it is a parliamentary way. The poverty of the nation, and how to increase its riches, is always one head, in considering the State of the Nation: prevent a consumption and general fears of the nation: wounds are not to be cured without being searched: if they are skinned over only, and not searched, they break out into blotches and boils. God give a blessing to what you are about!

Sir *Harbottle Grimstone* knows not how he shall please other men, but would have one ingredient: an application to the king to set a period to this parliament, and to allow us some time to pass bills now on the anvil, for the good of the nation. But would not bound the king. There is a great mischief in the length of this parliament, as if there were no parliament. A Standing Parliament is as inconvenient as a Standing Army. Would address the king, &c.

Sir *John Birkenhead.* God Almighty has put a period to half of the first men of this parliament, by removes and death. Hopes he shall never see a Rump again. But when he sees sons and brothers of those, who were undone by the Rebellion, and paid so dear for loyalty, put and thrust out to have a new set, he declares he is afraid of a Dissolution, because God is his witness, he is afraid the next will be worse. [Laughed at.] Would have gentlemen consider the new and the old. The kingdom so weak, is it time to make it weaker by dissolution of this parliament? Cannot but think that the end of this parliament will be the beginning of confusion.

Sir *Tho. Lee* cannot think the matter moved proper at this time. Is one of those that think this parliament may have good effect. Perhaps he is one of those that hope better of this parliament than, it may be, of the rest that come after. Would have one gentleman from our side of the house that can say, rents are improved, that has no other way of support. Sees no other cause that wool sells not, though after the rot, unless that money is crept into a few hands, and then you must expect rents to fall every day. And money is a commodity, as well as other things, and the engrossment of it into one hand governs trade. Would make some representation of your poverty, and why you comply not now, and likewise the sums we have given the king this parliament: tells the story of lord treasurer Salisbury's showing king James a great heap of money he had given away, &c. By his skill a great deal of money was saved. If you show the king what you have given (he fears the remembrance of it is out of mind) as a reason why money runs not round, hopes that will give full satisfaction in our non-compliance with his desires. Hopes the effect may be, that trade may be bettered, and money circulate, that we may be better able to give for the future. Is afraid, by the sums that are asked, that the king sees not how poor we are in the country, but how rich in other places. Would have him advised by the poor as well as the rich.

Mr. *Williams* looks into titles of Acts under that of 'aid.' Finds the preambles and arguments still to be 'necessity.' The same thing, though in other phrases. But what is become of all this money? Possibly accounts may have been kept, but he has seen none. Were it possible to give as much as has been given, may we not be told still 'that the king is not at ease, and there is a necessity, and if the king be not supplied, extremities must be used?' This frightens him. So he would be gladly told, when there will be an end of Anticipations; when, of giving. What account can be given to the country? It is said that rivers run into the sea, but that ebbs and flows, but this of giving money flows and never ebbs. In his country, they are selling bread to buy bacon, but fears that, at this rate, we shall be reduced to water. As we have given without measure, so we have without method. In the rolls of H. iv. Grievances precede Aid, but at the opening a session now, Money is the thing asked, and we have done it without computation. 1st James, there was a solemn protestation in parliament, 'that they could not give Supply, till a commutation for Grievances, and to go home and consult their electors whether they deserved Supply;' but now we give without that. It is said, 'prepare your grievances.' But it is not a commutation; by that protestation the king is obliged by his coronation oath. We are not obliged to give money for it. Observes it was said the other day, 'We are not to give money of courtesy; it is matter of right.' At this rate, the commons will be in the condition of deans and chapters; a congè d'elire their bishop, for form's sake only, sent for and asked. Finds not, in all this parliament, money denied when asked, and now, in 14 years time, it may be a precedent upon us for futurity and posterity; therefore let us deny it now, for precedent's sake. The king is willing to enter into a strict correspondence with us, and will relieve our necessities; as he tells us his wants, so we are to tell him the necessity of the country. Our duty to the king is to remove the country's fears and jealousies. Let us leave some records behind us, that we are true representatives of the people.

Sir *Lionel Jenkins.* To the representation spoken of, 1st James. It was after the ancient manner. Legal and illegal grievances. There were two rises for it. The one was wardship, the other purveyance, which were both grounded in law. A representation is to move and persuade, and why should the king be moved and persuaded to what he tells us he will do? Had bills been denied, and unfrequency of parliaments: but when the king can say, the parliament is continued, and no public bills, to which the king has said, le roi s'avisera, knows not any need of such representation, when the king is before hand with us. Would have Williams show what decay of trade, or religion, has been represented to the king, and not redressed. The parliament never did it, but when there was a clear obstruction; therefore would wave representation.

Mr. *Sacheverell.* The question is, whether you will make a representation of the present State of the Nation to the king, or no. Would now know what you will debate this matter for, if not to represent it to the king. It is said no such thing has been done before, but takes it plainly to lay before the king, the reason of impiety and atheism, and leave it with him, and how poor the nation is, and how we came into it, and leave it with him to amend it. Will tell you precedents that have been. 50 E. iii. Where the commons tell the king;

'They had given him so much, and, if well managed, he had been the richest king in the world. 25. E. i. 'By reason of such impositions they were brought to that poverty, that they could give no more.' And conclude, 'These have brought poverty on the king,' and then left it to the king, as he would do now. If any gentleman thinks there is no such thing as prophaneness and impiety in the government, and if he thinks not so much money is drawn into France from us, let him give his negative, and he will give his affirmative.

The *Speaker* is of opinion, that what is preferred deserves your consideration. When he considers the bills provided for Religion and Trade, ready to be reported, he cannot but think them worth consideration. To bills for Religion he concurs, but to make Religion by remonstrances is of most dangerous consequence. Could not believe that, after so long sitting in parliament and no public bills returned with le roi s'avisera: thinks there is no necessity of a remonstrance, which is in the nature of appeal to the people. Whoever will tell the people they are not well governed, he fears that people will give them too favourable an audience. The reformed, meek, humble men were the disturbers of the nation, in the last age, and he fears are so now. How low, how humbly, how dutifully they represented! it was they that acted all the villainies of the former age, and fears they are active for the disturbance of this. If the subject was violated of his right, and justice was but an empty name, then there was some countenance for such a thing. Could wish that the prudence of those gentlemen that had indemnity, would pardon the slips and failings of the government, and those occasioned by the necessity of the times. If all this while we had represented the undoing men for their loyalty, if we had so represented this. But since it is our misfortune to have omitted it, let us not now conclude that all was well done before the Act of Indemnity. That being slipt, let us not take this representation up at such a time, when it will be fatal, and tend to our destruction. There is a strict conjunction between the Fanatic and Papist, to dissolve this parliament, and wonders at that motion from a person who has had so little a share in the attendance of the house *. But when this parliament shall be dissolved, he fears the shaking both of church and state. Thinks a representation destructive to us and the government, and would have it laid aside.

Sir *Tho. Meres* looks upon Grimstone's motion, as from an ancient man, with St. Paul's '*cupio dissolvi*,' and believes many abroad gape after it. The question urged of a representation of the state of the kingdom, he thinks to be the sense of the house: bills are preparing, but to some points there cannot be any; but if bills could be in every one, yet would rather have this representation. He slights all harsh expressions, in comparison of doing good. Five or six times bills have been cut to pieces by prorogations. We are tired with hearing them read. In this representation he is confident of the king's grace and favour. These frequent prorogations destroy all we can do by bill. This way of representation will remedy it. He has read that of 1 James, seven, eight, or nine material subjects that concern the State of the Nation—As privilege was mixed with them, excellent lessons for Englishmen to learn! if that method had been taken and followed, it was impossible to have made a rebellion. But it was the breaking parliaments: would not lose the word—calm we are now, and in good temper, but if let alone till some grow angry, it may be much worse. That of 1 James is a good precedent, and would follow it. This parliament has an instance of it; on this very head of religion, 5 years ago, you discoursed the danger of Popery, the cause and remedies: remedies are, where the cause is not, in the king: we are the eyes of the king, and present to him were the canker is, and he remedies it.

Sir *Wm. Coventry* wonders at this debate, and thinks it out of the way. It is not yet the subject matter of debate. Thinks, that, as Grimstone is not seconded in his motion, so the thing will go off—Meres quoted St. Paul for it, and so it may pass. He was not so very young, but can remember the calamities of the late times, and is not a little troubled at what fell from the Speaker, 'That if this parliament be dissolved, it will be the ruin of the nation.' The king's government sure stands on better foundations, the laws and loyalty of his subjects: and the miseries of the late times, for a man's own sake, as well as his loyalty, he would prevent. It is wholly unnatural now to make a representation, because it is not the matter before you. If you were upon Grievances, and if the matters arise where there is no law, then it would be proper for a Bill. But where bills are already, we send messages to quicken them, as those of Popery, and Trade, and another thing not by bill, but we represent by Declaration. We represented to the king what the law was, and desired it should be so no more. If slips be in the government, would not do it merely to represent them, but to remedy them. If administration has not followed the law, we should represent it to the king. But would first consider the matter, before you think of a representation.

Sir *Tho. Lee* is one of those who would represent to the king the present condition of the kingdom, but was none of those 'meek and humble reformers;' though he is one of those that would not shut the doors to such a representation. Did never think that all advices from hence were appeals to the people. Knows not how else the ill management of his counsellors shall be represented to him. Though things have been made an ill use of, yet ar-

* Sir Harbottle Grimstone, who had been Speaker. He was at this time 73.

ciently they have been good. A fine way to shut up all the gates of the court, and the king never to know when he is ill advised! Would not have every little slip of the government represented, but only when the king cannot know the mismanagements of his government by any other way, but representation: and therefore would have it now.

Sir *John Duncombe* fears that the defect of supporting the Church is in ourselves; not in this house, but among themselves. Some of them, he will not say, have too much, but many have nothing at all. Many places are so unprovided, that the parson must work for his living, and, at this rate, the Church will fall of itself. Ill use is made even of the power of the Church; it does the Church no good. Not for the ends intended by the ecclesiastical courts; speaks not to oppose them, or to lessen the authority of the Church: thinks it worthy your thoughts to open the doors to some men. These are his humble thoughts.

Mr. *Garroway* thinks that we run out of method. The order of the house is 'for the committee to consider the State of the Nation;' desires that, in this case, we may go on clearly and not kindle it up. If all can be remedied by Bill, let it go; what cannot, let us in all humble duty represent to the king. Let us hear what all these motions are, and then you may consider whether provided for already, and recommend it to the committee to have bills in hand.

Sir *Rd. Temple.* This motion will bring all into confusion. Under the general head of Religion descend to particulars: insist not upon what the law has already provided for, but what it has not. Scandalous livings will make scandalous ministers. Would consider Pluralities, and such Churchmen as are above their callings, and come only to collect their duties. The king of France has wounded the Protestants more by this way than any: and especially moves to consider the scandal of Pluralities.

Sir *Philip Mulgrave* would not have 'debauchery and prophaneness' represented in the State of the Nation.

Sir *Tho. Meres.* If we are ashamed to represent it, let us say so, and try it by a question. Thinks the thing is recommended to the committee, by order, to be the first head of the matter under consideration.

Sir *Tho. Clarges.* How can we see such a profusion of treasure as we have had, and not tell the king of it? (called to Order) Is Representation such a terrible word not to be mentioned? Knows no way of acquainting the king, but by representation.

Mr. *Mallet.* 'The promiscuous use of women'—would have that considered, for they betray the counsels of the nation.

Mr. *Vaughan.* Some sort of men have had the confidence to represent the State of the Nation to the king, and very wrongly. We complained, in the late times, of decimations, and have not we had the Bank violated, and persons against oaths brought up to the Council-table? Nothing has been wanting, except taking the king's head off. Not 'the humble' but 'the proud,' reformed the government, to usurp it. And thinks that these are causes of Representation, and can say more hereafter.

Resolved, "That it is the opinion of the committee, that Atheism and Debauchery be one branch of the consideration of this committee to be redressed."

Mr. Howard committed to the Tower.] Oct. 26. Mr. Howard, according to Order, attended at the door of the house. Being called in, he was allowed a chair, without the bar, because of his lameness of the gout. Then the Speaker delivered himself thus. "The occasion of your coming hither is a scandalous Paper, which the house has more than a common presumption was dispersed by your order, and subscribed by you. The house would know, whether the paper was signed by you, or dispersed by your order?" The Paper was brought to Mr. Howard by the clerk. Then Mr. Howard thus spoke:

"My respect always has been to this hon. house, and I hope you will excuse me from giving any answer to a thing of this nature, not knowing who charges me with the writing it. As to the resentment of my dead brother, I believe any man who had lost so dear a friend, as well as a brother, might be provoked to some passion. I will not excuse myself: I cannot equally bear such a loss. I am the more concerned, because I knew my brother so much an Englishman, as to go with the sense of the Votes of this house, so far as he understood them. I have met with a Paper very extraordinary, but, because it doth not immediately touch me, shall offer it to your better consideration. I shall always owe respect to this hon. house, as becomes me, and hope I have not done any thing to incur your displeasure; but if so unhappy as to rest under it, shall humbly submit to any punishment. I find the Paper so extraordinary a one, that I think fit to offer it to the house."

The *Speaker.* Have you any thing farther to say concerning the Paper?

Mr. *Howard.* Let any man prove that it is my hand.—He withdrew.

Mr. *Stockdale.* He has so far owned the the Paper, as to submit to your justice. They are words of high nature, and dangerous: would have him sent to the Tower, but, being a worthy gentleman, not to come upon his knees.

Mr. *Williams.* Howard has been asked, if concerned in the Paper: he has had as fair proceedings as may be. He was examined first by a committee, and did not answer the thing at all. Has had a long time to consider of an answer. An express confession could not be expected. He has behaved himself modestly. He, in a manner, owned the provocation that might make a man so express himself. The other day, when the Paper that was posted up was debated, your member, (lord Cavendish) was present and sat mute; he denied not the thing: and now it is the same thing in this gentleman. He has, in a manner, stood mute: would have him committed to the Tower.

Mr. *Streete*. Before you proceed to sentence, would read Mr. Howard's Paper. Possibly it may guide your judgment in the Paper.

Mr. *Mallet*. He has as much as confessed the matter, and it concerns not only these persons, but the Protestants in general.

Sir *John Knight*. It is fit you should read the Paper.

Col. *Birch*. Somewhat like 'Did you do this, or not,' was asked him. He answered. Knows not how to reconcile this Paper, he offers, and that he is accused of: the Paper may be part of his defence.

Sir *Tho. Lee*. Consider what the flames are, and what water you have thrown on them. He fears that the Paper may be yet worse. Had the Paper been his own, you might have read it; and now you ask him about the scandalous paper, he tells you 'he has met with a Paper of an extraordinary nature.' Now the question is, whether such a Paper shall be read, before he opens what it is.

Serj. *Maynard*. The Paper he offers you is not relating to his offence. Knows not what you may imagine in reading it, unless to hear news.

Mr. *Sawyer*. If the gentleman had opened the contents of the Paper, then the house might have judged whether concerned or not: we may have a ballad read else.

Mr. *Sawyer*. You must, upon sentence, pronounce guilty, or not. He was called in to know, whether he owned the Paper or not. At common law he is a mute. If the person denies it, then go to proofs; if he does not deny it, it is fair to put the question, whether he be the author of the scandalous Paper, and he must give his affirmative to it.

Sir *Rd. Temple* has much respect to this gentleman, but seeing he cannot excuse himself, neither will he do so. There is a suspicion that he was the promoter of the Paper, but since he has neither denied nor confessed it, but in a manner excuses it, neither can he excuse him: would have him sent to the Tower.

Col. *Birch* agrees with Sawyer, that, if Howard deny it, we are put upon proving it; if not, it is taken pro confesso, a constant Order—It is contrary to Order for the Speaker to discourse with any person. If the house thinks him worthy to be heard, so must the Speaker. Could not the Speaker require him to open the Paper, for then you had opportunity to let him know the justice of the house in condemning the Paper? The least that can be done for the honour of the kingdom is to send him to the Tower.

Mr. *Sawyer*. The house is to judge of their own evidence. It is of dangerous consequence for people without doors to be judges. Therefore he believes Howard to be the promoter and disperser of the Paper.

Mr. Sec. *Coventry* would give judgment in this as if all the world heard your evidence. Now, whether Howard be the author, is the matter of fact. But to say 'The thing appears, because a man denies it not,' is not for your honour.

Resolved, "That it is the judgment of this house, that Mr. Howard is the author, promoter, and disperser of the scandalous Paper." Ordered, That he be committed to the Tower.

Debate on lodging the Money for the Ships in the Chamber of London, instead of the Exchequer.] Sir *Nich. Carew* moves that the money to be raised for building the Ships you have voted, be put into the Chamber of London, and not be issued out thence without an order from the lord mayor, and common council, to be the more certainly applied to the use of the fleet.

Mr. *Sacheverell* is the rather for the motion, because the money formerly was not to put to the use of the Fleet, which it was given for.

Sir *Tho. Meres*. We cannot trust the Exchequer, and therefore would have the money put into the Chamber of London.

Mr. *Garroway*. This is not the first time of his jealousy, because not the first time obligations have not been made good. If this money is to go for ships, is as free as any man to appropriate it.

Sir *Wm. Coventry* would have satisfaction how this money shall be used; which may make gentlemen more satisfied in giving. The new imposition upon wines were given only to pay the king's debts, and here we had not only general assurance, but the particular undertaking of lord Clifford, and yet that money was turned to a revenue, and no debt paid. Notwithstanding all the engagements to the contrary, yet the Exchequer was stopped, and there is a more easy pretence of stopping the money there by the king's ministers, which cannot be in the Chamber of London. And therefore would obviate one objection, that the stop of the Exchequer was only for the king's revenue. Has heard it said, that, at the time sir John Bank's money was lent to the exchequer, upon the act of parliament, it was refused him, when he called for it, by sir Robert Long. Banks desired his friends he brought with him to witness that, his money was demanded and stopped, against law. Long persisted in not paying him, but, upon consideration, found it not fit to break the act, upon so small a sum. This shows you that money lent, upon the security of the act of parliament, has been near stopping in the exchequer. Therefore would have the committee consider this with liberty, if they have it not already.

Sir *John Duncombe*. What can there be of jealousy that ships should not be built? It is impossible for any man to think it. The money must build ships.

Col. *Birch*. Ill use may be made hereafter of what you have already done. Would have the people believe that this money is lodged securely. Few tons of timber are yet ready, and what you do must be speedy. Is sorry the proverb, 'sure as Exchequer' is gone. Hopes it may come again. If any man employed in building these ships ask for his money, and it is in the exchequer, who will meddle? The king has told you, 'He will be a better husband.' It is for us to chalk him out the way.

Mr. Secretary Williamson. Moves to enter into the matter, without umbrage. The thing we are doing is to bring a question, whether we shall do it, or not. Enter not here into particulars, but you may give general instructions to the committee.

Mr. *Vaughan*. Though not jealous of his wife's honour, yet should you, or any one, come out of her chamber in drawers, he must be jealous. The Exchequer has done no good in this; by experience we have found it.

Sir *Tho. Meres*. Will any man place his money where he has been so often deceived? The law was prefaced for it, and trusted the Exchequer with it. Some say, 'punish the officers;' but we have not hearts to punish, we are too good natured. He foresees they will not be punished by the house, and knows of no where else, where they will be punished.

Mr. *Love*. If you expect this money to be well employed, you must put it into the city's, or some secure hands, or you are never like to have it rightly employed.

Sir *Ch. Harboard*. The Exchequer has failed, and there is nothing worse for the government than the failure of it. The morning after the stop of the Exchequer was made, sir Robert Long told him of it. He believed it not. He told Long, was it his case, he would rather lose his life, or office, than suffer it; for an action of the case might be brought against him for the money. Thinks the Chamber of London the best security. You must have public, or private, security. The Chamber has great helps to make good what they do, and you are safe in their hands, and the act will bind them beyond all seals they can make.

Sir *Wm. Bucknall*. It is not what I know, but what the people think. If the people believe not the money will be paid, the people will not trust where they think they shall not be paid. The Chamber of London is good credit.

Sir *George Downing*. You are the restorers of the government, but this about the Chamber of London, is setting up a new government. What was done to stop the Exchequer, was by order of council, and by the great seal, not orders of the Exchequer. That place that gives accounts most sure and constantly, is the best place. Money was paid into London at the beginning of the rebellion, and dreads every thing that may have its likeness. Would devise from Hell to say, 'destroy the Exchequer, and take this way,' which is one of the best securities—With it you destroy property. The Exchequer is one of the fundamental pillars of monarchy, the easiest and the cheapest. In 1660, money was paid into the Chamber of London, not yet accounted for, for disbanding the army, and no man can ever find out how it can be accounted for, nor ever will. Had it been in the Exceequer, it might. Shall it be said, we put it into such hands, nay vote it into such hands? Some are hot enough that the Exchequer is not to be trusted; when that trust is gone, the government is gone. Has any thing been misplaced in the Exchequer? Mend it. Resolve that the money be appropriated, and refer it to the committee to make it effectual.

Sir *Nich. Carew*. He is concerned because he made the motion. Would have it known that he is no gainer by the wars. He is the poorer, and some others within these walls the richer, but sees we are now all Cavaliers. [Reflective.]

Sir *Tho. Meres*. One reflection begets another. The Speaker should have taken Downing down for reflection. If he (the Speaker) will not *give* us leave to answer reflections we will *take* it.

Mr. Sec. *Coventry* will not decide which of the offices, the Exchequer or the Chamber, may be the most easily governed. As to the Chamber, the placing of the money there imports a treasurer. Hopes never to see that day, for the parliament to have one treasurer, and the king another. He knows what will follow. Weigh it well, whether you cannot have as good security from the Exchequer as from the Chamber of London.

Sir *Henry Capel* has a favourable opinion of the City of London, but sees no need of so great caution in placing this money. It looks like some mistrust, for this one time to trust this one sum in the city's hands. The better London performs this trust, the more danger there will be for future sums to be lodged there. Fears it will come to this, Who will trust the city, and who will trust the king, here, whom we ought to trust?

Mr. *Waller*. If he had his own natural inclination and desire, he would have taken this occasion to reform the Exchequer, which for ought he sees, breaks loose from all acts of parliament, when the king, lords, and commons made orders assignable, and they are worth nothing, which would make farthings current money.

Mr. *Pepys* would have been silent, if what he intends to say in this business was not entirely new, or if so proper for any body to say as himself. Of all hands, he knows this money will be most properly in the king's single hand, and none else; but bonds may be put upon the lord treasurer's hands, and other officers, and the king's hand is the safest on this occasion. A retrospection of the ill management you have found in the navy, gives this jealousy now. Is the state of the fleet worse than when the king came in? No. In quality, rate, burthens, and force, men, and guns, it is in better. Let any man offer a contradiction, that it is not the best fleet the kingdom ever knew. There are 83 sail, great and small, more than in all his royal predecessors; and he has built more ships in 14 years, in burthen and value, of that fleet, notwithstanding the war—The most beautiful are the king's own growth and building. It is said 'of late they have been neglected;' but there have been more ships built since 1670, than in any 5 years from any time backward. Another justice, next to the king, he must do the lord treasurer. More ships have been built in this lord treasurer's time, than in any ten of his predecessors. All this said, why will you not trust the king? He has the honour of a near attendance upon the king, by his office; none of his subjects have so many thoughts, or take more pains in the navy, than this master of ours.

The question being put, "Whether the Money to be raised for the Ships should be lodged in the Chamber of London," it passed in the negative, 171 to 160.

Debate on a new Test against Members receiving Bribes for their Votes.] Oct. 27. Exceptions being taken at some words which fell from sir John Hotham, by sir Philip Musgrave,

Sir *Tho. Clarges* said, He would not have the authority of the Chair degraded. The words are to be set down and agreed.

Mr. Sec. *Williamson.* He has his liberty to take his exceptions at what was spoken by Hotham, as other gentlemen have theirs, viz. 'That Members have been drawn from us, and the sums we have given have been employed to that purpose.'

Sir *Nich. Carew* would have a committee appointed to enquire into these things, and clear your members from aspersions.

Sir *John Hotham* explained himself, 'That the revenue is collected by several of the members, and by it they are withdrawn from their service here.'

Sir *John Knight* would know 'what members' are drawn away from us.

Mr. *Garroway* knows no-body reflected upon, (Knight saying 'we' and 'us') unless he be the number, and has employment.

Mr. *Stockdale.* It is an excellent motion, to purge ourselves by a Test; and would have a committee to consider of it.

Sir *John Coventry.* Possibly, though the nation be poor, yet there may be talk of guineas: would have us purged of it. Members have had letters sent them from officers of the court, some time before this session, to hasten their coming up: would have that enquired into.

Sir *John Hotham* would know who has received such letters.

Sir *Chs. Wheeler.* It is hard for us to recover surmises, and suspicions, without doors: telling the Yeas and Noes, who they are, may be of ill consequence abroad; and whenever you are pleased to appoint such a Test shall be very willing.

Sir *Tho. Meres.* 'We' and 'us' are very good English words. We are agreed, as to appropriation of this money. Why should we lose the first person plural! But where it is applied to parties, there we may have exception. Your question is, for such a Test as is proposed. The thing is talked of without doors, and some such Test would be very seasonable. The last session, there was some such thing, and was proceeded on, very forward. Now is ready to think, that guineas are raised in their price: knows nothing, but believes these to be idle things; but would take off the report.

Mr. *Williams* has not seen these Letters spoken of. Perhaps they were sent by the king's command. They are illegal, and not justifiable: would have these letters produced, and you may then judge, whether they are justifiable or no.

Sir *John Coventry.* If letters are not justified, they ought to be corrected; and would have the letters produced.

Sir *Winston Churchill.* There can be no greater infamy than this Test, in casting reflection, suspicion, and self-condemnation: would rather pass a vote, that such reporters without doors, if taken, shall be severely punished.

Sir *Wm. Coventry.* It is said, 'there could be no greater reflection upon the house, than this Test. He knows one greater reflection; that is, refusing such a test. The last time we met, enquiry was made into 5000 guineas, but no report of it was made from the committee. It is impossible to silence men's reports, or to keep secret what is said in this house; and all such reports are equally disadvantageous to us all. The thing being cut off by prorogation, if not revived now, the people will think the majority of the house afraid of that Test. Grimstone's motion * was not thought seasonable, but nothing can tend to a Dissolution of this parliament, like the people's ill opinion of us, and then to be no more useful to the government, is an obloquy upon us, and we become abominable in the eyes of the people, though not parliaments in general—An herb, John, in the pottage. But when this Test comes thus far into debate and is rejected, what may be the consequence of it? Therefore is for the Test.

Sir *Tho. Lee.* Reports of guineas come up and down so generally, that he cannot tell who here heard it reported, that he is one of those who has had them. If he had any, he has taken pains for them; he has attended the service very closely.

Sir *Ch. Harbord.* If any have had, they have ill deserved them.

Lord *Cavendish.* If we lose the opinion of the people, we can neither serve the king, nor the country: would have one word added to the question: 'For the committee to enquire both after Letters and Money:' and letters have been received.

Sir *John Coventry* seconds the Motion; for he believes that both letters and money have been received.

Sir *John Hanmer* would have the committee

* See p. 764.

enquire as well who have had manors, as letters and money.

Col. *Birch.* We say in the country, that if a man intends to pay well, when he borrows money, he gives a bill, or a bond, or any thing else. Is mighty glad to find this debate. Thinks we are not in a capacity to give money to build these ships, unless this Test be done. He finds no reason in the world against it, therefore would direct the committee in it.

Sir *Edm. Jennings* would have every man declare what he has by offices, or any other way, and refund. The king has had much money of his, and if he has any of the king's, shall willingly refund it.

Sir *Henry Puckering.* What does that look like? Impeaching. Perhaps you may find half the house concerned in the giving motion. This neither becomes your prudence nor gratitude: these little things, to rip up into little offices! The king is a liberal prince, who rewards services.

Sir *Henry Capel* is sorry to differ from him, having served the crown: but is there any thing so dear in the world as the honour of this parliament? Wonders, when things are so spoken of abroad: moves, of all things in the world, to put this question.

Sir *John Hotham* differs from Jennings. Yourself, Mr. Speaker, have had good things from the king, and have deserved them. The labourer is worthy of his hire; and he would not have the question of refunding.

Mr. Sec. *Coventry.* He that has betrayed his trust, and his honour, in taking money, will be so wise as to deny it, for his honour.

Sir *Wm. Coventry.* As you put the question, Mr. Speaker, it is taken for granted that the house has swallowed it. But he would have the Test, for members to purge themselves from having received.

Col. *Titus* supposes it is the intention of the enquiry, 'That if any man, &c.' upon report that several members were corrupted. The last session you made an Order, and he would do the same thing now.

Sir *Tho. Lee.* The last session, there was particular complaint of a lawyer.

The paper of the Test the last session was read, and referred to a committee. The committee was instructed to enquire what Members have had Guineas, Promises, Rewards, or Letters, to corrupt their Votes*.

Debate on Letters sent to particular Members in order to secure their Votes.] The house was informed of certain Letters sent to particular members, to summon them to give their attendance upon the service of this house:

Sir *Hen. Goodrick* thinks that his family has served the king faithfully, and wonders that he has not received a letter, as well as his neighbours. He thinks himelf slighted in not being thought so well worthy. Would have the secretaries of state inform you, who they sent letters to, and by whose direction.

Mr. Sec. *Coventry.* The secretaries may reveal or not reveal it, as they have orders from their master. If they are unlawful, ignorance has led them into a fault, for obeying the king's particular command. His ignorance, if so, has betrayed him and his brother secretary. These Letters are not guilty of the inconvenience, mentioned, of making faction. Goodrick would have the committee to know, why not to one man as well as to another? Shall any man ask the king, why not to one man as well as to another? If for any such ill intention, as is mentioned, the style would be accordingly. Is sure from his conscience there is no reason to imagine surprize by it. A Cambridge scholar was asked, why he wore but one spur? He replied, 'That if his horse went on one side, he would be hanged if the other side would be left behind.' In case of surprizal, private orders might have gone, not thus publicly sending to gentlemen's houses.

Mr. Sec. *Williamson.* Neither he nor his brother are ashamed, nor ought to be, of these letters. They came from no ill intention nor distinguishing end. There was a report that the house would not meet; several came to him to know. The king commanded him to

* "A suspicion prevailing in the house of commons, that a party could not uniformly and steadily oppose every vote and every motion that leaned to the popular side, and as uniformly and steadily forward and support every motion and vote that was calculated to favour the court, unless they were under some influence, which was inconsistent with their trust, the following Test was introduced and entered in their Books, though it does not appear to have been administered to this day: 'I *A. B.* do 'protest before God and this house of parliament, that, directly nor indirectly, neither I, 'nor any for my use, to my knowledge, have, 'since the 1st day of Jan. 1672, had, or received any sum or sums of money, by ways 'of imprest, gift, loan, or otherwise, from 'the king's majesty, or any other person, by 'his majesty's order, direction or knowledge, or 'by authority derived from his said majesty, or 'any pardon, discharge or respite of any money due to his said majesty, upon account of 'any grant, pension, gratuity, or reward, or 'any promise of any such office, place or command, of or from his majesty, or out of any 'money, treasure or estate of or belonging to 'his majesty, or of, from, or by, any foreign 'embassador or minister, or of, or from, or 'by any appointment, or with the knowledge 'of his majesty, or any of them, otherwise 'than what I have now in writing faithfully 'discovered, and delivered to this house, 'which I have subscribed with my name; 'neither do I know of any such gift, grant, 'or promise so given or made since the said 'time to any other member of this house, but 'what I have also inserted in the said writings; nor have I given my Vote in parliament for any reward or promise whatever. 'So help me GOD.'" Ralph.

assure all his friends and acquaintance, that they should meet, and so discountenance this report. There was no distinction in these Letters amongst such as were of his conversation. Believes generally that these gentlemen might promiscuously acquaint their neighbours, that there might be a full house.

Sir *Tho. Meres*. There being a report that these Letters were sent, he cannot believe the king in the least concerned in this matter, nor the worthy secretaries. He has heard of an order of council; but reminds you that the council cannot meddle with meum and tuum: He heard they have done it, by reference, thereby terrifying causes fit for Westminster-hall: but much more they are not to meddle with matters of parliament. If then they have so mistaken the common law of parliaments, it is good law for the country. Not good to engage a fourth part, and leave the other three disengaged; and for the story, 'the horse and one spur' spoken of, if the literate and illiterate had been upon one horse, they would have come together.

Col. *Birch*. It is absolutely necessary to sit here on an equal foot. Never knew any thing of this nature not gone to the bottom of, that had good effect. Until this matter appears bare and naked, there will be jealousies. Therefore moves 'that the king may be moved to give leave that the Secretaries may produce these Letters, to see wherein they differ,' and believes this would give satisfaction.

Sir *Wm. Coventry* thinks there is a difference in the nature of the Letters, by the authority of the king, and that of the secretaries. There is a difference betwixt a private man's letter to a judge, and a privy seal or great seal sent him about a cause. Thinks these Letters strange and unequal. The ancient way was to give such notifications by proclamation. When parliaments have been assembled, and not many members come up, and not full, they have adjourned for some time. But if any man was declared governor of a town, or a captain, these employments were a dispensato to his attendance here. If other differences be made, it is a great reflection upon the house. These people principally refer to us for their liberty and money, and the king recommends Religion and Money to us in his speech, and he remembers not but when any bill has been depending concerning religion, against popery, that he has been as forward and zealous as any man—possibly not so forward in money. He is at a stand, having had no Letters as well as other men, but for the motion of 'sending to the king to have leave to inspect the secretaries books,' he is against it. You may attain your end another way, by representing the inconveniences of such Letters, from the inequality of it, for his majesty's service, and to prevent it for the future.

Mr. *Waller*. If to find a fault in this matter, a committee is very good for it. But there is a fault some-where, in not giving advice to the king about these letters. Privy seals are forbidden to walk abroad for money, as they have done formerly: they should not meddle with the private purse, nor the public purse. Writs call us hither *ad consulendum*, but he perceives these letters are *ad dandum*.

Col. *Titus* perceives by this, and many other experiments, that many things are too fine and subtle for his gross apprehension. Just before this session of parliament, the king seemed to be wonderfully enamoured with a parliament man; and would see them here with the first. There may be an inconvenience in sending these Letters to country juries; they may be imposed upon and frighted; but persons here having too much integrity to be imposed upon, it is not to be imagined.

Resolved, "That his majesty be humbly moved, that the Members of this house may be summoned to give their attendance on the service of the house by Proclamation only."

Debate on St. Germain's Assault on Luzancy.] Nov. 8. Mr. *Russel*. Coming through the Hall to day, he heard of a priest, one St. Germain, who forced one Mr. Luzancy (in company with an English jesuit, who spoke broken French,) a minister of the French Church, with a dagger in his hand, (threatening to stab him on refusal) to sign a Paper of recantation, containing many seditious things, and that the nation would turn to Popery, &c. *

* "About this time, an accident happened, which not only renewed the cry against Popery, but raised it louder than ever. One Luzancy, who from a French Jesuit became a convert to the Church of England, preaching in the French Church in the Savoy, took occasion to inveigh with great bitterness against the errors of the Church of Rome; and afterwards printed his sermon. This alarmed the Papists, and particularly one Dr. Burnet, otherwise called Father St. Germain, a Jesuit and confessor to the duchess of York, who finding him alone in his chamber, and having posted three men at his door, threatened to murder him if he did not make satisfaction for the injury, and speedily return to France. The man thus awed and terrified, not only promised faithfully whatever was required of him, but signed a formal retraction, in order to get his liberty. But no sooner was he safe and free, than he went to Dr. Brevall, another converted Jesuist, and told him the whole story: the doctor communicated it to sir John Reresby, and sir John to the house of commons, who immediately took fire upon it, appointed a committee to examine the matter, and ordered Reresby to produce Luzancy the next day; who confirmed all; adding, moreover, the following particulars: That the said St. Germain, in several conferences with him, had attested, that the king was a Roman Catholic in his heart, that the court was endeavouring to get a Liberty of Conscience for the Roman Catholics; and, that granted, in two years, most of the English would acknowledge the Pope; that he knew the king's intention concerning reli-

Sir *Henry Goodrick* has little to add, but matter of fact, the thing has been so well related by Russel. But thinks it his duty to take care that no discouragement be put upon persons that turn from Popery to our religion. M. Luzancy, is as learned a man, as any that has turned to our religion. The priest, St. Germain, belongs to the dutchess of York, and so gives an account of the matter. He had the account from Dr. Brevall.

Sir *Rob. Southwell.* That night the council met, and lord Holles was summoned to attend, and he believes the king has the matter under his particular cognizance.

Sir *Philip Musgrave.* This is so great an affront to the Church, that, if nothing be done in it, the Church will grow low in esteem. Pray proceed with all expedition in it.

Sir *Ch. Harbord.* This goes beyond all precedents, to persuade, not only with arguments, but poignards! he never heard the like way before. Moves that the chief justice may issue out a general warrant to take him 'ubicumque fuerit in Angliâ,' to be indicted for the king's honour, justice, and safety.

Sir *John Birkenhead.* He values the thing the more, because Luzancy, by coming over to our Church, has done great hurt to the Church of Rome. He has written against it. But this St. Germain is a Frenchman, and not within the statute of 3 James—Insinuando by poignards, and daggers, as the story goes, to renounce God, and then stab him, to be revenged both of body and soul! these strangers to come in this manner to the king's subjects! The king has taken cognizance of it, you are told, and believes you will have an effect of it suddenly. If not, do what you please.

Mr. Sec. *Williamson.* The fact is a violence offered to this convert, M. Luzancy. On Thursday the king sent for him, to the lords house; the king had a Paper in his hand, given him by lord Holles, relating the violence offered this Luzancy, on the fourth of Oct. last, (and so gives an account of the Paper.) The king sent to have Luzancy examined, and the parties were warned to be at the Council at five of the clock. At seven Luzancy comes, and was examined upon oath: the next day he promised to bring his witnesses. When he was examined upon oath, the bishop of Oxford went to hear the examination. The king was presented with the examiners in the afternoon, and, if it could be, he gave order for a special council, but it sat not, and this day there is a council extraordinary for the thing.

Sir *Tho. Clarges.* For ought he perceives, here is a failure of justice. Would know whether the Secretary, when he had this information, did send a warrant to attach St. Germain.

Mr. Sec. *Williamson.* He sent a messenger to attach this St. Germain, but he was not to be found. He gave his Papers to the king: he had his direction, and obeyed it.

Sir *Tho. Meres.* There is a motion made to apprehend these two priests, and he seconds it.

Mr. Attorney *Montagu.* The king, as you are informed, has taken early notice of it, and as much as can be done. But it will be very ill if we do not something in it. Moves that two of our members may go to the Lord Chief Justice for a warrant to apprehend them forthwith.

Col. *Sandys.* The Priest has done you a kindness. The nation is full of them, and would have a warrant to search for all Priests and Jesuits in general.

Resolved, "That the Lord Chief Justice be desired forthwith to issue his warrant in par-

---

gion, and that he was sure his majesty would approve of all he should do in that matter; that he laughed at the parliament, as being only a wave, that had but a *little time;* and said, that nobody was more welcome at court, or had greater intrigues with the nobility than he; that it was good, sometimes, to force people to Heaven; and that there were an infinite number of Priests and Jesuits in London, who did God a very great service.—When all these particulars, which Luzancy offered to attest upon oath, had been reported to the house, lord Cavendish called upon sir John Reresby to give an account of some other things which he had heard from Luzancy: one was, that two French Protestants, being merchants of great substance and credit, had been threatened by certain papists, that if they were not less severe upon the Romanists, they would ere long see the Protestant blood flow in London streets. A committee was appointed to enquire into the truth of this matter; and Luzancy being summoned, gave evidence to the very self same effect, and gave it under his own hand. The parties he had his information from, being sent for, appeared also, and declared such threats to have been used towards them by some French Papists; but, to what cause it was owing, is uncertain; they gave in only such names as were of persons either absent, or of no estimation; so that little came of this business. But these and other such informations, concerning the height and insolence of the Papists, did so exasperate the house, that many motions were made to humble them. Some were for a speedy confinement of them to the country, others for banishment, and some again for disarming them, and the like. His majesty also was pleased to issue his royal Proclamation, Nov. 10, signifying, that he had taken Luzancy into his royal protection; setting forth St. Germain's offence; offering 200*l.* reward for the apprehending of him; commanding all constables, &c. to use their best endeavours to that end; and declaring, that whoever harboured him should be proceeded against with severity. This affair shewed the necessity of an Union among Protestants; and, accordingly a door of hope was once more opened to the Dissenters; leave having been given, in both houses, for the introduction of a Bill in their favour." Ralph.

ticular to apprehend those Jesuits, and another to search for and apprehend all Priests and Jesuits whatsoever.

Debate on the regulating the Election of Members to serve in Parliament.] Nov. 18. Sir *Henry Ford.* In the Long Parliament the Court of Stannaries was taken away, because if the plaintiff brought a vexatious suit, and was cast, he paid no costs.

Mr. *Garroway.* There is a short way to remedy these excesses, without taking away civil hospitality, viz. 'that the person to be chosen shall have an estate in the proper county.'

Serj. *Maynard.* By law, every man that serves here, must have his wages from the county or borough he serves for, but now, generally, there are none taken. This bribing men by drink is a lay simony: 'electiones fiant libere.' What do men give hogs drink for? To be carried on the shoulders of drunken fellows? Thinks it a good limitation, 'that none be capacitated to be chosen, but such as have estates, or reside, in the county.' Exclude them that have no estates from being trusted in what they give; who, to serve a turn, will be made free of the borough, and it may be, never live nor trade in the borough hereafter.

Sir *John Bramstone.* Before you give directions to the committee for a Bill to regulate Elections, you will, in the first place, not exclude so great a county as Essex, if you alter the law: but three boroughs and two knights in the county: before you give a restraint, make us even with other counties. In Oliver's time there were 16. Before you alter the law, would make the distribution more equal.

Sir *Rob. Carr.* There are but 12 for the county of Lincoln. Would have no man a knight of the shire, that has not an estate in the county he serves for; but for a burgess, if his estate be in another county, would have him serve for a borough.

Mr. *Boscawen.* It is looked on as a privilege of their county (Cornwall) to have so many to serve in parliament, but strangers are chosen that look not after the county. It may be, Yorkshire has as many as Devon and Cornwall, and anciently the boroughs petitioned to be discharged from sending burgesses, for the charge it put them to for wages; but the world is so altered now, that some forget for what place they serve.

Mr. *Vaughan.* A man is obliged, in justice and gratitude, to serve the interest of the place and county he serves for. It is the same thing as if a man had no estate at all, if he have none in the county or borough.

Sir *Edw. Dering.* If they have estates in any other county, as in law they may be chosen, so they may in reason also. Would leave both the expence and the qualification to the committee.

Sir *Rd. Temple.* Anciently there was no vote in a borough, but by burgage tenure, borough-houses: we come now to freemen, and salesmen, scotters and lotters, but such only had voice as were able to maintain the charge of their burgesses. Would tie up elections to such as have estates to answer their actions to the place they serve for. Would not have one chosen that has not an estate of 500*l.* per ann. And restrain all charges, and expences, that elections may be free.

Mr. *Williams.* By statute of Hen. vi. the county is to chuse by freeholders, and the cities by citizens and burgesses: electors, and elected also. There is another statute, 'that elections shall be freely and indifferently made, notwithstanding letters, &c.' which he has felt to his cost.

Mr. *Swynfin.* You are on a good subject, and it deserves consideration. You have had several things moved, almost impossible to come to effect. It was never before thought of to make rules for boroughs, but to leave men to stand upon their ancient privileges. Some boroughs, by prescription, have a settled right by law. In some there is no burgage tenure: would therefore avoid these large considerations. If you make a general Vote, there will be as much doubt on the interpretation, and be as full of dispute when it comes to be applied, as now. If you go about it, it is as much as to say you will have a bill that shall never come to effect. But there is one thing: that exorbitant corruption, amounting to no less than bribery: and it is better to allow to give 1000*l.* than to expend it so disorderly. It makes the very parliament have reflections upon it; therefore would have a Bill to restrain this giving or spending money before the election be made.

Tho. Meres. As good make a coat for the moon, as alter the manner of elections; we have one burgess sits here upon one point, and another upon another. Doubts that what we are about to do is impracticable. Those who wish not the parliament well, impute these things as a scandal to us. Therefore something should be done against drinking and bribery, and would have the Committee directed in it.

The following form of a Vote or Order of the house was then read, and referred to.—N. B. The Committee of Privileges passed it, with a few alterations, the day before the session ended.* Statute of 7 Hen. iv. was read, at the committee, viz. "The Election of Members to serve in Parliament, shall be freely and indifferently made, notwithstanding any prayer or commandment to the contrary."

Resolved, "That if any person, or persons, hereafter to be elected, in a place for to sit and serve in the house of commons, for any county, city, town, port, or borough, after the test, or issuing out the writ of election, upon the calling or summoning of any parliament hereafter, or after any such place becomes vacant hereafter, in the time of parliament, shall by himself, or any other in his behalf, or, at his charge, at any time, before the day of his election, give

* Grey.

any person or persons, having voice in any such elections, any meat or drink, exceeding in their true value 5*l.* in the whole, in any place or places, but in his own dwelling-house or habitation, being the usual place of his abode for twelve months last past, or shall, before such election be made and declared, make any other present, gift, or reward, or any promise, obligation, or engagement, to do the same, either to any such person or persons in particular, or to any such county, city, town, port, or borough, in general, or to, or for, the use of them, or any of them, every such entertainment, present, gift, reward, promise, obligation, or engagement, being truly proved, is and shall be a sufficient ground, cause, and matter to make every such election void, as to the person so offending, and to render the person so elected incapable to sit in parliament, by such election, and hereof the committee of elections and privileges is appointed to take especial notice and care, and to act and determine matters coming before them accordingly."

Debate on Sir E. Jennings, a Member, being made High Sheriff of the County of York.] Nov. 16. The house being informed, That sir Edmund Jennings, a Member of this house, is made High Sheriff of the County of York, a debate arose thereupon:

Sir *Nich. Carew.* If a Sheriff of a County plead privilege, he may obstruct the justice of that whole county, and no man can have remedy against him. Would have you vote, that it is a breach of privilege to be made a Sheriff, &c. thereby withdrawing his attendance from his service here.

Sir *Cha. Wheeler.* If there be a voluntary acceptance of the office, what breach of privilege is it? You have never exercised your authority against absent members. A hundred men of the house are away, and why you should fall upon one member, and not all the rest that are absent, knows no reason.

Mr. *Waller.* It is something to want half our knights of the shire. About 40 years ago there was made sheriff a great father of the law, sir Edw. Coke, because he should not help us here. One was made Sheriff,* and sat here, and was fined in the Star-Chamber for going out of his county: they cannot sit here because they cannot come out of their county. They may make the Speaker sheriff.

Sir *Rob. Carr.* He thinks the king has not broken your privilege, though possibly it is construed so without doors. Sheriffs have sat in parliament. If you make an address to the king for prevention of it for the future, he gives his consent.

Mr. *Sacheverell.* The law stands expressly, that the Sheriff is to be nominated, at such a time, in the exchequer. In the next place, all actions brought against a sheriff are personal, for the money he receives, and his executors are not liable to make account. A sheriff shall receive all monies upon executions, &c. and the parliament sits, he pleads his privilege, and cannot be brought to account. Would therefore address the king to supersede this writ, and vote this a breach of Privilege.

Mr. *Wilde.* There are three names sent to the king from the Exchequer, and he sets aside, and chuses, whom he pleases. Put the case that there should be a new parliament; a sheriff in one county may be chosen in another. But is seems, when it serves one turn, it is one thing, and then another: because this parliament has lasted 15 years, shall it continue 15 more? This parliament is made such a precedent, that we are like to have no more so long again.

Sir *Wm. Coventry* speaks out of no prejudice to this gentleman that is appointed sheriff for Yorkshire. Hears it said, 'that precedents, if there have been any, not taken notice of, do not fortify the right;' but, if at any time, would now make an end of them. Would now address only to claim our right, and no more. It is said, 'the gentleman is willing to accept the office,' and must we therefore give away our privilege? Fagg's case, he thought good in the lords house, and therefore he appeared there, but you sent him to the Tower for breach of your privilege. It is said often here, that we cannot give away the privilege of any man; the reason given, 'about executions &c.' convinces him. The king enters not into a nice disquisition of their being parliament men: if one be made, 50 may be made, and so 50 settled in the country, and he need not tell you how 50 votes would have carried things as they are not now carried. This of pricking members Sheriffs, and the letters sent to gentlemen, may tend all to the same end. So it concerns the parliament, that you leave not the gap open, to root up all your privileges. Whether the parliament be longer or shorter, there will be so many absent, Sheriffs—And when the parliament set to work about any thing, it is quickly done. From these considerations, moves that you will prevent this for the future, not barely by a petition, but your right annexed to it. If you address the king only by petition, it may possibly not be granted, and so your right be precluded for ever.

Mr. *Sawyer.* It is strange, at this time of the day, to declare this a breach of privilege; it has been practised in all times. Must all your members be turned off that are in such offices? Though they are bound to attend their offices, yet they are bound to attend the kingdom in the first place.

Mr. *Vaughan.* Sawyer argues very well, but his reasons must be well fortified to argue against privilege of parliament. But by being sheriff, a man must be in two places at one time, and you fine him here for his absence.

Sir *Ch. Harbord.* It is no breach of privilege at all, the thing has been usually done, and always so done. He thinks it true that no member can be absent without leave of the

* Mr. Walter Long, fined (5 Charles) burgess for Bath, and sheriff for Wilts.

house. Suppose the sheriff should put the king's money into his own purse, the consequence is, the king indicts the party. The king makes a man sheriff, and he is then chosen a parliament-man, and he cannot attend the business of the county to pay the money according to his writs—And persons escape—He thinks it a wise and a good counsel, that for the time to come this be not drawn into precedent, and to move the king so.

Mr. *Streete.* It is the resolution of the judges, that this law mentioned does not deprive the king of his sovereign power, but only eases him of the trouble and labour. The day after All-souls, the king may prick sheriffs without them. Queen Eliz. king James, and the late king, have pricked sheriffs. It was not the opinion of the house in the case of sir Edw. Coke. Look on your own books, and you will find, in that case, the opinion of the house 'that a Sheriff of one county may be elected to serve for another, and the sheriff of his county may be returned for a borough in the same county,' and some now sit so. It was never thought but a sheriff may be here, and it disables him not to attend his service. There are 4 of your members that have served, this parliament, for that county we now debate.

Sir *Tho. Meres.* Coke's case was nothing to this now in debate, and to clear that repeats the question—'Care of our Privileges.' The making a member of this house sheriff is a breach of the privilege of this house. This case comes not up to the other. This case is, the house sitting, to make a member sheriff of a county; and all that is said against it is, 'That we have some sit here that have been sheriffs of that county.' But if the thing has been once or twice done, and therefore must be a precedent, then, by the same reason, the lords may try your members, because it has been once or twice done. It is said, 'That it is as fit members should be sheriffs, as justices of the peace.' If that be the case, we may all be made sheriffs. If it be as equal to make us sheriffs as justices, perhaps 40 or 50 may be made sheriffs hereafter.

Sir *Winston Churchill* agrees to the inconvenience of it, but thinks it not a breach of privilege. Put the case that another man's cattle make a trespass upon him, and eat up his grass, but if the gaps or gates be left open, it is his fault. This is no trespass, but our fault. Before you vote it a breach of privilege, would be satisfied whether the king taking somewhat that is not his right—To prick a sheriff—If that be not the point, it has respect to your member only. In his case, he should think it hard and reflective that he only should be the man excepted. Not a Yorkshire gentleman has yet offered any thing against it.

Col. *Birch* is afraid to speak to you in this matter, lest, if any gentleman should say here we fly in the king's face, he may tell the king so. He can never believe that the same men were called up in three parliaments in Edw. iiid's time, (In H. iv's time lawyers were excluded.) But it is said, Why a breach of privilege at this time, and in this case, and never so before? He is apt to think that things have been done here that will never be done again. Such sums, he believes, any man would be laughed at, that should move for them again. Would do the thing easily: it cannot reflect upon the king, and is far from thinking on a minister of state.

Sir *George Downing.* This is a breach of privilege, and the party concerned makes no complaint. It is taken up by other gentlemen, and not the party concerned. You are going to vote, That making a member sheriff is a breach of privilege, and you never saw any thing to the contrary, but that he might, &c. There is no question yet stated. Some say, 'The king has broken the privilege,' without any farther ceremony. Shall not a committee first examine it? In far less things than this we go by steps. Let records be searched first. He will else never vote it. He will have his tongue out of his head before he will do it.

Sir *Henry Capel* rather would not have this gentleman made a precedent, but he thinks himself beholden to him for being the occasion of this debate. If the question be of privilege, he must give his vote for it.

Mr. *Bennet.* As to trespass spoken of, it is time now to mend the hedge, and shut up the gate. He hopes Jennings will not suffer so much by it, there will be found somebody to officiate it, and be to have the best share of the profits: and that we are so fond of him, we will not part with him.

Sir *Edward Dering.* Let the gentleman concerned look to that, before he takes the office upon him. The danger of making one sheriff that is a member, and the consequence of making many, is but a remote reason, and weighs not with him. We have had three or four members sheriffs of that county, and no complaint made of it. The deputy-sheriffs do give security for performance of the office. In all cases, would have the king treated with all reverence, and in this most tenderly: would, therefore, only address the king, 'That, for the future, no Member of the house be made Sheriff.'"

Sir *Tho. Littleton.* By this means we strike off half our privileges; for writs of privilege a man can only have when the suit is begun. It is moved to temper the business: is sorry for the member concerned, for whom he has a respect; but, if you proceed no farther than an Address to the king, 'That it shall be so no more for the future,' you give up the cause. For he has observed, that when a thing has been voted to be no precedent, for the future, it proves often to be a precedent to do the same thing again.

Sir *Henry Goodrick* hears it said, 'that few, or none, of Jennings's countrymen are concerned in this matter.' Though he has been silent in the thing out of modesty, is concerned as a reflection on his person, and reputation, which he would have so saved, as that the house may attain their end—We all conclude for proceeding, by way of Address to the king, and would have it in as home terms as you can invent. Pricking of members sheriffs, you find an encroachment on privilege: moves therefore that the Address to the king be 'not to prick any Member that serves for county, city, or borough.'

The *Speaker*, upon some disorder said, If any man have a privilege to be disorderly, let me know it. Then he proposed the question, viz. "That it is a breach of Privilege for any Member to be made Sheriff, &c. during continuance of parliament."

Mr. *Sacheverell* moves that the lord keeper be sent to, to supersede Jennings's commission of sheriff.

The main question was then put, and passed, 157 to 101. And a Committee was appointed to consider of a proper way of superseding the Commission, and discharging the Sheriff from his office.

The Duke of Buckingham's Speech for a Toleration.] About this time the unusual activity of the Papists, and the discoveries which had been made by Coleman's Letters, gave the hint to both houses to be more moderate in their proceedings with respect to Protestant Dissenters.—In that of the Lords, especially,

The Duke of *Buckingham* thus expressed himself in favour of a Toleration: "My lords; There is a thing called liberty, which (whatsoever some men may think) is, that the people of England are fondest of; it is that they will never part with; and is that his majesty in his Speech has promised us to take a particular care of. This, my lords, in my opinion, can never be done without giving an Indulgence to all Protestant Dissenters. It is certainly a very uneasy kind of life to any man, that has either Christian charity, humanity, or good-nature, to see his fellow-subjects daily abused, divested of their liberties and birth-rights, and miserably thrown out of their possessions and freeholds, only because they cannot agree with others in some opinions and niceties of religion, which their consciences will not give them leave to consent to; and which, even by the confession of those who would impose upon them, are no ways necessary to salvation. But, my lords, besides this, and all that may be said upon it, in order to the improvement of our trade, and increase of the wealth, strength, and greatness of this nation, (which, with your leave, I shall presume to discourse of some other time) there is, methinks, in this notion of persecution a very gross mistake, both as to the point of government, and the point of Religion. There is so as to the point of Government, because it makes every man's safety depend on the wrong place; not upon governors, or a man's living well towards the civil government established by law, but upon his being transported with zeal for every opinion, that is held by those that have power in the Church that is in fashion; and I conceive it is a mistake in Religion, because it is positively against the express doctrine and example of Jesus Christ. Nay, my lords, as to our Protestant Religion, there is something in it yet worse; for we protestants maintain, that none of those opinions, which Christians differ about, are infallible; and therefore it is in us somewhat an inexcusable conception, that men ought to be deprived of their inheritance, and all the certain conveniences and advantages of life, because they will not agree with us in our uncertain opinions of religion. My humble motion therefore to your lordships, is, that you would give leave to bring in a Bill of Indulgence to all Protestant Dissenters. I know very well that every peer of this realm hath a right to bring into parliament any bill he conceives to be useful to this nation: but I thought it more respectful to your lordships to ask your leave before; but I cannot think the doing of it will be any prejudice to the bill, because I am confident the reason, the prudence, and the charitableness of it, will be able to justify it to this house, and the whole world." Accordingly, the house gave his grace leave to bring in a Bill to that purpose.

Dispute between the two Houses on Dr. Shirley's Appeal, revived.] But while this, and several other Bills were depending, the unfortunate Contest was revived between the two houses, concerning Dr. Shirley and sir John Fagg,* the former having continued his process against the latter; and the lords themselves adhered to their first hearing of his appeal. Upon which the commons proceeded as follows:

Nov. 13. An Order from the lords to hear sir John Fagg's Cause to-morrow morning, was this day read in the commons and debated, and the farther debate thereof adjourned till Monday.

Nov. 15. The house resolved, That the prosecuting Appeals in the lords house, by Dr. Shirley against sir John Fagg, a member of this house, is a Breach of the Privileges of this house; and that the said sir John Fagg do not make any defence at the lords bar, in the said Appeal; and the farther debate thereof was adjourned till to-morrow morning.

Nov. 18. Sir John Fagg's business was resumed, and it was resolved that a Conference be desired of the lords for avoiding Differences between the two houses.

* "Some thought that the king had consented to the renewal of this Appeal-dispute, as disliking the warm proceedings of both houses; of which opinion was Marvell. Others believed that the lords of the country interest had persuaded the doctor thereto, with a view thereby to kindle such a flame between the two houses, as should oblige the king either to prorogue or dissolve them; the said lords apprehending that if this parliament should sit much longer, the majority might be gained over by places and money, so as to become quite obsequious to the court; and this, Savile lord Halifax, then in the interest of lord Shaftsbury, his uncle, told sir John Reresby was his opinion." Ralph.

Nov. 19. Sir Wm. Coventry reports from the Committee, to whom it was referred, to prepare and draw up Reasons to be offered at the conference to be desired with the lords, for avoiding the occasions of reviving the Differences between the two houses; and a Paper of Reasons agreed by the said committee to be reported to the house, being read, and the same agreed to, is as followeth:—"His majesty having recommended to us, at the opening of this session, the avoiding this Difference, if possible; and if it could not be prevented, that then we should defer these debates till we had brought such public Bills to perfection, as may conduce to the good and safety of the kingdom: the commons esteem it a great misfortune, that, contrary to that most excellent advice, the proceedings in the Appeal, brought the last session against sir John Fagg, by Mr. Shirley, have been renewed, and a day set for hearing the Cause; and therefore the commons have judged it the best way, before they enter into the argument of defence of their rights in this matter, to propose to your lordships, the putting off the proceedings in that matter for some short time; that so they may according to his majesty's advice, give a dispatch to some Bills now before them, of great Importance to the king and kingdom; which being finished, the commons will be ready to give your lordships such Reasons against those proceedings, and in defence of their rights, as we hope may satisfy your lordships, that no such proceedings ought to have been."

Resolved, "That a Message be sent to the lords, to desire a Conference, to preserve the good correspondence between the two houses."

Resolved "That whosoever shall prosecute any Appeal before the lords, against any commoner of England, from any court of equity, shall be deemed a betrayer of the rights and privileges of the commons of England; and shall be proceeded against accordingly: and the Resolution ordered to be affixed in the lobby, Westminster-Hall-gate, and all Inns of Court and Chancery."

Nov. 20. Ordered, "That Dr. Shirley be taken into custody by the serjeant at arms attending this house, as also sir Nich. Stanton, for serving Mr. Onslow with an Order to attend the lords;" and then the house adjourned to the 22nd.

Lord Shaftsbury's remarkable Speech thereon.] The proceedings of the commons on this occasion threw the lords into a flame. Upon the debate for appointing a day for the hearing Dr. Shirley's Cause, among many other warm speeches,

The Earl of *Shaftsbury* expressed himself as follows: "My lords; Our all is at stake, and therefore you must give me leave to speak freely before we part with it. My lord bishop of Salisbury is of opinion, 'That we should rather appoint a day to consider what to do upon the petition, than to appoint a day of hearing;' and my lord keeper, for I may name them at a committee of the whole house, tells us in very eloquent and studied language, 'That he will propose us a way, far less liable to exception, and much less offensive and injurious to our own privileges, than that of appointing a day of hearing.' And I beseech your lordships, did you not, after all these fine words, expect some admirable proposal? but it ended in this, 'That your lordships should appoint a day, nay, a very long day, to consider what you would do in it:' and my lord hath undertaken to convince you, that this is your only course by several undeniable reasons; the first of which is, 'That it is against your judicature to have this Cause, which is not proper, before us, nor ought to be relieved by us.' To this, my lords, give me leave to answer, that I did not expect from a man professing the law, that after an Answer by order of the court was put in, and a day had been appointed for hearing, which by some accident was set aside; and the plaintiff moving for a second day to be assigned, that ever, without hearing council on both sides, the court did enter into the merits of the cause. And if your lordships should do it here, in a case attended with the circumstances this is, it would not only be an apparent injustice, but a plain subterfuge, to avoid a point you durst not maintain.—But my lord's second reason speaks the matter more clearly; for that is, 'Because it is a doubtful case, whether the commons have not privilege,' and therefore my lord would have you 'to appoint a farther, and very long day to consider of it:' which in plain English is, that you conceive it on second thoughts a doubtful case; for so your appointing a day to consider will do; and that for no other reason, but because my lord keeper thinks it so; which, I hope, will not be a reason to prevail with your lordships; since we cannot yet, by experience, tell that his lordship is capable of thinking your lordships in the right, in any manner against the judgment of the house of commons, it is so hard a thing, even for the ablest of men, to change ill habits.—But my lord's third reason is the most admirable of all, which he stiles unanswerable; viz. 'That your lordships are all convinced in your own consciences, that this (if prosecuted) will cause a breach.' I beseech your lordships, consider whether this argument, thus applied, would not overthrow the law of nature, and all the laws of property and right in the world: for it is an argument, and a very good one, that you should not stand or insist on claims, where you have not a clear right, or where the question is not of consequence and moment, in a matter that may produce a dangerous, and pernicious breach, between relations, persons, or bodies politic, joined in interest and high concerns together. So, on the other hand, if the obstinacy of the party in the wrong shall be made an unanswerable argument for the other party to recede, and give up his just rights, how long shall the people keep their liberties or the princes or governors of the world their prerogatives? How long shall the husband maintain his dominion, or any man his property, from his friends or his neighbours obstinacy? But, my lords, when I hear my lord keeper open so eloquently the fatal consequences of a breach, I cannot forbear to fall into some admiration how it comes to pass, that (if the consequences be so fatal) the king's ministers in the house of commons, of which there are several that are of the Cabinet, and, have daily resort to his majesty, and have the direction and trust of his affairs; I say, that none of these should press these consequences there, or give the least stop to the career of that house in this business; but that all the Votes concerning this affair, nay, even that very Vote, 'That no Appeal from any court of equity is cognizable by the house of lords,' should pass nem. con. And yet all the great ministers with us here, the bishops and other lords of greatest dependance on the court, contend this point, as if it were *pro aris & focis*. I hear his maj. in Scotland hath been pleased to declare against Appeals in parliament: I cannot much blame the court, if they think (the lord-keeper and the judges being of the king's naming, and in his power to change) that the justice of the nation is safe enough; and I, my lords, may think so too, during this king's time, though I hear Scotland, not without reason, complains already. Yet how future princes may use this power, and how judges may be made out of men of ability or integrity, but men of relation and dependance, and who will do what they are commanded; and all men's causes come to be judged, and estates disposed on, as great men at court please.—My Lords, the constitution of our government hath provided better for us; and I can never believe so wise a body as the house of commons will prove that foolish woman, who plucks down her house with her hands.—My Lords, I must presume in the next place to say something to what was offered by my lord bishop of Salisbury, a man of great learning and abilities, and always versed in a stronger and closer way of reasoning, than the business of that noble lord I answered before did accustom him to; and that rev. prelate had stated the matter very fair upon two heads. The 1st, 'Whether the hearing of Causes and Appeals, and, especially in this point where the members have privilege, be so material to us, that it ought not to give way to the reason of state, of greater affairs that pressed us at that time?' The 2nd was, 'If this business be of that moment, yet whether the appointing a day to consider of this petition would prove of that consequence and prejudice to your cause?'—My Lords, to these give me leave in the first place to say, that this matter is no less than your whole judicature; and your judicature is the life and soul of the dignity of the peerage in England; you will quickly grow burthensome, if you grow useless; you have now the greatest and most useful end of parliaments principally in you, which is not to make new laws, but to redress grievances, and to maintain the old land marks. The h. of commons business is to complain, your lordships to redress, not only the complaints from them, that are the eyes of the nation, but all other particular persons that address to you. A land may groan under a multitude of laws, and I believe ours does; and when laws grow so multiplied, they prove oftener snares than directions and security to the people. I look upon it as the ignorance and weakness of the latter age, if not worse, the effect of the designs of ill men, that it is grown a general opinion, that where there is not a particular direction in some act of parliament, the law is defective; as if the common law had not provided much better, shorter, and plainer for the peace and quiet of the nation, than intricate, long, perplexed statutes do; which has made work for the lawyers, given power to the judges, lessened your lordship's power, and in a good measure unhinged the security of the people.—My lord bishop tells us, 'That your whole judicature is not in question, but only the privilege of the house of commons, of their members not appearing at your bar:' My lords, were it no more, yet that, for justice and the people's sake, you ought not to part with: how far a privilege of the house of commons, their servants, and those they own, doth extend, Westminster-Hall may with grief tell your lordships. And the same privilege of their members being not sued, must be allowed by your lordships as well; and what a failure of justice this would prove, whilst they are lords for life, and you for inheritance, let the world judge: for my part, I am willing to come to a Conference, whenever the dispute shall begin again; and dare undertake to your lordships, that they have neither precedent, reason, nor any justifiable pretence to shew against us; and therefore, my lords, if you part with this undoubted right merely for asking, where will the asking stop? And, my lords, we are sure it doth not stop here, for they have already, nem. con. voted against your lordships power of Appeals from any court of equity: so that you may plainly see where this caution and reason of state means to stop; not one jot short of laying your whole judicature aside; for the same reason of passing the king's money, of not interrupting good laws, and whatever else, must of necessity avoid all breach upon what score soever: thus your lordships plainly see the Breach will be as well made upon your judicature in general, as upon this; so that when your lordships have appointed a day, a very long day, for to consider whether Dr. Shirley's Cause be not too hot to handle; and when you have done the same for sir Nich. Stanton, whose Petition I hear is coming in, your lordships must proceed to a Vote, to lay all private business aside for 6 weeks; for that phrase of private business hath obtained upon this last age, upon that which is your most public duty and business, namely, the administration of justice. And I can tell your lordships, besides the reason that leads to it, that I have some intelligence of the designing such a Vote; for on the second day of your sitting, at the rising of the lords house, there came a gentleman into the lobby, belonging to a very great person, and asked in very great haste, 'Are the lords up? Have they passed the Vote?' And being asked, 'What Vote?' He answered, The Vote of no private business for 6 weeks.'—My Lords, if this be your business, see where you are; if we are to postpone our judicature, for fear of offending the h. of commons, for 6 weeks, that they, in the interim, may pass the Money, and other acceptable Bills that his maj. thinks of importance. Are so many wise men in the h. of commons to be laid asleep, and to pass all these acceptable things; and when they have done, to let us be let loose upon them?—Will they not remember this, next time there is want of Money? Or may not they rather be assured by those ministers that are amongst them, and go on so unanimously with them, that the king is on their side in this controversy? And when the public businesses are over, our time will be too short to make a breach, or vindicate ourselves in the matter. And then I beg your lordships, where are you, if after you have asserted but the last session your Right of Judicature, so highly, even in this point; and after the h. of commons had gone so high against you on the other hand, as to post up their Declaration and Remonstrances on Westminster-Hall doors; the very next session after you postpone the very same causes; and not only those, but all judicatures whatsoever? I beseech your lordships, will not this prove a fatal precedent and confession against yourselves? It is a maxim, and a rational one amongst the lawyers, 'That one precedent where the case hath been contested, is worth a thousand where there hath been no contest.' My lords, in saying this, I humbly suppose I have given a sufficient answer to my lord bishop's second question; 'Whether the appointing a day to consider what you will do with this Petition, be of that consequence to your right?' For it is a plain confession, that it is a doubtful case, and that infinitely stronger than if it were a new thing to you, never heard of before; for it is the very same case, and the very same thing desired in that case, that you formerly ordered, and so strongly asserted; so that, upon time, and all the deliberation imaginable, you declare yourselves to become doubtful, and you put yourselves out of your own hands, into that power that you have no reason to believe on your side in this question.—My Lords, I have all the duty imaginable to his majesty, and shall with all submission, give way to any thing he should think of importance to his affairs: but in this point it is to alter the constitution of the government, if you are asked to lay this aside; and there is no reason of state can be an argument to your lordships to turn yourselves out of that interest you have in the constitution of the government; it is not only your concern that you maintain yourselves in it, but it is the concern of the poorest man in England, that you keep your station; it is your lordships concern, and that so highly, that I will be bold to say, the king can give none of you a requital or recompence for it. What are empty titles? What is present power, or riches, and a great estate, wherein I have no firm or fixed property? It is the constitution of the government, and maintaining it, that secures your lordships and every man else in what he hath; the poorest lord, if birthright of the peerage be maintained, has a fair prospect before him for himself or his posterity; but the greatest title, with the greatest present power and riches, is but a mean creature, and maintains those in absolute monarchies no otherwise than by servile and low flatteries, and upon uncertain terms.—My Lords, it is not only your interest, but the interest of the nation, that you maintain your rights; for let the h. of commons and gentry of England think what they please, there is no prince that ever governed without nobility or an army; if you will not have one, you must have the other, or the monarchy cannot long support, or keep itself from tumbling into a democratical republic. Your lordships and the people have the same cause, and the same enemies. My lords, would you be in favour with the king? it is a very ill way to it, to put yourselves out of a future capacity, to be considerable in his service: I do not find in story, or in modern experience, but that it is better, and a man is much more regarded, that is still in a capacity and opportunity to serve, than he that hath wholly deprived himself of all for his prince's service. And I therefore declare, that I will serve my prince as a peer, but will not destroy the peerage to serve him.—My Lords, I have heard of twenty foolish models and expedients to secure the justice of the nation, and yet to take this right from your lordships, as the king by his commission appointing commoners to hear Appeals; or that the 12 judges should be the persons, or that persons should be appointed by act of parliament, which are all not only to take away your lordships just right, that ought not to be altered any more than any other part of the government, but are in themselves, when well weighed, ridiculous: I must deal freely with your lordships, these things could never have risen in men's minds, but that there has been some kind of provocation that has given the first rise to it. Pray, my lords, forgive me, if on this occasion I put you in mind of Committee Dinners, and the scandal of it, those droves of ladies that attended all causes; it was come to that pass, that men even hired, or borrowed of their friends, handsome sisters or daughters to deliver their Petitions: but yet for all this, I must say, that your judgments have been sacred unless in one or two Causes; and those we owe most to that bench from whence we now apprehend the most danger.—There is one thing I had almost forgot to speak to, 'which is the conjecture of time, the hinge upon which our reason of state turns;' and to that, my lords, give me leave to say, if this be not a time of leisure for you to vindicate your privileges, you must never expect one. I could almost say, that the harmony, good agreement, and accord that is to be prayed for at most other times, may be fatal to us now; we owe the peace of these last two years, and the disengagement from the French interest, to the two houses differing from the sense and opinion of Whitehall, so at this time the thing in the world this nation hath most reason to apprehend is a general peace, which cannot now happen without very advantageous terms to the French, and disadvantageous to the house of Austria. We are the king's great counsellors, and if so, have right to differ, and give contrary counsels to those few that are nearest about him: I fear they would advance a general peace, I am sure I would advise against it, and hinder it at this time by all the ways imaginable. I heartily wish, nothing from you may add weight and reputation to those councils, which would assist the French. No money for Ships, nor preparations you can make, nor personal assurances our prince can have, can secure us from the French, if they are at leisure. He is grown the most potent of us all at sea: he has built 24 ships this last year, and has 30 more in number than we; besides the advantage, that our ships are all out of order, and his so exquisitely provided for, that every ship has its particular storehouse. It is incredible the money he hath, and is bestowing in making harbours; he makes nature itself give way to the vastness of his expence; and, after all this, shall a prince so wise, so intent upon his affairs, be thought to make all these preparations to sail over land, and fall on the back of Hungary, and batter the walls of Kaminitz? or is it possible he should oversee his interest in seizing of Ireland, a thing so feasible to him, if he be master of the seas, as he certainly now is; and which, when attained, gives him all the Southern, Mediterranean, East and West India trade, and renders him, both by situation, and excellent harbours, perpetual master of the seas, without dispute?—My Lords, to conclude this point, I fear the court of England is greatly mistaken in it, and I do not wish them the reputation of the concurrence of the kingdom; and this out of the most sincere loyalty to his majesty, and love to my nation.—My Lords, I have but one thing more to trouble you with, and that, peradventure, is a consideration of the greatest weight and concern, both to your lordships, and the whole nation. I have often seen in this house, that the arguments with strongest reason, and most convincing to the lay-lords in general, have not had the same effect upon the bishop's bench; but that they have unanimously gone against us in matters, that many of us have thought essential and undoubted rights: and I consider, that it is not possible, that men of great learning, piety, and reason, as their lordships are, should not have the same care of doing right, and the same conviction of what is right, upon clear reason offered, that other your lordships have. And therefore, my lords, I must necessarily think we differ in principles, and then it is very easy to apprehend, what is the clearest sense to men of my principles, may not at all persuade or affect the conscience of the best men of a different one. I put your lordships the case plainly as it is now before us. My principle is, 'That the king is king by law, and by the same law that the poor man enjoys his cottage;' and so it becomes the concern of every man in England, that has but his liberty, to maintain and defend, to his utmost, the king in all his rights and prerogatives. My principle is also, 'That the lords house, and the judicature and rights belonging to it, are an essential part of the government, and established by the same law:' the king governing and administering justice by his house of lords, and advising with both his houses of parliament in all important matters, is the government I own, am born under, and am obliged to. If ever there should happen in future ages (which, God forbid) a king governing by an army, without his parliament, it is a government I own not, am not obliged to, nor was born under. According to this principle, every honest man that holds it, must endeavour equally to preserve the frame of the government, in all the parts of it, and cannot satisfy his conscience to give up the lords house for the service of the crown, or to take away the just rights and privileges of the house of commons, to please the lords. But there is another principle got into the world, my lords, that hath not been long there; for abp. Laud was the first author that I remember of it; and I cannot find that the Jesuits, or indeed the Popish clergy have ever owned it, but some of the episcopal clergy of our British Isles; and withal, as it is new, so it is the most dangerous, destructive doctrine to our government and law, that ever was. It is the first of the Canons published by the Convocation, 1640, 'That Monarchy is of divine Right.' This doctrine was then preached up, and maintained by Sibthorp, Manwaring, and others, and of later years, by a Book published by Dr. Sanderson, bishop of Lincoln, under the name of abp. Usher; and how much it is spread amongst our dignified clergy, is very easily known. We all agree, that the king and his government is to be obeyed for conscience sake; and that the divine precepts require, not only here, but in all parts of the world, obedience to lawful governors. But that this family are our kings, and this particular frame of government is our lawful constitution, and obliges us, is owing only to the particular laws of our country. This Laudean doctrine was the root that produced the Bill of Test, last session; and some very perplexed Oaths, that are of the same nature with that, and yet imposed by several acts this parliament.—In a word, if this doctrine be true, our Magna Charta is of no use, our laws are but rules amongst ourselves during the king's pleasure. Monarchy, if of Divine Right, cannot be bounded or limited by human laws; nay, what is more, cannot bind itself: and all our claims of Right by the law, or constitution of the government, all the jurisdiction and privilege of this house, all the rights and privileges of the house of commons, all the properties and liberties of the people, are to give way not only to the interest, but the will and pleasure of the crown. And the best and worthiest of men, holding this principle, must vote to deliver up all we have, not only when reasons of state and the separate interest of the crown require it, but when the will and pleasure of the king is known, and would have it so. For that must be, to a man of that principle, the only rule and measure of right and justice. Therefore, my lords, you see how necessary it is, that all our principles be known; and how fatal to us all it is, that this principle should be suffered to spread any farther.—My Lords, to conclude, your lordships have seen of what consequence this matter is to you, and that the appointing a day to consider, is no less than declaring yourselves doubtful, upon second and deliberate thoughts, that you put yourselves out of your own hands, into more than a moral probability of having this session made a precedent against you. You see your duty to yourselves and the people; and that it is really not the interest of the house of commons, but may be the inclination of the court, that you lose the power of Appeals: but I beg our house may not be *felo de se*, but that your lordships would take in this affair, the only course to preserve yourselves, and appoint a day, this day three weeks, for the hearing Dr. Shirley's Cause, which is my humble motion."

Protest on appointing a day for hearing Dr. Shirley's Cause.] The debate being over, and the house being resumed, the question was put, Whether the 20th of Nov. shall be the day appointed for the hearing of the Cause between Dr. Shirley and sir John Fagg? It was resolved in the Affirmative.—Before the putting the said question, leave being demanded and given to such lords as thought fit (if the same were carried in the affirmative) to enter their Protestation and Dissent; accordingly this Protestation is entered against the said Vote, for the Reasons following:

1. "Because it seems contrary to the use and practice of this high court (which gives example to all other courts) upon a bare Petition of the plaintiff Dr. Shirley, in a cause depending last session, and discontinued by prorogation, to appoint a day for hearing of the cause before the defendant is so much as summoned, or appears in Court, or to be alive. 2. The defendant, by the rules of this court, having liberty upon summons to make a new Answer, as sir Jeremy Whitchcott was admitted, after summons, to do last session in Darrel's Cause against him, discontinued by prorogation, or to mend his Answer, or to plead, as he shall see cause, is deprived of this and other benefits of law, by appointing a day of hearing without these essential forms. 3. It appears, by the plaintiff's own shewing in his Petition, that his case against a purchaser is not relievable in equity; and therefore ought to be dismissed without putting the parties to a further charge. 4. It appears, by his own shewing, and the defendant sir John Fagg's Plea, that he comes hither *per saltum*, and ought to attend judgment in the inferior courts, if his case is relievable, and not to appeal to the highest court, till either injustice is done him below, or erroneous judgment given against him, and relief denied him upon review. 5. The danger of this precedent is so universal, that it shakes all the purchasers of England. ANGLESEA."

Nov. 20. Dr. Shirley appeared at the bar of the house of lords, and his council, Mr. Wallop, appearing, who would have excused himself, but was ordered to appear again on Monday morning next, to plead the Cause; and the other two council (one being in the country, and the other sick) were excused: and the said Dr. Shirley, sir Nich. Stanton, and Mr. Wallop, were ordered to have the protection of the house: and upon debate of the commons Vote made yesterday, it was Ordered, "That the Paper posted up in several places, signed by William Goldsbro, Cler. Dom. Com. against the Judicature of the house of peers, in Cases of Appeals from Courts of Equity, is illegal, unparliamentary, and tending to the dissolution of the government."

Debate in the House of Lords on a Motion for an Address to the King to dissolve the Parliament.] Upon consideration of the said Vote of the commons, it was proposed by lord Mohun, to Address his majesty to dissolve the Parliament. This gave rise to a vehement debate,* "in the course of which," says Mr. Ralph, "all imaginable arguments, that could either influence court or country, were made use of to procure an affirmative: the king was flattered with the hopes, or rather bribed with the promise, of a large sum to pay his Debts: and the Church received the warmest assurances, that, though Protestant Dissenters should find some favour and ease, her lands and dignities would be safe: and, on the popular side of the question, the conduct of the present house of commons was exposed with as much severity, as if the nation had not one true representative. From the length of time which the purse of the people had been in their hands, and the free use they had made of it, it was urged, that they were become 'more than lords.' They were charged with having violated the ancient rules of parliament, by not admitting the right of the lords to

* In the APPENDIX to the present volume, No. VII, will be found a curious Tract written by the Earl of Shaftsbury, entitled "The Debate or Arguments for Dissolving this present Parliament and the calling frequent and new Parliaments. As they were delivered in the House of Lords, Nov. 20, 1675."

reduce their grants. They were reproached for having several times rejected, with scorn, a Bill for the more fair and equal Trial of the Peers. It was said, seriously, that they had never met without exciting the greatest apprehensions in all sober and wise men, and ironically, that it was owing to the goodness of the prince, and the virtue of the members, that honours, offices, pensions, money, employments and gifts, had not been bestowed and accepted as a consideration for reducing the government to the model of France, Denmark, &c. where the will and pleasure of the prince had taken place of the laws. It was added, 'How easily this may be done in future ages, under such princes, and such an house of commons as may happen, if 'long and continued parliaments,' be allowed for law, may be made some measure of judging by this; where, though the prince had no design, and the members of the house of commons have shewed so great candour and self-denial, yet the best observers are apt to think, that we owe it to the strong and opposite factions at court, that many things of great alterations have not passed.—It was also observed, that in former times when parliaments were short and frequent, the members constantly received their Wages, both from their counties and boroughs; many of the poorer boroughs petitioned to be excused from sending members, as not being able to bear their charge, and were so: laws were made in favour of the gentry, that corporations should *compel* none but the freemen of their own town to serve for them; nay, that in all the ancient returns of writs for knights of the shires, their sureties for their appearance were returned with them. But that now the case was so altered, that 1500*l.* and 2000*l.* and lately 7000*l.* was a price that men paid to be *entrusted.* That it was to be hoped the charity of those worthy persons, and their zeal for the public interest, had induced them to be at this expence: but that it were better to be otherwise, there being a scurvy English Proverb, 'That men that buy dear, cannot live by selling cheap."—The debate continued till 8 o'clock, when it passed in the negative by two voices. Content, 48; not content, 50. At the head of the lords who were for the Address, appeared the duke of York, who by his conduct on this occasion has given much credit to the Politics in Mr. Coleman's Historical Letter to Father le Chaise. His royal highness, however, was not followed by the whole body of Catholic peers; for some of them divided against him, and in particular, the celebrated earl of Bristol, so often mentioned in the beginning of this reign. The Lists on this division were remarkable in several respects, but in nothing more, than to see the names of Buckingham, Shaftsbury, Essex, Wharton, Holles, Townsend, &c. follow in train, after that of the presumptive heir, whom they so soon after, with so much violence, endeavoured to set aside.—But though they joined in the measure, it was with very different views: the Duke wanted to get rid of this house of commons, because of their zeal against the catholics; and in hope, that, by a confederacy with the other nonconformists, such a change might be made in the representative part of the legislature, as might pave the way for a general toleration: the rest, because the two parties approached too near an equality; because the condescensions of the king, or the practices of his ministers, might, in a day's time, take the game out of their hands, and put the lurch upon them.

Protest against rejecting the Address for dissolving the Parliament.] Upon the rejection of this Address, the following Protest was entered:

"We whose names are underwritten, peers of this realm, having proposed that an humble Address might be made to his majesty from this house, That he would be graciously pleased to dissolve this parliament; and the house having carried the Vote in the negative: for the justification of our loyal intentions towards his majesty's service, and of our true respect and deference to this hon. house, and to shew that we have no sinister or indirect ends in this our humble proposal, do with all humility herein set forth the Grounds and Reasons why we were of opinion that the said humble Address should have been made: 1. We do humbly conceive, that it is according to the ancient laws and statutes of this realm, that there should be frequent and new parliaments; and that the practice of several hundred years hath been accordingly. 2. It seems not reasonable, that any particular number of men should for many years engross so great a trust of the people, as to be their representatives in the house of commons; and that all other the gentry and the members of corporations of the same degree and quality with them should be so long excluded: neither, as we humbly conceive, is it advantageous to the government, that the counties, cities, and boroughs, should be confined for so long a time to such members as they have once chosen to serve for them; the mutual correspondence and interest of those who choose and are chosen admitting great variations in length of time. 3. The long continuance of any such as are intrusted for others, and who have so great a power over the purse of the nation, must, in our humble opinion, naturally endanger the producing of Factions and Parties, and the carrying on of particular interests and designs, rather than the public good.—And we are the more confirmed in our desires for the said humble Address, by reason of this unhappy Breach fallen out betwixt the two houses, of which the house of peers hath not given the least occasion; they having done nothing but what their ancestors and predecessors have in all times done, and what is according to their duty, and for the interest of the people, that they should do; which notwithstanding, the house of commons have proceeded in such an unprecedented and extraordinary way, that it is in our humble opinion become altogether impracticable for the two houses, as the case stands, jointly to pursue those great and good ends for which they were called. For these Reasons, we do enter this our Protestation against, and Dissent unto, the said Vote: Buckingham, Shaftsbury, Dorset, Newport, Westmoreland, P. Wharton, Delamer, Grey de Rollestone, Salisbury, Mohun, Stamford, H. Sandys, Howard E. of Berks, Clarendon, Townshend, J. Bridgewater, F. Fauconberg, Halifax, Winchester, Yarmouth, Chesterfield, William Petre."

The Parliament prorogued for 15 Months.] The above were all the lords who were in the house early enough to set their names, before the king came to prorogue the parliament; which he did to the 15th of February twelvemonth.

Principal Occurrences during the long Recess—Coffee Houses suppressed by Proclamation—Congress of Nimeguen—Campaign of 1676—Uncertain Conduct of the King.] "Soon after the prorogation," says Mr. Hume, "there passed an incident, which in itself is trivial, but tends strongly to mark the genius of the English government, and of Charles's administration, during this period. The liberty of the constitution, and the variety as well as violence of the parties, had begotten a propensity for political conversation; and as the Coffee-Houses in particular were the scenes, where the conduct of the king and the ministry was canvassed with great freedom, a proclamation was issued to suppress these places of rendezvous. Such an act of power, during former reigns, would have been grounded entirely on the prerogative; and before the accession of the house of Stuart, no scruple would have been entertained with regard to that exercise of authority. But Charles, finding doubts to arise upon this proclamation, had recourse to the judges, who supplied him with a chicane, and that too a frivolous one, by which he might justify his proceedings. The law, which settled the excise, enacted, that licenses for retailing liquors might be refused to such as could not find security for payment of the duties. But coffee was not a liquor subjected to excise; and even this power of refusing licenses was very limited, and could not reasonably be extended beyond the intention of the act. The king therefore, observing the people to be much dissatisfied, yielded to a petition of the coffee-men, who promised for the future to restrain all seditious discourse in their houses; and the proclamation was recalled.—This campaign proved more fortunate to the confederates than any other during the whole war. The French took the field in Flanders with a numerous army; and Lewis himself served as a volunteer under the prince of Condé. But notwithstanding his great preparations, he could gain no advantages but the taking of Huy and Limbourg, places of small consequence. The prince of Orange, with a considerable army, opposed him in all his motions; and neither side was willing, without a visible advantage, to hazard a general action, which might be attended either with the entire loss of Flanders on one hand, or the invasion of France on the other. Lewis, tired of so unactive a campaign, returned to Versailles; and the whole summer passed in the Low Countries without any memorable event.—The French, who, twelve years before, had scarcely a ship of war in any of their harbours, had raised themselves, by means of perseverance and policy, to be, in their present force, though not in their resources, the first maritime power in Europe. The Dutch, while in alliance with them against England, had supplied them with several vessels, and had taught them the rudiments of the difficult art of ship-building. The English next, when in alliance with them against Holland, instructed them in the method of fighting their ships, and of preserving order in naval engagements. Lewis availed himself of every opportunity to aggrandize his people, while Charles, sunk in indolence and pleasure, neglected all the noble arts of government; or if at any time he roused himself from his lethargy, that industry, by reason of the unhappy projects which he embraced, was often more pernicious to the public than his inactivity itself. He was as anxious to promote the naval power of France, as if the safety of his crown had depended on it; and many of the plans executed in that kingdom, were first, it is said, digested and corrected by him.—The successes of the allies had been considerable the last campaign; but the Spaniards and Imperialists well knew, that France was not yet sufficiently broken, nor willing to submit to the terms which they resolved to impose upon her. Though they could not refuse the king's mediation, and Nimeguen, after many difficulties, was at last fixed on as the place of congress; yet, under one pretence or other, they still delayed sending their ambassadors, and no progress was made in the negotiation. Lord Berkely, sir Wm. Temple, and sir Lionel Jenkins, were the English ministers at Nimeguen. The Dutch, who were impatient for peace, soon appeared: Lewis, who hoped to divide the allies, and who knew that he himself could neither be seduced nor forced into a disadvantageous peace, sent ambassadors: the Swedes, who hoped to recover by treaty what they had lost by arms, were also forward to negotiate. But as these powers could not proceed of themselves to settle terms, the congress, hitherto, served merely as an amusement to the public.—It was by the events of the campaign, not the conferences among the negotiators, that the articles of peace were to be determined. The Spanish towns, ill fortified and worse defended, made but a feeble resistance to Lewis; who, by laying up magazines during the winter, was able to take the field early in the spring, before the forage could be found in the open country. In the month of April he laid siege to Condé, and took it by storm in four days. Having sent the duke of Orleans to besiege Bouchaine, a small but important fortress, he posted himself so advantageously with his main army, as to hinder the confederates from relieving it, or fighting without disadvantage. The prince of Orange, in spite of the difficulties of the season, and the want of provisions, came in sight of the French army; but his industry served to no other purpose than to render him spectator of the surrender of Bouchaine. Both armies stood in awe of each other, and were unwilling to hazard an action, which might be attended with the most important consequences. Lewis, though he wanted not personal courage, was little enterprising in the field; and being resolved this campaign to rest contented with the advantages which he had so early obtained, he thought proper to intrust his army to mareschal Schomberg, and retired himself to Versailles. After his departure, the prince of Orange laid siege to Maestricht; but meeting with an obstinate resistance, he was obliged, on the approach of Schomberg, who in the mean time had taken Aire, to raise the siege. He was incapaple of yielding to adversity, or bending under misfortunes: but he began to foresee, that, by the negligence and errors of his allies, the war in Flanders must necessarily have a very unfortunate issue.—On the Upper Rhine, Philipsbourg was taken by the Imperialists. In Pomerania, the Swedes were so unsuccessful against the Danes and Brandenburghers, that they seemed to be losing apace all those possessions, which, with so much valour and good fortune, they had acquired in Germany.—About the beginning of winter, the Congress of Nimeguen was pretty full, and the plenipotentiaries of the emperor and Spain, two powers strictly con-joined by blood and alliance, at last appeared. The Dutch had threatened, if they absented themselves any longer, to proceed to a separate treaty with France. In the conferences and negotiations, the dispositions of the parties became every day more apparent.—The Hollanders, loaded with debts and harrassed with taxes, were desirous of putting an end to a war; in which, besides the disadvantages attending all leagues, the weakness of the Spaniards, the divisions and delays of the Germans, prognosticated nothing but disgrace and misfortune. Their commerce languished; and what gave them still greater anxiety, the commerce of England, by reason of her neutrality, flourished extremely; and they were apprehensive, lest advantages, once lost, would never thoroughly be regained. They had themselves no farther motive for continuing the war, than to secure a good frontier to Flanders; but gratitude to their allies still engaged them to try whether another campaign might procure a peace, which would give general satisfaction. The prince of Orange,* urged by motives of honour, of ambition, and of animosity against France, endeavoured to keep them steady to this resolution.—The Spaniards, not to mention the other incurable weaknesses into which their monarchy was fallen, were distracted with domestic dissensions between the parties of the queen regent and don John, natural brother to their young sovereign. Though unable of themselves to defend Flanders, they were resolute not to conclude a peace, which would leave it exposed to every assault or inroad; and while this made the most magnificent promises to the States, their real trust was in the protection of England. They saw that, if that small but important territory were once subdued by France, the Hollanders, exposed to so terrible a power, would fall into dependance, and would endeavour, by submissions, to ward off that destruction to which a war, in the heart of their state, must necessarily expose them. They believed that Lewis, sensible how much greater advantages he might reap from the alliance than from the subjection of the republic, which must scatter its people and depress its commerce, would be satisfied with very moderate conditions, and would turn his enterprises against his other neighbours. They thought it impossible but the people and the parliament of England, foreseeing these obvious consequences, must at last force the king to take part in the affairs of the continent, in which their interests were so deeply concerned. And they trusted, that even the king himself, on the approach of so great a danger, must open his eyes, and sacrifice his prejudices in favour of France, to the safety of his own dominions.—But Charles here found himself entangled in such opposite motives and engagements, as he had not resolution enough to break, or patience to unravel. On the one hand, he always regarded his alliance with France as a sure resource in case of any commotions among his own subjects; and whatever schemes he might still retain for enlarging his authority, or altering the established religion, it was from that quarter alone he could expect assistance. He had actually in secret sold his neutrality to France, and he received remittances of a million of livres a-year, which was afterwards increased to two millions; a considerable supply in the present embarrassed state of his revenue. And he dreaded lest the parliament should treat him as they had formerly done his father; and after they had engaged him in a war on the continent, should take advantage of his necessities, and make him purchase supplies by sacrificing his prerogative and abandoning his ministers.—On the other hand, the cries of his people and parliament, seconded by Danby, Arlington, and most of his ministers, incited him to take part with the allies, and to correct the unequal balance of power in Europe. He might apprehend danger from opposing such earnest desires: he might hope for large supplies if he concurred with them: And however inglorious and indolent his disposition, the renown of acting as arbiter of Europe would probably at intervals rouse him from his lethargy, and move him to support the high character with which he stood invested.—It is worthy of observation, that, during this period, the king was, by every one, abroad and at home, by France and by the allies, allowed to be the undisputed arbiter of Europe; and no terms of peace, which he would have prescribed, could have been refused by either party. Though France afterwards found means to resist the same alliance, joined with England, yet was she then obliged to make such violent efforts as quite exhausted her; and it was the utmost necessity which pushed her to find resources, far surpassing her own expectations. Charles was sensible, that so long as the war continued abroad, he should never enjoy ease at home, from the impatience and importunity of his subjects; yet could he not resolve to impose a peace by openly joining himself with either party. Terms advantageous to the allies must lose him the friendship of France: the contrary would enrage his parliament. Between these views, he perpetually fluctuated; and from his conduct, it is observable, that a careless, remiss disposition, agitated by opposite motives, is capable of as great inconsistencies as are incident even to the greatest imbecility and folly."

FIFTEENTH SESSION OF THE SECOND PARLIAMENT.

The King's Speech on opening the Session.] Feb. 15, 1676-7. The Parliament met according to prorogation, after a recess of nearly 15 months, when the king opened the session with the following Speech to both houses:

"My Lords and Gentlemen; I have called you together again, after a long prorogation, that you might have an opportunity to repair the misfortunes of the last session, and to recover and restore the right use and end of parliaments. The time I have given you to recollect yourselves in, and to consider whither those differences tend which have been so unhappily managed and improved between you, is enough to leave you without all excuse, if ever you fall into the like again. I am now resolved to let the world see, that it shall not be my fault, if they be not made happy by the consultations in parliament. For I declare myself very plainly to you, that I come prepared to give you all the satisfaction and security in the great concerns of the Protestant Religion, as it is established in the Church of England, that shall reasonably be asked, or can consist with Christian prudence. And I declare myself as freely, that I am ready to gratify you in a further securing of your Liberty and Property (if you can think you want it) by as many good laws as you shall propose, and as can consist with the safety of the government; without which, there will neither be liberty nor property left to any man.—Having thus plainly told you what I am ready to do for you, I shall deal as plainly with you again, and tell you what it is I do expect from you. First, I do expect and require from you, that all occasions of Difference between the two houses be carefully avoided; for else, they who have no hopes to prevent your good resolutions, will hope, by this reserve, to hinder them from taking any effect. And let all men judge who is most for arbitrary government, they that foment such Differences as tend to dissolve all parliaments; or I, that would preserve this and all parliaments from being made useless by such dissentions. In the next place, I desire you to consider the necessity of building more Ships, and how much all our safeties are concerned in it. And since the additional Revenue of Excise will shortly expire, you that know me to be under a great burden of Debts, and how hard a shift I am making to pay them off as fast as I can, I hope, will never deny me the continuance of this revenue, and some reasonable Supply to make my condition more easy.—And that you may be satisfied how impossible it is (whatever some men think) to support the government with less than the present Revenue, you may at any time see the yearly established Charge; by which it will appear, that the constant and unavoidable charge being paid, there will remain no overplus towards the discharging those contingencies which may happen in all kingdoms, and which have been a considerable charge to me this last year. To conclude: I do recommend to you the peace of the kingdom, in the careful prevention of all differences; the safety of the kingdom, in providing for some greater strength at sea; and the prosperity of the kingdom, in assisting the necessary charge and support of the government. And if any of these good ends should happen to be disappointed; I call God and men to witness this day, that the misfortune of that disappointment shall not lie at my doors. The rest I refer to the Chancellor."

The Lord Chancellor Finch's Speech.] Then the Lord Chancellor spake as followeth:

"My lords; and you the knights, citizens, and burgesses of the house of commons; By the most gracious pleasure of the king, you are here again assembled to hold another session of this parliament, wherein the king expects your advice and your assistance; your advice in matters of the highest deliberation, your assistance in matters of extreme and pressing difficulty. Your deliberations will chiefly be exercised about those things which do belong unto your peace, the peace of the Church and the peace of the State; two considerations of so close a connection between themselves, that in the very original writ of summons, by virtue of which you still sit here, they are jointly recommended to your counsel and your care. The peace of the Church is harder to preserve than the peace of the State; for they that desire innovations in the State most commonly begin the attempt upon the Church. And by this means it comes to pass that the peace of the Church is so often disturbed, not only by those poor mistaken souls who deserve to be pitied, but by malicious and designing men who deserve to be punished. And while things continue in this estate, it cannot be avoided, but that the laws which are necessary to restrain the malicious must and will sometimes disquiet and wound those that are weak. What Remedies are fit for this disease; whether the fault be in the laws or in the men, in the men that should obey, or in the men that should execute; whether the cure be a work of time and patience, or of zeal and diligence; or whether any new expedient can be found, to secure the ship from that storm which the swelling of two contrary tides seems to threaten; is wholly left to your advice. The king hath called you for that end, and doubts not but your counsels will be such as shall tend to safety and to establishment. The peace of the State requires as much of your care and vigilance too, our peace at home, and our peace abroad. As for that abroad, we are at this time, blessed be God for his mercy to us, and blessed be the king for his care of us, in perfect peace with all the nations upon earth; such a peace as makes us the envy of the Christian world, and hath enabled us to do ourselves right against the Infidels; such a peace as brings with it all the fruits of peace, and deserves not only our prayers for the continuance of it, but our best and most watchful care that nothing may be done on our part to give it an interruption. But then we must consider again, that our peace abroad will not subsist any longer than while we do maintain our peace at home; for, without this, no kingdom can be able to act in its full strength; and without that, the friendship or enmity or any nation ceases to be considerable to its neighbours.—Now it is a great and a dangerous mistake in those who think the peace at home is well enough preserved, so long as the sword is not drawn; whereas, in truth, nothing deserves the name of peace, but unity; such an unity as flows from an unshaken trust and confidence between the king and his people; from a due reverence and obedience to his laws and to his government; from a religious and an aweful care, not to remove the ancient landmarks, not to disturb those constitutions which time and public convenience hath settled; from a zeal to preserve the whole frame and order of the government upon the old foundations; and from a perfect detestation and abhorrency of all such as are given to change: whatever falls short of this, falls short of peace too.—If therefore there be any endeavours to renew, nay, if there be not all the endeavours that can be to extinguish, the memory of all former provocations and offences, and the occasions of the like for the future; if there be such divisions as begets great thoughts of heart; shall we call this peace, because it is not war, or because men do not yet take the field? As well we may call it health, when there is a dangerous fermentation in the blood and spirits, because the patient hath not yet taken his bed. And yet, as evident as it is that all we have or hope for depends upon the preservation of our peace and unity at home, as certain it is that no care to preserve it will be wanting here.—Nevertheless it remains still to be wished, that even this very point were no part of those difficulties we are now to struggle with; for there are many more, which without your aid and your assistance can never be overcome. One is, the weakness of our Fleet: for strength and weakness can no otherwise be judged of than by comparison; and by this measure we may truly judge our fleet to be less considerable than it was, because ours stands at a stay, while our neighbours round about us are improved. This is an affair wherein no time would be lost; because, whenever we set about it, it will take up some considerable time before it can be finished.—Another weight there is, which lies very heavy upon the Revenue; and that is, the Debts which incumber it. Justice and honour oblige the king not to forsake those who have assisted with their estates in the defence of the public. And although the necessary issues of his revenue, in the many new and chargeable emergencies of state, did for a while postpone their satisfaction, yet his maj. hath now gone very far in it, and hath provided for the security and payment of an immense sum, with such difficulties as none but a just and generous prince would ever have undergone.—And now, should the rest of his revenue fail, or fail to be unloaden in some degree, the inconvenience to the public and the insecurity of all our affairs would quickly be too manifest.—One difficulty more there is, without which all the rest were none; and that is, the strange diffidence and distrust, which, like a general infection, begins to spread itself into almost all the corners of the land. Much of this arises from the artifice of ill men, who create and nourish all the suspicions which they can devise; but the cure of it lies perfectly in your hands: for all this will presently vanish, as soon as men shall see your acquiescence, and the fruits of it, in a chearful concurrence with his maj. to all those good and public ends which he hath now so earnestly recommended to you. It would be somewhat strange, and without all example in story, that a nation should be twice ruined, twice undone, by the self-same way and means the same Fears and Jealousies. Would any man, that doth but give himself leave to think, refuse to enjoy and take comfort in the blessings that are present, only for fear of future changes and alterations? Surely it is enough for any kingdom, and more than most kingdoms in the world can boast of, to have their affairs brought into such a condition, that they may in all human probability, and unless it be their own default, continue for a long time safe and happy. Future contingencies are not capable of any certain prospect; a security beyond that of human probability no nation ever did, or ever shall, attain to. If a kingdom be guarded by nature against all dangers from without, and then will rely too much upon what nature hath done for them; if a kingdom be warned and cautioned against all dangers from within by former experiences, and then will either forget or make no use of those experiences; if a kingdom be powerful in shipping and navigation, and then see their neighbours endeavouring to overpower them that way, without being solicitous enough to augment and reinforce their own naval strength; if a kingdom be happy in the frequent assemblies of their great councils, where all that is grievous may be redressed, and all that is wanting may be enacted, and then will render those councils useless and impracticable, by continuing endless distractions: who can wonder if their affairs should begin to be less prosperous; when otherwise, humanly speaking, and in all common probability, their condition would have been out of the reach of fortune, and their security in a manner impregnable?—My Lords and Gentlemen; If the presaging malice of our enemies should pretend to foretel any such fate as this to befal us, the wisdom and the magnanimity of this great council will quickly be too hard for all their auguries. The honour and the loyalty of this august and venerable assembly will leave no kind of room for any such divinations. You that have the happiness to live under so excellent a monarchy, so admirable a constitution, and temper of government; you that remember what the want of this government cost us, and the miserable desolations which attended it; have all the motives, and are under all the obligations, that can be, to secure and advance the interest of it.—The king on his part meets you with so open and so full a heart, and is so absolutely resolved and determined to do all that in him lies to glad the hearts of his people, that it must be the strangest infelicity in the world, if either he or his subjects should meet with any disappointments here. For the king hath no desires but what are public; no ends or aims which terminate in himself. All his endeavours are so entirely bent upon the welfare of all his dominions, that he doth not think any man a good subject, who doth not heartily love his country; and therefore let no man pass for a good patriot, who doth not as heartily love and serve his prince. Private men, indeed, are subject to be misled by private interests, and may entertain some vain and slender hopes of surviving the misfortunes of the public: but a prince is sure to fall with it; and therefore can never have any interest divided from it. To live and die with the king, is the highest profession a subject can make; and sometimes it is a profession only, and no more: but in a king it is an absolute necessity, it is a fate inevitable, that he must live and die with his people. Away then with all the vain imaginations of those who labour to infuse a misbelief of the government! away with those ill-meant distinctions between the Court and the Country, between the natural and the politic capacity! and let all who go about to persuade others that these are two several interests, have a care of that precipice to which such principles may lead them: for the first men that ever began to distinguish of their duty never left off, till they had quite distinguished themselves out of all their allegiance. My Lords and Gentlemen; The king hath so long had, and still retains, such honourable thoughts of these assemblies, that we ought to make it one great part of our business to deserve the continuance of his majesty's grace and good opinion. Let no contention then come near this place but that of a noble emulation, who shall serve his country best, by well serving of the king: let no passion enter here, but that of a pious zeal to lay hold upon all opportunities of promoting the honour and service of the crown, till our enemies despair of ever profiting by any disorders amongst us. And let all who pray for the long life and prosperity of the king add their endeavours to their prayers; and study to prolong his sacred life, by giving him all the joys of heart which can arise from the demonstrations of the lively and the warm affections of his people." *

---

* "What the king had said so well, the Lord Chancellor, as usual, spoiled by straining to do it better; and, had not the Lord Treasurer used *a far more effectual way of persuasion* with the commons, there had been the same danger of the ill success of this meeting, as of those before. Concerning his lordship's Applications to Members, sir John Reresby has left us the following Memorial; which, whether it contains the whole truth, or not, let the understanding and impartial reader judge: Having kept my Christmas in the country, I no sooner returned to London, than my Lord Treasurer sent to speak with me. I waited on him therefore, and found him very open in his discourse upon several subjects, but for the most part lamenting that his countrymen would not allow him an opportunity to be of service to them with the king, and making many protestations that the jealousies of those who called themselves of the Country Party, were entirely groundless and without foundation: that to his certain knowledge, the king meant no other than to preserve the religion and government by law established; and, upon the whole, wished that neither himself or his posterity might prosper, if he did not speak what he really believed: that if the government was in any danger, it was most from those who pretended such a mighty zeal for it; but who under that pretence were endeavouring to create such discontents between the king and the nation, as might produce confusion in the end; and intreated me to be careful how I embarked myself with that sort of people. My reply was, That I hoped I was not one to be wilfully misled: that I should have no rule to go by in that house but my reason and conscience, and that so I could be of no particular faction or party: that as much as I yet understood of the duty of a member of the house of commons at this time, suggested to me a moderation between the two extremes, and to have an equal regard for the prerogative of the king and the liberty of the subject. True it is, till now, that

*Debate in the House of Lords on the Question, Whether the Parliament was not dissolved by the Prorogation of 15 Months?**] Instead of entering upon business, as usual, a Question was started in each house, Whether they had any Right to enter upon business at all? in short, Whether they were a Parliament?

The Duke of Buckingham's Speech on that Occasion.] As soon as the commons were withdrawn, and a Bill offered to be read, the duke of Buckingham rose up and desired to be heard first; which request being complied with, he moved "That this house would consider, whether this Parliament be not dissolved,

---

the Treasurer used such solemn asseverations, with regard to the king's good intention, and pretty clearly convinced me that some of the chiefs of the Country Party had most at heart their own private interest, whatever they asserted in favour and defence of the public, that I had great notions of the truth and sincerity of the Country Party." p. 36. 37. And again, p. 43. "The session had gone on smoothly and sedately enough in both houses; my Lord Treasurer having so ordered it, that the King's Party encreas'd rather than the other; but it was much feared, that some Votes were obtained more *by purchase* than affection." Ralph.

* This long Prorogation of fifteen months occasioned at that time much disquiet, and produced the following Arguments, which it has been thought proper to annex. It does not appear who was the author.

The Question is, Whether a Prorogation of the Parliament extended beyond twelve months, be not, in construction of law, dissolution?

"It seems evidently that the law cannot intend one thing, and, at the same time, permit another to be legal, which destroys its own purpose and intent. Wherefore if there be laws in force which intend and require the yearly sitting of parliament, the law cannot admit of Prorogation exceeding the compass of a year, for that were to make the law felo de se and to divest itself of capacity to take effect, or to be executed, since during a prorogation, which is legal, no other parliament can be called. The law cannot contradict itself, and if it requires the sitting of a parliament within a year, then the not sitting of a parliament within a year, must be contrary to law; and so a prorogation above a year, must be illegal. But if a prorogation beyond a year be illegal, it follows that it is no prorogation, but a discontinuance, or dissolution, of such parliament, so prorogued, in the same manner as an illegal commission is no commission. For since parliaments sit by the king's writ, and since the force and power of those writs must have a legal continuance, to keep and preserve the parliament in being, (as appears in the case of adjournments) therefore when a prorogation ceases to be legal, the legal continuance of the parliament also ceases, and so there is a discontinuance, viz. a dissolution. I think that we may take it for granted, that if these laws of Edw. iii. which require the annual calling of parliaments, be still in force, then a prorogation exceeding the compass is a discontinuance, or dissolution. It remains, therefore, to see whether those laws of Edw. iii. be still in force, and that they are so, appears, because they have not yet been repealed by any subsequent act of parliament.—We need not much insist upon the act 16 Cha. i. for triennial parliaments, because that act is repealed by Cha. ii. but we may affirm that that act of Cha. i. does no way repeal the laws of Edw. iii. but it rather puts the king upon a necessity of executing that trust in a reasonable time, which was incumbent upon him by the laws of Edw. iii. And this, perhaps was done (though in a way indecent to the crown) because former kings had not well executed their trust, in calling parliaments accordingly; and here, by the way, we may observe the different manner of the law, towards the king, and towards the subject, for when the law requires any thing to be done, by the subject, it commonly annexes a penalty for the not doing of it, but when the law requires the king to do any thing, (in respect to his majesty) it is without a penalty, and in the nature of a trust; but yet the law requires the performance of the thing enacted equally from them both.—The act then in force concerning this matter of calling parliaments is the 16th Cha. ii. which, in the first place, repeals that of Cha. i. and, by the way, gives us a very good precedent, showing how an act of parliament ought to be repealed. In the next place it recites, and (we may say) confirms the laws of E. iii. in these words. 'And, because, by the ancient laws and statutes of this realm, made in the reign of K. Edw. iii. parliaments are to be held very often, &c.' Here we are to observe that by the present tense 'are' these laws of Edw. iii. are affirmed still to be laws, for had the parliament intended or understood those laws to be repealed, they would certainly have said 'were,' and not 'are to be held' &c. This seems to be a judgment in the case, and a judgment of the highest nature; for who can presume to say those are no laws, which the parliament calls 'the ancient laws and statutes of this realm?'—This alone is evident against all that can be said to prove that K. Edward's laws, by a long disuse, were obsolete, and antiquated; but, for farther satisfaction, it is answered, that a law, or trust imposed by a law, is not therefore abrogated, because it is not broken, or not executed. How often has Magna Charta been broken since it was made, yet that does not at all invalidate the force of it, no more than the not affixing a penalty to a law does make the law less binding; since no penalty, nor constraint neither, is affixed to Magna Charta; besides, it may be said, that no prescription lies against the whole kingdom, any more than against the king, and because the Prorogation of this parliament for 15 Months is contrary to the statutes of 4 Ed. iii. and 36 Ed. iii." After which the duke of Buckingham made the following extraordinary Speech :*

"My lords; I have often troubled your lordships with my discourse in this house; but I confess I never did it with more trouble to myself, than I do at this time, for I scarce know where I should begin, or what I have to say to your lordships: on the one side, I am afraid of being thought an unquiet and pragmatical man; for, in this age, every man that cannot bear every thing, is called unquiet; and he that does ask questions, for which we ought to be concerned, is looked upon as pragmatical. On the other side, I am more afraid of being thought a dishonest man; and of all men, I am most afraid of being thought so by myself; for every one is the best judge of the integrity of his own intentions; and though it does not always follow, that he is pragmatical whom others take to be so, yet this never fails to be

---

that in the general maxims, 'Nullum tempus occurrit regi nec ecclesiæ,' and under the word 'regi, respublica' is also included. Since in a government, especially monarchical, and essentially free, the head is never to be taken without the body, nor the body without the head; because that either, separately taken, would be a monster. So that prescription only lies against particular persons, or communities. And, lastly, against the plea of prescription it is answered, that although these laws of E. iii. have not been duly executed to save a prescription against them, yet parliaments have ever since been sitting much within the compass of 60 years, and every sitting of parliament is an executing in part that trust which the law of E. iii. imposed upon the king. Else, in the case of a yearly rent, demanded upon an ancient deed produced in court, if it be proved, that the rent has been often paid within memory, though not duly and yearly, the rent will be still due in law, and no prescription will lie against it.—It may be objected, that, according to the maxims, 'Leges posteriores priores contrarias abrogant,' the last part of this act of Cha. ii. wherein it is enacted, 'that parliaments shall be held at least every three years,' is contrary to those of E. iii. which say 'that parliaments shall be called yearly,' and therefore repeals them. Now to this the answer is plain; that there is no contrariety in all those laws, because all of them, at once, may be executed. For if the king shall call parliaments yearly, the act of Cha. ii. is no less exempted than the acts of E. iii. Besides, this last part of the act of Cha. ii. is not exemptable, nor does it take effect till after the expiration of this present parliament, which clearly appears in the very letter of the act, wherein the word 'hereafter,' in the enacting part of that law, has a reference to the subsequent words, 'within three years from and after the determination of this present parliament.'—We shall close this discourse with these three short observations. 1. That no parliament, that is not antecedently so, can make itself a parliament by vote, for every thing must be before it can act, and nothing can be the cause of itself. 2. That nothing can be more prejudicial to the king and kingdom than to have a convention under the name of a parliament. 3. That a matter of such high importance ought not to be left dubious when it may be made certain."

Reasons to prove the last Prorogation of the Parliament to be illegal.

"It is a fundamental and unquestionable maxim in the law of England, that the kings of England are so bound by all statutes made for the public good, that every command, order, or direction of them, contrary to the substance, scope, or intent of any such statute, is void and null in law.—But the last prorogation of parliament is an order, or direction, of the king's, contrary to two statutes, the one in the 4th, the other in the 36th of Ed. iii. made for the greatest and chiefest common good; namely, the maintenance of our laws, and the redress of mischiefs and grievances which daily happen; for they both do positively appoint the meeting of parliament once within a year, and the king, by this last prorogation of parliament, has, contrary to both these statutes, ordered the parliament not to meet within a year, but some months after.—Wherefore this last prorogation of parliament is void and null in law, and, consequently the parliament is at an end, because the parliament cannot meet by virtue of a prorogation, which is void and null in law, and because that by the essential forms of parliamentary proceedings, the parliament having been dismissed without any legal prorogation, or adjournment, there is an impossibility of its meeting at any other time. —This ought to be seriously considered of by every Englishman, and whether, if any of the members of the parliament, begun the 8th day of May, 1661, should act by virtue of this Order of the king's, or prorogation, they do not admit and justify that particular Order of the king, though contrary to an act of parliament, of what importance soever, is yet, notwithstanding, good in law, and thereby allow of what would at once subvert the whole ancient government of England by law. For if a particular Order of the king's, upon this present occasion, about the assembly of a parliament, contrary to the intent of two laws, enacted for the maintenance of all the statutes of this realm, can be in force against those two laws; then a particular Order of the King's, upon some other occasion, about the raising of moneys, contrary to the intent of the act *de tallagio non concedendo*, and another against the taking away of any man's liberty, estate, or life, contrary to the intent of Magna Charta, must also be in force against those two other laws."

* State Tracts, vol. i. p. 237.

true, that he is most certainly a knave who takes himself to be so. Nobody is answerable for more understanding than God Almighty has given him; and therefore, though I should be in the wrong, if I tell your lordships truly and plainly what I am really convinced of, I shall behave myself like an honest man: for it is my duty, as long as I have the honour to sit in this house, to hide nothing from your lordships, which I think may concern his majesty's service, your lordships interest, or the good and quiet of the people of England.—The question, in my opinion, which now lies before your lordships, is not what we are to do, but whether at this time we can do any thing as a parliament; it being very clear to me that the parliament is dissolved: and if, in this opinion, I have the misfortune to be mistaken, I have another misfortune joined to it; for I desire to maintain the argument with all the judges and lawyers in England, and leave it afterwards to your lordships to decide whether I am in the right or no. This, my lords, I speak not out of arrogance, but in my own justification, because if I were not thoroughly convinced that what I have now to urge, is grounded upon the fundamental laws of England, and that the not pressing it at this time might prove to be of a most dangerous consequence, both to his maj. and the whole nation, I should have been loth to start a notion, which perhaps may not be very agreeable to some people. And yet, my lords, when I consider where I am, whom I now speak to, and what was spoken in this place about the time of the Prorogation, I can hardly believe what I have to say will be distasteful to your lordships.—I remember very well, how your lordships were then displeased with the house of commons; and I remember too as well, what reasons they gave to you to be so. It is not so long since, but that I suppose your lordships may call to mind, that, after several odd passages between us, your lordships were so incensed, that a motion was made here for an Address to his majesty, about the Dissolution of this Parliament (p. 802.); and though it failed of being carried in the affirmative by two or three voices, yet this in the debate was remarkable, that it prevailed with much the major part of your lordships that were here present; and was only overpowered by the Proxies of those lords who never heard the arguments. What change there has been since, either in their behaviour, or in the state of our affairs, that should make your lordships change your opinion, I have not yet heard. And therefore if I can make it appear (as I presume I shall) that by law the parliament is dissolved, I presume your lordships ought not to be offended at me for it.—I have often wondered, how it should come to pass that this house of commons, in which there are so many honest, and so many worthy gentlemen, should yet be less respectful to your lordships, as certainly they have been, than any house of commons that were ever chosen in England; and yet if the matter be a little enquired into, the reason of it will plainly appear. For, my lords, the very nature of the house of commons is changed; they do not think now that they are an assembly that are to return to their own homes and become private men again (as by the laws of the land, and the antient constitution of parliaments they ought to be) but they look upon themselves as a standing senate, and as a number of men picked out to be legislators for the rest of their lives. And if that be the case, my lords, they have reason to believe themselves our equals. But, my lords, it is a dangerous thing to try new experiments in a government: men do not foresee the ill consequences that must happen, when they go about to alter those essential parts of it upon which the whole frame depends, as now in our case, the customs and constitutions of parliament: for all governments are artificial things, and every part of them has a dependence one upon another. And with them, as with clocks and watches, if you should put great wheels in the place of little ones, and little ones in the place of great ones, all the movements would stand still: so that we cannot alter any one part of a government without prejudicing the motions of the whole.—If this, my lords, were well considered, people would be more cautious how they went out of the old, honest, English way and method of proceeding. But it is not my business to find fault, and therefore, if your lordships will give me leave, I shall go on to shew you why, in my opinion, we are at this time no parliament. The ground of this opinion of mine is taken from the antient and unquestionable statutes of this realm; and give me leave to tell your lordships, by the way, that statutes are not like women, for they are not one jot the worse for being old. The first statute that I shall take notice of, is that in the 4th of Edw. iii. c. 14. thus set down in the printed book: item, 'It 'is accorded that a Parliament shall be holden 'every year once, and more often, if need be.' Now, though these words are as plain as a pike staff, and no man living, that is not a scholar, could possibly mistake the meaning of them, yet the grammarians of those days did make a shift to explain, that the words, 'if need be' did relate as well to the words 'every year once,' as to the words 'more often;' and so by this grammatical whimsey of theirs have made this statute to signify just nothing at all. For this reason, my lords, in the 36th of the same king's reign, a new act of parliament was made, in which those unfortunate words, 'if need be,' are left out, and that act of parliament relating to Magna Charta, and other statutes, made for the public good. Item, 'For maintenance of these Articles and Statutes, and the 'Redress of divers Mischiefs and Grievances, 'which daily happen, a Parliament shall be hol- 'den every year,' as at other time was ordained by another statute. Here now, my lords, there is not left the least colour or shadow for mistake, for it is plainly declared, that the kings of England must call a parliament once within a year; and the reasons why they are bound to do so, are as plainly set down, namely, 'for 'the maintenance of Magna Charta, and other 'statutes of the same importance, and for pre'venting the mischiefs and grievances which 'daily happen.'—The question then remaineth, Whether these statutes have been since repealed by any other statutes or no? The only statutes I ever heard mentioned for that, are the two Triennial Bills, the one made in the last king's, and the other in this king's reign. The Triennial bill, in the last king's reign, was made for the confirmation of the two abovementioned statutes of Edw. iii. for parliaments having been omitted to be called every year according to those statutes, a statute was made in the last king's reign to this purpose, 'That if the king should fail of calling a parliament, according to the statutes of Edw. iii.' then the third year the people should meet of themselves, without any writs at all, and chuse their parliament-men. This way of the people's chusing their parliament of themselves, being thought disrespectful to the king, a statute was made in this last parliament, which repealed the Triennial bill; and after the repealing Clause (which took notice only of the Triennial bill made in the last king's reign) there was in this statute a paragraph to this purpose: 'That 'because, by the antient statutes of the realm, 'made in the reign of Edw. iii. parliaments 'are to be held very often, it should be enacted, 'that within 3 years after the determination of 'that present parliament, parliaments should 'not be discontinued above 3 years at most, 'and be holden oftener if need required.' There have been several half kind of arguments drawn out of these Triennial bills, against the statutes of Edw. iii. which I confess I could never remember, nor indeed those that urged them to me ever durst own: for they always laid their faults upon some body else, like ugly, foolish children, whom, because of their deformity and want of wit, the parents are ashamed of, and so turn them out on the parish.—But, my lords, let the arguments be what they will, I have this short Answer to all that can be wrested out of these Triennial bills, 'That the first Triennial bill was repealed, before the matter now disputed of was in question; and the last Triennial bill will not be in force till the question be decided, that is, till the parliament is dissolved.' The whole matter, my lords, is reduced to this short dilemma; either the kings of England are bound by the acts above-mentioned of Edw. iii. or else the whole government of England by parliaments, and by the laws above, is absolutely at an end: for if the kings of England have power, by an order of theirs, to invalidate an Act made for the maintenance of Magna Charta, they have also power, by an order of theirs, to invalidate Magna Charta itself; and if they have power, by an order of theirs, to invalidate the statute itself, *de Tallagio non concedendo*, then they may not only, without the help of a parliament, raise money when they please, but also take away any man's estate when they please, and deprive every one of his liberty, or life, as they please.—This, my lords, I think, is a power that no judge or lawyer will pretend the kings of England to have; and yet this power must be allowed them, or else we that are met here this day cannot act as a parliament: for we are now met by virtue of the last Prorogation, and that prorogation is an order of the king's, point-blank contrary to the two acts of Edw. iii. for the acts say, 'That a parliament shall 'be holden once within a year,' and the prorogation saith, 'A parliament shall not be held within a year, but some months after;' and this (I conceive) is a plain contradiction, and consequently that the prorogation is void. Now, if we cannot act as a parliament, by virtue of the last prorogation, I beseech your lordships, by virtue of what else can we act? shall we act by virtue of the king's proclamation? pray, my lords, how so? is a Proclamation of more force than a Prorogation? or if a thing that hath been ordered the first time be not valid, doth the ordering it the second time make it good in law? I have heard, indeed, That two negatives make an affirmative;' but I never heard before, 'that two nothings ever made any thing.'—Well, but how then are we met? is it by our own adjournment? I suppose no body has the confidence to say that: which way then is it? do we meet by accident? That, I think, may be granted, but an accidental meeting can no more make a parliament, than accidental clapping a crown upon a man's head can make a king. There is a great deal of ceremony required to give a matter of that moment a legal sanction. The laws have reposed so great a trust, and so great a power in the hands of a parliament, that every circumstance relating to the manner of their electing, meeting, and proceeding, is looked after with the nicest circumspection imaginable. For this reason the king's writs about the summons of parliament are to be issued out verbatim, according to the form prescribed by the law, or else that parliament is void and null. For the same reason, if a parliament summoned by the king's writ, do not meet the very same day that it is summoned to meet upon, that parliament is void and null. And, by the same reason, if parliaments be not legally adjourned, de die in diem, those parliaments must be also void and null.—Oh! but some say, There is nothing in the two acts of Edw. iii. to take away the king's power of prorogation, and therefore the prorogation is good. My lords, under favour, this is a very gross mistake; for, pray examine the words of the act: the act says, 'A parliament shall be holden once a year;' now to whom can these words be directed, but to them who are to call a parliament? And who are they but the kings of England? It is very true, this does not take away the king's power of proroguing parliaments, but it most certainly limits it to be within a year. Well, then; but it is said again, if that prorogation be null and void, then things are just as they were before, and therefore the parliament is still in being. My lords, I confess, there would be some weight in this, but for one thing, which is, that not one word of it is true: for if, when the king had prorogued us, we had taken no notice of the prorogation, there is an impossibility of our meeting and acting any other way. One may as properly say, that a man that is killed by assault is still alive, because he was killed unlawfully, as that the parliament is still alive, because the prorogation was unlawful. The next argument that those are reduced to, who would maintain this to be yet a parliament, is, that the parliament is prorogued sine die, and therefore the king may call them again by proclamation. In the first part of this proposition I shall not only agree with them, but also do them the favour to prove, that it is so in the eye of the law, which I never heard they have yet done; for the statutes say, 'That a parliament shall be holden once in a year;' and the prorogation having put them off till a day without the year, and consequently excepted against by the law, that day, in the eye of the law, is no day at all, that is, sine die; and the prorogation might as well have put them off till so many months after dooms-day; and then, I think, no body would have doubted, but that had been a very sufficient dissolution.—Besides, my lords, I shall desire your lordships to take notice, that, in former times, the usual way of dissolving parliaments was to dismiss them sine die; for the king, when he dissolved them, used to say no more, but that he desired them to go home, till he sent for them again, which is a dismission sine die. Now if there were 40 ways of dissolving parliaments, if I can prove this parliament has been dissolved by any one of them, I suppose there is no great need of the other 39. Another thing, which they much insist upon, is, that they have found out a precedent in queen Elizabeth's time, when a parliament was once prorogued three days beyond a year: in which I cannot chuse but observe, that it is a very great confirmation of the value and esteem all people ever had of the forementioned acts of Edw. iii. since from that time to this, there can 'but one precedent be found for the proroguing a parliament above a year,' and that was but for 3 days neither. Besides, my lords, this precedent is not of a very odd kind of nature; for it was in time of a very great plague, when every body, of a sudden, was forced to run away one from another; and so being in haste, had not leisure to calculate well the time of the prorogation, though the appointing it to be within 3 days of the year is an argument to me, that their design was to keep within the bounds of the acts of parliament. And if the mistake had been taken notice of in queen Elizabeth's time, I make no question but she would have given a lawful remedy.—Now, I beseech your lordships, what more can be drawn from the shewing this precedent, but only that because once upon a time a thing was done illegally, therefore your lordships should do so again now; though my lords, under favour, ours is a very different case from theirs; for this precedent they mention was never taken notice of, and all lawyers will tell you, that a precedent that passes sub silentio, is of no validity at all, and will never be admitted in any judicial court where it is pleaded. Nay, judge Vaughan says, in his reports, 'That in cases which depend upon 'fundamental principles, for which demonstra- 'tions may be drawn, millions of precedents 'are to no purpose.' Oh! but, say they, you must think prudentially of the inconveniencies which will follow upon it: for if this be allowed, all those acts which were made in that session of parliament will be then void. Whether that be so or no, I shall not now examine; but this I will pretend to say, that no man ought to pass for a prudential person, who only takes notice of the inconveniencies of one side. It is the part of a wise man to examine the inconveniencies of both sides, to weigh which are the greatest, and to be sure to avoid them: and, my lords, to that kind of examination I willingly submit this cause, for I presume it will be easy for your lordships to judge which of these two will be of the most dangerous consequence to the nation; either to allow that the statutes made in that particular session, in queen Eliz.'s time, are void, (which may easily be confirmed by a lawful parliament) or to lay it down for maxim, 'That 'the kings of England, by a particular Order 'of theirs, have power to break all the laws of 'England when they please.'—And, my lords, with all the duty we owe to his majesty, it is no disrespect to him to say, that his maj. is bound up by the laws of England; for the great king of Heaven and Earth, God Almighty himself, is bound by his own decrees: and what is an act of parliament, but a decree of the king, made in the most solemn manner it is possible for him to make it, that is, with the consent of the lords and commons? It is plain then, in my opinion, that we are no more a parliament; and I humbly conceive, your lordships ought to give God thanks for it, since it has thus pleased him, by his providence, to take you out of a condition wherein you must have been entirely useless to his majesty, to yourselves, and the whole nation: for, I do beseech your lordships, if nothing of this I have urged were true, what honourable excuse could we find for our acting again with the h. of commons? Except we could pretend such an exquisite art of forgetfulness, as to avoid calling to mind all that passed between us the last session; and unless we could have also a faculty of teaching the same art to the whole nation. What opinion could they have of us, if it should happen, that the very same men, who were so earnest the last session for having the house of commons dissolved, when there was no question of their lawful sitting, should be now willing to join with them again, when without question they are dissolved? Nothing can be more dangerous to a king or a people, than that the laws should be made by an assembly, of which there can be a doubt, whether they have a power to make laws or no; and it would be in us inexcusable, if we should overlook this danger, since there is for it so easy a remedy, which the law requires, and which all the nation longs for.—The calling a new parliament it is, that only can put his majesty into a possibility of receiving Supplies; that can secure your lordships the honour of sitting in this house like peers, and your being serviceable to your king and country; and that can restore to all the people of England, their undoubted rights of chusing men frequently to represent their grievances in parliament; without this, all we can do would be in vain; the nation may languish a while, but must perish at last: we should become a burthen to ourselves, and a prey to our neighbours.—My motion therefore to your lordships shall be, That we humbly address ourselves to his majesty, and beg of him, for his own sake, as well as for the people's sake, to give us speedily a New Parliament; that so we may unanimously, before it is too late, use our utmost endeavours for his majesty's service, and for the safety, the welfare, and the glory of the English Nation."

The Answers to this extraordinary Speech * were, "That those Acts have not been so understood, nor hath the usage been to regulate the holding of parliaments upon that foot, ever since the laws were made; and it is a rule of law that ancient statutes are to be construed by the general usage. That the words, 'if need be,' go as well to the 'holding every year,' as to the 'more often;' and, repeating them accordingly, it runs thus: 'a parliament shall be holden every year, if need be, or more often, if need be;' and the king is judge of the need. That it is ridiculous to say the parliament is *sine die*, when a day stands appointed by the prorogation. And, if the king were by law obliged to hold a parliament every year, and doth it not, but seldomer; it may be construed a misgovernment, or grievance, to be redressed in the ordinary way, by petition, but not to vacate future parliaments, and their acts. And, farther (what is not argumentative, but express) the time of parliamentary vacation is altered by later laws; as the before-quoted Triennial Act Car. i. and 16 Car. ii. which repeals the other. It is thereby enacted, 'That, hereafter, the sitting and holding of parliaments shall not be intermitted, or deferred, above 3 years;' which amounts to an allowance of a vacation not exceeding 3 years. That parliament had then been continued above 4 years: and this question, if it should turn upon the reasoning on the other side, would avoid all the acts of parliament made after the year expired; which would make strange work with the laws of this and other parliaments.

The Duke's Speech supported by the Lords Shaftsbury, Salisbury, and Wharton.] The duke's Speech was thought so bold and shocking, by the lords in the ministry, that one of them moved that the duke might be called to the bar: but the earl of Shaftsbury, who was fully prepared, opposed this motion, as improper and extravagant; and did with great courage and sharpness of application, second and enforce the duke of Buckingham's argument; and the earl of Salisbury and the lord Warton fell in briskly on the same side. While one of them was speaking, the duke took a pen and wrote the following Syllogism "It is a maxim in the law of England, that the kings of England are bound up by all the statutes made pro bono publico; that every order or direction of theirs, contrary to the scope and full intent of any such statute, is void and null in law: but the last prorogation of the parliament was an order of the king's, contrary to an act of king Edw. iii. made for the greatest common good, viz. the maintenance of all the statutes of England, and for the prevention of the mischiefs and grievances which daily happen: *Ergo*, the last Prorogation of parliament is void and null in law," after which he appealed to the Bishops, whether it was not a true Syllogism; and to the Judges, whether the propositions were not true in law.

The four Lords ordered to the Tower.] The debates arose to that height, that all the four lords were ordered to be sent to the Tower, for contempt of the authority and being of the present parliament, there to remain during the pleasure of his majesty and the house of peers. In the mean time the duke of Buckingham took the opportunity of slipping out of the house, while the lord Anglesey was arguing against the committing them. The house finding he had withdrawn himself, were in a rage, and designed to address the king for a Proclamation against him; but the duke foreseeing the event, would not give them so much trouble, and appearing the next day in his place, the court lords immediately cried out, 'To the Bar!' But his grace, who could readily turn any thing serious into jest, and extricate himself out of any difficulties, rose up, and said, 'He begged their lordships pardon for retiring the night before: that they very well knew the exact oeconomy he kept in his family, and perceiving their lordships intended he should be some time in another place, he only went home to set his house in order, and was now come to submit to their lordships pleasure,' which was to send him to the Tower, after the earls of Shaftsbury and Salisbury, and the lord Wharton *.

* North's Examen. p. 65.

* "The duke desired he might have his servants to wait on him, and the first he named was his cook; which the king resented highly, as carrying in it an insinuation of the worst sort. The earl of Shaftsbury made the same demand. But lord Wharton did not ask for his cook. Three of the lords lay in the Tower for some months; but they were set at liberty on their petitioning the king. Lord Shaftsbury would not petition." Burnet.

The lords, further to shew their resentment, ordered one Dr. Cary to be brought to the bar of the house, and to be questioned, concerning a Book he had carried to the press, treating of the Illegality of the Prorogation; and because he would not satisfy them in some interrogatories, they fined him 1,000*l.* for his contempt, and kept him close prisoner till the payment of the money.—Nor did they stop here, but made an order, "That the serjeant at arms attending that house should take into his custody Aaron Smith, and bring him to the bar of the house, there to answer for speaking certain dangerous and seditious words against the being of this present Parliament." And Mr. Smith having upon this absconded, they immediately presented their humble desires to his majesty, "That he would by his royal proclamation strictly charge and command, that the utmost and most effectual endeavours should be used for apprehending the person of the said Aaron Smith, and bring him before the said house of peers (if the parliament should be sitting at the time of his apprehension) or in case the parliament should not be then sitting, before one of his majesty's principal secretaries of state, to the intent that the said Aaron Smith might be secured, in order to his appearance before the house of peers, to answer for his said offence." To which his majesty complied by a proclamation issued out two or three days after the parliament broke up. And it is believed, the more effectually to chastise him and other like offenders, that the parliament was this year continued by adjournments rather than by prorogation, as was most commonly practised.

Debate in the Commons on the long Prorogation.] Feb. 15. Mr. Sec. *Williamson* said, When the king's Speech has been read, it has usually some place given it; and would have it considered the first thing after reading a Bill.

Sir *Tho. Lee* cares not how soon the king's Speech is taken into consideration, but would not lose the method and order of parliament. You always begin with reading a Bill. The king's Speech is usually about Supply, and that ought to be the last thing considered here. He takes this occasion to put in a claim to method. He is transported with the king's Speech as much any man; but would keep method.

Mr. Sec. *Coventry*. Nobody opposes the consideration of the king's Speech, but because of custom of respect. As the king speaks to us, so we to him, without compliment. There are all things in the king's Speech that can be spoken of in this house, Religion and Property, &c. Would look upon the genus before the species: supposes thanks to the king, with due consideration of his Speech, very proper.

Sir *John Mallet*. Mr. Speaker; since we were last in this place, there having been much discourse abroad, and some considerable doubts concerning our coming hither again, it is my duty (having always had as true loyalty and affection to his majesty's service, as any within these walls, or nation, hath or can have) humbly to offer my advice in this matter of so great weight and moment. That I conceive, before we enter upon any other business, it will be the best way for removing the doubts, which are, or may hereafter, arise, concerning this last prorogation; without letting so tender a matter remain under any doubt or question, and also that it will be the safest and speediest way for satisfying his majesty, with satisfaction to all his people, and that they may be assured of such good laws as shall be made (for his maj. is so gracious, as he accounts as great satisfaction to himself, to give us the good laws we desire of him, as to receive the Supply we shall give him) humbly to present our desires to his majesty, 'that he will be pleased to dissolve this, and very quickly call another parliament.' For I verily believe, whatsoever he would have in this, may more conveniently, in a very short time, be had and done in another parliament. Sir, I could present you with several reasons for it, but I humbly crave leave to forbear mentioning them till you please to admit of this my humble motion.*

Sir *Philip Monckton*. No man is more rejoiced to see you here, than he is. It would be a great satisfaction to the nation to have the two Acts of Edw. iii. about annual Parliaments, cleared; and moves it.

Sir *John Morton*. Would do all things regularly. Would first read a bill, and then consider the king's Speech.

Sir *Tho. Meres*. Though forms seem but little things, yet they are of great consequence. He will thank the king as much as any man. When a Bill is read, then we are fit for any motion.

Lord *Cavendish*. The motion is of no light nature, since we are told it is a doubt, all over the nation, whether the Prorogation be legal: thinks it not for our credit to pass it over without a question. Though the doubt may easily be removed, yet it is fit to be removed. We are told of two Acts of Edw. iii. and this Prorogation is contrary to them. Desires, that, since these acts are known, we may see how far these acts limit the king in his Prorogation. Moves for a question, Whether the two Acts mentioned be repealed, or not.

Mr. Sec. *Coventry* moves to order. If you admit that question, you may lay down your mace, you are no more a parliament. Who shall dissolve it? Who shall end it? We have nothing to do here.

Lord *Cavendish* desires to explain himself. Moves to order; to clear a doubt. There are books printed of an odd nature. Moves only to know, Whether those two Acts, mentioned, are in force against the king's prerogative.

Serj. *Maynard*. The question determines what you cannot determine, viz. That you are

* The above Speech was given to the Compiler (Mr. Grey) by sir John Mallet himself.

an unlawful assembly. The question will be, Whether, as a parliament, you cannot dissolve yourselves. No question, Whether those laws are in force, or not, can be put; for you read the very question as a parliament.

Sir *Harbottle Grimstone*, (Master of the Rolls.*) If we appear here in either capacity, by the proclamation, or by the king's writ, it does not therefore follow, that because we appear, we are a parliament. [Being called upon to look towards the Chair, when he spoke, he said, 'He had almost forgot the Chair, it was so long since he saw it.'] If by freedom of debate we may obviate doubts, which have troubled worthy and learned men, why should we not? He denies Maynard's logic, 'That the king's proclamation will justify our assembly,' though we had no more to show for it on the table. This may be a question somewhere else, as well as here, and would remove moot points and doubts in succeeding parliaments.

Mr. *Sacheverell* doubts not but we are as much a parliament, as at our last prorogation, and believes that gentlemen, upon debate of it, will be as fully satisfied in the matter as he is. He looks upon this prorogation as illegal, but yet that it is a good parliament still, and that we properly stand upon an adjournment. Would look back to the time those statutes mentioned were made in, and you shall see then Prorogations and Adjournments were all one, and for hundreds of years they went on to the same business they left, without beginning again as we have done in adjournments in later times. There have been prorogations before the parliament had once met, and for some reasons, as the king being detained by business, that he could not in person open this parliament, or for want of a full appearance of members, put off to a longer day. In E. i. E. iii. E. iv. it runs thus. 'Sic Dom. Rex adjournavit et prorogavit,' &c. And he takes this to be an adjournment. Adjournment is the act of the two houses, prorogation of the king only; and so by adjournment, your business remains where it did.

Sir *Rob. Howard*. You are upon the most dangerous debate that may be, and from which no good consequence can arise. If we meet upon an adjournment now, then all privileges of members stand good, and you lay all people by the heels that have arrested any of your members. If you debate upon deducible arguments, you set the town at work, and enter the lists, at the coffee-houses. If you run once to countenance great things by deducible arguments, you shake laws and mighty things. Moves to lay aside this dangerous debate.

Mr. *Sawyer*. You ought to begin the session with reading a Bill, and you meet in no capacity but as a parliament, not as a Convention. Your vote will not mar nor mend the matter. There have been books written about this question. He hopes you will not give countenance to such libels, that say, 'we are traitors in meeting, and acting as a parliament'.*

* Speaker of the parliament that restored the King. He died in 1684, aged 82.

* "It is remarkable" says Mr. Marvell, "that shortly after, upon occasion of a discourse among the commons concerning Libels and Pamphlets, first one member of them stood up, and, in the face of their house, said, 'That 'it was affirmed to him, by a person that might 'be spoke with, that there were among them '30, 40, 50, God knows how many, outlawed.' Another thereupon rose, and told them, 'It 'was reported too, that there were divers of 'the members Papists:' a third, 'That a mul'titude of them were bribed, and Pensioners.' And yet all this was patiently hushed up by their house, and digested, being, it seems, a thing of that nature which there was no reply to."

Under the head of BRIBERY, the same Author gives us the following dreadful particulars: "It is too notorious to be concealed, that *near a third part* of the house have beneficial Offices under his majesty, in the privy council, the army, the navy, the law, the household, the revenue both in England and Ireland, or in attendance on his majesty's person. These are all of them indeed to be esteemed gentlemen of honour, but more or less according to the quality of their several employments under his majesty; and it is to be presumed that they brought along with them some honour of their own into his service at first, to set up with. Nor is it fit that such an assembly should be destitute of them to inform the commons of his majesty's affairs, and communicate his counsels, so that they do not by irregular procuring of elections in places where they have no proper interest, thrust out the gentlemen that have, and thereby disturb the several counties; nor that they crowd into the house in numbers beyond modesty, and which instead of giving a temper to their deliberations, may seem to affect the predominance.—Yet common discretion would teach them not to seek after, and ingross such different trusts in those bordering interests of the king and country, where from the people they have no legal advantage, but so much may be gained by betraying them. How improper would it seem for a privy counsellor, if in the house of commons he should not justify the most arbitrary proceedings of the Council Table, represent affairs of state with another face, defend any misgovernment, patronize the greatest offenders against the kingdom, even though they were too his own particular enemies, and extend the supposed prerogative on all occasions, to the detriment of the subject's certain and due liberties? What self-denial were it in the learned council at law, did they not vindicate the misdemeanours of the Judges, perplex all remedies against the corruptions and encroachment of Courts of Judicature, word all acts towards the advantage of their own profession, palliate unlawful elections, ex-

The *Speaker*. The session is not begun till a bill be read; it is the ancient Order, and if so, your question is, Whether you will break that Order, or not.

Mr. *Garroway* thinks we may safely read the Bill, and yet the debate may be reserved. He is one who believes this as good a parliament as when we first sat. Though yet he is not very fond of it neither.

Col. *Birch* does not see you can go on in safety under a prorogation. One gentleman, tells you, 'of books and pamphlets abroad on

---

tenuate and advocate public crimes, where the criminal may prove considerable, step into the Chair of a Money bill, and pen the Clauses so dubiously, that they may be interpretable in Westminster-hall beyond the house's intention, mislead the house, not only in point of law, but even in matter of fact, without any respect to veracity but all to his own further promotion? What Soldier in pay but might think himself fit to be cashiered, should he oppose the increase of Standing Forces, the depression of Civil Authority, or the levying of Money by whatsoever means, or in what quantity? Or who of them ought not to 'abhor that traiterous position, of taking Arms by the king's authority against those that are commissionated by him in pursuance of such commission?' What Officer of the Navy, but takes himself under obligation to magnify the expence, extol the management, conceal the neglect, increase the debts, and press the necessity of rigging and unrigging it to the house in the same moment, and representing it all at once in a good and a bad condition? Should any member of parliament and of the exchequer omit to transform the Accounts, conceal the Issues, heighten the Anticipations, and in despight of himself oblige whosoever chance to be the lord treasurer; might not his *Reversioner* (sir Robert Howard) justly expect to be put into present possession of the office? Who, that is either concerned in the Customs, or of their brethren of the Excise, can with any decency refuse, if they do not invent all further impositions upon merchandize, navigation, or our own domestic growth and consumption: and if the charge be but temporary, to perpetuate it? Hence it came, that, instead of relieving the crown by the good old and certain way of Subsidies, wherein nothing was to be got by the house of commons, they devised this foreign course of Revenue, to the great grievance and double charge of the people, that so many of the members might be gratified in the farms or commissions.—But to conclude this digression: Whatsoever other Offices have been set up for the use of the members, or have been extinguished upon occasion, should they have failed at a question, did not they deserve to be turned out? Were not all the Votes, as it were in fee farm, of those that were intrusted with the sale? Must not Surinam be a sufficient cause of quarrel with Holland, to any Commissioner of the Plantations? Or who would have denied money to continue the War with Holland, when he were a Commissioner of Prizes, of Sick and Wounded, or transporting the English, or of starving the Dutch, prisoners? How much greater then would the hardship be for those of his majesty's houshold, or who attend upon his royal person, to forget by any chance vote, or in being absent from the house, that they are his domestic servants? Or that all those of the capacity abovementioned are to be looked upon as a distinct body under another discipline; and whatsoever sin they may commit in the house of commons against the national interest, they take themselves to be justified by their circumstances; their hearts indeed are, they say, with the country; and one of them (Hervey, vice chamberlain) had the boldness to tell his majesty, 'That he was come from voting in the house *against his Conscience*.'—And yet these gentlemen being full, and already in employment, are more good-natured and less dangerous to the public, than those that are hungry and out of office, who may by probable computation make *another third part* of this house of commons. Those are such as having observed by what steps, or rather leaps and strides, others of their house have ascended into the highest places of the kingdom, do, upon measuring their own birth, estates, parts, and merit, think themselves as well and better qualified in all respects as their former companions. They are generally men, who by speaking against the French, inveighing against the debauches of court, talking of the ill management of the Revenue, and such popular flourishes, have cheated the countries into electing them; and when they come up, if they can speak in the house, they make a faint attack or two upon some great minister of state, and perhaps relieve some other that is in danger of parliament, to make themselves either way considerable.—In matters of Money they seem at first difficult, but *having been discoursed with in private*, they are set right, and begin to *understand it better* themselves, and to convert their brethren; *for they are all of them to be bought and sold*; only their number makes them cheaper, and each of them doth so overvalue himself, that sometimes they outstand or let slip their own market.—It is not to be imagined, how small things in this case, even members of great estates, will stoop at; and most of them will do as much for hopes, as others for fruition; but if their patience be tired out, they grow at last mutinous and revolt to the country, till some better occasion offer. Among these are some men of the best understanding, were they of equal integrity, who affect to ingross all business, to be able to quash any good motion by parliamentary skill, unless themselves be the authors, and to be the leading men of the house, and for their natural lives to continue so. But these are men that have been once fooled, most of them, and discovered, and slighted at court; so that till some turn of state this subject.' It may be, he is of that courage, as not to heed them; but he does. Those in the Long Parliament were willing to keep their places, and he never yet met with any that were willing to part with theirs. But he would prevent dogs barking, 'that we do contrary to law by sitting as in a prorogation,' and would be provided against this, not knowing what this may overturn hereafter.

Mr. *Harwood.* Discourse of people abroad is a great thing, and not to be slighted: we are not safe from the law taking hold upon us.

---

shall set them in their adversaries place, they look sullen, make big motions, and contrive specious Bills for the subject; yet only wait the opportunity to be the instruments of the same counsels, which they oppose in others. —There is *a third part* still remaining, but as contrary in themselves as light and darkness; those are either the worst, or the best of men; the first are most profligate persons that have neither estates, consciences, nor good manners, yet are therefore picked out as the necessary men, and whose votes will go furthest: the *Charges of their Elections are defrayed*, whatever they amount to; *tables are kept for them* at Whitehall, and through Westminster, that they may be ready at hand, within call of a question: all of them are received into pension, and know their pay-day which they never fail of: insomuch that a great officer (the Lord Treasurer) was pleased to say, '*That they came about him like so many jack-daws for cheese, at the end of every session.*' If they be not in parliament, they must be in prison; and as they are protected themselves, by privilege, so they sell their protections to others, to the obstruction so many years together of the law of the land, and the public justice; for these it is that the long and frequent Adjournments are calculated; but all, whether the Court or the monopolizers of the Country party, or those that profane the title of Old Cavaliers, do equally, though upon differing reasons, like death, apprehend a Dissolution. But notwithstanding these, there is an handful of salt, a sparkle of soul, that hath hitherto preserved this gross body from putrefaction; some gentlemen that are constant, invariable, indeed Englishmen, such as are above hopes or fears, or dissimulation, that can neither flatter nor betray their king or country; but being consious of their own loyalty and integrity, proceed through good and bad report, to acquit themselves in their duty to God, their prince, and their nation; although so small a scantling in number, that men can scarce reckon of them more than a quorum; insomuch that it is less difficult to conceive how fire was first brought to light in the world, than how any good thing could ever be produced out of an house of commons so constituted; unless, as that is imagined to have come from the rushing of trees, or battering of rocks together, by accident, so these by their clashing with one another, have struck out an useful effect from so unlikely causes. But whatsoever casual good hath been wrought at any time by the assimilation of ambitious, factious, and disappointed members, to the little, but solid, and unbiassed, party, the more frequent ill effects and consequences of so unequal a mixture, so long continued, are demonstrable and apparent. For while scarce any man comes thither with respect to the public service, but in design to make and raise his fortune, it is not to be exprest the debauchery and lewdness, which upon occasion of Elections to parliament, are now grown habitual throughout the nation. So that the vice and the expence are risen to such a prodigious height, that few sober men can endure to stand to be chosen on such conditions. From whence also arise feuds and perpetual animosities, over most of the counties and corporations, while gentlemen of worth, spirit, and ancient estates and dependances, see themselves overpowered in their own neighbourhood, by the drunkenness and bribery of their competitors. But if, nevertheless, any worthy person chance to carry the election, some mercenary or corrupt sheriff makes a double return; and so the cause is handed to the Committee of Elections, who ask no better, but are ready to adopt his adversary into the house if he be not legitimate: and if the gentleman aggrieved seek his remedy against the sheriff, in Westminster-hall, and the proofs be so palpable that the King's Bench cannot invent how to do him injustice, yet the major part of the twelve judges, shall, upon better consideration, vacate the Sheriff's Fine, and reverse the judgment; but those of them that dare dissent from their brethren are in danger to be turned off the bench, without any cause assigned. While men therefore care not thus how they get into the h. of commons, neither can it be expected that they should make any conscience of what they do there; but they are only intent how to reimburse themselves (if their elections were at their own charge) or how to bargain their Votes for a Place or a Pension. They list themselves straightways into some Court-faction; and it is as well known among them, to what lord each of them retains, as when formerly they wore coats and badges. By this long haunting so together they are grown too so familiar among themselves, that all reverence of their own assembly is lost; that they live together, not like parliament-men, but like so many goodfellows, met together in a public house, to make merry. And, which is yet worse, being so thoroughly acquainted, they understand their Number and Party; so that the use of so public a council is frustrated; there is no place for deliberation, no persuading by reason; but they can see one another's votes through both throats and cravats, before they hear them.—Where the cards are so well known, they are only fit for a cheat, and no fair gamester but would throw them under the table. Hereby it is, that their house hath lost all the ancient

No man has the impudence to break the king's prorogation, and yet he would not part with the people's liberty.

Sir *Ch. Harbord.* All parliaments are in being till dissolved by death of the king, or by word of his mouth. There have been several prorogations of 15 months.

Mr. *Russel* is no great reader of statutes, and therefore is no competent judge of those mentioned, but since it is a question, whether they be in force, or no, men must be satisfied. Therefore he moves for an Address to the king, That we may (to put all things out of doubt) be dissolved.

Sir *Rd. Temple.* Because the legality of our meeting is questioned by libels without doors, must we therefore make it a question within doors? Heretofore, at the opening a session, the Speaker chose some Bill to be read, that would probably take up least debate; and would punish those who have dispersed these libels.

Sir *John Coventry* would have the house, in the least of our actions, express our loyalty. He believes this to be a parliament, and as good as ever it was, but hopes we sit not by proclamation-law. He plainly sees we have sat so long that the people are weary of us; and seconds the motion for an Address to the king to dissolve us.

Mr. *Williams* is of opinion, that the parliament is in being, but whether by prorogation or adjournment, is the question. He is against reading that Bill, because it will stop the mouths of gentlemen in the debate, and by it we must admit ourselves to meet now under a prorogation, and, for the like reason, is for reading the other bill, and reserving the farther debate. He hears discourses abroad that we are dissolved by this long prorogation. We cannot constitute ourselves a parliament, if we be none; but by our solemn debates, with reason, we may, in some measure, satisfy the world. Therefore moves for the Bill to be read a 2nd time.

Sir *George Reeves* offers a bill 'for regulating Elections of Members of Parliament,' ordered to be brought in the last session.—Which was read accordingly, and ordered a 2nd reading.

Sir *Tho. Meres* A Bill is now read, and, before it, the king's Speech was read; doubts not of hearts full of thanks for the king's gracious expressions in his Speech: no man doubts but the matters of it are of great weight, and we should have, at least, two or three days time to consider it; therefore moves for Tuesday to take it into consideration.

Mr. *Neale* thinks Tuesday a great while to defer the consideration of the king's Speech, considering you give him no thanks for it in the mean time. Moves for Monday, and no business to intervene, no, not privilege, till the safety of the nation be provided for.

Resolved, "That the king's Speech be taken into consideration on Tuesday."

Feb. 17. The debate was resumed, and the question being propounded, That the house do proceed to name their Grand Committee, it was carried 193 to 142.

Debate on Sir T. Strickland's Conviction of Popery.] Feb. 19. The house having been informed of sir Tho. Strickland's conviction of Recusancy, and been moved for a writ to be issued out to chuse a knight for Westmorland, in his stead, Ordered the record of his Conviction to be brought in by the clerk of the crown: and

The *Speaker* informed the house, That, by the record, it appears that he stood convicted of Recusancy, according to the form of the statute, but whether he be the same sir Tho. Strickland, member of the house, appears not.

Sir *Wm. Coventry* has known this gentleman many years before he sat here. For common respect, especially for one who has sat so long amongst us, would give him some time, though not by way of summons. It may else possibly be an inconvenience to his fortune; but if he come not, in some reasonable time, to give an account of himself, would send out a new writ, to chuse another member in his stead; but would do it without summons to him.

Mr. *Powle.* We cannot be too careful, when we are about to expel a member, especially when we remember that a minor part has once expelled a major in the Long Parliament. This gentleman may be convicted, and possibly know nothing of it. As for summoning of him, and that attested here at the bar, there can be no inconvenience; for he may absent himself, and you may take it pro confesso; and go solemnly to summoning him, and, if he appear not, then send a new writ to elect a member in his stead.

Sir *Tho. Meres.* It is properly no 'summons,' but 'notice,' to give the thing a more easy word.

Mr. *Whorwood* is as tender as any man for

weight and authority; and, being conscious of their own guilt and weakness, dare not adventure, as heretofore, the impeaching of any man before the lords, for the most heinous crimes of state, and the most public misdemeanors; upon which confidence it is that the conspirators have so long presumed, and gone unpunished. For although the conspirators have sometimes (that this house might appear still necessary to the people, and to make the money more glib) yielded, that even their own names should be tossed among them, and grievances be talked of, yet, at the same time, they have been so prevalent, as to hinder any effect; and, if the house has emancipated itself beyond instructions, then by chastizing them with Prorogations, frighting them with Dissolution, comforting them with long, frequent, and seasonable Adjournments; now by suspending or diminishing their Pensions, then again by increasing them; sometimes by a scorn, otherwhiles by a favour, there hath a way been found to reduce them again under discipline."

this gentleman, but thinks such scruples strange. He is fortunate that he has escaped this enquiry so long, and sat here without expulsion: would therefore have a summons plainly sent to him, and if thereupon he comes not, he wishes him gone.

Sir *John Birkenhead.* Strickland has taken the oath of Allegiance and Supremacy here, at his first admission, and the former he will take, and the lords are not obliged to the other.

Sir *Tho. Lee.* It is strange that Birkenhead should proffer you any thing against law. Both oaths are to be taken here.

The Speaker was ordered to give sir Tho. Strickland notice by letter accordingly.

A Supply of 600,000l. voted.] Feb. 21. Sir Rd. Temple reported from the Committee of the whole house, That it is the opinion of the committee, that a Supply be given to his majesty for the Building of Ships not exceeding 600,000*l.*; to which the house agreed.

Debate on the Bill to encourage the planting of Hemp and Flax.] March 1. A Bill to encourage the planting and sowing of Hemp and Flax was read the 2nd time.

Sir *Tho. Mompesson.* The bill is not practicable. Some lands cannot bear hemp.

Mr. *Sacheverell* would have the committee consider what countries the bill will be proper for. It is for ours, and would commit it.

Col. *Birch.* He brought the Bill in. In a body natural, if all the blood be brought up into the head, there will follow a dissolution. All the money is brought to London, and little left in the country but clipt and worn money. If it be so in fact, what will England come to in a short time? The country is almost depopulated for want of employment, and the people will follow employment. Employment is either from husbandry or trade. Want of people has forced the farmer to thrash himself. He cannot keep servants, corn is so cheap; and when it is got, there is nobody to eat it, and yet when we reap it, there is 18*d.* or 2*s.* a day for workmen, so few are there to be got. He is far from thinking this bill to be a present advantage to the nation this year: but where land is proper for it, in most towns some is sown. This is the end of this bill; if it pass, not one poor person will be in England that will but work. This half acre (enjoined in the Bill) is as much as most of the poor of a parish can dress. A poor woman that can get 3½*d.* a day will work, but you have not work for them without such a bill, not for one in ten: 20*s.* worth of linen takes up more hands to make it, than ten pounds-worth of woollen. Though there is a statute to set the poor to work, it rather increases the poor, than tends to a diminution. They allow them money weekly. If wool should fail, this would set the poor to work. You pay 150,000*l.* per ann. for foreign linnens: possibly, you may clap some of the money to be raised upon it. Possibly, you may employ all the poor, and whether you will continue this expensive trade of linen, and be pestered with poor for a year or two's inconvenience on gentlemen's lands, till this be settled, leaves it to you.

Mr. *Swynfin* thinks it a great confidence in Birch to teach all gentlemen and farmers in England how to husband their land. If there be any profit in planting hemp and flax, there needs no law to compel men to it, but that of necessity, all ways else failing. Flax and hemp are no strangers here. The sowing of it goes out, because people make no profit of it. If it were for their advantage, men would turn all their lands to it. Birch tells you, 'he has sown none these 7 years, though he has land fit for it.' He believes he can make no profit of it. Is it imaginable this can take any effect? By experience, we find, flax is at so low a rate that they sow it no more, and persons will pay a penalty rather than do it, and so the act may be an universal penalty. It may possibly breed some surveyors, and make officers break their oaths. How can he swear to so many acres? Can this then help the poor, or the farmers, who, by this law, must groan under the penalties? This bill is, upon a supposition only, to put all husbandmen upon new experiments. Let us have no more trouble with this bill, to hinder us from greater affairs.

Sir *George Downing* believes that for French linen there goes alone 500,000*l.* per ann. besides other linen. He is for the bill, but utterly against the imposing the half acre in a 100 acres to be planted with hemp and flax under a penalty. He knows a hundred parishes that have not one acre fit for it. Would move for planting olives, oranges, or pomegranates, as practicable as this. Hemp and flax can only be planted on mellow ground. You may as well plant Canary wine, under as specious pretences, as hemp and flax. By this bill, we bring in a law to wipe away all covenants and jointures, &c. nay, to plough up old pasture, and meadows, and perhaps in 20 years no grass will come up again. Consider what this charitable pretence of relieving the poor has been. But so much tax upon your lands.

Sir *Wm. Coventry* desires that encouragement may be given to the planting hemp and flax. But the only material objection is, the compulsatory parts of the bill. They are not usually well executed; mens hearts go not along with it. He would have the committee think of an inducement and encouragement to do it, as well as compulsion.—The Bill was ordered to be committed.

Complaint against the Clerk.] Sir *Tho. Lee* finds no Order for the business of the day, for the house to go into a Grand Committee for Grievances; and, he believes, no Order will be entered for the future, but what shall be acceptable to the Clerk.

Mr. *Garroway* moves for a new Clerk, this clerk having several times abused us; and would have him removed.

Sir *Wm. Hickman.* The clerk has served you so very often, and at this time he puts gentlemen into committees whom he knows to be in Lancashire.

Mr. *Sacheverell* thinks, if you let this pass, you may as well burn all your Journals. He has been one of the Committee for inspecting the Journals, and has had a Report ready in his hand these 4 sessions. In the session of 1672, the sense of the house was declared so, and entered otherwise. He moves for a new clerk, and that the king may be desired it. The two first pages of that session may much call in question the privilege and right of this house.

Col. *Birch* is for a new clerk. He has heard complaints of him these 7 years, of these miscarriages. When Birkenhead says, 'Rolls and Records,' he tells you they are so of his knowledge, and not one print agrees with the Rolls in matter and form. He takes thus the law to be. If any printed Act agrees not with the Record, a person tried may appeal to the Record, whether the law be so or not. Judge then the danger of false entering things in our books.

The Order for the day not being entered into the Journal by the Clerk, the consideration of Grievances was adjourned to Saturday next; and a Committee was appointed to inspect the Journal of the year 1672, and to examine and report the matter of the entry.

Debate on Dr. Cary's Commitment by the Lords.] March 2. Lord *Cavendish* moved to consider of the manner of Dr. Cary's Commitment to the Tower by the lords, &c.* And produced a copy of the lords Order of commitment.

Sir *Tho. Clarges* moves that a Committee may be appointed to search the Lords Journal, to state the matter of fact; the king having particularly recommended it to the lords care, not to occasion any difference between them and the commons.

Mr. Sec. *Coventry*. Dr. Cary is committed for bringing a libel to the press, which maintains 'that you sit wrongfully and have no right to sit as a parliament.' Whether this be not cognizable by the lords, as well as you, is the question. He has refused to give any satisfaction to the lords from whom he had the libel, and so they have committed him for libelling them, as you would have had cognizance, if he had violated or struck any lord or member.

Sir *Tho. Lee* fears that the lords will encroach precedents upon you; possibly the thing moved for is too early. But crimes against the government are not to be immediately punished in parliament for the law is open.

Mr. *Sacheverell*. For the seasonableness of the motion he will not speak, but the thing being come before you, the matter is, how to get off from it. 21 and 22 R. ii. a statute was made to rule that power, just as the lords do now exercise it, to prevent taking off commoners heads at their pleasure. This was the ground of all your first difference with the lords; they taking a cause originally before them. If the power of the lords be to examine a commoner against himself, and to condemn him for not answering, he knows not what condition we all are in. He would therefore have the matter looked into, and if it appear to be as it is represented, would proceed in it; and moves for some persons to be appointed to search the lords Journal.

Mr. Sec. *Coventry*. If this house, and the lords house, can find no way to punish such seditious libellers, you may be pulled out of your Chair; and as they brought the late king to the block, at this rate they may do this also. And moves to proceed no farther in this thing, and the lords punishment of Dr. Cary is just.

Mr. *Williams*. He hears this thing of the lords commitment of Cary justified from the bar, before we know what it is. Moves to have Ernly's paper read.

Sir *Wm. Coventry* was ever before for a moderate course with the lords. We are told how terrible the meddling with this matter might be, but he knows not the terror of it in the enquiry. Would have you proceed to the business of the day, and inform yourselves better in this matter.

Mr. *Powle* has seen a copy of this Order from the lords, for the commitment of Dr. Cary. It seems a matter of that weight, that, at least, as it is put, it deserves mature consideration. If this be so, no commoner of England but is at the lords mercy. This came not criminally yet before the lords; but they take it originally. Whether Dr. Cary be criminal is not the question; but the manner of his condemnation. What a man says against the government in particular is not cognizable in the lords house, any more than in another place. This is a crime no more particularly affixed to the lords than to this house. The lords examine him, and require him to accuse himself, or somebody else. By this means, any thing in the king's bench may be proceeded upon in the lords house. In this he would show that we are only upon the defensive part, and that we seek no occasion of difference with the lords. It is our desire that the precedent of 21 R. ii. may be prevented. This is so tender a point, that he would not let it go without a day to consider it farther; and would not have the world think the house so cold in so great a matter.

* "One Dr. Cary was brought to the bar of the house of lords, and questioned concerning a MS. treating of the illegality of the Prorogation, which he had carried to the press; and because he declined answering such questions as were put to him, and took sanctuary in the laws, which oblige no man to accuse himself, they fined him 1000*l.* and sent him close prisoner to the Tower till it was paid. That the lords, who had made so free with their own privileges, by submitting the liberty of four of their body at once to the pleasure of his majesty, should make thus free with both the liberty and property of a commoner, is perhaps scarce to be wondered at." Ralph.

Mr. *Sawyer*. Shall any member here undertake to know what the lords do? You have only the bare information of this matter before you of one member of this house, and no more. He is much afraid to give countenance to things of this nature. One book now abroad concerns us. It calls us 'traytors and rebels for meeting as a parliament,' and either house may enquire into such incendiaries. You passed the same sentence upon Mr. Howard, the last session; he would not say he did or did not write the letter, and you took it, pro confesso, and committed him to the Tower.*

Lord *Cavendish*. If this be a crime against the government, as is alledged, he would know whether the lords can judge it without a jury.

Mr. *Sawyer*. Invading our privileges, is invading the government, and such matters may be tried in either house, and this matter more especially in the lords house. Other courts may be timorous. In point of law you punish no man but as he offends against the government.

Sir *Wm. Coventry* will not contend matter of law with Sawyer, but would enter his claim, that we do not take ourselves to be part of the government, for then the government is no monarchy. We are only a part of the legislature: and would enter his claim against any such doctrine to be delivered here.

Mr. *Sawyer*. Explains himself. He acknowedges judgment and legislature, &c.

Sir *Wm. Coventry* takes the government to be as much, and more the ministerial part, as the legislature.

The *Speaker*. No cognizance can be taken of the lords proceedings unless they come regularly before you. It is the first instance of this kind. You judge them in their judicature of what is not before you. You may do it to any part of their judicature, as well as this. You may else raise what you cannot lay. But he is always for the privilege of this house.

Sir *Tho. Lee* remembers one man (Fitton) punished by the lords for making application to this house. It is a proper and regular way, and this matter may be brought before you by information of a member, as well as by petition from the party grieved. The question is not about the crime, but whether Dr. Cary be regularly brought to punishment. Here a man is committed without impeachment; you are the jury, and all men ought to be tried per pares. He thinks this properly represented to you, and would farther consider of it.

Sir *H. Goodrick*. In this matter we are under so great a restraint, that he knows not how we shall deliver ourselves. The eyes and prayers of the country are that we may have no difference with the lords. But when he considers the cries of the people, and the king's advice to us, in his Speech, not to entertain differences with the lords, and that it is not a time of day to do it, they that press this, he declares, are no friends to the good of the nation: explains what he has said, and will make it good. But submits it to the judgment of the house, and farther, whoever proceeds so is no friend to the nation. He has thought of it, and hopes to make it good.

Lord *Cavendish*. Is sorry to hear so great a reflection from Goodrick upon all gentlemen concerned in this debate, and upon himself who brought the debate in. No gentlemen that debated this but are as good 'friends to the nation,' and would not proceed, as little as Goodrick, to a difference with the lords; and must say, That from Goodrick was an indiscreet expression. He was taken down to Order.

Col. *Birch*. By order of the house, the words whereby lord Cavendish was offended must be written down, and asserted. Thinks that Goodrick said, 'they that press this business are no friends to the nation.'

Sir *Philip Harcourt*. The business is of a great nature, and he would have you, Mr. Speaker, declare, by order, whether the words are not to be asserted, and written down, before any explanation be admitted of them.

Mr. *Garroway*. Goodrick owned his words, and brought them to his own explanation. Your order is, 'those words that gave exception ought to be written down,' and you debate whether those words were said, or not. He believes Goodrick will so explain himself as to give you satisfaction.

Serj. *Maynard* apprehends the words were very bad, but let them be what they will, if you go to censure the person for the words, they must be written down. It was his own case twice, long ago, but he had liberty first to explain himself: for a man may sometimes outgo himself, and it may be every man's case.

Sir *H. Goodrick*. He is ready to give satisfaction to the house, and every particular member. He intended no reflection upon any gentleman. His words were: 'He that promoted this difference betwixt the lords and us was an enemy to the nation.' That was his intention, whatever were his words.

Sir *Tho. Meres* doubts that the words were otherwise, but would have them accepted as the gentlemen says he intended them. He would have us all bear with one another. We have always borne with the interpretation of the man that spoke the words, and without doubt, 'he is no friend to the nation, that promotes differences between the lords, and us.' But to go on, he believes that lord Cavendish brings the Order for Dr. Cary's commitment, by the lords, regularly before you; it is by the very same method as you went in sir John Fagg's case. You were informed of it by a member then, and no otherwise, and the farther consideration thereof was adjourned till Monday. To-morrow is the day appointed to consider of grievances; and this is the greatest. No man here, he believes, values Dr. Cary in prison, neither the man nor the punishment; but the manner of laying the punishment is

* See p. 770.

what we have reason to except against. This is not the privilege of a particular lord.

Lord *Cavendish* called Meres to Order, viz. That Goodrick meant particularly what he said to reflect upon himself, and not generally speaking.

Sir *Wm. Coventry.* What he heard Goodrick speak was, 'That they are no friends to the nation that promote a difference between the lords and us.' We have great reason, in these cases, to give grains of allowance to one another. In ancient times but a few persons spoke in the house, and their speeches were ready penned. The powder and shot was ready made up in cartridges; ready cut and dried, and a man had then time to think; but now we speak on a sudden, and therefore would have some grains of allowance given.

Lord *Burleigh** thinks that Goodrick's words particularly reflected upon lord Cavendish,† and would have them set down.

Sir *Henry Goodrick.* He should speak much against both his obligations and judgment, if he intended lord Cavendish, in what he said, or any other gentleman, in particular.

Sir *Tho. Meres* is glad that an end is made of this matter, as to lord Cavendish, who, he thinks, has satisfaction from Goodrick. But he would consider the manner of this judgment (upon Dr. Cary) of the lords, on a commoner. We ought to have as great and as good a privilege as the lords, but would not go on this, without being extremely clear, and perhaps we may find out more privilege than we know of already. Will press no question, but that the matter stands fair for another consideration.

Serj. *Maynard.* If there be public breaches on the liberty of the people, it is not strange to enquire into them. He fears this commitment of Dr. Cary has raised more dust than can be laid. He must come into a court where he may be indicted, and no man must be accused but by writ 'from some of the king's courts.' It will be one question, Whether Dr. Cary has offended before the parliament sat, or since; in or out of parliament? if a man be brought here for words spoken against this house, will not you commit him? if a man contemns any court, that court may fine any man. If the matter will hold you may go on, else it is a very ill thing to contend in this matter. If he be committed for contempt of an order, see what it is; and then consider whether you will go through or not.

Mr. *Garroway.* If Dr. Cary be committed for contempt indefinite, and we desire to know the cause from the lords, and they tell you it is for a breach of their privilege, then there is an end of it. The king, in what he said of avoiding controversy with the lords, never intended thereby to cut you off from your just privileges. No man will think so irreverently of the king. And you, Mr. Speaker, may go out of the chair without any question, in this matter, and he will move it again when we are better informed.*

* Son of the earl of Exeter, to which title he succeeded, on his father's death, in 1687. He died in France in 1700;

† He married lord Cavendish's sister.

Debate on a Bill to repeal the Statute of Wages to Members of Parliament.] March 3. Sir *Harbottle Grimstone,* (Master of the Rolls) moved, that he might have leave to bring in a Bill for the Indemnifying the Counties, Cities and Boroughs from paying any Wages now due to Members that serve in Parliament, and desired it might be in particular for Colchester, the place he serves for. For a writ had gone down from sir John Shaw, (his fellow burgess) to receive his wages for service done in parliament.†

Mr. *Williams.* The statute of limitations will cut off all the Wages, but of the last six years. He is against removing old land marks; what is an evidence betwixt man and man, electors and elected, he would not remove. He is not for imposing any thing upon corporations; he will trust his own corporation, but not every little borough. The Wages will not be due for a whole year, but for the days only that we sit here. He would trust the generosity of the members, in this of their Wages, and not have a bill for it. He has already released his wages.

Mr. *Powle.* The statute of limitations cuts not off a debt, but from six years after it is due; and this is not due till the parliament is ended, and therefore not cut off by that statute. Williams says, 'That wages are not due but for the days you sit here.' But for those that come from Cumberland, and such remote places, they have had sometimes 14 days allowed them, and to all the members, morando, redeundo, eundo. And if wages be demanded accordingly, it will ruin many poor boroughs. We are now estimated to have sat in this parliament 3000 days, which will be 600*l.* and the question is, whether Wages are not due in prorogations, as well as adjournments. For the ill use that may be made of this, when this parliament is at an end, he would have wages cut off. For debts, when they are grown old, are very heavy when paid, and consider how we load them now by this tax we have granted. But he would have this discharge of Wages for no more than what is already incurred, and not forward.

Mr. *Sawyer.* You have been offered the statute of limitations. That of Wages is not an action, but in the nature of a judicial writ, unto which the statute of limitation is not to be pleaded, being matter of record. Some wages have been already paid, and some persons are but lately come in. But he looks upon it for

* There is no mention of this debate in the Journal.

† Andrew Marvell, who was member for Kingston upon Hull, is said to have been the last who received these wages.

the honour of the house, that, where wages have not been received, we may imitate the statute of limitations; excepting the two last years.

Mr. *Boscawen* knows not why Sawyer, that has been here but two years, should give away his wages that has been here 16 years. It is generally promised at elections, in boroughs, to serve freely, and why an act should not be to confirm those promises, he knows not. He thinks it worthy your consideration to put the boroughs out of fear. For hereafter they will chuse their own burgesses, blue aprons, and gentlemen no more.

Mr. *Finch* is not for this bill, though thus magnified to you. All Wages are limited to eundo, morando, redeundo, and expressly limited by the writ to levy it. By 6 H. viii. 'No person that departs from parliament without leave of the Speaker and house, entered first into the Journal, shall have his Wages.' And Prynne's Register of Writs goes so far as to prove attendance here every day—but by this bill you take away from every gentleman an opportunity of obliging his corporation.

Sir *Wm. Thompson* intimated, that the city of London paid Wages formerly. He has received no wages, though the city is able to pay them.

Mr. *Love.* He never received any Wages from the city, nor demanded any, because he thinks he never deserved any at their hands.—A Bill was ordered to be brought in accordingly.

Sir Tho. Strickland expelled.] March 6. Sir Tho. Strickland sent a Letter to the Speaker, in answer to the notice which the Speaker had sent him by Order of the house, (p. 835) by way of excuse for his non-attendance in parliament, &c.

Resolved, "That whereas it doth appear to this house, that sir Tho. Strickland, a member of this house, is convicted upon record of Popish Recusancy, that he be from henceforth disabled from being any longer a member of this house." And a new writ was ordered for Westmoreland.

Debate on the Bill to repeal the Statute of Wages to Members of Parliament, resumed.] March 13. The Bill for releasing the Counties, &c. from all Wages due to Members, &c. was read the first time.

Mr. *Powle.* Now there is so great an arrear run into by boroughs to their burgesses, that the payment will be inconvenient to many, and will ruin some; and may have such an influence that if the borough will not make such a man an officer, or chuse such a man member, &c. they will sue them for Wages, and so they may be subjected to particular persons.

Sir *John Birkenhead.* It is dishonourable in the house to do this, when no petition is sent from any borough to desire it, representing it as prejudicial to them. Let them that desire it have that self-denying ordinance; boroughs complaining not of it. The best remedy for the fears of the boroughs is, for every man to forgive the Wages they owe him. The loss of wages is the only punishment the law has made for the absence of parliament-men from their attendance. He fears there is a worse end in it, that men should be posted who are against the bill. We may, by the next post, oblige our boroughs, by a letter, to release wages, without this bill, and, he supposes that unless we demand wages by a writ, after the session is over, we cannot have it.

Sir *Tho. Meres.* There is a jealousy that you will take wages, if you throw the bill out, and it will be very ill taken by those you represent.

Mr. *Crouch.* He never received wages for the place he serves for, and never will: but the bill is not fit to pass. Will you take away any man's land? Why will you take away his wages?

Sir *Philip Warwick* moves that as many gentlemen as will may release their wages.

Sir *Rd. Temple.* It is a reflection on the house, to discharge the wages by law; but he would have it a free-will offering.

Mr. *Swynfin.* If you think of casting this bill out, then he would have a bill brought in to make a law that Wages shall be taken. He is sure, now the thing is here in question, it will put such an awe upon corporations, for fear of having wages called for, who never thought of it before, that he thinks it a point of honesty in the house to declare they will not call for wages from the corporations, who else would be so universally deceived in so much expectation they should not pay wages. If we should now lay aside this bill, it would be scarce honourable, or honest. These 80 or 100 years wages have been scarce received, and now, that, for 14 years and upwards, members have not called for any, this is an intimation between man and man that they will never call for it. As if no rent has been paid for 80 years, and now we will fall on with all that weight. It is an implied promise, that they will not be called for, and that they are forgiven; and the throwing out the bill will revive a jealousy that they will be demanded. That which obliges corporations, in this, must oblige as the king's act, by act of grace, by taking away the punishment of penal laws. You would take it as a danger, if asked and denied.

Sir *Tho. Lee* knows not how long the parliament will last, and he knows not how his executors will deal with the borough he serves for, when he is dead; and therefore he is for the bill.

Mr. *Waller.* By this bill, we ask the lords leave to be bountiful to the people; by making it a law, we do it. We have ordered money for the servants here that attend us; he had rather forty times give it to the boroughs, than ask the lords leave. Some in the house are so poor, and some of the boroughs, so rich, that to force men not to take Wages would not be equal justice.

Address to the King on the Growth of the power of France.] March 15. Both houses presented the following Address to his majesty:

"May it please your majesty; we your majesty most loyal subjects, the lords spiritual and temporal, and the knights, citizens, and burgesses, in parliament assembled, find ourselves obliged, in duty and faithfulness to your majesty, and in discharge of the trust reposed in us by those whom we represent, most humbly to offer to your majesty's serious consideration, That the minds of your majesty's people are much disquieted, with the manifest danger arising to your majesty's kingdoms by the Growth and Power of the French king, especially by the acquisitions already made, and the further progress likely to be made by him, in the Spanish Netherlands; in the preservation and security whereof, we humbly conceive, the interest of your maj. and the safety of your people are highly concerned. And therefore we most humbly beseech your maj. to take the same into your royal care and to strengthen yourself with such stricter alliances as may secure your majesty's kingdoms, and preserve and secure the said Netherlands, and thereby quiet the minds of your majesty's people."

The King's Answer.] To the above Address the king gave the following Answer: "That he is of the same opinion with his two houses of parliament, that the conservation of Flanders is of great importance to England; and that therefore he assured them, that he will take all the care for the preservation of Flanders that can possibly consist with the peace and safety of the kingdom.

Debate on Mr. Harrington's Commitment by the Council.] March 16. Mr. Sacheverell presented a Petition, subscribed 'John Harrington'*. The warrant of Commitment on the back side of the Petition was read, viz. 'You are to take into your custody John Harrington, for suspicious practices, &c.'

Mr. Sec. *Williamson.* The ground of this

* "One Mr. Harrington, the son of a Cavalier who had suffered much in the royal cause, while the house was sitting, happened to meet with two Scotchmen, returned from abroad, who complained, that they had been pressed out of Scotland into the French king's service; and that there were several hundreds of their countrymen, as well as themselves, who had been forced from their houses, wives and families, bound together; and so, like galley-slaves, secured in the public gaols; their friends and relations not being suffered to come near them; and from thence put on shipboard, and transported into the service of France, contrary to the Addresses of parliament, his majesty's Answers thereunto, proclamation thereupon, and, what is of more authority than all, the privilege of nature itself; that exempts every man alike, from being forced into a danger, in which he has no concern.—Mr. Harrington was touched with their case, and thinking himself happy in an opportunity that bid fair to put a stop to those supplies which were sent almost daily to France, brought these Scotsmen to several members of parliament, to whom they evidenced the same things: his view was to have them examined at the bar of the house, when time should serve; and, in the mean while, fearing that endeavours might be used to corrupt them, he carried them to a master in Chancery, who took their depositions upon oath.—This was scarce done, before he was seized by a messenger, carried before the king and council, and accused of suborning those Scotsmen to disturb his majesty's government. While under examination, he was not well treated by the lord chancellor (these are his own words) and extremely ill by the lord treasurer; and, upon the issue, was committed close prisoner to the Tower (the cause assigned in the warrant being for Subornation of Perjury, tending to the defamation of his maj. and his government; and for contemptuously declaring, he would not answer his majesty any question, which his majesty, or his privy council, should ask him); debarred the use of pen and ink, the access of his friends, confined in such a place over the Tower ditch, as threw him into a dangerous sickness; and denied the assistance of either physician or divine: after all this, he made a hard shift to get a Petition presented to the house of commons; which produced an order for his being brought before the house; before whom he gave a clear account of the whole matter, and of his behaviour at the council-board.—But of the two Scots soldiers, the one made himself perjured, without being suborned by Harrington; denying, or misrepresenting to the house, what he had sworn formerly: and the other, the honester fellow it seems of the two, only absented. However, divers members of that house attested voluntarily, that the soldiers had affirmed the same thing to them: and indeed the truth of that matter became notorious, by several other soldiers that came over afterwards, and by further account from Scotland. Mr. Harrington also carried himself towards the house with so much modesty, that it seemed inseparable from him; so that a disposition appeared in the members to have concerned themselves for his liberty; when Mr. Secretary Williamson stood up, having been a principal instrument in committing him, and, because the other crimes rather deserved thanks and commendation, and the warrant would not justify itself, he insisted upon his strange demeanour towards his majesty; deciphered his very looks, says Mr. Marvell; and but that his majesty and the house remained still living flesh and blood, it might have been imagined, by his discourse, that Mr. Harrington had the head of a Gorgon. But this story so wrought with, and amazed the commons, that the prisoner found no redress, but might thank God that he escaped again into close prison." Ralph.

proceeding against Harrington was, an Oath by one Harriot, Lemmon, and Murray, Scotchmen, at the instigation of Fonseça, (the Spanish ambassador's secretary) who had engaged Harriot, &c. to the utmost disturbance of the government, to create jealousy between the king and this house, clandestinely seeking out informations from Scotland. Harriot he found out, and examined him upon oath. The purport was this: Harriot was one of the 500 men carried into Ostend, by one of their frigates, where he was not willing to serve, but was put in mind, that if he would pass into England, he should have his liberty. He got an address to Fonseça, and this Harrington was to have the care of him, and gave him money; but took care to ask him about men pressed in Scotland, and other transactions there, and took notes; which Harrington transcribed fair, and took him to a master in chancery, where he swore to that paper, though he never read it. But he said to the master in chancery 'he had read it,' but to him (Williamson) he deposed otherwise. This fellow said, 'he swore not conjointly what the other deposed, but for himself only, and not to the cutting off ears.' Says Harrington, 'I will get money for you to go thither: that will be good news to duke Hamilton.' This practice was so indirect, and by Harrington's carriage at the council, he appeared to be the most grown young man in his impudence, and he believes, in his loyalty: he stands committed for contempt: he used that style, that air, and mien to the king, as 'it may be so:' 'I will answer you no more' and the king said, 'I will ask you no more.' and for this he was committed by the lords of the Council's order.

Mr. *Garroway* rises not up to justify Harrington's deportment to the king, but he has heard that the last day the committee of grievances sat, these people waited at the door to tell you what they petition now, and, he believes, Williamson will tell you what is become of Harriot, &c. now not to be found; taken out of his lodgings: would ask Williamson about the commitment being brought hither to give evidence.

Mr. Sec. *Williamson.* He never saw him, since the deposition in his house. Harrington said to Harriot, 'go off; what you have said may cost you your own ears.'

Sir *Tho. Lee.* Williamson tells you of 'oath made of seditious practices.' Harrington brought them to be examined about men pressed, contrary to the king's proclamation. Harriot informed a master in chancery of it upon oath, and was not committed for contempt of the king. See now, the crime is to go to a master in chancery, before the king, and he is committed to a messenger before he was brought to the king, and there as a criminal, and asked questions, and he would not inform against himself. This, it seems, is 'unmannerly' and 'sedition.' No wonder we have so little account of Miscarriages, when things are thus managed in Council.

Mr. Sec. *Williamson.* His commitment was for going where he ought not to go, in matters of state, to give information, which belongs not to a master in chancery to examine. He should have come to those whom he ought. He wants breeding indeed, the best part of breeding, that of the mind, but for the other, he is a well fashioned man.

Lord *Cavendish* is far from excusing any man that has failed in good manners to the king; but he hears nothing alledged against his deportment at the lords of the Council 'but his looks, air, and mien.' Nothing apparent against him, but that he is unwilling to answer against himself. Williamson said, 'he was committed for carrying men to depose before a master in chancery, in matters of state, before he came to the king's council,' which he might justify, the parliament sitting; especially apprehending that some of the king's council are highly guilty of what we are about to remedy.

Sir *Francis Winnington.* He attended the Council when Harrington was brought. He observes, that the weight of exception is put upon it; that he was committed that so he might be prevented coming here to inform you. If he knows the matter of fact, it is his duty to acquaint you with it. Harrington, with another, was summoned to attend the Council, and came. Harrington was fairly asked questions about disturbances of the government, and what he knew of such a man. That no man is brought thither to accuse himself, is their rule; but to ask if he knew such a man, and what is become of him. Any man that owes allegiance to the king, ought not to refuse answering there. He looked not like an uneducated rustic man. No man behaves himself with more humanity than the king. But he never saw any gentleman more rude to another; throwing his head about—These were only questions concerning other persons, asked fairly by my lord chancellor. And he answered, 'Ask what questions you will, I will answer you none.' Those common questions that he was asked, no man will deny to another. The Privy-Council may do what a court-leet may, *quia male se gessit.* It is a common thing to commit upon rude deportment; and his commitment was, because he was of an ill behaviour before his prince—the law allows reverence to the king. He being present when this passed, he thought it his duty to acquaint you with it.

Mr. *Williams* stands not up to vindicate ill behaviour, but the rights of our liberties. He expected some particular certain cause from the great minister (Williamson) of this man's commitment: he finds only suspicion of seditious practices: so general an allowance is not to be admitted. Men are not to be imprisoned upon notions. If he were committed on the account of seditious practices, this is not the manner. No man is imprisoned but by 'lex terræ et judicium parium suorum;' by the king's writ, not by verbal commandment from the king's ministers. He does complain, and is in great fear of arbitrary proceedings. This way of commitment has been usual, but no authority for it by statute or common law: but many complaints of it. 'The King's presence!' How far that may intrench upon the liberty of the subject, ought to be examined. He doubts. It is said, 'He was judged by his eye and mien.' Every man has not *bonne mine*. Persons ought not to be committed for that in that place.

Sir *Wm. Coventry* fears that the business before you, the more you handle it, will run the more into your fingers. He could heartily wish the respecting part to the king declined, as it is not to be handled without pricking your fingers. Liberty is a tender thing, and may concern himself as well as another man. A secretary of state may call a man before him, and if he refuses to answer, he may put him in custody; and when he has him, the king may have notice of it; but the crime of the Chancery-Affidavit, and the disrespect to the king intervening, he is committed for that. It seems, Harrington is in custody, and if he be of any use to you he will not be refused, if you send for him to know what is become of Harriot; but as to the disrespect-part, he would leave that.

Sir *Henry Capel*. This is an unhappy debate, and he desires we may be rid of it as soon as we can. He would preserve a good correspondence with the king, and seconds the motion, to be tender to meddle with this person. If a common justice of the peace may commit him in this case, much more the council board. We are gone and lost for ever, if we pay not respect to our prince, and if ever to any prince, to this. We know the tenderness of his nature: he would send for Harrington, and interrogate him what you please, as to the other business.

Mr. *Vaughan*. No man that understands his duty to his prince, but will say that Harrington's gesture deserves censure. Remember your own stations: when your laws are contemned, justice is violated, and expected to be relieved at a committee of grievances; and if a person be so used that comes hither, you must enquire into it. He would adjourn the business to to-morrow, and let the Petitioner come then to the bar to give you an account of the grievance.

Col. *Birch*. If we slumber over this day's work, we shall never remedy it again. Such things as these come bye ways: but this shall not fright him: but the warrant of commitment must tell you what this is. Williamson ought to have secured the person that gave information, as well as have committed Harrington.

Mr. *Sacheverell* loves plain English, and hopes other gentlemen do so too. As this case seems to him, if this be allowed, there needs neither Star-chamber, nor oath, ex officio—Not only the Council table but the lords house commit for 'Contempt,' (A very brave word!) He asks whether any commitment can be without specifying special matter of crime, and not mere contempt? Would know, how Harrington stands committed? Whether upon the 1st, 2nd, or 3rd Commitment? In the 1st, the lords of the Council charge crime—aggravate that to misbehaviour, and that holds water, and they commit him to the Tower. Suppose all the case be true of misdemeanor, he asks, Whether for misdemeanor a man may be committed close prisoner? And whether they are not to take bail, if it be tendered? He would have them speak out, and then he will tell you more what he has to say.

Serj. *Maynard*. Harrington may be brought to the bar, if he desires it. He may be indicted or bailed. The countess of Shrewsbury complained to the Council-table, that the lady Arabella was treating with foreign ministers. The lady Arabella refused to answer. By the advice of the judges (at common law) she was committed, and it was no new thing. Ed. 1. A clerk forged a fine; the lord chancellor examined him; he was convicted, but removed to the exchequer, and there tried, and was convicted. Some matters of state must be looked after, in another manner than the common way: he cannot but justify the Secretary's warrant-general, 'for misbehaviour.' But that about 'pressing the men in Scotland, he does not.

Lord *Cavendish* moves for this other person, Harriot, to be brought likewise.

Mr. Sec. *Williamson* said, on his honour and sincerity, he knew not where he was, nor where to find him.

Mr. Harrington was ordered to be brought to the bar to-morrow.

March 17. The debate was resumed.

Sir *F. Winnington* humbly conceives the jurisdiction of the council to be this: the case may happen, that they may commit a person to custody: if he be not bailable, he may be committed till delivered by due course of law: the magistrate cannot force bail. 17 Cha. i. reports it not as to this man, but to all: the council cannot punish the estate, or the person, in giving bail. He is to have an indictment, or information, preferred against him, and he pleads to it.

Sir *Tho. Lee*. Winnington tells you plainly, 'That the Lords of the Council may commit a man;' but it must be in order to trial, not punishment. The matter stands now avowed by the deputy constable of the Tower, that Harrington stands committed close prisoner in the Tower: what greater hardship can he have? it takes away preparation for his defence, if on suggestion only; and that it is so close, no man can come to him. He may be sent beyond the sea, or put to torture, and if the warder of the tower keeps counsel, the man can have no remedy. He moves, therefore, that complaint may be made to the king, for keeping this person a close prisoner, and desire redress.

Mr. Sec. *Williamson*. The king (and for

weighty considerations) commanded verbally the constable of the Tower to keep Harrington close prisoner. This young fellow, for many months, and some years, has held correspondence with persons, (and there is reason to commit him to the Tower) and goes deep to subvert the whole government. The thing is laid on this side the sea, and beyond foreign ministers are concerned. This is one of their instruments who meddled with public matters. He questions, 'whether this be a parliament, or no parliament?' he holds, 'That rebellion must be against the three states, and not against any one of them.' This has been said by this man, and good witness of it. He said, 'That those hanged at Charing-Cross were hanged by the opinion of 12 men only.' The servants of these lords, now in the Tower, enquired for this man, and whether they might have access to him? he leaves you to judge, if that be our interest and concern, when he meddled with foreign ministers, which every man abominates.

Sir *Tho. Lee* never saw the man, nor knows any relation of his. But he moves not for his sake, but for those we represent. He shall go as far as any man to impeach him, if accused; but would not punish the worst of men (that may concern the innocentest most) without accusation. Let not the nature of the man take you off from that which may concern any man.

Sir *John Ernly*. If the king cannot do this, (imprison, &c.) his government is a straw. Every man then may talk, or preach any thing. He would be a king of clouts, if this cannot be.

The *Speaker*. He stands committed for contempt, &c. and by the king's verbal order to the constable, he is kept close prisoner. The warrant runs thus: 'To take into your custody Mr. Harrington for subornation of perjury, and stirring sedition in the government, and contempt of the king in council.'

Sir *Wm. Coventry* thinks it against law to restrain the person close prisoner, without warrant for so doing; and he thinks the constable to blame in it, and not the king: else how shall be come to have his Habeas Corpus? He desires you would declare that it ought not to be so now, nor for the future. Certainly the observation of our law deserves a sheet of paper for a warrant; if it be not worth that, it is very little worth. If the constable had desired it, the king would not have denied it; and it is his fault. For the future, if such commitments be, in God's name, let them be in writing; and he hopes you will discountenance this.

Mr. Harrington was then call in to the bar, where he spoke thus: "I am sensible of the honour the house has done me on this occasion, in receiving my Petition, and permitting me to come to make it out. It is my opinion, and I hope I am not in an error, that the liberty of being tried 'per judicium parium suorum' is the undoubted right of the subjects of England. Parliaments are called for urgent and weighty affairs, concerning the king and defence of the state, and against the mischiefs which daily happen. These are the proper subjects of debate; and it is proper for the members of this house to apply themselves to subjects, and they to you, on occasions of this nature. I am come to fling myself upon the protection of this house, and I hope for it. I met with some Scotchmen, who came from Ostend, taken by the Spaniards, pressed out of Scotland, &c. and I did what I thought was my duty. I acquainted several members of the house, that they could make it appear, how they were pressed for the French service in Scotland, after the king's Proclamation, &c. They did agree that I had reason and justice in such an application: one of them, Redcastle, a preacher, and a favourite of the duke of Lauderdale, was offered 20*l.* (it was an inconsiderable sum for a man of his quality) to forbear giving in evidence, &c. I took in writing what the Scotchman informed me, and carried it to sir John Coell, a master in chancery, where the Scotchman made affidavit of what I had written. The next day, I was committed to a messenger, for dangerous and seditious practices, where I was kept in durance, with one Lemmon, and Mr. Murray. When I was brought before the king and council, the lord treasurer acquainted the king, 'That this was a whipster, and a dangerous fellow to the king and government.' The chancellor asked me several questions, 'Whether I knew Harriot?' The treasurer said, 'I told you what he was; he will give you no direct answer.' I was asked, 'Whether I went with Harriot to a master in chancery, and who that master was?' I said, 'Possibly his name might be Coell.' The chancellor was studying more questions; but I desired him 'to think of no more questions, for I was resolved to give no answer; but, being come thither accused, I would answer according to law.' But this was construed a contempt, and, though for nothing else, I suffered imprisonment. My father and grandfather were particular servants to the king, and I owe obedience to the king, and hope, for the particular actions I am accused of, to be justified by the parliament, and submit myself to his majesty. I have given you as just an account of the matter as I can. From the Council I was sent close prisoner to the Tower, and forbid pen, ink, and paper. I was locked up, and no person admitted to me, but the person of the house where I was kept was civil to me. I had what meat I would, but was not suffered to walk upon the leads. I do not desire bail, but the benefit of the law."—He then withdrew.

Col. *Birch*. Harrington tells you, 'That for doing his duty as a commoner of England, and for privilege of this house, going to a master in chancery, &c. he was clapped up close prisoner.' He would have the Affidavit made before the master in chancery, annexed to the Petition, read.

The *Speaker*. There was no affidavit annexed to the Petition, and you (Birch) cannot make affidavit of it.

Col. *Birch.* He would not make affidavit, lest he mistake, as the Speaker did in declaration of the law about Petitions.

The *Speaker.* He mistook only the fore part of the law for the latter; and he hopes his mistake will never cost the house so much as Birch's has done [in something relating to a Tax-bill.]

Col. *Birch.* Whatever his mistake has cost the house, he is sure the marks were not upon the bags—[meaning that the Speaker had lost money at play, and the king's marks were upon the bags he sent the money in, being the Navy-bags.]

Harriot the Scotchman, and Murray, were next called to the bar and examined. After which, Mr. Harrington was dismissed, and the farther debate of the thing was left, sine die.*

Debate on a Bill for securing the Protestant Religion, by educating the Children of the Royal Family therein.] March 20. Sir *Harbottle Grimstone.* He has heard of this bill,† and liked the report of it well, but never read it. He finds, that it intends 'securing the Protestant Religion, &c.' but he would not, under pretence of providing against Popery, do things against the legal and monarchical power of the kings of England. He wonders that it passed the lords house, and made no more noise than it has done. He thinks there is a vizard upon the face of this bill; and he hopes every gentleman here will give his helping hand to pull it off; and then we shall see the spots on the face of this fair bill. In the last session, the lords were very busy in framing a Test for people to take, to secure the government, &c. which miscarried; now here is a Test provided for the king, and no man has less cause to be suspected.

Mr. Sec. *Williamson.* This is the first time of reading this bill, and it is of an extraordinary nature; and because the case is extraordinary, therefore it is an argument for a 2nd reading. The purport of it is this: 'That should the misfortune befall the kingdom of a prince of the Romish religion, that then you may endeavour to preserve the Protestant religion as one man. By what means, to have a Protestant clergy, three are to be presented to the king, by the bishops, to fill up vacancies; and the king is to take one.' If that objection be valid, 'That this is out of our power to do,' it is no purpose to make any laws. Though this bill comes not up to the whole of the cure, yet this house and the lords may make it up. Though the Church of England be in a body of professors of the Protestant religion, yet to be taught they must be sent; and whilst we have Protestant teachers, he hopes we shall be so ourselves. It is said, 'this Bill is to raise a faction between the laity and the clergy.' He thinks this Test proper to be given by such persons as may be supposed uncorrupt and untainted in religion.

Mr. *Vaughan.* We owe a natural allegiance to the king, as well as a political. He thinks this bill will be an unfortunate stain upon the nation. The king was once deprived of this kingdom by arms, and that was by the power of some few persons. But now this bill will do it by law, which is the sense of the whole nation. The laws since H. viii. contended to settle the supremacy on the crown, that you would now take away. Shall the king give this power away, and lodge it in the ecclesiastics? When the king once passes this into a law, he divests himself of his right, and puts it into the bishops.

Mr. *Finch.* This bill is for the security of the Protestant religion, and though this will not totally do it, yet it will go a good way towards it. The popish lords and papists abroad are against it, and therefore he is for it. He thinks it strange, that so many gentlemen, eminent for the profession of the Protestant religion, should concur with the Papists against this bill; but they apprehend encroachments on royal prerogative. This is not a total deprivation of the king's disposing of ecclesiastical promotions; but what he may take off when he pleases.

Serj. *Maynard.* The general end of the bill is, to keep us a Protestant clergy. No man can withstand that. But, to throw out the bill for what he has heard, amazes him to hear it. We must not think ourselves secured against all accidents of Popery, if we may not suppose a change. There is no mention in

* "That the commons, who are the express guardians of the people, and who had so lately taken arbitrary commitments, by his majesty and the privy council, into their consideration, in order to make a better provision for their security, should all at once grow so negligent of their trust, as to suffer any one individual to apply to them in vain for protection and deliverance, can never be wondered at enough; and yet the session before us produces an instance [the above] remarkable enough, on all accounts, to challenge a place in the History of England." Ralph.

† "This bill was called by one party, 'A Bill against Popery;' and, by the other, 'A Popish Bill.' It was of the Janus kind; for under the pretence of educating the Children of the Crown in the Protestant Religion, it admitted the kings of England to be successively Papists. They were, indeed, required to make a Declaration upon Oath, 'That they did not believe in transubstantiation;' but if they refused it, they might. And all they were to pay for this licence was, the parting with so much of their power as regarded the filling all ecclesiastical vacancies, (but such as were in the gift of the lord chancellor) which were then to devolve to the bishops, under certain limitations, as expressed in the bill itself; (to be found in Marvell's Growth of Popery) so that, in effect, this bill was no better than a compromise between the Church and the Duke, by which the latter passed a sort of fine to the former for being of what religion he pleased." Ralph.

scripture, but where a true king, true religion. It is said, 'This changes the king's prerogative.' If it should fall out to manacle the king's prerogative, we shall not, and the king may not, be short-sighted in that, before he passes it.—The Bill was ordered to be read a second time.

Mr. Hatcher's Petition was, upon the Question, rejected.

March 27. The Bill from the lords for educating the Children of the Royal Family in the Protestant Religion, &c. was read the second time. The house sat some time very silent, whereupon,

Mr. Sec. *Williamson* said, this bill is of great weight, by the silence in the house. He remembers, at the first reading, a remark upon one part of it: for the education of the children, it was thought the time was too narrow, 'from 7 to 14 years of age.' He thinks it reasonable to enlarge it, and moves that it may go to a committee for amendment, at least for that.

Mr. *Mallet*. In this bill there are interlineations, and figures, which is unparliamentary. He is against the commitment of the bill: it will blow up the government, it states an interregnum and an oligarchy. It is now a thesis amongst some churchmen, that the king is not king but by their magical unction. He knows not what the bill is—no interregnum can be by law—it sets up nine mitres above the crown —Monstrum horrendum!

Mr *Vaughan*. The king by this bill is made capable of error; and if once an offence be sheltered under error of the king, you may seek impeachments elsewhere than in the house of commons. He finds not the great rights amongst the bishops, which the Romanists say—If Popery come in, they and their books must burn together. It is said, 'The king's children are to be taught the Lord's Prayer, &c. and the rudiments of religion;' but as parrots, &c. 'Liberavi animam meam.' The bill is fatal to the crown, and so little in it to be retained, and so much to be rejected that he would throw it out.

Mr. *Marvell* wonders to see this bill so ready to be committed, that the consequence may be no likelihood of the king's consent. But it is an ill thing, and let us be rid of it as soon as we can. He could have wished it had perished at the first reading rather than have been revived by a second. He is sorry the matter has occasioned so much mirth. He thinks there was never so solemn and sad an occasion, as this bill before you; but he is glad the house is returned into that temper, which the gravity of the matter requires. The bill seems very unseasonable; the beginning is of two things not of mature consideration. First, it supposes 'the death' of the king. It might have had a more modest word to have disguised it from the imagination ('Demise.') Secondly, it supposes 'that possibly the crown may devolve on a Popish government;' which ought not to be supposed easily and readily. God be thanked for the king's age and constitution of body! The king is not in a declining age; and if we intermeddle in things of this consequence, we are not to look into it so early, as if it was the king's last will and testament. The law makes it treason, 'to imagine the death of the king that is'—A word more in it—The true and proper sense is not to imagine the king's death —His age may confirm you in no danger suddenly of the consequences of the bill, but as for that of 'a Popish Successor,' he hopes it is a matter remote in the event, and would not precipitate that evil, no, not in a supposition. For some reason, without doubt, this matter has been thought of in the house of lords, and next to the king living, he would cast as little umbrage on the successor, as might be. There is none yet in sight, but whose minds are in the hands of God, 'who turns them like the rivers 'of water.' Whilst there is time there is life, and whilst life, time for information, and the nearer the prospect is to the crown, information of judgment will be much easier. When God 'takes him on high and shows him the glory of the world, and tells him, 'All these things will I give thee, if thou wilt fall down and worship me,' he thinks these will be no temptation. Those who change for conscience-sake will have so much self-denial, that the crown will not make them alter the thing. It is unseasonable; it may be proper some other time, but not now. This bill is a great invasion on prerogative: to whom ever God shall dispose the kingdom, it is entire to the king. He does not love to reflect on the persons of those who represent the Protestant religion—(the bishops.) But it is said, 'This invasion is not made by the prelates; they were but passive in it.' But he will not speak of such reverend persons, with any thing of severe reflection, but will only suppose this power of the bishops given to any other order of men; to nine physicians, and they administer the Test to the king. Having altered the property of the persons, to speak with a little more freedom, he knows no body of men, if the parliament please, but may do it as well as they. The College of Physicians have a charter from the king, and are his sworn servants; let these come to the king to administer the Oath. It is a pretty experiment. Just a trial, whether the loadstone will attract the iron, or the iron the loadstone. Who can think that any body of men, that must depend upon the king, &c.? Which way, think you, it draws? We have seen (and he hopes we shall never see it again) in Henry viii.'s Edw. vi.'s, queen Mary's, and queen Eliz.'s time, all sorts ready to turn, one, one way, another, another. It is appointed by the bill, 'that the bishops should wait upon the king at Whitehall, &c.' He thinks not but physicians may be thought by a Popish king, as proper a cure for his soul, as bishops. The chevalier de Menevicette, physician to the Great Turk, was by him made Patriarch of Antioch. He thinks this power not fit to be lodged in any sort of persons whatsoever. Whatever prince

God gives us, we must trust him. Let us not, in prevention of future things so remote, take that immoderate care in this bill. Sufficient to the day is the evil thereof. Here is pricking of bishops, as if pricking sheriffs. If the king does not, they must. Here bishops make bishops; (as inherent a right to the crown as any think possible.) He desires, that, during this king's reign, we may apply ourselves to preserve the people in the Protestant Religion, not only in the profession of it, but that men may live up to it, in morality and virtue of religion, and then you establish men against the temptation of Popery, and a prince that may be popishly affected. If we do not practise upon ourselves, all these Oaths and Tests are of no use; they are but phantoms. The bill has a very good title, and a good intention, but nothing but the title is urged to be of the least validity. This puts him in mind of a private bill: you would not countenance the pretence of 'no people to make compact for themselves.' It is said, 'the bishops promoted not the bill, but they were under fear, in the lords house*.' Promotions make some men much better, and it is power that makes Popery: So great a power assembled upon such a body of men! The bill he spoke of, pretended, that the dean and chapter of Durham would have benefit by a ballast shore to be erected at Yarrow-Sleake, on Newcastle side. Says one, 'it will narrow the river.' Says another, 'it will widen it.' It was then said, 'that gentlemen love not to play tricks with navigation' much less should the nation play tricks with religion. But whether this bill will prevent Popery, or not, this will secure the promotions of the bishops; it will make them certain. He is not used to speak here, and therefore speaks with abruptness. Closes all with his motion that the bill may have the same fate others have moved for, 'not to be committed.'

Serj. *Maynard.* Nothing is more desirable than the end of this bill, but to the means to attain that end, he knows not how far he can consent, or whether at all. But he is not for desperate remedies. He would not have any thing propounded prejudicial to the crown. He has some difficulties upon him, but would commit the bill.—The Bill was then committed, 127 to 88.†

* This gentleman, in his Growth of Popery, expresses himself thus: "That the bishops were either the contrivers or promoters of this bill, is a scandalous falsehood, and devised by the authors to throw the odium off from themselves upon the clergy, and (the bills that aimed at the ruin of the Church of England having miscarried) to compass the same end by this defamation. A sufficient warning to the Clergy how to be intrigued with the statesmen for the future!"

† "This notorious Bill,' as Marvell calls it, after being committed, died of neglect, the committee either disdaining, or not daring publicly, to enter upon it." Ralph.

Debate on Mr. Andrew Marvell's striking Sir Philip Harcourt.] March 29. Mr. Marvell, coming up the house to his place, stumbling at sir Philip Harcourt's foot, in recovering himself, seemed to give sir Philip a box on the ear. The Speaker acquainting the house, 'That he saw a box on the ear given, and it was his duty to inform the house of it,' this debate ensued.*

Mr. *Marvell.* What passed was through great acquaintance and familiarity betwixt us. He neither gave him an affront, nor intended him any. But the Speaker cast a severe reflection upon him yesterday, when he was out of the house, and he hopes that, as the Speaker keeps us in order, he will keep himself in order for the future.

Sir *John Ernly.* What the Speaker said yesterday, was in Marvell's vindication. If these two gentlemen are friends already, he would not make them friends, and would let the matter go no farther.

Sir *Job. Charlton* is sorry a thing of this nature has happened, and no more sense of it. You in the Chair, and a stroke struck! Marvell deserves for his reflection on you, Mr. Speaker, to be called in question. You cannot do right to the house, unless you question it; and moves to have Marvell sent to the Tower.

The *Speaker.* I saw a blow on one side, and a stroke on the other.

Sir *Philip Harcourt.* Marvell had some kind of a stumble, and mine was only a thrust; and the thing was accidental.

Sir *H. Goodrick.* The persons have declared the thing to be accidental, but if done in jest, not fit to be done here. He believes it an accident, and hopes the house thinks so too.

Mr. Sec. *Williamson.* This does appear, that the action for that time was in some heat. He cannot excuse Marvell who made a very severe reflection on the Speaker, and since it is so enquired, whether you have done your duty, he would have Marvell withdraw, that you may consider of it.

Col. *Sandys.* Marvell has given you trouble, and instead of excusing himself, reflects upon the Speaker: a strange confidence, if not an impudence!

Mr. *Marvell.* Has so great a respect to the privilege, order, and decency, of the house, that he is content to be a sacrifice for it. As to the casualty that happened, he saw a seat empty, and going to sit in it, his friend put him by, in a jocular manner, and what he did was of the same nature. So much familiarity has ever been between them, that there was no heat in the thing. He is sorry he gave an offence to the house. He seldom speaks to the house, and if he commit an error, in the manner of his speech, being not so well tuned, he hopes it is not an offence. Whether out, or in the house, he has a respect to the Speaker. But he has been informed, that the

* There is no mention of this in the Journal.

Speaker resumed something he had said, with reflection. He did not think fit to complain of Mr. Seymour to Mr. Speaker. He believes, that is not reflective. He desires to comport himself with all respect to the house. This passage with Harcourt was a perfect casualty, and if you think fit, he will withdraw, and sacrifice himself to the censure of the house.

Sir *Henry Capel*. The blow given Harcourt was with his hat; the Speaker cast his eye upon both of them, and both respected him. He would not aggravate the thing. Marvell submits, and he would have you leave the thing as it is.

Sir *Robert Holmes* saw the whole action. Marvell flung about three or four times with his hat, and then gave Harcourt a box on the ear.

Sir *Henry Capel* desires, now that his honour is concerned, that Holmes may explain, whether he saw not Marvell with his hat only give Harcourt the stroke 'at that time.' Possibly, 'at another time' it might be.

The *Speaker*. Both Holmes and Capel are in the right. But Marvell struck Harcourt so home, that his fist, as well as his hat, hit him.

Sir *R. Howard* hopes the house will not have Harcourt say, he received a blow, when he has not. He thinks what has been said by them both sufficient.

Mr. *Garroway* hopes, that, by the debate, we shall not make the thing greater than it is. Would have them both reprimanded for it.

Mr. Sec. *Williamson* submits the honour of the house to the house. Would have them made friends, and give that necessary assurance to the house, and he, for his part, remains satisfied.

Sir *Tho. Meres*. By our long sitting together, we lose, by our familiarity and acquaintance, the decencies of the house. He has seen 500 in the house, and people very orderly; not so much as to read a letter, or set up a foot. One could scarce know any body in the house, but him that spoke. He would have the Speaker declare that order ought to be kept; but as to that gentleman (Marvell) to rest satisfied.

Address to the King concerning Alliances.] Sir John Trevor reported the Address to his majesty, which is as follows:

"We your majesty's most loyal subjects, the knights, citizens, and burgesses, in parliament assembled, do, with unspeakable joy and comfort, present our humble thanks to your majesty, for your majesty's gracious acceptance of our late Address, and that your maj. was pleased, in your princely wisdom, to express your concurrence in opinion with your two houses, in reference to the preservation of the Spanish Netherlands: and we do, with most earnest and repeated desires, implore your majesty, that you would be pleased to take timely care to prevent those dangers that may arise to these kingdoms, by the great power of the French king, and the progress he daily makes in those Netherlands, and other places: and therefore that your maj. would not defer the entering into such Alliances as may attain those ends. And in case it shall happen that in pursuance of such alliances, your maj. shall be engaged in a war with the French king, we hold ourselves obliged, and do, with all humility and chearfulness, assure your majesty, that your most loyal subjects shall always be ready, upon the signification thereof in parliament, fully, and from time to time, to assist your maj. with such Aids and Supplies, as, by the divine assistance, may enable your majesty to prosecute the same with success. All which we do most humbly offer your majesty as the unanimous sense and desire of the whole nation."

Debate on the Address.] Sir *John Ernly*. You are already in Alliances defensive, and farther alliances must be war, and so you will expose yourselves to depredations of the French at sea, upon your merchant-ships, and give the French a million by putting the king upon this Address. He declares, that the king's entering into farther Alliances is a war.

Mr. Sec. *Williamson*. The question is, whether this addition of 'farther Alliances' in this Address be a repetition, or to make the former address more effectual? the middle period of your paper is quite other matter, which was laid by, and set aside by the house. 'To preserve the Netherlands from the growing power of France, and to enter into stricter Alliances for that purpose.' He begs leave only to observe that exception for a question, and to leave it out.

Sir *Tho. Meres*. This Address is not good sense if it has not reference to the former, and the king cannot but think of the former. We are told, 'That stricter Alliances import war;' but if any thing saves Flanders, it will be 'stricter Alliances;' and he doubts not but that the parliament having resolved it, it will be of weight. He will not say what alliances the king should enter into, but doubts not but they will be good when made.

Mr. *Vaughan*. Is not our men going into France as much a declaration of war, as the motion of sending money into Germany? He would agree to the Address.

Mr. *Powle* expects no farther Answer from the king. The design of the house is to give the king thanks for what he thinks so. This goes no farther than the other Address, and extends not the thing at all. It is said, that this will incense the French king into a present war with us; but this only enables the king for a present war, if there shall be occasion. When the world knows that the king and his people are together, he is as formidable as any king; and he would agree to the Address.

Col. *Birch* was not at the drawing up of this address, and therefore it is not a brat of his own, to be fond of it. He takes the Address to be good. The king said, 'He agreed with the opinion of the house of commons,' and you thank the king for agreeing with your opinion, and you desire him 'not to defer entering into Alliances, &c.' It has been said, 'This puts a force upon the king, presently to do it.' But this shows the opinion of the house, and their zeal in it. 'From time to time' we will stand by the king. He never saw, but when things came on unitedly, it was the likeliest way to be quiet. What has this great man on the other side of the water done? the jealousies he has sown between the king and his people have given him that confidence. It is said, 'That ships are not ready, and therefore such a declaration of the king, as we desire in the Address, is improper.' But he believes that the danger was as much for want of ships 18 months since, as now, when we would have given money for ships, and it was not accepted. Now, or never, is the time to let the king of France see, that breaches are made up between the king and his people.

The Address was agreed to by the house; the question for its being recommitted being carried in the negative, 131 to 122.

Debate on the Bill for preserving the Protestant Religion.] April 4. A Bill from the lords was read, entitled, 'An Act for preserving of the Protestant Religion, and the more effectual conviction and prosecution of Popish Recusants.'*

Mr. *Sacheverell.* This bill from the lords is a toleration of Popery, and puts but 12*d.* a Sunday difference betwixt the best Protestant, and severest Papist. The lords sent us a Bill lately, wherein they thought fit to transfer the king's Supremacy into other hands;† to take it away, unless the king undergo a Test, &c. By this bill, the parliament may be chosen Papists, for the sheriffs and mayors may be so too: though Catholics may not, and are under an incapacity, yet another person, their deputy, may, who may set aside all but Romanists. It sets aside all the laws against Popery, but the Act for the Test; and any man may act three months without a test; and your work may be done in that time. The bill intends to put Protestant Recusants into a worse condition than the Popish: by express words in the bill, he is subject to all the penalties the Popish are. The laws have declared Priests and Jesuits dangerous to the government, and yet they shall not suffer death, &c. He fears not the danger of this bill, in this king's time, but, hereafter, one inclinable to Popery will not execute the Priests and Jesuits. This bill is a bare toleration of Popery, and he would throw it out.‡

Mr. *Garroway* is glad to see, that the zeal of the house will embrace nothing of this nature. We may, by it, see the influence of the Popish lords in their house. He rises to second the motion.

Mr. *Williams* desires that the question upon the bill may not be put suddenly. He would see any gentleman, that will speak for the bill.

Lord *Obrien* desires that something of the bill may be retained, which is the title of the bill only: something, as a mark, that you throw not out barely 'a Bill of Popery.'

Sir *Tho. Meres.* If you throw out this bill, then read your own Bill of Popery: would observe, two years, and above, to pass most things in this bill. Your bill is firm, and strong, and good. These in the lords bill are slight, and good for nothing: to destroy all your laws against Popery, in one bill! Whatever is good in this bill, is in yours; and this is to choak all you did good in that. Posterity will be fully satisfied of it.

Mr. Sec. *Coventry* would not, by too quick a severity, lay aside this bill. To throw this bill out, and immediately to send up your own to the lords, is not the way to have it pass; the Popish lords sitting in that house. He hopes that, in time, so great jealousies may pass over; but it is a great encouragement to the Catholics, for such a body to stand by them, and the king of France's provocation; therefore would not throw the bill out.

Sir *Tho. Lee* has reason to believe, that our sharp bill against Popery will be rejected by the lords, because we have rejected theirs of Toleration. Lord Clarendon's bill of banishment passed in two or three days, and yet was laid by, as this is moved to be. He fears that this may have the same fate, and would throw it out.

Sir *John Mallet* hopes gentlemen will not wonder, if his zeal against this bill be not equal to others, in throwing it out. This bill has a disarming the Recusants in it. He likes the clause of educating their children; but, as for repealing the Statute of Mortmain, he likes not that.

Sir *Harbottle Grimstone.* On the bill from the lords for establishing of Protestant Ministers in England, lately sent us down, when he differed from the lords judgment, he suspected his own. He believes gentlemen design mending this bill, to attain the end; but when it comes back, it will prove an unsavoury thing, stuck with a primrose. He would lay it aside. We are told of 'the danger that we may pass it in a thin house, as we did the Sale of the Fee-farm Rents.' It is not possible to be imagined, that a bill of this nature could come from the lords, to repeal all the laws against Popery. If our laws were executed, there

* "This bill, with a most plausible title, had a most pernicious tendency. It had an easy and undisputed passage through the house of lords, but from the commons it met with very different treatment." Ralph.

† The Bill for educating the children of the Royal Family, &c. See p. 853.

‡ "No sooner was it read, than a Member rose up, and, in a short speech, unmasked it so effectually, that a second moved, 'that it might not only be thrown out, but with some particular mark of infamy.' The question being called for, a third demanded, 'That they would stay a while, to see whether there was any man to be found hardy enough to speak one word for it.' Which no man presumed to do." Ralph.

would not have been this growth of Popery; and he fears the danger will be greater. As for 'breeding the children of Papists,' we have laws in force for that; they ought not to have the education of them; that is already provided for. He wishes a law would be sent us from the lords, that the good laws we have already may be put in execution. Is this the way to prevent Popery? We may as soon make a good fan out of a pig's tail, as a good bill out of this.

Sir *John Hanmer*. Our David against this Goliath; our bill against the lords bill. Ours will go up to the lords triumphant in throwing out this, and warm your party in the lords house.

Sir *Wm. Coventry* will only say this one little thing, that the readiness of the house of commons to throw a bill out, without debate, is not usual: this bill being, seemingly, only to feel our pulse for a Toleration. He is not afraid of the success of our bill with the lords. When the nation sees the zeal of this house against Popery, it will put courage into magistrates, to put the laws in execution. Would nor give it the countenance of a debate but throw it out.

Mr. *Sacheverell* would have something on our books, not only of the title of the Bill, but something that it meant a Toleration of Popery.

Sir *Wm. Coventry*. The bill has so good a title, that it would be a reflection upon us to cast it out, upon our books: but he would cause some entry to be made, 'That finding, upon reading the bill, that it repealed many laws against Popery, we have thrown it out."

The *Speaker* proposes this to be upon your books, viz. 'That a bill coming from the lords, so entitled, was rejected at the first reading.' That is the ordinary way of entry. But if you please to let it be thus, viz. 'The house, upon reading and opening the bill, sent from the lords, entitled, &c. finding it much otherwise, have rejected it.'

Mr. *Waller*. If we enter it so, this will teach the lords to make notes upon our bills. If we do this, it will remain upon record. Would have you content yourselves with a nem. con. in throwing out the bill, and have it so entered.

Sir *John Trevor*. When we send such a bill up to the lords, he would have the lords do so by us.

Resolved, "That the Entry be made as the Speaker proposed, viz. Upon reading the said bill, and opening the substance thereof to the house, it appeared to be much different from the title; and thereupon the house, nem. con. rejected the same.*—The house then read, the 3rd time, their own Bill for suppressing the Growth of Popery; and sent it up to the lords for their concurrence.

The King's Message for an Adjournment.] April 11. Mr. Sec. Williamson delivered to the house the following Message from his majesty:

"C. R. His majesty, having considered your last Address, and finding some late alteration in the affairs abroad, thinks it necessary to put you in mind, that the only way to prevent the danger which may arise to these kingdoms, must be, by putting his majesty timely in condition to make such fitting preparations, as may enable him to do what may be most for the security of them. And if, for this reason, you shall desire to sit any longer time, the king is content you adjourn now, before Easter, and meet again suddenly after, to ripen this matter, and to perfect some of the most necessary Bills now depending."

Debate thereon.] Mr. Sec. *Williamson*. He said, 'adjourn;' but the king means, by short adjournments, to Oct. to have the parliament within call, upon emergencies.

Lord *Cavendish*. The king, in his Message, does signify 'an alteration in affairs;' but not what, nor what influence it has had, or change upon his council. When he does, we shall do what the king can desire of us, upon this occasion. Till then, we are not ripe for the matter.

Mr. *Stockdale*. 'To sit after Easter to ripen things;' that is, in plain English, to grant Money.

Mr. *Stanhope*. It is not possible that any reasonable time can dispatch the bills depending before us; and the king may suffer, by the Commissioners not putting the act for the Tax in execution, by their stay here, and 500 of us being reduced to 140. It is not parliamentary, nor safe, to sit with so few; and he would move the king for a recess for some longer time.

Mr. Sec. *Williamson* knows not whether he did express himself clear enough. He said, 'The king intended a recess by adjournment;' and though the king means not so as to sit till Oct. yet, by short adjournments, to meet as occasion should require.

Mr. *Powle* cannot concur with the motion, to meet again after Easter. The session already has been a great labour to us, and our occasions require our presence; and he desires to have no other meeting, for few will attend it, being gone into the country. On the other side, this Message from the king respects our Address, concerning the French king's Greatness. If the king has entered into Alliances, and if he declared them, he would assist the king to support them. As for the other bills, they may keep till Oct. by adjournment. He would not have the house make an Address to the king, as if we affect sitting. But he believes, if there be occasion for us to meet, we will be ready to come up, upon reasonable summons.

* "It was rejected, with this censure added in the Journal; 'Because the body of the Bill was contrary to the Title.' A method of proceeding so totally different from the stated rules of intercourse between the two houses, that nothing but the crimes of the bill could have rendered it excusable." Ralph.

Sir *Tho. Lee.* What with the writing, and the verbal Message delivered by sec. Williamson, it puts him to a stand. If there be a necessity for taking arms immediately, then there may be a proclamation to call up your members. He would have the Message farther explained.

Col. *Birch* cannot make the Messages agree with one another. He remembers our Address; and, to be clear, would have this Message, by word of mouth by the secretary, entered, with that on paper, into our books, as an explanation of it. Adjournment must be with a house; and the Message says, we are to do no business. If it be cleared, that no business is to be done, then we may sit more quietly at home.

Sir *John Ernly.* There was not an apprehension of the loss of Flanders, till this repulse of the prince of Orange at the battle of Montcassel. Reparation now will not be seasonably asked. The king has neither stores, nor money, nor ships: 20 or 30 privateers may easily burn all our ships, and master the Channel.

Mr. Sec. *Coventry.* The Message does not speak to press you to any thing; but it lays before you the king's condition, and that he will take his measures according to the proportion that you will help him. Your Address is, 'That you will stand by him in such Alliances as he shall make, &c.' But what if the king make alliances with one hand, and offend with the other, and be not provided with defence! a man would have his servant go a journey, but will not have him engage in it, till he be provided with boots and horses, &c. Make what use of it you please.'

Sir *Edm. Jennings* would request from the king an adjournment, for some short time, to perfect the bills depending; that the world may not say, we have passed the Money-Bills, and no more. He would have something entered on the Journal, that there may be nothing reflecting upon us, as passing Money-Bills, and no more.

Mr. *Hopkins.* Are we assured that that servant whom Coventry spoke of would go that journey, when he has boots and horse provided him?

Mr. Sec. *Coventry.* Would it be wisdom in the king to tell you what journey he would go, or that he would go a journey, without being provided for it?

Mr. *Boscawen* would not have us address the king to meet soon again, upon account of the bills. It seems, it is not a fit time, or place, to tell you if any thing be done, as to your Address, here. If the king intends to give an Answer to the Address, then we may meet, but not as to the Bills; and he would address the king accordingly.

Sir *Philip Warwick.* It is the king's great wisdom, that he gives you no more light, in his Answer to your Address. It looks like a night-piece, under that shade which is fitting for it. If we will give no Supplies, till the king make such engagements, &c. we put him upon hardships; and if we vote farther engagements to supply him, he knows not how the country will take it.

Sir *Henry Capel.* When the king sends us word 'that there is an Alteration of affairs,' he would take some notice of it in our books, with some Resolution upon it. He would pass a vote, 'That, because the king is convinced, by the defeat of the prince of Orange, that he should make Alliances, &c.' And therefore this Vote is pursuant to our former Addresses.

Sir *Henry Ford* knows not what farther security we can give the king, in this case, than we have done. He would address, 'That we humbly accept of the king's intimation of a short Adjournment.' For our preservation, if our house was on fire, we would give some, to save all.

Sir *John Hotham* knows it his duty never to suspect the king; but has reason to suspect elsewhere. The Address before was, 'That we hold ourselves obliged in prosecuting such Alliances, &c. to assist the king.' If gentlemen would speak clear out, neither his estate nor person should be spared, whilst he has a drop of blood, or a penny in his purse, to support them.

Mr. Sec. *Coventry.* The king doubts not the constancy of this house. The king of Spain has good Alliances. The Hollander is firm to him, and he has great engagements. Valenciennes and St. Omers are taken, and were not provided for, and yet no failing in the Alliances. You will come too late, 'with lives and fortunes,' if you engage the king in a war, before he be provided for it. The thing is, let us consider, whether we be safe at home, before we go abroad: that we be provided with stores and necessaries.

Sir *Wm. Coventry.* The matter is, the king seems to think that affairs are so altered abroad, that it is necessary we should be stricter in the matter we desired of him. He seems to intimate, that he is not in a condition to do what we desire of him, and expects something from us, according to our promise, in the Addresses, 'to aid and assist him.' Now the question is, How far we should go forwarder? If we were not at the end of a session, he would never stick at it. But moving for a tax, now gentlemen are gone down, and after an intimation from the king, 'that we should rise suddenly,' there is so much consequence in such a surprize, that he will never move you to it. We hear abroad, with both ears, of the prince of Orange's ill success; but he hopes your Address has heartened the confederates; and, the king complying, he would be loth the thing should fall flat in our hands. He would be loth the French counsellors should say to the king, 'They that advised you, shrink and slacken their hands.' He would not therefore strengthen those French counsellors—Would not be thought so pusillanimous a nation, that, when, three weeks ago, we addressed the king, on this success of the French, we should shrink from it. The more the danger is, it is ten times more necessary that you should do something; and it is never too late, till all be gone. He is raw and imperfect in what to move; but wishes, from his soul, this Message had been sent 3 days ago. You have given the king Money for 30 Ships, and that cannot be laid out for that purpose under 3 years. He hears it talked of, 'that Oct. may be soon enough to meet again.' But the day before to-morrow is not soon enough. You are in danger of being lost before Oct. If it concur with the rules of the house, he would make no scruple to move, 'That the king may have power to make use of some part of that Money, with our promise to reimburse it again, upon this occasion.' The king seems to be willing we should sit after Easter, that we may be witnesses, in a short time, how far he has gone in our Addresses; and hopes he meant to ripen that matter, that you may be witnesses he has done his utmost. He desires we may adjourn before Easter, with this reservation, 'That, if the king see cause sooner than Oct. he may call us by proclamation, at 20 days notice, to give him farther aid.' A little of that already given may help him and the confederates. A little money may go a great way: but he will not go farther than 200,000*l.*

Sir *Tho. Lee.* As for the motion of 200,000*l.* it is not possible to be done; for you must have a prorogation for altering the day in the Tax-bill; as it may be of dangerous consequence for the lords to do it. The king may destroy your Adjournment by proclamation. He is informed there must be a special act of parliament for doing it, viz. for calling that parliament in the interval of adjournment.

Sir *Eliab Harvey.* Is our Fleet, that we have given money to let out, and the Excise, a secret to the king of France? And is not that making war? Can the Fleet go incognito? He would have nothing said of secrecy. If occasion be, we may meet particularly on that account, and none else.

Sir *Tho. Lee.* It is said, 'We should meet after Easter, in relation to Public Bills;' but he is against it, unless, withal, the Money-Bills may lie on the table. He speaks against the offer of any Public Bills whatever. We are embarrassed in foreign business, and all for want of confidence, lest the money should be for some ill intent, and not have the direct fruit of it. If, on the other hand, we show coldness or tergiversation in the house, it is the ruin of us all. He is in suspense what to do, and how. He could have wished the paper from the king had been sent sooner. He shall, for the present, move, 'to consider the thing farther to-morrow morning.' The Paper has been considered, and well weighed, by the king's council; he would do so too here; and hopes we shall do like Englishmen.—The farther debate was adjourned till to-morrow.

April 12. After having resumed the adjourned debate on the king's Message, it was resolved, "That a Clause be added to the Bill for continuing the additional Duty of Excise, to enable his majesty to borrow 200,000*l.* at 7 per cent.

Resolved also, "That the Thanks of this house be presented to his majesty, for laying before them his majesty's sense of the posture of affairs abroad; and to let his majesty know, that, in order to his majesty's Preparations, in pursuance of the Address of this house, for the Safety of the Kingdom, they have provided a security of 200,000*l.* And that whatsoever of that sum shall be expended accordingly, shall be by them reimbursed: and whensoever the posture of his majesty's affairs shall require their attendance in parliament, they will be ready to aid and assist him, as the nature of his majesty's Affairs shall require." And a Committee was appointed to draw up an Address, pursuant to the said Vote."

The Commons' further Address respecting Alliances.] April 13. Sir John Trevor reported the Address, which was read, and agreed to by the house, and is as follows:

"May it please your most excellent majesty; We, your majesty's most dutiful and loyal subjects, the commons in this present parliament assembled, do, with great satisfaction of mind, observe the regard your majesty is pleased to express to our former Addresses, by intimating to us the late Alteration in Affairs abroad; and do return our most humble Thanks for your majesty's gracious offer made to us thereupon, in your last Message. And having taken a serious deliberation of the same, and of the Preparations your majesty hath therein intimated to us, were fitting to be made, in order to these public ends, we have, for the present, provided a security in a Bill for an additional Duty of Excise, upon which your majesty may raise the sum of 200,000*l.* And if your maj. shall think fit to call us together again, for this purpose, in some short time after Easter, by any public signification of your majesty's pleasure commanding our attendance, we shall, at our next meeting, not only be ready to reimburse your majesty what sums of money shall be expended upon such extraordinary Preparations, as shall be made in pursuance of our former Addresses; but shall likewise, with most chearful hearts, proceed both then, and at all other times, to furnish your maj. with so large proportions of Assistances and Supplies, upon this occasion, as may give your majesty, and the whole world, an ample testimony of our loyalty and affection to your majesty's service; and may enable your majesty, by the help of Almighty God, to maintain such stricter Alliances, as you shall have entered into, against all opposition whatsoever."

The King's Answer.] April 16. Mr. Sec. Williamson delivered the following Message from his majesty:

"C. R. His majesty, having considered the Answer of this house to his last Message, about enabling him to make fitting Preparations for the security of these kingdoms, finds by it, That they have only enabled him to borrow

200,000*l.* upon a Fund given him for other uses: his majesty desires, therefore, the house should know, and hopes they will always believe of him, that not only that Fund, but any other within his power, shall be engaged to the utmost for preservation of his kingdoms.—But as his majesty's condition is, (which, he doubts not, but is as well known to this house as to himself) he must tell them plainly, that, without a sum of 600,000*l.* or credit for such a sum upon new Funds, it will not be possible for him to speak or act those things which should answer the ends of their several Addresses, without exposing the kingdoms to much greater dangers.—His majesty does farther acquaint them, that, having done his part, and laid the true state of things before them, he will not be wanting to use the best means for the safety of his people, which his present condition is capable of."

Another Address from the Commons.] The Commons fell into an immediate consideration of an Answer to the above Message, and after a short debate, agreed to the following Address:

"May it please your majesty; Your majesty's most loyal and dutiful subjects, the commons, in this present parliament assembled, having considered your majesty's last Message, and the gracious expressions therein contained, for employing your whole Revenue, at any time to raise Money for the preservation of your majesty's kingdoms, do find great cause to return our most humble Thanks for the same; and to desire your maj. to rest assured, that you shall find as much duty and affection in us, as can be expressed by a most loyal people to a most gracious sovereign. And whereas your maj. is pleased to signify to us, 'That the sum of 200,000*l.* is not sufficient, without farther Supplies, to enable your maj. to speak and act those things which are desired by your people,' we humbly take leave to acquaint your majesty, that, many of our members being (upon an expectation of Adjournment before Easter) gone into their several countries, we cannot think it parliamentary, in their absence, to take upon us the granting of Money; but do therefore desire your maj. to be pleased, that this house may adjourn itself for such short sime (before the sum of 200,000*l.* can be expended) as your maj. shall think fit; and, by your royal proclamation, command the attendance of all our members at the day of meeting: by which time, we hope your maj. may have so formed your affairs, and fixed your Alliances, in pursuance of our former Addresses, that your maj. may be graciously pleased to impart them to us in parliament.—And we no ways doubt, but, at our next assembling, your maj. will not only meet with a compliance in the Supply your maj. desires, but with all such assistances, as the posture of your affairs shall require: in confidence whereof, we hope your maj. will be encouraged in the mean time to speak and act such things, as your maj. shall judge necessary for attaining those great ends we have formerly represented to your majesty*."

The Parliament adjourned.] The king had no sooner received this Address, but finding the Money Bills ready, the same evening, he came suddenly to the house of peers, and being seated on his throne with the usual solemnity, he sent for the commons, and gave his royal assent to the several Bills presented to him. After which the Lord Chancellor, by his majesty's command, acquainted the two houses, that they had leave to adjourn themselves till the 21st of May next.

The Parliament meet.] May 21. The parliament met, according to his majesty's proclamation. The king made no Speech, but ordered one of the Secretaries to acquaint the house of commons, "That he would have them consider the substance of his last Message as soon as they could; for that he intended a recess very suddenly."

Debate on the King's Message respecting Alliances.] It was then moved, that the king's last Message be read.

Mr. *Sacheverell.* He has not heard the Message, for he was not here when the Address was made; but, if he understands it right, the Message seems to be, and he hopes it is, 'for Alliances, &c.' that when we came back, we might see our Money laid out; before we came hither again. Before we come to a question, several things are to be taken into consideration; as, whether the nation may be preserved by peace, before we think of war; and how far either is for England's interest? And, if gentlemen enter into debate, what our interest is, then it is time to speak, whether to give, or not; and how much. He would know, what Alliances we have made since we met last, and whether the Money be laid out according to your intention.

Mr. Sec. *Coventry.* If Alliances are made, or not made, they are not to be talked of in public. The king has Alliances with Spain, Denmark, Sweden, and many others. He would know what Sacheverell means.

Mr. *Sacheverell.* If the case stands there, he would know what new Alliances have been made. He thinks the nation may be preserved without expence of blood, or treasure. He proposes, fairly and calmly, that the thing may be opened, and that we may take the safest and securest way for the nation, either by peace or war. Unless such Alliances are made as we addressed for, it is in vain to make war, and run into hazard with potent neigh-

* "If Don Bernard de Solinas, the Spanish minister at London is to be depended on, the king was so angry with these Addresses against France, that he called the authors of them, 'A Company of Rogues.' It appears in sir Wm. Temple's Memoirs, that Don Bernard made no secret of this story to his friends in the house of commons; which his majesty so highly resented, that he ordered him to depart the kingdom within certain days." Ralph.

bours, as we did before, when we wanted alliances. He moves, that we may go into a committee of the whole house, for the more free and full debate of the thing; and that it may be scanned where our interest lies. As to France's growing greatness, it being greater than is consistent with the interest of England, he would know how he came by that power, that, as he has it, he may be reduced back again. As to his number of shipping, his purse is too big for us; and if an Alliance with Holland be not secured, we can never combat both their fleets. It is the interest of Holland to be ready to join with us, and we with them; and, if joined, France can never come up to us, in number or force; and so we may preserve the Netherlands. He would have the house go into a grand committee, fairly and calmly to debate of Alliances; and if, that way will not do, he will go what way you please.

Mr. Sec. *Williamson.* He is not against the motion, if the thing were not already done. We are off of that 'of Alliances.' It has been already debated, and addressed to the king, and a return of Answer upon it; and the matter is gone beyond debating. The last return from the king to your Address, was, 'He would do what you advised him; and without such a sum of money, or credit for it, he could not speak nor act the request of your Addresses.' This being a continuation of parliament, Sacheverell's motion is over entirely. The question is, plainly and nakedly, What will you do? in matter of Alliances, the king tells you, 'He cannot act nor speak of it, without being farther in a condition of owning it abroad.' And the thing can admit of no other Answer than is already given by the king.

Sir *Wm. Coventry* hopes no time has been lost, since we met last; and hopes that what we then desired is done, though not told us in what manner. He finds himself to have the same inclinations he had before, and has ever since persisted in them, and hopes he shall never waver. The thing is rightly stated. To enquire what Alliances we have entered into, since we met last, is not our question; or whether peace be properly Alliances; but our present purpose is, whether the Alliances, that require the assistance of the house to maintain them, are proportionable to our ends in our Address; and if they appear to be so, he will then not be wanting to support them. It has been said, 'The matter requires more time to finish, than this intermission of 5 weeks.' But our first Address was a longer time before than since the recess. He has heard, that the Triple Alliance was made in 5 days, when Holland had peace, and no more need of our alliance than France had. Can any man think that Holland requires your Alliance less now, than when they were in peace? he cannot imagine it hard, in time of war, to admit of a confederate, the Triple Alliance being done in 5 days. The king's ministers know their time best; therefore we mentioned no time for our recess; and, by the time we met, we expected Alliances to be made; and we needed not have met, if Alliances were not fit to be declared, nor ripe to be told us; being not fit to alarm our neighbours, but so that all may enter into the war together; for it is feared it should alarm France. If it were in his choice, he would rather have him alarmed in summer than in winter, when his armies are in the field, and employed. In winter, the French king has no other employment. Is it a less alarm to give money to support Alliances, than to declare war? if Alliances are not made, we are come too soon. Perhaps a post or two may ripen Alliances fit for imparting; and moves to adjourn to Thursday.

Sir *John Ernly* hears it said, 'If we are entered into war, we know what to give.' The king tells you, 'he cannot stir one step farther without 600,000*l.*' He wishes that Alliances might be made without blood; but he understands them not. With Spain you cannot make one step farther than is upon you already, but what must produce blood. That step is a war. He comes not here to ask money, but we cannot be insensible of our own weakness. We want ships and stores, and the king has used all his credit, but cannot get any thing from the city, but doubtful answers from the lord mayor. There are 42 ships ready, and there are 30 more preparing; and if all you have given had been in ready money, there could not have been taken a better course: all 30 ready in 12 weeks; and stores, as far as credit will go, are taken care for; and if, in this case you are in at this present time, you will go farther, you must assist the king.—Whereas gentlemen say, You are, as to ships, in as good a posture as you were a year ago, he knows that ships are forced to beg press-warrants, by reason of many seamen being gone out, having no other employment than in merchant-ships.

Mr. Sec. *Coventry.* The king says, 'without a Fund of 600,000*l.* he cannot act nor speak, &c.' And we cannot farther urge the thing, unless we give the king a reason for what we advise. It is the happiness of the kingdom, that the king either by reason brings us to his opinion, or we bring him to ours in this thing.

Mr. *Mallet.* All we do is insignificant, if we know not what Alliances are made. The king may 'act and speak' out, if he pleases; and we may have assurance mutual, that it is to support the Protestant cause.

Sir *Tho. Littleton* remembers, Grotius says, in his book 'De Jure Belli et Pacis,' on the causes of making war, 'If a prince makes extraordinary preparations, or any thing tending to it, it is not only a just cause for his neighbouring prince to arm, for jealousy of his safety, but, unless he desists that preparation, to make war upon him.' The use he makes of it is this; that the king of France has a vigilant council, and a watchful eye upon the king, and our Messages to him, and his Answers, and on the king's demand of 600,000*l.* When this was on foot, it is not to be imagined but that this expostulation being made, either the French ministers are told, that this is not against France, or are left doubtful where it is intended. Why, then, is this darkness to the king's subjects, when the matter is clear to the king of France one way or the other?—The further debate was then adjourned to the 23d.

The King's Speech to the Commons at Whitehall, respecting Alliances.] May 23. The king sent for the commons to Whitehall, and made the following Speech:

"Gentlemen; I have sent for you hither, that I might prevent those mistakes and distrusts which I find some are ready to make, as if I had called you together only to get Money from you for other uses than you would have it employed.—I do assure you, upon the word of a king, that you shall not repent any trust you repose in me, for the safety of my kingdoms; and I desire you to believe, I would not break my credit with you.—But as I have already told you, That it will not be possible for me to speak or act those things, which should answer the ends of your several Addresses, without exposing my kingdoms to much greater dangers; so I declare to you again, that I will neither hazard my own safety, nor yours, until I be in a better condition than I am able to put myself, both to defend my subjects, and offend my enemies.—I do farther assure you, that I have not lost one day since your last meeting, in doing all I can for our defence; and I tell you plainly, it shall be your fault, and not mine, if our security be not sufficiently provided for."*

Debate on the King's Speech.] As soon as the commons returned to their house they proceeded to take the king's Speech into conderation.

Sir *Edw. Bainton.* Here are two things before you, Money and Alliances. He is so much dissatisfied that we did precipitately enter into Money, that, he believes, if it had not been done, you would have had Alliances before now. He is for Alliances, but not upon implicit faith. No one man is certain of every thing. The French ambassadors were civilly treated; and, they say, had a good desert at parting, when they were lately here. There is a truce proposed at Nimeguen; and we have a potent neighbour upon us. He would have us go into a grand committee; not because one, two, or three may speak twice, but not precipitately to jump into Money. He would be informed by freedom of debate, which, by order of parliament, is not to be restrained in a committee to speak but once. For Alliances, in the first place; and what Alliances are to be entered into, that the whole kingdom, as one man, may be against him that shall advise the contrary. He means 'this house.'

[Exception was taken at his words, "rise as one man, &c."]

Sir *Tho. Meres.* Bainton said not a word of war, in what he said. 'If any single man dare advise Alliances, contrary to this house, the whole body of the nation, 'as one man,' may be against him.' As they are against you, you must be against them; and if we may not say so, farewell all! But he will give words to the question: he would have it be, 'to go into a grand committee, to consider of an Answer to the king's Speech.'

Sir *Philip Warwick.* Let us make Alliances among ourselves. When we are debating them abroad, let us not quarrel with ourselves. He would rather quench the flame, than increase it. Bainton's words were, 'rise, as one man, against him that should advise the contrary.' The words are sounding a trumpet of war; words not fit to be said here. What will the world think of us, to fall so particularly into a diffident Answer to the king's Speech? Though we are his great council, we are not his directors. He has been at his master's elbow (the late king) when the hatchet was almost at his head: He would leave off these heats, and would have that caution, that the committee may proceed with confidence in the king.

Sir *Tho. Littleton* observes some exception taken at what fell from Bainton. He would therefore go into a grand committee, for more freedom of debate. But since Warwick called it 'a trumpet of sedition in Bainton's mouth,' which words can have no other explanation than 'Rebellion,' (which words Bainton did not say) he desires an explanation from Warwick: he would therefore, for more freedom of debate, go into a grand committee.

The house then resolved into a Grand Committee, on the king's Speech. Sir John Trevor took the chair.

Sir *Eliab Harvey* moves, 'That we may enter into an Alliance, offensive and defensive, with the States of Holland.'

Sir *Robert Howard.* War is not a necessary consequence of Alliances. Trusting the king, or not trusting the king, is a word of a strange nature: will not be put to it, trust or not trust. No man can bring it up so strictly. He speaks this upon grounds that are deep, and not strange. Some, he hears, say, 'Alliances *may* produce a war;' and some say, '*must* produce a war.' To put the king upon Alliances with the Dutch—Is that all? One is slow-paced necessity, and another a quick suspicion. Consideration is best for every body; and he would adjourn to Friday.

Sir *John Hotham* ever thought it fit for us to

* "Had the word of a king never been forfeited, it is reasonable to suppose, that, upon this great occasion, it would have been taken: or, if all appearances had not been utterly irreconcileable with these professions, those who contended so warmly for the end, must have granted the means. But, as the case was, opposition was not only countenanced but applauded; and the majority, both of the parliament and people, acted as if there was more reason to dread the designs of their own monarch, than even of his brother of France." Ralph.

'abate the pride, assuage the malice, and confound the devices' of the king of France. Plainly, he desires, as Harvey has moved, 'That we may make an Address to the king, to make a league, offensive and defensive, with the States of Holland, against the king of France.'

Mr. Sec. *Coventry* hears a proposition made, that he never heard of before, 'To enter into a league, offensive and defensive,' without any treaty ever made; and another gentleman moves 'for a league to be made with the confederates.' You will never see a precedent of any such vote.

Mr. Sec. *Williamson*. Some are jealous, as if the king does call for Money for other ends than you desire. The king tells you, 'That, in the interim of your parting, he has not lost one day in doing what you have desired.' He takes notice of one motion 'for a league with Holland, offensive and defensive,' and another 'with the Confederates, &c.' He knows not how this can be made any part of the king's Speech. It is a great goodness, that the king has so graciously answered us; and let us not go farther than becomes this loyal house of commons; that we may expect to be gratified in a thing we strain not too much. Under 600,000*l.* the king can do nothing; and that is the naked thing before you, and proper for your consideration.

Mr. *Sacheverell*. The honour of the house is always to be preserved, and the good opinion of the king and people; and it will be so, to go by the same steps as when you were here last: to tell the king what Alliances you mean. In delay there will be danger, and the season of the year will be spent. When the king imparts those Alliances to us, then we may assist him in the support of them.

Sir *Christ. Musgrave*. Can the king make you any other Answer than what he has done already? There is no proper question before you, but, how to enable the king to enter into Alliances.

Sir *Tho. Meres* is not for a negative. The house has already declared how Money may be had; 'by declaring Alliances.' But it has been answered twice, 'No; Alliances cannot be declared till we give Money.' He would know what we are called together for now, by proclamation. He conceives we are now here to give an Answer to the king's Speech when we were here last.

Mr. Sec. *Coventry*. When you rose last, you were not a sufficient number to answer for the whole kingdom; therefore you then were adjourned. So that you are at a stand, till you enable the king 'to act and speak,' as he tells you.

Sir *Tho. Meres* believes, the king will be convinced by our reasons. We were, when we met last, willing to give the king credit, till 200,000*l.* was expended, in maintaining the Alliances we desired. And by this time we expected Alliances should be told us. But he finds not one step of Alliances made.

Mr. *Sacheverell* would gladly have shown him how they can employ 600,000*l.* in making such Alliances. Whilst this Alliance is making, do they think to be ready by winter, and fight in the spring, and let Flanders be lost, and then be put to get it again? Is this the meaning? Give 600,000*l.* to be in the hands of that Council, which broke the Triple League, and greatened France! What instance can be given, that those gentlemen have changed their principles? Men are still sent out of Ireland and Scotland, and arms out of the stores in England; and they persuade the king, that nothing can be done without 600,000*l.* Let them not dally with us, and put us off thus with fair promises, as they have done. When peace was made with Holland, we desired it exclusive to France. It was said then, 'trust the king;' and you were deceived then: will you be deceived twice? Let them own Alliances, and we are for them. If not, he would not give them a penny.

Mr. *Williams*. What has been said to us in speech, discourse, or message, is not to be looked upon as the king's. He gives them their true weight; they are the product of councils. Therefore he would begin where we ought, from whence it comes. We agree, in the main, for the safety of the kingdom. In some measure, the king is of our opinion. The thing we are to do, is to stop the power of France, which intimidates every man. We have addressed, but, it seems, too generally about Alliances. But let us be against the Growth and Power of France, this day, or never. And he will give all he has to defend us, expressly in opposition to the French greatness; either for an Alliance with Holland, or the Confederates. Till then, he will not give a penny.

Mr. *Mallet*. King James was said to be 'the Solomon of his age.' Our king is heir to his virtues. There is something more recorded of Solomon; he fell to strange Counsels *by strange women*. And we cannot repose any confidence in the king, if he puts his counsel into 'strange women.' If they be left, God will bless his Counsels.

Sir *Tho. Meres*. There are but two ways, either to defend ourselves from France, or comply with him. When we are afraid of a man, we either get his good-will, or take away his power. There are but these two ways. He would fain let his good-will alone a year or two longer.

Lord *Cavendish* hears it called 'the king's Speech,' though he thinks it rather the product of ill counsel: 600,000*l.* is demanded to enter into and declare Alliances, because the king, by chance, may be engaged into a war. It is an ill precedent to charge the people, because the king may have a war; they may be so charged for the future. If the consequence of such Alliances must be a war, it is better now the French bands are full, and no danger of invasion, if the king makes those Alliances that we would now make. He hears 'great difficulty in making these Alliances;' and 'not to be done without a great sum of money.' The parliament said, 'they will support alliances' and since we met, nothing has been done in pursuance of our Address, for stopping the growing Greatness of France. There is a great deal of Money asked; and how it may influence our counsels, he examines not; but he expected Alliances against we met. He moves now, 'That we may make Alliances with Holland and Spain.'

Mr. Sec. *Williamson* is glad to see us come towards some end. We have had many pauses. If the king's hands are not to be trusted with the Money, clear that. But that question carried, that is moved for, viz. 'An address to the king,' is but calling for another question, and is not to the point in question before you. If you distrust putting the Money into the hands of those who have so little satisfied you already, then it is proper to remove those who have had it in management, before you can go into any Alliance. It has been said, 'That there are some who would be as glad of a refusal, as of our giving money:' he would have no such reflections here. He knows no such persons. But hitherto this motion is an untrodden path; and he would not come by precipitation to that first, but have it well thought of first.

Sir *Tho. Meres.* Can it be imagined but that the question of Money will have a negative? therefore press it not.

Col. *Birch.* It has been said, 'We have had several pauses.' But he will set the cart on wheels, if he can, whilst he is here. But if 'there have been pauses,' it is because you find no Alliances made. Is any thing clearer, than that, if the king would but make the Alliances we desire, we would not only give that sum, but more? he would have us adjourn from 3 days to 3 days, till it be done; and he will move it. Chuse whether you will take his counsel, or not. Your safety depends upon this question, What to be done, and when? every gentleman says, 'he would have Alliances made against the king of France.' If ever, the time is now to declare. If gentlemen can show him that we are in inevitable danger, and cannot resist the king of France, then they say something. But, in six weeks time, he will find a way to raise a million of money, upon occasion of these Alliances. He thinks that nothing under heaven can hinder raising the Money, if these Alliances were entered into; and what can hinder the alliances? in short, there is no money to be had without alliances; and, till then, we have no security of our lives or religion. He is for ready money, and this may easily be done. Your extravagances will raise this money. He mistrusts not the king's ministers, and would have this great action wipe away their miscarriages. He hopes they will over-strive and over-do one another, as we shall do; and would appoint a committee, 'to draw up Reasons for an Alliance with Holland and Spain.'

Mr. *Sawyer.* As long as that door of France is open, our wealth will creep out at it, and their religion will come in. War and peace are in the king's breast; but he never found it successful but when with the concurrence of the parliament. The king has told you, 'That, till something be done to enable him to enter into Alliances, he cannot move farther than he has done already.' But he admits your advice. In the Palatinate war, in king James' time, the commons advice was not taken in time, and their hearts were dead, when afterwards their advice was called for. But he sees not why there should be a competition between the king and this house. Whilst we go on in preparing your money, Alliances may be preparing and finished. But he hears it said, 'This is a hardship put upon the king; the Hollanders and Spaniards will stand more upon terms, by our forwardness:' but you may be ready to alter your opinion, upon occasion. He would have the thing to be doing, whilst you are sitting, and would have them go hand in hand.

Sir *Wm. Coventry.* Our interest is to keep Holland fast to us, upon whom the danger is great, and our assistance from them may be great also. It is our good fortune that the house is not all of one opinion, so that truth may come better out by argument. Ernly said, 'our declaring to desire union will make Holland and France readier to agree.' But if any thing make them agree, the being tired out, and not seeing those, who are equally concerned, give them help, he is afraid, will make them agree. It may cause a despondency in them. If he was of the states of Holland, he could not find one word to say of safety for them, to continue the greatness of the king of France. 'We have tried the people of England,' they may justly say, 'but they do nothing.' But if they think themselves unable to help themselves, and persons concerned do it not, they must shift as well as they can. When the danger had not pressed them so near, and Flanders was a better bulwark to them than now, the consideration of this made De Wit, who loved not England, join with us against the greatness of France. Shall we think that the prince of Orange, at the head of their affairs, will have less success than De Wit had? and can we expect but that, if we give them help, considering all circumstances, France's progress in his conquests may be stopped? if we continue to neglect this, what can secure Holland? is it dangerous to provoke France, now Holland is his enemy? will it not be much more when they are both friends? France gave warrants for fishing to Holland, and that joined them. As for preparations, there need not six millions to keep the French out, by fortifications. He found Papers and Lists in sir Robert Long's office, of Fleets and estimates, in the Scotch war, in the late king's time; it seemed to him, as if things were managed then on purpose to ruin that good king. He was advised to set out second rate ships against Scotland, and the king had got a good sum of money by the lord treasurer Juxon's means; some of it was spent on the Army, but much on a great Fleet: great ships to catch small Scotch vessels; lobsters to catch hares. If therefore we go about to stop France's progress by a war, 600,000*l.* would not make necessary preparations. In our mutual league with Holland, we wish them to bear the brunt. A provision of 40 ships of a side, he thinks, would keep France pretty well in order; and for these 40 ships being kept out a whole year, 600,000*l.* will do that whole year's business. There needs little charge in embassies; a good-will will do that cheap. He would clear that suspicion out of the way, of falling upon ministers; we know, there has been little effect of that. But he hopes, whether there be faults or errors (he knows none unless that to subvert our religion) the king has passed a general pardon, and he hopes every gentleman will give them oblivion in his own heart, if they will redeem what is past, by their good deportment in this great business.

Mr. *Vaughan* has heard, that the lords of the council have sent to the body of the City to borrow Money.

Sir *Nich. Carew.* It is said, that the lord mayor and the city would not lend the king any money, because they could not do it upon a security that was already another's; for the Excise was anticipated, and farmed out.

Sir *Tho. Clarges.* As for Money borrowed of the city, the aldermen say, that it is the usual and ordinary way to be done by the common-council, and not by 20 particular men, (the aldermen;) but he believes there is no anticipation upon the additional duty of excise; for nobody would take tallies of anticipation upon a security not yet begun.

After further debate, it was resolved, 1. "That an humble Address be made to the king, that his majesty would be pleased to enter into a League, offensive and defensive, with the States General of the United Provinces; and to make such other Alliances with such other of the Confederates as his majesty shall think fit, against the Growth and Power of the French king, and for the preservation of the Spanish Netherlands." [To which there was not a negative but Mr. Secretary Williamson.] 2. "That a Committee be appointed to draw up the Address, with Reasons why this house cannot comply with his majesty's Speech, until such Alliances be entered into; and farther showing the necessity of the speedy making of such Alliances; and when such Alliances are made, giving his majesty assurances of speedy and cheerful Supplies, from time to time, for the supporting and maintaining those Alliances."

The Commons' Address to the King, declining a further Supply till his Majesty's Alliances are made known.] May 25. Sir John Trevor reported the said Address, which was read as follows:

"May it please your most excellent majesty; Your majesty's most loyal and dutiful subjects, the commons, in parliament assembled, having taken into their serious consideration your majesty's most gracious Speech, do beseech your maj. to believe it is a great affliction to them, to find themselves obliged, at present, to decline the granting your majesty the Supply that your maj. is pleased to demand; conceiving it is not agreeable to the usage of parliament, to grant Supplies for the maintenance of Wars and Alliances, before they are signified in parliament; which the two wars against the States of the United Provinces, since your majesty's happy Restoration, and the League made with them in Jan. 1668, for Preservation of the Spanish Netherlands, sufficiently prove, without troubling your maj. with instances of greater antiquity. From which usage if we should depart, the precedent might be of dangerous consequence in future times; though your majesty's goodness gives us great security during your majesty's reign; which we beseech God long to continue.—This consideration prompted us, in our last Address to your maj. before our late recess, humbly to mention to your maj. our hopes, that, before our meeting again, your majesty's Alliances might be so fixed, as that your maj. might be graciously pleased to impart them to us in parliament; that so our earnest desires of supplying your maj. for prosecuting those great ends we had humbly laid before your majesty, might meet with no impediment or obstruction; being highly sensible of the necessity of supporting as well as making the Alliances humbly desired in our former Addresses; and which we still conceive so important to the safety of your maj. and your kingdoms, that we cannot, without unfaithfulness to your majesty, and those we represent, omit, upon all occasions, humbly to beseech your majesty, as we now do, to enter into a League, offensive and defensive, with the States General of the United Provinces, against the Growth and Power of the French king, and for the Preservation of the Spanish Netherlands; and to make such other Alliances with such other of the Confederates as your maj. shall think fit and useful to that end. In doing which, that no time may be lost, we humbly offer to your majesty these Reasons for the expediting it: 1. That, if the entering into such Alliances should draw on a War with the French king, it would be least detrimental to your majesty's subjects at this time of the year; they having, now, fewest effects within the dominions of the French king. 2. That though we have great reason to believe the power of the French king to be dangerous to your maj. and your kingdoms, when he shall be at more leisure to molest us; yet, we conceive, the many enemies he hath to deal with at present, together with the situation of your maj.'s kingdoms, the unanimity of your people in this cause, the care your maj. hath been pleased to take of your ordinary Guard for the Sea, together with the credit provided by the late Act, entitled 'An

Act for an additional Excise for three years,' make the entering into and declaring Alliances very safe; until we may, in a regular way, give your maj. such farther Supplies, as may enable your maj. to support your Alliances, and defend your kingdoms. 3. Because of the great danger and charge which must of necessity fall upon your majesty's kingdoms, if through want of that timely encouragement and assistance (which your majesty's joining with the States of the United Provinces, and other the Confederates, would give them) the said states, or any other considerable part of the Confederates, should this next winter, or sooner, make a peace or truce with the French king (the prevention whereof hitherto must be acknowledged to be a singular effect of God's goodness to us;) which if it should happen, your maj. must afterwards be necessitated with fewer, perhaps with no alliances or assistances, to withstand the power of the French king, which hath so long and so successfully contended with so many and potent adversaries; and, whilst he continues his over-balancing greatness, must always be dangerous to his neighbours, since he would be able to oppress any one confederate before the rest could get together and be in so good a posture of offending him as they now are, being jointly engaged in a war. And if he should be so successful as to make a peace, or disunite the present confederation against him, it is much to be feared whether it would be possible ever to re-unite it; at least, it would be a work of so much time and difficulty, as would leave your majesty's kingdoms exposed to much misery and danger.—Having thus discharged our duty, in laying before your maj. the dangers threatening your majesty, and your kingdoms, and the only remedy we can think of for preventing it, and securing and quieting the minds of your majesty's people, with some few of those Reasons which have moved us to this, and our former Addresses, on this subject; we most humbly beseech your maj. to take this matter into your most serious consideration; and to take such resolutions, as may not leave it in the power of any neighbouring prince to rob your people of that happiness which they enjoy under your majesty's gracious government; beseeching your maj. to rest confident and assured, that, when your maj. shall be pleased to declare such Alliances in parliament, we shall hold ourselves obliged, not only by our promises and assurances given, and now with great unanimity renewed in a full house, but by the zeal and desires of those whom we represent, and by the interest of all our safeties, most chearfully to give your maj. from time to time such speedy supplies and assistances, as may fully and plentifully answer the occasions; and, by God's blessing, preserve your majesty's honour, and the safety of your people. All which is most humbly submitted to your majesty's great wisdom."

Debate on the Address.] Mr. Sec. *Coventry.* This Address is to the king, to stop the great and over-balancing power of the French king, &c. He hopes it will not be interpreted ill-will to this Address, when the means desired may attain your end. The king has returned you an Answer, declaring consent to the substance of the thing you desire, 'but cannot speak nor act a step farther till you enable him.' This is the main question upon which the whole depends. Unless you come to the king, or the king to you, the danger that you apprehend may remain, and the people lose their remedy against their fears and apprehensions of the power of the king of France. Enquire what the reason is, why we should persuade the king to desert: he finds but one; it is, you will grant no Money till Alliances be declared. He asks then, whether you have not given 200,000*l.* upon the Excise, towards this Alliance? And he thinks this a precedent; and that is the only argument; which does destroy itself. The king is furnished with another argument, if by way of precedent—'To tell the king the manner of his Alliances, offensive and defensive, &c.' The king may tell you, 'there was never such a precedent, as to tell the king terms of Leagues, offensive and defensive.' Very little is wanting, but sending the king a Treaty ready-made; the king made the Triple Alliance, not from any motion of this house; it was his own. This is another thing, you tell the king, 'Whether he be in a condition or not, you will have him do it.' He knows it may be answered from the nature of the writ of summons of parliament; but that is 'ad 'consulendum et deliberandum de quibusdam 'arduis regni negotiis,' not 'omnibus, &c.' The nation is concerned in this; but when formerly the house of commons desired queen Eliz. to marry, you know what she said; 'If you name the person whom I am to marry, it is unsufferable.' But, in your case, to nominate terms to the king, he thinks not proper for you. Does any man think that the king will go about to make Alliances against the growth and over-balancing power of France, and leave out Holland? It cannot be imagined. Consider another thing in this Address, in point of decorum; he has all the apprehensions of the greatness of France that you have, to the utmost, but you come and declare the house of Austria averse to a peace; but they never yet published it at Nimeguen. What kind of figure will you have of your sovereign, who sends to mediate, and has the secret depositums of all princes, and you put him upon this overt declaration, 'For preservation of Flanders from the king of France, &c?' The king, and all the world, cannot but understand your meaning, and it is needless to particularize either. He would have you therefore comply with the king, or give him stronger Reasons why you will not.

Sir *John Birkenhead.* Here are precedents in this Address, that he never saw before; he would have the points of it read, one by one.— Several called out, 'Agree! agree!'

Sir *Ch. Wheeler.* We are called upon, he

hears, 'to agree,' but would be sorry, without some farther consideration, to agree. The paper reported, has three parts, 1. The Address, &c. 2. The Reasons why we cannot comply with the king, &c. 3. Assurances of Supply, if the king will make Alliances, &c. The Reasons which are short, he expected longer, for they are no more than what we gave before; they ought to arise from the debate of Wednesday. Few were given in the last debate, and he expected some more at the private committee. Of that kind, there is one short one: 'A precedent of the Palatinate war.' Those of late time, not troubled with ancient. 'That of the Dutch war formerly.' He would have it derived from history, ancient and prophane, how the people can be entitled to the consideration of war and peace: it never belonged to the commons of England. When the king engages us in a war, he knows how we are to pray and petition, but this Address seems to extend farther than our province extends to. By this Address, the war is declared. Perhaps you may come into a war, and then he shall declare himself farther; but he is not for an Alliance with the Dutchmen. We are the greatest people at arms in the world, and we must trust all to the conduct of a Dutch army! He looks for popular arguments: we have soundly paid for a Dutch war. As to the last point of 'Assurances of Supply, &c.' he takes that to be the short of what we have said already. We say, 'We will do it liberally and largely.' But what is that? Some gentlemen say, 'some privateers and a squadron of ships for the present;' and some are of another opinion. But this Address, as it is penned, is not large enough, or else we take the conduct of the war upon us, from the beginning to the end.—There was a great cry, 'Agree! agree!'

Mr. Sec. *Williamson* says, he 'agrees' as far in the end of the Address as any gentleman does, but he fears that the success will show, that this way will not do it. He cannot but think this a new thing, and that it will be far from acknowledging the king's condescension; and that we encroach upon his prerogative. Let men be ever so hasty, yet if this Paper-Address must go to the king, he yet thinks some parts of it must be mended. The king tells you, 'He must have preparatives;' and you must show precedents why preparations have not been granted, before particular Alliances have been declared. Why must Alliances, offensive and defensive, be the matter of the Address? The people cannot consider it; that is proper only for the royal breast. 'Defensive' consideration is more proper for the people. He never knew an 'offensive' league declared here before. You are told, 'That the parliament advised the Palatinate War.' There is nothing too great for this house, but he never knew any thing done of this nature, but the house was first called up to it. They were called to consult of the Palatinate war, and of the late Dutch war. If there be no precedent of it, and if but one, he begs of gentlemen to consider what reception this Address will have, though from the best and kindest of princes, from such a house of commons. You desire freedom of speech and privilege of parliament. The king has but few prerogatives, as coining money, and making peace and war, and they are as land marks, and are known; they are but few, and a curse is upon him that removes them. You are told of the Alliances that saved Holland, &c. He will not compare those with the fears upon you at present; but in queen Eliz.'s time, before she could be brought to a league offensive and defensive with them, we had two cautionary towns, and a fort, put into our hands. You, by this hasty Address, are cut off from all hopes of any such caution from them. He has acquitted himself, as his allegiance and duty to this house obliges him, and he knows not what to advise you. But would have Reasons as strong in the thing as may be, before you go to the king with this Address.

Mr. *Neale* is for these Alliances, and therefore would not put the king upon hardships: he would know whether this is not an intrenchment upon the king's prerogative, to advise him where to make leagues offensive and defensive.—There was another great cry, 'Agree, agree.'

Sir *Jonathan Trelawney.* To cry 'agree, agree,' savours to him like Club-Law. You will never offer at precedents that the worst of times did never attempt.

Sir *Tho. Meres.* What has been said comes not home to this Address. When there is occasion, he shall answer those points alleged, 'of the unprecedentness of it.' But as for 'naming the States of the United Provinces,' in this Address, it was the Vote of the house, spoken to seventeen times, and but few negatives to it, and he wonders that it should be called 'Club-Law.'

Sir *John Ernly* agrees to the end of the Address, but he cannot fully to the means. He must put you in mind, that it does so clash with the prerogative of the crown, that he cannot agree to it. If he thinks there is no more difference than the word 'Holland,' and saying only 'such Alliances against France,' he hopes the king will agree to it. If the people desired a parliament, if they asked a day and place for its meeting, he believes it would not be granted. Refers it to your consideration, if the thing be asked in a way not fit to be granted, whether it is not probable it will be denied. It is directing the crown to make this league.

Sir *Rob. Carr* would not have any intrenching on the king's prerogative, in this Address. He would leave out 'a league with Holland, offensive and defensive.' Those words may give offence; and he would not give his Vote to that which may retard the thing, and would have it so amended as to be acceptable to the king.

Sir *Tho. Lee.* To the Orders of the house.

He appeals whether ever, when any committee was ordered expressly to bring in a thing, that thing, being voted to be part of the Address, shall again be put to the question?

The *Speaker*. You read a Bill thrice, and nothing is brought into the committee, but must be debated again.

Sir *Wm. Coventry*. The good intention and necessity of this Address will carry so much weight with it, that he hopes it will have acceptance from the king. The committee you appointed to draw it had not done their duty, if they had not gone according to the sense of the house. We have made many and many Addresses to the king, and there has been some reason for it: because we have not been rightly understood. There seemed to be general moderation, moved by some gentlemen in the Address, without naming particular Alliances; but that being not acceptable to the house, this is made more particular, to clear our meaning. A reason was given why we should supply the king, without naming Alliances, that we urge not usually in parliament; our own act was quoted against our affirmation, viz. 'The credit we gave the king upon the Excise, at our last meeting, before Alliances were spoken of.' But yet there is no precedent spoken of, when Money has been given for a war or alliances before they have been declared in parliament. It has been the constant usage of the crown to signify it in parliament, which gave such confidence in the commons, that it never doubted of the commons supply. He then read a passage of the king's Speech formerly about the Triple Alliance, viz. 'The Fleet had began something, but if not speedily supported by Alliances, he should want means to go on;' which shows that the constant method of parliament is, that Alliances have always been declared in parliament, and then Supply has been granted to support those Alliances. There was more said then for the first Dutch war; the second was signified in parliament, and owned by them so far, that they gave Money to maintain it. If methods of parliament be an obstacle to this Address, he thinks that is cleared. He would be 'fortiter in re, et suaviter in modo,' and he thinks the Address is so, and would agree to it.

Sir *Rd. Temple*. This of pressing the king to declare Alliances, and advising them by parliament, is no rule of parliament, and a dangerous precedent. He agrees to move the king 'To make farther Alliances;' and then you will have attained your end. It is not for the interest of the nation, for the king to name Alliances, which will give them opportunity to ask higher terms.

Col. *Birch* thinks the Paper is penned with as much modesty and duty as can be. If there be other Reasons to make the Alliances more particular, he would have them forborn. Our main business is, that the Religion and the interest of the nation be supported.

Mr. *Sacheverell*. The question is now, Whether we shall again put these Alliances into the same hands, to keep you off from such Alliances as you address for; and whether the king shall be advised by his privy council, and not by parliament. You give him advice, and submit it to him; and the privy council daily practise the contrary. It is said, 'That this is a breach of the king's prerogative.' We move him to a League with Holland, &c. and it is no breach at all of his prerogative, it seems, in the Council, to move him to a war. Our whole security depends upon a League with Holland against France, without whom we are never able to contend with him. All Counsel tends to make Alliances. And you are left wholly single to contend against that powerful prince.

Mr. Sec. *Coventry* is not afraid of any counsel he has ever given the king; as a privy counsellor he has taken his oath, and as a parliament-man, he has his opinion; and he is of opinion, that the king is not obliged to follow either his privy council, or parliament, if his opinion and reason be against it. Hen. iv. sent to his parliament for their advice concerning peace and war: they referred it to the king, and his council, and declared, 'They had nothing to do with it.' He hopes you will not do a thing to prejudice the thing you intend to do. He may probably be let into this prince's door when he scrapes,* but not when he knocks. Perhaps he shall be kept out. To deal in the rougher way with our prince is not the means to make him incline to your opinion. If any man is persuaded that he is wanting in his duty, if he name not 'Holland' in the Address, then it cannot be left out. The general way is more regular and decent, and he moves to leave out 'Holland.'

Sir *Tho. Lee*. If there be irregularity or indecency in this expression of 'Holland,' he is far from its being in the Address. But this is far from 'a knock at the Prince's door,' and cannot be gathered from the expressions in the Address. It is but advice and persuasion only. It is hard that the house shall not declare their opinion. The first occasion, perhaps, to get out of our misery, is to know how we came into it. The first step to it was our conjunction with France, against Holland; the first step we got out of it by was to make a separate Peace with Holland; but we find that the bare going out of it had not the effect we desired. What next? Is it not reasonable, that, if we still had kept that Alliance, we had suppressed Holland totally? Is it not the same thing now? Perhaps some greater advice is requisite. If it be a single question, he knows not what the consequence may be, in leaving it out, now it is put in. It is but plainly and barely showing your opinion, that you are not safe without an universal agreement with the Confederates. Flanders could not be preserved by a defensive Alliance in the Triple League, and therefore it is dangerous to leave 'Holland' out.

* The custom of the Court.

Lord *Cavendish.* There is the greatest mischief that can be, for Holland to make a separate peace with France. The danger is not great with Spain, therefore to prevent that, we specify an Alliance with Holland.

Mr. *Powle.* The sum of the debate is leaving Holland out of the Address. Though he did not expect to meet with this opposition, yet, upon recollection, he can show precedents wherein the king has been advised to particular Alliances. In the 18th of k. James, the parliament advised him to break the Match with Spain, and to make a war, and they then advised stricter Alliances with the States of Holland. In E. iii, R. ii, H. v, the parliament advised to make a League with the emperor, and it was signed and ratified in parliament. He will not wave these precedents, but he speaks these a little timorously, having not lately perused them. As for the argument of 'these Addresses being against the prerogative,' kings have always laboured to invite this house to peace and war, because their judgment did import Supply, and they could not excuse giving money to support it, where they had advised it. Our necessity of affairs brought us once to another course, but if there were new precedents, new dangers must create new precedents, and a new way. But let any man show him a precedent, that we ever assisted a neighbour too potent for us already. Would have a precedent shown him, where, after a representation in parliament of the greatness of the French king, still sending men to his assistance has been continued, and they were not ill received at court, when they returned home. He knows not what reason we have to leave Holland out of the Address, unless we have no intention to have Alliance with them at all. It is for the crown's advantage, and this is far from intrenching upon the prerogative. Carew told you, 'There were more reasons for this Address than were expressed;' and they were, why should we not trust the king? It is not fit to give them; but if they be pressed too much, he must give them. Though he will not say, 'We are not to trust the king,' yet he will say, 'We are not to trust counsellors.'

Mr. *Williams.* When the king and council shall see the opinion of the house for an Alliance with Holland, he believes it will remove counsellors, or stop the mouths of them.

Mr. Sec. *Williamson.* King James called for an opinion, in his Speech, from the house. He invited them to it, and the lords, that opened that parliament, said, 'The Temple of Janus must be opened, which has been long shut.' If that be the case, he has reason to doubt that the obstacle in the manner may hinder the matter of the Address. The king asked your advice in the separate peace with Holland mentioned, but that is not the case You are told, 'We would have it, because general Alliances may do no good, and not produce change of counsellors.' But what effect, do you think, this will have, when such exceptions are taken at it, as are likely to frustrate the end? Do you mean to treat so as not to leave your prince any latitude, but that he must grant, or not grant?

Mr. *Harbord* would ask a question: Is there no danger of our religion and property, but from France? And then when France is in peace, this startles him, that these Alliances may not be pursued. England is not safe, but by Alliance with Holland. Suppose there should be peace, the government of Flanders cannot support itself. To suppose the Spanish Netherlands, and Lorrain restored; Brisac destroyed; Alsace and Maestrich restored; would you then be safe? No more than now; because the French hands are full hands, and money makes power. The French hath both. But suppose all these places lost by the French, yet they abstract one million sterling from us yearly, in trade, and he will govern your councils every where. There is nothing to keep him from hence, but making him poor, and who can help you to do it, but the dutch? Make a law to prohibit French trade; you need no wine, and few of his commodities; and France will grow poor, and we shall grow rich, and if you send no forces into France, and support Holland, the first hour you do this, your money will increase; and then we can put the king at ease, and pay his debts; and never till then.

Mr. *Mallet.* When the king is here, he is in his imperial seat; but when in his other council, he is in his ministerial.

On a division, 182 were for the Address, and 142 against it. About forty or fifty members were in the Speaker's chamber, and Court of Requests, &c. who gave no voices at all. The Question was, for leaving out the words 'offensive and defensive, with the States of the United Provinces.'

Ordered, That the Secretaries of State, and Privy Counsellors of the house, be desired to know his majesty's pleasure, when he will be pleased to be attended with the Address.

May 26. His majesty appointed the house to attend him with their Address, at 3 in the afternoon, and the house being acquainted with the king's commands, they only passed the Bill for recalling his majesty's subjects out of the French king's Service, and ordered it to be carried up to the lords, with an express Order to their messengers to put the lords in mind of their Bill of Popery, which lay before their lordships. And so adjourned presently after ten o'clock till two in the afternoon, and then met and attended the king in the Banqueting House with their Address. To which his majesty, after hearing it read by the Speaker, said, "That the contents of it were long, and the matter of importance; and that he would take it into his consideration, and, with all convenient speed, return an Answer to it."

The King's Answer to the Address.] May 28. The house being met, the Speaker acquainted them with what the king had said to them, upon their Address, on Saturday; and immediately Mr. Secretary Coventry told the Speaker, That the king commanded the house to attend him presently in the Banqueting House at Whitehall. Upon which the house went accordingly.

Some members rising from their seats, and going to the door, before the Speaker had reported the king's command, viz. Mr. John Grey, member for Leicester, and sir Wm. Blacket, member for Newcastle upon Tyne, the Speaker reprimanded them in this manner: "The burgesses of Newcastle and Leicester are in great haste to be gone, before the king's Message is reported, as if they went to get places at a show, or a play." *

The King spoke as follows. "Gentlemen; Could I have been silent, I would rather have chosen to be so, than to call to mind things so unfit for you to meddle with, as are contained in some part of your Address; wherein you have intrenched upon so undoubted a right of the crown, that I am confident it will appear in no age (when the sword was not drawn) that the prerogative of making peace and war hath been so dangerously invaded. You do not content yourselves with desiring me to enter into such Leagues, as may be for the safety of the kingdom, but you tell me what sort of Leagues they must be, and with whom: and, as your Address is worded, it is more liable to be understood to be by your leave, than your request, that I should make such other Alliances as I please with other of the Confederates.—Should I suffer this fundamental power of making peace and war to be so far invaded (though but once) as to have the manner and circumstances of Leagues prescribed to me by parliament, it is plain, that no prince, or state, would any longer believe, that the sovereignty of England rests in the crown; nor could I think myself to signify any more to foreign princes than the empty sound of a king. Wherefore you may rest assured, that no condition shall make me depart from, or lessen, so essential a part of the monarchy: and I am willing to believe so well of this house of commons, that I am confident these ill consequences are not intended by you.—These are, in short, the reasons why I can by no means approve of your Address. And yet, though you have declined to grant me that Supply, which is so necessary to the ends of it, I do again declare to you, that, as I have done all that lay in my power, since your last meeting, so I will still apply myself, by all means I can, to let the world see my care both for the security and satisfaction of my people; although it may not be with those advantages to them, which, by your assistance, I might have procured.—† I would have you return to your house, and I require that you immediately adjourn to the 16th of July next; but I do not intend you shall sit till winter, unless there should happen any urgent occasions, in which case you shall have notice by proclamation."

The Parliament adjourned.] The commons then returned to their own house, where the Speaker reported the King's Speech as above.

Mr. Powle standing up to speak, the Speaker interrupted him, and said, 'I must hear no man speak, now the king's pleasure of adjourning the house is signified.'

Sir *Tho. Lee.* The act of adjourning the house cannot be yours, Mr. Speaker, but the act of the house; and no question can be put, when a gentleman stands up to speak. Pray, let us keep methods, however.

The *Speaker.* When there is a command from the crown to adjourn, we are not to dispute about it, but to obey, and adjourn. After a command of this kind, there remains nothing for you to do but to execute it. Unless any man can show me a precedent to the contrary, you will put a hardship upon me to do otherwise.

And so the Speaker adjourned the house to the 16th of July next, without naming place, or hour, and suddenly sprung out of the chair. Many called him again to the Chair, some cried 'stop the Mace upon the table.' Others would have put him again into the chair, or some body else. But the Speaker was soon surrounded by several of his party, and the Mace secured, and he went away with it before him, but not without reproachful speeches; as bidding him 'remember Lord Finch's case, of the like nature.'—And That he should be called to an account for it *. Upon the in-

* Grey.

† This last paragraph is not in the Speech, as inserted in the Journal, but only 'his majesty's pleasure for adjournment was afterwards signified by the Speaker.'

* "The members returned to the house, several of them rose up probably to express their sense of this cavalier treatment, but were overborne by the Speaker, who took upon him to play the dictator too, by insisting vehemently, that, after the king had required the house to adjourn, there was no more liberty of speech: this being, however, contested, and those who had stood up, demanding still to be heard, the Speaker had the confidence, without any question put, and of his own motion, to pronounce the house adjourned; and therewithal stepped down on the middle of the floor, leaving the members astonished at so flagrant a violation of their inherent privileges." Marvell.

"They had also the additional mortification to see this chiding Speech of the king's made public in the Gazette † of the next day, being the first which had ever appeared in that paper, to point them out, both to their own, and all other nations, as refractory, disobedient subjects, who had lost all respect to majesty: care being at the same time taken to suppress even the written copies of the proceedings of the house, that nothing might appear in their justification." Ralph.

† Upon this occasion, Marvell adds: "Thus were they well rewarded for their itch of perpetual sitting and of acting; the parliament being grown to that height of contempt, as to be gazetted among run-away-servants, lap-dogs, strayed horses, and highway-robbers."

stant of the Speaker's going out of the Chair, lord Cavendish proffered to show some precedents of debates after the king's signification of Adjournment; as at that meeting soon after Chatham business, when an Address was voted to the king for disbanding the new raised forces.*

The Parliament adjourned a second time.] July 16. The parliament met in pursuance of the late adjournment, and were again adjourned by the king's command, till the 3rd of December; though some of them seemed dissatisfied with the manner of this, as much as they were with the late adjournment. In particular,

Lord *Cavendish* moved, that the house might see the Journal by what order, and in what method, they were adjourned last.

Mr. *Williams* seconded the motion.

But some cried out 'Adjourn, Adjourn,' others called for the question. But the Speaker told them, 'That he had received Orders from the king, by Mr. Secretary Coventry, to adjourn the house till the 3rd of Dec.' and pronounced the house adjourned accordingly.

Principal Occurrences during the Recess—Marriage of the Prince of Orange with the lady Mary—Plan of Peace—Negotiations.] "It is certain," says Mr. Hume, "that this was the critical moment, when the king both might with ease have preserved the balance of power in Europe, which it has since cost this island great expence of blood and treasure to restore, and might by perseverance have at last regained, in some tolerable measure, after all past errors, the confidence of his people. This opportunity being neglected, the wound became incurable; and notwithstanding his momentary appearances of vigour against France and popery, and their momentary inclinations to rely on his faith; he was still believed to be at bottom engaged in the same interests, and they soon elapsed into distrust and jealousy. The secret memoirs of this reign, which have since been published, prove beyond a doubt, that the king had at this time concerted measures with France, and had no intention to enter into a war in favour of the allies. He had entertained no view, therefore, even when he pawned his 'royal word' to his people, than to procure a grant of money; and he trusted, that, while he eluded their expectations, he could not afterwards want pretences for palliating his conduct.—Negotiations meanwhile were carried on between France and Holland, and an eventual treaty was concluded; that is, all their differences were adjusted, provided they could afterwards satisfy their allies on both sides. This work, though in appearance difficult, seemed to be extremely forwarded, by farther bad successes on the part of the confederates, and by the great impatience of the Hollanders; when a new event happened, which promised a more prosperous issue to the quarrel with France, and revived the hopes of all the English, who understood the interests of their country.—The king saw, with regret, the violent discontents which prevailed in the nation, and which seemed every day to augment upon him. Desirous by his natural temper to be easy himself, and to make every body else easy, he sought expedients to appease those murmurs, which, as they were very disagreeable for the present, might in their consequences prove extremely dangerous. He knew that, during the late war with Holland, the malcontents at home had made applications to the prince of Orange; and if he continued still to neglect the prince's interests, and to thwart the inclinations of his own people, he apprehended lest their common complaints should cement a lasting union between them. He saw that the religion of the duke inspired the nation with dismal apprehensions; and though he had obliged his brother to allow the young princesses to be educated in the protestant faith, something farther, he thought, was necessary, in order to satisfy the nation. He entertained, therefore, proposals for marrying the prince of Orange to the lady Mary, the elder princess, and heir apparent to the crown (for the duke had no male issue), and he hoped, by so tempting an offer, to engage him entirely in his interests. A peace he proposed to make; such as would satisfy France, and still preserve his connections with that crown: and he intended to sanctify it by the approbation of the prince, whom he found to be extremely revered in England, and respected throughout Europe. All the reasons for this alliance were seconded by the solicitations of Danby, and also of Temple, who was at that time in England: and Charles at last granted permission to the prince, when the campaign should be over, to pay him a visit.—The king very graciously received his nephew at Newmarket. He would have entered immediately upon business; but the prince desired first to be acquainted with the lady Mary: and he declared, that, contrary to the usual sentiments of persons of his rank, he placed a great part of happiness in domestic satisfaction, and would not, upon any consideration of interest or politics, match himself with a person disagreeable to him. He was introduced to the princess, whom he found in the bloom of youth, and extremely amiable both in her person and her behaviour. The king now thought that he had a double tie upon him, and might safely expect his compliance with every proposal: he was surprised to find the prince decline all discourse of business, and refuse to concert any terms for the general peace, till his marriage should be finished. He foresaw, he said, from the situation of affairs, that his allies were likely to have hard terms; and he never would expose himself to the reproach of having sacrificed their interests to promote his own purposes. Charles still believed, notwithstanding the cold, severe manner of the prince, that he would abate of this rigid punctilio of honour; and he protracted

* Grey.

the time, hoping, by his own insinuation and address, as well as by the allurements of love and ambition, to win him to compliance. One day, Temple found the prince in very bad humour, repenting that he had ever come to England, and resolute in a few days to leave it: but before he went, the king, he said, must chuse the terms on which they should hereafter live together: he was sure it must be like the greatest friends or the greatest enemies: and he desired Temple to inform his master next morning of these intentions. Charles was struck with this menace, and foresaw how the prince's departure would be interpreted by the people. He resolved, therefore, immediately to yield with a good grace; and having paid a compliment to his nephew's honesty, he told Temple, that the marriage was concluded, and desired him to inform the duke of it, as of an affair already resolved on. The duke seemed surprised; but yielded a prompt obedience: which, he said, was his constant maxim to whatever he found to be the king's pleasure. (23d Oct.) No measure, during this reign, gave such general satisfaction. All parties strove who should most applaud it. And even Arlington, who had been kept out of the secret, told the prince, 'That some things, good in themselves, were spoiled by the manner of doing them, as some things bad were mended by it; but he would confess, that this was a thing so good in itself, that the manner of doing it could not spoil it.'—This marriage was a great surprise to Lewis, who, accustomed to govern every thing in the English court, now found so important a step taken, not only without his consent, but without his knowledge or participation. A conjunction of England with the allies, and a vigorous war in opposition to French ambition, were the consequences immediately expected, both abroad and at home: but to check these sanguine hopes, the king, a few days after the marriage, prolonged the adjournment of the parliament from the third of December to the fourth of April. This term was too late for granting supplies, or making preparations for war; and could be chosen by the king for no other reason, than as an atonement to France for his consent to the marriage. It appears also, that Charles secretly received from Lewis the sum of 2,000,000 of livres on account of this important service.—The king, however, entered into consultations with the prince, together with Danby and Temple, concerning the terms which it would be proper to require of France. After some debate, it was agreed, that France should restore Lorrain to the duke; with Tournay, Valenciennes, Condé, Aeth, Charleroi, Courtray, Oudenarde, and Binche, to Spain, in order to form a good frontier for the Low Countries. The prince insisted Frachecomté should likewise be restored; and Charles thought, that, because he had patrimonial estates of great value in that province, and deemed his property more secure in the hands of Spain, he was engaged by such views to be obstinate in that point: but the prince declared, that to procure but one good town to the Spaniards in Flanders, he would willingly relinquish all those possessions. As the king still insisted on the impossibility of wresting Franchecomté from Lewis, the prince was obliged to acquiesce.—Notwithstanding this concession to France, the projected peace was favourable to the allies; and it was a sufficient indication of vigour in the king, that he had given his assent to it. He farther agreed to send over a minister instantly to Paris, in order to propose these terms. This minister was to enter into no treaty: he was to allow but two days for the acceptance or refusal of the terms: upon the expiration of these, he was presently to return: and in case of refusal, the king promised to enter immediately into the confederacy. To carry so imperious a message, and so little expected from the English court, Temple was the person pitched on, whose declared aversion to the French interest was not likely to make him fail of vigour and promptitude in the execution of his commission.—But Charles next day felt a relenting in this assumed vigour. Instead of Temple he dispatched the earl of Feversham, a creature of the duke's and a Frenchman by birth: and he said, that the message being harsh in itself, it was needless to aggravate it by a disagreeable messenger. The prince left London; and the king, at his departure, assured him that he never would abate in the least point of the scheme concerted, and would enter into war with Lewis, if he rejected it.—Lewis received the message with seeming gentleness and complacency. He told Feversham, that the king of England well knew that he might always be master of the peace; but some of the towns in Flanders it seemed very hard to demand, especially Tournay, upon whose fortifications such immense sums had been expended: he would therefore take some short time to consider of an answer. Feversham said, that he was limited to two days stay: but when that time was elapsed, he was prevailed on to remain some few days longer; and he came away at last without any positive answer. Lewis said, that he hoped his brother would not break with him for one or two towns; and with regard to them too, he would send orders to his ambassador at London to treat with the king himself. Charles was softened by the softness of France; and the blow was thus artfully eluded. The French ambassador, Barillon, owned at last, that he had orders to yield all except Tournay, and even to treat about some equivalent for that fortress, if the king absolutely insisted upon it. The prince was gone, who had given spirit to the English court; and the negotiation began to draw out into messages and returns from Paris.—By intervals, however, the king could rouse himself, and show still some firmness and resolution. Finding that affairs were not likely to come to any conclusion with France, he summoned, notwithstanding the long adjournment, the parliament on the 15th of Jan, an unusual measure, and capable of giving alarm to the French court. Temple was sent for to the council, and the king told him, that he intended he should go to Holland, in order to form a treaty of alliance with the States; and that the purpose of it should be, like the triple league, to force both France and Spain to accept of the terms porposed. Temple was sorry to find this act of vigour qualified by such a regard to France, and by such an appearance of indifference and neutrality between the parties. He told the king, that the resolution agreed on, was to begin the war in conjunction with all the confederates, in case of no direct and immediate answer from France; that this measure would satisfy the prince, the allies, and the people of England; advantages which could not be expected from such an alliance with Holland alone; that France would be disobliged, and Spain likewise; nor would the Dutch be satisfied with such a faint imitation of the triple league, a measure concerted when they were equally at peace with both parties. For those reasons, Temple declined the employment; and Lawrence Hyde, second son of chancellor Clarendon, was sent in his place.—(1678.) The prince of Orange could not regard without contempt such symptoms of weakness and vigour conjoined in the English counsels. He was resolved, however, to make the best of a measure which he did not approve; and as Spain secretly consented that her ally should form a league, which was seemingly directed against her as well as France, but which was to fall only on the latter, the States concluded the treaty in the terms proposed by the king."

Dec. 3. The house met, when Mr. Secretary Coventry delivered the following Message from his majesty, which was read by the Speaker:

"C. R. His majesty, having giving notice by his Proclamation, that he intended the houses should be adjourned till the 4th of April,* hath now, for weighty considerations, thought fit to meet with both houses sooner; and therefore his pleasure is, that this house be adjourned to the 15th day of Jan. next."—The house adjourned accordingly.

Jan. 15. 1677-8. The house being met, his majesty sent the following Message by Mr. Secretary Coventry, which was read by the Speaker:

"C. R. His majesty hath matters of very great importance to communicate to both houses, in order to the satisfaction of their late Addresses, for the preservation of Flanders. But it so happening that matters are not yet so ripe, as within a few days they will be, therefore his majesty's pleasure is, that this house be immediately adjourned till Monday, the 28th of this instant January."*

Several members proffered to speak, but the Speaker would not suffer them, but adjourned the house.

The King's Speech to both Houses.] Jan. 28. This day his majesty came to the house of peers, and sending for the commons, made this remarkable Speech:

"My lords and gentlemen; When we parted last, I told you, that before we met again, I would do that which should be to your satisfaction: I have accordingly made such Alliances with Holland, as are for the preservation of Flanders; and which cannot fail of that end, unless prevented either by the want of due

* "Before the meeting appointed for the 3d of Dec. his majesty's Proclamation was issued, signifying 'that he expected not the members attendance, but that those of them about town should *adjourn themselves* till the 4th of April, 1678.' These words, 'that the house may adjourn themselves' were very well received by those of the commons who imagined themselves thereby restored to their right, after Mr. Speaker Seymour's invasion: when, in reversal of this, (he probably desiring to retain a jurisdiction that he had twice usurped, and to add this flower to the crown, of his own planting) Mr. Secretary Coventry delivered a written Message from his majesty, on the 3d of Dec. of a contrary effect, though not of the same validity with the Proclamation, viz. 'That the houses *should be adjourned* only to the 15th of Jan. 1677;' which as soon as read, Mr. Seymour would not give leave to a worthy member, offering, to speak; but abruptly, now the third time, of his own authority, adjourned them without putting the question; though sir John Finch, for once doing so, (3 Ch.) was accused of high treason. This only can be said perhaps in his excuse, That whereas that in 3 Ch. was a parliament legally constituted, Mr. Seymour did here do as a sheriff that disperses a riotous assembly. In this manner they were kicked from adjournment to adjournment, as from one stair down to another; and when they were at the bottom, kicked up again, having no mind yet to go out of doors." Marvell.

* One reason for this adjournment was, to know if the Spaniards would comply with a demand that the king had made of Ostend, and Portmahon, for the accommodation of his ships and troops, and which Mr. Godolphin was in this interval soliciting at Brussels: and another is given by the lord treasurer Danby in a Letter to Mr. Montagu ambassador at Paris dated Jan. 17, viz. 'To see if any expedient for the peace could be found out in that time." Ralph.

"It appears however from sir Wm. Temple, that the true reason of this Adjournment was to have time to receive the news of a League with Holland, which was signed Jan. 16, but being properly defensive, to prevent the king of France from pursuing his conquests in the Netherlands, it was very far from answering the desires of the parliament. The king believed, nevertheless, that this league would be capable to impose upon them; and therefore deferred their meeting to receive the news of its conclusion." Rapin.

assistances to support those Alliances, or by the small regard the Spaniards themselves must have to their own preservation.—The first of these I cannot suspect, by reason of your repeated engagements to maintain them; and I know you are so wise as to consider, that a war, which must be the necessary consequence of them, ought neither to be prosecuted by halves, nor to want such assurances of perseverance as may give me encouragement to pursue it. Besides, it will not be less necessary to let our enemies have such a prospect of our resolutions, as may let them see certainly that we shall not be weary of our arms, till Christendom be restored to such a peace as shall not be in the power of any prince alone to disturb.—I do acknowledge to you, that I have used all the means possible, by a mediation, to have procured an honourable and safe peace for Christendom; knowing how preferable such a peace would have been to any war, and especially to this kingdom, which must necessarily own the vast benefits it has received by peace, whilst its neighbours only have yet smarted by the war: but, finding it no longer to be hoped for by fair means, it shall not be my fault, if that be not obtained by force, which cannot be had otherwise.—For this reason I have recalled my troops from France; and have considered, that although the Dutch shall do their parts, we cannot have less on ours than 90 sail of capital ships constantly maintained, nor less than 30 or 40,000 land men (with their dependencies) to be employed upon our Fleets and elsewhere. And because there shall be no fear of misemploying what you shall give to these uses, I am contented that such Money be appropriated to those ends as strictly as you can desire. I have given testimony enough of my care in that kind, by the progress I have made in building the new ships; wherein, for the making them more useful, I have directed such larger dimensions, as will cost me above 100,000*l.* more than the act allows. I have gone as far as I could, in repairing the old Fleet, and in buying of necessary Stores for the Navy and Ordnance; and in this, and other provisions for better securing both my foreign plantations and the islands nearer home, I have expended a great deal more than the 200,000*l.* you enabled me to borrow upon the Excise, although I have not found such a credit as I expected upon that security. I have borne the Charge both of a rebellion in Virginia, and a new war with Algiers. I stand engaged to the prince of Orange for my niece's portion *: and I shall not be able to maintain my constant necessary Establishments, unless the new Impost upon Wines, &c. be continued to me, which would otherwise turn only to their profit to whom we least intend it.—I hope these things will need little recommendation to you, when you consider your promises in some and the necessity of the rest. And to let you see that I have not only employed my time and treasure for your safety, but done all I could to remove all sorts of jealousies, I have married my niece to the prince of Orange, by which I hope I have given full satisfaction that I shall never suffer his interest to be ruined, if I can be assisted as I ought to be to preserve them.—Having done all this, I expect from you a plentiful Supply, suitable to such great occasions; whereon depends not only the honour, but (for aught I know) the being of an English nation, which will not be saved by finding faults afterwards, but may be prevented by avoiding the chief fault of doing weakly and by halves what can only be hoped from a vigorous and thorough prosecution of what we undertake.—These considerations are of the greatest importance that ever concerned this kingdom; and therefore I would have you enter immediately upon them, without suffering any other business whatsoever to divert you from bringing them to good resolutions."

Resolved, nem. con. "That the king's Speech be taken into consideration to-morrow."

Debate on the irregular Adjournments of the House by the Speaker.] Mr. *Sacheverell.* I was unwilling to give interruption to this business, as long as I see the way before me, and now we have done the king right, it is time to right ourselves upon you, Mr. Speaker. I was present when you adjourned the house twice,* and you would not suffer any gentleman to speak. Because I would reduce things to a certainty, and leave no umbrage betwixt the king and us, of his majesty's power of adjourning us, I will state the case betwixt the house and you, Mr. Speaker. It seems you will undertake to be bigger than the house, and, contrary to four known rights of the house, will undertake to violate them upon your own authority. I have drawn up the heads of them, and I offer them, not as an impeachment, but a charge, and I offer them to be read, the substance whereof is, 'That it is the standing Order and undoubted right of the house, that the house be not adjourned by the Speaker, but by consent of the house, and not by the Speaker only.' And 'that when any gentleman stands up to speak, the person is not to be silenced, unless the house over-rule him.' But you, Mr. Speaker, contrary to your duty, after several members stood up to speak, would not suffer them to go on, and, though you acknowledged

* "The Prince of Orange arrived in England Oct. 9, 1677. On the 24th, the match between his highness, and lady Mary, the duke of York's daughter, was declared at the committee, on the morrow to the council, which was, upon that occasion, extraordinarily assembled, and in the next Gazette to the whole kingdom. Wherever the news spread, joy accompanied it. It was looked upon as a deliverance from the French, and no man, at that time, dreaded any other slavery." Ralph.

It was celebrated November the fourth, the prince's birth day. The prince's portion was 40,000*l.*

* See p. 890.

the right of Adjournment to be in the house, yet you hindered the house from proceeding in their debates.

Sir *John Ernly*. If I thought that the crown was not concerned in these Adjournments, and had a right to command it, and the only business was chastising the Speaker for not doing his duty, I should be for maintaining my right as much as any man. But if there be a Message from the king, sent by one of the secretaries, to adjourn, or the king sends for the house by the black rod, and signifies his pleasure of adjournment, it is the undoubted right of the king, and you are, according to his pleasure signified, to adjourn immediately. Mr. Sacheverell stood up to speak, and you obeyed the king's Order, and the house universally called out 'Adjourn! adjourn!' and it was done accordingly. Though it is the undoubted right of every member to speak, yet if the universal cry be to adjourn, you do it every day, 'till to-morrow 8 o'clock,' though gentlemen stand up to speak.

Sir *Rob. Carr*. It has been the general sense of the house to-day, that no interruption be given to the consideration of the king's Speech. I move that a time may be taken for the consideration of this matter of adjourning the house by the Speaker, &c. and I believe the Speaker will submit to the house, if he cannot satisfy the house therein.

Lord *Cavendish*. It did not appear to me, that, in the adjournment of the house, in May last, it was the opinion of the house to adjourn. Here is a charge against the Speaker, and, according to order of the house, if a charge be brought against a member, it ought to be read. It is a business of so great importance, that you are not fit to sit in the chair whilst it is debating, it concerning yourself. The gentleman that brought it in, has laid it upon the table, and I would have it read.

Sir *Cha. Wheeler*. Are we not imposed upon to have that Paper thrown upon the table, without the consent of the house by a vote? The charge is, Whether you can adjourn the house? But the adjournment was the king's adjournment, and I desire to have it fairly stated, and the king's Message for adjournment read. But supposing it was not the king's adjournment, the thing is done every day, and you take the sense of the house by the noise of the house calling 'adjourn! adjourn!' Three parts in four of the house, in May last, were for adjourning, and your declaration of it was good, till excepted against. When the king sends to adjourn, the question is between the king and us, and not between the Speaker and us. Therefore I move that a day may be set apart to debate this thing, that gentlemen may be ready to speak to it. The whole world will know this debate to-day, and will be apt to say, Why did not the house debate the great business in the king's Speech? They put that off always for weighty considerations, and now (they will say) 'The commons fall into other matters.'

Mr. Sec. *Coventry*. I am sorry for this debate, without making a compliment to you, Mr. Speaker, or any other. The matter in question is concerning the charge delivered in by Sacheverell, and I will speak only to what can be the issue of the debate of it in this house. The king's power of adjourning the house is denied by no man. The question is then, *de modo* only. If you put the king upon other ways of adjournment of the house, than by the Speaker, there is disadvantage on the other side. The consequence will be delay of your proceedings; and the French king's advantages are so great in this conjuncture, that if we should be left alone, we are no equal match for him. He is now upon his campaign, and if the Confederates hearts fail, by our delay, and the king of France takes two or three more important places, he may quickly end his campaign, before the Spaniards begin theirs. This debate will draw many circumstances along with it. And, whilst we come to our privileges, we shall, I hope, be tender of the king's prerogative. In the 19th of king James, there was a jealousy, in the parliament, of the power of the Spanish ambassador, Gondamar, at court, concerning the Spanish Match, then depending. The house of commons sent a very rough Message then to the king, and the king did adjourn the parliament by writ. The commons sent to the lords, 'that they could not adjourn unless the writ was read in their house,' and they entered a protestation into their books accordingly. King James was offended at it, and sent for the Journal, and in the privy council tore out the protestation with his own hands. I desire only to show you, by this, how great jealousy and discontent it occasioned betwixt the king and the commons. A year and a half after, the king called a parliament, and altered his councils about the Spanish Match, and told the parliament how he was abused by Spain, and made other complaints about breaking the Treaty of the Match, and of war in the Palatinate. Did the commons then go back to all those things of privilege about their adjournment of their house? No; they went on to the matter of the Palatinate war. They were not a body of men too easy to give up their privileges and the liberties of their country, but they laid them aside for that time, and entertained themselves about the Palatinate. At the Diet of Ratisbon, the electors themselves met. The elector of Mentz was their Speaker. The duke of Lunenburgh sent his credentials to the bishop of Cologn, by his secretaries; but being no elector, he was not received by his deputation; for the Diet said, 'he must come himself, for they would not receive them.' Upon which, Lunenburgh made his protest, that nothing should stand good to oblige him in that Diet, which occasioned a great disorder and delay in the proceedings of that Diet. I speak this so much from the bottom of my heart, that I think these delays, which this debate will occasion, extremely dangerous; and, I vow to God, though

I hate murder, yet I had rather be guilty of 20 murders than hinder our proceedings now;"* and I would be guilty of all the cruelties of Alsace rather than hinder our progress in this great conjuncture. Therefore I humbly move that this debate be laid aside.

Sir *Henry Capel.* There is nothing of so great importance as to keep ourselves, in a body, of one sense. What will be the end of this, if you enter into the debate to-day of this difference? What will the consequence be? Naturally it will be to see precedents of adjournments of the house, and a committee must sit, and you have tacitly implied, that no committee shall sit, because you have ordered to-morrow for the consideration of the king's Speech, and some time must be to think of it. I am for the setting this thing of Adjournment right, and believe it will corroborate us in what we shall do. When we parted last, we addressed the king to enter into Alliances with the Dutch, &c. to prevent the growth of the power of France. When we were adjourned, if the king had sent for us, and told us his pleasure, I believe nothing else would have intervened.

Mr. *Garroway.* I am sorry to hear some honourable persons put so great stress upon two days time. We have been 14 days in town; and when our liberties are concerned, and this matter of money must go abroad, for reputation's sake, I would willingly have had time to consider, whether we shall be undone by peace or war. If this great affair had been taken in time, according to our reiterated advices, something might have been done. But still we are put off to the last moment. A Paper is now offered, and I am sorry it is a Charge against yourself, Mr. Speaker. I mean clearly, as the gentleman said who brought in the Paper, the point of adjournment is not betwixt the king and us, but betwixt you and us. Therefore put a question to lodge it fairly, before we adjourn the debate. I think, that, if it appear to be your encroaching upon the house, it may be of as ill consequence as the war with France; if your power encroach upon us more than ever was intended you. If you will put the question, Whether the Paper shall be read, and adjourn the consideration of it to Thursday, I am well contented.

Sir *Rd. Temple.* For order sake, I would not have the question put for the reading the Paper given in by Sacheverell. It is a Charge and no Impeachment, against the Speaker. I never saw any thing of this nature before. If the gentleman that brought it in will recall it, and give it in as an Impeachment, it is another thing. The question about this matter of adjourning the house will necessarily arise betwixt the king and the house. The giving in the Paper is not regular; and no person can go about to make that the Speaker's case, which is wholly the king's.

Mr. *Powle.* He that delivered this Paper in, did well to make a difference in the case betwixt the king's and the Speaker's adjournment of the house. In the king's Speech, in the Gazette of the 28th of May, 1677, his majesty directed himself to the 'Gentlemen of the House,' and not to 'Mr. Speaker.' How has the Speaker then the authority of adjourning the house? If this be admitted, I need not tell you how dangerous the consequence would be. The former practice of adjournment was, that the king did do it in the lords house, and we were called up to that bar. The king may grant away a manor under his signet, but Westminster-hall will void that grant, being not under the great seal. If we do not preserve form, we shall lose substance. The question is plainly, by what authority you assume to yourself to do what the king commands us to do? I am sorry to have seen us on a precipice, and that that should be an argument against us of losing no time in preventthe growing greatness of the French king, which might have been prevented, in a great measure, had our advice been taken in time. The fault is somewhere. I never yet saw a pocket-order of adjourning the house admitted, and the whole liberty of the house is concerned, By the same reason that you adjourned the house, you may put by any question. It is in vain to think of conquests abroad, when we lose our liberty at home. Suppose to-morrow we come to a question in this great affair: we have adjourned, you may adjourn the house to Friday, and prevent the question. The gentleman that brought in the Paper, does not call it an Impeachment, because it is not to be sent up to the lords. He calls it a Charge, because we have liberty to judge of the misdemeanors of our own members. By word of mouth, or in writing, the Charge may be given in. Let the Paper be read, and admitted, and then adjourn the debate of it, if you please.

The *Speaker.* What is charged within doors, by word of mouth, against any member, or what is charged without doors, is at the election of the gentleman that brings it, to take his own method. I assure you, I sit uneasily till I answer to any thing relating to this Charge. As many artifices have been used as may be, to report me to have spoken what I never did, and to have done what I never did. But, I hope, no discourses will make impression upon the house, of things neither said nor done. I have received many undeserved favours from the house, which I acknowledge with all thankfulness. My coming to this place at first was as unexpected as your displeasure in what I did. Whatever my proceedings were in adjourning the house, when duly considered, the house, I believe, will see nothing in them inconsistent with the Order of the house. That power, which is lodged in the

* "Coventry in some heat said, 'The king was engaged, and he would rather be guilty of the murder of 40 men than do any thing to retard the progress of the war.' The oddness of the expression made it often to be objected afterwards to him." Burnet.

Chair, is not to be dislodged until the house dislodge it. When the king commands an Adjournment, it is the house's right to adjourn themselves. But, I say, the house has always exercised adjournment in that method I did it. The reason is, because, in executing the king's commands, the house goes out of the ordinary method. The king seems not to doubt any obedience in the house; which, putting a question for adjournment, after the king's command signified, will do. I desire to have your Order for what I shall do. There was never any debate, but once, of Adjournment, and then it was about executing a commission of adjournment not directed to the house; and I ought to continue in the practice of what I have done, till you have altered it; else I should commit a greater offence than I am now charged with.' Matter of form is only the case. If I have the honour to serve you, I must observe the same method I have done, till you order it otherwise.

Sir *Tho. Clarges.* You state not the case right. When any doubt, or question, arises about a thing, it is otherwise than when the thing goes off fairly by consent. This adjourning the house has been usurped by you, more than by any Speaker before you; and gentlemen stand up to speak, and you adjourn the house, and will not hear them; and you adjourn. He who was Speaker before you, would not patter out of the Chair with that precipitancy. He would sit till eight or nine o'clock at night, as long as any gentleman would speak. If the opinion of the Speaker must be the sense of the house, the ships and men the king speaks of may be doubled. It is our birth-right to speak; and we are not so much as a part of a parliament, if that be lost. Many worthy men, who are the king's servants, went on fast for Money; but when Privilege was but mentioned, all was laid aside. The then Attorney General, (Finch) now lord chancellor, when the king's Declaration, &c. was excepted against here, and the king told us, 'he would not have the Declaration touched upon,' did worthily give his opinion of it. Though his zeal, at that time, was great for money; yet he laid all that aside, and did bravely defend it at a conference. If it had been so in the Declaration, &c. freedom of speech had gone off; and if we cannot debate things with freedom, all is gone. The black rod knocked the last session, and then we must go to attend the king. 'But hold, (said you, Mr. Speaker) we cannot stir without the Money-Bill:' and the Money-Bill was sent down to you from the lords, before you would go up. The king may adjourn us in person, or by his commission. 1 Ch. i. there was a commission of adjournment sent to the lords house, and it was signified to the commons; but the commons answered, 'if the commission be sent down to their house, they would consider of it.' It was then debated, though under the broad seal; which is above all Paper commands. And the house was set in order first. And must you assume to yourself to adjourn without debate? 'to adjourn immediately' is with a *salvo jure*, that we may sit that day to set the house in order. 19 James, there was a kind of Protestation before the house adjourned; and when the king razed the Protestation out of the Journal, there was no privilege lost. The Adjournment is only obeyed here, where we have freedom of speech. When any exception is taken at words that fall from a gentleman, they are to be put into writing, and you snapped us off by your usurpation; so that there was no time to debate the exception we had against it. I move it, because it lies hard upon my heart; for, without this freedom, we are no house of commons; and I would have the Paper read.

The *Speaker.* I sent up for the Tax-bill, and the bill was actually brought down before the black rod knocked at the door. The 11th of July, 1 Ch. i. the house desired the lords to join with them in an Address to the king for a Recess; a commission accordingly was sent to the lords house by the king. The lords sent to the commons, to come up to their house to hear the commission read; the commons returned, 'That they would send Answer by messengers of their own.' The commission was sent down to the commons, and they did adjourn themselves to Oxford. Their adjournment was by the king's command; and so is this complained of now; and I will put upon that the issue of the cause. In all the Journals, I cannot find, that, when the king commanded an immediate Adjournment, the house proceeded in one tittle of business.

Mr. *Sacheverell.* If any such thing as a commission, &c. had been, I had done you, Mr. Speaker, much wrong in complaining. But I have precedents to show, when the matter comes to be debated, that the course of parliament is quite otherwise.

Mr. *Waller.* The gentleman that spoke last tells you of precedents, &c. but I have sat here 50 years, and never saw the matter done as you, Mr. Speaker, speak of. There is a confusion in the debate, whether the matter in question be betwixt the Speaker and us, or the king and us. When a man speaks against his duty, or we speak against one another, or the king, the words are stated, and the person is to withdraw. You, Mr. Speaker, bring us precedents overgrown with weeds. I believe the matter must be stated betwixt the king and us, or else 'the trumpet will give an uncertain sound.' No tribunal can judge of the privilege of this house but itself. I will tell you the practice for 50 years here. The king, without doubt, has the sole power of calling and suspending the states of the kingdom. But if the king should descend so low as to come to us, and adjourn us, I never knew but that we complied with the king. For writs to supply defects of members, a committee has been sent to desire leave of the king to sit on. And when the king would have prorogued, the house has interposed to sit on. Besides, we have obscured our own light by our own fault. We should have called the Speaker to the chair again We send the Speaker to the chair, when we chuse him, to show you that you are 'in potestate Senatus,' both in the chair, and out of it. The measure of our obedience to the king in all things is law; and I move that a committee may be appointed to recover our ancient right. We say, 'hear the chair;' but no body says, 'obey the chair.' I would have precedents searched betwixt the crown and us, that we may not play a lesson before we tune the instrument.

Mr. *Williams.* There is no such matter as prerogative in the case. The king's Message was, 'That the house should adjourn itself.' The question is between the Speaker and the house, whether you have not imposed upon the house, by adjourning, without their consent by a question. You have declared the right to be in the house, and yet you have done the contrary. When a member stood up to speak, you silenced him, and would not suffer him to go on. The Paper delivered in at the table ought to be read presently. You, Mr. Speaker, have repeated this adjournment, without a question, or consent of the house, four times over. The privileges of the house are, by course of parliament, first to be considered; and there can be no greater privilege than this of freedom of speech. I have heard and read of propositions to bridle parliaments, and they were censured in the Star-Chamber. This action of yours, Mr. Speaker, is gagging the parliament; and you, by skipping out of the chair, prevented speaking in parliament. I desire the Paper delivered in may be read.

Sir *Tho. Lee.* We are all out of the way in matter of order. Here is a Paper tendered, and called for to be read; and it is moved below to be adjourned to Thursday; and now the debate is entered into, which is moved to be on Thursday. Your proper question is, first, Whether the Paper proposed to be read, shall be now read; and the next question, Whether Thursday shall be appointed to debate the manner of your adjourning the house.

Sir *Rob. Thomas.* Mr. Speaker, you have gone about to answer the Paper, before the house was possessed of it.

Lord *Cavendish.* The Speaker put us first out of order, by answering the Paper before it was read. I doubt not but precedents are to the contrary of what you, Mr. Speaker, pretend. In this parliament there have been several to the contrary, and you yourself was of a contrary opinion formerly to what you are of now. I desire the Paper may be read; and when that is done, I will give reasons why this debate should not be adjourned, but proceeded in now.

Sir *Tho. Meres.* The debate is, whether the Paper shall be read, or no. My opinion is, that all forms in this house ought to be cautiously preserved, else we destroy the commons of England. Whenever you search into this matter, I believe you will find there have been mistakes. I know that the matter lies in a short compass. When the king commands us to adjourn, may we not bring it to a question? If our books show it, and that we divided upon that question, the matter in question is out of doors. But by no means would I have this debate adjourned, to lose it. Men may let it alone now, and take it up another time, to do mischief in unquiet times. As for laying it by as a troublesome thing, it may be laid asleep to trouble you more. Near precedents of things are better than those of an hundred years since. If you think fit, let seven or eight gentlemen search books for precedents, else you may be put to it on Thursday.

Mr. Sec. *Williamson.* I look upon the thing particularly as between the house and the crown, and not the Speaker; I move for Thursday to debate it.

Col. *Birch.* Whether the matter be betwixt the house and the Speaker, or the crown and the house, it is of absolute necessity to be determined. If it had been determined in May last, we had not been troubled with it now, to lose our time. I remember the precedent of the Tax-bill, that Clarges mentioned, &c. It is for the service of the crown and us, in uniting us; and I would have this thing set right. If the banks be good, the channel will go right. I would have such steps made in this as would give it dispatch. The question the Speaker put is a fair question, viz. Whether the Paper delivered at the table shall be read. I would have that put to the question; but I would have any one show me a precedent, whether a Paper given in at the table, and not then read, was read ever after. Then if any gentleman be of opinion not to have the Paper read, and be of opinion to adjourn to Thursday, and in the mean time would have you search Precedents, you will lose Thursday. Read the Paper now, and after that search Precedents.

The Question being put for reading the Paper now, it passed in the negative.—Ordered, "That this debate of the irregular Adjournment of the house, by the Speaker, be adjourned till Thursday."

The session opened with an unexpected strain of loyalty,* for before the House had

* "The Constitution of the present house of commons, that had sat near 17 years, was now more manifestly grown into two Parties, which were called by the name of the Court and the Country: the former were grown numerous, by a practice introduced about five years before this time, by the lord-treasurer Clifford, of downright buying off one man after another, as they could make the bargain. The Country Party still continued the majority and retained more credit upon the corruption of others, and their profession of adherence to the true interests of the nation, especially in points of France and Popery: where these came in question, many of the Court Party voted with those of the country, who then carried all before them; but whenever the court appeared

considered any part of his majesty's Speech, having sat on part of the 30th of Jan. the Anniversary Fast, upon the motion of lord O'Brian, whose son had lately married the Lord-Treasurer's daughter, they voted, "The sum of 70,000*l.* for a solemn Funeral of his late majesty king Charles i. and to erect a Monument for the said prince of glorious memory; the said sum to be raised by a two months tax, to begin at the expiration of the present tax for building Ships."

The Commons Address of Thanks to the King.] The house next proceeded to take the king's Speech into consideration, and in return presented the following Address to his majesty at Whitehall:

"We your majesty's most humble and loyal subjects, the commons in this present parliament assembled, do in all duty and gratitude render our most humble Thanks to your most sacred maj. for the great care your maj. hath expressed for the preservation and encouragement of the Protestant Religion, by concluding a Marriage between the lady Mary, your majesty's niece, and the prince of Orange, being a prince professing the same religion with us, and engaged in arms for the defence of the common cause of Christendom: for the promoting of which we do, in all humility, and with the highest zeal to your majesty's honour, and the safety of your people, beseech your maj. not to admit of any Treaty of Peace, whereby the French king shall be left in the possession of any larger dominions and territories, or of any greater power than what he retained by the Pyrenean Treaty; less than which, we conceive, cannot secure your majesty's kingdoms, and the rest of Europe, from the growth and power of the said king, but that he alone may be able to disturb the peace thereof, whensoever he is minded to attempt it; the places reserved by that treaty to the king of Spain in the Netherlands being advantageous, as well by the vicinity of some important towns and garrisons to the kingdom of France, as by the extent of the territory. And we do most humbly desire that, in all treaties, articles and confederations, in order to the obtaining that end, your maj. would be pleased to provide that none of the parties that shall join with your maj. in making war for that purpose, may lay down their arms, or depart from their Alliances, till the said king be reduced at least to the said Treaty: and we do farther desire, as one of the most effectual means to attain those ends, that it may be agreed between your maj. and the Confederates, that neither ourselves nor any of them shall hold any commerce or trade with the French king, or his subjects, during such war; and that no commodity of the growth, product, or manufacture of France, or of any of the territories or dominions of the French king, be admitted to be brought into your majesty's, or any of their countries and dominions, either by land or sea, or to be sold within the same; but that they be seized and destroyed wheresoever they be found, and days to be limited for the same, in as short time as the nature of such affairs will permit: and that in all treaties, articles, and confederations, made in order to or for the prosecution of such war, it may be agreed and declared, that no vessel of any nation whatsoever shall be permitted to enter into or come out of the ports of France, but that the ship and men shall be seized, and the goods destroyed.—We do therefore most humbly desire your maj. to proceed in making such Alliances and Confederations as shall be necessary for the attaining those ends; and though we believe your maj. can never doubt of the affections of your people, yet, upon this occasion, we do, with all alacrity, and with one unanimous consent, renew our former promises and engagements, beseeching your maj. to rest confidently assured of our perseverance in the prosecution of the said war; and that when your maj. shall please to impart such Alliances and Confederations to us in parliament, we shall, upon all occasions, give your majesty such ready assistances and supports as may, by the blessing of God, bring the said war to a happy conclusion."

Debate on Sir Solomon Swale's Recusancy.] Feb. 1. Sir Wm. Smith complained of sir Solomon Swale's being convicted for Popish Recusancy, upon record, in the county of Middlesex.

Mr. *Sacheverell.* I would have you see the record of conviction. The most innocent of mankind may be convicted of Recusancy by surprize, but the law gives men time to set themselves free from their conviction by conformity. It is my opinion to have the record of his conviction sent for, and time allowed him to attend you here. I would not hastily turn this gentleman out of the house for recusancy, unless it be certainly known whether he be convicted or not.

The *Speaker* reads the Record. By this Conviction, any dissenter in opinion may be convicted, as sir Solomon Swale is, it being 'for not coming to his parish Church.'

Mr. *Powle.* I like not gentlemen bringing records hither, but I would have you command the officer to bring the record; and then you proceed as you think fit.

Sir *Ch. Harbord.* It is not for the honour of the house, whilst we make laws against Popery, to suffer a member convicted of recusancy to sit amongst us, and suffer it here. But when such a thing is represented to you, you can do no less than examine it, and send for Swale to appear, and there will be no surprize at all, as you formerly did in the case of sir Tho. Strickland.—The officer was ordered to attend with the Record on Monday.

to fall in with the true interests of the nation, especially in those two points, then many of the Country Party, meaning fairly, fell in with the court, and carried the Votes, as they soon did upon the king's pretence to grow bold with France, and resolve upon a war, if the peace was refused." Echard.

Debate on the frequent and irregular granting of Paper Protections.] The *Speaker*. Pursuant to the Order of the house, I have sent out an order to supersede all Paper Protections. I find about 100 in London and Middlesex.

Mr. *Powle*. This, of Protections, is another abuse that these long sessions of parliament produce. We are adjourned from day to day without doing business, and privilege continues long. Formerly, when there was an end of the session, there was an end of the privilege and protections. I hope we shall now do our business, and be prorogued, and so have an end of these protections.

Sir *Courtney Poole* moves for a search, all England over, that gentlemen may answer, in their places, whether they have granted out any protections under their hand.

Sir *Tho. Lee*. It has always been the custom of parliament, than we can protect no more than our menial servants. But that which frights people from complaining is your not declaring how far privilege extends. If you make publication, 'That men may arrest persons, notwithstanding Paper Protections;' that will remedy the thing, and men may be safe, and the law may go forward.

Mr. *Garroway*. I hear the lords are before hand with us in this of Protections; they have registered, and numbered their menial servants. If you find gentlemen have extraordinary numbers, you may find out the abuse, and vindicate your honours in it.

Col. Wanklyn expelled for granting an improper Protection.] A Petition was presented from Mrs Cottington, complaining 'that col. Wanklyn, a member of the house, protected Mr. Cottington, her husband, as his menial servant, against her hearing a cause depending between her and her husband, about the validity of their marriage at Turin in Italy, (she being of that country) and humbly desiring the favour of the house, that the said Protection may be withdrawn.

The *Speaker*. Col. Wanklyn was with me about it, and he promised me that he would withdraw the Protection.

Col. *Wanklyn*. I did withdraw the Protection, according to my promise; but the bishop of Lincoln said, 'That Mr. Cottington had received a sentence in the court of arches against the law of God, and that the gentleman was under a hard censure;' and so I granted him my Protection, but revoked it on Thursday last.

Mr. Sec. *Coventry*. This gentleman, Cottington, it seems, is protected by your member, because he thinks he has a righteous cause, and the judges in the ecclesiastical court think he has a wrong cause. If you give your members leave to protect persons against judgments and sentences, when they think the judges are in the wrong, the house of commons will be a great place.

Col. *Wanklyn*. I do aver that Mr. Cottington was my servant, and had done me very acceptable service.

Sir *John Birkenhead*. Whenever a day of hearing came, then Mr. Cottington had his protection from col. Wanklyn ready. The judge of the spiritual court sent to col. Wanklyn, and I spoke to him six times about it, and he promised me to revoke the Protection. Then he certified his Protection, and a public notary entered it, 'recalled,' and soon after col. Wanklyn revoked his revocation. Let him prove Mr. Cottington to be his menial servant. A man of Mr. Cottington's estate to be his servant! let him give it under his hand, that now he is his menial servant.

The Speaker reads an old Order sir Edw. Turner made when he was Speaker: viz. Resolved, That all Protections and written certificates under the hand of any member of this house, be void, and called in according to law; and that menial servants be protected only, according to law; and that this Order be printed and published.

Sir *Tho Lee*. This case, complained of, is only a particular instance of a member; therefore you are to proceed upon it, when the member that offends has made his defence in his place, and judge it. Then you may make a general Order as to Protections.

Sir *R. Sawyer*. Col. Wanklyn signed a protection, which is filed in the exchequer, directed, 'to all mayors, bailiffs, sheriffs, &c.' in as high a style as a proclamation, neither to stir hand nor foot, and threatening what penalty would ensue for breaking his privilege.

Mr. *Waller*. One example against an offender of this nature has done more than all your talk and orders. In king James's time, it was proved, that one made these Protections and sold them, and he was turned out of the house for it. This was done when parliaments were short; much more ought it to be severely punished now parliaments are long. The Romans had a Justitium that stood still for a time, but now for justice to stand still 17 or 18 years, is not a thing to be suffered; and I would have col. Wanklyn answer this giving Protections.

Col. *Wanklyn*. As to this Protection that Sawyer speaks of, it is concerning Dry Hill in Kent. We had a verdict for it, and judgment; and by a writ of possession, we were legally put into it, and we ought not to be disseized. In the Exchequer there was a bill of discovery; the bill was answered, and, upon a trial, we had legal possession, and I will satisfy the committee of privileges farther in it, if you please to refer it to them.

Sir *Rob. Sawyer*. Wanklyn was never in the cause, nor heard of in it, before the writ of possession.

Col. *Wanklyn*. Jones has a good title to Dry Hill; be has had a verdict. In time of war, Jones was my quarter-master, and went often to make his claim, but, because he was of the king's party, in these times, could not have his legal course, for his right. I have a concern in it of 300*l.* which I lent Jones, and he has given these lands in security for it; and

I am concerned for supporting the title, and have been so all along.

Mr. *Williams.* The writ of possession was awarded to Jones, for Dry Hill in Kent. Jones was the lessor, and the feigned lessee delivered the possession to the sheriff, and possession was taken accordingly. He alledged, that the writ with the possession, was unduly obtained; therefore the lord chief justice awarded the party to be put out of possession, and restitution to be made. Complaint was made of the under-sheriff for not doing it, and it appeared that he durst not do it, because there was a protection from your member, Wanklyn, to Jones. Wanklyn himself was in court, and, upon a motion that there being privilege in the case, proceedings might stop, the feigned person, Jones, assigns his title over to Wanklyn 3 or 4 days within term. The court was so far satisfied of the abuse, that the court did order the under-sheriff, at his peril, to satisfy the court of the execution of the writ by Saturday; but the writ was not executed. The Protection Wanklyn gave Jones was read in court, and it was directed, 'To all officers, &c.' in very positive words, 'not to dare to disturb the possession, because of privilege.' The court was abundantly satisfied, but out of respect to privilege of parliament, they gave farther time for the execution of the writ; and this day, under colour of this protection, a motion was made in court; and I advised Wanklyn to withdraw his Protection. I would have right done in this matter for your honour.

Mr. *Sacheverell.* Whether the title was transferred to Wanklyn before the controversy, and before the writ of restitution was granted, is the question; and I would have Wanklyn asked, whether he was present in court, when the rule of court was given? I would have him asked that question by the Speaker.

Sir *Cha. Harbord.* Ask him, when the conveyance was made, and upon what consideration?

Col. *Wanklyn.* Jones was legally in possession of the estate before I granted him my protection. [He withdrew.]

Mr. *Hale.* This suit of Jones has been always reputed a vexatious suit, and no man that knows Jones will trust him for any thing; he is not worth a groat, nor has been for these 20 years. Such a man as Wanklyn, that is guilty of what has been made appear to you, is not fit to keep us company; and I humbly move that he may be turned out of the house.

Sir *Cha. Wheeler.* That which concerns us to consider is, whether a member be legally in possession of an estate, and whether his debt upon it be a legal and true debt, and the estate fairly transferred to him; and whether he would defend himself in his possession by privilege. We have privilege because we cannot attend two services, the law, and here. Let Wanklyn fairly prove the debt, from Jones, and that the estate was transferred to him, in consideration of that debt, and then you may judge the matter.

Sir *Tho. Clarges.* The case is for granting a Protection to support a litigious title; thereby laying the honour of the house at stake, for his private advantage. As for the Protection of Cottington, a man of 1,000*l.* a year, to keep him as a menial servant! And that protection to Jones, so high-penned a protection! You must remove the scandal from the house, and not suffer him to sit here.

Mr. Sec. *Williamson.* The question is about turning out this member. I hope the thing will be well weighed, before you turn him out. There is the honour of the house in the case, and the compassion of those that suffer. But I would go by such steps, as may consist with justice. It has been said, it matters not what the title is. If he had given maintenance to a litigious title, or had assumed an interest where he has none, then I abominate it. But all order, rule, and practice of granting protections has been overlooked in the house; and this man is an unfortunate man, that he must fall for two errors. There may be many looked into, and in case that be the meaning of your Order for turning men out of the house, I know not where it will stop. There is a great difference in punishment between a mulct on the purse, and hanging; and seeing you will not go through with the business where you find it, pray consider well of this case.

Sir *Courtney Poole.* This gentleman has been a gallant man, but now he is in poverty. I would make him an example, but no farther than asking the pardon of the house upon his knees. But as for turning him out of the house, I know not where that will end.

Mr. *Sacheverell.* To buy a title, pendente lite, is highly criminal in law. The getting this very writ of possession was a bad practice, and I hope this house will never protect such a man in what he has done, and I would have him turned out of the house.

Mr. *Finch.* It is not the protection of menial servants, which we call Paper Protections; that is the particular privilege of every member. This is a great offence of Wanklyn's, if he made use of his privilege, as is said, pendente lite. But Wanklyn had not the title, till he saw Jones in possession. I would not condemn Wanklyn before we know the case thoroughly. I would refer it to the committee. I fear it will be as foul as it is represented. The ancient custom was, that a member came into the court of chancery, and, upon oath, declared the person to be his menial servant, and it was there recorded, but no Paper Protections were anciently. The thing itself is cruel, and the length of this parliament aggravates it. It is not proper to expel your member, unless you do the same justice to all in the same case with him. It may be the case of 10, 20, or 30 members and some of your worthiest members. I would have a vote posted up, to show your dislike of these Protections; and then, if any member transgress it, let him be expelled the house; and I shall readily give my consent to it.

Mr. Sec. *Coventry.* The gentleman that spoke last desires you would not proceed to expel col. Wanklyn till you have made a public declaration, how far you will punish members that give Protections, as this gentleman has done. In the case of one of your members, Mr. John Ashburnham, you made no declaration that you would punish him, &c. Your Journal said only, 'That he had dishonoured the house.' There was no law against his taking that bribe of 500*l.* from the merchants, about soliciting the king concerning the French wines. He was a worthy gentleman, and yet you expelled him the house. He was no judge, and you judged that taking a bride. For the honour of the house, either do justice upon col. Wanklyn, or expunge that sentence against Mr. Ashburnham out of the Journal, if you pardon this.

Mr. Solicitor *Winnington.* I am unwilling to stand up, because I know something of this matter. Finch says, 'he hopes you will not proceed against Wanklyn, till you know what the offence is.' I hope no man here will do what col. Wanklyn has confessed. You asked Wanklyn, 'whether Mr. Cottington was his menial servant?' He answered you, 'That Cottington had an ill sentence in the court of delegates, and he did protect him from it; but that he did afterwards revoke it.' What he has done is a great scandal upon the house; and Wanklyn's confession of it makes me take it for truth. Finch tells you, 'it may fall out to be the case of many worthy members.' But I cannot call them so. If any are guilty of such crimes, I am sorry they should represent here, to bind me and my posterity in the weighty affairs of the kingdom. If the matter charged upon Wanklyn were questionable, or doubtful, it were another thing; but the matter is so plain, that it admits no dispute. The measure lies only in the mercy of this house to the gentleman, and, in that, I would go as high as any man.

Mr. *Waller.* Mr. Ashburnham's case was hard, and very dangerous. I have seen 20 members, in a morning put out of the house. Some have disputed that power in the house. Some say, 'Wanklyn has been a soldier, and a commander, and therefore perhaps the lawyers are against him.' I would, for the future, go by some Order about Protections, as has been mentioned. The gentleman has been in employment for the king, and for this offence I would reprove him at the bar only.

Mr. *May.* I discoursed with col. Wanklyn about these Protections, and told him, I wondered he would protect a servant that he never had. I told him, I feared his doom would be to be turned out of the house, and it is my opinion he should be turned out of the house.

The question proposed was, "That col. Wanklyn has dishonoured the house, in granting Protections to Mr. Cottington, and Mr. Jones, not his menial servants."

Mr. *Garroway.* I would not have you make more points upon what you do. Judge it in particulars, but do not assign it in the question.

Mr. *Powle.* I would not have expulsions out of the house too large, I would have the question 'contrary to justice, and the honour of the house.'

Sir *Rd. Temple.* I will be no advocate for the person, nor his case. But I would have the thing done, as your predecessors have done; never without particular cause assigned upon your books. If you make the case general, it will never be a justification to you to posterity. To protect a gentleman of 2000*l.* a year, for a man's menial servant, is an extraordinary thing. That servant rather kept his master than the master him. I would go as high in this censure as any man, but would be uniform in it. If any member has protected any person that is not his servant, he deserves your censure, but not so highly as in this case. I would have the case such as you may measure your justice by to posterity.

Sir *Ch. Harbord.* This offence is not only contrary to an Order of the house, but to the ancient order, constitution, and justice of the house. That sentence you passed upon Mr. Ashburnham, was for taking 500*l.* of the merchants, for service he had done them to the king, in a matter depending in this house. For this gentleman's punishment, I would give it him only in a reproof at the bar; and hereafter the house may take the matter of such Protections, as he has granted, into consideration. But for the first offender of this nature, I am utterly against having him expelled the house.

Sir *Tho. Dolman.* I would have this gentleman that has offended sent prisoner to the Tower, and that you make a standing Order, for the future, against offences of this nature.

Resolved, 1. "That granting Paper Protections to persons not menial servants of members of this house, is against the justice and honour of the house. 2. That col. Wanklyn is guilty of granting Paper Protections, against the justice and honour of this house."

Mr. Sec. *Williamson.* This is but altogether to make a judicial sentence against the man, and this is a judicial cutting off a man from us; and therefore let us do all that may be, for clearing the justice of the house in particular; and that the nature of the crime may appear, I would have Jones and Cottington, and some of the persons he has protected, named in the vote. It is the first time that ever a capital judgment was applied to that fact, that had not a precedent in law for it. Therefore in order to make it a just and honourable sentence, you must say that every dishonour of the house should be punished with expulsion, which is a cutting off your member from us. Therefore I would not do it, in this case, without naming the persons, and 'that col. Wanklyn, for granting Protections to Cottington and Jones, not being his menial servants, hath violated the justice and honour of the house.' Thus I would have your vote.

Resolved, "That col. Wanklyn, for granting such Protections shall be expelled the house."

Mr. Sec. *Coventry.* You have said, in your former Order, about Protections, 'That they are against law.' This is a greater offence done by this gentleman than that of Mr. Ashburnham's taking 500*l.*

Mr. Sec. *Williamson.* It was said, 'If you begin not with this gentleman, you will never begin.' Therefore I would go on with punishing other offenders of this nature; but, as this case is put, I cannot give my consent to expel him.

Col. *Birch.* I hear the case of this gentleman distinguished from other cases, and I have heard that of protecting menial servants disputed. As the question is penned in your paper, nothing appears on your paper, 'that he has protected persons not his menial servants according to law;' but only expressed 'menial servants.' But I would not have this house, in their zeal to punish this gentleman, make such a slip as never to be recalled. I would have it referred to a Committee.

The three Votes passed. On the last the house divided, 140 to 109.

The *Speaker* informed the house, that col. Wanklyn ought to receive his sentence on his knees.

Col. *Titus.* When pardons are read in courts of justice, the pardoned persons hear them read on their knees. But no man, condemned to be hanged, receives his sentence on his knees. The sentence ought to be received standing. I have given my vote against the gentleman, because I could not give it for him.

Sir *Tho. Littleton.* Wanklyn is none of you now; he is cut off from you, and therefore it is not proper to bring him on his knees to receive his sentence.

Col. Wanklyn, was brought to the bar, the mace by him, to receive his Sentence of expulsion, standing.

The *Speaker.* Col. Wanklyn, I am commanded by the house to pass sentence upon you, for the dishonour you have done the house in granting Protections. Your sentence is hard, and my task harder, who am to pronounce it. If you had taken my advice in private, you had not come to this disgrace in public. The house thinks it a great blemish to them, that Protections should be granted to persons who are not their menial servants, and you are in a great measure guilty of that crime. Mr. Cottington has brought the greatest misfortune upon you imaginable, to be the occasion of your being cut off from this glorious body. I am commanded to tell you, that you are expelled the house for what you have done, and the house has done you a favour that you receive not your sentence on your knees.

Col. Wanklyn, after the sentence was passed upon him, was conveyed to the door by the serjeant with his mace. He received his sentence and went away weeping.

The King's Answer to the Commons' Address of Thanks.] Feb. 4. Mr. Secretary Coventry delivered the king's Answer to the last Address, which was read by the Speaker, as follows.

"C. R. His majesty hath received and perused the late Address of this house, and thereunto returneth this Answer:—He is not a little surprised to find so much inserted there of what should not be, and so little of what should. In the first place, his majesty's Speech was to both houses jointly; and, the matter being of so public a concern, it is certainly very convenient the return to that Speech should be made jointly. For to receive several Addresses, and possibly very different, cannot but administer matter of distraction to his counsels, and consequently to the affairs of the nation. Nor is the house of peers reasonably to be left out in transacting those things which at last must needs pass by them.'—In the next place, he observes in the Address of this house of the 20th of May last, you invite his majesty to 'a league offensive and defensive with Holland, against the growth and power of the French king, and for the preservation of the Spanish Netherlands;' and, upon his declaration of such Alliances, you assure his majesty of 'such speedy Assistances and Supplies, as may fully and plentifully answer the occasions.' His majesty hath made accordingly the Alliances offensive and defensive with Holland, and declared it to you in parliament; so his part is performed. But, as to that of this house for Supplies, though he asked it in his Speech, you give no answer, nor the least hint of affording him any thing to support the Treaties he hath made. Only the old promises are put to new conditions; and so he may be used to eternity, should he seem satisfied with such proceedings.—You are not to think that either his majesty, or the States General, being to embark in so great a design, would deprive themselves of the other so considerable Alliances. Some ministers of the most concerned princes have known and approved his Treaty with the States General; and, that he hath not formally concluded one with them, the reason is, that the distance of the places the princes concerned reside in would not give time to perfect so many Treaties, to be ratified in places so remote; and, laying well the foundation in Holland, there could not be much doubt of their consent, for whose interest that Treaty is made. But nothing can delay, or indeed disappoint these treaties, more than the failing of this house to support these his maj. hath made. He must acquit his credit there, and see his word shall be maintained, before he can engage it elsewhere a-fresh.—In his majesty's Answer to the Address of this house of the 20th of May, he told you how highly he was offended at that great invasion of his prerogative: but you take no notice of it, but, on the contrary, add to your former ill conduct; new invasions, equally offensive to his majesty's authority, as contrary to his, and, he thinks, most other men's judgments.—This house desires his maj. to oblige his Confederates never to consent to a peace, but upon condition the the most Christian king be reduced to the Pyrenean Treaty at least. A determination fitting only for God Almighty! For none can tell what will be fitting conditions for a peace, but he that can certainly foretell the events of the war.—You advise his majesty to enjoin not only his allies, but all the world, not to let a ship of theirs go to, or come from France, upon pain of loss of goods, capture of ships and men, not excepting either ally, prince, or ambassador, (if amongst them:) he doth not believe that ever any assembly of men gave so great and public a provocation to the whole world, without either having provided, or so much as considered how to provide, one ship, one regiment, or one penny towards justifying it, (at least as far as you have acquainted him.) However, to show how willing his maj. is to give all reasonable satisfaction to this house, how unreasonable soever the propositions made him are, he doth again repeat to you what he said on the 28th past, 'That if, by your assistance, he may be put into arms sufficient for such a work, his majesty will not be weary of them till Christendom be restored to such a peace, as it shall not be in the power of any prince alone to disturb.'—This is, in the consequence of it, as much as a prince that values his word can say to you: and he is such a one. But to say he will make no other peace, than such a particular peace, whether able or not able, whether abandoned by his allies or not, is not to be said upon solemn engagement, because not certainly to be performed.—In sum, gentlemen, the right of making and managing war and peace is in his maj.; and if you think he will depart from any part of that right, you are mistaken. The reins of government are in his hands; and he hath the same resolution and concern to preserve them there, as he hath to preserve his own person; and he keeps both for his people's protection, and safety; and will employ them so as far as he can. If this house encourage his maj. to go farther in Alliances, by supplying him in maintaining those he hath made, his care and utmost endeavour will be employed for you. If this house doth intend this, it must be speedy. The time and conjuncture afford not leisure to consult long; and therefore his maj. desireth that, without farther loss of time, you apply yourselves to the consideration of that Supply; for from thence he must take his measures."

Debate on the King's Answer.] Mr. Sec. *Coventry.* The king has showed you, in his Answer to your Address, his dissatisfaction in pressing upon what belongs to him. He omits no care at all for the public, for all that, and endeavours to give you satisfaction, he tells you, 'he hath made Alliances, offensive and defensive, with Holland.' But it is in vain to make new Treaties, when we are put back to old ones. 'If the king has arms sufficient,' he tells you in his Answer, 'he will not be weary of them till he has restored Christendom to such a peace, &c.' No body but God Almighty can tell the event of the war. Would not the affront you received at Catham, in firing your ships, have augmented, if, after that, you had voted never to lay down your arms, till you had revenged yourselves? And yet now you would make peace, and have the Pyrenean Treaty calculated purely between the French and the Spaniards, and no part of Europe else concerned in it; no, not Holland. When the king of Spain, or any of that league comes into a war, the king is a party in the Treaty of Aix la Chapelle, and by that you are not obliged to the Pyrenean Treaty. Now the king finds France go on to conquer Flanders. The case stands thus; here is great advantage to the Confederates by your sitting; we hear of nothing done, though great preparations have been made by the French in Alsace and in Flanders, and the Confederates are in a low and sad condition; but by the addition of the king's strength, they may hold up their heads, unless this Treaty with Holland be ruined by you; and then you will quickly hear very fatal news in the consequence. Allow that the project sent to France should be accepted, and that those conditions are not so great as you would have had, yet you will have the guarantee of the Confederates—That peace the king of France has by the king of England; not that England makes that peace, but that he consents to it. If the king agrees not to it, of consequence the king of England is left alone. If the king be not helped, can he make it alone? If the king be left out, what kind of peace the king of France will give you alone, I leave you to think. I desire you to have assurance, that what the king can do, he will do. If his arms are weak, he can do nothing. If it were lawful for me to show you letters that I can produce, all the house would be of my mind. One cheerful vote will end all this.

Lord Obrien. In that Address to his majesty (in May) we pointed at 'Alliances with the States General, and other Alliances, and for support of them his majesty might rest assured, we would assist him.' These Alliances, he tells you, he has made, the consequence whereof is war; and have you not brought him into a war? When monarchies insult and conquer, the subjects may have conditions, but the monarchs never. Therefore, without delay, I would go into a committee of the whole house, to consider of a Supply for the king to support these Alliances.

Sir Tho. Clarges. The king's Message is large, and consists of many parts. There are many expressions in it that grieve me. If we have given just offence to his majesty, in our Address, and former precedents, instruct us, and we ought to be sorry. Whatever we do, it becomes us, in duty, to give the king satisfaction, and be ashamed, and ask his pardon and forgiveness. Preparatory to that, I would have the king's Paper considered to-morrow. I am not satisfied that the Alliances mentioned are made according to our former Addresses. Formerly, upon our Addresses, we have had satisfaction, and have given Supply thereupon. In all former Alliances there was a quota expressed for Lorrain, Spain, Holland, &c. This 40,000 men and 90 ships, in the king's Speech, is a doubt to me, what quota Holland must come up to. Formerly we saw all before us—And when we know what our parts are to bear, in this confederacy, or whether we are to bear the whole burden of the war, then it is time to talk of aids to support the war.

Mr. *Mallet*. One false step made by this parliament in this great afair, and England is lost for ever. What is done in it, I would have done with true light and good understanding, and I am for the consideration of it to-morrow.

Col. *Birch*. I have such a difficulty upon my spirits, as I never had since I was born. As the union of the house, in our last Address, gave me great rejoicing, so dividing of opinion, in this matter, makes me tremble. A right understanding amongst ourselves will prevent the greatness of the king of France, above all things. We were all of a mind, the other day, in the Address, and I wonder it is not so now. Surely it is for some great reason, and I would know what reason. Whatsoever we resolve of, I would not have a negative.

Sir *George Downing*. I have seen sadder days here than Birch speaks of, which he knows as well as I; but let that pass. I hope there will be no cause of division amongst us, and that, in what we do, we shall have no negative. I saw the other day the meaning was good to engage the kingdom in the Pyrenean Treaty: but that treaty was never brought to the table. I saw the meaning was good, and therefore I said nothing. The thing is wholly mistaken; the king's Speech is entire. After you have voted Supply, the rest is gradual, and you may go by steps. Consider, is France to be dallied with? Threaten him, and not dare to strike him? We may be stricken before we are ready strike. When I consider what has been called, 'the grievances of French counsels amongst us,' they are departed, since the time the prince of Orange a protestant prince, was married to the heir of the crown; and now we demur in going into a grand committee.

Mr. *Powle*. If I could be satisfied that we are wholly departed from French counsels, I would not be backward to go into a grand committee, to consider his majesty's Message. But these four years, Addresses have been made to prevent the growing greatness of the French, and the ministers declare against him, and yet France grows great under these counsels. I fear some inclination is still amongst the ministers to France, and they have brought us to the brink of ruin. And we may lay all considerations aside, if we suffer this;—ever by urgent necessity to be driven from Religion and Property. The apple of contention in the king's Message is as if the house had no interest to concern themselves in war and peace. If we look not to the interest of this house, it is in vain to think of any thing abroad. The king may make war and peace, and the house may advise war and peace; and this might have been done sooner, if you, Mr. Speaker, had not leaped out of the chair, and would not suffer gentlemen to speak, but adjourned the house. I can show precedents out of my small store, that the constant practice of the house has been otherwise. Now we are told, 'that here is a league offensive and defensive made with Holland, for preservation of Flanders.' And Money is called for to maintain that Treaty, and we know not one word of it. Must we be kept thus in the dark! When an Aid was desired in parliament for supporting the Triple Alliance, Mr. Secretary Morris opened every particular of it to the house. In the last war with the Dutch, the king offered to show us all the League with France. We are told in the king's Paper, 'he has communicated this Treaty to several of his Allies, and they approved it;' and why must we only be kept in the dark, who are called upon for money to support it? We have not brought Christendom into this danger; therefore we should not be alone to bring it out. I would see this Treaty, and then will support it as far as any man. I would adjourn the house now, that in the mean time the honourable persons who may know our desires, may come better instructed to inform us farther.

Mr. Sec. *Williamson*. It is moved, that the debate be adjourned to see how things stand, as to the Alliances his majesty hath entered into. And not to enter into the matter, unless the house go into a grand committee. But because something has been spoken, as to the king's ministers, I will answer. I will say, I know not the alliances, allies, nor the quota. For the terms we are upon, as much has been said as is fit to tell you. The king has spoken it out. It is a League with Holland, offensive and defensive, and that is spoken out; and after this is known, I take war to be declared, and that our neighbour, the French king, is at liberty, by the law of God and man, to take advantage upon us, when the king has so said to his people. Those Alliances are made, that you asked for, and which the nation longed for, and groaned for, and it is a cause for the French king to enter into war with us, and to seize our merchants. Let God and the world judge now, should this thing rest here, where the fault lies. This is, in sum, to answer all intermediate doubts of what Alliances are produced by the king; and there is a great difference between what you ask of the king to do, and what the king does of himself. The thanks of this house did not go to the Alliances the king told you he had entered into, and that is a great arrear of thanks. I move that the house will go now into a grand committee.

Mr. Sec. *Coventry*. I find it insisted upon, that we should see the Treaty. I ask this only, why is not this Treaty published in Holland, as well as here? Showing it, or not showing it, depends upon the nature of the treaty. Showing the treaty is when the king pleases, but it is not always to be showed upon demand. If 40 precedents of showing treaties in this house, be better than 500 to the contrary, I leave it to you. If the condition be of part of a treaty to be published at the parliament of Paris, or here, it must be by both parties so agreed. There may be things in the treaty not fit to be communicated to 500 men.

Mr. *Jones.* I am sorry we are compared to the parliament of Paris, or the States of Holland. I am but raw in the matter of the king's Message, and would fully consider of it. If there be reason for it, I should supply the king to support the Alliances, but I doubt surprize in it, it is so hastily moved for.

Lord *Cavendish.* The honourable person at the bar put it to you, 'that this Treaty was not fit to be communicated to 500.' But I think it very fit to be communicated to 500 that must give Supply to maintain it. By the great delays of counsels, wherein we are kept in a dark mist, I cannot but suspect that, if we blindly give Supply, without knowing for what, it will be too late to consider any thing. All agree we owe so much respect to the king as to consider of his Message, besides the importance of the thing. Therefore I would have to-morrow for it.

Mr. Solicitor *Winnington.* I rejoice at the unanimity of the house, in preventing the growing greatness of the French king, that he may not destroy us. I observe that the present question is about the time of consideration, not of the Supply itself: to delay it till to-morrow will seem some dissatisfaction to the king. I find still we are unanimous for Supply, to suppress the greatness of the French king. Delay will look as if there were not full satisfaction in every man, in the king's Speech. The nature of the Alliances is not, indeed, set out by the king. Peace and war, it was never doubted, was the authority of the crown to determine. But all instruments of Treaties of that nature, in the Crown Office, show that the king makes peace and war for the people's good, and parliaments are to give assistance to the king's good intention. Though kings resolved it, yet parliaments voided it.

Sir *Tho. Meres.* If this treaty, that the king's ministers tell us of, be so good and desired by the confederates, and we may not see it, it may be good for them, and not for us. However, if we must be urged, upon our words, to stand by his majesty in these Alliances, pray let it be upon our own terms, for we never promised the supporting them, but upon our own terms; and let us see whether the Treaty be good for us. I have read the king's answer to our last Address, I see nothing new in it. I thought we should have seen Alliances. We said, in our Address to the king, 'No, unless Alliances were imparted to us.' I would willingly hear a new thing said. It is past over in silence that we have a right to the defence of England. Though I would not move an angry point, yet I must say, that it is the call of our writ; by it, you are 'to consult of such arduous and difficult affairs as shall fall before you.' You have a right then to discourse it, and you have a right to pay for it. We have always spoke for it. There is not a step we have made but is all wrong, if we have not a right to the defence of the nation. Our ancestors have protested to their right of this. Your privileges are, never the less, for burning the Journals of this house; your right is good.

Mr. *Finch.* When we are told that the king has given us a bone of dissension, in his Message, it is no wonder if we have one here in the house, and are told of French councils. The king has married his niece to the prince of Orange—I would know what those steps are so spoken of, 'still towards French councils,' that occasion these dissensions amongst us. I would let the world know the reason why we apprehend French councils. If we have suffered damage by the ministers delay in concluding these Alliances, we ought not to increase jealousies, by letting it be longer in their hands, but dispatch it. A sharp sword must do now what a cudgel might have done formerly; and, by the same reason, it will cost more hereafter, if we delay it now. We have been told by some gentlemen that they would see the particulars of these Treaties. To that it has been answered, how inconsistent would that be in so great an assembly! There was a time, (and I hope there will never be such another) when the king and lords were put out of the government, and the commons only retained. Yet they thought not themselves fit to manage affairs of state; but made a council of state for that purpose. I would not abase the prerogative in this great affair, now so useful to our safety as well as the king's honour. But it is said, 'That other princes know these Treaties, and we must not.' To that I answer, they are a supreme power, and we are not. We are told likewise, 'That there are many precedents that the king has anciently advised with his parliament, in Treaties.' But we need not ancient precedents for that; the king has communicated his to you now; and now that our neighbour's house is on fire, and it is coming to our own, a punctilio of Order of our house may stop the affairs of all Christendom. There is no force in Christendom able to withstand the French. The hazard of the war is great, and the expence is as certain. We are unfit to partake the prerogative with the king, though he may please in his grace and favour sometimes to descend to us. Do you expect the thanks of the country for delay? their rage, rather, and the discontent of Christendom; and I hope, the Order of the house will never obstruct this great affair.

Mr. *Sacheverell.* I know not what answer to give, but I know what mind the country are of. They will not be pleased if we thrust a sum of money blindly into those hands that have so ill managed affairs. It is but to strengthen the hands of those who have ill managed things for the interest of the nation. They, by virtue of their places, may reconcile themselves to the king, which I cannot, being a private person; but I must, in public, ask those gentlemen, when the house has branded them for doing wrong, when ever the house has sat down tamely under it? the same influence from those men has branded the parliament, to make it odious. As to the king's prerogative, we have done it wrong in nothing, and such as persuade the king that we have done so, deserve not to have the management of this great affair. How should those counsellors see this now, that have gone 7 years another way? four years together the parliament addressed Hen. vii. about the loss of Britany. They gave a Supply for it, and they trusted the ministers, and as long as they gave nothing was done, and when Britany was lost, much about the 3d of Dec. just at that time, the king, council, and chancellor, all moved the parliament for a Supply, or all was lost. In Edw. ivth's time, he desired to make his Will, for he would go over to succour Burgundy *. And he went over when all was lost. The great men about the king had pensions then from the king of France, on record in the parliament of Paris, for life, all but the lord Hastings, lord chamberlain, who would give no acquittance for it. When Hen. vii. was first moved by the duke of Britany for assistance, the king of France sent to him to sit still. His council advised him to mediate a peace, and they mediated so long till all the dukedom of Britany was gone—12 Edw. iv. The ministers pursued this practice. A war, and an alliance was made with the duke of Burgundy, in all haste, and, when that was done, the ministers found it a fine game to receive pensions from the French, and raise money at home, and always were in haste, and they must have money from the parliament for this war to save Burgundy from the French; but all Burgundy was lost by it. What end can our ministers now have in not showing us these articles, but their being conscious to themselves who made the French Alliance, that they are faulty? the very same steps are taken now as were then, in all things, but taking pensions. The king's prerogative of making peace and war, is always allowed, as I will vouch, when there is an entire compliance between the king and parliament, and no division, as in 6 Edw. iii. The king called a parliament for a particular end, to consider of the French affairs; they met on Monday, and adjourned to Thursday, without taking any intimation from the king. They advised him to consider of the affairs of Scotland and Ireland, though they were not at all recommended to them. The commons advised by themselves, and the bishops and lords by themselves, and it was called 'a new advice.' The commons desired prorogation, because all their members were not come up—they met, and the commons gave by themselves, and the lords by themselves. I can never pass by that; nor ever will give a penny of money till the Treaties are produced.

* Phil. Comines. Lib. vi. cap. 2.

Sir *John Ernly*. Misfortunes of a later date did arise, more lately, by a difference between the lords and commons. I have heard to day such language of 'French councils and French money,' as I never heard before. Where any such are to be found, let them be hanged, and the money melted, and put down their throats. The king has done in the Alliance more than you ask, and has given the best security in nature. He has chosen the best alliances, and it is at your door to have them supported. Can it be thought you can have help, if this alliance be not embraced? shall Spain, or the confederates help you? are you told of this war, and will you not enter into it? this war will not keep cold. The French may seize your money now in their kingdom, and your Leeward Islands. Is your house on fire, and will you not quench it, but run to enquire who made it, by thus exclaiming against privy-counsellors? go into a grand committee to consider of supporting these alliances, the best course you can take.

Mr. Sec. *Coventry*. If you will allow these discourses, there is the same freedom for me, as for Sacheverell. It is 'evil counsel,' I am sure, to defer aiding the king to supply these Alliances, and it is as desperate counsel as France can give. If there be any traitor in the king's councils, let him be found out.

Mr. *Sacheverell*. I desire to explain myself. The distance of the place from me to those gentlemen, that have taken exception at what I said, might make me misapprehended. They apprehended, 'that I seemed to charge the present council with taking French money.' I said, 'there are all the steps now taken as in the precedent I mentioned, except taking pensions.'

Sir *Edw. Baynton*. Did I think that putting off the consideration of the king's Message till to-morrow would retard the main business, I should not be for it. To be unanimous, is more than in the time of to-day, or to-morrow. Presently to go into the great business' I doubt much that we are in the dark, as much as when we came out of the country. I am so still. Formerly, upon great occasions, when Aids were demanded, we went down to consult our country, and had nothing but a day's time to consider the matter; that we must leap into money, from managing our country affairs! Whip a vote for two millions in the Dutch war, for Ships, and we never have been strong at sea, since; such temptation that money gave to be profuse. Pray let the consideration be to-morrow.

The question for resolving into a Grand Committee, to consider of his majesty's Supply, was then carried, 193 to 151.

Feb. 5. The house in a grand committee on the Supply, came to this Resolution, "That the house doth agree with the committee, that a Supply be given to his majesty for the support of his present Alliances made with the States General of the United Provinces, for the preservation of the Spanish Netherlands, and lessening the power of France."

Feb. 6. Resolved, "That 90 ships are necessary for the support of his majesty's present Alliances," &c. Which was agreed to by the house.

Further Debate on the Speaker's irregular Adjournments of the House.] Feb. 9. The debate on the Speaker's Adjournments of the House was resumed.

The *Speaker*. After the king's command of adjournment of the house, I declared the house (as I thought was my duty) adjourned accordingly.

Sir *Tho. Clarges*. Lord Coke, in his Institutes, speaks at large of Adjournments of parliaments; where he declares the house of commons to be a court, and says, 'that adjournment of the house is not the single act of any one person, but of the whole court. Prorogations and adjournments were formerly convertible terms (as he tells you) but altered since. That of adjournment is always by general consent of the house, and if any one scruple arises, the Speaker cannot adjourn till it be removed, and the method is so in both houses of parliament.' I did enquire whether the lord chancellor, in the house of lords, did ask the lords pleasure, whether they would adjourn? and he had it in direction from the lords to adjourn. And in one of the late adjournments, the lords had a writ of error recorded before they adjourned. The lord chancellor is a man of great experience, and learned in parliament affairs, and would not do contrary to the lords commands, which he received. Now, whether will you read those records, which, you say, Mr. Speaker, will satisfy us in your proceedings? I would either have it done, or refer them to a committee to examine the authenticity and weight of them. And I move that the lawyers may be sent for from Westminster Hall, as is usual in such cases. There is one learned gentleman has studied the point, and may be of great help to us.

Sir *John Ernly*. I hear this house called 'a court' but we are no judicature, we cannot give an oath, our clerk is but 'Subclericus.' The lords clerk is 'Clericus Parliamentorum.' Full parliament is 'a Court.'

The *Speaker*. I had not all my precedents when this matter was last touched upon. I have since searched farther; and it is the doctrine I have learned from my predecessors, that when the king commands an adjournment of the house, it is your duty to obey it without any matter intervening; and till you declare the contrary, I shall continue to do what I have done formerly. If it be your pleasure, I shall open the nature of the thing, and leave it to your consideration.

Sir *Phil. Warwick*. A thing you would not have debated I will not begin to debate, since it is the king's authority. Consider the nature of the thing, whether the king cannot adjourn this house at his pleasure; and, after that, whether you can enter into any debate. I would see precedents of the thing, as has been moved, and those Records, the Speaker says, he has, to justify himself in what he has done.

Sir *Tho. Meres*. I observe, that when a troublesome matter comes before the house, and is once put off, it is seldom taken up again. But now we are come to our day, and we begin to debate it, I will wholly wave the present debate of the king's prerogative. This matter of adjourning the house is a question very requisite to be determined, which way soever it be, and I would by no means have you let it go, but settle it. I desire that those who are conversant in things of this nature, may be sent for, to attend, and the mace sent to call them up. And, I hope, in an hour or two, to find it a very clear case. Prorogation is not the point in question, and if you debate what is convenient, there will be no end of that; but let us go upon custom of parliament, which is the easiest way, and the matter will be quickly decided.

The Gentlemen of the Long Robe were sent for by the mace.

Mr. *Powle*. I allow the king's prerogative to call, adjourn, and prorogue parliaments. The question is not that, but the manner of exercising that power. That being premised, I conceive this is the right, and ought to be, of the house, adjourning themselves. Calling and dissolving parliaments is an act relating to the government of the nation; but adjourning the house, from time to time, relates to the affairs of the house, and is lodged in the house; and ought not to be communicated to the king, but by the mouth of the Speaker. It is a power always to reside in the house, who knew best how their affairs stand, and may be very inconvenient if in the king. The way of doing it by the king, is either by himself in person, in *pleno parliamento*, or it is done by commission, or writ, under the great seal, and no private message by the secretary or message under the signet is of authority, to adjourn us, unless, in *pleno parliamento*, as I have said. The king cannot call a parliament under his signet, nor any other way but by his writ, under the great seal. Though the house does take notice of Messages from the king, yet we are not bound by them. It has been said 'we are a court,' but the powers are diminished since the two houses separated themselves: though I can bring several precedents that we are a court of record. I take the lords house, and the commons to be but one court in judgment of law; and that is the high court of parliament. It must follow then, that the king must adjourn the whole court; either he must take the whole, or leave the whole, as in the courts of Westminster. If the king should adjourn the house of commons, and leave the lords sitting, or the lords, and leave the commons sitting (their actings mutually relating to each other as to the legislature) it would breed a confusion; and no man knows how far the lords court would extend itself upon lives and estates. Little now is left farther to be said; for if the power of adjournments be not in the crown, it cannot be in the Chair. The Speaker is called 'the mouth and tongue of the house,' which speaks the conceptions of the mind. Not that he is to make those conceptions, but pronounce what he has in command from the house. Lenthal, the Speaker, (upon an occasion known to most) told the late king 'He had neither tongue, eyes, nor ears, but what the house gave him*.' And having said all this, I think I have showed you some kind of reason for my assertion, that it is the right of the house to adjourn themselves. Now how this matter of Adjournment has been in practice; I am not so well versed in precedents, as other gentlemen. I have a book in my hand, of all the main precedents in Rushworth's Collections, which I shall rather make use of than those in particular cabinets. In 3 Charles, the king sent a Message to the house, not to adjourn the house for the Easter holidays, which by reason of the departure of many members they intended to do, but to continue sitting†. Sir Rob. Philips excepted first against this Message of non-recess, and took notice that in the 12th and 18th of king James, upon the like intimation, the house resolved that it was in their power to adjourn, or sit, and moved for a committee to consider thereof, and of our right herein, and to make a declaration; and accordingly it was appointed. And resolved, that it being now yielded unto, in obedience to his majesty, it might not turn to prejudice in time to come. Sir R. Philips and sir Edw. Coke both urged then, that the business of the house is always done by the house itself. Coke then cited a case of a Corrody, &c. The king sends his writ for a Corrody to an abbot, for a vallet; if it be ex rogatu, though the abbot yields to it, it binds not, but if without it, the abbot is charged by such a pension, for life of the vallet. So Coke desired that the Adjournment of the house might be entered upon the books, 'Ex rogatu, non ex mandato, Regis.'

The *Speaker* then asked Mr. Powle, Whether the Records he had recited agreed with the original?

Mr. *Powle* answered; Those in private hands agreed with Rushworth, and proceeded. In the 18th of king James§, the king had a mind to adjourn the house by commission: some then checked it in the house, for they found the commission was not directed to them; and therefore took no notice of it, but adjourned themselves. The next thing I shall mention is the strongest case of all, though not in all respects; and that is the case of lord Finch. The declaration, and causes of dissolving that parliament, which he was Speaker of, and the whole matter is in print, which sufficiently justifies me in the precedent. The 23d. of Feb.* the king sent to the house of commons to adjourn themselves for ten days. (The house was then in a Grand Committee. The Speaker signified the king's pleasure, and asked leave of the house to attend the king as he had commanded him; they gave him leave. The Speaker then delivered the king's command of adjourning the house, without a question, or admitting any farther speeches. Sir John Elliot then presented the house a Remonstrance against the lord treasurer Weston, to be read. The Speaker then leaped out of the chair, (as you, Mr. Speaker, have several times done) but offered not to adjourn the house, but would not suffer any man to proceed, and refused to put questions, and alledged he had the king's command for it: for had he supposed himself in that power, he needed not to have refused to put questions but might have adjourned the house without a question. Then a long time intermitted till that parliament, called 'the three weeks Parliament,' met. And although an intermission of 12 years, and Finch was removed into the lords house, yet the thing was revived, and debated. The short parliament was much better than that which succeeded, for the house then consisted of learned and worthy men, and therefore I lay the more weight upon it. And if the king had complied with that parliament, much of the misfortunes which afterwards happened, might have been prevented, in all human probability. The Vote they then made, was 'That the Speaker (sir John Finch) refusing to put a question, being thereunto required, or to adjourn the house upon any command whatsoever, without the consent and approbation of the house itself, are breaches and violations which highly impeach the privilege of parliament.' When the king had made a verbal command of adjournment, and signified it, and no adjournment shall be made; I dare venture the cause upon that issue. The Long Parliament came after, and lord Finch was impeached the 27th of Dec. Whilst the house was in debate upon the Impeachment, lord Finch asked leave of the house, and obtained it, to make his defence, and made the Speech in the printed paper.† This was done very early in that parliament, before any disturbances began, and, without question, that was an assembly of knowing and learned men. And his adjournment of the house by the king's command was voted a crime, and was the second Article in his Impeachment. For the Speaker to forbid a man to speak, is an offence of a high nature. For if that Speaker could have pretended power of adjournment, he might have done it, without forbidding gentlemen to speak. The lord keeper made this apology for himself, amongst several others in print, at large, 'humbly to beseech you all to consider that if it had been any man's case, as it was his, between

* See vol. ii. p. 1010. † Vol ii. p. 277.
§ See vol. i. p. 1262.

* Vol. ii. p. 488. † See vol. ii. p. 686.

the displeasure of a gracious king, and the ill opinion of an honourable assembly, he beseeched them to lay all together, lay his first actions with the last, and he would submit to the honourable construction of the house.' Now, for a more recent precedent, you will find in the king's two printed Speeches in the Convention, (though that was no parliament) yet one very like it. The king sent to the commons, when they had passed the Act of Oblivion, to adjourn themselves; and the king, in his speech, then did direct them to adjourn. The king could not think he had it in his power, he might else have as well done it then himself. In 1670, the king tells the commons, 'because they had been a long time from home, he was content they should adjourn themselves.' Oct. 26, 1677, The king in his Speech, says 'he intends the house of peers may, and the commons may adjourn themselves.' Whoever advised the king to do that, took it not for the king's prerogative to adjourn the house, but for the house to adjourn itself; and so it would have been the last time, if the house had been let alone by the Speaker. The house of lords has a Roll of Record of their standing Orders, and amongst them there is one 'That the chancellor shall not adjourn the house without Order from the house.' You may remember, Mr. Speaker, that motions were made for printing your Speech, and it was debated, and all that, after the king had signified his pleasure of adjournment of the house. This is all that I have to say in this matter. I have only opened it to give occasion to the gentlemen of the long robe to inform you farther, that the thing may be set right.

Mr. *Sacheverell.* This debate began first upon a charge in writing that I, some time since, delivered against the Speaker, (p. 898). The question now before us is not betwixt the house and the crown, in matter of Adjournment, but betwixt the Speaker and us. I have sought writings and records, to justify the right of the house in this matter. I am willing to part with that Charge I brought in, and since the house has waved it, I shall do so too; and will acquiesce in what the house shall determine.

Sir *Tho. Meres.* As Powle has mentioned the constitution of parliament in precedents from 60 years downwards, I would yet come lower. He said, 'As the lords have thought good not to be under that difficulty of adjournment by the chancellor, so we may be set out of it also by the Speaker, and may declare that the house is not to be adjourned without their own consent.' If the point be so put down upon your books, our day of debate upon this matter is ended, and the thing rests quiet. Every act here is by the consent of the house, two ways: it is had either upon the question, or by common consent. If entered, 'Ordered, upon the Question,' then it has been a debate. If the thing pass by common consent, it is entered, 'Ordered, only. So for Adjournment, if no question of it be made, then it is very frequent for the chair to order it upon the universal cry, 'adjourn, adjourn.' But if the Speaker be moved for a question, he cannot deny it. The thing itself is sufficiently declared when no man contradicts it. Generally the thing is thus entered by skilful clerks; possibly new clerks may do otherwise; yet they should not. The 20th of Dec. 1661, after the house was called up by the black rod to attend the king, who signified his pleasure of adjournment, the house came down, and resolved upon matters to be done at their next meeting, after that adjournment was signified. The king's pleasure of adjournment does but signify that day; but so that no minutes must be spent to set your house in order, cannot be the intention. As if a member should be beaten, coming from the lords house hither, will you not consider that breach of privilege? When the king signifies his pleasure of adjournment, it is not to be refused, and no parliament will ever refuse adjourning. In 1661, the adjournment was entered into the books, upon the question put, and the house adjourned, &c. by the consent of the house, which the entering the question plainly shows. In 1668, after the king's pleasure signified of adjournment, the house adjourned itself; though it was not entered 'by a question,' yet it is 'by Order,' which implies consent. The 1st of April, 2 Ch. i. the king desired the house would adjourn, and they debated the reason of it, and they divided upon the question, though it was carried as the king would have it; and the Speaker adjourned the house accordingly. These precedents are all plain upon your books. What I say is for the interest of king and parliament, and I would have the question easily wound up, as the lords have done, viz. 'That the house is not to be adjourned by the Speaker without their own consent.'

Mr. *Mallet.* The great minister of state, the earl of Clarendon, once attempted to have all powers involved upon a committee of lords and commons, upon pretence of a Plot, which was plainly for setting up a Standing Army; and what the king did was by the instigation of that minister. I desire, that the Order moved for, which the lords have made, may be a standing Order, and as perpetual as that of the Medes and Persians.

The *Speaker.* I have taken out of the Journal Books what I shall represent to you, in this matter of Adjournments, and leave it to your consideration. Prorogations and adjournments may be done by the great seal, the king absent, by commissioners; and, by the king present, 'ex mandato regis.' Adjournments from day to day are sometimes by the desire of the king, and sometimes by the desire of the house. That of adjournment by commission is a prorogation to some uses, though not to all, all bills remaining in statu quo, &c. and all committees ceasing, and privilege also. If the king be present at the adjournment, it is then entered into the book, 'ex mandato domini regis.' In Edw. i's time, the commons desired to consult their country upon an Aid demanded, before they granted it, and they were adjourned by the king. When that king was absent, they were adjourned by the queen, and the chancellor, and all bills were left, in statu quo. But not committees. No entry is made, in the lords Journals, of the houses adjourning themselves from Edw. vi's time, and from Hen. viii's time, to the end of the Long Parliament by a question. No entry is made of the commons adjournment, unless when the king commanded the adjournment, as in the case now before you. In king James's time, the ordinary adjournments, from day to day, were not entered into the Journal. That of the 12th James was not a parliament, for nothing was done in it; no bills passed. But in that Journal there are no footsteps of this matter. In the 13th James, all the king's adjournments were made by commission, and then the king signified his pleasure of the intended adjournment. The commons were dissatisfied with it, and desired to sit some time longer, till the bills before them were brought to some perfection; the commons sent a Message to the lords, to join with them in a Petition to the king for leave to sit longer, and the lords refused to join with them, and declared, 'that the adjourning, calling, and dissolving parliaments was the sole right of the crown.' But, at a conference afterwards, they acquainted the commons, 'that, by this Adjournment, the king had declared to them, that the Bills depending in each house should not be cut off by the adjournment;' and the commons rested satisfied. But king James told the commons, in harsh terms, his dislike of their proceedings, and commended the duty of the lords. The commission then for adjourning the parliament the commons avoided reading in their house, because not directed to them, but they obeyed the king's pleasure in adjourning, though not by that commission; and several adjournments afterwards succeeded one another. But it is noted in that Journal, 'That a motion being offered for writs to issue out to supply vacancies, the house refused to make any Order in it, being to adjourn, and would hear no motion that day.' I speak this to show that no question was ever put, nor business ever done, after the king's pleasure of adjournment was signified. 1st Ch. i. the lords sent to the commons to come up to the lords house, to hear the king's commission of Adjournment read. The commons sent the lords this Answer to their message, 'That it was according to ancient precedents, that the house of commons always adjourned themselves.' Now the question was only, whether the commons should be adjourned in the lords house, or here; and the commons then adjourned to Oxford to the 1st of August. 3rd Ch. i. the Speaker brings a Message from the king, to require the house to make no farther proceedings in business, and that the house should adjourn all committees; and the house was adjourned accordingly. A Message was sent from the lords, to signify 'that the king gave leave to the houses to sit a few days longer, to perfect the Petition of Right, and the Bill of Subsidies, and that they might go hand in hand.' I speak this to declare Adjournment, by commission, to be in the nature of prorogation. 5th Ch. i. Feb. 25. A Remonstrance was prepared by some members, after an adjournment of that day to the 2nd of March, which being proposed, sir John Finch, the then Speaker, said, 'He had a command from the king to adjourn the house to the 10th of March,' and put no question of adjournment, and refused to put any question. Mr. Sec. Coke delivered the Message of the house adjourning on the 25th of Feb. till the 2nd of March, and the Speaker adjourned the house accordingly, without a question, or particular command from the house. The house being met according to that adjournment, some called to the Speaker to put the question about the protestation, or remonstrance. He refused to put the question, and proffered to go out of the Chair, and the riot thereupon followed. The Little Parliament, in 1640, was not a parliament in law, having done no act. Though a parliament met not till ten years after, they fell into examination of the breach of privilege the last day of the sitting of the former parliament, by the Speaker. The matter of fact was stated, and the house came to a resolution in this vote, 'That the Speaker, (sir John Finch) refusing to put a question, being thereunto required, or to adjourn the house upon any command whatsoever, without the consent and approbation of the house itself, are breaches and violations which highly impeach the privileges of parliament.' I observe, that the house was then possessed of a debate, and the Speaker refused to put a question, and that was the thing complained of, and the particular article relates to nothing else, but the matter of fact depending in the house; and I make no question, nor ever did, that when the king commands an adjournment, it is the act of the house, and the Speaker can do no otherwise. But this always has been the form of doing it, when the king commands you to adjourn, and it is because you receive the king's command, and execute it after another kind of method than other things are done. The king sent a Message to the house, by the attorney general, and a question arose how the Message should be received: the attorney was ordered to come to the bar, and the Speaker and the house to be bare during the time of the delivery of the message, that no disrespect should be given to the king's command. No man that is not a member, but is called into the house by a question. But it was never known that a question was ever put for calling in the black rod, the king's messenger. We met here, upon an adjournment, and there was a motion for a writ to be issued out to fill up a vacancy, and you ordered no question to be put, the black rod knocking at the door. I say all this to show, that, in receiving the king's command, and executing it, it is not done as in other cases. For adjournment, upon the king's command, there is never any question put, because the obedience to it is never doubted, and where there is no room for a doubt, there is none for a question. 'The king commands the house to adjourn, and they will not.'—There is no precedent of any such thing. A gentleman did rise up to speak, when I adjourned the house, and all the house called out, 'Adjourn! adjourn!' and none 'Not adjourn.' I think I did then what I ought to do, in adjourning the house, and shall do it again, till I am otherwise ordered by the house.

Lord *Cavendish* If you had not adjourned the house the last time, the next question would have been, to put another in your place. I was at the first against bringing a charge against the Speaker, but I desire that the privilege of the house may be asserted. I thought, Mr. Speaker, you yourself was once of another opinion. In the last April adjournment, when the house came from the lords, a gentleman moved, 'That the Speaker might print his speech, which he made at the lords bar.' You, Mr. Speaker, did not say then, 'That no man could speak after the king's pleasure of adjournment was signified.' You made a modest reply, but said not, 'That no man could then make a motion.'

The *Speaker*. Mr. Secretary Coke presented the Remonstrance to the king, 2 Ch. i. and the king said, 'he would consider of it.' But there was no command then that the house should adjourn.

Sir *Tho. Meres*. The king in his proclamation says, 'The house may adjourn themselves.'

Mr. *Powle*. That precedent you mention, Mr. Speaker, of 2 Cha. i. shows no difference then between the Speaker and the house about Adjournment; you seeming to put by the blow, by that precedent. Had the Speaker then adjourned the house, there had been no room to call for the question. But take the Vote in sir John Finch's case, it is one thing what is done ill *de jure* and another out of respect to the king; and in that I would go as far as any man. But for the Speaker to adjourn the house *de jure*, may be dangerous to the very government. If you will observe that declaration for dissolving the parliament of 5 Ch. i. it tells you the Speaker took the command, &c. from the king, and he cannot do it by a verbal command, which does not imply that the king cannot do it by commission. The king made his command of Adjournment, in May last, to the house, and not to you, Mr. Speaker; and that I insist upon.

Mr. *Waller*. I like the question proposed very well, viz. 'That the house is not to be adjourned by the Speaker, without their consent.'

Mr. Sec. *Williamson*. Though this is not immediately the king's prerogative, yet it stands upon the confines of it. This point must not be upon matter of convenience, but perfectly upon matter of fact. We have heard precedents from learned gentlemen, and from yourself, Mr. Speaker, there are many, but if the question be rightly stated, and one word taken into it, viz. 'immediately,' no one precedent comes up to it. But when the king's pleasure is signified of an 'immediate' adjournment, nothing intervened of debate in the house, and it was not executed by a question. The whole hinge of the thing depends upon that single word. It is no doubt nor question, but that Adjournment is the single act of the house, but no business is to intervene before the adjournment. It appears by all precedents, when ever the king has signified his pleasure of adjournment, the house has done as the king directed, nothing intervening. I hope, that, as this is the authority of the crown, you will not make an order to take any of that power away, therefore, in order to the question, it may pass, so as it may not be construed hereafter to take the power out of the crown; that adjournment may not stand in opposition to prorogation, and not leave the government lame and impotent, in whatever emergency may occur.

Mr. *Waller*. In the word 'immediately' the king is extremely concerned, and more than the house, and I see not, without this question, how the king can be obeyed. If the Adjournment is 'immediately' to be made upon the king's command, then it is to be done sine medio. But yet the message of Adjournment was not sent to the Speaker, but to us, to adjourn ourselves so that if the Speaker does it, without direction from the house, we cannot obey the king, and I say it for the king's sake. The schoolmen say, 'God cannot make a thing to be and not to be at the same time.' This freedom of speech here could never be taken away. If a man be speaking, and the Speaker will not hear him, this is not to hear the house speak. The house is adjourned either by general consent, no man opposing, or in order to it, by a question, and if we cannot speak after signification of the king's pleasure of adjournment, we have no way left of complying with the king's desires. Plainly, in a prorogation of the parliament in the lords house, the lord keeper says, 'My lords and gentlemen, it is the king's pleasure to prorogue this parliament;' but then we are nothing but passive; we are not so in an adjournment. Great bodies must be moved with great majesty. In the act of recognition of the king's title, in king James's time, one bishop gave a great No to it, and it had like to have cost him his life. That instance given by the Speaker, of the black rod knocking at the door, is a perfect mistake, for in that we are perfectly passive. We were called by the king to dissolve us, in the Little Parliament before the Long Parliament. The king calls us to the lords house, and we must go. But in this of a command to the house to adjourn, the king bids us to be active, and shall we disobey him? As to the word 'immediately,' it is a new word, and if new words should throw away old privileges, we shall never want new words, and we shall want old privileges. In this question we are now in for all we are worth, and should it go to the people's ears that we that represent them, are all shrunk into the Chair, and that the Speaker only represents the commons of England, they would not think themselves secure of their lives and fortunes, and would very hardly raise the money you intend. If the Speaker be bigger than us, what bulwark are we of the lives and fortunes of them that sent us hither? You, Mr. Speaker, may be mistaken, and so may the house too, and I would willingly pass it by as to the crime in the Speaker, and put the other question of securing our privileges.

Mr. *Finch.* I conceive that when the king is in parliament, in person, or by commission, he may adjourn us, and that, to all intents and purposes, in some sense, is a prorogation; but I think the king cannot adjourn this house alone, without the adjournment of the lords also. For every commission of adjournment, or done by himself, in his royal person, is in law a prorogation, and all business ceases. 14 queen Eliz. the commons were sent for to the lords house, where the 'Custos Sigilli privati' adjourned the parliament, and you will find the adjournment entered from May to June. But though 'Custos Sigilli privati ex mandato Dominæ Reginæ adjournavit Parliamentum,' I cannot conclude from thence, that, because the king cannot call a parliament by the privy seal, yet by single command the lord chancellor, or lord keeper, &c. may not adjourn the house. From the reason of the thing done, it is your duty to obey the command, and it is no way derogatory to your privileges. If a question be put for an adjournment, it is no adjournment, till the Speaker pronounces it. You cannot adjourn yourselves above an ordinary time, without the king's leave. We are called by the king's writ, and should we adjourn the house for a week, or a month, and the lords do not adjourn, the confusion would be great; and to prevent it, our obedience to the king's command is necessary. Therefore in the king's printed Speeches, the king gives us leave, he directs it, and his consent to it infers that the king's leave is necessary. When sir John Finch refused to put the question, for reading the Remonstrance against the lord treasurer Weston, he was held in his chair, and how could he adjourn the house when held in his chair? the present debate is upon this point; whether, after the king's Message to command us to adjourn, we can proceed to debate any business? I believe we cannot. To that objected of 'a member's being beaten in his return from the lords house,' I thus answer: if adjournment be but one day in law, when the house meets again they may redress that violation of privilege. Suppose the king sends a Message to the house to adjourn at such a time, and in confidence of that adjournment, gentlemen go into the country, will you put it into the power of any numbers of gentlemen about the town to keep on debates, and proceed in business? if so, it will always necessitate the king to prorogations, and not adjournments, and so cut off all bills and business depending, and at your next meeting you must begin all again.

Serj. *Maynard.* I am sorry to hear things put in this debate neither for the advantage of the crown, nor this house. By the debate, the matter is thus: the king's pleasure of adjournment, being signified to the house, the house must immediately adjourn, without proceeding farther in any business whatsoever. I have attended all the precedents the Speaker has cited, with great care, diligence, and fidelity. I find not, in any proceedings, after king James, this case put into the books in terminis. But we speak not now of the king's power of adjourning and proroguing the parliament, which is always done by record by the great seal, or done in the lords house, by the king in person, where it is entered as a record. The power of pronouncing the Adjournment is certainly not in the Speaker. If it were so, black may be made white, and white black. May not the house, in great humility, after the king has signified his pleasure of adjournment offer him reasons for sitting a longer time? and how can you do that, if adjournment must be made 'immediately' upon signification of the king's pleasure? there is no way of adjourning or dissolving the house but by record. I am bound, as I am the king's serjeant, by oath, to maintain the prerogative, and I am under another obligation here, as a member of this house, to maintain your privileges, which I will do with my tongue. If this be, shall the house be adjourned, and not adjourned? shall the Speaker do it, and the house not do it? when the king opens a parliament, what does the Speaker first crave? liberty of speech. The king calls us, by writ, 'Nobiscum consulendum,' and how can treating be without speaking? the case may be of such an importance, after adjournment signified, as to induce an humble Address to the king from the house; and how can that be done, if the house cannot speak? I have heard say, in former times (though not in so good ones) 'What if the Speaker have a dormant Message to adjourn the house?' I am obliged to speak what I have done, come what will come of it. If the whole house conclude the thing, there is no wrong done. I have sat here in several tormenting debates, and never so unnecessary as when started between the king's prerogative, and the people's liberty, which I take not to be the true state of the question before you.

Mr. Solicitor *Winnington.* I am obliged to maintain the king's prerogative by the place I hold, and the privileges of this house as a member of it. I will first state that which we all agree to, and then that wherein we differ. The king's prerogative is undeniable, of adjourning, proroguing, and dissolving of parliaments. The lords house is a court of record, as to writs of error, &c. This house is no ourt of record, because it can give no oath, but I am unwilling to say what this house cannot do. The present case is a tenderness about our privileges. All are satisfied that the debate concerning ourselves is not worth the while. As to the king's power of Adjournment, &c. he may do it in person, and by commission; and that adjournment will be to our disadvantage, as many learned men say, it amounts to a prorogation,' and so you may lose the advantage you now enjoy by adjourning yourselves, by the king's command. I find the matter thus stands upwards of 50 or 60 years. It is hard to find any adjournment by the king's command, but always by the great seal, by commission under the broad seal, not by way of message, the king speaking then by record. This adjournment by message is for expedition sake. Though several ages may differ in form, yet the rule of right is still the same. Many times a message of adjournment is sent by sign manual only, to prevent the ceremony and state which (being done under the great seal, in the lords house,) it would occasion. The king's pleasure under his sign manual, is represented as a 'Summum jus,' and to be obeyed as a matter sent by the great seal, for in half an hour's time the great seal may be had to do it. I find that Mr. Waller puts great weight upon liberty of speech, and says, 'Would you have the house melt their privileges into the Speaker's chair?' It is possible you may not adjourn upon the king's command, but it is probable you will, because the king in a short time may compell it. If this question be put, that has been proposed, it must be for some good end, or to some purpose. No ancient parliament-man can say that ever such a question was proposed. I fear it will prevent good correspondence betwixt the king and us. To say that the parliament is willing to sit some days longer than the king has signified they should, looks as if we would take a liberty to do what the king would not have done, and so the consequence must be the adjournment by the great seal, (and not by message) or the king in person. Therefore I press for a good correspondence, that we may always comply with the king's message for Adjournment, having always done it. As for sir John Finch's case, should the Speaker say, 'he had a Message from the king, and he would adjourn the house,' or say 'That he had a private command from the king to do it,' there would be no end of that. But when the king sends a Message for Adjournment, under his sign manual, when was it ever denied? All that I propose is that jealousies may be laid aside betwixt the king and parliament. The manner of the king's proceedings in these cases is not as between man and man; which makes many a plausible argument in this case fall to the ground. The thing was never contradicted, and we argue but for what is not *tanti*. It looks as if there was a difference betwixt the king and parliament, and I would have no question put upon it.

Mr. *Williams*. Though I have not a gown on with tufts, [reflecting upon the Solicitor's gown,] and am in no office of the crown, yet I am bound as much by my allegiance to preserve the prerogative of the crown, as if I had. It is agreed on all hands, that the king may adjourn, prorogue, and dissolve parliaments. So there needs no dispute of adjournment and prorogation; it is well understood, so that the king cannot adjourn one house, and suffer the other to sit. Every step the king makes in an adjournment, is matter of record. The king may adjourn the terms, but it must be in form regularly, by writ under the great seal, read in the court sitting, and then the adjournment is pronounced, and nothing can be done afterwards. But this is still by matter of record. But consent is implied by it, express or tacit. That which provoked gentlemen at these last adjournments was, that several gentlemen stood up to speak, and the Speaker would not hear them speak. I am for the question.

Col. *Birch*. Those that spoke most to the point have industriously avoided the sore place, relating to the king's power. But if this matter perpetually must be a difference, the argument goes the other way. It was told us, upon making our last Address to the king, 'That there was no such thing ever done, but when swords were drawn;' but we might then have showed precedents of such an Address, if they had been required. Had we then presented the king with these precedents, to clear ourselves in that matter, we possibly might not have had such a Message at last. Suppose any gentleman can tell us of any exploit of the French king, and an adjournment is commanded, must we not debate it? The word of 'adjourning immediately' has been used but twice in my time; and I am always jealous of a new word. Must the king and kingdom be in danger, and we not debate it? No doctrine can be more dangerous to create a misunderstanding betwixt the king and us. I have heard here, formerly, that the lords and we sat together, and one adjournment, or prorogation, served the turn for us both. If the lords cannot be adjourned without their own consent, (as, it seems, they have entered it into their books) and if we may be adjourned without our consents, then there is a clear alteration of the government. We cannot be supposed to disobey the king's command, but if it be to save the king and kingdom may we not debate it? I would not have the lords and us upon two bottoms in this matter.

Sir *Philip Warwick*. I believe it not intended, but this may prove *insidiosa quæstio*; this has made me in my heart against this question. The lords did never, in any age, refuse to adjourn, when the king signified his pleasure to them by a minister of state. It can never be found that the lords denied it. I would avoid the question, and adjourn the house.

Sir *Wm. Coventry*. I am glad that this debate is separated from your own person, Mr.

Speaker. If the debate has held so long, it is some excuse to the Speaker, that it was a doubtful case. The king who calls us hither by record, sends us not away but by record. If the king required so immediate an adjournment after signification of his pleasure, as some gentlemen would have it, we needed not have come hither, but it might have been done in the Banquetting-House. That point of the king's power of adjourning the house is out of doors, and yielded on all hands. But I hope the king has never had, nor will have occasion to suspect the obedience of this house to his commands. Those kind of adjournments from day to day, and time for eating, and drinking, and keeping holidays, are as ancient as ever since parliaments have sat. But it must be understood, that the house has that power *cum grano salis*. We cannot adjourn for any long time. The point then is, that the act of adjourning is purely the act of the house, when done here. That we must obey the king is clear, but how this obedience is to be performed is the question. If by the pronunciation of the Speaker alone, without direction from the house, it is dangerous to the whole constitution of parliament. If after 12 of the clock no new business is to be started (which is an Order, and the Speaker has the house on his side) and the Speaker rises up to adjourn, and will hear no man speak, though the matter be of ever so great an importance, or the consequence extraordinary, surely you would not suffer it. Any inconvenience of refusing an adjournment, when commanded by the king, is answered by a gentleman of the long robe, viz. 'The king in half an hour may do it, by commission under the great seal.' Suppose an Act of Recognition should pass, or the taking the Oath of Allegiance and Supremacy, the question must be put three times, according to order; and can any man imagine there will be a negative? There will be terrible inconveniences, if it be the other way. Some gentleman may rise to speak, not to hinder nor oppose the command of adjournment, but if heard speak, would have moved for the adjournment. It is a fundamental rule of the house, 'that the house cannot be concluded in any thing as long as any gentleman stands up to speak.' That respect is had to the gentleman that stands up, to suppose, that possibly he may say something to give you new light into the matter coming to the question, so as to change the whole thing. It is not known what a gentleman will say, till he speaks. But if the Speaker will not give leave to the house to vindicate their obedience, here is such a power taken from you, that the Speaker, by the same reason, may take the thanks to himself that the whole house deserves for their obedience to the king's commands. I desire that the question may be put.

Mr. *Waller*. 'Abusus juris non tollit jus,' Much more the imagination of it does not. I would willingly have these shackles from our heels, before we go about to defend our neighbours. This is not the way to have a good understanding betwixt the king and us. Will the Speaker make children of us in the Adjournment? They are asked, 'Will you be baptized into this faith?' But not without godfathers. The king says, 'we shall adjourn ourselves,' and the Speaker does it.

The house was then adjourned, on a division, 131 to 121, but not the debate, and no question was passed upon the matter of the debate.

Debate on a Supply for carrying on the War with France.] Feb. 13. The house went into a grand committee of Supply.

Sir *George Downing*. You have voted that the house will give the king a Supply, to support his Alliances. Now the question is, what is to be given to carry on 90 sail of ships, and 30,000 landmen. This being so, charge so much, (that that lies before you is not a mere speculation,) for what time you will make provision for this charge. I wish our end may be obtained by a peace, but I would as little get into a bad peace, as any man here. If now we go away, and provide not for the whole charge, and come back again for the remainder, will that be done like provident men? I would provide for the whole charge of the thing. Christmas seems a more rational time to calculate to, for then the measures of princes are changed for the following year, and it is not prudent to run into arrear till then.

Mr. *Waller*. I look upon union betwixt the king and his people to be of as much consequence, as the sum to be given; therefore, for God's sake, let us lay aside all distrust of the king. The rule of the government is for us to assist, and the king to make peace and war: let us rely upon him, and I hope for good success. I hope that tomb we have voted to be erected for the late king will bury all the jealousies betwixt the king and us.—There was a great silence for some time.

Mr. Sec. *Williamson*. Whilst we sit still and say nothing, you must do something in the Chair, or we shall do nothing; you must either come to a question, as the Estimates are given in, or go upon a sum in gross. I have said something to day, and on other occasions, for the king's Supply to maintain his alliances, and the king would not have it, at present, nor will more be taken than in reason shall be seen necessary to keep this great force on foot, but till you may meet again. But a less sum (to the ensnaring the hand that takes it) than the king can comfortably proceed, and go on with in this great thing, I hope you will not think of. If there be such a lethargy upon men, they must be waked. The sun shines, sets, and rises, and things go on, as if we were careless, and understand it not. If this war must cost us so much per mensem, the first day's journey is always the longest, and if you consider so much for the months forward, let some gentleman come to a sum by the months, or a gross sum upon the months, as you shall see cause for it hereafter.

Mr. *Powle.* I wonder not at the silence of the committee, if every man is in the dark as well as I. I am so much in the dark, that I see not whether we shall have war or peace. The complection of affairs seems rather inclined to peace; and I see not the end of the war, by what fell from the honourable persons the other day, only in making this war to impose peace upon the world. If that be so, the question is, who is our enemy? If the confederates refuse to join with us in it, for ought I know, we shall have war against them. If that matter be not clear, I know not what to give. The honourable persons know what is spent, and is likely to be spent. If they will charge themselves on their reputations, that it will be such a war as will please us, then I would give to maintain it. But I think there seems some flagging in what was formerly told us. When that is cleared, I shall be as ready as any man to give Supply.

Sir *Thomas Meres.* I hear it complained, 'That nothing is said in this matter of Supply, &c.' You were told of 500,000*l.* as a motion. If the nation be in war, and at stake, no doubt but those here will go through stitch with it. And I doubt not but that some will do it. But to show frankness, and discharge my conscience, if it shall be a war to purpose, (but, as it is said, in case of refusal of the French to give towns, it may be a peace for Holland) because I will not spend your time idly, if we give 500,000*l.* in case there be war, we give to purpose.

Mr. *Garroway.* I hear it said, That there is no proposition made, &c. but we have sat so long, and if the danger be so great as is told us now, gentlemen should have told us of it sooner, and we would have named a sum. We have made the French king an idol, and we must worship him, and he must scourge us. If 250,000*l.* be too little if we have war, if it be peace it is every penny too much.

Mr. Sec. *Coventry.* I aver to you that we are not a hair's breadth towards a peace with France, and the king has not consented to a cessation of arms, nor any thing.

Sir *Henry Capel.* I would not give such a sum as may make a peace, and pin the basket there. Till we have a war, let us give in some proportion to the noise abroad. I move therefore to cut the thing in the middle. 600,000*l.* may happen to be intended, when 500,000*l.* was moved for and a million moved for. Therefore I move for 800,000*l.*

Col. *Birch.* I would have a word put into the question, viz. 'For maintaining a war against the French king.' I believe the money will be for a war, or kept for some other use. It is too great a thing to be jested with, and you cannot be looked in the face, if it be not done according to the bill.

Mr. Sec. *Williamson.* The purport of those words is no more than what is understood to be the sense of the words and intention of the order you sit by. Though I take not the words to be of a different sense, and I am not against them, yet you must go to the house for leave for the addition of them to the question. 'To enter into a war with the French king," is no more than 'to support the alliances.' If the words be insisted upon, we must go to the house for power to add them to the question.

Sir. *Tho. Clarges.* It is not fit to have the words in the question, 'to support Alliances with the States General,' because you are told that the Treaty is not yet confirmed, and it is strange to have it in an act of parliament.

The *Speaker.* I think it will consist with your order, though it be not in the words of your order. If you will give me leave to take notice of the order of your proceedings, the debates have been upon two sums, &c. I could have wished you had proceeded in another method. In this there is but one way of raising this. When several sums are proposed, and these, debated, the least sum is first put to the question; and then the other sum likewise in competition with the greater sum. So then the competition in the debate is between 600,000*l.* and a million. The other sum of 800,000*l.* interloped. I am never for so great a sum as will fright the people, nor so little a sum as is not to be depended upon by our allies. Shall the ships and men be raised in earnest? That will cost 3 millions, and you give but 600,000*l.* The king has made those Alliances upon our actual engagement and assurances of assisting him only, and, after a computation of so much, you come on with 600,000*l.* There would be no difficulty in this, if the question was betwixt the king and the people only; but others are to take measures too by it, and if you lessen it, they must seek it elsewhere. No man that hears me but will say, that it is an unnatural step to lower the king of France by distrust amongst ourselves. Distrust is a weed apt to grow here, and those, not under the duty we are will despise him; and therefore I never think it will proceed from this house. The greatest consent has been to a million, and will the king part with this duty and loyalty for a million? The king must never look you in the face again upon this cheat, that no particular man would go about to get money by. I will say nothing of the willingness of the nation to lend money, so bit by public faith, but they would caution such a sum of money as to make your coming again necessary. I would have this his act, not ours, not the result of his necessity but your duty, and not to perpetuate ourselves. We must trust the king, and you injure your question by sticking on it so long, and therefore I would have you put it.

Sir *Tho. Meres.* I affirm it to be order, that, if several sums be put to the question, you must put the least sum first, and so on; but if gentlemen would put 700,000*l.* afterwards, I do not say that question must be put. If I may have leave, I will say a short word to matter of trust. We may be trusted by the seamen. Foreigners may trust us; they have no cause to distrust us: betwixt the king and us it is the most valuable and worthy thing. I recommend it to the ministers, that, when the king has said it, though in a little matter, I am glad it is thought of such a value, and I hope no man thinks much to hear me, but if this has not been so formerly, it is none of our fault. I shall never lay it to the king. I could instance in three points they are ill plants. I shall not mention them. I could rather wish there was no appropriation of this money for ships. I should be rather glad of it. Trust is the best and noblest jewel of the crown.

Mr. *Mallet.* I agree not with the Speaker, that a sum, having been named, may be waved, and not put to the question. As to all other parts of the Speaker's discourse, in florid language, he says, 'Alliances are made;' but yet there is no discovery of them; but by woeful experience we have found vast deviations of money, and that makes me more cautious. I will say no more.—The question being put for 600,000*l.* it passed in the negative. The question for 800,000*l.* passed also in the negative.

Resolved, "That the sum of one Million be raised, for enabling his majesty to enter into an actual War against the French king." Which was agreed to by the house.

Debate on raising the Million—Tax upon New Buildings.] Feb. 19. In a grand committee on the Supply, on the manner of raising the Million, &c. A motion was made to lay part of the Tax upon New Buildings, &c.

Sir *Tho. Clarges.* I would know what new foundations have been since 1672. Lately, upon trial at law, lord chief justice Hale did declare it legal to build, where foundations were laid. And why may not a man make the best of his own land?

Sir *Tho. Littleton.* You eased London, and laid the tax upon Middlesex, by reason of these New Buildings; and so they are taxed already.

Sir *Nick. Pedley.* New Buildings were declared general nuisances in king James's time. They would in time make London too big for the whole body. You may well give a year's value upon them towards this charge.

Mr. *Garroway.* Young gentlemen, come lately into the house, flatter themselves that this may save their land in this tax. It is now 16 years experience that when we come to result, the thing, I believe, will be upon land; and that is ready calculated for you.

Mr. Sec. *Williamson.* These New Buildings are one of the banes of the country; they draw away all your tenants, and must not these lands supply your present occasion by way of penalty? Buildings may give something, &c. Those that hire them pay dear, and those that buy them. The owners having made profit of them, to the nation's injury, ought to bear some part of the burden. To lay not more upon land than what will come in upon land, is a necessary caution for this great work.

Serj. *Maynard.* The question is, where you will lay this tax. A certain sum is most certain to be raised, and most equal. Ever since I have known the law, and practised at the King's Bench, I never knew any general, but this of New Building declared a nuisance. Building itself is no nuisance, but it being an inconvenience to the civil government, is the greatest nuisance that ever was. Though the court of Star-Chamber in some things was a grievance to the nation, and the king could not make a thing unlawful to be lawful by prerogative, yet the Star-Chamber construed the increase of New Buildings to be a contempt, to do an unlawful thing, when there was a proclamation to the contrary.

Col. *Birch.* If I were sure we should have no war, I would charge land without any more ado. But if gentlemen have a clear sight in this great matter, there is nothing to make you low and contemptible to your enemies, but charging your land. If once you make a concurrent tax upon land, the French king will not be afraid of what you can do. I am for charging land, when we come shoulder to shoulder with the enemy. Till then it will be but vain to charge land. In the body politic it is as in the body natural. If the money does not circulate, all will fly to the head, like the blood, and kill presently. If those at the helm do not consider to bring the blood round again, the many consequences will be fatal. If you lay this tax upon land, the first six months perhaps may come in, but the second six months will sink a third part of the value of the land: and cattle and corn will give nothing. I would have this seriously thought of; there can never be war, if this money be raised by land-tax. I take this as before you; let New Buildings go as the least of evils; keep the tax from lands. I was here in a Convention in 1654, about paying some debts contracted for the navy. (I never saw so many wise men together.) And then it was said, and said again, 'that New Buildings were nuisances,' when all was fair green fields at St. James's.

Mr. Solicitor *Winnington.* I stand up, in the main, to ease land. But I think there is a mistake in this of new buildings, &c. It is the interest of the house to establish the durable interest of the nation, the freeholder. This debate is charging new buildings, and the reason in the debate is, 'that they are a common nuisance.' Though I am not of the coif, yet I will presume to offer my reasons. A common nuisance is not dispensible but by act of parliament, and is 'a detriment to all the king's subjects.' 27 Eliz. 'No buildings were to be within such a distance of London whatsoever.' But that was but for a number of years. I never knew a nuisance enacted perpetual, but that of exportation of leather, and importation of Irish cattle. When the act was expired, notice was taken of the contempt of it, against a proclamation. When Essex-House was to be pulled down, the society of the Middle Temple thought it an inconvenience. They had the best counsel they could get, but were forced to sit down with as good a composition as they could get. The first cause I ever was of was that between lord Clare, and Clement's Inn. Now they are not a nuisance. Yet there is reason why they should be charged. I think, a very young man may remember the increase of buildings about London. Nothing decays rents in the country like new buildings about London. Labourers in the country, at 6d. and 8d. a day, come here, and turn coachmen and footmen, and get a little house, and live lazily; and in the country the farmer is constrained to pay 16 or 18d. a day through the fewness of workmen, and therefore can pay less rent. They will leave the country for better wages. Sumptuous houses are a great invitation to gentlemen of quality, and their wives, to come to London, where they live better, and more at their ease and content, than with a greater number of servants and expence in the country.

Mr. *Garroway.* I look upon this tax as unjust, and therefore I am against it. I am taxed to the utmost in the country. If you will say, 'Tax them at the rate of the city of London by reason of their trade, but if for their monies because they have built houses,' I know not, but by the same reason, you will tax all men that have raised estates since the king came in and had nothing before, as if they were Rosicrucian Knights that had got the Powder of Projection.

The first question was put, "Whether one half of the full yearly value should be charged upon all the Buildings erected upon new foundations, without the city of London, and within the weekly Bills of Mortality, since 1630, except such as were demolished by the late fire;" which passed in the negative. The second question, "Whether upon Buildings, &c. since 1640;" passed also in the negative. The third question, "Whether upon Buildings, &c. since 1656;" passed in the affirmative, and was agreed to by the house.

Debate on the Re-assumption of Crown Lands.] Feb. 20. In a grand committee on the Supply—On the Re-assumption of Crown-Lands.

Sir *Cha. Wheeler.* The duke of Buckingham had 30,000*l.* a year of the crown-lands granted to his father, &c.

Serj. *Maynard.* King Ch. i. granted many lands to the city of London. Those that bought these lands were so wise as not to keep them. Consider from what time you will make this Re-assumption. That is one consideration. As to tenants that have bought those lands, will you make a distinction of service? Some have done great services for the crown, and have had those lands for a reward: and have not those that purchased been invited by you? 80,000*l.* a year was sold, by act of this parliament, of the king's Fee Farm Rents. If you shall undo the owners of these lands, without any way of consideration, it will be very hard.

Sir *Tho. Mompesson.* To put this in a method, will take more time than you have to spare. There is a stronger consideration for this of Re-assumption, &c. than the other of New Buildings, and I would have some consideration of that.

Col. *Birch.* They were chiefly rents bought in the late king's time: but I can show forty times the value now upon improved value. What has been disposed of by act of parliament cannot be touched, and I lay that aside, and it is not considerable in comparison of the others. Kings rarely come to parliament to enter into war: formerly they entered first into war, and then came to the parliament for aid to maintain it. I have heard from serj. Maynard, 'That acts of parliament confirm sales, &c. from such a time:' but none from the 1st of James. Now to make an Act of Re-assumption, from so long a time, would make an earthquake. We have found that deans and chapters' lands were sacred; they were restored, &c. I had bought some, but now I have none: the crown lands are in so many hands now, that it is not practicable to re-assume them, from 1st king James; and not one part in ten is alienated for the tenth part of the value. If you please to put those lands, at a two years value, towards this tax, with a non obstante, where there is an act of parliament for confirmation of them, I think it reasonable.

Mr. Sec. *Coventry.* Either these men that have these crown lands came lawfully by them, or unlawfully. It is not fair dealing to take from the king, &c. and confirm it to parties: if they are lawfully seized of these lands, I know not why they should be taxed for them.

Sir *Tho. Meres.* Those that have got on a sudden into great wealth and rents, I would have taxed.

Sir *Tho. Lee.* I think it as great a crime to take away the support of the crown, as to do a thing against the government, like that of New Buildings. The state of the case is quite altered. The king, at his coming in, was possessed of a great quantity of land: I think, of 150,000*l.* per annum. This, together with Excises, and 1,200,000*l.*: and then the solicitor, general Finch said, 'it was all you had to give, and all the king could ask of you;' and since that, the king has had the Chimney Act. An estimate was then brought into the house, it seems for no other purpose than for people to beg them, and the other revenues. And now the king 'cannot speak nor act, &c.' because all the Revenue is gone away. These are arguments why you always must give, and it always must be begged. These lands cannot be given without act of parliament, but re-assuming entirely is a great consideration; but this is only to take from them that have got it, out of what you have paid. Put the question then, 'Whether these lands shall bear any part of the tax;' and how much, is an after consideration.

Mr. *Sacheverell.* I think these revenues are not to be alienated on any terms, and if gentlemen look upon the grants as good, I am not for charging them to confirm them by it. If you intend to re-assume all the crown revenue, not granted by act of parliament, I am for it. But I would have an act also, to make it penal for the future to obtain such grants, and to make the crown lands unalienable for the future: I am for that.

Sir *John Knight*. Some would willingly give three years purchase to have these lands confirmed to them, and I would have them re-assumed that they may ease us in the burden of our taxes. In Cornwall there is 30,000*l.* a year of old rents, 100,000*l.* per annum. That is gone out of the crown, which was for the safety of it. You will find 30 several acts of parliament, in former kings times, for Re-assumption of the Crown Lands, and I would have it so now.

Sir *Tho. Meres*. I would not, by taxing those who have these grants in the crown lands, make a worse or a better title, but leave them in statu quo. I desire to take some profit of them now, and some another time. They may well contribute, for all their lands ought to go to the crown; but by this Act I would have them neither make a better nor worse step than before.

Mr. *Williams*. This charge you lay upon them is in respect of the profits they have already received. They have intruded into the king's possessions, therefore you do well to right the crown.

Mr. *Finch*. I am against the question, as it is stated. But neither myself nor any relation I have, has the least interest, direct nor indirect; not one foot of these lands I have, or am likely to have, and so I have no interest in the question, and may speak with the more freedom to it, because I am impartial. The king has an absolute right to these lands; he may sell, or give them—It is said, 'They have been given to deceivers, and obtruders. And this will confirm them—and the only intent 'to strengthen some letters patents.' If those letters patents are good already, they need no act to confirm them. Purchasers since 1660 have alienated those lands, by indefeasible title, and paid a consideration. Shall these pay for reversions that never have received the profits?

Sir *Edmund Wyndham*. Since this of Re-assumption, &c. has been started, I would have something done; people else will sell them, and then you cannot touch them again, when you meet. Therefore I would charge them now.

Sir *Gilbert Gerrard*. I would go farther than England: I would have the lands given away in Ireland re-assumed, and am ready to give my vote to the question.

Mr. *Powle*. This debate seems to me as if you had given so much the other day, that now you go a hunting where to find it. What may pass for good grants in Westminster-Hall, may yet be judged otherwise here. To take away the 'patrimonium sanctum,' was always esteemed a crime, and punished no where but here; legislatively, by acts of Re-assumption. But then they have come with fresh pursuit after them. Parliaments may have intervened. Formerly it has been upon a hot scent. Something of crime there is in it; but not such as to make the intruder punishable in Westminster-Hall. When multitudes offend, general punishment is not thought convenient in government. When the king came in, how many hundred thousand pounds were pardoned, which the crown had a right to! But when it is so populously concerned, viz. the whole government, it would do well that they paid a year's value, and that we confirm their titles. If you will go to a total Re-assumption of these lands, you will destroy thousands of families; and, I hope, by putting a year's value upon them, to have some account of them. In the late Convention, there was a question, that satisfaction should be made by the purchasers of the king's lands. It was then undertaken, that the king might have 100,000*l.* a year, and the purchasers be satisfied for what they had paid for the lands. There are not many hundred pounds a year of that left now in the crown. Now, if you will go back to king James's time, antiquity of possession does make a kind of right. There is always a distinction between the ancient patrimony of the crown, and lands which have fallen to the crown by escheats. That is a casual revenue, which the king has to give for reward of services done him. A year's value of lands given from the crown, from 1660, and a half years value of lands given, &c. from king James's time, I shall agree to.

Mr. *Waller*. I have heard that all lands were first in the crown, as in Doomsday book. Land-tax is a Re-assumption; we give back to the crown what came out of it. I cannot imagine how, if the common law cannot secure a man, an act of parliament should. Many men talk of Non obstante's, &c. The common law of England is of a second nature, a custom. I think, an act of parliament is no better than the common law, and I wonder at it, that, in king Stephen's great wars, there was not one tax laid upon the people. The reason was, because land was so in the crown; but at last land coming so out of the crown into the commons hands, they grew considerable. There may be extremities in all things. What a world of land would have come to the crown, if the Act of Oblivion, that sacred act, had not been made! I would have a committee to consider of such restrictions in this matter as may be equitable and just, and I shall approve of it.

Mr. *Garroway*. In this matter, I would stir nothing that may be any occasion of discontent from the people to the crown, as this may do. It may be of dangerous consequence, and I would be tender in it.

Sir *Ch. Harbord*. I have, both before and since I was the king's servant, endeavoured to prevent grants of the Crown Lands. But when they are passed, I would not have the king less just nor honest than another man. You would not pass them by act of parliament, by charging them as has been moved. There are two sorts of alienations of the Crown-Land, either by gifts and grants, or sales. In case of gifts and grants, you have confirmed some by acts, &c. And they are good grants in law. If you can in justice improve the crown-land, you may. But make justice equal, not to undo a million of persons. There were mighty grants formerly to the duke of Buckingham and the earl of Somerset. They were mighty things. Lord Dunbar had mighty things. All these were alienated to purchasers, freeholders, and the law cannot dispossess them. I would go no farther than those grants, &c. from 1660. But still that will not do your business to what these may bear. I would futurely easeland, but for the present this will raise you little or nothing.

Sir *Robert Sawyer*. Excepting two grants to the duke of Albemarle and the earl of Sandwich, I think there are no grants sold or given of the crown-lands that will in any measure do any thing. Grants that have reserved the old rents, I suppose, you intend not to meddle with. I believe they come not to above 10 or 15,000*l*. per annum, and to brand them criminal!—As the king has rewarded those who have suffered for him, will you let them who have bought and sold bishops lands, &c. go free? Will you let them alone? Whether are you going to raise 10, or 12,000*l*.? So small a thing! There are two sorts of patrimony of the crown. The ancient patrimony of the crown, and casual attainders and escheats. Escheats may be granted away. The ancient patrimony, &c. is of above 400 years, and it is a great difficulty to bring that back to memory. When the Conquest was, all lands were in the crown. And in the wars of York and Lancaster, the next succeeding king called all in question. When a weak prince had granted away the crown-lands, those sales have been called in question. And an act of such oppression as this will be cannot pass without some reflection upon us, who for some few instances of rewards, that the crown has given to persons of desert, &c. What is law, is law every where. When I consider how little this will raise, and what reflection it will be upon the government, I am against it. That casual revenue of escheats is kept separate in the exchequer from the rest of the revenue. I think it fit not to stir this matter, at this time of day.

Sir *Rd. Temple*. To say that no revenue of the crown is alienable, is strange; and if all the forfeitures in England were to be still in the crown, it would have all England in time. Ancient Demesne in the crown was never alienable. The late king Charles, out of a worthy resolution to pay his father's debts, sold some of the crown-lands, and, perhaps, he was deceived in the value. But since this king's time, you will find little alienated. You are now to consider, if it be reason to charge crown-land, sold since 1660, to be taxed distinctly from other lands. The king's revenue in 1660, then stated, was a great work. All that was done then was, not that the crown-lands should not be alienated, but that leases should be let upon improved value, and your Address to the king was accordingly. So that revenue made up, with the rest, 1,200,000*l*. a year. But I fear you will not find the moiety of the improved value reserved, upon leasing those lands. If you intend to see and examine that revenue, it will be a great trouble, and not to be done. Till I hear why these lands should be taxed more than others, I cannot give my consent. I would have you go on funds that you can raise money upon.

Sir *Ch. Harbord*. The king has granted me four manors of 400*l*. per annum each, not a farthing profit to me, as long as the queen lives. [This sir Charles said, upon Mr. Goring's alleging he had Crown-Lands given him.] As I have saved the crown 80,000*l*. at a time, I desired only a mark of my service, and that is all.

Sir *Tho. Meres*. Where the king's Revenue is alienated, I would have all that out, wheresoever it is.

The *Speaker*. This debate must end in a question. I am one of those that welcome all propositions that have a tendency to ease lands. That of the New Buildings, which you voted yesterday, if of as great a value as apprehended at first, may do something towards easing land, but this to-day will do less than nothing from a retrospect to 1660 only. I desire gentlemen to consider the bottom this stands upon, and the charge upon that alienation. The whole is not above 100,000*l*. a year, and some is disposed of by act of parliament. Some to the duke of Albemarle, and to the earl of Sandwich for his early repentance. Several lands, by act of parliament, have been commuted. Cast your thoughts a little, and remember that never any king came into his kingdom with such a debt of bounty as the king had to reward. Though their interest was given up for the public peace, yet some compensation they might expect of their lost fortunes, for preservation of the government; and you now lay upon them a charge for that loyalty. If you lay the charge on these gentlemen, it is unjust; if on the purchasers, it is so too. It will raise nothing, or worse than nothing, I would lay this debate aside.

Upon a division, &c. the Reassumption was laid aside*.

Feb. 23. Resolved, "That part of the million to be raised to enable his majesty to enter into an actual War against the French king, shall be raisedby a Poll-Bill." And a bill was ordered in accordingly†.

---

* This being in the committee is not mentioned in the Journal.

† The heads of this Bill were as follows: "All debts and ready money were taxed together with all persons exercising any public

Debate on the State of the Nation—War with France—Removal of Evil Counsellors, &c. *] March 14. Sir *Gilbert Gerrard.* The king has had unhappy counsels. I will not exasperate matters, nor ravel into counsels. I will only say, that if the advice of the parliament had been taken, we had not been in this condition. The strength of the French king, both by sea and land, is far beyond his neighbours. He has, at this time, no less than 100,000 fighting men under his banners. I am sorry we have neglected the Militia of the nation so long as we have done. Now things are mainly at the stake, and they might preserve us. Our out-works are already taken taken, the Spanish Netherlands, and, I fear, the French army is so great, that the prince of Orange cannot make head against it, and the worst of all is, we have jealousies amongst ourselves. Unless their be balsam to heal us, we are in a sad condition. I hope the wisdom of the house will resolve on such things as may give us cure; and I hope the lords, who are part of the government, will consider the State of the Nation as well as we. I will not sit down therefore without a motion, viz. "That we may humbly move his majesty to declare War against the French king." The consequence whereof will be the bringing in our allies, and we will venture our hearts and lives, and our purses will be open like Englishmen; and I hope for good success.

Lord *Russel.* * The gentleman that spoke

---

office, place, or employment, or receiving any pensions or stipends from his majesty; all judges, serjeants at law, counsellors, attorneys, solicitors, and scriveners; all advocates, proctors, and public notaries; and all persons practising the art of physic; all servants receiving wages; all persons other than such as receive alms of the parish, and their children under 16 years; all dukes, marquesses, earls, viscounts, barons, and their eldest sons; all baronets, knights of the bath, and knights bachelors; all esquires, or reputed esquires; all gentlemen, and reputed gentlemen; all widows according to the dignity of their husbands; every gentleman having an estate of 300*l.* all the dignified clergy; all persons holding two or more benefices with cure of souls, amounting together to the clear yearly value of 120*l.* all merchants, strangers, and Jews; all doctors of divinity, law, and physic, except doctors of divinity which have no ecclesiastical benefice; all merchants trading in the port of London, and not being free of the city; all merchants and others using any trade or manual occupation, and holding a house of 30*l.* per annum within the city of London, and bills of mortality; and all members of the East India and Guinea companies, for their share in the joint stocks of the two said companies."

* The commons, however, resolved that a day should be appointed to consider of the State of the Kingdom with respect to Popery. "And three days afterwards," says sir John Reresby, "my lord treasurer sent for several members of the house, and me among others, to the treasury chamber. His lordship there told us, it became all good subjects, to withstand all such motions and proceedings, which tended only to perplex the minds of men, and disturb the public tranquillity; in short, to raise jealousies of the government. The duke also among other things told me, it would be to disarm all Popish Recusants which he thought a ridiculous thing."

"We are farther told by sir John Reresby, that, on this day, several speeches were made in the house, full fraught with jealousies and fears; and particularly with regard to the Army at this time levying, as if it was rather intended to erect absolute monarchy at home, than infest the enemy abroad. Complaints were also made of evil councel, and counsellors; but nobody was named. It is reasonable to think that the immediate business of the day, was the farther consideration of the Supply, the far greatest part of which was still unprovided for; but the wayward disposition of the house inclined them to postpone the means, though they contended as warmly as ever for the end; making it a point to have the court at their mercy, rather than submit themselves and the nation to the mercy of the court. The debate was long, and gave rise to an Address containing the advice of the house, that the king would declare war with France. It was also stiffly contended for, that a part of this Address should be to intreat the king to put away those evil counsellors from about him, who had advised him to adjourn the parliament in May last, and thereby prevented a war with France all this time. But this being put to the question, it was carried in the negative by five votes only: and, whereas, the king had before reprimanded them for giving their Advice, without the concurrence of the lords, they resolved to remove that cavil by calling upon them to join in it: but whatever endeavours were used for that purpose, their lordships suffered the Address to lye before them, if not without notice, at least without answer." Ralph.

* Son of the earl of Bedford, who for his inviolable attachment to the Protestant Religion, by warmly promoting the Bill of Exclusion (as will appear hereafter), being tried and condemned for a pretended conspiracy against the king, was beheaded in Lincolns Inn Fields, on July 21, 1683. Bishop Burnet's character of him is as follows: "Lord Russel was a man of great candour, and of a general reputation; universally beloved and trusted; of a generous and obliging temper. He had given such proofs of an undaunted courage, and of an unshaken firmness, that I never knew any man have so entire a credit in the nation as he had. He quickly got out of some of the disorders into which the court had drawn him, and ever after that his life was unblemished in all respects. He had, from his first education, an

last, has made a good motion. I hope in time we shall justify ourselves from the aspersion that we did not give Money sooner. I would set the saddle on the right horse, and I move that we may go into a committee of the whole house, to consider of the sad and deplorable condition we are in, and the apprehensions we are under of Popery, and a Standing Army; and that we may consider of some way to save ourselves from ruin.

Mr. Sec. *Coventry*. I have been always as jealous of the greatness of France, as any man. There are already 48 companies of foot, sent over into Flanders: but what advantage shall we have more by a sudden declaring of war against the French king, before we are prepared? We have more merchant ships out, at this time, than any other nation. And this sudden Declaration will but give occasion to the king of France to fall upon us, before we are provided. What is it you can do by it? You are in treaties now, and will you overrun your allies? I would do as the Romans, who made Declarations of war jointly with their allies. That one thing I would know; what advantage we can have immediately to declare war, before we are in a posture for it? War will be declared, when we are ready for it; but if you advise the king as is moved, consider well what you have to do.

Sir *John Hotham*. I will not talk now like a Sophister, but like an Englishman. If our advice had been taken, which we gave honestly and worthily, things had not been at this pass. I am not worthy to sit here, if I do not second that noble lord's very worthy motion of going into a grand committee to consider the deplorable condition we are in.

Sir *Nich. Carew*. Coventry would know, why we are so hasty to enter into war. If we really declare war, we animate the confederates. If we go into a grand committee, I hope we shall find out the instruments of our long prorogations, and French counsels, as if they had been pensioners to the French king. Then the confederates will see that we are in good earnest. Let us enquire if we have not the same Counsels and Counsellors that we had before, and clear ourselves, and set the saddle on the right horse.

Sir *Philip Monckton*. I did not complain of my imprisonment in the Tower: I desired no man to complain of it. Neither shall I complain of my lord chancellor's putting me upon a recognizance. I will not complain of the king to his people: I would not be thought a man of petulancy, or a malecontent. It is said 'it is not now time to declare war.' Just at the beginning of these times, the late king was persuaded by his council that all was quiet in Scotland, and he never knew the Scotch army was marching, till they were upon the borders. I concur therefore with the motion for the house to go into a grand committee.

Sir *Ch. Wheeler*. It is moved, 'That you enquire into the king's Counsels.' I am old enough to remember that the enquiry into evil Counsellors began the late war, took off lord Strafford's head, and was followed by such an effusion of blood that I hope the like will never be again. I fear the consequence of this enquiry. I will not trouble you with old stories: if any person has any thing to say against Counsellors, he may now; but to go into a grand committee to set up a *si quis*, and make a noise abroad—if any gentleman will name persons, he may do it here.

Mr. *Vaughan*. Converse with persons without doors and within, and you will find dangers proclaimed at home and abroad. So sad an effect cannot be without ill causes. According to Wheeler's argument, let the consequence be ever so ill, of evil Counsellors, you must not examine them, because it had once ill-effect; and so the nation will never have remedy. I think we must see how we came into these misfortunes, before we get out of them.

Sir *John Ernly*. If I thought we were in jest, as some do, in this great affair of war, I would say nothing. The king is in actual war with the king of France, and will go, as far in it as you will enable him. He has at present no money, nor credit. I will say nothing to excuse any man. Let every tub stand upon its own bottom. I have a clear heart; our house is on fire, and will you not quench it, but enquire who set it on fire? I see no fruit of this proceeding you are upon, but confusion and misery.

Lord *Cavendish*. I am not of the opinion, 'that we are in jest.' I think some have been in good earnest. I would go into a grand committee, that we may enquire whether we shall go into a war, or no; for we are in the dark.

Sir *Philip Warwick*. I would rather that you took this matter moved into consideration to-morrow, than press it to day. I have feared this greatness of the French king these 40

---

inclination to favour the Nonconformists, and wished the laws could have been made easier to them, or they more pliant to the law. He was a slow man, and of little discourse: but he had a true judgment, when he considered things at his own leisure. His understanding was not defective: but his virtues were so eminent, that they would have more than balanced real defects, if any had been found in the other." His father was created by king William and queen Mary, marquis of Tavistock, and duke of Bedford, and among other reasons for conferring those honours, "This was not the least, that he was father to lord Russel, the ornament of his age, whose great merits it was not enough to transmit, by history, to posterity, but they were willing to record them in their royal patent, to remain in the family, as a monument consecrated to his consummate virtue, whose name could never be forgot so long as men preserved any esteem for sanctity of manners, greatness of mind, and a love to their country, constant even to death." See the Patent.

years; and in my last master's time, they had great correspondence in court, and found casements to look in at. If we apprehend our army's terrors to ourelves (and I have seen war to the ruin of the nation, and destruction of the prince) I have not a word distracted enough to express it. I am as willing (like Balaam's Ass) to crush my master's foot, when an angel stands in the way, as any body; but I am not for this question now.

The house then resolved itself into a committee, to consider the State of the Nation, and to present Remedies to prevent the Dangers thereof.' The question being put for making the Removal of those who had advised his majesty to the Answer of the Address in May last, from his Councils, part of the Address, it passed in the negative, 135 to 130, and a committee was ordered to draw up the Address.

Sir John Trevor afterwards reported from the said Committee, That they had taken the matter into their consideration; and had agreed to a vote: and the Vote being delivered in at the clerk's table, and twice read; was, upon the question, agreed; and is as follows. Resolved, &c. "That an Address be presented to the king, humbly to advise his majesty, That his majesty, to quiet the minds of his loyal subjects, and to encourage the princes and states confederated against the French king, will be graciously pleased, immediately to declare, proclaim, and enter into an actual War against the French king; and to give his majesty assurance, that this house will constantly stand by, and aid his majesty in the prosecution thereof, with plentiful supplies and assistances: and that his majesty be graciously pleased to recall his ambassadors from France and Nimeguen; and to send home the French king's ambassador."

The Commons' Address of Advice, that the King would declare War against France.] March 15. The said Address was reported, and is as follows:

"We your majesty's most humble and loyal subjects, the commons in this present parliament assembled, do, in all duty and faithfulness to your majesty's service, humbly present your maj. with this our Advice: that for the satisfying the minds of your good subjects, who are much disquieted with the apprehensions of the dangers arising to this kingdom from the growth and power of the French king; and for the encouragement of the princes and states confederated against him; your maj. would graciously be pleased immediately to declare, proclaim, and enter into an actual War against the said French king: for the prosecution whereof, as we have already passed a Bill of Supply, which only wants your royal assent, so we desire your maj. to rest constantly assured that we will from time to time proceed to stand by, and aid your maj. with such plentiful supplies and assistances, as your majesty's occasions for so royal an undertaking shall require. And because your majesty's endeavours, by way of mediation, have not produced those good effects your maj. intended, we do most humbly beseech your majesty, that you would graciously be pleased to recall your ambassadors from Nimeguen and France and to cause the French ambassador to depart from hence; that your maj. being publicly disengaged from acting as a mediator, or upon such terms and conditions as were then proposed, your maj. may enter into the war to no other end than that the said French king may be reduced into such a condition, as he may be no longer terrible to your majesty's subjects; and that Christendom may be restored to such a peace, as may not be in the power of the said king to disturb."

The Address was, upon the question, agreed to by the house. And it was resolved, That the concurrence of the lords be desired thereto. The Address was sent up accordingly, but it never proceeded further.

March 18. Resolved, "That such members as are of his majesty's privy council, do acquaint his majesty, that there is a Bill of Aid passed both houses, and ready for his royal assent."

March 19. Mr. Sec. Coventry delivered to the house the following Answer from his majesty:

"C. R. His majesty hath received the notice sent him by this house, that the Poll-Bill was now ready for the royal assent; which his maj. was well pleased to hear, and resolves to pass it to-morrow. His maj. desires this house to dispatch the rest of the Supply promised him, with all expedition. The sea and land preparations run great danger of being disappointed, if these supplies be retarded: and it would be a satisfaction to his maj. to hear from this house, that no more time should be lost in a work so necessary for the safety and reputation of the nation, as the finishing those supplies."

A Short Recess.] March 20. On a Message from the king, the house went up to attend his maj. in the house of lords; where he gave his assent to the Poll-Bill, &c. and made the following Speech;

"My lords, and gentlemen; I am so zealous for the good of the nation, that it shall be your fault, and not mine; if all be not done as should be, for the honour and safety of it: and I must tell you, there must be no time lost."

March 26. The house addressed the king for a short Recess; to which his majesty agreed, and appointed them to adjourn to April 11.

Sir Robert Sawyer chosen Speaker.] April 11. The house being met, Mr. Hen. Seymour, one of his majesty's bedchamber, and uncle to Mr. Seymour, the present Speaker, acquainted the house, That he had received information by a Letter by appointment from Mr. Speaker, who at present is at his house in the country in the interval of the sitting of the house; that he was there suddenly seized with a sickness and distemper, so violently, that he was confined to his bed, and not able to write himself; but so soon as it should please God to restore him, he would return to their service. And Mr. Secretary Coventry acquainting the house, That his majesty had received advertisement, that Mr. Speaker laboured under so great an indisposition of health that he could not possibly, for a long time, attend the service of the house; and to the end the public affairs might receive no delay; his majesty gave leave to the house to chuse a new Speaker; and to present him to his majesty on Monday next: and the house being satisfied, that, by reason of the Speaker's great indisposition, uncertainty of return: and in order to public affairs, it was very necessary a new Speaker should be chosen: thereupon Mr. Sec. Coventry proposed, and recommended, sir Robert Sawyer as a person fit, for his ability and learning, to be Speaker. And sir Robert Sawyer standing up, and making a speech to excuse and disable himself; and some other person being in nomination; and a debate arising; and a question demanded to be put, Whether sir Robert should be chosen Speaker or not; and who should put that question; a precedent was then produced out of the Journal of 1. Jac. where the clerk of the house, in like case with this, did, by direction of the house, make and put the question; and the present clerk being now directed and demanded so to do; and the mace not being in the house; he did humbly leave it to their consideration, whether it could be so regularly done, till the mace were brought into the house: and upon some debate had, it was thought fit, and the mace was, by their command, brought in by the serjeant, and laid under the table: and the house then again directed the clerk to make, and put the question: which he did, pursuant to the former precedent; viz. 'All that will have sir Robert Sawyer Speaker, say, yea:' Which being carried in the affirmative, by much the greater number of voices, without any division of the house, sir Robert was thereupon conducted to the chair by Mr. Sec. Coventry and Mr. Sec. Wililamson: and being there placed, and the mace then upon the table; after some pause, he stood up, and made a gratulatory speech to the house for their favour and respect to him; desiring their leave to intercede with his majesty to excuse him from undertaking so great and difficult an employment; which, by reason of his indisposition of body, and want of experience, he conceived himself not able to perform: but, if his excuse should not be admitted, he would serve them with all integrity, to the utmost of his capacity and ability: and desired the help and assistance of the members, who had been long versed and experienced in the proceedings of the house. And the house, having upon the question, ordered the clerk to enter the manner of chusing the Speaker; without proceeding to any other business.

The King proposes an Adjournment.] April 15. The house, on a Message from the king, attended him in the house of lords, where the Speaker elect was approved and allowed of by his majesty. Being returned, the Speaker, having taken the chair, acquainted the house, That it was his majesty's pleasure that both houses should adjourn themselves till the 29th.; and that the reason of such Adjournment was to this effect: "That the Dutch ambassador had not at present full instructions; and that the affairs concerning the Alliances were not yet so ripe, or fit to be imparted to both houses as it was expected they might have been upon the last adjournment."

Debate on the proposed Adjournment.] Several motions were made, after this signification of the king's pleasure of Adjournment, as it were to gain that point, controverted in the former Speaker's time, upon this new Speaker: as that of bringing in sir W. Killigrew's Bill; another by sir Edw. Jennings relating to the Durham Election, and that the Committee of Elections might be adjourned, by Order, to prevent witnesses coming up, &c. But because the point might be thoroughly gained, the house fell into the following debate.

Col. *Birch.* I have been at many choices of Speaker's and am heartily sorry for the loss of Mr. Seymour. Though I have an honour for you, Mr. Speaker, (Sawyer) I hope Seymour may be well enough to come again to the chair. I must take notice that the Speaker ought to report the four things the king usually grants the Speaker, which he requests in behalf of the house, &c. I hoped not for a fortnight's adjournment; I feared it; but seeing that it is the king's pleasure, I humbly submit to it.

Sir *Tho. Meres.* This adjournment for a fortnight is hard. When we desired it for three weeks, it was not granted. The last recess, there were 18 private bills passed, and no public bills; and this fortnight might have been for public bills, and the Popery matter is upon the anvil, and adjourned to this afternoon by order, and by order we may sit, but we cannot go through with it to day. Therefore I would send to the king, before the lords rise, that he may be moved to let us sit. These are things which concern the nation vitally, to be done, and I would have something done of the concern of the nation.

Mr. *Sacheverell.* As I stand informed, our Message to the king was, 'to adjourn to as long a time as his occasions would permit. And now his great occasion is not ready for you, I suppose this adjournment to be an Answer to your Message. The king's occasion is not fit. But I doubt not, but if you signify to the king, that you have public business in your eye, which may come on till his great affairs are ready, he will give you leave to sit, And I move to desire the lords to concur with you in still sitting, That of Popery is so necessary to be considered, that it looks as necessary as the Army itself. I fear there is Money in this Adjournment, and I move that the lords concurrence may be desired.

Mr. Sec. *Coventry.* We are to adjourn

presently, upon signification of the king's pleasure, and I do not remember that, when the king has signified it, this was ever done before, unless in the Long Parliament.

Sir *Tho. Lee.* (Upon some calling to adjourn) Gentlemen know me too well to sit down, because they call 'Adjourn.' In king Charles's time, what is moved was not so unusual a thing moved as Coventry says. It was done twice. Country gentlemen's affairs will call upon them. We shall better understand who counselled the king to this, about midsummer, than now; and if there is nothing to be done, but giving Money, then it is very well argued for adjournment now. But I am sure it is for the king's service, that things depending should be pursued. And because the lords are not up, I would put the question.

Mr. *Williams.* It is said by Coventry, 'There is no precedent of this but in the Long Parliament,' In the Journal you will find that, 2 or 3 Ch. i. an Address was made to the king to prolong the time of sitting of the house; and the king granted it in some part. Something, surely, we may proceed upon for the public, as Popery, &c. without meddling at all with the affairs of the war. If what was represented at our last sitting, relating to Popery be true, for this very purpose I would address the king, that we may sit to examine this matter, it being so much for the safety of Religion.

Mr. Sec. *Williamson.* I can easily pardon the resentment of country gentlemen for their disappointment by this adjournment. But the king has not known this change of his mind four days. Saturday was the last day he despaired of keeping his mind in this matter. The king had it in his mind to alleviate and soften this disappointment, by speaking to you himself. We ought certainly to clear this matter of Popery, and time may be for that. Some complaints have been of this, and this afternoon something may be done. My reading is little, and my experience less, in the nature of this motion of an Address to the king for sitting a longer time. In the 18th of king James, there was something of this kind, but the lords did refuse to join with this house. I am extremely sorry that this happens in such a conjuncture, when there is need of all possible harmony. This is a disappointment that puts as much trouble upon the king, as upon any gentleman here. But I hope, by the time you meet again, the king will be able to finish the matter, so as to lay it open to you. For the king cannot make them certain. For the present, they are as bad as bad can be. But I hope gentlemen will excuse the disappointment, and adjourn.

Mr. *Vaughan.* This is matter of that fatality that I fear it will take up all your time, and none will be left for the concerns of the king and kingdom. It is an ill thing for us to go back into the country, and they to tell us, 'we must go again to make War, and give Money.' There is a precedent of addressing for farther time, in the 9th and 13th of king James, and I doubt not but you will have the same return from this king that you had from king James.

Mr. Sec. *Coventry.* (They called out, 'He had spoke, spoke') No man can say I have spoke, when I stand up to explain myself. I have read that precedent of king James: the commons did represent to the king, 'That the time was not sufficient between the holidays, &c. to do the business before them, &c. But when the king has declared his pleasure for a speedy adjournment, the house never proceeded any farther.

Mr. *Powle.* I will only tell you what amazes me extremely. On the 28th of Jan. the king told you, 'He had made Leagues with Holland, &c.' And Williamson tells you, 'Things are as bad as bad can be.' I would know how that comes about?

Mr. Sec. *Williamson.* It is better to have things upon certainty than uncertainty. There was a treaty, and is a treaty. Now we have made it with Holland, and come to the rest of the allies, Holland flies off from us; and that made me say, 'things were as bad as bad can be.'

Sir *John Coventry.* These kind of adjournments are very strange things, and this proceeds from your counsels to raise men against Magna Charta, and set up Popery. No man can bear this. If the king thinks we are not fit to serve him, I desire he may be moved for a new parliament, and new counsellors.

Sir *Tho. Lee.* The matter being so, that the lords are up, it is in vain to address the king. I shall observe, that now there is an alteration from former times; for then all the study was to make parliaments meet and rise with complaceny; but now it is quite otherwise. That is all the observation I will now make, and let us adjourn.

Sir *John Hotham.* Since it is concluded that the lords are up, we lose time to debate farther; only before we adjourn, I would remind you that, about a fortnight ago, there was a committee appointed to send the lords Reasons for present declaring War against the French, &c. I desire this, that we may not enter into a war merely because there are jealousies, &c. but that the Reasons may be obvious. I move that, seeing the house is of a mind for their Religion, a committee may sit in this interval to prepare those Reasons, about Popery, &c. that the nation may see that we come for something besides gratifying particular people.

Sir *Tho. Littleton.* I think, Hotham has made you a good motion. It was said 'that it was a Long Parliament precedent to have a committee sit in the interval of sitting, &c.' We still have a recourse to that topic; but the lords have sat upon several businesses, besides the trial of lord Pembroke; and it is dangerous for one house to sit, and not the other. A committee to sit, is not so dangerous, and we may have a committee to sit, if the lords sit.

Sir *Gilbert Gerrard.* There are such a

multitude of Papists, and strangers, of all nations, that I would have a committee to sit, and draw up Reasons of our apprehensions of Popery, in this interval: and the house to be called over on Tuesday come fortnight.

Sir *Tho. Clarges.* If there be any doubt of a committee sitting in a recess of adjournment, there are divers precedents of it; and there is no doubt but they may sit.

Ordered, "That the Committee appointed to draw up Reasons for the Conference to be had with the Lords, concerning the danger the Nation is in by the Growth of Popery, do sit during the interval of the sitting of the house, to perfect the matters referred to them."

The Lord Chancellor Finch's Speech, demanding the Advice of both Houses relative to a League Offensive and Defensive with Holland.] April 29. The commons attended the king in the house of peers, where the Lord Chancellor, by his majesty's command, made the following speech to both houses:

"My lords; and you the knights, citizens, and burgesses of the house of commons; His majesty, having made a League offensive and defensive with Holland, and endeavoured to improve that league by entering into further and more general Alliances for the prosecution of the war, hath nevertheless thought fit, before he make his last step, to take the further Advice of both his houses of parliament, and resolves to govern himself by it. And to the end his parliament may be able to give a clear and certain judgment in this matter, his maj. hath commanded that the present State and Condition of Affairs should be fully and plainly opened to you. And this I shall do in a few words: —The first Address to his majesty from both houses was upon the 16th of March, 1676, wherein the dangerous Growth of the French monarchy being observed, and the conquests made in Flanders, together with the ill consequences arising from thence, his majesty is desired to strengthen himself by such stricter Alliances as may secure his own kingdoms and preserve the Spanish Netherlands. But this Address did neither desire, nor seem to intend, that his majesty should so suddenly and so abruptly depart from his figure of mediator, as immediately to become a party in the war, before any such Alliances were made. For this Address was followed with several other Addresses from the commons, in the months of March, April, and May following; all of them pressing his majesty to hasten this entering into such Alliances; and one of them particularly pointing at a League Offensive and Defensive with the States General.—And in truth, as no Alliances could well be made till we had consulted with Holland, so no entry could be made upon any alliance with Holland until the mind of the prince of Orange were perfectly known; for upon him would depend much of that certainty and secrecy, which was absolutely necessary to bring such a treaty to perfection: but the prince was in so great a hurry of business, and such a heat of action, that no time could possibly be found all that summer to enter upon this Treaty.—And yet, that no time might be lost, his majesty did all he could at home, to fit and prepare himself for such an alliance when the time should come: he repairs his old Fleet, buys in necessary stores for the Navy and Ordnance; and in this and other provisions for better securing his foreign Plantations and Islands nearer home, expended a great deal more than the 200,000*l.* which he was enabled to borrow upon the Excise; and if he could have then prevailed to have had the 600,000*l.* compleated as he desired, the expence of that in other stores and provisions, both for land and sea, would by this time have given an universal content and satisfaction.—Nor did his majesty rest here; but he continued still, during all the rest of that summer, to make all the steps he could towards an Alliance with Holland: to this end he did, in the month of June, send for his ambassador sir Wm. Temple to come to him from Nimeguen, in order to his being employed to negotiate with the prince of Orange, touching those measures which were necessary to be taken for the common safety; but the prince's continual action caused it to be deferred: and yet, in August following, the king appoints his ambassador Mr. Hide to wait upon the prince, and to know of him what course he thought best to be taken as things then stood; and to desire him, that he would either write his own mind, or send some person hither instructed with it, or come himself. The prince was pleased to chuse the latter.—By that conversation with his highness, his majesty quickly understood to what a low estate the affairs of Holland were reduced, and in what great disorder the rest of the Confederates were; they in Flanders totally desponding, and the people in Holland being violent for a peace; so that there seemed to be no other remedy or expedient left, but for his majesty to try whether a peace could be obtained upon reasonable conditions.—This being the main and principal point to which the king had all that year been earnestly solicited by the States, that is to say, in the months of Jan. May, and Sept. last, just before the prince came over; and his majesty had reason to believe that such endeavours would be grateful to the States, and took thereby an opportunity to engage the States, that, in case of refusal, they should enter into such an Alliance with his majesty, as might enable him to obtain his desires by force of arms; for his majesty did well perceive, that the States of Holland, whom he had so long found weary of the war, would never enter into any alliance with his majesty for the prosecution of this war without a prospect of a peace.—And, to convince the world that his majesty was resolved to espouse the interests of the States General to the uttermost, his majesty (who could not but see that the happiness and prosperity of the prince did very much depend upon the quiet and repose of those countries) did, in the time of their most pressing dangers, give his own niece in Marriage to the prince; which act alone was enough to extinguish the fears of all at home, and raise the hopes of all that were abroad. And with this assurance, and this evidence of the king's good intentions to the States, the prince returned.—And now, to the end it might be known whether his most Christian majesty would consent to such conditions of peace as might be grateful to the States, and that such measures might be taken as were fit, in case of refusal, conditions were prepared, and sent to Paris by the earl of Feversham in Nov. last; and in Dec. following, the earl returns with an Answer very dissatisfactory.—This ill answer being returned, the king his majesty hastened the meeting of the parliament, and proceeded to close up the Treaty with the States General for obtaining of those conditions by force of arms, which could not be obtained by fair means. And this is the League Offensive and Defensive made with Holland, and concluded in the beginning of Jan. last, which his maj. is graciously pleased may be communicated to the parliament, if they shall desire to see it.—And his maj. at the same time, and for the fuller satisfaction of his parl. and the better securing of his kingdoms in all events, did further take care to conclude another perpetual Defensive Treaty with the States General.—In execution of the Offensive and Defensive League, his maj. sent to the States, to have the number of forces by sea and land adjusted, and did agree what his own quota by sea should be, and sent over some forces into Flanders; and had sent more, but some difficulties were made on that side, which his majesty for the friendship's sake which he hath with them does not think fit to remember.—The next thing absolutely necessary to be done was, to have one common alliance for all parties to enter into, for the carrying on of the war, by disposing the several stations of the joint forces, by the general prohibition of commerce, and by providing against all possibilities of any separate peace.—For which causes, his majesty appoints his own commissioners to meet and treat with the foreign ministers: but, to the king's great disappointment, it appeared that the Dutch ambassador had no power to treat, which made the other ministers refuse to enter upon any discourse: and therefore, to obtain these powers to be sent, his majesty, besides the repeated and pressing instances of his own ambassador in Holland, was pleased to write himself to the states very earnestly in this matter.—At last, powers come; but then the ambassador wants Instructions, so that nothing at all could be concluded touching those points which were most essential and necessary to be settled between us, and which the king hath never ceased to press for to this very day. But hitherto the king finds, what he always feared, that the Dutch are making haste to get out of the war; and are so far from disposing themselves to enter into any new alliance for the more vigorous prosecution of it, that whether they will persevere in the League Offensive and Defensive which they have made with the king, or to what degree they will act if they should persevere, depends upon very many and very great uncertainties: for they are at this very time entered upon considerations of accepting such a peace as the Most Christian king hath thought fit to offer lately at Nimeguen, though it be without his majesty's consent or privity, and contrary to that league by which they stand obliged to him to prosecute the war, till a much better peace can be obtained.—To prevent this, the king hath sent an express, on purpose to know what they intend by this manner of proceeding, and to dissuade them from it, by letting them see that this will be as ill a peace for themselves and the rest of Christendom as their enemies could wish.—But the king as yet can receive no other account from them, but complaints of their great poverty, and utter inability to be at any further charge in carrying on the war. And the king is informed, by his ambassador, that they intend to send over an envoy extraordinary to his majesty, to beg his maj. to accept of these Propositions, to excuse themselves for this, upon the general impatience of their people. This is the state of the case; and thus it stands at this day between us and Holland, from whom we have little hopes now, that they should ever so far enter into this new and common Alliance as to make it quadrupartite. And now, upon the whole matter, the king demands your Advice, what may be fit for him to do in this difficult conjuncture; and resolves to pursue it: and therefore desires you to take this matter into your most speedy and most serious considerations."*

Ordered by the commons, "That the members of this house, that are of the privy council do desire his majesty, that he will be pleased to communicate to this house all such Leagues and Treaties as are mentioned in the Chancellor's Speech, or relating thereunto."

Reasons of the Growth of Popery.] The house then resumed the consideration of the State of the Kingdom, with regard to Popery, and received and approved the following

REASONS, to be offered at a Conference to be had with the Lords, concerning the Danger the Nation is in by the growth of Popery.

"The house of commons, taking into serious

* "No doubt, if ever his majesty was in earnest provoked against France, it was now; when they had not only belied him in their Declaration, all over Europe, but trifled with him in his Money Treaty. We are therefore to give so much the more attention to the scope of the lord Chancellor's Speech, which is very imperfectly touched on by Mr. Echard, and totally suppressed by Rapin, and every other historian. It is remarkable too, that Mr. North, when correcting the omissions of bishop Kennet, either overlooked it, or had no intelligence of this remarkable Speech." Ralph.

consideration the Dangers arising to this kingdom, from the restless endeavours of priests and jesuits, and other popish recusants, to subvert the true religion planted amongst us, and to reduce us again under the bondage of the Romish superstition and idolatry: and finding how great boldness they have assumed to themselves from the great remisness and connivency of his majesty's officers and ministers of justice, both civil and ecclesiastical; whereby so many good and necessary laws, heretofore made against them, have not of late times been put in any effectual execution: they do therefore think it requisite to apply some Remedy to this growing evil, especially at this time, wherein the unity of affections, and the mutual confidence between his maj. and his people does so much conduce to the preservation of the whole kingdom: and because they have found by experience, that all those applications they have formerly made upon this subject have not produced any effects answerable to their expectations; they have endeavoured to discover the Causes and Grounds thereof; which they conceive are principally these.—The difficulty to convict popish priests, by proving their Ordination by authority derived from the see of Rome, makes them more confident to appear in public, and perform their offices and functions without fear of punishment.—That Justices of peace are discouraged, because several of those that have been forward in executing the laws against papists, in such counties where they do most abound, have been turned out of commission, without any apparent cause; whilst others, suspected to be popishly inclined, have been continued in commission, or put in de novo.—That, in several counties, many protestant dissenters have been indicted, under the notion of popish recusants; and the penalties of the law levied upon such protestant dissenters; when the papists there have been either totally, or for the most part, discharged.—That the papists do evade the penalties of the law, by making over their estates by secret trusts, and fraudulent conveyances; and receive the profits of them to their own use and benefit.—Whereas in former times considerable sums of money were raised by the forfeitures of popish recusants, that now, by the remisness of some, and discouragement of others of his majesty's officers and ministers of justice, little or nothing is levied upon them, or likely to be levied hereafter, unless the care thereof be committed to particular commissioners in the several counties; and the money arising thence applied to some public use, for the advancement of the protestant religion; which may encourage persons to see it executed.—That persons are not discouraged to breed up their children, or to suffer them to be bred up in the popish religion; because they are as capable of inheriting the estates of their parents and relations, as any other of his majesty's protestant subjects.—The commons do therefore most earnestly desire your lordships to consider of the Dangers and sad Consequences that may befal this kingdom, by the spreading of that religion amongst us; and seriously and cordially to join with them, in removing these and all other impediments which obstruct the course of justice, and the due execution of the laws, either by expediting those Remedies which have been offered by them to your lordships, or by proposing such other as may be more effectual: and that this may be done with all expedition; because the commons cannot think it suitable to their trust, to consent to lay any further charge upon the people, how urgent soever the occasion be that require it, till their minds be satisfied, that all care and diligence is used to secure the kingdom, and prevent the dangers that may arise from the prevalency and countenance that is given to that party, by some more effectual course than hath been already provided."*

Debate on some Words that fell from Mr. Goring.] May 3. During the debate on the Treaties,

Mr. *Goring* said, 'I have heard many gentlemen on this side of the house make many complaints against the ministers of state for mismanagement: I desire they will first give a Test, that they do not desire to creep into their places; or that they may give security, that they will act better, if they come into their places. For my part, I see no ill these have done.'

Sir *Tho. Lee.* I would have that gentleman explain himself. He speaks of 'gentlemen on this side of the house having a Test.' They desire not to come into another man's office. I desire that Goring, who seems to like and know these counsels so well, will tell you who were against them.

Col. *Birch.* I was in hopes that Goring would have said something to have allayed this matter. When gentlemen, in this nick of time, and this vast business in hand, have such an affront cast upon that side of the house (though I was not on that side) it may be next on this side. Gentlemen must not say, as some did, 'No, no,' as if they were laughing in a play-house. I would have the house lay aside all debates, till they have satisfaction in this point.

Sir *Henry Capel.* I would not let these words pass, but write them down, and then afterwards proceed upon them.—The Words were then asserted, as Goring spoke them before.

Mr. *Goring* thus explained himself. I meant by what I said no particular person; and I am sorry if I gave the house offence.

---

* Sir W. Temple charges sir Tho. Clarges with having been the author of 'this peevish vote,' as he calls it, in spleen to the lord treasurer. He adds, 'it is certain no Vote could ever have passed more unhappily, or in such a counter season.' And again, 'in short, there was such a fatal and mutual distrust, both in the court and parliament, that it was very hard to fall into any sound measures between them.'

There was some debate whether his Explanation was satisfactory.—Sir Tho. Meres recriminating something that Goring had said, the other day, of the Committee of Popery,

Sir *John Talbot* said, If we call a gentleman to account for things said the other day, why may not the king call members hereafter to account for what they have said here? I will not justify what Goring has said, but I believe his excuse is satisfactory. I am for his withdrawing, but would have a question for it. I could not bear the misfortune to be under the displeasure of the nation. I think it is a misfortune. We must bear with one another, and not be extreme to mark what is done amiss.

Sir *Tho. Meres.* When Talbot condemns me for recriminating, and tells you of another thing likewise of this nature that he misliked, it is not orderly. I urged it not at all to the gentleman's prejudice, but to remind the Speaker and the house of the too great frequency of these things.

Sir *Rob. Howard.* I hear it said, 'It is a punishment and disgrace to withdraw.' If there be a disputable election depending, the gentlemen concerned must withdraw, and no man will say it is a punishment. I am on this side of the house, and I myself am in an office. This side is the major part of the house, and, for ought I know, here is a reflection on the whole house. The thing was ill done, and Goring tells you, 'he has liked all that the ministers have done,' when the commons of England have not liked it. For the indiscretion he has asked your pardon, and I heartily desire the house would give it him.

Mr. Sec. *Williamson.* These things are incident to any man, but should all things be taken notice of in great debates, business would never go on.

Sir *Tho. Lee.* There is more in this than in all the matter of the debate; but it must be a precedent for the future. Where the words are once written down, you cannot show me a precedent in the Journal that a question has been put for withdrawing; but it is done by direction of the Chair. I would not have it a precedent for future parliaments.

Sir *Geo. Downing.* So long as a gentleman will speak to it, he is not to withdraw. The gentleman is well descended, and but young in years and experience; and I desire the thing may go over.

The *Speaker.* If it be insisted upon, whether the house be satisfied, &c. he must withdraw.

Sir *Tho. Meres.* You state the question well, and then you go off from it. If the house be satisfied, there is no need then of withdrawing. You cannot let him be here present when the question is put. He may then vote to it, and it may come to a question, and therefore he must withdraw.

Sir *Wm. Coventry.* The words are stated and agreed, and the next thing is to consider the crime, and it is a most natural thing that the gentleman should not be present at the debate of this supposition of a crime.

Mr. *Goring* then said; 'I am sorry I have given the house occasion of this dispute, but since I find that my company is troublesome to the house, I will withdraw without a question.' And he withdrew.

Sir *Tho. Meres.* Alderman Foote said some words in the passing the Militia act, which gave offence; he had acknowledged the words, and was called in to his place, and the house admitted his excuse, 'that he was sorry he had given occasion of offence, &c.'

Sir *Chris. Musgrave.* As it was a great offence that Goring has committed, so he has given the house satisfaction by asking their pardon. I think it is satisfactory, and I would have you pardon him.

Sir *Tho. Littleton.* Alderman Foote was judged to have his reprimand on his knees at the bar; but in this I would not go so far. This gentleman (Goring) sat a great while in his place, smiling and laughing. (Some say, it is his custom.) One said, 'his words were not so black as those he reflected on.' It is an odd way this of excusing. The young gentleman is forward and zealous, but I would have no more said to him, but an admonition in his place to forbear the like for the future.

Mr. *Powle.* The words that fell from the gentleman were spoken immediately after what I had said; but I declare, that you may pass it over; and as Goring desires, 'there may be a Test against Offices,' so I desire there may be a Test against receiving Pensions.

Mr. *Howe.* I am glad to hear the word 'Pensions.' We are named to be the greatest rogues and villains, and it is said commonly, 'we are the greatest in nature, and that we take Money to betray our country.' I would have some committee to draw up a Test, about persons that receive Pensions.

Mr. *Boscawen.* You are to ask Goring no more questions, but to reprimand him in his place, and no more.

Mr. Goring being come to his place,

The *Speaker* said, "The house has considered your words, Mr. Goring, and, as they are displeased with your words, so they are pleased with your submission; and I admonish you to forbear the like for the future."

Vote and Address respecting the Treaties.] May 4. After several days-debate on the Treaties, the following Resolution was carried in the affirmative, 166 to 150. Resolved, "That the League offensive and defensive with the States General of the United Provinces, with the Articles relating thereunto, are not pursuant to the Addresses of this house, nor consistent with the good and safety of the kingdom."

It was next resolved, "That it is the opinion of this house, that his majesty be humbly advised, and desired forthwith to enter into the present Alliances and Confederations with the Emperor and the king of Spain, and the States General of the United Provinces, for the vigorous carrying on of the present War against the French king and for the good and safety of his majesty's kingdoms; and particularly, that effectual endeavours be used for continuing the States General in the present Confederation; and that it be agreed by all the parties confederate to prohibit all trade between their subjects and countries, and France, and all other the dominions of the French king: and that no Commodities of France, or any of the dominions of the French king, be imported into their countries, from any place whatsoever: and also, that all endeavours be used to invite all other princes and states into the said Confederation: and that no truce, or peace, be made with the French king, by his majesty, or any of the Confederates, without general consent first had therein."

Mr. Seymour re-chosen Speaker.] May 6. The commons being met, and sir Robert Sawyer, the present Speaker, being indisposed in his health, and having last night sent a Letter to the clerk of the house to be communicated to the house: which letter, being read by the clerk to the house, is as followeth:

"Mr. Goldesbrough; My long sitting the two last days, especially yesterday, hath so disabled me to attend my service in the chair of the hon. house of commons, that I can not longer attend it, without apparent hazard of shortening my life. I find myself already under great pain, and reduced to great weakness of body; from whence I apprehend severe fits of the stone. I have endeavoured this day, by physic, to prevent them, to the end I might be able to come to the house to-morrow; but my pain and weakness rather increase upon me this evening: so that there will be a necessity for me to enter into a course of physic; and I know it will be some time before I can possibly be restored to a competent measure of strength to attend that service. No person should be readier to serve the house than myself, would the constitution of my body give me leave: but it is too apparent it will not; and therefore I do humbly beg of the hon. members of that house, that they would not only excuse me for my non-attendance to-morrow, but discharge me from that duty they have commanded me to; and that they would please to pitch upon some person in my room, more fit for that employment. I do assure you, that in case it should please God in few days to restore me to strength enough to return to that Chair, yet I am assured that, without an extraordinary providence, I should in a few days after impair it by that service. Pray present my humble service, with this my humble and hearty excuse, to the hon. members of the house of commons; and you will oblige, your friend and servant, ROBERT SAWYER. Lincoln's-Inn-Fields, May 5. 78."

After the reading of which Letter, Mr. Sec. Williamson acquainted the house, That his majesty had also received intimation from the Speaker, to the same effect: and to the end the public may receive no delay, his majesty did give leave to the house to chuse another Speaker. And it having pleased God to restore Mr. Edward Seymour, the former Speaker, to his health again; and he being present in the house; Mr. Sec. Williamson did thereupon propose him to the house, as the fittest person, both for his ability, and long experience for that service: of which the house was so sensible and satisfied, that Mr. Seymour was unanimously called upon to the chair; and was afterwards approved of by his majesty.

The King's Answer to the Vote and Address.] Mr. Sec. Williamson acquainted the house, That the persons appointed to attend his majesty with the Votes of this house, of the 4th, did yesterday wait upon his majesty, and presented the said Votes to his majesty; and did desire his majesty's excuse, that they were not presented to him in the usual form: and that his majesty's Answer was, That he would consider of it, and return an Answer: and that he had accordingly received an Answer from his majesty, as followeth:

"*C. R.* His majesty having been acquainted with the Votes of this house, of the 4th instant, was very much suprised, both with the matter and form of them: but if his majesty had had exception to neither, yet his majesty, having asked the Advice of both houses, does not think fit to give any answer to any thing of that nature, till he hath a concurrent Advice from both houses."

An Address voted to remove Evil Counsellors.] May 7. The house resolved on a division of 154 to 139, "That an Address be presented to his majesty to remove those Counsellors who advised the Answers to the Addresses of the 26th of May, or 31st of January last, or either of them."

Address against the Duke of Lauderdale.] It was next resolved, on a division, 137 to 92, "That an Address be presented to his majesty to remove the duke of Lauderdale from his presence and councils;" and a committee was ordered to draw it up.

May 10. Mr. Powle read the Address for the second time, and the question being put whether the house should proceed on the said Address, it passed in the affirmative: Noes 174, Yeas 176. The house divided on the fourth and sixth paragraphs, the first of which was carried by six, and the last by three voices. The Address was as follows:

"We your majesty's most humble and loyal subjects, the commons in this present parliament assembled, do, in all duty and thankfulness, acknowlege your majesty's great grace and favour, in demanding our Advice upon the State of your majesty's Affairs in this present juncture, wherein your majesty's honour and the safety of the kingdom is so nearly concerned: according to which command of your majesty, we did immediately enter into consideration of what was imparted to us by your majesty's order; and after serious examination and weighing of the matter, we did resolve upon an Advice, which, because of the urgency of affairs, and the expedition they required, we did present in that form that was not usual in a matter of so great importance, and which we then directed to excuse to your majesty, upon that consideration.—And because we apprehended that the dangers were so imminent, that the delay of the least time might be of great prejudice to your majesty's service, and the safety of the kingdom after so much time already lost, we thought it necessary to apply immediately to your majesty by ourselves; which, in matters of this nature, is wholly in the choice of this house, and hath been frequently practised by us. And because these occasions are so pressing upon your majesty, and the whole kingdom so deeply sensible thereof, we most humbly beseech your majesty to communicate to us the resolutions your majesty has taken upon our said Advice, that thereby these imminent dangers may be timely prevented.—And whereas the commons conceive, that the present inconveniences and dangers, under which the kingdoms now lies, might have been either totally or in a great measure, prevented, if your majesty had accepted of that Advice, which, in all humility and faithfulness, we presented to your majesty on the 26th of May last, and which we re-iterated to your majesty on the 31st of Jan. ensuing; the refusing of which Advice, and dismissing of the parliament in May last, was the occasion of those ill consequences, which have since succeeded both at home and abroad; all which hath arisen from those misrepresentations of our proceedings, which have been suggested to your majesty, by some particular persons, in a clandestine way, without the participation and advice (as we conceive) of the Council-board; as though we had invaded your majesty's prerogative of making peace and war; whereas we did only offer our humble Advice in matters wherein the safety of the kingdom was concerned; which is a right was never yet questioned in the times of your royal predecessors, and without which your majesty can never be safe. Upon which grounds your majesty was induced to give us such Answers to those two Addresses, rejecting our Advice, as thereby your majesty's good subjects have been infinitely discouraged, and the state of your majesty's affairs reduced to a most deplorable condition: we do therefore most humbly desire, that, for the good and safety of this kingdom, and the satisfaction of your subjects, your majesty would be graciously pleased to remove those Counsellors, who advised the Answers to our Addresses of the 26th of May, and the 31st of Jan. last or either of them. And we do farther most humbly desire your majesty favourably to accept this our humble Petition and Address, as proceeding from hearts entirely devoted to your majesty's service; and that as we have never yet failed of giving testimonies of our affection and loyalty to your majesty's person, and government, so your majesty may rest confidently assured that we shall never be wanting to support your majesty's greatness and interest, whilst your majesty relies upon our counsels; which can have no other end than what sincerely tends thereunto, notwithstanding any sinister or self-interested endeavours to make impressions on your majesty to the contrary."

After this Address had been read, a motion was made to adjourn the house, which was over-ruled on a division; Yeas 150. Noes 156. A motion was then made and agreed to, "That the matter of the Address concerning the duke of Lauderdale be added to the Address this day agreed, in these words following: 'And we farther humbly beseech your majesty, That the duke of Lauderdale may be removed from your councils and presence*.'"

The King's Verbal Message to quicken the Supply.] May 11. Early, when the house was thin, by surprize, Mr. Secretary Williamson moved the house to supply the king with Money, Ships, &c. on a verbal Message from his majesty, "That the Charge was so great, that he must be forced to lay up several of the great Ships, already provided, and to disband many of the Forces newly raised, if he were not speedily supplied†."

Debate thereon.] Mr. *Mallet.* I desire that the mace may be sent into Westminster Hall, and the Court of Requests, for your members to attend.

Mr. *Boscawen.* I wonder that Money should be moved for before we have an Answer from the king to our Address. I would know of the hon. person that moved it, whether we are like to have peace, or war; for hitherto we are dealt with like children. By my consent, not a penny of money till we are plainly dealt with.

Mr. Sec. *Williamson.* Gentlemen ask, whether we shall have war, or not? If the thing must have its issue by the way and manner we have proposed, we can expect little. The Dutch ministry were in great trouble at our proceedings yesterday. I pacified them as well as I could, but upon the whole they feared some things that passed here would have that effect. I say, they desire to go deeper with you, and go higher. I told you formerly how peremptory they were: Van Leuen, is another sort of man, than Van Bennegen. It is so far from true, that they would be brought over to the French Alliance as the other was, that they would be brought to carry on the war: to for these two towns, the prince declared, he knew his uncle's mind; comparing things together, he could make conjecture: but whether it be peace, or war, Spain must be paid: and fear not to be outdone in the Supply: that nothing may be in the king's hand: and I would this day be upon it.

* It appears by the Journal, that lord Obrien and sir Tho. Chichley were this day ordered into the custody of the serjeant at arms, for a quarrel that had happened between them on a division of the house, in which blows were given.

† Grey.

Sir *Tho. Clarges.* I wonder that gentlemen will move you against a Vote of the house, 'for securing Religion, &c. before you go upon any other matter.' We now are in ready way for Money; but Popery, a bill of a half a dozen sheets, has lain with the lords 12 months. Till we be rid of those Counsels, that have so misled us, we have nothing to give the king. Common fame says, that some gentlemen have been turned out of their places, for their voting, and just upon their voting against the ministers. [Mr. Saville, &c.] A man that comes out of a room where one is killed, with a knife bloody, the Jury will find guilty, when no other man appears to have done the fact.

Mr. *Goring.* I would know, how that gentleman knows they are turned out of their places, for giving their votes here.

Sir *Tho. Clarges.* I said Common fame says so.

Sir *Cha. Wheeler.* He said, 'we are reduced to slavery.' I would have those words written down.

Sir *John Hotham.* More than common fame will make that out. That you are very near slavery is more than common fame. If these pranks go on, we shall be 'reduced to slavery.'

Sir *Tho. Meres.* It is said, 'That members are turned out of their places for giving their votes here.'. I know not for what other reason they are turned out. I would have some other cause assigned, if they know it. Just upon such an occasion they are turned out; one may make a probable conjecture though no demonstration, of it; and as the consequence, if the house be used to it, it will lose its liberty and freedom; and what makes people free but liberty to give their votes here?

The *Speaker.* If it be insisted upon, 'That the words spoken gave exceptions,' before you go on in the debate, they must be written down.

Sir *Tho. Littleton.* I would have the words written down. Clarges gave a comparison of a Jury that would find it murder in the person that came out of a house, with a bloody knife, &c. and no other cause appear.' I would have the words written down.

Sir *Tho. Lee.* If my worthy friend, Wheeler, had known what his soldiers had done in Southwark, he would not have been so forward in this.

Mr. *Garroway.* These gentlemen, that would have the words written down, would not be so forward, if they heard of what I shall tell you: what those soldiers are, and what they have done. Then you will judge whether it is fit to give Money to support them in their carriage. I would, in this unlucky juncture, do any thing for your service. Let gentlemen go on in the report, and wave this motion. If you will go on, let the words the gentleman spoke be asserted in writing, and do what you please upon them.—The thing went off.

The *Speaker* reported the substance of the king's Message by Sec. Williamson, viz. "That, by reason of the Expence and Charge his majesty has been, at for equipping and furnishing his Navy, and raising soldiers, &c. he desires that the house would immediately enter into consideration of a Supply for him; for his majesty must either disband the men, or pay them." *

Mr. *Garroway.* Pray let us be plain and see; for, as things are, we can make no judgment of them. Let us know our Answer from the king to our Address; and do like reasonable men. They have had great time to consider; we have had none. Pray let this Message alone till Monday. We know not why we should disband these forces, or keep them up, for we know nothing of war, or peace. Whatever we do, will else be by chance; it may be very well, or very ill. I would therefore consider of it.

Mr. *Powle.* There is one word in the king's Message which I take notice of, the word 'immediately.' To enter into the debate, I will always show as much respect to the king's Message, as any man: but I think that word 'immediately' over-rules the debate, and intrenches upon the privileges of this house. I am sorry those about the king will impose these things upon his majesty. It will be time to take up this debate, when our Grievances are redressed, and our Address answered. And then, giving Money ought to be the last thing considered. Why was the Army so hastily raised? Which was no good sign of good intention to the public. Let those about the king set things right and straight. Till then it is too raw and fresh to go upon Money. And I would let fall the debate now, and go upon other business.

Sir *John Ernly:* You must disband these men that are raised, or pay them. If it be a war, these men are ready for you, and I am glad we are in so much readiness towards it. I am no more for a standing army than any gentleman here; but I would give the king some resolution of his Message. If we consider it not now, that we would do it some other time. You cannot leave it thus, without great dissatisfaction to the nation.

Col. *Birch.* This was a work of darkness, from the beginning. We gave Money for what we see now not a word of it true: a bargain performed on the one side, and not on the other. We were told, 'that we must trust the king with the Treaties, because the thing could not be well discovered to us.' No doubt but the king knows the bottom of all this, and if he disband the men, and discharge the Ships, he knows why he does it. But still we have no Answer to making of Leagues, that we advised. If the king enter into this league, we shall see all the quotas of the Con-

* In the Journal, the words are the same with those in the Secretary's first Speech. The former part of the Message was, 'That his majesty had appointed 4 o'clock in the afternoon for their attending him with the Address.'

federates; but will any man give Money till he knows for what? But I find it is still designed for a peace with the French king, and whenever you leave that king with 100 sail of ships, and 100,000 men, you are in a worse condition than any war can make you. Upon the whole, this is like a question, that a man cannot tell whether to give his affirmative or negative to. Therefore, I would not adjourn it, but let it fall.

Mr. *Sacheverell.* I wish I could see a bottom to go upon: that which I insist upon is, not to give Money in time of war, to wheedle us into a peace; and next, I will not give money upon false suggestions. I would not put any marks upon this Message, but let that fall. If we see they will go into a war, I will be as ready as any man to give money; but seeing all this is for a peace, Clarges's words might be admitted.

Sir *Edm. Jennings.* The king cannot give an Answer to your Address, till he has an Answer to the Message he sent us to-day. Common fame says, we talk of war: yet we can go little towards it without Supply. Can an army be raised one day, and sent over into Flanders another? Unless the king be supplied, he cannot proceed.

Sir *Wm. Coventry.* I differ in opinion from those gentlemen that thought it too hasty to raise the army; for else it would have been undisciplined; and I am for Money to maintain the war. But why should we proceed now we have no light to go by? Will any man be satisfied to give money for war, when we see nothing but a face of peace? 100,000*l.* would disband this army. And if we should give a small sum of Money, the Confederates will leave you. If you stay till all Flanders be gone, you will do as king James did in the Palatinate war, treat, and treat, till all was gone, and no body to treat with him. If people urge us upon Money now, it must be answered in the negative; which I would not give the king. If the war really be, he must be a madman who will not give Money; and if it be a peace, no Englishman will be for keeping up the army. Till we have more light, we know not what to say, and I would decline a negative upon the king which all our souls abhor.

Col. *Titus.* There is a Vote already against this question. And, in short, by this question, either we give our money we know not why, or else we put a negative upon the king; neither of which I would do; and therefore I would not have the question put.

Mr. *Pepys.* When I promised that the Ships should be ready, by the 30th of May, it was upon the supposition of Money for the 90 ships proposed by the king, and voted by you, their sizes, and rates; and I doubt not by that time to have 90 ships; and if they fall short, it will be only from the failing of the Streights ships coming home, and those but two. I would have Clarges's harsh words explained, viz. 'cheated of another sum of Money.' There has not been one penny of it spent, but towards a war with the French king. If there has been 'a cheat,' it is on the king's side, who has debarred himself of all of it. Peace itself is war with France. Peaceful counsels and warlike preparations cannot subsist. Supplies are not in your hands, to have them when you please. This is the time of the year to send to the Baltic for stores, and this is the time for that Supply.

Sir *Rob. Howard.* Pepys here speaks rather like an admiral than a secretary, 'I' and 'we.' I wish he knows half so much of the navy as he pretends. Now the king of France is greater at sea than we, with all the preparations that are pretended. I hear the name of the king so often used, that I am sorry for it. We that are against their opinion, are as much for the king's service as they.

Mr. *Boscawen.* I know not the ground of asking Money, now we are halting between two opinions; peace and war. If we were in a grand committee, to consider of giving Money upon proposals, the debate would be more proper. But I would adjourn the house, that the honourable person who brought the Message for Money, &c. may be free to tell you whether we are to be in peace, or war.

Sir *Tho. Lee.* I think it well moved to adjourn the house now, because the house is put upon difficulties that the house was never upon before. You have had an Answer of 'surprizing,' only, and no more. I would have you severely punish those who misrepresent you to the king; it is absolutely necessary. When things come clearly before you, it will be hard to be excused, that an Army should be raised, and no war. I wonder gentlemen will say, 'you expect management of the war, &c.' If, as some have put it, the nation is at as much charge in peace as war, I am therefore for war. If you become not fatal to them that endeavoured to ruin you, they may be fatal to undo you.

Sir *Henry Capel.* If the question pass in the negative, then it will be a disrespect to the king, and, in effect, a negative to Money; and the French king will make his advantage of it. If this be carried in the affirmative, by two or three voices, the consequence will be Money coming heavily on. If we disband the Army, there must be Money. I hope the king will take care of a good peace, and if we have war, we shall stand by him in either.

Mr. *Garroway.* Perhaps they will disband a few men troublesome to them, and leave the rest to be troublesome to us. And that I fear of the peace. In 9th Hen. iv. you will find it in the record, it is against your privileges, and you will have it made out, 'That none of your debates are to be disclosed.' If the house be told the thing; it may be left indefinite, and I would adjourn.

Mr. *Vaughan.* If all the delusions of the last session were forgotten, then this might have been moved; but now we have the same stories repeated, and more would rejoice against giving Money than for it; because they would heighten still the king's displeasure against you. These proceedings are a brand upon the ministers, and I would have them pay for it.

Col. *Birch.* This Message must plainly be a late result. Whoever put the house upon this question, could not expect a smooth Answer; they could not but expect a negative on this of Money. Some of the king's council are good, and I am apt to believe some are bad; and you have said so. There are twins in the womb. If you adjourn till Monday, there is the same snare still, if we have no more light, neither Peace nor War.—The previous question for adjourning the debate passed in the negative, 178 to 177.

The King's angry Answer to this Address.] May 11. p. m. The house attended the king with the Address, to which his majesty was pleased immediately to return this Answer:

"This Address is so extravagant, that I am not willing speedily to give it the Answer it deserves."*

The King makes a Speech to the Lords, and prorogues the Parliament.] May 13. His majesty prorogued the parliament till May 23. Before the commons were sent for up to the lords house, by the black rod, the king spoke thus to the lords:

"My lords; I have received an Address of such a nature from the house of commons, as I cannot but resent very highly, from the ill consequences I have lived to see from such Addresses. I intend therefore to prorogue them for some short time, in hopes they will consider better what they ought to do at their return. I have chosen to tell this to you first, because I would have you know I am very well satisfied with the dutiful behaviour of this house, and you will by that time be more enabled to give me your Advice."

SIXTEENTH SESSION OF THE SECOND PARLIAMENT.

The King's Speech on opening the Session.] May 23. The parliament met again, when the king opened the session with the following Speech to both houses:

"My Lords and Gentlemen; When I met you last, I asked your Advice upon the great conjunctures abroad. What return you gentlemen of the house of commons made me, and whether it was suitable to the end I intended (which was the saving of Flanders), I leave it to yourselves, in cold blood, to consider. Since I asked your Advice, the conjunctures abroad and our distempers (which influenced them so much) have driven things violently on towards a peace; and where they will end, I cannot tell; but will say this only to you, that I am resolved, as far as I am able, to save Flanders, either by a war or a peace, which way soever I shall find most conducing towards it; and that must be judged by circumstances, as they play from abroad. For my own part, I should think, being armed, were as necessary to make peace, as war; and therefore, if I were able, would keep up my army, and my navy at sea, for some time, till a peace were concluded, if that must be; but, because that will depend upon your Supplies, I leave it to you to consider whether to provide for their subsistence so long, or for their disbanding sooner, and to take care, in either case, not to discourage or use ill so many worthy gentlemen and brave men, who came to offer their lives and service to their country upon this occasion; and in pursuit of your own Advices and Resolutions. I must put you likewise in mind of a branch of my Revenue, which is now expiring; and of another greater, which is cut off by a Clause in the Poll Bill; as also of the 200,000*l.* taken up upon the credit of the Excise at your request. And I desire your Resolutions may be speedy, because the present necessity requires it. And I shall consent to any reasonable Bills you offer me for the good and safety of the nation.—My Lords and Gentlemen; I shall say no more, but only to assure you (whatsoever some ill men would have believed) I never had any intentions but of good to you and my people, nor ever shall; but will do all that I can for your safety and ease, as far as yourselves will suffer me. And since these are my resolutions, I desire you will not drive me into extremity, which must end ill both for you and me, and (which is worst of all) for the nation, which we ought all to have equal care of; therefore I desire we may prevent any disorders or mischiefs that may befal them by our disagreement; and in case they do, I shall leave it to God Almighty to judge between us, who is the occasion of it.—One thing more I have to add; and that is, to let you know, That I will never more suffer the course and method of passing laws to be changed; and that if several matters shall ever again be tacked together in one bill, that bill shall certainly be lost, let the importance of it be never so great. The rest I leave to my Lord Chancellor."

The Lord Chancellor Finch's Speech.] Then the Lord Chancellor made this Speech following:

"My lords; and you the knights, citizens, and burgesses of the house of commons; That which remains to be said by his majesty's command will fall under these considerations; the present State of Christendom in reference to a general peace, then the influence that peace is like to have upon us; and the necessity of returning to some better kind of intelligence amongst ourselves than we had when we parted last.—The advances which have been made abroad towards a peace, though they may have been hastened by some late occurrences, yet they were long since meditated and prepared there; for when the States

* This Answer is not entered in the Journals of the house, but is preserved in sir Thomas Webster's "Collection of certain Extracts of this Session," and is also confirmed by sir John Reresby, in his Memoirs, p. 62.

General did perceive, that though they had strained themselves to the utmost, and exceeded all the proportions which by their Treaty they were bound to furnish, yet the Spaniards failed them in every point, not only in the Subsidies they were obliged to pay, but in the very strength and forces they stood engaged to set out; insomuch that all their towns and garrisons were so far from being in any tolerable posture to receive an enemy, that they remained as perfectly defenceless as if they were intended to be abandoned; the States resolved to seek all the occasions they could of coming out of the war and to lay hold on the first that should offer itself.—To this end, they did all the last year solicit his maj. to endeavour a peace; and they would then have taken such a peace as now they seek. But his maj. thought he had done great service to the Christian world, when he had gained two points upon them; first, to model and concert with him the Terms and Articles of a better peace; and then, in prospect of that peace (and without which it could never have been gained), to enter into a League Offensive and Defensive with his majesty, to obtain that peace by force, if it could not be had otherwise.—And while things stood upon this foot, and some preparations were making towards it, there was no small hopes of putting a considerable stop to the Growth of the Power of France.—For though the Dutch were still inclined to accept of peace, and were hearkening after the French Propositions at Nimeguen; yet such were his majesty's resolutions to hold them to their league, and so constant were all his refusals to hearken to such a peace, or to have any part in it, that they must of necessity at last have been obliged to continue in the war some way or other.—But when once it was heard abroad, that this league, which was the only thing by which his majesty could oblige the States, had been so ill understood at home, as to meet with some very unfitting and very undeserved reflections; as soon as it had taken air, and they understood that there was a resolution to give no money until satisfaction given in matters of religion, which in all countries are the longest debates that can be entered upon, and at this time above all others should least have been stirred; and when at last the king had received an address which they took to be of such a nature as was never seen or heard of before in any state or kingdom in the world, and had proceeded so far as to express his resentment of it!—Then they concluded with themselves, that it was in vain to rely any longer upon England, for England was no longer itself: then all sides began to wish for peace, even Spain as well as Holland; and if the cessation which is endeavoured to be made in order to it take effect, as in all likelihood it will, we may conclude that the peace will soon follow.—The influence such a peace will have upon our affairs is fitter for meditation than discourse; only this is evident, that, by the preparations we have made for war, and the prohibitions we have made of trade, we have given no small provocations to a mighty king, who may be at leisure enough to resent them if he please. And therefore it will import us so to strengthen ourselves, both at home and abroad, that it may not be found a cheap or easy thing to put an affront upon us.—The first step in order to this is, to preserve a state of peace and unity at home, which is now more necessary than ever: he that foments divisions now, does more mischief to his country than a foreign enemy can do, and disarms it in a time when all the hands and all the hearts we have are but enough to defend us.—No fears of arbitrary government can justify, no zeal to religion can sanctify, such a proceeding.—It hath been so stale a project to undermine the government, by accusing it of endeavouring to introduce popery and tyranny, that a man would wonder to see it taken up again.—Have we forgotten that religion and liberty were never truly lost, till they were made a handle and pretence for sedition? Are we so ill historians as not to remember when prelacy was called popery, and monarchy tyranny; when the property of nobility and gentry was held to be destructive of liberty; and that it was a dangerous thing for men to have any sense of their duty and allegiance?—Do we know all this, and suffer men without doors to hope by our divisions to arrive at the same times again? Can we endure to see men break the act of oblivion every day, by reviving the memory of forgotten crimes in new practices?—If fears and jealousies can ever become wise and good men, it is only then when there is danger of a relapse. No caution can be too great against the returns of that fatal distemper from which we have been so lately recovered, especially when some symptoms of it begin again to appear in printed libels, and in several parts of the nation.—It might perhaps be worth our while to consider, whether we do not bring some kind of scandal upon the Protestant religion, when we seem so far to distrust the truth and power of it; that, after so many laws that have been passed to guard it, after all the miraculous deliverances from the attempts which have been made against it, we should still be afraid of its continuance.—It is, no doubt, a duty which we owe to God and to ourselves, to the present age, and to posterity, to improve the opportunities God gives us of fencing our vineyard, and making the hedge about it as strong as we can. And the king hath commanded me to tell you, that he is ready to concur with us in any thing of this kind, which shall be found wanting, and which the Christian prudence and justice of a parliament can propose as expedient.—But why then do we suffer those abroad to complain of the dangers of religion, who complain only for complaining sake? Hath not the late act made it impossible, absolutely impossible, for the most concealed Papist that is, to get into any kind of employment? And did ever any law, since the reformation, give us so great a security as this?—As little cause there is to be jealous of our liberties and properties; nor do they believe themselves, who pretend to be afraid of either.—Can there be a greater evidence of the moderation of a prince, and his tenderness of the subjects, than to suffer, as he does every day, so much licentious and malicious talk to pass unpunished. If there be not one instance to be found in a whole reign of a man that hath suffered against law, and but very few examples of those that have suffered by it, shall we endure them that dare say, in coffee-houses, and in other public places, that the nation is enslaved?—Let it be lawful to provoke and challenge the most discontented and the most unsatisfied spirit in the kingdom, to shew that time, if he can, since the world began, and this nation was first inhabited, wherein there were fewer grievances, or less cause of complaint, than there is at this present; nay, give him scope enough, and let him search all ages, and all places of the world, and tell us, if he can, when and where was ever found a happier people than we are at this day.—And if malice itself ought to blush when it makes this comparison, what strange ingratitude both to God and man are they guilty of, who behave themselves so, as if they could be ill at ease under so temperate a government?—My Lords and Gentlemen; The king will not suffer himself to believe it possible that you should ever forsake him, when any difficulties or distresses are near him; and therefore he doth with great assurance expect your care to preserve him in the affections of his people, as well as your concurrence to his present Supplies.—The forces which have been raised, and the ships which have been set out by your advice, have been at a vast charge; and yet it will be no small expence to disband them again, and to pay them till they be disbanded.—That two hundred thousand pounds which was borrowed at your request remains as a debt upon the king, unless you acquit yourselves of the obligation which lies upon you to pay it.—That branch of the revenue which expires next month will leave the crown in great want, if it be not continued; and yet the continuance of it will not prove so considerable a support as it ought to be; for the Poll Bill hath extinguished the duty upon French wines, and all other customs arising upon trade with France; and it is worthy of the care of a parliament, to make this up some other way, that so his majesty may see and know that nothing can be lost by trusting his parliament.—But the king hath so far expressed himself this day, that it is evident the manner of your proceedings is to him as considerable as the matter; and that he will not accept a good bill, how valuable soever it may be, unless it come to him in the old and decent method of parliaments.—The late way of tacking together several independent and incoherent matters in one bill, seems to alter the whole frame and constitution of parliaments, and consequently of the government itself.—It takes away the king's negative voice in a manner, and forces him to take all or none, when sometimes one part of the bill may be as dangerous for the kingdom as the other is necessary.—It takes away the negative voice of the house of peers too by the same consequence; and disinherits the lords of that honour they were born to, the liberty of debating and judging what is good for the kingdom.—It looks like a kind of defamation of the government, and seems to suppose the king and house of lords to be so ill affected to the public, that a good bill cannot carry itself through by the strength of its own reason and justice, unless it be helped forward by being tacked to another bill that will be favoured.—It does at last give up the greatest share of legislature to the commons, and by consequences the chief power of judging what laws are best for the kingdom.—And yet it is a privilege that may be made use of against the commons, as well as by them; for, if this method hold, what can hinder the lords at one time or other from taking advantage of a bill very grateful to the commons, and much desired by them, to tack a new clause to it; of some foreign matter, which shall not be altogether so grateful, nor so much desired; and then the commons must take all or none too.—Thus every good bill shall be dearly bought at last; and one chief end of calling parliaments, the making of good laws, shall be wholly frustrated and disappointed; and all this by departing from that method which the wisdom of our ancestors prescribed on purpose to prevent and exclude such inconveniencies. These innovations the king resolves to abolish; and hath commanded me to say to you, 'State super vias antiquas.'—My Lords and Gentlemen; There never did, there never can again, so much depend upon the happy success of any one meeting, as there does upon this.—If this session do not repair the misfortunes, and amend the faults of the last, it will look like a fatality upon the nation. If we do not now strengthen the hands of the government, and shame the enemies of it, by banishing all manner of distrust, we shall be in danger to become, not only the most miserable, but the most unpitied nation under Heaven.—Let not the whispers, or evil surmises, of those who lie in wait to deceive, make any man the unhappy occasion of endangering the safety of the government, by mistrusting it. He whose house is destroyed by fire, would find but little consolation in saying the fire did not begin by his means; but it will be matter of perpetual anguish and vexation of heart to remember, that it was in his power to have extinguished it. Let the world now see, that your zeal to preserve the government is the same it was when you were ready to die for its restoration; and know, it is an act as meritorious, and an act of as great duty and loyalty to stand between the king, and all these practices of libelers which tend to create a misunderstanding between him and his parliament, as it is to fight for him in a day of battle. Embellish the history of this parliament, by shewing us the healing virtue of this session. So shall your service be acceptable to the king, who never forgets any thing but injuries; so shall you recommend yourselves to posterity, by transmitting to them the same peace and happiness you are trusted with. And the God of peace and unity prosper all your consultations to the honour and happiness of the king, and the joy and comfort of all his good subjects."

Vote for an Address to the King to declare War against France.] May 25. A motion was made for an address to the king, to know whether we shall have Peace, or War. After a long debate, a motion was made, to adjourn; which was carried in the affirmative, Yeas, 195. Noes, 176.

May 27. The commons agreed to the following Vote, which was sent to the king by the members of the privy council; "Resolved, That this house, taking into consideration the state of his majesty's affairs, and the great charge and burden that his majesty and the nation lies under by the Army now in being, are humbly of opinion, that if his majesty pleases to enter into a War against the French king, this house is, and always will be, ready to support and assist him in that war: but if otherwise, then they will proceed to the consideration of providing for the speedy disbanding of the Army."

The King's Answer.] May 28. Mr. Sec. Coventry delivered to the house the king's Answer to yesterday's Vote, as follows:

"C. R. His majesty having perused the Vote of this house of the 27th hath thought fit to return this Answer; That the most Christian king hath made such offers for a Cessation, till the 27th of July, as his majesty does not only believe will be accepted, but does also verily believe will end in a general peace: yet since that is not certain, his maj. does by no means think it prudent to dismiss either fleet or army before that time; nor does he think it can add much to the charge; because the raising the money, and paying them off, would take as long a time as that, although the speediest disbanding that is possible were intended. That, in the mean time, his majesty desires that some Supply may be provided for their subsistance; that as hitherto they have been the most orderly Army that ever were together, they may be encouraged to continue so. That there is another thing which presses his maj. with very great inconveniences in his domestic affairs; which is the want of the 200,000*l.* you promised to repay him at your next meeting after: and which does affect that whole branch of his revenue, by having a fifth part taken out of every payment, which should be applied to the necessary uses of his houshold: he does therefore desire you will immediately apply yourselves to the repayment of that money to him."

On the receipt of this Message the house resolved; "That it is the opinion of this house, that all the Forces that have been raised since the 29th of Sep. last, except those which have been sent to the Plantations, be forthwith paid off and disbanded."

Debate on an Affidavit annexed to an Election Petition from Aldborough.] Sir *Tho. Littleton.* I have a Petition concerning Aldborough.* There is annexed to it an Affidavit, which is rather a work of supererogation, but what will not vitiate the Petition.

Sir *Rd. Temple.* We are not to receive Affidavits here. I would have it struck out.

The *Speaker.* If the Affidavit be fixed to the Petition, if you receive the Affidavit you receive the Petition.

Sir *John Talbot.* If a member can aver, that he knows the hands that have subscribed the Petition, or if any without doors will aver it, you may receive the Petition. But you cannot receive an Affidavit of the subscription of the Petition.

Sir *Tho. Littleton.* I know the hands very well.

Sir *Tho. Meres.* Sir Wm. Wentworth undertakes that Mr. Wentworth will prosecute the Petition, and I would have the Petition read, but not the Affidavit.

Sir *Wm. Coventry.* The matter of the Petition becomes already very burthensome to the corporation. The other day a petition was delivered, and it was a question whether it was not signed all by one man's hand; now here is an Affidavit of the subscriptions sent with the petition, by the mistaken zeal of the gentleman. If we are not impowered to receive Affidavits here, it is no affidavit, and you may receive it. If they lapse any more time in their petition, they may be nonsuited again, as they have been twice already, and so their business is done for this parliament. I would therefore have the clerk read the Petition, and connive at the Affidavit.

The *Speaker.* If you will put the sitting member (sir John Reresby) to these unnecessary disturbances, and admit every irregularity, &c.

Sir *Tho. Lee.* I would publish rules, that all persons must come from all parts of England to avow Petitions, and so weary men out, that the mayors and bailiffs will chuse you all the parliament-men. The case of sir James Langham, for Northampton. He was first chosen by the commonalty, and secondly by the mayor and aldermen, and thirdly by both, and yet he missed it at last. There was something of a communion-table in the case.

Mr. *Powle.* Whilst we are gratifying a particular gentleman, let us not lose an essential privilege; that whenever a member avers the Petition, you never refuse it. Sir Wm. Wentworth tells you, he knows the hands, and un-

* This was a Petition of several of the burghers, setting forth, "That sir John Reresby had procured himself to be returned for that borough, though he was not duly elected."

dertakes they will prosecute the petition. If any member presents a petition to abuse you, and the petitioners will not avow the petition, it is in your power to punish that member, and send him to the Tower. A member has sat here four years, and the petitioners say he has sat wrongfully. Let us not begin new customs to hinder complaints of people coming to us. Let the petition be read, but not the Affidavit.

Mr. Sec. *Coventry.* By this Petition, the town complains of one that sits, that is not a representative of them, as a grievance. It must be owned by somebody, and I would have it now.

Sir *Edm. Jennings.* Since the Petition is insisted upon, I must say something, that I otherwise would not: I believe it to be fictitious. That letter could not come to Mr. Wentworth till Sunday morning, and he lives 20 or 30 miles from Aldborough, and sending to and again that Affidavit, which was made at Wakefield on Monday, and this is 26 miles farther, how it is possible this Affidavit could be made in such a time, I leave you to consider.

Sir *Wm. Coventry.* It is no compliment to your member to be the hander of a fictitious Petition to you. I presume the member has had caution. If it be fictitious, I wonder gentlemen should call for adjourning, and not enquire into it: every scrivener may else put these slurs upon you, and by calling it fictitious, and not proving it, the corporation may be slurred out of their right too. I would therefore refer the enquiry into it to the committee of privileges.

The question being put, That the Petition be read, it passed in the affirmative, 139 to 115, and the Clerk was ordered to blot out the Affidavit. The Petition was referred to the committee of privileges.

May 31. Resolved, "That a Supply be granted to the king towards the paying and disbanding of all the Forces raised since the 29th of Sept. last."

A Supply given to disband the Army by a certain Day.] June 4. The commons voted 200,000*l.* to be raised by a monthly tax, in six months, after the Land-tax, then in being, should be expired; with an appropriating clause, that this should be for disbanding the Army by the end of the present June: they also voted 200,000*l.* towards defraying the Expences of the Fleet; and seemed inclinable to throw in such another sum for the king's extraordinary occasions.

A Message from the King to prolong that term.] June 7. His majesty sent them another Message, signifying "That his mind was still the same with what he delivered in his Speech the 23d of May last, viz. That the Army and Fleet ought to be kept up till the expected peace be concluded: and he further recommended to their consideration, whether it were not dishonourable for him to recall his Forces in Flanders, from those towns which he had taken into his protection, before they could provide themselves of other succours."

Resolution to admit no further Motions for new Supplies.] The reason assigned in this Message was irresistible; and produced a Resolution to extend the time, as to the Forces in Flanders, till the 27th of July: but shortly after, viz. the 15th, as if an apprehension began to prevail, that the house was falling back into its old complaisance, it was moved, "That, after the Tuesday following, which was the 18th, no motions should be made for any new Supplies of Money, till after the next recess;" and carried in the affirmative: the courtiers losing the previous question by six, and the question itself by 9 voices: 314 members being present at the first division, and 317 at the last.

Debate on sir S. Swale's Conviction of Popery.] June 8. Sir Solomon Swale sent the Speaker a letter to excuse his attendance on the house, by reason of a quartan ague, that had reduced him to great weakness. He desired to be heard by his counsel, at the bar, by reason of his unwarrantable prosecution to conviction of Popery, at the sessions at the Old Bailey.

Mr. *Williams.* Dismembering a member is a very tender point. It is suggested that Swale is a convicted Recusant. The question before you is, not whether he be convicted, or not convicted, of recusancy, but whether he be truly convicted or not in the exchequer, or king's bench; and till it be voided there, it is a legal conviction. That a Popish Recusant cannot be a member, you have determined in sir Tho. Strickland's case.

Sir *Wm. Coventry.* It is said to be done by matter of record, which is always credited here. If a man come with the record of his return, he sits here by that record, and you can hear no counsel in Swale's case. No man sits here upon a false return, till first the Record be mended: and because you have not the trial of conviction of a member before you, the law has made this of recusancy easy. For he may be taken off, by his conformity. The Test of the new Act is not required to take off conviction, for that is only for offices. If he takes the Oaths of Allegiance and Supremacy, and conforms to the Church, &c. that is easily taken off. But to have counsel, in a thing that is not judgeable here; I would not have you meddle with it.

Sir *Tho. Clarges.* I would have the officers of the exchequer acquaint you how the thing stands, as to Swale's conviction. Suppose a member, after he is chosen, &c. takes not the oaths of allegiance and supremacy, and petitions you to sit here, without taking them. I would have the officers of the exchequer bring you the record of the process.

The clerk of the crown brought in the Record of the Conviction at the Old Bailey, but this gave no satisfaction, and so the Exchequer officers were called for, but were not at the door.

The *Speaker.* The method here of Swale

may be the case of any member. There needs nothing more to convict a Popish Recusant than not being at his parish church, &c. for the space of a month, without reasonable excuse, when perhaps he goes to another church elsewhere. Therefore pray be very tender in this.

Sir *John Trevor*. The matter has been depending these nine months, and how easily might Swale have reconciled himself in that time! Pray give not countenance to a papist to sit in the house.

The Officers of the Exchequer were ordered to attend on Monday next, with the Record of Conviction.

The question being put, "That there remains an obligation upon this house to repay his majesty the 200,000*l.* charged on the credit of the Act for additional Excise," it passed in the affirmative, 177 to 162.

Debate on a Standing Army.] June 11. The house, according to order, took into consideration his majesty's Message.

Mr. Sec. *Coventry*. The Speaker ought to have read the king's Message, and not the clerk.

Sir *Wm. Coventry*. I have observed, that the king's Message, always, at the first reading, is read by the Speaker, but if read again, by the clerk. The Speaker reads it the first time, and we are all uncovered; the clerk the second time, and we are all covered.

Mr. Sec. *Williamson*. The question is, Whether you will go into a committee with instructions relating to the Bill, or Whether you will go upon the Message, in the house? The parting with your Forces before the peace be beyond doubt or certainty of the possibility of a war, may be of ill consequence. I will beg leave to acquaint you with one thing that happened. On Sunday they had a new Memorial of the danger of the Confederates disbanding. Now whether you will proceed in the house, or by way of instruction to the committee, along with the Bill, is to be considered.

Mr. Sec. *Coventry*. In this interim, the Confederates have time to come in and accept of the peace. It may prove a dead child; it may be abortive; it is a thing that depends upon other men; a little time will tell you; but till then, I am not able to say any thing.

Mr. *Powle*. I see not, either from the state of affairs at home or abroad, that a Standing Army is a convenient thing for us, especially for home. We are told, 'we are in the state of mediators, indifferent between both parties; and neither to assist the king.' We hear of great jealousies the Dutch government has of us; and if so, they care not to see our Army on the other side of the water; and the Spaniards are jealous of us, as to France; and if we are in no condition to make war with the French, and that we cannot, &c. I would willingly make peace with them. If they be not your friends, prevent them from being your enemies. These new Forces may engage us in new broils, and we shall have nobody to assist us. As for giving advice in this case, I know not what to say, we having been so sharply reprimanded for it already. For my share of it, as to the protection of the king of Spain, remembering that when we advised the king about a French war, we were checked for it, therefore I move to answer the king's Message, 'that we leave it to him.' And if there may be any clause in the Bill, to continue the Forces in Flanders, that are there, I am not against it.

Mr. Sec. *Williamson*. It is not intended to keep those Forces up. But this is what we have been wishing and advising this year; and it is offered, for their sakes, to keep those men on foot only in Flanders, till a peace be settled. And their interest for so much is ours.

Mr. *Garroway*. If Holland and Spain have accepted of peace, then we are out of doors. They have taken care of themselves, and where is the dishonour, and where is the inconvenience, of recalling those Forces out of Flanders? If the peace be a good peace, why do not we come into it? If bad, why do we not protest against it? It is a strange intricate thing, that such and such a thing may happen, therefore we must keep up an Army. If you recall them out of Flanders, they and these here may be disbanded. The cessation of arms may be for three years. I would know whether we are under an obligation to keep the Army up for three years. I see nothing new before us, therefore, according to the first advice, you may very well go on with the Bill for disbanding the Army.

Col. *Birch*. Keep up the Army for fear of the king of France, and keep it up for ever. To my capacity, we are still in the same darkness as when we first raised this Army. If we had more clearness and plainness, the thing would succeed much better. It is pressed to know on which side we fall, and where is our benefit, by the peace? To which I hear not one word of answer. What do we get? What is our advantage? The *cui bono*? I doubt not, the honourable persons, if they please, could tell you. Shall we hire merchant ships and fire-ships for nothing? The war was intended against France, but, instead of that, this is to make war against ourselves, by the great charge. It cannot be thought that this is undertaken for Sweden, &c. Every man knows these great ships must do something before the 10th of Aug. for it is not safe to keep them longer out*. If it be for our fears of France, &c. that will never be at an end, and those fears will be hotter and hotter upon us, and the king of France cannot disband his army. He must keep his people in order. Either we have assurance with the Confederates, or with France. Having no more light

* It may not be amiss to observe here, that navigation is now so much improved, that the largest ships (larger than any that were built in those days) are able to keep the sea all the winter.

I know nothing you can farther do, than to proceed upon the Bill for disbanding.

Lord *Cavendish*. Could the king of France ever have had a more glorious peace than this, his Army we have raised has augmented his glory. It is too much to keep up these ministers, who have so much abused the nation, and the army both. Therefore I would disband the army.

Mr. *Bennet*. I am more afraid of French ministers than a standing Army.—He then told a story, reflecting upon lord treasurer Danby. When he was in France last, being to fight with a French marquess, he desired an English gentleman to be his second, who came in great haste to do him that service from Rouen. When the gentleman came, &c. he told him, 'He had killed the marquess in a rencounter the day before.' But soon after, the gentleman going to court saw the marquess there, &c. He made his comparison of raising the Army, to Danby's killing the marquess. The story occasioned much mirth in the house, and afterwards some libels.]

Sir *John Hotham*. I differ from Littleton, for I think those forces went into Flanders in time of peace, and not of war. If gentlemen had foreseen peace, no man would have been enticed to have raised them. But these forces in Flanders may be a nest-egg, &c. and since we have no war, and they have been raised by tricks and deceits upon you here, I would not have them kept up by tricks and conceits that we understand not.

Mr. *Vaughan*. The crown of England is established by laws; and had it not been so, king John's resignation to the pope had been good. If any man is so hardy as to advise the king to govern by a standing Army, he would subvert law; and it is against the government of the nation. The king has his Posse Comitatus, and the Militia, to oppose invasion and rebellion; and he may raise arms for defence of an alliance. These are all the ends to answer just government, and I believe the king will do no otherwise. But the keeping this Army up, is certainly in terrorem populi; and the laws abhor all arms but legal arms. These forces are upon free quarter, and if you let them stand against law, you will have little use of law—when their strength is above law. The longer you keep them here, the longer you must pay for them, and so you give up the liberties of the people you represent. You cannot keep them one hour longer, without giving up those you represent.

Mr. *Swynfin*. The account we can give of all the money that has been raised is, that it has been totally lost, for the end we gave it. If a man can give no other account to him that trusts him with his money, but 'that he was deceived, and outwitted,' will it not make a man careful in the rest of his reckonings? Possibly, at a committee, something may arise out of it, to bring in some new motion; but I would sit from day to day, till we have finished the bill.

Mr. *Sacheverell*. This is a strange debate, such as I never heard before, and, no farther reason assigned, we must renounce what we have passed upon a solemn debate. Let gentlemen remember what was spoken the other day, when, the last of June was proposed for disbanding, &c. It was said, 'the forces abroad could not be paid under a month's time.' And if that averment be true, we are under an impossibility of doing it. It looks as if an essay is made upon us, in time of peace, how we shall admit a Standing Army by consent. The same argument may be used, one, two, or three months hence. If it be for the honour of the king, &c. that is as good a reason as for the Army in Scotland. No man can think these forces are kept up for the safety of Flanders. At a month's end you may be told, that the cessation will be for three months more, and as good a reason for the precedent then, as now. Is it that we should increase jealousies in Holland, and they leap into the king of France's arms? therefore I can never give consent to one day's enlargement of the time of disbanding the army.

Mr. *Powle*. I move for an accommodation, as to those forces that are beyond the sea. That the question may be, 'whether the time shall be enlarged for disbanding the forces raised since the 29th of September last, not exceeding the 27th of July?'

The first question being put, 'That the time be enlarged for disbanding the forces that have been raised since the 29th of Sep. last, not exceeding the 27th of July,' it passed in the negative, 167 to 164.

The second question, 'That the time shall be enlarged for disbanding the forces now beyond the sea only, not exceeding the 27th of July,' passed in the affirmative, 172 to 166.

This was as instructions to the committee.

Debate on the Bill for hindering Papists to sit in Parliament.] June 12. A Bill for hindering Papists to sit in either house of parliament without taking the Oaths of Allegiance and Supremacy, and the Test against Transubstantiation, was read the 2nd time.

Sir *John Trevor*. I would no more speak against this bill, than for idolatry. But it is a vain thing to send this bill up to the lords. It has been three times sent up already, and you have had no dispatch of it, there are so many lords papists in that house. There runs an opinion without doors, that it makes a disinherison to pass this bill. But if the lords will not pay their duty to the king, and renounce those treasonable positions, they are not fit to sit there. I wish this bill may look forward, that you let not every tree be there to bear fruit, &c. The statute of queen Eliz. is, 'That the members of the house of commons shall take the oaths of Allegiance and Supremacy, forasmuch as the queen is already satisfied with the duty and loyalty of the lords temporal, they shall sit without taking the Oaths, &c.' And because of this statute of the 5th of the queen, and there are so many popish lords, they will throw it out of their house. Therefore I would have this bill look forward that no lords shall sit there, for the future, either by descent, or be called by writ, that shall not take the Oaths prescribed in the bill for the better suppression of popery.

Sir *Tho. Littleton.* If this bill will not pass, no bill that you can ever make against Popery can hold. Trevor's argument is, as if a man were ready to die of an acute distemper, and a physician should give him a remedy to operate 7 years hence. I have heard that the lords, in former bills for educating the children of Popish parents in the Protestant religion, called it 'the greatest inhumanity in the world.' Like Turks, that take away children of tribute from the Christians, the sharpest thing in the world! They had rather you would hang them. But this bill breaks no bones, it is consistent with the rules of the government, and it is reasonable that they should be excluded from part of the legislature, &c. It carries no cruelty in it. It is a fair and a just bill, and if it pass not the lords house, it will be the fault of the commons, for we may make it pass if we please.

Mr. *Wm. Harbord.* I am sorry to hear any arguments for jealousies and apprehensions that this bill should not pass the lords house. Look upon our neighbours; see what they have done in France and Holland. In queen Eliz.'s time, the Protestants were favoured in France; their judges and parliament were mixed with them; they called it 'Chambre mipartie.' But since that, in France, &c. they have made laws so severe against them, as to root them quite out; and surely it is as wise for us, as for that great monarch, to be tender of our religion. Holland is full of sects, but they suffer no religion in the government but Calvinistical. If we cannot support our religion, it is a wonder we should be contrary to all the world.

Col. *Birch.* I believe, verily, popery to be idolatry; but I had rather you would look forward than backward, and not let popery grow up to a tree in the education of their children. It has been such a practice in France in either party; if parents have been Catholics, their children have been taken away to be educated. The reason of this bill may turn against us another time. At such a jump, to turn so many lords and commons out of parliament! You know what I mean by this, should religion be changed. And I would give no countenance to any thing that looks like that.

Sir *Ch. Wheeler.* I desire our government may be preserved as we have found it. Let those that come after us struggle as well as we, without these extreme and violent ways. Cannot a lord that is not a Protestant, give a vote whether leather shall be transported, as well as a commoner? Saying 'it is in our power to make the bill pass,' is an innovation as well as all the rest. We may save ourselves from the growth of Popery, in punishing those that go off from us. The danger is, we know not what may be hereafter. I believe the Catholic Religion is idolatry. Bread in substance, transformed and transmuted into the body of our Saviour, &c. is intrinsic idolatry. As for that, spoken of, about 'their courts of justice in France and Holland,' no measure can be taken betwixt them and us. But I can name a Protestant now, a counsellor of the parliament of Rouen. He is sir Wm. Scott's son. So that holds not that is alleged.

Mr. *Powle.* I cannot be of Wheeler's opinion, 'to leave the kingdom as we found it.' That is, never to mend it. Had your predecessors been of that opinion, we had Popery long since established. I think the bill is very well calculated for this time. It meddles with nothing but keeping Papists out of the government. I wish that the Protestants, all the world over, had no more severe treatment than to be excluded out of the government. They are men so obnoxious to the penalty of the law, that they have not freedom of votes; and I am against any man's sitting here, that has not that freedom. As for the children, &c. I think that a cruelty to take away your child to have him damned, as that way in Turkey, &c. which is the worst sort of the Christian slavery. As for passing of this bill, there is much of it in our power. Within 12 months we have given great sums; and if we part with our money, and have not some good bills, it is in vain to sit here.

Sir *Tho. Littleton.* I desire to explain myself. This is called by Wheeler an innovation. But we know it was the ancient course of parliament to have Grievances redressed, before Money was given. But the 'innovation' is to give money first, before grievances are redressed.

Mr. *Wm. Harbord.* I know a lord lieutenant and a colonel that are Papists still. [He was called to name them; but the question was put, and carried for committing the Bill.]

Debate on the Speaker's reproving sir Tho. Meres for sitting up late.] June 15. On the Speakers touching upon sir Tho. Meres, by way of reproof, for sitting up so late at night that he came not timely in the morning to make his Report from the Committee of Privileges,

Sir *Tho. Meres* said, It is not true, that I sat up so late last night.

Several took exceptions at his reply to the Speaker.

Sir *John Hotham.* I think both the Speaker and Meres were to blame, for what they said I would have the thing rest, and go no farther. I have respect for them both.

Mr. Sec. *Coventry.* I would have Meres explain himself in this, as one gentleman would do to another.

The *Speaker.* If I said 'that Meres sat up late last night,' I hope it is no crime to say so. What is said to the Speaker, is said to you all; and if you will put it up, I will.

Sir *Tho. Meres.* It is the first occasion I have given to mispend your time, these 18 years. I grant I might have said it in the words, 'it is not so.' If there was heat in you, or me, I am sorry for it. But I must say I did not sit up late, for I was not well, and so went home late. When the house declares the words not fit to be said, I will say so too. Upon the whole matter, I desire I may not be the occasion of mispending the time of the house.

Sir *John Ernly*. Though Birch tells you, 'That among friends such words may pass,' yet it is the way to lose friendship by such words. I think Meres has asked the pardon of the house, and I would pass it over.

Sir *Tho. Meres*. So many of the words as are applicable to the Order of the house, I am sorry for. But for the other, of the reflection, hereafter instead of saying 'it is not *true*,' I must say 'it is not *so*.'

Sir *Tho. Littleton*. If the words had been said without a provocation, the house would have been warm upon it; but you, Mr. Speaker, gave the occasion. And I desire there may be forbearing on all hands for the future. If we have liberty to debate fairly without provocation, you, Mr. Speaker, will have no reflection upon you.

Mr. Sec. *Williamson*. As to the measure of the words 'true, or false,' in common conversation the words are not allowed to one another. I should much wonder if Meres should make a difficulty of asking your pardon, and that of the house, for what he said in heat. And I think it reasonable he should do it.

Mr. *Sacheverell*. I was not here, when the words past betwixt the Speaker and Meres. Though I would have the thing laid aside, yet not without some declaration; for till then, if any man says any thing of me that is not true, I shall tell him 'it is not true.'

Mr. *Garroway*. I hope the Speaker will not pretend to so absolute a command over the house as to say sharp things, and no man be permitted to reply upon him. The custom of the words 'it is not true' is more sharp than they are in their own nature.

Sir *Christ. Musgrave*. I will say something to the words I heard; they were 'I hope you will speak truth whilst you are in the Chair.'

Mr. *Goring*. I am not against putting these words up here, if we may have liberty to demand satisfaction without doors. To which,

Sir *John Hotham* replied; I like the motion well, if we were all upon the same foot, and if there might be no pardons so easily obtained, &c.

Sir *Tho. Meres*. If it may be acceptable to the house, I will speak. [His friends cried, 'No! No!']

Mr. *Garroway*. If you, Mr. Speaker, will not own the words that Meres supposed you said, Meres will quickly explain himself in the thing, and there is an end of it.

Sir *Tho. Meres*. I say it over again, I am sorry for your expence of time. I own the thing was sudden, and without any sort of ill-nature. I own all that, and that we have been long acquainted and familiar. And I apply my being sorry, as you apprehend it.

Sir *Wm. Coventry*. I am unwilling to speak, till I have heard the Speaker's and Meres's words perfect. The less we repeat the words of exceptions on both sides, the better. Meres saying 'his words were mistaken' goes a great way towards satisfaction. Some gentlemen seem to think that Meres saying 'he was sorry, &c.' was not applied the right way; but it seemed to me then that he applied the word 'sorry' right. I would have it passed over. It looks like an ill omen abroad, that here has been more clashing at words this session, than in seven, eight, or ten sessions before. But I hope the Speaker has had his full satisfaction, and I will proceed no farther in it.

Sir *Tho. Meres*. Most certainly Coventry has repeated my sense, and I own what I said to be his.—And so the thing went off.

The King's Speech, demanding an Additional Revenue of 300,000*l. per Ann.*] June 18. The king went to the house of peers, and made the following Speech to both houses:

"My lords and gentlemen; I know very well that the season of the year requires this session should be short; and that, both for my health and your occasions, we may all have liberty to go into the country by the middle of the next month at farthest. I think it a matter of yet more importance, that we part not only fairly but kindly too, and in perfect confidence one of another; since nothing else can render us either safe and easy at home, or considered so far abroad as this crown has ever been, and is now more necessary than ever, both for the safety of christendom and our own: therefore I shall at this time open my heart freely to you, in some points that nearest concern both you and me; and hope you will consider them so, because I am sure our interest ought not to be divided; and for me they never shall. I told you at the opening of this session, how violently things abroad were driving on towards a peace, and that I could not tell where they would end; but that I was resolved to save Flanders, either by a war or a peace; in which I am still fixed, as in the greatest foreign interest of this nation. I must now tell you, that things seem already to have determined in a peace, at least Spain and Holland; who have so far accepted the terms offered by France, that my ambassador at Nimeguen writes me word, he expected to be called upon to sign by the last of this month. My part in it will be not only of a mediator, but to give my guaranty to it, which the Confederates will call upon me for, and I am resolved to give in the strongest manner they themselves will desire, and I am able. How far this will go, I cannot tell; but they send me word already, that unless England and Holland will both join in the charge of maintaining Flanders, even after the peace, the Spaniards will not be in condition of supporting it alone, and must fall into other measures. On the other side, they think France will be left so great, that nothing abroad can treat with them hereafter upon an equal foot, without the hopes of being supported by this crown; and, to this end, I am sure, it will be necessary not only to keep our navies constantly strong at sea, but to leave the world in some assurance of our being well united at home, and thereby in as great an opinion of our conduct hereafter as they are already of our force. Upon this occasion, I cannot but say, that though, after our joint resolutions of a war, and the Supplies you have given towards it, you may think the peace an ill bargain, because it will cost you money, yet perhaps you will not believe it so, if you consider that by it so great a part of Flanders is like to be saved; whereas, without the paces we made towards war, there is nothing so certain as that the whole of it would have been absolutely lost this campaign, if not by this very time; and I believe you would give much greater sums than this will cost you, rather than the single town of Ostend should be in the French hands, and 40 of their men of war in so good an haven over against the river's mouth. Besides, both you and I (as we are true Englishmen) cannot but be pleased, and understand the importance of that reputation we have gained abroad, by having in 40 days raised an Army of near 30,000 men, and prepared a navy of 90 ships, which would have been now ready at sea, if we had gone into a war. Now, my lords and gentlemen, I know that in so great conjunctures you desire that I should keep the honour of my crowns, and look to your safety, by some balance in the affairs abroad; and I should be very glad I were able to do it: but I do not see how it will be possible for me, even in a time of peace, with a revenue so impaired as mine is by my debts long since contracted, and the present Anticipations, and at the best so disproportioned, not only to that of the kings my neighbours, but even to that of the United Provinces themselves (though of no larger extent than two or three of our counties): therefore, as I said I would open my heart freely to you, so I must tell you, that if you would see me able in any kind to influence the great conjunctures abroad, wherein the honour and safety of the nation are so much concerned, and wherein the turns are sometimes so short as not to give me leave to call in time either for your advice or assistances; if you would have me able but to pursue such a war as this of Algiers with honour, and at the same time keep such fleets about our own coasts, as may give our neighbours the respect for us that have been always paid this crown; if you would have me pass any part of my life in ease or quiet, and all the rest of it in perfect confidence and kindness with you and all succeeding parliaments; you must find a way of settling for my life, not only my Revenue, and the additional Duties as they were at Christmas last, but of adding to them, upon some new funds, 300,000*l.* a year: upon which, I shall consent that an Act may pass, for appropriating 500,000*l.* a year to the constant maintenance of the Navy and Ordnance, which I take to be the greatest safety and interest of these kingdoms; and I will at the same time (as I do now) assure you, that I shall not only, this or any other session of parliament, consent to such reasonable and Public Bills as you shall offer me, but shall employ my whole life to advance the true and public good and safety of my people, and endeavour, while I live, that none else shall ever be able to do them harm. I did not in my last Speech mention the 40,000*l.* I am engaged to pay to the prince of Orange for my niece's portion, because I had recommended it to you so lately before; but, the first payment being already due, and demanded by him, I must again put you in mind of it, and desire you will enable me to keep my word with him."

Debate on the King's Speech.] Mr. *Mallet.* Here are gracious expressions in his majesty's Speech, and if it fall out in the event as well as in the expression, it will be very well. I see we have peace, &c. and, in some measure, from counsels here. As for the guarantee, &c. I know not how it is made out to us. Yet we may give good Thanks 'for the gracious expressions in his majesty's Speech.'

Mr. Sec. *Williamson.* The king's Speech has matter of great weight in it. I suppose it is the order of parliament to set apart a time for the consideration of it. And in the mean time, to give his majesty Thanks, 'for the gracious expressions in his Speech.'

Sir *Robert Thomas.* I move that Williamson may carry the Thanks.

Lord *Cavendish.* (In ridicule) I move that Mallet, who firsted, and Williamson, who seconded the motion, may carry the Thanks to the king.

Mr. Sec. *Williamson.* I have no other exception to it, but that the thing is extraordinary. I desire, that, in the circumstances you do the Message, you would not lose the merits of it.

[Usually the Privy Counsellors carry the Message. Mallet was not one.]

Sir *George Hungerford.* At the latter end of a session, now we are going into the country, this demand of the king's is the most extraordinary thing that ever was done.

Lord *Cavendish.* All members are alike here, and as good as a privy counsellor to carry a Message to the king. These two persons moved for, have been firsted and seconded; and put it to the question.

Sir *Tho. Littleton.* I remember an Address of this house to the king, 'for wearing of English manufactures in the court, by his majesty's example, &c.' sent by sir Ch. Harbord, who was no privy counsellor. This is an answer to what is urged, 'that none but privy counsellors carry Messages to the king.'

Sir *Tho. Lee.* As to what is said of 'Messages by privy counsellors only, &c.' that is calling them only by their names. They go as a committee only from the house. If the custom has been that privy counsellors propose Speakers, and they are chosen, it does not therefore follow that privy counsellors chuse them. What you will do is one thing, and what you ought to do is another.

Sir *Edm. Jennings.* This is a reflection upon the whole house.

Sir *Tho. Meres.* The question is, Whether you will add any to the privy counsellors, as you have done upon other Messages. I have been added twice or thrice myself for one. But for sending the king Thanks, I remember none that have carried the Message but privy counsellors.

Ordered "That the Thanks of this house be returned to his majesty, for his gracious expressions in his Speech."

Mr. *Garroway.* If the privy counsellors, or the house go in a body, I am not against it.

Mr. *Bennet.* When this is over, I would enquire who it is that advised the king to demand so great a sum of us, and a Revenue that the nation is not able to bear. But I am as willing to give Thanks for the gracious expressions in his majesty's Speech as any man.

Mr. *Garroway.* Here are a great many points to be observed in the king's Speech. I think you have but little money to give. I remember, the present lord chancellor, when he was in this house, upon the making the king's Revenue 1,200,000*l.* a year, said, 'We had given all we had to give.' We have paid dear now for talking of a war with France, and our answer to this demand is, 'that it is beyond our abilities; we have it not to give.' I would first know where this 300,000*l.* is to be had, to make up the Revenue, &c? I would know where, or what it is? I know no such thing. I cannot imagine how so much as to think of it. I have heard it said, 'That the Revenue should never be so big as to destroy amity betwixt the king and us;' and, 'that it is fit for us to keep something always in reserve to present his majesty with.' This looks to me, of a strange nature, as if the house of commons were never to come here more. I know not how to comply with it.

Sir *Tho. Lee.* I would do all things with decency. You have made an Order, 'that no more motions for Money shall be made this session.' And if any gentleman can show a reason why you should retract your Order, and consider the king's Speech, he says something to the purpose.

Sir *Tho. Littleton.* Increasing the king's Revenue 300,000*l.* per ann. ought to be directly from a motion arising from the king's Speech in the house, before you go into a grand committee.

The *Speaker.* The reason of it is, the house avoids a question upon any thing of Money in the king's Speech, but it must arise from a motion in the house, referred to a grand committee to consider, &c.

Mr. *Swynfin.* I desire, we may not make day longer delay, but come to some resolution to-day, whether you will consider the several things in the king's Speech, or not. I am sorry the motion is made to us now from the king, and am sorry we can give the country so little account of what we have done already. We have complied with all things at the opening of the session, and it is a most unusual thing to have new demands for Money at the latter end of a session. I know not any precedent before of it. At the opening of the session, there was Money given for an Army by land, and a Navy by sea, for a French War. And all the latter part of the session has been spent in raising a great charge on the kingdom, for disbanding that Army; and it will lie very hard upon the people.

Sir *John Knight.* Consider the poverty of the nation, and fall of rents; it is impossible we should grant what is desired. Here are Pensions upon the Revenue, and we must still supply it. I would have an act of parliament to annul them all. At this rate we shall be Normans, and wear wooden shoes. I move, therefore, 'That there be no farther addition to the Crown Revenue, but that the Revenue may be better managed.' Which will sufficiently do the business of the crown without addition.

Lord *Cavendish.* There is no slavery like that under a form of law. This is so formidable a demand, in the king's Speech, that the first impression I can make of it is, to remove those who advised the king to demand it. 'The king would be at ease, if his Revenue was,' and as long as these ministers manage it, he never will; and I would have them removed. Our liberality has brought upon us the fears of Popery and arbitrary power. I would not have our sleeps disturbed with this demand in the king's Speech; and whilst the house is full, I would see an end of these demands.

Sir *Francis Drake.* Our Saviour was followed by a great many for the loaves, and so was the king's father. Great sums are asked. Is it from without us, or within us? Let us, however, get these men removed from the throne, that have endeavoured to break trust and confidence betwixt the king and us. They are uneasy with a parliament, and would have such a Revenue granted the king, that they may have no more. No Englishman can give this money demanded; and I would give none.

Mr. *Booth.* It is said 'that the Revenue cannot maintain the charge of the government.' If it be not enough, it is because there are so many privy seals; they are so numerous, and the Revenue is so ill managed; and it is very hard that the nation should supply the defects of ill management. The Speech tells you, 'That the Revenue is not so great as that of other princes.' If it was so great as that of France, I fear it would be to make the king as absolute as the king of France. As to the princess of Orange's Portion, I hope we shall not pay all the portions the king engages for. I hear there are great expences in lodgings as

Whitehall, [the dutchess of Portsmouth.] Still for more expences. I move, therefore, 'That we may give no farther addition to the king's Revenue.'

Sir *Tho. Meres* enumerates the king's Revenue, and the charges upon the people, now amounting to about two millions; and here is a request of 300,000*l.* for the king's life, which, at seven years value, amounts to two millions! Pray put a question whether you shall set a day for this motion. And I pray you will give a negative question. I will give a negative.

Mr. *Sacheverell.* There is more in this question than in any I ever heard, since I sat here. The States of France gave the king power to raise money upon extraordinary occasions, 'till their next meeting,' and they never met more. This sum is asked 'because of the Algiers war;' and another reason is, 'the king will give you 500,000*l.* per annum for the Fleet.' And we gave 700,000*l.* per ann. for it in the Customs. Those that move you now for a Supply, I believe, intend not to perpetuate it upon your land. Trade is already overcharged, and where will they have it? Home Excise; that way has lost them their liberty in France. Just as the calculation was made for the war, and disbanding the Army, and the Revenue demanded is calculated for an army of 20,000 men. I would ask any gentleman, whether he would make the Revenue so big, as there should be no use of a parliament for supplying the king? And whether ever the ministers will call a parliament again, should you grant such a Revenue as is asked? Consider this too; when we are upon any good laws, we are prorogued, and can do nothing but give Money. I will trust the ministers no more; and will give my negative to increasing the Revenue 300,000*l.* more.

Mr. *Powle.* I take this increase of the Revenue to import no less than the change of the government. Either we shall not need parliaments any more, by good husbandry of the crown, or else the crown must still have Aids, and the nation be not able to bear it. In the Revenue now, there are all the marks of superfluity; as Pensions on the Customs, and other branches of the Revenue, besides 80,000*l.* paid out of the exchequer for *secret service*, within these few months. And I have seen accounts in the Secretary's Papers, for Intelligence, &c. that come not near up to that sum. Now, we are required to inspect the Revenue, &c. a most unreasonable thing, at the latter end of a session! I know not how this Revenue can be granted, but upon a Home-Excise; and then what use can there be of so much revenue, but for keeping up the Army? I would have all men consider this question, of increasing the Revenue 300,000*l.* for the whole fate of Parliaments depends upon it.

Mr. Sec. *Williamson.* Unless you acquiesce in the reason of giving this Revenue, I would never press the house beyond their temper. I am willing that, for this time, the thing be laid aside.

Mr. *Vaughan.* By Williamson's argument, since the house does not willingly entertain the motion now, &c. that is to say, it may be taken up again. Some are dissolving this bond betwixt the king and his people, by this. I could not think that there was so much guilt in any person in the kingdom, to make such efforts. You have had strange judgments in the Exchequer chamber, in the case of Barnardiston and Soames. Such Judges may be prepared for judgments against you in the Exchequer-chamber for what you do here, when these doors are shut. Vassalages hereafter will not be confined to particular tenures, but this will be throughout the whole nation. I have seen men rise from nothing, within these walls. And when they are task-masters within these walls, they are task-masters to ruin the nation, with raising themselves. You have but one more addition to your misfortune, and that is, to give this 300,000*l.* increase to the Revenue. And I will give my negative to it.

Sir *Wm. Coventry.* I rise only to speak to the previous question. It is become a very parliamentary thing, but a word sometimes slips into it, that wakes a doubt. The word 'now' being not put in it, it may be a fortnight, or a month hence; but if you please to leave out the word 'now,' then the question will be, 'Whether you will consider of the motion of increasing the Revenue 300,000*l.* per an.'

Sir *Job Charlton.* I move that you will give the officers of the treasury time to make it out, whether the government cannot be supported without this addition to the Revenue. The king denies you no bills you present him, only 'le Roi s'avisera.' And I would not have you do any indecent thing to the king. [He was laughed at.]

The Commons refuse the King an Additional Revenue.] The question being put, "That the house will go into a grand committee, to consider of the motion for raising 300,000*l.* per annum, for an additional Revenue to the king," it passed in the negative, without a division.*

Debate on Members receiving Pensions.] Sir *Wm. Coventry* said, I take ourselves to be useful, not to say necessary, to the government, and till those scandals are taken away from us, mentioned in a book, of receiving pensions for our votes (which, it seems, has been thought fit to be amongst the advertisements in the Gazette, and a reward promised to the discoverer of the Author or Publisher),† I say, since this is made public, till this scandal be taken away, we cannot serve the nation

* "It was said, 'That there was a demand for a Revenue, which would furnish the Court so well; that there would be no more need of parliaments.' The Court party thought such a gift as this would make them useless, so the thing was, upon one debate, rejected without a division." Burnet.

† This very curious Tract will be found in the Appendix to the present volume, No. III.

as we ought. 'Money,' Solomon says, 'will blind the eyes of the wise.' If a man be in poverty, he need not be ashamed of his majesty's bounty. I say, he need not be ashamed of the bounty of his prince. But that man, whoever he be, that goes about to corrupt members of parliament for their votes, be he ever so great, should be ashamed of it. If a man be so base as to receive 500*l*. for his vote here, he, in time, will raise it up to 1500*l*. And that trick will be spoiled at last. If a man has been so transported by any pressures, let not the reputation of all your members lie under scandals; else the very laws you make will not meet with that chearful obedience they ought to have. I hope, therefore, that this house will do something in vindication of themselves, the thing now being made Gazette-matter, in the face of the whole world. I am not a man prepared to prescribe you a method to purge yourselves; but now that the jealousy has got so much strength as to be in print, and since it deserves the notice of the government, which has put it in print, seeing the ill fame of it has gotten abroad, I would have the good fame of our endeavouring to detect it get abroad likewise.

Sir *Tho. Clarges.* The Auditor of the Receipts of the Privy Seals can inform you, what money has been issued out since May 1677, upon extraordinary occasions.

Mr. *Wm. Harbord.* Whoever attempts the enslaving, and making the legislative power subservient to any particular subject, is guilty of the greatest crime that can be. Therefore I will explain myself thus. I would have every gentleman of the house come to the table, and protest that he has received no reward for any thing he has done in parliament, or for giving his vote. Or if any gentleman be in employment in the government, and has been put out of his place for giving his vote here according to his conscience, or has been threatened, this is a great crime. And I would have it as comprehensive as you can.

Whereupon several proposed these following Tests, &c. as they stood inclined to one party, or the other.

1. "Whether any members have received money to give their Votes, &c.? 2. Whether any members have been turned out of their places for giving their Votes, &c.? 3. Whether any members are guilty of Popery, and come not to the Sacrament, &c.? 4. Whether any members have been dealing with, or conversing with foreign ministers, or receiving money from them, to forward any business relating to parliament? 5. Whether any members have received money for giving counsel for any Bills depending in the house? 6. If any committees have received gratuities? 7 If any members have solicited voices in any business depending in parliament? 8. If any members have offered their service to any great persons to vote in parliament, and have been refused? 9. If any members have received money for granting Protections, &c.? 10. If any have kept public tables for Members, and at whose charges, &c.? 11. How many members sit in the house out-lawed, before judgment as well as after? 12. Enquiry to be made of those who go to Conventicles. 13. That a Test be given for discovery of the libel of the Catalogue of the Pensioners names, &c. who was the Author of it, and who promoted the dispersing, &c.?"

Of all these Articles it was proposed that every Member should purge himself; and a Vote passed accordingly, viz. Resolved, &c. "That an Account be taken, of what Pensions have been charged upon the Revenue; and what Privy Seals have issued for Secret Service, since May 1677: and that there be a Test concerning Bribery of Members for giving their Votes: and concerning Popery, and taking the Sacrament: and concerning conversing with foreign Ministers, or transacting with them, in relation to the proceedings of this house; and receiving money from them: and concerning such as have received any Money, as counsel for any bill depending in the house, or any reward for being chairman of a committee: and concerning such as have solicited for voices, in any cause depending before the house: and concerning such as have offered their service to great persons to give their Vote in parliament, and have been refused: and concerning such as keep public Tables; and at whose charge; and concerning such as have taken Money for granting Protections: and that inquiry be made, how many members are outlawed, as well before as after judgment: and that there be an inquiry made of such members as have gone to Conventicles or mass." But after it was thought that all was done and settled, and the house was about to rise, so many went away before a committee was appointed to draw up the said Tests, that the Court Party took advantage to put the question, Whether a Committee should be named, or no, which was carried in the negative, 100 to 86, and so the thing ended*.

Complaint against the Clerk.] June 19. Complaint was made, by several members, of the Clerk's non Entry of the Enquiries yesterday, concerning Moneys issued out by privy seals, and that he deserved to be turned out of his place for his misdemeanor.

The *Speaker.* You meddle with what you have nothing to do with, in displacing the Clerk, he being a patent officer.

Mr. *Hampden.* The clerk assistant is your own officer, and you may put him out, and displace him, upon misdemeanor.

Mr. Goldsborough, the clerk, was ordered to give an account of the pasting of the leaves together, in the Journal of the year 1663, and defacing it. The other allegation against the clerk, of the not entering yesterday's Order perfectly, was passed over with some reflection on the clerk; and he was ordered to perfect the Journal.

* Grey.

Sir Solomon Swale expelled.] A Letter was sent from sir Solomon Swale to the Speaker, to excuse his receiving the Sacrament * till Sunday sevennight, being prevented the last Sunday, by reason there was no Sacrament at St. Martin's Church, and after next Sunday come sevennight he hopes to be here to give his attendance.

Mr. *Wm. Harbord.* This is a mere trick; for Swale hopes by that time you will be up, and no farther enquiry be made after him. But I will take care to inform you of this trick.

Mr. *Williams.* A certificate of his repairing to divine service, and hearing it orderly, is a fair inducement to the Diocesan to certify. For the Order is nothing about receiving the Sacrament, only 'his conformity,' 3 James. And his 'allegation about receiving the Sacrament' is an insignificant thing, to delay time only.

The *Speaker* reads the Statute. 'He is to repair to his parish church where is the most of his abiding; and his receiving the Sacrament there shall undo the indictment.'

Lord *Gorges.* If Swale would have conformed he might have conformed in all this time, and it is a contempt of your Order.

Sir *Tho. Meres.* Since Swale has had two or three admonitions, for these five months last past that you have sat, and he has been convicted a year and a half, there's no farther forbearance can be, but you must do something with him.

Mr. *Daniel Finch.* The not receiving the Sacrament does not disable Swale from sitting in parliament, but the not taking the oaths of Allegiance and Supremacy. I move, that, if before Monday he receive not the Sacrament, and take not the Oaths of Allegiance and Supremacy, he shall not be permitted to sit here; and that a writ be sent out to chuse another member to serve in his place.

Sir *Robert Sawyer.* A Popish Recusant convict cannot come near the king's person, and, à fortiori, he cannot be of the great council of the nation. Whoever disables himself (as this case of Swale's is) from his attendance in parliament, you ought to discharge. And now you have fears and jealousies of Popery, to let such a man be one of you, that wilfully stands out of the church! You cannot answer it. I hope you will discharge him.

Then this question was put, and carried, viz. "That whereas it appears to the house, that sir Solomon Swale is convicted of Popish Recusancy; and having been divers times called upon by this house to signify his conformity to the Church of England, which he hath not done, in pursuance to a peremptory order of this house; ordered, That the said sir S. Swale be discharged from the service of this house; and that a new writ be issued out for the choice of another member to serve in his place, for the Borough of Aldborough, in the county of York."

* By an Order of June 10, he had been required to bring a Certificate by this day, of his conformity to the church of England.

The King's Message for continuing the Army longer on foot.] June 20. The Lord Treasurer, by his majesty's command, acquainted the lords, "That his majesty did yesterday receive a letter from his ambassador at Nimeguen, sir Lionel Jenkins, dated the 15th of June, which gave him an account, that the French ambassadors had declared to the Dutch ambassadors there, that they would not void any one of the places they held in the Spanish Netherlands, till Sweden be effectually restored to the places taken from them; no, notwithstanding that the peace was already signed and ratified between them. That upon this is arisen a difficulty on the side of the Spaniards, whether they will accept of the French conditions. That M. Beverning, one of the States ambassadors there, had thereupon earnestly enquired of him, whether the Army of England was presently to be disbanded; because nobody could tell what end things would come to; for if France will keep all the places in the Netherlands filled with their troops, it is in vain that the States have taken so much pains about their Barrier; for they will have none, when all is done. And the said M. Beverning was very anxious, till he did hear out of England, that the Army might not yet be disbanded.—That the Imperial ministers had been to visit him that day; and that their principal business was to learn what they could from him, in what state our Army was, things being in this doubtful condition."

The above was the same day communicated to the Commons, at a conference, and the lords delivered them a copy of the Message. The commons, after the conference, had some debate upon the said Message, but did nothing thereupon; but Resolved, "That a Message be sent to the lords, to remind them of the Bill for disbanding the Army."

The house then went into a committee of the whole house, and Resolved, "That the new imposts on Wines and Vinegar be granted to his majesty for three years, from the 1st of Aug. next, upon such Wines and Vinegar as may now be legally imported."

The question being put, "That the sum of 200,000*l.* which was borrowed on the credit of the Excise, shall be charged on the Bill for Impost on Wines," it passed in the negative, 179 to 168.

Vote on the Supply.] June 21. Resolved, "That a Supply, not exceeding 414,000*l.* shall be granted to his majesty, for paying off the extraordinary charge of the Navy and Ordnance; and for paying the princess of Orange's Portion; and for the repayment of the 200,000*l.* borrowed upon the credit of the additional Excise. And that the people be charged with no more money this session of parliament."

Controversy between the Houses.] June 22. The lords believing it impossible to disband the Army by the days the commons named in the Bill, changed the last of June to the 27th of July, for that part of the Army in England; and for those abroad, they changed the time from the 24th of July to the 24th of August. And the Bill, with these amendments, being returned to the commons this day, they were on debate, disagreed to by the house.'

June 25. The commons at a conference gave several reasons for their not agreeing with the lords in the above Amendments. The main one was, 'It being a Bill of Money, they cannot allow their lordships any manner of power, to add, or diminish, to, or from it, &c.' And they offered a Proviso, by way of expedient.

The same day several ways were proposed for raising the said sum of 414,000*l.* as upon Buildings erected since 1656, upon new foundations, within ten miles of London, but this was rejected, 117 to 88; by the old way of Subsidy, &c. but at last it was concluded by Land Tax. The house grew so thin, that, upon a division for adjourning the debate the Ayes were but 74, and the Noes 71.

June 26. The lords, at a Conference, gave several reasons for insisting on their Amendments to the Bill of disbanding, and for rejecting the Proviso offered by the commons. But to all the amendments but one the commons disagreed, and adhered to their proviso.

June 28. The lords voted that they adhered to their Amendments, and disagreed to the Proviso. And the commons voted è contra.

Vote on the Commons' Right of granting Money.] July 3. The commons resolved, "That all Aids and Supplies to his majesty in parliament, are the sole Gift of the commons; and all Bills for the granting of any such Aids and Supplies ought to begin with the commons; and that it is the undoubted and sole right of the commons to direct, limit, and appoint, in such Bills, the ends, purposes, considerations, conditions, limitations, and qualifications of such Grants; which ought not to be changed by the house of lords."

The Money Bill passed.] The same day the commons resolved, "That provision be made in the Bill now depending, for raising 414,000*l.* for raising 206,462*l.* 17*s.* 3*d.* for disbanding the Army; and that they be tacked together to be ingrossed in the same Bill." And this expedient ended the controversy between the lords and commons, about the lords alteration of the times of disbanding the Army, &c. in the Bill the commons sent up. And the former bill of disbanding the Army was laid aside.

July 8. The grand Money Bill passed, and was entitled 'An Act for granting a Supply to his majesty of 619,388*l.* 11*s.* 9*d.* for disbanding the Army, and other uses.'

The Parliament prorogued.] July 15. The house attended his majesty in the house of peers, where the royal assent was given to the Money Bill, and eight others; after which the Lord Chancellor made the following Speech:

"My lords; and you the knights, citizens, and burgesses of the house of commons; His majesty doth very graciously accept the service you have done him this session; and is as well pleased with your worthy and dutiful carriage towards him, as with the noble and liberal present you have made him.—He doth now consider, that some recess is necessary for your health and refreshment after all your labours; and he would be glad it might be for some longer time than his affairs at present will admit: for his majesty doth not know how soon he may be engaged in a war; and when he shall be so, he is sure that he can by no means want the counsel and assistance of his parliament; and therefore he hath resolved, never to put off this parliament too far from him.—For this cause, his maj. hath resolved to keep his parliament always in view, by making several, but very short, prorogations of it; but with an intention, however, that the parliament shall not sit till towards winter, unless his majesty's pressing and important occasions shall call for your advice sooner; and if they do so, his majesty will be sure to give timely notice thereof by his proclamation, to the end there may be a full appearance.—At this present, his majesty's pleasure is, to prorogue this parliament no further than till the first of August next; and this parliament is prorogued until the 1st of August next ensuing."*

Aug. 1. Both houses met, and were farther prorogued to August 29th; from thence to October 1st; and from thence to October 21.

PRINCIPAL OCCURRENCES DURING THE RECESS—THE POPISH PLOT—OATES'S NARRATIVE——COLEMAN'S LETTERS——GODFREY'S MURDER.] "The English nation," says Mr. Hume, "ever since the fatal league with France, had entertained violent jealousies against the court; and the subsequent measures adopted by the king, had tended more to increase than cure the general prejudices. Some mysterious design was still suspected in every enterprise and profession: arbitrary power and popery were apprehended as the scope of all projects: each breath or rumour made the people start with anxiety: their enemies, they thought, were in their very bosom, and had gotten possession of their sovereign's confidence. While in this timorous, jealous disposition, the cry of a PLOT all on a sudden struck their ears: they were wakened from their slumber; and like men affrightened and in the dark, took every figure for a spectre. The terror of each man became the source of terror to another. And an universal panic being diffused, reason and argument, and common sense, and common humanity, lost all influence over them. From this disposition of men's minds we are to ac-

* "Thus ended the 16th session of this parliament; and thus England saw herself engaged in an expence of 600,000*l.* to pay an Army and Fleet, which certainly had not been prepared to make war with France, or for the security of England." Rapin.

count for the progress of the POPISH PLOT, and the credit given to it; an event, which would otherwise appear prodigious and altogether inexplicable.—On the 12th of August, one Kirby, a chemist, accosted the king, as he was walking in the park: 'Sir,' said he, 'keep within the company: your enemies have a design upon your life; and you may be shot in this very walk.' Being asked the reason of these strange speeches, he said, that two men, called Grove and Pickering, had engaged to shoot the king, and sir George Wakeman, the queen's physician, to poison him. This intelligence, he added, had been communicated to him by doctor Tongue; whom, if permitted, he would introduce to his majesty. Tongue was a divine of the church of England; a man active, restless, full of projects, void of understanding. He brought papers to the king, which contained information of a plot, and were digested into forty-three articles. The king, not having leisure to peruse them, sent them to the treasurer, Danby, and ordered the two informers to lay the business before that minister. Tongue confessed to Danby, that he himself had not drawn the papers, that they had been secretly thrust under his door and that, though he suspected, he did not certainly know, who was the author. After a few days he returned, and told the treasurer, that his suspicions, he fonnd, were just; and that the author of the intelligence, whom he had met twice or thrice in the street, had acknowledged the whole matter, and had given him a more particular account of the conspiracy, but desired that his name might be concealed, being apprehensive lest the papists should murder him.—The information was renewed with regard to Grove's and Pickering's intentions of shooting the king; and Tongue even pretended, that, at a particular time, they were to set out for Windsor with that intention. Orders were given for arresting them, as soon as they should appear in that place: but though this alarm was more than once renewed, some frivolous reasons were still found by Tongue, for their having delayed the journey. And the king concluded, both from these evasions, and from the mysterious, artificial manner of communicating the intelligence, that the whole was an imposture.—Tongue came next to the treasurer, and told him, that a pacquet of letters, written by jesuits concerned in the plot, was that night to be put into the post-house for Windsor, directed to Bennifield, a jesuit, confessor to the duke. When this intelligence was conveyed to the king, he replied, that the pacquet mentioned had a few hours before been brought to the duke by Bennifield; who said, that he suspected some bad design upon him, that the letters seemed to contain matters of a dangerous import, and that he knew them not to be the hand-writing of the persons whose names were subscribed to them. This incident still further confirmed the king in his incredulity.—The matter had probably sleeped for ever, had it not been for the anxiety of the duke; who, hearing that priests and jesuits, and even his own confessor, had been accused, was desirous that a thorough inquiry should be made by the council into the pretended conspiracy. Kirby and Tongue were inquired after, and were now found to be living in close connection with Titus Oates, the person who was said to have conveyed the first intelligence to Tongue. Oates affirmed, that he had fallen under suspicion with the jesuits; that he had received three blows with a stick, and a box on the ear from the provincial of that order, for revealing their conspiracy: and that, overhearing them speak of their intentions to punish him more severely, he had withdrawn, and concealed himself. This man, in whose breast was lodged a secret, involving the fate of kings and kingdoms, was allowed to remain in such necessity, that Kirby was obliged to supply him with daily bread; and it was a joyful surprise to him, when he heard that the council was at last disposed to take some notice of his intelligence. But as he expected more encouragement from the public, than from the king or his ministers, he thought proper, before he was presented to the council, to go with his two companions to sir Edmonsbury Godfrey, a noted and active justice of peace, and to give evidence before him of all the articles of the conspiracy.—The wonderful intelligence, which Oates conveyed both to Godfrey and the council, and afterwards to the parliament, was to this purpose.—The pope, he said, on examining the matter in the congregation de propaganda, had found himself entitled to the possession of England and Ireland on account of the heresy of prince and people, and had accordingly assumed the sovereignty of these kingdoms. This supreme power he had thought proper to delegate to the society of jesuits; and de Oliva, general of that order, in consequence of the papal grant, had exerted every act of regal authority, and particularly had supplied, by commissions under the seal of the society, all the chief offices, both civil and military. Lord Arundel was created chancellor, lord Powis treasurer, sir William Godolphin privy seal, Coleman secretary of state, Langhorne attorney general, lord Bellasis general of the papal army, lord Peters lieutenant-general, lord Stafford paymaster; and inferior commissions, signed by the provincial of the jesuits, were distributed all over England. All the dignities too of the church were filled, and many of them with Spaniards and other foreigners. The provincial had held a consult of the jesuits under his authority; where the king, whom they opprobiously called the Black Bastard, was solemnly tried and condemned as a heretic; and a resolution taken to put him to death. Father le Shee (for so this great plotter and informer called father la Chaise, the noted confessor of the French king) had consigned in London ten thousand pounds to be paid to any man who should merit it by this assassination. A Spanish provincial had expressed like liberality the prior of the Benedictines was willing to go the length of six thousand: the Dominicans approved of the action; but pleaded poverty. Ten thousand pounds had been offered to sir George Wakeman, the queen's physician, who demanded fifteen thousand, as a reward for so great a service: his demand was complied with; and five thousand had been paid him by advance. Lest this means should fail, four Irish ruffians had been hired by the Jesuits at the rate of twenty guineas a-piece, to stab the king at Windsor; and Coleman, secretary to the late dutchess of York, had given the messenger, who carried them orders, a guinea to quicken his diligence. Grove and Pickering were also employed to shoot the king with silver bullets: the former was to receive the sum of fifteen hundred pounds; the latter, being a pious man, was to be rewarded with thirty thousand masses, which, estimating masses at a shilling a-piece, amounted to a like value. Pickering would have executed his purpose, had not the flint at one time dropped out of his pistol, at another time the priming. Coniers, the Jesuit, had bought a knife at the price of ten shillings, which he thought was not dear, considering the purpose for which he intended it, to wit, stabbing the king. Letters of subscription were circulated among the catholics all over England to raise a sum for the same purpose. No less than fifty Jesuits had met in May last at the White-horse tavern, where it was unanimously agreed to put the king to death. This synod did afterwards, for more convenience, divide themselves into many lesser cabals or companies; and Oates was employed to carry notes and letters from one to another, all tending to the same end, of murdering the king. He even carried, from one company to another, a paper, in which they formally expressed their resolution of executing that deed; and it was regularly subscribed by all of them. A wager of a hundred pounds was laid, and stakes made, that the king should eat no more Christmas pyes. In short, it was determined, to use the expression of a Jesuit, that if he would not become R. C. (Roman Catholic) he should no longer be C. R. (Charles Rex). The great fire of London had been the work of the Jesuits, who had employed eighty or eighty-six persons for that purpose, and had expended seven hundred fire-balls; but they had a good return for their money, for they had been able to pilfer goods from the fire to the value of fourteen thousand pounds: the Jesuits had also raised another fire on St. Margaret's Hill, whence they had stolen goods to the value of two thousand pounds: another at Southwark: and it was determined in like manner to burn all the chief cities in England. A paper model was already framed for the firing of London; the stations were regularly marked out, where the several fires were to commence; and the whole plan of operations was so concerted, that precautions were taken by the Jesuits to vary their measures, according to the variation of the wind. Fire-balls were familiarly called among them Teuxbury mustard pills; and were said to contain a notable biting sauce. In the great fire, it had been determined to murder the king; but he had displayed such diligence and humanity in extinguishing the flames, that even the Jesuits relented, and spared his life. Besides these assassinations and fires; insurrections, rebellions, and massacres, were projected by that religious order in all the three kingdoms. There were twenty thousand catholics in London, who would rise in four and-twenty hours, or less; and Jennison, a Jesuit, said, that they might easily cut the throats of a hundred thousand protestants. Eight thousand catholics had agreed to take arms in Scotland. Ormond was to be murdered by four Jesuits; a general massacre of the Irish protestants was concerted; and forty thousand black bills were already provided for that purpose. Coleman had remitted two hundred thousand pounds to promote the rebellion in Ireland; and the French king was to land a great army in that island. Poole, who wrote the Synopsis, was particularly marked out for assassination; as was also Dr. Stillingfleet, a controversial writer against the papists. Burnet tells us, that Oates paid him the same compliment. After all this havoc, the crown was to be offered to the duke, but on the following conditions; that he receive it as a gift from the pope; that he confirm all the papal commissions for offices and employments; that he ratify all past transactions, by pardoning the incendiaries, and the murderers of his brother and of the people; and that he consent to the utter extirpation of the protestant religion. If he refuse these conditions, he himself was immediately to be poisoned or assassinated, 'To pot James must go;' according to the expression ascribed by Oates to the Jesuits.—Oates, the informer of this dreadful plot, was himself the most infamous of mankind. He was the son of an anabaptist preacher, chaplain to colonel Pride; but having taken orders in the church, he had been settled in a small living by the duke of Norfolk. He had been indicted for perjury; and by some means had escaped. He was afterwards a chaplain on board the fleet; whence he had been dismissed on complaint of some unnatural practices, not fit to be named. He then became a convert to the catholics; but he afterwards boasted, that his conversion was a mere pretence, in order to get into their secrets and to betray them. He was sent over to the Jesuits' college at St. Omer's, and though above thirty years of age, he there lived some time among the students. He was dispatched on an errand to Spain; and thence returned to St. Omer's; where the Jesuits, heartily tired of their convert, at last dismissed him from their seminary. It is likely, that, from resentment of this usage, as well as from want and indigence, he was induced, in combination with Tongue, to contrive that plot, of which he accused the catholics.—This abandoned man, when examined before the council, betrayed his impostures in such a manner, as would have utterly discredited the most consistent story, and the most reputable evidence. While in Spain, he had been carried, he said, to don John, who promised great assistance to the execution of the catholic designs. The king asked him, what sort of a man don John was: he answered, a tall lean man; directly contrary to truth, as the king well knew. He totally mistook the situation of the Jesuits' college at Paris. Though he pretended great intimacies with Coleman, he knew him not, when placed very near him; and had no other excuse than that his sight was bad in candle-light. He fell into like mistakes with regard to Wakeman.—Notwithstanding these objections, great attention was paid to Oates's evidence, and the plot became very soon the subject of conversation, and even the object of terror to the people. The violent animosity, which had been excited against the catholics in general, made the public swallow the grossest absurdities when they accompanied an accusation of those religionists: and the more diabolical any contrivance appeared, the better it suited the tremendous idea entertained of a Jesuit. Danby likewise, who stood in opposition to the French and catholic interest at court, was willing to encourage every story, which might serve to discredit that party. By his suggestion, when a warrant was signed for arresting Coleman, there was inserted a clause for seizing his papers; a circumstance attended with the most important consequences. Coleman partly on his own account, partly by orders from the duke, had been engaged in a correspondence with father la Chaise, with the pope's nuncio at Brussels, and with other catholics abroad; and being himself a fiery zealot, busy and sanguine, the expressions in his letters often betrayed great violence and indiscretion. His correspondence, during the years 1674, 1675, and part of 1676,* was seized, and contained many extraordinary passages. In particular he said to la Chaise, 'We have 'here a mighty work upon our hands, no less 'than the conversion of three kingdoms, and 'by that perhaps the utter subduing of a pes-'tilent heresy, which has a long time domi-'neered over a great part of this northern 'world. There were never such hopes of 'success, since the days of queen Mary, as 'now in our days. God has given us a prince,' meaning the duke, 'who is become (may I 'say a miracle) zealous of being the author 'and instrument of so glorious a work; but 'the opposition we are sure to meet with is 'also like to be great: so that it imports us to 'get all the aid and assistance we can.' In another letter he said, 'I can scarce believe my-'self awake, or the thing real, when I think of 'a prince in such an age as we live in, con-'verted to such a degree of zeal and piety, as 'not to regard any thing in the world in com-'parison of God's Almighty glory, the salvation 'of his own soul, and the conversion of our poor 'kingdom.' In other passages the interests of the crown of England, those of the French king, and those of the catholic religion, are spoken of as inseparable. The duke is also said to have connected his interests unalterably with those of Lewis. The king himself, he affirms, is always inclined to favour the catholics, when he may do it without hazard. 'Money,' Coleman adds, 'cannot fail of persuad-'ing the king to any thing. There is nothing 'it cannot make him do, were it ever so much 'to his prejudice. It has such an absolute 'power over him, that he cannot resist it. 'Logic, built upon money, has in our court 'more powerful charms than any other sort of 'argument.' For these reasons, he proposed to father la Chaise, that the French king should remit the sum of 300,000*l.* on condition that the parliament be dissolved; a measure to which, he affirmed, the king was, of himself, sufficiently inclined, were it not for his hopes of obtaining money from that assembly. The parliament, he said, had already constrained the king to make peace with Holland, contrary to the interests of the catholic religion, of his most christian majesty: and if they should meet again, they would surely engage him farther, even to the making of war against France. It appears also from the same letters, that the assembling of the parliament so late as April in the year 1675, had been procured by the intrigues of the catholic and French party, who thereby intended to show the Dutch and their confederates, that they could expect no assistance from England.—When the contents of these letters were publicly known, they diffused the panic, with which the nation began already to be seized on account of the popish plot. Men reasoned more from their fears and their passions than from the evidence before them. It is certain, that the restless and enterprising spirit of the catholic church, particularly of the Jesuits, merits attention, and is, in some degree, dangerous to every other communion. Such zeal of proselytism actuates that sect, that its missionaries have penetrated into every nation of the globe; and, in one sense, there is a POPISH PLOT perpetually carrying on against all states, protestant, pagan, and mahometan. It is likewise very probable, that the conversion of the duke, and the favour of the king, had inspired the catholic priests with new hopes of recovering in these islands their lost dominion, and gave fresh vigour to that intemperate zeal by which they are commonly actuated.—Their first aim was to obtain a toleration; and such was the evidence, they believed, of their theological tenets, that, could they but procure entire liberty, they must infallibly in time open the eyes of the people. After they had converted considerable numbers, they might be enabled, they hoped, to reinstate themselves in full authority, and entirely to suppress that heresy, with which the kingdom had so long been affected. Though these dangers to the

* See Appendix, No. viii.

protestant religion were distant, it was justly the object of great concern to find that the heir of the crown was so blinded with bigotry, and so deeply engaged in foreign interest: and that the king himself had been prevailed on, from low interest, to hearken to his dangerous insinuations. Very bad consequences might ensue from such perverse habits and attachments; nor could the nation and parliament guard against them with too anxious a precaution. But that the Roman pontiff could hope to assume the sovereignty of these kingdoms; a project which, even during the darkness of the eleventh and twelfth centuries, would have appeared chimerical: that he should delegate this authority to the Jesuits; that order in the Romish Church, which was the most hated; that a massacre could be attempted of the protestants, who surpassed the catholics a hundred fold, and were invested with the whole authority of the state: that the king himself was to be assassinated, and even the duke, the only support of their party: these were such absurdities as no human testimony was sufficient to prove; much less the evidence of one man, who was noted for infamy, and who could not keep himself every moment from falling into the grossest inconsistencies. Did such intelligence deserve even so much attention as to be refuted, it would appear, that Coleman's letters were sufficient alone to destroy all its credit. For how could so long a train of correspondence be carried on, by a man so much trusted by the party; and yet no traces of insurrections, if really intended, of fires, massacres, assassinations, invasions, be ever discovered in any single passage of these letters? But all such reflections, and many more, equally obvious, were vainly employed against that general prepossession with with which the nation was seized. Oates's plot and Coleman's were universally confounded together: and the evidence of the latter being unquestionable, the belief of the former, aided by the passions of hatred and of terror, took possession of the whole people.—There was danger, however, lest time might open the eyes of the public (17th Oct.); when the murder of Godfrey completed the general delusion, and rendered the prejudices of the nation absolutely incurable. This magistrate had been missing some days; and after much search, and many surmises, his body was found lying in a ditch at Primrose-hill: the marks of strangling were thought to appear about his neck, and some contusions on his breast: his own sword was sticking in the body; but as no considerable quantity of blood ensued on drawing it, it was concluded, that it had been thrust in after his death, and that he had not killed himself: he had rings on his fingers, and money in his pocket: it was therefore inferred, that he had not fallen into the hands of robbers. Without farther reasoning, the cry rose, that he had been assassinated by the papists, on account of his taking Oates's evidence. This clamour was quickly propagated, and met with universal belief. The panic spread itself on every side with infinite rapidity; and all men, astonished with fear, and animated with rage, saw in Godfrey's fate all the horrible designs ascribed to the catholics; and no farther doubt remained of Oates's veracity. The voice of the nation united against that hated sect; and, notwithstanding that the bloody conspiracy was supposed to be now detected, men could scarcely be persuaded that their lives were yet in safety. Each hour teemed with new rumours and surmises. Invasions from abroad, insurrections at home, even private murders and poisonings, were apprehended. To deny the reality of the plot, was to be an accomplice: to hesitate was criminal: Royalist, Republican; Churchman, Sectary; Courtier, Patriot; all parties concurred in the illusion. The city prepared for its defence, as if the enemy were at its gates: the chains and posts were put up: and it was a noted saying at that time of sir Thomas Player, the chamberlain, that, were it not for these precautions, all the citizens might rise next morning with their throats cut.—In order to propagate the popular frenzy, several artifices were employed. The dead body of Godfrey was carried into the city, attended by vast multitudes. It was publicly exposed in the streets, and viewed by all ranks of men; and every one, who saw it, went away inflamed, as well by the mutual contagion of sentiments, as by the dismal spectacle itself. The funeral pomp was celebrated with great parade. The corpse was conducted through the chief streets of the city: seventy-two clergymen marched before: above a thousand persons of distinction followed after: and at the funeral-sermon two able bodied divines mounted the pulpit, and stood on each side of the preacher, lest, in paying the last duties to this unhappy magistrate, he should, before the whole people, be murdered by the papists.—In this disposition of the nation, reason could no more be heard than a whisper in the midst of the most violent hurricane. Even at present, Godfrey's murder can scarcely, upon any system, be rationally accounted for. That he was assassinated by the catholics seems utterly improbable. These religionists could not be engaged to commit that crime from policy, in order to deter other magistrates from acting against them. Godfrey's fate was no-wise capable of producing that effect, unless it were publicly known that the catholics were his murderers: an opinion which, it was easy to foresee, must prove the ruin of their party. Besides, how many magistrates, during more than a century, had acted in the most violent manner against the catholics, without its being ever suspected that any one had been cut off by assassination? Such jealous times as the present, were surely ill fitted for beginning these dangerous experiments. Shall we therefore say, that the catholics were pushed on, not by policy, but by blind revenge against Godfrey? But Godfrey had given them little or no occasion of offence in taking Oates's evidence. His part was merely an act of form, belonging to his office; nor could he, or any man in his station, possibly refuse it. In the rest of his conduct, he lived on good terms with the catholics, and was far from distinguishing himself by his severity against that sect. It is even certain, that he had contracted an intimacy with Coleman, and took care to inform his friend of the danger to which, by reason of Oates's evidence, he was at present exposed.—There are some writers, who finding it impossible to account for Godfrey's murder by the machinations of the catholics, have recourse to the opposite supposition. They lay hold of that obvious presumption, that those commit the crime who reap advantage by it; and they affirm that it was Shaftesbury, and the heads of the popular party, who perpetrated that deed, in order to throw the odium of it on the papists. If this supposition be received, it must also be admitted, that the whole plot was the contrivance of those politicians; and that Oates acted altogether under their direction. But it appears that Oates, dreading probably the opposition of powerful enemies, had very anxiously acquitted the duke, Danby, Ormond, and all the ministry; persons who were certainly the most obnoxious to the popular leaders. Besides, the whole texture of the plot contains such low absurdity, that it is impossible to have been the invention of any man of sense or education. It is true, the more monstrous and horrible the conspiracy, the better was it fitted to terrify, and thence to convince, the populace: but this effect, we may safely say, no one could beforehand have expected; and a fool was in this case more likely to succeed than a wise man. Had Shaftesbury laid the plan of a popish conspiracy, he had probably rendered it moderate, consistent, credible; and, on that very account, had never met with the prodigious success, with which Oates's tremendous fictions were attended.—We must, therefore, be contented to remain for ever ignorant of the actors in Godfrey's murder; and only pronounce in general, that that event, in all likelihood, had no connection, one way or other, with the popish plot. Any man, especially so active a magistrate as Godfrey, might, in such a city as London, have many enemies, of whom his friends and family had no suspicion. He was a melancholy man; and there is some reason, notwithstanding the pretended appearances to the contrary, to suspect that he fell by his own hands. The affair was never examined with tranquillity, or even with common sense, during the time; and it is impossible for us, at this distance, certainly to account for it.—No one doubted but the papists had assassinated Godfrey; but still the particular actors were unknown. A proclamation was issued by the king, offering a pardon and a reward of five hundred pounds to any one who should discover them. As it was afterwards surmised, that the terror of a like assassination would prevent discovery, a new proclamation was issued, promising absolute protection to any one who should reveal the secret. Thus were indemnity, money, and security, offered to the fairest bidder: and no one needed to fear, during the present fury of the people, that his evidence would undergo too severe a scrutiny. While the nation was in this ferment, the parliament was assembled."

SEVENTEENTH SESSION OF THE SECOND PARLIAMENT.

The King's Speech on opening the Session.] Oct. 21. The parliament met, and his majesty opened the session with the following Speech to both houses:

"My Lords and Gentlemen; I have thought the time very long since we parted last; and would not have deferred your meeting by so many prorogations, if I could well have met you sooner. The part which I have had this summer in the preservation of our neighbours, and the well-securing what was left of Flanders, is sufficiently known and acknowledged by all that are abroad: and though for this cause I have been obliged to keep up my troops (without which our neighbours had absolutely despaired); yet both the honour and interest of the nation have been so far improved by it, that I am confident no man here would repine at it, or think the money raised for their disbanding to have been all employed in their continuance; and I do assure you, I am so much more out of purse for the service, that I do expect you should supply it.—How far it may be necessary (considering the present state of Christendom) to reduce the land and sea forces, or to what degree, is worthy of all our serious considerations.—I now intend to acquaint you (as I shall always do with any thing that concerns me), that I have been informed of a Design against my person by the Jesuits;* of which I shall forbear any opinion,

* It may be proper briefly to repeat, that on Sept. 28, Titus Oates had given information, before the Council, of many discourses he had heard among the Jesuits, of their design to kill the king, naming persons, places, and times almost without number; upon which many Jesuits were seized that night and the next day; and in particular, having accused Coleman, the Duke's Secretary, of a strict correspondence with Father le Chaise, the French king's Confessor, adding, 'that he was acquainted with all their designs,' Coleman was immediately apprehended, and from his letters, which were seized and examined, the story gained great confirmation. Add to this, that sir Edmundbury Godfrey, an eminent Justice of Peace, who had attested Oates's Depositions, was found, on Oct. 17, with his own sword thrust through his body, in a ditch near Primrose-hill, in the way to Hampstead, having been missing ever since the 12th. And as it had been taken for granted that Coleman's Papers confirmed every thing that Oates had sworn, so it was no sooner known that Godfrey was

lest I may seem to say too much, or too little: but I will leave the matter to the law;* and, in the mean time, will take as much care as I can to prevent all manner of practices by that sort of men, and of others too, who have been tampering in a high degree by foreigners, and contriving how to introduce Popery amongst us.—I shall conclude with the recommending to you my other concerns. I have been under great disappointments by the defect of the Poll Bill. My Revenue is under great Anticipations, and at the best was never equal to the constant and necessary expence of the government, whereof I intend to have the whole state laid before you; and require you to look into it, and consider of it with that duty and affection which I am sure I shall always find from you.—The rest I leave to the Chancellor."

The Lord Chancellor Finch's Speech.] Then the Lord Chancellor made the following Speech:

"My lords; and you the knights, citizens, and burgesses of the house of commons; How much the king relies upon the advice and assistance of his parliament, how necessary he accounts it to him, and how safe he thinks himself in it, is evident by this, that he hath not suffered you all this year to be out of his reach; but hath continued you from time to time, by a succession of little and short prorogations; and without all peradventure we had sooner met, if it had been possible for us to take right measures here, without a full knowledge of the state and condition of our neighbours.—The close and period of the last Session is very memorable; for it may seem perhaps to some to have ended with very different, if not contrary, counsels and supplies, tending both to war and peace; but yet they who look more nearly into the matter shall find, that this incertainty proceeded not from any unsteadiness at home, but from the mutability of affairs abroad, every week almost producing several and contrary appearances.—The same incertainties of counsels and events abroad continued for the most part of the summer. One while the parties, exhausted by the war, seemed to be willing to accept any peace their enemies would give; and there wanted not those among them who made use of the impatience of their people to necessitate them to it.—Another while the performance of the conditions offered became so doubted, and was at last explained in a manner so vastly different from the first proposals, that despair begot new resolutions of continuing the war.—In the midst of these miserable perplexities and confusions, his maj. was daily solicited, with the highest importunities and the most earnest supplications that were possible, not to disband the troops he had raised; and not only so, but that he would still continue to send over more and more of his troops, and to augment the forces which he had already abroad. They did as good as tell him plainly, That it was from the reputation of his alliance, that any overtures of peace had been made at all; and that it was from the continuance of his arms that any fair performance could be expected. —They prayed his maj. to consider, That if he thought it expedient to obtain some kind of respite, or breathing-time, for the Spanish Netherlands, or to secure any kind of frontier or barrier between them and their too powerful neighbours; all this, and more, very much more, perhaps no less than the safety of Christendom, would entirely depend upon his majesty's preserving himself in that considerable posture both by sea and land wherein he then was.—There was no resisting such repeated intercessions; and though his maj. saw well enough that his complying with these desires would engage him in an expence far beyond what he was then provided for, yet he could not possibly decline the charge, nor refuse to undergo the difficulties. And now, whatever the cost of all this may amount to, yet neither his maj. nor his people will have any cause to repent it, when they shall consider, that it hath already produced such great and good effects to his majesty's allies, and so much honour to the whole nation; that whatsoever is saved of Flanders, is now acknowledged by all the world to be wholly due to his majesty's interposition.—And though the peace, which since hath followed, be very far from such a peace as his maj. could have wished, yet it is such a peace as his neighbours were resolved to have. No obligations they lay under to insist upon a better peace, no conjunction with his majesty, no, nor the offers to declare war on their behalfs if they desired it, could prevail with them, or keep them from being wrought upon by the ill arts of those who first raised unreasonable jealousies amongst them, and then caused them to precipitate themselves into a peace.—Thus you see at once, not only the necessity which his majesty had to continue his troops in pay,

killed, than by the general voice the Papists were charged with the murder; for the discovery of which a reward of 500*l.* was offered by Proclamation on October 20, the day before the parliament reassembled.

* "The king, knowing the disaffection of the commons, was resolved, if possible, to prevent this affair from coming before them: he feared, very justly, that they would examine into the bottom of this Plot, and, under a pretence of taking care of his person, discover many things which were yet to be concealed. For this purpose he expressly commanded the earl of Danby not to acquaint the two houses with what had passed through his hands, and resolved so to order it, that every thing concerning the Plot should be left to the law, in the belief that it would be much easier for him to manage the Judges than the parliament. But the earl of Danby broke all his measures, by communicating, the very first day, Oates's Narrative to the commons. The king was highly provoked with a procedure so contrary to his orders and designs, and gave him a severe reprimand; but the thing was without remedy." Rapin.

but likewise the benefits and advantages which have come of it.—Let no man wonder then, if the Money given toward this Disbanding have been applied toward the payment of the Army, as far as it would go: there needs no excuse for that which was inevitable. The provision which was made for paying off the Army went no further than till the last of June for part, and the last of August for the rest: but the Fleet was provided for only till the 5th of June; so that the continuation of the Fleet and Army from that time was wholly upon his majesty's charge.—And as this was an expence so absolutely necessary to our own interest, in the preservation of our neighbours; that his maj. could not with any honour or safety to himself have avoided it: so the service which hath been done by this means to a great part of Christendom is so universally acknowledged, that you cannot but be well pleased to have your share in the honour of it, and will be willing to defray the rest of the charge, which hath far exceeded all that was given by that Act.—And his maj. hath found himself in greater streights than he could have imagined, by the unexpected deficiency of the Poll Bill; for whereas it was made a fund of credit for 800,000*l.* besides a further credit for Stores, the product of that Act hath fallen so strangely short of what the parliament expected from it, that it hath not raised that sum of money, by a great deal, which was allowed to be borrowed upon it; and by this means, they who have furnished Stores upon the credit of that Act will be in danger to be very great losers, unless you are pleased to take some care of them.—Thus you have shortly an Account of what hath been doing Abroad, and the Charge of it: it is now high time to look a little nearer Home; and surely, in that state of things to which they are now reduced, it is visible and plain enough what must be our business for the time to come. First, we must look to ourselves, and provide for our own safety; for that which the Confederates acknowledge with thanks, we may be sure hath a quite different resentment in other places. And, in order to this, care must be taken so to strengthen ourselves, both at home and abroad, that they who see us in a firm and well-settled estate may have no hopes to surprize, nor any temptation to make an attempt upon us. —And herein it will be necessary to take notice of what his maj. recommended to you, and to weigh very well the importance of reducing the Sea and Land Forces, and the consequences which may attend such a reducement; for, this be assured, that nothing in the world would more gratify our enemies, than to see us afraid of maintaining ourselves in a posture of defence, which is the only posture they are afraid to find us in.—And that the fears of Popery may not too much disquiet you, be pleased to consider, that you have one security more; since that which was always the interest of his majesty's honour and conscience is now become the interest of his person too, to protect the Protestant Religion, and to prevent the swarming of Seminary Priests; for his maj. hath told you, that he hath lately received information of Designs against his own life by the Jesuits; and though he doth in no sort prejudge the persons accused, yet the strict enquiry into this matter hath been a means to discover so many other unwarrantable practices of theirs, that his maj. hath reason to look to them.—Nor are these kind of men the only factors for Rome; but there are found among the laity also some, who have made themselves agitators to promote the interests of a foreign religion, who meddle with matters of state and parliament, and carry on their pernicious designs by a most dangerous correspondency with foreign nations.—What kind of process the proof will bear, and to how high a degree the extent and nature of these crimes will rise, is under consideration, and will be fully left to the course of law.—In the next place, let us carefully avoid all Differences amongst ourselves, all manner of clashing about Jurisdictions, and all disputes of such a nature as can never end in any accommodation; for this is still what our enemies would wish, who would be glad to see us ruined, without their being at the charge of it.—And therefore we must now above all other times labour to shew the world the most effectual significations of our loyalty and duty that we are able to express; for nothing in the world can more discourage our enemies, as on the contrary nothing does or can so ripen a nation for destruction, as to be observed to distrust their own government. Be pleased then now to take occasion to manifest such a zeal for the government, as to look into the state of that Revenue which should support the constant and necessary Charge of it, and to see that it be made equal to it. There are many motives to oblige us to this inspection. First, you see, the king expects it; and then again you cannot but see that nothing is, or can be, of a more public consideration, than to support the dignity of the crown, which is in truth the dignity of the nation: besides, it is unsafe, as well as dishonourable, that the king's Revenue should fall short of his most necessary and most unavoidable Expences.—And, if upon a due examination, it shall be made appear to you, that though there had been no diminution of the Customs, yet no thrift or conduct in the world could ever make the Revenue able to answer the certain Charge of the government, much less to discharge those Anticipations which lie heavy upon it; how can it be possible for it to supply those contingencies which happen even in times of peace, and which can never be brought under any regulation or establishment? —You may be sure, a great and generous prince would be glad, by good managery, to have wherewithal to exercise his royal bounty. But our neighbours have found a way to prevent all that: for their vast preparations put his maj. upon a vast expence, to preserve himself and us.—My Lords and Gentlemen; You now find the king involved in difficulties as great, and without your assistance as insuperable, as ever any government did labour under. And yet his maj. doth not think that there need many words to bespeak your zeal and industry in his service; for the things themselves now speak, and speak aloud. The public and the private interest do both persuade the same things; and are, and ought to be, mighty in persuasion. If the honour and safety of your country, and, which is next to that, the concerns of your own families and posterities, cannot awaken your utmost care to preserve that govt. which only can preserve you and yours, all other discourses will be to no purpose. There can be no difficulties at all to them who take delight in serving of the king and their country, and love the occasions of shewing it. Such are all here: but though the king have had for many years a large and full experience of your duty, yet there never was a time like this to try your affections. There is so strange a concurrence of ill accidents at this time, that it is not to be wondered at, if some very honest and good men begin to have troubled and thoughtful hearts; yet that which is infinitely to be lamented is, that malicious men too begin to work upon this occasion, and are in no small hopes to raise a storm that nothing shall be able to allay. If you can rescue the king's affairs from such a tempest as this; if you can weather this storm, and steer the vessel into harbour; if you can find a way to quiet the apprehensions of those who mean well, without being carried away by the passions of others who mean ill; if you can prevent the designs of those without doors, who study nothing else but how to distract your counsels, and to disturb all your proceedings: then you will have performed as great and as seasonable a piece of service to the king, as ever he stood in need of. —And when the world shall see, that nothing hath been able to disappoint the king of the assistance he had reason to hope from this session, but that there is a right understanding between the king and his parliament, and that again strengthened and increased by new evidences of your duty and affection, and raised above all possibility of being interrupted; then shall the king be possessed of that true glory, which others vainly pursue, the glory of reigning in the hearts of his people; then shall the people be possessed of as much felicity as this world is capable of; and you shall have the perpetual honour and satisfaction of having been the means to procure so much solid and lasting good to your country, as the establishment of the peace and tranquillity of this kingdom, and consequently of all his majesty's dominions."

Address of both Houses for a solemn Fast.] The first Resolves of the house of commons were, That a committee be appointed to consider of Ways and Means for the preservation of his majesty's person: That an humble Address be presented to his majesty, for removing Popish Recusants from London; and that a Committee be appointed to enquire into Sir Edmundbury Godfrey's Murder; as likewise into the Plot. The same day the house agreed with the lords in an Address to his majesty, to appoint a solemn Fast; which was to the following effect: "That Information had been given of a horrible Design against his sacred life, and being very sensible of the fatal consequences of such an attempt, and of the dangers of the subversion of the Protestant Religion and government of this realm, they humbly beseech his majesty, that a solemn day of Fasting and Humiliation may be appointed, to implore the mercy and protection of Almighty God to his majesty's royal person, and in him to all his loyal subjects; and to pray that God will bring to light, more and more, all secret machinations against his majesty and the whole kingdom." All which was accordingly done by Proclamation dated the 25th of October, requiring, that Wednesday the 13th of November should be kept for a general Fast. On the 24th both Houses again agreed on another Address, and,

Address concerning Popish Recusants.] Oct. 26. Both houses presented the following Address to the king:

"We your majesty's most dutiful and loyal subjects, the lords spiritual and temporal, and commons in parliament assembled, having taken into our serious consideration the bloody and traiterous Designs of Popish Recusants, against your majesty's sacred person and government, and the Protestant Religion, wherewith your maj. hath been graciously pleased to acquaint us: for the preventing whereof, we do most humbly beseech your majesty, that your maj. would be graciously pleased, by your royal proclamation, to command all and every person and persons being Popish Recusants, or so reputed, forthwith, under pain of your majesty's highest displeasure, and severe execution of the law against them, to depart and retire, themselves and their families, from your royal palaces of Whitehall, Somerset-house, St. James's, the cities of London and Westminster, and from all other places within ten miles of the same. And that no such person or persons, do, at any time hereafter, repair or return to your majesty's said palaces, or the said cities, or either of them; or within ten miles of the same, other than housholders, being tradesmen exercising some trade or manual occupation, and settled for 12 months last past in houses of their own, and not having an habitation elsewhere, giving in their own names, and the names of all other persons in their families to the two next justices of the peace: and that it may be inserted in the said proclamation, that, immediately after the day limited for their departure, the constables, church-wardens, and other the parish officers, go from house to house in their several parishes, hamlets, constableries and divisions, respectively; and there to take an Account of the names and surnames of all such persons as are Popish Recusants or suspected so to be, as well householders, as lodgers and servants; and to carry a List of their names to the two next justices of the peace, who are to be thereby required and enjoined to send for them, and every of them; and to tender to them and every of them the oaths of Allegiance and Supremacy; and to commit to prison, till the next succeeding session of the peace, all such persons as shall refuse the said Oaths; and at the said session, to proceed against them according to law: and that your maj. will be pleased to direct commissions forthwith to be issued under the great seal of England, to all Justices within the Cities of London and Westminster, and within ten miles of the same, to authorize and require them, or any two of them, to administer the said Oaths accordingly. And that your maj. would farther please to command that no Warrant or Licence be granted by the lords of your maj.'s Privy-Council, or otherwise than at the Council-Board, to be signed by six lords of the privy council, whereof the lord chancellor, the lord treasurer or principal secretary of state to be one, for the stay, return, or repair of any such person or persons, in, or to any of the said places, till some more effectual law be passed for preventing the said Popish Conspiracies, and for the preservation of your majesty's sacred person, and the religion and government by law established; for which, we your majesty's most dutiful and loyal subjects will always employ our utmost endeavours and daily prayers. [The same day and the next, Mr. Oates,* Mr. Michael Godfrey, and Mr. Mulys, having given in certain Information to the house, (who on this occasion sent for Lord chief justice Scroggs from off the bench to sign certain Warrants) concerning the Plot, and the Death of Sir Edmundbury Godfrey, the following Clause was added to the Address.] And whereas the safety and preservation of your majesty's most sacred Person, is of so great a consequence and concernment to the Protestant Religion, and to all your subjects; we do farther most humbly beseech your majesty to command the lord chamberlain and all other officers of your majesty's houshold, to take a strict care that no unknown or suspicious persons may have access near your majesty's person: and that your maj. will likewise please to command the lord mayor, and the lieutenancy of London, during the session of parliament, and likewise, the lord-lieutenants of Middlesex and Surrey, to appoint such guards of the Trained-Bands in Middlesex, Westminster and Southwark, and other places adjacent, as shall be thought necessary."

To which his majesty was pleased to reply to this purpose: "That you shall have the effect of your desires, and that he would give speedy orders for putting the same in execution."

The house then proceeded to scrutinize farther into the Murder of Sir Edmundbury Godfrey, as likewise into the particulars of the Popish Plot; and ordered their Speaker to wait upon his majesty, and communicate to him the Informations the house had received of the dangers that his majesty and the nation lay under. To which his majesty was pleased to return: "That he acknowledged the great care of the house for the preservation of his person and government, &c."

A Bill passed to disable Papists from sitting in Parliament.] The following days, the house was almost wholly employed in examining Witnesses and Papers relating to the Plot, in the unravelling of which they testified a very extraordinary zeal; and Oct. 28, to prevent mischiefs in the interval, passed a Bill to disable Papists from sitting in either house of parliament.

Report of Coleman's Examination.] They likewise appointed a committee to examine Mr. Coleman, in Newgate, of which Mr. Sacheverell was chairman; who reported on the 30th, "That the prisoner Coleman denied any Design against either the king's life or authority, or that he ever knew or heard of any commissions to raise an army. That he likewise denied, that he ever designed or endeavoured to change the established Religion, or introduce Popery; but confesses, he did attempt to get this parliament dissolved, in order to procure liberty of conscience, which he thought they would never grant. In order to which, he solicited 300,000*l.* from France; adding, that there were not three men in England acquainted with his Designs, or Correspondence; of which the duke of York was one, who, he believes, communicated them to lord Arundel of Wardour.—That he farther confessed, that his first Correspondence in France, was by certain Letters he had addressed to sir Wm. Throckmorton, by which means he commenced a second with la Ferrier, on whose death, he sent three or four Letters to la Chaise. That he had also confessed a Correspondence with the Pope's Nuncio at Brussels, which was occasioned by a Proposal from the Pope, to furnish the king with a great sum of money, provided the Catholics here might receive proportionable favour.—That upon this, he was dispatched by the duke of York to Brussels to the said nun-

* "Titus Oates was the son of an Anabaptist teacher, who afterwards conformed, and got into orders, and took a benefice, as this his son did. He was proud and ill natured, haughty, but ignorant. He had been complained of for some very indecent expressions concerning the mysteries of the Christian Religion. He was once presented for perjury. But he got to be a chaplain in one of the king's ships, from which he was dismissed upon complaint of some unnatural practices." Burnet.

The picture of this noted man is also drawn with the like features by Mr. North, L'Estrange, and all the court writers of those times, with this only difference, that they are set forth by the last with bolder strokes and stronger colours.

cio, for a farther explanation of that proposal: who then disowned that he had any authority from the court of Rome to make it; but that he had made it as a private man; offering however, his services at his return to bring it about: that notwithstanding, he had not corresponded with him for three or four years.—That the Cypher, with the provincial's mark, was that used between him and father St. Germain: that he used no Cypher to the provincial: that he used another Cypher to Rouvigny's secretary, but not in public concerns.—And being then asked, Whether he knew of any other sum proposed or treated on, he answered: That he believed there was, to keep the king from joining the confederates, but could not affirm that any had been paid."

Mr. Wright, a Member, examined and acquitted.] Oct. 31. Mr. Robert Wright, a member, was accused by the Speaker, of having corresponded with Coleman: on which he was examined by the house, and his Papers searched; but acquitted with honour.

Mr. Coleman's Letters were then read; of which three were entered in the Journals by Order of the House, viz. one from Mr. Coleman to father le Chaise, a second to the same, and a third from le Chaise, acknowledging the receipt of the two former.*

Resolution of the Commons with regard to the Plot.] Upon the Evidence already arisen with regard to the Plot, the house came to a Resolution, and appointed a committee to prepare matters for a conference with the lords upon it; who, the next day, Nov. 1. by sir Robert Sawyer, their chairman, delivered in their Report as follows: "That the house of commons, after examination of several persons, Papers, many of which his majesty did acquaint the house had been communicated to your lordships, and deliberate consideration had thereupon, came to this unanimous Resolution: Resolved, 'That, upon the Evidence, that has 'already appeared to the house, that this house 'is of opinion, that there hath been and still is 'a damnable and hellish Plot, contrived and 'carry'd on by popish recusants, for the assassinating and murdering the king, and for 'subverting the government, and rooting out 'and destroying the Protestant Religion;' The house of commons, being very sensible of the imminent danger both the king and kingdom are in, do think it their duty to acquaint your lordships therewith, and do pray your lordships will be pleased to take it into your serious consideration, what Remedies are fit and suitable to be applied for the preserving the king's person and government; to which the commons shall readily concur, as they doubt not of your lordships concurrence to such Remedies as have, or shall be by them proposed to your lordships for effecting this great end."

A Conference thereon.] These Reasons being agreed to by the house, a Conference was immediately desired and obtained; an account of which was, in the afternoon of the same day, delivered to the house from the committee, by sir Tho. Meres, viz. That my lord Chancellor managed the Conference, and that what was delivered, was as follows: "The lords have considered the Votes of the house of commons, communicated to them at the conference, and have most readily and unanimously concurred with them in it, nem. con. And their lordships are very glad to see that zeal which the commons have shewed upon this occasion, and do fully concur with them: that the most speedy and serious consideration of both houses is necessary for preventing these imminent dangers. In order whereunto, their lordships have resolved to sit die in diem, forenoon and afternoon, and desire the house of commons would do so too. And when their lordships shall have well considered of it, and proper Remedies for these dangers, they will be ready to communicate them to the commons, and will also take in good part, whatever shall be communicated to them by the commons; and will suffer nothing to be wanting on their parts, which may preserve a good correspondence between both houses, which is absolutely necessary to the safety of the king and kingdom."

Nov. 2. It was ordered, that Mr. Speaker do address his majesty from the house, That Mr. Coleman may be pardoned on a full discovery, and that otherwise, neither pardon nor reprieve might be granted him; to both which requests, his majesty was pleased the same day to accord. It was likewise ordered, that Mr. Speaker should signify what had passed to Mr. Coleman in Newgate, who replied: "That he was very sensible of the miserableness of his condition; for that he knew there was enough already known to take away his life, and that he did not know enough to save it."

Debate on a Motion for removing the Duke of York.] Nov. 4. Lord *Russel* moved to address the king, That the duke of York might withdraw himself from the king's person and councils.

Mr. *Booth* seconded the motion.

Mr. Sec. *Coventry.* We ought to have no consideration of persons, when the king and the government are concerned, though the thing ought to be done with all the decency that is possible. It might move some gentlemen, methinks, as it has done me, that his royal highness has desired the king that he may remove from his councils; therefore I hope you will not press that farther. Consider the consequence, when one house addresses the king for one thing, and the lords for another, and they neither are of the opinion of the king. An Address is a temporary declaration, and for the present, and I think this Address not good for the present. The king has sent his Proclamation for Catholics to go out of town: why will you talk of sending the

* For the Letters themselves, see Appendix No. VIII.

duke to them, when they are sent from him? You ought to use a decorum, for fear precedents may be made use of upon light occasions. The Letters of Coleman's penning tell you of 'providing a place for him in France, &c.' Consider what it will be to send the heir of the crown to the king of France. I go along with lord Russel, that the king is not safe, and we ought by all ways and means to secure the king's person. Your advice is good for the king's guards to be near him; but shall he have them every step he takes, to be weary of them? As long as it is the Catholics' interest to plot the king's death the Jesuits will make it their conscience. Make a law to secure the king's person, and that will cease.

Mr. *Bennet*. I like that law Coventry mentions; but till such a law be made, I am for the motion of removing the duke, &c. because before that law may pass, the influence of the duke, being near the king, may hinder it.

Mr. Sec. *Williamson*. I know that nothing can lie in the balance with the government, religion, and the king's person; yet this must bear proportionable respect to him who has exposed his person for the honour of the nation. I confess, if nothing but removing the duke would do, were he yet nearer the king, were he his son, I should be for it. His mixing in the king's affairs with the king may give presumption of jealousy and suspicion. The duke, as we have been told, has prevented our asking his being removed out of the king's councils. The other part is, Whether his personal absence will be the cure, and the only cure of our fears. It is impossible to put them any where, but there may be a communication by letters or secondary hands. To have no influence where there is tenderness of nature and affection, betwixt the two brothers! This will not remedy the thing. I think nothing will provoke the duke to a resentment in his own person; but this is a cutting of him from the stock: this Plot when represented to posterity! Such a villainous design to precipitate and hasten nature, to bring the duke to the crown, by murdering the king? This is a villainy never to be forgotten: there is a time in nature when the duke has his time to be upon the throne, (pray God make it safe!) The fears are these; if possible, by any kind of foresight, that when that comes, the heir of the crown may not disturb Religion, or the Government; the other, to keep off violent hands that would hasten the king's death. Now, it is apprehended that the removal of the duke leaves you at full ease and security, that you may act for the safety of Religion and the king's person. But how far is this from helping you! I see it rather endangers a desperation of that party. Though the whole party be in such a despair, they would seek hell to bring about their designs. Where should the duke be removed? Is not the king in less danger by having the duke in his eye, when he sees all company and addresses that are made to him? The duke would not be suffered to attempt the least hair of the king's head. No countries are to be trusted with the duke, in this case, and it cuts off no possibility of a degree of the duke's influence upon the king, if at a distance, as when he is in the same room. I have sat here, with trouble for Popery, several sessions, but I never suspected this horrible Plot, &c. and what was done at every meeting, principally aims at it. And I agree with lord Russel's motion. Humanly what you can do may come too late: but these will be violences that are needless, and let every man lay his hand upon his heart, and God direct us all!

Col. *Birch*. I agree, that if this session will not establish the Protestant Religion, and secure the king's person, it will never be to any purpose to do more. Williamson tells us, 'that, by reason of the rising Sun, Popery comes on;' and, it may be, you may have a majority here; and, by what I heard from the two Secretaries, I think what is moved is absolutely necessary. Observe Coleman's Papers, and let every man answer to God, and his own conscience, whether this motion is not necessary. If I was one near his highness, I honour him so much, that I would advise him to retire, &c. till the nation was secured in their fears. As for the laws that Coventry moved, we may all stand still, and have our throats cut whilst they are making; but till laws are made to begin in the next king's time, that, whoever he is, he may not be able to destroy the Protestant Religion, nor our Property, we can never be safe.

Mr. Solicitor *Winnington*. I think we are in as great difficulty in this debate, as ever we or our forefathers were. I stand obliged to the duke above all persons, though I have declared myself for the Protestant Religion; so that I am to do two things, not to show ingratitude to the duke, and yet to shew myself for the Protestant Religion. I find that all gentlemen that speak in this case are of one mind for the Protestant Religion; not one division, nor opposition; we differ in mediums, but are unanimous in the end. But I confess the thing you are upon has not that import to do you good, as it has to do you prejudice. As to what has been moved to-day by the honourable lord Russel; I believe, had he known what he did of the duke in the lords house, the motion had not been made; but seeing it is for the Protestant Religion, I would not have it receive a baffle. After the happy conjunction with the lords in all things relating to the Plot, the house then began to think of the obstructions the duke might make to their proceedings. I will not say that the duke is a Papist, but I believe it. The lords thought, if the duke was removed things would go on. The duke has complied and satisfied the lords. I say, such an Address as this may occasion a dissimulation, I mean a dissention, between the two houses, and it may divide us; which if so, I look upon the Protestant Religion to be gone. You make an Address different from the sense of the lords house: the commons would, by this Address, banish the duke, one of the house of peers. It is a judgment in law against him, and shall the king's brother be in a worse capacity than the meanest subject? Is it imaginable that the king will do it, when he has the authority of the house of lords, to back him? And would you have the king put so severe a punishment on the duke as the law allows not? You cannot expect that the king will comply with it.

Sir *Tho. Meres.* This last discourse weighs with me; the Solicitor and I shall find these Bills, &c. obstructed, and then we shall be both of a mind, that the king may be addressed to, to remove the duke, &c. Have not all our bills hitherto been obstructed? It will be objected (he tells you) 'That to take a lord from parliament will be a hard thing;' but if you do not a great and difficult thing, you will never save yourselves: as to indifference, methinks if there be a God and Salvation among us: the Papists take Scripture from us; they take sense from us in transubstantiation, and communion in both kinds; Popery sets up another government, imperium in imperio; it is against the interest of the nation; and as it is, it carries away our coin out of the kingdom, and if it be settled, much more. If the thing be tolerable, let us hear why; if intolerable, pray let us do this. We changed religion pretty well in Hen. viii's time, and Edw. vi. and in queen Mary's time all the clergy turned popish except about 160. About 40 years ago the church was in its height; and then we had changes in the late times of rebellion, and now we have a church of England again if we can keep it. We are a mutable people, and the Papists number is great. We see an Army of 20,000 men listed in the Plot; I am really afraid then, when such a day comes, that two-thirds of the nation will stand neuter, and so but one third part will engage for the Protestant Religion. They will save their stakes. After all, I end where I began. Let any gentleman show me that there will be no solicitations to hinder the passing of our laws, and that there will not be a proviso put in, that the execution of it will not be worth a halfpenny; let any man show me, that unless you do something that is substantial and difficult, you do nothing. We know not what the lords have done as to the duke, and we cannot take notice of it. We are satisfied, both lords and commons, that there is a Plot; let us do our part. If this be not done, farewell any attempts to preserve the Protestant Religion!

Mr. *Finch.* I fear the unanimity of the lords with us will be interrupted by this Address, and I cannot be for the removal of the duke. I hope and expect gentlemen will not think my opinion is for partiality, and my reasons are, that nothing is to be done to impeach the succession; and if the motion tends to that end, every man will be afraid of those means. One unkindness begets another, and if we think this prince not fit to be near the throne, &c. this being so fatal a consequence, let us avoid this first step—It is pretended, 'that the removal of the duke, &c. is the only means to facilitate the passing the laws we shall make,' but if by his presence he can obstruct those laws, how much more can he obstruct the Address! Meres says, 'that not one good law has passed, by the duke's influence upon the king;' but I will tell you one; the Test upon all that bear Office, &c. I believe the designs of the Papists, &c. and I believe they leave nothing unattempted to destroy the Protestant Religion. If the duke's interest be so great, why should you press the thing you may reasonably think you cannot accomplish? Therefore I move to lay aside the motion.

Mr. *Laurence Hyde.* It is objected, 'that the laws now passing may not pass, by the duke's influence.' I think I have ground to say, that any laws now in agitation, or others that may be prepared for the security of the Protestant Religion, will not be opposed by the duke. The two sons of the martyred king, the only surviving sons, now to be torn from one another by such a parliament as this! I speak for the king, and not for the duke. I move against the Address.

Lord *Cavendish.* I fully agree that we provide for the safety of the king, religion, and our liberties, by good laws. But it sticks with me. I know not whether those laws will pass, till the obstruction be removed. The same reason I had before, that the duke is the obstruction, &c. will make me think so still, and take away all encouragements from our enemies, and therefore I am against the continuance of a standing Army; for it is easier with it, than without it, to change the government. I have an extreme veneration for the duke, for I think the duke had not the least hand in the Plot. I think his loyalty to his brother is without example; but his being next of blood to the succession of the crown, and what encouragement that may give the Papists, to take away the king. If I had the honour to be near the duke, I would advise him to withdraw. It has been said, 'that the duke has declared, in the lords house, that he will do it.' But we cannot take notice of what is said in the lords house. Since we have been making laws against Popery, the duke has still been in the councils. It is said, 'the duke may still influence the king by letters;' but surely not so easily as by his presence. I think we cannot answer our duty to the king, nor our country, if we do not address.

Sir *Robert Sawyer.* For the duke to depart from that Religion his father signed with his blood! I can assign no other cause for this dismal attempt that has been discovered, but the hopes the Papists have of the duke's religion. The preservation of the present prince, and the establishment of the government, is the great consideration; and I never knew it denied by the supreme council; but certainly we are to deal with a great prince, and therefore we are to make as wise steps, as may be, in it. The effect of my motion is this; the encouragement the Recusants have taken, from his royal highness's change of his religion, has been the cause of these hellish attempts against the king, the government, and religion. When that is destroyed, you will see another kind of government. I would therefore have an Address to the king, to acquaint him, 'That, his royal brother being a Papist, is the cause of all this confidence in the Papists, and that the king be humbly desired to prevail with his brother to declare, in open parliament, whether he be a Papist, or not.'

Sir *Nich. Carew.* I fully concur with Sawyer, at the beginning of his speech, 'That the opinion the Papists have of his royal highness coming to the crown, is the cause of all their insolencies;' and that is the reason why I would have this Address, &c. made now, that his royal highness, by his presence, may not hinder the laws against Popery, you are about now; for hereafter, all the laws you can make will be to little purpose. When the Papists see they have such advocates for them, what will they not attempt? Sink under this Address, and farewell all; the safety of the king's person, our religion, and government!

Mr. *Waller.* I think gentlemen speak their hearts in this debate. I think him a Papist in his heart, that gives an Aye, or a No, in this matter, that has not the thoughts in him of preservation of the king's person, religion, and government. The duke not only was abroad in the Protestant Religion, but his father was of it too. I have studied the Protestant Religion, and I believe that Christ founded the religion we profess, at his first coming into the world; and I hope Christ will find it here at his second coming. I would let this debate alone. There may be more danger in removing the duke, than in letting him alone. Some of the brothers of France went away in discontent to Brussels, and they said then, 'that Brussels did breed the children of France;' but they were all glad in France when they came back again. Absalom asked his father leave to go out of his court, and you know what followed. At court the duke will keep none but good company, abroad Catholics. I would pause upon this motion. I am not satisfied whether to give my Aye, or No, to this question, yet; therefore I move that you would consider of it.

Mr. *Harwood.* He that moves to defer this question one minute longer, I believe him to be an enemy to his king and country.

The *Speaker* interrupted him, and said, 'Such conclusions as these are uncharitable, and wonderfully unparliamentary.'

Mr. *Harwood* goes on. The weight of the thing has so transported me, that I hope gentlemen, not of my opinion, will pardon me. I respect the duke as duke; but as he is a Papist, let every man lay his hand upon his heart, whether his being a Papist has not given encouragement to the Plot, &c. The duke has houses in the country, and loves fox-hunting; I would have him retire to some of them, to be out of the influence of these damned Jesuits. I am his friend, and out of good intention I would have him out of occasion of doing ill.

Sir *Tho. Clarges.* I take this to be the greatest debate that ever was in parliament. Here is on the one side our Religion and Liberties concerned; and the duke on the other. But I believe this had never been, if the duke had not been a Papist. He is a good, wise, and virtuous prince, but that which grieves me is, that his goodness is made use of by the Papists. When that unhappy stroke is struck, that the Papists intended, he is king; and are not we all concerned to prevent that stroke? We see that the Protestant Religion has been attempted for some years. Address upon address has been made against Popery and the French interest; and the duke had engaged for the French interest against Holland and the Netherlands; one the bulwark of our religion, the other of our safety from the French greatness; and it is but eight months ago (as appears by Coleman's Letters) that the duke's eyes have been opened; but the duke's locks are cut by the Papists. One great Plot has taken; the duke is turned Papist. The king is king, and the duke is but a subject, and I would have the duke stay his time to come to the Succession. Act after act has been made to secure religion, and this act, now sent up to the lords, the duke may hinder. The two brothers have parted formerly; one was at York, the other at Salisbury, in the plague-time; and, God be thanked! they came together again. I am told of five or six and thirty Papists, the other night, in the withdrawing-room; and this still will be more if not prevented. I see several of the house that eat the king's bread, that are his servants; I hope they will be for the preservation of the king's person; for so long as the duke is about the court, Papists will flock thither; therefore pray put the question for the Address.

Sir *John Ernly.* As Coleman's Papers tell you of the duke's compliance to dissolve the parliament, so they tell you of money that has been given for that purpose. I would know to whom this money has been paid? I hope all Coleman's Papers are not evidence, though Mr. Oates's is, who cleared the duke in the matter of the Plot. As to liberty of conscience, you know who are for that. He that is above water will hold him down that is under. The duke's hand and seal have been counterfeited. Consider what you do. If you turn the duke thus away, you put him at the head of 20,000 men, and then it will be much more in his power to do you hurt. The Address may be granted, or refused; if granted, yet there may be correspondence betwixt such relations; and, if not granted, possibly you will be discontented. Therefore you know not what this day's debate may produce in the duke, by a voluntary removal of himself from the king. Therefore I would consider longer of this matter.

Sir *George Downing*. You begin with punishment, before examination. Do not do that to the king's brother, which you would not have done to another. We once named a great person here, to be removed from the king, &c. and no crime was assigned against him. Another time there was a crime named, and no person, and you had effect accordingly in those Addresses. These wicked men in the Plot will expose themselves to your justice, and you may meet with them; but, at this time, lay by this Address, that will touch the lords too near.

Serj. *Maynard*. Two things are propounded; sequestration of the duke from the king's council, and sequestration of him from the king's person. He has of himself abstained from being admiral of England, and exercises that office as to the Plantations only; and he has promised in the lords house to absent himself from the king's councils. I should be loth, after such a concurrence amongst ourselves and the lords, to give any occasion of discord betwixt the lords and us. Suppose you vote to sequester the duke from the king's person; this Address, as it is no law, works nothing. You make no confinement of him by sequestration from the king's person. But I would not lose all this debate. The duke has promised he will retire, &c. He may dispense with that promise; the Vote of sequestration may do you hurt. The Address, &c. is not punishment for a crime. The Address is a prudent caution, and, I fear, if made, and not granted, this will discourage people abroad in this way of proceeding. I think verily, the great encouragement of the papists is from the duke. The Council of Lateran, and 4 or 5 councils agree, 'that killing of kings that are hereticks, is meritorious.' I will not go far into that matter; but in case there should be a division between the two houses upon this, it will put a great discouragement upon people as to the prosecution of the Plot, and in their fears of popery.

Sir *Philip Warwick*. I believe popery is a confederacy against God, and against the kingdom. I believe, if this horrid Plot had come to effect, it might have converted the duke to our religion. He is our king in presumptive succession, and let us use him like such a one.

Sir *Henry Capel*. The duke has made the advance to the parliament by his behaviour, in informing the lords he will retire. Let us not cast him out of our arms. It is entirely necessary that we be unanimous. If we once divide, we give him all the advantage against us imaginable. I have great respect for his person. His father, with my father *, suffered in the Rebellion; but if I cannot separate my interest from his person, I must divide from him. We all agree as to making such laws, that, should the duke be king, it might not be in his power to prejudice the protestant religion. I move, therefore, not to lose the fruit of this debate; and as you have been told, he has removed himself from the king's councils, you may agree to that; and as for removing him from the king's person, adjourn that debate to another time.

Col. *Titus*. There are ways to make things look tragical. We are told of 'tearing the duke from the king;' but that is not the question, but 'Whether the duke shall withdraw from the king's person, for some time, till some laws are passed, which we fear he may obstruct.' If I suspected that my father would set my house on fire, I would take the brand out of his hand, but I would not cut his throat; and if he, that is at the helm, would run the ship upon a rock, I would take him from it.

Mr. *Sacheverell*. If this be so tender a matter, I wonder, now the safety of the kingdom is in danger, we should put it off for two or three days. I have read a little in the law, but I would have the gentlemen of the long robe tell me, whether any degree or quality whatsoever, of any subject, can patronize any correspondence with the king's enemies? or whether the king and the parliament may not dispose of the succession of the crown? and whether it be not præmunire to say the contrary? let them resolve this question, whether there has not been a male-management? if not in the king's ministers for some years past, let them name the persons who have had the influence over affairs. But as to the point of the Address, I am not satisfied whether it be our interest; but if it be, I will go higher and higher.

The debate was adjourned to the 8th.

Nov. 8. Sir *John Coventry*. We talk here of Popery, and the heir of the crown protects papists. I move for the business of the day, about removing the duke. There are papists now walking about the court of requests.

Mr. Sec. *Coventry*. I know not what that gentleman would have. There is all the care taken imaginable to clear the court of papists, night and day, by the council. One man drops a letter in an entry at Whitehall as a papist, another as a protestant, and takes liberty to impute any crimes to any man or woman whatsoever. I know not what can be more done than is done already.

Mr. Sec. *Williamson*. When it shall please God (as in the course of nature) that we lose the king, you may be fortified with such laws as may be for yours and his safety. The king, I may say, will say something to you of this nature to-morrow.

Sir *Tho. Meres*. I think those papists walking in the Hall is a contempt of the king's proclamation. It is no great matter for them to go ten miles out of town. If you do not something immediately, you will show remissness. Suppose the case had not been a papist, but a fanatic; he would have been otherwise used. This ought, this very hour, to be punished, or we cannot sit here with honour or safety.

Sir *Wm. Hickman*. If the papists intend mischief, they will strike presently; therefore,

* Lord Capel.

as Meres has moved, I would not be baffled in the proclamation, but take present remedy to secure yourselves from these mens attempts. You cannot else be safe.

The debate was again adjourned to the 14th.

Coleman's further Examination.] Sir Henry Capel reported from the Committee, appointed to examine Mr. Coleman in Newgate, "That the said Coleman received of M. Rouvigny 300*l.* and of M. Courtin, * 360*l.* for intelligence of every day's debates in parliament, and for keeping a good table. That he received last session of M. Barillon* 2500*l.* to be distributed among members of parliament, which he had converted to his own use: that M. Barrillon had, on the occasion, pointed at several members; and that he had told M. Barrillon, he had complied with his Instructions. That, at the end of the last session, he received of M. Barrillon 260*l.* more for Parliament Intelligence. That M. Rouvigny, believing the parliament was inflamed by the Confederates against France, did therefore encourage him to pursue a Correspondence with members: to render which more effectual, he did treat with St. Germain, about a sum of crowns to be disposed of amongst them. That none of that money was received: that he entered no foreign Letters in his books, after his correspondence with le Chaise ceased: that he was to receive 30,000*l.* on procuring a security for the Banker's Debt, which was afterwards reduced to 7000*l.* in silver, and 5000 guineas: of which he received but the moiety of the silver only. And that this contract made between himself and sir Robert Viner, Alderman Bakewell, and Mr. Whitehall, was verbal only. Signed Edward Coleman."

The King's Speech to both Houses, relating to the Succession.] Nov. 9. The king went to the house of peers, and made the following speech to both houses:

"My lords and gentlemen; I am so very sensible of the great and extraordinary care you have already taken, and still continue to shew for the safety and preservation of my person in these times of danger, that I could not satisfy myself without coming hither on purpose to give you all my most hearty thanks for it. Nor do I think it enough to give you my thanks only, but I hold myself obliged to let you see withal, that I do as much study your preservation too as I can possibly; and that I am as ready to join with you in all the ways and means that may establish a firm security of the Protestant Religion, as your own hearts can wish: And this not only during my time, of which I am sure you have no fear, but in future ages, even to the end of the world. And therefore I am come to assure you, that whatsoever Bills you shall present, to be passed into laws, to make you safe in the reign of my Successor, (so they tend not to impeach the Right of Succession, nor the descent of the crown in the true line; and so as they restrain not my power, nor the just rights of any Protestant Successor,) shall find from me a ready concurrence. And I desire you withal, to think of some more effectual means for the conviction of Popish Recusants, and to expedite your councils as fast as you can, that the world may see our unanimity; and that I may have an opportunity of shewing you how ready I am to do any thing, that may give comfort and satisfaction to such dutiful and loyal subjects."

Nov. 9: p. m. The commons went to the banquetting-house at Whitehall, and, by their Speaker, returned his majesty their humble and hearty Thanks, for his most gracious Speech: To which his majesty was pleased to give this Answer: "Gentlemen, It shall always be my study to preserve the Protestant Religion, and to advance and support the interest of my people."

Bedlow's Narrative.] Nov. 10. Mr. W. Bedlow * gave the commons an account concerning the Murder of sir E. Godfrey, as also concerning the Plot. Then Bedlow read a narrative, which he had presented to the lords †. All

* Embassadors of France.

* "This Wm. Bedlow had formerly been a servant to lord Bellasis, afterwards an ensign in Flanders. About Michaelmas 1674 he was sent for over by Harcourt, recommended by the English abbess at Dunkirk, and so by degrees became acquainted with the Jesuits, and was at last generally employed as an agent for them, and sent frequently with letter's into foreign parts." Hist. of the Plot, p. 127.

Burnet says, "Bedlow had led a very vicious life; he had gone by many false names, by which he had cheated many persons. He had gone over many parts of France and Spain, as a man of quality, and he had made a shift to live on his wits, or rather by his cheats. He was apprehended at Bristol, by his own desire, and brought to London, Nov. 6, where a guard was immediately assigned him for his security, and a pension for his subsistence, with a lodging at Whitehall." Rapin.

† "In regard to the murder of Godfrey, he swore before the two secretaries (Nov. 7.) in presence of his majesty, 'That it was committed in Somerset-house, by Walsh and Le Phaire, Jesuits, and two laymen;' at the same time declaring also upon oath, 'That he could say nothing at all as to the plot that was then in question.' But, on the very next day, being brought before the lords, by the king's directions, to give the same account he had done the evening before to his majesty, (that is to say, concerning the Murder of Godfrey) he all at once made a transition to the Plot, 'that two of the persons he had named as the murderers, viz. Walsh and Le Phaire, had informed him, that the lord Bellasis had a commission to command forces in the north, the earl of Powis in South Wales, and that lord Arundel of Wardour had a commission to grant commissions to whom he pleased; that Coleman was a great agitator in the designs against the

the Information he then gave at the bar, relating to the Plot, is fully mentioned in the Trials of the Murderers of sir E. Godfrey, and others of the Traitors.

Address for tendering the Oaths of Allegiance and Supremacy to his Majesty's Servants.] Nov. 12. The commons resolved, "That, there being an accusation of High-Treason against sir Wm. Godolphin, his majesty's ambassador in Spain, an humble Address be presented to his majesty, to desire him to call him home, to answer the accusation." To which his majesty was pleased to answer, "That he had already ordered his letters of revocation: and that he had a person in his eye, who he designed should succeed him in that service." And on the same day the commons presented another Address to his majesty, praying, "That a special commission may be issued forth, for tendering the Oaths of Allegiance and Supremacy to all the servants of his majesty and royal highness; and to all other persons (except his majesty's Portugal servants) residing within the palaces of Whitehall, St. James's and Somerset house, and all other his majesty's houses; and that there may be likewise special commissions issued forth, for tendering the said Oaths to all persons residing within the two Serjeants Inns, all the Inns of Court, and Inns of Chancery."

The King's Answer.] To which his majesty returned an Answer in writing two days after:

"That as to all his majesty's own Servants, all the servants of his royal highness, all other persons residing in Whitehall, St. James's, Somerset-house, or any other of his majesty's houses, except the menial servants of the queen and dutchess; as also all persons within either of the Serjeants Inns, or any of the Inns of Court, or Chancery, his majesty grants it. But as to the queen's menial servants, who are so very inconsiderable in their number, and within the Articles of marriage, his majesty does not think it fit. And his maj. cannot but take notice, that in a late Address from the house of peers, the menial servants of the queen and dutchess are excepted; and his majesty hopes that this house will proceed with the same moderation as to that particular."

Another Address to the same effect.] This Answer not being thought satisfactory, on the 15th the house proceeded to another Address, in which they humbly advise his majesty, and renew their desires, that the persons excepted in his majesty's message may be comprehended in the same commission; for which they do, in all duty, lay before his majesty the Reasons following. "1. For the quieting of the minds of your majesty's good Protestant subjects, who have more than ordinary care and solicitude for the safety of your majesty's person, by reason of the notorious conspiracy of the Popish Party at this time, even against the life of your sacred majesty. 2. By your majesty's Proclamation, set forth upon the Address of both houses, for banishing Popish Recusants ten miles from London, there is no such restriction. 3. The discouragement it would be to this kingdom, to see so great a neglect; and the occasions that Papists would take to say from thence, that all our fears were groundless. 4. It is too great a countenance to the dangerous factions which are already come to that height, that it renders all manner of discouragement on that side necessary. 5. It is against the laws and statutes of the realm; which, as they are preserved and maintained by your majesty's authority, so we assure ourselves, you will not suffer them to be thus violated by your family and royal presence, upon the account of Popish Recusants."

Mr. Secretary Williamson sent to the Tower.] Nov. 18. The commons being informed, that there were several Commissions to Popish Recusants, and Warrants also that they should be mustered, notwithstanding they had not taken the Oaths, and subscribed the Declaration, according to the act of parliament, and that they were countersigned by sir Joseph Williamson, Secretary of State; the notice of this raised such a heat in the house, that they immediately sent sir Joseph, as a member of their house, to the Tower.

The King releases him.] This much offended the king, who the next day sent for the house of commons to attend him in the Banquetting-House, where, in a speech to them, he told them plainly, "That though they had committed his servant without acquainting him: yet he intended to deal more freely with them, and acquaint them with his intentions, to release his Secretary:" which accordingly he did that very day.

An Address to the King that he might not be discharged.] Upon which the commons immediately drew up an Address to his majesty to present to him these Reasons of their proceedings, in the commitment of sir Joseph Williamson, as a member of their house, viz. "1. That divers Commissions were granted to Popish Officers, and countersigned by the said sir Joseph, and delivered out in Oct. last, since the meeting of this house, and discovery of the present Popish Conspiracy. 2. Divers Warrants have also been produced before us, of Dispensations, contrary to law, for Popish officers to continue in their commands, and to be passed in muster, notwithstanding they have not taken the oaths of allegiance and supremacy, and received the blessed Sacrament of the Lord's Supper according to the act of parliament in that behalf: all which said warrants were likewise countersigned by the said

king; that he asking them, 'Why he had not been sooner let into the secret concerning the king's death,'—they answered, 'None were permitted to know it, but such as lord Bellasis nominated.' Here he stopped short, desiring time to put his whole Narrative in writing, which he said he had begun. And being asked 'if he knew Titus Oates?' answered in the negative, without any reservation." Ralph.

sir Joseph; which being complained of to us, and confessed by the said sir Joseph, we your majesty's most dutiful subjects, having the immediate consideration before us, of the imminent danger of your majesty's person, the safety whereof is above all things most dear, and likewise the dangers from Popish Plots, so nearly threatening the peace and safety of your majesty's government, and the Protestant Religion, were humbly of opinion, we could not discharge our duty to your majesty and the whole kingdom, without the committing the said sir Joseph; and therefore most humbly desire, That he may not be discharged by your majesty. And we do farther most humbly desire your majesty, to recal all Commissions granted to all Papists within the kingdom of England and Ireland, or any other of your majesty's dominions and territories."

Debate on the Lords Proviso in the Popery Bill, exempting the Duke of York.] Nov. 21. The lords sent down the Bill for disabling Papists to sit in either house of parliament, &c. with some Amendments, and a Proviso, exempting the duke of York from taking the Oaths of Allegiance and Supremacy, and the Declaration, &c.

Sir *Rob. Markham.* I am glad that the lords have sent us the Bill again, and am not sorry for the Proviso in it, exempting the duke, &c. If the duke's relation to the Crown be considered, there is a difference between him and other subjects, and I move you to pass the Proviso.

Sir *John Ernly.* This was a *salva conscientia* to myself. I make a difference betwixt this peer (the duke) and all the rest. The lords have made a great step in this bill, that they have exempted no other persons; and I cannot but say there is great reason why this person should not be comprehended in the common calamity with the rest. If the duke should be banished, or removed (he is out of the king's councils already) from the king's person, in the circumstances he is in, whether would it be better, to be removed, or continue in the king's eye, to be observed? Foreign aid, we see, has been treating for with the French king by Coleman. If the Jesuitical party should despair, and fall upon any person, I know not the consequence. I fear not what can come to us, if the duke be amongst us. But I think in conscience, that if we banish the Papists, and have the duke under the king's eye, there will be no danger. There is but this one person exempted by the lords, &c. and no great danger of him but what is in your power to remedy.

Sir *Winston Churchill.* Upon this disadvantage, when I hear so loud a cry, 'To the Question,' I should not speak, but to discharge my conscience. Though I think not to prevail, when I heard so loud a cry against what I am moving. The lords are so near the government, that they see more than we. They have not so slight stakes as to oversee their game. I think that the monarchy of England is concerned in this. Consider the consequence, if you reject this Proviso. How far will you force so great a prince to declare? You will give your adversaries great advantage. Suppose the duke takes not the Oaths. All that do not take them, &c. will you make them Papists? There were some at your bar that were Quakers, who would not take them; will you drive all that herd of swine into the sea of Rome at once? If those that sit in parliament must take them, those out of parliament must too. [And so he sat down abruptly.]

Sir *Ch. Wheeler.* I agree to the Proviso. If the duke be in a capacity to sit in the lords house, then the debate you have adjourned, about removing the duke from the king's presence and councils, you cannot proceed in. If the duke remains in the lords house, he cannot singly and solely, on his own vote, stop any bill there, and this very bill has passed that you favoured so much.

Mr. Sec. *Coventry.* You have the greatest matter before you that ever was in this house. The danger of disturbance of Religion, is one of the most pernicious apprehensions imaginable. If this prince should go into another place, it must cost you a Standing Army to bring him home again. These things to be done upon the heir of the crown were never before. It was in the power of queen Mary to see queen Elizabeth, and of Edward vi th to see queen Mary. Suppose the king on his death-bed; must he not see the duke, to give any order about the affairs of the kingdom? It is a hardship not to be offered to a condemned person. You are losing this bill, by casting out the lords' Proviso. And these Popish peers sit in the lords' house. You lose that thing too, and it cannot be remedied, and the lords will carry any other provision you shall make against Popery. Deny it to be in the king's power to see his brother, and he him, and the consequence will be fatal.

Sir *Edm. Jennings.* You have not yet made any steps towards the safety of the kingdom. The head-ach coming from an ill stomach, to cut off the hair and apply oils to the head will do no good, when the way is to cleanse the stomach. It is not removing Popish lords out of the house, nor banishing Priests and Jesuits, nor removing the duke from the king; but it must be removing Papists from the nation.

Sir *Allen Apsley.* When the house is all of a mind, as to the duke's valour and exposing himself for the honour of the nation, we cannot, without ingratitude, throw out this Proviso.

Sir *John Hanmer.* If you throw out this Proviso, you endanger the nation. You know what you have done in rejecting the duke's servants. You had better impeach the duke than throw out this Proviso, and take him from his brother. Keep him here, and you may breathe the wholsome doctrines of the Church of England into him.

Sir *Jonathan Trelawney.* The consequences may be so fatal, if you throw out this Proviso, that I am for agreeing with the lords in it. The scope of the bill is not only to suppress persons that may propagate the growth of Popery, but to break their future hopes. This before you is of the greatest moment and concernment, that ever came before a house of parliament. I speak sincerely; by throwing out this Proviso, give you not the greatest advantage to the Papists to drive the duke into Popish hands? Should that day come, of the king's death, what disobligation do you put upon the duke! For God's sake accept the Proviso.

Those against the Proviso sat silent.

Earl of *Ancram*. This debate looks as if it was not upon good ground and reason, but a resolved business. Nobody opens his mouth to answer any thing that is said, but only to call for the Question. If so, put it to the common fate of Aye and No. I think this is a subject for another man's brains and tongue better than mine. But pray consider; the duke is the king's only brother, the son of that martyr who died for his religion. The duke is said to be 'but a subject;' but he is another kind of subject than lord Carrington (lately secured about the Plot) It is said, 'the duke is not heir apparent;' but I am sure he is apparent heir. Generations to come will curse this day's work; therefore pray consider of it.

Sir *Wm. Killegrew*. I dread taking the duke from the king—(and weeps.)

Sir *John Birkenhead*. In Henry vi.th's time, when all the peers were sworn to the Great Charter, and not to take up the difference between the duke of Norfolk and the earl of Warwick, the 'make-king,'* 'propter celsitudinem et excellentiam Domini principis,' he was not obliged to take the oath—to make a law that the king shall not go to his brother, I understand not; it is the same thing as that his brother shall not come to him. Do you think the king will give his consent to this bill, to restrain himself thus? Cannot the king go to see Mr. Coleman, if he will? And not go see his brother! You here will make a law, that the duke shall be removed from the king's presence. Whither shall he go? Into the country? Or will you force him beyond sea? If he was a pusillanimous prince, of weak capacity; but he is one of the most magnanimous princes in the world. He renounced the French interest, that used his brother ill in his exile: drive him into French hands! I speak in the presence of God, I think, if you pass this Proviso it will be the greatest means to get him to our religion. For God's sake pass this Proviso.

Sir *George Downing*. I am one of those that will agree to this Proviso, and I will give you my reason for it, for my own justification. I had rather have half a loaf than no bread. I say not that the duke is a Papist; I know nothing of that; but if he be a Papist, I had rather he sat alone in the lords house, than with all the Popish lords. Next consider, whether it is not better in prudence, for the good of the kingdom, that the duke sit in the house of York [He meant 'the House of Lords.'] I had rather have him amongst Protestants than Papists, in the heap of Papists. It is better in prudence to endeavour to keep him amongst us, than to thrust him amongst others: the duke is a person to be led and not driven, to be won and not to be frighted, to be persuaded and not compelled.

Sir *Tho. Higgins*. Let gentlemen, who are so earnest against this Proviso consider, should the duke think himself disobliged, and go beyond the sea, and the French king support him with 100,000 men; could a greater blow be given to the Protestant Religion?

Sir *Rd. Temple*. Would you break all the wheels of this design, is it not better to keep the duke here alone with us? That is the way to make him ours. Wherever the duke goes, his title to the crown goes along with him. The matter of Popery will go on, the duke absent, better than when the king sees all things. If you will take off all the wheels of this pernicious design, make the duke yours, and keep him with you.

Sir *Edw. Dering*. The dignity of the persons makes the greatness of the thing. If we disagree with the lords in this Proviso, and leave it out, and the king give not his consent to the bill, your bill must fall, or runs a great hazard. I would agree, &c. and when that is done, move the king to give an immediate consent to the bill. You have then but one Popish peer in the lords house, (if the duke be one.) You may have great advantage in other bills of Popery, by getting this.

Mr. *Waller*. I am much perplexed in this business. The debate of removing the duke, has been adjourned several days, and always put off, but now blown in by a side-wind. Still the debate has been put off; that was some sign you would lay it aside. I am sorry for the Proviso, I wish we had had the bill without it. But you expound that which I never understood, that the duke, by it, should be removed from the presence of his brother. From my experience abroad, and what I have read at home, I have ever observed, that princes of the duke's magnitude are like fire out of the chimney, and put in the middle of a room; it makes a great blaze, but sets all on fire. Edw. iv. did not agree with his cousin the duke of Hereford. The princes of the blood in France are generally of a different opinion with the ministers of state: they went away, but the king did all he could to get them to court again. When the Civil Wars were in France, Hen. iii. sent for the king of Navarre to marry his sister to be a help to him. David himself was a holy and a good man, but Absalom would not stay at court. David was afraid of his life, for his servants ran away from him to

* "The earl of Warwick had the honour of restoring Henry vi. to the throne, after having deposed him, and of pulling down Edw. iv. who had been raised entirely by his means; therefore he was commonly called 'The king-maker.'" Rapin.

Absalom, as Jonathan told him. Foreign princes will make use of the discontents—'multis utile bellum.' This removal of the duke is of vast consequence. Gentlemen are in earnest against Popery. If I thought this Proviso was not, I would be against it. There are laws against Papists. This will make them shuffle again, and the Papists can have no hope but by disorder or despair. By union in one vote, when we were at Peace amongst ourselves, we gave Spain a kingdom, viz. Sicily. What can we not do if we have glory at home, and peace abroad? I would lay aside this Proviso, as the most dangerous thing in the world.

Sir *Tho. Meres.* On one side, the reason against the Proviso is, prudence and safety. On the other, civility, gratitude, and compliment. I would be on the civil side, were not the safety of the nation concerned. No doubt but sir E. Godfrey was civil to go to Somerset House, &c. and he was civil to Mr. Coleman to compare notes with him: but he lost his life by it. I think that the bill, as we sent it up to the lords, names not the duke; and I would avoid naming him in the proviso. The lords name him. I am afraid to name him so, as if possibly he may be a rebel, as if possibly a Papist. This Bill names him not. I had rather this bill had never been brought into the house, than that this Proviso should name the duke. I name him not so, but if the Proviso will name him so, it is a beginning of Toleration. I am against the Proviso for the duke's sake.

Sir *Philip Warwick.* At the beginning of the Long Parliament, no moderation could be had between the king's prerogative and the subjects liberty. Nothing was more unjust, nothing more unfortunate. I would rather consider that a Popish successor may not be, but a Protestant of our religion.

Sir *Henry Capel.* It is said by Warwick, 'no moderation could be had in the Long Parliament,' but it was neither imprisonment of the members, though that broke into laws and liberties, it was not the violation of property by illegal taxes, but it was the unhappy hand of Popery which brought that disorder in, and possibly shed the blood I came of—(his father, lord Capel.) Since the king's Restoration, Popery has played in court, in our negotiations of war and peace, of setting up ministers and taking them down; and God knows where it will end. I have a representation as other men have; wife and children, and all is at stake. Will not this startle a great man? I hope it will. Were it not for hope, the heart would break. I hope yet that this great prince will come into our Church. But will you, by admitting this Proviso, have all our tongues tied, and by law declare the duke a Papist? Shall this be done by a law? If it must come from us, this is not the time. If once I can separate the duke's interest from his person, I would serve him. Press down that Popish interest more and more by law, and when the duke is naked, and clear from Popish interest, then it is time to offer our services to him. It is in his hands to save this whole nation, but I will never allow an argument, as this Proviso implies, that a peer shall do any thing against his country. When he is naked and alone, I will serve him, and he may serve himself.

Sir *Wm. Coventry.* A gentleman on the other side of the house has said one word that has awakened me. In point of gratitude, I need not tell you my obligations to the duke.* I will not deny a great deal of what has to-day been started. The danger of the Proviso is only reasons from the presumption of the goodness of this Prince's disposition. I shall say but one word, though, I apprehend, not any thing I can say can prevail in this matter. Consider whether this prince has not been useful to you. Whether he has not made a greater step to the Protestant Religion, by marrying his daughter to the prince of Orange, which had his concurrence. From that instance, he is so far from danger, that he has been a help to us: this is the reason why I am for the Proviso.

Several cried out, "Coleman's Letters, Coleman's Letters."

Sir *Rob. Howard.* Capel's father would have fought for the crown, whatever devil had raised the storm against it. This Proviso is a single disposing of a person for the security of the nation. Excluding the duke from the presence of the king, is it meant eternally? (It is granted he may stay 30 days, &c. by warrant from the privy council.) What will hold of all you have done, if the crown come to him? What will become of you, if an exasperated prince come to govern, though not of so great a spirit as the duke? I, in my extremity, would scorn to do an act so low, that I would not have disdained to do in my prosperity. The proposition of doing good by this, &c. is to do nothing, for it is but the shape of a thing, and not the thing itself. He is not a man in ordinary condition of other peers. He is separate from other subjects, and by a title. The duke sees no Catholic lords come to the house of peers more. He sees he is separated from them by this Proviso; and will a man in his condition, preserved by a parliament, put himself upon mischief? Will that be his gratitude, think you? We all respect his person, and may hope, that, when he sees his own temper so different from us, he will embrace that here which he will never find in the popish religion. He is safe, when others are rejected, he is preserved, and may return more useful to the king and us.

Lord *Cavendish.* I cannot agree to the duke's being declared a Papist by act of parliament, till I hear the lords Reasons for the Proviso. If we agree to the Proviso, we cannot hear the lords Reasons. Possibly I may be convinced by the lords, but I am not by any thing I have heard yet.

---

* He had been his Secretary.

The Proviso was agreed to, 158 to 156 *.

Resolved, "That Reasons be drawn up to be offered at a conference for not agreeing with the lords in their 2nd and 3rd Amendments, &c." relating to the Servants of the Queen and Dutchess of York.

Debate on sir J. Trelawney's calling Mr. Ash a Rascal.] A breach of the peace happening in the house, between sir Jonathan Trelawney and Mr. Ash:

The *Speaker* said, I know not who was the author, or occasion, of this disturbance, but be my relation ever so near to them,† I must tell you who they are that have given blows in the house: they are sir Jonathan Trelawney and Mr. Wm. Ash.

Mr. *Williams*. I saw something that passed betwixt these two gentlemen. I am sorry I saw what I did see. There was such a case once in Westminster-Hall, and it puzzled the Judges. I am sorry for this case, now we are securing the nation by the Militia, that the peace should be broken amongst ourselves. What has passed looks like an unhappy omen.

Sir *Jonathan Trelawney*. I rise up the earlier to speak, because I wish this had been in another place; but perhaps in a more sacred place than this, if any man should call me 'rascal,' I should call him 'rebel,' and give him a box on the ear. The cause of the quarrel that happened was this. Col. Birch was saying, 'lose this question (about the Proviso) and he would move for a general toleration.' 'No,' said I, 'I never was for that.' And Ash said, 'I am not for Popery.' Said I, 'Nor I for Presbytery.' I came to Ash, and told him 'he must explain his words.' Said Ash, 'I am no more a Presbyterian than you are a Papist.' Upon which I said, 'Ash was a rascal,' and I struck him, and should have done it any where; but I am sensible it was in heat, and I humbly ask the pardon of the house for it.

Sir *Wm. Harbord*. He has behaved himself like a man of honour. I must say this, I saw Trelawney strike a stroke.

Sir *Wm. Portman*. Here has been a just account given of the thing. I pray God there be no ill consequence of it.

Mr *Sacheverell*. I have a great respect for the two gentlemen, but more for the preservation of the peace of your councils. If you put up this, and make not an example, you do not justice to yourselves.

Lord *Cavendish*. I allow both the gentlemen to be in the fault extremely. There can be no excuse made for ill language, nor blows, here, but you must make distinction. You ought, in your censure, to go first on the aggressor, who has done so great a fault contrary to the peace at this time. You can do no less than send him to the Tower, and expell him the house.

Mr. *Williams*. By the Orders of the house, if you debate the censure they ought to withdraw.

The *Speaker*. If you go on in the debate, they must withdraw.

Mr. *Ash*. You have a relation from the gentleman, which is, in a great measure, true. I hope you will allow that the provocation was great. I do acknowlege I have done a great fault, and I humbly ask the pardon of the house.

Mr. Sec. *Coventry*. There can be no debate who shall be punished, or who not, till they are both withdrawn.

Sir *Tho. Meres*. Who provoked, or who followed the provocation must be an after debate. But neither of them ought to sit; it will be voting in one another's case.

Sir *Tho. Lee*, upon the Speaker's motion, 'That both of them should be in custody of the serjeant,' said, You must commit them before judgment be passed upon them, and then they ought to come upon their knees to the bar, before they be discharged.

Sir *Tho. Littleton*. It is not an equal way of proceeding. The Speaker says, only, 'in safe custody.' It may be others think they do not deserve commitment at all, or one to be committed to the serjeant, the other to the Tower.

The *Speaker*. There is nothing more equal than to put them both in the same condition, and to order it upon your Books, 'that it is for security, till the house consider how to proceed.'

Ordered, "That sir Jonathan Trelawney and Mr. Ash be secured by the serjeant at arms, for having committed a breach of the peace in the house, until the matter be examined and determined by the house."

Lord *Cavendish*. I move, that Trelawney, as being the aggressor in this breach of the peace, may be expelled the house.

Mr. *Booth*. Trelawney came to Ash and reflected upon his family for being Presbyterians and rebels. You can do no less than send him to the Tower, and expell him the house.

Mr. *Bennet*. When I consider the noise without doors, and how your members are reflected on for what they do here: and that when I had the ill luck to displease the court, they said, 'there goes such a rogue, he is for a commonwealth?' and when families are reflected upon, notwithstanding an act of indem-

* "The duke spoke on this proviso in the house of lords with great earnestness, and with tears in his eyes. He said 'he was now to cast himself on their favour in the greatest concern he could have in this world.' He spoke much of 'his duty to the king, and of his zeal for the nation;' and solemnly protested, 'that, whatever his religion might be, it should only be a private thing between God and his own soul; and that no effect of it should ever appear in the government.' The Proviso was carried for him by a few voices. And, contrary to all mens expectations, it passed in the house of commons." Burnet.

† Mr. Ash and the Speaker married two sisters, and sir Jonathan Trelawney married the Speaker's aunt.

nity and pardon, what will be the end of all this! Though I can justify myself from all this. My father and grandfather were for the king, yet I have heard myself called 'fanatic,' where I durst not answer again. Whoever calls a man 'rebel' here deserves to be expelled the house, and I would have but that one punishment for Trelawney.

Sir *John Talbot.* Your first question must be 'whether Trelawney was the first aggressor.'

Sir *Ch. Wheeler.* He that strikes again, makes himself his own judge. Both have broken your order. [He was mistaken, and out, and so sat down.]

Sir *Rob. Dillington.* It was my chance to be by, when the difference happened between these two gentlemen. Col. Birch said, 'he was an old soldier, and was for making a safe retreat, and the best way now was for a bill of Toleration.' Trelawney said, 'I am not for tolerating presbytery.' 'Nor I,' says Ash, 'for popery.' And this was all the provocation that Ash gave to Trelawney.

Sir *Tho. Meres.* Trelawney names 'presbytery' first, and strikes first; pray determine that, and then come to the rest.

Earl of *Ancram.* Where the honour of the house is concerned, I will speak my mind freely. I will not come to the provocation, but the action. It is one way to do an act out of the house, and another in. A blow struck in the house of commons is a blow struck at all the commons of England; all are struck, and it may go farther. Private persons must not wound all the commons of Englnad. I leave it to you.

Mr. *Williams.* I hope you will not make your own court less than Westminster-Hall. I would punish Trelawney by expelling him the house.

Sir *John Ernly.* I move 'that Trelawney may be sent to the Tower, and then that you will consider what to do with Ash.—I would not consider the provocation on one side or the other. We saw the blows, but heard not the words. Both struck, and pray send them both to the Tower.

Mr. Sec. *Coventry.* If you expel Trelawney, you take away the freehold of them that sent him hither. The law considers mediums, when things are done with intention and in cold blood. I would know, what a gentleman should do, in such a case as this. But the fact is done; put therefore such a question, as you have examples and precedents of. Send them both to the Tower.

The *Speaker.* I must do right to the house. The first question moved for was, 'whether Trelawney should be expelled the house.'

The previous question for expelling Trelawney passed in the negative, 130 to 110.

Sir J. Trelawney sent to the Tower.] The *Speaker.* I will make you a motion, 'that sir J. Trelawney may be sent to the Tower, there to remain during this session.' The person of Mr. Ash is nearest in relation to me, and I would be nearest in my service to him. But pray regard your own honour, regard yourselves.

Sir *Tho. Meres.* What you have moved is most worthy, and I am for it.

Resolved, "That sir Jonathan Trelawney be sent to the Tower, there to remain during this session of parliament."

Mr. Ash reprimanded.] Mr. *Williams.* Where the law acquits him, I suppose you will not condemn him, here. It being true that Trelawney said the words, you have punished Mr. Ash by commitment to the serjeant. It is true, a man may strike in his own defence; it is lawful. It is plain, the first provocation was from Trelawney. What happened from Ash is justifiable in law.

Serj. *Gregory.* I hope you will not punish a man that has committed no fault. If the second blow appears to be in Ash's own defence, the law, upon an action brought, makes him not guilty. He had worse words than 'rascal' given him, before he gave any. Ash being guilty of no crime, I hope you will inflict no punishment.

Sir *John Birkenhead.* I wonder that a man should take the sword out of the magistrate's hand, and that should be no crime, and the long robe should say 'it is no offence.' The blow was given in the king's house, and, by the Saxon law, it was death, and, by a continuando, 23 Hen. viii. drawing of blood. Let Ash be punished by you, lest he have greater punishment.

Serj. *Gregory.* The affront was not given to the walls of the house, but to the Speaker, sitting in the chair of the house.

Sir *John Birkenhead.* By the 28th Hen. viii. if a man strikes in an integral part of the king's palace, he might as well strike in the king's bed-chamber.

Earl of *Ancram.* I have known that misfortune of words, amongst brave men. Words may make reparation for words: but blows are for a dog, and not a quarrel to be taken up. Here has been a blow given in the house of commons. A man that sits here should have his understanding so far about him, that a word should not bring him so in passion, as it would do in another place. Truly I think Mr. Ash pardonable in this case; and I would have him reprimanded only in his place.

Which being ordered, Mr. Ash was called in.

The *Speaker.* Mr. Ash, the house has considered the disorder you committed, and the provocation that was given you. They have a tenderness for every gentleman that is a member; therefore they have thought fit to proceed tenderly with you, only. When you make the house judge, &c. you make yourself no way justifiable, but by extraordinary provocation and passion. And you are to proceed no farther in this quarrel with sir J. Trelawney, and the house requires you to declare it.

Mr. *Ash.* I acknowledge that I have committed a great fault, but there was a great provocation to it. And I shall humbly acquiesce in the determination of the house. I shall proceed no farther in the matter, and I acknowledge the great favour of the house.

Sir *Tho. Littleton.* I move for the same engagement from Trelawney; for else, when the session is ended, there may be disorders, and he not in your power to punish. And I move that the Speaker require him in obedience to your commands, not to pursue the quarrel. And I believe he will give obedience to it.—It was ordered accordingly.

The King's third Speech to both Houses.] Nov. 25. The king made the following Speech to both houses:

"My lords and gentlemen; I told you in the beginning of this session, how much I had been obliged to keep up my Forces in Flanders: That without it our neighbours had absolutely despaired, and by this means, whatever has been saved of Flanders, is acknowledged to be wholly due to my interposition. And I shewed you withal, that I had been forced to employ that Money which had been raised for the disbanding those troops, in the continuance of them together; and not only so, but that I had been much more out of purse for that service; a service by which the honour and interest of the nation have been so much improved, that as I am confident no man would repine at it, so I did not doubt but you would all be willing to supply it. I have now undergone this expence so long, that I find it absolutely impossible to support the charge any longer; and did therefore think of putting an end to that charge, by recalling my troops with all possible speed, who are already exposed to the utmost want and misery, being without any prospect of farther pay or subsistence. But whilst I was about to do this, I have been importuned by the Spanish ministers to continue them a little longer, until the ratifications of the peace be exchanged; without which, all that hath been hitherto saved in Flanders, will inevitably fall into the hands of their enemies. And now, between this importunity to keep up those troops, and my own inability to pay them any longer, I find myself in great difficulties what to resolve. If you do not think that the public safety may require the continuance, I do wish as heartily as any man, that for the public ease, they may be speedily disbanded, and paid off. I have thought fit thus to lay the matter before you; and having acquitted myself to all the world, by asking your advice and assistance, I desire it may be speedy, and without any manner of delay."

The Commons resolve to disband the Army.] Nov. 27. The commons proceeded to the consideration of the state of the nation, in relation to the Army; and resolved, nem. con. "That it is necessary for the safety of his majesty's person, and preservation of the peace of the government, that all the forces that have been raised since the 29th Sept. 1677, and all others that since that time have been brought over from beyond seas from foreign service, be forthwith disbanded." And farther in these words resolved, "It is the humble opinion and desire of the house, that the Forces which are now in Flanders, may be immediately called over, in order to their disbanding."

An Address to remove the Queen from Court.] Nov. 28. Mr. Sec. Coventry acquainted the house, that the Vote with relation to the disbanding the Army, had been presented to his majesty; which being a matter of great moment, he would consult and advise with his house of lords, before he would give an Answer. After which, Mr. Oates having delivered certain Informations to the house against the Queen *, the following address was immediately prepared, and ordered to the lords for their concurrence:

"We your majesty's loyal and dutiful subjects, the and commons in parliament assembled, having received Information, by several witnesses, of a most desperate and traiterous Design and Confederacy against the life of your most sacred majesty, wherein, to their great astonishment, the Queen is particularly charged, and accused; in discharge of our allegiance, and out of our affection and care for the preservation of your majesty's sacred person, and, consequently, of the whole kingdom, do most humbly beseech your majesty that the Queen, and all her family, and all papists, or reputed or suspected papists, be forthwith removed from your majesty's court at White-hall."

* "It was a known thing that his majesty was not over fond of his consort; and it was generally believed that he would have been glad of another, as well for the sake of issue, as variety. Here then was the fairest opportunity imaginable laid before him, to do what he was thought to desire most: A charge of high treason, brought home to her majesty's life by an overt-act, and supported by a brace of witnesses (Oates and Bedlow;) and all this at a time when the people were so exasperated against the presumptive heir, that any expedient, of any kind, to set him aside, would have met with a hearty welcome. But to the king's honour it ought to be remembered, that, instead of embracing it, he attended to the depositions with indignation; and was heard to say, 'They think I have a mind to a new wife; but, for all that, I will not see an innocent woman abused.' Certain it is, that, upon this occasion, he caused Oates to be clapped up in close confinement, his papers to be seized, his servants to be dismissed, and nobody to be admitted to converse with him, unless one of the clerks of the council was present." Ralph.

Oates had, in the same manner, charged the Queen upon oath before Mr. sec. Coventry, Nov. 24; which he also confirmed upon oath, the next day, before the king and council. Bedlow was before the council on the 27th. On which day Coleman was tried and convicted, on the evidence of Oates and Bedlow and his own letters. He was executed Dec. 3, and died without any confession.

Quarrel between the Lords Pembroke and Dorset.] This day, the lords being informed of a Quarrel which happened lately betwixt the earls of Pembroke and Dorset, It is ordered, that the gentleman usher of the black rod do give notice to the earl of Pembroke, that he attend this house presently; and that Mr. Lloyd and the footman be summoned to appear presently, to give this house an account thereof. In the mean time the earl of Dorset gave the house an account, That on Wednesday last, late at night, the earl of Pembroke sent one Mr. Lloyd, who told him that the earl of Pembroke desired of him to speak with him at Mr. Locket's house: the earl of Dorset asked, whether the earl of Pembroke was sober; and was answered, yes; and when his lordship came, he found the earl of Pembroke in a low room; who told him, 'That he had done him an injury, therefore he would fight him:' the earl of Dorset asked him 'Where, and when?' The earl of Pembroke told him, 'Now in this room;' and then laid violent hands upon him; and the earl of Pembroke's footman took away his sword from his side; but Mr. Lloyd closed in and parted them, and so his lordship got loose from him.—The earl of Pembroke being come, standing in his place, the lord chancellor told him what an account the earl of Dorset had given to the house: the earl of Pembroke said, 'He remembered no such thing;' but confessed, 'he desired to speak with the earl of Dorset about business, and had no intent of fighting; and that the earl of Dorset had two men with him; and that his own servant took his sword away.' The house directed the earl of Dorset to relate again, in the presence of the earl of Pembroke, what passed betwixt them; then both these lords withdrew themselves.—The house taking this business into consideration, and how much the honour of this house was concerned therein, made the Order following: "For the better preservation of the peace, and preventing any mischiefs which may happen between the earl of Pembroke and the earl of Dorset, It is ordered, That the earl of Pembroke and the earl of Dorset be and are hereby confined to their respective houses or lodgings, till farther orders; and that they, or either of them, send not any message, or write to the other, during this confinement."—The next day they were both released on an intimation by the duke of Bucks that the Quarrel was made up.

Misunderstanding between the Marquis of Winton and the E. of Clarendon.] The same day the earl of Clarendon, being speaking in the debate the house was in concerning Titus Oates, took notice, that the marquis of Winton said, 'he lies, he lies;' of which words the house required the marq. of Winton to give an account: the marquis denied not the words, but begged the pardon of the house, that he was talking of other things whilst the house was in debate; and he said, he did not intend the words against the earl of Clarendon, and if he have offended the house he was sorry for it, and begged pardon for it.—Ordered, "That the marquis of Winton and the earl of Clarendon do not go out of the house until the house be adjourned." After which, the house laid their commands upon them not to carry their resentments any farther, concerning the business which happened that day.

The King refuses to pass the Militia Bill even for half an hour.] Nov. 30. The King came to the house and gave the royal assent to the Test-Bill against Popery, called 'An Act for the more effectual preserving the King's Person,' &c. of which he pleaded the merit, to excuse himself from passing the Militia-Bill, presented at the same time; which, he said, put the Militia for so many days out of his power, and that was what he would not comply with, though but for half an hour."

Address resolved on the State and Danger of the Nation.] Dec. 2. The commons ordered, "That an humble Address be presented to his majesty, containing a representation of the present State, and Dangers of this Nation, to be grounded on the following Heads, viz. 1. On the Misrepresentation of the Proceedings of this house. 2. On the dangers that have and may arise from private Advices, contrary to the advice of parliament. The house divided on this Article, and it was carried in the affirmative, Yeas 138, Noes 114. 3. On the great Danger the Nation lies under from the Growth of Popery. 4. On the Danger that may arise to his majesty and the kingdom, by the non-observation of the laws, that have been made for the preservation of the peace and safety of the king and kingdom*."

The King's Message concerning the Militia Bill.] Mr. Sec. Coventry delivered the following Message from his majesty:

"C. R. His majesty, to prevent all misunderstandings that may arise from his not passing the late bill of the Militia, is pleased to declare, that he will readily assent to any bill of that kind, which shall be tendered to him, for the public security of the kingdom by the Militia, so as the whole power of calling, continuing, or not continuing of them together, during the time limited, be left to his majesty to do therein as he shall find it to be most expedient for the public safety."

Resolved, "That a committee be appointed,

* 'This' says sir J. Reresby, p. 73, 'aimed at my Lord Treasurer, and some others of the Cabinet Council. This was carried by two-and-twenty votes, and even some of the courtiers were for it; whence it was by some surmised, that the duke, being no longer in council, was grown jealous of the Treasurer, and had a mind he should be removed. It was now said the duke had been persuaded (but unjustly) that his lordship endeavoured to insinuate into the king, that there was something of probability in the accusation against the queen, purely that he might hearken to a divorce, and marry another, more likely to bring children to the crown.'

to inspect precedents touching the methods and proceedings of parliament in passing of Bills; and to enquire, Whether, according to the methods of parliament, a Bill may be brought in, for making the Militia more useful; and to report their opinion to the house."

Five Popish Lords impeached, and committed to the Tower.] Dec. 5. The commons impeached the lord Arundel of Wardour, the earl of Powis, the lord visc. Stafford, the lord Petre, and the lord Bellasis, of High Treason, and other crimes and misdemeanors.—The Lord Chief Justice had in Oct. issued out his warrant for apprehending the said lords at the instance of the commons; which the lords being informed of by the said Chief Justice, they committed the said lords to the Tower by an Order of their own.*

A Supply granted for disbanding the Army.] Dec. 16. The house resolved, "That the Bill for granting a Supply to his majesty, for paying off, and Disbanding the Forces, &c. should pass; and that it should be entitled, 'An Act for granting a Supply to his majesty, of 206,462*l.* 17*s.* 3*d.* for the effectual Paying off, and Disbanding the Forces raised, or brought over from foreign parts, into this kingdom, since September 29, 1677."

A committee was then appointed, instantly to wait upon the king with this vote, who, upon their return, informed the house, That they had been to wait upon his majesty, according to order, who had sent them word out of the house of lords, that he was at that time very busy, and that his majesty had rather they would attend him at Whitehall, when the house was up.

Sir Jonathan Trelawney, prisoner in the Tower, (see p. 1048.) petitioned the house for leave to go into the country for recovery of his health; which was granted.

The King's Message informing the Commons that he had ordered Mr. Montagu's (a member) Papers to be seized.] Sir John Ernly, chancellor of the exchequer, acquainted the house, That he was commanded by the king to deliver this Message. "That his majesty having received Information, that his late Ambassador in France, Mr. Montagu †, a member of this house, had held several private Conferences with the pope's nuncio there, has, to the end that he may discover the truth of the matter, given order for the seizing Mr. Montagu's Papers *."

Debate thereon.] Serj. *Maynard.* I wish the like proceedings had been in other cases. Coleman had time to sort his Papers, and this diligence would have prevented it. I would let this matter alone awhile. The charge of corresponding with the pope's nuncio, borders upon treason very near; at least looks that way. Quicquid necessitas cogit, defendit. Correspondence of this nature sometimes may be justifiable.

Sir *Tho. Lee.* This is a high charge against your member. I would hear him in his place. Because he is a member he is not exempt from crimes.

Mr. *Powle.* No man can defend an ambassador's having correspondencies, or conferences, with the pope's nuncio. Montagu is a member of parliament; and it is an old rule, that, in treason, no private man, nor member's person, can be seized, before the accusation be given in upon oath: if not, any member may be taken from parliament. I would know, whether any legal information has been given against your member. This was a fatal case in the last king's time, of seizing members and their papers. I hope never to see the like again. If a great minister has a quarrel against a gentleman, and one go and tell the king a story of him to his prejudice, and his papers thereupon must be seized, I know not whither that will go. In the first place, I would be instructed from Ernly, whether there be any legal Information against your member? and, if there be not, then you may consider what to do.

Mr. *Hampden.* I would have the notice from the king, by the honourable person, written down, as the very words delivered by him, by the clerk.

Sir *John Ernly.*] I said, 'the king had com-

* The accusation against these lords was, upon the evidence of Titus Oates, for accepting commissions from the Pope. See Burnet, vol 1. p. 430.

† Son of lord Montagu of Boughton, to which title he succeeded (on his father's death) in 1683: he was afterwards, for his eminent services, created by king William earl, and by queen Anne duke, of Montagu. He had been twice ambassador to the court of France, and in the house of commons was as zealous in promoting the Bill of Exclusion, as he was in the house of lords in forwarding the Revolution; soon after which he was appointed Master of the Great Wardrobe. He died in 1708.

* "The earl of Danby had broke with Montagu, but knowing what Letters he had wrote to him, and with what secrets he had trusted him, was apprehensive Montagu might accuse him; so he resolved to prevent him. Jenkins, who was then at Nimeguen, wrote over (according to a direction sent him, as was believed) 'that he understood Montagu had been in a secret correspondence, and in dangerous practices, with the pope's nuncio at Paris.' Montagu, it seems, had made use of him, and given him money, which he loved, for such secrets as he could draw from him. Upon Jenkins's letter the king sent the above Message. This was a device of lord Danby's, to find his own letters, and destroy them; and then to let the prosecution fall. But Montagu understood the arts of a court too well to be easily catched, and had put a box, in which those letters were, in sure hands, out of the way. A great debate arose upon this matter in the house of commons." Burnet.

manded me to let you know, that he having received information from abroad, that Mr. Montagu, his late embassador, contrary to his Instructions, had held private Conferences with the pope's nuncio, he had caused his Papers to be seized, to the end that he may discover the matter.'

Sir *Tho. Clarges.* I am glad to hear that the ambassador had Instructions not to correspond with the pope's nuncio. I am very glad to hear it indeed, (jeeringly.) Sir Wm. Godolphin, the Spanish ambassador, is accused of high treason by Mr. Oates, and yet we hear nothing of him. Montagu's instructions will appear in the secretary's minutes. I would have Ernly answer, whether this Information be upon oath?

Sir *John Ernly.* I have told you what the king has commanded me; but I cannot be free to say farther, without leave. I do not say 'contrary to any Instructions,' but 'without any Instructions,' from his majesty.

Sir *Wm. Coventry.* The whole business will turn upon this hinge. The devil is as bad as the broth he is boiled in, the proverb is. Some of us, it may be, have sons at Rome, and they have kissed the pope's toe, and may be guilty of treason for that. I would have that explained.

Mr. *Powle.* I shall acquaint you from Mr. Montagu, that he will deliver all his own Papers himself; else papers for his own private defence may be embezzled. He will resign them to any hand this house shall appoint.

Mr. *Bennet.* If his Papers are seized, papers may be put into his cabinet, as well as taken out, to his great prejudice.

Mr. *Powle.* Five or six gentlemen, from Whitehall, have seized all the passages to Mr. Montagu's house, and his lady has sent him a letter of it.

Col. *Birch.* This is a mighty mystery, and the greatest business I have heard here. I should be very loth to make a wrong step in it here. I have always taken it for granted, that no member's Papers can be seized. I know not what haste they are in, in this matter, nor where it will end. Forty more members papers may be seized, at this rate, and the house garbled; and then the game is up. You have Information from Ernly of the thing, &c. and you may have as good information as this, against another member. The kingdom of France is in secretary Coventry's province; and I would have members to go to his office, to search the minutes for ambassador Montagu's Instructions, when he was sent into France.

Sir *Tho. Lee.* I would, in this matter, make tender steps. I see there is no harm in making an Address to the king about it, 'That he may let the house know whether there is any Information upon oath against Mr. Montagu.'. If there be such information as the law warrants, I would sit down under it; if not, I would look to our privileges.

Col. *Titus.* If there be no Information upon oath, then it is a breach of privilege.

Sir *Wm. Coventry.* If we address the king, to know whether the Information be upon oath, it will so turn the thing upon us, that we shall know it. I agree with Birkenhead, that it is a great fault in an ambassador, an omission to give the king an account of public transactions that have passed through his hands. It may be through forgetfulness; but unpardonable, if the king calls for it, and the person does not give it. I have been abroad myself in popish countries, and may have conversed with nuncios. I have had the king's pardon, and my share in the last act of indemnity. An ambassador has nothing for his justification, but his papers; and his neck may go for it, if he has not his papers to justify himself. I should be loth to have my papers seized, though but for matter of reputation. I had rather have my shirt, than my papers, taken from me. Montagu desires only sorting of his papers, and that he may mark them, and he will deliver them to such as you shall approve of, and that he may mark them, and set them in order, to make his defence the better. Otherwise any minister, employed in foreign negotiations, is in a desperate condition.

Mr. *Powle.* I would not have his Papers tumbled and tossed about, before you know whether the Information against him be upon oath. The ministers heretofore answered for ill actions in the government, but now they put them all upon the king.

Mr. *Vaughan.* If Papers are seized at this rate, a great many of your members papers may be seized, because some men are guilty of high treason.

The *Speaker.* The thing is of great moment, and the king has told you why he has caused the Papers to be seized; and Montagu has told you, 'he has received a letter from his lady, that his house is guarded, &c.' but they are not to be seized till Montagu comes to his house to sort the papers. You concern not yourselves in matters of state, but matters of privilege. Till you know that his charge is not upon oath, you ought to believe that the matter is upon oath. It is a nice thing, and I know the stress and consequence of it. It may be, I know the thing and matter of it. And if no-body is more capable to advise than myself, I would have you expect the issue.

Mr. *Powle.* What I moved is, because the thing yet is in possibility of recall. It is plain that his Papers are sent to be seized. The rights and privileges of parliament are the greatest strength and security of the king and the nation. I think it a very dutiful way to know what the thing is. Therefore you cannot go a better than to send to the king, &c. before we rise.

Mr. *Williams.* If you adjourn, you submit your privilege to the king's pleasure. I cannot give my opinion, whether it is a breach of privilege, or not, till you have the thing entirely before you. I would know what this Information is against your member. I know, by the aw of England, there is no distinction of state reason, felony, or breach of the peace, against which there is no privilege. It is not every breach of the peace that a member may be seized upon, &c. where there is no more required than security, &c.—And he ought to have the privilege of an Englishman. He that will be ridden shall be ridden. Therefore I would address, &c.

Sir *Rob. Howard.* Suppose you go to the king, and say, 'What is it you know of Montagu?' That is too early, and yet your member has his house seized. In this there is difficulty every way. It seems, a reference is made by Montagu to see whether the charge be true in his Papers. Shall your member forbear, and give up his Papers? That you will not do. Your member has offered to give up his Papers, and to mark them, that they may be no injury to him. Therefore I would have some of your members accompany Montagu, that he may sort his Papers.

Col. *Titus.* If the Information be upon oath, and it be neither felony, treason, nor breach of the peace, your privilege is violated. With this Message moved for, I would have another, viz. 'Of what nature this conference with the pope's nuncio was.'

Sir *John Knight.* Conferences have been held at Whitehall with Father Patrick, and Father Howard, and other priests. I would have that enquired into likewise.

Sir *Tho. Meres.* Whoever has had private conference with the pope's nuncio, now in the Tower, I would seize all their Papers, one and all—of whom I will tell you tomorrow; some of their Papers, upon what I say, will be laid aside. Let it go where it will; let the subject-matter against Montagu be seen, if proved true; that this may not be a precedent upon this house for the future. I would therefore beseech the king to suspend any farther proceeding upon Montagu, till this house be satisfied whether the Information be given upon oath; and whether the subject of that conference was treason.

Sir *Wm. Coventry.* I am against the whole thing; either sending to the king to know what the crimes are, or whether upon oath. I believe there are persons that put the king upon this (as I believe it done by advice) and I believe it is not treason he is charged with, because they have not seized Mr. Montagu's person, as well as his Papers, which was the properest thing to be done. He may be guilty, he may be innocent; possibly the thing will be put farther. But to take away his armour that must defend him, a little thrust will destroy him. The very law gives him his Papers to justify himself by, not only for his commissions but omissions. His Papers to be delivered out of his hands clearly away, is a very dangerous thing. I would be glad to hear something from Montagu himself. It has been proposed, 'that some of the members may go with him to sort his Papers.' If there be any Papers relating to the pope's nuncio, they may be copied out, and Montagu may keep the originals and the rest of the Papers.

Sir *John Ernly.* Montagu knows something of the nature. In all these cases there are warrants of the same nature. You may send for the warrant, and you will find these Papers are to be seized before reasonable evidence, and that the Papers be so scheduled, as that the gentleman may have no prejudice.

Sir *Tho. Lee.* The Papers being seized by the king's warrant, may be looked upon as in the king's actual possession. By the king's order so much appears, that persons are at Montagu's house, &c. This is your tenderness to them that have advised the king to this, or some others, that may hereafter, that you may avoid all occasion of offence. You are told of a conference with the pope's nuncio, that he has had. Therefore the Papers were ordered to be seized, to know the truth of the matter. Then it seems, those Papers are seized to see whether those Informations are treason, or no; therefore in this you go the most moderate way. The consequence will be, you will see your member tried, and sit still till it be done; and no matter how soon you see Montagu guilty or not guilty. And so there will be nothing upon your Books to hurt parliaments in eternal consequence. Therefore I would have this Message sent to the king, to prevent declaring what your privileges are in this matter.

Mr. *Powle.* You are past that consideration. Now the question is, Whether you will go with this second part. It is not so decent to go often to the king. You are not yet ripe to desire the king to desist proceeding, for you know not what the thing is yet, and that may be quickly done, when you know.

Mr. Harbord was sent to Mr. Montagu's house to inform the house of the proceedings, &c. who gave this account: "That, by order of council, Montagu's cabinets were seized, but were not to be opened till Montagu was present. And that they were taken away, and set in a chamber near the council chamber."

Mr. *Montagu.* I believe, that the seizing my cabinets and Papers was to get into their hands some Letters of great consequence, that I have to produce, of the designs of a Great Minister of State.*

Mr. *Harbord.* This has been intended 3 or 4 days, but, I believe, they have missed of their aims; and I would not for 40,000*l.* they had those Papers. And, freely, this was my great inducement to stir so much to make Mr. Montagu a member of this house†. In due time

* See the last Note.

† "Mr. Montagu aspiring to the office of Secretary of State, took it very ill that the Treasurer had engaged to bring in sir Wm. Temple. Mr. Montagu was the Treasurer's most dangerous enemy, because he had private Letters in his hands from that minister; and though he could not divulge them without great injury to the king, this gave him no uneasiness, because resolving to throw himself

you will see what those Papers are. They will open your eyes, and though too late to cure the evil, yet they will tell you who to proceed against, as the authors of our misfortunes. I desire that some persons of honour and worth may be present at the opening these Cabinets, lest some of these Letters should be there. For they are of the greatest consequence that ever you saw.

Mr. *Bennet.* The sum the gentleman speaks of, 40,000*l.*, is a great deal of money. But pray let these Papers be forth-coming for your use. As for the breach of our privileges, &c. this thing was thrown in to blind us. I know my share of transactions too, and you shall in time know of it.

Sir *Gilbert Gerrard.* This business is of great consequence, and I hope may save us. I would address the king, 'That these Cabinets may not be opened, but may be produced here to-morrow, that we may proceed upon them.'

Col. *Titus.* To seize Papers thus is very illegal. Any man's may be seized at this rate. I look upon this as one of the wisest actions the ministers have done. Were I one of them, right or wrong I would have seized Montagu's Papers. I second the motion, 'That the Papers, &c. may be produced here to-morrow.' And then I believe you will see why those Papers were seized.

Sir *Nick. Carew.* I would sit on, and let the Papers in Montagu's hands be brought now, and if they concern any man, under his majesty himself, I would prosecute the thing now. I know not whether we shall be here to-morrow morning, or no. It may be, we shall be all clapped up by to-morrow. Let Montagu therefore be commanded to bring in his Papers now, before you rise.

Sir *John Lowther.** For ought I know, Montagu may be served as sir E. Godfrey was; therefore I would not have him go out of the house for the Papers. He knows by what practices these negotiations with France have been done. I am of opinion that we shall not sit here to-morrow. I move therefore to have the Papers sent for now.

Sir *Henry Capel.* I second that motion. We know what practices have been in the late times, &c. how Papers of members have been seized. The king has power on his subjects, but it is according to law. I wondered at the proceeding of the Sheriff of Northamptonshire at Montagu's election; but now it is all out; we know the reason of it. He may give us much light into transactions. Lowther has awakened you with the case of Godfrey, which is of great importance. I know not what may become of us to-morrow; therefore I would have Montagu's Papers brought to-night.

Lord *Cavendish.* I believe, it will appear by those Papers, that the war with France was pretended, for the sake of an Army, and that a great man carried on the interest of an Army and Popery; and Montagu gives you the convenience of this discovery. I move therefore, 'That he bring the Papers in as soon as can be.'

Col. *Titus.* I suppose Montagu has those Papers in his custody; else neither he nor his friends would have informed you of them. I would therefore have some members go with him to fetch them.

Lord *Russell.* Montagu has imparted some of the contents of those Papers to me; and I was required by him not to impart them to any body; but now it is no secret. Montagu cannot come at the originals, for the present, but he has a copy of them.

Lord Danby's Letters produced.] Mr. Harbord and some others were ordered (Mr. Montagu having acquainted the house that he had in his custody some Papers which concern the Peace of the Government) to receive directions from Mr. Montagu where to find those Papers. The house sat till the gentlemen returned with Mr. Montagu's Papers. Then Mr. Harbord reported, 'That they had repaired to the place where Mr. Montagu directed them, and had brought the Box of Papers which he mentioned; but that the key is carried to Whitehall, locked up in the Cabinets; and that they have sent for a smith to break it open." Mr. Montagu went up to sort the Papers.

Mr. *Montagu.* I am sorry that so great a minister has brought this guilt upon himself. It was my intention (making reflections upon your apprehension of a standing Army) to have acquainted Mr. sec. Coventry with the Papers. I will now only tell you, that the king has been as much deluded as the Dutch or Spain; and you have been deluded too by this great minister. This I should not have done, out of duty and respect to the king, but by command of the house.

The Box being ordered to be opened, Mr. Montagu selected and presented to the house two Letters, which were read by the Speaker, the one dated Jan. 16, 1677-8; the other March 25, 1678. The principal matter therein is contained in these words: "In case the conditions of peace shall be accepted, the king expects to have six millions of livres (300,000*l.*) yearly, for 3 years, from the time that this agreement shall be signed between his majesty and the king of France; because it will be 2 or 3 years before he can hope to find his parliament in humour to give him supplies, after

into the party against the court, which was most prevalent in the parliament, he knew he should be protected even against the king himself. To this end he got himself elected member for Northampton, and suddenly leaving Paris without the king's consent or knowledge, came to London, and took his seat in the house." Rapin.

* Created lord visc. Lonsdale by king William, in 1696, having been very instrumental in the Revolution, by securing the city of Carlisle, and bringing over the counties of Cumberland and Westmorland. He was also in that reign vice-chamberlain of the houshold, lord privy seal, &c. and died in 1700, aged 45.

your having made any peace with France, &c." Subscribed "DANBY." "To the Secretary you must not mention one syllable of the money." [At the bottom of this Letter were these words: "THIS LETTER IS WRIT BY MY ORDER. * C. R."]

Debate thereon.] Mr. *Bennet.* I wonder the house sits so silent when they see themselves sold for six millions of livres to the French. Some things come home to treason in construction. I would have the lawyers tell you, whether this you have heard be not worthy impeaching the Treasurer of Treason. Now we see who has played all this game; who has repeated all the sharp Answers to our Addresses, and raised an Army for no war. You know now who passes by the secretaries of state. I would impeach the Treasurer of high treason.

Mr. *Williams.* Will any member aver this to be the Treasurer's letter?

Mr. *Montagu.* I conceive it to be the Treasurer's hand. I have had several letters from him of the same hand.

Mr. *Williams.* If this be his Letter, there cannot be a more constructive Treason than is contained in it. You have heard of Religion and Property apprehended in danger, in several speeches. But when your laws are contemned by a Great Minister, and they miscarry and are laid dead—(A great cry of the house, 'Name him, name him.') The letters name the person sufficiently. Nothing ought to be imputed to the king, but this man, unless he clears himself upon somebody else, must take this crime upon him. This project of peace is what you have prophesied all along. This agrees with Coleman's Letters, this great engine Money. Now when this great person is on this point to make parliaments useless, it is Treason. And the parliament may declare a treason, without making any. For any minister to destroy a confederacy, and to make the king a pensioner to France, I would impeach him of Treason.

Mr. *Harbord.* I hope now gentlemen's eyes are open, by the design on foot to destroy the government and our liberties. I believe, if the house will command Mr. Montagu, he will tell you more now. But I would not press it now upon him, because poisoning and stabbing are in use. Therefore I would not examine him farther now, but let him reserve himself till the matter comes to trial before the lords. As to the danger of the king's person, there is something much more extraordinary. But I will not name him yet. The thing has taken wind. A witness has been taken off with 300*l.* and denies his hand. I protest, I am afraid that the king will be murdered every night. A peer, and an intimate of this earl's, said, 'There would be a change in the government in a year.' He has poisons both liquid and in powders. But I would ask Montagu no more questions now, but have an Impeachment drawn up, and I doubt not but this great man will have condign punishment, when the matter comes before the lords.

Sir *Henry Goodrick.* We now come upon Impeachment of a noble peer, who deserves well of the nation, and, I assure you, has promoted the protestant religion, and has honour for the government. I put Harbord upon it, that all the evidence against him may be produced, and make it out who converses with this nobleman, that has 'the poisons' he mentions. For the king's security, I would have the persons named.

Mr. *Bennet.* I accuse my Lord Treasurer of High Treason, and I will bring other matters against him.

Sir *John Hanmer.* The king's life is concerned, and I cannot sit still when I hear 'poison' spoken of. I would find this poisoner out; else he betrays the nation and the king.

Mr. *Harbord.* If you please, I will tell Mr. sec. Coventry who it is; but I assure you, it is told the king already.

Sir *John Knight.* This Army was raised for a French war, and so many hundred thousand pounds given for that purpose, and yet we had no war! Money given to disband the Army, and that not done! The popish Plot discovered at that time! And all runs parallel. Take such evil counsellors from the king, that have done these things, and he, and his posterity, and we all shall flourish: else we shall be destroyed.

Sir *Edm. Jennings.* As to the matter in the Lord Treasurer's letter, thus I will state the question: 'Whether there be matter in that Letter to ground an Impeachment against this lord.' As to the other thing, "of poisoning," the king's person is so nearly concerned, that I would have the person known for the king's sake, and all our own sakes. If not, then let us adjourn.

Mr. *Harbord.* If I was not well satisfied that the king had known of it, I would have found means to acquaint the king. But the design of moving this is to divert the question. The design I had, in not naming the person, was, that it might be impossible for the person to avoid being taken off, since the king knows it already, and a member knows the thing, and I have seen the things. But the party fell off from his evidence. The king knows it, and if you will know him too, I am not afraid to name him. He had the poison, and tried it upon dogs with good success. The first thing I said was, 'Does the king know of it?' He told me 'he did, and he had been offered a sum of money to conceal it.' There has been 200,000*l.* in 12 months paid out of the exchequer, for secret service; and vast sums of money diverted out of the course of payment in the exchequer.

Col. *Titus.* I find it a hard matter, and very dangerous, to accuse a Treasurer. The righteous or unrighteous mammon makes

* "These last words made very much for Mr. secretary Coventry; since now it appeared that he was not trusted with these ill practices." Burnet.

friends. There has been 197,000*l.* issued out of the 200,000*l.* we gave, by one person that is a member. This lord had once an Impeachment against him upon an illegal patent. First, we could get no witnesses, &c. And all we got by it, was to vote, 'That this patent was not illegal.' Never any thing prospered in his ministry. There is not a penny of money in the exchequer, and I am sure he is Treasurer. Now whether this lord, with the interest of France, has not carried on his own? When the king of Spain was in the circumstances the king of France now is, if Walsingham and Burleigh, instead of supporting H. iv. of France, had supported the League, and made the king of Spain greater than he was, (who was ten times too great for us,) had not they been good counsellors for Philip ii. and ill counsellors for queen Elizabeth? It was said by Philip de Comines, 'That all king Lewis of France's ministers did ride upon one horse.' Now we were told of 'a war,' and 'an actual war with France,' an army was raised for it, and a shameful peace made up with France. And the Lord Treasurer thinks he deserves six millions of livres for doing it; and so no occasion for the parliament to meet in 3 years. The Lord Treasurer, it seems, was of one opinion; the parliament and the law of another. His crime is great, and tends to the subversion of the nation, and so it is, when the king shall have no parliaments. Some fear the Treasurer, and some love him; I do neither, and would impeach him.

Mr. *John Ernly.* Titus tells you, 'That nothing has prospered under the Lord Treasurer's ministry.' He has paid, I am sure, a great part of the debt of two millions upon the exchequer. As for his ministry, pray God send we have no worse French counsellors! And if we had war then, God knows what would have become of us. If this lord has hatched these councils, France is not for him. But I am the most mistaken, if he has not been opposite to France. Now for the Letter that speaks of the Money; if it had been ten times as much, I could have wished it with France. As for the peace, it was made by the Confederates, and not the king. The Confederates have, all along, importuned the king not to lay aside the Army, for all Flanders would be lost. I am as little for an Army as any man; and am for having it disbanded, if the king had money to pay them off. Does not this Letter come by way of recrimination? It is necessary to see Mr. Montagu's Answer to this Letter. I would have the lawyers debate it, before you come to this matter as a charge against this lord; barely given you by recrimination. The king's safety is concerned; and I desire, that the person that should have poisoned him, be named. You cannot absolve yourselves from it.

Mr. *Cha. Bertie.* I affirm that my Lord Treasurer paid 600,000*l.* of old arrears out of the Exchequer. And I appeal to the Speaker's Office in the Navy. So in this he has not squandered the Treasury in secret service.

Mr. *Montagu.* My Lord Treasurer has my Answer to his Letter. And let him, if he please, produce a copy of that letter, and you find, that if my advice had been followed, the army had not been raised, and a better peace made. And I aver, that the French king offered our king some money, and more towns, than when we were in conjunction with France. 'I find my Lord Treasurer has so much the sweet of being treasurer of England, that he would be treasurer of France too.' This the king of France said, and so would treat no longer. I was for peace, because I saw no intention of our ministers for war, and so would have had no army. I brought the conditions so far as that the French should deliver Valenciennes and Conde to the Spaniards; far better conditions than now they have; but after the army was raised, they were for peace. If I have done ill in this, impeach me for it.

In the other Letter which was read, subscribed "Danby," were the following passages: "Your intelligence concerning M. Rouvigny has not been the least of your favours. For my part I will contribute to the friendship of the two kings. We depend upon an Adjournment of 13 days, to see if there can be any expedient for the peace in that time. And the effect of that Adjournment has been, that every body apprehended peace, &c."

Lord *Dumblain**. Montagu, in his discourse in France, has given the nation great discommendations. I have heard him say, 'the house of commons had a company of loggerheads and boobies in it.' For what my father is accused of, if proved, I would not spare him nor pardon him more than the greatest rascal that had done me the most injury.

Mr. *Peregrine Bertie.* Put the question first, about "poisoning the king."

Sir *Henry Capel.* I have no article against any man, but only from my observations of the government. We have sat here all seasons of the year to no purpose. I have something to say, let it fall where it will; and I will serve no man here, but my king and my country. We that are of common understanding, know not foreign notions, nor mysteries of state at home. If Religion, the Government and Property be safe, we sit down and enjoy what we have, and thank God for it. If foreign negotiations have been prosperous, let it be spoken of. Has the Protestant Religion gone forward? I would gladly know, whether the Exchequer is in good order as we have been told. I know what sums we have given; but if it be not in such order, are we to sit still? Does not France increase upon us? We were no sooner got out of the War with Holland, but assistances of men were sent into France to

* The Lord Treasurer's son; called up to the house of lords in 1690, by the title of lord Kiveton. He succeeded to the dukedom of Leeds (on his father's death) in 1712, distinguished himself in the sea-service, being vice admiral of the red, and died in 1729, aged 71.

reaten the French king. We can get no bills of Popery passed. These last four or five ears, we have had nothing but Prorogations nd Adjournments of the parliament, without oing any thing to purpose. If we had lived ell with this great man, and not made the ote the last session, 'That till the Tax, &c. e expired, and the Protestant Religion secured, and ill Ministers, &c. removed, we ould give no more Money, &c.' But the king as been persuaded that a prince must depend pon a party, and he is told that we proceed s in 1641 and 1642. Is any thing more clear han the concurrence of the Letters, that have een produced you by Montagu, with Coleman's Papers? This minister has let the French ing grow upon us, and let our king take money from him, to lay aside his people; this has een Danby's advice. If the gentlemen of he long robe will say this is Treason, I say so no, and shall think this a ground to impeach im.

Mr. Solicitor *Winnington*. Before I meddle with the Treasurer's Letters, I will speak o the point of declaratory Treason. I have wife and children, and some estate, and loyalty to my prince, and I hope to leave it to my osterity. In this matter I shall deliver my pinion, and I fear no man alive, let it fall where it will. By 25 E. iii. declaratory Treason, is only in parliament, where those things hall be declared Treason, for the Judges to roceed upon, and no other. I will put you familiar example: the killing of John Imperial, the Genoa ambassador, was declared reason. It was treason at common law beore, but after that statute they had recourse o parliament for the same crime, and they delared it so. It has been the wisdom of pariament to keep the power of declaring Treason in themselves, to bridle great men, who y friendship and authority, may avoid jusice. Since I came into this house, which is bout three years since, I have been present t several Addresses, &c. and I would not how unkindness, in the post I am in, to my uperior officer. If a member does undertake o prove an Article, &c. though it be but proable, it is a ground for a grand jury to find he bill, (and in Impeachments you are of that ature,) but the judgment is still in the lords. If any subject impeach any man, it is our duty o receive it, as a grand jury. But gentlemen put a hard thing on the long robe, in this case. The Treasurer, in his Letters to Mr. Montagu, says, 'He must not communicate it to the Secretary of State. He must not know of the six millions of livres yearly, &c. that so there may be no need of a parliament.' If this be given as a case to a lawyer, and if this be to destroy parliament, and the fundamental laws of the kingdom; if there be concomitant evidence that the thing was done eâ intentione; if you have power of declaratory Treason, and do not declare this to be treason, you will declare nothing. I have heard Montagu say be has more Letters to produce. Suppose you should vote not to impeach the Treasurer upon these Letters; the common people will say, 'Have not the house impeached him?' How can any member look the world in the face? finding that this is in order to trial, and in order to impeachment. The Lord Treasurer is my superior, but if you pass by this, you may have more such Letters and such practices. There have been other matters alleged against this lord, as diverting the Money, &c. from the usual course of payment in the Exchequer, &c. This is but a small matter in comparison of Treason: but such as have done these things, the parliament has either broken their backs, or they have ran for it. As for giving Money to Members, to vote in this house, he will have the shame of it, and I hope it will be seen by the vote this night, that no man has received any money. Certainly these things are not so mean as to be put off. Without probable evidence, you have no ground of accusation. As for conviction, that is to be done in another place. And I am for impeaching him.

Mr. *Sacheverell*. I have observed the debate; and I take notice that no fault is found out that it is too forward. No man denies these Letters to be the Treasurer's, and yet gentlemen say, 'There is no matter of charge in them against him.' I have not been a man much for shifting hands in the ministry: I see all that come after are as bad as those that went before. By way of defence of the Treasurer, it is said, 'That he found much debt upon the crown, and has paid off a great deal.' It is true. But there was 1,250,000*l.* granted to the king, &c. before he came in to be Treasurer, but he received a great share of it. I would not now charge him singly upon these Letters, but upon the whole pursuance of the thing: he shows you, that, as the rest of the ministers have done great kindness to France, he will do nothing to break that friendship. When we had given a great sum of money for a war with France, then he takes Coleman's way. And it was a great sum of money for England to pay. Give money hastily and no war, and there will be no need of a parliament. This is the only difference; Pensions are not now matter of record. It seems by the Treasurer's Letter, that it is the king's ease to have no parliament. Hereafter let us keep our purses, and we shall have good ministers in time. And let us remember we shall not then have ministers to prorogue us at their pleasure, at the same time that the king was told that war was necessary; and that he might have had a better peace, and an Army was raised, to the great charge of the nation. Let gentlemen give their No to the Impeachment, I will give my Aye to it.

Mr. *Vaughan*. I envy no man's greatness nor fortune that lessens not his prince's. From the grounds of this Letter of the Treasurer, on the 20th of March, the king passed an Act for a war with France, and an Army was raised accordingly. This Letter is dated the 25th of

March, to stipulate peace with the French. And is this matter of recrimination by Montagu, as is said? You give money for an actual war, and the Treasurer stipulates for a peace, and the ministers make peace. The Papists would have a dissolution of the parliament, and these men make it useless. I know very little difference in it. King John's ministers made him a pensioner to the Pope, and it is as great a crime to make our king pensioner to the French king. I am therefore for impeaching the Treasurer.

The question being put, "That there is matter sufficient in these Letters, &c. to impeach Thomas earl of Danby;" the previous question was put and carried, 179 to 116. The main question was then carried in the affirmative, and a committee was appointed to prepare and draw up Articles of Impeachment.*

Resolved, "That Mr. Speaker shall not, at any time, adjourn the house, without a question first put if it be insisted upon. And that this be entered in the Journals as a Standing Order of the house."

Articles of Impeachment against the Earl of Danby.] Dec. 21. Mr. Williams reported the Articles of Impeachments against the Lord Treasurer Danby, as followeth:

Articles of Impeachment of High Treason, and other High Crimes, Misdemeanors, and Offences, against Thomas earl of Danby, Lord High-Treasurer of England.

I. "That he hath traiterously encroached to himself regal power, by treating in matters of Peace and War with foreign princes and ambassadors, and giving Instructions to his majesty's ambassadors abroad, without communicating the same to the secretaries of state, and the rest of his majesty's Council; and against the express declaration of his majesty and his parliament; thereby intending to defeat and overthrow the provisions which had been deliberately made by his maj. and his parliament, for the safety and preservation of his majesty's kingdoms and dominions.—II. That he hath traiterously endeavoured to subvert the ancient and well-established Form of Government in this kingdom; and instead thereof to introduce an arbitrary and tyrannical way of government. And the better to effect this his purpose, he did design the Raising of an Army, upon pretence of a War against the French king; and then to continue the same as a Standing Army within this kingdom: and an army being so raised, and no war ensuing, an act of parliament having passed to pay off and disband the same, and a great sum of money being granted for that end, he did continue this army contrary to the said act, and misemployed the said money given for disbanding, to the continuance thereof; and issued out of his majesty's revenue divers great sums of money for the said purpose; and wilfully neglected to take security from the paymaster of the Army, as the said act required; whereby the said law is eluded, and the army is yet continued, to the great danger and unnecessary charge of his maj. and the whole kingdom.—III. That he, traiterously intending and designing to alienate the hearts and affections of his majesty's good subjects from his royal person and government, and to hinder the Meeting of Parliaments, and to deprive his sacred maj. of their safe and wholesome councils, and thereby to alter the constitution of the government of this kingdom, did propose and negotiate a Peace for the French king, upon terms disadvantageous to the interest of his maj. and his kingdoms: for the doing whereof he did endeavour to procure a great sum of money from the French king, for enabling of him to carry on and maintain his said traiterous designs and purposes to the hazard of his majesty's person and government.—IV. That he is popishly affected; and hath traiterously concealed, after he had notice, the late horrid and bloody Plot and Conspiracy contrived by the Papists against his majesty's person and government; and hath suppressed the evidence, and reproachfully discountenanced the king's witnesses in the discovery of it, in favour of popery; immediately tending to the destruction of the king's sacred person, and the subversion of the Protestant religion.—V. That he hath wasted the king's Treasure by issuing out of his majesty's Exchequer, and several branches of his revenue, for unnecessary Pensions and Secret Services, to the value of 231,602*l.* within two years: and that he hath wholly diverted, out of the known method and government of the Exchequer, one whole branch of his majesty's Revenue to private uses, without any account to be made of it to his majesty in the exchequer, contrary to the express act of parliament which granted the same: and he hath removed two of his majesty's commissioners of that part of the revenue, for refusing to consent to such his unwarrantable actings therein, and to advance money upon that branch of the revenue, for private uses.—VI. That he hath by indirect means procured from his majesty for himself, divers considerable Gifts and Grants of

* "The next day the Lord Treasurer sent Mr. Montagu's Letters of the 11th and 18th of Jan. likewise before quoted; the first giving notice of young Rouvigny's Journey to England, and his practices among the malcontents: and the last, among other things, mentioning old Rouvigny's maxim, That they (the French) must first diminish the Lord Treasurer's credit, before they could do any good in England. These Letters, his lordship himself affirms, the house of commons would not permit to be read: but John Reresby affirms the contrary, in his Memoirs, as doth also one of his lordship's own Apologists; and even the Journals of the House of commons. But if they were read, they had no weight: Mr. Montagu had all the favour usually shewn to those who impeach their accomplices, and was thought to act so meritoriously in the discovery, that no body cared to reflect that he himself was the chief promoter of the guilt." Ralph.

inheritance of the ancient Revenue of the crown, even contrary to acts of parliament."

On reading the first Article a second time, the question was put, that the Articles be committed, which passed in the negative, Yeas 137, Noes 179. The house divided next on a motion for Candles, which passed in the affirmative, Yeas 165, Noes 115. The house again divided on a motion to leave out the word 'traitorously' in the first Article, which passed in the negative, Noes 179, Yeas 141. On a Resolution that lord Danby should be impeached on the above-recited Articles, a motion was made to adjourn, but over-ruled, Yeas 142, Noes 170. The last division during this grand debate, was on a motion whether the said lord should be impeached, on the 4th Article, and it was carried in the affirmative, Yeas 143, Noes 119 *.

The Earl of Danby's vindicating Speech in the House of Lords.] Dec. 23. The commons carried up the Impeachment to the lords. Upon the reading of which, a motion being made for his lordship to withdraw, it was over-ruled by a majority of 20; after which, his lordship rose up and made a formal Speech in his own vindication, in substance as follows:

"My Lords; I know this is not the time for me to enter regularly upon my Defence, because I know your lordships will first order me a copy of my Charge, and appoint me a time for my vindication; when I doubt not to do it to the full satisfaction of your lordships, and all the world. In the mean time I will only beg leave to observe to your lordships, that those Articles in this Charge which seem to have any thing of Treason in them, have their Answer so obvious, that there is very little in them, which may not be answered by many others, as well as myself, and some of them by every man in the kingdom. The 1st, which is the assuming of Regal Power, I confess, I do not understand; having never in my life done any thing of great moment, either at home, or relating to foreign matters, for which I have not always had his majesty's command. And though I am far from having been the most cautious man in taking care of my own security, (which perhaps my great innocence hath been the cause of,) yet I have not been so wanting of common prudence, as in the most material things not to have had his majesty's orders and directions under his own hand, and particularly for the letters now made use of against me. The 2d, I think, does scarce need my giving any Answer to; it being obvious, that the Army was no more raised by me, than by every lord in this house: and whoever is in that station which I hold, must certainly be a fool, to desire any thing which creates a want of Money, especially so great a one, as the Charge of an Army must necessarily and immediately produce. And so for one part of the Article concerning the Pay-Master of the Army, it is in fact otherwise; for security from the pay-master has been taken in the sum of 400,000*l.* The 3d, is of the same nature with the first, and comes from the same foundation, which is, what a gentleman hath thought fit to produce to the house of commons. I will not now censure his actions, I think it will do enough for itself; I will only say, that though I take it for one of the greatest misfortunes which can befal a man, to lie under such a Charge of the house of commons, yet I would much sooner chuse to be under that unhappiness, than under his circumstances. The 4th Article is not only false in every part of it, but it is not possible to believe it true, without my being the greatest fool on earth, as well as the blackest villain. For were I capable of such wickedness, yet the more wicked any man is, the more he is carried to his own interest; and is it possible any thing under heaven can agree less with my interest, than the destruction of this king? Can I possibly hope to be better than I am? And is it not apparent, that there is not one man living, whose happiness depends so much as mine upon the preservation of his person? My lords, I know there is not one man in the world, that can in his heart think me guilty of that part of the Article, if I should say nothing to it. But, besides, I was so far from concealing this hellish Plot, that it is notoriously known, his majesty sent me the first notice of it, together with 43 Heads of the Information, before I knew a syllable of it from any body else: and it hath been owned at the bar of the house of commons by him, from whom only I had the intelligence, 'That he had all the encouragement and dispatch from me, that I could give him.' Besides, when it was disclosed to the Council board, he told some of the clerks of the council, as he had done me divers times before, 'That it would have been much better, and more would have been discovered, if it had been longer kept private.' Besides this, I had the fortune to be particularly instrumental in seizing Mr. Coleman's Papers, without which care, there had not one of them appeared; and consequently, the best and most material evidence which is yet of the Plot, had been wholly wanting. And certainly this is the first time that any man was accused to be the concealer of that Plot, whereof he hath been the principal means of procuring the discovery. For that part of the Article that says, I am 'popishly affected,' I thank God, that the contrary is so well known to all the world, that even some of those that voted against me, did own their knowledge of the falsity of that allegation; and I hope I have, through my whole life, given so good testimony of my religion, both in my own fa-

* While this last question was under dispute, a younger son of the earl's, who had a seat in the house, joined issue with the persecutors of his father, and made it his request, that this part of the Charge might be permitted to stand: that, from thence it might appear with what sort of zeal the whole affair had been conducted. See the Earl's Defence, p. 1071.

mily, and by my services to the Church, whenever it hath laid in my power, that I shall not need much vindication in that particular: and I hope your lordships will forgive me my weakness, in telling you, that I have a younger son in the house of commons, whom I shall love the better as long as I live, for moving to have that part of the Article to stand against me, 'That by that pattern it might appear, with what sort of zeal the whole hath been carried on to my prejudice.'—The fifth Article will, upon examination, appear to be as ill gounded as any of the rest; and I am sorry I am able to give one reason; which is, That I have known no treasure in my time to waste, having entered upon an empty Treasury, and never seen one farthing given to his majesty, in almost six years, that hath not been appropriated to particular uses, and strictly so applied by me, as the acts have directed. And there hath not been one of those Aids, which, instead of giving the king money, hath not cost him more out of his own purse to the same uses, as doth appear by the larger dimensions of the new ships, and so in other things: Insomuch, that I take upon me the vanity to say, that, by the payments I have made to the navy and seamen beyond former times; the paying off the greatest part of the debt which was stopped in the Exchequer before my time, by my punctuality in the course of payments, and by other things which I am able to shew, I doubt not to appear meritorious, instead of being criminal upon that Article.—As to the 6th Article, which mentions my 'great gettings,' I cannot deny but that I serve a master, whose goodness and bounty hath been a great deal more to me than I have deserved, and to whom I can never pay gratitude enough by all the services of my life. But when the particulars of those gettings shall appear, it will be found very contrary to what is suggested abroad; and that, in near six years time in this great place, I have not got half that, which many others have got in lesser places in half that time. And from the examination of this, which I desire may be seen, there will arise matter to accuse my prudence, in not having done for my family what justly I might; but nothing to arraign my honour, my conscience, or my faithful service to the crown. —My Lords, If my obedience to the king shall not be my crime, I think nothing else will stick upon me from these Articles: for my own heart flatters me to believe, that I have done nothing but as a Protestant, and a faithful servant, both to my king and country. Nay, I am as confident, as that now I speak, that, had I been either a Papist, or friend to the French, I had not been now accused. For I have reason to believe, that the principal informer of the house of commons hath been assisted by the French advice to this accusation; and if that gentleman were as just to produce all he knows for me, as he hath been malicious to shew what may be liable to misconstruction against me, or rather against the king, as indeed it is, no man could vindicate me more than himself; under whose hand I have to shew, 'how great an enemy to France I am thought; how much I might have been otherwise; and what he himself might have had for getting me to take it.' But I do not wonder this gentleman will do me no right, when he does not think fit to do it to his majesty, upon whom chiefly this matter doth reflect: Though he knows, as will appear under his hand, 'That the greatest invitations to his majesty for having money from France, have been made by himself; that, if his majesty would have been tempted for money, he might have sold towns for as much as if they had been his own, and the money have been conveyed as privately as he pleased; that his majesty might have made Matches with France, if he would have consented to have given them towns;' and yet, that the king hath always scorned to yield the meanest village, that was not agreed to by the Spaniard and Hollander. That gentleman hath often pretended 'how much his own interest in France was diminished, only by being thought my friend.' And, besides divers other instances, I have under his hand to shew the malice of the French court against me, I sent two of his Letters to the house of commons, which shew how M. Rouvigny was sent hither on purpose to ruin me; which, I am well assured, at this time, they would rather see, than of any one man in England. Besides what that gentleman could say of this kind, if he pleased, I hope his majesty will give me leave, in my defence, to say in his presence, and in the hearing of divers lords, with whom I have the honour to sit in the committee of foreign Affairs, that which, were it not true, his majesty must think me the impudentest and worst of men, to affirm before him, That, ever since I had the honour to serve his majesty, to this day, I have delivered it as my constant opinion, 'That France was the worst interest his majesty could embrace; and that they were the nation in the world from whom, I did believe, he ought to apprehend the greatest danger; and who have both his person and government under the last degree of contempt. For which reason alone, were there no other, I would never advise his majesty to trust to their friendship.—'"

The Lords debate Whether the Impeachment should be received as an Impeachment of High Treason?] When the earl had ended his Speech, a great debate arose, on the question, Whether the Impeachment should be received as an Impeachment of High Treason only, because the commons had added the word High Treason in it? It was said, the utmost that could be made of it, was to suppose it true. But even in that case, they must needs say plainly, that it was not within the Statute. To this it was answered, That the house of commons that brought up the Impeachment, were to be heard to two points, viz. to the nature of the crime; and the trial of it. But the lords could not take upon them to judge of either of these, till they heard what the commons could offer to support the Charge: They were bound therefore to receive the Charge, and to proceed according to the rules of parliament, which was to commit the person, so impeached, and then give a short day for his trial. So it would soon he over, if the commons could not prove the matter charged to be High Treason.

The Earl of Carnarvon's remarkable Speech thereon.] The debate* was carried on with much heat on both sides, and, among the speakers on this occasion, was the earl of Carnarvon, a lord who is said never to have spoken before in that house; who, having been heated with wine, and more excited to display his abilities by the duke of Buckingham, (who meant no favour to the Treasurer, but only ridicule) was resolved, before he went up, to speak upon any subject that should offer itself. Accordingly he stood up, and delivered himself to this effect:

"My Lords; I understand but little of Latin, but a good deal of English, and not a little of the English history, from which I have learnt the mischiefs of such kind of prosecutions as these, and the ill fate of the prosecutors. I could bring many instances, and those very antient; but, my lords, I shall go no farther back than the latter end of queen Elizabeth's reign: at which time the earl of Essex was run down by sir Walter Rawleigh. My lord Bacon, he ran down sir Walter Rawleigh, and your lordships know what became of my lord Bacon. The duke of Buckingham, he ran down my lord Bacon, and your lordships know what happened to the duke of Buckingham. Sir Thomas Wentworth, afterwards earl of Strafford, ran down the duke of Buckingham, and you all know what became of him. Sir Harry Vane, he ran down the earl of Strafford, and your lordships know what became of sir Harry Vane. Chancellor Hyde, he ran down sir Harry Vane, and your lordships know what became of the chancellor. Sir Thomas Osborne, now earl of Danby, ran down Chancellor Hyde; but what will become of the earl of Danby, your lordships best can tell. But let me see that man that dare run the earl of Danby down, and we shall soon see what will become of him."

This being pronounced with a remarkable humour and tone, the duke of Buckingham, both surprised and disappointed, after his way, cried out, 'The man is inspired! and claret has done the business.'—The majority, however, was against the commitment; "upon which it was visible," says Dr. Burnet, "that the commons would have complained, that the lords denied them justice. So there was no hope of making up the matter; and upon that the parliament was first prorogued and then dissolved."

The King prorogues the Parliament.]. Dec. 30. His majesty, in the house of lords, spoke as follows to both houses:

"My lords and gentlemen; It is with great unwillingness that I come this day to tell you, I intend to prorogue you. I think all of you are witnesses that I have been ill used; the particulars of it I intend to acquaint you with at a more convenient time. In the mean time, I do assure you, that I will immediately enter upon the disbanding of the Army, and let all the world see, that there is nothing that I intend but for the good of the kingdom, and for the safety of Religion. I will likewise prosecute this Plot, and find out who are the instruments in it: and I shall take all the care which lies in my power, for the security of religion, and the maintenance of it, as it is now established. I have no more to say to you at this time, but leave the rest to my Lord Chancellor to prorogue you*."

Then the lord chancellor said, "His majesty hath commanded this parliament to be prorogued to the 4th of Feb. next, and this parliament is accordingly prorogued to the 4th of Feb. next."

The Long Parliament dissolved.] On the 24th of Jan. 1678-9, the parliament was dissolved by Proclamation†. And in the same

* "And here I cannot but take notice, that the king observing the lord Stafford to be very violent in the house against the lord Danby, (which, it seems, took birth from a personal pique to him, for obstructing a pension he had from the crown) told me, He wondered at it much, seeing his father came to the unfortunate end he did, by the very self-same method of procedure." Sir John Reresby.

* "Immediately after the prorogation, Mr. Secretary Williamson resigned the seals, which were delivered by the king to the earl of Sunderland, though he had given hopes of the place to sir Wm. Temple, then ambassador in Holland, and had called him over for that purpose. But Temple, at his arrival, found the post filled, the earl of Sunderland having paid Williamson 6000*l.* and 500 guineas, which Temple was not able or willing to give. Shortly after, the king dismissed the earl of Danby, and put the Treasury into commission." Rapin.

Sir Wm. Temple, in his Memoirs, contradicts what Rapin asserts: he says, "That the king sent for him over from the Hague, where he was ambassador, to take possession of the office of secretary of state in the room of secretary Coventry; but on his arrival he declined the accepting it, though greatly pressed by the king, representing to his majesty how necessary it was for him to have one of the secretaries in the house of commons, (where it had been usual to have them both) and that consequently it was very unfit for him to enter upon that office before he got into the house, which was attempted, and failed."

† "Some think this parliament was dissolved, on purpose to protect the Popish Lords in the Tower, and divert, if possible, the noise of the Popish Plot; or else to cover the duke of York from the resentment of the commons, and the general indignation of the people." Kennet.

proclamation notice was given of his majesty's intentions of calling another parliament to meet the 6th of March following.

PRINCIPAL OCCURRENCES AFTER THE DISSOLUTION—TRIAL OF COLEMAN AND IRELAND—NEW ELECTIONS—DUKE OF MONMOUTH—DUKE OF YORK RETIRES TO BRUSSELS.] "Thus came to a period a parliament," says Mr. Hume, "which had sitten during the whole course of this reign, one year excepted. Its conclusion was very different from its commencement. Being elected during the joy and festivity of the restoration, it consisted almost entirely of royalists; who were disposed to support the crown by all the liberality which the habits of that age would permit. Alarmed by the alliance with France, they gradually withdrew their confidence from the king; and finding him still to persevere in a foreign interest, they proceeded to discover symptoms of the most refractory and most jealous disposition. The popish plot pushed them beyond all bounds of moderation; and before their dissolution, they seemed to be treading fast in the footsteps of the last long parliament, on whose conduct they threw at first such violent blame. In all their variations, they had still followed the opinions and prejudices of the nation; and ever seemed to be more governed by humour and party-views than by public interest, and more by public interest than by any corrupt or private influence. During the sitting of the parliament, and after its prorogation and dissolution, the trials of the pretended criminals were carried on; and the courts of judicature, places which, if possible, ought to be kept more pure from injustice than even national assemblies themselves, were strongly infected with the same party-rage and bigoted prejudices. Coleman, the most obnoxious of the conspirators, was first brought to his trial. His letters were produced against him. They contained, as he himself confessed, much indiscretion: but, unless so far as it is illegal to be a zealous catholick, they seemed to prove nothing criminal, much less treasonable, against him. Oates and Bedloe deposed, that he had received a commission, signed by the superior of the Jesuits, to be papal secretary of state, and had consented to the poisoning, shooting, and stabbing of the king: he had even, according to Oates's deposition, advanced a guinea to promote those bloody purposes. These wild stories were confounded with the projects contained in his letters; and Coleman received sentence of death. The sentence was soon after executed upon him. He suffered with calmness and constancy, and to the last persisted in the strongest protestations of his innocence. Coleman's execution was succeeded by the trial of father Ireland: who, it is pretended, had signed, together with fifty Jesuits, the great resolution of murdering the king. Grove and Pickering, who had undertaken to shoot him, were tried at the same time. The only witnesses against the prisoners were still Oates and Bedloe. Ireland affirmed, that he was in Staffordshire all the month of August last, a time when Oates's evidence made him in London. He proved his assertion by good evidence, and would have proved it by undoubted, had he not, most iniquitously, been debarred, while in prison, from all use of pen, ink, and paper, and denied the liberty of sending for witnesses. All these men, before their arraignment, were condemned in the opinion of the judges, jury, and spectators; and to be a Jesuit, or even a catholic, was of itself a sufficient proof of guilt. The chief justice, in particular, gave sanction to all the narrow prejudices and bigoted fury of the populace. Instead of being counsel for the prisoners, as his office required, he pleaded the cause against them, brow-beat their witnesses, and on every occasion represented their guilt as certain and uncontroverted. He even went so far as publickly to affirm, that the papists had not the same principles which protestants have, and therefore were not entitled to that common credence, which the principles and practices of the latter call for. And when the jury brought in their verdict against the prisoners, he said, 'You have done, gentlemen, 'like very good subjects, and very good Christ-'ians, that is to say, like very good protest-'ants: and now much good may their 30,000 'masses do them:' Alluding to the masses by which Pickering was to be rewarded for murdering the king. All these unhappy men went to execution, protesting their innocence; a circumstance which made no impression on the spectators. (1679. 14th Jan.) The opinion, that the Jesuits allowed of lies and mental reservations for promoting a good cause, was at this time so universally received, that no credit was given to testimony delivered either by that order, or by any of their disciples. It was forgotten, that all the conspirators engaged in the gun-powder treason, and Garnet the Jesuit, among the rest, had freely on the scaffold made confession of their guilt. Though Bedloe had given information of Godfrey's murder, he still remained a single evidence against the persons accused; and all the allurements of profit and honour, had not hitherto tempted any one to confirm the testimony of that informer. At last, means were found to complete the legal evidence. One Prance, a silversmith, and a catholic, had been accused by Bedloe of being an accomplice in the murder; and upon his denial had been thrown into prison, loaded with heavy irons, and confined to the condemned hole, a place cold, dark, and full of nastiness. Such rigours were supposed to be exercised by orders from the secret committee of lords, particularly Shaftesbury and Buckingham; who, in examining the prisoners, usually employed (as it said, and indeed sufficiently proved) threatenings and promises, rigour and indulgence, and every art under pretence of extorting the truth from them. Prance had not courage to resist, but confessed himself an accomplice in Godfrey's murder. Being asked concerning the plot, he also thought proper to be acquainted with it, and conveyed some intelligence to the council. Among other absurd circumstances, he said, that one le Fevre bought a second-hand sword of him; because he knew not, as he said, what times were at hand: and Prance expressing some concern for poor tradesmen if such times came, le Fevre replied, that it would be better for tradesmen if the catholic religion were restored: and particularly, that there would be more church work for silversmiths. All this information with regard to the plot, as well as the murder of Godfrey, Prance solemnly retracted, both before the king and the secret committee: but being again thrown into prison, he was induced, by new terrors and new sufferings, to confirm his first information, and was now produced as a sufficient evidence. Hill, Green, and Berry, were tried for Godfrey's murder; all of them men of low stations. Hill was servant to a physician: the other two belonged to the popish chapel at Somerset-house. It is needless to run over the particulars of a long trial, it will be sufficient to say, that Bedloe's evidence and Prance's, were in many circumstances totally irreconcilable; that both of them laboured under unsurmountable difficulties, not to say gross absurdities; and that they were invalidated by contrary evidence, which is altogether convincing. But all was in vain: the prisoners were condemned and executed (Feb. 21st and 28th). They all denied their guilt at their execution; and as Berry died a protestant, this circumstance was regarded as very considerable: but, instead of its giving some check to the general credulity of the people, men were only surprised, that a protestant could be induced at his death to persist in so manifest a falsehood.—As the army could neither be kept up, nor disbanded, without money, the king, how little hopes soever he could entertain of more compliance, found himself obliged to summons a new parliament. The blood, already shed on account of the popish plot, instead of satiating the people, served only as an incentive to their fury; and each conviction of a criminal was hitherto regarded as a new proof of those horrible designs imputed to the papists. This election is perhaps the first in England which, since the commencement of the monarchy, had been carried on by a violent contest between the parties, and where the court interested itself, to a high degree, in the choice of the national representatives. But all its efforts were fruitless, in opposition to the torrent of prejudices which prevailed. Religion, liberty, property, even the lives of men were now supposed to be at stake; and no security, it was thought, except in a vigilant parliament, could be found against the impious and bloody conspirators. Were there any part of the nation, to which the ferment, occasioned by the popish plot, had not as yet propagated itself; the new elections, by interesting the whole people in public concerns, tended to diffuse it into the remotest corner; and the consternation, universally excited, proved an excellent engine for influencing the electors. All the zealots of the former parliament were re-chosen: new ones were added: the presbyterians, in particular, being transported with the most inveterate antipathy against popery, were very active and very successful in the elections. That party, it is said, first began at this time the abuse of splitting their freeholds, in order to multiply votes and electors. By accounts, which came from every part of England, it was concluded, that the new representatives would, if possible, exceed the old in their refractory opposition to the court, and furious persecution of the catholics.—The king was alarmed, when he saw so dreadful a tempest arise from such small and unaccountable beginnings. His life, if Oates and Bedloe's information were true, had been aimed at by the catholics: even the duke's was in danger: the higher, therefore, the rage mounted against popery, the more should the nation have been reconciled to these princes, in whom, it appeared, the church of Rome reposed no confidence. But there is a sophistry which attends all the passions; especially those into which the populace enter. Men gave credit to the informers, so far as concerned the guilt of the catholics: but they still retained their old suspicions, that these religionists were secretly favoured by the king, and had obtained the most entire ascendant over his brother. Charles had too much penetration not to see the danger, to which the succession, and even his own crown and dignity, now stood exposed. A numerous party, he found, was formed against him; on the one hand, composed of a populace, so credulous from prejudice, so blinded with religious antipathy, as implicitly to believe the most palpable absurdities; and conducted, on the other hand, by leaders so little scrupulous, as to endeavour, by encouraging perjury, subornation, lies, impostures, and even by shedding innocent blood, to gratify their own furious ambition, and subvert all legal authority. Roused from his lethargy by so imminent a peril, he began to exert that vigour of mind, of which, on great occasions, he was not destitute; and without quitting in appearance his usual facility of temper, he collected an industry, firmness, and vigilance, of which he was believed altogether incapable. These qualities, joined to dexterity and prudence, conducted him happily through the many shoals which surrounded him; and he was at last able to make the storm fall on the heads of those who had blindly raised, or artfully conducted it.—One chief step which the king took towards gratifying and appeasing his people and parliament, was, desiring the duke to withdraw beyond sea, that no farther suspicion might remain of the influence of popish counsels. The duke readily complied; but first required an order for that purpose, signed by the king; lest his absenting himself shoud be interpreted as a proof of fear or of guilt. He also desired, that his brother should satisfy him, as well as the public, by a declaration of the illegitimacy of the duke of Monmouth.—James duke of Monmouth was the king's natural son by Lucy Walters, and born about ten years before the restoration. He possessed all the qualities which could engage the affections of the populace; a distinguished valour, an affable address, a thoughtless generosity, a graceful person. He rose still higher in the public favour, by reason of the universal hatred to which the duke, on account of his religion, was exposed. Monmouth's capacity was mean; his temper pliant: so that, notwithstanding his great popularity, he had never been dangerous, had he not implicitly resigned himself to the guidance of Shaftesbury, a man of such a restless temper, such subtle wit, and such abandoned principles. That daring politician had flattered Monmouth with the hopes of succeeding to the crown. The story of a contract of marriage, passed between the king and Monmouth's mother, and secretly kept in a certain black box, had been industriously spread abroad, and was greedily received by the multitude. As the horrors of popery still pressed harder on them, they might be induced, either to adopt that fiction, as they had already done many others more incredible, or to commit open violation on the right of succession. And it would not be difficult, it was hoped, to persuade the king, who was extremely fond of his son, to give him the preference above a brother, who, by his imprudent bigotry, had involved him in such inextricable difficulties. But Charles, in order to cut off all such expectations, as well as to remove the duke's apprehensions, took care in full council to make a declaration of Monmouth's illegitimacy, and to deny all promise of marriage with his mother. The duke, being gratified in so reasonable a request, willingly complied with the king's desire, and retired to Brussels."

FIRST SESSION OF THE THIRD PARLIAMENT OF KING CHARLES II.*

List of the House of Commons.] March 6, 1678-9. This day the New Parliament met. The following is a List of the Members of the House of Commons:

A LIST OF THE HOUSE OF COMMONS, IN KING CHARLES THE SECOND'S THIRD PARLIAMENT, WHICH MET MARCH 6, 1678.

Abingdon,
John Stonehouse.
Agmondesham,
Sir Roger Hill,
William Drake.
St. Albans,
Thomas Blount,
John Gape.
Aldborough, (Suffolk)
Sir Richard Haddock,
Hen. Johnson.
Aldborough, (Yorkshire)
Sir John Reresby,
Sir Godfrey Coply.
Allerton North,
Sir Gilbert Gerrard,
Sir Henry Claverly.
Andover,
Francis Pawlet,
William Withers.

* The whole of the proceedings of this short Session are erased from the Commons' Journals.

Anglesea,
Rich. Ld. Visc. Bulkley.
Appelby,
Richard Tufton,
Anthony Lowther.
Arundel,
William Garraway,
James Butler.
Ashburton,
Thomas Raynell,
William Stawell.
Aylsbury,
Richard Ingolsby,
Thomas Lee.
Bambury,
Sir John Holman.
Barnstaple,
Sir Hugh Acland,
John Basset.
Bath City,
Sir William Basset,
Sir George Speke.
Beaumaris,
Richard Bulkley.
Bedfordshire,
William Lord Russel,
Sir Humphry Monoux.
Bedford Town,
Sir William Franklyn,
John Keyling.
Bedwin,
Francis Stonehouse,
John Dean.
Berkshire,
Sir Humphry Foster,
William Barker.
Berwick,
John Rushworth,
Sir Ralph Grey.
Beverly,
Michael Wharton,
Sir John Hotham.
Bewdley,
Philip Foley.
Bishops Castle,
William Oakley,
Edmund Warring.
Bletchingly,
George Evelyn,
Edward Harvy.
Bodmin,
Nicholas Glynn,
Hender. Roberts.
Boralston,
Sir William Bastard,
Sir Joseph Maynard.
Boroughbridge,
Sir Richard Meleverer,
Sir Henry Goodrick.
Bossiny,
William Coriton,
John Treagle.
Boston,
Sir Philip Harcourt,
Sir William Ellis.
Brackley,
William Lisle,
Thomas Carew.
Bramber,
Nicholas Eversfield,
Henry Goring.
Brecon County,
R. Williams.

Brecon Town,
John Jefferys.
Bridgwater,
Sir Henry Tynt,
Robert Stawell.
Bridport,
William Young,
John Strangeways.
Bristol,
Sir Robert Cann,
John Knight.
Bridgenorth,
Sir Thomas Whitmore,
Sir Will. Whitmore
Buckinghamshire,
Thomas Wharton,
John Hampden.
Buckingham Town,
Lord Latimer,
Sir Richard Temple.
Calne,
Sir George Hungerford,
Walter Narbon.
Cambridgeshire,
Ferdinand Russel,
Edward Patrick.
Cambridge Town,
Lord Arlington,
Sir Tho. Chichley.
Cambridge University,
Sir Thomas Exton,
James Vernon.
Camelford,
Sir James Smith,
William Harbord.
Canterbury,
Edward Hales,
William Jacob.
Cardiffe,
Robert Thomas.
Cardigan County,
Edward Vaughan.
Cardigan Town,
Hector Philips.
Carlisle,
Sir Philip Howard,
Sir Christ. Musgrave.
Caermarthen County,
Lord Vaughan.
Caermarthen Town,
Altham Vaughan.
Caernarvon County,
Thomas Bulkley.
Caernarvon Town,
Thomas Moystin.
Castle-rising,
Sir Richard Howard,
James Hoste.
Chester County,
Henry Booth,
Philip Egerton.
Chester City,
William Williams,
Thomas Grosvenor.
Chichester,
Richard May,
John Bramen.
Chippenham,
Sir John Talbot,
Edward Hungerford.
Chipping,
Thomas Lewis,
Sir John Borlace.

Christ's Church,
Sir Thomas Clarges,
Henry Tulse.
Cirencester,
Henry Powle,
Sir Robert Atkins.
Clifton,
John Upton,
Nat Hern.
Clithero,
Sir Thomas Stringer,
Sir Ralph Ashton.
Cockermouth,
Sir Richard Graham,
Orlando Gee.
Colchester,
Sir Walter Clarges,
Sir Henry Grimstone.
Corfcastle,
Visc. Dumblain,
John Tregonel.
Cornwall,
Francis Roberts,
Richard Edgcomb.
Coventry,
John Beak,
Richard Hopkins.
Cricklade,
Edmund Webb,
Henry Dunch.
Cumberland,
Sir John Lowther,
Richard Lamplugh.
Denbighshire,
Sir Thomas Middleton.
Denbigh Town.
Sir John Salisbury,
Derbyshire,
William Sacheverell,
Lord Cavendish.
Derby Town,
Anthony Grey,
George Vernon.
Devizes,
Sir Walter Ernly,
Sir Edward Bainton.
Devonshire,
Sir William Courtney,
Edward Seymour.
Dorchester,
Sir Francis Hollis,
Nicholas Gold.
Dorsetshire,
Thomas Strangeways,
Thomas Freak.
Dover,
William Stokes,
Thomas Papillon.
Downton,
Maurice Buckland,
Sir Joseph Ash.
Droitwich,
Samuel Sandys,
Henry Coventry.
Dunwich,
Sir Philip Shippon,
Sir Thomas Allen.
Durham County,
Matthew Fetherston,
William Bowes.
Durham City,
Sir Richard Lloyd,
William Blackston.

Eastlow,
Sir Jon. Trelawny,
Henry Seymour.
Edmunds Bury,
Sir Thomas Harvey,
Thomas Jernegan.
Essex,
Sir Eliab Harvey,
Henry Mildmay.
Evesham,
Henry Parker,
James Rushout.
Exeter,
Peter Glyde,
Malachi Pyne.
Eye,
Sir Charles Gaudy,
Sir Robert Reeve.
Flintshire,
Mutton Davies.
Flint Town,
Roger Whitley.
Fowey,
John Trefry,
Jon. Rashleigh.
Gatton,
Sir Nicholas Carew,
Thomas Turgis.
Germans,
Richard Elliot,
Daniel Elliot.
Glamorgan,
Bussey Mansel.
Gloucestershire,
Sir John Guise,
Sir Ralph Dutton.
Gloucester City,
William Cook,
Evan Seys.
Grampound,
Sir Joseph Tredenham,
Charles Trevanion.
Grantham,
Sir William Ellis,
John Newton.
Grimsby,
William Broxholm,
George Pelham.
Grimstead,
Thomas Pelham,
Edward Sackville.
Guildford,
Thomas Dalmahoy,
Richard Onslow.
Harwich,
Sir Anthony Dean,
Sir Thomas Pepys.
Haslemere,
Sir William More,
James Gresham.
Hastings,
Sir Robert Parker,
John Ashburnham.
Haverford West,
William Wogan.
Helston,
Sir Vial Vivian,
Sir Peter Killegrew.
Herefordshire,
Herbert Crofts,
John Scudamore.
Hereford City,
Peter Harford,

Paul Foley.
Hertfordshire,
William Hale,
Silas Titus.
Hertford Town,
Sir Charles Cæsar,
Sir Thomas Bide.
Heydon,
Henry Guy,
Hugh Bethel.
Heytesbury,
Richard Reeves,
William Trenchard.
Higham,
Sir Rice Rudd.
Hindon,
Richard How,
Thomas Lambert.
Honiton,
Sir Walter Young,
Sir Thomas Putt.
Horsham,
Anthony Whitfield,
John Mitchel.
Huntingtonshire,
Ralph Montagu,
Robert Aprees.
Huntingdon Town,
Sidney Wortly,
Nicholas Pedley.
Hythe,
Sir Edward Deering,
Julius Deeds.
Ilchester,
Robert Hunt,
Edward Philips.
Ipswich,
John Wright,
Giles Lynfield.
Ives, (St.)
James Praed,
Edward Noseworthy.
Kellington,
Sir John Coriton,
Samuel Roll.
Kent,
Sir Vere Fane,
Thomas Deering.
Kingston,
Lemuel Kingdon,
William Ramsden.
Knaresborough,
Sir Thomas Slingsby,
William Stockdale.
Lancaster County,
Charles Gerrard,
Peter Bold.
Lancaster Town,
Richard Bold,
Richard Harrison.
Lanceston,
Bernard Greenville,
Sir Charles Harbord.
Leicestershire,
Lord Sherrard,
Lord Roos.
Leicester Town,
Sir Henry Beaumont,
John Grey.
Leominster,
James Pitt,
John Duttoncolt,
Leskard,

John Buller,
John Conock.
Lestwithiel,
Sir John Carew,
Walter Kendal.
Lewis,
William Morley,
Edward Bridges.
Lincolnshire,
Sir Robert Carr,
Sir George Castleton.
Lincoln City,
Henry Monson,
Thomas Meers.
Litchfield,
Sir Henry Littleton,
Michael Bidulph:
Liverpool,
Richard Wentworth,
John Dubois.
London,
Sir Robert Clayton,
Thomas Player,
Christopher Love,
Thomas Pilkington.
Ludlow,
Thomas Neal,
John Smith.
Luggershall,
Thomas Neal,
John Smith.
Lyme,
Sir George Strode,
Henry Henley.
Lymington,
John Button,
Benjamin Bunkley.
Lynn,
John Turner,
Simon Taylor.
Maidstone,
Sir John Tufton,
Sir John Deering.
Malden,
Sir John Graham,
Sir William Wiseman.
Malmsbury,
William Estcourt,
Joseph Long.
Malton,
Walter Payser,
William Palmes.
Marlborough,
Thomas Bennet,
Edward Goddard.
Marlow,
Sir Humphry Winch.
John Borlace.
Mawes,
Sidney Godolphin,
Henry Seymour.
Melcomb,
Thomas Brown,
Michael Harvey.
Merioneth,
John Wynne.
Midhurst,
Sir William Morley,
John Alford.
Middlesex,
Sir William Roberts,
Sir Robert Peyton.
Milbourn,

John Hunt,
William Lacy.
Minehead,
Sir John Mallet,
Francis Lutterel.
Michael,
Sir John St. Aubin,
Walter Vincent.
Monmouthshire,
Lord Herbert,
William Morgan.
Monmouth Town,
Sir Trevor Williams.
Morpeth,
Lord Morpeth,
Sir George Downing,
Montgomeryshire,
Edward Vaughan.
Montgomery Town,
Matthew Price.
Newark,
Lord Deincourt,
Sir Robert Markham.
Newcastle, (Staffordsh.)
Sir Thomas Bellot,
William Gower.
Newcastle, (Northum.)
Sir William Blacket,
Francis Anderson.
Newport, (Cornwall)
John Coriton,
Ambrose Pudsey.
Newport, (Hants)
Sir Robert Holmes,
Sir Robert Dillington.
Newton, (Lancashire)
Sir John Chichley,
Andrew Fountain.
Newton, (Hants)
Sir John Holmes,
John Churchill.
Norfolk County,
Sir John Hobart,
Sir Peter Glyn.
Northamptonshire,
Sir Roger Norwich,
John Park.
Northampton Town,
Sir William Farmer,
Edward Montagu.
Northumberland County,
Sir John Fenwick,
Ralph Delaval.
Norwich,
Lord Paston,
Augustus Briggs.
Nottinghamshire,
Sir Scroop How,
John White.
Nottingham Town,
Richard Slater,
John Hutchinson.
Okehampton,
Sir Arthur Harris,
John Calmady.
Orford,
Lord Huntingtower,
Sir John Duke.
Oxfordshire,
Sir Edward Norris,
Sir Anthony Cope.
Oxford City,
William Wright,
Benjamin Whorwood.
Oxford University,
John Edisbury,
Sir Heneage Finch.
Pembrokeshire,
Sir Hugh Owen.
Pembroke Town,
Arthur Owen.
Penryn,
Sir Robert Vivian,
Francis Trefusis.
Peterborough,
Francis St. John,
Hugh Orme.
Petersfield,
Sir John Norton,
Leonard Bilson.
Plymouth,
John Spark,
Sir John Maynard.
Plimpton,
George Treby,
Richard Hillersden.
Pool,
Thomas Trenchard,
Thomas Chaffin.
Pontefract,
Sir Patience Ward,
Sir John Dawney.
Portsmouth,
George Legg,
John Kempthorn.
Preston,
Sir Robert Carr,
Edward Rigby.
Queenborough,
James Herbert,
Edward Hales.
Radnor County,
Row. Gwynn.
Radnor Town,
Sir Edward Harley.
Reading,
Nathan Knight,
John Blagrave.
Retford,
Sir Edward Nevill,
William Hickman.
Richmond,
Thomas Craddock,
Hugh Wharton.
Rippon,
Richard Stern,
Edmund Jennings.
Rochester,
Richard Head,
John Banks.
Rumney,
Paul Borret,
Sir Charles Sedley.
Rutlandshire,
Sir Thomas Mackworth,
Philip Sherrard.
Rye,
Thomas Frewen,
Henry Morley,
Ryegate,
Dean Goodwyn,
Roger James,
Salop County,
Sir Vincent Corbet,
Richard Newport.
Salop Town,
Sir Richard Corbet,
Edward Kynaston.
Saltash,
Bernard Greenville,
Nicholas Lawney.
Sandwich,
Sir James Oxenden,
James Thurbane.
Sarum New,
Thomas Mompesson,
Alexander Thistlethwait.
Sarum Old,
Sir Eliab Harvey,
John Young.
Scarborough,
Francis Thompson,
William Thompson.
Seaford,
Herbert Stapley,
Sir Thomas Dyke.
Shaftsbury,
Thomas Bennet,
Henry Whitaker.
Shoreham,
Sir Robert Fagg,
John Hale.
Somersetshire,
Sir John Sydenham,
Sir Hugh Smith.
Southampton County,
Edward Noell,
Richard Norton.
Southampton Town,
Sir Richard Ford,
Thomas Knowles.
Southwark,
Sir Richard How,
Peter Rich.
Staffordshire,
Sir Walter Baggot,
Sir John Bowyer.
Stafford Town,
Walter Chetwynd,
Stephen Armstrong.
Stamford,
Sir Richard Cust,
William Hyde.
Steyning,
Henry Goring,
John Fag.
Stockbridge,
Henry Whitehead,
Oliver St. John.
Sudbury,
Sir Robert Cordel,
Jervis Elwys.
Suffolk County,
Sir Harvey Elwys,
Sir Samuel Barnadiston.
Surry County,
Arthur Onslow,
George Evelyn.
Tamworth,
Thomas Thynn,
John Swinfen.
Tavistock,
Sir Francis Drake,
Edward Russel.
Taunton,
John Trenchard,
Sir William Portman.
Tewkesbury,
Sir Francis Russel,
Sir Henry Capel.
Thetford,
William Harbord,
Sir Joseph Williamson.
Thirsk,
Nicholas Saunderson,
William Stanley.
Tiverton,
Sir Henry Ford,
Samuel Foot.
Totness,
Sir Edward Seymour,
John Kelland.
Tregony,
Charles Trevanion,
Hugh Boscawen.
Truro,
William Boscawen,
Edward Boscawen.
Wallingford,
John Stone,
Robert Packer.
Warwickshire,
Sir Richard Bowton,
Robert Burdet.
Warwick Town,
Robert Beak,
Richard Hopkins.
Wareham,
Thomas Erle.
George Savage.
Wells,
Edward Berkley,
William Coward.
Wendover,
Edward Blackwell,
Richard Hampden.
Wenlock,
Sir John Weld,
William Forrester.
Weobly,
William Gray,
John Birch.
Westbury,
Thomas Trenchard,
Edward Norton.
Westlow,
Jonathan Trelawney,
John Trelawney.
Westminster
Sir Stephen Fox,
Lewis Putt.
Westmoreland,
Sir John Lowther,
Allen Bellingham.
Weymouth,
Winston Churchill,
Sir John Coventry.
Whitchurch,
Richard Ayloffe,
Henry Wallop.
Winchelsea,
Christopher Draper,
Thomas Austin.
Winchester,
Lord Annesly,
Sir John Cloberry,
Windsor,
Sir John Ernley,
John Powney.
Wilton,
Thomas Huist,
Thomas Penradock.

Wiltshire,	*Worcester City,*
Sir Richard How,	Sir Francis Winnington,
Thomas Thynn.	Thomas Street.
Woodstock,	*Yarmouth, (Norfolk)*
Sir Littleton Osbaldiston,	Lord Huntington,
Nicholas Bainton.	William Coventry.
Wooton Basset,	*Yarmouth, (Hants)*
Laurence Hyde,	Sir Richard Mason,
John Pleydell.	Richard Lucy.
Wygan,	*Yorkshire,*
Roger Bradshaw,	Lord Clifford,
Lord Antrim.	Lord Fairfax.
Worcestershire,	*York City,*
Thomas Foley,	Sir Henry Henley,
Samuel Sandys.	Henry Thompson.

SPEAKER, Serjeant Gregory.

The King's Speech on opening the Session.] His majesty opened the Session with the following Speech to both houses:

"My lords and gentlemen; I meet you here with the most earnest desire that man can have to unite the minds of all my subjects, both to me, and to one another. And I resolve it shall be your faults, if the success be not suitable to my desires. I have done many great things already in order to that end; as, the Exclusion of the Popish Lords from their seats in parliament; the execution of several men, both upon the score of the Plot, and of the Murder of sir Edmondberry Godfrey: and it is apparent that I have not been idle in prosecuting the discovery of both, as much further as hath been possible in so short a time.—I have disbanded as much of the Army as I could get money to do; and I am ready to disband the rest, so soon as you shall reimburse what they have cost me, and will enable me to pay off the remainder: and, above all, I have commanded my Brother to absent himself from me, because I would not leave the most malicious men room to say, I had not removed all causes which could be pretended to influence me towards Popish Counsels.—Besides that end of union which I aim at (and which I wish could be extended to Protestants abroad, as well as at home), I propose, by this last great step I have made, to discern whether Protestant Religion and the peace of the kingdom be as truly aimed at by others, as they are really intended by me; for, if they be, you will employ your time upon the great concerns of the nation, and not be drawn to promote private animosities, under pretences of the public; your proceedings will be calm and peaceable, in order to those good ends I have recommended to you; and you will curb the motions of any unruly spirits, which would endeavour to disturb them. I hope there will be none such amongst you; because there can be no man, that must not see how fatal differences amongst ourselves are like to be at this time, both at home and abroad.—I shall not cease my endeavours daily to find out what more I can, both of the Plot and Murder of sir Edmondberry Godfrey; and shall desire the assistance of both my houses in that work.—I have not been wanting to give orders for putting all the present laws in execution against Papists; and I am ready to join in the making such further laws as may be necessary for securing of the kingdom against Popery.—I must desire your assistance also in Supplies, both for disbanding the Army (as I have already told you) and for paying that part of the Fleet which hath been provided for by parliament but till the 5th of June last; as also that Debt for Stores which was occasioned by the Poll Bill's falling short of the sum which that act gave credit for.—I must necessarily recommend to you likewise the discharging of those Anticipations which are upon my Revenue, and which I have commanded to be laid before you; and I have just cause to desire such an increase of the revenue itself, as might make it equal to my necessary expences: but, by reason of those other Supplies which are absolutely necessary at this time, I am contented to struggle with that difficulty a while longer; expecting for the present, only to have the additional duties upon Customs and Excise to be prolonged to me; and that you will some way make up the loss I sustain by the prohibition of French Wines and Brandy, which turns only to my prejudice, and to the great advantage of the French.—I must needs put you in mind, how necessary it will be to have a good strength at sea this summer, since our neighbours are making naval preparations; and, notwithstanding the great difficulties I labour under, I have taken such care as will prevent any danger which can threaten us, if your parts be performed in time. And I do heartily recommend to you, that such a constant establishment might be made for the Navy as might make this kingdom not only safe, but formidable; which can never be whilst there remains not enough besides to pay the necessary Charges of the crown.—I will conclude, as I begun, with my earnest desires to have this an healing parliament; and I do give you this assurance, that I will with my life defend, both the Protestant Religion and the laws of this kingdom; and I do expect from you, to be defended from the calumny, as well as danger, of those worst of men, who endeavour to render me and my government odious to my people. The rest I leave to the Lord Chancellor."

The Lord Chancellor Finch's Speech.] Then the Lord Chancellor spake as followeth:

"My lords; and you the knights, citizens, and burgesses, of the house of commons; You are here assembled, by virtue of his majesty's most gracious writs of summons, to hold a parliament; the great, the wise, and the powerful council of this kingdom. From the wisdom of this council, the king is sure, he shall receive the best advice; from the duty and loyalty of this assembly, he can never want a chearful assistance: and the king resolves to meet you all with so much grace and goodness, that he hopes this parliament shall end in no disappointment of any, but our enemies.—It may seem strange perhaps to some, that his majesty, who had so long and large an experience of the duty of the last parliament, should now, and in this present conjuncture, think fit to call a new one. But the king hath so equal a confidence in the affections of all his good subjects, that he intends to be acquainted with them all, and to have many and frequent consultations with them; and hopes by this means to attain, first, a true and right understanding of the desires of his people; and, next to that, to be rightly understood by them.—The considerations which are now to be laid before you, are as urgent and as weighty as ever were yet offered to any parliament, or indeed ever can be: so great and so surprizing have been our dangers at home, so formidable are the appearances of danger from abroad, that the most united councils, the most sedate and the calmest temper, together with the most dutiful and zealous affections that a parliament can shew, are all become absolutely and indispensably necessary for our preservation. At home we had need look about us; for his majesty's royal person hath been in danger, by a Conspiracy against his sacred life, maliciously contrived, and industriously carried on, by those Seminary Priests and Jesuits, and their adherents, who think themselves under some obligation of conscience to effect it; and, having vowed the subversion of the true religion amongst us, find no way so likely to compass it, as to wound us in the head, and to kill the defender of the faith.—His maj. wanted not sufficient evidence of his zeal for our religion, without this testimony from his enemies, who were about to sacrifice him for it: but it hath ever been the practice of those votaries, first, to murder the fame of princes, and then their persons; first, to slander them to their people, as if they favoured Papists, and then to assassinate them for being too zealous Protestants. And thus, by all the ways and means which our law calls treason, and their divinity calls merit and martyrdom, they are trying to set up the dominion and the supremacy of the Pope, as if the dignity of his triple crown could never be sufficiently advanced, unless these three kingdoms were added unto him, and all brought back again under that yoke, which neither we nor our fore-fathers were able to bear.—The inquiry into this Conspiracy hath been closely pursued, and the lords of the council have been careful to prosecute the discovery, ever since the rising of the last parliament; and the king doth now recommend it to you to perfect: more evidence hath been already found out, and more malefactors discovered, some in hold, some fled: justices of peace have been quickened in the execution of their duty, the negligent have been reproved and punished, the diligent encouraged, and assisted in doubtful cases by the opinions of the Judges; active and faithful messengers have been sent into all the corners of the kingdom where there was any hope of service to be done. The very prisons have been searched, to see whether any had fled thither to hide themselves there, and under pretence of debt to escape the pursuit: and if any have desired leave to go beyond sea, they have first given security not to go to Rome, nor send their children to be bred in any Foreign seminaries, and then they have been obliged to give in a List of all their menial servants, and those servants too have been examined upon oath; and order is given that they be again examined at the ports, and make oath they are the same persons were examined above: so that all possible care hath been taken that no malefactors might escape us in disguise. And though the Priests themselves do not keep the confessions of their proselytes more secret than these keep the injunctions of their priests, yet enough hath appeared to bring some capital offenders to public justice, and to convict them of the crime: some of the traitors have been executed; several priests have been arrested and imprisoned; all are hiding themselves, and lurking in secret corners like the Sons of Darkness. The murderers of sir Edmondberry Godfrey have been condemned, and suffered death; some Papists have banished themselves out of the kingdom; others are imprisoned for not taking the oaths; all are prosecuted towards conviction; and the very shame and reproach which attends such abominable practices hath covered so many faces with new and strange confusions, that it hath proved a powerful argument for their conversion; nor is it to be wondered at that they could no longer believe all that to be Gospel which their priests taught them, when they saw the way and means of introducing it was so far from being Evangelical.—In a word, so universal is that despair to which the Papists are now reduced, that they have no other hopes left but this, that we may chance to overdo our own business; and by being too far transported with the fears of Popery, neglect the opportunities we now have of making sober and lasting provisions against it.—And it is not to be doubted, but that it would infinitely gratify the Papists in the revenge they wish for this discovery, if they could see us distracted with jealousies incurable, and distrusting the government to such a degree as should weaken all that reverence by which it stands: for then the Plot would not be altogether without effect; but those whom they could not destroy by their conspiracy, they should have the satisfaction to see ruining themselves after the discovery; so that, though we had escaped that desolation which they intended to have brought upon us, nothing could save us from that destruction which we should bring upon ourselves.—But their expectations of this are as vain, as their other designs were wicked; for his maj. hath already begun to let them see with what severity he intends to proceed against them. He hath passed a law to disable all the nobility and gentry of that faction ever to sit in parliament; and, not content with that, he did offer to the last parliament, and does again renew the same offer to this parliament, to pass any further laws against Popery which shall be desired, so as the same extend not to the diminution of his own prerogative, nor to alter the descent of the crown in the right line, nor to defeat the succession. He hath refused the Petition of the lords, who, during the interval of parliament, desired to be brought to their trial; and, after so long an imprisonment, might reasonably enough have expected it: but his maj. thought it fitter to reserve them to a more public and conspicuous trial in parliament; for which cause, their trial ought now to be hastened, for it is high time there should be some period put to the imprisonment of the lords.—But that which the king hath been pleased to mention to you this morning surpasses all the rest, and is sufficient of itself alone to discharge all those fears of Popish influences which many good men had too far entertained: for now, you see, his maj. of his own accord hath done that which would have been very difficult for you to ask, and hath deprived himself of the conversation of his royal and only Brother, by commanding him to depart the kingdom; to which command his r. h. hath paid a most humble and most entire submission and obedience. This separation was attended with a more than ordinary sorrow on both sides. But he that for your sakes could part with such a brother and such a friend, you may be sure, hath now no favourite but his people. Since, therefore, his maj. hath shewn so much readiness to concur with, and in a manner to prevent, the desires of his parliament, it is a miserable refuge our enemies trust to, when they hope to see our zeal outrun our discretion, and that we ourselves should become the unhappy occasion of making our own councils abortive. —Not only the care of the State, but the care we ought to have of the Church too, will preserve us from all errors of this kind: for, as there neither is, nor hath been these 1500 years a purer Church than ours, so it is for the sake of this poor Church alone that the State hath been so much disturbed: it is her truth and peace, her decency and order, which they labour to undermine, and pursue with so restless a malice; and, since they do so, it will be necessary for us to distinguish between Popish and other Recusants, between them that would destroy the whole flock, and them that only wander from it: and among the many good laws you shall think fit to provide, it may not be amiss to think of some better remedy for regulating the press, from whence there daily steal forth Popish Catechisms, Psalters, and Books of Controversy. And it may be another good fruit of such a law, to hinder schismatical and seditious Libels too; for certainly it were much better for us to make such laws as will prevent offences, rather than such as serve only to punish the offenders.—From the dangers which we know at home, and have already in a great measure overcome, be pleased to carry your considerations abroad, and weigh the dangers which may come from thence. We all see and know the posture of our neighbours; and that, the general peace of Europe being once made, there must needs be great fleets and armies unemployed, and ready for an occasion. And it is as visible that some of our neighbours are so wasted by the war, that they are unable to give us any help, if we should stand in need of it. And when we consider withal the afflicted condition of the Protestants abroad, we may be sure that every calamity they suffer is in some measure a weakening of the Protestant interest, and looks as if it were intended to make way for a general extirpation.—These dangers would not be so considerable as they are, if the present wants of the crown were not too well known. The king doth not intend to press you at this time with the full consideration of them all; for, as the king cannot hope in any one session to do all that may be good for his people, so neither doth he expect from them all that may be necessary for himself; but hopes the good understanding between him and his people shall be for ever maintained, by a perpetual reciprocation of grace and favour on his part, and duty and affection on yours.—That which doth most press the king at present is, the want of that treasure which he hath exhausted by going as far as he could in the disbanding of his Army; which is very much, but not fully done. The Charge of a great Fleet at sea, now ready to be paid off after a long service, and the necessity of setting out another this summer; the defects of the Poll Bill, which fell short of that sum which was allowed to be borrowed upon it, and by that means hath deceived those who did furnish stores upon the credit of that Act, unless you relieve them; together with the continuation of some additional Duties of Custom and Excise; and it were much to be wished, that, since the Revenue at the best was always short of the necessary charge of the government, a way may be found to take off those Debts and Anticipations, and to supply that Diminution of the Customs which makes it much narrower than it was.—My Lords and Gentlemen; There are so many things to do, and so little time to do them in, that there ought not to be one minute lost. The season of the year is not yet so far advanced, as to make it too late to set out a Fleet this summer; for most of the Preparations are ready, if we go about it with that diligence which is requisite: and therefore it doth infinitely import us all to husband time. —The best way of doing this will be, to avoid all long and tedious consultations, which sometimes do as much harm as ill resolutions; and above all, to take heed of such questions and debates as tend to raise heat, or may create any kind of disturbance; nor does any thing in the world so much contribute to dispatch, as a quiet and orderly proceeding; for they who are in haste and attempt to do all their business at once, most commonly hinder themselves from bringing any thing to perfection.—You have now an opportunity of doing great things for the king and kingdom, and it deserves your utmost care to make a right use of it; for it is not in the power of a parliament to recover a lost opportunity, or to restore themselves again to the same circumstances, or the same condition, which they had once a power to have improved.—Would you secure Religion at home, and strengthen it from abroad, by uniting the interests of all the Protestants in Europe? this is the time. Would you let the Christian world see the king in a condition able to protect those who shall adhere to him, or depend upon him? this is the time. Would you extinguish all our Fears and Jealousies? Would you lay aside all private animosities, and give them up to the quiet and repose of the public? This is the time. Would you lay the foundations of a lasting peace, and secure the Church and State against all the future machinations of our Enemies? this is the time.—My Lords and Gentlemen; the present face of things, and the state wherein we now are, is so well known and understood abroad, that the whole world is in great expectation of those resolutions which shall be taken here. The results of this council seem to be decisive of the fate of these kingdoms for many ages; and are like to determine us either to happiness or misery of a very long duration. We use to say, and say truly, That the king, when seated in parliament, is then in the fulness of his majesty and power, and shines forth with the brightest lustre: let no exhalations from beneath darken or obscure it. Foreign nations say, and say truly, That a king of England, in conjunction with his parliament, is as great and dreadful a prince as any in Europe. Shew them the sight they are afraid of: and, since they have laid it down for a maxim in their politics, That England can never be destroyed but by itself, and that it is in vain to make any attempt upon this nation, until they be in some great disorder and confusion among themselves; make the ambitious despair betimes; and establish so perfect an intelligence between all the parts of this great body, that there may be but one heart and one soul among us.—And let us all pray, That He who hath once more miraculously delivered the king, the church, and the state, would be pleased still to continue His divine protection, and give us thankful and obedient hearts. And when we have offered up those hearts to God, let us in the next place offer them again to the king, and lay them down at the footstool of His throne: that so the king may see himself safe in your councils, rich in your affections, victorious by your arms, and raised to such a height by your loyalty and courage, that you may have the honour of making him the greatest king, and be the glory of making you the happiest people. I have but one thing more in command; and that is to the gentlemen of the house of commons: That they proceed immediately to the choice of a Speaker; whom his maj. will expect to be presented to him here at three of the clock to morrow in the afternoon.

Mr. Seymour chosen Speaker.] After most of the members had taken the oaths of Allegiance and Supremacy before the lords commissioners, in the inward court of wards, they chose Mr. Seymour*, Speaker, with little or no contest, and he was led to the chair by sir Tho. Lee and Mr. Hampden. [He hung back, and acted his unwillingness very well †.] He then spoke to the house to this effect: "No satisfaction could be greater to me than the honour thus freely and unanimously to be called to the chair: and as you have been so obliging to me, so I will be careful that your favour tend not to the prejudice of your service. My errors are so many arguments to excuse me from this employment, because I see so many persons judgments fall into such mistakes as lead them into errors, by too favourable an opinion of me. I have been master of much better health than I now enjoy, so that I cannot attend your service as I ought. These considerations, I hope, will induce you to proceed to another choice, that your service may be better performed. Dangers threaten religion and the state by the horrid Plot. Do not gratify your enemies by stumbling at the threshold, in your choice of me. But since you are pleased to sequester your judgments, in this choice, give me leave to present my excuse to the king, and I hope the king will have no cause to disagree with you in any thing but your choice of me."

The Speaker's Speech to the King.] March 7. The Speaker thus chosen, the commons went up to the lords bar to present him to his majesty, where Mr. Seymour spoke to this effect "May it please your majesty, the knights, citizens, and burgesses, in Parliament assembled, in obedience to your majesty's command, have made choice of a Speaker, and have unanimously chosen me: and now I am come hither for your majesty's approbation, which if your majesty please to grant, I shall do them and you the best service I can."

The Speaker rejected by the King.] The lord chancellor made this Answer: "Mr. Seymour, The approbation which is given by his majesty to the choice of a Speaker, would not be thought such a favour as it is and ought to be received, if his maj. were not at liberty to deny as well to grant it. It is an essential prerogative of the king to refuse, as well as approve of, a Speaker. This is a matter which by mistake may be liable to misrepresentation, as if the king did dislike the persons that chose, or the person chosen. As to the first, there can be no doubt. They are old representatives of his people, whom he hath a desire to meet; and

* "Seymour and lord Danby had fallen into some quarrellings, both being very proud and violent in their tempers. Seymour, had in the last session, struck in with such heat against popery, that he was become popular upon it. So he managed the matter in this new parliament that, though the court named Meres, yet he was chosen Speaker." Burnet.

† Grey.

there can be no doubt of the latter; nor has his maj. any reason to dislike you, having had great experience of your ability and service. But the king is the best judge of men and things. He knows when and where to employ. He thinks fit to reserve you for other service, and to ease you of this. It is his majesty's pleasure to discharge this choice; and accordingly, by his majesty's command, I do discharge you of this place you are chosen for; and in his majesty's name command the house of commons to make another choice, and command them to attend here to-morrow at 11 o'clock *."

Debate thereon.] The commons then came back to their house; where

Sir *John Ernly* said, I shall propose a gentleman of experience, and without exception, sir Thomas Meres.

Mr. *Sacheverell.* I take it to be a great misfortune, that, after a house had made choice of a Speaker, the king, by any information, to promote and carry on the designs of particular persons, should gratify them, rather than this house in their choice of Seymour. And I am the rather induced to believe it, because no exceptions have been made against Seymour in the Chancellor's Speech. But if it be proved that the king has always granted, and never denied the choice, I suppose the thing will be given up. There is but one precedent of the king's denial, and that was in the case of Thorp. It is strange that this house must be made a second. I see many worthy faces that were not here the last parliament: and therefore I shall say, it is very hard, there having, for an 100 years together, never been so much as one excuse made by a Speaker chosen by the commons, nor one allowance or disallowance made in parliament, that it should be so now. It was usually excused by compliment, and this parliament has complimented itself out of its right. But I would not lose a hair's breadth of the king's right, nor the subjects. They are enemies to the nation, that, at this time, throw a bone betwixt the king and us. After all this danger and distraction we are in, must this house be made the next precedent? I move, 'that the clerk may put the question for adjourning the house till to-morrow,' and in the interim the records may be searched for precedents in this matter, and then we may inform the king how much this manner of proceeding is to his prejudice and yours.

Mr. *Williams.* This is now a question of right. I am sorry that our time, at the beginning of a session, should be thus lost, by the starting this question. Here is a worthy person named, sir Tho. Meres, and we named and presented to the king a worthy one too. The commons have been without a Speaker, nor was their having a Speaker originally from the crown, but by the commons. Till Hen. iv's time, not one precedent of presenting a Speaker, &c. The chancellor tells us, 'That the king's favour may not turn to his prejudice, &c.' This being put to a question of right, we must stand upon our right. There is no reason from the electors or the elected, why he should be rejected; therefore I adhere to Mr. Seymour.

Sir *Tho. Clarges.* I desire to inform the house, because there are a great many new members that were not of the last parliament; that we have power of adjourning ourselves by the clerk. In time of sickness of the Speaker, it has been done from day to day. Gentlemen, our lives and liberties are preserved by this house, and the privileges of it are inheritable to us. I must inform you, that Mr. Seymour attended the king yesterday, and he acquainted his majesty with the unanimous choice of him to be the Speaker, 'and that he hoped to have the king's good liking.' The king said, 'he liked very well the choice.' If so, this alteration of the king's mind must be from evil-disposed people about the king, who would create discontent between the king and his people. The king said once, 'he would have no favourites but the commons of England.' If you will not think fit to cause Mr. Seymour to declare what the king said to him, I acquiesce. But I move that you will adjourn.

Mr. *Garroway.* I am one that have sat here long, and have seen great miscarriages, prorogations, and dissolutions. I am not afraid of it now, and I hope no man else here is afraid of it. I would not give the king offence, but not part with one hair of our right. If you will not stand to it here you will have a great many things put upon you. I am satisfied that we could not fix upon a fitter person for Speaker than Mr. Seymour; he is a privy counsellor, treasurer of the navy, and has done the king very good service here, which makes me wonder he should not be approved of by the king. I thought we could not have obliged the king more. The king said, 'he would have no favourite but his people.' And thus to have your Speaker rejected, what will you think of it! Pray, gentlemen, let us sleep upon

* Concerning this transaction Ferguson writes as follows: "There being a council that night, and notice coming that Mr. Seymour was chosen, the Treasurer persuaded the king from accepting him, to shew his prerogative right of rejecting; so that the next day, when the house came to present their Speaker, he was rejected; but the house having some intimation that he would be rejected, ordered him, or he himself resolved, not to make the common formal apology of insufficiency, at the lords bar, but instead thereof he roundly told the king, 'That he was unanimously chosen, by the suffrages of all the commons of England, to be their Speaker; and that he was resolved to serve his majesty in that station, to the utmost of his power.' So that the Chancellor, who had orders to accept of his excuses, now had not a word to say: at last, upon deliberating and whispering, he recollected himself, and told the house," &c. Growth of Popery, part ii. p. 235.

it, and let the clerk put the question for adjourning till to-morrow.

Sir *Tho. Lee.* I see it is the universal opinion to adjourn, therefore I shall say but a little. Before the prorogation, information was given the house of the danger of the king's person, and the house addressed the king, 'to have a care of his person, &c.' The Answer was, 'the king was then busy, but we should have an account of our Message;' but for 3 weeks we heard nothing, and we were prorogued. I take notice only how things grow by degrees. We came up to this parliament with great joy, and expectation of doing good, and now we are thus interrupted! This being our condition, and we having precedents plain in the case for us, I would adjourn till to-morrow, and then make a Representation of the thing to the king.

Col. *Birch.* I am heartily sorry this has happened. This is an unlucky stumble at the threshold, before we get into the house. I came hither with an intention (God is my witness) to make this a 'healing parliament.' I have always heard here, that it is the undoubted right of this house to chuse their Speaker, &c. I have reason to believe Mr. Seymour very proper for the employment, and that he would be acceptable to his majesty; but he that did this with the king may do more. I would adjourn till to-morrow, and make a Representation of our right to the king.

Mr. *Powle.* This gives me apprehension that there is some person too near the king, who is afraid of this parliament. I have observed that, of late, those things of the greatest moment are done without any council at all; done in a corner. As for the prorogation and the dissolution of the last parliament, there was not one word of the advice of the privy council in it. I fear no advice was asked, but given for supporting the designs of private men. I have ever taken the record to be, that no man was ever refused being Speaker when presented to the king, but for some disability of body; as in sir John Popham's case, who desired to be excused from that service by reason of disability of body from wounds he had received in the wars, 28 Hen. vi. And lately sir Job Charlton, not being able to endure the employment, by reason of disability of body. But nothing of this can be objected against Mr. Seymour. Must any private person inform the king of his unfitness, without any cause assigned? I know not what may come of it. Corruption, in the former parliament, was complained of for private malice, but I doubt not but gentlemen come to this with clear thoughts. I do protest before God, that I think the greatness of the nation is under the privileges of this house. A people can never heartily support that government that does not protect them. A slavish people can never heartily support the government. Those that come after us, here, if we are dissolved upon this point, will speak the same language. I fear not dissolution. Let us adjourn till to-morrow, and consult our own hearts what is fit to be done.—Then the Clerk put the Question for adjourning.

March 8. Sir *Tho. Lee.* It is now 11 of the clock, and it is necessary we propose what to do before the black rod comes; whether you will do something previous; whether you will acquaint the king what we suffer for want of a Speaker; or whether you will propose somebody to say something at the lords bar to the king? I move you to consider which you will do.

Sir *Harbottle Grimstone.* I second that gentleman. Some of the Long Robe, I believe, have taken pains to search for precedents. My eyes are not good, and I am infirm, and not able to search. But thus much I shall say to the rational part. The question is, Whether the king's approbation of a Speaker is the substance and essence of the matter? For my part I never took it to be so. When you wait upon the king with your Speaker, he is your Speaker so soon as you have chosen him, and you may lay the mace upon the table. When you go up with the Speaker to the lords house, you go up to tell the king that, according to his direction, you have chosen a Speaker. It has been a thing of course to give the king notice of the person you have chosen, that he may know him; and we stand by, and give the Speaker leave modestly to deny, and exercise his oratory. If the king's approbation must be the essence of your choice, if you part with this, you part with all. Shall we not have the liberty to chuse our own servant, fit to do our own work? Other people would destroy our work, if we part with that which must enable us to do the work of them that trusted us and sent us hither. If any one man may be imposed upon us, who will not do our work, it may be he will put what question he pleases, and tire you out. This I have seen done. I would ask any man, who has influence upon this action, now we have chosen a Speaker, that he should be refused? Whoever broke the last parliament, without the desire of this house, or the advice of the privy council, that man or men, that broke that parliament, will break this too, to the utter undoing of the nation. Our time is short, if you please to think of it. If Seymour be not in the lords house (as it is said he is) or if he be in the country; if the person be in the country and not here, that we shall choose, then let us set up another to rule for him till he comes, as in the absence of a knight of the shire that is chosen. Mr. Seymour is a person of great experience for the place, and he is the fittest to go on where you left off; but he being not here, let somebody sit in his chair to represent his person, till he comes. And then we will offer our Reasons to the king, why we cannot recede from our first election.

Sir *Tho. Clarges.* I was glad yesterday to find that moderation in this great matter. Though we were then satisfied in our right, yet, by this night's consideration, gentlemen have looked over precedents. But though one of the long robe be more proper for Speaker, yet there are precedents of others that have been in that place. I find anciently that the commons have chosen their Speaker without presenting him to the king for approbation. Some have made excuses to the king, and some none (1 Hen. iv.) and 7 Hen. viii. he was presented before the ordinary privileges were asked. But it is notorious that all these things were our birthrights before. But if this argument be used against our right, because, in respect to the king, we make a formality of the king's approbation, all our rights will fall with that. This matter before us is that which all the commons of England have a right to, and I hope we shall not impair those rights that they have entrusted to us. R. ii. sir John Cheyney was chosen Speaker, and went up to the king, &c. to be confirmed. The next day he fell sick, and desired the house to chuse another, and they chose Dorwood, and notified it to the king that they had chosen him. Popham was chosen 28 Hen. vi. (a troublesome time.) He was sick and unable to perform the office, and the commons had leave granted to chuse another. But there are upon record many Speakers that have been chosen, and were ready to serve, without making any excuse. It is a strange thing that we should hear nothing of this for 200 years, and now the kingdom is in danger, that this parliament should have an interruption. I hope that in the consideration of this matter, we shall take such steps as are worthy of the great trust reposed in us.

Mr. *Sacheverell.* This matter is of great importance, and therefore we ought to take wary steps in it to the king, that those who advised him to this, may have no colour against us. The first question stands thus, 'Whether a Speaker chosen stands good to the service of the house, before he has the king's approbation?' The second question is, 'If the king can reject a Speaker, chosen by the house, and qualified?' If that be so, there is an end of your business. 1st James, after sir R. Philips was chosen Speaker by the commons, he sent out warrants for writs, as Speaker, without the king's approbation of him; and I can tell many more precedents. But perhaps we may have papers pinned upon our backs, as the former parliament had, and be sent home. I move, that we may have some persons nominated, of eminence about the king (though not privy counsellors, for they have not the sole privilege of carrying our Messages) humbly to acquaint the king, 'That the matter delivered by my Lord Chancellor, in his name, is of so great importance, that we desire some farther time to consider of it.' And then, no doubt, but we shall acquaint ourselves as we ought to do. I move that sir Robert Carr, the Chancellor of the Duchy, may go with the Message; and I doubt not but we shall make out our rights with all duty to the king.

Sir *R. Carr.* I humbly move you, that the privy counsellors may carry the Message. I was one, but I am not now. I hope you will dispense with me. There are none of the council here now, but I suppose they will be here.

Mr. *Sacheverell.* If you stay for the privy counsellors, the black rod will come to call you up. We have sent those to attend the king formerly who were no privy counsellors, and I would have Carr for one now.

Mr. *Leveson Gower.* I would know, whether ever the house made an Address to the king when they had no Speaker? I would have Sacheverell inform the house, whether there be any precedent of that.

Sir *W. Portman.* There is no precedent of a Speaker presented to the king by the house, that has been rejected: and let us make a precedent of addressing the king without a Speaker.

Mr. *Leveson Gower.* I would have any man cite a precedent, whether ever any Address was made to the king without a Speaker? [He spoke it roughly, and several younger gentlemen called aloud, 'To the Bar.']

Mr. *Vaughan.* Something must be done; and in this case we must create a precedent *primæ impressionis.* Was there ever any precedent that so many met together and did nothing? It is fit to make a precedent, when such a body of men are met together, and do nothing. I move you to make an Address to the king.

Sir *Eliab Harvey.* Our time is but short, and pray let us not mispend it. I will name another to go to the king with Carr, lord Russel.

Sir *Christ. Musgrave.* I conceive your proper question is, 'Whether an Address shall be made to the king for some longer time, &c.?' And when that is over, then you are to nominate persons to attend the king; and I shall name a third.

Mr. *Powle.* I would have the question be, 'That an application shall be made to the king that the matter delivered by the Lord Chancellor yesterday is of such great importance relating to the Speaker, that we desire some time to consider of it.'

The Commons apply to the King.] The Message was this: "That the matter delivered by the Lord Chancellor yesterday is of such great importance, that this house cannot immediately come to a Resolution therein; therefore do humbly desire that his majesty would graciously be pleased to grant some farther time to take the matter into consideration." — Ordered, "That lord Russel, lord Cavendish, sir Henry Capel, and sir Rob. Carr, do attend his majesty with this Message."

The King's Answer.] Being returned, Lord Russel, reported, That, according to command, they have attended the king, and his majesty was pleased to make this Answer to the Message, viz. "I have considered your message, and do consent to a farther time for you to consider, till Tuesday next: and as I would not have my prerogative encroached upon, so I would not encroach upon your privilege; if a third person cannot be found out for an expedient in the mean time."

Debate thereon.] Serj. *Streete.* When the difference was between the lords and commons, in the case of sir S. Barnardiston, which you laboured under, the king found out an expedient. That being the case, I will presume to name a third person for Speaker. (But he was not suffered.)

Mr. *Garroway.* You have had a gracious Answer from the king. If in this time we have not lessened his prerogative in what we have done, we may consider farther of it; and as long as the king has given us time, I would certainly consider of it, and you may consider of it.

Mr. *Williams.* I wonder that now it should be proposed to name a third person, since the king has given you great time for deliberation. If you name a third person, you give up your right. I am as ready for Mr. Powle (named by Streete) as any man; but your Answer yesterday from the Chancellor was about rejecting your Speaker by the king's Prerogative. And will you sit down and give up your right for a compliment? If so, farewell chusing a Speaker for the future! Mr. Powle is a gentleman of great value; but let every man consider the right of the commons of England.

Sir *John Knight.* It is all one, if you name a second or third person; it is equally giving up your right to name a third or a second. Here were two in contest, and both were equally named. I move, therefore, that, as the king is pleased to give us till Tuesday next, to chuse some person, that we may draw a Petition to the king, to set out our right in chusing a Speaker.

Mr. *Sacheverell.* I am not for any question at this time; because many gentlemen know not what was said by the Chancellor to us yesterday. In this case, I would send to search the Lords Books, to know whether a refusal or dismissing our Speaker is there entered. And as the king has given you time, so I would make use of it to search the Lords Books for what the king has said by the Chancellor, to shape your Answer accordingly.

Mr. *Williams.* The very words were, 'That the choice of the Commons of their speaker was dismissed.'

Mr. *Hampden.* I went to look into the Lords Journal, and there is no entry made yet of any thing, but in the Minute-Book only; and what you do must be a debate grounded upon that.

So the house adjourned till the 10th by the clerk, as before.

The Search of the Lords' Journal reported.] March 10. Sir *Tho. Lee.* I am one of those whom you commanded to search the Lords' Journal, and, according to the order of the house, we went to the lords house, where we searched the Journal, but we found no Entry made, but, some Minutes of the Lord Chancellor's Speech in a Paper; but the lord chancellor had taken the paper to correct, and we should have them as soon as they were done.

Mr. *Sacheverell.* Seeing you can do nothing with these minutes, I would do something without them, and not sit still till the lords have adjourned till Tuesday. Though I am confident of our right, yet at this time I would give the least occasion of offence that might be; and proceed by such gentle steps as may give the king no cause of offence; nor those near the king, to possess him that we have done so. I would look a little back, yet put no question upon it. For this reason, I have taken some pains to look back how the house has proceeded in things of this nature; and of those, the gentlest proceedings. This is owned on all hands, that anciently the Speaker made no excuse, nor had the house order from the king to chuse a Speaker. 5 Rich. ii. and 2 Hen. iv. was the first excuse that was made. But I would take notice of one thing. Though, of late, Speakers, it is true, have made excuses, &c. yet it is as true, that the king has admitted them Speakers. But they have made none, but by leave of this house of commons. 1 James, out of the Journal: before the Speaker was approved by the king two or three days, the house not only made an Order to elect another Speaker instead of sir Francis Bacon, but in this session 1 James, the king was advised, 'That freedom of speech, and the use of the rest of the privileges of the house of commons, were *ex gratiâ*, and not *ex debito*;' and the king sent them a Letter, 'That he was satisfied with it.' But the commons addressed farther, by way of Representation, how the usage of parliament had been, in that matter, in an humble Petition, 'That their privileges might be continued by way of decency, but not to yield their right.' But as to the matter now before us, I would only state the case to the king, by way of Representation, 'how usage of parliament has been,' and wait his gracious Answer; and I doubt not but the king will see that he is wrongfully informed in the matter, and will give such an Answer as will satisfy the kingdom.

Mr. *Hampden.* The right of election of our Speaker no man can contradict. If the king has a right to chuse our Speaker, it had been most proper when we were before the king. But there is no distinction of privy counsellors from others in the house, that their presence is necessary when a Speaker is chosen, or that they must propose him; unless they make a distinction of themselves. You have now chosen a gentleman for your Speaker unanimously; one whom you thought qualified for the employment, and who, you had reason to think, would have been acceptable to the king. But if privy counsellors must propose a Speaker, and necessarily be present at the choice, if there be no privy counsellors of the house, by that consequence you must have no Speaker. But the Chancellor said 'The king had other employment for him.' Surely that was an extemporary excuse, for a member of parliament ought not to be employed elsewhere. I hope that in this matter you will make such a Representation to the king, as may have a favourable Answer, and so you may be let into the service of the king and kingdom; and I would have some gentlemen withdraw and pen it.

Sir *John Ernly.*' You have an undoubted right of election of your Speaker. It was hinted here, and confirmed by practice, 'That no man was ever named here for Speaker by the secretaries of state, or the privy counsellors, in the king's name;' for the choice is in the commons, and it is undoubted that the refusal of a Speaker, when chosen, is of right in the king.

Mr. Goring. Some worthy persons have taken pains to search precedents. I would know, whether any person but a privy counsellor usually proposes a Speaker? And then the king, without doubt, knows before-hand who the Speaker is. I have heard gentlemen formerly allege it, as an exception against Mr. Seymour, that he was a privy counsellor, and therefore excepted against him for being Speaker.

Sir *John Cloberry.* I am glad to see the house in so excellent a temper to hear a debate of as great a concernment as can come before you. 1. It is said, 'That the Speaker ought to be presented by some of the privy council,' but I take it to be the right of every member to present whom he pleases. 2. 'Whether it be our undoubted right?' That is undubitable, the *modification* of the choice. It has been asserted by the Master of the Rolls, and he is pleased to call the presenting of a Speaker to the king 'a compliment only;' which doctrine, if true, then we have a *consummate* Speaker; as in *materia prima* there is a capacity of receiving various forms. The choice of the Speaker is our undoubted right, but the manner totally and integrally in our choice. I will begin with Mr. Seymour, who sat in the chair but a while; he made a modest excuse, and then said, 'The house cannot make a Speaker but by the king's approbation, and he hoped that would be the only thing the king would deny this house.' Then, as soon as the king's negative came down upon Mr. Seymour, it was thought an infringement of your privileges. There were never any such precedents as for us to adhere to our first choice. In Hen. vi.th's time, the Speaker was refused, at his own request (Popham.) The law is tendered of creating a difference between the king and his people, and it may be the king will not deny any law you advise him, only under this *modification*, 'That he has employment for Mr. Seymour.' The ceremony of excusing was omitted by Mr. Seymour. Now you will reduce the king to such a strait, as either to give up his Prerogative, or discontent his people. I will not say that we have power in this matter; but that we have right is not yet proved. I had rather give my eyes, hands, and head, than part with this power, if it be your right; but if it be a flower of the Crown, I would rather die than take it away. A blot is no blot till it be hit. Therefore I move, that the thing may be thoroughly debated, and see our own title to it, and not carry a *doughbaked* representation to the king, that we cannot maintain.

[Soon after sir John Cloberry had made an end of his speech, some merrily-disposed gentlemen sent a Note from hand to hand about the house, sealed up, with this superscripton: "To the right honourable lord *Cloberio*, baron *Dough-baked*, earl *Consummation* and *Modification*, marquis of *Materia Prima*, Frank *Danby*."*]

Sir *Harbottle Grimstone.* Something fell from Cloberry that does a little concern me, of a word slipped from me, 'That the presenting the Speaker to the king was a compliment, &c.' I spoke what I meant, viz. 'That the choice of a Speaker is an act done by the house, and there needed nothing more to be done.' When we are called by the authority of the king's writ, surely it is to do some work, and I believe there never was more work to do than now. Nothing but an act of omnipotence can carry us through it. We carry the Speaker up to the lords bar, to let the king know whom we have made choice of; and he is as much accomplished to do our work, to collect debates for a question, that every man may say Aye or No, clearly to the question, as if he was presented to the king, &c. It is not how things will be construed elsewhere, but naturally here. When I had the honour to serve here as Speaker, in the Convention, [1660] (though the king called it a parliament, it has not had since so great a reputation,) I was then weak in my health; but thus much I remember, that when we were in debates, before the king came hither, I was commanded to wait upon the king with the submission of the house, and after I had been at the lords bar, &c. we had occasion to carry up votes. If ever the Speaker had made excuse, and presented himself for the king's approbation, the transport of joy for the king's coming might have put us upon it. Mr. Wm. Pierpont took exceptions at what I then said at the lords bar, viz. 'That I had not full order for what I said, and was too lavish of my tongue.' If a Speaker, carried up to the lords house, as Mr. Seymour was, and though he excused not the accepting of the employment, yet said, 'He stood for the king's approbation,' which he was not instructed to do, he might well be reprimanded. I am willing to comply with any expedient in this matter; but I would not part with our right.

Serj. *Maynard.* Gentlemen, I will tell you what I have observed in my time. Cloberry did well to distribute what he had to discourse of; but it is not now seasonable to make a formal determination of the thing. When I heard the question first, I thought it out of all question, but it is not so clear and satisfactory to me, though I am the king's serjeant, and so

* Grey.

sworn to maintain the king's prerogative. 'Hannibal ad portas, Catilina intra mœnia.' In Haman's conspiracy against the Jews, Ahasuerus gave them liberty to speak for themselves, and Haman was hanged upon the same gallows he had prepared for Mordecai. But as to the point in question, I had a clear opinion, led by my lord Coke, of 200 years practice, that in that time there was no such thing as a public Speaker till 15 Edw. iii. He said so, but I find it not. 5 R. ii. there was a presentment of a Speaker. I do but observe this, though I do not make any conclusion on one side or other. Sometimes it is found that the Speaker goes up to the lords house, and exercises his oratory in excusing himself, and sometimes not: but never that the Speaker desired the king's approbation, anciently. This Speaker, Seymour, after you have chosen him, makes his excuse, and you refuse it, and he goes up to the king and makes it, and carries his excuse to another place. This is a breach of your privilege. That of sir John Popham was a real excuse, and there was a necessity to constitute another Speaker, for it is impossible that a body of this nature can be without a Speaker.

Ordered, "That an humble Representation be made to his majesty, in the matter relating to the Speaker contained in the Lord Chancellor's Speech."

The Commons' Representation to the King.] March 11. Mr. Powle reported the Representation to the king as follows:

"We your majesty's most loyal and dutiful subjects the commons in this present parliament assembled, do, with all obedience, return your majesty most hearty thanks for the favourable reception and gracious Answer your majesty was pleased to return to our late Message, wherein your maj. was pleased not only to allow us longer time to deliberate of what was delivered to us by the Lord Chancellor, relating to the Choice of a Speaker, but likewise to express so great a care not to infringe our privileges: and we desire your majesty to believe, that no subjects ever had a more tender regard, than ourselves, of the rights of your majesty, and your royal prerogative; which we shall always acknowlege to be vested in the crown, for the benefit and protection of your people. And therefore, for the clearing all doubts that may arise in your royal mind, upon this occasion now before us, we crave leave humbly to represent to your majesty, that it is the undoubted right of the commons to have the free election of one of their members to be their Speaker, and to perform the service of the house, and that the Speaker, so elected, and presented, according to custom, hath, by the constant practice of all former ages, been continued Speaker, and executed that employment, unless such persons have been excused for some corporal disease, which hath been alleged by themselves, or some others in their behalf, in full parliament. According to this usage, Mr. Edward Seymour was unanimously chosen, upon the consideration of his great abilities and sufficiency for that place, of which we had large experience in the last parliament, and was presented by us to your majesty as a person we conceived would every way be most acceptable to your maj.'s royal judgment. This being the true state of the case, we do in all humility lay it before your majesty's view, hoping that your maj. upon due consideration of former precedents, will rest satisfied with our proceedings, and will not think fit to deprive us of so necessary a member, by employing him in any other service; but to give us such a gracious Answer, as your majesty and your royal predecessors have always done heretofore, upon the like occasions; that so we may, without more loss of time, proceed to the dispatch of those important affairs, for which we were called hither, wherein we doubt not but we shall so behave ourselves, as to give an ample testimony to the whole world of our duty and affection to your majesty's service, and of our care of the peace and prosperity of your kingdoms."

The King's Answer.] To this Representation the king immediately gave this short Answer:

"Gentlemen; All this is but loss of time: and therefore I command you to go back to your house, and do as I have directed you."

Debate thereon.] Mr. *Sacheverell.* I never knew before that such a Representation was 'loss of time.' I took this Representation to be as modest and dutiful as could be. Divers Representations have been formerly made to his majesty, upon several occasions, and I did expect that we should have such an Answer to this; and we might reasonably expect as gracious an answer as formerly, there being nothing but duty in it. But the gentlemen that gave us this answer, would not let the king give us a direct answer, because it would be under examination here. Therefore they have taken this course. It seems, they think it 'loss of time' to inform his majesty of the state of the case about a Speaker. But I would address the king again. In the case of the Declaration, some time since, we did not make one Address, but three, and had some rougher Answers from his majesty than this. Let us justify it to the world, that we have done nothing, but in all duty to maintain our rights. And I move, that we may address the king, that he would please to take our Representation into farther consideration, and give us a gracious Answer.

Lord *Cavendish.* I am not of opinion that this interruption proceeds from the same counsels, &c. The last dissolved parliament was uneasy to them; and in this, here are too many men of quality and estates to diminish the rights of the crown. On the one side, I do not fear this will break this parliament; and on the other side, I would not gratify the designs of ill men. It is most proper for us now to consider, whether this thing will admit an expedient. The

Speaker may be made a lord, a judge, or an ambassador; and that ends the dispute. Whereas some men fancy that the Speaker is not made without the king's approbation; if so, we give up our right. Till the king approves, or rejects, it is his choice of the Speaker, and not ours. I would have some gentlemen propose whether there may not be an expedient in this case.

Mr. *Bennet*. This is playing at French hotcockles. I would not, in this, gratify the designs of ill men, who have thrown this bone amongst us. This is to back and mount the colt with a snaffle, and then to bring him on to a bitt and curb. This great assembly is not to be bought nor sold, but, I fear, the last was. It is an expedient, that Mr. Seymour comes not to the house; his absence is an expedient; but still assert your right. I would not have him that is named by the privy council, (Meres) but some other.

Sir *Tho. Lee*. I never took that for an expedient, that was a total quitting of your right. I think, time is precious; but I do not think that if this matter be not quieted, the parliament will be dissolved. I have seen Answers from the king much blacker than this. This case is of a very great nature, and if once things of this kind come to be refined by distinctions in debate, we may refine away the greatest privileges we have. One parliament called so soon after another has not been for some time. That called in 1640 sat but three weeks, and the king repented half an hour after he had dissolved it, and then another was called; and there is no danger to the kingdom though we are sent away. And wherein does a new parliament differ? They are the people still in another parliament, and I hope no man will be alarmed with that. I wonder not that Mr. Seymour is absent; he knows not what place to sit in, without displeasing the king. The king answers your Representation, 'that this is losing time,' and there is nothing remaining upon your books whom you have chosen for Speaker (for till you are qualified by the Tests you can enter nothing;) but it is entered upon the Lords Books, 'That your choice of Mr. Seymour is discharged, and you are directed to chuse another man.' And what privilege will you gain by an expedient? When the practice has been always with you of chusing, you will get no reputation by an expedient. I would address the king again in this, and hope for success.

Mr. *Vaughan*. Your question is not now, whether you shall insist upon Mr. Seymour for Speaker, &c. but your being called hither to consult 'de arduis regni negotiis.' When your privileges are invaded, what way have you to do what you came hither for? I speak now because the parliament is ruining. Perhaps our prince is misinformed, and he does not look upon our paper, nor consider it. Whatever you do afterwards, press your paper now; but at the beginning of a parliament, do not give up your right.

Mr. *Williams*. This is no 'loss of time,' but will be 'loss of right,' if you insist not upon your privileges. And plainly, if the right be with us, shall we sit still, and let it be invaded? And you, in parliament, give away the right of parliament? Acquiesce in your right, one way or other, and have a fair question for it, and part not with it so easily.

Col. *Birch*. I speak at this time under some disorder and great fear. This matter before us requires as great and serious consideration as any thing that has happened in my time. When the last parliament left things, many things concerning the gentlemen in the Tower were undiscovered; and many were under the fear of it.—This is so plain a thing, that scarce a man but will be descanting upon this point. Undoubtedly your Speaker is chosen, and ought not to be rejected without cause shown why; but those are not true consequences, 'That the king may, by the same reason, refuse all Speakers and Bills too.' I desire to do that here, that, if any mischief follows upon it, we may answer it. We have shown our opinion of Mr. Seymour, and have stuck to him as long as we could. It seems, the king has occasion for him, and you may chuse a third person; whoever does this, I am apt to think, will do more. I desire none will prejudge. Greater things than this must be debated. Whoever threw in the bone, the king will see that we step over this to oblige him. I hope he will let us go currently in our business. The king's Answer to me looks as if something was resolved on, and then I doubt whether we are able to answer to God and those that sent us hither, in the result, if we too much insist upon our right. In the choice of a third person, it loses not our liberty, but, I believe, gains a step.

Mr. *Wm. Harbord*. I was never reduced to so great a strait how to give my opinion, as I am now. Did I think this was giving up your rights, I would be the last man that should give my consent to it. I think the king has power to deny his approbation of a Speaker. Suppose it should so fall out that any parliament should make choice of a Speaker to-day, and that gentleman should be so unhappy as to wound any man, and that man be in danger of his life, and the king should say, 'I am informed of such a thing?' or that the Speaker you had chosen had had a hand in this Conspiracy of the Papists:—he was taken down to Order by

Sir *Harbottle Grimstone*. Really we are in great disorder, as to Arguments, on both sides. The point in debate is the king's approbation and reprobation of a Speaker chosen. As well give it up and *monstrari digitis*. The Speaker we have chosen, Mr. Seymour, has declared his abilities; and some Speakers may so spoil a question that you may never do any business. If the king has such a prerogative, that the king may say 'no' to our choice, it may serve a turn to knock another Speaker down, as well as this, and so we shall become utterly useless to the intent we were sent hither for. In this great strait, if an expedient could be found out, if we could make our claim on record, as well as the king's refusal on the Lords Books; but that appears there, and ours does not, and is no where for us. As this now stands, were there not something else in the case, we would easily part with it. It is a great advantage for the king to set up his throne in the hearts of his people. There will be great difficulty in an expedient in this matter; and that must be with great patience and kindness to hear one another. If the king pleases to call Mr. Seymour to the lords house, all is free and at liberty, and we may proceed to the choice of another, and our privileges will be safe. But since we are between two rocks, it becomes prudent men to go where the least danger is. But I know not what to propose.

Sir *Edw. Dering*. I am not so superstitious that, because we stumbled at the threshold, we should leave off our journey: and I hope we shall be at our journey's end. I hoped, that, after two or three days, and the consideration of the merits of the person, and our choice, the king would have admitted Mr. Seymour. But seeing he does not, I would proceed to another choice. There is no precedent directly in the case, of our power. In this doubtful case, I would consider in prudence what is to be done. All know our dissatisfactions at home, and that we have a powerful enemy abroad. We have a restless faction at home of Papists. We are in a very bad and helpless condition. Suppose the king should dissolve this parliament, upon this point, and call another, it will be a discouragement to gentlemen to come again; and if there be no other consequence of our pains than to sit but a week, gentlemen will not be ambitious of that trust. Consider, whether we can answer it to the country, if we break upon this point. If it be said, 'That if the king refuses one Speaker, he may refuse 500, and has not refused any, these hundreds of years,' that is a strange inference. I think it the best expedient to chuse a third person.

Mr. *Garroway*. I am not much frighted, nor much invited to sit, since I find, at the beginning, what entertainment you are likely to have at the latter end of the parliament. We are only unhappy that the king does not consider our Representation. Let us try the king whether he will or no, for one day. I would not yield up our right, and, I believe, the king will find out an expedient, and neither infringe your liberty nor his own prerogative. I have known whole sessions defeated in a day, by a prorogation; and if this be done, by the same counsel it may be again. I pray that, with all duty imaginable, the king may be farther addressed in the matter; and if he will not give us an Answer, then I would put the question of our right.

Sir *Tho. Clarges*. This point of prerogative, that has stuck these hundreds of years, will raise that other scruple to break you. There is great difference betwixt matters of grace and matters of right. This of chusing our Speaker, is so much of the essence of parliament, that we cannot part with it. When was any Speaker, that was presented, ever refused? If nothing of that be, but absolute power in the king; suppose five or six Subsidies should be demanded, and you make application to the king, and represent, 'That the commons are poor and cannot raise them all,' and the king should answer, 'Go your ways, consider what I have said, and raise them.' I am afraid that, when you have chosen your Speaker, and that is over, still you will have blocks and interpositions in the way, and ill counsellors will be encouraged to advise yet worse. The same Answer may be given to our three requests of Freedom of Speech, &c. If my borough that I serve for should ask me, 'Why we did not chuse another Speaker?' I will answer, 'Because I will not part with their right.' I advise, therefore, that we do as was done in the former king's time, in the Petition of Right; that we apply to the king for a better Answer to our Representation.

Serj. *Maynard*. This is not a question to put the ruin of a nation upon. The last parliament, pursuing things with zeal and truth, yet were dissolved. I could not have believed it. I believe that gentlemen have in this matter spoken their hearts, and I believe I shall speak mine too. What is your evidence for this right that you pretend to? From R. ii.'s and Hen. iv.'s time, there has been no denial of the Speaker that you have chosen. Because it has not been denied, cannot it be denied? why do you let the Speaker excuse himself at the lords bar, and not accept his excuse here: if a man can show the fruits of his ancient possession, though his evidence be lost, yet that goes a great way. It is said, 'by this we shall lose our privilege, and Speakers may be rejected without end.' It cannot be presumed that our Speakers will be rejected till one be got for the turn; that will be too gross. We come here for the good of the king's crown, and the government, and posterity, as well as for our own present good. If we demand just laws of the king, he grants or rejects them, and it is matter of grace, and not of right; and that is a greater prerogative than rejecting or accepting a Speaker. That which astonishes me is, we have dangers at home and abroad. This matter of right is not clear to me. But it is clear that we shall be ruined by a breach with the king.

Mr. Solicitor *Finch*. I think it a good expedient to chuse a third person for Speaker, and I think it not fit to represent to the king what he has twice denied us. The king's negative power is as much as chusing a Speaker.

Mr. *Vaughan*. What higher testimony can a subject have for all he has than records? I would not show the way here to cancel records. When we consider that 30 laws were broken by the Declaration for Liberty of Conscience, and money given for a Fleet, and we had no Fleet, money for an Army, and no war, what cannot we suppose? what remedy can we have, when the king will not so much as look upon our Petition, that has all our rights? the same counsel put him upon this. This is but beginning to ride a parliament. Languishing persons to take physic, not out of hopes to be cured, but to prolong their life some time. I fear that may be our case.

Col. *Titus*. There are not worse counsels than have been given by those about the king, and I expect no better from them. Nobody will deny that the choice of a Speaker is in the house. This matter is not of that last importance as to venture the kingdom upon it. If the king denies one or two Speakers, he may deny ten, till he have one to serve a turn: it is possible, but not probable. The words of the writ that calls us hither are, 'to consult de quibusdam arduis regni negotiis'—and all that is to give Money: an empty Exchequer, and a full house! will the king lose his Money, do you think, by putting by 40 Speakers? I would not have that argument pass, that if we chuse not another Speaker, we shall be dissolved. When once a parliament is so fond of their places, and so fearful of a dissolution, that parliament did never do any good. Gentlemen did not expect such an Answer from the king; but when I consider who was the counsellor of it, I wonder not at all at it. I move you to adjourn till to-morrow.—The debate was accordingly adjourned by the Clerk.

March 12. Sir *John Cloberry* moves, that the question may be put for the chusing another Speaker.

Mr. *Trenchard*. The king has no right to reject our Speaker, but ancient usage has been to the contrary. Consider the nature of the thing; if the case be doubtful, we ought to insist upon it. It is a great inconvenience to the house to have no Speaker; and more for the king; and where it is so, it ought to turn the scales. We are told of 'dangers abroad and at home.' But that is more to give warrant for us to give our rights away. Those persons who formerly have made misunderstandings betwixt the king and parliament, I see, will continue it: as yet you cannot honourably admit of an expedient. At present, you have humbly addressed the king by way of representation of your case; and the king has given you such an Answer as was never yet given to any house of commons. You expose the honour of the house to censure, if you give up your right upon such a slight answer. I would therefore address the king for a farther answer.

Sir *Hugh Cholmondeley*. As far as I can guess, this question is better to be left undetermined than determined. If the king can refuse a Speaker, he may refuse several. If the king has not liberty, &c. he cannot displace, upon excuse of infirmity. We had better begin anew, and leave it as it was. It was moved, 'That the king might cause nothing of this matter to be entered upon the Lords Journal.' I propose that way as most expedient.

Sir *Harbottle Grimstone*. It has been our work four or five days to find out an expedient in this matter, and we cannot. The king has been so advised, that we chuse any member but one; which is as much as to say, 'chuse whom you will but 20.' Except one, and except 20. It was a saying of king James, 'That when he called a parliament, he let down his prerogative to his people; but when he dissolved a parliament, he took it up again; not for his pleasure, but for his power.' If one Address will not do, I am for a second and a third to the king.

Sir *John Reresby*. If you put the king upon a dissolution of the parliament upon this point, though some gentlemen say, 'they do not fear it, because of the king's necessity for Money;' the king's necessity is his people's necessity; and if we have so little consideration of the king's necessity, the king may have as little as our's; therefore I move that you will nominate a third person.

Sir *Thomas Exton*. I shall not enter into the debate of the king's prerogative in this matter. I am not of opinion, that to wave it now is to give it up for ever. The city is on fire, and one comes and blows up my house, which is my right, but upon that extremity I wave it. No man will say that this is our right; and as the king has given up his right by our free choice of a Speaker, as he has directed you, it is no yielding the point.

Mr. *Williams*. Prerogative does and must consist, and the essence of it, as much in custom as any of our privileges. Now the business of the five days is to make a precedent in your house against yourselves as it were. Dr. Exton, who is in another orb of the law, would let your right sleep now, to resume * it another time. Now popery and foreign fears are upon us! I have ever observed, that prerogative once gained was never got back again, and our privileges lost are never restored. What will become of you when a popish successor comes, when in king Charles ii.'s time, the best of princes, you gave up this privilege? When you have the oppression of a tyrant upon you, and all ill counsels upon you, what will become of you? Now you have none to struggle with, but ill counsellors and a good prince. I will lay this as heavy upon counsellors as any man can lay it upon man. I am as willing to heal as any man, but can you lay this aside with honour, having represented it already? He that made this question cannot want another to play with, and then you will be sent home maimed in your privileges, wounded in your body. This is gagging the commons of England, and like an Italian revenge, damning the soul first, and then killing the body. The Representation you have delivered, is very mode-

* See sir Thomas Exton's speech above. He was a member for the University of Cambridge, and LL. D.

rately penned; and will you receive this manner of answering? When you have presented an humble Petition, what sort of Answer do you receive? Do you not, by laying this aside, set up a worse precedent than you have had an Answer? I have that in my mind which I cannot so well express, but gentlemen may easily imagine. By good counsel, the king may heal all this, but it will never be in the power of the house of commons to retrieve it, if you give up your right.

The Commons' Second Representation to the King.] The commons then agreed upon the following humble Representation to his majesty:

"Most gracious sovereign: Whereas by the gracious Answer your maj. was pleased to give to our first Message in council, whereby your maj. was pleased to declare a resolution not to infringe our just rights and privileges, we, your majesty's most dutiful and loyal commons, were encouraged to make an humble Representation to your majesty upon the choice of our Speaker, which on Tuesday last was presented to your maj. by some of our members: we do, with great trouble and infinite sorrow, find by the report that was made to us, by those members at their return, that your maj. was pleased to give an immediate Answer to the same, without taking any farther consideration thereof; which, we are persuaded, if your maj. had done, what we then offered to your maj. would have so far prevailed upon your royal judgment, as to have given your maj. satisfaction, as to the reasonableness thereof, and preserved us in your majesty's favourable opinion of our proceedings: and since we do humbly conceive, that the occasion of this question hath arisen from your majesty's not being truly informed of the state of the case, we humbly beseech your maj. to take the said Representation into your farther consideration, and to give us such a gracious Answer, that we may be put into a capacity to manifest our readiness to enter into those consultations which necessarily tend to the preservation and welfare of your maj. and your kingdoms."

The King's Answer.] To this Representation the king immediately gave this quick reply, "I will return you an Answer to-morrow."

The King prorogues the Parliament for two days.] March 13. The commons being met, in expectation of his majesty's Answer, about 11 of the clock the king sent the black rod for them to attend him in the house of lords, which they did; where the Lord Chancellor said, "That it was his majesty's pleasure that this parliament be prorogued to the 15th instant. And accordingly it is prorogued to that time."

SECOND SESSION OF THE THIRD PARLIAMENT.

The King's Speech on opening the Session.] March 15, 1678-9. The house met, according to the prorogation, when his majesty, in the lords house, spoke to this effect:

"My lords and gentlemen; Though this hath been a very short recess, yet there are some doubts whether you can take notice of what I said at the opening of this parliament, in point of form; therefore it is necessary that I recommend to you what I and my Lord Chancellor said to you the other day, as if we said it now. The rest I refer to the Lord Chancellor."

The Lord Chancellor then spoke as follows:

"My lords, and you the knights, citizens, and burgesses of the house of commons; Since it hath pleased the king to refer you all to what he lately said at the opening of this parliament, it will concern us all to take it into our most serious thoughts, and to enter upon the matter therein recommended to us, that so we may proceed effectually in that great work for which we were called, without being diverted from it by any consideration whatsoever. For if this parliament succeed not well, if it do not quiet and compose the minds of all the people; it will be thought the most unaccountable thing in the world, considering the great preparations the king hath made for it, and those excellent dispositions of mind he brings towards it. Wherefore, that no time may be lost, his majesty commands you, gentlemen of the house of commons, to proceed immediately to your choice of a Speaker, and his maj. will expect that he be presented to him on Monday next."

Serjeant Gregory chosen Speaker.] The commons then returned to their house to chuse their Speaker.

Lord *Russel.* Gentlemen, I hope the occasion of the late unhappy difference about the choice of our Speaker is removed by the prorogation. And I hope now that no ill persons, by tricks, can create a misunderstanding betwixt the king and his people, and hinder the happy effects of this session. And since the first step we are to make is to chuse a Speaker, I shall humbly recommend Mr. Serj. Gregory as a fit person.

Mr. *Sacheverell.* I stand not up to oppose the motion, but for what every honest gentleman ought to do. I blame no man that differs from me, or goes according to his judgment. I differ from those who think that this point of right, of chusing our Speaker, is now quiet, and I stand up only to give my reason for it, why I differ, and then I will withdraw. I differ, because that in honour we cannot leave Mr. Seymour, since he may suffer by being named Speaker by us. Next, if our right be not maintained, we have a precedent upon us. Next, if there be no expedient, then the motion is warrantable; but I know not of any.

Lord *Cavendish.* By the last prorogation, the king seemed rather to yield to us, by admitting that the point in difference could not be decided any other way. The king's denial of the Speaker that we chose is not entered into the lords Books. Therefore in respect to the affairs of the nation, let us chuse our Speaker, and I second the motion for serj. Gregory.

Serj. *Gregory.* I humbly thank you for your good opinion of me; but when I consider the weight of your debates, which require a person of the greatest experience and parts, my time of sitting here has not been above a year, and my experience so little that you may suffer in your affairs; and I come with the greatest disadvantage imaginable to succeed a person of so much experience. Pray consider of it and chuse a more experienced person.

Then lord Russel and lord Cavendish took him by the arms, and led him to the Chair; which he did not in the least resist.—On the 17th he was presented to the king, who without hesitation approved of the choice.

A committee of Secrecy appointed.] March 20. The commons resolved, "That a Committee of Secrecy be appointed to take informations, and prepare Evidence, and draw up Articles against the lords that are impeached, and that are now in the Tower, and to take such farther Informations as shall be given, relating to the Plot and Conspiracy against his majesty and the government, and the Murder of sir E. Godfrey."

The Commons remind the Lords of the Impeachments against the E. of Danby.] They next resolved, "That a Message be sent to the lords to put them in mind of the Impeachment of High-Treason, exhibited against Tho. earl of Danby, in the names of the commons of England, and to desire that he may be committed to safe custody."

Oates and Bedloe's Informations.] March 21. Dr. Tongue and Mr. Oates were called before the commons, to give in their Informations concerning the Plot, &c. and the latter gave in an Information, not only against the earl of Danby, but also against sir John Robinson, col. E. Sackville, and capt. H. Goring, all three members of the house of commons: which raised a new flame in that place.—Bedloe likewise delivered in his Information; upon which the house Resolved, "That an humble Address be made to his majesty, that the 500*l.* reward, promised by his proclamation for the discovery of the Murder of sir E. Godfrey, may be forthwith paid to Mr. Bedloe, who, this house is satisfied to be the first discoverer thereof: and that his majesty would farther be pleased to order, that the 20*l.* reward, for the discovery of every Priest, may be effectually paid to the Discoverers of them."—In another Address, they desired his majesty, That the care of Mr. Bedloe's Safety may be immediately recommended to his grace the duke of Monmouth." To which the king gave a present Answer: "That he would take immediate care for the payment of the 500*l.* and the 20*l.* they desired: that he had hitherto taken all the care he could of Mr. Bedloe, and that he knew how considerable his Evidence was, and that he would see hereafter that he should want for nothing, and that he would be responsible for him, whilst he remained in Whitehall; but that he could not be answerable for him when he went abroad."

The Plot voted to be real.] They next came to this Resolve, "The house doth declare, that they are fully satisfied by the Proofs they have heard, that there now is, and, for divers years last past, hath been, a horrid and treasonable Plot and Conspiracy, contrived and carried on by those of the Popish Religion, for the murdering his majesty's sacred person, and for subverting the Protestant Religion, and the ancient and well-established government of this kingdom." To this Vote they desired the concurrence of the lords, which was granted.

Message against the E. of Danby.] March 22. The commons ordered a Bill to be brought in, to secure the king and kingdom against the Danger and Growth of Popery. And being commanded, at the same time, to attend his majesty in the house of peers, the king spoke to them in favour of the earl of Danby: but returning to their house, they presently Resolved, "That a Message be immediately sent to the lords, to remind their lordships of the last Message sent them from this house, relating to Tho. earl of Danby; and, to demand that he may be forthwith sequestered from parliament, and committed to safe custody." Upon this request the lords desired a Conference: but the commons returned answer, "That it was not agreeable to the usage and proceedings of parliament, for either house to send for a conference, without expressing the subject matter of it."—Upon a second Message, wherein the earl of Danby was mentioned, they met the lords in the Painted-Chamber, where the duke of Monmouth spoke as follows: "I am commanded by the lords to acquaint you, that their lordships, having taken into their consideration matters relating to the earl of Danby, together with what his maj. was pleased to say upon that subject, have ordered that a Bill be brought in, by which Tho. earl of Danby may be made for ever incapable of coming into his majesty's presence, and of all offices and employments, and of receiving any gifts or grants from the crown, and of sitting in the house of peers."

The King grants the Earl a Pardon.] In the mean time, the commons, hearing that the king had signed a Pardon for the earl, appointed a committee to repair to the several offices, (at neither of which no entry of it had been made) and particularly to the Lord Chancellor, to enquire into the manner of suing out that Pardon. Whereupon the Lord-Chancellor, (after premising, that he neither advised, drew, or altered it) informed the committee, "That the said Pardon was passed with the utmost privacy, at the desire of the earl, who gave this reason for it, That he did not intend to make use of it, but to stand upon his innocence, except false witnesses should be produced against him; and then he would make use of it at the last extremity. That he advised the earl to let the Pardon pass in the regular course; but, after consulting with the king, his maj. declared he was resolved to let it pass with all privacy: and, suddenly after, the king commanded the Lord-Chancellor to bring the seal from Whitehall, and, being there, he laid it upon the table; thereupon his majesty commanded the seal to be taken out of the bag, which his lordship was obliged to submit unto, it not being in his power to hinder it; and the king wrote his name upon the top of the parchment, and then directed to have it sealed: whereupon the person that usually carried the purse, affixed the seal to it." The Chancellor added, "That, at the very time of affixing the seal to the parchment, he did not look upon himself to have the custody of the seal."

The Commons resolve to demand Justice against him, and declare his Pardon illegal.] Upon reading this Report, the house fell into a violent heat and debate; and of those that spoke, we must not omit Mr. Powle's severe Speech, who naming the earl of Danby, proceeded thus: "The person to whom we owe the dangers and fears of the French king against us: the person to whom we owe the threats and severe Answers to those humble Addresses we made the last session of parliament: the person to whom we owe the ruin of this nation, and exhausting the king's Revenue: the person to whom we owe the expence of 200,000*l.* a year unaccounted for: the person to whom we owe the raising of a Standing-Army, to be kept up by the Receipt of six millions of livres yearly, for three years, to enslave us and our Religion: the person to whom we owe the late bone that was thrown in on the sitting of the last parliament, to hinder the good issue that might have come by their proceedings; who is now laying down his staff, and making up his accounts in the Treasury as he pleases, to enrich himself out of the spoils of the people, and so depart." At the conclusion of the debate, Resolved nem. con. "That a Message be sent to the lords to demand Justice, in the name of the commons of England, against Thomas earl of Danby; and that he may be immediately sequestered from parliament, and committed to safe custody." They likewise resolved, "That an humble Address be made to his majesty, representing the irregularity and illegality of the Pardon, mentioned by his majesty to be granted to the earl of Danby, and the dangerous consequence of granting Pardons to any persons that lie under an Impeachment of the commons of England."

The Earl of Danby makes his Escape.] March 25. The lords sent a Message to acquaint the commons, "That they had sent to apprehend the earl of Danby both to his house here in town, and to his house at Wimbleton; and that the gentleman usher of the black rod had returned their lordships Answer, that he could not be found."*

The Commons resolve to attaint the Earl of Danby.] 'Whereupon the commons ordered, 'That a bill be brought in to summon Tho. earl of Danby to render himself to justice by a certain day, to be therein limited; or in default thereof, to attaint him.'

The Earl of Shaftsbury's Speech on the State of the Nation.] March 25. It was moved in the house of lords, "That inquiry may be made into the State of the Nation,"; upon which occasion,

The Earl of *Shaftsbury* made the following Speech: "My lords; You are appointing the consideration of the state of England, to be taken up in a committee of the whole house, some day next week. I do not know well how what I have to say may be received, for I never study either to make my court well, or to be popular; I always speak what I am commanded by the dictates of the Spirit within me.—There are some considerations abroad, that concern England so nearly, that without them you will come far short of safety and quiet at home: 'We have a little Sister, and 'she hath no Breasts; what shall we do for our 'sister in the day when she shall be spoken 'for? if she be a Wall, we will build on her a 'Palace of Silver; if she be a door, we will inclose her with Boards of Cedar.' We have several little sisters without breasts, the French protestant churches, the two kingdoms of Ireland and Scotland; the foreign protestants are a wall; the only wall and defence to England; upon it you may build palaces of silver, glorious palaces. The protection of the protestants abroad is the greatest power and security the crown of England can attain to, and which can only help us to give check to the growing greatness of France. Scotland and Ireland are two doors, either to let in good or mischief upon us; they are much weakened by the artifice of our cunning enemies, and we ought to inclose them with boards of cedar.—Popery and slavery, like two sisters, go hand in hand, and sometimes one goes first, sometimes the other; but wheresoever the one enters, the other is always following close at hand.—In England, popery was to have brought in slavery; in Scotland, slavery went before, and popery was to follow.—I do not think your lordships, or the parliament, have jurisdiction there. It is a noble and ancient kingdom; they have an illustrious nobility, a gallant gentry, a learned clergy, and an understanding, worthy people: but yet, we cannot think of England as we ought, without reflecting on the condition they are in. They are under the same prince, and the influence of the same favourites and councils; when they are hardly dealt with, can we that are richer expect better usage? for it is certain that in all absolute governments, the poorest countries are always most favourably dealt with.—When the an-

* "Though the gentleman usher reported, that the bird was flown, yet the contrary was true; for though his servants denied him, both at his house in town and at Wimbleton, sir John Reresby saw him come out of his closet at midnight, from a consultation with his intimates the 24th, which was the very day the lords made the order for his commitment; and when he did disappear, it was only to take sanctuary at Whitehall." Ralph.

tient nobility and gentry there cannot enjoy their royalties, their shrievaldoms, and their stewardries, which they and their ancestors have possessed for several hundreds of years; (but that now they are enjoined by the lords of the council, to make deputations of their authorities to such as are their known enemies) can we enjoy our Magna Charta long under the same persons and administration of affairs? if the council-table there can imprison any nobleman or gentleman for several years, without bringing him to trial, or giving the least reason for what they do; can we expect the same men will preserve the liberty of the subject here?—I will acknowledge, I am not well versed in the particular laws of Scotland; but this I do know, that all the northern countries have, by their laws, an undoubted and inviolable right to their liberties and properties; yet Scotland hath outdone all the eastern and southern countries, in having their lives, liberties, and estates subjected to the arbitrary will and pleasure of those that govern. They have lately plundered and harrassed the richest and wealthiest counties of that kingdom, and brought down the barbarous Highlanders to devour them; and all this without almost a colourable pretence to do it: nor can there be found a reason of state for what they have done; but that those wicked ministers designed to procure a rebellion at any rate, which, as they managed, was only prevented by the miraculous hand of God, or otherwise all the papists in England would have been armed, and the fairest opportunity given, in the just time for the execution of that wicked and bloody design the papists had; and it is not possible for any man that duly considers it, to think other, but that those ministers that acted that, were as guilty of the Plot, as any of the lords that are in question for it.—My lords, I am forced to speak this the plainer, because till the pressure be fully and clearly taken off from Scotland, it is not possible for me, or any thinking man to believe, that good is meant to us here.—We must still be upon our guard, apprehending that the principle is not changed at court; and that these men are still in place and authority, who have that influence upon the mind of our excellent prince, that he is not, nor cannot be that to us, that his own nature and goodness would incline him to.—I know your lordships can order nothing in this, but there are those that hear me can put a perfect cure to it; until that be done, the Scotish weed is like death in the pot, 'mors in olla:' but there is something too, now I consider, that most immediately concerns us; their act of 22,000 men to be ready to invade us upon all occasions. This, I hear, that the lords of the council there have treated as they do all other laws, and expounded it into a Standing-Army of 6000 men. I am sure we have reason and right to beseech the king that that Act may be better considered in the next parliament there. I shall say no more for Scotland, at this time; I am afraid your lordships will think I have said too much, having no concern there; but if a French nobleman should come to dwell in my house and family, I should think it concerned me to ask what he did in France? for if he were there a felon, a rogue, a plunderer, I should desire him to live elsewhere; and I hope your lordships will do the same thing for the nation, if you find the same cause.—My lords, give me leave to speak two or three words concerning our other sister, Ireland: thither, I hear, is sent Douglas's regiment, to secure us against the French. Besides, I am credibly informed, that the Papists have their arms restored, and the Protestants are not many of them yet recovered from being the respected party; the sea-towns, as well as the inland, are full of Papists: that kingdom cannot long continue in the English hands, if some better care be not taken of it. This is in your power, and there is nothing there, but is under your laws; therefore I beg that this kingdom at least may be taken into consideration, together with the state of England; for I am sure there can be no safety here, if these doors be not shut up and made sure."

Col. Sackville expelled.] This day, Oates gave his testimony against col. Sackville, a Member of the house formerly mentioned, declaring that he said, "That they were sons of whores, who said there was a Plot, and that he was a lying rogue that said it." Whereupon the colonel was immediately sent to the Tower, and ordered to be expelled the house, with a Petition to the king to be made incapable of bearing any office. But in a short time, upon his submission, he was discharged from his imprisonment, but not restored to his seat.

A Conference about the Earl of Danby.] April 4. A conference was held between the two houses, in the Painted Chamber, concerning the Bill sent up against the earl of Danby; where the earl of Anglesey, lord Privy Seal, delivered himself to this effect, being the chief manager for the peers; "That the lords chose to deliver back this Bill by conference, rather than Message, to preserve a good understanding, and prevent debate and controversy between them. The lords observe, that the greatest affairs of the nation are at a stand, at a time of the greatest danger and difficulty that this kingdom ever laboured under; that the king hath always in his reign inclined to mercy and clemency to all his subjects: therefore to a king so merciful and compassionate, the first interruption of his clemency they did desire should not proceed from the two houses pressing the king to an act of the greatest severity; therefore they have passed the Bill with some amendments, which he delivered to them."—The commons were no way satisfied with the lords proceedings, therefore drew up Reasons against them, to be offered in another conference, which were as follow: "The addition of the title does shew, that the Amendments made by your lordships to the Bill do wholly alter the nature of it, and from a Bill of Attainder have converted it to a Bill of Banishment, which the commons cannot consent to for these Reasons: 1. That banishment is not the legal judgment in cases of High-Treason, and the earl of Danby being impeached by the commons of high-treason, and having fled from justice, hath hereby confessed the Charge, and therefore ought to have the judgment of high-treason for the punishment. 2. That banishment being not the punishment the law inflicts upon those crimes, the earl of Danby might make use of this remission of his sentence as an argument, that either the commons were distrustful of their proofs against him, or else that the crimes are not in themselves of so high a nature as treason. 3. That the example of this would be an encouragement to all persons that should be hereafter impeached by the commons, to withdraw themselves from justice, which they would be always ready to do, if not prevented by a commitment upon their Impeachment, and therefore hope to obtain a more favourable Sentence in a legislative way, than your lordships would be obliged to pass upon them in your judicial capacity."

An Address for a Proclamation to apprehend the Earl of Danby.] Upon the reading of this Paper, they immediately resolved, "That an Address be presented to his majesty that he would issue out his royal proclamation for apprehending of Tho. earl of Danby; and to command all ministers of justice to use deligence to apprehend him; and to forbid all subjects to harbour him; and to require all officers of the houshold to take care that no person suffer him to conceal himself in any of the king's palaces."

A second Conference on the Bill of Attainder.] On the same day, the commons had a second conference with the lords upon the same case, where the earl of Huntingdon managed for the house of peers, and what he delivered was to this effect: "The lords have desired this conference with the commons, not so much to argue and dispute, as to mitigate and reconcile: They have already observed, That the debates of this Bill have given too long, and too great an obstruction to public business; and therefore they desire you to believe, that that is the reason which hath chiefly prevailed with their lordships in a matter of this nature. And upon this ground it is, that if a way may be found to satisfy and secure the public fears, by doing less than the Bill you have proposed, the lords do not think it advisable to insist upon the utmost and most rigorous satisfaction to public justice, which might be demanded. To induce you to this compliance, the lords do acknowledge, that Banishment is so far from being the legal judgment in case of high treason, that it is not the legal judgment in any case whatsoever, since it can never be inflicted but by the legislative authority: But they see no reason why the legislative authority should always be bound to act to the utmost extent of its power; for there may be a prudential necessity sometimes of making abatements, and it might be of fatal consequence, if it should not be so. And the lords, to remove all jealousies of the precedents of this kind, do declare, that nothing which hath been done in the earl of Danby's case, shall ever be drawn into example for the time to come, and will so enter it upon their Journal. And thereupon their lordships insist upon their Amendments so far, as to exclude all Attainders; and do promise themselves the commons will in this point comply with their lordships, who do again assure them, That their Resolutions are grounded only upon their tenderness, and the consideration of the public."

A third and free Conference.] This being not satisfactory, a third and free conference was held two days after, in which the Lord Privy-Seal said: "That the house of commons might see by the present quick free Conference, which the lords desired, that their lordships did shew their willingness, by using all means possible, to reconcile both houses, and to come to such an understanding, as to pass the Bill with all expedition. He owned the cogency of the commons reasons, and therefore the lords were content to make the Bill absolute, without giving the lord Danby any day to appear, and the penalties to continue. He observed, that, by the passing of this Bill, he would not only be ruined, together with his family, but likewise those acquisitions which he got by the marriage into a noble family, would be lost. And if the commons would have any other penalties added to the Bill, their lordships would leave it to them, provided they run not to the absolute destruction of the lord impeached." He took notice, "That although reason and justice were of the commons side, yet in a legislative capacity, they were to consider circumstances with relation to the good of the public. That in this affair they had gained two great points; the first was, 'That Impeachments made by the commons in one parliament, continue from session to session, and parliament to parliament, notwithstanding prorogations or dissolutions:' the other point was, 'That in cases of Impeachment upon special matter shewn, if the modesty of the party impeached directs him not to withdraw, the lords admit that of right they order him to withdraw, and that afterwards he must be committed.' But without special matter alledged, he said, he did not know how many of their lordships might be picked out of the house of a sudden."

The earl of Shaftesbury, now in a way of preferment in court, declared, "They were as willing to be rid of the earl of Danby, as the commons; but he let them know, That the expression which was sent with Reasons from the lords the other day, namely, That the lords would not draw into example the proceedings of the earl of Danby, but would vacate them; they intended that to extend only to the points of not withdrawing and not committing. He likewise declared, That the way now proposed would be a means to have the Bill pass; for the commons might have other penalties if they would, as confiscation of estate, loss of honours, &c. Therefore he desired the commons to consider, that there were weighty Reasons, which were better understood than expressed, that proved it necessary for the good of the public, that this Bill should speedily pass."

The commons replied, "That they hoped their lordships did not think, they took it as if they had now gained any point; for the points, which their lordships mentioned as gained, were nothing but what was agreeable to the ancient course and methods of parliament."

The Bill of Attainder passes against him.] Then they delivered the Bill again to the lords, with their Amendments, with expression of hopes and desire of their concurrence with them, that justice may have its course, and the great affairs of parliament be no longer obstructed, by spending more time on him, who hath brought the kingdom into so sad a condition.—And thus they so immoveably adhered to their own Bill of Attainder, that, within two or three days time, the lords thought fit to pass the Bill, in which the 21st of April was appointed for the earl's surrendering himself to trial.

The Earl surrenders himself.] The earl finding himself reduced to this extremity, rather than risk the mischiefs that might happen to himself, or to the king, if he should refuse to pass the Bill, on the 15th of April surrendered himself to the usher of the black rod, which was signified to the commons the next day.

The five Popish Lords put in their Answers.] April 16. The house was informed by a Message from the lords, That all the five Peers, lately committed to the Tower, had brought their Answers to the Impeachments against them, in person, except the lord Bellasis. Upon which a debate arose, Whether the said lord Bellasis, having not in person delivered his Answer, was actually and legally arraigned? And a committee was ordered to inspect the Entries that had been made in the Lords Journals touching the appearance and arraignment of the five Lords, and give in their report the next day.

A Supply voted and appropriated.] The same day, the house resolved, "That a Supply be granted to his majesty of 206,462*l.* 17*s.* 3*d.* for the paying off and dismissing all the Forces then in arms, raised or brought over from foreign parts, to be raised by six months tax."—The next day, a Clause was ordered to be added to the said Resolution, to appropriate the Money to that use only, with penalties upon such persons as should divert the same: and, a motion being made, That the said Supply should be paid into the Exchequer, the house divided, and it passed in the Affirmative, Noes 131, Yeas 191.

Report of the Contents of the Lords' Journals, relating to the five Popish Lords.] April 17. The Report of the committee appointed to inspect the Lords Journals was delivered in by Mr. Hampden, in effect as follows: "That April 8, the lord Shaftsbury reported from the committee of privileges, That their lordships were of opinion, that the lords now prisoners, ought to be brought to the bar, and kneel there, and then stand up, and hear the Articles against them read. Which was ordered by the house accordingly; That April 9, the lords Powis, Stafford, Petre, and Arundel of Wardour did appear at the bar of the house, where they heard the Articles against them read, and were told, his majesty would appoint a lord high steward for their trials: That, then, the lords, having put in several requests, withdrew, and being called in again, were told by the lord-chancellor, That the house had ordered the several indictments brought against them by the grand jury, should be brought into that court by writ of certiorari, that their lordships should be allowed copies of the Articles against them, that till the 15th would be given them for their Answers, and farther time, in case any new Articles were alledged: with liberty to take out copies of records, journals, &c. That, then, they find notice taken, that lord Bellasis had not appeared at the bar. And that Tho. Plessington, and Robert Dent, being sworn, had attested that his lordship was so ill of the gout, that he could not turn in his bed without help: which reasonable excuse being allowed, the said Tho. Plessington, in behalf of his lordship, desired a copy of the Articles exhibited against his lordship, with council, &c. which particulars were all granted: That April 15 being appointed for the said lords to put in their Answers, they were ordered to be brought to the bar of the house, for that purpose, and that lord Bellasis was permitted to deliver in his Answer in writing."

The commons then ordered the Answers of the said lords to be inspected by the Committee of Secrecy: who were farther to consider the methods of proceeding upon Impeachments, and give in their Report accordingly.

The King's Speech to the Parliament, on declaring a new Privy-Council.] April 21. His majesty, by message, commanded the commons to attend him in the house of peers, where he expressed himself, as follows:

"My lords and gentlemen; I thought it requisite to acquaint you with what I have done now this day; which is, that I have established a new Privy Council, the constant number of which shall never exceed 30 *. I have made choice of such persons as are worthy and able to advise me; and am resolved, in all my weighty and important affairs, next to the advice of my Great Council in parliament (which I shall very often consult with), to be advised by this Privy council. I could not make so great a change, without acquainting both houses of parliament. And I desire you all to apply yourselves heartily, as I shall do, to

* The former Council was composed of 50.

those things which are necessary for the good and safety of the kingdom, and that no time may be lost in it*."

Report from the Committee, concerning the Answers of the five Popish Lords.] April 23. Sir John Trevor gave the following Report, from the Committee appointed to inspect the Answers of the five Lords, and the methods of proceeding upon Impeachments: "That it is the opinion of the committee, that the lord Bellasis being impeached of high-treason, cannot make any Answer but in person. That the several writings, put in by the lords Powis, Stafford, and Arundel of Wardour, are not Pleas, and Answers, but argumentative, evasive, and to which the commons neither can, or ought to reply: That, if the Answers of the said lords, as well as that of the lord Petre, were sufficient, proceedings ought to be stopt, till the lord Bellasis had also put in a sufficient Answer in person: That the commons do demand of the lords, that their lordships would forthwith order the said lords to put in their perfect Answers; or, in default thereof, that the commons may have justice against them."

April 24. The said Report being approved of by the house, a Conference was desired with the lords, at which, the Answers of the five Peers were returned, together with the Reasons of the commons for their insufficiency: to which was added by Order that the house

* "At last the king was prevailed upon to dismiss the Council, which was all made up of lord Danby's creatures; and the chief men of both houses were brought into the new Council. This was carried with so much secrecy, that it was not so much as suspected, till the day before it was done." Burnet.

"It does not appear that either house acknowledged the compliment of this speech by Address, which is now become almost a matter of course on much less considerable occasions, or even, that any such acknowledgment was moved for." Ralph.

"The house of commons received it with most coldness, where the contrary was most expected, and the pretended knowers among them, who were not of the Council, pretended now to know nothing of it, to expect new revelations, to doubt it might be a new court-juggle, and to refer it to time to tell what it was in truth; in the mean time to suspend their judgments." Temple.

"Sir William Temple had lately been recalled from his foreign employments; and the king, who, after the removal of Danby, had no one with whom he could so much as discourse with freedom of public affairs, was resolved, upon Coventry's dismission, to make him one of his secretaries of state. But that philosophical patriot, too little interested for the intrigues of a court, too full of spleen and delicacy for the noisy turbulence of popular assemblies, was alarmed at the universal discontents and jealousies which prevailed, and was determined to make his retreat, as soon as possible, from a scene which threatened such confusion. Meanwhile, he could not refuse the confidence with which his master honoured him; and he resolved to employ it to the public service. He represented to the king, that, as the jealousies of the nation were extreme, it was necessary to cure them by some new remedy, and to restore that mutual confidence, so requisite for the safety both of king and people: that to refuse every thing to the parliament in their present disposition, or to yield every thing, was equally dangerous to the constitution, as well as to public tranquillity: that if the king would introduce into his councils such men as enjoyed the confidence of his people, fewer concessions would probably be required; or if unreasonable demands were made, the king, under the sanction of such counsellors, might be enabled, with the greater safety, to refuse them: and that the heads of the popular party, being gratified with the king's favour, would probably abate of that violence by which they endeavoured at present to pay court to the multitude. The king assented to these reasons; and, in concert with Temple, he laid the plan of a new privy-council, without whose advice he declared himself determined for the future to take no measure of importance. This council was to consist of thirty persons, and was never to exceed that number. Fifteen of the chief officers of the crown were to be continued, who, it was supposed, would adhere to the king, and, in case of any extremity, oppose the exorbitancies of faction. The other half of the council was to be composed, either of men of character, detached from the court, or of those who possessed chief credit in both houses. And the king, in filling up the names of his new council, was well pleased to find that the members, in land and offices, possessed to the amount of 300,000*l.* a year; a sum nearly equal to the whole property of the house of commons, against whose violence the new council was intended as a barrier to the throne. This experiment was tried, and seemed at first to give some satisfaction to the public. The earl of Essex, a nobleman of the popular party, son of that lord Capel who had been beheaded a little time after the late king, was created treasurer in the room of Danby: the earl of Sunderland, a man of intrigue and capacity, was made secretary of state: viscount Halifax, a fine genius, possessed of learning, eloquence, industry, but subject to inquietude, and fond of refinements, was admitted into the council. These three, together with Temple, who often joined them, though he kept himself more detached from public business, formed a kind of cabinet council, from which all affairs received their first digestion. Shaftsbury was made president of the council; contrary to the advice of Temple, who foretold the consequence of admitting a man of so dangerous a character into any part of the public administration." Hume.

desired their lordships would appoint a short day for the said peers to put in their effectual Answers.—The 25th, the lords, by Message, acquainted the house, that the earl of Danby had put in his Plea, and the lord Bellasis his Answer, in person, at the bar of the lords; which said Plea, and Answer, the lords sent down at the same time, desiring they might be returned with all convenient speed.

The same day, the lords, by Message, acquainted the house, that the lords Stafford, Arundel of Wardour, and Powis, had that day retracted the former pleas, and put in others, which were sent down with a request, that they might be returned with all convenient speed.

Debate on the Duke of York's Succession to the Crown.] April 27, (Sunday). Several artifices were used to divert the business of this day, which was, 'To consider how to preserve the King's Person from the attempts and conspiracies of the Papists, &c.' by engaging the house into other debates. Which being apprehended, occasioned several loud cries, 'To the business of the day;' which was thus introduced by

Mr. *Harbord.* Mr. Speaker, these several things started being off from your hands, I shall say something to the occasion of your meeting upon this extraordinary day. It is, 'for the security of the King's Person, and for the preservation of the Protestant religion established by law.' Nothing can be so fatal to our religion, and by consequence our laws and liberties, as the danger of the first. Should his maj. fall by any unhappy stroke, it would not be in our power to defend the Protestant religion long. The way to do it, is to take away those men that are likely to destroy him, which are the Papists. Many Catholics will now take the Oaths, and, under the notion of inhabitants, creep into houses. Now since the danger of the King's Person is so great, by reason of their villainous conspiracies, I move, that there may be an order for bringing in a Bill, to banish all Roman catholics from this city, &c. for some time, and I hope that, in the interim, we may make such laws as may put power into such hands as may preserve us.

Mr. *Bennet.* The duke of York has as much right to succeed his brother, if he die without heirs, (which God forbid!) as my son, has to inherit my estate after me. Therefore I desire that by some law we may have power to arm ourselves against him, if he would bring in Popery amongst us. If the king have a son then we are out of fear; but if a way cannot be found out that the king may have a son, then we are to go another way to work.

Sir *John Knight.* What will signify banishing the Papists out of town for four or five months, unless you secure a Protestant Succession? When idolatry was set up in Israel, then they were led away captive. What we aim at is only for posterity, and but for our souls; and this is a proper day for that consideration, that we may overcome those persons that would subvert our religion, which the very 'gates of Hell cannot prevail against.' I think it not safe to let the duke be out of the nation. I would address the king, therefore, to let him see how much it is for his interest to persuade the duke to be a Protestant, and to order the duke to return into England.

Sir *Hugh Cholmondeley.* I have a heart full of sorrow for the occasion of our meeting today. It is a sad supposition, that the presumptive heir of the crown should change our religion. The short question is, whether there is any safety for the crown, whilst the Papists wish the king dead. We can never be safe, till it be the Papists interest to have the king amongst the living, that their condition may be never the better for having a king of their own religion. Therefore till you make it the interest of the Catholics to wish the life of the king, you do nothing.

Sir *Tho. Player.* We are come to that pass now, that Protestants and Papists cannot live together in England; and whilst the Papists have a prospect of a Popish successor, they will never be quiet, but be always making attempts upon the king's person. What has been transacted lately by lord Danby, in having Money given from France that England might be governed without parliament, and so enslaved for ever? And this was done, during the duke's prevalency upon the ministers. Now, I move that you will chuse a Committee to examine all the Papers that can be had, relating to the duke, and to extract all things done by the duke, in setting up popery and arbitrary government, and report it to the house.

Mr. *Bennet.* If you will have the duke of York come to the crown, as other kings do, speak plain English. If you intend that, I will prepare to be a Papist.

Col. *Birch.* Are we come here to give money, for some few new men being put into the Privy Council; and shall we do such things as we have done before? I hope the king will not leave one of the Council that was at the giving such advice as we have had. I would not give a penny for such advice.. I am the weakest in this great assembly, but on this point I cannot stay myself. I would support the government to the highest; but this plaistering and patching spoils all. It must not be the addition of four or five persons to the Council that will do it; it must be thoroughly done. When there are no reserves, and when the king fears nobody, when that is done, we shall answer the rest. Till you admit no claim to the crown, till there be an examination of the king's death in parliament, you may be safe. As for the duke of York, I can scarcely speak of him without tears. I hope he will come over to us; but I shall never desire to see that day he should be king without it. I have a kindness for the duke, but I have bowels of compassion for the kingdom too. I move therefore, 'That a Bill may be brought in, that at the fall of the king by any violent stroke (which God forbid!) no person come to the crown of England till that be examined.'

Mr. *Sacheverell.* Now a Bill has been moved, pray make it effectual. It was moved, 'to banish the papists 20 miles from London, and every one of them not to stir 5 miles from home.'

Sir *Fr. Russel.* I move for an explanatory vote, 'That the duke of York is the occasion of all these jealousies of the papists;' and so have the lords concurrence to it, and then you will have some ground to go upon.

Lord *Russel.* I think we are but trifling hitherto. If we do not something relating to the succession, we must resolve, when we have a prince of the popish religion, to be papists, or burn. And I will do neither. We see now, by what is done under a protestant prince, what will be done under a popish. This is the deciding day betwixt both religions. I am transported, I confess, both with spiritual and temporal concerns. I have abbey-lands, but I protest before God and man, I could not be more against popery than I am, had I none. I despise such a ridiculous and nonsensical religion—A piece of wafer, broken betwixt a priest's fingers, to be our Saviour! And what becomes of it when eaten, and taken down, you know. The king, I believe, will do his part in this matter, if we do ours. In the last parliament, I moved something of this nature, which was not a house to do great things; but I hope this house will neither be bribed, corrupted, nor cajoled, nor feasted, into the giving up the grand concerns of our Religion and Property. Therefore I desire 'That a committee may be appointed to draw up a Bill to secure our Religion and Properties in case of a Popish Successor.'

Mr. *Hampden.* I shall humbly propose, that this may be the question, viz. "That the duke of York being a papist, and the hopes of his coming such to the Crown, have given the greatest countenance and encouragement to the present Conspiracies and Designs of the Papists against the king, and the Protestant Religion."

Which Question passed nem. con.; and the lords concurrence was desired to it *.

April 28. The commons resolved, "That a Message be sent to the lords, to desire their lordships to demand of the earl of Danby, Whether he will rely upon, and abide by the plea of his pardon."

The King's second Speech to both Houses relative to the Succession.] April 30. The king came to the house of peers, and made this short Speech to both houses:

"My lords and gentlemen; The season of the year advancing so fast, I thought it necessary to put you in mind of three particulars: 1. Prosecution of the Plot. 2. Disbanding of the Army. 3. Providing a Fleet for our common Security. And to shew you, that, whilst you are doing your parts, my thoughts have not been misemployed; but that it is my constant care to do every thing that may preserve your Religion, and secure it for the future in all events; I have commanded my Lord Chancellor to mention several Particulars, which I hope will be an evidence that in all things that concern the public Security I shall not follow your zeal, but lead it."

The Lord Chancellor's second Speech.] Then the Lord Chancellor spake as followeth:

"My lords; and you the knights, citizens, and burgesses of the house of commons; That royal care which his majesty hath taken, for the general quiet and satisfaction of all his subjects, is now more evident, by these new and fresh instances of it which I have in command to open to you. His maj. hath considered with himself, that 'tis not enough that your Religion and Liberty is secure during his own reign; but he thinks, he owes it to his people, to do all that in him lies, that these blessings may be transmitted to your posterity, and so well secured to them, that no succession in after-ages may be able to work the least alteration.—And therefore his majesty, who hath often said in this place, 'That he is ready to consent to any laws of this kind, so as the same extend not to alter the descent of the crown in the right line, nor to defeat the Succession,' hath now commanded this to be further explained.—And, to the end it may never be in the power of any Papist, if the crown descend upon him, to make any change either in church or state, I am commanded to tell you, that his maj. is willing that provision may be made; first, to distinguish a Popish from a Protestant Successor; then, so to limit and to circumscribe the authority of a popish successor, in these cases following, that he may be disabled to do any harm.—First, in reference to the Church, his maj. is content, that care be taken, that all ecclesiastical and spiritual benefices and promotions, in the gift of the crown, may be conferred in such a manner, that we may be sure the incumbents shall always be of the most pious and learned protestants; and that no popish successor, while he continues so, may have any power to controul such presentments.—In reference to the State, and civil part of the government; as it is already provided, that no papist can sit in either house of parliament; so the king is pleased, that it be provided too, That there may never want a parliament, when the king shall happen to die; but that the parliament then in being may continue indissoluble for a competent time; or if there be no parliament in being, then the last parliament which was in being before that time may re-assemble, and sit a competent time, without any new summons or elections.—And as no Papist can by law hold any place of trust; so the king is content, that it may be further provided, That no lords or others of the privy

* Mr. Sidney says, "That the lords gave their consent to it, with the addition of the word 'unwillingly;' that is to say, 'that the duke, being a papist, had made him unwillingly the occasion of the plot.'"

council, no judges of the common law or in chancery, shall, at any time during the reign of any Popish Successor, be put in, or displaced, but by the authority of parliament; and that care also be taken, that none but sincere protestants may be justices of peace.—In reference to the military part, the king is willing, that no lord lieut. or deputy lieut. nor no officer in the navy, during the reign of any Popish Successor, be put in or removed, but either by authority of parliament, or of such persons as the parliament shall entrust with such authority.—'Tis hard to invent another restraint to be put upon a Popish Successor, considering how much the Revenue of the successor will depend upon consent of parliament, and how impossible it is to raise money without such consent: but yet, if any thing else can occur to the wisdom of the parliament, which may further secure Religion and Liberty against a Popish Successor, without defeating the Right of Succession itself, his maj. will most readily consent to it.—Thus watchful is the king for all your safeties: and if he could think of any thing else, that you do either want or wish, to make you happy; he would make it his business to effect it for you. God Almighty long continue this blessed union between the king and his parliament and people!" *

The Commons vote the Earl of Danby's Pardon illegal and void, and demand Judgment against him.] May 5. The commons resolved, "That it was the opinion of this house, that the pardon pleaded by the earl of Danby was illegal and void, and ought not to be allowed in bar of the Impeachment of the Commons of England." After which, Mr. Speaker, with the whole house, went up to the lords bar, and demanded Judgment against the earl in these words:

"My lords; the knights, citizens and burgesses, in parliament assembled, are come up to demand Judgment, in their own names, and the names of all the commons of England, against Tho. earl of Danby, who stands impeached by them before your lordships of High-Treason, and divers high Crimes and Misdemeanors; to which he has pleaded a Pardon: which Pardon the commons conceive to be illegal and void; and therefore they do demand Judgment of your lordships accordingly."†

The Commons' Address against the Duke of Lauderdale.] May 8. The following Address against the duke of Lauderdale was agreed to; with the Resolution that it should be presented by the whole house:

"We your majesty's most loyal and dutiful subjects, the commons in parliament assembled, finding your majesty's kingdoms involved in imminent dangers, and great difficulties, by the evil designs and pernicious councils of some who have been, and are in high place, and trust and authority about your royal person; who, contrary to the duty of their places, by their arbitrary and destructive counsels, tending to the subversion of the Rights, Liberties and Properties of your subjects, and the alteration of the Protestant Religion established, have endeavoured to alienate the hearts of your loyal subjects, from your maj. and your government. Amongst whom we have just reason to accuse John duke of Lauderdale, for a chief promoter of such counsels; and more particularly for contriving and endeavouring to raise jealousies and misunderstandings between your majesty's kingdoms of England and Scotland; whereby hostilities might have ensued, and may arise, between both nations, if not prevented. Wherefore, we your majesty's loyal subjects, could not but be sensibly affected with trouble, to find such a person (notwithstanding the repeated Addresses of the last parliament) continued in your councils at this time, when the affairs of your kingdom require none to be put into such employments, but such as are of known abilities, interest and esteem, in the nation, without all suspicion of either mistaking or betraying the true interest of the kingdom, and consequently of advising your majesty ill. We do therefore most humbly beseech your most sacred majesty, for taking away the great jealousies, dissatisfactions, and fears among your good subjects, that your maj. will graciously be pleased to remove the duke of Lauderdale from your majesty's councils, in your kingdoms of England and Scotland, and from all offices, employments, and places of trust, and from your majesty's presence for ever."

To this the king only made this cold Reply: "That he would consider of it, and return an Answer."

May 9. The commons resolved, "That no Commoner whatsoever should presume to maintain the validity of the Pardon pleaded

* Bishop Burnet affirms, "That the duke was struck with the news of the king's concessions, when it reached him at Brussels, and that he (the bishop) saw a letter written by the dutchess the next post, in which she wrote, 'That as for all the high things that were said by their enemies, they looked for them, but that Speech of the Lord Chancellor's was a surprise, and a great mortification to them.'"

† "Nothing could be more artificial than the proceedings of the commons. It was manifest, that, in condemning the Pardon; they, in effect, condemned the man; and yet they seemed to leave the peers in full possession of their privilege of judgment. The lords, on the other hand, had their expedients and resources as well as the commons, and resolved not only to center the whole authority of decision in themselves, but to make sure of such a decision as should be favourable to the Prerogative. In order to which, they made an Order, the same day, 'That the house, on the morrow, would take into consideration, whether the lords spiritual were to give their Vote in judicature, in Cases of Blood, or upon Bill of Attainder,' as a preliminary to the demand of the Speaker, concerning the earl of Danby." Ralph.

by the earl of Danby, without the consent of this house; and that the persons so doing, shall be accounted betrayers of the liberties of the commons of England."

Mr. Bertie examined as to 252,467l. received by him for Secret Service.] May 10. Mr. Bertie (entrusted by patent, with the disposal of 20,000l. per ann. Secret Service Money out of the Excise) was called in, and examined on several questions; and being withdrawn, it was resolved that the house was not satisfied with his Answers. After which, sir Robert Howard, auditor of the exchequer, informing the house that from Lady Day 1676, to March 26, 1679, 252,467l. 1s. 9d. had been paid to the said Mr. Bertie for Secret Service; an Order was issued, "That Mr. Bertie be committed to the custody of the serjeant at arms, for his contempt to this house."

Debate on the Bill of Exclusion.] May 11. (Sunday.) The business of this day was, to take into consideration that part of the king's and the lord chancellor's Speech which relates to 'the best ways and means of preserving the Life of his sacred majesty, and of securing the Protestant Religion, both in the reign of his majesty and his successors.' Several interruptions happened to this day's proceedings, which seemed designed.* The debate was thus opened by

Mr. *Bennet.* Mr. Speaker, we have trifled away too much time to-day; pray, let us improve the rest, and do our duty. Seeing that the duke of York is gone out of the kingdom, that he may not bring Popery with him to be established at his return, I will make you a short motion, viz. 'To make an Address to the king, that the duke may not come over again without the consent of the king and the two houses of parliament; and that we will stick to the king with our lives and fortunes against him, or any of the popish party that shall attack us.'

Mr. *Pilkington.* I would humbly pray the king, 'That the duke may come over, that we may impeach him of High Treason.'

Sir *John Knight.* It is impossible that the Protestant religion should be preserved under a popish prince; as inconsistent as light and darkness. The king's coronation Oath is to maintain religion, and that is the Protestant religion. The king's subjects are bound by law to take the Oaths of Supremacy and Allegiance—*Rex nunquam moritur.* How impatient are the Papists till the king be out of the way, that the Protestants may be destroyed. How is it possible that the kingdom should be satisfied under these oppositions so contrary? O Lord, what will the people say to us, if we do nothing? If the Pope gets his great toe into England, all his body will follow. Something must be done, but I dare not venture to propose what.

Mr. *Dubois.* The king offers us many gracious things in his Speech and somewhat more, viz. 'To secure the Protestant religion.' The king's life will be so much the more in danger, by how much the Papists think their case desperate. There is no way to defeat their execution of this Plot, like taking away their hopes; and unless, by some Vote, you determine the Succession, you will never put the Papists out of hopes of accomplishing their design.

Sir *Geo. Hungerford.* As long as the duke is heir to the crown, the kingdom is unsafe; and I believe that the queen will never be capable of children; for when she came into England she had something given her to be always a red-lettered woman. But something must be done.

Sir *Tho. Player.* I join with the motion that has been made for a Bill for an eternal banishment of the duke of York; but yet, that it might go farther, I would pursue the great end of our sitting to-day, to consult the safety of the king's person. This Bill will not set the king safe; therefore, besides the duke's Banishment, I propose, 'a Bill for excluding the duke of York by name, and all Papists whatsoever, from the crown of England.'

Col. *Birch.* If we can have no safety by a popish prince, it is your duty to take some resolution. Whilst the law of the militia is in being, which obliges a declaration, &c. we cannot fight against any commissioned by a popish Successor. When it is their interest to do a thing, the desperate Papists will do it, and till you change the Papists interest to keep the king alive, you do nothing.

Mr. Sec. *Coventry.* I think, the King's Person is to be considered how to be preserved, which is the proper consideration of the day, as well as the rest that has been moved, and to show the Papists, that it is not their interest to take the king away by violence; and what better way to do it than that proposal in the Chancellor's Speech, That the Papists may be in ten times a worse condition by doing it than they were before? If the Catholics be under a popish prince that cannot pardon them, they are in a worse condition than under a prince that can pardon them. The propositions I have heard moved to-day are the most ruinous to law and the property of the subject imaginable. Will any man give the duke less law than the worst felons have, to banish and disinherit him without so much as hearing him? The precedent will be the greatest inconvenience to ourselves in the world. Consider, the king is vigorous, in very good health, and but a year or two older than the duke; the king is not of such an age but that he may have children, and the duke is not so settled and grafted into the Romish religion, but that he may return to our religion again. Acts of parliament, we know, have not kept Succession out of the right line, but brought in blood and sword. Must you banish a young prince, and a young princess? He is now abroad, and may procure help to contend his title to the crown, to the end of the world; and no prince that ever

* Grey.

came to the crown, by a wrong title, but must maintain it by a standing army.

Mr. *Hampden.* For us to go about to tie a Popish Successor with laws for preservation of the Protestant Religion, is binding Sampson with withes; he will break them when he is awake. The duke is the presumptive heir of the crown, indeed; but if a man be likely to ruin the estate he may be heir to, we disinherit every day. But I find it a principle amongst a great many, 'That if the prince be great, it is no matter how low the people are, if his greatness be kept up.' I think that a prince is made for the good of the people, and where there is a Popish prince that may succeed, I think we ought to secure ourselves against that Succession. There is great inconvenience that may be assigned in every proposal I have heard to-day, but there is the least inconvenience in 'a Bill to exclude the duke from the crown,' and therefore I move for it.

Lord *Cavendish.* In all this debate, I see nothing certain but our danger; the remedies moved for are uncertain. A Bill of Banishment has been moved for the duke, but no man at this time will think it convenient for the duke to come into England, for he may come, and you cannot deny him to be heard by his counsel, before such a Bill pass. If you pass it, it may put him upon getting assistance from some foreign prince, and make a party here or in Ireland, and you ought to consult therefore the safest remedy, before the desperate. If you say, 'a Popish prince cannot be limited,' you may as well say, 'No law can keep the duke out.' I would therefore know first, whether what is proposed in the king's and chancellor's Speech may not go a great way in what you aim at. Consider therefore the safest ways, and if they will not do, then go the desperate.

Sir *F. Winnington.* I shall say a few words to this debate, though I must confess, I am the unfittest man to meddle in it, considering the relation I have had to this great prince, the duke of York. But when I consider, that the greatest thing in the world is at stake, I must argue to defend it. You have been told of doubts and fears from several hands, but have had no resolute motions. As they have been of different natures, so, if the house divide upon this great thing, you give the greatest blow to the protestant religion imaginable; therefore, whatever we do, let it be with unanimity, as Protestants, and I hope all here are so. Therefore I propose, that, in giving our opinions, all gentlemen that are not pleased to speak to the business, may have as visible actions as they that do. I think we are not ready for the main question, but I propose that we may consider the danger of the nation. It is easy to argue, that we are inevitably ruined if there be a popish Successor, but it is hard to say what will save us. The prospect of the duke's being a Papist has brought upon our hands enough to overwhelm us. The disease seems desperate. The five popish lords are in the Tower, on account of the plot, and another lord is there, though not under that name, yet centered on that bottom, and has made his greatness upon it. The lords in the Tower, if we divide upon this great thing, will think themselves saved; and now within a few days, they are to be tried. If what I shall say be not acceptable to the house, I protest I speak it not out of favour to the duke, but for the preservation of the Protestant cause. Now that this thing is brought on, let us do like honest men, and Protestants. If we divide upon the question, the Papists will have more encouragement than the duke ever gave them. Now we are steady, I would not lose one mite of advantage; therefore I would have the debate adjourned, and no question now put upon it, and go on upon it, as soon as the Lords in the Tower are tried, and no business whatsoever to be interposed; and when we are once come again to this debate, whoever is here may personally say, he owns or disowns the Resolution, and not leave it to a few gentlemen to debate and argue, and the rest to slip away, but that every man may have his share in it; and if we part with this debate, we do not wisely. If the Judges see the commons faint and tender in this matter, the Judges will be so too in judging this law, and the lords will shrink and be tender too. As this Bill will be hard for the duke, so it is hard for us to be deprived of our civil liberties, which will be at the power of a prince that governs as the pope shall give his determination. When popery is introduced, but for one prince's reign, the pope will dispose of the royal family as well as us; therefore when I speak against Popery, I speak for the royal family; and in speaking this, I speak for all good and virtuous men. If it be Exclusion, or Banishment, of the duke, let the Resolution be what it will, it is for our security.

Mr. *Boscawen.* I do not take this matter we are upon, but with all the circumstances that attend it, and then I take it for granted, that if there be any more probable means to preserve the protestant religion amongst us, than what have been proposed, I shall not differ at all. But if you consider the horrible Plot which has made the papists an irreconcileable party, and that a protestant king is in danger of his life, much more will religion be in danger when a papist comes to the crown. By being willows, and not oaks, men have kept their places at court; which makes me expect little effect from what has been proposed in relation to the king's and chancellor's Speeches. No confession of faith binds a man to any allegiance to a prince secluded the crown by law. As for Hen. IV. there was no law to seclude him from the crown, and he was but a private person, and the people ought not to have taken up arms against him. But where there is a law for it, they are betrayers of the protestant religion, if they do it not when in their power. We ought to consider the chancellor's first Speech, and not that last Speech. Now you have an opportunity to secure the protestant religion, do it; else, posterity will curse you in your graves. The whole protestant religion in Europe is struck at, in a Popish Succession in England. If the protestant religion keeps not up its head now, under a protestant king, it must be drowned under a popish. Suppose the succeeding prince should be a lunatic, as the king of Portugal was, and they had no way of securing the government, but by pretermitting him—Much more in our case, if the security of an act of parliament be as good as any security for the right of the crown. Queen Eliz. had no right to the crown, but by act of parliament, and she made it Præmunire, by law, for any man to hold the contrary, &c. and yet some gentlemen say, 'it is against law.' We must have a law to secure this law, else you will be infamous. I am clearly of opinion, that till we go against popery, beyond retreat, we shall have no happy days; and then, I hope, we may see happy days. But popery and French government are almost check-mate* with us. There is no probability of security the other way proposed. Would you have parliaments make laws without a prince? or would you have the government in conservators hands, such as we may confide in? That would look like a commonwealth, and I know no such great men that we can trust upon such an account; besides, they have no power, and will be insignificant. Making clergymen and justices of the peace will signify nothing. A troop of horse, and a file of musketeers, will easily turn us all out of doors. Let us know what we have to trust to. But the several proposals made to secure the King's Person, and the Protestant Religion (except this Bill proposed) look like gold, but are but leaf-gold when you touch them. Whatever becomes of us, let us preserve the protestant religion, and pray put the question for the bill.

After further debate, and some contest, for candles, or no candles, the Vote was carried in these words: Resolved, "That a Bill be brought in to disable the duke of York to inherit the Imperial Crown of this Realm." The house divided, those for the Bill went out, and those within soon removed from their seats, and would not be counted, but yielded the question. And a committee was appointed to draw it up.

The Commons resolve to stand by the King with their Lives and Fortunes.] Resolved, nem. con. "That in defence of the King's Person, and the Protestant Religion, this house doth declare, That they will stand by his majesty with their Lives and Fortunes; and that, if his majesty shall come by any violent death (which God forbid!) that they will revenge it to the utmost upon the papists." And an Address was ordered to be drawn up accordingly.

* A phrase at chess, implying that the game is lost, by the king's being in such a situation, that he cannot move, without being taken.

May 15. The Exclusion bill was called for and read the first time. It set forth, after the particulars of the execrable Conspiracy, "That the emissaries, priests and agents for the pope, had traitorously seduced James duke of York, presumptive heir to these crowns, to the communion of the church of Rome; and had induced him to enter into several negotiations with the pope, his cardinals and nuncios, for promoting the Romish Church and interest; and by his means and procurement, had advanced the power and greatness of the French king, to the manifest hazard of these kingdoms. That by descent of these crowns upon a papist, and by foreign alliances and assistance, they might be able to succeed in their wicked and villainous designs." Then, after another Preamble, they enacted to this effect: 1. "That the said James, duke of York, should be incapable of inheriting the crowns of England, Scotland, and Ireland, with their dependencies; and of enjoying any of the titles, rights, prerogatives and revenues belonging to the said crowns. 2. That in case his majesty should happen to die, or resign his dominions, they should devolve to the person next in Succession, in the same manner as if the duke was dead. 3. That all acts of sovereignty and royalty that prince might then happen to perform, were not only declared void, but to be high-treason, and punishable as such. 4. That if any one, at any time whatsoever, should endeavour to bring the said duke into any of the fore-mentioned dominions, or correspond with him in order to make him inherit, he should be guilty of high treason. 5. That if the duke himself ever returned into any of these dominions, considering the mischiefs that must ensue, he should be looked upon as guilty of the same offence; and all persons were authorized and required, to seize upon and imprison him; and in case of resistance made by him or his adherents, to subdue them by force of arms."

May 21. The Bill was read a 2nd time. Upon which, the question being put, whether the Bill should be committed, the house divided, and the Yeas ordered to go forth, were 207, and the Noes who staid were but 128, the majority 79; and so the Bill was committed to a committee of the whole house: but the parliament being soon after prorogued, it proceeded no farther.

Debate on Money paid to Members by Sir Stephen Fox.] May 23. Sir *Francis Drake*. It is generally reported, that the last parliament had sold the nation; as if they came up to give Money to betray their public trust. I am of opinion that such were amongst us then. I would have the committee report what they are informed of it, though Bertie's book is not yet known.

Sir *John Holman*. If my name be there, I would have you know it.

Sir *Nich. Carew*. Though nothing can be got out of Mr. Bertie, yet the secret committee knows something. I know not how long we shall last; and I would have the world know it.

Mr. Sacheverell. The Committee will be able to produce several persons, who can prove Moneys paid. But you have a member within your walls, (if you will go to it in good earnest) that can discover to whom Money and Pensions were paid; and if he will not, he is not fit to be here. It is sir Stephen Fox, who, though he has delivered up the private Books, yet has several books that can discover it; his Ledger, and other books of Pensions, &c. before Bertie came in. I move you, that, if he will not give you an account, you will deal with him accordingly.

The house being informed of several sums of Money paid to some of the Members of the last parliament by sir Stephen Fox, and that he has Books of Accounts to evidence the same; ordered, "That he be immediately sent for to attend the house, and do bring with him all the Books, and Papers of Accounts, of any Money that he has paid to such Members, and others, for keeping public tables."

Sir Stephen Fox. 'I came but just now from my lodgings, by water, and I was told of the Order.' The Order was read to him. He proceeded, 'I know not whether I can do what you command me in any time. I have paid much Money for 'Secret Service,' but for these four years I have paid none. I have paid it as 'the King's Bounty,' and under such other titles, but not as 'Members of Parliament.' It is absolutely necessary that I have some time to peruse my Books.'

Mr. Williams. Your design is to have his Books, and you to judge whether the Pensions given, be 'the King's Bounty,' or to what other purpose.

Mr. Garroway. I would know, whether Fox kept the book of Secret Service apart, or mixed with other accounts. Formerly, when the Committee of Accounts was, sir Philip Warwick brought in 60,000*l.* pensions, and in a little book 'for Secret Service,' in one folio, there were fifty items of Money 'for Secret Service,' for members of the house.

Sir Stephen Fox. If your design be to know the Money 'for Secret Service,' I desire I may have time to ask leave, &c. When I was discharged, my Books were commanded from me.

Mr. Whorwood. I think it not fit that any person should ask leave to do his king and country service. I hope he will better consider of it. I hope this gentleman will be so ordered, that he must bring his Books hither. He has no dependence more upon that unfortunate person now under the obloquy of the nation.

Mr. Boscawen. Fox has acknowledged that he has such books. You have been told by a learned gentleman (Maynard) 'of corrupting the Fountain of Justice and Law.' If this place has been corrupted, it is God's great mercy that such a house had not delivered up the nation to arbitrary government. I will not stick to move you, if Fox will not do it, for a law to confiscate his estate, and to take off his head.

Sir Stephen Fox. This is an entire surprize to me. I have made a Book 'of Secret Service,' but I have delivered up my books; but I have other books. I was a great accountant, and this 'of Secret Service' is mixed with other accounts. What is meant is, time to ask leave to have those books I have delivered. It will give no satisfaction to the house to bring my Ledgers. They are great vast books. I desire that I may have time to ask leave to recover that book of 'Secret Service' I extracted out of the books. All that ever I paid in my life are in that book; but they are so intermixed, that you will have no satisfaction. What I desire, is leave. This, 'of Secret Service,' is of divers natures, and the Ledger is of several millions. That for Secret Service is mingled. When I delivered up my Books, that particularly 'of Secret Service' I delivered up likewise. I kept no transcript of the Account 'for Secret Service,' but it is within that Ledger. The Ledgers will not satisfy you, but if I can obtain leave, I will bring the Book, or extract of what is 'for Secret Service' out of the Ledger. It was my own care to keep an exact Account, to satisfy the master I serve. This was not an employment I desired. I never spoke, nor was adviser, but I was directly to issue out Money, as I was ordered. I hope to obtain leave to bring that book; but I would be understood that I have not that book.

Mr. Williams. Entries of Monies may be under disguised names, and so you are never the nearer. As for Fox, he fences with you; he is no Exchequer Officer, here are no footsteps of his payments. This is a cunning insinuation. Let him answer plainly, if the book he showed the king, be exactly what is entered into the Ledger Book?

Sir Stephen Fox. Nothing will satisfy the house but the Book 'of Secret Service;' the other is so mixed. I will endeavour to bring that book.

Mr. Garroway. Fox has given you a shifting answer, and no ways satisfactory. I would have his answer plainly, whether those in the Ledger be the same sums and circumstances?

Sir Nich. Carew. Ask Fox no more questions, but send some gentlemen to seize all his books and papers that he has, and to bring them hither.

Mr. Williams. If gentlemen will suppose this book to be with the rest, you may find it; but if in a dark and close hand, you will not find it. Ask him whether this book is in his hand, and let him declare it sincerely.

Sir Stephen Fox. This book lies not among my other books, but I delivered it up to lord Danby, but I will endeavour to bring this book. It lies in the king's closet, and I will obtain it, if I can; if not, I will bring you the best copy I can.—Being asked about the Acquittances, he answered, 'I certainly always took Acquittances, and they are with my books and papers at home.' I was not so careful as to enter the Receipts into books, but in loose papers. This business went on by degrees, 2 or 3000*l.* per ann. and I am not an accountant by law. But could I have foreseen so long an employment, I would have been more exact; but I have them in loose papers.

Sir *John Hotham.* Remember the place you are to go to (Whitehall) and make no Order to seize, nor search for Books or Papers, but take such as he will deliver to you. He knows your mind, and what is for your purpose; and if he will not deliver them, you may take an Order with him.

Mr. *Williams.* Whitehall may be a sanctuary for these concealments, but no place is sacred against your search. I would not have that pass for doctrine.

Sir *John Hotham.* If it be your Order to search, I will go as far in obeying it, as any man.

Mr. *Swynfin.* I would not use your power, till you have occasion for it. Spend no farther time, but let Hotham go.

Sir *John Hotham.* If Fox desire to speak with any body, or go from us, (in this nice point, I desire to understand you fully, and I will serve you fully,) whether are we to permit it, or not?

Sir *Stephen Fox.* My Cash-keeper and Book-keeper are gone to the Exchange; and if I am not so ready in it, you will excuse me, and have no ill thought of me, for I protest I never knew of this before.

Ordered, "That sir John Hotham, sir Rob. Peyton, and sir John Holman do accompany sir Stephen Fox to Whitehall, and that he do bring his Ledger Book, Cash Book, and Journal, and his Receipts for Money by him paid, 'for Secret Service;' and he is enjoined not to go out of the company of the said members, before they return to the house; and that no member do depart the service of this house, until sir Stephen Fox and the other members do return."

Report of the Committee appointed to seize sir S. Fox's Papers.] Sir John Hotham, and the rest, return from Whitehall, and report, That according to Order, they attended Fox to Whitehall. They were not half a quarter of an hour there, but Fox called his servants to bring such Books as they had in their custody, and sent for other servants that had the rest. Some great books were brought into the room; but whilst he sent for the Acquittances, the Lord Chamberlain (the earl of Arlington) came in, and spoke to Fox. Fox said, 'These gentlemen are some members of the house, and I shall not speak without their hearing.' My Lord Chamberlain said, 'I take notice that you are employed to search for Books and Papers, but you shall not take any away out of Whitehall.' I replied, 'some it seems, do make friends of the unrighteous Mammon.' Your lordship has quick information of what we came about, for our house-doors were shut.' My Lord Chamberlain saw the mistake, and would have debated some things, but I said, 'I was not sent to argue this, or that, but to obey my order.' (He had been so taught.) My Lord Chamberlain was very desirous to tell us why those Books were not to be taken out of Whitehall; but I said, 'let me have what your lordship would say in writing, and I will inform the house of it.' But what he said was, 'That he dared not consent that any Books should go out of Whitehall, without the king's orders, nor that we should inspect any Books, without the king's command.' I had forgot one thing that my Lord Chamberlain said, viz. 'I would not do any thing that should look like the displeasure of the house of commons; but I believe if the house address the king, they may have their desire.

Several moved, "That Fox should tell the house, upon his memory, when, and what Monies he had paid to Members of the former parliament, and if the house find that he omits any thing wilfully, that they will take an Order with him."

Sir *S. Fox.* I hope the house will not lay this upon me, that no man could have imposed upon me. It is so easy a way to ask the king's leave for the Books, that I hope you will take that way. What you desire to know is 4 years ago, and I cannot charge my memory with it.

Mr. *Sacheverell.* I hope he can remember to acquaint the house, what he told the committee. He has named some gentlemen of the last parliament, whom he has paid Money to.

Ordered, "That sir S. Fox do, upon his memory, name to the house such Members of the last parliament as he paid Money to, for Secret Service."

Mr. *Sacheverell.* I desire to know of him, during the time he paid Money 'for Secret Service,' whether he cannot remember a name? If he cannot, I can.

The *Speaker.* Who did you pay Money to, of the Members of the last Parliament, 'for Secret Service?'

Sir *S. Fox.* These are hard circumstances I am under, either to disobey the house, or to divulge a secret by the king's command. I can name so few persons, that it will give no satisfaction to the house. I named none but what the committee named to me, and my memory is not good enough to repeat it. It may be, the persons may have an action against me. Upon my memory I cannot tell who I paid Money to 'for Secret Service,' and who upon other accounts. I humbly pray, that I may not be put to answer.

Mr. *Williams.* They that will be ridden shall be ridden—You have been strangely used at Whitehall. Let him withdraw, and then you will consider what to do with him.

Sir *Rob. Howard.* The list of all the Members, is a way proposed to do your business. Will you not assist your own Order, by letting him have a list to help his memory? If it be so great a thing as you apprehend, let not Fox pick and chuse whom he will to accuse.

Mr. *Boscawen.* For Fox to be the first accuser seems hard. But let the clerk read the list of the names of the last parliament, and Fox will be careful to tell you no untruth in those he shall name to have received Money, and not forfeit his reputation.

The clerk was ordered to read the names of the Members, one by one, in the catalogue, beginning with the Speaker, &c. Fox charged Mr. Seymour, Speaker, at the end of every session to have received 1500*l.* as Sir Edward Turner had received before him.

Mr. *Seymour* somewhat affrontively answered, I would have Fox answer you, whether I received any Money before I was Speaker? In the presence of God I speak it, I never directly nor indirectly, disposed of any Money 'for Secret Service.' I told the king, 'That my fortune was not sufficient for that service (of Speaker,) and I was paid the Money out of the exchequer; but that was so troublesome, I desired it might be paid another way; and it was the only favour lord Danby ever did me, to let me receive it out of the Money appointed 'for Secret Service.'

Sir Stephen Fox names the Pensioners.] Sir *Stephen Fox.* Neither clerk nor agent of mine, to my knowledge, paid any to Seymour. I might have paid some to counterfeit names I did not know. I paid

1. Sir Charles Wheeler 400*l.* per ann. upon the account of Secret Service. 2. Sir Jonathan Trelawney 4 or 500*l.* per ann. upon account of being put out of the employment of the Excise. 3. Robert Roberts, esq. 500*l.* per ann. upon account of Secret Service. 4. Sir Philip Howard upon account of a Farm he had of the Excise, 4 or 500*l.* per ann. 5. Sir Courtney Poole 1000*l.* per ann. upon account of Secret Service. 6. Sir Rd. Wiseman 400*l.* per ann. as the king's bounty. 7. Tho. King esq. had some money, but I know not how much. 8. Thomas Price, esq. 400*l.* per ann. 9. Herbert Westphaling, esq. 200*l.* per ann. 10. Humphry Cornwall, esq. 200*l.* per ann. 11. Sir John Barnaby 200*l.* per ann. 12. Sir Lionel Walden upon account of a Farm of the Excise, 300*l.* per ann. 13. Daniel Collingwood, esq. upon the same account, 2 or 300*l.* per ann. 14. Somerset Fox, esq. had a Pension paid out of the exchequer, but what I cannot remember. 15. Sir Job Charlton had 1000*l.* pension whilst he was Speaker. 16. Mr. Knowles 200*l.* per ann. upon account of the Excise. 17. Robert Philips, esq. had 300*l.* per ann. upon the Excise. 18. Randolph Egerton, esq. 4 or 500*l.* per ann. upon the Excise. 19. Sir George Reeves had several sums of 500*l.* paid him at a time. 20. Sir Tho. Woodcock had 200*l.* per ann. out of the Excise. 21. Henry Clerk, esq. of Wiltshire, ever since he was out of the prize commission, 400*l.* per ann. 22. Sir John Talbot 500*l.* per ann. upon account of 'Secret Service,' paid out of the Excise. 23. Sir Philip Monckton 300*l.* Pension out of the Excise. 24. Sir Gilbert Gerrard 300*l.* per ann. on account of his Farm in the Excise. 25. Mr. William Robinson 200*l.* per ann. 26. Mr. Edw. Progers 400*l.* per ann. 27. Col. Roger Whitley 300*l.* per. ann. on account of a Farm in the Excise *.

Report from the Committee of Secrecy relative to Money given to Members.] May 24. Sir Francis Winnington reports, from the Committee of Secrecy, Money given to Members of the Last Parliament, for Secret Service. "I have brought every particular information, and you shall see whether your members have any wrong. There was 20,000*l.* per ann. paid quarterly by the Commissioners of Excise, for Secret Service, to members, &c. mostly by Mr. Bertie, whereof no account was given to the Exchequer, but 'for Secret Service.' Bertie was examined at the committee, whether he paid any of the 20,000*l.* to members of parliament. He answered, 'That he had a privy seal to pay it without account, and he was not at liberty to tell how he disposed of the money, till he had the king's command.' Next, though sir Stephen Fox has taken a great deal of matter out of my hands, yet, there are some more than he has acquainted you with, who have received Money, viz. to sir Rd. Wiseman, and one Knight, which Wiseman paid, by a false name, each of them 400*l.* per ann. Mr. Roberts, at one or two payments, 500*l.* and Mr. Price 400*l.* Sir John Fowell at twice had 500*l.* of Fox. Poole, Talbot, and Wheeler, as before. Now that I have summed up the substance of other evidence from payments in Danby's time, there came in tallies of 20,000*l.* per annum, 'for Secret Service,' out of the Excise. Major Huntington and sir John James paid the money. Sometimes the money was paid before the quarter-day, and when tallies were struck, papers were delivered back. A Book of Names there was, to whom money was paid; and Bertie had an agent, who says, 'That after the Treasurer was impeached, about the 24th Dec. Bertie came in great haste to him for that Book with all Letters and Acquittances, and that book has many false names in it. And if he saw the book, he could tell what members were concerned, and under what head he stands.' The Book of 20,000*l.* was increased by Danby in his time, for formerly it was not above 12,000*l* per ann. for Pensions. Farther, there was paid out of the Exchequer for Mr. Chiffins, who delivered about a 100 Acquittances to Bertie. Before the parliament did sit, there were greater sums paid, than at other times. The Paper the Committee took, &c. mentions other persons. Sir Joseph Tredenham had 500*l.* per ann. and Mr. Piercy Goring 300*l.* per ann. Sir Rob. Holt had several sums to maintain him in prison. Sir Wm. Glascott, and sir John Bramstone had several sums, but we could not discover the particulars. Wiseman, King, and Trelawney offered to sell their Pensions to the Commissioners of Excise, and did pretend, that they might have money before-hand, and the commissioners had a discount of 12 per cent."

* The above list is given by Mr. Grey. It is not inserted in the Journal.

Ordered, "That sir Rd. Wiseman and Mr. Knight be immediately sent for to attend this house."

Debate thereon.] Sir *Tho. Clarges.* I move, that persons who have received any Money the last parliament, may be incapable of any trust in the government, and refund what they have had.

Sir *Fr. Winnington.* I found several witnesses very willing to make discoveries, but in reality they were threatened. I move, that there may be some way, or method, to know the bottom of this; whether you will call witnesses to the bar, or to the committee. Apply your remedy, when you know the disease. I do say, that if any man takes Money to sell his country, I would use the utmost power of punishment, that parliaments may not be lost.

Mr. *Bennet.* Here is good evidence against Mr. Bertie. If you have no farther account of this matter, proceed upon him. If you get the Book out of him, you have all. If not, make an example of him, and you will have the rest.

Sir *John Trevor.* If these Papers be left in the clerk's hand, a superior power may command them from him; therefore let them be in the hands of the chairman.

Sir *Fr. Winnington.* I would not be used as sir Edmundbury Godfrey was, whilst I have such Papers about me, as I have reported. Really, I believe the Papers are of that nature, that they ought to be in the custody of the house, and let the Speaker keep them.

Mr. *Garroway.* Enter them upon your Books, and they will be as safe as all the rest of your transactions.

Sir *Joseph Tredenham.* I move that they may not be entered upon your Books, till gentlemen that are named have justified themselves. If you will enter upon their justification, I will now proceed to my own.

Mr. *Boscawen.* According to my observation, the Order of the house is, that immediately they be heard; and, in justice, do not enter it into the Journal till they be heard.

Sir *Tho. Meres.* Your question is, Whether the Papers shall be entered; but if these gentlemen named think the entry will be detrimental to them, it is but reasonable that they should be heard.

Sir *Fr. Winnington.* There are very honourable persons named. Some say 'enter the Papers.' But it is one of the hardest things in the world for a man to have papers entered upon him; it is a kind of passing judgment. The Votes will be sent all England over. Suppose those gentlemen of honour and quality vindicate themselves, you will tear your Book sure, and not suffer them to be upon Record.

Lord *Cavendish.* It will be no hardship upon them to have the Papers entered, for if they justify themselves, their innocence will be entered too.

Col. *Titus.* It is no crime at all to have money, nor pension, but to have it for an ill use. Therefore let every member concerned be heard in his place. He may justify himself.

Mr. *Garroway.* I am not against entering the Report. But before you give your judgment, hear your members in their place. This is parliamentary; and then they are to withdraw, and you judge whether you will acquit, or condemn them.

Sir *John Talbot.* I confess to you, I am afraid what I shall say always, but more now I am in confusion, and shall speak my thoughts very indigestedly. I beg I may speak more than once if I have occasion. This is a great crime of betraying a trust: though this day I am more unfortunate to be in suspicion. But I desire I may be distinguished when I know the integrity of my own heart. Yesterday this was mentioned, &c. and is got about the town, and my reputation is exposed to censure. Let every man lay his hand upon his heart. I say, with great assurance, that directly or indirectly I never took one shilling as a gift, or begging, from the time the king came in. I do disown any thing by way of 'Secret Service' to influence my vote here. I will submit myself to the censure of the law, to be tried by that law. I will submit it to any judicial way of proceeding. Give me leave to open this matter to you. I desire to justify myself, and to live no longer than I can do it. Some gentlemen, besides those, have been mentioned, their number not great. When the act passed for the Excise to be made a Revenue, when the king came in, it was thought an advantage to the Revenue, and ease to the country, for gentlemen to manage the Excise. For that clause was put into the act, to impower the king to let it for three years, that such contracts might be good in law, and another shall not proceed, but such as is recommended at the quarter sessions, and be shall have the refusal, and not to be let under the rate he refused it at. When the rate was put, we had the refusal, and this was my case: I paid the rent. At last lord Clifford, when the Farm was just going out, made a private contract, without our knowledge, and disposed of all those Farms to four or five other persons, without our knowledge. I will not censure lord Clifford, but I will say this, that the king's Revenue never was kept up, till it was in that method again. One of the farmers told me, 'That the Treasurer made a contract to other persons, and let us go, and offered 10,000*l.* a year more than they were to give, and advanced it at 6*l.* per cent. and no more, and so made the proposition better.' But he told us, the king was resolved, and wanted Money. (I think about this time the Triple League was broke.) I said to lord Clifford, 'That no man will turn out a tenant that pays his rent well: I hope the king will be no worse than other men.' Lord Clifford replied, 'The king intends not to use you ill, that have served him and his father well.' Upon this the king said, 'He would not put us upon hardships, but we should have some consideration for our Farm.' I appeal to sir Stephen Fox, whether I am not in the list of names of those to whom the king intended to give compensation for their Farms taken out of their hands; and I appeal to him, whether I had not the Pension under that consideration. But had it been a gift, or grant, and not under any consideration whatsoever, the king has employed me in several trusts; if I have changed my principles, or been guilty of the practices of any immorality, I beg that consideration, not to be exposed to that cruelty, not to be exposed to public censure.

Col. *Whitley.* I am one under that unfortunate list of Pensions. I was one of those in the recommendation of the country, for the farming the Excise. I had a covenant of 10,000*l.* from Dashwood not to supplant me. We fell into suit, and at last into an award, and till such time I never touched a penny of the money. I had in all 900*l.* which I received at several times. This is the true state of the case. If I did betray my country, I am not only fit to be turned out of the house, but out of the world. I have had money a long time due to me, and can get none of it. Be pleased to examine what relates to me as publickly as you please.

Sir *Stephen Fox.* I did distinguish carefully, of the lists of persons lately concerned in farming, &c. and in it, several members had pensions; and some had that were not members. Talbot was careful in expressing the reason in the receipt of the money. He would not receive it till he had it entire, and then received it, as a person lately concerned in the Excise.

Sir *Philip Howard.* If my case be distinct from others, I hope I shall be so judged. I am one of those to be considered under the head of 'Farmers of the Excise;' and I desire I may come under the head of those who came in upon a valuable consideration.

Mr. *Harbord.* This may well admit of a distinction, but not till you have farther heard the matter. If you find that the king's bounty went to one sort of parliament-men, and not to another, you may guess by that, for I could in the last parliament have told you how the question would go. If a pensioner went not well, slash he was put out of his pension.

Sir *Joseph Tredenham.* A Pension to betray one's country is a detestable thing to receive by any body, and I do utterly deny to have received any. I had the honour of the favour of my prince, and I had his favour when I made application for it. Avarice was never my humour. A gentleman having a small government called Cheade Castle, which lay nearer me, upon a reversionary patent, I was put upon it to get him to resign his government. He had 250*l.* and 250*l.* for quitting that Castle. I have had the honour here to be a zealous asserter of the Protestant religion, and in the country so too. As for my vote here, I gave it for Money, that the king should not supply his necessity by extraordinary means.

Sir *Fr. Winnington.* As for what Tredenham says of the nature of the Secret Committee, he need not reflect on the secret committee, but that it borders upon 'secret service,' I have heard that Tredenham has reported, 'That because he defended the duke of Lauderdale, I would be revenged of him.' As for this Castle, &c. when I was Solicitor General I passed a warrant, &c. but I appeal to him whether he told me of the 500*l.*? because he has given some sparring blows towards me, I desire he may name the person.

Sir *Joseph Tredenham.* I desire that grace for my passion which I must allow for others. This putting me in the van of the Report of these gentlemen, does look like something of pointing at me. I have had considerable places offered me, but I would not have gentlemen turned out for me. As for this of Lauderdale, it is but a hearsay.

Sir *Fr. Winnington.* He dwindles this of Lauderdale to a flying report. There are thirty before him in the list, but had he been last you would have found him out.

Mr. *Harbord.* This is a hardship, that a private person should use one so, that has done you service. If Tredenham got a castle one way, Winnington lost one of the best places in England, (Solicitor General,) for doing his duty here, and I hope God will reward him.

Sir *Henry Capel.* It is no wonder, if the Committee of Secrecy go new ways to work, (as Tredenham alleged,) you must consider that never such new things were done before. Winnington has most dexterously and prudently made enquiry into this matter of the Pensioners, and it becomes you to be very severe to any man that makes such reflections. [Many called Tredenham to the Bar.]

Sir *Tho. Clarges.* What need you call for proof? Tredenham has confessed 'That he had 500*l.* to enable him to buy a Castle.' He called to Winnington, 'Prove it, prove it,' very peremptorily, and you ought to censure him.

Sir *Joseph Tredenham.* I beg pardon for being too ready to give credit to a report, but when I consider the smallness of this matter of the Castle, which I did buy only for convenience of the situation near my estate, I submit to your censure, and beg your pardon. Pray consider how difficult it is for me to speak, I have had no time to prepare myself.

Sir Richard Wiseman at the bar.

The *Speaker.* The house is informed that you have disposed of several Pensions, of four times 400*l.* per ann. From whom did you receive the Money, and to whom did you pay it, and for what use?

Sir *R. Wiseman.* Those I received and paid I will give an account of in writing. I never employed it for a Mr. Knight, nor received it for Mr. Knight. I know one Knight, sir John Knight's son; when I saw him last, he was of the Temple; he had no transactions in the Money. I named him, because you, Mr. Speaker, named him.

The *Speaker*. Not long since, in the last session of parliament, you kept a good table; of whom had you the money to maintain it?

Wiseman. My Tenants gave me my money to keep my Table. I had no money from sir Stephen Fox, nor Mr. Bertie, nor by his order; nor from Mr. Chifinch, nor by his order. [This he spoke rudely and surlily. The Speaker asking him, 'Whether he had no Money for keeping a Table but from his tenants?' in a very preremptory manner he answered, 'No.' —He withdrew.

Sir *Tho. Lee*. This answer of Wiseman, and the manner of it, is not usual. If you allow this to any may at the bar, to give what he is asked in writing, you will lose your authority, and make an ill example for the future. If once you be put off with writing Answers to your questions at the bar, he will have counsel. You must tell him, 'He contemns the commons of England, if he makes no Answers to the questions you ask him."

Wiseman again at the Bar.

The *Speaker*. The house is not satisfied that you shall give your Answer in writing. They require a direct Answer from you to what questions they shall ask you; I ask you, what annuity or pension you have received upon your account from the Excise, or any other person, for your particular use?

Wiseman. If I might have ever so much, I cannot tell you. I ask but a reasonable thing, to give my Answer in writing, and I will justify it by witnesses, and authentic testimony. But to a thing I am not prepared to answer, my reputation will be lost without reparation. I say not, I will not answer, but I will make a reasonable Answer, like a reasonable man.

To the Speaker's Questions.—*Answ.* I remember no sum whatsoever. I have received Money from the Excise, by a letter from Mr. Bertie. The last sum I received was five or six years ago. I cannot remember how much any of the sums were.

The *Speaker*. Did not you receive money in the name of a knight, or for one Mr. Knight? —*Answ.* I received none of the king's money, for any other person, I aver it. I appointed nobody to do it. I never gave any money to pay bills for housekeeping, I stand upon it. —He withdrew.

Sir *Stephen Fox*. I did say Wiseman received 400*l.* per ann. from me, till Michaelmas 1675, and I did so at the committee. I said I could give no answer to Knight, but Wiseman could, and for him 400*l.* per ann. was paid, and three other persons more. I charge not Wiseman with receiving this always, but some of it to him I never failed to pay.

Wiseman again at the bar.

The *Speaker*. You have had time given you to consider the questions proposed. The house does expect a more direct Answer. This does so nearly concern you, that they expect you provided to give an answer, and therefore have sent for you down again, before they give their judgment.

Wiseman. I received no money from sir Stephen Fox, and I know nothing of 'secret service' received by the king's order. Give me time, and I will tell you the exact sums I received.

The *Speaker*. In this you are disproved by Fox, and if you will run the hazard of the displeasure of the house, you must expect what will follow.

Wiseman. I have told you, I remember not to have received 400*l.* per ann. from Fox. I cannot remember other sums. I persist in it. none by the king's order. So far as I am able, on the sudden, I will give you an account. When the Excise was let by lord Clifford, it was for 500,000*l.* per ann. Some friends put me upon it to farm the Excise. We gave 20,000*l.* per annum more, and 70,000*l.* advance money, for which service the king directed I should receive some money, but I remember not the particulars; there was but one contract. I acted by another party. I cannot tell whom. I do now remember the man, it was alderman Ford. I know not whether I received 7, 8, or 900*l.*

The *Speaker*. Did you receive any money from Mr. Bertie?

Wiseman stood mute some time, and then answered, 'I have not received any money from Mr. Bertie this year and a half. I had no order for continuance of my Pension out of the excise. That which the king gave me was annual, but I received it in a gross sum. I sold the annual pension the king gave me for 7, 8, or 900*l.* The pension was not granted me for life, but till the king declared otherwise. The assignment of the pension was made to the commissioners, or farmers; I believe it was assigned to major Huntington, Mr. Dawson, and sir John James.' This he spoke drawningly, and withdrew. The further consideration of the Report was adjourned to the 27th.

The Habeas Corpus Act passed.] May 26. Sir Robert Clayton was just giving an account of members who had Pensions out of the excise, upon consideration of their farms, when the black rod knocked at the door, and commanded the house to attend the king in the house of lords, where his majesty passed the Habeas Corpus Bill.*

* "The great, essential, and inestimable service done to the people of England, by this parliament, was in perfecting the Habeas Corpus Bill; which had been so long in agitation, and by which many wholsome provisions were made, to preserve the liberty of the subject from the invasions of the prerogative. Abuse of power, and the prevention of such abuses for the future, are the causes assigned in the preamble of the Bill for the enacting clauses it is composed of: The most material of which are, 1. To oblige all sheriffs, gaolers, ministers, or others, when served with a writ of Habeas Corpus, to obey it, within 3 days after the said service, by carrying up the body of the person therein named to the court, or judge, by whom

The Parliament dissolved.] After passing the said Bill, his majesty made this short speech to both houses:

"My lords and gentlemen; I was in great hopes that this session would have produced great good to the kingdom, and that it would have gone on unanimously for the good thereof. But to my great grief, I see there are such differences between the two houses, that I am afraid very ill effects will come of them. I know but one way of remedy for the present, assuring you, that, in the mean time, I shall show my sincerity with the same zeal I met you here. Therefore, my lord chancellor, I command you to do as I ordered you."

His lordship accordingly prorogued the parliament to the 14th of August. But before that day, it was dissolved by proclamation *.

the said writ was granted; and before him to certify the true causes of his detainer and imprisonment, on the penalty of 100*l.* for the first offence, and 200*l.* and to be made incapable of holding his office, for the second: As also, under the like penalties, to grant the prisoner a true copy of the warrant of commitment and detainer, within six hours after demand. 2. To provide that no person shall be re-committed, for the same offence, after being enlarged by order of court, on the penalty of 500*l.* Also, 3. That if any judge, either in term-time, or vacation, refused any prisoner their Habeas Corpus, upon application, he should forfeit 500*l.* to the said prisoner. And 4. That no subject of this realm should be any longer liable to illegal imprisonments, in prisons beyond the seas.—Ferguson in his 'Growth of Popery,' with some bitterness, affirms, that this Bill met with great opposition from the lords; that it gave rise to several conferences between the two houses; and that, though it was far short of what it ought to have been, it was almost a miracle that their lordships suffered it to pass at all: And so much of truth there is in these assertions, that the committees of the two houses met several times upon it, without coming to any agreement; insomuch that the completing of the Bill was put off to the last hour of the sessions; and, even then, the commons were glad to admit of the lords' Amendments, that they might have the merit, and their fellow-subjects the benefit, of so useful a law." Ralph.

* Shortly after the Dissolution a singular pamphlet made its appearance, intitled, 'An Appeal from the Country to the City, for the preservation of his majesty's Person, Liberty, Property, and the Protestant Religion.' For a copy of it see Appendix No. IX.

"The impeachment of the five popish lords in the Tower, with that of the earl of Danby, was carried on with vigour. The power of this minister, and his credit with the king, rendered him extremely obnoxious to the popular leaders; and the commons hoped that, if he were pushed to extremity, he would be obliged, in order to justify his own conduct, to lay open the whole intrigue of the French alliance, which they suspected to contain a secret of the most dangerous nature. The king, on his part, apprehensive of the same consequences, and desirous to protect his minister, who was become criminal merely by obeying orders, employed his whole interest to support

PRINCIPAL OCCURRENCES AFTER THE DISSOLUTION—STATE OF THE MINISTRY—MEAL-TUB PLOT—WHIG AND TORY.

"The general affection," says Mr. Hume, "borne the king, appeared signally about this time. He fell sick at Windsor; and had two or three fits of a fever, so violent as made his life be thought in danger. A general consternation seized all ranks of men, increased by the apprehensions entertained of his successor. In the present disposition of men's minds, the king's death, to use an expression of sir William Temple, was regarded as the end of the world. The mal-contents, it was feared, would proceed to extremities, and immediately kindle a civil war in the kingdom. Either their entire success, or entire failure, or even the balance and contest of parties, seemed all of them events equally fatal. The king's chief counsellors therefore, Essex, Halifax, and Sunderland, who stood on bad terms with Shaftesbury and the popular party, advised him to send secretly for the duke, that, in case of any sinister accident, that prince might be ready to assert his right against the opposition which he was likely to meet with. When the duke arrived, he found his brother out of danger; and it was agreed to conceal the invitation which he had received. (2d Sept.) His journey, however, was attended with important consequences. He prevailed on the king to disgrace Monmouth, whose projects were now known and avowed; to deprive him of his command in the army; and to send him beyond sea. He himself returned to Brussels; but made a short stay in that place. He obtained leave to retire to Scotland, under pretence still of quieting the apprehensions of the English nation; but in reality with a view of securing that kingdom in his interests. Though Essex and Halifax had concurred in the resolution of inviting over the duke, they soon found that they had not obtained his confidence, and that even the king, while he made use of their service, had no sincere regard for their persons. Essex in disgust resigned the treasury: Halifax retired to his country seat: Temple, despairing of any accommodation among such enraged parties, withdrew almost entirely to his books and his gardens. The king, who changed ministers as well as measures with great indifference, bestowed at this time the chief confidence on Hyde, Sunderland, and Godolphin. Hyde succeeded Essex in the treasury. All the king's ministers, as well as himself, were extremely averse to the meeting of the new parliament, which they expected to find as refractory as any of the preceding. The elections had gone mostly in favour of the country party. The terrors of the plot had still a mighty influence over the populace; and the apprehensions of the duke's bigoted principles and arbitrary character weighed with men of sense and reflection. The king therefore resolved to prorogue the parliament, that he might try, whether time might allay those humours, which, by every other expedient, he had in vain attempted to mollify. In this measure he did not expect the concurrence of his council. He knew that those popular leaders, whom he had admitted, would zealously oppose a resolution, which disconcerted all their schemes; and that the royalists would not dare, by supporting it, to expose themselves to the vengeance of the parliament, when it should be assembled. These reasons obliged him to take this step entirely of himself; and he only declared his resolution in council. It is remarkable, that, though the king had made profession never to embrace any measure without the advice of these counsellors, he had often broken that resolution, and had been necessitated, in affairs of the greatest consequence, to control their opinion. Many of them in disgust threw up about this time; particularly lord Russel, the most popular man in the nation, as well from the mildness and integrity of his character, as from his zealous attachment to the religion and liberties of his country. Though carried into some excesses, his intentions were ever esteemed upright; and being heir to the greatest fortune in the kingdom, as well as void of ambition, men believed that nothing but the last necessity could ever engage him to embrace any desperate measures. Shaftesbury, who was, in most particulars, of an opposite character, was removed by the king from the office of president of the council; and the earl of Radnor, a man who possessed whimsical talents and splenetic virtues, was substituted in his place. It was the

the validity of that pardon which had been granted him. The lords appointed a day for the examination of the question, and agreed to hear council on both sides: But the commons would not submit their pretensions to the discussion of argument and inquiry. They voted, that whoever should presume, without their leave, to maintain before the house of peers the validity of Danby's pardon, should be accounted a betrayer of the liberties of the English commons. And they made a demand, that the bishops, whom they knew to be devoted to the court, should be removed, not only when the trial of the earl should commence, but also when the validity of his pardon should be discussed. The bishops before the reformation had always enjoyed a seat in parliament: but so far were they anciently from regarding that dignity as a privilege, that they affected rather to form a separate order in the state, independent of the civil magistrate, and accountable only to the pope and to their own order. By the constitutions, however, of Clarendon, enacted during the reign of Henry ii. they were obliged to give their presence in parliament; but as the canon law prohibited them from assisting in capital trials, they were allowed in such cases the privilege of absenting themselves. A practice, which was at first voluntary, became afterwards a rule; and on the earl of Strafford's trial, the bishops, who would gladly have attended, and who were no longer bound by the canon law, were yet obliged to withdraw. It had been usual for them to enter a protest, asserting their right to sit; and this protest, being considered as a mere form, was always admitted and disregarded. But here was started a new question of no small importance. The commons, who were now enabled, by the violence of the people and the necessities of the crown, to make new acquisitions of powers and privileges, insisted that the bishops had no more title to vote in the question of the earl's pardon than in the impeachment itself. The bishops asserted that the pardon was merely a preliminary; and that, neither by the canon law nor the practice of parliament, were they ever obliged, in capital cases, to withdraw till the very commencement of the trial itself. If their absence was considered as a privilege, which was its real origin, it depended on their own choice, how far they would insist upon it. If regarded as a diminution of their right of peerage, such unfavourable customs ought never to be extended beyond the very circumstance established by them; and all arguments from a pretended parity of reason, were in that case of little or no authority. The house of lords were so much influenced by these reasons, that they admitted the bishops' right to vote, when the validity of the pardon should be examined. The commons insisted still on their withdrawing; and thus a quarrel being commenced between the two houses, the king, who expected nothing but fresh instances of violence from this parliament, began to entertain thoughts of laying hold of so favourable a pretence, and of finishing the session by a prorogation. While in this disposition, he was alarmed with sudden intelligence, that the house of commons was preparing a remonstrance, in order to inflame the nation still farther upon the favourite topics of the plot and of popery (27th May). He hastened, therefore, to execute his intention, even without consulting his new council, by whose advice he had promised to regulate his whole conduct. And thus were disappointed all the projects of the malcontents, who were extremely enraged at this vigorous measure of the king's. Shaftesbury publicly threatened that he would have the head of whoever had advised it. The parliament was soon after dissolved without advice of council; and writs were issued for a new parliament (10th July). The king was willing to try every means which gave a prospect of more compliance in his subjects; and in case of failure, the blame, he hoped, would lie on those whose obstinacy forced him to extremities." Hume.

favour and countenance of the parliament, which had chiefly encouraged the rumour of plots; but the nation had gotten so much into that vein of credulity, and every necessitous villain was so much incited by the success of Oates and Bedloe, that, even during the prorogation, the people were not allowed to remain in tranquillity. There was one Dangerfield, a fellow who had been burned in the hand for crimes, transported, whipped, pilloried four times, fined for cheats, out-lawed for felony, convicted of coining, and exposed to all the public infamy which the laws could inflict on the basest and most shameful enormities. The credulity of the people, and the humour of the times, enabled even this man to become a person of consequence. He was the author of a new incident, called the Meal-tub Plot, from the place where some papers, relating to it, were found. The bottom of this affair it is difficult, and not very material, to discover. It only appears, that Dangerfield, under pretence of betraying the conspiracies of the presbyterians, had been countenanced by some catholics of condition, and had even been admitted to the duke's presence and the king's: and that, under pretence of revealing new popish plots, he had obtained access to Shaftesbury, and some of the popular leaders. Which side he intended to cheat, is uncertain; or whether he did not rather mean to cheat both: but he soon found that the belief of the nation was more open to a popish than a presbyterian plot; and he resolved to strike in with the prevailing humour. Though no weight could be laid on his testimony, great clamour was raised; as if the court, by way of retaliation, had intended to load the presbyterians with the guilt of a false conspiracy. It must be confessed that the present period, by the prevalence and suspicion of such mean and ignoble arts on all sides, throws a great stain on the British annals. One of the most innocent artifices practised by party men at this time, was the additional ceremony, pomp and expence, with which a pope-burning was celebrated in London: (17th Nov.) The spectacle served to entertain, amuse, and inflame, the populace. The duke of Monmouth likewise came over without leave, and made a triumphant procession through many parts of the kingdom, extremely caressed and admired by the people. All these arts seemed requisite to support the general prejudices, during the long interval of parliament. Great endeavours were also used to obtain the king's consent for the meeting of that assembly. (1680.) Seventeen peers presented a petition to this purpose. Many of the corporations imitated the example. Notwithstanding several marks of displeasure, and even a menacing proclamation from the king, petitions came from all parts, earnestly insisting on a session of parliament. The danger of popery, and the terrors of the plot, were never forgotten in any of these addresses. Tumultuous petitioning was one of the chief artifices by which the malcontents in the last reign had attacked the crown: and though the manner of subscribing and delivering petitions was now somewhat regulated by act of parliament, the thing itself still remained; and was an admirable expedient for infesting the court, for spreading discontent, and for uniting the nation in any popular clamour. As the king found no law, by which he could punish those importunate, and, as he deemed them, undutiful solicitations, he was obliged to encounter them by popular applications of a contrary tendency. Wherever the church and court party prevailed, addresses were framed, containing expressions of the highest regard to his majesty, the most entire acquiescence in his wisdom, the most dutiful submission to his prerogative, and the deepest abhorrence of those who endeavoured to encroach upon it, by prescribing to him any time for assembling the parliament. Thus the nation came to be distinguished into Petitioners and Abhorrers. Factions indeed were at this time extremely animated against each other. The very names, by which each party denominated its antagonist, discover the virulence and rancour which prevailed. For besides petitioner and abhorrer, appellations which were soon forgotten, this year is remarkable for being the epoch of the well-known epithets of Whig and Tory, by which, and sometimes without any material difference, this island has been so long divided. The court party reproached their antagonists with their affinity to the fanatical conventiclers in Scotland, who were known by the name of Whigs: the country party found a resemblance between the courtiers and the popish banditti in Ireland, to whom the appellation of Tory was affixed. And after this manner, these foolish terms of reproach came into public and general use; and even at present seem not nearer their end than when they were first invented.—' As the kingdom was regularly and openly divided into two zealous parties, it was not difficult for the king to know, that the majority of the new house of commons was engaged in interests opposite to the court: but that he might leave no expedient untried, which could compose the unhappy differences among his subjects, he resolved at last, after a very long interval, to assemble the Parliament."

FIRST SESSION OF THE FOURTH PARLIAMENT OF KING CHARLES II.

List of the House of Commons.] October 7, 1679. The New Parliament met, but was prorogued to the 17th, and then was adjourned to the 30th. At last, after seven more prorogations, they met for the dispatch of business on the 21st of Oct. 1680. The following is a List of the Members of the House of Commons:

A LIST OF THE HOUSE OF COMMONS, IN KING CHARLES THE SECOND'S FOURTH PARLIAMENT, WHICH MET OCTOBER 21, 1680.

Abington,	*Agmondesham,*
Sir John Stonehouse.	Sir Roger Hill,

Sir William Drake.
St. Albans,
Thomas Pope Blount,
Samuel Grimstone.
Aldborough, (Suffolk)
John Bence,
John Corrance.
Aldborough, (Yorkshire)
Sir Godfrey Copely,
Sir B. Stapleton.
Allerton, North,
Sir Gilbert Gerrard,
Sir Henry Calverly.
Andover,
Francis Powlet,
Sir Robert Henley.
Anglesea,
Richard Bulkley.
Appelby,
Richard Tufton,
Anthony Lowther.
Arundel,
William Garraway,
James Butler.
Ashburton,
Thomas Raynell,
Richard Duke.
Aylsbury,
Sir Richard Ingolsby,
Sir Thomas Lee.
Bambury,
Sir John Holman.
Barnstaple,
Richard Lee.
John Basset.
Bath City,
Sir William Basset,
Sir George Speke.
Beaumaris,
Henry Bulkley.
Bedfordshire,
William Lord Russel,
Sir Humphry Monoux.
Bedford Town,
Sir William Franklyn,
Pawlet St. John.
Bedwin,
William Finch,
Francis Stonehouse.
Berkshire,
William Barker,
Richard Southbey.
Berwick,
John Rushworth,
Sir Ralph Grey.
Beverly,
Michael Wharton,
Sir John Hotham.
Bewdley,
Philip Foley.
Bishops Castle,
Richard Scriven.
Edmund Waring.
Bletchingly,
George Evelyn,
John Morris.
Bodmin,
Nicholas Glynn,
Hender. Roberts.
Boralston,
Sir William Bastard,
Sir John Trevor.
Boroughbridge,
Sir Thomas Meleverer,
Sir John Brooke.
Bossiny,
Charles Bodvile Roberts,
Narcissus Lutterel.
Boston,
Sir Anthony Irby,
Sir William York.
Brackley,
Richard Wenham,
Sir Wm. Egerton.
Bramber,
Henry Sidney,
Henry Goring.
Brecon County,
R. Williams.
Brecon Town,
John Jefferys.
Bridgwater,
Sir Haswel Tynt,
Ralph Stawell.
Bridport,
Sir Robert Henley,
William Bragge.
Bristol,
Sir Robert Cann,
John Knight.
Bridgenorth,
Sir Thomas Whitmore,
Sir Will. Whitmore
Buckinghamshire,
Thomas Wharton,
John Hampden.
Buckingham Town,
Lord Latimer,
Sir Richard Temple.
Calne,
Sir George Hungerford,
Lionel Ducket.
Cambridgeshire,
Sir Levinus Bennet,
Sir Robert Cotton.
Cambridge Town,
Lord Arlington,
Sir Tho. Chichley.
Cambridge University,
Sir Thomas Exton,
Sir W. Temple.
Camelford,
Sir James Smith,
Robert Russel.
Canterbury,
Edward Hales,
Sir Thomas Hardress.
Cardiffe.
Sir Robert Thomas.
Cardigan County,
Edward Vaughan.
Cardigan Town,
Hector Philips.
Carlisle,
Sir Philip Howard,
Sir Christ. Musgrave.
Caermarthen County,
Lord Vaughan.
Caermarthen Town,
Altham Vaughan.
Caernarvon County,
Thomas Bulkley.
Caernarvon Town,
Thomas Moystin.
Castle-rising,
Sir Robert Howard,
James Hoste.
Chester County,
Henry Booth,
Sir Robert Cotton.
Chester City,
William Williams,
Sir Thomas Grosvenor.
Chichester,
Richard Farrington,
John Bramen.
Chippenham,
Samuel Ash,
Sir Edward Hungerford.
Chipping Wycombe,
Thomas Lewis,
Sir John Borlace.
Christ Church,
Sir Thomas Clarges,
George Fulford.
Cirencester,
Henry Powle,
Sir Robert Atkins.
Clifton,
John Upton,
Edward Yard.
Clithero,
Sir Thomas Stringer,
Sir Ralph Ashton.
Cockermouth,
Sir Richard Graham,
Orlando Gee.
Colchester,
Sir Walter Clarges,
Sir Harbottle Grimstone.
Corf-castle,
Nathaniel Bond,
Sir Nathan Naper.
Cornwall,
Francis Roberts,
Sir Richard Edgecomb.
Coventry,
John Stratford,
Richard Hopkins.
Cricklade,
Edmund Webb,
Hungerford Dunch.
Cumberland,
Sir John Lowther,
Edw. Lord Morpeth.
Denbighshire,
Sir Thomas Middleton.
Denbigh Town,
Sir John Salisbury,
Derbyshire,
William Sacheverell,
Lord Cavendish,
Derby Town,
Anchitel Grey,
George Vernon.
Devizes,
Sir Giles Hungerford,
John Eyles.
Devonshire,
Sir William Courtney,
Samuel Rolle.
Dorchester,
James Gould,
Nicholas Gould.
Dorsetshire,
Thomas Strangeways,
Thomas Freak.
Dover,
William Stokes,
Thomas Papillon.
Downton,
Maurice Blockland,
Sir Joseph Ash.
Droitwich,
Samuel Sandys, jun.
Henry Coventry.
Dunwich,
Sir Philip Shippon,
Sir Robert Kemp.
Durham County,
Tho. Fetherston Hough,
William Bowes.
Durham City,
Sir Richard Lloyd,
William Blakeston.
East Low,
Sir Jon. Trelawny,
Henry Seymour.
Edmunds Bury,
Sir Thomas Harvey,
Thomas Germyn.
Essex,
John Lemot Honeywood,
Henry Mildmay.
Evesham,
Henry Parker,
Sir James Rushout.
Exeter,
William Glyde,
Malachi Pyne.
Eye,
Charles Fox,
George Walch.
Flintshire,
Mutton Davies.
Flint Town,
Roger Whitley.
Fowey,
John Trefry,
Jon. Rashleigh.
Gatton,
Sir Nicholas Carew,
Thomas Turgis.
Germain's,
Richard Elliot,
Daniel Elliot.
Glamorgan,
Bussey Mansel.
Gloucestershire,
Sir John Guise,
Sir Ralph Dutton.
Gloucester City,
Sir Charles Berkeley,
Evan Seys.
Grampound,
Nicholas Hearle,
John Tanner.
Grantham,
Sir William Ellis,
Sir John Newton.
Grimsby,
William Broxholm,
George Pelham.
Grimstead,
Goodwyn Wharton,
Wm. Jephson.
Guildford,
Morgan Randyl,
Richard Onslow.
Harwich,
Sir Philip Parker,
Sir Thomas Mydleton.

Haslemere,
Dennis Onslow,
Francis Dorrington.
Hastings,
Sir Robert Parker,
John Ashburnham.
Haverford West,
Thomas Owen.
Helston,
Sir Vial Vivian,
Sidney Godolphin,
Herefordshire,
Sir Edw. Harley,
Viscount Scudamore.
Hereford City,
Bridstock Harford,
Paul Foley.
Hertfordshire,
Sir Jonathan Kent,
Sir Charles Cæsar.
Hertford Town,
Sir Thomas Birde.
Sir Wm. Cooper.
Heydon,
Henry Guy,
Sir Hugh Bethel.
Heytesbury,
William Ash,
Edward Ash.
Higham,
Sir Rice Rudd.
Hindon,
Richard How,
Sir R. Grobham How.
Honiton,
Sir Walter Young,
Sir Thomas Putt.
Horsham,
Anthony Eversfield,
John Mitchel.
Huntingdonshire,
Sir Thomas Proby,
Silas Titus.
Huntingdon Town,
Sidney Wortly,
Lionel Walden.
Hythe,
Sir Edward Deering,
Edward Hales.
Ilchester,
William Strode,
John Speke.
Ipswich,
John Wright,
Sir J. Barker.
Ives, (St.)
Edward Noseworthy,
Edward Noseworthy.
Kellington,
Richard Carew,
William Treviza.
Kent,
Sir Vere Fane,
Edward Deering.
Kingston,
Sir Michael Wharton,
William Gee.
Knaresborough,
Sir Thomas Slingsby,
William Stockdale.
Lancaster County,
Lord Brandon,
Sir Chas. Houghton.
Lancaster Town,
Richard Kirby,
William Spencer.
Lanceston,
Sir John Coriton,
Sir Hugh Pyper.
Leicestershire,
Lord Sherrard,
Sir John Hartop.
Leicester Town,
Sir Henry Beaumont,
John Grey.
Leominster,
Thomas Coningsby,
John Dutton Colt.
Leskard,
John Buller,
Sir Jonathan Trelawney,
Lestwithiel,
Sir John Carew,
Walter Kendal.
Lewes,
Richard Bridget,
Thomas Pelham.
Lincolnshire,
Sir Robert Carr,
Lord Castleton.
Lincoln City,
Henry Monson,
Sir Thomas Meres.
Litchfield,
Daniel Finch,
Michael Biddulph.
Liverpool,
Ruishee Wentworth,
John Dubois.
London,
Sir Robert Clayton,
Sir Thomas Player,
William Love,
Thomas Pilkington.
Ludlow,
Francis Charlton,
Thomas Walcot.
Ludgershall,
Thomas Neal,
John Gerrard.
Lyme,
Thomas More,
Henry Henley.
Lymington,
John Button,
John Burrard.
Lynn,
John Turner,
Simon Taylor.
Maidstone,
Sir John Tufton,
Thomas Fane.
Malden,
Sir Thomas Darcy,
Sir William Wiseman.
Malmsbury,
Sir William Estcourt,
Sir James Long.
Malton,
Sir Watkinson Payler,
William Palms.
Marlborough,
Thomas Bennet,
Lord Bruce.
Marlow,
Thomas Hobby,
John Burlace.
Mawes, (St.)
Sir Joseph Tredenham,
Henry Seymour.
Melcomb,
Thomas Brown,
Michael Harvey.
Merionethshire,
Sir John Wynne.
Midhurst,
John Lewkener,
John Alford.
Middlesex,
Sir William Roberts,
Sir Robert Atkins.
Milbourn,
John Hunt,
Henry Bull.
Minehead,
Thomas Palmer.
Francis Lutterel.
Michael, (St.)
Sir John St. Aubin,
Walter Vincent,
Monmouthshire,
Sir Trevor Williams.
William Morgan.
Monmouth Town,
John Arnold.
Morpeth,
Daniel Collingwood,
Sir George Downing,
Montgomeryshire,
Edward Vaughan.
Montgomery Town,
Matthew Price.
Newark,
Sir Richard Rothwell,
Sir Robert Markham.
Newcastle, (Staffordsh.)
Sir Thomas Bellot,
William Leveson Gower.
Newcastle, (Northum.)
Sir William Blacket,
Sir Ralph Carr.
Newport, (Cornwall)
William Coriton,
Ambrose Manaton.
Newport, (Hants)
John Lee,
Sir Robert Dillington.
Newton, (Lancashire)
Sir John Chichley,
Andrew Fountain.
Newton, (Hants)
Sir John Holmes,
Lemuel Kingdon,
Norfolk County,
Sir John Hobart,
Sir Peter Glyn.
Northamptonshire,
John Packhurst,
Miles Fleetwood.
Northampton Town,
Sir William Laugham,
Ralph Montagu.
Northumberland County,
Sir John Fenwick,
Sir Ralph Delaval.
Norwich,
Lord Paston,
Augustus Briggs.
Nottinghamshire,
Sir Scroop How,
John White.
Nottingham Town,
Richard Slater,
Robert Pierrepoint.
Okehampton,
Sir Arthur Harris,
Josias Calmady.
Orford,
Henry Parker,
Sir John Duke.
Oxfordshire,
Thomas Hoard.
Sir John Cope.
Oxford City,
William Wright,
Broom Whorwood.
Oxford University,
Sir Leolin Jenkins,
Dr. Perrot.
Pembrokeshire,
Sir Hugh Owen.
Pembroke Town,
Arthur Owen.
Penryn,
Charles Smith,
Sir Nich. Slannig,
Peterborough,
Francis St. John,
Charles Orme.
Petersfield,
Sir John Norton,
Leonard Bilson.
Plymouth,
Sir William Jones,
Sir John Maynard.
Plimpton,
George Treby,
John Pollexfen.
Pool,
Henry Trenchard,
Thomas Chaffin.
Pontefract,
Sir Patience Ward,
Sir John Dawney.
Portsmouth,
George Legg,
Richard Norton,
Preston,
Sir John Otway,
Edward Rigby.
Queenborough,
William Glanvile,
Sir Edward Hales.
Radnor County,
Row. Gwynn.
Radnor Town,
Griffith Jones.
Reading,
Nathan Knight,
John Blagrave.
Retford,
Sir Edward Nevill,
Sir William Hickman.
Richmond,
Thomas Craddock,
Humphrey Wharton.
Rippon,
Richard Stern,
Christopher Wandesford,
Rochester,
Francis Barrell,
Sir John Banks.

Rumney,
Paul Barret,
Sir Charles Sedley.
Rutlandshire,
Sir Abel Barker,
Philip Sherrard.
Rye,
Thomas Frewen,
Sir John Dorrel,
Ryegate,
Dean Goodwyn,
Roger James,
Salop County,
Sir Vincent Corbet,
Richard Newport.
Salop Town,
Sir Richard Corbet,
Edward Kynaston.
Saltash,
Sir John Davy,
Nicholas Lawney.
Sandwich,
Sir James Oxenden,
James Thurbane.
Sarum New,
Sir Thomas Mompesson,
Alexander Thistlethwait.
Sarum Old,
Sir Eliab Harvey,
Lord Coleraine.
Scarborough,
Francis Thompson,
William Thompson.
Seaford,
Herbert Stapley,
Sir William Thomas.
Shaftsbury,
Thomas Bennet,
Sir Matthew Andrews.
Shoreham,
John Cheale,
John Hales.
Somersetshire,
Sir William Portman.
George Speke.
Southampton County,
—— Jarvis,
Sir Francis Roll.
Southampton Town,
Sir B. Newland,
Sir Chas. Wyndham.
Southwark,
Sir Richard How,
Peter Rich.
Staffordshire,
Sir Walter Baggot,
Sir John Bowyer.
Stafford Town,
Sir Thomas Wilbraham,
Sir Thomas Armstrong.
Stamford,
Sir Richard Cust,
William Hyde.
Steyning,
Philip Gell,
Sir John Fagg.
Stockbridge,
Henry Whitehead,
Oliver St. John.
Sudbury,
Sir Jervis Elwys,
Jervis Elwys.
Suffolk County,
Sir W. Spring.
Sir Samuel Barnadiston.
Surry County,
Arthur Onslow,
George Evelyn.
Sussex,
Sir John Pelham,
Sir Nicholas Pelham,
Tamworth,
Thomas Thynne,
Sir Andrew Hacket.
Tavistock,
Sir Francis Drake,
Edward Russel.
Taunton,
John Trenchard,
Edmund Freeman.
Tewkesbury,
Sir Francis Russel,
Sir Henry Capel.
Thetford,
William Harbord,
Sir Joseph Williamson.
Thirsk,
Nicholas Saunderson,
Sir Wm. Frankland.
Tiverton,
Sir Henry Ford,
Samuel Foot.
Totness,
Sir Edward Seymour,
Edward Seymour.
Tregony,
Charles Trevanion,
Hugh Boscawen.
Truro,
William Boscawen,
Edward Boscawen.
Wallingford,
W. Lenthal,
Scorie Barker,
Warwickshire,
Sir Edward Boughton,
Robert Burdet.
Warwick Town,
Thomas Lucy,
Richard Booth.
Wareham,
Thomas Erle.
George Savage.
Wells,
John Hall,
William Coward.
Wendover,
Edward Backwell,
Richard Hampden.
Wenlock,
John Woolryche,
William Forrester.
Weobly,
John Booth,
John Birch.
Westbury,
William Trenchard.
Edward Norton.
West Low,
Jonathan Trelawney,
John Trelawney.
Westminster
Sir Wm. Pulteney,
Sir Wm. Walker.
Westmoreland,
Christ. Philipson,
Allen Bellingham.
Weymouth,
Sir John Morton,
Sir John Coventry.
Whitchurch,
Richard Ayloffe,
Henry Wallop.
Winchelsea,
Creswel Darper,
Thomas Austin.
Winchester,
Lord Annesly,
Sir John Cloberry.
Windsor,
Richard Winwood,
Samuel Starkey.
Wilton,
Thomas Herbert,
Sir John Nicholas.
Wiltshire,
Sir Walter St. John,
Thomas Thynne.
Woodstock,
Sir Littleton Osbaldiston,
Nicholas Bainton.
Wooton Basset,
Laurence Hyde,
Henry St. John.
Wygan,
Earl of Ancram,
—— Banks.
Worcestershire,
Thomas Foley,
Samuel Sandys.
Worcester City,
Sir Francis Winnington,
Thomas Street.
Yarmouth, (Norfolk)
Richard Huntington,
Geo. England.
Yarmouth, (Hants)
Sir Richard Mason,
Thomas Wyndham.
Yorkshire,
Lord Clifford,
Lord Fairfax.
York City,
Sir Henry Hewley,
Sir Henry Thompson.

SPEAKER—Serj. Williams.

The King's Speech on opening the Session.] Oct. 21, 1680. The king opened the session with the following Speech to both houses:

"My lords and gentlemen; I have many particulars to open to you; and because I dare not trust my memory with all that is requisite for me to mention, I shall read to you the particulars out of this paper; viz. My lords and gentlemen, the several prorogations I have made have been very advantageous to our neighbours, and very useful to me; for I have employed that time in making and perfecting an Alliance with the crown of Spain, suitable to that which I had before with the States of the United Provinces, and they also had with that of Spain, consisting of mutual obligations of succour and defence.—I have all the reason in the world to believe, that what was so much desired by former parliaments must needs be very grateful to you now; for, though some perhaps may wish these measures had been taken sooner, yet no man can with reason think that it is now too late; for they who desire to make these alliances, and they who desire to break them, shew themselves to be of another opinion.—And as these are the best measures that could be taken for the safety of England, and the repose of Christendom; so they cannot fail to attain their end, and to spread and improve themselves farther, if our divisions at home do not render our friendship less considerable abroad.—To prevent these as much as may be; I think fit to renew to you all the assurances which can be desired, that nothing shall be wanting on my part, to give you the fullest satisfaction your hearts can wish, for the security of the Protestant religion; which I am fully resolved to maintain, against all the conspiracies of our enemies; and to concur with you in any new Remedies which shall be proposed, that may consist with preserving the Succession of the crown in its due and legal course of descent.—And, in order to this, I do recommend to you, to pursue the further examination of the Plot, with a strict and an impartial enquiry. I do not think myself safe, nor you neither, till that matter be gone through with; and therefore it will be necessary that the Lords in the Tower be brought to their speedy Trial, that justice may be done.—I need not tell you what danger the city of Tangier is in, nor of what importance it is to us to preserve it: I have, with a mighty charge and expence, sent a very considerable relief thither: but constantly to maintain so great a force as that war will require, and to make those new works and fortifications without which the place will not long be tenable, amounts to so vast a sum, that without your support it will be impossible for me to undergo it. Therefore I lay the matter plainly before you, and desire your advice and assistance.—But that which I value above all the treasure in the world, and which I am sure will give me greater strength and reputation both at home and abroad than any treasure can do, is, a perfect union amongst ourselves.—Nothing but this can restore the kingdom to that strength and vigour which it seems to have lost; and raise us again to that consideration which England hath usually had. All Europe have their eyes upon this assembly; and think their own happiness or misery, as well as ours, will depend upon it. If we should be so unhappy as to fall into such a misunderstanding amongst ourselves as would render our friendship unsafe to trust to; it will not be wondered at, if our neighbours should begin to take new resolutions, and perhaps such as may be fatal to us. Let us therefore take care, that we do not gratify our enemies, and discourage our friends, by any unseasonable disputes. If any such do happen, the world will see it was no fault of mine; for I have done all that was possible for me to do, to keep you in peace while I live, and to leave you so when I die. But from so great prudence, and so good affections, as yours, I can fear nothing of this kind; but do rely upon you all, that you will use your best endeavours to bring this parliament to a good and happy conclusion."

Mr Williams chosen Speaker.] After this Speech, the lord chancellor, by his majesty's command, directed the commons to return to their house, and to proceed to the Choice of a Speaker, when W. Williams, esq. was unanimously elected; and was approved the next day by his majesty.

Oct. 26. Mr. Dangerfield was brought to the bar of the commons, where he gave an account of the new Sham Plot, as it is printed in the Trials.*

Debate on the Means of suppressing Popery, and preventing a Popish Successor.] Oct. 26. Lord Russel rose and said:—Mr. Speaker; sir, seeing by God's providence, and his majesty's favour, we are here assembled, to consult and advise about the great affairs of the kingdom, I humbly conceive it will become us to begin first with that which is of most consequence to our king and country, and to take into consideration how to save the main, before we spend any time about particulars. Sir, I am of opinion, that the life of our king, the safety of our country and Protestant religion, are in great danger from Popery; and that either this parliament must suppress the power and growth of popery, or else that popery will soon destroy, not only parliaments, but all that is near and dear to us. And therefore I humbly move, that we may resolve to take into our consideration in the first place, how to suppress Popery, and to prevent a Popish Successor; without which all our endeavours about other matters will not signify any thing, and therefore this justly challengeth the precedency.

Sir *Henry Capel.* I stand up to second that

---

* "Dangerfield, a subtle and dexterous man, who had gone through all the shapes and practices of roguery, and in particular was a false coiner, undertook now to coin a Plot for the ends of the Papists. He was in jail for debt; and was in an ill intrigue with one Cellier, a Popish midwife, who had a great share of wit, and was abandoned to lewdness. She got him to be brought out of prison, and carried him to the countess of Powis, a zealous managing Papist. He, after he had laid matters with her, got into all companies, and mixed with the hottest men of the town, and studied to engage others with himself to swear, 'That they had been invited to accept of commissions; and that a new form of government was to be set up, and that the king and the royal family were to be sent away.' He was carried with this story first to the duke, and then to the king, and had a weekly allowance of money, and was very kindly used by many of that side; so that a whisper ran about town, that some extraordinary thing would quickly break out. Dangerfield having some correspondence with one col. Mansel, he made up a bundle of seditious but ill contrived Letters, and laid them in a dark corner of his room; and then some searchers were sent from the Custom-House to look for some forbidden goods, which they heard were in Mansel's chamber. There were no goods found, but as it was laid, they found that bundle of Letters; and upon that a great noise was made of a discovery. But upon enquiry it appeared the Letters were counterfeited, and the forger of them was suspected: so they searched into all Dangerfield's haunts, and in one of them they found a Paper that contained the scheme of this whole fiction, which, because it was found in a Meal Tub, came to be called the "MEAL-TUB PLOT." Dangerfield was upon that clapped up, and he soon after confessed how the whole matter was laid and managed: In which it is very probable he mixed much of his own invention with truth, for he was a profligate liar. This was a great disgrace to the Popish party, and the king suffered much by the countenance he had given it." Burnet.

motion, and to give some reasons, why I agree in it; not doubting but other persons will be of the same opinion, if they have the same sentiments of what influence the Popish party have had in the management of most of our affairs both at home and abroad, for many years last past; and how that party hath increased, and been encouraged. Sir, I remember, that, after his majesty's happy Restoration, it was thought convenient that an Act of Uniformity should pass, as the best law that could be invented, to secure the Church from the danger of Popery and Fanaticism, and accordingly it did pass in 1662; but in 1663, some, that then managed the great affairs of state, or at least had great interest with his majesty, were of another opinion: for they had prevailed with him to grant a Toleration and Indulgence, and to make a Declaration to that purpose. The parliament assembling soon after, thought it very strange, that in one year an Act of Uniformity should be the best way to preserve the Church, and that in the next year a Toleration and Indulgence: therefore, after a serious debate about it, in Feb. 1663, they made an Address to his majesty, humbly representing how it would reflect upon the wisdom of that parliament, to have such an Alteration made so soon; and that such proceedings, for aught they could foresee, would end in Popery. Upon which his majesty, out of his great goodness, stopped the issuing out of the said Toleration; hearkening rather to the advice of his parliament, than to any private counsellors. Sir, I cannot inform you who it was that gave that Advice to his majesty, nor certainly affirm they were popishly affected; but, if I may take the liberty to judge of a tree by its fruit, I have some reason to think so; because I find by Coleman's Letters, and other discoveries, that a Toleration and Indulgence should be one of the great engines they intended to use for the establishing of Popery in this nation. But the project thus failing at this time, they were forced to wait with patience until they could have another opportunity; employing in the mean time their diabolical counsels, in weakening the Protestant Interest, (in order to a general destruction of it) by engaging us in a war with Holland. In which the French acted the same part in the behalf of the Dutch, as they did afterwards in our behalf against them 1672; very fairly looking on both times, while we poor Protestants with great fury destroyed one the other. But this was not so strange, nor so plain as the dividing of our Fleet under the command of prince Rupert and gen. Monk, and the Design of destroying them as well as their Ships, and the rest of our navy royal at Chatham. And as they thus acted their part at sea, so they did not forget to do their best ashore; in April 1666, some persons that were then hanged, fairly confessed they had been treated with, and had treated with others, to burn the City of London in Sept. following, of which confession we then took as little notice, as we have of other discoveries against Papists since: however, accordingly in Sept. 13,000 houses of the city of London were burnt; and those that were taken in carrying on that work generously discharged without any trial; and one papist, that confessed that himself and others did set the city on fire, was in great haste hanged, and so the business was hushed up as completely as the late great Plot is like to be now, branding Hubert, that then made that confession, with madness; as now these last witnesses with perjury, sodomy, and what not. However, these businesses were not so carried, but his maj. discerned some of the intrigues of them, which made him alter his councils, and, contrary to the endeavours of that party, enter into new Alliances, by making up that excellent League, usually called the Triple League; which put a stop to these men's designs as to affairs abroad, but not to their designs here at home. For having obtained the Oxford Act, and some others against the Dissenters, great endeavours were used to have them executed severely, in expectation that the Dissenters would soon be made weary of living quietly under them, and in the end be glad of a toleration; but the Dissenters deceived them, and submitted to the laws; insomuch that in 1670 to 1671, there was hardly a conventicle to be heard of in England; and might never have been more, if that party had not been afraid of a great disappointment thereby: wherefore to revive our divisions, and to bring in (as they hoped) their own religion, they employed all their force again to get a Toleration. I say they did it; because it cannot be imagined it could be from any Protestant interest; both church-men and dissenters publickly declaring their detestation of it. And in 1672, was obtained, printed, and published. After we had, in order to the carrying it on, broke that never to be forgotten Triple League, sacrificed our honour to the French, not only by making a strong Alliance with them, but by seizing the Dutch Smyrna Fleet, and then afterwards proclaiming war with them. Which war continued in order to ruin us both; for the French proved but lookers-on at sea, (as they had done when engaged with the Dutch in 1665,) though great conquerors at land, especially of the Protestants in Germany and Holland. And as this Toleration was accompanied with these great alterations in affairs abroad, so it was backed, 1. With a great minister of state at the helm at home, who was so confident of the refixing Popery here, that he could not forbear to declare himself to be of that religion; I mean my lord treasurer Clifford: as also, 2. With a great Army at Blackheath, ready upon all occasions: and, 3. With the greatest violation on the Property of the subject, that ever happened in this nation, the seizing of one million and an half, or thereabout, in the Exchequer. All which indeed made our condition desperate, and, as many thought, past retrieve. But, Mr. Speaker, here again the goodness and wisdom of his maj. saved us refusing to follow such pernicious counsels; upon which Clifford not only lost his place, but his life too, breaking his heart (as is by most believed) to see himself so disappointed in this great design. And here, as we can never too much detest my lord Clifford, and such others, who contrived our ruin; so we can never sufficiently admire his majesty's royal care, in working out our security, by refusing to follow any advice that tended to those ends. And therefore, to the great disappointment of that party, at the request of the house of commons, at their next meeting, he recalled the said Toleration, disbanded the Army, and in convenient time made a peace with Holland. But though this party were thus defeated of their design, yet not so discouraged as to give it over. They changed their measures, but not their principles; and although they desisted from farther aiming at a Toleration, yet they no ways neglected pursuing a Reformation; but in order thereto, prosecuted a correspondence formerly begun for that purpose with the French king, and, by promising him considerable Supplies, to carry on the war he was then engaged in, secured themselves, as they thought, of his assistance for settling of Popery here. Accordingly, it is not unknown, what a party of men, what quantity of ammunition, and other necessaries for war, were sent to the French king, during the war he was then engaged in; and how it was done contrary to the advice of the parliament, and the solicitations of most of the princes in Europe, and true interest of England, to the astonishment of all good men; especially because it was contrary to his majesty's own Proclamation, and when the French had declared they made that war for Religion, endeavouring to force the Dutch to allow of Popish Churches. However, such was the strength of this Party, that this assistance was continued until the French king was willing to make a peace, and then who more instrumental than our ministers to effect it? Several ambassadors, and plenipotentiaries too, being sent as well to the court of Spain, as Germany and Holland, for that purpose. And at last, the Dutch being weary, and consumed with the War, they were persuaded to be willing for a Peace, and accordingly the 10th of Jan. 1676, entered into a Treaty with us for a general peace, to be accomplished by such ways and means as are therein prescribed. Which League was kept private for some time, and instead of any discovery thereof, about the end of Feb. following, (the parliament being then soon after to assemble) a great noise was made of entering into a war with France, it being concluded, that nothing like that would incline the parliament to give Money, nor the people freely to part with it, because it was the only way to extinguish those Fears they lay under, by reason of the growing greatness of France. At the meeting of the parliament, the project was set on foot with all the art and industry imaginable; and so far were the major part of the members persuaded of the reality thereof, that they were inclinable to give a great sum of Money for the carrying on of the war; but while they were in consultation about it, the League formerly mentioned, agreed at the Hague, was unluckily made (in some measure) public, and occasioned a great jealousy of the reality of the pretended war. And the greater, because upon an enquiry, they could not find there were any Alliances made to that purpose. And yet, notwithstanding this, and the great endeavours of some worthy members of that parliament, (now of this;) an Army of 30,000 men were raised, and a Tax of above 1,200,000*l.* was given. And then, instead of a War, a general Peace, according to that Treaty agreed with Holland, was presently made. By which that Party thought they had secured, not only the power of France, but the men and money here raised at home, to be made serviceable for their ends; there wanting nothing but a Popish king to perfect all these Designs. For which we have great reason to believe they had made all necessary preparation, as well by employing men and money, to find out wicked instruments to take away the king's life, as by providing one Cleypole to be a sacrifice, to make an atonement for the Act, and to cast the wickedness thereof on the Fanatics. To which purpose the said Cleypole was really imprisoned some time before in the Tower, upon the evidence of two witnesses, that he should say, that he and 200 more had engaged to kill the king, the next time he went to Newmarket. For which, in all probability, he had as really been hanged, if the breaking out of the Plot had not prevented their designs. Then was Cleypole, the next term after, publicly cleared at the King's-Bench bar, the witnesses appearing no more against him. Thus were we again reduced to a miserable condition; but it pleased God, by the discovery of the Plot by Dr. Oates, once more to save us; whose Evidence (he being but one witness) they thought at first to have out-braved; but some of them being so infatuated as to kill Justice Godfrey, and Coleman so unfortunate as to leave some of his important Papers in his house, notwithstanding the time he had to convey them away, it wrought so great a fermentation in the people, as that there was no remedy, but that the farther pursuit of the Plot must be again laid aside, and a fair face put upon things. And so accordingly, there was for a few months; but how, after Wakeman's Trial, things turned again, what endeavours have been since used to ridicule the Plot, to disparage the old witnesses, to discourage new ones, to set up Presbyterian Plots, and to increase our divisions, I suppose must be fresh in every man's memory here, and therefore I shall not offer to trouble you therewith.—But, sir, I cannot conclude without begging your patience, while I observe how things have been carried on in Scotland and Ireland, answerable to what was done here. In Ireland, the Papists are at least five to one in number to the Protestants, and may probably derive from their cradle an inclination to massacre them again: at least the Protestants have no security, but by having the militia, arms, and the command of towns and forts in their hands. But about the same time, or a little before that the Toleration came out here, in 1672, an Order went from hence, which, after a long preamble of the loyalty and affection of the Papists to his majesty, required the lord lieut. and council to dispense with the Papists wearing of arms, and living in corporations, and a great many other things in their favour; of which they have made such use, as that the Plot there was in as good readiness as that here: but how carried on, and how endeavours were there also used to stifle it, will appear when your leisure may permit you to examine those witnesses.—In Scotland, the government is quite altered, the use of parliaments in a manner abolished, and the power of that government lodged in a commissioner and council, a standing army of 22,000 men settled, all endeavours used to divide the Protestant Interest, and to encourage the Papists. By which we may conclude, that the same interest hath had a great hand in the management of affairs there also.—And, sir, may we not as well believe, that the world was at first made of atoms, or by chance, without the help of an Omnipotent Hand, as that these affairs in our little world have been thus carried on, so many years together, so contrary to our true interest, without some great original cause, by which the Popish Interest hath so far got the ascendant of the Protestant Interest, that, notwithstanding all his majesty's endeavours, things have been strangely over-ruled in favour of that Party; how and which way, his majesty's Declaration made in April 1679, is to me a great manifestation.—Sir, I hope the weight of the matter I have discoursed on, will plead my pardon with the house for having troubled you so long: I submit what I have said to your judgment, humbly desiring a favourable construction; and although I have said some things that are very strange, and other things grounded only on conjectures, yet I believe that no man will have just reason to doubt the probability of the truth, if they will but consider what a potent friend the Papists have had of James duke of York, and how emboldened by the hopes of having him for king. And as it is not to be doubted but that they have had his assistance, so they have had the French ambassador's too; who, by his frequency at the Palace, had seemed rather one of the family and king's houshold, than a Foreign ambassador; and by his egress and regress to and from his majesty, rather a prime minister of state of this kingdom, than a counsellor to another prince. And the truth of all hath been so confirmed by Coleman's Letters, making the duke's Interest, the French Interest, and the Papists Interest so much one, and by the many witnesses that have come in about the Plot, that I think we may rather be at a loss for our remedy, than in doubt of our disease. And therefore, though I know the difficulties I may bring myself under, by having thus laid open some men's designs; yet seeing my king and country have called me to this service, I am resolved, that as my father lost his life for king Ch. i. so I will not be afraid to adventure mine for king Ch. ii. and that makes me expose myself in his service in this place.—Sir, I think (seeing things are thus) without neglecting our duty to our king and country, nay to our God too, we cannot defer endeavouring the securing the king's Person, and Protestant Religion, by all lawful means whatsoever; and therefore I second the motion that was made, that we may, in the first place, take into our consideration, how to suppress Popery, and prevent a Popish Successor; that so we may never return again to superstition, idolatry and slavery, but may always preserve that pure religion, to be the religion of this nation, for which so many of our fore-fathers have suffered martyrdom, I mean the Protestant Religion, as long as the Sun and Moon endures.

Sir *Fr. Winnington*. Sir, the Popish party have not only had a great influence on the management of our affairs, both foreign and domestic, while they could do it under a disguise; but notwithstanding the discovery of their whole Plot, have ever since gone on triumphant, as if they were not afraid of any opposition that can be made against them. Although the most part of Dr. Oates's Discovery was no news to most men; and the great Correspondence which Coleman had held with foreign parts, had been generally observed for some years: yet what difficulties were there raised against believing of Oates's testimony, and against apprehending of Coleman's person, and seizing of his Papers; by which he had opportunity to carry away the most part, and by that means prevented a great deal of evidence, which we should otherways have had against that party; though by chance he left enough to hang himself. And as their power, or the respect which was borne them, appeared in this; so their great confidence in the never-to-be-forgotten death of sir E. Godfrey, which doubtless they accomplished, (as to conceal evidence, so to intimidate justices and others from doing their duty,) with great assurance, that those who did it should never have been brought to justice. And I must confess, we took a strange unheard-of way, either to do that, or prevent the going on of the Plot: for in Oct. after the Plot broke out, no less than 57 Commissions were discovered for raising soldiers, granted to several popish recusants, with warrants to muster without taking the Oaths of Allegiance and Supremacy or Test; countersigned by the then secretary of state. Of which the parliament taking notice, they were soon after dissolved, in the midst of the examination of the Plot. And the next that called, though composed of true English gentlemen, as soon as they fell severe upon popery, had no better success; certainly, sir, not by the prevalency or advice of any true English rotestants; and who then may be presumed o have given such advice, I leave to your udgment. These two parliaments being thus lissolved, a third was summoned, but was not ermitted to sit, but, on the contrary, put off y several prorogations. At which the people eing discontented, their Fears and Jealousies rising from the papists increasing, from which hey knew they could not be effectually secured but by a parliament; several counties and ities joined in petitioning his maj. for a parliament. But it being foreseen that every thing hat tended to make way for the meeting of arliaments, was dangerous, such was the influence of that party, as that they obtained a 'roclamation, penned I think by Coleman imself, or by somebody that had no more love or the protestant religion than he, forbidding etitioning as seditious and tumultuous. And hat nothing should be wanting to shew their ower, at length, by the endeavours of some reat men, some credulous and ambitious men rere drawn in to be Abhorrers. Good God! there were these men's senses, that in a time vhen the nation was in such imminent danger, here should be any good protestant that should bhor petitioning for a parliament? But I ope this house will have a time to speak with hose gentlemen, and mark them with the rand they deserve. And now that it was ound, that there were a good, easy sort of redulous people that might be wrought upon, was thought high time to have a Counter-'lot that might swallow up that of the papists, nd restore them to their former credit. How r this was carried on by good men and bad, am loth to particularize; but I cannot but bserve, that Dangerfield had more money and ncouragement given, while he was carrying on f that Plot, than I could ever hear he hath ad since the discovery of it. But though it e not strange, that the papists should be so icked, as to contrive such a design, for the asting of the Plot upon the protestants, though ith the loss of so many honest men's lives, as as intended; yet it is strange to see how illing many protestants, especially of those ho have reason to think themselves of the est sort, were to believe it; and how little leased with Dangerfield, for the great service e did in discovering that wicked Plot. So owerful and so lucky are the popish party, in ifusing of animosities amongst us, tending to ivide us, and so willing are we to entertain iem to our destruction. And as the popish arty have been very industrious in the con-'iving of Reports and Plots, to remove the ill eports they lie under, and have had a great ifluence in managing of parliamentary affairs; we may presume they have had in the dispensing of justice, as may appear by considering what hath been done by our judges of late. —At Wakeman's Trial, those persons who at ormer trials had been treated with that repect that is due to the king's evidence, and those credit and reputation had stood clear rithout exception in all other trials, were now not only brow-beaten, but their evidence presented to the jury as doubtful, and not to be depended on; and so at all other trials of papists from that time forward. By which many of the greatest offenders were quitted and cleared as to the Plot, and those that were brought for defaming the king's evidence, and suborning witnesses in order thereto, very kindly treated, and discharged with easy sentences, especially if papists; but if protestants, though only for printing or vending some unlicensed Book, were imprisoned and largely fined, But I beg leave to particularize in the case of one Carr, who was indicted for printing a Weekly Intelligence, called, 'The Packet of Advice from Rome; or, the History of Popery.' This man had a strange knack of writing extraordinary well upon that subject, and the Paper was by most persons thought not only very ingenious, but also very useful at this time, for the information of the people, because it laid open very intelligibly the errors and cheats of that church. However, upon an Information given to the court of King's-Bench against this Carr, this Rule was made: 'Ordinatum est, quod liber intitulat, 'The Weekly Packet, &c. non ulterius imprimatur, vel publicetur, per aliquam personam quamcunque. Per. Cur.'—I think it amounts to little less than a total prohibition of printing any thing against popery.—The true English protestants being thus prevented of having parliaments to redress their Grievances, and to secure them against the fears of popery, as also from petitioning for parliaments, or writing for the protestant religion, they had recourse to their old way of presenting grievances by juries. But advice being given, that some great papists were concerned in the presentment, particularly the duke of York, the jury was dismissed in an extrajudicial manner, and so no remedy in the world allowed for poor protestants. What an unhappy star were we born under, that things should be thus carried against us, in the whole course of our government, whilst we have a wise protestant king over us? What may not be expected under a popish king, if it should be our misfortune to have any? And therefore, I think, sir, we ought to endeavour to prevent it, by consulting in the first place how to suppress popery, and prevent a popish successor, which is my humble motion.

Mr. *Montagu.* Sir, you have heard what an influence the Popish party hath had in the management of all our affairs of greatest importance, almost ever since his maj.'s happy Restoration; how the making of peace, or war, or foreign alliances, hath been over-ruled by that party, to the great danger of the nation, and Protestant Religion both at home and abroad: insomuch as it may be justly feared, that there is a general design to root out that religion from the face of the earth; which may not be difficult to be done, if by establishing Popery here, assistance to the Protestants abroad may be prevented; or by destroying the Protestants abroad (which are so many bulwarks to us) we should be left to resist alone. You have also heard how that party hath influenced the resolutions made touching parliaments and affairs here at home. The truth is, sir, that interest is crept into our court, and hath a great power in our councils; it is crept into our courts of justice, and hath a great command in our army, our navy, our forts, and our castles, and into all places upon which our security depends. And it is impossible it should be otherwise, as long as we have a Popish Successor, and that party the hopes of a Popish king. And I humbly conceive that it is very obvious, that as long as that party hath such a power, not only our religion, but the life of his majesty, and the whole government, is in danger. And therefore I think we cannot better comply with our duty to our king and country, than in resolving to use our utmost endeavours to extirpate Popery, and prevent a Popish Successor; and therefore I would desire you would be pleased to put the question.

Resolved, nem. con. "That it is the opinion of this house, that they ought to proceed effectually to suppress Popery, and prevent a Popish Successor."

Resolved, "That an Address be made to his majesty, declaring the Resolution of this house, to preserve and support the king's Person and Government, and the Protestant Religion at home and abroad."

Petitioning the King, voted to be the Right of the Subject.] Oct. 27. Sir *Gilbert Gerrard.** Mr. Speaker, I crave leave to mind you of a great infringement which hath been made of the liberty of the subject, since the last session of parliament. Sir, many good Protestants thinking it very strange, that two parliaments should be dissolved, without doing any thing material against Popery, and a third so often prorogued in a time of such imminent danger; and foreseeing the ruin such delays might bring upon them, resolved to petition his majesty; and accordingly in several counties and corporations, Petitions, humbly praying his majesty to let the parliament sit, were drawn up, and signed by many thousands of good subjects, in a peaceable and quiet way, and delivered to his majesty by no greater number of persons than is allowed. But although this was conformable to law, and the duty of good subjects, considering what danger his majesty's person and the Protestant Religion was in, yet it was traduced to his majesty as seditious and tumultuous, and forbidden by a Proclamation, and great affronts and discouragements given to such, as either promoted or delivered the said Petitions; and at last several persons in many places were set up to declare at the assizes, and other public places, an Abhorrency and Detestation of such petitioning.

Mr. *Sacheverell.* Sir, I humbly conceive the subjects of England have an undoubted right to petition his majesty for the sitting of parliaments, and redressing of Grievances; and, that considering the circumstances we are under, we have no reason to lose it. If it should be our unhappiness to have a popish king, may be

* "In the beginning of Jan. sir Gilbert Gerrard, and one Mr. Smith, accompanied by eight other gentlemen, presented a Petition to his majesty, for the sitting of the parliament, in the name of some thousands of his subjects, inhabitants of London, Westminster, and the places adjacent; but met with a very ungracious reception; his maj. declaring, 'That he looked upon himself to be the head of the government, and the only judge of what was fit to be done in such cases; and that he would do what he thought most for the good of himself and his people.' His majesty likewise expressed his concern to find one of sir G. Gerrard's name, and particularly sir Gilbert himself, in such a thing; and, when sir Gilbert would have replied, turned away in displeasure. But this mortifying reception did not deter others from treading the same path. They were now sensible, that the laws had no hold of them; and frowns they did not fear. Tho. Thynne, esq. accompanied by sir Walter St. John, and sir Edward Hungerford, presented a Petition in the name of the county of Wilts: sir Rob. Barrington, col. Mildmay, Mr. Honeywood, &c. another for Essex: and certain other gentlemen a third, for Berkshire. All were alike discountenanced: except that the king made a jest of the Berkshire application: whereas he treated that of Wilts as coming from a company of 'loose, disaffected people,' because it had not the sanction of the Grand Jury: and as to that of Essex, he took occasion to reproach col. Mildmay, though indirectly, with the mercy he had received by the Act of Oblivion; to which he added a caution, 'That such as had stood in need of that Act would do well, not to take such courses as might need another.' But, notwithstanding all this severity, still several other Petitions were presented, though from persons of less eminence; and, in particular, one from Taunton, as the king was coming out of the house of lords, the day he had in person declared to both houses his resolution to postpone the session; and his majesty asking the presenter, 'How he dared do that?' 'Sir,' said he, 'my 'name is DARE.'" †

A most humourous description of the manner of procuring these Petitions is thus given by Mr. North, in his Examen, p. 542: "But,

† This person was a goldsmith of that town, and was selected to be made an example of: not for petitioning, though in spite of the Proclamation; that could not be done: but for speaking seditious words: for which he was first sent for up to Council, in custody; and afterwards prosecuted, and fined 500*l.* And the town of Taunton, profiting by his example, took occasion soon after, to disown his Petition publicly in the Gazette, No. 1501.

not be surrounded with popish counsellers, so as that poor Protestant subjects may be debarred of all other ways whatsoever of making known our complaints to him; and must we lose this too? Sir, I think it is so necessary, and material a privilege to the subject, as that we ought, without loss of time, to assert our rights to it: and therefore I humbly move you to make some Vote to that purpose.

Sir *F. Winnington.* Sir, I am not only of opinion with that worthy member that spoke last, as to making a Vote for asserting the Right of the subject to petition their prince, but also for chastizing of those who have been so wicked and abominable as to traduce it and abhor it. And to that purpose, I think, sir, it will be convenient that we find out who advised or drew that Proclamation against it, and examine how a Petition that was made in Berkshire, was ordered to be taken off the file at a Quarter-Sessions, if worthy to be so called, there being but four Justices of the Peace, and two of them such obscure persons as I cannot get their names. And also make some inspection into those Addresses that have been made against Petitioning, and by whom contrived, signed, or delivered. But this must be a work of time; for the present, I humbly move you to pass one Vote to assert the Right of the Subject to petition the king, another of censure on those persons that have traduced it, and to appoint a committee for your farther proceeding herein.

It was then Resolved, "1. That it is, and ever hath been, the undoubted Right of the Subjects of England to petition the king, for the calling and sitting of Parliaments, and redressing of Grievances. 2. That to traduce such Petitioning as a violation of duty, and to represent it to his majesty as tumultuous or seditious, is to betray the Liberty of the Subject, and contributes to the design of subverting the antient legal constitution of this kingdom, and introducing arbitrary power. 3. That a committee be appointed to enquire after all such Persons, that have offended against the Right of the Subject."

Col. *Titus.* Sir, I am very glad these Votes have past so unanimously; for Popery and Arbitrary Government can never be set up in this nation, if we could be sure of frequent parliaments. And therefore the asserting of the right of the subject in any thing which tends to that, may be of great use to this nation. But, sir, seeing you have taken this business into your consideration, I think we may do well to go a little farther with it, even at this time. I am informed some members of the house are guilty of having acted contrary to those Votes; and I am of opinion, that as they were not willing that we should sit here; so that we should be as willing not to have them sit amongst us. For, if it were a great crime in others, much more in those that were chosen to assert the rights and liberties of the people. It is very unlikely that men of such principles should make good parliament-men; and I think it will very well consist with the justice of the house, to begin with a reformation amongst ourselves; and therefore I humbly move we may first proceed against such. Being commanded to name such Members, he named sir Francis Withins, who not being in the house, was ordered to attend the next day.

Sir R. Cann expelled.] Oct. 28. It having been proved, That sir Robert Cann, a Member, had publickly declared, That there was no Popish-Plot, but a presbyterian plot: and having, in his Defence, uttered several reflecting words against sir J. Knight, another Member, who confirmed the Evidence against him, the said sir R. Cann was first ordered to the Tower, and then expelled the house.

Sir F. Withins expelled.] Oct. 29. The commons resolved, "That sir F. Withins, by promoting and presenting to his majesty an Address, expressing an Abhorrence to petition his majesty for the calling and sitting of par-

---

for the effecting so great a work as this, it was necessary to institute a method of proceeding, and to retrench the laborious part as much as they could. And thus it was done: Petitions in form, as had been authentically prepared for the sake of the unlearned, were written, or, as I take it, printed upon parchments of a prescribed width, with large blanks underneath; and these were put into the hands of agitants and sub-agitants in the countries about, branching forth so nice as into hundreds, towns, and villages, if any thing populous, or affording confiding persons to negociate. And these Agitators, being choice party-men, and well instructed, went to every free voter, and indeed every one, as they came in their way, demanding their hands to the Petition; and did it in such a manner, as a plain man knew not well whether it was lawful for him to refuse or no. And when this hand-tax was gathered, the parchment-petition was sent up to a select assembly or club, who had this administration in charge. And there the bead-roll of hands and marks was cut off the several Petitions out of one county, except one; and to that all the rest were glued. So there appeared a fair Petition, intituled, 'From all the Freeholders, &c.' And, the roll being opened and extended, there appeared more shapes than ever dreams presented, looking as if they were alive, and, like insects, crawling about, or as the half-formed equivocal vermin in the mud of Nile; but looking closer, they all shewed themselves no other than hieroglyphics of clowns. And, rather than want a due number of these monsters, it was common for the Agitators, or their masters, to forge marks and names, as they would have, and so save a great deal of trotting about, without so much as seeing the parties, or caring whether they approved it or no. But, for certain, the work was carried on with such pragmatical impertinence and impetuosity, as well as insolence and scandal to the government, that words can scarce represent the true genius of the proceeding."

liaments, hath betrayed the undoubted rights of the subjects of England." They then Ordered, "That the said sir F. Withins be expelled the house, for this high crime. And, that he do receive his Sentence at the bar of this house, upon his knees, from Mr. Speaker," which was done accordingly.

The Votes first ordered to be printed.] Oct. 30. The house Resolved, for the first time, "That their Votes should be printed, being first perused and signed by the Speaker: and, that the Speaker nominate and appoint persons to print the same."

Votes against the Duke of York.] Nov. 2. Sir F. Winnington made a Report of what was found in the Lords Journal relating to the horrid Popish-Plot. Mr. Treby reported what by order of the secret committee he reported to the last parliament relating to the Popish-plot. After some debates thereupon, it was Resolved, "That the duke of York's being a Papist, and the hopes of his coming such to the Crown, hath given the greatest countenance and encouragement to the present Designs and Conspiracies against the King and Protestant Religion." 2. "That, in defence of the King's Person and Government, and Protestant Religion, this house doth declare they will stand by his majesty with their Lives and Fortunes; and that if his majesty should come to any violent death, which God forbid, they will revenge it to the utmost on the Papists."

Debate on bringing in the Bill of Exclusion.] Col. *Titus.* Sir, I have observed from the Reports that have been read, and all the Evidence that I have heard about the Popish Plot, that it hath its original, as you have voted, from James duke of York; and it is not probable, in my opinion, that the popish interest can ever decline, as long as there is a Popish Successor, and they have such hopes of his coming to the crown; and therefore I humbly move you, that a Committee be appointed to draw up a Bill to disable James duke of York from inheriting the imperial Crown of this realm.

Lord *Russel.* Sir, if we consider the train of ill consequences that attend the having of a popish successor, and the certain miseries that must fall on this nation, if ever we should have a popish king; and how impossible the one, or improbable that the other can be prevented, but by disinheriting the duke of York; I think that as we cannot disagree, as to the sadness of our condition, so it will be hard to find out any other way to secure us; and therefore I second the motion.

Mr. *Harbord.* Sir; we shall do ill to be mealy-mouthed, when our throats are in such danger; therefore I will not be afraid to speak out, when speaking plain English is necessary to save our king and country. Have we not heard, and is it not apparently true, that peace and war, foreign alliances, meetings, dissolutions, and prorogations of parliaments, trials at Westminster-Hall, resolutions in council, and other things of importance, have been influenced by a popish party or interest? And can we, sir, imagine that these great things should be done by a less man than James duke of York; Hath not the examination of the Plot, in which the king's life and all our safeties is so much concerned, been kept off to admiration, and the witnesses discouraged even to despair? Have not counter-plots been set up, and carried on with a strong hand, and false witnesses in abundance, to destroy the true ones? From what cause can such strange, unheard of effects proceed, but from the power and influence of a Popish Successor? And we have no great reason to admire it, if we consider how usual it is for politicians to be given to flattery, and to be led by ambition, and how natural it is for courtiers and great ministers of state to worship the rising sun. And, sir, is it not easy to foresee what great miseries may come to this kingdom by such kind of managements? Can any man imagine, that, as long as there is a Popish Successor, there will not be a Popish Interest, and that by his assistance it shall not be strong enough to contest with the Protestant Interest? Or rather, have we not seen it for many years already? And how can it be otherways, as long as no office, small or great, is disposed of without his approbation; no, not so much as preferment in our Protestant Church? And I think, unless you can destroy that in which the interest centers, you will never destroy the interest itself.—Sir, I have no ill-will for the duke's person, but rather a great veneration, as he is descending from our past, and as brother to our present king. But I think it ought not to stand in competition with my duty to my king and country, which can never be safe as long as this interest is so predominate. And I think there is no other way to suppress it, but by going to the roots first: and therefore I agree in the motion that hath been made, for appointing a committee to bring in a Bill to disinherit James duke of York.

Mr. *Garroway.* Sir, I agree with those worthy members, that have spoke to this present business, that Popery hath for a long time had a great influence in the management of our affairs; and that the Protestant religion and government of the nation is much in danger thereby. But I hope that the prudence of this house may find out some expedient to secure the nation, more likely to be brought to perfection, than this of the Exclusion Bill. We all know that his maj. in his speech at the opening of the session, and formerly, hath declared, that he will consent to any thing you shall offer for the security of the Protestant religion; provided it consist with preserving the Succession in the due legal course of descent. As his maj. is gracious to us, so I know we are all willing to carry ourselves with all respect and duty to him; he offers you to consent to all other ways you can propose, but seems resolved not to consent to this way you are now upon. For my part, sir, I am more afraid of an army without a general, than of a general without an army; and therefore I think, that if, instead of ordering a committee to bring in a Bill for disinheriting of the duke, you bring in a Bill for banishing all the Papists out of the nation, and other bills for the having of frequent parliaments, and to secure good judges and justices, that so the laws you have already, as well as what more you may make, may be duly executed, it may do as well, and be more likely to have good success. And therefore I would humbly move you, that we may try these other ways, and not offer to put this hardship upon his majesty, seeing he hath declared against this Bill, lest, by displeasing his majesty, we should interrupt all other affairs, which at this time may be very unfortunate to this nation, and our neighbours too. The eyes of Christendom are upon the success of this meeting, and the peace, quietness, and honour of the nation much depends thereon; and therefore, if the going on with this Bill should occasion a breach, (which for several reasons I am much afraid of) it may prove one of the greatest misfortunes that could befal us. Sir, moderation in all things will always become this house, but especially in a business of so high a nature. The duke hath not yet been either heard or found guilty, how can we then answer the passing of so severe a sentence? We ought to be very careful in a business of this nature, that we do nothing but what we may be able to answer to the whole world. And therefore sir, I think that seeing his maj. hath declared, that he will not agree with us in this Bill, and other bills may be as effectual; I would humbly move you to think of some other way, and for that purpose to appoint a day to have it debated in a committee of the whole house.

Sir *Henry Capel.* I cannot agree with that worthy member that spoke last, and yet I have formerly given some proof that I have been for moderation, and, God willing, shall always be for it, when it may do good. In the two last parliaments I did so argue for moderation, that many of my friends told me, that I had deserted the true interest of my king and country; but as the loyalty which I pretend to derive from my birth, made me slight such surmises, so it shall always preponderate with me in all my actions. Sir, I am of opinion that this is a case, in which there is no room for moderation, if by moderation be meant the making of any other law for the security of our religion, because, according to the best judgment I can make, upon a full consideration of the matter, all other bills that can be desired without this Bill, will not prove effectual; but will leave us in that unhappy condition, of contesting with the influence of a Popish Successor, during the king's life, and the Power of a Popish king hereafter. Of what danger this may be to his majesty's person at present, and the Protestant Religion for the future, I leave to every one to judge. It hath been said, that take away the army, and you need not fear the general; but I say, that a general that hath the power of a king, will never want an army. And our condition is so bad, that I am afraid we shall not be safe, without being free of the general and army too; which I think, sir, as the case stands, we ought in prudence to do, or else I am afraid we shall give but a bad account to our country, of having done any thing to the purpose for the securing of our religion. And therefore I am of opinion you are under a necessity of having this Bill brought in.

Mr. *Boscawen.* How often I have been for expedients and moderation it is well known. But we are now come to that pass, that we must be either Papists or Protestants, one or other, and I see no expedient in the case. We know, when the Bill of Exclusion was brought in, the last parliament, it was of no long extent, and has the first, second, and third reading, and gentlemen may offer provisoes if they please. But why should we go back to a committee after a Report made of the Letters, &c. and the Votes you have passed? Why we should go shorter than in the last parliament, I know not any reason.

Sir *Fr. Winnington.* Our difference, I find, is by notions only; to the manner, and not the thing. I would not vote one thing one day, and throw it down another. In our Vote the other day, about a Popish Successor, I did understand that the house was unanimous, and did think, that a person of the duke's principles was not fit to come to the crown, to destroy us (and it was the sense of that Vote.) When I speak of this great prince, whom I have a great respect for, and had once a relation to, I do it with great reluctance. I supposed it the true intent of the house, by that Vote, that you would not have a Popish Successor to the crown; and if that was the meaning of it, then your debate will be short, viz. Whether you will order a Bill to be brought in for that purpose, or whether you will go into a Grand Committee to consider of the means of preserving the king's Person and the Protestant Religion. You have made steady motions and gradations for this Bill already, and if your meaning is to debate over again your last Vote, that is irregular. If any man will stand up and say, 'That the Duke is not a Papist,' it will be a great comfort to us all here, and to all England. But the duke's being a Papist, and the hopes of his coming such to the crown, is the occasion of all our misfortunes. It is painful to me when I speak of this great prince, but there are degrees in things, and as my bowels yearn towards him, so they do likewise towards my wife and children. Seeing then that this Vote is already passed, and that the nation is in expectation from us for their security, and that I converse with men of consideration, you have put another kind of consideration into them. Pray do not throw out what you have already voted.

Col. *Titus.* I observe that the arguments that have been offered against the bringing in of this Bill, are founded on his majesty's Speech, and on a supposition that other bills may be as sufficient for our security, and more facilly obtained, seeing his maj. hath so often declared, that he will not consent to the altering the Succession from its legal course of descent. Sir, the king calleth his parliament to give him advice, and they cannot therein be restrained, but may give any advice which they think may be necessary for the security of his person and government. And it hath oftentimes happened, that parliaments before now have many times offered such advice to the kings of this nation, as hath not been grateful to them at first, and yet, after mature deliberation, hath been well-received, and found absolutely necessary. When Clifford, or who else it was, had persuaded his maj. to grant a Toleration in 1672, and to tell the parliament in his Speech then made to them, that he would stand by it, and make it good; yet that house of commons finding it of dangerous consequence, and humbly offering such their Advice to his majesty, he was pleased, notwithstanding the said Speech, to cancel the said Toleration. And if he had not, as we are in a bad case now, so we might have been in a worse then. For aught I know, if that house of commons had been so great courtiers, as not to have concerned themselves in that Toleration, because of his majesty's Speech, the nation might have been ruined by Papists before this. And I think we are now under as great danger, and I hope we shall not be less courageous, nor true-hearted. If a man were sick of a pleurisy, and nothing could save his life but bleeding, would it not be strange if his physician, after having pretended that he is hearty for his cure, should allow him all other remedies but bleeding? Nothing like this can be presumed of his majesty, of whose wisdom and goodness we have had so great experience. And as to the second branch of the supposition, that other laws may secure us as well, I have not heard any arguments offered to make it good, and I must confess I cannot apprehend there can be any. I am sure the experience of former times shews us the contrary. It is plain from them, that Popish princes have not thought themselves bound by any laws against the interest of the Church; and our fore-fathers have found to their sorrow, that the strength of our laws were not sufficient to defend them against Popish tyrannies. For no prince of that religion ever yet thought himself bound to keep faith with Heretics. After queen Mary had seriously pledged her royal word to the Suffolk-men, to allow them their religion, by which they became the greatest instruments of putting the crown on her head; did she not in return put the crown of martyrdom on theirs? All other laws that you can propose in this case, must be grounded on some trust or fidelity that must be reposed in that party, for which no argument can be given, but that they never kept any faith with heretics, and therefore that we may do well to try what they will do. We are advised to be moderate, and I think we ought to be so; but I do not take moderation to be a prudent virtue in all cases that may happen. If I were fighting to save my life, and the lives of my wife and children, should I do it moderately? If I were riding on a road to save my throat from thieves, and I should be advised to ride moderately, lest I spoiled my horse, would not such advice seem strange at such a time? And so certainly would it be, if I were in a ship, (which may well be compared to a Commonwealth,) and it were sinking, would not the advice to pump moderately, for fear of a fever, seem strange? But, sir, I admire, seeing moderation is so much talked of, of late, and so much recommended, why there cannot be other objects found out, on whom to place it, as well as on the Papists. I know not why it should not be as agreeable to Christian charity, and more for the Protestant Interest at this time, because it may tend to union, to place it on the Protestant Dissenters, seeing we agree with most of them in points of faith, and only differ about a few ceremonies. The moderatest and meekest man that ever was, seeing an Egyptian struggling with an Israelite, slew the Egyptian; but at another time seeing an Israelite struggling with an Israelite, it is recorded in Holy Writ, he parted them, saying they were brethren. Of late many are at work to persuade us, that the Church hath no weapons but prayers and tears; this is a notion come up amongst us since the breaking out of the Plot, and, as far as I can observe, is only to hold good against Popery, for against Protestant Dissenters we have always had, and can still find, other weapons.

Mr. *H*——— made a speech reflecting on the duke and lord Clarendon, for making up the Match for the king, as if they did it because they foresaw that the queen would have no children, and particularly on the duke, for the loss of my lord Sandwich, for clearing of persons taken in the Fire of London, the death of sir Ed. Godfrey, &c.

Mr. *Laurence Hyde.* 'Mr. Speaker, I am sorry to see a matter of so great importance managed in this house with so much bitterness on the one hand, and with so much jesting and mirth on the other; I think it is a serious thing we are about, and that more gravity would very well become, not only this house, but the subject of the debate also. It is to me very unpleasant, to hear a prince, that hath so well deserved of this nation, by fighting our battles, and so often appearing for us in war, so upbraided. I am apt to think he was far from being of opinion, the queen would have no children, and that he scorned any of those other actions that have been laid to his charge; and therefore to hear such things said, is a great provocation. But, being I know where I am, I will lay my hand upon my mouth. But I hope you will pardon me, if, to comply with the obligation of nature, I declare myself much concerned to see the ashes of my dear father thus raked out of the dust, and to hear his memory blasted by an affirmation which cannot be proved: because I am confident he was not guilty. He and his family suffered enough by his misfortunes, occasioned by dark interests and intrigues of state. Many hink he was severely chastised while living; I ,m sorry to see that some others cannot spare ,im though dead. But, for my comfort, I have ,eard that he was a good Protestant, a good Chancellor, and that we have had worse ministers of state since. But I will not trouble ou farther, but apply myself to the business nder debate. I am of opinion, that the bringig in of this Bill will be a great hindrance to be business of the nation, and not attain your nd. And also, I am concerned for the justice f the house; for though the duke deserve reat mortifications, because he hath given so rent a suspicion of his being inclined to that eligion, and I believe doth not expect to come ow to the crown, on such terms as formerly, ut with such limitations as may secure the 'rotestant religion; yet I think it very hard or this house, to offer at so great a condemnaion without hearing the person concerned, or aving had any preceding process. For my wn part, I make it a great question, whether : would be binding to him, or a great many ther loyal persons of this nation; and if not, : may occasion hereafter a civil war. And ithout any just fear, or cause; for the king nay very well out-live the duke, and then all hat we are about would be unnecessary; and hy should we, to prevent that which may ever happen, attempt to do that which we can ever answer, either to our king or country? cannot apprehend that our case is so despeate, but that we may secure ourselves some ther way, without overturning foundations. cannot fear a general without an army. By idding ourselves of all other Papists, we may e safe, making such other laws to bind the uke, as may be necessary, by the name of ames duke of York; which, and the small evenues which belong to the crown, without he assistance of parliaments, with such other aws as may be contrived, I humbly conceive nay be sufficient for our security; and therefore it ought to be considered in a committee f the whole house, that such as are for these xpedients, may have more freedom of debate.'

Col. *Titus.* I must beg your leave to speak gain, being reflected on. I can assure you, ir, that what I have said upon this subject, is o far from proceeding from a merry, jolly humour, that it is rather from as great sorrow as ver my heart endured; being very sensible hat dangers we have undergone, and what niseries we may hereafter suffer, by means of he duke's being of this religion. I hope, sir, hat offences that proceed from natural infirmiies, will always find a favourable construction n this house. If that hon. member had but onsidered, that all men have not that good ortune to be born, with such a grave, majestic, ober aspect as that (let them say what they ill, it looks serious and weighty) he would not ave been offended at my discourse; but, sir, or the satisfaction of the house, that I am not n jest in this business, I do declare, that I hould be very sorry to be thus jested with myelf.

Sir *L. Jenkins.* Sir, the question that ariseth from this debate is, whether we had best proceed by an extremity, or by expedients. For I look on this Bill to be of the highest nature that ever was proposed in the house of commons, and the greatest extremity imaginable, which I humbly conceive we ought not to proceed to, until we have made some trial of expedients, which will be very useful. For it will give a great satisfaction, not only to his majesty, but to all other persons in general that are against this Bill, by which the world will see that we were very cautious, how we offered at such an extremity, and that we did not do it, until we had found all other ways and means whatsoever insufficient. I must confess, sir, I think such a Bill would be against law and conscience, and that nothing less than an army will be necessary to support it; and therefore I humbly move you, that we may debate this business in a committee.

Col. *Birch.* I admire to hear that hon. member make a doubt as to the legality of this Bill; certainly, sir, our legislative power is unbounded, and we may offer to the lords, and so to his majesty, what Bills we think good. And it can as little be doubted, that the legislative power of the nation, King, Lords, and Commons, should want a law to make laws; or that any laws should be against what laws they make; otherways they cannot be legally opposed. And as I think it cannot be against law, so neither against conscience, unless it could be made out, that we ought in conscience to bring in Popery. I should be very glad to hear any arguments to make good what hath been offered about expedients; but I am afraid, when they come to be examined to the bottom, they will be found very insufficient, and that we may as well think of catching a lion with a mouse-trap, as to secure ourselves against Popery by any laws without the Exclusion Bill. Have we not to do with a sort of people, that cannot be bound by any law or contract whatsoever? Much less can their words or promises be depended on. Are they not under all the obligations that can be offered, from the temptations of this life, as of that to come, not to keep faith with Heretics, but to break it when it may tend to the promoting of the Catholic cause? And if laws cannot bind other persons, much less will it princes that are of the Catholic religion? Did they ever keep any league or contract that was made with Protestants, longer than was necessary, in order to cut their throats? What use did the Papists make in Ireland of the favours granted them by king Ch. i.? Did they not make use of it to the destruction of the Protestants, by rising up in rebellion, and massacring 100,000? Sir, I see things go hard against Popery, I know not what to say to it, but I am afraid that if we should be so infatuated, as to let it creep on more and more upon us, and at last let it ascend the throne again, that we shall soon have the same miserable fortune our fore-fathers had in queen Mary's days, and be burnt in Smithfield for our indiscretion. Sir, we are upon a business of as great importance as ever was debated within these walls; for either we must suppress Popery, or be suppressed by it. For although that interest do not look so big as that of the Protestants, yet I plainly see, that it hath wrought like a mole under ground for a long time, and that it hath eaten into our bowels, and will soon come to the vital parts of the Protestant religion, and destroy it too, if great care be not taken, and that speedily. I hear some say, that our cares are needless at this time, because the king may outlive the duke; which is as much as to say, there is no need of laws against Popery, until we see whether we shall have occasion to make use of them, or no. But they do not tell us how we should be sure then to obtain them. I must confess such arguments are so far from weighing with me, as that they increase my fears, because it discovers a strange, easy, careless, indifferent humour among us Protestants. Must our lives, liberties, and religion depend upon 'may-be's?' I hope it is not come to that yet: I am sure it will not consist with the prudence of this assembly to leave it so, but rather to endeavour to settle this matter upon such a foundation, as may (with as much probability as human things are capable of) secure us. I am of opinion, that such an engine may be contrived, as should give such a whirle to the popish interest, as that it should never rise up against us again; I know of no difficulty but the same which happened to Archimedes, where to fix it. And I am not altogether at a loss for that neither; for so long as we have a good king, I will not despair. And, sir, I cannot fear any of those things that are objected against this Bill, that it is against law, and therefore will occasion a civil war: for my part I never will fear a civil war in favour of idolatry, especially when we have gotten a law on our side to defend our religion. Therefore I move you that the Bill may be brought in.

Sir *Rob. Markham.* If you intend to exclude the duke, I desire you will take the prince of Orange's children into consideration.

Mr. *Bennet.* Could any expedient be found out to preserve the protestant religion, I should be glad not to exclude the duke. In the last parliament, no expedient could be found out; and one reason for this Bill was the preservation of the king's life. The duke being looked upon as heir apparent to the crown, the king's life is still in danger; the papists, I believe, would still knock him on the head. This Bill will put it in our power to defend ourselves; and when the duke is once out, by law, from the Succession, no doubt but the parliament hereafter will keep him out. The taking away the general will leave the army alone. When a catholic king has places to bestow, and power, he will have temptation enough for ransacking the city of London to maintain an Army. And we sit patiently here for an expedient! Therefore I move for the Bill as before.

Sir *Tho. Player.* Sir, I have read in Scripture of one man dying for a nation, but never of three nations dying for one man; which is like to be our case. There hath been already so much said on this matter, and the reasons that have been given for bringing in of the Bill are so plain, that I should not have troubled you to have said any thing about it, but that I knew not how to have answered it to that great city (London) for which I serve, not to have appeared in this business, in which the protestant religion is so much concerned. But, sir, being I am up, I will beg leave to acquaint you, that I have been lately in company with a great many persons, where I have heard the duke cried up, and the king so slighted, that I must confess they made me afraid, they had thoughts of acting over here what was lately done in Portugal. Believe it, sir, many are very industrious to make an interest for the duke; if we should not use our endeavours to keep up the king's interest, and that of the protestant religion, I am afraid they will be encouraged to embroil us in blood before we are aware of it. I have no patience to think of sitting still, while my throat is cutting; and therefore I pray, sir, let us endeavour to have laws that may enable us to defend ourselves. And I know not how we can have any that are like to prove effectual, without this for excluding James duke of York; and therefore I humbly move it may be brought in.

Sir *Christ. Musgrave.* This is a business of great weight, and I desire the house may go into a grand committee. I am of opinion, that now we must free ourselves from popery, or submit to it. I wonder that expedients are now called for, when a man cannot do that in the house (where he can speak but once to a thing) which he may do at a grand committee. To extirpate the duke, and at the same time not to declare his Successor, will be strange, and you will make the thing perplexed. It is not orderly to proceed in the house. A grand committee will put you in a way to prepare Heads to draw up a Bill upon, which will be better digested there than can be in the house, without those restrictions and limitations. This you are upon, is no less than taking away a right, and you are told, 'It may endanger a Civil War, by putting the duke from his Succession to the crown of England;' which nevertheless cannot exclude him Scotland. And I should be glad to have the Borders secured, for my own concern, for I live near them.

Mr. *Edw. Seymour.* Sir, I have by many years experience observed, that it is very agreeable to the custom, prudence, and justice of this house, to debate all things very well before a question is put, but especially of great importance. It hath formerly been thought a great thing, and hard to be borne by some princes, that any thing relating to the prerogative of the crown should be debated any where but in the privy council; and I have observed, that former parliaments have done it with a great deal of tenderness. And if so, well may a Bill that tends to the alteration of the Succession, pretend to the right of having a full and fair debate, which I hope this solemn assembly will not deny; many being to take their resolutions from it in as great a point as ever was debated in a house of commons, for which we shall be answerable to our own consciences, as well as to our king and country. It is these great considerations make me trouble you at this time, otherwise I might haply have been silent, because I am one of those that have been shot at by wind-guns, which have prejudiced my reputation; and therefore, until I should have had an opportunity to vindicate myself, and to shew that I am an enemy both to popery and arbitrary government, I was more inclined to have been silent, and should not have troubled you, if the nature of this business had not laid on me a more than ordinary compulsion. I do not doubt but every one that sits here is willing to take notice of what arguments may be offered *pro* and *con*, it being the only way to pass a right judgment in this matter, which is very necessary, because what resolution you may take upon this debate, will be examined not only within his majesty's dominions, but by most princes and politicians in Europe. And therefore that you ground your resolution on such solid reason, that may endure the Test of a plenary examination, will be very necessary for the securing the credit of this house, of which I know you are very tender.—Sir, I must confess I am very much against the bringing in of this Bill; for I think it a very unfortunate thing, that, whereas his maj. hath prohibited but one thing only, we should so soon fall upon it. I do not see there is any cause, why we should fear popery so much, as to make us run into such an extreme. We are assured there can be no danger during his majesty's life; so, upon an impartial examination, we shall find there can be no great reason to fear it after his death, though the duke should outlive and succeed him, and be of that religion. Have we not had great experience of his love for this nation? Hath he not always squared his actions by the exactest rules of justice and moderation? Is there not a possibility of being of the church, and not of the court of Rome? Hath he not bred up his children in the protestant religion; and shewed a great respect for all persons of that profession? Would it not be a dangerous thing for him (I mean in point of interest) to offer at any such alteration of the religion established by law? Can any man imagine that it can be attempted, without great hazard of utterly destroying both himself and his family? And can so indiscreet an attempt be expected from a prince, so abounding in prudence and wisdom? But though we should resolve to have no moderation in our proceedings against papists, yet I hope we shall have some for ourselves. It cannot be imagined, that such a law will bind all here in England, or any in Scotland; and it is disputed whether it will be binding in Ireland: so that in all probability it will not only divide us amongst ourselves, but the three kingdoms one from the other, and occasion a miserable civil war. For it cannot be imagined, that the duke will submit to it. And to disinherit him for his religion, is not only to act according to the popish principles, but to give cause for a war with all the catholic princes in Europe; and that must occasion a standing Army, from whom there will be more danger of popery and arbitrary government, than from a Popish Successor, or a popish king. Sir, it is very agreeable to the weight of the matter, and the usual proceedings of this house, that this business should be fully debated; and therefore I humbly move you it may be in a committee.

Sir *Rd. Graham* made a long discourse, shewing the dangers and miseries of a civil war, by a large account of those between York and Lancaster: That this Bill, if it should pass, would lay a foundation for such another: That it would not be binding either to Scotland or Ireland, and so consequently occasion a division between the three kingdoms, which had formerly been the occasion of wars and miseries, as well as our own divisions amongst ourselves. He then gave an historical account, to make out how fatal divisions had proved to other nations, and instanced in Theodosius, and others. That he thought it absolutely necessary, (if this Bill must be brought in,) to prevent a civil war, that the Successor should be named; which would need a great deal of consideration; and if to debate business of smaller importance, it is usual for the house to resolve itself into a committee, how could it be answered, that it should not be done in a business of so great importance, that so expedients might be offered and debated, with more freedom and satisfaction than it was possible they could be in the house.

Sir *Wm. Pulteney*. Sir, I am of opinion, that expedients in politics are like mountebank-tricks in physic; as the one does seldom good to bodies natural, so not the other to bodies politic. Government is a weighty thing, and cannot be supported nor preserved but by such pillars as have neither flaws nor cracks, and placed on a sure foundation. And I am afraid, that all expedients will be found to have far different qualifications. I cannot foresee how the excluding of one person, who hath a right to the Succession depending upon contingencies upon such an account as this, should occasion a civil war; but rather do think there is a great deal more danger, not only of a civil war, but of our religion and liberty too, if we should not do it, and so have a popish king. For I do believe, that such a king would soon have a popish council. For if there be 11 to 7 now for the interest of a Popish Successor, what may you not expect when you have a popish king? And should you not then soon have popish judges, justices, deputy-lieutenants, commanders at sea and land; nay, and popish bishops too. For if there be none put into those places now, that are for acting against a Popish Successor, well may we expect that none shall be put in then, but what are for a popish king. And therefore I am astonished to hear any man, that pretends to be a Protestant, argue, that in such a case we need not fear Popery; for it is indeed to argue for Popery, and must proceed from an opinion that the Protestant Interest is very low, and not able to bear up any longer against popery, or else that Protestants are credulous and inconsiderate, and may be brought to destroy themselves with their own hands. Must our religion and liberty have no security but what depends on the virtues and goodness of a prince, who will be in subjection to the Pope, and probably influenced by none but jesuits and such creatures? Will it seem strange that such a prince should compose his privy council of persons inclined to that religion; or that he should employ none others as judges, justices, sheriffs, or commanders in any place of trust either at land or sea? And can we think that by the many endeavours which will be used, that the common people will not be debauched, and either be misled, or made indifferent, in a little while? Is it not in the power of the king to nominate his counsellors, judges, sheriffs, commanders at sea and land? And can it be imagined, that he will not take care to nominate such as shall be for his turn? Certainly, sir, no man can imagine that the Protestant religion can long be preserved under such a king, but such as cannot or will not see at a distance, what a change such a scheme of government would soon produce, and how likely it is that it will be set up and practised, if ever we should have a Popish king. And as I do think that our religion never can be secured without this Bill, so I do not fear that it will occasion any civil war, or any division between this kingdom, Scotland or Ireland; but rather, I believe it will be a means to reconcile the Protestant interest, and to settle the government upon such a bottom as will prove invincible. In Scotland the major part of the people hate Popery as well as we, and so do the Protestants in Ireland; and therefore certainly it will be their interests to join with us against a common enemy, and not to divide. And whereas it hath been suggested, that this Bill will engage us in a war against all Catholic princes, I look upon it as a bugbear, and do believe that we shall gain many friends by being settled, as we may by having this Bill; because then we may be formidable to our enemies, and serviceable to our allies; but never without it. And, sir, this is not to disinherit a man for his religion, but because he hath rendered himself uncapable to govern us, according to our laws, which, whether it proceed from his religion, or any thing else, is all one to us. His being uncapable, is the ground for our proceedings, having no other way to preserve ourselves. Upon the whole matter, I do conclude, that a Popish king and a Protestant religion are irreconcilable, and have no reason to fear a civil war, so long as we have a law for our defence, and a Protestant king to head us; which we cannot expect without passing some such Bill as this under debate.

Mr. *Daniel Finch.* Sir, the business you are debating is of so high a nature, that I cannot tell how to speak to it, without fear and trembling. To go about to alter the Succession of the crown, must be of great concernment to all Englishmen, and therefore ought to be considered with a great deal of deliberation, for which the justice, prudence and usage of this house calls aloud, there never having been any business debated in this house, in which so much care was required. Sir, I am unsatisfied with myself, how we can in justice pass any such Bill as is proposed; for I never heard of any law, which made an opinion in religion a cause to be dispossessed of right: in former times it was not so, though there were princes and emperors that were apostates. And queen Elizabeth would not allow of putting any such thing in practice, but rather chose to proceed against Mary queen of Scots, according to the settled laws of the nation. This nation hath been so unfortunate as to cut off one king already, let us have a care how we cut off the right of another. There is a possibility that the duke may return to the Protestant religion, let us not exclude him from such temptations as may be convenient to reduce him. But, whatever should be your resolution at last, I humbly conceive there can be no reason given, why a business of this weight should not be debated in a committee, before you vote the bringing in of the Bill, that so the validity of such other expedients as may be proposed, may be examined, and the reasons for and against this Bill be digested as they ought to be. How shall we otherwise answer it to his majesty, who hath offered you every thing but this? If there were a motion made for a Bill to give Money, would it not probably be debated in a committee? By this bill we are going to give away the right of a crown, which I take to be more than Money; and therefore, I humbly move you that it may be farther debated in a committee.

Mr. *Hugh Boscawen.* Mr. Speaker, Have not the Papists always proceeded against the Protestants with a barbarity surmounting the worst of heathens? And must we be so mighty careful how we proceed to hinder them from ruling over us, as that we must stumble at every straw, and be afraid of every bush? A man that is in an house that is on fire, will leap out at a window, rather than be burnt. I do admire how any person, that doth know with what treachery and inhumanity the Papists behaved themselves in the massacres of Piedmont, Paris, and Ireland; their cruelties in queen Mary's days, lately on sir E. Godfrey, and what they had designed against the king, and all of us, can offer any thing to delay, much more to hinder what is so precisely necessary for the good of the king and kingdom; especially seeing in this we shall do nothing, but what may be justified by many laws and precedents. And if there were none, of which I know there are a great many that are liable to no objection; yet I take it, that the law of nature and self-preservation would afford us sufficient arguments. I think the sun is not more visible at noon-day, than that the Papists have a design to extirpate our religion; and that they have done great things in order thereto, even now while we live under the government of a Protestant king, by some invisible power that hath strangely acted its part in favour of that interest, in all our councils and resolutions in affairs of greatest importance; and it is as plain that this is so, because there is a Popish Successor; and that their interest will never decline as long as there is such a successor, and the hope of a Popish king. And now, that by the watchful providence of God, these things have been made so plain to us; is it not strange, that any man should go about to persuade us to be so neglectful and inconsiderate, as to sit still and look on, while the Papists are putting their chains about our arms, and ropes about our necks? Which must be the consequence of permitting a Popish king to ascend the throne; against which there can be no law to secure us but this. In Edw. vi.th's and queen Mary's, and Elizabeth's days, was not the religion of the prince the religion of the nation? Did not most of the privy counsellors, and great ministers of state, and some bishops too, change with the times? Is it not customary for great men to insinuate and flatter their princes, by being of their religion? On what must we ground our hopes of security, in such a case? On nothing, sir, but on a civil war, which such a prince must certainly occasion. But I do not fear it from this Bill, but rather think it the only way to prevent it; not doubting but that there will be people enough that will give obedience to it, sufficient to execute the law on such as may be refractory, if any, which can only be Papists, and such as may be Popishly affected; the objections as to a civil war, and disobedience to this law, may as well be made against any other severe law that we may attempt to make against Papists: and must we therefore let them all alone? I hope we shall not be so inconsiderate; but as we have discovered that their weapons are near our throats, so we shall not acquiesce in any thing less than what may secure us; that so, if possible, we may not fall into the hands of such a bloody, merciless people; which must infallibly be the consequence of having a Popish king.

Mr. *John Trenchard.* Mr. Speaker, have not popish kings, as well in other countries as here, always brought in a popish religion? and have we any reason to suppose the like will not happen here, if ever we should have a king of that religion? Have we not undeniable proof, that the great thing designed, by endeavouring at a popish king, is the rooting heresy out of these three nations? And are not Rome and France engaged to give their assistance therein, as well as the great parties at home, not only of professed papists, but of some who profess themselves protestants, but are so but in masquerade? And do they not say, that they have so clenched and riveted their interest, as that God nor man cannot prevent their accomplishing their design? And shall we be so indiscreet as to let it creep on thus upon us, and not endeavour to remedy ourselves? Let it never be said of this house of commons, that they were so stupified or negligent of their duty to their country, or so indifferent in their religion, or preservation of their liberties, as to forget so great a concern. If, when we have done what we can, we should be conquered by force, or deceived by such little arts and tricks as may be used, a patient submission to God's providence must follow. But to be the occasion of our own destruction, by being supine and inconsiderate, will never be answered to posterity.

Resolved, "That a Bill be brought in, to disable the duke of York to inherit the imperial Crown of the Realm."

Nov. 4. The said Bill was read the first time.

Sir *Leoline Jenkins.** I have spent much of my time in studying the laws of this land; and I pretend to know something of the laws of foreign countries: and, I have upon this occasion well-considered of them; but cannot find how we can justify the passing of this Bill, rather much against it. 1. I think it is contrary to natural justice, that we should proceed to condemnation, not only before conviction, but before we have heard the party, or examined any witnesses about him; I am sure, none in his defence. And to do this, by making a new law on purpose, when you have old laws in being, that have appointed a punishment to his crime, I humbly conceive, is very severe; and contrary to the usual proceedings of this house, and the birthright of every Englishman. 2. I think it is contrary to the principles of our religion, that we should dispossess a man of his right, because he differs in point of faith. For it is not agreed by all, that dominion is founded in grace. For my part, I think there is more of popery in this Bill, than there can possibly be in the nation without it; for none but papists, and Fifth-monarchy-men, did ever go about to disinherit men for their religion. 3. I am of opinion, that the kings of England have their right from God alone; and that no power on earth can deprive them of it. And I hope this house will not attempt to do any thing, which is so precisely contrary, not only to the law of

* "Jenkins, now made Secretary of State in Coventry's place, was the chief manager for the court. He was suspected of leaning to popery, though very unjustly; but he was set on every punctilio of the Church of England to superstition, and was a great assertor of the Divine Right of monarchy, and was for carrying the Prerogative high. All his speeches and arguments against the Exclusion were heard with indignation." Burnet.

God, but the law of the land too. For if this Bill should pass, it would change the essence of the monarchy, and make the crown elective. For, by the same reason that this parliament may disinherit this prince, for his religion, other parliaments may disinherit another, upon some other pretence which they may suggest; and so consequently, by such exclusions, elect whom they please. 4. It is against the oath of allegiance, taken in its own sense, without jesuitical evasions. For by binding all persons to the king, his heirs and successors, the duke, as presumptive heir, must be understood. And I am of opinion, it cannot be dispensed withal. Sir, I will be very cautious how I dispute the power of parliaments, I know the legislative power is very great, and it ought to be so. But yet I am of opinion, that parliaments cannot disinherit the heir of the crown; and that if such an Act should pass, it would be invalid in itself. And therefore I hope it will not seem strange, that I should offer my judgment against this Bill, while it is in debate; in which I think I do that which is my duty, as a member of this house. Henry iv.th of France was a protestant, his people most Papists, who used some endeavours to prevent his coming to the crown; but when they found they were not like to perfect their design, without occasioning a civil war, they desisted; concluding, that a civil war would probably bring on them more misery than a king of a different religion, and therefore submitted. Sir, I hope, we shall not permit our passion to guide us instead of reason; and therefore I humbly move you to throw out the Bill.

Mr. *Ralph Montagu.* Sir, the hon. member may understand very much of the laws of other countries, and foreign affairs; but I am apt to think, not much of the laws of this nation; or else he would not argue, that this is a popish Bill, when it is the only thing that can save his king, the kingdom, and the Protestant Religion; which I hope will never come to that extremity, as to need any thing that is popish to save it. For my part, I am so far from thinking that this Bill is so unreasonable as hath been argued, that I think this house of commons will get as much credit by passing of this Bill, as that in 1660 did, by passing that which brought home the king. For as the one restored him; so the other may preserve him, and nothing less.

Mr. *John Hampden.* Sir, I do not understand how it can be construed, because we go about to disinherit the duke, that therefore it must be for his religion. For my part, I do approve of the Bill; but it is because the opinions and principles of the Papists tend to the alteration of the government and religion of this nation: and the introducing, instead thereof, of superstition and idolatry, and a foreign, arbitrary power: If it were not for that, I am apt to think, the duke's being a Papist would not be thought a sufficient cause for this house to spend time about this Bill. And I cannot see the danger of reducing the government to be elective by it; for why should we presume that any thing but the like cause should have the like effect? Though the Succession of the crown hath been formerly often changed by acts of parliament, yet hitherto it hath not made the crown elective; and why must we fear it now? Neither can I apprehend, that the passing of this Bill is contrary to natural justice: because we have not heard what the duke hath to say for himself. The precedents that might be offered to make out, that the parliaments have, when they thought good, condemned persons by bill, are numerous, and without any hearing too. But if there were none, to doubt the power of the legislative authority of the nation in that or any other case, is to suppose such a weakness in our government, so inconsistent with the prudence of our ancestors, and common reason, as cannot well be imagined. And I do not think we are about going to do any such strange thing neither, but what would be done in other countries upon the like occasion; but do believe, that if the dauphin of France, or the infant of Spain, were Protestants, and had, for nearly twenty years, together endeavoured the setting up of another interest and religion, contrary to the interest of those kings and the catholic religion; especially if such endeavours had been accompanied with such success as here, and those nations had been so often, by such means, reduced so near to ruin, as we have been, by divisions, tolerations, burnings, plots, and sham-plots at home, and by wars and foreign alliances, over-ruled in their favour abroad; but that they would have been more impatient than we have been for this remedy. And for my own part, I cannot but admire more at the long delay there hath been, in seeking out a remedy against this great evil, than at our offering at this Bill. For notwithstanding what hath been said, I cannot think our danger so remote or uncertain, as some would suppose it. Can the king be safe, as long as the Papists know that there is nothing but his life stands in their way, of having a king to their mind? Which is the only thing they want, to go on with their designs and to accomplish their expectations. Will it then be an easy thing to withstand such an enraged, barbarous people? The more false and unreasonable their religion is, the more cruelty will be necessary to establish it. Can it be imagined we shall not pay severely, for having shed so much blood of their martyrs, as they call them, and for having enjoyed their Holy-church-land so long? Or that they will not do all that they shall think necessary, to secure an entire and quiet possession to themselves? For my own part, I cannot imagine that the pride of these Church-men will be satisfied with any thing less, than an utter ruin and extirpation of us and our posterities. And I think that nothing can save us but this Exclusion Bill.

Resolved, "That the said Bill be read a 2d time on the 6th inst."

Nov. 6. The Bill was read a 2d time.

Sir *Rd. Temple* made several objections against the tenor of the Bill, as not answering the intention of the house; shewing how (if not altered) it would occasion an inter-regnum; and that the Clause for limiting the Exclusion to the person of the duke only, was not well drawn.

Sir *Leoline Jenkins.* In my humble opinion, the body and whole tenor of this Bill carries with it a great reflection on the whole English nation. For to suppose that one person is able to turn us about to Popery, is to suppose that we are either very imprudent, or irresolute, or that we have no great love to, but are rather very indifferent in our religion. And if we may thus disinherit the presumptive heir, not only the royal family, but the whole nation, will be subject, by such a precedent, to many inconveniencies. For by the same reasons the like may be done hereafter upon any other pretence. For, sir, though we know that this house is composed of persons that have a great veneration for the royal family; yet we know not what may happen hereafter: but, if some such Bill as this must pass, I humbly conceive there is a great necessity of naming a Successor, and not leave that in dispute, lest an inter-regnum, or civil war, happen thereupon.

Mr. *Henry Booth.** I wish I could have been silent, and I wish there had not been an occasion for this day's debate: but since we are brought into this condition, it behoves every man to put it to his shoulders to support this tottering nation: and in this matter that is now before us, we ought to consider very well, for a great deal depends upon it, and therefore I hope that every gentleman will speak and vote as God shall put it into his heart, without any prejudice or prepossession. A Bill to exclude all Papists from the crown will produce a great many inconveniencies on both hands, because his r. h. being a Papist, it will set him aside: therefore we are to consider which is the lesser evil, and to chuse that. If the duke be excluded, you are told how unjust it is to take away his right from him: that the crown is his inheritance if he survive the king, and besides you provoke him and all the Papists in England to rise and cut our throats.—On the other hand, it is in plain, that when we shall have a Popish king, our religion and laws are not secure one moment, but are in continual danger. So that the case in short is this: Whether we shall sit still and put it to the venture of having a Popish Successor, then we must either submit our heads to the block, or fight and be rebels: or else to have a law that will justify us in the defending our religion and laws: in plain English, whether we would fight for or against the law. I think I have put it right; and now let every man make his choice, that loves either his God or his country.—As to the duke's right to the crown, I wish it were clearly known what sort of right it is he claims, and whence he derives it: he is not heir apparent, neither do I think that our law knows any such thing as an heir to the crown, but only as a Successor: and therefore the duke, nor any other whatever, can pretend the same title to the crown, as the son of a subject can to his father's estate after his decease; for with subjects they do not succeed but inherit. It is not so as to the crown, for there they succeed: and it is from a not rightly considering the word Heir, as it is a synonymous term with that of Successor, that has made so many to be deceived in the duke's title to the crown: for this word Heir to the Crown was not heard of till arbitrary power began to put forth. Before Wm. the Conqueror's time it would have been a senseless word, when the people set up and pulled down as they saw cause: and till queen Eliz. it was not much in fashion, when the crown was so frequently settled by act of parliament, and the next of blood so often set aside; when the son seldom followed his father into the throne, but either by election in the life-time of his father, or else by act of parliament. So that to make the duke either heir apparent or presumptive to the crown, it must be proved either by the constitution of the government, or by some law or act of parliament. If therefore he has a title to the crown, it is necessary to know what it is, and whence he has it; but if he has none, it is not unjust to pass the Bill, or any other where he shall be particularly named: but I will say no more of this, lest I may seem to be against kingly government, which I am not.—If the duke be excluded because he is a Papist, yet it is no justice: why will he be of that religion that the law endeavours to suppress? The subjects who are of that religion forfeit two parts in three of their estates, and shall any subject by reason of his quality be exempted from the law? I hope not; besides, if a subject forfeit two parts, it is reasonable that the next of blood, or any that is of that religion, should be excluded from the crown: because the law has prohibited all Papists from having any Office civil or military, because their principles are inconsistent with the government; and then how preposterous would it be to make him the Head of the Church, and the Preserver of our Laws and Liberties, whose Religion obliges him to ruin and destroy both? So that if the duke had not by his practices given us just causes to except against him, yet barely as he is a Papist he ought to be excluded: but when it is considered that he has held a correspondency with the Pope and the French king, to subvert our religion and laws, what protection can we expect from him if he be king? It is a senseless thing to imagine, that he will not disturb us in our religion and laws, seeing whilst he is a subject he is practising to destroy us and them: therefore for my part, I think we betray both our religion and laws if we do not pass this Bill.—There is one opinion which

* Afterwards earl of Warrington. The Speeches of this gentleman are taken from his Works, which were published in 1694.

prevails much in the world, which as it is false, so it does a great deal of hurt, and that is this; that every government in the world was constituted by God himself: but that cannot be so; for it would follow, that God is unjust, which he cannot be. There neither is nor was any government of that sort but only that of the Jews; the rest of the world were left to themselves, to frame such a government as suited best their inclinations, and to make such rules and laws as they could best obey and be governed by.—Ours is compounded of an absolute Monarchy and a Commonwealth, and the original of it we have from the Saxons: but be it what it will, or whence it will, it is without question that the first original of our kings was, that the people found it for their advantage to set one over them, because of his wisdom, valour, and justice, and therefore they gave him several prerogatives above the rest of the people, that he might be the better able to govern and defend them: for there is none of the king's prerogatives, but are for the good of the nation if rightly employed. But it will be a strange conclusion to suppose, that the people obliged themselves to submit to the posterity of that man whom they first chose for their king because of his extraordinary endowments, let them be what they would, and never so unfit for the government: for the next of blood may be incapable of governing in several respects; suppose a fool or lunatic; by his principles, if he aim at arbitrary power; by his religion, if he be a Papist or a Heathen; or by his practices, before he comes to the crown, to destroy the religion and government by law established.—Now this I do not say, to argue that the election of the king is in the people, though, I think, much might be said in that case, neither is it now the question; but that which I speak for is, to prove that the next of blood has not so absolute an inherent right to the crown, but that he may for the good of the nation be set aside.—There is yet another inconvenience to allow the next of blood to have so absolute a right to the crown, because the possession of the crown takes away all disabilities, but only such as are by act of parliament; which being so, every king must thank his successor for every moment that he lives; if he kill him himself, he cannot be questioned for it, because as soon as the one is dead the other is king, for here the king never dies.—If therefore the next of blood has so absolute a right, the king is very unsafe: for though the duke be not inclined to shorten his brother's days, nay though he be averse to it, yet in obedience to the Pope and his Priests, it must be done either by himself or some other hand, and then how long may we expect his majesty's life?—If kings were good men, an absolute monarchy were the best government; but we see that they are subject to the same infirmities with other men, and therefore it is necessary to bound their power: and by reason that they are flesh and blood, and the nation is so apt to be bad by their example, I believe was that wherefore God was averse to let the Jews have a king; till they had kings, they never revolted so wholly from him: when their kings were good, they were obedient to him; but when they were idolatrous, then the people went mad of idols. I hope it is no regis ad exemplum that makes our nation so lewd and wicked at this day.

Sir *Henry Ford.* The king told us, in his Speech, 'That the eyes of all Europe were upon us.' This Bill is a thing of the greatest consequence. If you make a law, who shall not succeed to the crown, the regular way is next to declare who shall. I shall never think that dominion is founded in grace, or nature, but from a power ordained you know by whom: 'by me kings reign.' They say, no man is born with a crown on his head, or a saddle on his back. The end of this Bill is great, and I hope you will come to it by lawful means. I am as fond, as any man, of the Protestant religion; but I offer to your consideration, how far the legality of this Bill will be.

Sir *Wm. Hickman.* Here is nothing in the Bill that the crown may devolve to the next successor. Suppose that two Protestants lay claim to the crown; if they divide, they may let in Popery at the end of it. Princes often leave those things doubtful, but parliaments should leave them plain. I would have it left to the next right heir in succession.

Sir *Nich. Carew.* I would add a Clause to the Bill, to exclude all other Popish Successors.

Sir *Tho. Lee.* Perhaps there may rise a difficulty, who is a Popish Successor? Who must judge that?

Mr. *Harbord.* I have a great mind that this Bill should pass, and I approve of gentlemen's zeal for future security. I would have it provided in the Bill, 'That no king shall marry a Popish queen,' if we be so happy that this Bill should pass. It is from thence all our miseries come. I have been told, that we owe our misfortunes, of the duke's being perverted, to his mother; from her we derive that wound. If this Bill should exclude the duke's children from the crown, that are Protestant, I am against it; it is unjust.

Sir *Christ. Musgrave.* Nothing is more natural, than in this Bill to declare a Successor. When you take off this prince from the succession, the danger is great, and much more without this clause of declaring who is to be the successor.

Col. *Birch.* Consider what we are doing: not only securing the Protestant Religion, but the king's life, and, I hope, long life; and till this Bill pass, it is the interest of every Papist to do, what I hope God will never permit. I remember the answer queen Eliz. gave the parliament, when they pressed her to declare her Successor;* a thing I would by no means have done at this time.

Mr. *Daniel Finch.* The excluding the duke

* Viz. "That the naming her Successor, would be digging a grave for her."

will not give a right to the next heir, to take possession of the crown while the duke is living; and therefore unless you name a successor, it will either prove ineffectual, or cause a great disturbance in the nation, by an interregnum. And, sir, as this part of the Bill is too weak, so the other is too strong: for, as it is now penned, it may probably exclude all the duke's children, at leastwise leave it so, as that it may prove a great question, which I suppose you do not intend.

Col. *Titus*. Sir, I do not see how you can name a Successor, unless you can in the same act prohibit the queen from having of children, the king from marrying again, the duke from having sons, which would not be more preposterous, than the many provisos which otherwise the act would require, to secure such issue their right; which would probably make the remedy worse than the disease. And I think, sir, that in a case of this importance, you will be careful how you make laws, that shall be liable to so many difficulties and disputes. And therefore you had better rely on the old laws you have, than make new ones to perplex the case. And I do not see how the excluding of the duke only can any way infect the right which his children may have to the succession. And therefore I think there is no need of naming a Successor.

Sir *Robert Howard*. Sir, I tremble to hear so much discourse about the king's death, and naming him a successor; certainly the like was never known in any former age, but rather it was looked on as so dangerous a thing to be discoursed of, as that none durst attempt it, whatever the occasion were. Queen Eliz. concluded, that the naming a Successor to the crown, would be digging a grave for her; and therefore I hope we shall never go so far as to put it into an act. I am for shewing a great respect for the duke, and his children; but I think we are first bound in duty to the king; and therefore ought first to shew our respects to him. Some persons, in my poor opinion, have shewed so much zeal for the duke's interest, that I am afraid they have forgot their allegiance to the king. Can he ever be safe, as long as it is the interest of every Papist in England to kill him? Which it will be, as long as there is hopes of a Papist to succeed to the throne.

Resolved, "That the Bill be committed to a committee of the whole house: That it be an instruction to the said Committee, that the Exclusion in the said Bill do extend to the person of James duke of York only: That this house do resolve into a committee of the whole house on the 8th inst."

Nov. 8. The house resolved into a committee of the whole house, to proceed in the consideration of the Bill, to disable James duke of York, to inherit the Imperial Crowns of England and Ireland, and the Dominions and Territories thereunto belonging; and after many debates about several Amendments, and Clauses to be added, the Bill was agreed, and reported to the house.—Resolved, "That the said Bill, with the several Clauses and Amendments, be engrossed."

Message from the King relating to the Exclusion Bill.] Nov. 10. His majesty's Message to the house was read.

"His majesty desires this house, as well for the satisfaction of his people, as of himself, to expedite such matters as are depending before them, relating to Popery and the Plot; and would have them rest assured, that all Remedies they can tender to his majesty, conducing to these ends, shall be very acceptable to him; provided they be such as may consist with preserving the Succession of the Crown in its legal course of descent."

Debate thereon.] Mr. *Boscawen*. Sir, I look on all his majesty's Speeches to parliaments, and Messages to this house, to be acts of state, and the results of serious councils; and therefore the more deserving our consideration: but also I think we may in some respects look on them as we do on letters patent, or other grants in the king's name; if in them there be any thing against law, the lawyer or officer that drew them is answerable for it. So if his Speeches be the product of council, if there be any mistake in them, it must be imputed to the council, and we may and ought to conclude the king never said it, for he can do no wrong. I cannot, sir, but much admire what neglect of ours, as to Popery and the Plot, hath occasioned this message. Hath not most of our time been spent about examination of witnesses about the Plot, and in making inspections into the proceedings of the last parliaments as to their transactions about it, that so we may proceed upon such grounds as we ought? Hath there any day past, in which we have not done something as to the Plot and Popery, besides what we have done about the duke's Bill? Which alone is sufficient proof of our endeavours to discover the Plot and Popery, because it plainly appears that all the Plot centers in him, and that we can never prevent Popery, but by preventing that power to rule, which is derived from a Popish Successor, and the having of a Popish king. It is true, we have spent some time also, in asserting the right of the people to petition the king for parliaments, or other grievances; but I do not take that to be so remote to this affair; for can the Plot ever be searched to the bottom, or Popery prevented, as our case stands, but by parliaments? And seeing there were so many prorogations of this parliament, when there were occasions so urgent for their sitting, in order to search the Plot to the bottom, and to make laws against Popery, have we not great reason to believe, that it was from that party that such strange endeavours were used to prevent the meeting of parliaments, from whom they know nothing but ruin can attend them? Do we not see, by Coleman's Letters, what contrivances they always had for to manage the meetings, sittings, prorogations, and dissolutions of parliaments? And why should we not believe they exercise the same arts still? Seeing it is plain that the dissolutions of the last two parliaments, and many prorogations of this, did not proceed from any Protestant interest; and therefore well may we conclude from whom. And for the same reason that they fear parliaments, have not the people reason to be fond of them, being the only legal way to redress Grievances? And could we have answered the neglecting of the asserting our rights in that particular? Sir, I think that, next to the duke's Bill, the asserting of the People's Right to petition, is the most necessary affair we could have spent our time about, in order to have the Plot examined to the bottom, by conveying to his majesty the desires of his people, to have parliaments sit in order thereto. And therefore I am jealous that the Advice given for this Message, doth proceed rather from a fear that we are doing too much, than from our doing too little against Popery. However, sir, seeing the Message comes in his majesty's name, let us, according to our duty, give all the compliance we can to it; and therefore I humbly move you, that a Message be sent to the lords, to desire them to appoint a day for the Trial of William visc. Stafford.

Mr. *John Hampden.* Sir, I cannot but observe, that his majesty in his Speech made to us at the opening of this session, recommended to us the Examination of the Plot, and the making laws for the security of the Protestant religion, which is not yet above 20 days ago. And therefore it is very strange, in my opinion, that we should so soon receive another Message to the same purpose, especially considering how we have spent our time ever since our meeting, in that which we have reason to think tends as much to the preventing of Popery, as any thing we could invent. The truth is, sir, I am fully persuaded, that the advice for this Message proceeds from the same men that advised the Dissolution of the two last parliaments, and the many prorogations of this; for though it may look like a contradiction, that going fast or going slow should tend to one and the same end, yet it doth so in this case: for by the dissolutions of those parliaments, and many prorogations of this, time was gotten for the disheartening of some witnesses, and tampering with others, and the death of the most material one; and now, by pressing upon this parliament to make great haste, other witnesses may be prevented from coming in, for which his maj. hath declared he will give two months time by his proclamation. So that it plainly appears, that the farther Examination of the Plot must be prevented some way, if they can do it; and that rather than fail, your endeavours to go to the bottom of the Plot shall be turned upon you, and made use of to their advantage. Sir, we are under great difficulties, and therefore we must be careful what we do. By the contents of this Message we may plainly see, that our enemies are at work to represent our proceedings ill to the king, that so if possible there may be some plausible pretence found out that may serve to gull the people, if they should procure a Dissolution. But I hope his maj. will not hearken to such advice; in order to prevent it, let us, until we have an opportunity to express our duty to him by actions, do it by words, to satisfy him, that we have spent most of our time in examining the Plot, and in contriving how to secure his person and government against the dangers arising from Popery; and to assure him, that we will lose no time till we have done what lies in our power in order thereto; and that we may withal give some farther instance of our endeavours, let us vote that we will immediately proceed to the Trial of lord Stafford.

Mr. *Harbord.* Sir, I am well content to understand that part of the Speech, which recommends to us a speedy examination of the Plot, to proceed from his majesty's goodness, on a supposition that he is now more sensible than ever of the danger his person and government is in by papists. And I hope it is from that, and not from any other reason, that he hath been pleased to send us this Message so soon after his Speech, notwithstanding our endeavours as to the Plot and Popery. But, sir, what I am most concerned at, is the latter part of the speech, that about the Succession; for it looks like the difficulty that was put upon the Israelites, of making bricks without straw. For seeing all the discoveries about the Plot make it clearly out, that it all centers in the duke, and that all their hope is derived from a Popish Successor, and expectation of a popish king, how can we do any thing that can be effectual in pursuance of the first part of that proposition, without contradicting the latter, it being impossible to secure the protestant religion under such limitations? However, sir, I hope that none of these things will put the house out of that temper and moderation which becomes this place; for I hope that at last his maj. will either convince us, or be advised by us, that so we may come to a fair understanding, and this session have a happy conclusion. Let us be careful not to give our enemies any just advantage to misrepresent us: And then I hope all will do well at last, maugre all the endeavours of our back-friends. That we do vote that we will proceed to Trial of some of the lords, and appoint a committee to draw up an Address in answer to this Message, is, I conceive, what is necessary at this time.

Col. *Titus.* Sir, his majesty's Message is a tacit reprehension of this house, for not having done their duty, as to the Plot and Popery. And as well by this Message, as by his Speech at the opening of the session, he doth now seem much concerned, that the Examination of the Plot, and the securing of the nation against the danger of Popery, hath been so long deferred; for my part, I think he hath a great deal of reason for what he saith, and I am glad to hear it. For I hope he is now truly sensible what strange advice he followed in dissolving the last parliaments, and so often proroguing this; and that he will now permit the parliament to sir, until they have done their duty in that particular. But, sir, though his majesty may now be very sensible of the miscarriages there have been in the management of this business already, yet I think we may not do amiss (seeing his maj. hath given us this occasion) to particularise to him, how the Examination of the Plot, and the securing us against Popery, hath been prevented. Sir, was not the late Long Parliament, after the Plot broke out, in a fair way to have tried the Lords, and to have examined the Plot to the bottom? And did not the dissolution of them frustrate all their proceedings? Did not the next parliament fall upon the same subject, and were they not advanced very far towards it? And did not the prorogation and dissolution come, and make all void? Hath this parliament, though called to meet the 17th Oct. was 12 months, ever sat till now? And have they not ever since their meeting employed most of their time about the Plot and Popery? And can there lie any just complaints against us? The truth is, sir, it is plain to me, that if this Message proceeds from his majesty's own judgment, as I hope it doth, (for how can it be presumed that his maj. should not see how we proceed against the Plot and Popery as well as every body else?) or if it proceed from such counsel, as do really intend we should do something against Popery, then we may be permitted to sit until we have done something for the security of our religion, and good of our country; but, on the other side, if this Message do proceed from the same counsel that advised the dissolutions of the last parliaments, and many prorogations of this, then we may take it as a clear discovery, that there are persons at work to represent us ill to the king, and to find some such pretence for our dissolution, as may pass with the people; and such I take to be enemies both to the king and kingdom, and therefore hope you will take a time to find them out, and proceed against them as they deserve.

Sir *Fr. Winnington.* Sir, though I know that we are under an obligation from duty to make a good construction of all his majesty's Speeches and Messages to this house, yet because they generally do proceed from some advice and counsel taken on such occasions, therefore, I think, we may, without offence, when any thing is irreconcileable in them, attribute it to the ministers; though all that which is good, and agreeable to that wisdom and prudence which is inherent in his majesty, ought to be attributed to himself; and, as the case stands with us, I think only from him can it proceed. What is said in this Message, that neither his maj. nor the people can be satisfied, unless we expedite such matters as relate to the Plot, I believe it proceeds from his majesty's own genius, it being so agreeable to that love which he hath always professed for the protestant religion; but that tacit imputation that we have neglected the Examination of the Plot, and proceedings against Popery, appears to me like a kind of infatuation in those ministers that advised it. For, sir, is there any thing more obvious, than that this parliament have spent most of their time in matters relating to the Plot and Popery, and to make such laws as may prevent the coming in of Popery upon us? And did not both the last parliaments do the same, from the time the Plot broke out? And if I may take the liberty to prophesy, I am apt to think, that the next, and the next, will proceed in the same steps, until such laws be made as are precisely necessary for the hindering of Popery from coming in upon us: And I pray God it may not be a cause why we shall have no parliaments to sit and act for a while. But, sir, as this is plain, so to our grief it is, that there are those about the king in great power, who are against the Examination of the Plot to the bottom, or making laws against Popery. Hath not this appeared by the great endeavours that have been used to stifle the Plot; the menacing and discouraging of the true witnesses, and setting up and encouraging of false ones? I mean, by the great power that accompanied those endeavours; but above all, by the great authority and interest, which that party have shewed in the dissolution of the last two parliaments, (though as to the first I heartily forgive them) and the many prorogations of this. And must they now, after they have stopped or smothered all proceedings that tended to destroy Popery, for above two years, find fault that we have not brought all to perfection in two weeks? Sir, this looks like such a profound piece of policy, as that of killing Justice Godfrey. But I am not sorry that their politics run so low. Such a pretence as this can only pass with persons that have a mind to be deceived. I will never doubt the prudence of the major part of the nation in this particular, who know that the non-prosecution of the Plot is the great grievance which the nation groans under; and the making of such laws which may secure us against Popery, the greatest reason why they have so longed for a parliament, and adventured so much, as some did, in petitioning for one. And, sir, I think, that accordingly this house have not been wanting to do their duty therein; and therefore do believe that such representations to his maj. are made by such, as aim at the destruction of parliaments, and bringing in of Popery. But the better to prevent their taking any such advantage for the future, I could wish that we may not spend more mornings about Irish cattle, nor East-India trade, until the business of the Plot and Popery be more off our hands. But in order to satisfy his maj. of our obedience to his commands, I agree both for the committee, and Trial of the lord Stafford.

An Address voted.] Resolved, "That a committee be appointed, to draw up an humble Address to his majesty upon the debate of the house, in answer to his majesty's gracious Message."

Lord Stafford's Trial resolved on.] Resolved, "That this house will proceed in the prosecution of the Lords in the Tower, and will forthwith begin with Wm. visc. Stafford."

The Commons' Address, in Answer to the King's Message.] Nov. 11. Sir Wm. Jones* reported from the committee appointed to draw up an Address to his majesty, upon the debate of the house, in answer to his majesty's gracious Message; which being read, was agreed to by the house, as follows:

"We your majesty's most loyal and obedient subjects, the commons in this present parliament assembled, having taken into our most serious consideration your majesty's gracious Message, brought unto us the 9th day of this inst. Nov. do with all thankfulness acknowledge your majesty's care and goodness, in inviting us to expedite such matters as are depending before us, relating to Popery and the Plot. And we do, in all humility, represent to your majesty, that we are fully convinced, that it is highly incumbent upon us, in discharge both of our duty to your majesty, and of that great trust reposed in us by those whom we represent, to endeavour, by the most speedy and effectual ways, the Suppression of Popery within this your kingdom, and the bringing to public justice all such as shall be found guilty of the horrid and damnable Popish Plot. And though the time of our sitting (abating what must necessarily be spent in the chusing and presenting a Speaker, appointing grand committees, and in taking the oaths and tests enjoined by act of parliament) hath not much exceeded a fortnight; yet we have in this time not only made a considerable progress in some things which to us seem, and (when presented to your maj. in a parliamentary way) will, we trust, appear to your maj. to be absolutely necessary for the safety of your majesty's person, the effectual Suppression of Popery, and the security of the religion, lives, and estates of your majesty's protestant subjects: but even in relation to the Trials of the five Lords impeached in parliament for the execrable Popish Plot, we have so far proceeded, as we doubt not but in a short time we shall be ready for the same. But we cannot (without being unfaithful to your majesty, and to our country, by whom we are entrusted) omit, upon this occasion, humbly to inform your majesty, That our difficulties, even as to these Trials, are much increased by the evil and destructive counsels of those persons who advised your majesty, first to the prorogation, and then to the dissolution of the last parliament, at a time when the commons had taken great pains about, and were prepared for those Trials. And by the like pernicious counsels of those who advised the many and long prorogations of the present parliament, before the same was permitted to sit; whereby some of the Evidence which was prepared in the last parliament, may possibly (during so great an interval) be forgotten or lost; and some persons, who might probably have come in as witnesses, are either dead, have been taken off, or may have been discouraged from giving their evidence. But of one mischievous consequence of those dangerous and unhappy counsels, we are certainly and sadly sensible, namely, that the testimony of a material witness against every one of these five Lords (and who could probably have discovered, and brought in much other evidence about the Plot in general, and those lords in particular) cannot now be given viva voce; for as much as that witness is unfortunately dead, between the calling and the sitting of this parliament. To prevent the like, or greater inconveniences for the future, we make it our most humble request to your most excellent majesty, that, as you tender the safety of your royal person, the security of your loyal subjects, and the preservation of the true protestant religion, you will not suffer yourself to be prevailed upon by the like counsels, to do any thing which may occasion, in consequence, (though we are assured never with your majesty's intention) either the deferring of a full and perfect discovery and examination of this most wicked and detestable Plot, or the preventing the conspirators therein from being brought to speedy and exemplary justice and punishment. And we humbly beseech your maj. to rest assured, (notwithstanding any suggestions which may be made by persons, who, for their own wicked purposes, contrive to create a distrust in your majesty of your people,) that nothing is more in the desires, and shall be more the endeavours of us, your faithful and loyal commons, than the promoting and advancing of your majesty's true happiness and greatness."

Debate on the 3d Reading of the Exclusion Bill.] Mr. *George Vernon.* Sir, I hope this Address will satisfy his majesty, that this house hath not been negligent in the prosecution of the Plot and Popery, and that it will create in his majesty a good opinion of our proceedings, that so we may not meet with any interruption in the perfecting of those Bills which are necessary for the good of the king and kingdom, and may have the glory of having been instrumental in accomplishing that security which the nation so much desires in point of Religion, and in making his majesty's government not only more easy to him, but so formidable, as that he may become a terror to his enemies, and in a capacity to give assistance to his friends both at home and abroad; and, if possible, so reconcile all divisions, as that there may be no distinction but of Papists and Protestants, nor of that neither, if there could be a way found out to prevent it. For I know this house wants nothing but opportunity to express their loyalty to the king, and love to the Protestant Religion, and their country;

* "This Address was drawn up under the sanction of sir Wm. Jones, who was that very day introduced into the house, as also appointed of the Committee, and by them placed in the chair, out of a peculiar compliment." Ralph.

ut I am afraid that all our endeavours will rove ineffectual, unless we can remove from is majesty all counsellors that advise him in avour of the Popish interest, and such as influence him in favour of that party. I do not nean little ones, but such as by experience we ad found, have in the time of our greatest langer exercised a kind of uncontrolable power. The Witnesses which you have heard this day it the bar, as to the wicked Plot of the Papists n Ireland, and in what a dangerous condition he poor Protestants are there, how exceeded n numbers by their enemies, and deserted by heir friends, added to the Evidence we have of the Plot in England, hath given to me a new rospect of the deplorable condition we are n; and therefore, although it be a little late n the day, seeing here is a full house, and of such persons as I believe will never think any hing too much, that is so necessary for the good of their king and country; I hope you will not think it unseasonable, that I should now move you, that the ingrossed Bill, for disinheriting James duke of York, be read.

The Bill, amended as the house had ordered, was then read, entitled, 'An Act for securing 'of the Protestant Religion, by disabling James 'duke of York to inherit the imperial Crown 'of England and Ireland, and the dominions 'and territories thereunto belonging.'

Sir *Leoline Jenkins.* Sir, this great business cannot be too well considered, before you come to a final resolution therein. I will not now offer you any prudential arguments against this Bill; because I did offer several at the last reading. But, sir, I would desire you to consider, that this prince is brother to our present king, and son to our late pious king Ch. I. for whose memory this nation hath a great veneration: that this prince is enriched with excellent endowments, which he hath employed in the service of this nation, by fighting our battles, and defending us from the oppression of our enemies; and is only guilty of this one crime, which, I hope, upon mature deliberation, will not deserve so great a condemnation. Sir, I knew it is usual for this house to proceed in affairs of less importance, with all the calmness, justice, and prudence, that can be imagined; and therefore I hope you will be careful how you deviate from those measures, in a business of this nature. I would once more remember you, that there are laws already for the punishment of the crimes he is accused of; and therefore humbly conceive, you ought not to chastise him, by making a new law; especially with that severity, which is, by this bill, now intended, before any hearing.—Sir, for my part, I have taken the oath of allegiance, and think myself therein bound to him, as heir, until it please God that his majesty have children. I know of no power on earth, that can dispense with my oath; and therefore I cannot (so much as by being silent) give my consent to this Bill, lest I therein wrong my conscience; seeing I have the honour to be a member of this house.—I do not doubt but most here have a great esteem for the Church of England, as members thereof: I could wish they would consider what a great blow this Bill will give to our religion, and to our Church. To disinherit a prince for no other cause, but for being of a different opinion in some points of faith, is, I think, quite contrary to the principles of the religion we profess, and also to the established laws of this land. And if such an act, when made, should be of any validity, I do conclude, that you will thereby change the constitution of this monarchy, and make it in a manner elective; and therefore I humbly move you, that the Bill may be thrown out.

Sir *Rob. Markham.* Sir, I think there ought to be a Proviso, That if the duke should turn Protestant, that then the Bill should be void, and he not excluded from his right; that so we may not leave him without some temptation to return to the Protestant Religion. And I think there ought to be a proviso, that in case the duke should have a son, after either of his daughters (if it should be their fortune) have ascended the throne, for the reserving of him a right. For there is a possibility, that if the duke should out-live the king, he may have a son, after that his daughters, by virtue of this act, may have taken the crown. I suppose, as there is no intent to chastise the daughters for the father's sake, so not the son; and therefore I humbly move you, that some proviso may be added, to secure him his Right, if any such thing should happen.

Mr. *Goodwin Wharton.** I have not yet troubled you since I had the honour to be here, and should not at all upon any other matter. I know my own inabilities, in comparison of many abler and wiser men than myself, but I cannot be silent when I hear the justice of the house questioned. If those things be true which are suggested in the Bill, the duke has forfeited his life upon it. Passing this bill is in order to our security only, and therefore it is just. The duke has done his utmost endeavour to ruin this nation, and to destroy us all. It is said, 'that the duke has fought our battles;' but I think he did not when he fell asleep.† It was not fair in the duke to let our ships fight with the Dutch, and to suffer the French to stand still. At the great fire, when London was burnt, certain men were taken, actually firing houses, and delivered to the guards, who let them escape, and the officer that set them at liberty was afterwards one of his greatest favourites. It was a sign of a very ill principle in the duke, that, when the duke of Monmouth was sent into Scotland to suppress that Rebellion, it was thought amiss by the duke, that they were not all destroyed. I do not think that you will chuse a prince that will not speak truth, to inherit the crown. When Bedlow gave in his information of the murder of sir E. Godfrey, and accused one Le Phaire to have been one of the murderers, and one of the

* A younger son of lord Wharton.

† See p. 406.

queen's servants, I heard the duke say to those about him, 'There was no such man in the world, nor about the queen.' And within three or four days after, there was a bond found, under his hand. A prince not to speak truth! I cannot express what to call it. This is plain, that the duke did hinder the discovery of the Plot. Is such a prince fit to succeed? Never were worse things done, nor a worse man in betraying the French Protestants, by placing the French ambassador behind the hanging when he made some overtures—

Here lord Castleton interrupted him, to the Orders of the house. 'To hear a prince thus spoken of, I am not able to endure it!'

Mr. *Wharton* went on. It is not my business to make a speech, but what I know, and think to be real truth, ought to be taken notice of. But since these things are so odious, I will not touch any more upon them now. As for the prudential part of the Bill, an hon. person told you, 'he would not speak to it,' and he has kept his word very exactly. And whereas another member before him objected, 'That it was possible the Duke might turn Protestant,' I will only answer, that I do not think it possible, that any person that has been bred up in the Protestant Religion, and hath been weak enough (for so I must call it) to turn Papist, should ever after (in that respect) be wise enough to turn Protestant. And therefore, upon the whole matter, my motion is, That the Bill may pass.

Mr. *Laurence Hyde.* Sir, I do not know that any of the king's murderers were condemned without being heard; and must we deal thus with the brother of our king? It is such a severe way of proceeding, that I think we cannot answer it to the world; and therefore it would consist much better with the justice of the house, to impeach him, and try him in a formal way; and then cut off his head, if he deserve it. I will not offer to dispute the power of parliaments; but question whether this law, if made, would be good in itself. Some laws have a natural weakness with them. I think, that by which the old long parliament carried on their Rebellion, was judged afterward void in law; because there was a power given, which could not be taken from the crown. For aught I know, when you have made this law, it may have the same flaw in it; if not, I am confident there are a loyal party, which will never obey, but will think themselves bound, by their oath of allegiance and duty, to pay obedience to the duke, if ever he should come to be king, which must occasion a civil war. And, sir, I do not find that the proviso, that was ordered to be added for the security of the duke's children, is made strong enough to secure them, according to the debate of the house; it being liable to many objections; and the more, because the words, 'presumptive heir of the crown,' are industriously left out, though much insisted on when debated here in the house. Upon the whole matter, my humble motion is, that the Bill may be thrown out.

Sir *Wm. Jones.** Sir, I am very unfit to speak in this place, being a member but of yesterday, but I will rather adventure to draw a censure on myself, than be wanting to serve my country (seeing they have called me hither) in a business of so great importance, I think, as great as ever was debated in an house of commons. I can truly affirm, that I have a great respect for the duke; and therefore, as well for the preservation of the Protestant Religion, I am for this Bill. For I take it for granted, that it is impossible that a Papist should come to the possession and quiet enjoyment of this crown, without wading through a sea of blood, and occasioning such a war as may, for aught I know, shake the monarchical government of this nation, and thereby not only endanger himself, but his children too. For no man can foresee what may be the end of such a war, nor what miseries it may bring on the nation: but, in all probability, it may prove the deepest tragedy that ever was acted on this great theatre. For it cannot be imagined, that the great body of Protestants which are in this nation, will tamely submit to the Popish yoke, which they will see in time must be the consequence of submitting to a Popish king, without some struggling. And wars begun upon the score of religion are generally attended with more fatal and bloody consequences than other wars; and this may exceed all others that ever yet were made. And I see no way to prevent it, but by passing this Bill, which, so long as it excludes only him, and secures the crown to his children, is, I think, (as the case stands) the greatest kindness we can do him. Sir, I do much admire to hear some hon. and learned members say, that this Bill is against natural justice, because it condemns a man before he is heard; and that it is too severe a condemnation; that it is against the oath of allegiance and principles of our religion; that it will be a scandal to our Church, to exclude a man of his right, for his opinion in religion; that it is a law that will be void in itself, and that there are a loyal party which will never obey it; that it will make the crown elective, and occasion a civil war; and that the Proviso, as to the duke's children, is not strong enough, because the word, 'presumptive Heir,' is left out.—Sir, the first objection.

* This was the first time he spoke in parl. "Sir Wm. Jones, the late Attorney General, at his first entrance into the house, espoused the Bill with a warmth and vehemence which were not natural to him. And this person having the fame of being the greatest lawyer in England, and a very wise man; being also known to be very rich, and of a wary or rather timorous nature, made people generally conclude, that the thing was safe and certain, and would at last be agreed on all hands, whatever countenance was made at Court." Temple's Memoirs.—In the Appendix to the present volume, No. XV. will be found an excellent Tract written by this gentleman.

I think, is a great mistake; for this Bill is not intended as a condemnation to the duke, but a security to ourselves; and is so far from being against natural justice, that the passing of it is agreeable to the very foundation not only of natural justice, but natural religion too; the safety of the king and kingdom depending thereon, which, according to the rules of justice and religion, we are bound to use our endeavours to preserve, before any one man's interest. That about the oath of allegiance I do a little admire at; for it is the first time I ever heard that oath pleaded in favour of Popery. I have oftentimes had occasion to scan the meaning of that oath, but never found it extended to the successor during the king's life; and therefore no need of any dispensation in that point. And I cannot understand, how it can be any scandal as to our Church or Religion, if by Church be meant our Protestant Church. Can our Church, or churchmen, be scandalized because we endeavour to secure ourselves against Popery by all lawful means? I rather think the very supposition an high reflection on our churchmen, as rendering them willing to let in Popery, which I am confident they are not. As to what is said, that the law will be void in itself, and that there will be a loyal party that will never obey it, and that it will occasion a civil war; I must confess these are strange arguments to me: for, to doubt that the legislative power of the nation, king, lords and commons, cannot make laws that shall bind any, or all the subjects of this nation, is to suppose there is such a weakness in the government as must infallibly occasion its ruin. And therefore I am of opinion, that what laws you make in this case, will carry as much right and strength with them, not only now, but after the king's death, as any law whatsoever. And how then, can there be a loyal party that will not acquiesce therein, unless the word loyal have some other signification than I know of? I take it to be a distinction that can only be given to such as obey laws; and, I think, we need not doubt, but if once this law were passed, there would be Protestants enough, whose interest it will be to defend it, that would compel an obedience to it. And we have much more reason to fear a civil war without it, than with it; for if we can get this Bill, we may be thereby so united, and enabled to defend ourselves, as that the Popish party may never have the confidence to attempt us; but without it we shall not be in any capacity to defend ourselves; which above all things, may encourage a civil war. As to the Proviso, for securing the right to the duke's Children, if it be not strong enough, I am ready to give my vote it should be stronger; but I take it to be as full and comprehensive as can be made; at least, I take the leaving out the words, 'presumptive Heir to the crown,' to be no objection against it: for there is no such word in our Law-Books, nor no such term in treating of the Succession; and therefore I hope you will be careful how you make a precedent in that case.—And, sir, as I do not find there is any weight in the arguments that have been made against this Bill; so I think, that if the preservation of our king, our government, our lives, and our religion, be things of moment, that there is much to be said for it. For although the malignity of men cannot deface his majesty's goodness; yet by assisting the Popish Faction, they have spoiled the beautiful face of the best government in the world, by breaking that good correspondence there ought to be between the king and his people; by dividing us in points of religion; and by being the cause of just Jealousies and Fears: by which his maj. is reduced to great difficulties and trouble, in the administration of his regal authority; and the credit, peace, and tranquillity of the nation almost irrecoverably lost, As to all which, the art of man cannot find out any remedy, as long as there is a Popish Successor and the fears of a Popish king; and therefore I humbly move you this Bill may pass.

Sir *F. Winnington.* Sir, the arguments that have been used against this Bill may be very excellent to lull us into a fatal security, by possessing us with opinions, that there is no need of taking so much care about popery; or that we ought not to oppose it; or that it will be to no purpose, because we have no power to hinder it. But I do not see what weight they have in them, grounded on any other consideration, to hinder the passing this Bill. Rather, for the same reason that such arguments as these are here offered against this Bill, and such endeavours used abroad to reconcile the people to have a better opinion of popery than formerly, I think we ought to be the more zealous for this bill; because nothing can give a greater encouragement and assistance to popery, than the growth of such opinions, nor prevent their design who are industrious to infuse them, than the passing of this Bill. Whoever will consider how this monarchy hath declined in grandeur, honour, and reputation abroad, by the destruction of our Navy in 1666, and the little appearance we have ever since made, of being formidable at sea; but above all, our ministers double-dealing in the making of Alliances, or performing of them, (in order to keep up our interest with France.) How from being umpire to all this part of the world, according to the advantage which we have by our situation, we are become the despicablest nation in Europe. How the government is weakened at home, not only by Fears and Jealousies, but by the debaucheries and divisions which have been promoted amongst our people; how narrowly we escaped ruin when the city of London was burnt, as well as when the Toleration came out, and the Army was at Black-Heath? as lately by the horrid Plot, if it had not been discovered; how there is nothing stands between us and death, but the king's life; and how all these dangers, past and present, do arise from Popery: and how impossible it is it should be otherwise, as long as there is a Popish Successor, we may justly admire there should be any arguments offered in this place to lessen our care for preventing the growth and power of Popery. I cannot tell how these learned members understand natural justice; but I am of that opinion, that self-preservation, and the preservation of our religion, and the life of our king, by all lawful ways, is very agreeable to natural justice. And I do admire to hear such a construction made of the oath of allegiance, that it binds all persons to the next heir, as well as to the king. For it is a most dangerous maxim, and may be of ill consequence, if ever the next heir of the crown should make a rebellion; for he may thereby challenge allegiance from the people, as well as the king; which might be of pernicious consequence. And I do not see wherein our Church or Religion can be scandalized by this bill. For we do not disinherit this prince for his religion, but to save our own, and to prevent the manifest ruin of the nation. And therefore I think it is a kindness to the Church, above all acts whatsoever; because the only way to preserve it, I mean the Protestant Church. And those objections that have been made against the lawfulness and validity of this act, do not weigh with me; but, notwithstanding what hath been said, I do believe it will be as good in law, if once it be passed, and will be as well observed too, as any act whatsoever. The king hath his right from God, and, as supreme, is accountable to none; his person sacred, and, by our laws, can do no wrong. If we should give all these qualifications to a successor, as hath been, in some measure, insinuated, it would make a strange confusion in the government. Life itself, to which a man hath as much right, as any successor can pretend to have to the crown, is taken away upon some forfeitures for the public good. And as there may be a forfeiture for life, so there may be a forfeiture of a right to the Succession. And to doubt that there is not an unlimited, uncontrolable power, residing somewhere in all governments, to remedy the exigencies that may happen, is to suppose there is such a weakness in this, or any other government, as that it must fall when a powerful faction shall endeavour it. In this nation, this power is in the king, lords, and commons; and I hope they will make use of it to preserve the government upon this occasion. And I do not doubt, but if the Bill pass, all will obey it heartily, that wish well to the Protestant Religion.

Col. *Legge*. Though I am talked of abroad to be a papist, yet, I thank God, I am none. And for an instance that I am not any, I will not pay that respect to Peter's Chair, as to 'deny my master*.' Many laws have been made about the Succession of the crown, but none without blood and misery. My father was twice condemned to die for asserting the right of the crown, and I hope I shall never forsake it. There has been a talk in the world of another Successor than the duke, in a Black Box*; but if Pandora's Box must be opened, I would have it in my time, not in my childrens, that I may draw my sword to defend the right heir. Has any happiness ever come to princes, who came to the crown, and the lawful heir thus put by? After Edw. vi. Jane Grey was proclaimed, but it proved unfortunate to her. If my master the duke be popish, God's curse be on him that was the cause of it! I hope you will take a course, that misery may not fall on posterity. I have Church-Lands, and reason to apprehend Popery coming in as other men—I cannot recollect what I had farther to say; but this Bill will set us all together by the ears.

Sir *H. Capel*. Sir, I do observe, and am glad to see it, that all that have spoken in this business, pro or con, seem to agree, that we ought to do all we can to preserve the present government, and prevent a civil war; but we differ about the way: some think, that this Bill is the only way; and others are of a contrary opinion, I cannot tell for what good reason. For there being nothing intended by this Bill, but the Exclusion of the duke only, in order to prevent the great danger we lie under, by reason of his great influence at court at present; and those we fear, if ever a Popish king should ascend the throne. There being nothing in the Bill that tends any way to prejudice the next heir, it cannot, in my poor opinion, weaken, much less tend to alter, the present government, or be any prejudice to the royal family, more than in the Exclusion of this one person intended by the Bill. From whom there can be no fear of a civil war; unless we should imagine, that the people of this nation, when they have a law, upon the observation and execution whereof their lives, liberties, and religion depend, they should be so great brutes as not to value themselves thereon; but rather embrace a blind, superstitious religion, and submit to all the slavery imaginable. We may as well think that, after the king's decease, the people will be willing to submit to the government, and pretended authority of the pope himself, though they should be never so well able to defend themselves. The worthy member that spoke last, did in a manner affirm, that all the precedents that have been mentioned, as to the Succession of the crown by act of par-

* He was master of the horse, and gentleman of the bed-chamber, to the duke of York; and afterwards lord Dartmouth.

* "A report was industriously propagated, that a Marriage had been solemnized, or at least a contract had passed, between his majesty, while abroad, and Mrs. Walters otherwise Barlow, his grace of Monmouth's mother; that the late bishop of Durham had consigned a writing in a Black Box, relating thereto, into the custody of sir Gilbert Gerrard, and that the said writing had been communicated to several persons of distinction, and had fully satisfied them that the fact was so." Ralph.

liament, have been accompanied with blood. If he would but take the pains to peruse the Histories of England, I think he would be of another opinion. But I am sure, none ever equalized the short reign of queen Mary. The barbarities which were exercised in her reign, by fire and faggot, may be put into the balance with all the inconveniencies that ever happened by any Exclusion Act. But, sir, if it had been so, which I utterly deny, it would not have signified much as to our case; for in those days, matter of right was always so confounded, (I mean, as to the understanding of the people) by the many arguments that were imposed on them by each party, that neither point of right, nor any consideration, as to any thing of interest, came fairly before them. Whether A. or B. should be king, was their only question, without being loaden with any difficulties; as to which the common and major part of the people in those days might probably be very indifferent. And yet, sir, upon a full examination it will be found, that most of those acts of parliament, touching the succession, had the effect they were designed for; and did serve as expedients, to prevent those miseries which were feared, and were the occasion of them. But, sir, the case will be now much otherwise, if ever you should be so unfortunate, as that the duke should out-live the king, and you should come to try the strength of this Exclusion Bill: for the question in this case will not be only whether A. which is excluded; or B. which is the next heir, shall, according to this act, be king; but whether it shall be a Papist or a Protestant. Upon which it will plainly appear, the safety of their estates, lives, and religion, doth depend. Sir, I have heard and read of strange things done by Popish miracles; and I must confess, I have seen much of it, even amongst many that pretend to be good Protestants, since the Plot broke out; I mean, as to their believing any thing against Popery. If some such omnipotent power should hereafter over-rule in such a conjunction, haply this Bill, if it should pass into an act, may be slighted and neglected; but otherwise I humbly conceive, it cannot be presumed, that the Protestants should omit to make use of it, to save themselves from popery and slavery, which would be the consequence thereof; and thereby not only prevent a civil war, but support the government established in the right line. The truth is, sir, the most material observation that I can make of the arguments against this Bill is, that it is thought too good for us; and that it may probably be effectual for the securing of the Protestant religion. And I am afraid, sir, that this is the fatal consideration that hath prevailed with some, to advise the king not to grant it. If we consider how all other laws, which have been hitherto made against the duke, have been defeated; we may, with some reason, fear the like success of all others that shall be made; unless you can do something that may tend to changing of the interest; which can never be done without this Bill.

Mr. *Daniel Finch*. Sir, I will not say, that acts of parliament cannot dispose of the Succession; because it was made treason, by a statute 13th Eliz. which I do not remember was ever repealed. But I will deny, that the kings of England rule by virtue of any statute-law, as was suggested; for their right is by so ancient a prescription, as that it may justly be said, to be from God alone; and that no power on earth ought to dispute it. And I am of opinion, that the Succession of the crown is inseparably annexed to proximity of blood; and therefore am not yet altered in my opinion, that if this Bill should pass into a law, it would be in itself invalid. Which, with what hath been already said, that we cannot in justice answer the inflicting of this severe condemnation without hearing the party concerned; and the improbability of ever attaining this bill, doth very much weigh with me for my opinion against this bill.

Mr. *John Trenchard*. Sir, I have hearkened to the objections that have been made against this Bill, which have not convinced me, that we want either a just cause, or a legal power, for the making of this Bill. If the Popish interest be grown too strong for the Protestant, then any of these arguments may serve; for force and power will supply the defect of them. Otherwise I think they have been so fully answered, as that there is no need more should be said about this matter; but I am sorry to see, that the Protestant Religion, and our lives and liberties, must have nothing to depend on, but the continuance of the king's life, and the good-nature of the Popish party afterward. And this, after such demonstration as we have of the interest of that party in France, Scotland, and Ireland, as well as here; and after a full direction of the growth of that interest, by means of the duke's; and of the endeavours that are used to possess the Protestants, with several opinions that will tend very much to the strengthening of it; and a clear discovery, that the Plot in favour of Popery goeth on as much as ever. It hath created in me an opinion, that Popery is too strong to be subdued by laws; and that, after this king's life, the Protestant religion must either be overcome by Popery, or defend itself by the sword. At least, I believe, that this is the design of some men now about the king; but I hope he will at last hearken to the advice of his parliament, and prevent the nation from falling into so miserable a condition. The objection made about the duke's son, if he should have any, after either of his daughters have taken possession of the government, may, in some measure, be made against the course of Succession observed in all kingdoms: If a king die, leaving a queen, the next heir is presently proclaimed, to prevent an inter-regnum; though there be a possibility of the queen's being with child, to whom the right should, in the first place, belong. If any such should be born, such a settlement as is designed by this Bill may destroy the French and Popish interest, but can never be a gratification to them. Our ancestors, upon many occasions, settled and changed the Succession: of which he gave many instances, and concluded for the Bill.

The Exclusion Bill passed.] After which, it was resolved, That the said Bill do pass; and that the lord Russel do carry it up to the lords for their concurrence; which he did on the 15th.*

Proceedings against Lord Stafford renewed.] Nov. 12. The house resolved, that a Message be sent to the lords, to acquaint them with the Resolution of this house to proceed to the Trials of the Lords in the Tower, and forthwith begin with the lord Stafford, and to desire their lordships to appoint a convenient day for the Trial of the said viscount; and, likewise, that the lords in the Tower may be confined and kept from correspondence one with another, as usual in the like cases.—To which their lordships replied the same day, "That as to the confinement of the lords, they had already given orders as the house desired; and that as to the trial of the lord Stafford, they had appointed Tuesday come fortnight for the said Trial."

Proceedings against sir G. Jefferies.] Nov. 13. Several citizens of London having before delivered in a petition against sir G. Jefferies*, the Recorder of the said city; and having made good their allegations before the committee appointed to enquire after persons who had offended against the right of the subject to petition, &c. the house resolved, "That the said sir G. Jefferies, by traducing and obstructing petitioning for the sitting of this parliament, hath betrayed the Rights of the Subject."—Ordered, "That an Address be made to his majesty, to remove sir G. Jefferies out of all public offices; and that the members for London do communicate the Vote of this house, relating to him, to the court of aldermen for the said city."

Debate on his Majesty's Message concerning Tangier.] Nov. 17. His majesty's Message about Tangier was read. 'His majesty did, in his Speech at the opening of this session, desire the advice and Assistance of his parliament, in relation to Tangier: the condition and importance of the place obliges his majesty to put this house in mind again, that he relies upon them for the support of it; without which it cannot be much longer preserved. His majesty doth therefore very earnestly recommend Tangier again, to the due and speedy care and consideration of this house.'—A long debate ensued, in the course of which

Sir *Wm. Jones* said, Sir, I am very sorry that the business of Supply for Tangier is now moved; because I take it to be a place of great importance, and that, as well for the honour of the nation, as benefit of trade, it ought to be preserved. But, sir, we have now things of greater importance to look after, of so pressing a nature, and of so dangerous consequence, if delayed, that we cannot answer, either to our king or our country, the preferring of this before it. It is a duty incumbent on us, to secure things at home, on which our all depends, before we enter into an expence of time about securing things abroad. If an enemy were but coming to invade us, it might be proper to fortify Dover-Castle, Portsmouth, or Plymouth, or any of our Port-Towns: but if an enemy were actually landed, it would be more proper to strengthen London, or other in-land cities or

* "The Exclusion Bill was quickly brought up to the lords. The earls of Essex and Shaftsbury argued most for it; and the earl of Halifax was the champion on the other side. He gained great honour in the debate; and had a visible superiority to lord Shaftsbury in the opinion of the whole house: and that was to him triumph enough. In conclusion, the Bill was thrown out upon the first reading. The Country Party brought it nearer an equality than was imagined they could do, considering the king's earnestness in it, and that the whole bench of bishops, except three, was against it." Burnet.

"Till 11 o'clock at night the rage of altercation and the lust of superiority kept up the contest, the king being present all the while, and the whole house of commons attending, who had adjourned their own proceedings to indulge their curiosity in observing the progress and event of this." Ralph.

"This was one of the greatest days ever known in the house of lords, with regard to the importance of the business they had in hand, which concerned no less than the lineal Succession to the Crown. Great was the debate, and great were the speakers: the chief of those for the Bill was the earl of Shaftsbury; against it, lord Halifax. It was matter of surprize that the latter should appear at the head of an opposition to the former, when they were wont always to draw together; but the business in agitation was against lord Halifax's judgment, and therefore he opposed it with vigour; and being a man of the clearest head, finest wit, and fairest eloquence, he made so powerful a defence, that he alone, so all confessed, influenced the house, and persuaded them to throw out the Bill." Reresby.

The numbers on the division were 63 to 30. A Protest was entered on the occasion by lord Carew.

* This over-bearing lawyer, being afterwards made Lord Chief Justice, &c. was notoriously distinguished in the succeeding annals of this and the following reign, for his arbitrary proceedings on the bench, and particularly for his cruelties in the West, after the duke of Monmouth's defeat in 1685. At the Revolution, being then Lord Chancellor, having disguised himself in a sailor's habit, in order to escape to Hamburgh, he was accidentally discovered by the mob, and by the lord mayor sent to the Tower, where he soon after ended his days under great misery and affliction.

towns. I am afraid, sir, this is too much our case; I am afraid we have got an enemy within our bowels, and a great one too; and that it is high time to make preparation to oppose him. We have been already careless and inconsiderate too long; and shall we now go about Tangier, instead of continuing our endeavours about that? Tangier may be of great importance to trade; but I am afraid, hath not been so managed, as to be any security to the Protestant religion. The Portuguese, when they delivered it up, did covenant to have one popish church remain there, for the conveniency of some priests and friars, and others of that nation that were permitted to stay there; but it was then agreed, That their mortality should not be supplied, that so, after the decease of those persons, the said popish church might be demolished, or converted to a Protestant use: but I am well informed that it hath been otherwise managed; and that the Papists there are now more than ever. And was not my lord Bellasis, now a prisoner in the Tower for the Plot, governor of Tangier? And, I think some others of that religion; if not, I am sure the soldiers and commanders are most of that religion; which makes me conclude, it is a kind of nursery for popish soldiers; and haply for that reason, as much as for the advantage of trade, may the advice given his majesty, in reference to Tangier, proceed. But, sir, there is another consideration, which will make the debate of Tangier improper at this time; it must end in Money, and not a little sum neither, enough to raise an Army; which, although in time I doubt not but this house will be willing to advance, as far as his majesty's occasions shall require? yet I think, sir, we are not ready for it as yet. We must be better satisfied into whose hands it will go; whether to such persons as for the popish interest, or Protestant; that so we may not be afraid, that, instead of going to the support of Tangier, it should be employed to the destruction of the Protestant religion. When these things have been looked into, and secured, then it will be time to take care of Tangier, and of all other his majesty's dominions. In the mean time, our duty binds us to give his maj. all the satisfaction we can, as to our proceedings; and therefore I humbly move you, that a committee may be appointed to draw up an Address for that purpose.

Mr. *L. Hyde.* Sir, every one that knows how advantageously Tangier is situated, to command the greatest thoroughfare of commerce in the world, and how by advantage of the mole, it is like to prove an excellent receptacle for our merchant ships, to further and secure them in their trading voyages into the streights, and for our men of war, when they may be employed in those parts, to check or oppose the Turks, or other enemies; how advantageous it is for carrying on a trade with Spain, in cases of extremity; and what hopes we have of opening a trade into Barbary that way, will, I suppose have reason to conclude, that it is a place of great importance, and not to be slighted. And I cannot believe that it is a nursery for popish soldiers, for it is well known under what a regulation our soldiers are, not only herein England, but Ireland too, of taking such oaths and tests as secures them to be Protestants.

Mr. *John Hampden.* Sir, among the rest of the regiments that have been sent to Tangier, I think there is my lord of Dunbarton's; haply that air might have changed them, but I am sure they were looked upon as rank Papists all the while they were here, and I believe, in Ireland too. I have heard that one argument, that was lately given elsewhere against a Bill which we passed in this house, was, that the duke had all the Papists in England ready for his assistance; that his particular friends had the command of all the places of strength in this nation; that he had an Army of 22,000 men in Scotland at his command; that in Ireland the Papists were six to one for the Protestants; and that most of the princes of Christendom were combined for his assistance; add to this, that the government of Tangier is also at his command, and, I think, we shall have no great reason to give money as yet; I am very well satisfied, sir, that we ought, and must put a trust in the king; an argument much used in former parliaments, I do admire hath been so long forgotten in this. I am sensible too, that this nation cannot be happy, unless there be such an understanding between the king and his people, as that Money may be given. But, sir, how shall we be sure, that what Money we give shall ever go to the king? May it not be intercepted by the mighty power we have been speaking of? May it not be a great temptation for carrying on the Plot, especially as to that part of it that refers to his sacred life? If there were no other reason to be given but this, why we cannot at this time give money, I think it enough.

Col. *Birch.* Sir, I think we cannot answer to God nor man the giving of Money, until there be a great reformation all over the nation, as to persons in trust and command. Not but that there are very worthy men in several places; but I am afraid, no where without being overpowered by such who are for the duke's interest: and for my part, I desire to speak plain, I cannot make any distinction between the duke's interest and the popish interest. If there be any body that can split that hair, I wish he would do the house that service; for I take it to be a material point, and fit to be agreed some way. And if it be so, sir, can we give money, as long as there are 11 to 7 in some places certainly known, and all in others, and in places of great importance too? Sir, I am very sensible that this session can never be successful, nor the nation happy, unless we come to have so fair an understanding with his majesty, as that we may freely give him Money; which seeing it cannot be done with any security to the king or his government, as long as the great affairs of this nation are thus influenced, that there may be no just cause of having any imputation lie at our door, I agree in the motions that have been made for an Address.

Lord *Russel.* Sir, if ever there should happen in this nation any such change, as that I should not have liberty to live a protestant, I am resolved to die one; and therefore would not willingly have the hands of our enemies strengthened, as I suppose they would be, if we should give Money while we are sure it must go to the hands of the duke's creatures. Doth not the duke's interest endanger the king's life? And are not our lives and fortunes in danger to be swallowed up by his power? And shall we yet make them stronger by putting Money into their hands? No sir, they are too strong already; but whenever his maj. shall be pleased to free us of the danger of a Popish Successor, and remove, from his council and places of trust, all those that are for his interest, (because there can be no distinction made between the duke's interest and popish) then, sir, I will conclude, that what Money we shall give, will be disposed of according to his majesty's own royal pleasure, and for the true protestant interest. And I shall be ready to give all I have in the world, if his maj. should have occasion for it; but in the mean time I pray, sir, let us not endeavour to destroy ourselves by our own hands. If we may not be so happy as to better the condition of the nation, I pray, sir, let us not make it worse. And until the king shall be pleased to give us encouragement to express our duty and loyalty to him, by giving him Money, let us do it by making an Address.

Sir *W. Temple.* Sir, this debate hath more of weight in it, than the business of Tangier, I think. As affairs now stand, the most part of Christendom is concerned in it, I am sure all the protestants. And therefore I hope your patience will hold out, to have the whole circumstances of it fairly examined: For the arguments that have been offered in the consideration of this Message, have inlarged the debate farther than was at first intended, and have brought the whole State of the Nation in some measure before you, instead of that one particular business of Tangier; so that now what resolve you make will be a discovery of your inclinations, not only as to what you intend to do as to a Supply for Tangier, but as to giving Money for Alliances and all other occasions, upon which result, the good or bad success of this parliament doth depend. As to Tangier, I do agree with that worthy member that spoke before, that it is not of any great use to us upon the account of any advantage we shall make by it. But however, I think it is very well worth our keeping, because of the disadvantages we should receive by it, if it should fall into the hands either of the Turk, or Spaniard, but especially the French; who will not only be thereby enabled to fetter us, as to our trade in the Levant, but to curb also all other nations whatsoever, and be such an addition to the too great power he hath acquired, both by sea and land already, that I am of opinion, we ought to be very cautious how we weaken the security we now have that it shall not fall into his hands. But if the Mole and the Town could be blown into the air, or otherwise reduced into its first chaos, I think, considering the charge it will cost keeping, England would not be much the worse for it; but to move you to consider any thing about that, at this time, cannot be proper, because the Moors have so besieged it, that the first thing that must be done, whether in order to keep it, or destroy it, is, to beat them off, by some speedy supplies which must be presently sent, or else the town, according to the best information come from thence, is like to be lost. And, sir, I think this single consideration may be persuasive to move you to give some such Supply, as may be precisely necessary for the defence and protection of this place. A small sum of money, in comparison of what this house hath formerly given, may be sufficient to satisfy his majesty's expectation, and secure the place too. But I must confess, sir, it is not the consideration of Tangier that makes me press you to it; but the deplorable estate of the protestants abroad. Sir, I have had the honour to serve his maj. in some public employments, and by that means may be a little more sensible of the state of affairs in reference to our neighbours, than others may be, having not only had the advantage of information, but was under a necessity of using my best endeavours to get a true account of them. Sir, I am confident the eyes of all Europe are upon this parliament; and not only the protestants abroad, but many Catholic countries, (who stand in fear of the power of France) do think themselves as much concerned in the success of this parliament, as this house, and will be as much perplexed to hear any ill news thereof. This, sir, as well as the necessities of our affairs at home, makes me trouble you at this time, to desire you to be careful what you do, that we may not occasion, in his maj. any dislike to this house. Whatever you do as to the business of Money for Tangier, I pray, sir, let there be no notice taken in your Address, of the lords having cast out your Bill; for we have no reason to think the king was any ways concerned therein. To throw out a Bill of so great importance, without a conference, was, in my humble opinion, very strange, and contrary to the usual proceedings of that house. But pray, sir, let it lie at their doors that did it, for the king could not be concerned in a parliamentary way. For by this means we may obviate all misunderstandings with his maj. about this affair, and I hope, create in him a good opinion of this house, upon which the welfare not only of this nation, but of Europe, doth much depend.—Sir, his maj. in his Message puts you in mind of giving Advice as well as Money. I think if we make that expression the ground of our Address, we may naturally graft very good things thereon, especially what may conduce to the preservation of a fair correspondence. Sir, though a king alone cannot save a kingdom, yet a king alone can do very much to ruin it: and though a parliament alone cannot save this kingdom, yet parliaments alone may do much to ruin it. And therefore we cannot be too circumspect in what we do. It is our fortune to sit here in a critical time, when not only the affairs of this nation, but the Protestant Religion abroad, need our continuance; and for the same reason we may justly fear, that there are those who endeavour to contrive the putting off this parliament. I pray, sir, let us not give them any advantage, and then I doubt not but his majesty's care and goodness will at last overcome all difficulties, and bring this session to a happy conclusion.

Mr. *Edward Deering.*] Sir, I think his majesty may easily send succour to Tangier without any great charge. Here are three or four regiments of soldiers about this town, which do rather hurt, than good to the nation; and therefore may very well be spared; and then that Money which pays them now here, may pay them there, and so I suppose there will be no need of money, save only for their transportation. I hope there will be great care taken in drawing this Address, that so our enemies may not have any ground to represent us as a stubborn parliament, that have no intention to give Money upon any terms whatsoever. I think, sir, we may be plain with his majesty, and give him as full assurance as ever any house of commons did, that when we have those things granted, which are unavoidably necessary for the preservation of our religion, that we will freely and heartily give money for the supply of his occasions; and I cannot but hope, that such fair proceedings will occasion a happy issue to this parliament. For it cannot be doubted, but that the king is very sensible, That he owes more to his people in general, than to any one man, be he brother, or any other relation; and that he cannot, without much trouble to himself, because of his coronation oath, longer permit that our laws and religion should be in such imminent danger. And therefore I hope that we shall not only have a fair correspondency continued, but also gracious compliance, in what we have desired for the effectual security of our religion, and therefore would desire you to put the question for a committee.

Resolved, "That a committee be appointed to draw up an Address to be presented to his majesty, upon the debate of the house, humbly representing to his majesty the dangerous State and Condition of the Kingdom, in answer to his majesty's Message."

Proceedings against the Earl of Halifax.] The same day, a debate arising in the house, on a motion for an Address to his majesty to remove George earl of Halifax from his maj.'s presence and councils for ever; the question was put to adjourn the said debate, and passed in the Negative, Yeas, 95, Noes 219. After which the said Address was voted.

Nov. 20. This day, in the house of lords, the question being propounded, Whether there shall be a Committee appointed, in order to join with a committee of the commons, to debate matters concerning the State of the Kingdom? it was resolved in the affirmative.*

Articles of Impeachment against Edw. Seymour, Esq.] The same day, sir Gil. Gerrard acquainted the house, That he had Articles of Impeachment of High Crimes, Misdemeanours and Offences, against Edw. Seymour, esq. a Member, and Treasurer of the Navy; the contents of which were to the following effect:

I. "That whereas 584,978*l.* was appropriated by act of parliament for the building 30 Ships of War, and it was enacted that the Treasurer of the Navy should keep all Monies paid on that Account distinct and apart from all other monies, and should issue the same by warrant of the principal officers and commissioners of the Navy, to the said specified use, and to no other whatever: the said Edw. Seymour, being Treasurer of the Navy, contrary to his duty, had lent the sum of 90,000*l.* at 8 per cent. part of the sum above-mentioned, towards the support and continuance of the Army, after such time as by act of parliament the said Army ought to be disbanded; whereby the said two several Acts were eluded, and the said army was kept on foot, to the great disturbance, hazard, and danger of the peace and safety of this kingdom; and the nation was afterwards put to a new Charge of raising 200,000*l.* for the disbanding the said Army. II. That whereas a Poll-Tax was granted to enable his majesty to enter into an actual War with France, and for the repayment of any such persons as should furnish his majesty with Money or Stores for that end: and whereas certain East-Land Merchants did supply great quantities of Naval Stores, on being assured that 40,000*l.* part of the Money raised by the said Act, was at that time actually in the hands of the said Edw. Seymour, which he likewise acknowledged, and did promise to pay the said Merchants in part of satisfaction for the said Stores; he the said Edward Seymour did issue out the said sum to the victuallers of the navy by way of advance for provisions not brought in, contrary to the meaning of the said Act, and of which the said merchants did complain in parliament. III. That the said Edw. Seymour being Treasurer of the Navy, and then, and still having a salary of 3000*l.* per ann. clear for the same, during the time he was Speaker for the late Long Parliament, did receive out of the Monies appointed for Secret Service the yearly sum of 3000*l.* over and above the said salary, which was constantly paid to him, as well during the intervals, as the sessions of parliaments; and particularly during the prorogation of 15 months. IV. That during the Dutch War, the said Edw. Seymour being one of the Commissioners of Prizes, did frau-

* See Appendix, No. X and XII.

dulently and unlawfully unlade a Prize-Ship, without order or authority, and did house the lading of the said ship, and lock up; and afterwards, without the presence of any storekeepers, did sell the same for Muscovado Sugars, and did account with his majesty for the same as such; when, in truth, the said ship was laden with cochineal, indigo, and other merchandizes of a great value."

Ordered, "That sir Edw. Seymour have a Copy of the said Articles; and that he do put in his Answer on the 25th."

Address to remove the Earl of Halifax.] Nov. 22. Mr. Trenchard reported the Address to his majesty to remove the earl of Halifax,* when a motion was made to re-commit the said Address, but it passed in the negative, Yeas 101, Noes 213. After which, it was agreed to by the house, as follows:

"We your majesty's most dutiful and loyal subjects, &c. being deeply sensible of the manifold dangers and mischiefs that have been occasioned to your kingdom by the Dissolution of the last parliament, and by the frequent Prorogations of the present parliament, whereby the Papists have been greatly encouraged to carry on their wicked and damnable conspiracies against your royal person and government, and the Protestant Religion now established amongst us, have had many opportunities to contrive false and malicious Plots against the lives and honours of several of your loyal Protestant subjects; and having just reason to believe, that the said Dissolution was promoted by the evil and wicked councils of George earl of Halifax, do, therefore, most humbly pray your majesty, for the taking away all occasion of distrust and jealousies between your majesty and us your loyal commons; and that we may with greater chearfulness, proceed to perfect those matters now before us, which tend to the safety and honour of your sacred person and government, and the preservation of the true Protestant Religion, both to ourselves and our posterity, That you would be graciously pleased to remove the said George earl of Halifax from your presence and councils for ever."

The King's Answer.] To this Address, his majesty sent the following Answer:

"C. R. His majesty, having received the Address of this house, relating to the earl of Halifax, has thought fit to return this Answer: That he conceives the said Address to be liable to several exceptions: but, having a great desire to preserve all possible good understanding with this house, he chuses to decline to enter into particulars, to avoid all occasions of dispute. He, therefore, thinks fit to tell them, That he doth not find the grounds in the Address of this house to be sufficient to induce him to remove the earl of Halifax. But he answers them at the same time, that whenever the house shall, in a due and regular course, prove any crime either against the said earl or any other person, who either now is, or hereafter shall be in his council, he will leave him or them to their own legal defence, without interposing to protect them.'

Debate on discharging a Middlesex Grand Jury.] Nov. 23. Lord *Russel.* 'There are some persons at the door, who can give you an account of the illegal proceedings of my lord chief justice Scroggs, in discharging the Grand Jury of Middlesex.'—Whereupon, several of the Grand Jury were called in, and some other persons, who gave an account of the carriage of that matter, as will be at large recited in the Articles against the lord chief justice Scroggs.

Sir *Wm. Jones.* Sir, the preservation of the government in general, as well as our particular safeties, have a dependance upon the matter that is now before you; in which there are so many miscarriages so complicated, as there ariseth some difficulty how to examine them. I cannot but observe, how the Proclamation is here again mentioned; by which you may conclude there lieth a great weight on the people's right to petition by means thereof; and that the best way to remove it is, to find out the advisers and contrivers of that Proclamation, in order to proceed against them according to their deserts. Without which, what you have done in asserting the right of petitioning, will remain with some doubt; and those that advised the proclaiming to the people, that it is seditious to petition the king, without that chastisement they deserve. And therefore I humbly conceive, you will do well to consider of it as soon as you can. It is not strange, that the Proclamation shall be made use of with country gentlemen, to get Abhorrers to petitioning; seeing the Judges themselves have made use of it to that purpose: they should have known, that though a Proclamation might be of great use, to intimate the observation of a law; yet it had never been used instead of a law. But yet I do not admire so much at this, as I do at the Discharge of the Grand-Jury, before they had finished their presentments. It tends so much to the subversion of the established laws of this land, that I dare pronounce that all the laws you have already, and all that you can make, will signify nothing against any great man, unless you can remedy it for the future. I observe, there were two reasons why the Grand Jury were so extra-judicially discharged; one, because they would otherwise have presented the duke of York for a Papist; the other, because they presented a Petition to be

* Created marquis of Halifax in 1682, and soon after made Lord Privy Seal, and upon king James's accession appointed Lord President of the Council; but upon refusing to consent to the Repeal of the Test, he was dismissed from all his employments. In the Convention-Parliament he was chosen Speaker of the house of lords, and was again made Lord Privy Seal by king William, but being attacked in parliament in 1689, he quitted that post, and died in 1695.

delivered to the king, for the sitting of the parliament; which they said it was not their business to deliver. Though I cannot but observe, how, upon other occasions, they did receive petitions, and delivered them to the king; and all the difference was, that those petitions so delivered, were against sittings of parliaments. The truth is, I cannot much condemn them for it; for if they were guilty of such crimes as the witnesses have this day given you information of, I think they had no reason to further petitions for the sitting of a parliament. But, sir, this business will need a farther information; and therefore I humbly pray it may be referred to a committee.

Sir *Henry Capel.* This matter is of the greatest moment. We are under the security of parliaments for redressing our grievances, and another, out of parliament, that the law have its course, that the Judges obstruct not the law. I observe that these Judges are grown omnipotent. 'They have done those things which they should have left undone.' This is very fine, that Judges, who must be upon the Bench, must be dropped at Whitehall, before they come to Westminster-Hall; and I know what law we must have, if they take instructions from those that advised the Proclamation against Petitioning. See the consequence; is it not as much as to say, that the Judges know all the grievances of the country, and the Judges must redress them, and we sit here but for form-sake? All misdemeanors, and what is amiss in the nation, the Judges must rectify. This is such a presumption, that they must answer it. If this be done in Westminster-Hall, how dare grand juries in the country represent any thing that is amiss? Suppose there should be an indictment of murdering a man's father or brother, &c. and the Judges take upon them to discharge the jury; this stops all justice, and the consequence will be, men will murder us, and we kill them again. I move, therefore, that you will proceed to punish the offender in this great matter, and remedy the miscarriage for the time to come.

Sir *F. Winnington.* Sir, I think we are come to the old times again, when the Judges pretended they had a rule of government, as well as a rule of law; and that they have acted accordingly. If they did never read Magna Charta, I think they are not fit to be Judges; if they had read Magna Charta, and do thus so contrary, they deserve a severe chastisement. To discharge Grand-Juries, of purpose to disappoint them of making their presentments, is to deprive the subject of the greatest benefit and security the law hath provided for them. If the Judges, instead of acting by law, shall be acted by their own ambition; and endeavour to get promotions, rather by worshipping the rising sun, than by doing justice, this nation will soon be reduced to a miserable condition. Suppose that after the discharge of this Grand-Jury, some person had offered to present some murder, treason, or other capital crime, for want of the Grand-Jury there would have been a failure of justice. As faults committed by Judges are of more dangerous consequence than others to the public; so there do not want precedents of severer chastisements for them, than for others. I humbly move you, first, to pass a Vote upon this business, of discharging Grand-Juries; and then to appoint a Committee to examine the Miscarriages of the Judges in Westminster-Hall, and to report the same with all speed to you.

Col. *Titus.* Sir, as it hath been observed, that this business hath some reference to the Proclamation; so I believe, there is something of the Plot in it too. And therefore I think if this Plot does not go on, it will have the worst luck that ever Plot had; seeing the Judges, as well as most other persons in public places, have given it as much assistance as they could. But whereas some have spoken ill of these Judges, I desire to speak well of them in one thing: I am confident they have herein shewed themselves grateful to their benefactors; for I do believe, that some of them were preferred to their places of purpose, because they should do what they have done. Laws of themselves are but dead letters; unless you can secure the execution, as well of those you have already, as of those you are now making, we shall spend our time to little purpose.

Mr. *Sacheverel.* Sir, the business of this debate is a great instance of our sick and languishing condition. As our ships, forts, and castles, are for securing us from the danger of our enemies from abroad, so our laws from our enemies at home; and if committed to such persons as will turn their strength upon us, are equally dangerous. Sir, we all know how the government of Scotland hath been quite altered since his majesty's Restoration, by some laws made there; pray let us have a care that ours be not altered, by the corrupt proceedings of Judges, lest we be reduced to the same weak condition of defending ourselves against Popery and arbitrary government here, that they are there. If Judges can thus prevent the penalties of the law, by discharging Grand-Juries before they have made their presentments, and can make laws by their rules of court, the government may soon be subverted; and therefore it is high time for this house to speak with those gentlemen. In former times several Judges have been impeached, and hanged too, for less crimes than these; and the reason was because they had broke the king's oath as well as their own. If what hath been said of some of these Judges be fully proved, they shall not want my Vote to inflict on them the same chastisement. The truth is, sir, I know not how the ill consequences we justly fear from judges can be prevented, as long as they are made *durante bene-placito,* and have such dependencies as they have. But this must be a work of time: in order to remedy our present Grievances, let us pass a Vote upon this business of discharging Grand-Juries; and that it may be penned as the case deserves.

Mr. *H. Sidney*, sir, I would beg leave to observe to you, because I think it may be necessary to be considered by your committee what an opinion was giving not long since by some of these Judges about Printing; which was, that printing of news might be prohibited by law; and accordingly a Proclamation issued out. I will not take on me to censure the opinion as illegal, but leave it to your farther consideration. But I remember there was a consultation held by the Judges a little before; and they gave their opinion, that they knew not of any way to prevent printing by law; because the act for that purpose was expired. Upon which, some Judges were put out, and new ones put in; and then this other opinion was given. These things are worthy of a serious examination. For if Treasurers may raise money by shutting up the Exchequer, borrowing of the bankers, or retrenchments; and the judges make new laws by an ill construction, or an ill execution of old ones: I conclude, that parliaments will soon be found useless; and the liberty of the people an inconvenience to the government. And therefore, I think, sir, you have been well moved to endeavour to pass your censure on some of these illegal proceedings by a vote.

Mr. *Powle*. Sir, in the front of Magna Charta it is said, 'nulli negabimus, nulli differemus justitiam;' we will defer, or deny justice to no man: to this the king is sworn, and with this the Judges are entrusted by their oaths. I admire what they can say for themselves; if they have not read this law, they are not fit to sit upon the bench: and if they have, I had almost said, they deserve to lose their heads.—The state of this poor nation is to be deplored, that in almost all ages, the Judges, who ought to be preservers of the laws, have endeavoured to destroy them: and that to please a Court-Faction, they have by treachery attempted to break the bonds asunder of Magna Charta, the great treasury of our peace. It was no sooner passed, but a chief justice (Hubert de Burg) in that day, persuades the king he was not bound by it; because he was under age when it was passed. But this sort of insolence the next parliament resented, to the ruin of the pernicious Chief Justice. In the time of Rd. ii. an unthinking dissolute prince, there were Judges that did insinuate into the king, that the parliament were only his creatures, and depended on his will, and not on the fundamental constitutions of the land: which treacherous advice proved the ruin of the king, and for which all those evil instruments were brought to justice. In his late majesty's time, his misfortunes were occasioned chiefly by corruptions of the long robe; his Judges, by an extra-judicial opinion, gave the king power to raise Money, upon any extraordinary occasion, without parliament; and made the king judge of such occasions: charity prompts me to think they thought this a service to the king; but the sad consequences of it may convince all mankind, that every illegal act weakens the royal interest; and to endeavour to introduce absolute dominion in these realms, is the worst of treasons: because whilst it bears the face of friendship to the king, and designs to be for his service, it never fails of the contrary effect.—The two great pillars of the government, are Parliaments and Juries; it is this gives us the title of free-born Englishmen: for my notion of free Englishmen is this, that they are ruled by laws of their own making, and tried by men of the same condition with themselves. The two great and undoubted privileges of the people, have been lately invaded by the Judges that now sit in Westminster-Hall; they have espoused Proclamations against law; they have discountenanced and opposed several legal acts, that tended to the sitting of this house; they have grasped the legislative power into their own hands, as in that instance of printing; the parliament was considering that matter, but they in the interim made their private opinion to be law, to supersede the judgment of this house. They have discharged Grand-Juries, on purpose to quell their presentments, and shelter great criminals from justice; and when juries have presented their opinion for the sitting of this parliament, they have in disdain thrown them at their feet, and told them they would be no messengers to carry such Petitions; and yet in a few days after, have encouraged all that would spit their venom against the government: they have served an ignorant and arbitrary faction, and been the messengers of Abhorrences to the king.—What we have now to do, is to load them with shame, who bid defiance to the law: they are guilty of crimes against nature, against the king, against their knowledge, and against posterity. The whole frame of nature doth loudly and daily petition to God their Creator; and kings, like God, may be addressed to in like manner, by petition, not command. They likewise knew it was lawful to petition: ignorance can be no plea, and their knowledge aggravates their crimes; the children unborn are bound to curse such proceedings, for it was not Petitioning, but parliaments they abhorred. The atheist pleads against a God, not that he disbelieves a deity, but would have it so. Tresilian and Belknap were Judges too; their learning gave them honour, but their villainies made their exit by a rope. The end of my motion therefore is, that we may address warmly to our prince against them: let us settle a Committee to enquire into their crimes, and not fail of doing justice upon them that have perverted it; let us purge the fountain, and the streams will issue pure.

Resolved, 1. "That the discharging of a Grand Jury by any Judge, before the end of the Term, Assizes, or Sessions, while matters are under their consideration, and not presented, is arbitrary, illegal, destructive to public justice, a manifest violation of his Oath, and is a means to subvert the fundamental laws of this kingdom. 2. That a Committee be appointed to examine the Proceedings of the Judges in Westminster-Hall, and report the same, with their opinion thereon, to this house."

Impeachment ordered against Lord Chief Justice North.] Nov. 24. Mr. Attorney-General being called in, and examined touching the manner of issuing forth the Proclamation, stiled, 'A Proclamation against tumultuous Petitioning;' and giving account to the house, that sir Francis North, Chief Justice of the Common-Pleas, was advising and assisting at the said drawing and passing the said Proclamation: it occasioned a debate, which terminated in the following Resolution: "That the Evidence this day given to this house against sir Francis North, Chief-Justice of the Common-Pleas, is sufficient ground for this house to proceed upon an Impeachment against him for high Crimes and Misdemeanors;" and the heads of an Impeachment were ordered to be prepared accordingly.

Nov. 26. The house resumed the Impeachment of Mr. Seymour. Resolved nem. con. "That there was matter sufficient to impeach the said Mr. Seymour, on every Article exhibited against him; and ordered, that a committee be appointed to prepare the said Impeachment."

Trial of the Earl of Stafford.] Nov. 30. The commons proceeded to the Trial of the earl of Stafford; of which the following is an Abstract: The Managers for the commons, among whom were the most considerable lawyers in the house, as serj. Maynard, sir Wm. Jones, Mr. Treby, &c. opened the cause with great copiousness and eloquence: 'They began with the Plot in general, and laid open the malice, wickedness and horror of so dreadful, bloody and hellish a design: they strenuously insisted on the express positive oaths of the witnesses, upon whom the credit of the Plot chiefly depended: they expatiated upon Coleman's Letters, and others, clearly proving the designs and activity of the writers: they pressed home the execrable murder of sir E. Godfrey, charged upon the Papists, as well by the oaths of self-acknowledged partners in the fact, as by a Letter sent from London to Tixall, intimating this very murder the 3rd day after it was committed: they fully displayed the Sham-Plots and Counter-Contrivances, whereby the Papists would have suborned the king's evidence, and turned all the guilt upon his majesty's most loyal subjects: they urged the firing the City, the burning the Navy, the calling in French Armies, Wild-Irish, Spanish-Pilgrims, &c. They recapitulated the several Trials of Ireland, Whitebread, Langhorn, &c. and alledged the Votes of both houses declaring the Plot. To corroborate all which, they repeated the cruelties of queen Mary, the French and Irish Massacres, the Powder-Plot, &c. and they anatomized the wicked principles and practices of murdering, lying, equivocating, forswearing, faith-breaking, &c. imputed to the Papists as held by them lawful and meritorious. In sum, nothing was omitted, or neglected through the whole process, but the least circumstance fully enforced and advanced, with such art and acuteness, as well answered to so great a cause, prosecuted by so high an authority, before so illustrious judges, and so august an assembly. —Some Witnesses were first produced to prove the reality, or at least the probability, of the Plot in general; but chiefly three appeared against the lord in particular, namely, Dugdale, Oates, and Turberville, the last said to be both a profligate and an indigent person. 1. Dugdale swore, 'That at a certain Meeting held at Tixall in Staffordshire, about the end of Aug. or beginning of Sept. 1678, the lord Stafford, with lord Aston and others, did, in the presence of the witness, give his full consent to take away the king's life, and introduce the Popish Religion. That on the 10th or 21st of Sept. this lord sent for the witness to his chamber, while he was dressing; and turning his servants out, offered him 500*l.* for his charges and encouragement, to take away the king's life; and further told him, he should have free pardon of all his sins, and be sainted; for the king had been excommunicated, and was likewise a traitor and a rebel, and an enemy to Jesus Christ.' 2. Oates swore, 'That in 1677, both in Spain, and at St. Omers, he saw several letters, signed Stafford, wherein his ldp. assured the Jesuits of his fidelity and zeal in promoting the Catholic Cause. That in 1678, being in London, his ldp. came to the chamber of father Fenwick, since executed, and there in his presence received a Commission from him, to be Pay-Master-General to the army: whereupon his ldp. said, he must of necessity go down into the country to take account how affairs stood there; and did not doubt but at his return, Grove should do the business. And, speaking of the king, he further added, He hath deceived us a great while, and we can bear no longer.' 3. Turberville gave an account, of disobliging his friends by leaving his friar's habit at Doway; and thereupon went into France, in 1675, where at Paris getting acquaintance with his ldp. he proposed to the witness a way, both to retrieve his credit with his friends, and make himself happy; and this was by taking away the life of the king, who was a heretic, and a rebel against God Almighty. That when he took leave of him, his ldp. appointed to meet him at London; but he soon after returned into France, not being willing to undertake the proposals, and was discountenanced by his friends, and reduced to poverty.'—The accused lord in his Defence, alledged many things to invalidate the credit of the Plot, and particularly the Reputation of these three witnesses.—It would be too long to mention all the particulars of this Trial, which lasted a whole week, and in which great skill and dexterity was used by the managers to support the credit and reputation of the witnesses, among whom they believed there was no contrivance or confederacy. They argued, 'That they had made it plain and apparent in the beginning of the Trial, by the testimony of six witnesses, by the Declarations of both houses, by Coleman's Letters, by the Trial and conviction of other traitors, that there was a general design amongst the Papists, to introduce their religion, by raising of armies, murdering the king, and subverting the government. And as to his lordship's particular case, they had three witnesses, which sufficiently proved him guilty; and so expatiated upon the danger of Popish principles,' &c. Sir William Jones exerted his skill and eloquence in a long speech, as much to prove the reality of the Plot, as the guilt of the prisoner; and thus especially argued: 'So that I think now none remain that do pretend not to believe it, but two sorts of persons; the one, those that were conspirators in it; and the other, those that wished it had succeeded, and do desire it may so still.' And by way of conclusion he said, 'The Evidence is so strong that I think it admits of no doubt; and the offences proved against my lord and the rest of his party are so foul, that they need no aggravation. The offences are against the king, against his sacred life, against the Protestant religion, nay against all Protestants. It is a design that appears with so dreadful a countenance to your lordships, to this great assembly, and to the whole nation, that it needs not any words I can use to make you apprehend. His lordship made two several pathetic speeches, besides his Answers to the witnesses, and in conclusion declared, in the presence of God, of his Angels, of their lordships, and all who heard him, that he was intirely innocent of what was laid to his charge; that he left it to their lordships to do justice, and with all submission resigned himself to them.

Dec. 6. The lords, by Message, acquainted the house, that they had appointed the next day to give judgment on lord Stafford; on which the house resolved nem. con. "That this house will then go, together with their Speaker, to the bar of the house of lords, to demand Judgment against the said lord."

Dec. 7. The commons resolved, "That the Managers of the Impeachment against the lord Stafford be empowered, in case the lords should, immediately after the fact found, proceed to Judgment, to insist upon it, that it is not parliamentary for their lordships to give judgment, until it be first demanded by this house."—Mr. Speaker then left the chair, and the committee of the commons were present at the court in Westminster-hall, when the peers found the said lord Guilty of High Treason. When the Lord Chancellor, now Lord High Steward, collecting the Votes, which were 55 guilty, 31 not guilty; the said High Steward pronounced lord Stafford guilty of High Treason, who replied, 'God's holy name be praised!' And then being asked, what he could say for himself, why Judgment of Death should not pass upon him, according to law? he added, 'My lord, I have very little to say; I confess I am surprised at it, for I did not expect it. But God's will be done; I will not murmur at it. God forgive those who have falsely sworn against me!'

After which, the commons, with Mr. Speaker and the mace, went up to the bar of the house of lords, and, by Mr. Speaker, in the name of the commons in parliament, and of all the commons of England, demanded Judgment of High Treason.—The house then returned, and the lords by Message signified, that they were going presently to give the said Judgment.

The managing committee then went into Westminster-hall, and were present when the lords gave Judgment, &c.—At which time, the Lord High Steward made the following Speech, "That which remains now to be done, is very sad on my part; I have never given Sentence on any man, and I am very sorry I must begin with your lordship, a person of your quality and fortune, descended of noble ancestors, a great sufferer in the late times, obliged to the government for the moderation you had in the exercise of your religion; obliged to the king's father, and so much to this king: yet you have gone about not only to consult his death, but even the destroying of three whole nations, both of body and soul, as far as in you lay; of which you stand impeached by the commons, and have been found Guilty by the lords. There have been many and great conspiracies against the life of the king for the destroying of the government; and they have been carried on by consults, letters, and otherways; by the burning of London, and the death of sir E. Godfrey, the Plot hath been carried on abroad, at White-hall, and London, and your ldp. hath been concerned in them all, with a mixture of malice: You have called the king 'heretic,' and said, 'he was an enemy to God Almighty;' here the proverb is verified, 'Curse not the king, though in the inward chamber, for the birds of the air will reveal it.' It hath pleased God to leave you to yourself, and you have digged a pit, and fallen into it yourself. God never leaves any man until they leave themselves; think not still well of your religion, and let not blind guides mislead you; true repentance is never too late, and be not persuaded not to confess that sin in public, which you possibly have been absolved of in private: for whatsoever value you set on the prayers of them you call Heretics, yet I am sure, that both they that cleared you, and those that condemned you, are sorry for your condition. I will pray for your ldp.; and this is the last time I must call you my lord." And so he pronounced Sentence of Death against him, according to the usual form in case of High Treason.*

* Many writers, and in particular Mr. Worth and sir John Reresby, are of opinion, that this nobleman was selected by the commons to bear the sins of the whole five, on the presumption that he was least capable of defending himself, and that his very spirits, as well as his parts, would fail him, under the weight of such a prosecution. He was old and infirm,

Sir Rob. Peyton expelled.] Dec. 14. It appearing to the house by the Report made at the bar, and by the Confession of sir Rob. Peyton (a Member) in his place, that the said sir Robert had negotiated with the duke of York, by the means of the earl of Peterborough, Mrs. Cellier, and Mr. Godfrey, at such time when they were turning the Popish Plot upon the protestants," Ordered, "That Sir Rob. Peyton be expelled the house, and that he be brought to the bar, and do receive the Censure of the house upon his knees." But not being to be found, the house afterwards ordered him to be taken into the custody of the serjeant at arms.

Dec. 15. Sir Rob. Peyton appeared at the bar upon his knees, to receive the Sentence of Expulsion.

The *Speaker*. Sir Robert Peyton: It is a long time that you have had reputation in the world, and that you have served as knight of the shire for the county of Middlesex. Two parliaments, the last and this, your county made a free election of you; your county had a great opinion of you; and now you are in that condition, that you have appeared to the world the man you really were not. You have made a show, and have acted a part against Popery and arbitrary power, yet really and inwardly you have sought your own advantage, and not that of your country. It is manifest, by the report from the committee, and your own defence makes it clear. Many gentlemen here, whose eyes are in their heads, their tongues and eyes have moved as well as yours. You have sat betwixt the Devil and the Witch, Mr. Gadbury and Mrs. Cellier. The dark ways you have taken show your ill designs; your company and conductors show your errand. You are fallen from being an angel to be a devil. From the beginning, you sought your own interest. To set up a common-wealth, you had '20,000 men' to make your interest the stronger. You were bustling, like the wind, in this house, and in coffee-houses. Your county chose you to this place, not only for your interest, but for an example to other men, not with noise and thundering, but to behave yourself without vanity or ostentation. You are one of them that have played your own game and part; and that all men may take notice, you are a warning for all other members, and I hope there are none such. It shows that this parliament nauseates such members as you are. You are no longer a part of this noble body. How you will reconcile yourself to your country, is another consideration. You are discharged this house, and the custody of the serjeant, paying your fees *.

The King's Speech to both Houses on Alliances, and the State of Christendom.] This day his majesty made the following Speech to both houses:

"My lords and gentlemen; At the opening of this parliament I did acquaint you with the Alliances I had made with Spain and Holland, as the best measures that could be taken for the safety of England, and the repose of christendom. But I told you withal, that if your friendship became unsafe to trust to, it would not be wondered at, if our neighbours should begin to take new resolutions, and perhaps such as might be fatal to us. I must now tell you, that our allies cannot but see how little has been done since this meeting, to encourage their dependance upon us. And I find by them that unless we can be so united at home, as to make our Alliance valuable to them, it will not be possible to hinder them from seeking some other refuge; and making such new friendships as will not be consistent with our safety. Consider that a neglect of this opportunity is never to be repaired.—I did likewise lay the matter plainly before you, touching the estate and condition of Tangier. I must now tell you again, that, if that place be thought worth the keeping, you must take such consideration of it, that it may be speedily supplied; it being impossible for me to preserve it, at an expence so far above my power.—I did promise you the fullest satisfaction your hearts could wish, for the security of the protestant religion; and to concur with you in any Remedies, which might consist with preserving the succession of the crown in its due and legal course of descent. I do again with the same reservations, renew the same promises to you; and being thus ready, on my part, to do all that can reasonably be expected from me; I should be glad to know from you, as soon as may be, how far I shall be assisted by you; and what it is you desire from me."

Resolved, "That this house will on Saturday next take into consideration his majesty's most gracious Speech."

Debate on Popery.] The house then resolv-

had been under confinement for above ten years; was timorous by nature; had the popular tide against him; had the ablest and most zealous members of the house of commons for his prosecutors; a large and considerable body of his judges, the peers, were on the same side; and his majesty, though he pitied the victim, had not resolution enough to prevent the sacrifice." Ralph.

* Grey. "The Speaker performed his office in such coarse terms, and thereby so highly exasperated him, that the session was no sooner over, than he challenged him; but, instead of answering it, Mr. Williams, with more propriety than gallantry, made his complaint to the privy-council, and Sir Robert was, in consequence thereof, again committed to the Tower." Ralph.

Sir Robert took care to have the most offensive part of this Speech printed, under the following Title, "A Specimen of the rhetoric, candour, gravity, and ingenuity, of William Williams, Speaker to the late house of commons, at Westminster, in his Speech to sir Robert Peyton, when he expelled him that house."

ed into a grand committee, how to secure the kingdom against Popery and Arbitrary Government. Mr. Powle in the chair.

Lord Cavendish. Sir, when I consider the immunities and advantages we enjoy by the excellent composure of our government both in Church and State: how the king, as sovereign, enjoys all the prerogative that can be necessary to make him either great or happy; and the people all the liberty and privilege that can be pretended for their encouragement to be industrious, and for securing to themselves and posterities the enjoyment of what they get by their industry; how the doctrine of the church is void of idolatrous, superstitious opinions; and the government of tyranny, or absolute dominion: I cannot but admire that there should be any body amongst ourselves, that should aim at any alteration, and be the occasion of this day's debate. But, sir, it is too evident that such there are; and that they have made a great advance to effect their design, by many contrivances which they have pursued for a long course of years, according to the results and consultations held by Jesuits for that purpose: but above all, by converting to their religion James duke of York; the presumptive heir of the crown; and by engaging him to espouse their interest with that zeal and fervency, which usually attends new converts: especially when so great a glory is proposed, as the rooting a pestilent heresy out of three nations; and the saving of so many souls as would depend thereon. The sad effect of this conversion we have felt for many years, it having had the same operations in our body politic, as some sorts of lingering poison hath in bodies natural; made us sick and consumptive, by infecting and corrupting all the food and physic which hath been applied in order to preserve us from popery and slavery, worse than death itself. From this fatal act, the declination of the grandeur of this monarchy may be dated; and to the consequences thereof, its absolute ruin (if not timely prevented) will be hereafter attributed. This being our case, I could not but admire to see this house so long coming to consider this weighty point: insomuch, that, I began to persuade myself, that either our dangers were not so great as our discourses, upon some other occasions, had represented them, or that we were not in good earnest to endeavour any redress. It is true, when we consider what ill fortune we have had with our Bill, lately sent up to the lords, in having it thrown out in such a heat, without so much as a conference, (though whenever they shall consider of it in cool blood, they will find there can be no other way to secure the Protestant Religion) we may with some reason be discouraged. But I hope, sir, that, seeing our country have thought us worthy to be their representatives, we shall not be so easily daunted in what so nearly concerns them: but be as indefatigable in finding out ways for our preservation, as our enemies are to find out means for our destruction; hoping we shall not meet always so bad success in the house of lords: for though the too much kindness of some men, who pretended to be for the Bill, but underhand made a party against it, did this time operate as fatally, as enmity disguised in friendship useth to do; yet I hope that on another occasion we may have better success; not doubting but a great many lords, when they are persuaded that they shall not be able to find out any other way (as I hear they begin to despair they shall) to secure the Protestant Religion, that they will join with us in the same, or some other Bill to the same purpose: especially my good lords the bishops, who cannot be presumed to have made peace with Rome, but to be ready to die for the Protestant Religion; and therefore, doubtless, will not long stick at joining in a Bill to save it. But seeing that, according to the course of parliaments, we are not like to bring this to a trial for a long time, I am of opinion, we had best try something else; and although I know not what other act can be made to serve instead of that, but will either prove too weak, or too strong: yet seeing we are put upon it, we must try, that so we may not be represented as stubborn. And therefore I humbly move you, That a Bill may be brought in for the association of all his majesty's protestant subjects.

Mr. Ralph Montagu. Sir, great things are expected from this day's debate; and we could not well have entered into it sooner; it now comes more seasonable than it would have done before, because of the opportunities we have had to feel the pulse of affairs since the beginning of the session; and the time we have spent in asserting the Right of Petitioning, by which the essence of parliaments, and the foundation of the people's Liberties were struck at. And the Trial of my lords Stafford, and the Disinheriting-Bill could not possibly have been avoided. And as our labour hath not been lost in all, so I hope that at last we shall have some benefit of that spent about the Succession-Bill. For, as it was said at the passing of the Bill, that there were a loyal party that would never acquiesce in it; so I do believe, there is a true Protestant party that will never acquiesce in any thing less, than what may be sufficient for the security of their Religion; which, I am apt to believe, will end in that Bill. But in the mean time, that we may shew that we are not humorists, let us try what strength we can muster up to oppose these great enemies by some other laws; as when a house is on fire, we make use of buckets and tubs for casting of water, until the great engines can be got. But I would move you to be cautious what you do; for I am afraid that the design of putting you upon finding out expedients, is it not in order to have any thing done that may be effectual against Popery; but in order to have you offer at something that may purchase a disrepute on the house, and give your enemies an advantage to pursue their designs of breaking us, by alledging that you aim at laws that will overturn the government. For my part, I am fully persuaded, that this is the design of those that have put the king so often to declare against altering the Succession, and to recommend other ways; and that, offer at what you will, if it be any thing that is like to prove strong enough to secure us against popery, you will see the house put off before it comes to any perfection; and that in time it will be made use of to arraign the proceedings of parliament, and to persuade the people, that this house did attempt to alter the government by such and such bills; and so by degrees possess the people, that parliaments are either dangerous, or inconsistent with the government, that, if possible, they may be well content to be without them. Sir, I am afraid that the Popish Party are more serious in this design than we are aware of; and that, next to the great endeavours they have used for many years to keep up our divisions in points of Religion; the next great artifice which they depend on is, the infusing into the people the dislike of parliaments; for they well know, that Popery can never be established in this nation, as long as parliaments are permitted to sit and act. Therefore, though I know it is below a house of commons to mind every little discourse; yet I think, if we conclude, that this powerful party, amongst their many designs, have this for one, that we ought to countermine it as much as we can. We cannot well comprehend what a Bill of Association will be before it be drawn up, nor what difficulties may be found in the contriving of it; and therefore I think no great debate will be necessary about it, before such a Bill be brought in. And I believe it will be found more likely to be serviceable, in case the Papists be banished; and therefore I conceive, a Bill for banishment of all the considerable Papists out of England, may be very necessary: and if at the same time that we endeavour to secure ourselves against popery, we do not also do something to prevent arbitrary power, it will be to little purpose; for the one will be sure to have a hand to bring in the other; and I think nothing can prevent that, or rather both, better than frequent parliaments. And therefore I humbly move you, that a Bill for securing frequent Parliaments may be taken into your consideration.'

Sir *G. Hungerford*. Sir, I think you are well advised, that the way to secure ourselves effectually against Popery, is to secure ourselves also against arbitrary government; and that the having of frequent parliaments is the best way to secure both; and therefore I think you may do well to move the house, that a Committee be appointed to inspect what old laws there are, for enforcing the sitting of frequent parliaments; that if they should be found deficient, some new laws may be made for that purpose. I do agree, that a Bill for banishing out of England the most considerable Papists, may do well; but I hope, sir, that if you banish the men, you will banish some women too; for I do believe, that some of that sex have been great instruments in bringing about our ruin. And if in time you will consider, how to prevent the royal family's marrying Popish women, it would be of great security for hereafter. For I am of opinion, that the late queen mother's zeal for her religion, was not only a great occasion (amongst many others) of the miseries that befel us in 41; but the great cause of all our miseries now, by perverting the duke from his religion, as is reported; and may reasonably be believed, if we conclude, that she had that motherly care for the salvation of her children, as other mothers usually have; for, according to her opinion, it was not to be obtained out of the pale of that Church: and no man can doubt, but that the Protestant interest hath been much prejudiced, by his majesty's marrying a princess of that religion: for we have plainly seen, since the discovery of the Plot, how some of the most material Jesuits, and Popish instruments, have sheltered themselves under her royal protection; and how they have helped to carry on the Plot, being so impudent, as to pretend they had her patronage, and by abusing her authority; but more especially by the duke's marrying the princess of Modena; because of her near relation to the Popes and Cardinals. All which was plainly foreseen by that parliament which met a little before that marriage in 1673, and therefore they made an Address to his majesty, representing the said ill consequences; desiring him not to permit it, because it would tend to the destruction of the Protestant Religion. But their endeavours were defeated by that party, as we may guess, seeing we find so much use of her name in Coleman's Letters; for well might they who have over-ruled in so many great affairs, as hath been instanced in this house, have an influence also in this, that so that party might not want so useful an instrument in so great a station; and so the parliament's Address miscarried; but that they had either a good judgment, or prophetic spirit, I hope will never miscarry, but remain upon record. And unless you believe, that these ladies are less compassionate than others usually are, how can it be otherwise, their principles considered? But, sir, I will not trouble you farther about it; but suppose it may be worth your consideration in due time. In the interim, I agree for the Bill of Banishment and Association too.

Mr. *Wm. Harbord*. Sir, it is not to be doubted, but that Popery and arbitrary government are so near of kin, that they cannot be separated; and therefore, if we destroy the one, we need not fear the destruction of the other. Before our late miserable wars, Popery was more in masquerade; and arbitrary power, the Loans, Monopolies, and Ship-money, more invisible; now Popery is more visible, except in the business of the Exchequer, which amounting to above one million of money, we may not admire we have not heard of more great things of that kind, since especially; being we know how averse the king is to hearken to such advice; but our fears of Popery are the stronger, because of the Popish Successor; and therefore I cannot but commend the policy of those who are tender in using arbitrary proceedings at this time, lest the fears and jealousies that might arise from both together should prove intolerable.—I must confess, sir, I am at a great loss what to offer to your consideration in this matter; for our danger is not only from the strength of the Popish party, but from the weakness of the Protestants by reason of the animosities which they sow amongst us, not only in points of religion, but of interest too. For of late they have not been content with carrying on the design of dividing the Churchmen and Fanatics, but of arraigning the last parliament as omnipotent and dangerous, for going about to disinherit the duke. They endeavour to divide the people in their opinions as to parliaments, and to render them incompatible with the government, that, so, if possible, they may keep the Protestant interest divided, and work them to destroy themselves, by engaging party against party, in hopes at last to have but one party to deal with, and to have an opportunity of gaining the weakest to their side by assurances of liberty of conscience, or otherways, which must certainly be the consequence of such a contest. And although I am very unwilling to detract from the merits of our churchmen, for whom I have a great veneration; yet I cannot but observe, how that ever since the Trial of Wakeman was over, but more about the time of the Presbyterian Plot, they preached up (especially in public assemblies) the danger of fanatics to be more than of Papists; and to disinherit the duke was against the law of God. Which said opinions, if they should be imbibed by the people, what will your Association-Bill signify, or any other law you can make against Popery? Sir, I do not mention these things to you without a great deal of regret; for I am well known to be a true friend of the church, and have (when I was thought worthy to be in commission) exprest myself a severe enemy to fanaticism. But however, I cannot but observe this strange contradiction, of pretending to keep out Popery, and yet at the same time to endeavour to divide the Protestant Interest, and to reserve a right to make a Papist king. I must confess, I am more distracted from the ill consequences I fear from such contrivances as these, than from the strength of the Papists themselves. They will certainly go on with their interest, as long as they are secure of such auxiliaries. These things must be considered in the drawing your Bill, that so the remedy you propose may be proportionable to your disease. For an Act of Association may be several ways evaded by such opinions as these, if they should grow amongst the people; and it will be an irreparable blow to the Protestant Interest to accept of such an expedient, if it should prove ineffectual. And therefore it ought to be so drawn, as may provide for all the contrivances of that party: for, sir, I cannot imagine that ever Popery will attempt to come into this nation bare-faced, but do expect that the design will always be carried on, as hitherto, under some disguise, either by a Toleration in favour of tender consciences, or in the name of churchmen, or a loyal party, for the defence of the church or government, to which some Presbyterian Plot would much conduce, and be an excellent pretence for raising of an Army, and apprehending or disarming of such persons as are most likely to oppose that interest. Unless you can change the interest at court, and remove these counsellors that are so much for the duke, I think you may justly fear all these stratagems, and that it will be impossible to contrive any Association-Bill that can provide against them. And therefore, that we may not spend our time in vain, I would humbly move you, sir, to go on with the Bill of Banishment, which is most likely to do you some service.

Col. *Birch.* Sir, I retain a good opinion of an Association-Bill, notwithstanding what hath been said, as to the weakness it may receive from our unhappy divisions in points of religion and interest, too much promoted by some of our clergy. For, sir, when I consider how the Laudean principles, as to raising of Money without parliaments in the late times, infected most of our clergy, so as that they not only preached up the king's absolute authority over men's properties, but branded with the title of rebels, and condemned to hell those that offered to argue against it: I do conclude, that it is usual for one or two bishops to give measures or directions to the rest of the bishops, and they to the clergy of their several dioceses: and that therefore the clergy derive their politics generally from one or two bishops in some great station. Yet, sir, when I remember how, after some little time, many of the clergy fell off, and would not follow such instructions; and how the people soon excused themselves from following the advice in such politics, and would not freely pay illegal taxes, notwithstanding all their endeavours; I am apt to think, sir, that as the people were not long then misled, so as to submit to lose their property, so they will not now to any thing that shall tend to the losing of their religion and property both. They will soon discover what is their interest, and how true interest will not lye. I have often told you within these walls they will soon apprehend that Popery will bring in slavery, and reduce them not only to an idolatrous superstitious religion, but to wear wooden shoes like the French, and to eat herbs like the Spaniard, because they will soon know that they shall not be long masters of any thing they have: and however they may be persuaded for a while, I am confident they will at last consult how to save their bacon. They will discern that the clergy may be good divines, but not so good politicians; and that there may be some difference in point of interest between them and the clergy, because clergymen may be in a possibility of being advanced by popery if they submit; but the laity under a probability of losing all, notwithstanding all submissions. Sir, I do not trouble you with this discourse out of a fear that our clergy will not shew themselves good Protestants; for I have that veneration for them, and opinion of them, as to believe that many of the bishops and clergy too would as soon die for the Protestant Religion as many persons in the nation. But I am jealous that there is some over-awing power got in amongst them, something answerable to that of a Popish Successor in the state; by whose means those Bills were so easily passed in the late Long Parliament, under a pretence that they were for the preservation of the Protestant Religion, which the commons then found, and any person that will now peruse them may find, would infallibly have brought in popery: and how, since the Plot, the danger of fanatics is cried up more than that of the Papists; and how tender they are in the point of a Popish Successor, or joining in any thing that is against him. But though these things make me jealous there is somebody that misleads them now in matters relating to Popery, as formerly in things relating to Property; yet I am of opinion that they will ere long see, that to stand up for the Interest of a Popish Successor, to have a Popish King, to weaken the Protestant interest, and speak ill of parliaments, is not the right way to preserve the Protestant Religion; but a plain contradiction, and an invention of Jesuits. And therefore, sir, I am for going on with the Association Bill.

Sir *Wm. Hickman.* Sir, I think you have been well moved, as well for the Association Bill as the Banishing-Bill. By the one, you will send your enemies out of the country; by the other be in a good condition to keep them out, which may go a great way to secure us.

Mr. *Leveson Gower.* I would banish all the Papists, lest they be like the court, in the Long Parliament; when they had taken off one active man from the interest of his country, another as considerable did start up. They take all the care to get the Protestant Papists into the administration of the government; they are encouraged, and true Protestants turned out. Next to Papists, I would consider to put out those popishly affected. When they are banished, next you may take into consideration how their estates shall be disposed of, and how to breed their children, and that the next heir be a Protestant. I would have a Bill to banish all considerable Papists, excepting no one man in England whatsoever.

Sir *Nick. Carew.* Sir, I am not against any of these Bills, because they may be all convenient for the present occasion; but if any man think that these Bills will do without the Succession Bill, I believe they will find themselves mistaken, for these Bills will signify nothing, unless you can remove your Popish Successor, and your Popish interest. These bills will not reach your Papists in masquerade, who will certainly continue as long as there is a Popish Successor, and make your Banishing-Bill, and Association-Bill too, as ineffectual as white paper. Let such as I could name to you have the command of the sea-ports, (as I suppose they will without my naming them) and in the lieutenancy, and commission of the peace, and when the present heat is over, let the Papists come back when they will, they will have no cause to doubt having a kind reception. For you must not expect to have plain rustic country gentlemen in such commands, but well bred courtiers, and some good, easy, credulous gentlemen that will soon be persuaded there is no danger in Popery; and then of what use will your banishing or Association-Bill be? As long as the duke hath so many friends at court, (between whose interest and Popery I cannot hear there is any distinction) I think no laws that we can make against Popery will do us any good, because all the laws we have already have done us none. For the same arts and power that have hitherto defeated all your other laws, will also defeat what you are now about. And therefore, sir, I am of opinion we are not now acting like the true physicians of the nation, but like mountebanks. For the most we shall be able to do this way, is to patch and plaister up our sores, and have them hereafter break out incurable upon us. But if you are resolved to go on with these bills that have been proposed, I will not offer to oppose the sense of the committee, but would move you, (that we may not forget, or lose in the croud, that which at last, I believe, must be pursued, if ever you will do any thing for your religion) that in the first place you pass a vote, "That it is the opinion of this Committee, that as long as the Papists have any hopes of the duke of York's succeeding the king, the King's Person, the Protestant Religion, and the Lives and Liberties of the People, are in apparent danger.

Col. *Titus.* Sir, I have read that a great minister of state of Spain, gave this short advice to a friend of his that was coming ambassador into England; that he should not always aim at the best. I think it may be convenient for us to follow that advice; for if we should not have something for our security, before we get the best, I am afraid it may happen to us, as it did to a man whose house was beset with thieves; he was so long arming his servants, and appointing them their distinct quarters, that the thieves broke in, and caught them all unprovided. I pray God it may not be our case; though I am very sensible that none of these Bills can effectually do our business; for nothing can secure us against this party, but being free of their principles as well as of their persons; which I conclude will always remain in some persons amongst us, notwithstanding your banishing of Papists, as long as there is a Popish Successor. For I remember what a great man of Swedeland told me, that all laws they could make had never any effect against them, until they not only banished them out of their country, but secured the government in the hand of princes of their own religion; and I am afraid, that nothing less than the same way will ever do our business here. For it is not so much the number of Papists, as their principles, and the danger of their getting the government into their hands, which we know they have been long aiming at, that may justly be feared, in which I am persuaded they will be so restless, as that we shall never be secure against them, unless we can banish their principles from court, as well as the people out of the country.

Sir *Fr. Winnington.* Sir, what my good friend that spoke last hath said, that we should get something, and not lose all, by aiming so earnestly at the best, is very well, if we were like to get any thing instead of it, that shall have the appearance of being serviceable in this case: but I have seen old parliament-men mistaken sometimes, and I am afraid that he will sooner see this parliament dissolved, than any thing granted that shall be material against Popery. And that the mentioning of these Bills shall afterwards arise in judgment against you; however, I think we must adventure. What this Association-Bill may be, I cannot tell, until it be drawn; but I see no opposition made to any of those Bills that have been proposed; and I believe there is much business yet behind for this day, and that you will do well to husband your time, and put this business out of your hands, by putting the questions.

Sir *Rd. Temple.* Sir, you have been very well moved for the bringing in of such Bills as may tend as much to the security of the Protestant Religion, as any that can be offered. That of Banishment will certainly go a great way to destroy, not only their power, but their interest and principles too, and be a great disheartening to their party abroad. That interest will not then have so many engines to work with here, as now they have. And the Bill of Association will be necessary, that we may have a law to defend ourselves.

Resolved, "That it is the opinion of this Committee, that one means to suppress Popery is, that the house be moved that a Bill be brought in immediately, to banish all the considerable Papists out of the kingdom."

Mr. *Ralph Montagu.* Sir, by offering at the Exclusion Bill, we may conclude we have offended the duke; by this Bill for Banishment, all the rest of the considerable Papists in England. As we have made many enemies, so it will be convenient, that we should endeavour to get some law to defend ourselves against their implacable designs. For which a Bill for an Association of all his majesty's Protestant Subjects may do well; and therefore I pray that we may move the house to have it brought in.

Mr. *Garroway.* Sir, as we are sick of complicated diseases, though all have their original from one cause, seeing we cannot be permitted to cure that cause, we must think of many remedies to cure the many evils that sprout from it. The Banishing of the Papists alone will not do it: and I am not willing to pass any judgment on the Association-Bill before I see it. But, sir, what fruit can you expect from your laws, unless you can secure good Judges in Westminster hall, and good men in commission in all other places? Is there at this time a judge, a deputy-lieut. or a justice of peace in commission, that you can expect shall act against the duke? Or if any such be in, are they for more than a colour? Are they not over-powered by such as are for the duke's interest? If this do not make all your laws invalid, by not executing them; is there not an Army of about 10,000 men under the name of Guards? And may not more be raised? And what then will your laws signify? Have we not already had some experience of this, when the Toleration came out in 1672, when there was that Army at Black-Heath, and Clifford had the management of the great affairs of state? If the king had not then hearkened to the advice of his parliament, what would all the laws that were then in force against Papists have signified? And may you not see the same again, if you do not take some care to prevent it? What great difference between Clifford and some of our present great ministers, only that he had that weakness to declare himself to be a Papist, and these the discretion to keep the knowledge of their religion to themselves. But we see they manage things as much in favour of Popery, as ever Clifford did. Did not that Toleration, that Army, and that minister of state, repeal all your laws as effectually, as if they had never been made? When I consider how the Triple-League was broke, after we had made laws for the keeping it, by giving near three millions; how the Peace was made up at Nimeguen, after we had made an Act for an actual War with France, and given above a million for entering into it; I will never believe that any law will be observed, make what you will, unless there be those about the king that may be for the keeping of it; otherwise you shall have such judges, justices, deputy-lieutenants, and other commissioned officers, as will repeal your laws at pleasure. And therefore I could wish you would consider well, how you possess those that sent you here, with an opinion that they may depend upon such laws as these. And at the same time, sir, that you are consulting the destruction of the Papists, I think you may do well to endeavour the preservation of the Protestants. Is this a time for the Church-men and Dissenters to quarrel? It is like two men riding upon a road, a highwayman coming to rob them, instead of uniting to defend themselves, they quarrel and disarm one the other, and so were both robbed. I pray God, this do not prove at last our case. For as that project of the Papists hath, since Wakeman's Trial, had strange success in dividing us; so no doubt but it will at last come to disarming us too; and how that will facilitate their conquest, may be easily calculated? Is this a time to weaken the Protestant Interest, by tearing us in pieces by the execution of acts made against Papists? That man who can believe, that that is the way to preserve the Protestant Religion, or Protestant Church, is fit to believe that St. Dennis walked many miles with his head under his arm, or any other Popish miracle whatsoever. And therefore I think you will do well to hasten the Bill for uniting of the Protestant Dissenters, that we may bring into the Church as many of them as is possible, and not longer be so infatuated as to gratify the Papists in that particular, by doing their business in destroying one another; but prevent them if possible by union, which will tend more to prevent Popery than all the Bills that have been proposed.

Mr. *Paul Foley**. Sir, I have read in scripture, 'What king going to make war against another, sitteth not down first, and consulteth whether he be able with ten thousand to meet him that cometh against him with twenty?' I take the denial of the Bill of Exclusion to be a plain demonstration, that the popish party should not be deprived of a right to govern us; and it is not to be doubted, that having that right, they will be sure to make use of all the power they can back it with. That we may be the better able to judge, whether we can fortify ourselves sufficiently against such a right, and the power that will naturally follow it, I pray, sir, let us follow our Saviour's advice, and consult, whether with ten thousand we can meet twenty thousand.—When I consider how the Triple League was broke, and now all Alliances and transactions relating to peace and war have been since managed in favour of the French interest, contrary to the true interest of England, and the pressing importunities of foreign nations, as well as our own, I think we cannot but conclude that the duke's interest, the French interest, and Popish interest, are all one. And that the duke's or Popish interest have some great dependance on the French king, for his assistance in the settling of popery here. And no man can doubt this, but he that will not believe Coleman's Letters, or that there was a peace made at Nimeguen, in order to put him in the better condition. If the Jesuits do manage all the affairs of Europe, as is said, it may be justly feared, that the French king will improve this argument so, as to get Flanders, if not Holland too, before he perform his promise of giving them the expected assistance; which, being it will conduce to the destroying of the protestants abroad, as well as here, we may justly fear the Jesuits will never obstruct.—Besides the dependance which the papists may have of assistance from this mighty monarch, in Ireland they are five to one for the protestants, and amount to many hundred thousands, full of bloody revenge, derived from their ancestors, wanting nothing but arms, (which they may have from France in a night) to be enabled to massacre all the protestants in Ireland, and to be ready to be transported hither. How the Plot hath been carried on there in order to it; how endeavours have been there used to stifle and counterplot it; who commands all the English coast opposite to Ireland, we know; and how our forts and castles are provided, the examination of the governor of Chepstow-castle may inform you.—And that they may not want a strength to compel us on every side, is not the government of Scotland quite altered, by some acts made within these few years? Is it not become very arbitrary, parliaments in a manner laid aside, and the power invested in a privy-council? And is there not a Standing Army of 22,000 men, settled by act of parliament, with a Declaration, that they shall be ready to come into England upon any occasion? And is not the duke now there, managing the government of that kingdom, and army too, by putting his own creatures into the council and into the command of the army, and using all other ways imaginable to improve his interest there.—And may we not conclude, that in England there may be 100,000 papists fighting men, and that Portsmouth, Plymouth, Sheerness, Tilbury-Fort, and Hull, and all other places of importance, shall, when that interest shall think it convenient, be in the hands of persons they may confide in, as well as the command of the militia and fleet.—And what now, sir, can any man say is wanting, to enable this party to make a great contest with us, but a popish king to head them? And does any thing stand in their way for that, but his majesty's life? And is it not strange, that though we see things never so plain, there is no remedy for poor protestants? Can it be imagined, that if this party should once have a king on their side, endowed with a valourous spirit, and vowing revenge, spurred on with a fiery zeal, to get not only three crowns on earth, but the crown of glory in heaven, by rooting a pestilent heresy out of three nations; that they will neglect so great an opportunity for the establishing of popery here? And will not the divisions they carry on amongst us, as to churchmen and fanatics, Plot or no Plot, be very useful to them; but especially their arraignments of parliaments, and all that speak against popery, as 41 men, and enemies to the government, occasion a great weakness on our side? I think, sir, all this put together makes a great strength for that party, enough to bring us into misery, whatever the issue may be. I would now, sir, give you some account how the protestants may be able in such a case to defend

* "The younger brother of one, who, from mean beginnings, had by iron-works raised one of the greatest estates that had been in England in one time. He was a learned, though not a practising, lawyer, and was a man of virtue and good principles, but morose and wilful; and he had the affectation of passing for a great patriot, by his constant finding fault with the government, and keeping up an ill-humour and a bad opinion of the court." Burnet.—He was twice chosen Speaker, and was uncle to the first lord Foley.

themselves; but I protest, sir, I know not what defence they will be able to make legally. It is true, sir, as long as our good king lives, we may live in quiet; but things being thus, are not the papists under great temptations to go on with their old damnable design, or set up a new one for the destruction of the king? And if it should so happen, either by their wicked counsels, or naturally, I think there is no way left us to oppose this party, but by a rebellion; and therefore I think we may conclude, that our lives, liberties, and religion, are to terminate with the king's life.—I confess, sir, this is a melancholy discourse, but I am afraid too true; and that the more you consider of it, the more reason you will have to believe, that there is such a net spread to catch poor protestants, as cannot fail to do it effectually, whenever the Jesuits shall be pleased to draw it. And our condition looks the more dismal, because though king, lords, and commons have so often declared, that there hath been a damnable, execrable, devilish, hellish, abominable Plot, carried on by the papists, yet that all remedies against the like for the future must be denied us; I mean such as can signify any thing: And we must now again be exposed, as we were before the Plot broke out, to all their barbarities, having only weakened that party by executing about 20 old men; but strengthened them much more, by having discouraged all witnesses from ever revealing more of their plots, and by the discoveries they had made of the strength of their party, in the stifling of this Plot. And yet all will not open the eyes of some protestants, that so, if possible, we might be so happy as to lay our divisions aside, and join against the common enemy, without which we must certainly be ruined.—And if this be our case, and there be nothing wanting but a popish king to complete our misery, and the art of man cannot find out any way to secure us against a popish king, without the Exclusion Bill; is it not strange it should be rejected in the house of lords? I cannot believe that the Fathers of the Church should join in that, which must infallibly give opportunity for the tearing out the bowels of their mother, and destroying her for ever. If so, well may we lie down and cry 'We have nobody to help us but only thou, O God.'

Resolved, "That it is the opinion of this Committee, that as long as the Papists have any hopes of the duke of York's succeeding the king in the kingdom of England and Ireland, and dominions thereunto belonging, the king's person, the Protestant Religion, and the Lives, Liberties, and Properties of all his majesty's Protestant subjects, are in apparent danger of being destroyed."

Sir *Gilbert Gerrard*. Sir, I am of opinion the Popish Plot goeth on as much as ever, and the Papists are so proud of it, that they cannot forbear bragging of their hopes to see better days speedily. I think, sir, seeing we are not like for one while to have the Exclusion Bill, we shall appear neglectful of our duty, if we do not try what security can be contrived by an Association-Bill: and therefore I humbly pray, that the house may be moved to appoint a Committee, to draw up and bring in a Bill for associating all his majesty's Protestant subjects.

Sir *Henry Capel*. Sir, the reason why we are now in this debate, is because a negative is passed on our Bill for excluding the duke. It is strange, seeing the danger of the Protestant Religion is so great (if there be any intent to save it) that the only bill which could serve for that end should be thought too much. I am of opinion, that no other bills can do us any service (for it will be pretended they are all void, because made against the right and prerogative of your lawful king) without this Exclusion-Bill. Yet, seeing his majesty hath so often in his Speeches recommended the Security of the Protestant Religion by other ways, I think it is our duty to try what other laws can be made, though it be only to give the king and the world satisfaction, and to enable us the better to judge, whether such Speeches proceed from his majesty's goodness, or from evil counsel. I must confess, I am afraid, (seeing the duke's interest is now as great at court as ever, and that there are so many of the privy counsellors for him, as well as most others in places of trust and command) that they that advise the king to put in that limitation in all his Speeches, do know, that without that law there can be none made that can prejudice the duke's interest, and so consequently not save the Protestant Religion, and therefore they advise it. For how can we reasonably presume otherways, seeing his interest is so fixed as it is, and the wheel within the wheel continues, which hath been so often complained of. When I ponderate on the good things his majesty always doth, when he is pleased to exclude the corrupt politics, and advice of others, I cannot but lament afresh our great misfortune in having a Popish Successor, that should be able to create such an interest, as to hinder us from the good effect thereof.

Sir *Fr. Winnington*. Sir; the many discourses you have heard this day, touching the strength of the Popish Interest at home, and how combined with foreign power, doth not so much startle me, as to see, that all the strength, upon which the Protestant Party must depend for security, is put into the hands of persons who are for the duke's interest, which we have reason to understand to be the same with Popery; not a person being employed in any place of command or trust, that ever declared against that interest. If I be mistaken in what I say, I desire to be corrected; I speak according to the best information I could have, and I believe all here know, what an exact scrutiny there hath been often made in all countries and corporations, for the finding out of men that way inclined, or otherwise so qualified, as are not fit to make any opposition to the designs carried on by the popish party. And if by chance any is put in, not fettered either by opinion or interest to that party, upon the first appearance he is presently discharged, as if he were a traitor to his country. And now, after a long interval of parliaments, and more and more discoveries of the reality and danger of the Popish Plot, what remedies are we like to obtain this session? I am afraid very few or none; for I must confess, I am still of opinion, there can be none without the Exclusion-Bill, which the lords have thrown out without so much as a conference; and therefore I am afraid that what the witnesses have said they were told by several Jesuits, is true; That Popery was so clenched and riveted, that it did not lie in the power of God, nor man, to prevent the settling of it in this nation. And if we consider what an interest that party hath now at present, and how things are prepared to afford them a greater assistance hereafter; how a popish king, as well as our divisions and animosities, will contribute to it, though I hope, God will make them liars; yet I conclude, they have a great deal of reason to be very confident. And I see not how we can help ourselves, seeing there are so many ministers of state about the king, who are as a partition-wall between him and his people. I find in Coke's Reports, that when the nation was in apparent danger, the people might go directly to the king with their Grievances, and make their Complaints and Petitions known. I think we may do well to consult this text, and see if we can find out any better way than what we have tried already, to convey our humble Supplications to his royal person. In the mean time, I think you had not best to go off from the Bill of Association.

Mr. *Leveson Gower*. Sir, I would not discourage you from going on with these Bills; but I am afraid they will fall far short of the power and strength that will be necessary to root out an Interest that hath been above 100 years riveting itself by all arts and ways imaginable, and hath now fixt itself so near the throne. I must confess, I am afraid we are at labour in vain, and that this interest hath so clenched itself, (as the Jesuits term it) that it will break not only this parliament, but many more, if not all parliaments, and the Protestant Religion too. It is too weighty to be removed, or perverted, by such little Bills as these: no, sir, you will find, that nothing less than a firm union amongst all the Protestants in this nation can be sufficient to give any check to this interest. As long as there are amongst us so many persons, as know not rightly how to apply the dangers of the Church and State, nor the miseries of 1641, but will be led by Popish projectors, I am afraid such Bills as these will not do our business: because they will not destroy that footing which they have at court, nor strengthen the Protestant Interest, which must have its original from union. It is strange that none but those who are for the duke's interest should be the only persons thought fit to be in places of trust! It is so strange a way to preserve the Protestant Church and Religion, that it raiseth with me a doubt, Whether any such thing be designed. Such persons may be proper to manage affairs in favour of the Popish interest; but it is to be admired, that they, and they only, should be thought fit to be intrusted with the Protestant interest. I think it as hard for them to do it, as to serve two masters. It is not usual in other countries, to retain their enemies in the government, nor such as are friends to their enemies; and it is strange that we, of all other nations, should fall into this piece of policy. But, sir, for these reasons you may conclude, that, unless what laws you make be strong and well-penned, they will signify nothing against so powerful a party as you have to do with.

Sir *Wm. Jones*. Sir; seeing there is a negative passed upon the Bill we had contrived to secure us from these great dangers, I think we may do well to try if we can get any thing else. But I am persuaded if this Association-Bill be made as it should be, that we shall have no better success with it than we had with the Exclusion-Bill: for I am afraid, that though we are permitted to brandish our weapons, yet that we shall not be allowed to wound Popery; but rather do believe, that they who advised the throwing out of that Bill, will also do the same by this, or dissolve the house before it come to perfection: for this Bill must be much stronger than that in queen Eliz.'s days; that was for an Association only after her death, but I cannot tell if such a bill will secure us now, the circumstances we are under being very different. In queen Eliz.'s days, the privy counsellors were all for the queen's interest, and none for the successor's; now, most of the privy-counsellors are for the successor's, and few for the king's. Then the ministers unanimously agreed to keep out Popery, now we have too much reason to fear, there are many that are for bringing it in. In those days they all agreed to keep the Popish Successor in Scotland, now the major part agreed to keep the Successor here; all which must be considered in drawing up of the Bill.

An Association Bill voted.] Resolved, "That it is the opinion of this Committee, that the house be moved, that a Bill be brought in for an Association of all his majesty's Protestant subjects, for the safety of his majesty's person, the defence of the Protestant Religion, and the preservation of his majesty's Protestant subjects, against all invasions and oppositions: and for preventing the duke of York, or any other Papist, from succeeding to the crown."

Proceedings on Mr. Seymour's Impeachment.] Dec. 17. The commons ordered, "That Mr. Seymour be taken into the custody of the serjeant at arms, for securing his forth-coming to answer the Impeachment of this house against him, until he shall have given security to this house, to answer to the said Impeachment; and that the serjeant at arms be empowered to receive security for the forth-coming of the said Mr. Seymour."

Votes to secure the Kingdom against Popery, &c.] The same day, the house resolved into a committee, farther to consider of ways and means to secure the kingdom against Popery and arbitrary Government; and after several debates, how ineffectual all laws would prove, without good Judges, Justices, and others in commission, that will execute them; and how frequent parliaments would conduce to have laws put duly in execution; 1. Resolved; "That it is the opinion of this house, that the house be moved, that a Bill be brought in, for the more effectual securing of the Meetings and Sittings of frequent Parliaments. 2. That this house do agree with the committee, that a Bill be brought in that the Judges hereafter to be made and appointed, may hold their Places and Salaries *quamdiu se bene gesserint*: and also to prevent the arbitrary proceedings of Judges. 3. That this house do agree with the committee, that a Bill be brought in, against illegal Exaction of Money upon the people, to make it High-Treason."

Debate on the King's Speech.] Dec. 18. His majesty's Speech, made to both houses on the 15th, was read.

Mr. *John Hampden.* Sir; the veneration that is due to all his majesty's Speeches doth require, that we should seriously debate them before we give any answer to them; but the circumstances we are under at this time challenge a more than ordinary consultation: for, by the tenor of the Speech, I conclude, that the success of this parliament depends upon our Answer to it; and consequently, the safety of the Protestant Religion, both at home and abroad. And therefore I think myself very unable to advise in this matter, and should not have attempted it, but that you have encouraged me by your leave to speak first. So that if I offer any thing amiss, those that come after will have opportunities to correct me. I would begin with the latter end of the Speech first; because that part of it is most likely to beget a fair understanding between his maj. and this house. But I cannot but observe, what great care is here again taken to preserve the Succession in the right line, as in all other his majesty's Speeches ever since the Plot broke out. I think more could not be done, though it were in behalf of the king's son, and a Protestant too. That limitation, and his majesty's offer of securing the Protestant Religion, (if by Succession in the right line be meant the duke) upon many debates in this house is found irreconcilable; and therefore must be imputed to those that have advised his maj. thereto. To preserve the right Succession in the duke, is to preserve something or nothing. The something must be no less than the crown, in case of his majesty's death; and so consequently the interest of the Popish party, who, after 100 years endeavours to have a prince of their own religion, the indefatigable industry of the Jesuits to obtain it, and the loss of so much blood spent therein, will, besides their principles and inclinations, lay on them great obligations, to make use of the opportunity to establish their religion again in this nation. So that I must confess, these reservations look to be like a perfect design to save the whole party, accompanied with a power and a pretence sufficient to enable them to accomplish their end. For to this the saving of the duke's right doth amount, and consequently the destruction of the Protestant Religion: which cannot be imagined to proceed from his majesty. In former times, the interest of no one man could ever bear up against the interest of the nation; now it seems, that the Religion, lives and liberties of all the people of this nation, nay, I may say, all the Protestants of the three nations, must be all lost, rather than one man be dispossest of his right; though by his act he hath made himself incapable to enjoy it. Certainly there must be more intended by this than the saving of one man; it must be the saving of a party: and therefore, sir, I am afraid we are but where we were two years ago: for it is plain to me, that there is a certain fatal scheme, which hath been exactly pursued these 20 years, in order to destroy the Protestant Interest, and hath had a strange secret operation in the management of all our affairs; and although now and then some accidents have happened, that have occasioned some alteration for a time, as by his majesty's recalling the Toleration, some transactions of parliaments, the breaking out of the Plot, and his majesty's Toleration of his Council in 1679; yet I observe, that after a little while there is no change in the main; all returns to the old scheme, as if there were a certain infallible balance that did preponderate. We have had so much experience of his majesty's goodness and inclinations, that we cannot but conclude that there is still some such thing, as a wheel within a wheel; whether Jesuits, (for it is like them) or who, I cannot tell, nor how the government is influenced, that the protestants should not be able to obtain any thing for their security. But we may guess and justly fear, that it will never be otherwise, as long as there is a Popish Successor. The truth is, we have a hard task to serve our king and country in such a time as this is. We may expose ourselves to the rage of a powerful party; but, I am afraid, get little to secure ourselves against their revenge. We are under the same inequality as fair gamesters that meet with those that use false dice; and are like to have the same ill luck at last, unless his maj. should be pleased to consider, who stands up most for his government, and who plays fairest; and accordingly, change his councils.—It is not to be doubted but that, as well for the security of the nation at home, as of Flanders against the power of France, and the Protestant Religion abroad, we are under a necessity to make Alliances; and that they cannot be made nor supported without money. But did we not give above 2 millions for the preservation of the Triple league? And were not the said 2 millions by the power of the French and Popish party employed to break it? Did we not a little while since give about a million and an half for an actual French war? And was there not presently a general peace made? Do not all foreign nations complain, that, notwithstanding all our treaties, pretences, and declarations, we have been only true to France? And what reason have we now to imagine, that if we should give Money for Leagues, that it would be employed otherwise than formerly? Is not the same scheme of government pursued still? Is not the French ambassador, and the French woman too, as great at court as ever? And have not the duke's creatures the management of all affairs? And if the duke's interest, the French interest, and the Popish interest, be all one, can you imagine, that your Money shall be employed to make any Alliances, that shall be for the advantage of the Protestant Religion? No, sir, though his maj. so intend it, yet the wheel within a wheel, which hath managed all other Alliances hitherto, will also manage these, and have the disposal of our Money too, and pervert it to our destruction. And, until things settle here at home on a true Protestant bottom, it cannot be imagined, that any foreign prince will depend on us, or make Alliances with us. And therefore as well for that, as because our Money may not probably be disposed of for any good end, it is in vain to treat of either Alliances or money. For, until the interest be changed at court, that so there may be a better understanding between the king and his people, it cannot produce any thing for our advantage.—I beg leave to add something about the latter part of the Speech, which doth a little comfort me, because I hope we may graft such an Answer thereupon, as may beget a right understanding with his majesty. I know this house is constituted of persons different from that of the Long Parliament, because of the many Pensioners that were in it; and that we need not now be afraid to talk of Money. I believe we all know, that without giving Money this session, the nation can never be happy, nor his majesty's government so formidable as it ought to be. And therefore I would humbly move you to appoint a committee, to draw up an Address to assure his majesty, that when his maj. shall be pleased to grant us such laws, as are necessary for the security of our Religion, which may be particularized in the address, that we will be ready to give him what Money his occasions may require, not only for the support of Tangier, and Alliances, but to enable him to have a good Fleet at sea, for the encouraging of Seamen, and security of Trade, and preservation of his dominions; that so we may shew we are ready to express our duty, as well by our acts as words.

Lord Russel. Sir, seeing it is so apparent that all our fears of Popery arise from, and center in the duke: and that is impossible the affairs of this nation should ever settle on a good Protestant bottom, as long as there is a Popish Successor, which cannot be prevented but by the Succession Bill: that there may be no ill construction made of our desires, I would humbly move you to offer to supply the king with what Money he may need for the support of Tangier and Alliances, upon his granting of the Succession Bill only, that so his maj. may have no reason to be diffident of us; not doubting, but that if we can once lay a foundation for a good correspondence, that his maj. will take so much content in it, beyond what he doth now enjoy, that to preserve it he will afterwards grant us what more Bills may be farther necessary for the security of the Protestant Religion. And therefore I am not for clogging this Address with any request for any thing more, than that one Bill.

Sir *Wm. Jones.* Sir, we have hitherto had so little success in our endeavours, that we may justly suspect, we are permitted to sit here, rather to destroy ourselves than to save our country. It is a matter of admiration to me, that those who have so often advised his majesty, to put this, and the former parliaments, upon finding out expedients for securing the Protestant Religion, without altering the Succession, should all this while find out none themselves; but still continue advising the king to put that upon us, which, after many debates, is found to be impossible. And that the king should always have at his elbow persons ready to remember him constantly to make this limitation, which, in all appearance, must tend to the final destruction of the Protestant Religion: and that there should be no body there to mind him of proposing some expedients to prevent it, only in general words, of which no use can be made. According to the opinion of three successive parliaments, the limitation in favour of the Popish interest is plain, intelligible, and practicable. I hope his majesty, against the next occasion, will require them that have so advised him, to make the expedients and other ways to secure the Protestant Religion, as plain and practicable, that so we may see if the security of the Protestant Religion be designed in good earnest by such advisers, which I cannot believe; because what they propose is, in my opinion, a contradiction in itself. Without the Exclusion Bill, there can be no expedient but what will leave us in that miserable condition, of having, first or last, a contest with our lawful king. And there can be no such thing as setting up a power to oppose him, but by putting a kind of supreme authority in the parliament; with a power to oppose, as well by making war as laws, which might prove the destruction of the monarchial government. The said trust or power (without the Exclusion-Bill) being not to be reposed in the next heir, or any single person, lest he should die before he come to have the power in him, or utterly refuse to act, if he should live to have a right, by virtue of such a settlement, to administer the government. In such a case, there would be no lawful power lodged any where else, to oppose such a king, and there must not be an Interregnum. By this short account you may see, what difficulties all expedients will be liable to; and may conclude, that those that advise the king to make this limitation, do intend it as an expedient to make the endeavours of parliaments ineffectual, and to bring in Popery. And if you had offered at such expedients as I have mentioned, as the last house of commons was arraigned for omnipotent and arbitrary, so would this with some worse character; as having attempted to destroy the monarchical government, that if possible the king and people might be put out of love with parliaments. But, sir, though it is plain, that things are thus out of order, yet let us not be wanting in our duty, but give such an Answer to his majesty, as may, if possible, create in him a good opinion of this house, and satisfy him of the necessity of the Bill of Exclusion; and that all other acts of grace will but serve to fatten us for the slaughter of our enemies.

Mr. *Garroway.* If you do not represent all your Grievances in this Address, as the condition of your giving Money, whatever you shall offer at afterwards will be looked upon as clamourous, and out of order. And therefore I would advise you, not to omit any one Grievance you expect any remedy in. And I am for enumerating all your Grievances, in the Address, which have been lately debated. And I do admire nobody takes notice of the Standing Army; which if not reduced to such a number as may be convenient for guards, and so limited, that they may not be increased, unless in case of a rebellion, or an invasion, all your laws may signify nothing. And I am not satisfied in the making such general offers of Money. For if you do, you will hear in time, that the Fleet needs one million; Alliances, as much more; and Tangier (though I think not worth keeping) little less.

Resolved, after further debate, "That a committee be appointed to prepare an humble Address to his majesty, upon the debate of the house, in answer to his majesty's Speech."

The Commons' Address, in Answer to the King's Speech.] Dec. 30. Mr. Hampden reported the Address; which was read and agreed to, as follows:

"We your majesty's most dutiful and loyal subjects, the commons in this present parliament assembled, having taken into our serious consideration your majesty's gracious Speech to both houses, on the 15th of this instant Dec. do, with all the grateful sense of faithful subjects and sincere Protestants, acknowledge your majesty's great goodness to us, in renewing the assurances you have been pleased to give us, of your readiness to concur with us in any means for the Security of the Protestant Religion, and your gracious invitation of us, to make our desires known to your majesty. But with grief of heart we cannot but observe, that, to these princely offers, your majesty has been advised (by what secret enemies to your maj. and your people, we know not) to annex a reservation, which, if insisted on in the instance to which alone it is applicable, will render all your majesty's other gracious inclinations of no effect or advantage to us. Your majesty is pleased thus to limit your promise of concurrence, in the Remedies which shall be proposed, that they may consist with preserving the Succession of the Crown in its due and legal course of descent. And we do humbly inform your maj. that no interruption of that descent has been endeavoured at by us, except only the descent upon the person of the duke of York, who, by the wicked instruments of the Church of Rome, has been manifestly perverted to their Religion. And we do humbly represent to your majesty, as the issue of our most deliberate thoughts and consultations, that for the Papists to have their hopes continued, that a prince of that religion should succeed in the throne of these kingdoms, is utterly inconsistent with the safety of your majesty's person, the preservation of the Protestant Religion, and the prosperity, peace and welfare of your Protestant subjects.—That your majesty's sacred Life is in continual danger, under the prospect of a Popish Successor, is evident, not only from the principles of those devoted to the Church of Rome, which allow, that an heretical prince (and such they term all Protestant princes) excommunicated and deposed by the Pope, may be destroyed and murdered; but also from the testimonies given in the prosecution of the horrid Popish Plot, against divers traitors, attainted for designing to put those accursed principles into practice against your majesty.—From the expectation of this Succession, has the number of Papists in your majesty's dominions so much encreased within these few years, and so many been prevailed with to desert the true Protestant Religion, that they might be prepared for the favours of a Popish prince, as soon as he should come to the possession of the crown; and while the same expectation lasts, many more will be in the same danger of being perverted.—This it is that has hardened the Papists of this kingdom, animated and confederated by their priests and Jesuits, to make a common purse, provide arms, make application to foreign princes, and solicit their aid, for imposing Popery upon us; and all this, even during your majesty's reign, and while your majesty's government and the laws were our protection.—It is your majesty's glory and true interest, to be the head and protector of all Protestants, as well abroad as at home: but if these hopes remain, what Alliances can be made for the advantage of the Protestant Religion and Interest, which shall give confidence to your majesty's allies, to join so vigorously with your majesty, as the state of that interest in the world now requires, while they see this Protestant kingdom in so much danger of a Popish Successor? By whom, at the present, all their councils and actions may be eluded, as hitherto they have been; and by whom (if he should succeed) they are sure to e destroyed.—We have thus humbly laid before your majesty some of those great dangers and mischiefs, which evidently accompany the expectation of a Popish Successor. The certain and unspeakable evils which will come upon your majesty's Protestant subjects, and their posterity, if such a prince should inherit, are more also than we can well enumerate.—Our Religion, which is now so dangerously shaken, will then be totally overthrown; nothing will be left, or can be found to protect or defend it.—The execution of old laws must cease, and it will be vain to expect new ones. The most sacred obligations of contracts and promises, (if any such should be given) that shall be judged to be against the interest of the Romish Religion, will be violated; as is undeniable, not only from argument and experience elsewhere, but from the sad experience this nation once had on the like occasion. In the reign of such a prince, the Pope will be acknowledged supreme, (though the subjects of this kingdom have sworn the contrary) and all causes, either as spiritual, or in order to spiritual things, will be brought under his jurisdiction. The lives, liberties, and estates of all such Protestants, as value their souls and their religion more than their secular concernments, will be adjudged forfeited.—To all this we might add, that it appears in the discovery of the Plot, that foreign princes were invited to assist in securing the crown to the duke of York, with arguments from his great zeal to establish Popery, and to extirpate Protestants (whom they call Heretics) out of his dominions; and such will expect performance accordingly.—We farther humbly beseech your majesty, in your great wisdom to consider, whether, in case the imperial crown of this Protestant kingdom should descend to the duke of York, the opposition which may possibly be made to his possessing it, may not only endanger the further descent in the royal line, but even monarchy itself.—For these reasons, we are most humble petitioners to your most sacred majesty, that, in tender commiseration of your poor Protestant people, your majesty will be graciously pleased to depart from the reservation in your said Speech; and when a Bill shall be tendered to your maj. in a parliamentary way, to disable the duke of York from inheriting the crown, your majesty will give your royal assent thereto; and as necessary to fortify and defend the same, that your maj. will likewise be graciously pleased to assent to an Act, whereby your maj.'s Protestant subjects may be enabled to associate themselves for the Defence of your maj.'s person, the Protestant Religion, and the security of your kingdoms.—These requests we are constrained humbly to make to your majesty as of absolute necessity, for the safe and peaceable enjoyment of our religion. Without these things, the alliances of England will not be valuable, nor the people encouraged to contribute to your majesty's service. As some farther means for the preservation both of our religion and property, we are humble suitors to your majesty, that from henceforth such persons only may be judges within the kingdom of England, and dominion of Wales, as are men of ability, integrity, and known affection to the protestant religion: And that they may hold both their offices and salaries, 'quamdiu se bene gesserint.' That (several deputy-lieutenants and justices of the peace fitly qualified for those employments, having been of late displaced, and others put in their room, who are men of arbitrary principles, and countenancers of papists and popery) such only may bear the office of a lord-lieutenant, as are persons of integrity and known affection to the protestant religion. That deputy-lieutenants, and justices of the peace, may be also so qualified, and may be moreover men of abilities, of estates and interest in their country. That none be employed as military officers, or officers in your majesty's fleet, but men of known experience, courage, and affection to the Protestant religion.—These our humble requests being obtained, we shall, on our part, be ready to assist your majesty for the preservation of Tangier; and for putting your majesty's fleet into such a condition, as it may preserve your majesty's Sovereignty of the Seas, and be for the defence of the nation.—If your majesty hath, or shall make any necessary Alliances for defence of the Protestant religion, and interest and security of this kingdom, this house will be ready to assist and stand by your majesty in the support of the same. After this our humble Answer to your majesty's gracious Speech, we hope no evil instruments whatsoever, shall be able to lessen your majesty's esteem of that fidelity and affection we bear to your majesty's service: but that your maj. will always retain, in your royal breast, that favourable opinion of us your loyal commons, that those other good Bills which we have now under consideration, conducing to the great ends we have before mentioned, as also all laws for the benefit and comfort of your people, which shall from time to time be tendered for your majesty's royal assent, shall find acceptance with your majesty."

Debate on the Bill for uniting his Majesty's Protestant Subjects.] Dec. 21. A Bill was read for uniting his majesty's Protestant Subjects *.

Mr. *Powle.* Sir, it is not to be doubted but that the happiness of this nation, and safety of our religion, doth depend very much upon preserving the well-constituted government of the church; and that the government in the state will not long stand, if that be pulled down, to which, I am afraid, this Bill will contribute very much. Sir, it is well known, how, notwithstanding all the endeavours of his majesty,

* "This Bill was not introduced till towards the latter end of Dec. when the close of the session was in view. And hence it may be concluded that it was one of those parliamentary fire-works that are occasionally let off, only to make a noise and expire." Ralph.

as well in parliament as otherwise, all the acts that are in force against Dissenters, all the endeavours of the fathers of the church, there are a sort of men, and great numbers too, who will neither be advised nor over-ruled; but, under the pretence of conscience, break violently through all laws whatsoever, to the great disturbance both of church and state. And if you should give them more liberty, you will encourage them to go on with more boldness; and therefore I think it will be more convenient to have a law for forcing the Dissenters to yield to the church, and not to force the church to yield to them; and I think we are going quite the wrong way to do the nation good. And therefore I am against this Bill.

Mr. *D——.* Sir, I would not open my mouth in favour of this Bill, if I thought it would any ways prejudice the church, or church-government; but I believe it may have a quite contrary effect, and tend more for the preservation and safety of the church and church-government, than any bill whatsoever that could be contrived. We have a church-government settled by law, to which the major part of the people, like good christians and loyal subjects, give obedience; but it is our misfortune that there are in the nation a great many, who will not submit to this government, who may be divided under three heads: 1. The Papists, who differ from us in points of faith, and will not give any obedience but to the church of Rome: 2. Independents, Presbyterians, and some others, who agree in points of faith, and differ only in points of doctrine and ceremonies: 3. Quakers, who disagree not only in points of doctrine and ceremonies, but in points of faith, and are a head-strong sort of unreasonable people, that will not submit to any laws made about religion, but do give obedience to the civil magistrates upon all other occasions. The church of England-men are not only the greatest number, but have the government of their side. What laws to make, that may tend most to the preserving of it, is your business. It is in danger from the Papists on the one hand, and the rest of the Protestant dissenters on the other, who in some measure agree in their enmity and disrespect to the church, and therefore the more care ought to be taken for its preservation.—Having thus, sir, discovered the danger of the church in general, it will be necessary, in order to find out a Remedy, to discourse a little of the strength and interest of each party in particular.—Sir, the Papists are not the greatest number, but yet, in my opinion, upon several considerations, are most to be feared, because of their desperate principles, which make them bold and indefatigable, and the assistance they may have from Rome, France, and Ireland; but above all, from the great share they have in the management of the government, by the means of a popish successor, and the fear of their getting the government into their hands hereafter by having a popish king: which of itself hath been sufficient in former times to change the religion of this nation, and, as may justly be feared, may have the same effect again, unless the Protestants be well united. The Presbyterians, Independents, and all other Dissenters, may be more in number than the Papists, and may be willing enough to have the church-government altered, if not destroyed; yet, being they cannot have any succour from abroad, nor from the government here at home, I cannot see any great danger from them: for, it is not probable they shall ever have a king of their own opinion, nor a parliament, by the discovery they made of their strength in the last elections: for, according to the best calculation I can make, they could not bring one in 20, and therefore, because they have not such bloody, desperate principles as the Papists, and because we agree in points of faith, and so there is no such great danger from them as from the Papists, I think we have reason to conclude, that the church is most in danger from the Papists, and that therefore we ought to take care of them in the first place; and we cannot do that by any way more likely to prove effectual, than by some such Bill as this.

Mr. *Finch.* Sir, this Bill is intended for the preservation of the church, and I am of opinion, is the best Bill that can be made in order thereto, our circumstances considered: but I know not what effect it may have, because you are to deal with a stubborn sort of people, who in many things prefer their humour before reason, or their own safety, or the public good. But, sir, I think this is a very good time to try, whether they will be won by the cords of love or no, and the Bill will be very agreeable to that Christian charity which our church professes; and I hope that in a time of so imminent danger as we are in of a common enemy, they will consider their own safety, and the safety of the Protestant religion, and not longer keep afoot the unhappy divisions that are amongst us, on which the Papists ground their hopes. But rather, seeing the church doth so far condescend, as to dispense with the surplice, and those other things which they scruple at, that they will submit to the rest that is enjoined by law, that so we may unite against the common enemy: but if this Bill should not have this desired effect, but, on the contrary, notwithstanding this condescension, they should continue their animosities and disobedience to the church, I think still the church will gain very much hereby, and leave that party without excuse, and be a just cause for the making of more coercive laws.

After further debate, it was resolved, "That the said Bill be committed." *

Queries relating to the Execution of Lord Stafford.] Dec. 23. Some Queries relating to the

* "The Bill was committed on the question, but afterwards dropped, no doubt on the same political principles which first made way for its admission; for though it was expedient to favour the non-conformists, it was not safe to wage war with the church." Ralph.

execution of Wm. late viscount Stafford, were offered to the house by the sheriffs of London and Middlesex. 1. "Whether the king, being neither judge nor party, can order the execution? 2. Whether the lords can award the execution? 3. Whether the king can dispense with any part of the execution? 4. If the king can dispense with some part of the execution, why not with all?"

Serj. *Maynard.* I cannot find fault with the king's mercy in remitting part of the sentence against this lord; but this question has arisen, I believe, that the lords and we may be at difference upon it. Either the Papists hope that, by it, this lord may be acquitted, or that we may so differ, that all business may be at a stand.

Sir *Wm. Jones.* I think that the proposal of this matter from the Sheriffs does not deserve blame, but thanks, and that they did well to apply themselves to this house. I have considered of it, and I think there is no reason to go to the lords about it; it will not prejudice us so much as some apprehend. The Impeachment is at our prosecution, and the Judgment at our suit. Death is the substance of the Judgment; the manner of it is but a circumstance. If a nobleman be judged to be hanged for felony, that he may be beheaded by the king's warrant lord Coke doubts; though the Judges argued that, in the case of lord Castlehaven, who was condemned to be hanged for bu——ry, and his Judgment was changed into beheading. The Judgment against a woman, for high-treason, is to be burnt; but we know frequently that they have been beheaded, as was Anne Bullen. I take it easy to show, that, if the substance be preserved, which is death, the circumstances may be varied. No man can show me an example of a nobleman that has been quartered for high-treason: they have been only beheaded. But now, what shall we do in this case? Shall we desire the lords to do what was never done before? By nature, Englishmen are not so severe; as if the substance could not be performed without the circumstances. What is then to be done? Either execution will be done by this writ, or by conference you will complain to the lords, that execution is not ordered according to Judgment, or that they have not done, in the upper house, what was never done before. To satisfy the Sheriffs, I would pass a vote, "That this house is content that Execution be done upon lord Stafford, by severing his head from his body."

Resolved, "That this house is content that the Sheriffs of London and Middlesex do execute William late Viscount Stafford, by severing his head from his body only."

Report relating to the Proceedings of the Judges.] The same day, sir Rd. Corbet reported the resolves of the Committee appointed to examine the Proceedings of the Judges in Westminster-Hall, touching the Discharge of the Grand Jury in the King's-Bench. Upon which, the house resolved, nem. con. 1. "That the discharging of the Grand Jury of the hundred of Oswaldston, in the county of Middlesex, by the Court of King's Bench, in Trinity Term last, before the last day of the Term, and before they had finished their Presentments, was arbitrary and illegal, destructive of public justice, a manifest violation of the oaths of the Judges of that court, and a means to subvert the fundamental laws of this kingdom, and to introduce Popery. 2. That the Rule made by the Court of King's-bench in Trinity Term last, against printing of a Book called, 'The weekly Pacquet of Advice from Rome,' is illegal and arbitrary, thereby usurping to themselves legislative power, to the great discouragement of the Protestants, and for the countenancing of Popery. 3. That the Court of King's-bench, in the Imposition of Fines on Offenders of late years, have acted arbitrarily, illegally, and partially, favouring Papists, and Persons Popishly affected, and excessively oppressing his majesty's Protestant Subjects. 4. That the refusing sufficient Bail in these cases, wherein the persons committed were bailable by law, was illegal, and a high breach of the Liberties of the Subject. 5. That the said Expressions in the Charge given by the said baron Weston, were a scandal to the Reformation, and tending to raise discord between his maj. and his subjects, and to the subversion of the ancient constitution of parliaments, and of the government of this kingdom. 6. That the said Warrants are arbitrary and illegal."

Resolutions for the Impeachment of the said Judges.] Resolved, 1. "That sir Wm. Scroggs, knight, Chief Justice of the Court of King's-bench: 2. Sir Tho. Jones, one of the Justices of the said Court of King's-bench; and sir Rd. Weston, one of the Barons of the Court of Exchequer, be impeached upon the said Report, and Resolutions of the House thereupon."

Ordered, "That the committee appointed to prepare an Impeachment against sir Fr. North, chief justice of the court of Common-Pleas, do prepare Impeachments against the said sir Wm. Scroggs, sir Tho. Jones, and sir Rd. Weston, upon the said Report and Resolutions."

*Debate on Mr. Sheridan's Habeas Corpus.**] Dec. 30. Mr. *Boscawen.* Mr. Sheridan stands committed, as a judgment of the house, for breach of privilege. It seems to me, that his commitment does run on the hinge of an act of court in a criminal cause, which we may suppose in execution, where a Habeas Corpus does not lie, and he is not bailable, and they will not discharge him in a court of criminal causes. I think his commitment stands good, and you are to consider the privilege of the house.

* "There was a bold forward man, Sheridan, a native of Ireland, whom the commons committed, and he moved for his Habeas Corpus. Some of the Judges were afraid of the house, and slipt out of the way; but baron Weston had the courage to grant it." Burnet.

The *Speaker*. The thing, in fact, stands thus. Sheridan and Day were committed by your Order the 9th of Dec.; they were brought to the bar the same day, and ordered to continue in custody during the pleasure of the house, and no person to be admitted to come to him unless it were with necessaries. Then that order was mitigated, and you ordered him to be taken into custody. Then you ordered a committee to examine him and Wilson. The Act directs, 'That the Judges, within such a time, grant a Habeas Corpus, when desired, and they are required to bail where the Act gives that liberty.' Now the question is, Whether a Habeas Corpus lies in case of any of your Commitments, the parliament sitting? [And he reads the Act.] In the Act here is nothing relates to Parliament-Commitments. The 'Head-Court' is the King's-bench, and this seems not to relate to the parliament. This is a commitment of parliament, and if so, the Judges cannot grant a Habeas Corpus.

Serj. *Maynard*. You are going upon a sudden to give an opinion in a thing not thought of before. As I take it, his Habeas Corpus is granted: now, what is to be done in this case? I desire not to be concluded in any thing I shall now say, but I will tell you my apprehension; where shall he go to be bailed, but to this house? Your remedy for breach of your privilege is commitment, and no action can be brought against either the lords or commons. When you commit a man, you do not always express the cause; if the Judges bail him, he is gone, and there is an end of him.

Serj. *Stringer*. This is a matter of great concern. I would consider whether a Judge can deny a Habeas Corpus. By the Act, the jailor is to pay the penalty of 500*l.* upon affidavit; 'That he is refused the copy of his commitment.' So far a Judge may safely go. But the great point is, Whether the judge can discharge him. If so, farewell all the privileges of the commons! When the matter comes to a Habeas Corpus, the judges may be informed how he stands committed. It is said, 'That this Sheridan is a second Coleman,' and, if so, let him be hanged as he was. I would take time to consider this, and I believe the opinion of this house will go a great way with the Judges.

Sir *Wm. Jones*. Sir, the privileges of both houses are concerned in this business, and in that the very being of parliaments: and therefore we must be careful what we do in it. I have perused the Habeas Corpus bill, and do find, that there is not any thing in it that doth reach, or can be intended to reach to any commitment made by either house of parliament during session. The preamble of the Act, and all the parts of it, do confine the extent of the Act to cases bailable, and directs such courses for the execution of the act, as cannot be understood should relate to any commitment made by either house. This house is a court of itself, and part of the highest court in the nation, superior to those in Westminster-hall; and what laws this house joins in making, are to bind inferior courts, but cannot be understood to bind themselves as a court; that would prove not only dangerous, but destructive to the dignity of parliaments, and level them with the courts in Westminster-hall. Great care ought to be taken how you allow of restraints and limitations to the proceedings of both houses, being so great a part of the legislative power of the nation, lest thereby you should by degrees render them useless. A commitment of this house is always in nature of a judgment; and the act is only for cases bailable, which commitments upon judgments are not; at least commitments by this house were never yet allowed to be bailable; and I suppose you will never grant them so to be. Can it be imagined that this house, who represent all the commons of England, should not be entrusted with as much power for the preservation of their constitution, upon which the support of the government so much depends, as ordinary courts and officers are entrusted with, which are only designed for the welfare of particular persons. I am of opinion, that no act can deprive this house of that power which they have always exercised, of committing persons without bail, unless in express words it be so declared: nor of discharging upon bail, after committed. The same reasons which may be given for discharging such as are not committed for breach of privilege, if it be grounded on the act for the Habeas Corpus, will hold as strong for the discharging of persons committed for breach of privilege; and so consequently deprive this house of all its power and dignity, and make it insignificant. This is so plain and obvious, that all judges ought to know it; and I think it below you to make any resolve therein, but rather leave the judges to do otherwise at their peril, and let the debate fall without any question.

Sir *F. Winnington*. All I move for is this, 'That no entry be made upon your books for the present;' but upon the whole frame of the act, I see no Habeas Corpus lies upon a commitment of parliament.—No entry was made in the Journal, and it was adjourned to tomorrow.

Debate on Placemen and Pensioners in Parliament.] What followed the same day, related to Placemen and Pensioners sitting in Parliament; on which occasion

Sir *Fr. Winnington* expressed himself thus: —Sir, the last house of commons being sensible how narrowly this nation escaped being ruined by a sort of monsters called Pensioners, which sate in the late Long Parliament, had entered into a consideration how to prevent the like from coming into future parliaments; and in order thereto resolved, that they would severely chastise some of those that had been guilty, and make the best laws they could to prevent the like for the future: and for that purpose a Committee was appointed, of which Mr. Serjeant Gregory, now Judge Gregory, was chairman: by which, many Papers relating to that affair came to his hands. Sir, I think it a business of so great importance, that it never ought to be forgotten, nor the prosecution of it deferred. I have often heard, that England can never be destroyed but by itself: to have such parliaments was the most likely way that ever yet was invented. I remember a great lawyer said in this house, when it was debated in the last parliament, that it was treason; and he gave many learned arguments to make it out. Whether it be so or no, I will not now offer to debate; but I think, that for those that are the legislators of the nation to take Bribes to undermine the laws and government of this nation, that they ought to be chastised as traitors. It was my fortune to sit here a little while in the Long Parliament; I did observe that all those that had Pensions, and most of those that had Offices, voted all of a side, as they were directed by some great officer, as exactly as if their business in this house had been to preserve their Pensions and Offices, and not to make laws for the good of them that sent them here. How such persons could any way be useful for the support of the government, by preserving a fair understanding between the king and his people, but on the contrary how dangerous to bring in arbitrary power and popery, I leave to every man's judgment. They were so far from being the true representatives of the people, that they were a distinct middle interest between the king and the people; and their chief business was to serve the end of some great minister of state, though never so opposite to the true interest of the nation. Sir, this business ought never to fall, though there should be never so many prorogations and dissolutions of parliaments, before any thing be done in it; I think it is the interest of the nation, that it should be prosecuted from parliament to parliament, as if there were an impeachment against them. And therefore, sir, I would humbly move you to send some members of this house to judge Gregory, for the Papers he hath taken in his custody relating to this affair, that so you may in convenient time proceed farther herein, as you shall think good. And, sir, being there is a report that some of this house have now made a bargain at court for great offices in order to vitiate and corrupt their Votes in this house, which though but a project to cast a reflection on such members, however to satisfy the world, I pray, sir, let there be a Vote past, 'That no Member of this house shall accept of any Office under the crown, during such time as he continues a member."

Mr. *Harbord.* So many artifices are used to asperse your members, against the public good, that I move that no person may have any place during the parliament without leave of the house, or else that he be incapable of being a parliament-man if he accept of it.

Col. *Titus.* As I came to the house this morning, I heard myself to be a great man, and that I had a place at court, and had so many compliments upon being a great minister, that I began to flatter myself that I was really so; but now I plainly discover that I have no such place at all. After you have so proceeded against sir Rob. Peyton for his truckling for a place, should I accept of a Pension, or a Place, it would be no wonder if I should be brought upon my knees, as he was. I never heard that man said to have kept a fort, for it was never assaulted. A woman with an ill face is seldom tempted. I protest, I never heard of any place till I came hither this morning. I met with another report, 'That I had been with the duchess of Portsmouth.' If any man can prove, whilst I was of the bed-chamber to his majesty, that ever I spoke a word to her, I will lie under all your accusations. I know not a better design, nor more dextrous, to carry on popery, than this of raising jealousies. Let me repeat that part of the litany, 'From envy, hatred, and malice, good Lord deliver us.' If my own actions will not justify me, my words never will. I think you have been regularly moved, 'That the Papers about the pensioners in sir Stephen Fox's hands may be reviewed.' If any man have no impediment for preferment, let him take it, but not be a parliament-man. If a man think himself qualified for a place, let him leave the parliament, and accept of the place. 'Lead us not into temptation,' we pray daily. The house will always have power over their members, and I move that they may have no employment during parliament.

Mr. *Vaughan.* There was something of this nature offered at in the Long Parliament, but it fell. Now I think this parliament consists of good men, able to maintain themselves. Prevent such ulcers in your own bowels. That Bill then offered provided, 'That upon acceptation of any such office, a new writ should issue out, to chuse another person.' I am not for gentlemen purging themselves. I believe them honest men.

Col. *Titus.* I have been congratulated for a great place, and I humbly desire Vaughan's leave to clear myself. I say that some of us were accused of Places, but not that Vaughan did.

Col. *Birch.* I have a place, and I had it before the Long Parliament was called, (I was one of the secluded members) and so I am beforehand. Though Vaughan has not gone much abroad, yet it is the talk of the town. I have sat in that corner amongst those gentlemen who have been talked of for Places, and had there been provender amongst them, I should have been crumping with them. But now there are no such places or bargain made, to the shame of them that reported it. Some corrupt judges formerly had their skins stuffed with hay, for an example; I desire those Gentlemen-Pensioners, if there be any, may be stuffed with straw, and I am content. If they received Pensions in the Long Parliament, I have heard that all done in such a parliament is null and void; that it has been so formerly.

Mr. *Garroway.* I think, a Vote in this case will not do your business, nor answer your end. Therefore I am for a Bill.

Mr. *Hampden.* I am now for a Bill, but I would have a vote first, and thus far a vote will be obligatory to men of worth and honour: If any man will say that he is not obliged by that vote, let him. Pass such a vote first, 'That during parliament we may have no Places nor Pensions to the scandal of the house.'

Sir *Wm. Jones.* I like both the questions, both for a Vote, and a Bill, but I am sorry that you have no means to bring things to light about the Pensioners. Mr. Bertie is gone abroad, and I am afraid will not return till this parliament be up. When men do not act for such Places, in time the world will be undeceived, and let that pass. 'Places of Profit' will be a word too general in your question; they may have places in corporations; but I would add to the vote, 'Not to exclude your Members from the magistracy, as lord mayor or sheriff of London, &c. It may be convenient to have them members of parliament. I would have them only excluded Offices from court, and Places from his majesty.

Col. *Titus.* Suppose his majesty should have occasion to send ambassadors, or admirals, it may be those are the ablest men for it. Suppose we should have a war, will you not let your members fight for you? The way to hinder a thing, is to clog it. Therefore pray pass the vote as it is moved.

Sir *Tho. Lee.* I had an office conferred upon me in parliament (commissioner-admiral), and got out of it out of parliament: my country habitation was of more satisfaction to me. No man knows what a man will be, but himself. I think you may leave out the words, 'Without leave of the house.' You will have no advantage by it.

Sir *Fr. Winnington.* What I moved this day, was not to vindicate the reputation of your members, but to prevent reflections without. I believe the people will be satisfied with any of your members having Places whom the house thinks well of.

Mr. *Henry Booth.* Sir; without doubt the last parliament had great matters in agitation, and the enquiry they made about the Pensioners of the preceding parliament was no small one, but rather one of the chief things they had in hand; for had they been permitted to have perfected that, it had been a good recompence for the disappointment which the nation sustained in their other expectations, by the sudden prorogation: and without all question, nothing is fitter for the thoughts of a parliament, than to take into consideration how to punish them that had proved the best, and had almost (if not altogether) ruined the nation; and how to prevent the like mischief for the future. The name of a Pensioner is very distasteful to every English spirit; and all those who were Pensioners I think are sufficiently despised by their countrymen: and therefore I will mention only two or three things that will lie at their doors, before I offer my advice what is to be done. Breach of trust is accounted the most infamous thing in the world, and this these men were guilty of to the highest degree; robbery and stealing our law punishes with death, and what deserve they who beggar and take away all that the nation has, under the pretence of disposing of the people's money for the honour and good of the king and kingdom? And if there were nothing more than this to be said, without doubt they deserve a high censure.—Besides the giving away such vast sums, without any colour or reasonable pretence; there is this great mischief will follow upon it: every man very well knows that it has put the king into an extraordinary way of expence: and therefore when he has not such great Supplies, it must of necessity bring the king into great want and need: and shall not only give him an ill opinion of all parliaments, that do not supply him so extravagantly, but perhaps put him to think of ways to get Money that otherwise would never have entered into his thoughts; so that whatever ill may happen of this sort, these Pensions are answerable for it.—Farthermore, they have laid us open to all our enemies; whoever will invade, may not doubt to subdue us: for they have taken from us the sinews of war, that is Money and Courage; all our money is gone, and they have exhausted the treasure of the nation, and when people are poor, their spirits are low, so that we are left without a defence; and who must we thank for bringing us into this despicable condition, but these gentlemen, who notwithstanding this had the face to stile themselves the king's friends, and all those who opposed their practices were factious and seditious. They had brought it to that pass, that debates could not be free; if a gentleman's tongue happen to lie a little awry in his mouth, presently he must be called to the bar; or if that would not do, whensoever any gentleman that had a true English spirit happened to say any thing that was bold, presently away to seek the king and tell him of it; and oftentimes more than the truth: and thus they endeavoured to beget an ill opinion in the king of his best subjects: and their practice was the more abominable, because their words and actions gave the occasion to force those smart expressions from the gentlemen that spoke them; for their honest hearts were fired with true zeal to their king and country, when they beheld the impudence and falseness of those Pensioners.—It is true we find that in or about the 10th of R. ii. it was endeavoured to get a corrupt parliament; for our English story says, that the king sent for the justices and sheriffs, and enjoined them to do their best, that none should be chosen knights and burgesses, but such as the king and his council should name; but we find it could not be effected.—The next that occurs to my thoughts is that in the 4th of Hen. iv. the parliament that was called at Coventry, named the Lay-Men's Parliament: for the sheriffs were appointed that none should be chosen knights or burgesses that had any skill in the laws of the land.—The next that I remember is that in Hen. vi.th's time, in 1449, or 50, when the duke of Suffolk was accused by the commons, and committed to the Tower; the king dissolved that parliament not far unlike our case of my lord Danby, but it differs in this, that Suffolk was committed to the Tower as of right he ought; but we were denied that justice against Danby; only Hen. vi. made the cases thus far even, that he set Suffolk at liberty after he had dissolved that parliament: soon after a parliament was called, wherein great care was taken in chusing of parliament men that should favour Suffolk; but they so far failed of their purpose, that his appearance at the parliament gave great distaste to the house of commons, and they were so far incensed, that they began the parliament with a fresh accusation against him and others; so that you may see that it was not in the power of the court to corrupt the house of commons.—In the time of Hen. viii. about the 20th of his reign, when the parliament was active against Pluralities and Non-residence, there was an Act passed to release to the king all such sums of money as he had borrowed at the loan, in the 15th of his reign; it is said that it was much opposed, but the reason that is given why it passed, is, because the house was mostly the king's servants; but it gave great disturbance to the nation: and this is the only case that I can remember that comes any thing near to our Pensioners; but we cannot find that they or any parliament took money to vote: so that we must conclude that there were never any Pensioners in parliament till this pack of blades were got together.—Therefore, sir, what will you do? Shall these men escape, shall they go free with their booty? Shall not the nation have vengeance on them, who had almost given up the government? It was they who had perverted the ends of parliaments: parliaments have been and are the great refuge of the nation, that which cures all its diseases, and heals its sores; but these men had made it a snare to the nation, and at best had brought it to be an engine to give money; if therefore these go away unpunished, we countenance what they have done, and make way to have Pensioners in every parliament; but far be any such thought from any man that sits within these walls: and having said this, I will in the next place humbly offer my thoughts what is to be done. In the first place I do propose, that every man of them shall on their knees confess their fault to all the commons, and that to be done at this bar one by one. Next, that as far as they are able, they refund all the money they have received for secret service. Our law will not allow a thief to keep what he has got by stealth, but of course orders restitution, and shall these proud robbers of the nation not restore their ill-gotten goods? And lastly, I do propose that they be voted incapable of serving in parliament for the future, or of enjoying any office civil or military; and order a Bill to be brought in to that purpose: for it is not fit, that they who were so false and unjust in that trust, should ever be trusted again: this, sir, is my opinion, but if the house shall incline to any other way, I shall readily comply, provided a sufficient mark of infamy be set on them, that the people may know who bought and who sold them.

Sir *Wm. Jones.* I would not have a question pass that cannot be well defended without doors. Shall the world say, 'you will make a vote (be the occasion ever so great, or the man ever so fit) that he must not accept of an office?' You will hardly find arguments against the unreasonableness of it. If you leave it in the power of your member to put himself out of office, then it is another thing. This parliament is not like to sit so long as to send members ambassadors out of it; besides, it would seem a very strange thing, that the house should ever mistrust itself so far, or has any gentleman so much authority as to persuade the house to it? I have put myself, and will, out of the possibility of it, and I desire the words may stand in the question.

Resolved, nem. con. "That no Member of this house shall accept of any Office, or Place of Profit, from the Crown, without the leave of this house: or any promise of any such Office, or Place of Profit, during such time as he shall continue a Member of this house; and that all offenders herein shall be expelled this house."

Mr. Booth's Speech for Parliaments and against Favourites.] About this time, Mr. Henry Booth, afterwards earl of Warrington, made the following Speech:

Sir, a king of England, at the head of his parliament, is in his full strength and power, and in his greatest splendor and glory: it is then that he can do great things, and without a parliament he is not very formidable. Therefore when kings leave off the use of parliaments, and rely upon the advice of particular favourites, they forsake their chiefest interest, they lay aside the staff that supports them, to lean upon a broken reed that will run into their hands; and this is proved by the example of former kings: what kings performed such enterprizes, and did such wonderful things, as those who still consulted their parliaments? And who had more the command of the people's purses than those kings who met the natives frequently in parliament? As witness Henry i. Edward i. Edward iii. Henry v. Henry viii. Q. Elizabeth; and what kings were so mean and obscure, despised by their neighbours, and abhorred by their subjects, as those who left off the use of parliaments and doted upon their favourites: as witness Will. ii. John, Henry iii. Edward ii. Richard ii. Henry vi. And I think it is undeniable that when the king leaves off parliaments, he forsakes his interest, he refuses the good and chuses the bad. I wish it could not be said that for two years last past, the use of parliaments has almost been laid aside: it is too true that parliaments have been delayed, and there is but a little between delaying and denying, and the first step to a denial is to delay: every man knows the great need we have had of a parliament these seventeen months, and why it has not met till now: it is very well known how earnestly it was desired by all good Protestants and true Englishmen, and what applications have been made to his majesty that it might sit; and it could not be obtained till now: and it is not to be forgotten how often it has been prorogued, and the notice that has been given to the nation of the several prorogations; the first time that we have heard of them was by the Gazette, in which is seldom any thing of truth, and then out comes a proclamation for a prorogation about a day or two before the day of meeting: when gentlemen have disposed their affairs that they may attend at the parliament, and possibly were on their journey towards London, upon the road they meet the news of the prorogation, (very good usage!) and there is nothing to be said in justification of such short notice, but that when his majesty by his proclamation had appointed a farther time for the meeting of the parliament, that in plain English no man must believe it would meet: for if gentlemen did believe it, they would prepare for it; and if they are prepared, it is but reasonable that sufficient notice should be given to prevent them: certainly they who advised the king in this matter, intended that none of his majesty's proclamations should have any credit: for his majesty put out several proclamations against Papists, and we see how they are regarded, not the least obedience yielded to them: and this giving of such short notice, was certainly done on purpose that those proclamations should neither be obeyed nor believed. Thus is the king abused, thus does he lose the hearts of the people, and thus is the nation abused: what will become of us when we cannot believe what his majesty says. Out of parliament the king cannot speak to his people in a more notable way than by proclamation, and as the matter is ordered, these are not regarded: in a subject nothing is more infamous, than to say of him, that his word is not to be relied on, he does not regard what he says: and therefore what villains are they, who by their advice, do bring the king but into the suspicion of it. This delaying of parliaments seems to portend the laying of parliaments aside; and if so, an army will follow: for the king must govern either by a parliament or an army, for one of them he must have; now the way to get rid of parliaments is this: first, although they meet sometimes, yet something must be started to hinder their success; or if that won't do, prorogue or dissolve them before any thing be finished; and thus parliaments will be made useless; and this being done, it will not be long before they become burdensome, and then away with them for good and all.—Kings only then grow out of conceit with parliaments, when their favourites are so overgrown, and their actions are so exorbitant, that they will not endure to be scanned by a parliament: and therefore to save themselves, they persuade the king to keep off the parliament, though it be to his great hurt: for the last Trump at the Day of Judgment will not be more terrible to the world, than the sound of an approaching parliament is to unjust ministers and favourites.—That state is sick of a grievous distemper, when kings neglect their parliaments, and adhere to favourites, and certainly that woe is then fallen upon the nation, which Solomon denounces; for says he, 'Woe to that nation whose king is a child;' and without question he meant a child in understanding, and not in years. We have had in England kings who, when they were children, by the help of a wise council, have governed very well: but after that they took matters into their own hands, it went very ill with England; as Rd. ii. Hen. vi. who whilst they were children, the government was steered aright; but their understanding not growing as fast as their years, they assumed the government before they were ready for it; and so managed matters, that it is better not to name them, than to reckon them in the catalogue of the kings.—And there is yet another reason why great favourites should advise against parliaments: kings that dote too much upon their favourites, do for the most part pick up mean men, people of no fortunes or estates, upon whom it is that they place their favour to so high a degree: and therefore it is for their interest to advise the king to govern by an Army, for if he prevails, then they are sure to have what heart can wish; or if he fail, yet they are but where they were, they had nothing, and they can lose nothing.—There is no man but very plainly sees, that there are people about his maj. who advise him to shake off the fetters of the laws, and to govern arbitrarily; and I wish that their advice has not prevailed for the most part; yet I think his majesty's own inclinations do not bend that way, for he seems to love quiet and ease, which no prince can have that rules by an Army: therefore, before we can expect that his maj. will come in to us, these people of arbitrary principles must be removed from his throne: for, whilst there are the same advisers, we must expect the same advice; whilst there are the same counsellors, we must expect the same results: and this alone will not do it, it is but the first step to our happiness; the principles or maxims of state must be removed, it is not taking away this or the other man, and putting in another to act by the same rules, that will cure our disease; but it is the change of principles that must do it.—You may remember in the last parliament the change that was made in the Privy Council, and Ministers, and upon the first news of it, I met with a gentleman that had a great service for White-Hall; says he, 'I hope now you are pleased, what can you expect more from his majesty? I replied, I like it well; yet not so very well; for, said I, all is well that ends well, for all is not gold that glitters: I am not sure, that these men that are put out, have not left their principles behind them; when those are gone, I shall like it very well.' The man was angry, and flung away, saying, you are hard to please; and says I, you are easy, and so we parted.—And I pray you, how much wool have we had after all this cry, what benefit have we reaped by that change? Do not we see, that unless they would act by the maxims of their predecessors, they must do nothing; and therefore several did desire leave to go off? Some of those worthy lords and gentlemen that did so are now in my eye, and I shall ever honour them for it: I cannot forget the promises made to the parliament at the same time, and how well they have been kept.—Therefore I think it is very plain, that till these principles are removed from White-Hall, that all our labour and pains will end in nothing: the way then as I conceive to do this, is to lay before his maj. the state of the case; let us shew him how unable these men are to serve him, and how destructive to his interest it is to follow their advices; and that he can be safe and great only by closing with his parliament.—Would his maj. be safe, alas, what can his creatures do? Just nothing, they have no power, nor have they will farther than it serves for their own advantage: but his maj. is safe in his parliament, for it is the interest of every man in England to preserve and defend his majesty's governing by his parliament.—Does he want Money to make him easy? I pray what can he expect from the caterpillars his favourites? Their care is not how to serve him, but to make their own fortunes: but from his parliament he need not want very plentiful supplies, to preserve the honour of himself and the kingdom. Would he maintain his dominions and rights, what can his creatures do? But when he closes with his parl. he can neither want the heads, hearts, nor purses of his people to serve him: so that whatever his maj. would have, it is only to be had by his parliament: for his favourites cannot in the least contribute to make him safe or honourable; or whatever else a king may want or desire: all the use a king can have from his favourites, is to have stories and lies to set him at variance with his people. I hope when the case is laid before his majesty, that he will close with us; but if his judgment is so prepossessed, that it will not convince him of his interest, then we must conclude, that it is with him as it was with Rehoboam, who forsook the council of the old men, and inclined to that of the young men, who counselled him to tell the people that his little finger should be thicker than his father's loins; and I pray what was the effect of that huffing speech? Why ten tribes were taken from him, and it was not his young men that could recover them for him again; neither was it without a parliament that his maj. was brought into England; I hope his maj. has not forgot it.—Let them advise what they will, but I am confident they will think on it a good while, before they will adventure to put those arbitrary councils into execution; it will prove a hot matter to handle: for though I hope no man here will lift up his hand against his majesty, yet we may oppose any man that does seek to invade our properties: and for my own part, I will pistol any subject, be he the greatest in England, that shall endeavour to deprive me of my just right: let us do what we can to effect an union between the king and his people, and leave the success to God Almighty, and his will be done.

Articles of Impeachment against Lord Chief Justice Scroggs.] Jan. 5, 1680-1. Sir Rd. Corbet reported the Articles appointed to be drawn up against sir Wm. Scroggs, lord chief justice of the king's-bench, which were as follows:

ARTICLES of IMPEACHMENT of High-Treason and other great Crimes and Misdemeanours against sir Wm. Scroggs, Chief Justice of the Court of King's-Bench, by the Commons in Parliament assembled, in their own name, and in the name of all the Commons of England.

I. "That he the said sir Wm. Scroggs, being then Chief Justice of the Court of King's Bench, hath traitorously and wickedly endeavoured to subvert the fundamental laws, and the established Religion and government of this kingdom; and, instead thereof, to introduce Popery, and an arbitrary and tyrannical government against law: which he hath declared by divers traitorous and wicked words, opinions, judgments, practices, and actions.—II. That the said sir Wm. Scroggs, in Trinity-term last, being then Chief Justice of the said Court, and having taken an oath duly to administer justice, according to the laws and statutes of this realm; in pursuance of his said traitorous purposes, did, together with the rest of the said justices of the said court, several days before the end of the said term, in an arbitrary manner discharge the Grand Jury, which then served for the hundred of Oswaldston, in the county of Middlesex, before they had made their presentments, or had found several bills of indictment which were then before them; whereof the said sir Wm. Scroggs was then fully informed, and that the same would be tendered to the court upon the last day of the said term; which day then was, and, by the known course of the said court, hath always heretofore been given unto the said jury, for the delivering in of their Bills and Presentments: by which sudden and illegal discharge of the said jury, the course of justice was stopped maliciously and designedly, the presentments of many papists and other offenders were obstructed, and in particular a bill of indictment against James duke of York, for absenting himself from church, which was then before them, was prevented from being proceeded upon.—III. That whereas one Henry Carr had, for some time before, published every week a certain Book, intituled,

'The Weekly Pacquet of Advice from Rome; or, The History of Popery;' wherein the superstitions and cheats of the Church of Rome were from time to time exposed; he the said sir Wm. Scroggs, then Chief Justice of the Court of King's-Bench, together with the other judges of the said court, before any legal conviction of the said Carr of any crime, did, in the same Trinity-Term, in a most illegal and arbitrary manner, make, and cause to be entered a certain Rule of that court, against the printing of the said book, in hæc verba: 'Dies 'Mercurii proxime post tres septimanas sanctæ 'Trinitatis, Anno 32 Car. ii. Regis. Ordina-'tum est quod liber intitulat, 'The Weekly 'Packet of Advice from Rome; or, the His-'tory of Popery,' non ulterius imprimatur vel 'publicetur per aliquam personam quamcun-'que. Per Cur.' And did cause the said Carr, and divers printers and other persons, to be served with the same; which said rule and other proceedings were most apparently contrary to all justice, in condemning not only what had been written, without hearing the parties, but also all that might for the future be written on that subject; a manifest countenancing of Popery, and discouragement of Protestants, and open invasion upon the right of the subject, and an encroaching and assuming to themselves a legislative power and authority.—IV. That the said sir Wm. Scroggs, since he was made Chief Justice of the King's Bench, hath, together with the other judges of the said court, most notoriously departed from all rules of justice and equality, in the imposition of Fines upon persons convicted of misdemeanors in the said court; and particularly in the term of Easter last past, did openly declare in the said court, in the case of one Jessop, who was convicted of publishing false news, and was then to be fined, that he would have regard to persons and their principles in imposing of Fines, and would set a fine of 500*l.* on one person for the same offence, for the which he would not fine another 100*l.* And according to his said unjust and arbitrary declaration, he the said sir Wm. Scroggs, together with the said other justices, did then impose a Fine of 100*l.* upon the said Jessop; although the said Jessop had, before that time, proved one Hewit to be convicted as author of the said false news. And afterwards in the same term did fine the said Hewit, upon his said conviction, only 5 marks. Nor hath the said sir Wm. Scroggs, together with the other judges of the said court, had any regard to the nature of the offences, or the ability of the persons, in the imposing of Fines; but have been manifestly partial and favourable to Papists, and persons affected to, and promoting the popish interest, in this time of imminent danger from them: and at the same time have most severely and grievously oppressed his majesty's protestant subjects, as will appear upon view of the several Records of Fines, set in the said court; by which arbitrary, unjust, and partial proceedings, many of his majesty's liege people have been ruined, and Popery countenanced under colour of justice; and all the mischiefs and excesses of the court of Star-Chamber, by act of parliament suppressed, have been again, in direct opposition to the said law, introduced.—V. That he, the said sir Wm. Scroggs, for the farther accomplishing of his said traitorous and wicked purposes, and designing to subject the persons, as well as the estates of his majesty's liege people, to his lawless will and pleasure, hath frequently refused to accept of Bail, though the same were sufficient, and legally tendered to him by many persons accused before him only of such crimes, for which by law bail ought to have been taken; and divers of the said persons being only accused of offences against himself; declaring at the same time, that he refused Bail, and committed them to goal, only to put them to charges; and using such furious threats as were to the terror of his majesty's subjects, and such scandalous expressions as were a dishonour to the government, and to the dignity of his office. And particularly, that he, the said sir W. Scroggs, did, in 1679, commit and detain in prison, in such unlawful manner, among others, Henry Carr, G. Broome, Edw. Berry, Benj. Harris, Fr. Smith, sen. Fr. Smith, jun. and Jane Curtis, citizens of London: which proceedings of the said sir W. Scroggs are a high breach of the liberty of the subject, destructive to the fundamental laws of this realm, contrary to the Petition of Right, and other statutes, and do manifestly tend to the introducing of arbitrary power.—VI. That the said sir W. Scroggs, in farther oppression of his majesty's liege people, hath, since his being made Chief Justice of the said Court of King's Bench, in an arbitrary manner granted divers General Warrants for attaching the persons, and seizing the goods of his majesty's subjects, not named or described particularly in the said warrants; by means whereof many of his majesty's subjects have been vexed, their houses entered into, and they themselves grievously oppressed contrary to law.—VII. Whereas there hath been a horrid and damnable Plot contrived and carried on by the Papists, for the murthering the king, the subversion of the laws and government of this kingdom, and for the destruction of the Protestant Religion in the same; all which the said sir W. Scroggs well knew, having himself not only tried, but given judgment against several of the offenders; nevertheless, the said sir W. Scroggs did, at divers times and places, as well sitting in court as otherwise, openly defame and scandalize several of the witnesses, who had proved the said treasons against divers of the conspirators, and had given evidence against divers other persons, who were then untried, and did endeavour to disparage their evidence, and take off their credit. Whereby, as much as in him lay, he did traiterously and wickedly suppress and stifle the discovery of the said Popish Plot, and encourage the conspirators to proceed in the same, to the great and apparent danger of his majesty's sacred life, and of the well-established government, and religion of this realm. VIII. Whereas the said sir W. Scroggs, being advanced to be Chief Justice of the Court of King's Bench, ought, by a sober, grave and virtuous conversation, to have given a good example to the king's liege people, and to demean himself answerable to the dignity of so eminent a station; yet he the said sir W. Scroggs, on the contrary, by his frequent and notorious excesses and debaucheries, and his prophane and atheistical discourses, doth daily affront Almighty God, dishonour his majesty, give countenance and encouragement to all manner of vice and wickedness, and bring the highest scandal on the public justice of the kingdom.—All which words, opinions and actions of the said sir W. Scroggs, were by him spoken and done, traiterously, wickedly, falsely and maliciously, to alienate the hearts of the king's subjects from his majesty, and to set a division between him and them; and to subvert the fundamental laws, and the established religion and government of this kingdom, and to introduce Popery, and an arbitrary and tyrannical government, contrary to his own knowledge, and the known laws of the realm of England. And thereby he, the said sir W. Scroggs, hath not only broken his own oath, but also, as far as in him lay, hath broken the king's oath to his people; whereof he, the said sir W. Scroggs, representing his maj. in so high an office of justice, had the custody: for which the said commons do impeach him the said sir W. Scroggs, of high-treason against our sovereign lord the king, and his crown and dignity, and other the high crimes and misdemeanours aforesaid.—And the said commons, by protestation saving to themselves the liberty of exhibiting, at any time hereafter, any other Accusation or Impeachment against the said sir W. Scroggs, and also of replying to the Answer that he shall make thereunto, and of offering Proofs of the premises, or of any other Impeachments or Accusations that shall be by them exhibited against him, as the case shall (according to the course of parliament) require; do pray, that the said sir W. Scroggs may be put to answer to all and every the premises, and may be committed to safe custody; and that such proceedings, examinations, trials and judgments, may be upon him had and used, as is agreeable to law and justice, and the course of parliaments. Upon which, the house came to this Resolution:

Resolved, "That the said sir Wm. Scroggs be impeached upon the said Articles, and that they be ingrossed, and carried up to the lords, by my lord Cavendish."

Several other Judges ordered to be impeached.] Ordered, "That the committee appointed to examine the proceedings of the Judges in Westminster-hall, and to prepare Impeachments against sir F. North, chief justice of the Common Pleas; sir Tho. Jones, one of the justices of the court of King's Bench; and sir R. Weston, one of the barons of the Court of Exchequer, do bring in such Impeachments with all convenient speed:"

But the parliament being soon after prorogued, this affair was dropped. However, the lord chief justice Scroggs was removed from his high station, and allowed a pension for life.

Resolution concerning the Irish Plot.] Jan. 6. Col. Birch made a Report of the Informations relating to the Irish Plot, and several Irish witnesses were examined. And a Message from the lords about the Irish Plot read: Resolved, "By the lords spiritual and temporal in parliament assembled, That they do declare, that they are fully satisfied that there now is, and, for divers years last past, hath been a horrid and treasonable Plot contrived and carried on, by those of the Popish religion in Ireland, for massacring the English, and subverting the Protestant Religion, and the ancient established government of that kingdom; to which Resolution their lordships desire the concurrence of this house." Upon this, a debate ensued, after which, it was resolved, "That this house doth agree with the lords in the said Vote, with the addition of these words, 'That the duke of York's being a Papist, and the expectation of his coming to the crown, hath given the greatest countenance and encouragement thereto, as well as to the horrid Popish Plot in this kingdom of England.'"

The Earl of Tyrone impeached.] A motion being made and seconded, for the impeaching of the earl of Tyrone, Resolved, "That Rd. Poure, earl of Tyrone in the kingdom of Ireland, be impeached of High Treason." Ordered, "That the lord Dursly go up to the bar of the lords, and impeach him of High Treason in the name of this house, and of all the commons of England, and do pray that he may be committed to safe custody."

The King's Message refusing to pass a Bill of Exclusion.] Jan. 7. A Message from the king, was read, as follows:

"C. R. His majesty received the Address of this house, with all the disposition they could wish, to comply with their reasonable desires; but upon perusing it, he is sorry to see their thoughts so wholly fixed upon the Bill of Exclusion, as to determine that all other Remedies for the suppressing of Popery will be ineffectual: his majesty is confirmed in his opinion against that Bill, by the judgment of the house of lords, who rejected it. He therefore thinks, there remains nothing more for him to say, in Answer to the Address of this house, but to recommend to them, the consideration of all other means for the preservation of the Protestant Religion, in which they have no reason to doubt of his concurrence, whenever they shall be presented to him in a parliamentary way: and that they would consider the present state of the kingdom, as well as the condition of Christendom, in such a manner as may enable him to preserve Tangier, and secure his Alliances abroad, and the Peace and Settlement at home."

Debate on the King's Message.] Mr. *H. Booth.* Sir, his majesty is pleased to say in his Message, that he is confirmed in his opinion against the Exclusion-bill, by the judgment of the house of lords; and that he is sorry to see that this house hath such an opinion of it, as to conclude all other ways and means insufficient. He is also pleased to say, that we have no reason to doubt his concurrence, in any other means that shall tend to the preservation of the Protestant Religion, when presented to him in a parliamentary way, which I do not doubt but he will comply with, whenever he shall be pleased to follow the dictates of his own judgment. But so long as there are so many persons about him, who have publicly declared for the duke's interest, we have good reason to doubt, that we shall hardly obtain any thing for the security of the Protestant Religion. We well know how many in the house of lords came to their honours, and by whose interest; and it is not strange, that those that are as servants should obey their master; but it is strange, that those who have prevailed with the king to reject this Bill, if Protestants, should be so unconcerned in the welfare of the Protestant Religion, as not to offer what Expedients they have, to secure it any other way; especially seeing the last parliament, as well as this, found it a task too hard for them. But to reject the Bill which we propose, and to offer no other to serve instead thereof, though they have had two years time for consideration, is to me plain demonstration, that nothing must be had against popery. That these difficulties should be put upon us, and our dangers thus prolonged in favour of the duke, after such full evidence that the Plot centers all in him, and that the original of our miseries is from him, when the immediate safety of the king, and our lives and religion, is concerned on the other hand, is a plain discovery of the great power of the Popish interest, and of the low ebb of the Protestants, and that it is impossible that any thing can be granted us in favour of the Protestant Religion, as long as those that are so much for the duke's interest, are about the king. And therefore seeing we are not like to do any thing by Bill, that those that sent us here may see we have done what we can, let us make such Votes as may be serviceable to our country, viz. 1. That neither the king's Person nor Protestant Religion, can be secured any way without the Exclusion-Bill. 2. That we can give no Money, without endangering the king's Person and Protestant Religion, until we have that Bill. And, 3. That seeing Supplies for all public Money ought to come from this house, there being no other way to supply the king with the love of his people, as well as with Money, let us pass a Vote to prevent Anticipations on the Revenue and other Supplies. And because I believe things are come to a point, and that there are those that have advised the Dissolution of this parliament, and the nation can never be happy as long as we have such counsellors, let us, while we may, pass our censures on such persons; for only God knows when we shall be permitted to sit here again.

Lord *Russel.* It appears plainly by the king's Message, what interest is prevalent at court, the duke's creatures; which is so great, that little good can be effected. Where Popery is so countenanced, we can do little good. Nothing can save the nation but union betwixt the king and the parliament. We have done our parts to procure it; the parliament will never be undisposed to do it; but unfortunately some get betwixt the king and us, to frustrate our good intentions, and to promote the duke's interest, though to the king's destruction. We know who have advised the king to these things, and that he should not pass the Bill of Exclusion. Therefore I am of Booth's opinion, to stick to the Bill, as our only security, and to brand those that have hindered it from passing.

Mr. *Montagu.* Sir, the truth is, we committed a great error in the beginning of this session; when we went about to look into the Popish Plot, we went into the Tower, whereas we should have gone to the court; for it is plain, that the duke's friends which are there, do still carry on the Plot against the protestant religion, as much as ever the lord Bellasis, Powis, or any of those lords in the Tower did. And we may reasonably conclude by the little success we have had against popery this session, that until we can remove that interest from about the king, we take pains to no purpose.

Sir *H. Capel.* Sir, I am ready to agree in those Votes that were moved: For it appears plain to me, that we are not like to have any laws against popery: for the truth is, the popish interest is too strong for us. If there were any intent that we should have the protestant religion secured any other way, it is strange that those who advise the king to oppose our way, should not at the same time prevail with him to propose his. I am afraid that this advice proceeds from those that think the king or kingdom are not in danger of popery, because they are of opinion, that popery cannot hurt the king nor kingdom; for otherwise they might plainly see it is like to have a contest with us: and that it would be convenient it should be prevented, and be induced thereby to offer some expedient, if there be any. And as we may conclude ourselves an unhappy people upon these accounts, so also in that the house of lords, after they had spent so much time about Expedients, and found them insufficient, should afterwards reject this Bill, without any farther care how to preserve the protestant religion; at least, not by sending any thing to this house, though we have heard from them of Mr. Seymour's Articles, and some trivial matters. And also in that some worthy members, who have the honour to serve in great places about his majesty, and have opposed this Bill, seeing this house in this great dilemma, should not offer to do the nation and this house that kindness as to propose them. If there be any such worthy member that has any such Expedient, I hope he will stand up, and then I will presently sit down. [After a little pause, and nobody offering to stand up;] The truth is, Sir, every day doth more and more discover our danger, and demonstrate, that this of Expedients is put upon us, in hopes that we should have offered at some Bill; of which advantage might be taken, to represent us as persons not well affected to the government, that so, if possible, even the people, as well as the king, might be brought out of love with parliaments. I do remember, that after the great endeavours which some ministers of state had used to bribe the late Long Parliament, and had come so near to perfection, as that the nation was in a manner saved but by two or three votes, this Dissolution was much admired at; and it was most men's business to cast about to find out the reason of it: Amongst other things it was concluded, That if the popish interest had any hand in it (as believed) that it was out of hopes, that they should thereby have an opportunity to make the king out of love with all parliaments, and so occasion some difference between him and his people. The little success which the last parliament had, the improbability of this, and the stumbling-blocks that are laid for the next, make me afraid that the Long Parliament was dissolved for this reason: I have heard that the Jesuits have at this time a great stroke in the management of all the affairs of Europe, and that it is by their advice and assistance, that the king of France goeth on so triumphantly, because they design to make him universal monarch, and in order thereto are true to him, though false to all the world besides. How far we have contributed already to the king of France his greatness, and how this breaking off parliaments, and keeping this nation in this unsettled condition, may conduce to his taking of Flanders and Holland, and his other designs, all here may judge: And how it agrees with the report of the Jesuits having the management of all the affairs of Europe: And how this can be prevented, without the Exclusion Bill, is a paradox to me. For I do still conclude, that so long as there is a Popish Successor, there will be a popish interest, and that as long as there is a popish interest and fears of a popish king, the nation will be divided, and there will be constant fears and jealousies, not only here at home, but with our allies abroad; which will frustrate all endeavours to oppose the French designs, because there can be no confidence between the king and his people. And this makes me conclude, we are under great difficulties; if we give money, we have reason to fear it may be employed to our destruction; if we do not, if Flanders or Holland should be lost, great endeavours will be used to lay it at our doors, though we have given such hearty assurances to his majesty, of our readiness to supply him with money for the support of it. And how we shall extricate ourselves out of these difficulties, I know not. —Sir, I have troubled you the longer, and with the more earnestness, because I am doubtful whether I may ever have another opportunity to speak in this place. Things are so out of order, and such prevalent endeavours are used to unsettle them the more, that I am afraid, not only of our religion, but of the very government and being of the English nation: for if these things should occasion blood, while the French king is so powerful, he may easily have the casting voice; and without that, only God knows what may be the end of such confusions as some men endeavour to occasion. All projects of settling the affairs of this nation without parliaments, have hitherto proved unsuccessful, and been attended with ill consequences. I have a great deal of reason to be sensible of the miseries of 41, and therefore am sorry to see such dissolutions of parliaments without success. I am afraid there are projectors again a-foot, that are for altering the government, as to the use of parliaments: I judge so by their proceedings, because I am of opinion, that popery must destroy the use of parliaments, before it can be settled in this nation. Seeing we are not like to have any act pass this session that may do the nation any good, I think you have been well moved to do what service you can by your votes.

Mr. *L. Hyde.* Sir, it is not only very strange, but, if I be not mistaken, contrary to the custom of parliaments, that after the lords have passed a negative upon a bill, we should still press for it, and declare ourselves resolved not to be satisfied without it, though it be well known that the king doth also intend to pass his negative upon it; and that it cannot be had this session, unless his majesty be pleased to prorogue the house, of purpose to give an opportunity to go on with it again, which is very unlikely, if the contents of his Speeches and Messages be considered, seeing the lords have confirmed him in his opinion of it. And therefore I should think it were much better to follow his majesty's directions in his Message, and to try some other way, which would be a great confirmation of our readiness to obey his majesty, in following his advice, which, I believe, is the best way to prevent any farther disagreement, that so this parliament may have a happy conclusion.

Lord *Cavendish.* Sir, I am fully persuaded, that we cannot be secure, neither of our religion nor peace and quietness, without this Bill; yet seeing we are not like to have it at this time, I am for going on with those other bills that are afoot, that we may try if we can get them. Seeing we cannot do all the good we would, let us endeavour to do all the good we can. But I am ready to agree in the vote that was proposed, That it is the opinion of this house, that neither the king's person, nor Protestant religion can be secured any other way, provided it be not intended to bind the house from trying what may be done by other laws, lest advantage should be taken thereof to break this parliament, which I tremble to think of, because it will be attended with a great ruin to our affairs both abroad and at home.

Sir *R. Markham.* Sir, being the house is inclinable to hear of Expedients, I will crave leave to offer you one. In case the duke should outlive the king, I think, if by an act of parliament, the prince of Orange were appointed to administer the government jointly with him, with such powers and limitations as might be thought convenient upon a serious debate, it might give great satisfaction, and probably secure the Protestant religion. [Laughed at.]

Mr. *Hampden.* You seem, by the debate, to incline to think that no other way can secure us, but the Bill, and I am still of opinion, I could wish I could hear Expedients; but none were offered this parliament; what were offered was the last parliament. When we go to fight, we are offered a bean-straw instead of a sword to fight with. Nothing was offered the last parliament like an Expedient. You found all the laws in being, made by the wisdom of your ancestors for your safety, frustrated by the duke: this is no new thing since 1670; Have not all things been so? 2,500,000*l.* was given to make a brave war with the Dutch; the money was got, and the peace made, but the Dutch would not. But it had another effect; it helped to ruin a Protestant neighbour. And so many more sums. Have you not had great fruit of all this? Is not France brought very low? All laws are put in execution except those against popery, when it comes to the highest. What has been done in the interval of parliament? A few apprentices, for pulling down bawdy-houses, were hanged for treason. And this in the reign of a Protestant prince! What must we expect under a Popish prince? Will your laws be better preserved? Do you think to live in England and be protestants? It is so absurd a thing, no man can imagine it. But I do not know whether parliamentarily the king can take notice of the lords rejecting our Bill of excluding the duke. The proviso in the Long Parliament, to exempt the duke from the oaths and test, was so little rectified here (I thought it would have passed without contradiction) that it was carried but by two voices. And now the Plot has been these two years discovered, and we have been handling it, and making sport with it; but I believe we have had, and have a Plot, and we are in more danger than ever. Secure the Protestant religion, else all things besides will be ineffectual. I will say nothing more to the ministers; but if we admit any remedy, without the Bill of Exclusion, we expose the kingdom and the Protestant religion to ruin.

Sir *Wm. Jones.* Sir, you have had several propositions made you, and the way to come to some speedy resolution, is not to debate too many together, but to keep close to that to which most have spoken; which, if I be not mistaken, is that which relates to the duke's Bill, which some have opposed, because of the difficulties arising from the Bill, and would rather have you go into a committee, and treat of Expedients. But I think it below the gravity of the house to be put out of their method, unless some Expedients were proposed. But notwithstanding all the provocations that have been given, we cannot hear of any expedients, only one, which hardly deserves any farther consideration in a committee; because crowned heads or lovers, do not willingly allow of rivals, but will be uneasy till they be rid of them. And I am afraid all other expedients will be liable to as strong objections; and that therefore it is that they are not proposed, though they have been so often discoursed of. If any person would offer any, that had any appearance of giving satisfaction, I should be ready to give my voice for going into a committee to debate them. But I know not why the house should lose that time, without some expedient be first offered; and if there could be any expedients found out, which were likely, really and effectually to prejudice the duke's interest, why should not the same argument arise against them, as against the Exclusion Bill? Why would not any such bill be also against natural justice, the oath of allegiance, be a severe condemnation, and not good in law, but liable to occasion a civil war? For I am not apt to think this great contest is all about an empty name; and if not, then the same arguments will hold against any other Bill, that will be sufficient to keep him from the government, if some such bill or bills could be contrived, as against the Bill of Exclusion: but the truth is, there can be no other bill that can serve us in this case, because all other bills will leave us in that miserable condition of opposing our lawful king, and all opposition in such a case, would be liable to be construed a rebellion. All other bills in this case would be no more for the security of our religion, than a great many leases, releases, and other writings, are in many cases of estates, without fines and recoveries. However, I am against the vote that was proposed, That the duke's being a Papist hath rendered him uncapable of the crown: for that were to take on us a legislative power; but let your question be, That it is the opinion of this house, that the king's person, and Protestant religion, cannot be secure without that Bill: that so the proceedings of the house may be justified, in demanding that Bill hereafter, though we should in the mean time go on with any other bills.

Mr. *D. Finch.* Sir, The question is at present, whether, seeing we cannot have this Bill, we shall not aim at something else, that so, if possible, we may prevent the breaking up of this parliament, without any effect, as to the great things they were summoned for, on which I cannot reflect without being much concerned; and I am afraid that it will be the consequence of persisting for this bill. I cannot be persuaded, notwithstanding all that hath been said, but that there are other Bills that may attain our end, or at least do us some good.

.nd we have no certain demonstration that ›is bill, if we should obtain it, will infallibly o what is desired. The acts made in Eliz.'s ays did not suppress that party totally: iough the queen of Scots was cut off, yet ıat interest continued, and even to this day ɛmains, and so it may probably though we ıould get this bill; and therefore why should e stand so much in our own light, as not to ıke what we can get? The Bill of Banish-ıent may be of great use, and some bills to mit the power of such a prince, by putting ıe power in parliaments and privy counsel-›rs; why should we lose all by being so eager ›r that we are never like to get? And there-›re, I humbly conceive, we may do better to › on with such other bills as may be thought onvenient, and not struggle nor persist for the btaining of this.

Col. *Birch*. Sir, I am not for adventuring ıy life upon rhetoric, which is all I can find ıere is in the discourses that are made for xpedients. We all know that a little thing ltered the government in France, and redu-ed the people of that kingdom to slavery: ray let us have a care that, for want of a ttle short act, we be not reduced to slavery nd Popery too. Will not all the expedients hat have been talked of, or can be imagined, ɛave us to contest with our lawful prince, and hat assistance which he is well assured of, not nly from the Papists here, but in Ireland, and rom France and Scotland, I am afraid, enough o make it a measuring cast? And is the Pro-estant interest so low, that though our dan-ers be so great, instead of a sword to defend urselves, we must be content with a sheath? am not for cheating those that sent me ere: I think it much more for the interest f the nation, that we should have no laws, han such as will but trepan us, by failing s like rotten crutches when we have occa-ion to depend on them; I had rather lose ıy life and my religion, because I were ıot able to defend them, than be fooled ut of them by depending on such laws. I ake it for granted, that seeing the Exclusion-Bill is thought too much for us, and such reat endeavours are used to preserve the trength and interest of that party, that we ıust either submit, or defend our religion by . sharp contest; and therefore I hope we shall ıot depend on laws that will tend to weaken s. I am confident, that if some ministers of tate did not stand as clouds between the king .nd us, we should have redress. For how can : consist with his goodness or coronation-oath, hat for the interest of one man, the bodies nd souls of the rest of his subjects should be n such danger of perishing, as they are in case f his death, if a popish king should succeed, ınd such popish counsellors, judges, justices, ınd bishops too, as we had in queen Mary's lays? For it cannot be doubted, but that hose that will be so loyal as to bring him in, vill be so loyal, as it will be called, to obey him n all things which may be for his interest. And the same argument, which queen Mary used, will supply the defect of all laws, that the execution of all ecclesiastical laws may be suspended by force, but could never be re-pealed by the power of parliaments; and there-fore commanded, that notwithstanding all laws to the contrary, they should be executed as in the beginning of her father's reign. The great endeavours that are used to ridicule the Plot, arraign parliaments, and divide the Protes-tant Interest, is a full confirmation to me, that the Plot goeth on as much as ever. And how can it be otherwise, unless we can get the king of our side, that so he may be more for us than he is for the duke, without which it is impossible that the Protestant In-terest can stand long. In order to do some-thing, I am ready to agree in the Votes that have been made.

Mr. *G. V.* (Probably Geo. Vernon.) Sir, it is clear to me, that all Expedients without this Bill cannot signify any thing for our defence against Popery. All our difficulty will be, to satisfy his majesty, that nothing else can save his people from the popish bondage. And if we could do that, I do not doubt but he will rather pass the Bill, than let three nations pe-rish. The king doth now rely on the judg-ment of the lords in the matter, yet haply will find upon an informatien, that he hath no good ground so to do. For I believe, if he would ask the lords why they were of that opinion, many of them would tell him, because he was of that opinion, and because they were awed by his presence. And it is my opinion, there wants nothing but a conference to have an agreement with the lords; in the mean time, that they may have occasion to consider better of it, let us by a Vote declare our resolution to stick to the Bill.

Sir *Wm. Pulteney*. Sir, by the debate which you have had about Expedients, it plainly ap-pears that the Popish Interest is so well fixed, that we are not like to obtain any thing against it, that will do us any good. And it is not strange, that we should meet with great oppo-sition. For we may reasonably conclude, that those, who had the power to instil those prin-ciples into the royal family, have not been neg-ligent to improve their interest, to secure those advantages they have long hoped for, and ex-pected, from such a proselyte. And therefore those arguments which some worthy members have used, as to the improbability that ever a popish king should attempt to change our re-ligion, as not consisting with his interest, are to me very preposterous, and a great demon-stration of the influence of that party, in be-ing able to broach such opinions, as are so useful to bring in that religion. For my part, I am of a different judgment, and do believe, that a popish head on a Protestant body, would be such a monster in nature, as would neither be fit to preserve, or be preserved; and that therefore it would as naturally follow, as night follows day, that either the head will change the body, or the body the head. Have we not already had sufficient experience, what a miserable thing it is for the king to be jealous of his people, or the people of their prince? Can it be imagined that there can be a popish king in this nation, without occasioning a constant noise of Plots and Popery, and that such reports, grounded on the king's inclinations, will not occasion such a fermentation in the people, as will end in misery? Or, if it should prove otherwise, that by such arts as may probably then be set on foot, the people should be lulled into a security? Can we think that the Papists, who have been so many ages at work for the opportunity, should not take advantage of that security, to fetter us with their popish bondage? We may as well think that they will all then turn Protestants, or be true to the Protestant Interest. No, sir, their great design of having a Popish Successor was in order to bring in Popery. And we may conclude, they will heartily and earnestly pursue it, whenever they shall have a popish king. And therefore, I think, it will never become the prudence of this house, to desist from endeavouring to get the Exclusion-Bill, which is the only remedy that can be in this case, that we may have a right to defend ourselves and our religion against a Popish Successor, without which, this nation will be in time ruined.

Sir *F. Winnington.* Sir, I have considered this Message with that duty and respect I ought; it doth so agree with all others which his maj. hath been pleased to send to this parliament, that I do believe that all proceed from the same council, and that our endeavours to prevail with his majesty, in that particular of changing councils, hath hitherto had no effect. The king is pleased to say, that he is confirmed in his opinion as to the Bill, by the house of lords having rejected it; I admire how the king should know it in a parliamentary way, so as to intimate so much to this house. Probably he might be present, as he hath generally been, ever since my lord Clifford had so great a share in the management of the affairs of this kingdom. And how things have gone there since, we all know. I do not doubt but his maj. takes that unparalleled trouble of attending there daily, chiefly for the good of the Protestant religion; but I cannot but observe, that it hath had little success. For, things, however, have gone with so much difficulty against the popish party, that it may be a question, whether his royal presence, or the influence of a Popish Successor were strongest. The Bill for Papists taking the Test, though accompanied with a great sum of money, passed with much difficulty, and so that for excluding the lords, and not without an exception as to his royal highness: and therefore we have no great reason to admire, that this about the Succession should be thrown out: and how can we expect it should be otherwise, as long as so many who sit there are in the possession of great places by the duke's means; and so many others who would come into great places, which cannot be had but by his means? And how this altogether makes an interest, may easily be imagined. Sir, I do not mention these things without regret; for I know my distance, and have a great veneration for the nobility of this land; and I know the lords have their freedom of voting, and that there are many sit in the lords house, who have all the qualifications necessary for that great station. But to see a Bill of this importance treated so contrary to the usual course of parliament, it is necessary that we should a little consider what may be the cause, in order to regulate our proceedings for the future: for if nothing must go in that house against the duke, I think the Protestant Religion is like to have little security from acts. If the duke had ever consulted the books writ by his grandfather or father, or their Declarations in matters of Religion, he would never have brought these difficulties upon his king and country. It is strange he should aim to get Heaven, by proceedings so contrary to what his father attested with his blood. But though he hath neglected to consult his interest, I hope we shall not neglect to consult ours, in pursuing this Bill, seeing there is no other remedy: though I am afraid it is a great work, and may break many parliaments, because it is so like to destroy all the Papists hopes of establishing their religion. However, I will not fear but, God granting the king life, it may be obtained at last; unless the project now a-foot, of representing parliaments as dangerous and useless, should prevent the meeting of any more: for even the old Band of Pensioners could slip their collars, when Popery came bare-faced before them. It is not to be admired, that, seeing the Jesuits have been 100 years at work to rivet their interest, by getting a prince of their religion, they should struggle hard to preserve it, that so they may have those blessed effects they expect from it, which the succession-Bill only can prevent. But it is strange, that, after such discoveries of the Plot here and in Ireland, and the certainty of our irrecoverable danger upon the king's death, that so many Protestants should be deluded by that party, and rather be led by artificial falsehoods, to their own destruction, than by naked truth, to join in that which only can save them. For Protestants to ridicule the Plot, and disparage the Witnesses, though their evidence is so confirmed, that a man may as well believe that bread may be made flesh by transubstantiation, as that the danger of our religion is not true, is as strange as to believe, that let the Papists carry on what Plots they will for the future, there will be ever any more discoveries made: but if there should, I am sure the witnesses will deserve the censure of being mad (as was passed on him that owned the burning of London) considering how those have been rewarded. It is plain to me, that, as the king was under great difficulties, arising from the solicitations and advices of private cabals, when he put out his Declaration in April 1679, so he is now, and that it will never be otherwise, until he take up the same Resolution again of following the Advice of his privy-council, and great council the parliament: till when, I expect no alteration of our affairs.

Sir *L. Jenkins.* Sir, I have hearkened with great attention to the debates you have had about this matter; and it is plain to me, that there can be no such thing as demonstration in this case, because this Exclusion Act, if obtained, may be liable to many objections, and probably not secure us. Why then, should we be so bent upon it, seeing the great difficulties of obtaining it are so visible? For my part, I think if it should pass, it would be void of itself, and be of no force at all: for which reason, and because we are not like to get it, it is strange to me, that no arguments will prevail to aim at some other things, that so we may get something, which must be better than to have this parliament be broken, for want of our taking what we may get. For supposing the worst, that we should not get any thing, that should be sufficient to prevent the duke's coming to the crown, yet we may get such laws as may be sufficient to secure our Religion, though he should come to it. And would it not be much better, to spend our time in making laws which may tend to that purpose, which we have reason to believe will be granted, than to spend our time in pursuing that we are not like to get? Some good laws added to what we have, and the number of people which we have in this nation Protestants, would in my opinion be an impregnable fence against Popery. And it is no such strange thing to have a prince of one religion and people of another. The late duke of Hanover was a Papist, yet lived in peace with his people, though Lutherans. The king of France, notwithstanding his greatness, permits a great proportion of his people to be Huguenots, and lives in peace with them. And seeing there is a great probability that we may do so too, and that we may have what laws we will, to secure our religion to us in such a case, why should we engage ourselves farther for the getting of an act, which the king and lords have both declared against, and will never be consented to by the king, as we may reasonably believe, because he hath often declared, that he thinks it an unlawful act, and that it is against his conscience?

Col. *Titus.* Sir; the great character this hon. member bears, the great employments he hath been in under his maj. abroad, as well as his education in the laws of this nation, do justly challenge, that what he saith, should be well weighed and considered, before any man should offer to contradict it. He is pleased to say, that this Act would be unlawful and invalid, if it should be obtained: and therefore, because we are not like to obtain it, and because the duke of Hanover, though a Papist, lived in peace with Lutherans, and the king of France with Huguenots, that we had better spend our time in contriving laws for the security of our Religion, if a Papist should come to the crown, which we may get; and not in contriving laws to keep him from the crown, which we are not like to have. If this be not in plain English, the sense of his discourse, I am willing to be corrected. But, sir, if it be, I do admire upon what foundation the first argument is grounded; I mean, that relating to the unlawfulness and invalidity of the Exclusion Bill. Was there ever any government in this world, that had not an unlimited power lodged somewhere? Or can it be possible that any government should stand, without such a power? And why such a power should not be allowed here, which is so essential for the support of the government, I think can only be in order (if I may say it without reflection) to have this government fall; and I am afraid even at this time, by this very business we are now debating. For it must be the consequence, of denying that the legislative power of the nation, king, lords, and commons, are not able to make the laws to prevent it. But as this opinion is strange, so are the politics drawn from the duke of Hanover, and king of France, to induce us to be willing to have a Popish king come to reign over us; when neither of the said examples come home to our case: but if they should, why must we be so willing to have a Popish king to govern us, as that we should be rather led by examples fetched so far from abroad, than by the miserable examples we had here in queen Mary's days; and by the undeniable arguments and reasons that have been offered to make out, that a Popish king will endeavour to bring in a Popish religion? And notwithstanding the example brought from France, I am afraid the French king is bound to assist the duke's interest therein; or otherways may be said of us, what the devil could not say of Job, that we have served him for nought, contrary to the true interest of England, these many years. But by these arguments, and all the king's Speeches and Messages, I plainly see, that this hon. member is in the right in one thing; that we struggle in vain to get any Act, that shall signify any thing to prevent the duke's coming to the crown: but that if you will aim at laws to secure your Religion after his coming to the crown, you may probably obtain them. If this be not plainly said, I think it is plainly inferred; for are not all his majesty's Speeches and Messages with an absolute prohibition as to any thing against the Succession? And I suppose will be as much understood against your Association Bill, or any other that tends to that purpose: and you may be sure, that when you come with any such, if so contrived as to signify any thing, that the same opposition shall be made to them as to the Exclusion Bill. For it is plain to me, that the king's offering to concur in any laws you shall propose for the securing of your Religion, compared with the other limitations, can only be so understood; which is a fair denial of all laws against Popery, at least those that advise it I the Penal Laws is at this time grievous to the subject, and a weakening to the Protestant Interest, and an encouragement to Popery, and dangerous to the peace of this kingdom."

The Parliament dissolved.] The same day the king came to the house of peers, and prorogued the parliament to the 20th of Jan.; but dissolved it on the 18th, leaving 22 bills depending, and eight more that were ordered to be brought in, but never came to be debated.*

PRINCIPAL OCCURRENCES AFTER THE DISSOLUTION—LONDON PETITION—LONDON INSTRUCTIONS TO THEIR MEMBERS—PETITION AGAINST SITTING AT OXFORD.] The prorogation being attended with some very extraordinary consequences, we cannot avoid laying some of the principal before our readers, as the most proper introduction to the meeting of the next. On the 13th of January, the lord-mayor of London, sir Patience Ward, with a court of common-council, ordered a Petition to be drawn up, and presented to the king, setting forth, "That whereas the parliament had convicted one of the five Popish lords in the Tower, and were about to convict the other four of high-treason; that they had impeached the chief justice Scroggs, and were about to impeach other judges; and all this in order to the preservation of his majesty's Life, the Protestant religion, and the government of England: that they were extremely surprized to see the parliament prorogued in the height of their business: that their only hopes were, that this was done only in order to bring such affairs about again as were necessary to the settling the nation. They therefore prayed, that his maj. would be pleased to let the parliament sit at the day appointed, and so continue till they had effected all the great affairs before them." To this effect was the Petition, which was further ordered to be delivered that night, or as soon as might be, by the lord-mayor, attended by the new recorder George Treby, esq. and certain members of the court of aldermen, and common-council. But this farther provoked the king, and hastened his resolution of finally parting with his parliament. Accordingly, two days before the time of their meeting, he by Proclamation dissolved the present parliament: and in the same Proclamation, he declared his intention of calling another parliament to meet on the 21st of March next. But, being offended at the city of London, and hoping to meet with better success by a removal, he appointed Oxford to be the place of their meeting, where he had formerly, in the year 1665, found the most imaginable harmony in and between both houses. —When the elections came on, the temper of the nation was soon discovered by their choice; both parties were extremely busy; and the city of London set the first example to the rest of the kingdom by returning their old members Clayton, Player, Pilkington, and Love; to whom, as soon as the election was over, an extraordinary Paper was presented in the name of the citizens of London then assembled in common-hall, containing, "A return of their most hearty Thanks for their faithful and unwearied endeavours, in the two last parliaments, to search into and discover the depth of the Popish Plot, to preserve his majesty's royal person, the protestant religion, and the well-tablished government of this realm, to secure the meeting and sitting of frequent Parliaments, to assert our undoubted rights of petitioning, and to punish such as have betrayed those rights, to promote the long wished-for union of his majesty's protestant subjects, to repeal the 35th of Eliz. and the Corporation-act; and more especially for their assiduous endeavours in promoting the Bill of Exclusion of James duke of York." In fine, they concluded, "That being confidently assured, that they, the said Members for the City, will never consent to the granting any Money-Supply, till they have effectually secured them against Popery and Arbitrary Power, they resolved, by God's assistance, to stand by their said members, with their lives and fortunes." In the like manner were the former members of parliament again chosen, in most places in the kingdom; and in many, such like Papers of Addresses were presented to them, in their respective countries, as had been done to their members by the commonalty of London. And the zeal was now so great, that, contrary to the custom of the members treating the country, now the country in most places treated them, or at least every man bore his own charges.—The greatest uneasiness and disappointment to the prevailing party in the elections, was the place of their meeting, Oxford, the distance of which might naturally cause a diminution of their power and influence. Therefore it was resolved by several of the nobility to draw up a formal Petition against that place; which was early delivered to the king by the earl of Essex himself, who introduced it by this following Speech: "May it please your majesty,

* "Though the king came privately to the house this day, the commons had a quarter of an hour's previous notice. In which short interval, in a loose and disorderly manner, they made a shift to pass the above extraordinary Resolves. They had not time to proceed any farther, if they had any farther matter to proceed upon. While the last Vote was yet passing, the usher of the black-rod came to the door, and ordered their attendance on his majesty. Those who are pleased to assume the venerable title of Patriots, have given large scope to their resentments against the king for this anti-constitutional proceeding; and those who value themselves as much on the glory of being Loyalists, have shed their gall as freely on the commons for their licentious Votes; and it may serve as a general key to the modern History of England, 'That parties have never so good a title to be believed as when they expose each other.'" Ralph.

The lords here present, together with divers other peers of the realm, taking notice that by your late Proclamation, your maj. had declared an intention of calling a parliament at Oxford; and observing from history and records, how unfortunate many assemblies have been, when called at a place remote from the capital city; as particularly the congress in Hen. ii's time at Clarendon; three several parliaments at Oxford in Hen. iii's, and at Coventry in Hen. vi's time; with divers others which have proved very fatal to those kings, and have been followed with great mischief on the whole kingdom: And considering the present posture of affairs, the many jealousies and discontents which are amongst the people, we have great cause to apprehend, that the consequences of a parliament now at Oxford may be as fatal to your maj. and the nation, as those others mentioned have been to the then reigning kings. And therefore we do conceive, that we cannot answer it to God, to your majesty, or to the people, if we, being peers of the realm, should not on so important an occasion humbly offer our Advice to your majesty; that, if possible, your maj. may be prevailed with to alter this (as we apprehend) unseasonable resolution. The Grounds and Reasons of our opinion are contained in this our Petition, which we humbly present to your majesty."—The Petition itself consisted of a recapitulation of the misfortunes attending the untimely prorogations, dissolutions, and discontinuations of parliaments of late, at a time when his majesty's person, and the whole nation, was in imminent danger from the papists: "And now at last his maj. had been prevailed to call another parliament at Oxford, where neither lords nor commons could be in safety, but would be daily exposed to the sword of the papists, and their adherents, of whom too many had crept into his majesty's guards: The liberty of speaking according to their consciences would be thereby destroyed, and the validity of their acts and proceedings left disputable: the straitness of the place no ways admitted of such a concourse of persons, as now followed every parliament; and the Witnesses which were necessary to give Evidence upon the Commons Impeachment, were unable to bear the charges of such a journey, and unwilling to trust themselves under the protection of a parliament, that was itself evidently under the power of guards and soldiers. In conclusion, they prayed that the parliament might, as usually, sit at Westminster, where they might consult and act with safety and freedom." This Petition was subscribed by 16 lords, viz. Monmouth, Kent, Huntington, Bedford, Salisbury, Clare, Stamford, Essex, Shaftsbury, Mordant, Evers, Paget, Grey, Herbert, Howard, and Delamer. The king gave no answer that we find, but frowned upon the deliverers of this Petition, and persisted in his resolution of holding the parliament at Oxford: whither the king repaired with a great train, March 14, as likewise the members to attend him.—Those for the city of London came with a numerous body of well-armed horse, having ribbands in their hats, with these words woven in them, 'No Popery, No Slavery!' And many others of the members were attended in the like manner, as apprehending some extraordinary designs of the papists against them; so that at length, the manner of their assembling, (says Mr. Echard), looked more like the rendezvous of a country-militia, than the regular meeting of a parliament.

FIRST SESSION OF THE FIFTH AND LAST PARLIAMENT OF KING CHARLES II.

List of the House of Commons.] March 21, 1680-1. The Fifth and last Parliament in this reign, was opened at the city of Oxford; where the Gallery at the Public Schools was prepared for the Lords, and the Convocation-House for the Commons. The following is a List of the Members of the House of Commons:

A LIST OF THE HOUSE OF COMMONS, IN KING CHARLES THE SECOND'S FIFTH AND LAST PARLIAMENT, WHICH MET AT OXFORD, MARCH 21, 1680-1.

‡ Those marked thus are doubtful.

Abington,
Sir John Stonehouse.
Agmondesham,
Sir William Drake,
William Cheney.
St. Albans,
Thomas Pope Blount,
Samuel Grimstone.
Aldborough, (Suffolk)
John Bence,
John Corrance.
Aldborough, (Yorkshire)
Sir Godfrey Copely,
Sir John Reresby.
Allerton, North,
Sir Gilbert Gerrard,
Sir Henry Calverly.
Andover,
‡ Francis Powlet,
‡ Sir Robert Henley.
Anglesea,
Richard Bulkley.
Appelby,
Sackvil Tufton,
Sir John Bland.
Arundel,
William Garraway,
James Butler.
Ashburton,
Thomas Raynell,
William Stawel.
Aylsbury,
Sir Richard Ingolsby,
Sir Thomas Lee.
Bambury,
Sir John Holman.
Barnstaple,
Richard Lee.
John Basset.
Bath City,
Sir William Basset,
Visc. Fitzharding.
Beaumaris,
Henry Bulkley.
Bedfordshire,
William Lord Russel,
Sir Humphry Monoux.
Bedford Town,
Sir William Franklyn,
Pawlet St. John.
Bedwin,
Sir Walter Ernley,
John Wildman.
Berkshire,
William Barker,
Richard Southbey.
Berwick,
John Rushworth,
Sir Ralph Grey.
Beverly,
Michael Wharton,
Sir John Hotham.
Beudley,
Philip Foley.
Bishops Castle,
Sir Richard Mason,
Richard Moore.
Bletchingly,
Sir William Guston,
George Evelyn.
Bodmin,
Nicholas Glynn,
Hender. Roberts.
Boralston,
Sir Duncombe Colchester,
John Elwell.
Boroughbridge,
Sir Thomas Meleverer,
Sir John Brooke.
Bossiny,
Charles Bodvile Roberts,
Sir Peter Colliton.

Boston,
Sir Anthony Irby,
Sir William York.
Brackley,
William Lisle,
Sir Wm. Wenham.
Bramber,
Pierce Goring,
Henry Goring.
Brecon County,
R. Williams.
Brecon Town,
John Jefferys.
Bridgwater,
Sir Haswel Tynt,
Sir John Mallet.
Bridport,
William Bragge,
John Michael.
Bristol,
Sir Richard Hart,
Thomas Earl.
Bridgenorth,
Sir Thomas Whitmore,
Sir Will. Whitmore
Buckinghamshire,
Thomas Wharton,
Richard Hampden.
Buckingham Town,
Sir Ralph Verney,
Sir Richard Temple.
Calne,
Sir George Hungerford,
Walter Norborn.
Cambridgeshire,
Sir Levinus Bennet,
Sir Robert Cotton.
Cambridge Town,
Lord Arlington,
Sir Tho. Chichley.
Cambridge University,
Sir Thomas Exton,
Robert Bradey.
Camelford,
Sir James Smith,
Robert Russel.
Canterbury,
Lewis Whatson,
Vincent Denn.
Cardiffe.
Bussy Mansel.
Cardigan County,
Edward Vaughan.
Cardigan Town,
Hector Philips.
Carlisle,
Lord Morpeth,
Sir Christ. Musgrave.
Caermarthen County,
Lord Vaughan.
Caermarthen Town,
Altham Vaughan.
Caernarvon County,
Thomas Bulkley.
Caernarvon Town,
Thomas Moystin.
Castle-rising,
Sir Robert Howard,
James Hoste.
Chester County,
Henry Booth,
Sir Robert Cotton.
Chester City,
William Williams,
Roger Whitley.
Chichester,
Richard Farrington,
John Bramen.
Chippenham,
Sir George Speke.
Sir Edward Hungerford.
Chipping Wycombe,
Thomas Lewis,
Sir John Borlace.
Christ Church,
Sir Thomas Clarges,
George Fulford.
Cirencester,
Henry Powle,
Sir Robert Atkins.
Clifton,
John Upton,
Edward Yard.
Clithero,
Sir Thomas Stringer,
Henry Marsden.
Cockermouth,
Sir Richard Graham,
Orlando Gee.
Colchester,
Samuel Reynolds,
Sir Harbottle Grimstone.
Corf-castle,
Sir Nathan Naper,
Richard Fownes.
Cornwall,
Francis Roberts,
Sir Richard Edgcomb.
Coventry,
John Stratford,
Richard Hopkins.
Cricklade,
Edmund Webb,
William Lenthal.
Cumberland,
Sir John Lowther,
Sir Geo. Fletcher.
Denbighshire,
Sir John Trevor.
Denbigh Town.
Sir John Salisbury,
Derbyshire,
William Sacheverell,
Lord Cavendish.
Derby Town,
Anchitel Grey,
George Vernon.
Devizes,
Sir Walter Ernley,
George Johnson.
Devonshire,
Sir William Courtney,
Samuel Rolle.
Dorchester,
James Gould,
Nathaniel Bond.
Dorsetshire,
Thomas Strangeways,
Thomas Freak.
Dover,
William Stokes,
Thomas Papillon.
Downton,
Maurice Blockland,
Sir Joseph Ash.
Droitwich,
Samuel Sandys, jun.
Henry Coventry.
Dunwich,
Sir Philip Shippon,
Sir Robert Kemp.
Durham County,
Tho. Petherston Hough,
William Bowes.
Durham City,
Sir Richard Lloyd,
William Tempest.
East Low,
Sir Jon. Trelawny,
John Kendal.
Edmunds Bury,
Sir Thomas Harvey,
Thomas Germyn.
Essex,
John Lemot Honeywood,
Henry Mildmay.
Evesham,
Edward Rudge,
Sir James Rushout.
Exeter,
Sir Thomas Carew,
Thomas Walker.
Eye,
Sir Robert Reeve,
Sir Charles Gawdy.
Flintshire,
Sir John Hanmer.
Flint Town,
Thos. Whitley.
Fowey,
John Trefry,
Jon. Rashleigh.
Gatton,
Sir Nicholas Carew,
Thomas Turgis.
Germain's,
Richard Elliot,
Daniel Elliot.
Glamorgan,
Sir Edward Mansel.
Gloucestershire,
Sir John Guise,
Sir Ralph Dutton.
Gloucester City,
Lord Dursley,
Lord Herbert.
Grampound,
Nicholas Hearle,
John Tanner.
Grantham,
Sir William Ellis,
Sir John Newton.
Grimsby,
William Broxholm,
George Pelham.
Grimstead,
Sir Cyrill Winch,
Henry Powle.
Guildford,
Morgan Randyl,
Richard Onslow.
Harwich,
Sir Philip Parker,
Sir Thomas Mydleton.
Haslemere,
Sir Wm. Moore,
Geo. Woodroffe.
Hastings,
Sir Robert Parker,
Thomas Mann.
Haverford West,
Thomas Howard.
Helston,
Charles Godolphin,
Sidney Godolphin.
Herefordshire,
Sir Edw. Harley,
Viscount Scudamore.
Hereford City,
Paul Foley,
Herbert Aubery.
Hertfordshire,
Wm. Hales.
Sir Charles Caesar.
Hertford Town,
Sir Thomas Birde.
Sir Wm. Cooper.
Heydon,
Henry Guy,
William Boynton.
Heytesbury,
William Ash,
Edward Ash.
Higham,
Sir Rice Rudd.
Hindon,
John Thynne,
Sir R. Grobham How.
Honiton,
Sir Walter Young,
Sir Thomas Putt.
Horsham,
John Machell,
John Mitchel.
Huntingdonshire,
Sir Thomas Proby,
Silas Titus.
Huntingdon Town,
Sidney Wortly,
Lionel Walden.
Hythe,
Sir Edward Deering,
Edward Hales.
Ilchester,
Sir John Barb,
Thomas Hoddy.
Ipswich,
John Wright,
Sir J. Barker.
Ives, (St.)
Edward Nosworthy,
James Praed.
Kellington,
Richard Carew,
William Coriton.
Kent,
Sir Vere Fane,
Edward Deering.
Kingston,
Sir Michael Wharton,
William Gee.
Knaresborough,
Sir Thomas Slingsby,
William Stockdale.
Lancaster County,
Lord Brandon,
Sir Chas. Houghton.
Lancaster Town,
Richard Kirby,
William Spencer.
Lanceston,
William Harbord,

Sir Hugh Pyper.
Leicestershire,
Lord Sherrard,
Sir John Hartop.
Leicester Town,
Sir Henry Beaumont,
John Grey.
Leominster,
Thomas Coningsby,
John Dutton Colt.
Leskard,
John Buller,
Sir Jonathan Trelawney,
Lestwithiel,
Sir John Carew,
Walter Kendal.
Lewes,
Richard Bridger,
Thomas Pelham.
Lincolnshire,
Sir Robert Carr,
Lord Castleton.
Lincoln City,
Sir Thomas Hussey,
Sir Thomas Meres.
Litchfield,
Daniel Finch,
Michael Bidulph.
Liverpool,
Ruishee Wentworth,
John Dubois.
London,
Sir Robert Clayton,
Sir Thomas Player,
William Love,
Thomas Pilkington.
Ludlow,
Francis Charlton,
Charles Baldwin,
Ludgershall, (dble. ret.)
Thomas Neal,
John Gerrard.
Sir J. Talbot,
Jno. Smith.
Lyme,
Thomas More,
Henry Henley.
Lymington,
‡ John Button,
‡ John Burrard.
Lynn,
Sir Henry Hobart,
Simon Taylor.
Maidstone,
Sir John Tufton,
Thomas Fane.
Malden,
Sir Thomas Darcy,
Sir William Wiseman.
Malmsbury,
Sir William Estcourt,
Sir James Long.
Malton,
Sir Watkinson Paylet,
William Palms.
Marlborough,
Thomas Bennet,
Lord Bruce.
Marlow,
Thomas Hobby,
John Burlace.
Mawes, (St.)
Sir Joseph Tredenham,
Henry Seymour, jun.
Melcomb,
Sir Jno. Coventry,
Henry Henning.
Merionethshire,
Sir Robert Owen.
Midhurst,
William Montagu,
John Cook.
Middlesex,
Sir William Roberts,
Nicholas Raynton.
Milbburn,
John Hunt,
Henry Bull.
Minehead,
Thomas Palmer.
Francis Lutterel.
Michael, (St.)
Sir Wm. Russel,
Henry Vincent.
Monmouthshire,
Sir Trevor Williams.
Sir Edward Morgan.
Monmouth Town,
John Arnold.
Morpeth,
Daniel Collingwood,
Sir George Downing,
Montgomeryshire,
Edward Vaughan.
Montgomery Town,
Matthew Price.
Newark,
Sir Richard Rothwell,
Sir Robert Markham.
Newcastle, (Staffordsh.)
Sir Thomas Bellot,
William Leveson Gower.
Newcastle, (Northum.)
Sir Nathaniel Johnson,
Sir Ralph Carr.
Newport, (Cornwall)
William Morris,
Ambrose Manaton.
Newport, (Hants)
‡ John Lee,
‡ Sir Robert Dillington.
Newton, (Lancashire)
Sir John Chichley,
Andrew Fountain.
Newton, (Hants)
‡ Sir John Holmes,
‡ Lemuel Kingdon.
Norfolk County,
Sir John Hobart,
Sir Peter Glyn.
Northamptonshire,
John Packhurst,
Miles Fleetwood.
Northampton Town,
Sir William Laugham,
Ralph Montagu.
Northumberland County,
Sir John Fenwick,
Sir Ralph Delaval.
Norwich,
Lord Paston,
Augustin Briggs.
Nottinghamshire,
Sir Scroop How,
John White.
Nottingham Town,
Richard Slater,
Robert Pierrepoint.
Okehampton,
Sir Arthur Harris,
Sir George Cary.
Orford,
Thomas Glemham,
Sir John Duke.
Oxfordshire,
Thomas Hoard.
Sir Philip Harcourt.
Oxford City,
William Wright,
Broom Whorwood.
Oxford University,
Sir Leolin Jenkins,
Dr. Perrot.
Pembrokeshire,
William Wogan.
Pembroke Town,
Arthur Owen.
Penryn,
Charles Smith,
Sir Nich. Slanning.
Peterborough,
Francis St. John,
Lord Fitz Williams.
Petersfield,
‡ Sir John Norton,
‡ Leonard Bilson.
Plymouth,
Sir William Jones,
Sir John Maynard.
Plimpton,
Sir George Treby,
John Pollexfen.
Pool,
Henry Trenchard,
Thomas Chaffin.
Pontefract,
Sir Patience Ward,
Sir John Dawney.
Portsmouth,
George Legg,
Richard Norton,
Preston,
Sir Robert Carr,
Sir Jervas Elwys.
Queenborough,
William Glanvile,
Gerrard Gore.
Radnor County,
Sir Row. Gwynn.
Radnor Town,
Sir John Morgan.
Reading,
Nathan Knight,
John Blagrave.
Retford,
Sir Edward Nevill,
Sir William Hickman.
Richmond,
John Darcy,
Humphrey Wharton.
Rippon,
Richard Stern,
Christopher Wandesford,
Rochester,
John Banks.
Sir Francis Clark.
Rumney,
Paul Barret,
Sir Charles Sedley.
Rutlandshire,
Edward Fawkener,
Philip Sherrard.
Rye,
Thomas Frewen,
Sir John Dorrel,
Ryegate,
Dean Goodwyn,
Ralph Freeman.
Salop County,
William Levison,
Richard Newport.
Salop Town,
Sir Richard Corbet,
Edward Kynaston.
Saltash,
Sir John Davy,
Bernard Greenville.
Sandwich,
Sir James Oxenden,
John Thurbane.
Sarum New,
John Windham.
Alexander Thistlethwait.
Sarum Old,
Sir Eliab Harvey,
Sir Thomas Mompesson.
Scarborough,
Francis Thompson,
William Thompson.
Seaford,
Edward Moutagu,
Edward Selwyn.
Shaftsbury,
Thomas Bennet,
Sir Matthew Andrews.
Shoreham,
Robert Fagg,
John Hales.
Somersetshire,
Sir William Portman.
George Speke.
Southampton County,
Earl of Wiltshire,
Sir Francis Roll.
Southampton Town,
Sir B. Newland,
Sir Chas. Wyndham.
Southwark,
Sir Richard How,
Peter Rich.
Staffordshire,
‡ Sir Walter Baggot,
‡ Sir John Bowyer.
Stafford Town,
Edwin Skrymsher,
Sir Thomas Armstrong.
Stamford,
Richard Cust,
William Hyde.
Steyning,
Sir James Morton,
Sir John Fagg.
Stockbridge,
‡ Henry Whitehead,
‡ Oliver St. John.
Sudbury,
Sir Jervas Elwys,
Jervas Elwys.
Suffolk,
Sir W. Spring,
Sir Samuel Barnadiston.
Surry County,

Arthur Onslow,
George Evelyn.
Sussex,
Sir William Thomas,
Sir John Fagg.
Tamworth, (doub. ret.)
Sir Thomas Thynne,
John Swynfen.
John Swynfen,
John Turton.
Tavistock,
Sir Francis Drake,
Edward Russel.
Taunton,
John Trenchard,
Edward Prideaux.
Tewkesbury,
Sir Francis Russel,
Sir Henry Capel.
Thetford,
William Harberd,
Sir Joseph Williamson.
Thirsk,
Sir W. Ascough,
Sir Wm. Frankland.
Tiverton,
Sir Henry Ford,
Samuel Foot.
Totness,
John Kelland,
Charles Kelland.
Tregony,
Charles Trevanion,
Hugh Boscawen.
Truro,
Henry Ashhurst,
Edward Boscawen.
Wallingford,
Scorie Barker,
Taverner Harris.
Warwickshire,
Richard Newdigate,
Thomas Marriot.
Warwick Town,
Thomas Lucy,
Thomas Coventry.
Wareham,
Thomas Erle.
George Savage.
Wells,
John Hall,
William Coward.
Wendover,
Edward Blackwell,
John Hampden.
Wenlock,
John Woolryche,
William Forrester.
Weobly,
John Booth,
John Birch.
Westbury,
William Trenchard.
John Ash.
West Low,
Jonathan Trelawney,
John Trelawney.
Westminster
Sir Wm. Pulteney,
Sir Wm. Walker.
Westmoreland,
Sir John Lowther,
Allan Bellingham.
Weymouth,
Michael Harvey,
Sir John Coventry.
Whitchurch,
‡ Richard Ayleffe,
‡ Henry Wallop.
Winchelsea,
Creswel Darper,
Sir Stephen Leonard.
Winchester,
Lord Annesly,
Sir John Cloberry.
Windsor,
Richard Winwood,
Samuel Starkey.
Wilton,
Thomas Herbert,
Sir John Nicholas.
Wiltshire,
Sir Walter St. John,
Thomas Thynne.
Woodstock,
Henry Bertie,
Nicholas Bainton.
Wooton Basset,
John Pledel,
Henry St. John.
Wygan,
Earl of Ancram,
Lord Colchester.
Worcestershire,
Thomas Foley,
Bridges Nanfan.
Worcester City,
Sir Francis Winnington,
Henry Herbert.
Yarmouth, (Norfolk)
Sir James Johnson,
Geo. England.
Yarmouth, (Hants)
‡ Sir Richard Mason,
‡ Thomas Wyndham.
Yorkshire,
Lord Clifford,
Lord Fairfax.
York City,
Sir Henry Hewley,
Sir Henry Thompson.

SPEAKER—Mr. Serjeant Williams.

The King's Speech on opening the Session.] Both houses being met, the king made this Speech to them:

"My lords and gentlemen; The unwarrantable proceedings of the last house of commons, were the occasion of my parting with the last parliament; for I, who will never use arbitrary government myself, am resolved not to suffer it in others. I am unwilling to mention particulars, because I am desirous to forget faults; but whosoever shall calmly consider what offers I have formerly made, and what assurances I renewed to the last parl.: how I recommended nothing so much to them, as the Alliances I had made for preservation of the general peace in Christendom, and the farther examination of the Popish Plot, and how I desired their advice and assistance concerning the preservation of Tangier; and shall then reflect upon the strange, unsuitable returns made to such propositions, by men that were called together to consult; perhaps, may wonder more, that I had patience so long, than that at last I grew weary of their proceedings.—I have thought it necessary to say thus much to you, that I may not have any new occasion given me to remember more of the late Miscarriages: it is as much my interest, and it shall be as much my care as yours, to preserve the Liberty of the Subject; because the crown can never be safe when that is in danger: and I would have you likewise be convinced, that neither your liberties nor properties can subsist long, when the just rights and prerogatives of the crown are invaded, or the honour of the government brought low, and into disreputation.—I let you see, by my calling this parliament so soon, that no irregularities in parliament shall make me out of love with them; and by this means, offer you another opportunity of providing for our security here, by giving that countenance and protection to our neighbours and allies, which you cannot but know they expect from us, and extremely stand in need of at this instant; and at the same time give one evidence more, that I have not neglected my part, to give that general satisfaction and security which, by the blessing of God, may be attained, if you, on your parts, bring suitable dispositions towards it: and that the just care you ought to have of Religion, be not so managed and improved into unnecessary fears, as may be made a pretence for changing the foundation of the government. I hope the example of the ill success of former heats, will dispose you to a better temper, and not so much inveigh against what is past, as to consider what is best to be done in the present conjuncture. The farther prosecution of the Plot; the Trial of the Lords in the Tower; the providing a more speedy Conviction of Recusants; and, if it be practicable, the ridding ourselves quite of that party, that have any considerable authority or interest amongst them, are things, though of the highest importance, that hardly need to be recommended to you, they are so obvious to every man's consideration, and so necessary for our security. But I must needs desire you, not to lay so much weight upon any one expedient against Popery, as to determine that all others are ineffectual: and, among all your cares for Religion, remember, that without the safety and dignity of the Monarchy, neither Religion nor Property can be preserved.—What I have formerly, and so often declared touching the Succession, I cannot depart from. But to remove all reasonable fears that may arise from the possibility of a Popish Successor's coming to the crown; if means can be found, that in such a case the administration of the government may remain in Protestants hands, I shall be ready to hearken to any such expedient, by which the Religion might be preserved, and the Monarchy not destroyed. I must therefore earnestly recommend to you, to provide for the Religion and Government together, with regard to one another, because they support each other: and let us be united at home, that we may recover the esteem and consideration we used to have abroad. I conclude with this one advice to you, That the rules and measures of all your Votes may be the known and established laws of the land; which neither can, nor ought to be departed from, nor changed, but by act of parliament: and I may the more reasonably require, That you make the laws of the land your rule, because I am resolved they shall be mine."

William Williams, Esq. chosen Speaker.] Upon finishing this Speech, the lord-chancellor, by his majesty's command, directed the commons to return to their house, and to chuse a Speaker. Which they accordingly did, unanimously electing W. Williams, esq. who had been Speaker in the last Parliament. When the commons presented him to his majesty, on the 2d, he made this Speech to the king:

"May it please your majesty, The knights, citizens and burgesses in parliament assembled, with duty and loyalty agreeable to themselves and the persons whom they represent, are in obedience to your royal pleasure, for the disposing of themselves in that great assembly for your majesty's service, considered of a Speaker: and, to manifest to your majesty, and the world, That they are not inclinable to changes, have with one voice elected me their Speaker, having had the honour to serve your maj. and the commons in that trust, in the last parliament. With all humility I presume again, by their commands, to stand before your majesty, to receive your pleasure, with a head and heart full of loyalty to your sacred person; armed with a settled resolution, never to depart from your well-known, ancient and established government."

Though the king was not pleased with the Speech, he thought fit by the lord-chancellor to approve of the election, in the usual form. Upon which the new Speaker made this farther Speech: "Most gracious sovereign, natural allegiance commands loyalty to your maj. from every subject. Your singular grace and favour to me, in the last parliament, continued by the honour I have in this, add more than dutifulness and obedience to my loyalty. I am set in the first station of your commons for trust and quality; an high and slippery place! It requires a steady head, and a well-poised body in him that will stand firm there. Uprightness is the safe posture, and best policy, and shall be mine in this place, guarded, with this opinion, That your majesty's service in this trust, is one and the same with the service of your commons, and that they are no more to be divided than your crown and sceptre. They truly serve the crown and country, which shall be my care and industry, who make the safety of your sacred person, the defence and security of the Protestant religion, the support of your majesty's government, the maintenance of the laws, and preservation of the ancient constitutions of parliament, one and the same undivided interest, one and the same safety, one and the same inseparable security for yourself and people. These are the desires of all good men, but must be the effects of good councils. For the enabling of your majesty's Great Council now in parliament assembled, to compleat this blessed establishment, with all humility I address to your majesty, in the name and on the behalf of the commons in parliament; 1. That we and our servants may be free in our persons and estates, from arrests, and other disturbances. 2. That in our debates, liberty and freedom of speech be allowed us. 3. That, as occasion shall require, your maj. will vouchsafe us access to your royal person. I take leave to join this humble Petition for myself, That nothing by me, in weakness, or through inadvertency, said or done, may turn to the prejudice of the commons: and that my behaviour and proceedings may receive a benign and favourable interpretation with your gracious majesty."

Upon this, the Lord Chancellor, by command from his majesty, made this return to the Speaker: "Mr. Speaker, All your Petitions are fully and freely granted by his majesty, in as large and ample a manner, as ever any house of commons yet enjoyed them: the king is very sure, the wisdom of this house of commons will make as prudent an use of them, as any of your ancestors ever did. Your own particular Petition is grateful to the king too; because he knows you will be as careful to avoid mistakes, as his majesty is ready to forgive them. And now, Mr. Speaker, these preliminaries being thus over, the king desires you would hasten to the rest that are necessary to be dispatched, before we can enter into business; that so we may husband time, which is now more necessary than ever; and he hopes that this parliament will come to a very happy and prosperous conclusion: and that it may do so, God Almighty direct and prosper all your consultations."

Though the Speaker had not the good fortune to please the king, on this occasion; he was ordered the Thanks of the house, and desired to print his Speech.

Debate on printing the Votes.] March 24, Sir *John Hotham.* What I am about to move concerns us all. The last parliament, when you were moved to print your Votes, it was for the security of the nation, and you found it so; it prevented ill representations of us to the world by false copies of our Votes, and none doubted your honour in the care of it;

and I am confident that this house will be no more ashamed of their actions than the last was. Printing our Votes will be for the honour of the king, and safety of the nation. I am confident, if it had been necessary, you would have had petitions from the parts I come from, that your actions might be made public. As I came hither, every body almost that I met upon the road cried, 'God bless you!' I move, therefore, 'That your Votes may be ordered to be printed, with the rest of your proceedings.' And I shall only add, that yourself has done so well in taking that care upon you the last parliament, that the house will desire you to continue them in the same method.

Sir *Wm. Cowper*. That which put me upon moving the printing your Votes, the last parliament, was false papers that went about, in former parliaments, of the votes and transactions of the house. Let men think what they please, the weight of England is the people, and the world will find, that they will sink Popery at last. Therefore I second the motion.

Mr. Sec. *Jenkins*. I beg pardon, if I consent not to the motion. Consider the gravity of this assembly; there is no great assembly in Christendom that does it. It is against the gravity of this assembly, and it is a sort of Appeal to the People. It is against your gravity, and I am against it.

Mr. *Boscawen*. If you had been a privy-council, then it were fit what you do should be kept secret; but your Journal-Books are open, and copies of your Votes in every coffee-house, and if you print them not, half votes will be dispersed, to your prejudice. This printing is like plain Englishmen, who are not ashamed of what they do, and the people you represent will have a true account of what you do. You may prevent publishing what parts of your transactions you will, and print the rest.

Mr. *L. Gower*. I find that those who write our votes and transactions, and send them all England over, are favoured, and I believe that no gentleman in the house will be against printing them, but Jenkins. I hope you will not be ashamed of what you do; therefore I am for printing your votes.

Colonel *Mildmay*. By experience we have found, that, when former parliaments have been prorogued or dissolved, they have been sent away with a Declaration against them. If our actions be naught, let the world judge of them; if they be good, let them have their virtue. It is fit that all Christendom should have notice of what you do, and posterity of what you have done; and I hope they will do as you do; therefore I am for printing the votes.

Sir *Francis Winnington*. Because what has been said by Jenkins is a single opinion, for he says, 'printing is an Appeal to the People,' I hope the house will take notice that printing our Votes is not contrary to law. But pray who sent us hither? The privy council is constituted by the king, but the house of commons is by the choice of the people. I think it not natural, nor rational, that the people, who sent us hither, should not be informed of our actions. In the Long Parliament it was a trade amongst clerks to write Votes, and it was then said, by a learned gentleman, 'That it was no offence to inform the people of Votes of parliament, &c. and they ought to have notice of them.' The Long Parliament were wise in their generation to conceal many things they did from the people; and the clerk, who dispersed the Votes, was sent away, and nothing done to him. The Popish party dread nothing more than printing what you do, and I dread that a man in Jenkins's post, (and such an accusation upon him, as is in the last parliament) should hold such a position, 'that printing your Votes was an Appeal to the People.'

Resolved, "That the Votes and Proceedings of this house be printed."

Mr. *Harbord*. Now you have passed this Vote, I would graft something upon it. I move, 'That the care of printing the Votes may be committed to the Speaker,' who so well acquitted himself in it the last parliament. —Which was ordered.

Debate on the Miscarriage of the Bill for Repeal of 35th Eliz.] Mr. *Hopkins* made a motion to enquire why the Bill of Repeal of a Statute of 35th Eliz. which, in the last parliament, had passed both houses, was not presented with the rest for the royal assent.

Mr. *Hampden*. I think the motion is to enquire after the slipping of that Act the last parliament, and not presenting it for the royal assent. For my own part, I look upon it as a breach of the constitution of the government. We are told that we are republicans, and would change the government: but such as are about to do so, it is a natural fear in them to be thought so, and they will cast it upon others. In a crowd, it is frequent for pick-pockets to cry out, 'Gentlemen, have a care of your pockets,' that they may be more safe themselves, and have the less suspicion upon them. I will not offer this to your consideration to-day, but move you to adjourn it till to-morrow.

Sir *F. Winnington*. I shall humbly put in this word. I doubt this matter will be too big for to-day; it is of great importance, and will not be forgotten. Be pleased to adjourn the debate of it.—Which was accordingly done.

Debate on bringing in the Bill of Exclusion.] Sir *Nich. Carew*. I move, That for the preservation of the Protestant Religion, and the king's Person, a Bill be brought in to prevent a Popish Successor, and in particular against James duke of York, the same Bill which passed the last parliament.

Mr. Sec. *Jenkins*. I must give my negative to this motion; and my reason why I do so, is, because the king has declared, in his Speech, 'That, as to the point of the Succession, he will not depart from what he has so often declared.' The king has given his vote against it; and therefore I must do so too.

Mr. *L. Gower*. The duke of York is in Scotland, and I hope the king will now come up to what he has said in his Speech. My liberty and property are dear to me, and I will support the king's prerogative too; and those people that are briars and thorns scratch you in your intentions against Popery; which, I see, we cannot prevent without this Bill.

Col. *Birch*. I am heartily glad to find that the zeal of the house still continues for the Protestant religion. My opinion is, that we cannot preserve the Protestant religion with a Popish successor to the crown, any more than water can be kept cold in a hot pot. But I would do it in all the decent ways to come at it. The king recommends to you, in his Speech, 'to look back to what he formerly said as to the Succession, &c.' If there be no other way to prevent Popery, my opinion is, that it will be more decent to our prince, and better for those who sent us hither, before the Bill be brought in, to give it the honour of a day, to consider of Expedients to save Religion, &c. for that I shall expect from some honourable persons; if none come, then you may proceed to this Bill with more honour; therefore appoint a day for consideration.

Sir *John Ernly*. I should not have troubled you but from what was spoken last. By all means just and lawful, we are to secure our religion and properties; we see the great attempts made upon us from Rome, and we must do something for our farther security. I will not speak of the former Bill against the duke, nor of the king's Speech; that give you latitude for Expedients, and I would not offer any if I thought they would not do as well as that Bill, which is but an Expedient; but because the king has declared against that Bill, and invited you to Expedients, I would not put that Bill any more to the hazard of rejection, but think of some Expedients.

Mr. *Harbord*. I can see no expedient to save religion, and preserve the king's person, but the Bill to exclude the duke, &c. All gentlemen, I believe, would be willing as to the manner, and save the matter, but when our prince is encompassed with all the duke's creatures, the duke's safety is because of their dependencies. The danger is not from Popery, but from the king's being encompassed with the duke's creatures. I would proceed in this matter with all decency; and since a day is moved for, pray let us have time to consider.

Sir *Christ. Musgrave*. You are invited, by the king's gracious motion, to consider how to preserve Religion, &c. I desire that we may not now put a question for bringing in a Bill to exclude the duke, else properly we cannot consider any expedients for preservation of Religion.

Mr. *Whorwood*. They who advised the king's Speech, must answer for it. I think those about the king have done enough to ruin him and us. But I would have the king see, that we are so far from putting him upon that stress, that we would help him out. I think that Speech, which the king did read to us, had nothing of the king's in it. He is a better man, and a better protestant, than to do it of himself; therefore I would not put on a Resolution, here, as flat and as short as the king's Speech. The king has gone as far as this Resolution comes to, in his Declaration about Dissenters formerly, and yet he was persuaded to revoke it. If persons have been so prevalent about the king, as to put the king upon this Speech, let me see those persons so forward to bring the king into a thing, to help him out; if they do not, I hope the king will lay the blame at their doors, and not at ours. If they could have told us what Expedients were necessary, they would have put them into the king's Speech, and the resolution-part, of 'not altering the Succession,' would have been left out. A little consideration, in this great matter, can do us no hurt, and will satisfy the people without doors. But if they about the king can find no Expedients, I hope he will lay them aside, and take their counsel no more.

Mr. *Powle*. Though I hear of Expedients abroad, yet I cannot conceive that a title or name can destroy the nature of expedients. But the king, in his speech, has held you out a handle, &c. and I would not give those about the king occasion to say, that this house is running into a breach with him.

Mr. *Hampden*. This is a matter of great weight, and I would adjourn it till to-morrow. As for the reason of proposing Expedients, I do not move to adjourn for that, for it is as little reason to me to expect any as it was the last parliament. That parliament gave reasons why no Expedients could be of any effect but this Bill of Exclusion, and that parliament saw enough of Expedients. There are a great many talked of abroad in the streets, and will not you hear Expedients? What can a man say less, with any modesty? But no man can say but that we are in danger, if the duke should come to the crown. But the question is, Whether you will put off this debate? Therefore I move, 'That the house will take into consideration the security of the Protestant Religion to-morrow.'

Sir *Fr. Winnington*. When this Bill passed the last parliament, it was nem. con. and most of this parliament were of the last. As for 'Expedient,' it is a word mightily used, and talked of, and willingly embraced; but none have been proposed. Let this matter be re-assumed on Saturday, and so taken into consideration, to secure the Protestant Religion, and not to let any thing appear upon your Books, relating to Expedients, or preventing a Popish Successor.

Mr. *Trenchard*. I was much surprized at the king's Speech, considering your weighty reasons for the Bill, &c. the last parliament, and that the lords found no Expedients effectual for preservation of Religion; but that the king may see that what we do is out of a real sense of the danger we are in, &c. and not in contradiction to him, and when nothing is found effectual to save us, that we may justify ourselves in what we do, therefore I am for adjourning the debate.

Resolved, nem. con. 'That this house will, on Saturday the 26th, consider of means for the security of the Protestant Religion, and for the safety of the king's Person.'

Thanks voted to Counties and Boroughs, for electing their Members without Charge.] March 25. Mr. *Swynfin.* When there has been a general corruption, and all have not done their duty, you should distinguish and give Thanks to them that have. As you have done to officers for doing their duty in suppression of Popery, when through the corruption of the times, some have not done their duty. Nothing is more parliamentary than to return thanks to those who have freely, and without expence, chosen you Members, and I desire that these Members so elected should send their Thanks to those who chose them.

Which was ordered accordingly as follows: "It being represented to this house by several members, That many counties, cities, and boroughs, have freely, without Charge, elected many of the Members in this present parliament, according to the ancient constitution of elections of members to serve in parliament; wherefore this house doth give their Thanks to such counties, cities, and boroughs, for the said elections."

Farther Debate on the Loss of the Bill for Repeal of a Statute of 35 Eliz.] Sir *Wm. Jones.* This matter deserves material consideration, whether in respect of the loss of the Bill, or the shaking the very constitution of parliament. The bill that is lost, is of great moment, and of great use to secure the country, and perhaps their lives too, in the time of a Popish Successor. Those men that hindered the passing that bill had a prospect of that, and if it be sent up again, we are like to meet with great opposition. But be the bill what it will, the precedent is of the highest consequence. The king has his negative to all bills, but I never knew that the clerk of the parliament had a negative, if he laid it aside, or not. But consider, if we send up many good bills, if this be not searched into, we may be deprived of them. No man that knows law or history but can tell, that to bills grateful and popular the king gives his consent; but if this way be found out, that bills shall be thrown by, it may be hereafter said they were forgotten and laid by, and so we shall never know whether the king would pass them, or not. If this be suffered, it is vain to spend time here, and it will be a great matter to find time to redress it. I move, therefore, 'That a Message be sent to the lords, for a conference, that some way may be found out to give us satisfaction in this great matter.'

Mr. *Boscawen.* I do concur with Jones, that parliaments are prorogued and dissolved by the king, and now here is a new way found out to frustrate bills. The king cannot take one part of a bill and reject another, but gives a direct Answer to the whole. But to avoid that, this bill was never presented to the king; a thing never done before! I desire that we may send to the lords for a conference, to represent this innovation, and that a committee be appointed to draw up Reasons for the managers.

Mr. *Garroway.* I was a friend to this bill, and I agree in all things concerning the weight of it. The laying this bill aside is such a breach of the constitution of parliament, that it is in vain to pass any bill if this be not searched into. By the constitution of parliament all bills, but Money bills, after they have passed both houses, are deposited in the lords hands, and it is below you to look after the clerks for this bill. If the lords give you no answer for the loss of this bill, that is satisfactory, I would then send to them to know the reason why the bill was not tendered to his maj. with the other bills.

Sir *Rob. Howard.* I would have you search the lords Journals, and if you find no account of the bill there, then it will be time for us to go to the lords.

Sir *Rd. Temple.* I fully concur in the weight and consequence of this matter, and you are to take all the care that can be to secure it for the future. Never any thing of this nature was done before, but the Bill for the better observation of the Sabbath, in the late Long Parliament; it was left upon the table, at a conference, and stolen away. (see p. 285) It is not proper to take notice of this in a Message to the lords, because the miscarriage of this bill was in another parliament. The matter must go upon the desire of a conference, concerning the rights and privileges of both houses of parliament, and then you may appoint a committee to inform you of the progress of this matter.

Mr. *Vaughan.* I think the passing over the enquiry after the loss of the Bill of the Sabbath was the great occasion of the loss of this. Consider how many interruptions parliaments have had, of late, in the greatest business, by prorogations and dissolutions; and another way to gratify your enemies is to stifle your laws when they have a mind the people should have no benefit of them, though they have passed both houses.

Sir *Henry Capel.* The lords are the depositaries of all Bills, but those of Money; and without any other words, I would send for a conference, to know what is become of the Bill. I know of but three negatives to bills, but by this, there is a fourth; which will destroy the government.

Col. *Titus.* In things of this nature, it is the best way to observe old methods, and the best method to know one another's mind is by conference. I remember, the lords once sent to us for a conference, where they told us the house was falling on our heads. The lords sent us not a Message, 'That the Roof was falling and dangerous,' but they sent for a conference 'on a matter of great consequence;' therefore I would send to the lords for a conference 'about matters relating to the nation.'

Mr. *Hampden*. I would say this in the Message; 'That we desire a conference with their lordships concerning the Constitution of parliaments in matter of passing Bills.'

Resolved, "That a Message be sent to the lords, desiring a conference with their lordships in matters relating to the Constitution of parliaments in passing of Bills:" and a committee was appointed to prepare the subject-matter.

Debate on Fitzharris's Examination.] Sir Wm. Waller gave an account of the discovery of Fitzharris's Plot; and sir George Treby read his Examination.*

Sir *J. Hartop* moves it may be printed, for the world to see the devilish conspiracies of the Papists.

Sir *Wm. Jones*. I like the motion well for printing Fitzharris's Examination.

Mr. Sec. *Jenkins*. The scandalous Paper reflecting upon the king was read over to his maj. by Waller; whereupon I issued out warrants to apprehend Fitzharris, &c. and Waller saw the execution of them.

Sir *Fr. Winnington*. This is of great importance, and in it we ought to acquit ourselves like wise men. We, that come out of the country, hear that the treasonable Paper should have been sent to many gentlemen, and then they should have been seized upon as traitors in the conspiracy in this Plot. All is now at stake; therefore how long or short a time we are to sit here, (the trooper, Harrison, that was seized, said, 'We should have other guards at Oxford, than we had at Westminster,') let not our courage lessen. This being our case, let us go to the bottom of this business. It has been moved, 'That he should be sent for hither;' but we have experience, that, when once an accusation in parliament is against a man upon record, and in the greatest court in the kingdom made known, malefactors have not been cleared, and have not had justice; therefore I move, 'That you will take care that this man be impeached of High-Treason,' and, it may be, then he will tell you all.

Sir *Rob. Clayton*. When Mr. Recorder and myself examined Fitzharris in Newgate, he asked us, 'Whether he had said enough to save his life?' We told him, 'We thought not; but if he would ingenuously confess what counsel he had for drawing and modelling his treasonable Paper, and be ingenuous in the whole, we would take his farther Examination;' and wished him to consider of it. But, the next day after he promised he would, he was removed out of our reach to the Tower.

Fitzharris impeached.] Resolved, "That Edw. Fitzharris be impeached of High-Treason, in the name of all the commons of England; and that Mr. Secretary Jenkins do, to-morrow morning, go up, and impeach him at the bar of the lords house."

Debate on Mr. Sec. Jenkins refusing to carry up Fitzharris's Impeachment.] Mr. Sec. *Jenkins*. The sending me up with this Impeachment reflects upon his majesty, my master, in the character I bear under him; and I

* "A few days before the king went to Oxford, Fitzharris, an Irish Papist, was taken up for framing a malicious and treasonable Libel against the king and his whole family. He had met with one Everard, who pretended to make discoveries, and, as was thought, had mixed a great deal of falshood with some truth; but he held himself in general terms, and did not descend to so many particulars as the witnesses had done. Fitzharris and he had been acquainted in France; so on that confidence he showed him his Libel; and he made an appointment to come to Everard's chamber, who thought he intended to trepan him, and so had placed witnesses to overhear all that passed. Fitzharris left the Libel with him, all writ in his own hand. Everard went with the paper, and with his witnesses, and informed against Fitzharris, who upon that was committed. But seeing the proof against him was like to be full, he said, 'the Libel was drawn by Everard, and only copied by himself.' But he had no sort of proof to support this. Cornish, the sheriff, going to see him, he desired he would bring him a justice of the peace; for he could make a great discovery of the Plot, far beyond all that was ever known. Cornish, in the simplicity of his heart, went and acquainted the king with this: for which he was much blamed; for it was said, by this means that discovery might have been stopped. But his going first with it to the court proved afterwards a great happiness both to himself and to many others. The secretaries and some privy-counsellors were, upon that, sent to examine Fitzharris; to whom he gave a long relation of a practice to kill the king, in which the duke was concerned, with many other particulars which need not be mentioned; for it was all a fiction. The secretaries came to him a second time to examine him farther: he boldly stood to all that he had said; and desired that some justices of the city might be brought to him. So Clayton and Treby went to him; and he made the same pretended discovery to them over again; and insinuated, that he was glad it was now in safe hands that would not stifle it. The king was highly offended with this, since it plainly showed a distrust of his ministers; and so Fitzharris was removed to the Tower; which the court resolved to make the prison for all offenders, till there should be sheriffs chosen more at the king's devotion. Yet the deposition made to Clayton and Treby was in all points the same that he had made to the Secretaries: so that there was no colour for the pretence afterwards put on this, as if they had practised on him." Burnet.

The Libel was entitled "The True Englishman, speaking plain English." It will be found in the Appendix No. XIII.

will not go on the Message.—A great cry, 'To the Bar, To the Bar.'

Sir *Tho. Lee.* I would not have said one word, but that the very being of the parliament is in the case. It is to no end to sit here any longer, if this be suffered. Jenkins had no ground or reason to bring the king's name in question, nor was there any reflection upon his majesty, or Jenkins, in sending him with the Impeachment. But, for Jenkins to say, 'Do what you will with me, I will not go with the Message!' Let his words be first asserted, and read to you, before he explain them, according to the order of the house.

Sir *Geo. Hungerford.* I never heard such words uttered in parliament before, 'That the whole house of commons should reflect upon the king in sending him with the Message,' and 'that he will not obey your commands.' Pray call him to the bar.—At which there was a loud cry, 'To the Bar.'

Mr. *Trenchard.* The house will grow contemptible to the extremest degree, at this rate. Such a thing was never before in parliament, that the whole house should reflect upon the king,' and for him to say, 'Do what you will with me, I will not go.'

Mr. Sec. *Jenkins.* I said no such thing, 'That the house reflected on the king,' but 'That I take it as a reflection upon the king, my master.'

His words were thus stated, 'This Message had not been put upon me, but for the character I bear. I value not my life nor liberty; do what you will with me, I will not go.'

Mr. Sec. *Jenkins.* I said 'That this is put upon me, to my apprehension, for the character I bear; and do what you will with me, I will not go.'

Sir *Wm. Jones.* I am sorry to see any member behave himself at this rate. This confirms me in the opinion of the design some men have to depress the honour of this house. A Book has been written by a member of this house* (which, in time, I hope, you will consider of) 'That the house of commons, in Hen. iii's time, sprung out of Rebellion.' This goes on this day in the same method. Let a man be of what quality he will, if he be too big to carry your Message, he is too big to be your member, and not fit to be chosen for one. Thus to scorn the commands of the house, and to be too big for a messenger of the house of commons! Secretaries are sent on Messages every day, and is he too big for this, to accuse a person of the Popish Plot? If this be so, sit no longer here, but go home. His character is great, but he may be privy to things hid from us, possibly, by this extraordinary carriage. Is it come to that pass, for us to be dealt withal as none of our predecessors ever were before. If my brother, or son, dealt with the house thus, I would have him made an example; and, for aught I see, he provokes you more by his explanation; therefore pray go on.

* Dr. Brady, who served for the University of Cambridge.

Mr. Sec. *Jenkins.* I am ready, and I think myself as much obliged as any man, to obey the commands of the house. The office I have under his maj. excludes me not; but the thing I stand upon is, that the motion was carried on in ridicule. I have an honour for this, and ever have had for all houses of commons, but in this Message I must and will be excused.

Sir *Hen. Capel.* Ridicule is not a word proper for a house of commons: what is appointed by them is with all gravity, especially where the life of a man is concerned, as it is in an Impeachment. We are in an unfortunate age; now things come to light, more than we were before; that now it must be said, 'Impeachments of treason strike at the king,' and 'the Bill of excluding the duke, &c. is levelled at the king,' I am sorry it is said here, as well as in other places. This that we put upon Jenkins is an employment for the king's service, and he tells us, 'It reflects upon the king, and he will not go.' All the commons do will be reversed, if this must pass for doctrine, 'That what we do reflects upon the king.' But, sir, we are in a ship, and we have to do with the master, and he with us. If this gentleman would make any sort of excuse for himself, I would, for my share, pass it by; but he has not taken it off, but rather aggravated it. If he has nothing farther to say for himself, he must withdraw, and then I shall make a motion, for the honour of the house.

Sir *Tho. Meres.* I know no difference of any persons here; if Jenkins said, 'I thought sending me with the Impeachment reflected on the king; and in case it be so, I will suffer any thing under that reflection,' a man may be mistaken in his thoughts: But, as I take it, he said, 'It was his thoughts that the Message was a reflection upon the king, and in that case he would suffer any thing rather than a reflection upon the king in the character be bears.'

Sir *John Ernly,* (after he had inspired Jenkins with a whisper, said,) It is an ill thing to stumble at the entrance. I do hope that Jenkins intended no disservice to the house, in what he said, but on a perfect mistake. I did apprehend, and so did some others, that he was put upon it, by the gentleman that moved it, in jest (Mr. Coningsby.) But be it in jest, or in earnest, he ought to obey your order; but every man cannot subdue his own heart. But I would know of Jenkins, whether, upon farther consideration, he will undertake this service, or no? I am the worst advocate in the world for an obstinate person; but I humbly offer it to your consideration to put the gentleman upon it, whether he will go, or no, before he withdraw.

Mr. Sec. *Jenkins.* Since the house is so favourable as to bear me, I must say I did apprehend it a reflection upon the king, which was the reason why I refused the Message; but if I apprehend it a reflection upon the king my master, I am heartily sorry I should incur the displeasure of the house, and I hope you will pardon the freedom of the expression, of reflecon upon the king. I had no other consideration whatsoever that induced me to say the words.

Mr. *Fleetwood.* I look upon this as so great reflection upon the house, from this gentleman, that he ought to come upon his knees, at the bar, to ask pardon.

Mr. *Boscawen.* We are all subject to infirmities. Seeing the thing is so, Jenkins could not apprehend any reflection upon the king in the Message, but he might upon himself. The king was a little smilingly moved; but since he has explained himself, I would have this passed by, as I should desire for myself, upon the like occasion.

Lord *Cavendish.* The gentleman's fault is a great one; but after he has now begged the pardon of the house, and that he is ready to obey the order of the house, I am willing to pass it over. Though it be a great fault, yet it is too little to give occasion for a breach, at this time.

Mr. Sec. *Jenkins.* I am ready to obey the orders of the house, and I am very sorry that the words which fell from me, gave the house offence.—And so the thing passed over, and he carried the Message.

Col. *Birch.* For the discovery of this Plot of Fitzharris we ought all to give God thanks, next to the discovery of the Popish Plot. This is a great service to the nation, and it is not the first service that sir Wm. Waller has done the nation. If ever the Thanks of the house were deserved, it is for this discovery; therefore I move, 'That he may have the Thanks of the house.' Ordered.

Farther Debate on bringing in the Bill of Exclusion.] March 26. Sir *Rob. Clayton.* I must confess, I have been full of expectation for an Expedient, in some measure to secure the protestant religion, and the king's person, in case of a Popish Successor, and my expectation has been from those gentlemen who opposed the Bill for excluding the duke of York from the Succession of the Crown, and I can call that no otherwise than 'an expedient.' I have, in my weak judgment, weighed all the expedients I have heard of, both in the lords house, here, and abroad, but they seem all to be a breach of the constitution of the government, and will throw us all into confusion and disorder. I have heard, that it has been an ancient usage for the members to consult their counties, cities, and boroughs, in any other matter of weight, as well as in giving Money; and the practice was good, and we can discharge our trust no better, than to observe the directions of those that sent us hither. We, who represent the city of London, have received an Address from the body of that city in the matter of the Bill for excluding the duke of York. I could heartily wish that some expedient may be found out rather than that Bill; but if there be none, I must pursue my trust, and humbly move, 'That a Bill may be brought in to disable James duke of York from inheriting the imperial crown of this realm.'

Lord *Russel.* I have the same obligation upon me, from the county I serve for, as the gentleman who spoke before me. I have been long of opinion that nothing but excluding the duke can secure us. In the last parliament, we were of opinion, 'That the duke's being a Papist gave all this encouragement to the Plot.' Should he come to the crown, his power will be more, and every day we see the sad consequences of his power. I should be glad if any thing else but this Bill would secure us from Popery, but I know of nothing else that will.

Mr. *Montagu.* The security of the Protestant Religion, and the safety of the king's person, are things of so great weight, that we should not have stayed so long as this day, to take into consideration the Exclusion of the duke. I am sorry to hear of the king's giving us expedients to secure the Protestant Religion: I am sorry to hear that language. This is not to be used as an English parliament, but French, to be told in the king's Speech what we are to do, and what not. The greatest arbitrary power that can be used in England, is to cow a parliament, and, it may be, that was the design in bringing us hither. But be we called to York, or all England over, we shall, I believe, be the same men, both as we are here and were at Westminster, in our opinions. When lord Danby dissolved the Long Parliament, he said, 'He had spoiled the old rooks, and had taken away their false dice.' Soon after him started in new ministers of state, and they shuffle and cut the cards again, and will dissolve and prorogue parliaments, till they can get one for their turn; and in this condition we are. As for the Bill of disinheriting the duke, were my brother or my son like to ruin my family, I would disinherit them, and turn away servants that would ruin me. If the bishops and the counsellors had spoken plain English to the king, things would not have been in this condition, and they cannot answer deferring our security so long. But neither these Ministers of the Gospel have endeavoured the preservation of the Protestant Religion, nor the ministers of state the government, both acting against Religion, and the preservation of the king's person. And seeing no expedient can serve us, but the Bill for excluding the duke, therefore I move for it.

Mr. *Hen. Coventry.* Several gentlemen tell us, there is no expedient, but none tell us what is. All men believe, that the religion of the duke is as fatal a thing as can be to the nation. What does he deserve, then, who perverted him? Let us consider, then, in what depends upon this house, to proceed like men. If it be our opinion that excluding the duke be the best way, this house cannot do it alone. If we cannot have that best way, we are guilty to our country of the consequences, if we take none. Suppose a man be sick, and nothing must be taken by him but by the order of three physicians; the Jesuits powder is by two of them thought fit to be given him, but one is against it, and does the duty of his opinion;

but because the other two do not agree to it, must the sick man take nothing? We are but one of the legislative power. I remember, in the Dutch war, several expedients were proposed to raise money, and the house, for the more freedom of debate, went into a grand committee: a man, whoever he be, that proposes an expedient, will desire leave to make good that expedient in a grand committee; but when it comes to that, if that man have no expedient, and loses your time, he will be trampled upon. A grand committee is most proper for this debate, and if it should happen which question should take place, if one be denied, the other may take place, but not any one to be put to exclude the rest, which, if you put a question for bringing in a Bill to exclude the duke, it will do. Let it be exclusion, limitation, or what it will, your order is general. Find out a way to secure us from Popery, and preserve the king's life, be it what it will. When men press on too fast, many times they tire their horses, and come late into their inn. Let a committee try expedients, else it is not *consultare* but *dicere*. I am of a contrary opinion, of debating this matter in the house, for this reason, and if gentlemen will do reasonably, the house should go into a grand committee.

Mr. *Swynfin.* You have had motions proposed for expedients, but there is not a word of expedients in the order of the day, and that answers it. The order is only, 'To consider of means for the security of the Protestant Religion, and for the safety of the king's person.' Those who were here present when the order was made, have left it free for a Bill, or any other thing, and therefore we are not tied to have bills, or to offer expedients against bills. As for the simile of 'the three physicians,' made by the hon. gent. that two were to administer nothing without the third, though one be for one thing, and another for another, yet if the case be such, that the two offer nothing but what is mortal to the patient, he ventures to his own disreputation, if he joins with them. However, in our case, the three physicians do not agree. We never saw any thing from the lords in answer to the Bill for excluding the duke, which they threw out, the last parliament. All the expedients have been to increase the fears of the kingdom, and to hasten our undoing; and when all was at stake, the parliament was dissolved, and that was an ill expedient. And those about the king who have come over to our opinion of the Bill, are all put away, and those about the king now are for expedients. The council of the Jesuits and all the Popish party have their end, by thus disappointing the kingdom; and the fears of the people are either that they must take up with a false security for their religion, as good as none, and so to impose Popery upon us that way, or to bring the kingdom into disorder; and when religion and the laws are at the duke's disposal, the kingdom will be in so great disorder, that the Protestants will not be able to enjoy themselves quietly; and no surer way for the Papists to effect their end. For the house to go into a grand committee, it is a motion of great weight; if you deny it, it will look as if you intended to precipitate, and deny free debate; if you accept it, you lie under delay, and who knows how long time we have to be together? If you were sure of your time to sit two, three, or four months, I would be willing to go into a grand committee; but as to the ill umbrage of refusing a committee, it is not like other cases. I would have an instance given me, if ever it was done in a thing of this weight. This matter in consideration to-day has been in two parliaments, and the whole kingdom is satisfied, that nothing but the Bill to exclude the duke can save us, and it was the opinion of the last parliament; what reason, therefore, is there to go into a grand committee for a thing so often debated? No man can deny, but that a grand committee, when there is something offered of an Expedient, is proper, to debate it with the more freedom: but to offer expedients generally, is as if the thing had never been consulted nor debated before. I never saw any expedient offered, but this of excluding the duke, and I never heard of any reason against the Bill, but 'set it aside, and think of Expedients.' Therefore I am for the Bill.

Mr. *Leveson Gower.* If any gentlemen have Expedients to preserve the Protestant Religion, without this Bill of Exclusion, they would do well to propose them, and they will deserve well of the house; and if they seem to them to give security, I should be glad to hear them.

Sir *John Ernly.* When the motion was first made for considering Expedients, I did then second it, because of the honour of the place I serve in. I did understand by the king's Speech, that there were Expedients. I am unwilling to determine the sense of any gentleman, who am myself of the weakest; but the motion was seconded, to go into a grand committee to consider Expedients; and if you please to do so, I then shall offer you something.

Mr. *Bennet.* Expedients that have been moved, already, are Jesuits powder for an ague; but our disease is a pleurisy, and we must let blood. Let the expedient go to what will do our business; and, it may be, you must have other expedients to fortify your Bill of Exclusion. I would have the house rightly understand, that those who are for going into a grand committee to consider expedients, are not for excluding the duke, and they who are not, are for it; and now put the question, if you please.

Sir *Fr. Russel.* A Bill for excluding the duke is a good expedient; let both that and others, as they are proffered, be considered.

Mr. *Hampden.* I must put you in mind that this Bill is no new nor strange thing; and now it is proposed to find out expedients to preserve the Protestant religion. Here is a way, by this Bill of Exclusion, that has passed two parliaments already; a way that had no reasonable objection against it; and a way rejected in gross by the lords, in the last parliament; but I doubt, if other expedients be tried, and they prove false, the Protestant religion will be endangered by it.

Sir *John Ernly*. If the house be of the mind not to go into a committee, I shall offer my little mite; and it is every man's duty to offer you his help. I doubt not but other men have expedients, and better than I have; but if you go not into a grand committee, I shall offer what I have. I do apprehend, that the Bill spoken of is a bar to the Succession of the duke, and to place the succession in the next heir. I humbly conceive, that, if you place the power of the government in a regency, and let the duke retain the name of king, it is no new thing. It has been done in Spain, France, and lately in Portugal, and God knows how soon it may be our case. If the administration be placed in a safe hand, that shall have no power to resign it, and shall have full power and authority, from the death of the king, to call again the last parliament that sat, and that that parliament shall have time to sit, to confirm this by parliament; if such a way can be contrived, I hope it may be done with safety.

Sir *Nicholas Carew*. This proposition is, 'That the government after the death of the king, may be in the hands of a regency.' I would be satisfied, if the duke will not submit to that, whether those who fight against him are not traitors by law?

Sir *Wm. Pulteney*. I think this, that has been proposed, is a matter of weight, and some expedient has been offered you, but I think as yet but a crude one. I can never imagine an effectual one. Ernly has told you, 'That this expedient, when drawn into better form, he hopes will satisfy.' It excludes the duke from the exercise of the government, and places the regency in the next successor, but the Bill for excluding the duke, &c. in the last parliament, left the Succession in the law. But pray consider what is a regency: A thing never heard of but in a prince in possession of the crown, in a minor, or a lunatic, but generally very unfortunate. But to talk of a regency *in futuro*, in condition and limitation of time, I never heard of before. This is an expedient that does not answer the king's Speech, nor your former Bill. By this expedient they make the king but a shadow, and divide the person from the power. Our law will not endure it to divide the person of the king from the power. Both the person and the power will be courted, and who that next heir will be, I know not. The king, in his Speech, leads you to consider expedients, but such as will consist with the safety and dignity of the monarchy. This expedient must be, to have two kings at the same time, one by law and another by right. In Portugal there has been some instance of this. That king was put into prison for some personal miscarriages, and his brother, the next heir, was made regent: but there is a vast difference betwixt these two cases; the king of Portugal was set aside for personal miscarriages, and not for being a Papist, and that was present, this to be. This expedient seems to me, to let the duke in, and then to make a question, Whether allegiance be due to him, or not? But I am afraid, that, unless we be true to those we serve, we shall deserve a just reproach; and by express directions of those I represent (Westminster) I am enjoined to adhere to the Bill of Exclusion. That Bill has been under the consideration of all the people of England, and perhaps of all the Protestants of Europe. All the wits of learned men have made their objections against it, and yet, notwithstanding, all the people are still of the same mind, that nothing but that Bill can save the Protestant religion; and now we run upon the most mishapen expedient, and, it may be, two or three years before we understand it: an expedient to have an operation no man knows when; of very little weight, unless it be improved by somebody!

Sir *Tho. Littleton*. We are flying at a great matter. All conclude, to fight against the duke, if he be king. God forbid! We have been told by three or four gentlemen, of directions they have from their principals to adhere to the Bill of Exclusion, and to be against all those things of Expedients. I would not have that way much cherished here. Those Addresses of the country are uncertain things, and no footsteps remain of any of those Papers from the countries. I take the meaning of that to be, to go down and consult their neighbours for direction what they shall do. I hear talk to-day of the parliaments of France, but this way is as dangerous; like the States of Holland, who are to consult with their principals before they resolve. It is a most unusual thing here, and of dangerous consequence. A regency has been proposed, to secure the administration of the government in Protestant hands, so as not to alter the constitution of the monarchy; and this alters the constitution of the monarchy the least imaginable, to have a regency in room of the king, and the monarchy goes on. We have had formerly a regent protector, call it what you please, in the nature of a protector, primus Consiliarius in the case of a minor king; but I propose not this. If you alter the government, I am against it; but here is offered a regent in place of a king, or a transferring the government. But it may be said, 'Where shall the duke be all this while?' That point is pretty well over. The lords, in the last parliament, proposed the banishing him 600 miles from England. The duke has an estate in England; he, as all men else do, loves it, and will not part with it by coming into England, against this law. But your Bill of Exclusion secludes the duke, and the crown then is to fall, as it does fall. What then will be the case? You must imagine either that his own daughter will take up arms against him, if he attempts to regain the crown, or somebody else will; and this will raise such an anger in the duke's mind, that where will the people shelter themselves? Not under the duke's daughter; they must naturally shelter themselves by running into arms. Cromwell's way to support himself in his usurpation was an army of 60,000 men. And he did do it, especially when his army was flushed with victory. And an army that has got power will keep it. The nation is not in the condition it was formerly, when great lords cherished their tenants, and by good leases could presently raise an army, and when they had accomplished what they designed, send them home again. But we are now in another way; raise an army, and they will think of their own interest how to keep themselves up. But if it fall out to be thus, your Bill will leave this very loose. As soon as this Bill of Regency shall pass, suppose the regency be established in the princess of Orange, and in case of her decease without issue, or issue in minority, then the lady Anne, the duke's other daughter, to be regent, and in the same law, commissioners to be forthwith sent to the prince and princess of Orange to take their oaths, that they will take upon them the execution of this Act, and that their oaths be recorded; you then are not left in that loose manner you will be by the Bill of Exclusion; and it is a far less matter for the princess to save a family, before misfortune come upon it, than to take the government upon her afterwards, in the height of trouble and disorder, which may ensue upon the Bill of Exclusion. But it may be said, 'what needs all this? It is just nothing but retaining the name of a king, in an exiled man.' But it is less violation for her, to govern in her father's name, than to have the kingdom given her, from him. It may be wondered why, in Portugal, when the king was to be removed from the government, there was a great debate amongst the three estates of that kingdom, (though they hold not proportion as they do here,) the commons were for don Pedro to be king; the nobility were for having him regent only; the ecclesiastics demurred: But at last both the ecclesiastics and the commons came over to the nobility: but Don Pedro stuck here, and would still leave his brother the title of king: he would leave nothing of shelter to force nature too far. I find that there are reserves in the king's Speech, if it be well observed. Another thing may be objected, which is, paying a difference to the crown for the sacredness of it, for the government's sake; and that looks like something; and how can we be secure, when it is treason to take up arms against the king? But the duke is like to be 500 miles off; and how came that law to be made, that the king and parliament may dispose of the Succession of the crown? It was then an opinion amongst lawyers, that the crown was unalienable: but when that law was made, for the king and parliament to dispose of the Succession of the crown, that opinion was damned under a penalty, though a standing maxim amongst lawyers. If so, this new Act of regency will be a warrant to what is proposed, as that was for the other. For my part, I have had the ill fortune to have the wind in my face; to be against the general opinion and stream of the world; and having had no share, for some time, in the government, I may speak my mind, possibly, more freely than they that have. It is a great crime to spy things too soon, which makes us apt to run from one extreme into another. I have proposed the best Expedient I can to preserve Religion, and quiet the minds of the people; but I am afraid, if we do nothing at all in this matter (I will grapple with neither of the Expedients) but if we do nothing, but let the thing lie loose, we shall gratify the Jesuits, on the one hand, by our confusion, and the Common-wealth's men to shuffle again, on the other hand; and if you go into some medium, both these men will be undone.

Sir *Wm. Jones*. I have heard with great attention this very able and learned gentleman, and am really of opinion that if any better Expedient could have been proposed, he, as soon as any gentleman, would have proposed it; but I am amazed that so learned a gentleman should not see through this Expedient. That which I take for the Expedient is, 'That, should the duke come to the crown, he should retain the name only of king, and that the next heir, under the title of regent, or protector, should have the administration of the government.' Who does he mean by 'next heir?' For any thing I know, or believe, it may be the duke's daughter, but, it may be, the duke may have a son. Either I have a great cloud on my understanding, or this is very strange; if the duke shall have a son, and shall he at a day, a month, or a year old, be regent? Suppose the princess of Orange come over to be protector to this young regent, and she die, and leave a child (the prince of Orange has no right) that child must have a protector, and so there will be a protector of a protector. But we are told, 'That it is for nothing, but to keep up the greatness of the government, that makes them go from the Bill of excluding the duke to this Expedient.' But pray, is it so great and pleasing a thing to wear a crown, and have no authority nor power? Is it not much worse than to lose the actual crown and possession? But if this Expedient pass into a Bill, and the duke be banished 500 miles off, it must be out of England, and if the name of king will please him in civility, beyond sea he shall be king, and it is as much to his purpose beyond sea to be called king only, as here: and to tell us, 'That the forfeiture of his estate upon his return will keep him there;' he that will venture the loss of a kingdom for his religion, will his estate too, and that is but a weak tye. It is less evil or injustice to take away from him both the crown and power than to leave him of both but the name. If you allow the duke the name of king, it will imply a right; therefore that to be used as an argument, is strange. But why is this contention, and all this ado, I wonder, for an empty name? But I am afraid this kind of Expedient is a kind of Jesuits powder. I do not think that Littleton's opinion or interest is for the Jesuits; but wise men may overdo things sometimes. But if you do not exclude the duke's title by law, the duke is king still, and then learned lawyers will tell you, that, by the 1st Hen. vii. all incapacity is done away by his being king. If you take not away the descent of the crown upon the duke, and the duke has a title to be king, then without doubt, all incapacities fail. But if this can be made effectual, I am as willing to exclude the duke's power as name; but lawyers will tell you it cannot be done. But there is a great difference betwixt the one and the other. When the lady comes to be regent, not only nature, but conscience, will bid her 'give unto Cæsar his due,' being not incapacitated to succeed, and perhaps that text some of our divines will preach upon. They will say, 'That the parliament, by what they have done, do acknowledge the duke to have a good title.' But if he be king, as the parliament allows him to be, in name and right of descent, an argument like this in queen Mary's time had like to have restored to her the first-fruits and tenths. Another thing, perhaps, came from those men who first proposed the Expedient (I will not believe that it originally came from Littleton,) 'That if we had passed the Bill of Exclusion in the last parliament, it would not have been submitted to;' but if this Expedient pass into law, and the duke have a right to be king, and be kept from the administration of the government, I doubt whether I shall fight against him. The Papists will say, we have got a law to separate what is inseparable; and I would, were I as the duke, have such a Bill to perplex my opposers, rather than a clear one. Littleton tells us of 'an army to maintain the Exclusion, and that that army will not soon be laid down.' But why an army? People will be sure that the lady will let her father in, if he have title; but will the people be sure of their religion, if he have title and power too? If there must be an army to maintain the Bill of Exclusion, there must be four armies to maintain the Expedient. There has been a protector proposed, &c. not like that of Edw. vi. who was little more than our lord president of the council: but certainly they who proposed this Expedient, intended the same power in the regent to let the duke in as to keep him out. Therefore pray lay aside this consideration, and take up that of the Bill.

Mr. *Leveson Gower*. I think it fit that you should present Reasons to the king for passing this Bill for excluding the duke, I do think that the administration of the government has been in such hands, since the king came in, that, though the ministers have been shifted, yet the same principles of government remain to this day. The Triple League has been broken, and the Smyrna Fleet seized, before we had open war with Holland. The king of France made war with Holland for his glory, and our ministers, to get taxes from us to make the king absolute: such violations, as never were done, upon the rights of the people!—He was called to order by

Mr. *Vaughan*. A question so extremely well spoken to as was the last, to be interrupted with any angry question, is not decent at this time. What the gentleman urges is a matter to be enquired into another time, though the gentleman, I believe, does it with a worthy intent. If any gentleman have any thing else to propose, of the matter now in debate, pray hear him.

Mr. *Leveson Gower* goes on. I intended, from what I said, to move you to present the king with reasons to pass the Bill of Exclusion. The shameful retrenchments in the king's family arise from the duke's creatures; and it is not safe for the king to part with any one of his ministers, unless he parts with them all. These that retrench the king's family, do it to get together a bank of money for a Popish Successor, and then will be their time to take away the king.

Sir *Tho. Meres*. I have heard this expedient debated with patience. This expedient has been well offered, and, I believe, mistaken by the gentleman that answered it. I must say, this is your question; your business is religion, and I have given as good testimony of sincerity to the Protestant religion, these 20 years, as any man has; and I have been for this Bill of Exclusion, and I am of opinion, that something must be done for the people, to quiet their fears of Popery. But for the point of law mentioned; if the law be such, that dominion must run with the name of king, that single reason is to carry the debate; but if they answer not to that, I am at an end. But, sure, those words that can disinherit a king may make this expedient law. I would not rise now to speak, if I thought that this Bill of Exclusion would pass the lords and the king. My grounds are but conjectures. The last parliament, I did believe that the Bill would pass, with greasing the wheels. Our condition of England is thus: we do need one another; the king and the people had need make use of parliaments to assist one another, to relieve us in the difficulties we are in. If the duke be king, he will need a parliament, and so will his people. In order to this, if there be any other expedient like this, though not the same, which no objection of law could destroy, if any gentleman would produce such a one, he would do the king and kingdom great service and advantage. In this necessity, we are like two great armies encamped upon two hills; and neither dares remove, not for their valour, but their reason: he that has the last loaf stays the longest, and necessity compells the other to go off. At last, it must be one side or other, or England will have the worst of it. But if none will venture, in point of law, to maintain the expedient, I am answered. If any gentleman could alter that Bill of Exclusion, that it may not be just the same as it was the last parliament, but have something of this expedient, I should like it; for this expedient is a Bill of Exclusion, and a strong one: if the duke were to chuse, he had rather have the first. I am for that nail that will drive, to do our business; and if gentlemen have other thoughts, pray so contrive it, that we may have one Bill or the other.

Mr. *Harbord*. All the expedients that I have yet heard have been like a cucumber; dress it, and then throw it away. This proposition of the expedient is either honest, or not. If it be honest, and without design, then all the dispute betwixt the king and us is, Whether the duke shall have a title to the crown? and I hope the king will rather gratify the nation than his brother, who has attempted the ruin both of it and him. If it be not honest, people about the king have done it to circumvent him, and will find ways, from day to day, to divert him from the advice of his people. Why was England so fond of Calais, but to have some footsteps in France? And so the duke's creatures are fond of this expedient, that the duke may still have a title to the crown, though the government be placed in a regency; and then all those gentlemen who depend upon the duke, if he comes to the crown, will change their measures, and show you of what religion they are.

Sir *Fr. Winnington*. As to the question, concerning the Bill of Excluding the duke; that that bill is lawful in conscience, no man will oppose, and after the great opposition it met with in the lords house, yet they agreed it lawful. So that we are not doing what wise men think unjust, and what *jure divino* is not unlawful, *concurrentibus iis qui concurrere debent*. Some gentlemen have told you, 'That their countries have given them intimations to press this Bill of Exclusion:' and Littleton has told you, 'It is dangerous to take instructions from the country.' But I say it is more so to take it from the court. Parliaments formerly, upon any weighty affair, stayed, and sent their members down to consult their countries. I am not subjected to what my country does propose. I have my trust to serve them here as well as I can. It is alleged, 'That consulting our country is like the states of Holland.' I am as much against a republic as he that fears it most, and I say, I know Littleton to be a man of that great reason, that if he go away satisfied with this day's debate, he will do all he can to satisfy the king in the post he is in. But to keep close to the question: it being allowed by law, that there may be an excision of the duke from the government, the next thing is to consider the expedient proposed of the regency. The same authority that makes a descent from the crown may modify it, and this was argued, to show that the regency would signify nothing in taking away the dig-y of monarchy. Now the question is, Which is most practicable, the regency or the exclusion? We lawyers are aptest to go on the strongest side, and to call every thing 'prerogative.' But I will put you a case that happened in king James's time; a sheriff had an exception in his commission, 'That he should not keep his county-court, but should have all other powers of his office;' but the judges resolved, 'That when once he had received his commission, and taken his oath, he was sheriff to all intents and purposes, and could not be deprived of keeping the county-courts.' Acts of parliament against common sense are void in themselves; to make a man king, and not suffer him to exercise kingly power, is a contradiction. Some clauses, in acts of parliament, have been flattering clauses, to satisfy the people, that they might not have the thing. This act of regency would be nonsense, and it would be said hereafter, 'That the house of commons were outwitted.' If the duke be king I owe him my obedience, and if he be king, and have no power to govern, he is king and no king. This I have urged the rather, to show that this of the Regency is no Expedient to save Religion; it blears the eyes of the people only, and is no solid security. To say, 'That the duke values his estate, and will not venture to come into England after the Act has banished him, for fear of forfeiting it,' as he loves his estate, so he loves a crown too, very well; therefore you need no farther to arm yourselves in point of conscience (that being yielded on all hands) but in point of reason. In the last parliament I did see, by the arguments of the Papists and the ministers, that without this Bill our ruin was irresistible. If the duke comes to the crown a Papist, he brings *merum imperium* along with him, and that made me fond of the Bill of Exclusion from the beginning. If by law the duke never was king, no case of conscience lies upon us in the matter. I shall only make this observation upon the king's Speech, wherein he says, 'If it be practicable to rid ourselves of the Popish party;' and next, 'If means can be found that, in case of a Popish Successor, the administration of the government may remain in Protestant hands;' so that we see the king doubts himself, and this, delivered by the king in great wisdom, is clipped off into this Expedient of Regency. You see, now we are come to Expedients, which the ministers have had two parliaments to consider of, what they are come to, and the proposition of the danger of a Popish Successor not at all lessened. We have no security in law by this Expedient: You take away no authority from the duke, should he be king. Therefore I hope the Bill of Exclusion will pass, and that reason, and not great offices, will take men off from a nem. con. I speak this as a dying man.

Mr. *Booth*. I have it in command from the county I have the honour to serve for (Cheshire), that they apprehend that no Expedient to preserve Religion, in case of a Popish

Successor, but makes the remedy worse than the disease, unless the Bill to exclude the duke from the Succession; and I have, as yet, heard no reason given by any man against it: but there is an *aliquid latet*. If the duke be not set aside, I am sure the government will be. Therefore I move for the Bill.

Sir *Tho. Meres*. What Bill soever we have, pray let us have the law on our sides, that, if the king should die, we may know whither to go. I think the king's Speech is penned as it ought to be penned, and should the king speak positively to what laws he would have, we are an Irish parliament, and not an English. But the king's words are tender words, and the thing lies fairly before you. If any thing of Expedient can be thought of to save Religion under a Popish Successor, not to destroy the monarchy; and if the next Expedient be not the best, pray refuse not the next to that.

Mr. *Vaughan*. You have had an Expedient offered of a Regency; pray consider what this Regency is. It is but the whole office of king, to place judges, constitute privy counsellors, call parliaments, make peace and war, &c. This they would take away, and reserve this empty name of king to the duke. This is perfectly to bring a war upon us, and for the duke to come in by conquest; and so farewell law, church, and all! The Regency must be supported by war, as well as the Bill of Exclusion. In 13th Eliz. the Crown could not be alienated but by king, lords, and commons, and then there was no successor named to keep king James in awe; and for the same reason, no Successor was named in the Bill of Exclusion the last parliament. Though we have been frighted by prorogations and dissolutions, it will not frighten them whose reasons go along with the Bill of Exclusion. I am for it because all men are for it, and have sent up the same parliament again; but if you lead the people into uncertainties, by such an Expedient as this of the Regency, both court and country will then be of a mind to lay aside parliaments, because they are become useless.

Sir *Hen. Capel*. By these conspiracies of the Papists, people's eyes are now enlightened, and, all the world over, they are an informed people. The Papists care not who is king, if he be a Papist. In the last parliament it was said, [by Hyde], 'There was a loyal party would stick to the duke, notwithstanding the Bill of Exclusion.' We see France has fallen upon the Protestant party there. The emperor has mastered them in Hungary, and what has been done in Bohemia, they say, broke the Prince Elector's heart. An universal design against the Protestant party—[The rest of his Speech was mostly what he had said in the last parliament.]

Col. *Legge*. I would not have spoken for the duty I owe my master, the duke of York, but for my duty to my country; and I own my obligation to the king for being the duke's servant; and farther, I am a Protestant, and was never out of England; and for the king's service my father bred me at sea. I know my own weakness in not having been bred to the law; but by enquiry I find, that the doctrine of deposing kings, and disposing of their kingdoms, is the damnable doctrine of the Church of Rome. In the 24th of Edw. iii. the king, I find, demanded advice of parliament in matters relating to the crown; the Answer of the whole parliament was, 'They could not advise any thing relating to the crown, nor of disinheriting him to whom they were sworn.' The fundamental and common-law of England has made the duke, as heir, to come to the crown, if the king have no sons. Hen. iv. came to the crown by parliament, but laid his claim to it by descent from Hen. iii. and so it continued to Hen. vi. and then the parliament declared, that those acts were not binding, but unjust and invalid, and so the right heir came in. Hen. viii. had power to dispose of the crown by his last will and testament; and though Jane Grey baited her title by Religion, yet right took place in the Succession; and since that, there has been an Act of Restitution in king James, as lawfully and justly the right and next heir to the crown; and to beseech the king to accept of their allegiance to him and his posterity. I think our ancestors were sworn to king James and his posterity, as well as we. It is a great happiness that the two lines of York and Lancaster are united, which has spent so much noble and royal blood in the barons wars. We have had an attempt of turning the government into a republic; and who knows but that, if we put by the right of the duke to succeed, that may be attempted again; and the crown revenue being much upon the people's gift, it may the more easily turn us into a republic. In the late times, when my father was in prison, an eminent person then in power, discoursing with him, said, 'I have obliged you, and when the king comes in (as I believe he will do, first or last) pray be my friend, and think of what I say; when the king's party shall be again in the saddle, if once you divide amongst yourselves, farewel monarchy for ever!' If by a law you keep out the duke, what must follow? An Act of Association. I speak now for England and for my posterity, (I have seven children.) How will this look? The king's father was murdered, and you take his brother from him. Sure this can take no effect with the king, and the lords, to make it a law. I wish the duke many happy days, but, from my heart, I wish the king more than the duke. The king is a healthy man, and the duke is not. What I have said is not as I am the duke's servant, barely out of pique of honour, but that I would not do any thing to destroy my posterity.

Col. *Birch*. This is the day of England's distress, and not only of England, but upon this day's resolve depends the good fate of the Protestant religion all the world over. Except we expect a miracle from Heaven, nothing else can save the Protestant religion. I think, I said this many years ago, 'That Popish Matches would bring in Popery at last.' But as to what is said to point of law, 'That the law will be interpreted according to the strength that maintains it;' I doubt not but if you do your endeavours, this great matter in debate may be settled; but if we have nothing left but prayers and tears to help us, we are in a miserable condition. All government begins either by conquest or compact; but it is interest that must defend this Bill of Exclusion, and not an army. We are the army. I have a family as well as others; and as for setting up idolatry, rather than my children should breathe in such an air, I had rather they were buried. All the mischiefs in the world that may ensue upon this Bill of Exclusion have been ingenuously offered you by Legge; but if you quit this bill, pray sit down and take up a Popish Successor, and renounce the Protestant religion. I would break this popish interest, and it will be our interest to maintain this bill. If once this bill pass, and, as in queen Eliz.'s time, Protestants are put into places of trust, you may be sure of the good effects of your bill. Where 10 were of the mind for this Bill a twelve-month ago, there are an 100 now that will bleed for it. In plain English, let us show the world that the Protestant religion is dear to us, and that we have the law on our sides to maintain it.

Sir *Tho. Littleton*. I was mistaken by some gentlemen, therefore I desire to be rectified. I shall be very short, and tender of you, having sat long. It is objected 'the uncertainty this Expedient will lie under, if the duke have a son;' which is thus answered; 'That then the princesses respectively shall succeed in the regency;' which obviates an incurable absurdity in the former Bill of Exclusion. For if the duke have a son, the lady cannot descend from the throne. This Bill of Exclusion is so weak a thing, that it will require all the props imaginable to support it; and a train of consequences will follow. What you have been told of Scotland is worthy your consideration: if Scotland is not consenting, I know not how you will obviate that; I fear it may unite the Papists of England and France.

Mr. *Boscawen*. Littleton may be convinced of the weakness of the Expedient by his own argument. For by so much the easier it is for the princess to descend from the Regency, so much the less is our security. And as for the objection of Scotland, the same interest which passes the Bill of Exclusion here, will do it in Scotland; and for Ireland there is no need of it. By the proposition of the Expedient, all commissions for sea, land, and the church must go from the regent in the duke's name; and if all dispatches, &c. must go under his name, there will be still no security, for the oaths of allegiance and supremacy must be taken to the duke; and if that be not a true proposition, 'That we are not to take up arms against the king, nor those commissioned by him,' I know not why it was by law obliged to be taken by all that execute the Militia; and if that be a true proposition, why must it be destroyed by this Expedient now? The thing lies loose to me. Methinks, this Expedient of the Regency seems to me as if a man that sat by the fire and burnt his shins, instead of removing himself farther off, should send for a mason to remove the chimney back farther from him. I have heard, that, if a man make a freehold lease to commence from the date thereof, it is void. It would be far more ingenuous for gentlemen to say, 'That if you do pass the Bill of Exclusion, they will not be bound by it, but will have the duke to succeed;' and then I wish they would tell us what will save the Protestant religion. If the duke do come in, will gentlemen chuse either to turn Papists, or to be burnt or hanged? If this proposition would keep out popery, I would accept of it. I have no disrespect to the duke; but if I am to leap over a river, I had better have no staff than a broken one; and this Expedient is no security. If it must be in the power of the council and the regent to dispose of the public treasury, to make war and peace, pray where is the government? Where is the monarchy? Either they will be faithful and keep this law of regency, and the duke shall be king but by name, and so take away the soul of the government, or they will let the duke in to govern as king.

The debate thus ended, and this Vote passed, viz. "The house having taken into solemn debate and consideration, the means for the Security of the Protestant Religion, and for Safety of the King's Person, doth resolve, That a Bill be brought in to exclude James duke of York from inheriting the Imperial crowns of England and Ireland, and the dominions and territories thereunto belonging; and that a committee be appointed to draw up the said Bill."

A gentleman moved, 'That this Bill might also exclude all other Popish Successors.' To which

Mr. *Hampden* answered, He believed the gentleman made the motion with a good intent; but this is a Bill for the purpose only of the duke's Exclusion, and that for all other Popish Successors may be done in another Bill hereafter; for the way to lose a Bill is to clog it with too many things.

Debate on the Lords refusing to proceed upon Fitzharris's Impeachment.] March 26. p. m. The commons were informed, 'That the lords had refused to proceed upon the impeachment of the commons against Edw. Fitzharris; and had directed, That he should be proceeded against at the common law.'*

* "The Commons' Impeachment against Fitzharris was rejected by the lords upon a pretence with which the lord Nottingham furnished them. It was this: Edw. iii. had got some commoners, the six murderers of Edward ii. to be condemned by the lords, of which when the commons complained, an Order was made,

Sir *Wm. Jones.* In a matter so very plain nd conspicuous, as the refusal of this Impeachment by the lords, I am unwilling to make unecessary doubts. If indeed an inferior court ad proceeded to Judgment in this matter of 'itzharris, then it might have been pleaded in ar against the Impeachment of the commons. 'here was an indictment against the lords in he Tower, in the King's-bench, found upon ecord, and yet that was no impediment to heir trial by the impeachment of the commons; but in this case of Fitzharris, here is no ndictment or prosecution begun in any inferior ourt of law. We have a precedent fresh in nemory of the Impeachment of a commoner t the lords bar, if the lords doubt that, which vas of my lord chief justice Scroggs; so that ve need not spend our time to search for precedents to maintain our right at a conference vith the lords. Perhaps the Lords Journals re not yet made up into form; but some nembers have taken notes out of their minutes, nd find that the lords have dismissed the Impeachment against Fitzharris, and left him to rial at common law, and have ordered it so by he lords spiritual as well as temporal; and in his case they have determined a great point, 'That the lords spiritual have power to judge n an Impeachment of capital matters,' which ve never own, nor ever shall, and here we are enied justice by those who have no right to ote it. In this the lords have done a double ct of injustice. Seeing then that the lords ave taken upon them to throw out this Impeachment, let us assert and declare our right f impeaching in capital causes, and that the ords have denied us justice in refusing the Impeachment against Fitzharris; and then, after aving asserted our privilege, let us draw up ur Reasons to maintain it, and make it part f our conference to show the lords, how unreasonable the lords actions have been in their 'roceedings.

Sir *Fr. Winnington.* If this refusal of the ords was an ordinary Impeachment of Monopolies, or the like, I should not press you in he matter; but this is not an ordinary consideration, but that which relates to our Religion nd Property; and how the bishops come in o stifle this Impeachment, let God and the vorld judge! I would know if there be an impeachment against a man from the commons, nd no indictment upon record against him in the courts below, only the attorney-general told the lords, that the king gave him directions to prosecute Fitzharris, and there is no Record against him. If the lords vote, 'That the commons shall not impeach this man,' they may as well vote, That we shall not be Protestants. But yet we will be Protestants. I take this to be a new Plot against the Protestant Religion, and we impeach this man, and the lords fairly say, 'We will not hear it.' If this be the case, I desire you will come to some vote. You are willing to discover this Plot if you could. If the attorney-general had prepared the prosecution of Fitzharris, and, as Jones said, if the inferior courts had proceeded to judgment against him, then that judgment is pleaded in bar against an Impeachment. But if our time be short to be here (as I believe it is) pray do not delay discharging your part in this matter. If the house be satisfied in it, pray make a vote, to assert your own right. A little while ago, we knew, that the Judges of the King's-bench discharged the Grand Jury, whilst the indictment against the duke of York, for a Popish Recusant, was depending: this proceeding of the lords, in rejecting the Impeachment of Fitzharris, seems as if the house of lords intended to justify that proceeding of the Judges by their own. It is a just reflection of weakness to doubt in a plain matter. If no gentleman doubts of our right of impeaching, pray vote it so.

Sir *Rob. Howard.* I am glad we are off from one great thing, viz. the Exclusion of the duke. I cannot believe but that, in this matter of rejecting the Impeachment of Fitzharris, the lords have cause for what they do. In this matter, precedents you need not search; you have instances of very late date: but this of Fitzharris seems to me to be a more dangerous breath than usual, a breath fit to be stifled. There is something in this more than ordinary. If this be a sacred respect in the lords to the common trials of England by juries in the inferior courts, it is strange that, in the case of Skinner, the lords should contend with the commons about the trial of it, though an original cause. This refusal of the lords seems to me to be no great value of the law of England, but a value of Fitzharris to keep him from us. When I have seen, in all the speeches to-day relating to the Duke's Exclusion, that the duke goes not single, but all along associated with Popery—I have heard such excellent discourses to-day of that matter, that I am loth to mingle my weakness with them; but these are such counsels from the lords, that I believe hereafter the king will have no cause to thank the lords, or those that were the originals, for involving him in the fatality of them. They will make the traiterous Libel of Fitzharris the copy of their counsels. Dangerfield was a man reputed most infamous, yet if he would discover what he knew of that sham Presbyterian Plot, nothing of mercy was too big for him; but Fitzharris, a man of no infamy, must be hurried away from Newgate to the Tower, when he

---

That no such thing should be done for the uture.' Now, that related only to proceedings t the king's suit; but it could not be meant, hat an Impeachment from the commons did ot lie against a commoner. Judges, secretaies of state, and the lord keeper, were often ommoners. So if this was good law, here was certain method offered to the court, to be roubled no more with Impeachments, by emloying only commoners. In short, the peers aw the design of this Impeachment, and were esolved not to receive it, and so made use of his colour to reject it." Burnet.

was disposed to confess the whole Plot to those gentlemen who examined him. Are you so lost, that there is no mercy left for the Protestant Religion? If the terror of his condition incline him to discover all, must he now be taken out of our hands? We hear of other things too; that the French ambassador had a hand in the contrivance of this Plot with him, and can that be enquired into by a common jury, who are to concern themselves in no more, than whether Fitzharris be guilty, or not guilty? I must confess, that with the carriage of this, I have enlarged my suspicion, and I must always expect unusual ways. We see that the worst of mankind has been pardoned, with all his villainies about him, upon an ingenuous confession; but what provocation has there been from Fitzharris, to be thus hurried away to trial at common-law in a disposition to confess all, and so be out of the reach of pardon, should that disposition continue upon him? But I am persuaded something depends upon this man, as well as upon the Bill we ordered to-day. When I saw the temper of the house, when Jenkins refused your Message (p. 1314) (and there was something in that too) that the house would make no breach upon it, and passed it over with great temper, that now we must lay down all prosecution of the Plot, and that the Protestant Religion shall have no mercy! Fitzharris may merit by his confession, where he may reasonably hope for the same intercession for his pardon, that much blacker offenders have obtained; but if his breath be stopped, I am sorry the people should have occasion to say, 'If it were not for the lords, the Protestant Religion might have been saved.' Therefore I move, that, in the wording of your Vote, you will not only say, 'That the lords rejection of this Impeachment is not only a subverting the constitution of parliament, but 'of the Protestant Religion' also; and I hope you will do this with the same calmness of mind that every man does wish that loves his religion.

Serj. *Maynard.* This damnable Popish Plot is still on foot in England, and I am sure in Ireland too; and what arts and crafts have been used to hide this Plot! It began with the murder of a magistrate (Godfrey,) then with perjury and false Subornation, and this of Fitzharris is a second part of that. We sent up an Impeachment to the lords against Fitzharris, and told the lords, 'That, in due time, we would bring up Articles against him,' and the lords refuse to try him. In effect, they make us no parliament. If we are the prosecutors, and they will not hear our accusation, their own lives, as well as ours, are concerned. This is a strange way of proceeding; the same day we impeach Fitzharris, they vote we shall not prosecute him: now, when all is at stake, we must not prosecute. If this be so, Holland must submit, and let the French run over all. This is a strange breach of privilege of parliament, and tends to the danger of the king's person, and the destruction of the Protestant Religion, and I hope you will vote it so.

Sir *Tho. Player.* I shall make you a motion, but first I shall say we have had a considerable discovery of the former Plot. I call it the old plot, but this of Fitzharris has been new upon us. This is still a confirmation of the intention of murdering the king, the duke consenting to destroy his own brother and our king. I have often heard it whispered, that the design of Madame's voyage to Dover was to promote the Popish Religion, but it is plain that Godfrey was murdered by the Papists, and that the army mustered on Black-heath was raised with intentions to destroy the protestants in Holland, and to awe the city of London. When Fitzharris gave intimation, that he would discover what he knew of this Plot, and that two or three hon. members of this house had examined him, this man was fetched the next day to Whitehall, and from thence hurried away to the Tower, and so we were deprived of all farther hopes of discovery from him. We now revive the information from an Impeachment, and now this man must not be brought hither to be tried: he must be tryed in an inferior court, that his mouth may be stopped, and put out of capacity to discover. This being the case, I move, 'That if any judges, justices of the peace, juries, &c. shall proceed upon the Trial of this man, that you will vote them guilty of his murder, and betrayers of the rights of the commons of England.'

Resolutions in the Case of Fitzharris.] The house then resolved, 1. "That it is the undoubted right of the commons, in parliament assembled, to impeach, before the lords in parliament, any peer or commoner for treason, or any other crime or misdemeanor; and that the refusal of the lords to proceed in parliament upon such Impeachment is a denial of justice, and a violation of the constitution of parliaments. 2. That, in the case of Edw. Fitzharris, who, by the commons, has been impeached for High-Treason, before the lords, with a declaration, 'That in convenient time they would bring up the Articles against him;' for the lords to resolve, 'That the said Edw. Fitzharris should be proceeded with according to the course of common-law,' and not by way of Impeachment in parliament, at this time, is a denial of justice, and a violation of the constitution of parliaments, and an obstruction to the farther discovery of the Popish Plot, and of great danger to his majesty's Person, and the Protestant Religion. 3. That for any inferior court to proceed against Edw. Fitzharris, or any other person lying under an Impeachment in parliament for the same crimes for which he or they stand impeached, is an high breach of the privilege of parliament."

Protest relative to Fitzharris's Impeachment.] On the question being put in the house of lords, Whether Edw. Fitzharris shall be proceeded with according to the course of the Common Law, and not by way of Impeachment in parliament at this time? It was resolved in the affirmative. Before the putting of the above-said question, leave was asked for entering Protestations; which was granted.

"Dissentient; Because that in all ages it hath been an undoubted right of the commons to impeach before the lords any subject for treasons, or any crime whatsoever; and the reason is, because great offences, that influence the government, are most effectually determined in parliament. We cannot reject the Impeachment of the commons, because that suit or complaint can be determined no where else; for if the party impeached should be indicted in the King's-bench, or in any other court, for the same offence, yet it is not the same suit; for an Impeachment is at the suit of the people, and they have an interest in it; but an indictment is at the suit of the king: for one and the same offence may entitle several persons to several suits; as, if a murder be committed, the king may indict at his suit; or the heir, or the wife of the party murdered, may bring an Appeal, and the king cannot release that appeal, nor his Indictment prevent the proceedings in the appeal, because the appeal is the suit of the party, and he hath an interest in it.—It is, as we conceive, an absolute denial of justice, in regard (as it is said before) the same suit can be tried no where else: the house of peers, as to Impeachments, proceed by virtue of the judicial power, and not by their legislative; and as to that act, as a court of record, and can deny suitors (especially the commons of England) that bring legal complaints before them, no more than the justices of Westminster-Hall, or other courts, can deny any suit or criminal cause that is regularly commenced before them. Our law saith, in the person of the king, 'Nulli negabimus justitiam,' We will deny justice to no single person;' yet here, as we apprehend, justice is denied to the whole body of the people. And this may be interpreted an exercising of an arbitrary power, and will, we fear, have influence upon the constitution of the English government, and be an encouragement to all inferior courts to exercise the same arbitrary power, by denying the presentments of grand juries, &c. for which at this time the chief justice stands impeached in the house of peers. This proceeding may misrepresent the house of peers to the king and people, especially at this time, and the more in the particular case of Edw. Fitzharris, who is publickly known to be concerned in vile and horrid treasons against his majesty, and a great conspirator in the Popish Plot to murder the king, and destroy and subvert the Protestant Religion. (Signed,) Kent, Shaftsbury, Macclesfield, Herbert, Sunderland, Essex, Crewe, Bedford, Stamford, Westmorland, Salisbury, P. Wharton, Mordaunt, Grey, Paget, Cornwallis, Huntingdon, Clare, Monmouth, J. Lovelace."

Debate on the first Reading of the Bill of Exclusion.] March 28. The Bill for excluding the duke of York, &c. was read the first time.

Sir *Leoline Jenkins.* This Bill before you is very extraordinary. There was never the like before in parliament. No bill was ever offered in parliament so much against the justice of the nation. Here is a great prince condemned before he is heard. Next, it is *ex post facto* very extraordinary, and against the justice of the nation; and not only so, but against the wisdom of the nation too; for it will introduce a change in the government. If the duke should try to cut this law with his sword, and he should overcome, the same power that can set aside this law will set aside all laws both of our Religion and Property; the power will be in the hands of a conqueror, and he will certainly change the government. This is against the religion of the nation. We ought to pay obedience to our governors, whether good or bad, be they ever so faulty or criminal. Heathen princes were obeyed by Christians *in licitis et honestis.* And we are 'not to do evil that good may come of it,' or for any prospect of good. One word more: this Bill is against the oaths of the nation, the oaths of Allegiance and Supremacy. We are bound by those oaths, in the eye of the law, to the duke, and I am consequentially sworn to him. Every oath is to be taken in the sense of the lawgiver; and if this bill pass into a law, who can dispense with me from that oath to the king? Possibly I am too tedious, and not willingly heard. This Bill is against our Religion, against the government and wisdom of the nation; and I hope you will throw it out. [Jenkins's argument being the same with that of the last parliament, which was then fully answered, passed off without notice.]

Mr. *Bennet.* Jenkins has moved to throw out this bill, and that he might be heard patiently. Nobody, it seems, seconds him; therefore pray let him go on, and second himself.

The Bill was ordered to be read a second time next day, in a full house.

Sir *Wm. Jones.* As to the Votes you passed on Saturday, upon occasion of the lords rejecting your Impeachment against Fitzharris, because there has been discourse of them in the town, and I believe will be, in time, in the nation, though what has been done will be made good, let us give all men satisfaction that we are in the right. Amongst our other misfortunes, in this place we are far from Records and Books, and so it will not be easy to prepare ourselves to argue this. But according to the little I have looked into this matter, I find that it is the undeniable right of the commons to bring Impeachments in parliament not only against lords but commoners; and Magna Charta says not only that Subjects shall be tried 'per judicium parium suorum,' but 'per legem terræ.' And Trial in Parliament is lex terræ. I have heard of a Record of 4. Ed. iii. where when a lord, the earl of March—

The Black-Rod knocked at the door, and gave notice that the king commanded the attendance of the house immediately in the house of lords.

The Parliament suddenly dissolved.] The house went up accordingly; where his majesty made a short Speech to this effect:

"My lords and gentlemen; That all the world may see to what a point we are come, that we are not like to have a good end, when the divisions at the beginning are such: therefore, my Lord Chancellor, do as I have commanded you."

Then the Lord Chancellor said; "My lords and gentlemen; His majesty has commanded me to say, That it is his royal pleasure and will, that this parliament be dissolved: and this parliament is dissolved*."

* "By the steps which the commons had already made, the king saw what might be expected from them; so, very suddenly, and not very decently, he came to the house of lords, the crown being carried between his feet in a sedan: and he put on his robes in haste, without any previous notice, and called up the commons, and dissolved the parliament; and went with such haste to Windsor, that it looked as if he was afraid of the crowds that this meeting had brought to Oxford." Burnet.

Ferguson asserts "That the Conspirators (meaning the Court) having received intelligence that Fitzharris's wife and maid were come to Oxford, in order to discover what they knew, resolved to put a stop to the career of the commons early on Monday morning by a dissolution; which was resolved on late the night before, in the cabinet-council at Christ-Church." Growth of Popery, part ii. p. 194.

And Mr. North gives the following detail both of the cause and manner of this extraordinary event: "The commons complained, that the Convocation-House was too strait for them to sit and transact in; and, at their desire, orders were given for the immediate fitting up the Theatre for their use. The king concerned himself much about the disposition of it, viewed the design, gave his judgment, and came in person among the workmen; and particularly, on Saturday, March 26, 1681, I had the honour of seeing him there, and observed his taking notice of every thing. On Sunday next his maj. was pleased, especially towards the evening, to entertain himself and his court with discourse of the wonderful accommodations the house of commons would find in that place; and by his observations and descriptions showed how it was to be. All this while the spies and eves-droppers could find no symptom of a dissolution, but rather of the contrary, that the parliament was likely to make a long session of it. The next morning, which was Monday, the king came to the house of lords, as he was wont, in a chair, and another chair followed with the curtains drawn; but instead of a lord, as was thought to be in it, there were only the king's robes. Thus they went and sat down in a withdrawing room. When the robe-chair was opened, a gross mistake appeared, for the garter robes were put up instead of the robes of state! so the chair must go back with an officer to bring the right. A lord happened to be in the room, who, upon this discovery, was stepping out (as they thought) to give the alarm: upon which, those with the king prevailed to continue his lordship in the room till the chair returned, and matters were fixed, and then he had his liberty." Examen. p. 104, 105.

SUMMARY OF THE REMAINING PART OF KING CHARLES II.'S REIGN.] This was the last Parliament called by Charles II.; though in a Declaration which he published, on the 8th of April, for satisfying his people, after reckoning up all the hard things that had been done in the three last parliaments, and setting forth their undutiful behaviour to himself in many instances, in conclusion, he assured them "That nothing should ever alter his affection to the Protestant religion as established by law, nor his love to parliaments: for he would still have frequent parliaments *."—Sir Francis Pemberton having succeeded Scroggs as Chief Justice, Fitzharris's Trial came on in Easter term. His Impeachment in parliament was over-ruled, the lords having thrown it out, and the proof was so full, that he was condemned. Upon this, seeing there was no hope, he charged lord Howard with being the author of the Libel, who was immediately sent to the Tower, and lay there till Michaelmas term, and then was discharged by the Habeas Corpus act; Fitzharris's wife and maid, who were the two witnesses against him, being so evidently forsworn, that the attorney-general withdrew the bill. Fitzharris was executed, and soon after College, a joiner, charged, by Dugdale, Turberville, and others, with being concerned in a Protestant Plot to kill the king at Oxford. The grand jury at London refused to find the bill. Upon which he was carried to Oxford, and there was tried, condemned, and executed, denying to the last all that was sworn against him. In like manner, the earl of Shaftesbury, upon the evidence of the Irish witnesses, being sent to the Tower, the grand jury, to the great chagrin of the court, rejected the bill. A few days after, Turberville, being seized with the small pox, persisted in his last moments in avowing the truth of all that he had sworn both against lord Shaftsbury and lord Stafford; so that the last words of dying men being opposed to the last words of those that suffered, must leave the impartial ever in the dark.—In Scotland, in 1682, the earl of Argyle, for refusing to take the Tests there enacted, without his own explanation, which he did not scruple unguardedly to avow, was immediately committed to Edinburgh castle, tried, and condemned, and had he not made his escape, would probably have suffered. The duke of York was now permitted to return to court, and seemed to have overcome all difficulties. And to remove all fears of future parliaments, the cities and boroughs of England were pre-

* For an Answer to this Declaration, written by sir Wm. Jones, see Appendix No. XV.

vailed on to surrender their charters, and take new ones, modeled as the court thought fit. The earl of Sunderland, who had been disgraced after the Exclusion Parliament, was restored, and lord Conway was made the other secretary *. And on the death of lord Nottingham, the seals were given to lord chief justice North, who was created lord Guilford. The city of London refusing to surrender its charter, judgment was given against it in the King's Bench.—The year 1683 will long be remembered for the fatal catastrophe of lord Russel and Algernon Sidney. That a rising was intended, and that lord Russel was present when it was discoursed of, cannot be denied; but that he was guilty of the treason alleged, of conspiring the king's death, or could have been condemned but by a packed jury and corrupt judges, is equally undeniable. In fact, the Bill of Exclusion was his death warrant. He was beheaded in Lincoln's Inn Fields in July. And the earl of Essex, for the same conspiracy, being sent to the Tower, was found in his room with his throat cut the very morning of his friend's trial. Col. Sidney was tried next, and upon the single evidence of lord Howard, added to an unfinished manuscript of his own writing, found in his closet, he also, by an unheard-of stretch of law, was condemned and executed. Need it be added, that he was one of the first that had moved for the Exclusion? Soon after this, the duke of Monmouth (who had made his escape) upon his confession was pardoned, but upon his recantation was again disgraced. Mr. Hampden, on lord Howard's evidence, was fined in the sum of 40,000*l.* (Feb. 6.) and Holloway, by the hopes of a pardon being induced to confess, and sir Tho. Armstrong, being seized in Holland (though the time of his coming in was not elapsed) were both executed. The earl of Danby and the popish lords were bailed, and Oates being prosecuted at the duke's suit for Scandalum Magnatum was fined 100,000*l.* To conclude, on Feb. 6, 1684-5, king Charles died, confirming on his death bed that attachment to popery of which he was suspected during his life.

JAMES II.

James II. proclaimed.] Immediately after the death of Charles II. such of the lords of the privy-council, together with such other of the lords spiritual and temporal as were in town, assembled together, to the number of above forty; and without hesitation signed an Instrument for proclaiming the duke of York and Albany king, by the name of James II. In which were these words; "We, the lords spiritual and temporal, assisted with those of his late majesty's privy-council, with numbers of other principal gentlemen of quality, with the lord-mayor, aldermen and citizens of London, do now, hereby, with one full voice and consent of tongue and heart, publish and proclaim, That the high and mighty prince James ii. is now, by the death of our late sovereign of happy memory, become our lawful, lineal, and rightful liege lord, &c. To whom we do acknowledge all faith and constant obedience, with all hearty and humble affection; beseeching God, 'by whom kings do reign,' to bless the royal king James ii. with a long and happy reign over us."

The King's first Speech in Council.] The same day, the new king made the following Speech to his privy-council, at whose request it was made public.

"My lords; Before I enter upon any other business, I think fit to say something to you. Since it hath pleased Almighty God to place me in this station, and I am now to succeed so good and gracious a king, as well as so kind a brother, I think it fit to declare to you, that I will endeavour to follow his example, and most especially in that of his great clemency and tenderness to his people. I have been reported to be a man for arbitrary power, but that is not the only story that has been made of me; and I shall make it my endeavour to preserve this government both in Church and State, as it is now by law established. I know the principles of the Church of England are for Monarchy, and the members of it have shewed themselves good and loyal subjects; therefore I shall always take care to defend and support it. I know too, that the laws of England are sufficient to make the king as great a monarch as I can wish; and as I shall never depart from the just right and prerogative of the crown, so I shall never invade any man's property. I have often heretofore ventured my life in defence of the nation, and I shall still go as far as any man in preserving it in all its just rights and liberties."

He likewise set forth a Proclamation signifying, "That all persons, who at the decease of the late King, were lawfully possessed of any office, whether civil or military, within the realms of England and Ireland, or any other of his dominions thereunto belonging, particularly all presidents, lieutenants, vice-presidents, justices of the peace, sheriffs, &c. should be continued in the said places and offices, as formerly they held and enjoyed the same, until the king's pleasure shall be further known. That all persons then in offices, of whatsoever degree or condition, shall not fail, every one according to his place, office, or charge, to proceed in the performance and execution of all duties thereunto belonging, as formerly appertained to them while the late king was living; and that all the king's subjects should be aiding and assisting to the command of the said officers and ministers in the performance of

* In the Appendix to the present volume, No. XVI. will be found a valuable Paper entitled "The Earl of Anglesey's State of the Government and Kingdom, prepared and intended for his majesty, King Charles ii. in the year 1682."

their respective offices and places, upon pain of the king's displeasure. Lastly, That all orders and directions made or given by the lords of the privy-council of the late king in his life-time, should be obeyed and performed by all and every person, as it should or had been obeyed in the life of the late king."

After which, the late king was no sooner buried, but his royal brother acquainted the world, that he died a Roman-Catholic, and publicly appeared at mass himself. He, likewise, by another Proclamation, declared, "That he had thought fit to call a parliament speedily to be assembled, in which he made no doubt but care would be taken for settling a sufficient Revenue upon the crown, for the support of the government; the necessities of which, in the mean time, required that the Customs and Subsidies, and other Duties upon Merchandizes, should be continued to be collected, as in the time of his dearest brother lately deceased."

The First and only Parliament held in the Reign of James II.

List of the House of Commons.] May 19, 1685. This day the Parliament met. The following is a List of the Members of the House of Commons:

A List of King James's Parliament, summoned to meet May 19, 1685; and dissolved by Proclamation July 2, 1686.

Abington,
Sir John Stonehouse.
Agmondesham,
Sir William Drake,
William Cheyne.
St. Albans,
George Churchill,
Thomas Dockwray.
Aldborough, (Suffolk)
John Bence,
Henry Bedingfield,
Aldborough, (Yorkshire)
Sir Michael Wentworth.
Sir Roger Strickland.
Allerton, North,
Sir David Fowlis,
Sir Henry Marwood.
Andover,
Sir John Collins,
Robert Phillips.
Anglesea,
Visc. Bulkley.
Appleby,
Sackvil Tufton,
Philip Musgrave.
Arundel,
William Garroway,
Wm. Westbroke.
Ashburton,
Edward Yard,
William Stawel.
Aylesbury,
Sir William Egerton,
Richard Anderson.
Bambury,
Sir Dudley North.
Barnstaple,
Sir A. Chichester,
John Basset.
Bath City,
Sir William Basset,
Visc. Fitzharding.
Beaumaris,
Henry Bulkley.
Bedfordshire,
Sir Villiers Charnock,
William Boteler.
Bedford Town,
Thomas Christie,
Sir Anthony Chester.
Bedwin,
Lemuel Kingdon,
Thomas Lowder.
Berkshire,
Sir Humphry Forster,
Richard Southbey.
Berwick
Philip Bickerstaffe,
Ralph Widdrington.
Beverly,
Michael Wharton,
Sir Ralph Wharton.
Bewdley,
Sir Chas. Lyttleton,
Bishops Castle,
Edmund Warring,
Francis Charlton.
Bletchingly,
Ambrose Brown,
Sir Marmaduke Gresham.
Bodmin,
Nicholas Glynn,
Hender. Roberts.
Boralston,
Sir John Maynard,
Sir Benj. Bathurst.
Boroughbridge,
Sir Thomas Meleverer,
Sir Henry Goodrick.
Bossiny,
John Cotton,
John Mountsteven.
Boston,
Lord Willoughby,
Peregrine Bertie.
Brackley,
Sir Richard Wenman,
James Griffin.
Bramber,
Sir Thomas Bludworth,
Wm. Bridgman.
Brecon County,
M. of Worcester, *waved*
Edw. Jones.
Brecon Town,
M. of Worcester, *waved*
John Jeffreys.
Bridgwater,
Sir Haswell Tynt,
Sir Francis Warre.
Bridport,
Hugh Hodges,
Thomas Chafe.
Bristol,
Sir Richard Crump,
Sir John Churchill.
Bridgenorth,
Roger Pope,
Sir William Whitmore.
Buckinghamshire,
Thomas Wharton,
Lord Brackley.
Buckingham Town,
Sir Ralph Verney.
Sir Richard Temple.
Callington,
Sir John Coriton,
William Coriton.
Calne,
Sir John Ernly,
Thomas Webb.
Cambridgeshire,
Sir Levinus Bennet,
Sir Robert Cotton.
Cambridge Town,
William Wren,
Sir Thomas Chichley.
Cambridge University.
Sir Thomas Exton,
Robert Brady.
Camelford.
Nicholas Courtney,
Hump. Langford, *(dead)*
Sir Charles Scarborough,
Canterbury,
Sir Wm. Honywood,
Henry Lee.
Cardiff,
Francis Gwynn.
Cardigan County,
John Lewis.
Cardigan Town,
Hector Philips.
Carlisle,
James Graham.
Sir Christ. Musgrave.
Caermarthen County,
Lord Vaughan.
Caermarthen Town,
Richard Vaughan.
Caernarvon County,
Thomas Bulkley.
Caernarvon Town,
John Griffith, *(dead)*
Castle-rising,
Sir Nich. L'Estrange,
Thomas Howard.
Chester County,
Sir Philip Egerton,
Thomas Cholmondeley.
Chester City,
Sir Thomas Grosvenor.
Robert Werden.
Chichester,
Sir Richard May.
George Gunter.
Chippenham,
Henry Baynton,
Sharring. Talbot *(dead)*
Richard Kent.
Chipping Wycombe,
Sir Dennis Hampson,
Edward Baldwyn.
Christ Church,
Sir Thomas Clarges,
Anthony Ettrick.
Cirencester,
Earl of Newburgh,
Thomas Master.
Clithero,
James Stanley,
Edward Ashton.
Cockermouth,
Sir Daniel Fleming,
Sir Orlando Gee.
Colchester,
Sir Walter Clarges,
Nathaniel Lawrance.
Corf-Castle,
Sir Nathan Napier,
Richard Fownes.
Cornwall,
Lord Bodmyn, *(removed)*
F. Roberts, *(in his room)*
Lord Lansdown.
Coventry,
Sir Roger Cave,
Sir Thomas Norton.
Cricklade,
Edmund Webb,
T. Freake, *(discharged)*
Charles Fox.
Cumberland,
Sir John Lowther,
Visc. Preston.
Dartmouth,
Roger Pomeroy,
Arthur Farewell.
Denbighshire,
Sir Richard Middleton.
Denbigh Town,
Sir John Trevor.
Derbyshire,
Sir Robert Coke,
Sir Gilbert Clarke.
Derby Town,
John Coke,
William Allestrey.
Devizes,
Sir John Talbot,

Walter Grub.
Devonshire,
Sir Bouchier Wrey,
Sir Copleston Bampfylde.
Dorchester,
Edward Miller,
William Churchill.
Dorsetshire,
Thomas Strangeways,
Thomas Freak.
Dover,
Arthur Herbert,
William Chapman.
Downton,
Maurice Blockland,
Sir Chas. Raleigh.
Droitwich,
Samuel Sandys, jun.
Thomas Windsor,
Dunwich,
Roger North,
Thomas Knyvett.
Durham County,
Robert Byerly,
William Lambton.
Durham City,
Sir Richard Lloyd,
Charles Montagu.
East Low,
Charles Trelawny,
Sir William Trumbull.
Edmunds Bury,
Sir Thomas Harvey,
William Crofts.
Essex,
Sir W. Maynard,
Sir Thomas Fanshaw.
Evesham,
Henry Parker,
Sir J. Matthews.
Exeter,
Edward Seymour,
James Walker.
Eye,
Sir John Rous,
Sir Charles Gawdy.
Flintshire,
Sir John Conway.
Flint Town,
Sir John Hanmer.
Fowey,
John Trefry,
Bevil Granville.
Gatton,
Sir Thomas Thompson,
Thomas Turgis.
Germain's,
Sir Thomas Huggins,
Daniel Elliot.
Glamorgan,
Sir Edward Mansel.
Gloucestershire,
Marquis of Worcester.
Sir Robert Atkyns.
Gloucester City,
John Wagstaffe.
John Powel.
Grampound,
Sir Joseph Tredenham.
Robert Foley.
Grantham,
Thomas Harrington,
John Thorold.
Grimsby,
Sir Edward Ayscough,
Sir T. Barnardiston.
Grimstead,
Simon Smith,
Thomas Jones.
Guildford,
Henry Finch.
Richard Onslow.
Harwich,
Sir Anthony Deane,
Samuel Pepys.
Haslemere,
Sir George Vernon,
Sir Geo. Woodrooffe.
Hastings,
Sir Dennis Ashburnham,
John Ashburnham.
Haverford West,
William Wogan.
Helston,
Charles Godolphin,
Sidney Godolphin.
Herefordshire,
Sir John Morgan,
Sir John Hoskyns.
Hereford City,
Thomas Geers,
Herbert Aubery.
Hertfordshire,
Ralph Freeman,
Thomas Halsey.
Hertford Town,
Sir Thomas Byrde,
Sir Fr. Boteler.
Heydon,
Henry Guy,
Charles Duncombe.
Heytesbury,
William Ash,
Edward Ash.
Higham,
Sir Lewis Palmer.
Hindon,
Robert Hyde,
Thomas Lambert.
Honiton,
Edmund Walrond,
Sir Thomas Putt.
Horsham,
Anthony Eversfield,
John Mitchel.
Huntingdonshire,
Sir John Cotton,
Sir Lionel Walden.
Huntingdon Town,
Oliver Montagu.
Lionel Walden.
Hythe,
Heneage Finch,
Julius Finch *(discharged)*
Wm. Shaw.
Ilchester,
Sir Edward Wyndham,
Sir Edw. Phillips.
Ipswich,
Sir Nich. Bacon.
Sir J. Barker.
Ives, (St.)
Charles Davenant,
James St. Amand.
Kent,
Sir William Twysden,
Sir John Knatchbull.
Kingston,
Sir Willoughby Hickman,
John Ramsden.
Knaresborough,
Henry Slingsby,
William Stockdale.
Lancaster County,
Sir Roger Bradshaw,
James Holt.
Lancaster Town,
Roger Kirkby,
Henry Crispe.
Lanceston,
John Greenville,
Sir Hugh Pyper.
Leicestershire,
Lord Sherrard,
John Verney.
Leicester Town,
Sir Henry Beaumont,
Thomas Babington.
Leominster,
Thomas Coningsby,
Robert Cornwall.
Leskard,
Chichester Wrey,
John Connock.
Lestwithiel,
Sir John Carew,
Walter Kendal.
Lewes,
Richard Bridger,
Thomas Pelham.
Lincolnshire,
Sir Thomas Hussey,
Lord Castleton.
Lincoln City,
Sir Henry Monson,
Sir Thomas Meres.
Litchfield,
Thomas Orme,
Richard Leveson.
Liverpool,
Sir Richard Atherton,
Thomas Leigh.
London,
Sir John More,
Sir Wm. Pritchard,
Sir S. Dashwood,
Sir Peter Rich.
Ludlow,
Sir Edw. Herbert,
Wm. Charlton, *(dead)*.
Sir Josiah Child.
Ludgershall,
Thomas Neal,
Henry Clarke.
Lyme,
John Pole,
Sir Winston Churchill.
Lymington,
Richard Holt,
John Burrard.
Lynn,
Sir John Turner,
Sir Simon Taylor.
Maidstone,
Sir John Tufton, *(dead)*
Edward Waytt,
Archibald Clincard.
Malden,
Sir Thomas Darcy,
Sir John Bramston.
Malmsbury,
Sir Thomas Estcourt,
John Fitzherbert.
Malton,
Thomas Fairfax,
Thomas Worsley.
Marlborough,
Sir J. Ernly,
George Willoughby.
Marlow,
Sir Humphrey Wynch,
Sir John Borlace.
Mawes, (St.)
Sir J. Tredenham, *waved*
Henry Seymour, jun.
Peter Prideaux.
Melcomb,
George Strangways,
Francis Mohun.
Merionethshire,
Sir John Wynn.
Midhurst,
Sir Wm. Morley.
John Lewknor.
Middlesex,
Sir Charles Gerrard,
Ralph Hawtry.
Milbourn,
John Hunt,
Henry Bull.
Minehead,
Nathaniel Palmer.
Francis Lutterel.
Michael, (St.)
Thomas Price,
John Vyvyan.
Monmouthshire,
Marquis of Worcester,
Sir Charles Kemeys.
Monmouth Town,
M. of Worcester, *waved*.
Sir James Herbert.
Morpeth,
Sir Henry Puckering,
Theophilus Oglethorpe.
Montgomeryshire,
Edward Vaughan.
Montgomery Town,
W. Williams, *(removed)*
Charles Herbert.
Newark,
Henry Saville,
Philip D'Arcy.
Newcastle, (Staffordsh.)
Edw. Maynwaring,
William Sneyd.
Newcastle, (Northum.)
Sir Nathaniel Johnson,
Sir William Blacket.
Newport, (Cornwall)
William Morice,
John Specott.
Newport, (Hants)
Sir Robert Holmes,
Sir Wm. Stevens.
Newton, (Lancashire)
Thomas Done.
Wm. Blathwaite.

Newton, (Hants)
Thomas Done,
Wm. Blaithwaite.
Norfolk County,
Sir Thomas Hare,
Sir Jacob Astley.
Northamptonshire,
Sir Roger Norwich,
Edward Montagu.
Northampton Town,
Sir Justinian Isham,
Richard Rainsford.
Northumberland County,
Sir John Fenwick,
William Ogle.
Norwich,
Robert Paston,
Sir Nevile Catelyn.
Nottinghamshire,
Sir William Clifton,
Reason Mellish.
Nottingham Town,
John Beaumont,
Sir Wm. Stanhope.
Okehampton,
Sir Simeon Leach.
William Cary.
Orford,
Thomas Glemham,
Lord Huntingtower.
Oxfordshire,
Viscount Falkland,
Thomas Tipping.
Oxford City,
Henry Bertie,
Sir George Pudsey.
Oxford University,
Sir Leolin Jenkins,
Dr. Perrot.
Pembrokeshire,
William Barlow.
Pembroke Town,
Arthur Owen.
Penryn,
Henry Fanshaw,
Sir Nich. Slanning.
Peterborough,
Charles Fitzwilliam,
Charles Orme.
Petersfield,
Sir John Norton,
Thomas Bilson.
Plymouth,
Bernard Greenville,
Earl of Ranelagh,
Plimpton,
Richard Strode.
Sir Christopher Wren.
Pool,
William Ettrick,
Thomas Chaffin.
Pontefract,
Viscount Downe,
Sir Thomas Yarborough.
Portsmouth,
William Legg,
Henry Slingsby.
Preston,
Sir Thomas Chichley,
Andrew Newport, *(dead)*
Edward Fleetwood.
Queenborough,
Sir John Godwyn,
Caleb Banks.
Radnor County,
Richard Williams.
Radnor Town,
Owen Wynn.
Reading,
John Breedon,
Thomas Coates.
Retford,
Sir Edward Nevill,
John Millington.
Richmond,
John D'Arcy,
Humphrey Wharton.
Rippon,
Gilbert Dolben,
Sir Edm. Jennings.
Rochester,
Sir John Banks,
Sir Francis Clark.
Rumney,
Thomas Chudleigh,
Sir B. Bathurst. *waved*
Rutlandshire,
Baptist Noel,
Sir Thomas Mackworth.
Rye,
Thomas Frewen,
Sir Thomas Jenner.
Ryegate,
Sir John Werden,
John Parsons.
Salop County,
Edw. Kynaston,
John Walcott.
Salop Town,
Sir Francis Edwards,
Edward Kynaston.
Saltash,
Sir Cyril Wych,
Edmund Waller.
Sandwich,
John Strode,
John Pepys, *(waved)*
Philip Parker.
Sarum New,
John Windham,
Sir Stephen Fox.
Sarum Old,
Sir Eliab Harvey,
Sir Thomas Mompesson.
Scarborough,
Sir Thomas Slingsby,
William Osbaldiston.
Seaford,
Sir Wm. Thomas.
Sir Edward Selwyn.
Shaftsbury,
Sir Henry Butler,
John Bowles.
Shoreham,
Sir Edw. Hungerford,
Sir Richard Haddock.
Somersetshire,
Sir John Smith.
George Horner.
Southampton County,
Sir Chas. Wyndham,
Sir Benj. Newland.
Southampton Town,
Sir B. Newland,
Sir Chas. Wyndham.
Southwark,
Sir Peter Daniel,
Anthony Bowyer.
Staffordshire,
Sir Walter Baggot,
Edward Littleton.
Stafford Town,
Walter Chetwynd,
Rowland Okeover.
Stamford,
Peregrine Bertie,
Charles Bertie.
Steyning,
Sir James Morton,
Sir John Fagg.
Sir H. Goring. *(dead)*
Stockbridge,
John Head,
Essex Strode.
Sudbury,
Sir John Cardelle,
Sir Geo. Weneive.
Suffolk,
Sir Robert Brooke,
Sir Henry North.
Surry County,
Sir Adam Brown,
Sir Edw. Evelyn.
Sussex,
Sir Henry Goring,
Sir Thomas Dyke.
Tamworth,
Richard Howe,
Sir Henry Gough.
Tavistock,
Sir James Butler,
John Beare.
Taunton,
Sir W. Portman,
John Sandford.
Tewkesbury,
Sir Francis Russel,
Richard Dowdeswell.
Thetford,
Wm. De Grey,
H. Hevingham, *removed*
Sir Joseph Williamson.
Thirsk,
Sir Hugh Cholmondeley,
Thomas Frankland.
Tiverton,
Sir Hugh Ackland,
William Coleman.
Totness,
John Kelland,
Sir Edw. Seymour,
Tregony,
Charles Trevanion,
Charles Porter.
Truro,
John Arundel,
Henry Vincent.
Wallingford,
John Stone,
John Holloway.
Warwickshire,
Sir Charles Holt,
Richard Verney.
Warwick Town,
Lord Digby,
Thomas Coventry.
Wareham,
Thomas Erle.
George Ryves.
Wells,
Thomas Wyndham,
Edward Berkeley.
Wendover,
John Beckwell,
Richard Hampden.
Wenlock,
Thomas Lawley,
George Weld.
Weobly,
Henry Cornwall,
Robert Price.
Westbury,
Richard Lewis,
James Herbert.
West Low,
Henry Trelawney,
James Kendall.
Westminster
Charles Benython,
Michael Arnold.
Westmoreland,
Sir John Lowther,
Allan Bellingham.
Weymouth,
Henry Henning.
Sir John Morton.
Whitchurch,
James Russell,
Henry Wallop.
Winchelsea,
Creswel Draper,
Earl of Middleton.
Winchester,
Roger L'Estrange,
Charles Hanseys.
Windsor,
William Chiffinch,
Richard Graham.
Wilton,
Oliver Nicholas,
Sir John Nicholas.
Wiltshire,
Viscount Cornbury.
Lord Bruce,
Woodstock,
Richard Bertie,
Sir Littleton Osbaldiston.
Wooton Basset,
John Pleydell,
Henry St. John.
Wygan,
Earl of Ancram,
Lord Murray.
Worcestershire,
Sir John Packington,
James Pitts.
Worcester City,
William Bromley.
Bridges Nanfan.
Yarmouth, (Norfolk)
Sir Wm. Cooke,
John Friend.
Yarmouth, (Hants)
William Hewer,
Thomas Wyndham.
Yorkshire,
Lord Clifford,
Sir John Kaye.
York City,
Sir John Reresby,
Sir Metcalfe Robinson.

SPEAKER—Sir John Trevor.

The Lord Keeper Guildford's Speech.] His majesty being come to the house of peers, commanded the black-rod to acquaint the house of commons, that it is his majesty's pleasure they attend him, immediately; who being come to the bar of the lords house, sir Francis North, baron of Guilford, and lord keeper of the great seal, having first received his majesty's pleasure, spoke to this effect:

"My lords; and you the knights, citizens, and burgesses of the house of commons; I have it in command from his majesty, to let you know, that he will defer his speaking to you until the members of both houses have taken the oaths appointed at the beginning of every parliament, the doing whereof will require some time. When that is over, his maj. will come again, and declare his mind to you concerning the causes of his calling this parliament.—And it being necessary there should be first a Speaker of the house of commons; it is his majesty's pleasure, that the gentlemen of the house of commons go apart to the usual place, and do proceed to the choice of a fit person to be their Speaker; his maj. doth appoint four of the clock this afternoon, to have him presented here for his royal approbation."

Sir John Trevor chosen Speaker.] The commons being returned to their own house, lord Middleton named sir John Trevor, as a fit person for their Speaker, and one that would be acceptable to his majesty; whereupon the commons unanimously made choice of sir John, who took the Chair, and the house adjourned till 4 of the clock: when he went up to the bar of the house of peers, and was approved of by his majesty.

Twenty Lords introduced in one day.] The same day the following lords were introduced, and took their seats in the house, viz. Francis lord North, lord keeper of the great seal, Laurence earl of Rochester, George marq. of Halifax, James duke of Ormond, Henry duke of Beaufort, Edward earl of Litchfield, Daniel e. of Nottingham, James e. of Abingdon, Edw. e. of Gainsborough, Tho. e. of Plymouth, Horatio, visc. Townsend, Tho. visc. Weymouth, Christ. visc. Hatton, Rd. lord Lumley, John lord Ossulston, George lord Dartmouth, Ralph lord Stawell, Sidney lord Godolphin, George lord Jeffreys, and John lord Churchill.

Proceedings in the Case of the Popish Lords.] The same day, the house of peers received the Petitions of the Lords who had lain under an impeachment several years in the Tower, and been admitted to bail about a year ago, viz. the earl of Powis, the lord Arundel of Wardour, the lord Bellasis, and the earl of Danby: the last having made their personal appearances, in pursuance to their bail, and delivered their Petitions, the house entered into consideration of the hardship of their cases, and came to this question, Whether the Order of the 19th of March, 1678-9, be reversed and annulled as to their several impeachments? which passed in the affirmative.

Protest thereon.] Four lords only entered their Dissent, namely, Radnor, Anglesea, Clare, and Stamford, with these following Reasons: 1. "Because it doth, as we conceive, extrajudicially, and without a particular cause before us, endeavour an alteration in a judicial rule and order of the house, in the highest part of their power and judicature. 2. Because it shakes and lays aside an Order made and renewed upon long consideration and debate, report of committees of precedents and former resolutions, without permitting the same to be read, though called for by many of the peers, and against weighty reasons, as we conceive, appearing for the same, and contrary to the practice of former times. 3. Because it is inherent in every court of judicature to assert and preserve the former rules of proceedings before them, which therefore must be steady and certain, especially in this high court, that the subject, and all persons concerned, may know how to apply themselves for justice; the very Chancery, King's-bench, &c. having their settled rules, from which there is no variation."—However, two days after, the matter was brought to a conclusion by this following Order; "Whereas several Indictments were found at the sessions held at Westminster against Wm. earl of Powis, &c. which are since brought into this house by certiorari, pursuant to an Order of the 9th of April 1678; the house being this day informed, by Mr. Attorney General, That his maj. hath sent a warrant to him directed, to enter a noli prosequi upon the said Indictments: It is ordered, That his majesty's said attorney general may have recourse to the said indictments, in order to the entering a noli prosequi thereupon pursuant to his majesty's warrant: and it is further ordered, That the bail given in the court of king's bench, for the appearance of the said Wm. earl of Powis, Henry lord Arundel of Wardour, and John lord Bellasis, be, and are hereby discharged.*

* "The upper house discussed, at the same time, the affair of the lords accused of high treason, and cancelled a rule of that house, which orders that the accusations entered by the lower house shall be in force from one parliament to another: this was done to perpetuate the accusations of the earl of Danby and the Catholic peers, who by this means would have always remained liable to condemnation upon the evidence given against them. They are now free from the accusation, and to prosecute them again would require both a fresh accusation and a fresh trial. This decision of the upper house repeals whatever was done respecting the pretended plot of the Catholics, which without it would have still subsisted. This is a very important matter in relation to his Britannic majesty. The earls of Devonshire, Anglesey, Clare, and Radnor opposed the measure, which only shewed their ill will." Barillon's Letters to the King of France. See Fox's James II. Appendix, p. lxxxvi.

The King's Speech on opening the Session.] May 22. His majesty opened the session with the following Speech to both houses:

"My lords and gentlemen; After it pleased Almighty God to take to his mercy the late king my dearest brother, and to bring me to the peaceable possession of the throne of my ancestors, I immediately resolved to call a parliament, as the best means to settle every thing upon those foundations as may make my reign both easy and happy to you: towards which, I am disposed to contribute all that is fit for me to do.—What I said to my privy-council at my first coming there, I am desirous to renew to you *, wherein I fully declare my opinion concerning the principles of the Church of England, whose members have shewed themselves so eminently loyal in the worst of times, in defence of my father, and support of my brother, of blessed memory; that I will always take care to defend and support it. I will make it my endeavour to preserve this government both in Church and State, as it is now by law established; and as I will never depart from the just rights and prerogatives of

* "The repetition of the words made use of in his first speech to the privy council, shews, that in the opinion of the court at least, they had been well chosen, and had answered their purpose; and even the haughty language which was added, and was little less than a menace to parliament, if it should not comply with his wishes, was not, as it appears, unpleasing to the party which at that time prevailed, since the revenue enjoyed by his predecessor was unanimously, and almost immediately, voted to him for life. It was not remarked, in public at least, that the king's threat of governing without parliament, was an unequivocal manifestation of his contempt of the law of the country, so distinctly established, though so ineffectually secured, by the statute of the 16th of Charles ii. for holding triennial parliaments. It is said, lord keeper Guildford had prepared a different speech for his majesty, but that this was preferred, as being the king's own words; and, indeed that part of it in which he says that he must answer once for all, that the commons' giving such proportions as they might think convenient, would be a very improper way with him, bears, as well as some others, the most evident marks of its royal origin. It is to be observed, however, that in arguing for his demand, as he styles it, of revenue, he says, not that the parliament ought not, but that he must not suffer the well-being of the government depending upon such revenue, to be precarious; whence it is evident, that he intended to have it understood, that, if the parliament did not grant, he purposed to levy a revenue without their consent. It is impossible that any degree of party spirit should so have blinded men, as to prevent them from perceiving, in this speech, a determination on the part of the king, to conduct his government upon the principles of absolute monarchy, and to those who were not so possessed with the love of royalty, which creates a kind of passionate affection for whoever happens to be the wearer of the crown, the vindictive manner in which he speaks of Argyle's invasion, might afford sufficient evidence of the temper in which his power would be administered. In that part of his speech he first betrays his personal feelings towards the unfortunate nobleman, whom, in his brother's reign, he had so cruelly and treacherously oppressed, by dwelling upon his being charged by Argyle with tyranny and usurpation, and then declares, that he will take the best care, not according to the usual phrases, to protect the loyal and well-disposed, and to restore tranquillity, but that the declaration of the factious and rebellious may meet with the reward it deserves; thus marking out revenge and punishment as the consequences of victory, upon which he was most intent.—It is impossible, that in a house of commons, however composed, there should not have been many members who disapproved the principles of government announced in the speech, and who were justly alarmed at the temper in which it was conceived. But these, overpowered by numbers, and perhaps afraid of the imputation of being concerned in plots and insurrections, (an imputation which, if they had shewn any spirit of liberty, would most infallibly have been thrown upon them,) declined expressing their sentiments; and, in the short session which followed, there was an almost uninterrupted unanimity in granting every demand, and acquiescing in every wish of the government. The revenue was granted, without any notice being taken of the illegal manner in which the king had levied it upon his own authority. Argyle was stigmatised as a traitor; nor was any desire expressed to examine his declarations, one of which seemed to be purposely withheld from parliament. Upon the communication of the duke of Monmouth's landing in the west, that nobleman was immediately attainted by bill. The king's assurance was recognized as a sufficient security for the national religion; and the liberty of the press was destroyed by the revival of the statute of the 13th and 14th of Charles ii. This last circumstance, important as it is, does not seem to have excited much attention at the time, which, considering the general principles then in fashion, is not surprising. That it should have been scarcely noticed by any historian, is more wonderful. It is true, however, that the terrour inspired by the late prosecutions for libels, and the violent conduct of the courts upon such occasions, rendered a formal destruction of the liberty of the press a matter of less importance. So little does the magistracy, when it is inclined to act tyrannically, stand in need of tyrannical laws to effect its purpose. The bare silence and acquiescence of the legislature is, in such a case, fully sufficient to annihilate, practically speaking, every right and liberty of the subject." Fox's JAMES II. p. 143.

the crown, so I will never invade any man's property; and you may be sure, that having heretofore ventured my life in the defence of this nation, I will still go as far as any man in preserving it, in all its just rights and liberties; and having given you this assurance concerning the care I will have of your Religion and Property, which I have chose to do in the same words which I used at my first coming to the crown; the better to evidence to you, that I spoke them not by chance, and consequently that you may firmly rely upon a promise so solemnly made.—I cannot doubt that I shall fail of suitable returns from you, with all imaginable duty and kindness on your part, and particularly to what relates to the settling of my Revenue, and continuing it, during my life, as it was in the life-time of my brother. I might use many arguments to enforce this demand, for the benefit of Trade, the support of the Navy, the necessity of the Crown, and the well-being of the Government itself, which I must not suffer to be precarious; but I am confident, your own consideration of what is just and reasonable, will suggest to you whatsoever might be enlarged upon this occasion.—There is one popular argument which I foresee may be used against what I ask of you, from the inclination men have for frequent parliaments, which some may think would be the best security, by feeding me from time to time by such proportions as they shall think convenient; and this argument, it being the first time I speak to you from the throne, I will answer once for all, that this would be a very improper method to take with me, and that the best way to engage me to meet you often, is always to use me well.—I expect, therefore, that you will comply with me in what I have desired; and that you will do it speedily, that this may be a short session, and that we may meet again to all our satisfactions.—My Lords and Gentlemen; I must acquaint you that I have had news this morning from Scotland, that Argyle is landed in the West Highlands, with the men he brought with him from Holland;* that there are two Declarations published, one in the name of all those in arms, the other in his own; it would be too long for me to repeat the substance of them, it is sufficient to tell you, I am charged with usurpation and tyranny, the shorter of them I have directed to be forthwith communicated to you.—I will take the best care I can, that this Declaration of their own faction and rebellion may meet with the reward it deserves, and I will not doubt but you will be the more zealous to support the government, and give me my Revenue as I have desired it without delay."

Both Houses return Thanks to the King.] The commons immediately resolved, nem. con. "That the most humble and hearty Thanks of this house be given to his majesty for his most gracious Speech, and that the lords' concurrence be desired thereto." To which the lords acceded.

The late King's Revenue granted for Life.] Resolved, nem. con. "That the Revenue which was settled on his late majesty for his life be settled on his present majesty during his life." —Ordered, That Mr. Solicitor do bring in a Bill for that purpose.*

* "The earl of Argyle, after having lived quiet in Friseland ever since the disappointment in 1683, resolved at last to go to his own country, where he hoped he could bring 5000 men together. Accordingly he landed with some of his country-men in Argyleshire, but the early notice the council had of his designs had spoiled his whole scheme; for they had brought in all the gentlemen of his country to Edinburgh, which saved them, though it helped on his ruin. Yet he got above 2500 men to come to him. But he lingered too long, hoping still to have brought more of his Highlanders together: so much time was lost. And all the country was summoned to come out against him. At last he crossed an arm of the sea, and landed in the Isle of Bute; where he spent 12 days more, till he had eat up that island, pretending still that he hoped to be joined by more of his Highlanders." Burnet.

* "As the grant of revenue was unanimous, so there does not appear to have been any thing which can justly be styled a debate upon it; though Hume employs several pages in giving the arguments which, he affirms, were actually made use of, and, as he gives us to understand, in the house of commons, for and against the question; arguments which, on both sides, seem to imply a considerable love of freedom, and jealousy of royal power, and are not wholly unmixed even with some sentiments disrespectful to the king. Now I cannot find, either from tradition, or from contemporary writers, any ground to think, that, either the reasons which Hume has adduced, or indeed any other, were urged in opposition to the grant. The only speech made upon the occasion, seems to have been that of Mr. (afterwards sir Edward,) Seymour, who, though of the Tory party, a strenuous opposer of the Exclusion Bill, and in general, supposed to have been an approver, if not an adviser, of the tyrannical measures of the late reign, has the merit of having stood forward singly, to remind the house of what they owed to themselves and their constituents. He did not, however, directly oppose the grant, but stated, that the elections had been carried on under so much court influence, and in other respects so illegally, that it was the duty of the house first to ascertain, who were the legal members, before they proceeded to other business of importance. After having pressed this point, he observed, that, if ever it were necessary to adopt such an order of proceeding, it was more peculiarly so now, when the laws and religion of the nation were in evident peril; that the aversion of the English people to popery, and their attachment to the laws, were such, as to secure these blessings from destruction by any other

The Earl of Argyle's Declaration.] The earl of Middleton delivered a Paper from his majesty, entitled,

The DECLARATION of Archibald earl of Argyle, Cowall and Campbel, Lorn, &c. Heretable Sheriff and Lieutenant of Argyle and Tarbet, and Heretable Justice General of the said Shires, and of the West Isles, and others; with his Orders to his Vassals and others in the said Shires, and under his jurisdiction, to concur for Defence of their Religion, their Lives and Liberties.

"I shall not mention my Case published in print in Latin and Dutch, and more at large in English, nor need I repeat the printed Declaration emitted by several noblemen and gentlemen, and others of both nations now in arms; but because the sufferings of me and my family are therein mentioned, I have thought fit to declare for myself, that as I go to arms with those that have appointed me to conduct them for no private or personal end, but only for those contained in the said Declaration, I have concorded with them and approved of their design, so I claim interest but in what I had before, the pretended forfeitures of my friends, and have sufficient right to.—And that I do freely, fully, and as a Christian forgive all personal injuries against my person and family, to all that shall not oppose, but join and concur with us in our present undertaking, for the mentioned reasons in the said Declaration. And hereby I oblige myself never to pursue them in judgment.—And I farther declare, that, obtaining the peaceable and quiet possession of what belonged to my father and myself before our pretended forfeitures, I shall satisfy all debts due from my father and myself, and as my faithfulness to his late majesty and his government hath sufficiently appeared to all unbiassed persons void of malice, so I do with grief acknowledge my former too much complying with, and conniving at the methods taken to bring us to the sad condition we are now in, though (God knows) never concurring in the design. I have now, with God's strength, suffered patiently my unjust sentence and banishment three years and a half, and have never offered to make any uproar or defence

---

instrumentality than that of parliament itself, which, however, might be easily accomplished, if there were once a parliament entirely dependant upon the persons who might harbour such designs; that it was already rumoured that the Test, and Habeas Corpus Acts, the two bulwarks of our religion and liberties, were to be repealed; that what he stated was so notorious as to need no proof. Having descanted with force and ability upon these, and other topics of a similar tendency, he urged his conclusion, that the question of royal revenue ought not to be the first business of the parliament. Whether, as Burnet thinks, because he was too proud to make any previous communication of his intentions, or that the strain of his argument was judged to be too bold for the times, this speech, whatever secret approbation it might excite, did not receive from any quarter either applause or support. Under these circumstances it was not thought necessary to answer him, and the grant was voted unanimously, without further discussion.—As Barilion, in the relation of parliamentary proceedings, transmitted by him to his court, in which he appears at this time to have been very exact, gives the same description of Seymour's speech and its effects, with Burnet, there can be little doubt but their account is correct. It will be found as well in this, as in many other instances, that an unfortunate inattention, on the part of the reverend historian, to forms, has made his veracity unjustly called in question. He speaks of Seymour's speech as if it had been a motion in the techuical sense of the word, for enquiring into the elections, which had no effect. Now no traces remaining of such a motion, and, on the other hand, the elections having been at a subsequent period inquired into, Ralph almost pronounces the whole account to be erroneous; whereas the only mistake consists in giving the name of motion to a suggestion, upon the question of a grant. It is whimsical enough, that it should be from the account of the French ambassador, that we are enabled to reconcile to the records, and to the forms of the English house of commons, a relation made by a distinguished member of the English house of lords. Sir John Reresby does indeed say, that among the gentlemen of the house of commons whom he accidentally met, they in general seemed willing to settle a handsome revenue upon the king, and to give him money; but whether their grant should be permanent, or only temporary, and to be renewed from time to time by parliament, that the nation might be often consulted, was the question. But besides the looseness of the expression, which may only mean that the point was questionable, it is to be observed, that he does not relate any of the arguments which were brought forward, even in the private conversations to which he refers; and when he afterwards gives an account of what passed in the house of commons, (where he was present,) he does not hint at any debate having taken place, but rather implies the contrary.—This misrepresentation of Mr. Hume's is of no small importance, inasmuch as, by intimating that such a question could be debated at all, and much more, that it was debated with the enlightened views, and bold topics of argument with which his genius has supplied him, he gives us a very false notion of the character of the parliament, and of the times which he is describing. It is not improbable, that if the arguments had been used, which this historian supposes, the utterer of them would have been expelled, or sent to the Tower; and it is certain, that he would not have been heard with any degree of attention, or even patience." Fox's JAMES II. p. 147.

ny arms, to disturb the peace, upon my private concerns. But the king being now dead, and the duke of York having taken off his masque, and having abandoned and invaded our Religion and Liberties, resolving to enter into the government, and exercising contrary to law, I think not only just, but my duty to God and my country, to use my utmost endeavours to oppose and repress his usurpation and tyranny. And therefore being assisted and furnished very nobly by several good Protestants, and invited, and accompanied by several of both nations to head them, I resolve, as God shall enable me, to use their assistance of all kinds towards the ends expressed in the said Declaration.—And I do hereby earnestly invite and oblige all honest Protestants, and particularly all my friends and blood relations to concur with us in the said Declaration. And as I have written several Letters, so having no other way fully to intimate my mind to others, I do hereby command all my vassals every where, and all within my several jurisdictions, with defensable men in their commands, to go to arms, and to join with us according to the said Declaration, as they will be answerable at their perils, and to obey the particular orders they shall receive from me, from time to time."

The Commons resolve to stand by the King, with their Lives and Fortunes.] The commons resolved, nem. con. "That this house will stand by and assist his majesty with their Lives and Fortunes, against Archibald Campbel the pretended earl of Argyle and his adherents, and all rebels, and traitors, and all others whatsoever, that shall assist them or any of them."

The King's Answer.] May 23, p. m. The house attended his majesty with the above Resolution, to which his majesty was pleased to make this Answer: viz.

"Gentlemen; I could expect no less from a house of commons so composed, as (God be thanked) you are: I rely on the assurances you have given me, which are the natural effects of Monarchical and Church of England men. I will stand by all such, and, so supported, have no reason to fear any rebels, or enemies I have or may have."

Resolutions concerning Religion.] May 27. Sir T. Meres reports from the grand committee for Religion, That the committee, having taken the matters yesterday to them referred into their consideration, had agreed upon the two following Resolves; viz. 1. "That it be reported to the house, as the opinion of this grand committee, to assist and stand by his majesty, according to our duty and allegiance, for the support and defence of the Reformed Religion of the Church of England, as now by law established, with our lives and fortunes. 2. That the house be moved, from this grand committee, to make an humble Address to his majesty to publish his royal Proclamation for putting the laws in execution against all Dissenters whatsoever from the Church of England." Both which, upon the previous question, being disagreed to by the house,

Resolved, nem. con. "That this house doth acquiesce, entirely rely, and rest wholly satisfied in his majesty's gracious Word, and repeated Declaration, to support and defend the Religion of the Church of England, as it is now by law established; which is dearer to us than our lives."*

* "The unanimous vote for trusting the safety of religion to the king's declaration, passed not without observation; the rights of the church of England being the only point upon which, at this time, the parliament were in any degree jealous of the royal power. The committee of religion had voted unanimously, "That it is the opinion of the committee, that this house will stand by his majesty with their lives and fortunes, according to their bounden duty and allegiance, in defence of the reformed church of England, as it is now by law established; and that an humble address be presented to his majesty, to desire him to issue forth his royal proclamation, to cause the penal laws to be put in execution against all dissenters from the church of England whatsoever." But upon the report of the house, the question of agreeing with the committee was evaded by a previous question, and the house, with equal unanimity, resolved, "That this house doth acquiesce, and entirely rely, and rest wholly satisfied, on his majesty's gracious word, and repeated declaration to support and defend the religion of the church of England, as it is now by law established, which is dearer to us than our lives." Mr. Echard, and bishop Kennet, two writers of different principles, but both churchmen, assign, as the motive of this vote, the unwillingness of the party then prevalent in parliament, to adopt severe measures against the Protestant dissenters; but in this notion they are by means supported by the account, imperfect as it is, which sir John Reresby gives of the debate; for he makes no mention of tenderness towards dissenters, but states, as the chief argument against agreeing with the committee, that it might excite a jealousy of the king; and Barillon expressly says, that the first vote gave great offence to the king, still more to the queen, and that orders were, in consequence, issued to the court members of the house of commons, to devise some means to get rid of it. Indeed, the general circumstances of the times are decisive against the hypothesis of the two reverend historians; nor is it, as far as I know, adopted by any other historians. The probability seems to be, that the motion in the committee had been originally suggested by some Whig member, who could not, with prudence, speak his real sentiments openly, and who thought to embarrass the government, by touching upon a matter, where the union between the church party and the king, would be put to the severest test. The zeal of the Tories for persecution, made them at first give into the snare; but when, upon reflection, it occurred, that the involving of the Catholics in one common danger with

The Speaker's Speech to the King on presenting the Revenue Bill.] May 30. His majesty being on his throne, the lords being also in their robes; the gentleman usher had command to signify to the commons his majesty's pleasure, that they come presently, with their Speaker, to attend him; who, being come, said,

"Most gracious sovereign; We the knights, citizens, and burgesses of the commons, assembled in parliament, do now come in all duty to present to your maj. the Revenue you pleased to demand at the opening of this parliament; wherein we proceeded with as much speed as the forms of passing bills of that nature would admit.—We bring not with it any Bill for the Preservation or Security of our Religion, which is dearer to us than our lives: in that, we acquiesce, intirely rely, and rest wholly satisfied, in your majesty's gracious and sacred word, repeated declaration and assurance, to support and defend the Religion of the Church of England, as it is now by law established.—We present this Revenue to your majesty, without the addition of any conditional Appropriating or Tacking Clauses, &c.; and we humbly beseech your maj. to accept of it; and along with it our hearty prayers, that God Almighty would bless you with a long life, and happy reign to enjoy it."

The King's Speech thereupon.] After passing the said Bill, his majesty made this Speech:

"My lords and gentlemen; I thank you very heartily for the Bill you have presented me this day; and I assure you, the readiness and cheerfulness that has attended the dispatch of it, is as acceptable to me as the bill itself. After so happy a beginning, you may believe, I would not call upon you unnecessarily for an extraordinary Supply. But, when I tell you, that the Stores of the Navy and Ordnance are extremely exhausted; that the Anticipations upon several branches of the Revenue are great and burthensome; that the Debts of the king my brother to his servants and family are such as deserve compassion; that the Rebellion in Scotland, without putting more weight upon it than it really deserves, must oblige me to a considerable expence extraordinary; I am sure, such considerations will move you to give me an Aid, to provide for those things, wherein the security, the ease, and the happiness of my government, are so much concerned: but, above all, I must recommend to you the care of the Navy, the strength and glory of this nation, that you will put it into such a condition, as may make us considered and respected abroad. I cannot express my concern upon this occasion more suitable to my own thoughts of it, than by assuring you I have a true English heart, as jealous of the honour of the nation as you can be. And I please myself with the hopes, that, by God's blessing and your assistance, I may carry the reputation of it yet higher in the world, than ever it has been in the time of any of my ancestors. And as I will not call upon you for Supplies but when they are of public use and advantage; so I promise you, that what you give me upon such occasions shall be managed with good husbandry: and I will take care it shall be employed to the uses for which I ask them."*

A Supply voted for the Navy.] A motion being made for a Supply, upon his majesty's Speech; the house, in a grand committee, Resolved, nem. con. 1. "That a Supply be given to his majesty towards the repairs of the Navy and Ordnance, and the Stores for the same; and for those other occasions in his majesty's Speech. 2. That, towards the said Supply, an Imposition to be laid on all Wines and Vinegar. 3. That the Imposition to be laid on Wines and Vinegar be the same that was laid thereon by an act of parliament, 22 Ch. ii. entitled, &c." Which being reported were agreed to by the house, and the Solicitor-General was ordered to prepare a Bill accordingly.

Bill to reverse Lord Stafford's Attainder.] June 3. The lords in a grand committee made some alterations in the title to a Bill for the reversing the Attainder of the lord visc. Stafford, a considerable Amendment in the Preamble, and a small Amendment in the enacting Clause, and then the Bill was engrossed: and the Reason of the Reversal was in these words; "Whereas it is now manifest, that the said Wm. late visc. Stafford, was innocent of the Treason laid to his Charge, and the Testimony whereby he was found guilty, was false: be it enacted, &c."

---

the Protestant dissenters, must be displeasing to the king, they drew back without delay, and passed the most comprehensive vote of confidence, which James could desire." Fox's JAMES II. p. 151.

* "Rapin, Hume, and Ralph, observe upon this speech, that neither the generosity of the commons' grant, nor the confidence they expressed upon religious matters, could extort a kind word in favour of their religion. But this observation, whether meant as a reproach to him for his want of gracious feeling to a generous parliament, or as an oblique compliment to his sincerity, has no force in it. His majesty's speech was spoken immediately upon passing the bills which the Speaker presented, and he could not therefore take notice of the Speaker's words, unless he had spoken extempore; for the custom is not, nor I believe ever was, for the Speaker to give, beforehand, copies of addresses of this nature. James would not certainly have scrupled to repeat the assurances which he had so lately made in favour of the Protestant religion, as he did not scruple to talk of his true English heart, honour of the nation, &c. at a time when he was engaged with France; but the speech was prepared for an answer to a money bill, not for a question of the Protestant religion and church, and the false professions in it are adapted to what was supposed to be the only subject of it." Fox's JAMES II. p. 160.

Protest thereon.] But before the question ·as put for engrossing the Bill, the earls of ·nglesea and Radnor, and two or three other ·rds, desired leave to enter their Dissents, for ·ese Reasons; 1st, Because the assertion in ·e Bill of its 'being now manifest that the ·te visc. Stafford died innocent, and that the ·stimony on which he was convicted was ·lse,' which are the sole grounds and reasons ·iven to support the Bill, were destitute of all ·roof, warrant, or testimony, or matter of ·ecord before us. 2. That the Record of the ·ing's-bench, read at the committee, con·erning the conviction, last term, of one of the ·itnesses for perjury, in collateral points of ·roof, of no affinity to the lord Stafford's Trial, ·nd given several years before, it is conceived ·an be no ground to invalidate the testimony ·pon which the said viscount was convicted, ·hich could never legally be by one witness, ·nd was in fact by the judgment of his peers, ·n the evidence of at least three. 3. It is ·onceived the said Judgment in the King's-·ench was unprecedented, illegal and unwar·anted, and highly derogatory to the honour, ·udicature and authority of this court, who ·ave power to question and punish perjuries of ·itnesses before them, and ought not to be ·nposed upon by the judgments of inferior ·ourts, or their Attainder of a peer invalidated ·y implication; and the Popish Plot so con·emned, pursued and punished by his late ma·esty and four parliaments, after public solemn ·evotion through the whole kingdom, by autho·ity of Church and State, to be eluded, to the ·rraignment and scandal of the government; ·nd only for the restoring of the family of one ·opish lord. And all this, being without any ·natter judicially appearing before us to induce ·he same; and the records of the Trial not ·uffered to be read, for the information of the ·ruth, before the passing of the bill. 4. For ·nany other weighty Reasons offered and given ·y divers peers in the two days debate of ·his bill, both at the committee, and in the ·ouse."

The next day, the Bill was read a third time, ·nd passed in the house of peers; but the fore·nentioned lords repeated their Protestations ·gainst it, and were seconded by the earls of ·tamford and Clare, and the lord Eure, be·ause the preamble of it was not amended, ·nd no defect in point of law alledged as a ·eason for the reversal of the Attainder. But ·hough the said Bill passed the lords, it was ·ropped by the commons.*

Account of the Duke of Monmouth's landing.] June 13. The earl of Middleton acquainted the commons from his majesty, "That his majesty had this morning received advice, as well by Letter from the mayor of Lyme in Dorsetshire, as by two messengers come from thence, who had been examined upon oath at the Council Table, That the duke of Monmouth, with the late lord Grey, was landed in a hostile manner, with many men and arms; and had seized the port and guns, setting up a standard in the town, and were listing others."*

Resolutions thereupon.] And the said Letter being produced, and read to the house; and the said messengers being called in, and testifying the truth of the matter at the bar of the house;

Resolved, nem. con. "That the most humble and hearty Thanks of this house be returned to his majesty, for his gracious Message to this house communicating the landing of the duke of Monmouth; and that this house will stand by and assist his maj. with their Lives and Fortunes against the said James duke of Monmouth, his adherents and correspondents, and all re-

---

* "The only matter in which the king's ·iews were in any degree thwarted, was the ·eversal of lord Stafford's attainder, which, hav·ng passed the house of lords, not without op·position, was lost in the house of commons; a ·trong proof that the Popish plot was still the ·ubject upon which the opposers of the court ·ad most credit with the public. Mr. Hume, ·otwithstanding his just indignation at the con·demnation of Stafford, and his general inclination to approve of royal politics, most unaccountably justifies the commons in their rejection of this bill, upon the principle of its being impolitic at that time to grant so full a justification of the Catholics, and to throw so foul an imputation upon the Protestants. Surely if there be one moral duty that is binding upon men in all times, places, and circumstances, and from which no supposed views of policy can excuse them, it is that of granting a full justification to the innocent; and such Mr. Hume considers the Catholics, and especially lord Stafford, to have been. The only rational way of accounting for this solitary instance of non-compliance on the part of the commons, is either to suppose that they still believed in the reality of the Popish Plot, and Stafford's guilt, or that the church party, which was uppermost, had such an antipathy to Popery, as indeed to every sect, whose tenets differed from theirs, that they deemed every thing lawful against its professors." Fox's JAMES II. p. 161.

* "As soon as lord Argyle sailed for Scotland, the duke of Monmouth set about his design with as much haste as possible, and was hurried into an ill-timed invasion. His whole company, with whom, after a prosperous course, he landed at Lyme in Dorsetshire, (on June 11) consisted but of 82 persons. Many of the country people came in to join him, but very few of the gentry. And he quickly found what it was to be at the head of undisciplined men, that knew nothing of war, and that were not to be used with rigour. His great error was, that he did not, in the first heat, venture on some hardy action, and then march either to Exeter or Bristol, where, as he would have found much wealth, so he would have gained some reputation by it. But he lingered in exercising his men, and stayed too long in the neighbourhood of Lyme." Burnet.

bels and traitors, and all others whatsoever that shall assist them, or any of them." And a committee was appointed to prepare the said Address.

Resolved, "That a Bill be brought in for Preservation of his majesty's Royal Person and government."*

Resolved "That a Bill be brought in for the Attainder of James duke of Monmouth of High Treason."

The Commons' Address to the King.] Mr. Solicitor-general Finch reports from the committee the following Address:

"We your majesty's most loyal subjects, the commons of England, in parliament assembled, do, with all duty, return our most humble and hearty Thanks for your majesty's gracious Message, communicated to us by the earl of Middleton, of the invading this your kingdom by that ungrateful rebel James duke of Monmouth; and do, with all duty and loyalty, and utter detestation of such rebels and traitors, assure your majesty, that we are, and always shall be, ready to stand by and assist your maj. with our Lives and Fortunes against the said James duke of Monmouth, his adherents and correspondents, and all rebels and traitors; and all others whatsoever that shall assist them, or any of them. And since the Preservation of your majesty's Person is of the highest concern to the peace and happiness of this kingdom, we your most dutiful and loyal subjects, do most humbly beseech your maj. to take more than ordinary care of your royal person, which we beseech God long to preserve."

The King's Answer.] Which Address being

* "Further to manifest their servility to the king, as well as their hostility to every principle that could by implication be supposed to be connected with Monmouth or his cause, the house of commons passed a bill for the Preservation of his Majesty's Person, in which, after enacting that a written or verbal declaration of a treasonable intention should be tantamount to a treasonable act, they inserted two remarkable clauses, by one of which, to assert 'the legitimacy of Monmouth's birth'—by the other, 'to propose in parliament any alteration in the succession of the crown,' were made likewise high treason. We learn from Burnet, that the first part of this bill was strenuously and warmly debated, and that it was chiefly opposed by serjeant Maynard, whose arguments made some impression even at that time; but whether the serjeant was supported in his opposition, as the word 'chiefly' would lead us to imagine, or if supported, by whom, that historian does not mention; and unfortunately, neither of Maynard's speech itself, nor indeed of any opposition whatever to the bill, is there any other trace to be found. The crying injustice of the clause, which subjected a man to the pains of treason, merely for delivering his opinion upon a controverted fact, though he should do no act in consequence of such opinion, was not, as far as we are informed, objected to, or at all noticed, unless indeed the speech above alluded to, in which the Speaker is said to have descanted upon the general danger of making words treasonable, be supposed to have been applied to this clause, as well as to the former part of the bill. That the other clause should have passed without opposition, or even observation, must appear still more extraordinary, when we advert, not only to the nature of the clause itself, but to the circumstances of there being actually in the house, no inconsiderable number of members who had, in the former reign, repeatedly voted for the Exclusion Bill.—It is worthy of notice, however, that, while every principle of criminal jurisprudence, and every regard to the fundamental rights of the deliberative assemblies, which make part of the legislature of the nation, were thus shamelessly sacrificed to the eagerness which, at this disgraceful period, so generally prevailed, of manifesting loyalty, or rather abject servility to the sovereign, there still remained no small degree of tenderness for the interests and safety of the church of England, and a sentiment approaching to jealousy upon any matter which might endanger, even by the most remote consequences, or put any restriction upon her ministers. With this view, as one part of the bill did not relate to treasons only, but imposed new penalties upon such as should by writing, printing, preaching, or other speaking, attempt to bring the king or his government into hatred or contempt, there was a special proviso added, 'that the asserting, and maintaining by any writing, printing, preaching, or any other speaking, the doctrine, discipline, divine worship, or government of the church of England as it is now by law established, against Popery or any other different or dissenting opinions, is not intended, and shall not be interpreted, or construed to be any offence within the words or meaning of this act.' It cannot escape the reader, that only such attacks upon Popery as were made in favour of the doctrine and discipline of the church of England, and no other, were protected by this proviso, and consequently that, if there were any real occasion for such a guard, all Protestant dissenters who should write or speak against the Roman superstition, were wholly unprotected by it, and remained exposed to the danger, whatever it might be, from which the church was so anxious to exempt her supporters.—This bill passed the house of commons, and was sent up to the house of lords on the 30th of June. It was read a first time on that day, but the adjournment of both houses taking place on the 2d of July, it could not make any further progress at that time; and when the parliament met afterwards in autumn, there was no longer that passionate affection for the monarch, nor consequently that ardent zeal for servitude, which were necessary to make a law with such clauses and provisos, palatable or even endurable." Fox's JAMES II. p. 154.

agreed to by the house, and presented in the afternoon, his majesty was pleased to answer, "That he did thank this house for their loyal Address, and particularly for their care of his person; that he would venture his life in defence of his people, and for their peace; and he did not doubt, but, with God's blessing, and the assistance of his loyal subjects, to repell all traitors and rebels."

The D. of Monmouth's Declaration ordered to be burnt by the Common Hangman.] June 15. A traiterous Paper entitled, 'The Declaration of James duke of Monmouth, &c.' * being sent from the lords, with an Order which that house had made thereupon; and the said Paper and Order being read to the house, resolved, nem. con. "That this house doth agree with the lords; and that the said traiterous Paper be burnt by the hands of the common hangman accordingly."

A Bill for the Attainder of James duke of Monmouth of High Treason was read the first and second time, ingrossed, and read the third time, and sent up to the lords for their concurrence. †

A Supply Voted.] June 17. A motion being made for a Supply to be given to his maj. towards his present extraordinary expence for suppressing the Rebellion of the late duke of Monmouth, and the pretended earl of Argyle; Resolved, That a Supply be given to his majesty, &c.

The King's Message desiring a Supply.] June 18. The following Message from his majesty was delivered in writing, by the earl of Middleton.

"James R. His majesty judges it necessary, for the good of his service, that the gentlemen of this house, (on whose loyalty and affection he depends, where-ever they are) should be present in their respective countries; and therefore designs there should be a recess in a very few days: but, because the Rebellion in the West will occasion an extraordinary expence, his maj. desires there may be a good fund of Credit provided for a present sum of money to answer the immediate charge his maj. must be at: and to the end none of the Bills now depending may be prejudiced, his maj. is pleased that this separation shall be an adjournment, and for some short time only."

£.400,000. voted.] Resolved, "That a Supply not exceeding 400,000*l.* be given to his majesty for his present extraordinary occasions."

June 22. The earl of Middleton acquainted the house from his majesty, That the grand rebel, Argyle, is taken, and now in safe custody *.

Resolved, "That the most humble and hearty acknowledgment and thanks of this house be presented to his majesty, for his gracious communication to them of the taking of that arch-traitor the late earl of Argyle: which this house received with all imaginable joy and satisfaction."

The Parliament adjourned.] July 2. The commons attended his majesty in the house of lords, where the Lord Keeper declared his majesty's pleasure; "That both houses should forthwith severally adjourn themselves till the 4th day of August next. That his majesty doth not at present intend there shall be then a session; but that the session be carried on by farther adjournments, by such members as shall be about the town, till winter, unless in case of some emergency that shall require it: in which case or whensoever he shall intend a session, he will give timely notice by proclamation."—The house accordingly adjourned to August the 4th, and from thence, by his majesty's pleasure, it was farther adjourned to November the 9th.†

* "The duke of Monmouth's Manifesto was long and ill penned; full of much black and dull malice. It charged the king with the burning of London, the Popish Plot, Godfrey's murder, and the earl of Essex's death; and, to crown all, it was pretended, that the late king was poisoned by his orders. It was set forth, that the king's religion made him incapable of the crown; that three subsequent houses of commons had voted his exclusion: the taking away the old Charters, and the hard things done in the last reign, were laid to his charge; the elections of the present parliament were also set forth very odiously with great indecency of stile: the nation was also appealed to, when met in a free parliament, to judge of the duke's own pretensions; and all sort of liberty, both in spirituals and temporals, was promised to persons of all persuasions." Burnet.

† "The alarm of Monmouth's invasion was brought hot to London; where, upon the general report and belief of the thing, an Act of Attainder passed both houses in one day; some small opposition being made by the earl of Anglesea, because the evidence did not seem clear enough for so severe a sentence, which was grounded on the notoriety of the thing. The sum of 5000*l.* was set on his head." Ibid.

* "Argyle had left his arms in a castle, with such a guard as he could spare: but they were routed by a party of the king's forces. And with this he lost both heart and hope. And then, apprehending that all was gone, he put himself in a disguise, and had almost escaped: but he was taken. Thus was this Rebellion brought to a speedy end, with the effusion of very little blood. Nor was there much shed in the way of justice. Argyle was carried to Edinburgh, where he was executed, pitied by all. His death, being pursuant to the sentence passed three years before, was looked on as no better than murder." Burnet.

† "With the duke of Monmouth's Attainder the session of parliament ended; which was no small happiness to the nation, such a body of men being dismissed with doing so little hurt." Burnet.

The King's Speech at the Meeting of Parliament.] Nov. 9 *. The parliament met, when his majesty in the house of lords made the following Speech to both houses: which was afterwards read by the Speaker:

"My lords and gentlemen; After the storm

Soon after the rising of the parliament, the duke of Monmouth, having marched from Lyme to Taunton, and from thence to Bridgewater, having in vain attempted Bath, and finding his men desert daily, resolved to attack the earl of Feversham (who was sent against him with the guards and regular troops) on the very first night of his encampment at Sedgmore, which was July 5, and had not his ill fate placed a battalion of Dumbarton's regiment in his way, he had in all probability surprized the king's army in their camp, and perhaps at that single blow decided the fate of England. As it was, he was entirely routed, having 3000 men killed on the spot, 1000 in the pursuit, and as many taken prisoners. Several parties being sent out after the duke, he was discovered, July 8, in a ditch, covered over with fern. He was brought to London, July 13, and two days after was beheaded on Tower-Hill. Lord Grey, who it was thought betrayed him, received a pardon, and was afterwards created by king William earl of Tankerville. The cruelties that followed, the legal massacres of Jefferies, and the military executions of Kirk, cannot be mentioned without horror.—"Such arbitrary principles had the court instilled into all its servants, that Feversham, immediately after the victory, hanged up above twenty prisoners; and was proceeding in his executions, when the bishop of Bath and Wells warned him, that these unhappy men were now by law entitled to a trial, and that their execution would be deemed a real murther. This remonstrance however did not stop the savage nature of colonel Kirke, a soldier of fortune, who had long served at Tangiers, and had contracted from his habitudes with the Moors, an inhumanity less known in European and in free countries. At his first entry into Bridgewater, he hanged nineteen without the least enquiry into the merits of their cause. As if to make sport with death, he ordered a certain number to be executed, while he and his company should drink to the king's health, or to the queen's, or to judge Jefferies's. Observing their feet to shake in the agonies of death, he cried that he would give them music to their dancing; and he immediately commanded the drums to beat and the trumpets to sound. By way of experiment, he ordered one man to be hung up three times, questioning him at every interval, whether he repented of his crime: but the man obstinately asserting, that, notwithstanding all the past, he would still willingly engage in the same cause, Kirke ordered him to be hung in chains. One story, commonly told of him, is memorable for the treachery, as well as barbarity which attended it. A young maid pleaded for the life of her brother, and flung herself at Kirke's feet, armed with all the charms, which beauty and innocence, bathed in tears, could bestow upon her. The tyrant was inflamed with desire, not softened into love or clemency. He promised to grant her request, provided that she, in her turn, would be equally compliant to him. The maid yielded to the conditions: but after she had passed the night with him, the wanton savage, next morning, showed her from the window her brother, the darling object for whom she had sacrificed her virtue, hanged on a gibbet, which he had secretly ordered to be there erected for his execution. Rage and despair and indignation took possession of her mind, and deprived her for ever of her senses.—All the inhabitants of that country, innocent as well as guilty, were exposed to the ravages of this barbarian. The soldiery were let loose to live on free quarter; and his own regiment, instructed by his example, and encouraged by his exhortations, distinguished themselves in a more particular manner by their outrages. By way of pleasantry he used to denominate them his lambs; an appellation, which was long remembered with horror in the west of England—The cruel Jefferies succeeded after some interval; and showed the people, that the rigours of the law might equal, if not exceed, the ravages of military tyranny. This man, who wantoned in cruelty, had already given a specimen of his character in many trials, where he had presided; and he now set out with a savage joy as to a full harvest of death and destruction. He began at Dorchester; and thirty rebels being arraigned, he exhorted them, but in vain, to save him, by their free confession, the trouble of trying them: and when twenty-nine were found guilty, he ordered them, as an additional punishment of their disobedience, to be led to immediate execution. Most of the other prisoners, terrified with this example, pleaded guilty; and no less than 292 received sentence at Dorchester. Of these 80 were executed. Exeter was the next stage of his cruelty: 243 were there tried, of whom a great number were condemned and executed. He also opened his commission at Taunton and Wells; and every where carried terror and astonishment along with him. The juries were so struck with his menaces, that they gave their verdict with precipitation, and many innocent persons were involved with the guilty. And on the whole, besides those butchered by the military commanders, 251 are computed to have fallen by the hands of justice. The whole country was strowed with the heads and limbs of traitors. Every village almost beheld the dead carcass of a wretched inhabitant. And all the rigours of justice, unabated by any appearance of clemency, were fully displayed to the people by the inhuman Jefferies." Hume.

* "Now that the parliament is on the eve of meeting, they begin in London to talk about the matters that will be agitated in that assembly; it is difficult yet to judge of their success;

that seemed to be coming upon us when we parted last, I am glad to meet you all again in so great peace and quietness; God Almighty be praised, by whose blessing that Rebellion was suppressed! But when we reflect, what an inconsiderable number of men began it, and how long they carried it on without any opposition, I hope every body will be convinced, that the Militia, which hath hitherto been so much depended on, is not sufficient for such occasions; and that there is nothing but a good force of well-disciplined troops in constant pay, that can defend us from such, as either at home or abroad, are disposed to disturb us: and in truth, my concern for the peace and quiet of my subjects, as well as for the safety of the government, made me think it necessary to increase the number to the proportion I have done: that I owed as well to the honour as the security of the nation; whose reputation was so infinitely exposed to all our neighbours, by having so evidently lain open to this late wretched attempt, that it is not to be repaired without keeping such a body of men on foot, that none may ever have the thought of finding us again so miserably unprovided.—It is for the support of this great charge, which is now more than double to what it was, that I ask your assistance in giving me a Supply answerable to the expences it brings along with it: and I cannot doubt, but what I have begun, so much for the honour and defence of the government, will be continued by you with all the cheerfulness and readiness that is requisite for a work of so great importance.—Let no man take exception, that there are some Officers in the Army not qualified, according to the late Tests, for their employments: the gentlemen, I must tell you, are most of them well-known to me: and, having formerly served with me on several occasions, and always approved the loyalty of their principles by their

for although the greater number of the members seem well disposed towards his Britannic majesty, yet the Test and the Habeas Corpus acts are considered by all Englishmen as the bulwarks of the Protestant religion, and the privileges of the nation. The king hopes to succeed in obtaining their repeal; otherwise it would be a very imprudent step to attempt it, and then find himself obliged to dissolve the parliament without having procured from it what he considers necessary for the firm establishment of his authority. The restitution of the Catholic peers, and the confirmation of those officers in the army and the household, who are Catholics, will be a consequence of the repeal of the Test act. All this is considered of great importance; and almost all the English see with much concern that the royal authority is daily gaining fresh strength, and that the existing laws against the Catholic religion cannot be put in force under a king who publicly professes that religion".—Again, "All the schemes and plans are forming with regard to the parliament; it is certain that very important matters will come under discussion, of the issue of which no judgment can yet be formed. The king of England thinks he will succeed in obtaining the greater part of what he shall ask, and he seems very determined not to relax any thing in what he is desirous of procuring for the benefit of the Catholics and the strengthening of his authority. There is great distrust in the Protestant party; they well know that the future safety of the Protestant religion depends upon the measures of this session. The Catholics are not entirely agreed among themselves; the most skilful, and those who have the greatest share in the king's confidence, know that the present juncture is the most favourable one that can be hoped for, and that if they let it slip it may be long before such another occur. The Jesuits are of the same opinion, which certainly is the most just. But the opulent and settled Catholics are alarmed for the future, and apprehend a change which may ruin them; they are therefore willing to admit of every possible modification, and to be content with the most moderate advantages there may be a wish to grant, as the revocation of the penal laws, without insisting on a repeal of the Test act, which renders the Catholics incapable of holding any office or employment.—This party is supported by those who secretly favour the prince of Orange; and their advice would prevail, did not the others use every means in their power to convince the king of England, that if he does not seize the present opportunity, and carry into effect his designs respecting the Catholics and his own power, he will find greater obstacles arise daily. The king's disposition leads him to pursue a firm and vigorous conduct; the influence of those of his ministers who entertain the same sentiments appears to increase. The fate of the marquis of Halifax has alarmed those who wished to act with moderation, and adopt temperate measures. All this creates much cabal, both in the court and parliament. The king often speaks to me about what he wishes to do, and seems resolved to profit of the present juncture. He always tells me, that peace abroad is of the last necessity to him, and charges me to represent this to your majesty as decisive for the benefit of the Catholic religion. I confine myself within those limits prescribed to me by your majesty, and without busying myself to inspire him with any thing too violent, I strengthen the resolution he seems to have taken to profit of the present occasion. I will be assiduous to discover all that takes place, and to send your majesty as exact a detail as I can. There has not been for many years a more important session of parliament. I foresee even that many things will be treated of respecting the future, which was not expected. I will spare no pains to be well informed." M. Barillon's Dispatches to the French King. See Fox's JAMES II. Appendix, p. cxxvi.

practice, I think them now fit to be employed under me: and I will deal plainly with you, that, after having had the benefit of their service in such a time of need and danger, I will neither expose them to disgrace, nor myself to the want of them, if there should be another Rebellion to make them necessary to me *.—I am afraid some men may be so wicked to hope and expect that a difference may happen between you and me upon this occasion: but when you consider what advantages have arisen to us in a few months, by the good understanding we have hitherto had; what wonderful effects it hath already produced in the change of the whole scene of affairs abroad, so much more to the honour of the nation, and the figure it ought to make in the world; and that nothing can hinder a farther progress in this way, to all our satisfactions, but Fears and Jealousies amongst ourselves; I will not apprehend that such a misfortune can befall us, as a division, or but a coldness, between me and you; nor that any thing can shake you in your steadiness and loyalty to me; who, by God's blessing, will ever make you returns of all kindness and protection, with a resolution to venture even my own life in the defence of the true interest of this kingdom."

Thanks voted by the Lords.] His majesty being withdrawn, the lords thought fit to debate, Whether they should give the king Thanks for his Speech or not? Some were for it, while others as warmly opposed it; but the marquis of Halifax, a man of a sharp satirical wit, said, by way of irony, 'They had 'now more reason than ever to give Thanks to his majesty, since he had dealt so plainly with them, and discovered what he would be at.' What he meant for a jest, was suddenly laid hold on by the courtiers for earnest, so the affirmative carried it, and an Address of Thanks was presented: to which his majesty returned this Answer:

The King's Answer.] "That he was very well satisfied that their lordships were well pleased with what he said; and that he would never offer any thing to their house, that he should not be convinced was for the good and true interest of the kingdom."

Debate in the Commons on the King's Speech, and on the Supply.] The earl of Middleton, a member of the house of commons, and one of his majesty's principal secretaries of state, moved, "That the house would immediately return their Thanks to his majesty, for his most gracious Speech." After some debate, it was resolved, "That the house resolve itself into a committee of the whole house, on Thursday the 12th instant, to take into consideration his majesty's Speech.

Nov. 12. The house resolved itself into the said committee, Mr. solicitor Finch in the chair. The king's Speech was read.

The Earl of *Middleton* moved to have it considered by paragraphs.

Sir *Winston Churchill.* Some other than the Militia is necessary to be found: I move a Supply for the Army.

Lord *Preston.* We have lately had an unfortunate proof, how little we are to depend upon the Militia, and therefore sure we must all approve of his majesty's increasing the Forces to what they are. France is formidable, now Holland's forces are greatly increased, and we must be strong in proportion, for preservation of ourselves and Flanders, and toward that, the good harmony betwixt the king and this house hath greatly contributed. It has had two other great effects abroad. 1. The French king's Army last spring was marching towards Germany; Crequi was far advanced; but when the king of France heard the kindness of this house to the king, and the defeat of Monmouth, he recalled them. 2. The French and Spaniards had also a difference about Haye and Fonterabia: the French advanced their troops, and recalled them on this news. This is the noble effect of the harmony between the king and this house, who have (I hope) brought the same heart and loyalty they had the last time here. Hence we may conclude, these levies made by the king are just, reasonable, and necessary. And so let us vote a Supply, to answer his majesty's present occasions.

The Earl of *Ranelagh.* The question is, Whether a Supply, or not? I do not intend to arraign the Militia, but seeing a soldier is a trade, and must (as all other trades are) be learned, I will show you where the Militia has failed; viz. at Chatham; and in June last, when the late duke of Monmouth landed, and had but 83 men, and 300*l.* in money, who, in spite of the Militia, nay, in spite of such other force as the king could spare hence, brought it so far as he did. If the king of France had landed then, what would have become of us? I say, the Militia is not insignificant, but an additional force is necessary, and so a Supply that is answerable to it.

Sir *Tho. Clarges.* If it shall appear to you, that the king's Revenue that he hath already, be sufficient to supply all the occasions, what then need we give him more? It is moved, That we should proceed by paragraphs. To come first to the Militia, who, let me tell you, did considerable service in the late Rebellion, and if a great nobleman of this kingdom had been supplied and assisted, it had soon been quelled. A confidence betwixt the king and his people is absolutely needful, let it come whence it will; our happiness consists in it. His majesty, on his first entrance on the crown, told us, 'he had been misrepresented, and that he would preserve the government in Church and State now established by law, and would maintain us in all our just Rights and Privileges.' Over-joyed at this, we ran hastily in to him; we gave four millions (reckoning what we added to him for life was worth) at

* "Thus the king fell upon the two most unacceptable points that he could have found out; which were a Standing Army, and a violation of the Act of the Test." Burnet.

once. The present Revenue is 1,900,000*l.* or two millions, yearly; the charge of the government (admitting this Army kept up) is but 1,300,000*l.* yearly: and pray let us not forget that there was a Bill of Exclusion debated in this house; I was here, and showed myself against it; the arguments for it were, "That we should, in case of a Popish Successor, have a Popish Army.' You see the Act of the Test already broken, but pray remember what the late lord chancellor told you, when the late king (of blessed memory) passed that Act: the words were to this effect: 'By this Act you are provided against Popery, that no Papist can possibly creep into any employment.' I am afflicted greatly at this Breach of our Liberties, and seeing so great difference betwixt this Speech, and those heretofore made, cannot but believe this was by some other advice. This, struck at here, is our all, and I wonder there have been any men so desperate, as to take any employment not qualified for it; and I would therefore have the question, 'That a Standing Army is destructive to the country.'

Sir *John Ernly.* The number of the standing forces is about 14 or 15,000 men, and they were about half so many before, and I conceive we are not safe without these forces to aid and help the Militia. I am not for laying aside the Militia, but I say, there is a necessity for a standing force. Half the charge of those forces, viz. about 300,000*l.* yearly, the whole being 600,000*l.* yearly, I conceive, is all we need to give for it: of that there remains 200,000*l.* unreceived of the 400,000*l.* given last, so the 200,000*l.* may go towards it, and the rest may be supplied by a tax on commodities as, for balancing of trade, may better be charged than not. I am for a Supply.

Sir *Hugh Cholmondeley.* I stand up for, and would not have the militia reflected on: it was very useful in the late Rebellion of Monmouth; it kept him from Bristol and Exeter, and is as good as any army we can raise against any at home.

Mr. *Coningsby.* I am for vindicating the Militia. There is just cause for a Supply, and I would give it, and reward the officers not qualified, or take them off some other way.

Mr. *Ashburnham.* I dread a Standing Army, but am for a Supply.

Mr. *Waller.* Kings, in old time, used to send, not only an account of their revenues, but of the charge they were going to be at, to the parliament, when they demanded aids. Hen. v. had but 56,000*l.* and queen Eliz. had 160,000*l.* and odd pounds, yearly. I am for a Bill for making the Militia useful, and would know, if we give money thus, whether it be not for setting up a Standing Army? I am for good Guards.

Sir *Wm. Trumbull.* The kingdom is guarded by law; we are now in perfect peace; the king is both feared and loved; an Army little needed; men justly afraid: that which made the last Rebellion as it was, the man that headed it was a favourite of the faction, and though he had got such a number, he was beaten by 1800 men only. I am against an Army.

Mr. *Seymour.* This last Rebellion has contributed to our future peace, and those engaged in it have sung their penitential psalm, and their punishment rejoiced at by all good persons. I do not commend the Militia, yet it is not to be rejected, but to be new modeled; and, for my part, I had rather pay double to these, [meaning for keeping up the Militia] from whom I fear nothing, than half so much to those, of whom I must ever be afraid; and, say what you will, it is a Standing Army. The last force preserved the peace, and was sufficient to do it, in the late king's time, and is now; all the profit and security of this nation is in our ships; and had there been the least ship in the Channel, it would have disappointed him. Supporting an Army is maintaining so many idle persons to lord it over the rest of the subjects. The king declared, 'That no soldiers should quarter in private houses;' but that they did; that they should pay for all things they took; but they paid nothing for almost all they took. And for Officers to be employed not taking the Tests, it is dispensing with all the laws at once; and if these men be good and kind, we know not whether it proceeds from their generosity, or principles: for we must remember, it is treason for any man to be reconciled to the Church of Rome; for the Pope, by law, is declared an enemy to this kingdom. A Supply given, as moved for, is a kind of an establishing an army by act of parliament; and when they have got the power into their hands, we are then to derive it from their courtesy; and therefore I would have the question be, 'That the safety of the kingdom doth not consist with a Standing force:' and this, it may be, will disappoint these persons, that make it their business this way, to make themselves useful.

Sir *Tho. Clarges* then moved for an Address.

Sir *Tho. Meres.* I am first for a Supply; that hinders not an Address: his majesty, in his Speech, only says, 'That the Militia is not sufficient.' The late Long Parliament always owned some force necessary: we are not to name the number, the king is best judge of that; a great soldier, and a good prince: I hear the number is 14 or 15,000; and I am for a Supply, and never saw, but money was always one part of the business of every parliament. There was a bitter spirit in the three last parliaments, not yet well allayed; and so I conclude a considerable force needful, besides the Militia. I call those raised, Guards, and would have a Supply given to support his majesty's extraordinary occasions. The Navy wants 6 or 800,000*l.* and I will give any reason for it; so a Supply may, without a negative, be given.

Serj. *Maynard.* There is already a law, that no man shall, on any occasion whatsoever, rise against the king: lord-lieutenants, and deputy-lieutenants, have power to disarm the disaffected: if you give thus a Supply, it is for an Army; and then, may not this Army be made of those that will not take the Test? Which act was not designed a punishment for the Papists, but a protection for ourselves; and giving this Money is for an Army: I am against it.

Sir *Rd. Temple.* I must concur with the king, that the Militia is not sufficient: I am for mending the Militia, and to make it such as the king and kingdom may confide in it; to trust to mercenary force alone is to give up all our liberties at once. If you provide a constant Supply to support them by setting up an Army, sir Tho. Meres has turned it into a Supply for the Navy. There is no country in the world, that has a law to set up an army. We have already made an ample Supply for the government. It is for kings to come to the house, from time to time, on extraordinary occasions; and if this army be provided for by law, they will never more come to this house. I am for giving for the extraordinary charge past. Armies are useful, when occasion is for them; but if you establish them, you can disband them no more. I am for a Supply, but not on this score of the Militia: there was not a company formed till 1588; and as soon as queen Eliz. had done with her army, she disbanded it. Armies have been fatal often to princes. The Army, in the late king's time, often turned out their leaders. I am for moving the house, for leave for a Bill to mend the Militia.

Sir *Winston Churchill.* The Beef-eaters, at this rate, may be called an Army.

Sir *Tho. Hussey.* The colonel may say what he will of the Beef-eaters, as he nicknames them; but they are established by act of parliament.

Mr. *Seymour.* I can make out, that the king's Revenue is sufficient to maintain the force on foot.

The question being put, "That a Supply be given to his majesty," Sir Tho. Clarges moved, "That the words, 'towards the support of the additional forces,' may be added: which was carried in the negative, 225 to 156; and then these votes passed:

Resolved, nem. con. "That a Supply be given to his majesty; and, that the house be moved to give leave to bring in a Bill to render the Militia more useful." Which were agreed to by the house.*

Nov. 13. A motion being made, by the earl of Middleton, "That the house should proceed to the farther consideration of his majesty's Speech;" The house thereupon resolved itself into a committee of the whole house; and the previous question being then put, for the house to go on with the Supply, or proceed to the next Paragraph; the house divided. For proceeding to the Supply, 182. For proceeding to the next Paragraph, 185.

* "The discussion in the house of commons on the 22d (12th) of this month, was very warm, and attended with much debate. The court party, however, carried the grant of a supply. When the question for this was put, the opposition had the address to propose, in addition, the words, 'That these supplies should be for the keeping up of the army,' which would have caused it to be rejected by a majority of votes. But, through the Speaker, and some other members, the question was confined to a grant of the Supply, without specifying for what purpose, and it passed by a small majority: but the house, at the same time, came to a Resolution, to represent to his maj. that the true force of the kingdom consists in the militia, and that it would take every possible means to render this force efficient. This was a plain declaration that the commons will not allow of a regular standing army. Many of the members spoke with great vehemence against the army and the Catholic officers, and asserted that the king's speech was a contradiction of what he had said in the proceeding session, since in this he openly declares himself against the established laws which are the safeguard of the Protestant religion. Messrs. Seymour and Clarges spoke in very harsh terms. One Jennins, a creature of the earl of Danby, and a new member, named Twisden, also spoke with much energy, and received great applause. All their speeches were directed against a standing army, and allowing of Catholic officers. One member said, he could not see that England made that great figure in Europe, which his majesty had talked of in his speech. To this lord Preston replied, that he knew, positively, your majesty would have attacked Spain, in some part or other, had not the king of England prevented it; and that you would not have been deterred from it, had you not thought that a rupture with Spain would have thrown England into the arms of your enemies. There were some other members, who maintained that the king of England only could stop the progress and increase of that power which makes all the others tremble, and that it is for the real interest of the English nation, that the king should be in a condition to oppose it, which cannot be done if he have not a sufficient force, always ready for service. This reasoning was indirectly combated by other members, who insisted that the true interests of Englishmen are to live in peace and tranquillity at home, with an assurance of their laws and property, as well as of their consciences in the exercise of their religion; and that when this should be the case, England would be of sufficient importance abroad. This discussion appeared so opposite to what his Britannic majesty could desire, that it has been already said that the parliament would be prorogued, or dissolved. Many meetings had taken place on the day preceeding, in which the old members who are not in the present parliament gave instructions to the new representatives." Barillon's Dispatches. See Fox's JAMES II. Appendix, p. cxxxii.

Resolved, "That it be an instruction to the grand committee, that the committee proceed first in the consideration of that Paragraph in his majesty's Speech, which next follows that of the Supply."*

Nov. 14. An Address was moved in the Committee, by sir Edmund Jennings. Others moved the inconveniency of it, if not granted, and so to let it alone. Others, to have the Catholics, who had been so useful and well known to his majesty, named and compensated. Some seemed to doubt his majesty's compliance. Others, that it was not to be doubted, when addressed by such a house.

Mr. Solicitor Finch reports from the Grand Committee [instructed as above] that the committee had agreed upon the two following Resolutions, viz. 1. "That the house be moved, That a committee be appointed to prepare an humble Address to be presented to his majesty, humbly showing, that those Officers of the Army, who are not qualified for their Employments by the acts for preventing Dangers which may happen from Popish Recusants, cannot by law be capable of their Employments: and that it be part of the said Address, '*That his majesty would be pleased not to continue them in their Employments.*' 2. That the house be moved to appoint a Committee to bring in a Bill to indemnify those persons unqualified, for the time past."—Which were agreed to by the house, with an Amendment in the first Resolve, by leaving out the words marked in Italics, and by adding, instead thereof, these words: 'That his majesty would be graciously pleased to give such directions, that no apprehensions or jealousies may remain in the hearts of his majesty's good and faithful subjects.'—And an Address was ordered to be prepared accordingly, and also a Bill to indemnify those persons unqualified.

Resolved, "That it be an instruction to the said committee, That, in the preamble of the said Address, the humble and hearty thanks of this house be returned to his majesty, for his great care in the Suppression of the late Rebellion.*

The Commons' Address against Popish Officers.] Nov. 16. Mr. Solicitor Finch reports, That the committee appointed had drawn up an Address to his majesty; which was read, and agreed to, as follows:

"Most gracious sovereign; We your majesty's most loyal and faithful subjects, the commons, in parliament assembled, do in the first place (as in duty bound) return your maj. our most humble and hearty Thanks for your great care and conduct in suppressing the late Rebellion, which threatened the overthrow of this government both in Church and State, and the utter extirpation of our Religion as by law established, which is most dear unto us, and which your maj. hath been pleased to give us repeated assurances you will always defend and support; which with all grateful hearts we shall ever acknowledge.—We farther crave leave to acquaint your majesty, that we have, with all duty and readiness, taken into our consideration your majesty's gracious Speech to us: and as to that part of it, relating to the Officers in the Army, not qualified for their Employments, according to an act of parliament made in the 25th of the reign of your majesty's royal brother, entitled, 'An Act for preventing 'Dangers which may happen from Popish Re'cusants,' we do, out of our bounden duty, humbly represent unto your majesty, That those Officers cannot by law be capable of

* "The house met again on the 23d, (13th) when the proceedings were still more violent; and on the question whether they should discuss the grant of the supplies, or take the king's speech into consideration, the opposition carried the latter by a majority of three: this was occasioned by several persons attached to, or dependent upon the court, being absent, and from some of those present even voting with the opposition, among others, Mr. Fox, paymaster of the Forces, whose father is an officer in the household, and formerly had the post of paymaster, in which he gained a large fortune; a lieutenant in the horse-guards, of the name of Darcy, a person of rank, also voted with the opposition. The language of the different speakers was more violent than on the day preceding, against a Standing Army and the Catholic Officers; and it seemed to be the almost unanimous sentiment of the house that no money should be granted for the support of the army, and that no Catholic officers should be suffered to remain in it." Barillon's Dispatches; See Fox's James II. Appendix, p. cxxxviii.

* "The day before yesterday (the 24th) the house again met, to consider the king's speech. It was expected that there would be still greater warmth and animosity than there had been on the two preceding days; but there was much more temper and moderation than was looked for. There was scarcely any repetition of what had been before said; but yet the discussion was conducted with great firmness, and the house seemed fully resolved not to allow the king to employ Catholic officers, since it is directly contrary to the laws. Different expedients were suggested to reconcile this difficulty; that of allowing those who are already appointed to remain, and of obtaining a promise from the king, that he would make no further increase in their number, was rejected, and the house concluded with moving an address to his majesty, praying him to remove the suspicions and jealousy which the non-execution of the laws has created in the nation. The temper shewn in this last discussion is attributed to a fear of giving an occasion for the dissolution of parliament. Others say it was caused by a club of old members, who have secretly inspired a firmness and obstinacy, under an outward display of moderation." Barillon's Dispatches: See Fox's James II. Appendix, p. cxxxiii.

their Employments; and that the Incapacities they bring upon themselves thereby, can no way be taken off but by an act of parliament. —Therefore, out of that great deference and duty we owe unto your majesty, who have been graciously pleased to take notice of their services to you, we are preparing a Bill to pass both houses for your royal assent, to indemnify them from the Penalties they have now incurred: and, because the continuing of them in their Employments may be taken to be a dispensing with that law without act of parliament, (the consequence of which is of the greatest concern to the rights of all your majesty's subjects, and to all the laws made for security of their religion) we therefore do most humbly beseech your majesty, that you would be graciously pleased to give such directions therein, that no apprehensions or jealousies may remain in the hearts of your majesty's good and faithful subjects."

A motion being made for going to the lords for their concurrence; some debated, 'That it would carry with it the greater weight, and be more likely to have good effect; and if the concurrence of the lords were asked, the Judges, in the lords house, would have an opportunity of speaking their opinion to it.' Others opposed it, 'for the lords having already given their Thanks to the king for his Speech, as being contented therewith, and that it would be more for the honour of the house of commons to address alone.' Those that were against the thing itself when it passed first, were for going to the lords for their concurrence. The house divided. For asking concurrence, 204. Against it, 216. So it passed in the negative.

Debate on the Supply, and the Way of raising it.] The house being resolved into a committee of the whole house, to consider of a Supply for his majesty; Mr. Solicitor took the chair.

Lord *Campden* moved 'for 200,000*l.* to be given to the king for a Supply, which, with 200,000*l.* confessed of what was given for suppressing the late Rebellion, makes 400,000*l.*' and was seconded.

Sir *John Ernly.* 1,200,000*l.* is needful, and such a sum has been given before in the same session, when there was an Address of this kind made to the late king.

Sir *Tho. Clarges.* We have this session already given Customs and Excises for his majesty's life: additional Duty on Wines eight years, 150,000*l.* yearly. Tax on Sugar and Tobacco, eight years, 200,000*l.* yearly. Tax on Linen and East-India Commodities, five years, 120,000*l.* yearly. In all, six millions. Let us give little now, to have opportunity to give more another time; for if we give too much now, we shall have nothing left to give; and if we proceed thus, what we have will be taken from us.

Sir *Edm. Jennings.* To give 1,200,000*l.* now, because such a sum has been given, is no argument; once 2,400,000*l.* was given here, and therefore should it be so now? 200,000*l.* with what is confessed to be in cash, makes 400,000*l.* and that will maintain the charge one year, and better; and giving all at once is doubting the affection of the people.

Lord *Preston.* You unanimously voted a Supply last night, and naming so little now is not so ingenuous a way of proceeding. We are told, six millions have been this session given; I would have you, gentlemen, take notice, the giving his maj. what the late king had, is but settling a Revenue that before was not sufficient for the support of the government; what was given besides, was part for the late king's servants, part for the Fleet and Stores, and part for suppressing the late Rebellion. To give so little now, is not to enable the king to defend and preserve us, which he has promised to do. I am for 1,200,000*l.*

The Earl of *Ranelagh.* The question is for 200,000*l.* or for 1,200,000*l.* What has been given in this matter already, ought not to be weighed at all; and what is called six millions, had all uses (when given) tacked to it. The Revenue his brother had, had uses enough, as the Wine and Vinegar act, rated at yearly 15,000*l.* for the Fleet, Stores, Ordnance, and Servants: The Sugar and Tobacco act, rated at yearly 200,000*l.* for the said Stores, Ordinary, and Fleet: and the additional duty on French linen and East-India commodities, rated at yearly 120,000*l.* for suppressing the late Rebellion. So there are uses for all that, and what is now given, must be taken for supporting the forces: and therefore I am for 1,200,000*l.*

Sir *Winston Churchill.* 200,000*l.* is much too little: Soldiers move not without pay. 'No Penny, No Paternoster.'

Mr. *Ettrick* moved for 700,000*l.* and mentioned to have it raised upon the new Buildings, which might produce 400,000*l.* and a Poll-Bill for the other 300,000*l.*

Mr. *Waller.* If I knew the king's Revenue were short, I would give as far as any man; but now we are going for this particular use, and if this 200,000*l.* will not do, how can we be sure that 1,200,000*l.* will? If we give too little now, hereafter, if we see occasion, we may give more; but if we now give too much, I do not see how we shall ever have it again, though I have heard of such a thing in queen Eliz.'s time. The king (reckoning what he had of his own into it) has 600,000*l.* yearly more than the late king had, and when there is need, I am for more, but now only 400,000*l.* and to raise that easy you will be put to it: how will you do it? If you lay it upon trade, that will make it revenue, and when once in the crown for some time, it will never get out again. I am for only 400,000*l.*

Lord *Campden.* If the king wants 200,000*l.* I would give him 200,000*l.* but I am for giving no more than he really wants.

Mr. *Waller.* We give, because we are asked. I am for the least sum, because for an army, and I would be rid of them as soon as I could; and am more now against it than I lately was, being satisfied that the country is weary of the oppression of the soldiers, weary of free quarters, plunder, and some felons, for which they have no complaint, no redress: and since I heard Mr. Blaithwayte tell us, how strict rules were prescribed them by the king, I find by their behaviour, the king cannot govern them himself; and then what will become of us?

Sir *Willoughby Hickman*. The Rebellion is suppressed, and the Army is urged to be small, but it is so thick of Officers, that by filling up the Troops, which is easily at any time done, increases their number to a third part more. I am for providing for them but one whole year only, and only for 400,000*l.*

Mr. *Coningsby*. I agree to the 400,000*l.* We owe besides a duty to our country, and are bound by that duty to leave our posterity as free in our liberties and properties as we can; and there being Officers now in the army, that have not taken the Test, greatly flats my zeal for it, and make me esteem the Militia; of which if well modeled, and placed in mens hands of interest in their country, we are certain, and so is the king secure; for there is no such security of any man's loyalty, as a good estate. Reasons I have heard given against armies, that they debauched the manners of all the people, their wives, daughters, and servants. Men do not go to Church where they quarter, for fear mischief should be done in their absence. Plough-men and servants quit all country-employments to turn soldiers; and then a court-martial, in time of peace, is most terrible. In peace, justices of it, and the civil magistrate, ought to punish, if applied to. And what occasion then can be for them? Is it to suppress a rebellion in time of an invasion? All then will go towards that. Or is it to assist his allies? The house will give aid, when wanted, on that score. The Guards I am not against; those showed themselves useful in Venner's business, and the late Rebellion; I am not against them: I only speak of those that have been new raised.

Col. *Ashton*. I will tell you the use of these forces; they expected the rising of a great party, and were not these forces standing, to prevent a a Rebellion, you would have one in a few days.

Mr. *Blaithwayte*. If any disorders have been committed, it is not yet too late to have them redressed; and martial law (if by that cleared) does not hinder proceeding at common law for the same thing: 400,000*l.* is not enough; no state near us, in proportion, but what exceeds this small number of men.

Sir *Tho. Clarges*. Seven millions of men in England; the strength of England consists in our marine, in which (for want of men) France can never equal us; their trade will not breed them; a ship of fifty tons will carry 100,000*l.* of their goods, linen and silks. Ours are bulky goods, and employ twenty times more, unless you (by burdening of trade) let them into the West-Indies. Armies are not manageable; commanders have been very often known to rebel: the measure of our Supply is our security. His majesty's Declaration says, 'If on complaint, the Officers give no redress, then complain to the king;' and so justice is baulked by this hardship put upon the complainant.

Sir *Wm. Trumbull** moved to have it temporary from year to year.

Sir *Christ. Musgrave*. Let it be, to enable his majesty to preserve us in peace at home, and to make his majesty formidable abroad, for 1,200,000*l.* as a Supply answerable to the loyalty of this house.

Sir *Hugh Cholmondeley*. This house was so forward to give last time, that the king's ministers gave their stop to it.

Sir *John Werden*. The use is to direct the quantum. I see a present necessity for continuing these Forces, till the Militia is made useful; I am for trying two years, and so for 400,000*l.* and so leave the door open for coming hither to give another time.

Sir *Tho. Meres*. The principle of the rebel party is never to repent. I am for 1,200,000*l.* and if so much be given, I would have you, gentlemen, to remember that the Fanatics are the cause of it.

Mr. *Pepys*. An island may be attacked, notwithstanding any fleet. Ours is much mended, a thousand men daily at work, ever since we gave money for it, and not one man in it an officer, that has not taken the Test.

Col. *Oglethorp*. New troops are not so good as old, and more subject to commit disorders, but will be less so, when they are longer under discipline. The king of France never sends troops to his Army, till they have been two or three years on foot in a garrison.

Sir *Tho. Clarges*. The Trained Bands at Newbury fight did brave things.

Then the question was, "That a sum, not exceeding 400,000*l.* should be given to the king. The previous question being put, it passed in the negative, 179 to 167. Then the question was put for 700,000*l.* and no more; which passed in the affirmative, 212 to 170.

Resolved, "That it is the opinion of this committee, That a Supply of 700,000*l.* be given to his majesty, and no more." Which was agreed to by the house with an Amendment, by leaving out the words 'and no more,' and, instead thereof, inserting these words, 'not exceeding the sum.†

* Afterwards Secretary of State to king William.

† "Yesterday, being Sunday, the house did not meet. To-day it considers the supplies. The general question is, whether the commons will grant them unconditionally, and content themselves with having shewn how much they abhor a regular standing army and the employment of Catholics, without insisting farther upon any previous satisfaction. If this be the case, the king will have obtained every thing

Nov. 17. The house resolved into a committee of the whole house, to consider the way of raising his majesty's Supply. Mr. North took the Chair.

Sir *John Ernly.* I move for an additional duty upon Wines to yield 400,000*l.* yearly; and other goods, &c. about 600,000*l.* yearly, which, with the continuance for some years of the late act of imposition on French linens, and East-India silks, &c. might make up the sum; and I propose this way, to avoid a land-tax. The goods I propose to be rated, are soap, pot-ashes, to pay 7½*d.* to treble; unwrought silks, deals, planks, and other boards, to double. Raisins and prunes 2*s.* per cent. to double. Iron, which now pays 7*s.* per cent. to double. Copperas 18*s.* per cent. to double. Oils to 8 or 10 per ton, pay now 30*s.* Drugs will bear two-thirds more than rated. Drugs and spices from Holland, salt, and all prohibited goods, 20*l.* per cent. And this, I hope, may do what is now intended to be raised at this time, supposing 4*l.* per ton on French wines.

Sir *Dudley North* moved much to the same effect, and enlarged on it, and said, The Book of Rates has been well considered, and these goods are capable of bearing the duties proposed; but if the king took the 40*l.* per ton on French wines at 20,000*l.* yearly, he would be a loser by it.—Other gentlemen insisted on having French linen higher charged.

Mr. *Neale.* The pepper that is expended here, paying 1d. a pound, might pay one penny more, and so yield 70 or 80,000*l.* yearly; and that bullion, exported to the Indies, might bear 5*l.* per cent. and encourage the sending of other goods (in some measure) instead of it thither.

Sir Rd. Temple moved Subsidies, or Land-Tax; but the house inclining to what was first proposed, and it being consented to by the king's ministers, seemed contented with it: so it was voted, "That an Act for laying an Imposition on French linens, East-India goods, brandy, &c. should be continued for five years, from Midsummer 1690, and be given to his majesty as 400,000*l.*' And that an additional imposition of 4*l.* per ton be laid upon all French wines, on which to be raised 300,000*l.* which makes up the 700,000*l.*"—The time how long this 4*l.* per ton shall be laid, is not yet determined, an account being first to be brought from the custom-house books, of what number of tons are yearly imported: it was said, 100,000 tons; others affirmed, there were near double so

---

essential; for the general discontent will not prevent him from keeping up his army, and having the means of paying it. This day's discussion will determine the length of the present session; for his majesty seems resolved not to relax in any thing; and his firmness astonishes those who thought that what had taken place in the house of commons, would have induced him to admit of some modifications, and not to persist in carrying in this session all that he desires.—From what I have the honour of sending to your majesty, you will see that the affairs of this country are greatly altered within these few days; some changes and ameliorations may take place in them: I know that money is employed to soften those most opposed to the court; but it is difficult to establish a perfect concert, and to remove entirely the great distrust which exists on all sides. The opposition party is that of the prince of Orange, whom a great number of persons secretly favour: there is even a division in the court; this I will explain to your majesty as clearly as I can, in the course of my letter. It seems to me, at the same time, that I have nothing to do in execution of the order contained in your last dispatch, but to take all possible care to obtain the fullest information, and to acquaint you exactly with what passes.—I have preserved a connexion with some of the leading persons in the preceding parliaments, and it would not be impossible to increase, if it were necessary, the divisions which seem to be rising. It would be for your majesty's interest, still to keep some persons dependent upon you; this might even, on certain occasions, be of use to the king of England, and the welfare of our religion. I see nothing urgent at present. Affairs seem, at this moment at least, to be taking of themselves that course which may be most advantageous to your majesty; it is, however, difficult to foresee the sudden changes and revolutions which happen in this country; and your majesty well knows that affairs are begun and terminated before there is time to receive fresh instructions.—The house of commons began this morning with reading the address which is to be presented to his majesty. I have been assured that it is conceived in very strong and positive terms against the Catholic officers; there was afterwards a motion for requesting the lords to join the commons in this Address; but it was rejected, and the court party prevailed. The supply was next taken into consideration; and after much debate, they agreed to grant 700,000*l.* at once. The king looked for 1,400,000*l.*; however, I believe he will not be dissatisfied, provided the sources from which it is to arise be secure, and the lower house do not insist upon the address which it is to present, as a previous condition: this is yet uncertain. We must wait till it is seen whether some incident may not happen to prevent the effect of the resolution which has deen adopted. If the money affair can be entirely separated from the other things which are agitated, the king will gain his end, and may dispense with the parliament, at least for a considerable time. The earl of Sunderland has just told me that he does not think the king and the parliament can agree, because their respective wishes are in direct opposition to each other." Barillon's Dispatches: See Fox's JAMES II. Appendix, p. cxxxiv.

many.—The house seemed to incline to 8 or 10 years, and that the duties already on it should still continue on the same time; which 4*l.* per ton, with the duty it already pays, is near 20*l.* per ton.

The King's Answer to the Address.] Nov. 18. The Speaker acquainted the house, That his majesty having been yesterday attended, in the Banquetting-house at Whitehall, with the Address of thanks from this house for his great care and conduct in suppressing the late Rebellion, and likewise concerning the Officers of the Army not qualified for their Employments, he was graciously pleased to return an Answer, to the effect following:

"I did not expect such an Address from the house of commons, having so lately recommended to your consideration the great advantages a good understanding between us had produced in a very short time, and given you warning of Fears and Jealousies amongst ourselves.—I had reason to hope, that the reputation God hath blessed me within the world, would have created and confirmed a greater confidence in you of me, and of all that I say to you: but however you proceed on your part, I will be steady in all my promises I have made to you, and be very just to my word in this, and all my other Speeches."

Mr. Coke's offensive Speech.] The said Answer was read with all due reverence and respect, and there being a profound silence in the house for some time after it,

Mr. *Wharton* moved, 'That a day might be appointed to consider of his majesty's Answer to the late Address of this house;' and named Friday next.

Mr. *Coke* stood up and seconded that motion, and said 'I hope we are all Englishmen, and are not to be frighted out of our duty by a few high words.'

Lord *Preston* took present exceptions against the words, which, as is usual, were written down by the clerk, and Mr. Coke was called upon to explain.

Mr. *Coke* said, 'He intended no ill by it; and that he did not believe these the words. And that if he had said any thing that had given the house offence, he was sorry, and would ask them pardon for it.'

Sir *Christ. Musgrave.* It is not enough to say these were not the words, but you are to say what the words were.

Mr. *Coke.* I do not make set speeches: I cannot repeat them; and if they did drop from me, I ask the king and your pardon.

So these being taken for granted to have been the Words, Mr. Coke, as the custom is in such cases, withdrew into the Speaker's chamber.

Sir *Joseph Tredenham.* Not our own honour, but the king is concerned in this. I move, that he be brought to the bar, and there receive a reprimand from Mr. Speaker for it.

Sir *Hugh Cholmondeley.* He is a gentleman of great loyalty, never before of the house; I desire he may have what favour he can.

Mr. *Ashburnham.* It is a great reflection upon this house, if this be let pass.

Several spoke of his loyalty, but none to excuse him for this.

Lord *Preston.* Send him to the Tower!

Lord *Middleton.* The meaning of this seems like an incendiary. The Tower! This needs no aggravation. A reprimand for an offence to this house might do; but this does not end there; and it is a question whether it be in the power of the house to pass it by, the offence being given to the king as well as you: I am for calling him to the bar in the first place.

Resolved, "That Mr. John Coke, a member of this house, for his indecent and undutiful reflecting on the king and this house, be committed to the Tower." And the Speaker was ordered to issue his warrant accordingly.

Mr. *Seymour.* Now this is over I cannot but consent to those that moved for a day, to consider of his majesty's Answer, nor think myself as honest as I should be, if I now hold my tongue. And if we do take this matter into consideration, I doubt not but that we shall behave ourselves with that decency to his majesty, that we may hope for a more satisfactory Answer than as yet this seems to be to me.

Sir *John Ernly.* I hope that acquiescence that was this morning in this house, on reading his majesty's Answer, has ended this matter. I do think the king will do all that he promised, and am for resting there.

Sir *Tho. Meres* moved to adjourn, and said, 'He did not know what to say to it.'

Sir *Tho. Clarges.* For that very reason I move for a day to consider of it; and I do not think we show that respect we ought to do to the king, if we do not.

The Lords take the King's Speech into consideration.] "By this time," says Mr. Ralph, "the danger of the public grew so apparent that the Lords grew ashamed of their first days work; and even the Bishops put in for their share of merit, by moving, 'That a day might be appointed for taking the King's Speech into consideration.' Compton of London, was the right reverend father in God, who, on this occasion, stood forth (courageously, says Echard) as the mouth of the Bench. Alarmed at this unexpected attack, the courtiers endeavoured to stave it off, by urging, That having already given Thanks for the Speech, they had thereby adopted the sentiments contained in it; and precluded themselves from finding fault with any part of it. This plea was, however, rejected with indignation, and put an end, says bishop Burnet, to the compliment of giving Thanks for a Speech, when there was no special reason for it. The lords Halifax, Nottingham, and Mordaunt, were the chief speakers; for as to the Bishops, they acquiesced in what his lordship of London was pleased to say for them: and though the point before them was only for setting a day, many things, we are told, escaped in relation to the merits of the case: as, that the Test was now the best fence they had for their religion: if they gave up so great a point, all the rest would soon follow; and if the king, might by his authority, supersede such a law, fortified with so many clauses, and above all with that of an incapacity, it was in vain to think of law any more. The government would become arbitrary and absolute. All which, it seems, Jeffereys undertook to answer, and that in as haughty and arrogant a tone, as he had used himself to on the bench. But he was soon taught to know his place; and that frowns, and noise, and menaces would not pass for arguments there. Upon the whole, the court-party finding themselves out-numbered, as well as out-argued, were forced to give way; and it was agreed, that, on the 23d the Speech should be taken into consideration."*

The Parliament dissolved, after many Prorogations.] Nov. 20. The king, by the usher of the black-rod, commanded the commons to attend him in the house of peers, where his majesty was pleased, by the lord chancellor Jeffereys, for many weighty reasons to prorogue the parliament to February 10;† when it met, and was farther prorogued to May 10, 1686, from thence to Nov. 22, from thence to Feb. 15, from thence to April 28, 1687, and from thence to Nov. 22, but before that day came the parliament was dissolved by Proclamation, dated July 2.

The King publishes a Declaration of Indulgence.] Previous to the Dissolution, namely, on the 4th of April 1687, the king published a Declaration of Indulgence,* setting forth "That there was nothing which his majesty so earnestly desired as to make his subjects happy, and to unite them to himself by inclination as well as duty, and that this could only be done by granting them the free exercise of their Religion, in addition to the perfect enjoyment of their Property, which had never been invaded by him, since his accession to the crown, and which should ever be preserved to them during his reign, as the truest methods of their peace and his glory." His majesty then proceeds to say in substance, "That though he could not but heartily wish, that all his subjects were members of the Catholic Church: yet he had always declared, That conscience ought not to be constrained, nor people forced in matters of mere Religion; that force was contrary to the interest of government, and never obtained th[illegible] end for which it was employed: that this was become manifest by the expe[illegible]nce of the four last reigns; and that this shewed the necessity of his present Declaration, which virtue of his royal prerogative, he had thought fit to issue forth, and which he made no doubt the two houses would concur with him in, when he should think it convenient for them to meet." Descending then to particulars, his majesty in the first place, declared, "That he would protect the archbishops, bishops, &c. of the Church of England in the free exercise of their Religion, as by law established, and in the quiet enjoyment of their possessions, without any molestation or disturbance whatsoever. 2. That the execution of all, and all manner of Penal Laws in matters Ecclesiastical, should be immediately suspended. 3. That he gave his free leave to all his loving subjects to serve God their own way either in public or private, provided they took special care that nothing was preached or taught among them tending to alienate the hearts of the people from his government. 4. That it was his command that no disturbance of any kind should be given to them, under pain of his displeasure, and of being proceeded against with the utmost severity. 5. That it was his royal will and pleasure, That the Oaths commonly called the Oaths of Supremacy and Allegiance, as also the several Tests and Declarations mentioned in the acts of parliament of the 25th and 30th

* "The king," says sir John Reresby, "happened to be present, as he was generally constant in the house of lords, and was much concerned at the freedom that was used upon this subject: and in truth it gave great dissatisfaction, that the law, in this point, particularly, should be thus invaded and set at naught; and the very best of the king's friends, as well as his officers, whether civil or military, except such as were Popishly inclined, were strangely alarmed thereat, and expressed themselves with great freedom, wherever it happened to be the topic of their discourse."

† "The king saw, that both houses were now so fixed, that he could carry nothing in either of them, unless he would depart from his Speech, and let the Act of the Test take place: so he prorogued the parliament, and kept it by repeated prorogations still on foot for about a year and a half, but without holding a session." Burnet.

"The parliament was prorogued this morning to the 20th of February. From what took place in the house yesterday, the king of England saw clearly that the opposition were daily gaining strength, and that there would be much inconvenience in suffering them to remain longer together. I learn that the surprise was very great, and that there was no expectation that the parliament would be prorogued before the money bill was passed. Every measure that has been brought forward in the house, and not completed, is rendered null by the prorogation; and the grant of the supplies is, of course, entirely done away. There is no likelihood that this step can produce any other effect than that of increasing the discontent of those who are already irritated. This occasions a great alteration in the affairs of England. I will take all due care to transmit to your majesty an exact account of every thing, in order that I may receive your instructions with respect to my future conduct." Barillon's Dispatches. See Fox's JAMES II. Appendix p. cxxxiv.

* For an Answer to this Declaration, written by the Marquis of Halifax, see Appendix No. XVII.

of Charles ii. should not for the future be required to be taken by any person, who was or should be employed in any place of trust: and, that it was his farther pleasure and intention, to grant his royal dispensations under the great seal to all persons so employed, who should not take the said Oaths. 6. That he did thereby give his free Pardon to all Nonconformists, Recusants, and other his loving subjects, for all crimes and things by them committed against the said Penal Laws: and that the pardon so given should be as good and effectual to all intents and purposes, as if every individual had been therein particularly named, or had received particular pardons under the great seal. And lastly, That he would maintain his loving subjects in all their properties and possessions, as well of Church and Abbey Lands, as any other."

On the 24th of August 1688, his majesty declared in Council that another parliament should be summoned to meet on the 27th of Nov. the Writs to bear date the 5th of Sept. but the said Writs were recalled or not issued, on the advice of the prince of Orange's designs. The violent attempts made during the remainder of this reign to introduce tyranny both in Church and State; the Judgments given for the Dispensing Power; the introduction of a Jesuit to the Council Board; the reception of the Pope's Nuncio; the sending an Ambassador to Rome; the attacks on both the Universities; the committing the Bishops to the Tower, &c. are all too well known to be here recited.

On the 10th of October 1688, the prince of Orange, who was now on the point of embarking his troops for this country, issued his first DECLARATION from the Hague: with which we shall commence our Fifth Volume.

APPENDIX.

Lightning Source UK Ltd.
Milton Keynes UK
UKHW02f0303250818
327756UK00009B/481/P

9 781528 001403